"As exceptional for the 2000's as Rashi was for the 1000's, this is the definitive Jewish commentary on the Five Books of Moses."

—BARUCH HALPERN,
Chaiken Family Chair in Jewish Studies, Pennsylvania State University

"Richard Elliott Friedman has created a pathbreaking translation and commentary. His intelligent use of biblical and archeological scholarship consistently yields new insights into the Bible, while his spiritual sensibility allows him to emphasize the rich religious meanings that inhere in Torah. Jews and Christians alike will hail this work!"

—RABBI DAVID ELLENSON, Ph.D.,
President, Hebrew Union College-Jewish Institute of Religion

"This is the way to study Torah! Friedman has produced a commentary that is both traditional and modern, drawing on the best of medieval commentaries and modern scholarship but adding his own perspective as well. He models for us the most intelligent—and traditional—way to make the Torah live in our own lives."

—RABBI ELLIOT N. DORFF, Ph.D.,
Rector and Distinguished Professor of Philosophy, University of Judaism

"A vast array of insights. Every page of the commentary shows Friedman's keen eye for subtle nuances and telling literary details. I would recommend this book to all Bible readers, but especially as a valuable resource for those who are engaged in serious, ongoing Torah study."

—ALAN COOPER,
Professor of Bible, Jewish Theological Seminary
and Union Theological Seminary

"A commentary that is both learned and engaging, consistently reaching out to the reader in order to make the Biblical text relevant to contemporary spiritual and ethical perplexity. Lucid, judicious, provocative; a major achievement."

—ARNOLD EISEN,
Professor of Religious Studies, Stanford University

"... ulminating work by a remarkable scholar. Friedman has had a place in the company of the great scholars of the recent past; now we find him another place of equal value and importance among an older generation of legendary commentators on the Hebrew Scriptures: Kimhi and Abarbanel, Rashbam and Nachmanides, and that perennial master of the written Word, Rashi. We will leave the comparison at that point, in order to emphasize the remarkable scope and depth, the brilliance and winsomeness of this new but constant Companion to the Holy Scriptures."

—DAVID NOEL FREEDMAN,
General Editor, The Anchor Bible

"Richard Friedman not only provides a fresh and exciting translation in the real language of ordinary people, he also presents a discerning and original commentary. With him as guide, the Five Books of Moses take on new life. Here we see, in his language, 'problems we had not seen, old problems that had not been solved,'—together with his always-compelling solutions. He lives up to his well-earned name as the single most interesting mind working on the Bible in any language today."

—JACOB NEUSNER,
Senior Fellow, Institute of Advanced Theology,
and Research Professor of Religion and Theology, Bard College

"Friedman's reading is close and keen—able to dig out half-hidden details and problems in the text and offer convincing explanations of them. Yet none of what he writes is remote and obscure; it is rather in easily accessible prose, which brings out the continuing vitality and power of the Biblical text in a compelling way. He has, especially, a deep and comprehensive grasp of the interconnectedness of the Bible, showing again and again how individual verses and passages echo and build on one another."

—PETER MACHINIST,
Hancock Professor of Hebrew and Other Oriental Languages, Harvard University

"At last—a translation of the Torah that finds a successful balance between the literal and the idiomatic. And at last—an accompanying commentary informed by the best classical and modern scholarship and also exquisitely sensitive to the questions and concerns of the contemporary student of Torah."

—CAROL MEYERS,
Professor of Biblical Studies and Archaeology, Duke University

"Richard Friedman's *Commentary on the Torah* is unique and wonderful—intelligent, courageous, creative, and playful. It could only have been created by a world class scholar. It could only have been crafted by a great lover of Bible. It could only have been written by Richard Elliott Friedman."

—RABBI BRADLEY SHAVIT ARTSON,
Dean, Ziegler School of Rabbinic Studies, University of Judaism

"Like the prototypical commentator, Rashi, Richard Friedman conveys a vast amount of learning with a light touch. His translations are fresh and vibrant. His masterful commentary blends scholarly precision, literary sensitivity, and spiritual reflection."

—DANIEL MATT,
author of *God and the Big Bang* and *The Essential Kabbalah*

"[A] masterful commentary that truly teaches how the Torah text might be read as a whole, and how it might 'teach' and inform the life of the religiously sensitive individual. His pedagogical skills—his ability to communicate in a clear and interesting fashion—are especially laudable. I know of no other work that has these merits, and I imagine that anyone from any background who reads this commentary will gain an enriched sense of the Torah, its meaning, and its significance."

—MARC BRETTLER,
Professor of Bible, Brandeis University, *Bible Review*

"*Commentary on the Torah* displays not only a scholar's mastery of biblical Hebrew but also a poet's ear for language."

—JONATHAN KIRSCH,
Los Angeles Times

"First-rate. . . .The rich library of Bible translations and commentary gets even richer with the arrival of the Friedman version."

—ELLIOT JAGER,
Jerusalem Post

"Jewish scholars have praised this modern, one-person treatise as 'the definitive Jewish commentary on the Five Books of Moses' and have called the new English translation 'a successful balance between the literal and the idiomatic.'"

—*The Houston Chronicle*

"[M]onumental. Friedman's translation is fresh and dynamic."

—*The Bible Today*

". . . Reflects modern research and scholarship as well as traditional sensibility. Friedman's own translation and his commentary . . . has won praise across theological lines."

—*Publisher's Weekly*, October 15, 2001

"Richard Elliott Friedman's new translation and commentary on the Torah provides profound routes of return for scholars and laypersons, Jew and Christians alike. [T]his voice of Friedman's, while clearly the voice of an academic scholar, speaks as if directly to our contemporary American English-speaking heart."

-PETER OCHS,
Books & Culture

COMMENTARY

ON THE

TORAH

WITH A

NEW ENGLISH TRANSLATION

RICHARD ELLIOTT FRIEDMAN

HarperSanFrancisco

A Division of HarperCollinsPublishers

Also by Richard Elliott Friedman

The Exile and Biblical Narrative

The Creation of Sacred Literature, Editor

The Poet and the Historian, Editor

The Future of Biblical Studies: The Hebrew Scriptures, Co-editor

Who Wrote the Bible?

The Hidden Face of God (originally published as *The Disappearance of God*)

The Hidden Book in the Bible

FIRST HARPERCOLLINS PAPERBACK EDITION PUBLISHED IN 2003

Library of Congress Cataloging-in-Publication Data
Friedman, Richard Elliott.
    Commentary on the Torah : Richard Elliott Friedman
       p. cm.
    ISBN 0-06-050717-9 (paperback)
     1. Bible. O.T. Pentateuch—Commentaries. I. Bible. O.T. Pentateuch. English.
Friedman. 2001. II. Title.
BS1225.3 .F7495 2001
222'.1077—dc21

                               00-031979

  06 07 RRD(H) 8 7 6 5 4

This book is dedicated with love to my daughter

Alexa Jaymie Friedman

who is a bright light in my life

TABLE OF CONTENTS

ACKNOWLEDGMENTS

I am fortunate. I owe thanks to

My father, Alex Sandor Friedman, and my mother, Reva Axelrod Friedman, who first taught me the Torah, by word and example.

My rabbi, Mayer Abramowitz, who sat with me, teaching me the Torah with commentaries, every Sabbath afternoon, year after year, as I grew up. His skill as a teacher, his feeling for the text, and his generosity with his time and attention were an unrepayable gift. When I was still a young boy, I told him that I wanted to write a commentary on the Torah when I grew up. Here it is. I hope that he will be pleased with what he has produced.

Professor Yohanan Muffs, my extraordinary teacher at the Jewish Theological Seminary, who brought me back to understand as an adult the greatness of the *Tanak* that I had felt as a child.

Professor G. Ernest Wright and especially Professor Frank Moore Cross, my incomparable teachers at Harvard, who showed me that the Hebrew Bible was both the treasure of the Jews and a source of blessing to all the families of the earth.

Professor David Noel Freedman, my senior colleague, friend, and teacher, who read every word of the commentary and translation and, with his well-known generosity, criticized and enriched it, from the tiniest point of punctuation to the largest concept. His *hesed* is present between the lines of every page of this book.

Professor William Henry Propp, my colleague, the world's most learned person on the book of Exodus, who read my own commentary on and translation of Exodus, and saved me from a number of errors, improved the work in many ways, and encouraged me.

Professor David Goodblatt and Professor Thomas Levy, my colleagues who come from other, related fields of expertise, but who contribute with a gracious spirit to those of us with whom they work.

My friend Irv Kass and my student Miriam Sherman, who also read and improved the work.

The superb community of biblical scholars in Jerusalem, where I spent a year working on the commentary. I was shown particular hospitality, kindness, and exchange of

learning by Shalom Paul, Menahem Haran, Moshe Weinfeld, Avi Hurvitz, Israel Knohl, Alex Rofé, Immanuel Tov, Edward Greenstein, and especially Moshe Greenberg.

Elaine Markson, my literary agent who does not just sell books and represent authors, but who loves books and is beloved by the authors she represents.

Randy Linda Sturman, my wife, my partner, my *basherta*.

Richard Elliott Friedman

I have come to realize that a book should list and acknowledge the persons at the publishing house and its associates who produce the work. This book had the fortune to be placed in the hands of persons at HarperSanFrancisco, a division of Harper-Collins, who have a combination of professionalism and personal, human qualities that make the inevitably complex process of publication a positive one. Stephen Hanselman, the President of HarperSanFrancisco, gave this book his personal attention. And it benefited from the skills of Mark Chimsky, Douglas Abrams, Terri Leonard, Renee Sedliar, Roger Freet, John Kohlenberger, Ann Moru, and June Gunden.

INTRODUCTION

*T*he first book to be printed on the printing press in Hebrew was not the Bible. It was the Torah with the commentary of Rashi. Why? Because the Torah is not to be read. It is to be studied. And at various times during one's studies, one needs a teacher. Studying the Torah with Rashi's commentary is a joy because he shows one what questions one can ask of a text. Look here! Is this a contradiction? Look here! This can have two opposite meanings. Which is right? Why does the Torah not tell us this piece of information that we need to understand the text? Why does it give us this fact that seems to be of no significance at first glance?

Rashi wrote his commentary nine hundred years ago. Commentaries for laypersons in recent times have changed. They have been written as introductory notes to help explain the text. They often collect comments from scholars of the past and from current biblical scholars. This is different from what Commentary meant classically. The purpose of Rashi's commentary and of Ibn Ezra's and Ramban's was to show the readers new things in the text, problems that they had not seen, or to address old problems that had not been solved—and then to offer the commentator's solutions to those problems. In this commentary, I mean to return to the classical purpose. I shall have some basic explanatory comments to be helpful to the new student, but, above all, I mean to make new contributions to the understanding of the Torah. I mean to try to offer explanations for old problems and to address new ones. I aim to shed new light on the Torah and, more important, to open windows through which it sheds its light on us.

The idea is to address the kinds of things that we treat in academic scholarship but in a manner that is accessible and interesting to laypersons as well. I still cling to the belief that has governed my last several books: that serious biblical scholarship is not over the heads of nonscholars. It is possible to discuss our findings in a way that intelligent people understand—and that shows them how interesting and valuable this learning is.

In this purpose, my fellow biblical scholars and I have new sources that were not available to the great medieval commentators. Through the archaeological revolution of the last two centuries, we have new knowledge of the biblical world, both of Israel and its neighbors. We know the languages that they spoke and wrote in addition to

Hebrew and Aramaic: Akkadian, Canaanite (Ugaritic, Phoenician, Moabite), Egyptian, and Sumerian. We have hundreds of sites and tens of thousands of ancient texts. We have manuscripts of the Torah and of the entire Hebrew Bible, the *Tanak*, from Qumran (the Dead Sea Scrolls) that are a thousand years older than those that Rashi had. We have the use of the Greek version (the Septuagint), which, together with the Qumran texts (and Samaritan and Aramaic and Latin texts), gives us a more precise knowledge of the original text. And we have the great commentators themselves. Their thinking and their conclusions are our starting point, already at our fingertips, enabling us to learn from them and then to go farther. And we have the work of great scholars of more recent times as well.

There has developed a kind of Rashi fundamentalism in recent years. Especially in orthodox communities, it is practically heresy to question whether Rashi was ever wrong. I think that Rashi himself might have been disappointed that it would come to that. The commentators who immediately followed him—Ibn Ezra and Ramban and Rashi's grandson Rashbam—knew better. They expressed respect for Rashi, but they disagreed with and offered alternatives to his comments. Rashi's commentary served for nearly a millennium. There is still much that is useful in it, and it can be valuable for millennia to come. But we also need new commentary for the coming generations, in the light of a world of new knowledge and new questions and new needs.

What Rashi and the other commentators taught us to do was to look at a text critically. They were teaching us to do philology: the art of reading well. Reading with care. Thinking about what the words mean. It is thus ironic that some people have become Rashi fundamentalists. They have learned not to read the Torah critically but to parrot the critical reading of Rashi. And they do not read Rashi critically. Although Ibn Ezra and Ramban questioned Rashi and pointed out where they thought he was wrong, more recent generations of teachers have lost faith in their own knowledge and judgment, and so they risk failing to relate the Torah to the lives of their people. But something has happened in the present generation. There have been great scholars, and they have acquired new sources of information: archaeology, knowledge of the ancient Near East, literary sensitivity, and knowledge of the social sciences. And so it is time for new commentaries—not to replace the classical commentators, but to join them.

My commentary is meant to do that: to be in the tradition of the classical commentaries but to use this new learning. There are many volumes of such new commentary, but they are mainly on single books of the Bible, sometimes gathered into collections of volumes on the Torah or on the whole Bible. There have been few that follow the tradition of being a single scholar's commentary on the Torah as a whole. Some take the form of introductory footnotes on a translation. I mean to do the opposite: precisely to show how united and connected the whole Torah is, and to try, like

the commentators who are our starting point, to relate it to life. In this respect the most useful part of my preparation for writing this commentary was to attend study groups for laypersons on the weekly reading of the Torah. Every week I attended one such group led by an orthodox rabbi and another led by a reform rabbi. And I had grown up studying with a conservative rabbi. Various commentaries were on the table when we studied. What I found was that none of those commentaries was answering the kinds of questions that the people at the tables were asking.

I have been attracted to synthesis. That is what I did in *Who Wrote the Bible?* and in *The Hidden Face of God.* A commentary, however, seems to be the opposite sort of human enterprise and thinking: a focus on the small, the individual insight, shedding light on the meaning of a single word, relating two adjacent passages. What I mean to do in this commentary is both: to interpret and shed light on individual words and passages—to try to find new solutions for classic problems, show cases of beauty of wording and profundity of thought—but also to show how intricately, how *essentially* connected all of it is, how logical its progression is, how essential the early stories are to what follows them, and how essential the *later* stories are to what precedes them!

The classical commentaries were a product of Europe, written before the discovery of the New World. My commentary is a product of that New World, coming at the end of the century in which that New World stepped into a prominent place in world history. And, extraordinarily, it was also the century in which Israel was reborn in its location on the tip of Asia. The classical commentaries came at the midpoint between the end of old Israel and the rebirth of new Israel. Rashi came about nine hundred years after the destruction of Israel, and we have seen the rebirth of Israel about nine hundred years after Rashi.

I shall make my comments in terms of the text itself, not in terms of the history of scholarship. That is, there is no apparatus of footnotes and citations of recent scholarly articles and books. I trust that I have done enough of that in my past books and articles to establish that I know and respect the scholarship of my field. But the purpose of this book is different. It is to make comments that reflect the conclusions I have reached in the light of the state of the field of biblical studies and in light of my own research. The exceptions will be the references to my teachers and to my colleagues (and visiting colleagues) here at my own institution, whose direct, personal communications must be acknowledged. I shall sometimes cite the classical commentators, mainly to set the work into the context that they formulated.

I stand between two poles of other kinds of commentary: midrash and critical scholarship. For example, in the case of the near-sacrifice of Isaac, at the end of the story it says "And Abraham returned to his servants." It does not mention Isaac. Some midrashim suggested that Isaac was in fact sacrificed (and later returned to life). Critical scholarship, too, has raised the startling possibility that in the original version of the text Isaac was actually sacrificed and that this story was changed by someone who

found such an ending inconceivable. I am familiar with both of these interpretations. They are intriguing and worthy of study and analysis, acceptance or rejection. But they are simply not the kind of commentary that I am doing in this book. Here I am doing my best to understand and to help others to understand the meaning of the text that we have called the Torah for two and a half thousand years. Like Rashi, I am trying to do what is known as *pěšaṭ* —pursuing the straightforward meaning of the text.

I shall comment on the usual textual, literary, historical, and linguistic matters that biblical scholars pursue, including meanings of terms and differences in the surviving versions of the text. But in making comments in these areas, I shall try to show why they matter. They are not arcane points, of interest only to scholars. They make a difference in what the Torah says and what it means. In any case, the matters I raise are not just about the text's literary and historical qualities but also about its moral messages.

Some readers will be surprised to find that I shall *not* comment on the Torah's authors and sources. I have already written two books on this subject (*Who Wrote the Bible?* and *The Hidden Book in the Bible*) and a number of articles. For those who are interested in those questions, I refer them to those works and to other works of scholarship of the last century that deal with those questions of how the Torah came to be written. But, the question for this commentary is: now that it has been written, what does it mean to us?

The idea is to be helpful both to beginners and to experienced students of the Torah, but not by providing the standard introductory points that can be found in any commentary or introduction. Rather, the aim is to show the readers new and interesting things: points they might miss, connections that are not readily seen, answers to old questions, and some new questions that have not been asked or answered before.

On my bar mitzvah my rabbi's gift to me was a copy of the Torah with a commentary. On the first page he inscribed a classic line: "Turn it over, and turn it over, because everything is in it." I do not know if everything is in fact in it, but I do know after spending a large part of my life turning it over and over that I am still finding something new all the time.

This commentary includes a new English translation of the Torah. I never had any desire to be a translator. I have done a new translation for the sole reason that none of the existing translations was adequate for my purpose. One of the recent translations uses English idioms and paraphrases a great deal, so that it reflects the translators' judgments of what the original Hebrew says. That is fine for some purposes, but, even when I agree with their judgments, I think that a translation that goes with a commentary should reflect more closely the words of the Hebrew. The commentator can explain any unusual Hebrew idioms in the comments when necessary. Another recent translation has as its stated aim to give an English reader the *feeling* of the original Hebrew. Whatever my judgment of how well it succeeds in giving the feeling of

Hebrew to a reader who does not know that language, such a project is still not the point of a translation that goes with a commentary. The purpose of a commentary's translation, rather, is the same as the purpose of the commentary itself: to make clear what the Torah says—and what it means—so one can learn from it for one's life today.

In addition to the divisions by chapter and verse, the translation and commentary are divided according to the traditional portions designated for weekly reading in synagogues. Each weekly portion—the parashah—is identified by its title at the appropriate place in the text. I hope that this will make this commentary useful to study groups who follow the weekly readings, and to individuals who wish to study the text with these comments on a weekly basis. I mean it to be useful to everyone who wants to study—and not just read—the Torah.

NOTES ON THE TRANSLATION

ranslation is an art, not a science. There have been long and tedious debates over whether a translation should be as literal as possible or should use the idioms of the language into which the text is translated. That debate has little to do with the reality of translation. There is no single rule. Some passages are clearest when translated literally. Some passages cannot possibly be translated literally without becoming misleading and sounding absurd. It is the art, the skill, and the sensitivity of the individual translator that make the difference. He or she must make the individual decision on each and every passage: how to capture it, how to convey what it means to someone who cannot read it in the original. Translation of the Bible is a string of decisions. The translator is always searching for the balance between literal and idiomatic. To get that balance exactly right is impossible. The closest any translation has come to it in English is the King James Version. All English translations since then have been steps in refining that balance, with varying degrees of success.

The translation here is my attempt at finding it. The following are some notes on a few basic points of this translation.

1. Mixing old and new English: Many translators eliminate old English terms—the whithers and thithers, whences and thences and hences, thees and thys and thous—to produce a contemporary translation; yet they still retain some archaic terms that do not have ready counterparts in contemporary English, such as "lest" and "in the midst." The result is unfortunately an English that no English speaker ever wrote or spoke. And so it just does not feel right. I have tried to produce a translation that is consistent in the English it employs. Sometimes there is simply no way to convey a Hebrew phrase's meaning in contemporary English, but I have tried for this consistency to the extent that it is possible while being true to the original.

2. Contractions: English translators rarely use contractions, even when translating discussions in common speech. But in normal spoken English, one almost never speaks for as much as five minutes without using a contraction. The result is that practically every conversation in the Bible sounds artificial in translation. I do not use contractions when translating *narration*; but, when translating *conversations*, I have used contractions where they would normally be used in English conversation.

3. Possessive case: English translators have tended to avoid the possessive case. They would rather say "the house of Moses" than "Moses' house"—even though the latter is the way people express this type of phrase ninety-nine out of a hundred times in English. The translators do this with a good intention: they are trying to capture the Hebrew, which uses a construct form to express such things. But this requires adding a word ("of"), which does not appear in the Hebrew, and it often makes an unnatural English. I freely use the possessive case. This is not an absolute rule. I still use the "of" form if it makes better sense, as, for example, in the case of a well-known phrase like "the children of Israel."

4. Starting verses with the word "and": The Hebrew conjunction begins almost every verse. It usually means "and," but it has a wider range of meanings as well, so translators make it "but," "since," "while," "then," and more. I usually leave it as "and" in English, but I do use the other terms in cases in which the context directs us to take it differently. Further, some recent translators simply leave it out altogether; so, unlike the KJV, RSV, and JPS, each sentence in these translations does not begin with the word "and." On this point, too, I prefer to preserve the feel of the original. I retain the word "and" where it occurs in the Hebrew.

5. Hebrew idioms: Sometimes I keep an idiom rather than translate it away—so long as its meaning is clear—because then my translation makes known to the reader of the translation how the Hebrew works. For example, in Gen 16:2 I translate the Hebrew quite literally as: And Abraham "listened to Sarah's voice," which is unusual and even a bit redundant in English, but I would rather have the reader of the translation see how this is expressed in the Bible than modify it to something like "listened to Sarah." Similarly in Gen 19:8 and many other places, I translate the expression "good in your eyes" literally because it is understandable in English even if it is not the common idiom.

6. Paragraphs: Separating a text into paragraphs is a basic part of writing and reading in English. It is now impossible to know for certain where the paragraphs began in the original text of the Torah. Some translations do not separate paragraphs at all. I have made decisions on where to begin new paragraphs based on the content, logic, and emphases of the stories. My divisions between sections likewise are based on these factors. They do not necessarily correspond to the points at which chapter breaks come in the text.

7. The name of God: I write it the same as it appears in the original, with the four consonants showing, thus: YHWH. This is known as the Tetragrammaton. In biblical times people would have read the name aloud. In the period following the completion of the Hebrew Bible, Jews began the practice of not saying the divine name out loud. Christians followed this practice as well. The practice for centuries was to say "the LORD" (Hebrew *'ădōnāy*) whenever one came to this word rather than to say what the four Hebrew letters actually spelled. Currently, some people have returned to the

practice of saying the name out loud. Readers should follow the same practice in reading this translation that they would follow when reading the original. If they do not pronounce the divine name aloud, then they should say "the LORD" whenever they see the four letters.

8. The gender of God: Even though, like most people, I do not conceive of a deity who is male or female, there is no way around the fact that the Torah does in fact present God in consistently masculine terms. Even the name of God is masculine. (The feminine would be THWH.) I have therefore conveyed the masculine Hebrew conception in the translation as well. My point is that in each case I am translating an original work that someone else wrote, and I do not seek to impose my theological conceptions on that person's work, nor do I want to hide that person's views by means of a translator's power.

9. The infinitive of emphasis: Hebrew sometimes has the infinitive of a verb placed before the verb itself in order to convey emphasis. Thus the Hebrew *môt yûmāt* would mean literally: "dying he shall be put to death." Most English translators use some formulation such as "he shall surely be put to death" or "he shall be put to death, yes, death" to convey it. Since the function of this infinitival formulation in Hebrew is to emphasize, I think that it is best translated by the usual mechanisms of emphasis in English. The usual ways to convey emphasis in English are the use of either italics or exclamation points. I therefore generally use italics to convey Hebrew infinitival emphatics. Occasionally I use an exclamation point to convey this emphasis. In a few cases in which neither of these English conventions properly conveys the Hebrew meaning, I leave the infinitive untranslated.

10. Cognate accusatives: Cognate accusatives (for example, "I dreamed a dream," "I did a deed") are fairly common and a hallmark of literary style in Biblical Hebrew. Cognate accusatives are not incorrect grammatically in English but are sufficiently rare as to be felt by English readers to be uncomfortable. And so, like nearly all translators, I convey cognate accusatives without repeating the cognate forms. Thus, for example, I translate *hălôm hālamtî* as "I had a dream" rather than the literal "I dreamed a dream."

11. Cohortatives: Like nearly all translators, I convey the cohortative as "let me" or "let us" or "may I" or "may we." Unfortunately, these English forms suggest permission, as if the person using the cohortative is asking to be allowed to do something. The reader should note that the Hebrew does not usually have such a connotation. It merely expresses the person's wish or intent, without necessarily implying that action or permission by anyone else is necessary.

12. Jussives: The same applies to the jussive, which I convey as "let it" or "let him" or "let them" or "let there be" or "may he" or "may they."

13. A redundant formulation: The formulation "And he said, saying . . ." occurs fairly often in the Hebrew text. Although it feels redundant and awkward in English, I still prefer to retain the extra word—"saying"—to reflect the original.

14. Etymologies of names: Often a story is told that explains the origin of a name of a person or place. For example, the name Isaac, Hebrew *yiṣḥāq*, means "he laughs" or "let him laugh," and it is derived in this story from the fact that Sarah laughs at the idea that she could give birth to a son in her old age (Gen 18:12–15). It is difficult to convey this in an English translation without adding a bracketed or footnoted comment. Similarly with the names Noah, Babel, Jacob, Moses, and so on, it is usually impossible to convey such Hebrew etymological material in translation. A note or bracketed insertion interrupts the story for the reader, and I did not want to do that. So, as most translators have done in the past, I have left the text itself alone, accepting the fact that this is one of the inherent limitations of translation, and I have explained some of the etymologies in the comments.

15. Words with multiple translations: Hebrew terms sometimes have a wider range of meaning than any single English counterpart. Hebrew *ăbādîm*, for example, can be "slave" or "servant" and therefore must be translated by different English words in different contexts. Hebrew *ʿāyēp* can be "tired," "exhausted," "faint," or "famished." Hebrew *gādōl* can be "big," "great," "high," or "old." Hebrew terms for groups of animals—flock, herd, sheep, oxen, cows, animals, domestic animals, wild animals—do not correspond exactly to English terms, and it is virtually impossible to translate each term consistently through the *Tanak*. Translators must make decisions in translating such terms individually in their contexts.

16. The text: The translation follows the Hebrew text that is beside it. That is, it is a translation of the Masoretic Text. I raise notable cases of differences in the Septuagint, Dead Sea Scrolls, and other versions in the comments below the text.

KEY TO TRANSCRIPTIONS OF BIBLICAL HEBREW

CONSONANTS		VOWELS	
Transcription	Hebrew Letter	Transcription	Hebrew Letter
ʾ	א	ba	בַּ
b	ב	bā	בָּ
g	ג	be	בֶּ
d	ד	bē	בֵּ
h	ה	bê	בֵּי
w	ו	bi	בִּ
z	ז	bî	בִּי
ḥ	ח	bō	בֹּ
ṭ	ט	bô	בּוֹ
y	י	bu	בֻּ
k	כ	bû	בּוּ
l	ל	bĕ	בְּ
m	מ		
n	נ		
s	ס		
ʿ	ע		
p	פ		
ṣ	צ		
q	ק		
r	ר		
š	שׁ		
ś	שׂ		
t	ת		

The Hebrew letter ו, commonly pronounced as a *v* (*vav*) at present, was pronounced as a *w* (*waw*) in the biblical period. Reduced (*ḥatep*) vowels are marked with breve. Vowels with *matres lectionis* (*waw, yod*) are marked with circumflex. The *hē* mater (for example, in the feminine ending -ah) is represented by the letter -h. Forms of the letters *b g d k p t*, which sometimes have a *daghesh* and sometimes do not, are not distinguished by different letters in transcription.

GENESIS

———— ✦ ————

בראשית

———— ✦ ————

TRANSLATION & COMMENTARY

*T*he first portion of the Torah has a double role: it conveys its own story, and it sets the context of the entire Torah. The Torah's stories have been observed to be rich in background, as opposed to, for example, the epic poems of Homer. In Homer each episode is self-contained: all the information that a reader needs is provided then and there, and all action is in the foreground. That is fine, but it is not the way of the Torah. To read the Torah at any level beyond "Sunday school," one must have a sense of the whole when one reads the parts. To comprehend what happens in the exodus and in the revelation at Sinai, you have to know what has happened in Genesis 1. Like some films that begin with a sweeping shot that then narrows, so the first chapter of Genesis moves gradually from a picture of the skies and the earth down to the first man and woman. The story's focus will continue to narrow: from the universe to the earth to humankind to specific lands and peoples to a single family. (It will expand back out to nations in Exodus.) But the wider concern with skies and the entire earth that is established here in the first portion will remain. When the story narrows to a singular divine relationship with Abraham, it will still be with the ultimate aim that this will be "a blessing to *all the families of the earth.*" Every biblical scene will be laden—artistically, theologically, psychologically, spiritually—with all that has come before. So when we read later of a man and his son going up a mountain to perform a fearful sacrifice, that moment in the history of a family is set in a cosmic context of the creation of the universe and the nature of the relationship between the creator and humankind. You *can* read the account of the binding of Isaac without being aware of the account of the creation or the account of the covenant between God and Abraham, but you lose something. The something that you lose—depth—is one of the essential qualities of the Torah.

The first portion initiates the historical flow of the Torah (and of the entire *Tanak*). It establishes that this is to be a related, linear sequence of events through generations. That may seem so natural to us now that we find this point obvious and banal. But the texts of the Torah are *the first texts on earth known to do this.* The ancient world did not write history prior to these accounts. The Torah's accounts are the first human attempts to recount history. Whether one believes all or part or none of its history to be true is a separate matter. The literary point is that this had the effect of producing a

text that was rich in background: every event carries the weight of everything that comes before it. And the historical point is that this was a new way to conceive of time and human destiny.

There is also a theological point: this was a new way to conceive of a God. The difference between the Torah's conception of God and the pagan world's conception is not merely arithmetic: one versus many. The pagan deities were known through their functions in nature: The sun god, Shamash, *was* the sun. If one wanted to know the essence of Shamash, the thing to do was to contemplate the sun. If you wanted to know the essence of the grain deity Dagon, you contemplated wheat. To know Yamm, contemplate the sea. But the God of the Torah was different, creating all of nature— and therefore not knowable or identifiable through any one element of nature. One could learn no more about this God by contemplating the sea than by contemplating grain, sky, or anything else. The essence of this God remains hidden. One does not know God through nature but by the divine acts in history. One never finds out what God *is*, but rather what God *does*—and what God *says*. This conception, which informs all of biblical narrative, did not necessarily have to be developed at the very beginning of the story, but it was. Parashat Bereshit establishes this by beginning with accounts of creation and by then flowing through the first ten generations of humankind. (Those "begat" lists are thus more important than people generally think.)

The Torah's theology is thus inseparable from its history and from its literary qualities. Ultimately, there is no such thing as "The Bible as Literature" or "The Bible as History" or "The Bible as . . . anything." There is: the Bible.

IN THE BEGINNING

בְּרֵאשִׁית

1 ¹In the beginning of God's creating the skies and the earth

1 ‏¹בְּרֵאשִׁית בָּרָא אֱלֹהִים אֵת הַשָּׁמַיִם וְאֵת

1:1. **In the beginning of God's creating the skies and the earth.** Rashi began his commentary with the remark that the Torah could have begun with the first commandment to Israel—the commandment to observe Passover—which does not come until Exodus 12, rather than with creation. He answered that it begins with creation in order to establish God's ownership of all the world—and therefore God's right to give the promised land to Israel. I suggest that the lesson that we learn from the fact that the Torah does not begin with the first commandment is precisely that the commandments are not the sole purpose of the Torah. The Torah's *story* is no less important than the commandments that it contains. Law in the Bible is never given separately from history. The Ten Commandments do not begin with the first "Thou shalt" but with the historical fact that "I brought you out of the land of Egypt . . ."

Another lesson is that, in the Torah, the divine bond with Israel is ultimately tied to the divine relationship with all of humankind. (Rashi did not refer to the first *commandment*, which is "Be fruitful and multiply" and is given to all humankind, but rather to the first commandment to *Israel*, which is Passover.) The first eleven chapters establish a connection between God and the entire universe. They depict the formation of a relationship between the creator and all the families of the earth. This relationship will remain as the crucial background to the story of Israel that will take up the rest of the Torah.

1:1. **In the beginning of God's creating the skies and the earth.** The Torah begins with two pictures of the creation. The first (Gen 1:1–2:3) is a universal conception. The second (2:4–25) is more down-to-earth. The first has a cosmic feeling about it. Few other passages in the Hebrew Bible generate this feeling. The concern of the Hebrew Bible generally is history, not the cosmos, but Genesis 1 is an exception. There is a power about this portrait of a transcendent God constructing the skies and earth in an ordered seven-day series. In it, the stages of the fashioning of the heavenly bodies above are mixed with the fashioning of the land and seas below.

The translation of the Torah's first phrase is a classic problem. Even at the risk of a slightly awkward English, I have translated this line literally, not only to make it reflect the Hebrew, but to show the significant parallel between this opening and the opening of the second picture of creation in Gen 2:4, thus:

In	the	beginning	of	God's	creating	the skies	and	the earth
In	the	day	of	YHWH God's	making	earth	and	skies

(The second line is translated slightly differently above because it is not possible to reproduce the doubled divine identification, YHWH God, with a possessive in English.)

—2when the earth had been shapeless and formless, and darkness was on the face of the deep, and God's spirit was hovering on the face of the water—

3God said, "Let there be light." And there was

הָאָֽרֶץ: 2וְהָאָ֗רֶץ הָיְתָ֥ה תֹ֨הוּ֙ וָבֹ֔הוּ וְחֹ֖שֶׁךְ עַל־פְּנֵ֣י תְה֑וֹם וְר֣וּחַ אֱלֹהִ֔ים מְרַחֶ֖פֶת עַל־פְּנֵ֥י הַמָּֽיִם: 3וַיֹּ֥אמֶר אֱלֹהִ֖ים יְהִ֣י א֑וֹר וַֽיְהִי־אֽוֹר: 4וַיַּ֧רְא אֱלֹהִ֛ים

Note that this first, universal conception puts the skies first, while the second, more earthly account starts with earth.

1:2. **the earth had been.** Here is a case in which a tiny point of grammar makes a difference for theology. In the Hebrew of this verse, the noun comes before the verb (in the perfect form). This is now known to be the way of conveying the past perfect in Biblical Hebrew. This point of grammar means that this verse does not mean "the earth was shapeless and formless"—referring to the condition of the earth starting the instant after it was created. This verse rather means that "the earth *had been* shapeless and formless"—that is, it had already existed in this shapeless condition *prior* to the creation. Creation of matter in the Torah is not out of nothing (*creatio ex nihilo*), as many have claimed. And the Torah is not claiming to be telling events from the beginning of time.

1:2. **shapeless and formless.** The two words in the Hebrew, *tōhû* and *bōhû*, are understood to mean virtually the same thing. This is the first appearance in the Torah of a phenomenon in biblical language known as hendiadys, in which two connected words are used to signify one thing. ("Wine and beer" [Lev 10:9] may be a hendiadys as well, or it may be a merism, a similar construction in which two words are used to signify a totality; so that "wine and beer" means all alcoholic beverages.) The hendiadys of "*tōhû* and *bōhû*," plus the references to the deep and the water, yields a picture of an undifferentiated, shapeless fluid that had existed prior to creation.

1:2. **God's spirit.** Or "wind of God." Words for "soul" or "spirit" in Hebrew frequently denote wind or breath (likewise in Greek: *pneuma* means both wind and spirit). This suggests that, in the ancient world, life was associated, in the first place, with respiration, as opposed to later determinations of life in terms of blood circulation or brain activity. Thus the animation of the first human will be described this way: "And He blew into his nostrils the breath of life, and the human became a living being."

1:2. **God's spirit/wind hovering on the face of the water.** The parallel with the ancient pagan creation myth of the wind god (Enlil, or Marduk) defeating the goddess of the waters (Tiamat; compare Hebrew *tĕhôm*, translated "the deep," in this verse) is striking. The *difference* between the two is striking, too: in the Torah the water and all other components of the universe are no longer regarded as gods. Nature is demythologized.

1:3. **Let there be light.** God creates light simply by saying the words: "Let there be" (the Hebrew jussive). Only light is expressly created from nothing (*creatio ex nihilo*). All other elements of creation may possibly be formed out of preexisting matter, that is, from the initially undifferentiated chaos. Thus God later says, "Let there be a space,"

light. 4And God saw the light, that it was good, and God separated between the light and the darkness. 5And God called the light "day" and called the darkness "night." And there was evening, and there was morning: one day.

6And God said, "Let there be a space within

אֶת־הָאוֹר כִּי־ט֑וֹב וַיַּבְדֵּ֣ל אֱלֹהִ֔ים בֵּ֥ין הָא֖וֹר וּבֵ֥ין הַחֹֽשֶׁךְ: 5וַיִּקְרָ֨א אֱלֹהִ֤ים ׀ לָאוֹר֙ י֔וֹם וְלַחֹ֖שֶׁךְ קָ֣רָא לָ֑יְלָה וַֽיְהִי־עֶ֥רֶב וַֽיְהִי־בֹ֖קֶר י֥וֹם אֶחָֽד: פ 6וַיֹּ֣אמֶר אֱלֹהִ֔ים יְהִ֥י רָקִ֖יעַ בְּת֣וֹךְ הַמָּ֑יִם וִיהִ֣י מַבְדִּ֔יל בֵּ֥ין

---

but the text then adds, "And God *made* the space." And God says, "Let there be sources of light," but the text adds, "And God *made* the sources of light." So we cannot understand these things to be formed simply by the words "Let there be." Now we can appreciate the importance of understanding the Torah's first words correctly: The Torah does not claim to report everything that has occurred since the beginning of space and time. It does not say, "In the beginning, God created the skies and the earth." It rather says, "In the beginning of God's creating the skies and the earth, when the earth had been shapeless and formless . . ." That is, there is preexisting matter, which is in a state of watery chaos. Subsequent matter—dry land, heavenly bodies, plants, animals—may be formed out of this undifferentiated fluid. In Greece, the first philosopher, Thales, later proposed such a concept, that all things derive from water. Examples from other cultures could be cited as well. There appears to be an essential human feeling that everything derives originally from water, which is hardly surprising given that we—and all life on this planet—did in fact proceed from water.

1:4. **God separated.** Initially there is only the watery chaos: shapeless and formless. Then creation is the making of distinctions: "And God separated between the light and the darkness," "And separated between the water that was under the space and the water that was above the space." Then more distinctions: between dry land and seas, among plants and animals "each according to its kind," between day and night, and so on. In each case, creation is the act of separating a thing from the rest of matter and then giving it a name.

1:5. **God called the light "day" and called the darkness "night."** The first day also includes the creation of the ordering of time. Before the invention of day and night, time no less than space would be undifferentiated: "formless." Light, the one thing that is totally *ex nihilo*, is thus essential to all that follows: the separating between light and dark in an ordered arrangement initiates a sequence of distinctions of time and space, and these distinctions embody creation.

1:5. **And there was evening, and there was morning.** It is sometimes claimed mistakenly that Genesis 1 is poetry. True, the wording is powerful and beautiful, and the recurring words "And there was evening, and there was morning" and the chronology that they reflect lend a formulaic order to the chapter. But that does not make the text poetry. It is prose.

1:6. **space.** The distinction between "the water that was under the space and the water that was above the space" is particularly important and was frequently confusing to readers who were not certain of the meaning of the old term for this space: "fir-

the water, and let it separate between water and water." ⁷And God made the space, and it sepa-

מַיִם לָמָיִם: ⁷וַיַּעַשׂ אֱלֹהִים אֶת־הָרָקִיעַ וַיַּבְדֵּל בֵּין

mament." As Rashi perceived, the text pictures a territory formed in the middle of the watery chaos, a giant bubble of air surrounded on all sides by water. Once the land is created, the universe as pictured in Genesis is a habitable bubble, with land and seas at its base, surrounded by a mass of water. Like this:

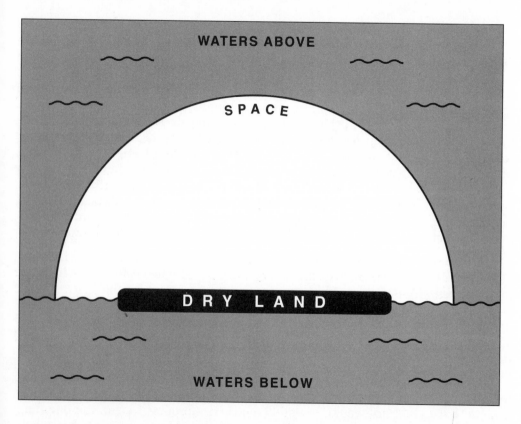

God calls the space "skies." "The skies" (or "heavens") here refer simply to space, to the sky that we see, and not to some other, unseen place where God dwells or where people dwell after their death.

The reference to "water that was above the space" presumably reflects the fact that when the ancients looked at the sky they understood from its blue color that there was water up there above the air. As when we look out at the horizon on a clear day and can barely distinguish where the blue sea ends and the blue sky begins, so they pictured the earth as surrounded by water above and below. The space was the invisible substance that holds the upper waters back. It is important to appreciate this picture of the cosmos with which the Torah begins or one cannot understand other matters that come later, especially the story of the flood. See the comment on Gen 7:11.

rated between the water that was under the space and the water that was above the space. And it was so. 8And God called the space "skies." And there was evening, and there was morning: a second day.

9And God said, "Let the waters be concentrated under the skies into one place, and let the land appear." And it was so. 10And God called the land "earth," and called the concentration of the waters "seas." And God saw that it was good.

הַמַּ֙יִם֙ אֲשֶׁר֙ מִתַּ֣חַת לָרָקִ֔יעַ וּבֵ֣ין הַמַּ֔יִם אֲשֶׁ֖ר מֵעַ֣ל לָרָקִ֑יעַ וַֽיְהִי־כֵֽן׃ 8וַיִּקְרָ֧א אֱלֹהִ֛ים לָֽרָקִ֖יעַ שָׁמָ֑יִם וַֽיְהִי־עֶ֥רֶב וַֽיְהִי־בֹ֖קֶר י֥וֹם שֵׁנִֽי׃ פ 9וַיֹּ֣אמֶר אֱלֹהִ֗ים יִקָּו֨וּ הַמַּ֜יִם מִתַּ֤חַת הַשָּׁמַ֙יִם֙ אֶל־מָק֣וֹם אֶחָ֔ד וְתֵרָאֶ֖ה הַיַּבָּשָׁ֑ה וַֽיְהִי־כֵֽן׃ 10וַיִּקְרָ֨א אֱלֹהִ֤ים ׀ לַיַּבָּשָׁה֙ אֶ֔רֶץ וּלְמִקְוֵ֥ה הַמַּ֖יִם קָרָ֣א יַמִּ֑ים וַיַּ֥רְא אֱלֹהִ֖ים כִּי־טֽוֹב׃

1:6. **Let there be a space.** The "firmament" is either the entire air space or, more probably, just the transparent edge of the space, like a glass dome (Ramban says "like a tent"), which is actually up against the water. It is difficult to say which. The Hebrew root of the word, רקיע, refers to the way in which a goldsmith hammers gold leaf very thin. This may suggest that the firmament is best understood to be the thin outermost layer of the air space. Still, we must be cautious not to commit the etymological fallacy. That means: *we should not automatically derive the meaning of a word from its root.* People commonly make this mistake because the Hebrew of the *Tanak* is so beautifully constructed around three-letter roots. Looking for root meanings is usually very helpful. But sometimes it can lead to misunderstandings. Words can evolve away from their root meanings over centuries.

1:8. **God called the space "skies."** The space (or "firmament") and the sky are the same thing. This appears to be an explanation of what the sky *is*. It is a transparent shell or space that holds back the upper waters.

1:8. **a second day.** The first day's account concludes with the cardinal number: "one day." All of the following accounts conclude with ordinal numbers: "a second day," "a third day," and so on. This sets off the first day more blatantly as something special in itself rather than merely the first step in an order. It may be because the first day's creation—light—is qualitatively different from all other things. Or it may be because the opening day involves the birth of *creation itself.* Or it may be that the first unit involves the creation of a *day* as an entity. A more mundane explanation—which is presumably the *pĕšaṭ* —would be that this simply is a known biblical form, which has no special meaning for the matter of creation, because it occurs elsewhere as well. See the numbering of the four rivers of Eden, which likewise uses the cardinal "one" and then the ordinals "second, third, fourth" (Gen 2:11–14; see also 2 Sam 4:2).

1:10,12. **God saw that it was good.** God observes the day's product to be good on every day except the second day. Instead, the text says "it was good" twice on the third day. Rashi suggested that this is because the task of the division of the waters was begun on the second day but not finished until the third. But, in that case, one might still ask why the task had to be thus split between two days. The reason why the second day's work—the formation of the space, with water above and below—is not pro-

11And God said, "Let the earth generate plants, vegetation that produces seed, fruit trees, each making fruit of its own kind, which has its seed in it, on the earth. And it was so: 12The earth brought out plants, vegetation that produces seeds of its own kind, and trees that make fruit that each has seeds of its own kind in it. And God saw that it was good. 13And there was evening, and there was morning: a third day.

14And God said, "Let there be lights in the space of the skies to distinguish between the day and the night, and they will be for signs and for appointed times and for days and years. 15And they will be for lights in the space of the skies to shed light on the earth." And it was so. 16And

11וַיֹּאמֶר אֱלֹהִים תַּדְשֵׁא הָאָרֶץ דֶּשֶׁא עֵשֶׂב מַזְרִיעַ זֶרַע עֵץ פְּרִי עֹשֶׂה פְּרִי לְמִינוֹ אֲשֶׁר זַרְעוֹ־בוֹ עַל־הָאָרֶץ וַיְהִי־כֵן: 12וַתּוֹצֵא הָאָרֶץ דֶּשֶׁא עֵשֶׂב מַזְרִיעַ זֶרַע לְמִינֵהוּ וְעֵץ עֹשֶׂה־פְּרִי אֲשֶׁר זַרְעוֹ־בוֹ לְמִינֵהוּ וַיַּרְא אֱלֹהִים כִּי־טוֹב: פ 13וַיְהִי־עֶרֶב וַיְהִי־בֹקֶר יוֹם שְׁלִישִׁי: פ 14וַיֹּאמֶר אֱלֹהִים יְהִי מְאֹרֹת בִּרְקִיעַ הַשָּׁמַיִם לְהַבְדִּיל בֵּין הַיּוֹם וּבֵין הַלָּיְלָה וְהָיוּ לְאֹתֹת וּלְמוֹעֲדִים וּלְיָמִים וְשָׁנִים: 15וְהָיוּ לִמְאוֹרֹת בִּרְקִיעַ הַשָּׁמַיִם לְהָאִיר עַל־הָאָרֶץ וַיְהִי־כֵן:

nounced "good" may rather be that God will later choose to break this structure (in the flood story, Gen 7:11). The double notice that "it was good" on the third day may be because (1) the formation of land and (2) the land's generation of plants are each regarded as creations worthy of notice.

This explanation is based on the Masoretic Text (MT). The Greek text (Septuagint), on the other hand, includes the words "And God saw that it was good" on the second day as well. It may be that these words were simply omitted from the MT by a scribe whose eye jumped from the first two letters of this line (Hebrew וי) to the beginning of the next line ("And there was evening . . ."), which begins with the same two first letters (וי). This is called haplography.

1:12. **vegetation that produces seeds of its own kind.** The fact that plants (and, later, animals) not only reproduce but also propagate offspring like themselves, rather than random production of new life-forms, is not taken for granted. It is treated as both fundamental and a wonder of life, which needed an explicit creative utterance by the deity.

1:13. **third day.** On the third day the divine attention turns from the cosmos to the world: first land, then the vegetation that the land yields. On the fourth day the attention turns back to the skies: the creation of lights in the sky. The alternation between skies and earth continues as the deity turns back to the earth on the fifth day. This conveys that the earth and the skies are not conceptually separate. Understanding the nature of the universe is essential to understanding our place as humans on earth. We have especially come to realize this through the discoveries in astronomy and physics of the last century.

1:15. **they will be for lights in the space.** Note that daylight is not understood here to derive from the sun. The text understands the light that surrounds us in the daytime to be an independent creation of God, which has already taken place on the first day.

10

God made the two big lights—the bigger light for the regulation of the day and the smaller light for the regulation of the night—and the stars. ¹⁷And God set them in the space of the skies to shed light on the earth ¹⁸and to regulate the day and the night and to distinguish between the light and the darkness. And God saw that it was good. ¹⁹And there was evening, and there was morning: a fourth day.

²⁰And God said, "Let the water swarm with a swarm of living beings, and let birds fly over the earth on the face of the space of the skies." ²¹And God created the big sea serpents and all the living beings that creep, with which the water swarmed, by their kinds, and every winged bird by its kind. And God saw that it was good. ²²And God blessed them, saying, "Be fruitful and multiply and fill the water in the seas, and let the birds multiply in the earth." ²³And there was evening and there was morning, a fifth day.

²⁴And God said, "Let the earth bring out living

וַיַּ֣עַשׂ אֱלֹהִ֔ים אֶת־שְׁנֵ֥י הַמְּאֹרֹ֖ת הַגְּדֹלִ֑ים אֶת־ ¹⁶
הַמָּא֤וֹר הַגָּדֹל֙ לְמֶמְשֶׁ֣לֶת הַיּ֔וֹם וְאֶת־הַמָּא֤וֹר הַקָּטֹן֙
לְמֶמְשֶׁ֣לֶת הַלַּ֔יְלָה וְאֵ֖ת הַכּוֹכָבִֽים: וַיִּתֵּ֥ן אֹתָ֛ם ¹⁷
אֱלֹהִ֖ים בִּרְקִ֣יעַ הַשָּׁמָ֑יִם לְהָאִ֖יר עַל־הָאָֽרֶץ:
וְלִמְשֹׁל֙ בַּיּ֣וֹם וּבַלַּ֔יְלָה וּֽלֲהַבְדִּ֔יל בֵּ֥ין הָא֖וֹר וּבֵ֣ין ¹⁸
הַחֹ֑שֶׁךְ וַיַּ֥רְא אֱלֹהִ֖ים כִּי־טֽוֹב: וַֽיְהִי־עֶ֥רֶב וַֽיְהִי־ ¹⁹
בֹ֖קֶר י֥וֹם רְבִיעִֽי: פ   וַיֹּ֣אמֶר אֱלֹהִ֔ים יִשְׁרְצ֣וּ ²⁰
הַמַּ֔יִם שֶׁ֖רֶץ נֶ֣פֶשׁ חַיָּ֑ה וְעוֹף֙ יְעוֹפֵ֣ף עַל־הָאָ֔רֶץ עַל־
פְּנֵ֖י רְקִ֥יעַ הַשָּׁמָֽיִם: וַיִּבְרָ֣א אֱלֹהִ֔ים אֶת־הַתַּנִּינִ֖ם ²¹
הַגְּדֹלִ֑ים וְאֵ֣ת כָּל־נֶ֣פֶשׁ הַֽחַיָּ֣ה ׀ הָֽרֹמֶ֡שֶׂת אֲשֶׁר֩ שָׁרְצ֨וּ
הַמַּ֜יִם לְמִֽינֵהֶ֗ם וְאֵ֨ת כָּל־ע֤וֹף כָּנָף֙ לְמִינֵ֔הוּ וַיַּ֥רְא
אֱלֹהִ֖ים כִּי־טֽוֹב: וַיְבָ֧רֶךְ אֹתָ֛ם אֱלֹהִ֖ים לֵאמֹ֑ר ²²
פְּר֣וּ וּרְב֗וּ וּמִלְא֤וּ אֶת־הַמַּ֨יִם֙ בַּיַּמִּ֔ים וְהָע֖וֹף יִ֥רֶב
בָּאָֽרֶץ: וַֽיְהִי־עֶ֥רֶב וַֽיְהִי־בֹ֖קֶר י֥וֹם חֲמִישִֽׁי: פ ²³
וַיֹּ֣אמֶר אֱלֹהִ֔ים תּוֹצֵ֤א הָאָ֨רֶץ֙ נֶ֣פֶשׁ חַיָּה֙ לְמִינָ֔הּ ²⁴

The sun, moon, and stars are understood here to be light *sources*—like a lamp or torch, only stronger. Their purpose is also to be markers of time: days, years, appointed occasions.

This also implies an answer to an old question: People have questioned whether the first three days are twenty-four-hour days since the sun is not created until the fourth day. But light, day, and night are not understood here to depend on the existence of the sun, so there is no reason to think that the word "day" means anything different on the first two days than what it means everywhere else in the Torah. People's reason for raising this is often to reconcile the biblical creation story with current evidence on the earth's age. But it is better to recognize that the biblical story does not match the evidence than to stretch the story's plain meaning in order to make it fit better with our current state of knowledge.

1:16. **the bigger light.** The sun.

1:16. **the smaller light.** The moon.

1:21. **sea serpents.** Hebrew *tannîn*. This is generally understood to refer to some giant serpentlike creatures that were formed at creation but later destroyed, associated with the monsters Rahab (Isa 51:9) or Leviathan (Isa 27:1). Later, Aaron's staff (and the Egyptian magicians' staffs) turns into such a creature (not merely a snake!) at the Egyptian court (Exod 7:9–12).

beings by their kind, domestic animal and creeping and creeping thing and wild animals of the earth by their kind." And it was so. 25And God made the wild animals of the earth by their kind and the domestic animals by their kind and every creeping thing of the ground by their kind. And God saw that it was good.

26And God said, "Let us make a human, in our image, according to our likeness, and let them dominate the fish of the sea and the birds of the skies and the domestic animals and all the earth and all the creeping things that creep on the earth." 27And God created the human in His image. He created it in the image of God; He created them male and female. 28And God blessed

בְּהֵמָה וָרֶמֶשׂ וְחַיְתוֹ־אֶרֶץ לְמִינָהּ וַיְהִי־כֵן: 25וַיַּעַשׂ אֱלֹהִים אֶת־חַיַּת הָאָרֶץ לְמִינָהּ וְאֶת־הַבְּהֵמָה לְמִינָהּ וְאֵת כָּל־רֶמֶשׂ הָאֲדָמָה לְמִינֵהוּ וַיַּרְא אֱלֹהִים כִּי־טוֹב: 26וַיֹּאמֶר אֱלֹהִים נַעֲשֶׂה אָדָם בְּצַלְמֵנוּ כִּדְמוּתֵנוּ וְיִרְדּוּ בִדְגַת הַיָּם וּבְעוֹף הַשָּׁמַיִם וּבַבְּהֵמָה וּבְכָל־הָאָרֶץ וּבְכָל־הָרֶמֶשׂ הָרֹמֵשׂ עַל־הָאָרֶץ: 27וַיִּבְרָא אֱלֹהִים ׀ אֶת־הָאָדָם בְּצַלְמוֹ בְּצֶלֶם אֱלֹהִים בָּרָא אֹתוֹ זָכָר וּנְקֵבָה בָּרָא אֹתָם:

1:26. **Let us make.** Why does God speak in the plural here? Some take the plural to be "the royal we" as used by royalty and the papacy among humans, but this alone does not account for the fact that it occurs only in the opening chapters of the Torah and nowhere else. Others take the plural to mean that God is addressing a heavenly court of angels, seraphim, or other heavenly creatures, although this, too, does not explain the limitation of the phenomenon to the opening chapters. More plausible, though by no means certain, is the suggestion that it is an Israelite, monotheistic reflection of the pagan language of the divine council. In pagan myth, the chief god, when formally speaking for the council of the gods, speaks in the plural. Such language might be appropriate for the opening chapters of the Torah, thus asserting that the God of Israel has taken over this role.

1:27. **He.** In the present age many people choose not to conceive of the deity as male or female. In the Torah, however, there are passages in which one cannot help but understand and translate a divine reference as masculine. The Torah depicts God as male. Rather than impose a present view on an ancient text, I feel bound to leave the masculine references to the deity as they are, although I urge those who study the Torah to contemplate what this has meant through the ages from the time of the writing of the Torah to their own respective times.

1:27. **in the image of God**. We argue but truly do not know what is meant: whether a physical, spiritual, or intellectual image of God. (Some light may be shed on this by Gen 5:3. See the comment there.) Whatever it means, though, it implies that humans are understood here to share in the divine in a way that a lion or cow does not. That is crucial to all that will follow. The paradox, inherent in the divine-human relationship, is that only humans have some element of the divine, and only humans would, by their very nature, aspire to the divine, yet God regularly communicates with them by means of *commands*. Although made in the image of God, they remain subordinates. In biblical terms, that would not bother a camel or a dove. It will bother humans a great deal.

them, and God said to them, "Be fruitful and multiply and fill the earth and subdue it and dominate the fish of the sea and the birds of the skies and every animal that creeps on the earth." ²⁹And God said, "Here, I have placed all the vegetation that produces seed that is on the face of all the earth for you and every tree, which has in it the fruit of a tree producing seed. It will be food for you ³⁰and for all the wild animals of the earth and for all the birds of the skies and for all the creeping things on the earth, everything in which there is a living being: every plant of vegetation, for food." And it was so.

³¹And God saw everything that He had made, and, here, it was very good. And there was evening and there was morning, the sixth day.

כח וַיְבָ֣רֶךְ אֹתָם֮ אֱלֹהִים֒ וַיֹּ֨אמֶר לָהֶ֜ם אֱלֹהִ֗ים פְּר֥וּ וּרְב֛וּ וּמִלְא֥וּ אֶת־הָאָ֖רֶץ וְכִבְשֻׁ֑הָ וּרְד֞וּ בִּדְגַ֤ת הַיָּם֙ וּבְע֣וֹף הַשָּׁמַ֔יִם וּבְכָל־חַיָּ֖ה הָֽרֹמֶ֥שֶׂת עַל־הָאָֽרֶץ: כט וַיֹּ֣אמֶר אֱלֹהִ֗ים הִנֵּה֩ נָתַ֨תִּי לָכֶ֜ם אֶת־כָּל־עֵ֣שֶׂב ׀ זֹרֵ֣עַ זֶ֗רַע אֲשֶׁר֙ עַל־פְּנֵ֣י כָל־הָאָ֔רֶץ וְאֶת־כָּל־הָעֵ֛ץ אֲשֶׁר־בּ֥וֹ פְרִי־עֵ֖ץ זֹרֵ֣עַ זָ֑רַע לָכֶ֥ם יִֽהְיֶ֖ה לְאָכְלָֽה: ל וּֽלְכָל־חַיַּ֣ת הָ֠אָרֶץ וּלְכָל־ע֨וֹף הַשָּׁמַ֜יִם וּלְכֹ֣ל ׀ רוֹמֵ֣שׂ עַל־הָאָ֗רֶץ אֲשֶׁר־בּוֹ֙ נֶ֣פֶשׁ חַיָּ֔ה אֶת־כָּל־יֶ֥רֶק עֵ֖שֶׂב לְאָכְלָ֑ה וַֽיְהִי־כֵֽן: לא וַיַּ֤רְא אֱלֹהִים֙ אֶת־כָּל־אֲשֶׁ֣ר עָשָׂ֔ה וְהִנֵּה־ט֖וֹב מְאֹ֑ד וַֽיְהִי־עֶ֥רֶב וַֽיְהִי־בֹ֖קֶר

1:27. **in the image of God; He created them male and female.** Both men and women are created in the divine image. If the physical image of God is meant, it is difficult to say what is implied about the divine appearance.

1:28. **Be fruitful and multiply and fill the earth.** This commandment has now been fulfilled.

1:28. **subdue it and dominate.** Incredibly, some have interpreted this command to mean that humans have permission to abuse the earth and animal and plant life—as if a command from God to rule did not imply to be a *good* ruler!

1:31. **everything that He had made, and, here, it was very good.** The initial state of creation is regarded as satisfactory. Things will soon go wrong, but it is unclear if that means that the "good" initial state becomes flawed, or if there is hope that the course of events will fit into an ultimately good structure in "the length of days." One of the most remarkable results of having a sense of the *Tanak* as a whole when one reads the parts is that one can experience the overwhelming irony of God's judging everything to be *good* in Genesis 1 when so much will go wrong later. The deity notes on every working day that what was created in that day is good (except on Monday, but it compensates, saying "God saw that it was good" twice on Tuesday; see the comment on 1:10,12). And at the end of the six days God observes that everything is *very* good. But before we are even out of Parashat Bereshit we read that God begins to see "that human bad was multiplied in the earth" (6:5). Above all, the struggle between God and humans will recur and unfold powerfully and painfully. The day in which the humans are created is declared to be good, but this condition ends very soon. No biblical hero or heroine will be unequivocally perfect. Individuals and nations, Israel and all of humankind, will be pictured in conflict with the creator for the great majority of the text that will follow. Parashat Bereshit is a portent of this coming story, which is arguably the central story of the *Tanak*, because its first chapter contains the

2 ¹And the skies and the earth and all their array were finished. ²And in the seventh day God finished His work that He had done and

creation of humans that is divinely dubbed *good,* and its last verses contain the sad report that God regrets making the humans in the earth (6:6ff.). Importantly, Parashat Bereshit ends not with the deity's mournful statement that "I regret that I made them" (6:7) but rather with a point of hope: that Noah found favor in the divine sight (6:8). And this note, that there can be hope for humankind based on the acts of righteous individuals, is also a portent of the end of the story. In the last installment in the narrative, the book of Nehemiah, God does not speak, there are no extraordinary reports of miracles, no angels, dreams, talking animals, or Urim and Tummim (see comment on Exod 28:30); but humans, now having to live without these things, behave better and appear to be more committed to the Torah than perhaps any other generation in the Bible. (Nehemiah comes last in the Leningrad Codex, the oldest complete manuscript of the entire *Tanak.* Printed editions of the Hebrew Bible generally have the books of Chronicles last, but the story ends with Nehemiah.) Nehemiah ends by asking his God to "Remember me for good" (13:31). The fact that the Hebrew Bible's story concludes with the word "good" is an exquisite, hopeful bookend to the opening chapter of Genesis, in which everything starts out being good.

2:1. **the skies and the earth and all their array were finished**. Attempts to reconcile this seven-day creation story with evolution and geological and cosmological evidence of the age of the universe are absurd, requiring a twisting of the words of the text in ways they never remotely meant. Arguments over whether the biblical or the scientific picture is correct are pointless. *Of course* the biblical picture is not a factual, literal account of the universe's origin. The evidence to this effect is overwhelming. It is, however, a meaningful, valuable, instructive account: It conveys a particular conception of the relationship between humans and the cosmos, of the relations between the sexes, of the linear flow of time, of the Sabbath. It sets the Bible's story in a context of a universe that starts out as *good,* with God being initially very close to humans. I have discussed the relationship among creation in the Bible, creation in Kabbalah, and what we know of the universe's origin through science in *The Hidden Face of God,* chapters 10–12.

2:2. **the seventh day.** The seven-day week is found in cultures around the world, presumably because of the association with the sun, moon, and five planets that are visible to the naked eye. Hence, the English Sunday (Sun-day), Monday (Moon-day; cf. French *lundi*), and Saturday (Saturn-day), and French *mardi* (Mars-day) and *mercredi* (Mercury-day). It is fundamental to creation in the Torah, again relating the ordering of time to the very essence of creation. The reckoning of days and years is established by the creation of the sun and moon on the fifth day. The reckoning of weeks is established by the very order of divine activity in the creation itself. This may suggest that the week is given a special status among units of time, and this appears to be confirmed by the singular status given to the Sabbath. It is blessed by the creator, sanctified, and later will be recognized among the Ten Commandments.

ceased in the seventh day from all His work that He had done. ³And God blessed the seventh day and made it holy because He ceased in it from doing all His work, which God had created.

⁴These are the records of the skies and the earth when they were created: In the day that YHWH God made earth and skies

אֲשֶׁר עָשָׂה וַיִּשְׁבֹּת בַּיּוֹם הַשְּׁבִיעִי מִכָּל־מְלַאכְתּוֹ
אֲשֶׁר עָשָׂה: ³וַיְבָרֶךְ אֱלֹהִים אֶת־יוֹם הַשְּׁבִיעִי
וַיְקַדֵּשׁ אֹתוֹ כִּי בוֹ שָׁבַת מִכָּל־מְלַאכְתּוֹ אֲשֶׁר־בָּרָא
אֱלֹהִים לַעֲשׂוֹת: פ ⁴אֵלֶּה תוֹלְדוֹת הַשָּׁמַיִם וְהָאָרֶץ
בְּהִבָּרְאָם בְּיוֹם עֲשׂוֹת יְהוָה אֱלֹהִים אֶרֶץ וְשָׁמָיִם:

2:2. **ceased.** The word (Hebrew שׁבת) means to "stop," not to "rest" as it is often taken. The explicit association of the Sabbath with rest will come later, in the Ten Commandments.

2:3. **made it holy.** (Hebrew קדשׁ) This word is commonly understood to mean "separated," in the sense of being set off from the usual, rather than denoting a special spiritual or even mysterious quality, but there really is little linguistic justification for that understanding. Holiness in the Torah seems indeed to be a singular, powerful quality that certain objects, places, and persons acquire. See comments on Leviticus 19. It means much more than just "separate."

2:3. **made it holy.** What does it mean to make a *day* holy? The creation of humans toward the end of the account is both a climax and, at the same time, a small component of the universe. Their creation is not the culmination of the story. The culmination, as the story is arranged, is the Sabbath, a cosmic event: the deity at a halt and consummation. A. J. Heschel wrote that the special significance of the concept of the Sabbath is that it means the sanctification of time. Most other religious symbols are spatial: sacred objects, sacred places, sacred music, prayers, art, symbolic foods, gestures, and practices. But the first thing in the Torah to be rendered holy is a unit in the passage of time. This powerfully underscores the Torah's character as containing the first known works of history. In consecrating the passage of time in weekly cycles, the institution of the Sabbath at the end of the creation account in Genesis 1 is itself a notable union of the cosmic/cyclical and the historical/linear flow of time. It sets all of the Bible's coming accounts of history in a cosmic structure of time, just as the story of the creation of the universe in that chapter sets the rest of the Bible's stories in a cosmic structure of space. Thus Genesis 1 is a story of the fashioning of a great orderly universe out of chaos in which everything fits into an organized temporal and spatial structure.

2:4. **These are the records.** A second account of creation starts here. What is the relationship of the two creation accounts: In the scholarship of recent centuries, the two creation stories have come to be attributed to different authors. On this and other matters of authorship, see my *Who Wrote the Bible?* There I addressed the story of how the Torah came to be written, and I identified the source texts that were combined to form it. I concluded that the combination of those texts produced a Torah that is greater than the sum of its parts. In this commentary I am more concerned with the point at which *Who Wrote the Bible?* leaves off: with the final product of centuries of

—5when all produce of the field had not yet been in the earth, and all vegetation of the field had not yet grown, for YHWH God had not rained on the earth, and there had been no human to work the ground, 6and a river had come up from the earth and watered the whole face of the ground— 7YHWH God fashioned a human, dust from the

וְכֹל ׀ שִׂיחַ הַשָּׂדֶה טֶרֶם יִהְיֶה בָאָרֶץ וְכָל־עֵשֶׂב הַשָּׂדֶה טֶרֶם יִצְמָח כִּי לֹא הִמְטִיר יְהוָה אֱלֹהִים עַל־הָאָרֶץ וְאָדָם אַיִן לַעֲבֹד אֶת־הָאֲדָמָה: 6וְאֵד יַעֲלֶה מִן־הָאָרֶץ וְהִשְׁקָה אֶת־כָּל־פְּנֵי־הָאֲדָמָה: 7וַיִּיצֶר יְהוָה אֱלֹהִים אֶת־הָאָדָם עָפָר מִן־הָאֲדָמָה וַיִּפַּח

history and composition, which came to be known and cherished as the Torah. In the case of the creation story, the combination of the from-the-sky-down and the from-the-earth-up accounts produces a much richer and much more whole conception of creation than we would have if there were only one account. Also, placing the cosmic conception first creates the impression of the wide camera view narrowing in. This feeling of narrowing in will continue through the coming stories, contributing to the rich-in-background feeling that will persist through the rest of the Bible.

2:4. **records.** This word has commonly been understood to mean "generations," but that translation is inadequate. The word is used both to introduce records of births (as in Gen 5:1) and to introduce stories of events within a family (as in Gen 37:2). (Its root meaning is "to give birth," but it acquired a much broader sense. Its broadest meaning is here in its first occurrence in the Torah, where it refers to the skies and earth and introduces the story of the early events of creation.) It thus means historical records, and usually *family* records.

This verse is sometimes taken to be the conclusion of the preceding seven-day account. That is wrong. The phrase "These are the records" always *introduces* a list or story. It is used ten more times in Genesis to construct the book as continuous narrative through history rather than as a loose collection of stories.

2:5. **not yet.** The word for "not yet," Hebrew *ṭerem*, occurs twice in this verse, followed by the explanation that God has not "rained," Hebrew *himṭîr*, on the earth. This kind of pun, based on rearrangement of root letters (metathesis), occurs frequently. This story is riddled with puns. They convey right from the beginning that the elegance of the Torah's wording is important even while it imparts important content. One might say: even though the ideas here could stand on their own feet, they are given chariots of gold in which to ride. Also, since puns are untranslatable, their presence here urges us all to learn to read the Torah in Hebrew.

2:6. **a river.** The Hebrew word, *ʾēd*, is probably related to Sumerian *ID*, which means a river, rather than meaning a mist, as it has frequently been understood.

2:7. **human.** Hebrew *ʾādām*. As in Gen 1:26, the word refers to the species, not to the male of the species. The word "man" (Hebrew אִישׁ) is not used until after the formation of woman (2:23), which implies that a sexual identification is meaningless so long as there is only one being. This may in turn imply something about the sexual identification of the deity in monotheism. On one hand, God is regularly identified

16

ground, and blew into his nostrils the breath of life, and the human became a living being.

8And YHWH God planted a garden in Eden at the east, and He set the human whom He had fashioned there. 9And YHWH God caused every tree that was pleasant to the sight and good for eating to grow from the ground, and the tree of life within the garden, and the tree of knowledge of good and bad.

וַיִּטַּ֞ע 8בְּאַפָּ֖יו נִשְׁמַ֣ת חַיִּ֑ים וַֽיְהִ֥י הָֽאָדָ֖ם לְנֶ֥פֶשׁ חַיָּֽה׃

יְהוָ֨ה אֱלֹהִ֤ים גַּן־בְּעֵ֙דֶן֙ מִקֶּ֔דֶם וַיָּ֣שֶׂם שָׁ֔ם אֶת־הָ֣אָדָ֔ם

אֲשֶׁ֥ר יָצָֽר׃ 9וַיַּצְמַ֞ח יְהוָ֤ה אֱלֹהִים֙ מִן־הָ֣אֲדָמָ֔ה כָּל־

עֵ֛ץ נֶחְמָ֥ד לְמַרְאֶ֖ה וְט֣וֹב לְמַאֲכָ֑ל וְעֵ֤ץ הַֽחַיִּים֙

בְּת֣וֹךְ הַגָּ֔ן וְעֵ֕ץ הַדַּ֖עַת ט֥וֹב וָרָֽע׃ 10וְנָהָר֙ יֹצֵ֣א

with masculine verbs and adjectives and has a masculine name. (See the comment on Gen 1:26.) On the other hand, what is the meaning of a sexual distinction when there is only *one* of something?! As in many other matters relating to God in the *Tanak*, the hiddenness of the deity leaves this question unanswerable. The ancient Israelites themselves were at least as uncertain about this as people in subsequent ages, for there were times when they conceived of their God as having a female consort. Thus the prophet Jeremiah criticizes the people for including "the Queen of the skies" in their worship (Jer 44:17ff.). And an inscription that was excavated at Quntillet 'Ajrud refers to "YHWH and His Asherah."

2:7. **a human, dust from the ground.** A pun: The word for human in Hebrew is *'ādām* (sometimes translated in English as "Adam"), and the story reports that he is formed from the ground (Hebrew *'ădāmāh*). And this in turn began with a river (*'ēd*) coming up. So we have in vv. 6–7 the sequence אד, אדם, אדמה.

2:9. **tree of life.** Ancient Israelites believed in an afterlife, but it will not come up in the Torah until later. It is not part of the creation account. Even in the combined picture of the two parts of the creation account there is no reference whatever to the creation of a realm for afterlife—no heaven or hell. On the contrary, there is a tree of life in the garden which enables one to live forever. Humans are not forbidden to eat from this tree. (Only the tree of knowledge of good and bad is prohibited.) So death, life after death, heaven and hell, eternal reward and punishment are not yet elements of the account. After the humans are expelled from the garden and thus cut off from the tree of life, death will enter the story. But there still will be no account of the establishment of any realm of afterlife.

2:9. **tree of knowledge of good and bad.** Not good and "evil," as this is usually understood and translated. "Evil" suggests that this is strictly moral knowledge. But the Hebrew word (*rā'*) has a much wider range of meaning than that. This may mean knowledge of what is morally good and bad, or it may mean qualities of good and bad in all realms: morality, aesthetics, utility, pleasure and pain, and so on. It may mean that things are good or bad in themselves and that when one eats from the tree one acquires the ability to see these qualities; or it may mean that when one eats from the tree one acquires the ability to make *judgments* of good and bad. Perhaps the meaning was clear to the ancient reader who knew the immediate connotations of the words. It is not clear to us in the text of the story as it has survived. The only immediate consequence of eating from the tree that the story names is that before eating

10And a river was going out from Eden to water the garden, and it was dispersed from there and became four heads. 11The name of one was Pishon; that is the one that circles all the land of Havilah where there is gold. 12And that land's gold is good; bdellium and onyx stone are there. 13And the name of the second river is Gihon; that is the one that circles all the land of Cush. 14And the name of the third river is Tigris; that is the one that goes east of Assyria. And the fourth river: that is Euphrates.

15And YHWH God took the human and put him in the garden of Eden to work it and to watch over it. 16And YHWH God commanded the human, saying, "You *may eat* from every tree of the garden. 17But from the tree of knowledge of good and bad: you shall not eat from it, because in the day you eat from it: you'll *die!*"

מֵעֵ֗דֶן לְהַשְׁק֖וֹת אֶת־הַגָּ֑ן וּמִשָּׁם֙ יִפָּרֵ֔ד וְהָיָ֖ה לְאַרְבָּעָ֥ה רָאשִֽׁים: 11שֵׁ֥ם הָֽאֶחָ֖ד פִּישׁ֑וֹן ה֣וּא הַסֹּבֵ֗ב אֵ֚ת כָּל־אֶ֣רֶץ הַֽחֲוִילָ֔ה אֲשֶׁר־שָׁ֖ם הַזָּהָֽב: 12וּֽזֲהַ֛ב הָאָ֥רֶץ הַהִ֖וא ט֑וֹב שָׁ֥ם הַבְּדֹ֖לַח וְאֶ֥בֶן הַשֹּֽׁהַם: 13וְשֵֽׁם־הַנָּהָ֥ר הַשֵּׁנִ֖י גִּיח֑וֹן ה֣וּא הַסּוֹבֵ֔ב אֵ֖ת כָּל־אֶ֥רֶץ כּֽוּשׁ: 14וְשֵׁ֨ם הַנָּהָ֤ר הַשְּׁלִישִׁי֙ חִדֶּ֔קֶל ה֥וּא הַֽהֹלֵ֖ךְ קִדְמַ֣ת אַשּׁ֑וּר וְהַנָּהָ֥ר הָֽרְבִיעִ֖י ה֥וּא פְרָֽת: 15וַיִּקַּ֛ח יְהוָ֥ה אֱלֹהִ֖ים אֶת־הָֽאָדָ֑ם וַיַּנִּחֵ֣הוּ בְגַן־עֵ֔דֶן לְעָבְדָ֖הּ וּלְשָׁמְרָֽהּ: 16וַיְצַו֙ יְהוָ֣ה אֱלֹהִ֔ים עַל־הָֽאָדָ֖ם לֵאמֹ֑ר מִכֹּ֥ל עֵֽץ־הַגָּ֖ן אָכֹ֥ל תֹּאכֵֽל: 17וּמֵעֵ֗ץ הַדַּ֙עַת֙ ט֣וֹב וָרָ֔ע לֹ֥א תֹאכַ֖ל מִמֶּ֑נּוּ כִּ֗י בְּי֛וֹם אֲכָלְךָ֥ מִמֶּ֖נּוּ

---

from the tree the humans are not embarrassed over nudity and after eating from it they are. This is not sufficient information to tell us what limits of "good and bad" are meant, nor does it tell us if absolute good and bad are implied or if it is the more relative concept of making judgments of good and bad. The wording, "the eyes of the two of them were opened, and they knew that they were naked," may imply awareness of an absolute value. On the other hand, great numbers of commandments, as articulated in later accounts in Genesis and especially in the following four books of the Bible, suggest that few things are treated as good or bad acts in themselves in these texts. Rather, there is only that which God commands or God prohibits.

2:13. **Gihon.** The name is a pun, because later the snake will be cursed that it (and all snakes) must crawl on its "belly," which in Hebrew is *gĕḥōn* (Gen 3:14). The names of the other rivers may contain puns as well, for the letters of Euphrates (Hebrew פרת) occur in the next words of the snake's curse: עפר תאכל; Pishon (Hebrew פישׁון) contains the same root letters as the word that describes the human's becoming "a living being" (Hebrew נפשׁ); and the letters of Tigris (Hebrew חדקל) occur in a similar jumble (a metathesis) at the end of the story: ידו ולקח (3:22). So the rivers that all derive from Eden both convey geography and hint at the coming events there.

2:16–17. **every tree of the garden but from the tree of knowledge of good and bad.** Only the tree of knowledge of good and bad is forbidden. The tree of life is not forbidden.

2:17. **in the day you eat from it: you'll *die!*** On first reading, most readers take this to mean that one's death will occur in the very day that one eats from the tree. In the absence of punctuation in the Hebrew text, however, one cannot be certain. Before eating from the tree of knowledge, humans have access to the tree of life and therefore

18And YHWH God said, "It's not good for the human to be by himself. I'll make for him a strength corresponding to him." 19And YHWH God fashioned from the ground every animal of the field and every bird of the skies and brought it to the human to see what he would call it. And whatever the human would call it, each living being, that would be its name. 20And the human gave names to every domestic animal and bird of the skies and every animal of the field. But He did not find for the human a strength corresponding to him.

21And YHWH God caused a slumber to descend on the human, and he slept. And He took one of his ribs and closed flesh in its place. 22And YHWH God built the rib that He had taken from the human into a woman and brought her to the human. 23And the human

מֹת תָּמוּת: 18וַיֹּאמֶר יְהוָה אֱלֹהִים לֹא־טוֹב הֱיוֹת הָאָדָם לְבַדּוֹ אֶעֱשֶׂה־לּוֹ עֵזֶר כְּנֶגְדּוֹ: 19וַיִּצֶר יְהוָה אֱלֹהִים מִן־הָאֲדָמָה כָּל־חַיַּת הַשָּׂדֶה וְאֵת כָּל־עוֹף הַשָּׁמַיִם וַיָּבֵא אֶל־הָאָדָם לִרְאוֹת מַה־יִּקְרָא־לוֹ וְכֹל אֲשֶׁר יִקְרָא־לוֹ הָאָדָם נֶפֶשׁ חַיָּה הוּא שְׁמוֹ: 20וַיִּקְרָא הָאָדָם שֵׁמוֹת לְכָל־הַבְּהֵמָה וּלְעוֹף הַשָּׁמַיִם וּלְכֹל חַיַּת הַשָּׂדֶה וּלְאָדָם לֹא־מָצָא עֵזֶר כְּנֶגְדּוֹ: 21וַיַּפֵּל יְהוָה אֱלֹהִים ׀ תַּרְדֵּמָה עַל־הָאָדָם וַיִּישָׁן וַיִּקַּח אַחַת מִצַּלְעֹתָיו וַיִּסְגֹּר בָּשָׂר תַּחְתֶּנָּה: 22וַיִּבֶן יְהוָה אֱלֹהִים ׀ אֶת־הַצֵּלָע אֲשֶׁר־לָקַח מִן־הָאָדָם לְאִשָּׁה וַיְבִאֶהָ אֶל־הָאָדָם: 23וַיֹּאמֶר הָאָדָם

---

can live forever. This verse may mean that in the day that humans eat from the tree of knowledge they become mortal, in the sense of: "If you stay away from it, you'll live; in the day you eat from it, you'll die." This general meaning of the expression "In the day you do you'll die" occurs elsewhere (1 Kings 2:37,42); and this is what in fact occurs in the story here.

Alternatively, if it does in fact mean that their death will occur in the very day that they eat from the tree, then we must understand what subsequently occurs to be a divine act of mercy or relenting: they do not die immediately but are rendered mortal.

2:18. **a strength corresponding to him.** Woman is usually understood to be created as a suitable "helper" (Hebrew '*ēzer*) to man in this account. The Hebrew root, however, can also mean "strength." (This was first proposed by R. D. Freedman. See cases of '*ēzer* in parallel with '*ōz*, another word for "strength," as in, for example, Ps 46:2. See also *Azariah* [2 Kings 14:21] and *Uzziah* [2 Chron 26:1] as alternative names of the same king.) The Hebrew phrase '*ēzer kĕnegdô* therefore may very well mean "a corresponding strength." If so, it is a different picture from what people have thought, and an intriguing one in terms of recently developed sensitivities concerning the sexes and how they are pictured in the Torah. In Genesis 1, man and woman are both created in the image of God; in Genesis 2, they are corresponding strengths. However one interprets subsequent stories and laws in the Torah, this essential equality of worth and standing introduces them.

2:19. **animal of the field.** This phrase refers to wild animals.

2:20. **the human gave names.** The human, who is created in the image of the creator, is now given a function that the creator performed in Genesis 1: bestowing names on parts of the creation.

said, "This time is it: bone from my bones and flesh from my flesh. This will be called 'woman,' for this one was taken from 'man.' "

24On account of this a man leaves his father and his mother and clings to his woman, and they become one flesh.

25And the two of them were naked, the human and his woman, and they were not embarrassed.

3 1And the snake was slier than every animal of the field that YHWH God had made, and

זֹאת הַפַּ֫עַם עֶ֫צֶם מֵעֲצָמַי וּבָשָׂר מִבְּשָׂרִי לְזֹאת יִקָּרֵא אִשָּׁה כִּי מֵאִישׁ לֻקֳחָה־זֹּאת: 24עַל־כֵּן יַעֲזָב־אִישׁ אֶת־אָבִיו וְאֶת־אִמּוֹ וְדָבַק בְּאִשְׁתּוֹ וְהָיוּ לְבָשָׂר אֶחָד: 25וַיִּהְיוּ שְׁנֵיהֶם עֲרוּמִּים הָאָדָם וְאִשְׁתּוֹ וְלֹא יִתְבֹּשָׁשׁוּ: 3 וְהַנָּחָשׁ הָיָה עָרוּם מִכֹּל חַיַּת הַשָּׂדֶה אֲשֶׁר עָשָׂה יְהוָה אֱלֹהִים וַיֹּאמֶר אֶל־הָאִשָּׁה אַף כִּי־אָמַר אֱלֹהִים לֹא תֹאכְלוּ מִכֹּל עֵץ הַגָּן: 2וַתֹּאמֶר הָאִשָּׁה אֶל־הַנָּחָשׁ מִפְּרִי עֵץ־הַגָּן נֹאכֵל: 3וּמִפְּרִי הָעֵץ

2:23. **bone from my bones and flesh from my flesh.** In addition to its literal meaning in this case—the woman is formed from the bone of the man—this expression has the figurative meaning of persons belonging to one another. It has this latter meaning in biblical episodes to come (Gen 29:14; Judg 9:2; 2 Sam 5:1 = 1 Chron 11:1; 2 Sam 19:13–14).

2:23. **will be called 'woman,' for this one was taken from 'man.'** The Septuagint and Samaritan read "*her* man" (Hebrew אישׁה), which makes the pun better, and that reading avoids both the grammatical problem and the social problem that Hebrew אשׁה is not in fact the feminine of Hebrew אישׁ. (Its root is אנשׁ and is related to Hebrew *'enōš*.) It also makes a better parallel to the coming reference in 3:20 to "*his* woman."

2:23. **man.** Now, after woman has been formed, the word "man" occurs for the first time instead of "human." Sexual distinction has no meaning unless there are two or more kinds of a species, so there is no male until there is a female.

2:24. **On account of this . . .** This is understood to be more than the story of two individuals. The acts of the first two humans are presented as having implications for the character and destiny of all their descendants. This fact is established here, prior to the events surrounding the tree of knowledge, so that it will be clear that the consequences of those events will be the fate of all humankind.

2:24. **and clings to his woman, and they become one flesh.** This may be taken as the origin of marriage or of sexual union or both.

2:25. **his woman.** The use of the word "his" may or may not imply possession of the woman or some dominant role for the male, because the text refers a few verses later to "her man" (3:6). Also, men's domination of women is pictured in this story as deriving from God's decree on woman after the episode of the tree of knowledge of good and bad, which has not yet occurred at this point.

3:1. **slier.** A pun: The snake is introduced as the most "sly" (*'ārûm*) of the animals (3:1). In the subsequent dialogue between God and the man, the man says, after eating from the tree, that he is *'ērōm*, naked. His condition is spelled with the same con-

he said to the woman, "Has God indeed said you may not eat from any tree of the garden?"

²And the woman said to the snake, "We may eat from the fruit of the trees of the garden. ³But from the fruit of the tree that is within the garden God has said, "You shall not eat from it, and you shall not touch it, or else you'll die.""

⁴And the snake said to the woman, "You won't *die!* ⁵Because God knows that in the day you eat from it your eyes will be opened, and you'll be like God—knowing good and bad." ⁶And the woman saw that the tree was good for eating and that it was an attraction to the eyes, and the tree was desirable to bring about understanding, and she took some of its fruit, and she ate, and gave

אֲשֶׁר בְּתוֹךְ־הַגָּן אָמַר אֱלֹהִים לֹא תֹאכְלוּ מִמֶּנּוּ
וְלֹא תִגְּעוּ בּוֹ פֶּן־תְּמֻתוּן: 4וַיֹּאמֶר הַנָּחָשׁ אֶל־הָאִשָּׁה
לֹא־מוֹת תְּמֻתוּן: 5כִּי יֹדֵעַ אֱלֹהִים כִּי בְּיוֹם
אֲכָלְכֶם מִמֶּנּוּ וְנִפְקְחוּ עֵינֵיכֶם וִהְיִיתֶם כֵּאלֹהִים
יֹדְעֵי טוֹב וָרָע: 6וַתֵּרֶא הָאִשָּׁה כִּי טוֹב הָעֵץ
לְמַאֲכָל וְכִי תַאֲוָה־הוּא לָעֵינַיִם וְנֶחְמָד הָעֵץ
לְהַשְׂכִּיל וַתִּקַּח מִפִּרְיוֹ וַתֹּאכַל וַתִּתֵּן גַּם־לְאִישָׁהּ

---

sonants as the snake's characteristic. The paronomasia may be purely a play on the root letters. Or it may be a pun of content, since the man now uses the word *ʿērōm* when he is in fact no longer naked but is attempting, like the snake, to mislead.

3:1. **Has God indeed said you may not eat from any tree of the garden?** A confusing formulation, conceivably to throw the woman off.

3:3. **and you shall not touch it.** But God is not reported to have said that they could not touch it (2:17). As Rashi notes, the dialogue appears to develop the principle that if one starts out by adding to a command one may come to take away from it in the end. We should also note that this principle is already introduced here at the beginning of the Torah, because it is an *essential* principle that Moses pronounces twice near the end of the Torah: "You shall not add to the thing that I command you, and you shall not take away from it" (Deut 4:2; 13:1).

Moreover: God is not quoted as having given *any* instruction to the woman. The natural understanding is that she has learned it from the man. So it may suggest that he adds it to protect himself (or her), or that she adds it herself. Either way, it is a caution concerning human oral transmission of a divine command.

3:5. **you'll be like God.** Whatever is meant by creation in the image of God, it means that humans are understood to participate in the divine in some way that animals do not. Only humans would *aspire* to the divine. And that is the basis of the snake's appeal to the humans here.

3:6. **its fruit.** The text does not say what kind of fruit. Rashi, following the Talmud (Sanhedrin 70b), suggested figs, so that it is ironic that they then cover themselves with fig leaves. Artists traditionally make it an apple. I have also heard pomegranate, citron (Hebrew *ʾetrog*), and wheat! I think it is meaningful that the text does not tell us what it is. This may suggest that it is a unique fruit, the fruit of this unique tree. Or it may convey that the kind of fruit is not mentioned because that is not the point. In

to her man with her as well, and he ate. 7And the eyes of the two of them were opened, and they knew that they were naked. And they picked fig leaves and made loincloths for themselves.

8And they heard the sound of YHWH God walking in the garden in the wind of the day, and the human and his woman hid from YHWH God among the garden's trees. 9And YHWH God called the human and said to him, "Where are you?"

עִמָּהּ וַיֹּאכַל: 7וַתִּפָּקַחְנָה עֵינֵי שְׁנֵיהֶם וַיֵּדְעוּ כִּי עֵירֻמִּם הֵם וַיִּתְפְּרוּ עֲלֵה תְאֵנָה וַיַּעֲשׂוּ לָהֶם חֲגֹרֹת: 8וַיִּשְׁמְעוּ אֶת־קוֹל יְהוָה אֱלֹהִים מִתְהַלֵּךְ בַּגָּן לְרוּחַ הַיּוֹם וַיִּתְחַבֵּא הָאָדָם וְאִשְׁתּוֹ מִפְּנֵי יְהוָה אֱלֹהִים בְּתוֹךְ עֵץ הַגָּן: 9וַיִּקְרָא יְהוָה אֱלֹהִים אֶל־הָאָדָם

---

its extraordinary economy of detail, the Torah gives us only what is crucial to the story. What matters is not whether the fruit is a grape or a banana—but that it is forbidden, that it gives one the knowledge of good and bad, and that the humans are attracted to take it. The kind of fruit is of concern only for picturing this story in art. My daughter Jesse, when she was nine years old, painted a picture of this story, and she made all different fruits grow from this same tree.

3:6. **gave to her man with her.** People frequently have claimed that this story blames the woman for persuading, enticing, or seducing the man to eat the fruit. But there is no reference to any act of persuasion. Indeed, the words "her man *with her*" may suggest that he should be pictured as having been there while the snake was speaking to her. And even the deity's words later—"you listened to your woman's voice" (3:17)—need not suggest seduction or persuasion on her part. They merely respond to the man's having tried to shift blame to her, and they affirm that he must bear the consequences of his own actions. Moreover, the snake speaks with plural verbs, suggesting that he is including the man.

3:7. **they picked fig leaves and made loincloths.** Humans do not yet fashion or invent anything new themselves. They do not actually make clothing. They only cover themselves with leaves. The first clothing is made by God (3:21).

3:9. **Where are you?** The conversation between God and the two humans in the garden is a masterpiece. God says, "Where are you?" (a strange thing for a deity to say). The man answers, "I hid because I was naked," and his creator pounces like an attorney who has caught a witness in a stupid mistake on the stand: *Who told you that you were naked?! Have you eaten from the tree . . . ?"* To which the man replies, unchivalrously, "The *WOMAN*," and ungratefully, "whom *YOU* placed with me," and trying to escape responsibility for his own actions: *"SHE gave me from the tree, and I ate."* The creator turns to the woman, who also tries to pass the responsibility down the line: "The *SNAKE* tricked me." God pronounces a curse on the snake (and on all snakes)— no dialogue, there's no one left for the snake to blame—but then God turns back to the woman and pronounces a painful fate for her (and all women) as well. During this pronouncement one should consider the tension in the man, who does not know if the pendulum of recompense will swing all the way back to him. Did his blaming the woman excuse him? Clearly not, as YHWH next turns back to the man and says,

22

10And he said, "I heard the sound of you in the garden and was afraid because I was naked, and I hid."

11And He said, "Who told you that you were naked? Have you eaten from the tree from which I commanded you not to eat?"

12And the human said, "The *woman*, whom *you* placed with me, *she* gave me from the tree, and I ate."

13And YHWH God said to the woman, "What is this that you've done?"

And the woman said, "The *snake* tricked me, and I ate."

14And YHWH God said to the snake, "Because you did this, you are cursed out of every domestic animal and every animal of the field, you'll go on your belly, and you'll eat dust all the days of

וַיֹּאמֶר מִי הִגִּיד 11וַיֹּאמֶר מִי הִגִּיד
לְךָ כִּי עֵירֹם אָתָּה הֲמִן־הָעֵץ אֲשֶׁר צִוִּיתִיךָ לְבִלְתִּי
אֲכָל־מִמֶּנּוּ אָכָלְתָּ: 12וַיֹּאמֶר הָאָדָם הָאִשָּׁה אֲשֶׁר
נָתַתָּה עִמָּדִי הִוא נָתְנָה־לִּי מִן־הָעֵץ וָאֹכֵל:
13וַיֹּאמֶר יְהוָה אֱלֹהִים לָאִשָּׁה מַה־זֹּאת עָשִׂית
וַתֹּאמֶר הָאִשָּׁה הַנָּחָשׁ הִשִּׁיאַנִי וָאֹכֵל: 14וַיֹּאמֶר
יְהֹוָה אֱלֹהִים ׀ אֶל־הַנָּחָשׁ

כִּי עָשִׂיתָ זֹּאת אָרוּר אַתָּה מִכָּל־הַבְּהֵמָה וּמִכֹּל
חַיַּת הַשָּׂדֶה

עַל־גְּחֹנְךָ תֵלֵךְ וְעָפָר תֹּאכַל כָּל־יְמֵי חַיֶּיךָ:

"Because *YOU* listened . . ." and pronounces a hard fate for him (and all men) as well. This first divine-human dialogue in the Torah is remarkable—at times humorous and at times fearfully serious—but the point is not merely a literary one; it is a psychological one (showing the sexes reacting to guilt and fear) and a spiritual one (showing divine-human confrontation) as well. This exchange is a powerful introduction to the coming account of the relationship between God and humans in the Torah.

3:14. **the *snake*.** Just a snake, not the devil or Satan as later Christian interpretation pictured. As the curse that follows indicates, this story has to do with the fate of snakes, not with the cosmic role of a devil. There is no such concept in the Hebrew Bible.

3:14. **you'll go on your belly**. Scholars often refer to the "economy" of wording in biblical stories, but even by the Bible's obviously economical standard the story of Eden stands out as a showpiece for accomplishing so much in just twenty-four verses. Stories in Genesis frequently develop etiologies—explanations of the origins of names and practices—but none comes close to the number of origins accounted for in Genesis 3. Namely:

1. It is the story of why snakes do not have legs. Contrary to the vast majority of depictions of this story in art—which have the snake coiled around the tree while addressing the woman—the text states explicitly in v. 14 that the fact that snakes crawl on their bellies is the punishment imposed on the snake (and its descendants) for the offense that it has committed. Before v. 14 the snake must be pictured as having legs.

2. The story is the etiology of what was perceived to be the natural enmity between humans and snakes (v. 15). Presumably, the human phobia even of

your life. 15And I'll put enmity between you and the woman and between your seed and her seed. He'll strike you at the head, and you'll strike him at the heel."

16To the woman He said, "I'll make your suffering and your labor pain great. You'll have children in pain. And your desire will be for your man, and he'll dominate you."

17And to the human He said, "Because you listened to your woman's voice and ate from the tree about which I commanded you saying, 'You shall not eat from it,' the ground is cursed on your account. You'll eat from it with suffering all the days of your life. 18And it will grow thorn and thistle at you, and you'll eat the field's vegetation. 19By the sweat of your nostrils you'll eat bread until you go back to the ground, because

15וְאֵיבָה ׀ אָשִׁית בֵּינְךָ וּבֵין הָאִשָּׁה
וּבֵין זַרְעֲךָ וּבֵין זַרְעָהּ
הוּא יְשׁוּפְךָ רֹאשׁ וְאַתָּה תְּשׁוּפֶנּוּ עָקֵב: ס
16אֶל־הָאִשָּׁה אָמַר
הַרְבָּה אַרְבֶּה עִצְּבוֹנֵךְ וְהֵרֹנֵךְ
בְּעֶצֶב תֵּלְדִי בָנִים
וְאֶל־אִישֵׁךְ תְּשׁוּקָתֵךְ וְהוּא יִמְשָׁל־בָּךְ: ס
17וּלְאָדָם אָמַר כִּי־שָׁמַעְתָּ לְקוֹל אִשְׁתֶּךָ וַתֹּאכַל
מִן־הָעֵץ אֲשֶׁר צִוִּיתִיךָ לֵאמֹר לֹא תֹאכַל מִמֶּנּוּ
אֲרוּרָה הָאֲדָמָה בַּעֲבוּרֶךָ
בְּעִצָּבוֹן תֹּאכְלֶנָּה כֹּל יְמֵי חַיֶּיךָ:
18וְקוֹץ וְדַרְדַּר תַּצְמִיחַ לָךְ
וְאָכַלְתָּ אֶת־עֵשֶׂב הַשָּׂדֶה:
19בְּזֵעַת אַפֶּיךָ תֹּאכַל לֶחֶם
עַד שׁוּבְךָ אֶל־הָאֲדָמָה כִּי מִמֶּנָּה לֻקָּחְתָּ

harmless snakes was as common at the time of this story's composition as it is to this day.

3. It is the etiology of man's domination of woman in the world in which this story was composed (v. 16).

4. It is the author's etiology of woman's being drawn to man (v. 16), and:

5. man's mating with woman ("On account of this a man leaves his father and his mother and clings to his woman, and they become one flesh," 2:24).

6. The story contains the etiologies of clothing (and embarrassment over nudity), 2:25; 3:7,10–11,21;

7. labor pain in childbirth (v. 16);

8. work (vv. 17–19);

9. knowledge of good and bad;

10. death. The humans have access to the tree of life initially, which would make them immortal (v. 22). They are denied only the tree of knowledge of good and bad. It is as a result of eating from the tree of knowledge that they lose access to the tree of life. They are driven from the garden of Eden, in which the tree of life is located, and cherubs and a flaming sword bar the way back.

3:17. **the ground is cursed on your account.** As a consequence of human behavior, the environment suffers. This phenomenon will recur in the Torah. See the comment on 4:11.

3:18. **thorn and thistle.** The environment now becomes hostile to humans.

24

you were taken from it; because you are dust and you'll go back to dust."

20And the human called his woman "Eve," because she was mother of all living.

21And YHWH God made skin garments for the human and his woman and dressed them.

22And YHWH God said, "Here, the human has become like one of us, to know good and bad. And now, in case he'll put out his hand and take from the tree of life as well, and eat and live forever:" 23And YHWH God put him out of the garden of Eden, to work the ground from which he was taken. 24And He expelled the human, and He had the cherubs and the flame of a revolving sword reside at the east of the garden of Eden to watch over the way to the tree of life.

כִּי־עָפָר אַתָּה וְאֶל־עָפָר תָּשׁוּב:
20וַיִּקְרָא הָאָדָם שֵׁם אִשְׁתּוֹ חַוָּה כִּי הִוא הָיְתָה אֵם כָּל־חָי: 21וַיַּעַשׂ יְהוָה אֱלֹהִים לְאָדָם וּלְאִשְׁתּוֹ כָּתְנוֹת עוֹר וַיַּלְבִּשֵׁם: פ 22וַיֹּאמֶר ׀ יְהוָה אֱלֹהִים הֵן הָאָדָם הָיָה כְּאַחַד מִמֶּנּוּ לָדַעַת טוֹב וָרָע וְעַתָּה ׀ פֶּן־יִשְׁלַח יָדוֹ וְלָקַח גַּם מֵעֵץ הַחַיִּים וְאָכַל וָחַי לְעֹלָם: 23וַיְשַׁלְּחֵהוּ יְהוָה אֱלֹהִים מִגַּן־עֵדֶן לַעֲבֹד אֶת־הָאֲדָמָה אֲשֶׁר לֻקַּח מִשָּׁם: 24וַיְגָרֶשׁ אֶת־הָאָדָם וַיַּשְׁכֵּן מִקֶּדֶם לְגַן־עֵדֶן אֶת־הַכְּרֻבִים וְאֵת לַהַט הַחֶרֶב הַמִּתְהַפֶּכֶת לִשְׁמֹר אֶת־דֶּרֶךְ עֵץ הַחַיִּים: ס

3:20. **Eve.** Hebrew *ḥawwāh*, the feminine form of the word for "life" (*ḥay*). Interestingly, this Semitic root elsewhere can mean snake! Again, the story is replete with puns.

3:22. **to know good and bad**. Together with the artistry of language (punning, dialogue) and the etiologies, the story merges insight into the human condition. Like the Greek myth of Prometheus, the first story of the Bible develops the notion that knowledge is a prize taken from the divine realm and that the price for this forbidden prize is suffering. What is particular to the Bible's story is the kind of knowledge that is at stake: knowledge of good and bad. As to what that means, see the comment on Gen 2:9.

3:22. **put out**. The text plays on forms of the verb שׁלח: rather than "put out" his hand (v. 22) the human is "put out" of the garden (v. 23).

3:22. **tree of life**. The comparative literature is intriguing. In the ancient Near Eastern epic of Gilgamesh, the hero, seeking immortality, goes to the bottom of deep waters and brings up a plant that is supposed to have the power to rejuvenate life. (If one eats from it, one becomes young again.) While he goes off to bathe, however, a *snake* steals away this "tree of life;" and this is the etiology of snakes' sloughing their skin and being rejuvenated (*Gilgamesh*, Tablet XII, lines 263–289).

3:22. **and eat and live forever**. The fact that there is no mention of afterlife being created at the time that death begins, in Genesis 3, is very suggestive. See the comment on Gen 2:9.

3:24. **cherubs.** Sphinxes. Creatures of mixed species, frequently with the head of a human, the body of a four-legged animal, and the wings of a bird. Cherubs guard the path to the tree of life. Later, statues of cherubs will be placed over the ark, seemingly guarding its contents, which are sources of wisdom and righteousness, which in turn

4 ¹And the human had known Eve, his woman, and she became pregnant and gave birth to Cain and said, "I've created a man with YHWH." ²And she went on to give birth to his brother, Abel. And Abel was a shepherd of flocks, and Cain was a worker of ground. ³And it was at the end of some days, and Cain brought an offering to YHWH from the fruit of the ground. ⁴And Abel brought, as well, from the firstborn of his flock and their fat. And YHWH paid attention to Abel and his offering ⁵and did not pay attention to Cain and his offering. And Cain was very upset, and his face was fallen.

⁶And YHWH said to Cain, "Why are you upset, and why has your face fallen? ⁷Is it not that if you do well you'll be raised, and if you don't do well then sin crouches at the threshold? And its desire will be for you. And you'll dominate it."

⁸And Cain said to his brother Abel. And it was

וְהָאָדָם יָדַע אֶת־חַוָּה אִשְׁתּוֹ וַתַּהַר וַתֵּלֶד 4
אֶת־קַיִן וַתֹּאמֶר קָנִיתִי אִישׁ אֶת־יְהוָה: ²וַתֹּסֶף
לָלֶדֶת אֶת־אָחִיו אֶת־הָבֶל וַיְהִי־הֶבֶל רֹעֵה צֹאן
וְקַיִן הָיָה עֹבֵד אֲדָמָה: ³וַיְהִי מִקֵּץ יָמִים וַיָּבֵא קַיִן
מִפְּרִי הָאֲדָמָה מִנְחָה לַיהוָה: ⁴וְהֶבֶל הֵבִיא גַם־הוּא
מִבְּכֹרוֹת צֹאנוֹ וּמֵחֶלְבֵהֶן וַיִּשַׁע יְהוָה אֶל־הֶבֶל
וְאֶל־מִנְחָתוֹ: ⁵וְאֶל־קַיִן וְאֶל־מִנְחָתוֹ לֹא שָׁעָה וַיִּחַר
לְקַיִן מְאֹד וַיִּפְּלוּ פָּנָיו: ⁶וַיֹּאמֶר יְהוָה אֶל־קַיִן לָמָּה
חָרָה לָךְ וְלָמָּה נָפְלוּ פָנֶיךָ: ⁷הֲלוֹא אִם־תֵּיטִיב
שְׂאֵת וְאִם לֹא תֵיטִיב לַפֶּתַח חַטָּאת רֹבֵץ וְאֵלֶיךָ
תְּשׁוּקָתוֹ וְאַתָּה תִּמְשָׁל־בּוֹ: ⁸וַיֹּאמֶר קַיִן אֶל־הֶבֶל

---

are pictured as ultimately the key to a return to the closeness with the deity that is lost here (Prov 3:18; 11:30; see my *The Hidden Face of God*, pp. 115–116).

4:1. **I've created a man with YHWH.** Hebrew *qānîtî*: one of the meanings of this word is "to create." It comes to explain the name Cain (Hebrew *qayin*); but Eve would not claim to have created a man herself, and so she says that she has created him together with God. Thus giving birth, the human act that imitates the divine more than anything else, is regarded here as being done by humans and God together.

And note: the first person to pronounce the name of God in the Bible is the woman. Adam, Cain, Abel, and Seth are never quoted as saying the name.

4:8. **Cain said to his brother Abel**. What did he say? The second half of the sentence seems to be missing. The Samaritan, Greek (Septuagint), and Latin (Vulgate) texts read: "And Cain said to his brother Abel, 'Let's go out to the field.'" Cain's words appear to have been skipped in the Masoretic Text by a scribe whose eye jumped from the first phrase containing the word "field" to the second.

The Masoretic Text (MT) is known from medieval Hebrew manuscripts (from the tenth century C.E. on), which were copied from manuscripts going back to the late centuries B.C.E. and early centuries C.E. The Greek text of the Torah, the Septuagint (LXX), is known from manuscripts of the fourth–fifth centuries C.E., which were copied from manuscripts of a translation of a Hebrew text going back to the same period as the sources of the Masoretic Text. In order to try to determine the original text of the Torah, we must read both the Masoretic Text and the Septuagint text, as well as the

while they were in the field, and Cain rose against Abel his brother and killed him.

אָחִיו וַיְהִי בִּהְיוֹתָם בַּשָּׂדֶה וַיָּקָם קַיִן אֶל־הֶבֶל

Qumran (Dead Sea Scrolls) texts, which are the oldest surviving manuscripts of the *Tanak*. Sometimes the Targum (Aramaic), Samaritan, and Vulgate (Latin) are helpful as well.

4:8. **it was while they were in the field**. What is the significance of informing us that they are in a field at the time? Early biblical commentators searched for the meaning of this seemingly inconsequential detail. But to understand it we must observe, first, that fratricide recurs repeatedly in the *Tanak*. It begins here with Cain and Abel and ends with King Solomon executing his brother Adonijah; and in between these the issue of fratricide comes up in the stories of Jacob and Esau, Joseph and his brothers, Abimelek killing *seventy* of his brothers (Judges 9), the war between Benjamin and its fellow tribes of Israel (Judges 20), the struggle between Israel and Judah (2 Sam 2:26–27), and King David's sons Absalom and Amnon (2 Samuel 13–14). Next, we must observe that the word "field" repeatedly occurs in these stories. Thus: Absalom has his brother Amnon killed. In an attempt to get David to pardon Absalom for this murder, a woman (the "wise woman of Tekoa") comes and tells David a fake story about her own two sons, claiming that one of them killed the other. In the course of her tale, she mentions a seemingly unrelated detail: they fought "in the field" (2 Sam 14:6). The same "inconsequential" detail that occurs in the Cain-Abel story occurs there. Likewise in the story of the rivalrous brothers Jacob and Esau, Esau comes to Jacob "from the field" (Gen 25:29). Indeed, Esau is introduced as "a man of the field" (25:27). And Joseph begins his report of his dream that offends his brothers with the words "here we were binding sheaves *in the field*" (Gen 37:7), which prompts his brothers to propose fratricide a few verses later (37:19–20). The story of the war between Benjamin and the rest of the Israelite tribes is also presented in terms of brothers killing brothers (Judg 20:13,23,28; 21:6); and there, too, the word "field" comes up twice. The recurring word, therefore, appears to be a means of connecting the many instances of brother killing brother. It recognizes that sibling rivalry is felt by nearly all humans, and it warns us to be sensitive to keep our hostile feelings in check—and to be sensitive to our siblings' feelings as well. This will be developed through this chain of sibling stories in Genesis, culminating in Joseph, who offends his brothers in his youth (Gen 37:2–11) but who learns to show them understanding and kindness in his mature years (50:15–21).

4:8. **Cain rose against Abel his brother**. It never tells why, exactly, he kills him. Many suggestions have been made. But it is significant that the text never tells what the reason is. It implies, of course, that it is his anger over God's favoring Abel's sacrifice, but it never says this explicitly. Sometimes a silence in the Torah is revealing. In this case it suggests that the concern is not Cain's immediate motive, but rather the deeper, essential fact of sibling rivalry. Everyone with children learns that it is not the specific content of their fights that matters so much as the *fact* of the fight. The issue is the *existence* of the sibling. As the first humans to *have* a sibling, Cain and Abel are the archetypes for sibling rivalry. The whole world was Cain's until Abel came along.

9And YHWH said to Cain, "Where is Abel your brother?"

And he said, "I don't know. Am I my brother's watchman?"

10And He said, "What have you done? The sound! Your brother's blood is crying to me from the ground! 11And now you're cursed from the ground that opened its mouth to take your brother's blood from your hand. 12When you work the ground it won't continue to give its po-

אָחִ֖יו וַֽיַּהַרְגֵֽהוּ: 9וַיֹּ֤אמֶר יְהוָה֙ אֶל־קַ֔יִן אֵ֖י הֶ֥בֶל
אָחִ֑יךָ וַיֹּ֙אמֶר֙ לֹ֣א יָדַ֔עְתִּי הֲשֹׁמֵ֥ר אָחִ֖י אָנֹֽכִי:
10וַיֹּ֖אמֶר מֶ֣ה עָשִׂ֑יתָ ק֚וֹל דְּמֵ֣י אָחִ֔יךָ צֹעֲקִ֥ים אֵלַ֖י
מִן־הָֽאֲדָמָֽה: 11וְעַתָּ֖ה אָר֣וּר אָ֑תָּה מִן־הָֽאֲדָמָה֙ אֲשֶׁ֣ר
פָּצְתָ֣ה אֶת־פִּ֔יהָ לָקַ֛חַת אֶת־דְּמֵ֥י אָחִ֖יךָ מִיָּדֶֽךָ: 12כִּ֤י
תַֽעֲבֹד֙ אֶת־הָ֣אֲדָמָ֔ה לֹֽא־תֹסֵ֥ף תֵּת־כֹּחָ֖הּ לָ֑ךְ נָ֥ע וָנָ֖ד

4:9. **Am I my brother's watchman?** It is hard to give up the famous English translation, "Am I my brother's keeper?" but I think it is important to convey the continuing play on forms of the word for "watch" (Hebrew *šmr*). Humans had been put in the garden "to watch over it" (2:15), but in the end the cherubs are put there "to watch over" the way to the tree of life (3:24). Now the first human to murder another questions cynically his responsibility to watch out for his brother. The development of this term climaxes when God declares that the promises to Abraham will be upheld, including that "all the nations of the earth will be blessed through your seed because Abraham listened to my voice and *kept my watch*" (26:4–5). This phrase (which in the Hebrew uses the root *šmr* twice, emphasizing it by using it in the verb and in its object) thereafter becomes a standard expression in the Torah for conveying loyalty to God.

4:10. **What have you done?** These are the same words that God had said to Cain's mother in the preceding story (3:13). By opening with a question (even if one already knows the answer!) one gives a person a chance to tell the truth and admit to a wrongdoing.

4:10. **The sound! Your brother's blood is crying.** Older translations make this "The voice of your brother's blood is crying," but that is wrong. The word for "voice" or "sound" is singular. The word for blood is plural and must therefore be the subject of the plural verb "crying." The word "sound" must be understood as an interjection.

4:11. **you're cursed from the ground.** Central again is the idea that the environment becomes hostile to humans as a result of human corruption, an idea to which our own age is becoming acutely sensitive. YHWH had said to Cain's father, "The ground is cursed on your account" (3:17). Whereas formerly the man had been able to feed freely from the fruits of the garden, hereafter he would have to work to get the earth's bounty, and it would produce thorns for him to cope with. Now Cain takes his brother Abel's life, and YHWH says to Cain, one step beyond what he had said to Cain's father, "You're cursed from the ground. . . . When you work the ground it will no longer give its bounty to you" (4:11–12). (In the first case the curse is on the ground; in this second case the curse is on the man.) The theme of alienation from the earth and its vegetation, reiterated in this story, continues and reaches a high point in the flood story.

tency to you. You'll be a roamer and rover in the earth."

13And Cain said to YHWH, "My crime is greater than I can bear. 14Here, you've expelled me from the face of the ground today, and I'll be hidden from your presence, and I'll be a roamer and rover in the earth, and anyone who finds me will kill me."

15And YHWH said to him, "Therefore: anyone who kills Cain, he'll be avenged sevenfold." And YHWH set a sign for Cain so that anyone who finds him would not strike him. 16And Cain went out from YHWH's presence and lived in the land of roving, east of Eden.

17And Cain knew his wife, and she became pregnant and gave birth to Enoch. And he was a builder of a city, and he called the name of the city like the name of his son: Enoch. 18And Irad was born to Enoch, and Irad fathered Mehuya-el, and Mehuya-el fathered Metusha-el, and Metusha-el fathered Lamech. 19And Lamech took two wives. The one's name was Adah, and the second's name was Zillah. 20And Adah gave birth to Yabal. He was father of tent-dweller and cattleman. 21And his brother's name was Yubal. He was father of every player of lyre and pipe. 22And Zillah, too, gave birth to Tubal-Cain, forger of every implement of bronze and iron. And Tubal-Cain's sister was Naamah. 23And Lamech said to his wives:

> Adah and Zillah, listen to my voice,
> Wives of Lamech, hear what I say.
> For I've killed a man for a wound to me
> And a boy for a hurt to me,
> 24 For Cain will be avenged sevenfold
> And Lamech seventy-seven.

25And Adam knew his wife again, and she gave birth to a son, and she called his name Seth

תִּהְיֶ֣ה בָאָֽרֶץ׃ 13וַיֹּ֥אמֶר קַ֖יִן אֶל־יְהֹוָ֑ה גָּד֥וֹל עֲוֺנִ֖י מִנְּשֹֽׂא׃ 14הֵן֩ גֵּרַ֨שְׁתָּ אֹתִ֜י הַיּ֗וֹם מֵעַל֙ פְּנֵ֣י הָֽאֲדָמָ֔ה וּמִפָּנֶ֖יךָ אֶסָּתֵ֑ר וְהָיִ֜יתִי נָ֤ע וָנָד֙ בָּאָ֔רֶץ וְהָיָ֥ה כָל־מֹצְאִ֖י יַֽהַרְגֵֽנִי׃ 15וַיֹּ֧אמֶר ל֣וֹ יְהֹוָ֗ה לָכֵן֙ כָּל־הֹרֵ֣ג קַ֔יִן שִׁבְעָתַ֖יִם יֻקָּ֑ם וַיָּ֨שֶׂם יְהֹוָ֤ה לְקַ֙יִן֙ א֔וֹת לְבִלְתִּ֥י הַכּוֹת־אֹת֖וֹ כָּל־מֹצְאֽוֹ׃ 16וַיֵּ֥צֵא קַ֖יִן מִלִּפְנֵ֣י יְהֹוָ֑ה וַיֵּ֥שֶׁב בְּאֶֽרֶץ־נ֖וֹד קִדְמַת־עֵֽדֶן׃

17וַיֵּ֤דַע קַ֙יִן֙ אֶת־אִשְׁתּ֔וֹ וַתַּ֖הַר וַתֵּ֣לֶד אֶת־חֲנ֑וֹךְ וַֽיְהִי֙ בֹּ֣נֶה עִ֔יר וַיִּקְרָא֙ שֵׁ֣ם הָעִ֔יר כְּשֵׁ֖ם בְּנ֥וֹ חֲנֽוֹךְ׃ 18וַיִּוָּלֵ֤ד לַֽחֲנוֹךְ֙ אֶת־עִירָ֔ד וְעִירָ֕ד יָלַ֖ד אֶת־מְחֽוּיָאֵ֑ל וּמְחִיָּיאֵ֗ל יָלַד֙ אֶת־מְת֣וּשָׁאֵ֔ל וּמְתֽוּשָׁאֵ֖ל יָלַ֥ד אֶת־לָֽמֶךְ׃ 19וַיִּֽקַּֽח־ל֥וֹ לֶ֖מֶךְ שְׁתֵּ֣י נָשִׁ֑ים שֵׁ֤ם הָֽאַחַת֙ עָדָ֔ה וְשֵׁ֥ם הַשֵּׁנִ֖ית צִלָּֽה׃ 20וַתֵּ֥לֶד עָדָ֖ה אֶת־יָבָ֑ל ה֣וּא הָיָ֔ה אֲבִ֕י יֹשֵׁ֥ב אֹ֖הֶל וּמִקְנֶֽה׃ 21וְשֵׁ֥ם אָחִ֖יו יוּבָ֑ל ה֣וּא הָיָ֔ה אֲבִ֕י כָּל־תֹּפֵ֥שׂ כִּנּ֖וֹר וְעוּגָֽב׃ 22וְצִלָּ֣ה גַם־הִ֗וא יָֽלְדָה֙ אֶת־תּ֣וּבַל קַ֔יִן לֹטֵ֕שׁ כָּל־חֹרֵ֥שׁ נְחֹ֖שֶׁת וּבַרְזֶ֑ל וַֽאֲח֥וֹת תּֽוּבַל־קַ֖יִן נַֽעֲמָֽה׃ 23וַיֹּ֨אמֶר לֶ֜מֶךְ לְנָשָׁ֗יו עָדָ֤ה וְצִלָּה֙ שְׁמַ֣עַן קוֹלִ֔י נְשֵׁ֣י לֶ֔מֶךְ הַֽאְזֵ֖נָּה אִמְרָתִ֑י כִּ֣י אִ֤ישׁ הָרַ֙גְתִּי֙ לְפִצְעִ֔י וְיֶ֖לֶד לְחַבֻּֽרָתִֽי׃ 24כִּ֥י שִׁבְעָתַ֖יִם יֻקַּם־קָ֑יִן וְלֶ֖מֶךְ שִׁבְעִ֥ים וְשִׁבְעָֽה׃ 25וַיֵּ֨דַע אָדָ֥ם עוֹד֙ אֶת־אִשְׁתּ֔וֹ וַתֵּ֣לֶד בֵּ֔ן וַתִּקְרָ֥א אֶת־

4:17. **Cain knew his wife**. Where did she come from?! See the comment on Gen 5:4.

"because God put another seed for me in place of Abel because Cain killed him." 26And a son was born to Seth, him as well, and he called his name Enosh. Then it was begun to invoke the name YHWH.

5 1This is the Book of Records of the Human. In the day of God's creating a human, He made it in the likeness of God. 2He created them male and female, and He blessed them and called their name "Human" in the day of their being created. 3And the human lived a hundred thirty years, and he fathered in his likeness—like his image—and called his name Seth. 4And the human's days after his fathering Seth were eight

שְׁמוֹ שֵׁת כִּי שָׁת־לִי אֱלֹהִים זֶרַע אַחֵר תַּחַת הֶבֶל כִּי הֲרָגוֹ קָיִן: 26וּלְשֵׁת גַּם־הוּא יֻלַּד־בֵּן וַיִּקְרָא אֶת־שְׁמוֹ אֱנוֹשׁ אָז הוּחַל לִקְרֹא בְּשֵׁם יְהוָה: פ

5 1זֶה סֵפֶר תּוֹלְדֹת אָדָם בְּיוֹם בְּרֹא אֱלֹהִים אָדָם בִּדְמוּת אֱלֹהִים עָשָׂה אֹתוֹ: 2זָכָר וּנְקֵבָה בְּרָאָם וַיְבָרֶךְ אֹתָם וַיִּקְרָא אֶת־שְׁמָם אָדָם בְּיוֹם הִבָּרְאָם: ס 3וַיְחִי אָדָם שְׁלֹשִׁים וּמְאַת שָׁנָה וַיּוֹלֶד בִּדְמוּתוֹ כְּצַלְמוֹ וַיִּקְרָא אֶת־שְׁמוֹ שֵׁת: 4וַיִּהְיוּ יְמֵי אָדָם אַחֲרֵי הוֹלִידוֹ אֶת־שֵׁת שְׁמֹנֶה מֵאֹת שָׁנָה

5:1. **Records**. This word has usually been understood to mean "generations," but that is inadequate. The word is used both to introduce records of births (as in this verse) and to introduce stories of events within a family (as in Gen 37:2).

5:1–5. **human**. In these verses, the Hebrew *'ādām* sometimes refers to the species, as in v. 2, where it applies to both male and female; and it sometimes refers specifically to the first male human, so that it also functions as his personal name: Adam.

5:3. **he fathered in his likeness—like his image**. The first man's similarity to his son is described with the same two nouns that are used to describe the first two humans' similarity to God (1:26–27). It certainly sounds as if it means something physical here. We surely would have taken it that way if we had read this verse without having read Genesis 1. Still, we must be cautious on such a classic biblical question. In any case, the significance of this verse is to establish that whatever it is that the first humans acquire from God, it is something that passes by heredity. It is not only the first two humans but the entire species that bears God's image.

5:3. **Seth**. With the birth of Adam's and Eve's son Seth, the text begins a flow of generations, narrowing to a particular family, that continues unbroken through the book of Genesis and ultimately through the rest of the Hebrew Bible. Ironically, the element that establishes this flow, that produces the continuity of Genesis, and that sets the history of the family into the context of the universal history is the "begat" lists. It is ironic because these lists are tedious to most readers. They therefore skip, skim, plow through, or joke about them. The result is that many (perhaps most) readers never get the feeling of Genesis as a book. It is a continuous, sensible work, filled with connections, ironies, puns, and character development—which are diminished or even lost when one reads it only as a collection of separate stories.

5:4. **he fathered sons and daughters**. This is the presumed answer to the question of where Cain's wife came from.

30

hundred years, and he fathered sons and daughters. 5And all of the human's days that he lived were nine hundred years and thirty years. And he died.

6And Seth lived five years and a hundred years, and he fathered Enosh. 7And Seth lived after his fathering Enosh seven years and eight hundred years, and he fathered sons and daughters. 8And all of Seth's days were twelve years and nine hundred years. And he died.

9And Enosh lived ninety years, and he fathered Cainan. 10And Enosh lived after his fathering Cainan fifteen years and eight hundred years, and he fathered sons and daughters. 11And all of Enosh's days were five years and nine hundred years. And he died.

12And Cainan lived seventy years, and he fathered Mahalalel. 13And Cainan lived after his fathering Mahalalel forty years and eight hundred years, and he fathered sons and daughters. 14And all of Cainan's days were ten years and nine hundred years. And he died.

15And Mahalalel lived five years and sixty years, and he fathered Jared. 16And Mahalalel lived after his fathering Jared thirty years and eight hundred years, and he fathered sons and daughters. 17And all of Mahalalel's days were ninety-five years and eight hundred years. And he died.

18And Jared lived sixty-two years and a hun-

וַיּוֹלֶד בָּנִים וּבָנוֹת: 5וַיִּהְיוּ כָּל־יְמֵי אָדָם אֲשֶׁר־חַי תְּשַׁע מֵאוֹת שָׁנָה וּשְׁלֹשִׁים שָׁנָה וַיָּמֹת: ס 6וַיְחִי־שֵׁת חָמֵשׁ שָׁנִים וּמְאַת שָׁנָה וַיּוֹלֶד אֶת־אֱנוֹשׁ: 7וַיְחִי־שֵׁת אַחֲרֵי הוֹלִידוֹ אֶת־אֱנוֹשׁ שֶׁבַע שָׁנִים וּשְׁמֹנֶה מֵאוֹת שָׁנָה וַיּוֹלֶד בָּנִים וּבָנוֹת: 8וַיִּהְיוּ כָּל־יְמֵי־שֵׁת שְׁתֵּים עֶשְׂרֵה שָׁנָה וּתְשַׁע מֵאוֹת שָׁנָה וַיָּמֹת: ס 9וַיְחִי אֱנוֹשׁ תִּשְׁעִים שָׁנָה וַיּוֹלֶד אֶת־קֵינָן: 10וַיְחִי אֱנוֹשׁ אַחֲרֵי הוֹלִידוֹ אֶת־קֵינָן חֲמֵשׁ עֶשְׂרֵה שָׁנָה וּשְׁמֹנֶה מֵאוֹת שָׁנָה וַיּוֹלֶד בָּנִים וּבָנוֹת: 11וַיִּהְיוּ כָּל־יְמֵי אֱנוֹשׁ חָמֵשׁ שָׁנִים וּתְשַׁע מֵאוֹת שָׁנָה וַיָּמֹת: ס 12וַיְחִי קֵינָן שִׁבְעִים שָׁנָה וַיּוֹלֶד אֶת־מַהֲלַלְאֵל: 13וַיְחִי קֵינָן אַחֲרֵי הוֹלִידוֹ אֶת־מַהֲלַלְאֵל אַרְבָּעִים שָׁנָה וּשְׁמֹנֶה מֵאוֹת שָׁנָה וַיּוֹלֶד בָּנִים וּבָנוֹת: 14וַיִּהְיוּ כָּל־יְמֵי קֵינָן עֶשֶׂר שָׁנִים וּתְשַׁע מֵאוֹת שָׁנָה וַיָּמֹת: ס 15וַיְחִי מַהֲלַלְאֵל חָמֵשׁ שָׁנִים וְשִׁשִּׁים שָׁנָה וַיּוֹלֶד אֶת־יָרֶד: 16וַיְחִי מַהֲלַלְאֵל אַחֲרֵי הוֹלִידוֹ אֶת־יֶרֶד שְׁלֹשִׁים שָׁנָה וּשְׁמֹנֶה מֵאוֹת שָׁנָה וַיּוֹלֶד בָּנִים וּבָנוֹת: 17וַיִּהְיוּ כָּל־יְמֵי מַהֲלַלְאֵל חָמֵשׁ וְתִשְׁעִים שָׁנָה וּשְׁמֹנֶה מֵאוֹת שָׁנָה וַיָּמֹת: ס 18וַיְחִי־יֶרֶד שְׁתַּיִם

5:5. **nine hundred years and thirty years**. The long life spans in the early portions of the Torah are an old question. Some assume that the ancients must have counted years differently. But that is not correct. (If we divide Adam's 930 years by ten to get it within normal range, then how shall we divide Moses' 120?) It is clear that this author thought of a year as a normal solar year because that is how long the flood lasts. The point to note is: life spans are pictured as growing shorter. The ten generations from Adam to Noah approach ages of 1,000. But the last one to live more than 900 years is Noah. The next ten generations start with Shem, who lives 600 years, and life spans decline after him. The last person to live more than 200 years is Terah. Abraham (175), Isaac (180), and Jacob (147) live long lives, but not as long as their ancestors. And Moses lives to be 120, which is understood to have become, at some point, the maximum for human life. (See the comment on Gen 6:3.)

dred years, and he fathered Enoch. ¹⁹And Jared lived after his fathering Enoch eight hundred years, and he fathered sons and daughters. ²⁰And all of Jared's days were sixty-two years and nine hundred years. And he died.

²¹And Enoch lived sixty-five years, and he fathered Methuselah. ²²And Enoch walked with God after his fathering Methuselah three hundred years, and he fathered sons and daughters. ²³And all of Enoch's days were sixty-five years and three hundred years. ²⁴And Enoch walked with God, and he was not, because God took him.

²⁵And Methuselah lived eighty-seven years and a hundred years, and he fathered Lamech. ²⁶And Methuselah lived after his fathering Lamech eighty-two years and seven hundred years, and he fathered sons and daughters. ²⁷And all of Methuselah's days were sixty-nine years and nine hundred years. And he died.

²⁸And Lamech lived eighty-two years and a hundred years, and he fathered a son ²⁹and called his name Noah, saying, "This one will

וְשִׁשִּׁים שָׁנָה וּמְאַת שָׁנָה וַיּוֹלֶד אֶת־חֲנוֹךְ: ¹⁹וַיְחִי־יֶרֶד אַחֲרֵי הוֹלִידוֹ אֶת־חֲנוֹךְ שְׁמֹנֶה מֵאוֹת שָׁנָה וַיּוֹלֶד בָּנִים וּבָנוֹת: ²⁰וַיִּהְיוּ כָּל־יְמֵי־יֶרֶד שְׁתַּיִם וְשִׁשִּׁים שָׁנָה וּתְשַׁע מֵאוֹת שָׁנָה וַיָּמֹת: פ ²¹וַיְחִי חֲנוֹךְ חָמֵשׁ וְשִׁשִּׁים שָׁנָה וַיּוֹלֶד אֶת־מְתוּשָׁלַח: ²²וַיִּתְהַלֵּךְ חֲנוֹךְ אֶת־הָאֱלֹהִים אַחֲרֵי הוֹלִידוֹ אֶת־מְתוּשֶׁלַח שְׁלֹשׁ מֵאוֹת שָׁנָה וַיּוֹלֶד בָּנִים וּבָנוֹת: ²³וַיְהִי כָּל־יְמֵי חֲנוֹךְ חָמֵשׁ וְשִׁשִּׁים שָׁנָה וּשְׁלֹשׁ מֵאוֹת שָׁנָה: ²⁴וַיִּתְהַלֵּךְ חֲנוֹךְ אֶת־הָאֱלֹהִים וְאֵינֶנּוּ כִּי־לָקַח אֹתוֹ אֱלֹהִים: פ ²⁵וַיְחִי מְתוּשֶׁלַח שֶׁבַע וּשְׁמֹנִים שָׁנָה וּמְאַת שָׁנָה וַיּוֹלֶד אֶת־לָמֶךְ: ²⁶וַיְחִי מְתוּשֶׁלַח אַחֲרֵי הוֹלִידוֹ אֶת־לֶמֶךְ שְׁתַּיִם וּשְׁמוֹנִים שָׁנָה וּשְׁבַע מֵאוֹת שָׁנָה וַיּוֹלֶד בָּנִים וּבָנוֹת: ²⁷וַיִּהְיוּ כָּל־יְמֵי מְתוּשֶׁלַח תֵּשַׁע וְשִׁשִּׁים שָׁנָה וּתְשַׁע מֵאוֹת שָׁנָה וַיָּמֹת: פ ²⁸וַיְחִי־לֶמֶךְ שְׁתַּיִם וּשְׁמֹנִים שָׁנָה וּמְאַת שָׁנָה וַיּוֹלֶד בֵּן: ²⁹וַיִּקְרָא אֶת־שְׁמוֹ נֹחַ לֵאמֹר

5:24. **Enoch walked with God**. This expression is used in ancient Near Eastern texts to express continuous fidelity. So here it would mean that Enoch was faithful to God.

5:24. **and he was not, because God took him**. I do not know what this means. It was traditionally understood to mean that Enoch does not die. Alternatively, it could be the report of his death. It comes at the point at which all the other entries in this list say "And he died." The same word is used later by Joseph's brothers to express the fact that he is gone (Gen 42:13). At that point, the brothers do not know whether he is alive or not. It may possibly mean something like that in the case of Enoch as well: his fate was unknown. At minimum, it means (as with the case of Elijah later) that there is something distinctive and unusual about the man, his relationship to God, and his departure from life among humans.

5:29. **Noah**. The name is connected here to the Hebrew root *nḥm*, meaning "console," though we would naturally connect it to a different root, *nwḥ*, meaning "rest," which matches the name Noah and does not have the extra *m* (Hebrew *mem*) at the end. Biblical names, like contemporary naming of Jewish children, are not necessarily based on precise etymologies, but rather may be based on similarity of sounds, involving only some of the root letters. See, similarly, the comment on the name Cain (Gen 4:1).

console us from our labor and from our hands' suffering from the ground, which YHWH has cursed." 30And Lamech lived after his fathering Noah ninety-five years and five hundred years, and he fathered sons and daughters. 31And all of Lamech's days were seventy-seven years and seven hundred years. And he died.

32And Noah was five hundred years old, and Noah fathered Shem, Ham, and Yaphet.

6 1And it was when humankind began to multiply on the face of the ground and daughters were born to them: 2and the sons of God saw the daughters of humankind, that they were attractive, and they took women, from all they chose. 3And YHWH said, "My spirit won't stay in humankind forever, since they're also flesh; and their days shall be a hundred twenty years." 4The Nephilim were in the earth in those

זֶה יְנַחֲמֵנוּ מִמַּעֲשֵׂנוּ וּמֵעִצְּבוֹן יָדֵינוּ מִן־הָאֲדָמָה אֲשֶׁר אֵרְרָהּ יְהוָה: 30וַיְחִי־לֶמֶךְ אַחֲרֵי הוֹלִידוֹ אֶת־נֹחַ חָמֵשׁ וְתִשְׁעִים שָׁנָה וַחֲמֵשׁ מֵאֹת שָׁנָה וַיּוֹלֶד בָּנִים וּבָנוֹת: 31וַיְהִי כָּל־יְמֵי־לֶמֶךְ שֶׁבַע וְשִׁבְעִים שָׁנָה וּשְׁבַע מֵאוֹת שָׁנָה וַיָּמֹת: ס 32וַיְהִי־נֹחַ בֶּן־חֲמֵשׁ מֵאוֹת שָׁנָה וַיּוֹלֶד נֹחַ אֶת־שֵׁם אֶת־חָם וְאֶת־יָפֶת:

6 1וַיְהִי כִּי־הֵחֵל הָאָדָם לָרֹב עַל־פְּנֵי הָאֲדָמָה וּבָנוֹת יֻלְּדוּ לָהֶם: 2וַיִּרְאוּ בְנֵי־הָאֱלֹהִים אֶת־בְּנוֹת הָאָדָם כִּי טֹבֹת הֵנָּה וַיִּקְחוּ לָהֶם נָשִׁים מִכֹּל אֲשֶׁר בָּחָרוּ: 3וַיֹּאמֶר יְהוָה לֹא־יָדוֹן רוּחִי בָאָדָם לְעֹלָם בְּשַׁגַּם הוּא בָשָׂר וְהָיוּ יָמָיו מֵאָה וְעֶשְׂרִים שָׁנָה: 4הַנְּפִלִים הָיוּ בָאָרֶץ בַּיָּמִים הָהֵם וְגַם אַחֲרֵי־כֵן

6:3. **My spirit won't stay in humankind forever**. Meaning: humans will not live forever.

6:3. **their days shall be a hundred twenty years**. God sets a maximum of 120 years for a human life. The reduction takes place gradually from a peak in the 900s (Methuselah and Noah) to ages in the 100s for the patriarchs. At the end of the Torah, Moses is said to have lived the full 120 years.

6:4. **Nephilim**. Some Bible stories are virtually self-contained. Even though they may have implications elsewhere in the *Tanak*, we can still read them as sensible, comprehensible individual units. But this account of the giants is an example of another type of story: those whose elements are widely separated, distributed across great stretches of the narrative. These stories provide the connections that make the *Tanak* a united work, telling a continuous story, rather than a patchwork of little tales.

The issue is that there are giants: uncommonly big, powerful persons, who are frightening. The first question is: from where did they come? Answer: *"běnê 'ĕlōhîm"* have relations with human women, and they give birth to giants, Nephilim. Whatever the biblical author thought *běnê 'ĕlōhîm* were, we can say at minimum that it refers here to some sort of (male) creatures from the divine realm (see my comment on Deut 32:8). As in an extremely common mythological theme, such mixed divine-human breeding produces beings who are bigger and stronger than regular humans.

This does not come up again in the story until thousands of years later. When Moses sends men to scout the promised land, they see the giants: "the Nephilim" (Num 13:33). That is what scares the scouts, and their fear infects the Israelites, changing the destiny of the wilderness generation. A generation later, Joshua eliminates all

days and after that as well, when the sons of God came to the daughters of humankind, and they gave birth by them. They were the heroes who were of old, people of renown.

⁵And YHWH saw that human bad was multiplied in the earth, and every inclination of their heart's thoughts was only bad all the day. ⁶And YHWH regretted that He had made humankind in the earth.

And He was grieved to His heart.

⁷And YHWH said, "I'll wipe out the human whom I've created from the face of the earth, from human to animal to creeping thing, and to the bird of the skies, because I regret that I made

אֲשֶׁ֣ר יָבֹ֜אוּ בְּנֵ֤י הָֽאֱלֹהִים֙ אֶל־בְּנ֣וֹת הָֽאָדָ֔ם וְיָלְד֖וּ
לָהֶ֑ם הֵ֧מָּה הַגִּבֹּרִ֛ים אֲשֶׁ֥ר מֵעוֹלָ֖ם אַנְשֵׁ֥י הַשֵּֽׁם: פ
⁵וַיַּ֣רְא יְהֹוָ֔ה כִּ֥י רַבָּ֛ה רָעַ֥ת הָאָדָ֖ם בָּאָ֑רֶץ וְכָל־
יֵ֙צֶר֙ מַחְשְׁבֹ֣ת לִבּ֔וֹ רַ֥ק רַ֖ע כָּל־הַיּֽוֹם: ⁶וַיִּנָּ֣חֶם יְהֹוָ֔ה
כִּֽי־עָשָׂ֥ה אֶת־הָֽאָדָ֖ם בָּאָ֑רֶץ וַיִּתְעַצֵּ֖ב אֶל־לִבּֽוֹ:
⁷וַיֹּ֣אמֶר יְהֹוָ֗ה אֶמְחֶ֨ה אֶת־הָֽאָדָ֤ם אֲשֶׁר־בָּרָ֙אתִי֙ מֵעַל֙
פְּנֵ֣י הָֽאֲדָמָ֔ה מֵֽאָדָם֙ עַד־בְּהֵמָ֔ה עַד־רֶ֖מֶשׂ וְעַד־ע֣וֹף

---

the giants from the land except from the Philistine cities, particularly the city of *Gath* (Josh 11:21–22). And later still, the most famous Philistine giant, Goliath, comes from *Gath* (1 Sam 17:4). And David defeats him.

We can read each of these stories without noticing that they are a connected account, building to a climactic scene, but obviously we miss something that way. Such widely distributed stories are there because the Bible is *not* a loose collection of stories. It is an intricate, elegant, exquisite, long work with continuity and coherence. When we know our Bible well, we read this story about the giants in creation, and we are aware that they will play a part in the tragedy of the wilderness generation, that Joshua will defeat them, and that David will face the most famous (and last?) of them.

This episode, coming at the end of the first parashah of the year, is a reminder that one cannot really learn the Torah without learning the rest of the *Tanak* as well.

6:6. **And YHWH regretted**. What could this mean? If God knows the future, how could God regret something once it has happened? Compare what the prophet Samuel says about God: "He's not a human that He should regret" (1 Sam 15:29); yet it says twice in that same chapter that God *does* regret making Saul the king of Israel (15:11,35)! This word is commonly understood to mean "repented," especially when referring to human beings, but the question still remains what it would mean for God. The problem may be more linguistic than theological, as a result of a lack of a satisfactory word in English to capture the wider range of the Hebrew word. It refers to a change of heart or making a reversal of direction. The nature of this change may vary according to the situation, so that it may mean "repent" or "regret" or "relent," and in biblical terms it may apply to either God or humans.

6:8. **Noah found favor**. Parashat Bereshit ends not with the deity's mournful statement that "I regret that I made them" (6:7) but rather with a point of hope: that Noah found favor in the divine sight.

6:8. **Noah found favor**. Note the artistry: This is the beginning of a chain of wordplay on the name Noah, as its two strong root letters, *N* and guttural *Ḥ*, recur frequently:

them." ⁸But Noah had found favor in YHWH's eyes.

הַשָּׁמָיִם כִּי נִחַמְתִּי כִּי עֲשִׂיתָם: ⁸וְנֹחַ מָצָא חֵן בְּעֵינֵי יְהוָה: פ

NOAH

נח

⁹These are the records of Noah: Noah was a virtuous man. He was unblemished in his generations. Noah walked with God. ¹⁰And Noah fathered three sons: Shem, Ham, and Yaphet. ¹¹And the earth was corrupted before God, and the earth was filled with violence. ¹²And God saw the earth; and, here, it was corrupted, because all flesh had corrupted its way on the earth. ¹³And God said to Noah, "The end of all flesh has come before me, because the earth is filled with violence because of them. And here: I'm de-

⁹אֵלֶּה תּוֹלְדֹת נֹחַ נֹחַ אִישׁ צַדִּיק תָּמִים הָיָה בְּדֹרֹתָיו אֶת־הָאֱלֹהִים הִתְהַלֶּךְ־נֹחַ: ¹⁰וַיּוֹלֶד נֹחַ שְׁלֹשָׁה בָנִים אֶת־שֵׁם אֶת־חָם וְאֶת־יָפֶת: ¹¹וַתִּשָּׁחֵת הָאָרֶץ לִפְנֵי הָאֱלֹהִים וַתִּמָּלֵא הָאָרֶץ חָמָס: ¹²וַיַּרְא אֱלֹהִים אֶת־הָאָרֶץ וְהִנֵּה נִשְׁחָתָה כִּי־הִשְׁחִית כָּל־בָּשָׂר אֶת־דַּרְכּוֹ עַל־הָאָרֶץ: ס ¹³וַיֹּאמֶר אֱלֹהִים לְנֹחַ קֵץ כָּל־בָּשָׂר בָּא לְפָנַי כִּי־מָלְאָה הָאָרֶץ חָמָס מִפְּנֵיהֶם וְהִנְנִי מַשְׁחִיתָם אֶת־

"This one will comfort us" (5:29) *yĕNaḤămēnû*

"He regretted" (6:6) *wayyiNNāḤem*

"I regret" (6:7) *NiḤamtî*

"Noah found favor" (6:8) *NōaḤ māṣā' HēN*

"And the ark rested" (8:4) *wattāNaḤ*

"pleasant smell" (8:21) *NîḤōaḤ*

6:9. **unblemished in his generations**. Is it not redundant to say "in his generations"? When else could he have lived?! The classic rabbinic interpretation of this is two-sided. It can be taken to his credit: that he could be good even in so corrupt an era. Or it can be taken as diminishing his credit: that he is good only in comparison to his corrupt era, but that he would appear less outstanding in a more moral generation. But really the word here means "without a blemish." It is used elsewhere to refer to a sacrificial animal, which can have no injury or else it would be disqualified for sacrifice. There are no degrees of "unblemished." One either is unblemished or is not. So the words "in his generations" do not diminish this. Noah's virtue is being established here. And it is important that a story composed by Jews emphasized the virtue of someone who is not a Jew—and who is the father of *all* people. (A related term is used to describe Job, another virtuous man who is not a Jew; see Job 1:8; 2:3.)

6:11. **the earth was corrupted**. The Hebrew word, *'ereṣ*, can mean "land" or "earth." Here it refers to all the earth but still applies just to the dry land, and not the sea. (Cf. Exod 8:20.) That is why there will be no destruction of sea creatures. It is the land that will disappear, and land creatures that will die.

stroying them with the earth. 14Make yourself an ark of gopher wood, make rooms with the ark, and pitch it outside and inside with pitch. 15And this is how you shall make it: three hundred cubits the length of the ark, fifty cubits its width, and thirty cubits its height. 16You shall make a window for the ark, and you shall finish it to a cubit from the top, and you shall make the ark's entrance in its side. You shall make lower, second, and third stories for it. 17And I, here: I'm bringing the flood, water on the earth, to destroy all flesh in which is the breath of life from under the skies. Everything that is in the earth will expire. 18And I shall establish my covenant with you. And you'll come to the ark, you and your sons and your wife and your sons' wives with you. 19And of all the living, of all flesh, you shall bring two of each to the ark to keep alive with you. They shall be male and female. 20Of the birds by their kind and of the domestic animals by their kind, of all the creeping things of the ground by their kind, two of each will come to you to keep alive. 21And you, take some of every food that will be eaten and gather it to you, and it will be for you and for them for food." 22And Noah did it. According to everything that God commanded him, he did so.

7 1And YHWH said to Noah, "Come, you and all your household, into an ark, for I've seen you as virtuous in front of me in this generation.

הָאָרֶץ: 14עֲשֵׂה לְךָ תֵּבַת עֲצֵי־גֹפֶר קִנִּים תַּעֲשֶׂה אֶת־הַתֵּבָה וְכָפַרְתָּ אֹתָהּ מִבַּיִת וּמִחוּץ בַּכֹּפֶר: 15וְזֶה אֲשֶׁר תַּעֲשֶׂה אֹתָהּ שְׁלֹשׁ מֵאוֹת אַמָּה אֹרֶךְ הַתֵּבָה חֲמִשִּׁים אַמָּה רָחְבָּהּ וּשְׁלֹשִׁים אַמָּה קוֹמָתָהּ: 16צֹהַר ׀ תַּעֲשֶׂה לַתֵּבָה וְאֶל־אַמָּה תְּכַלֶּנָּה מִלְמַעְלָה וּפֶתַח הַתֵּבָה בְּצִדָּהּ תָּשִׂים תַּחְתִּיִּם שְׁנִיִּם וּשְׁלִשִׁים תַּעֲשֶׂהָ: 17וַאֲנִי הִנְנִי מֵבִיא אֶת־הַמַּבּוּל מַיִם עַל־הָאָרֶץ לְשַׁחֵת כָּל־בָּשָׂר אֲשֶׁר־בּוֹ רוּחַ חַיִּים מִתַּחַת הַשָּׁמָיִם כֹּל אֲשֶׁר־בָּאָרֶץ יִגְוָע: 18וַהֲקִמֹתִי אֶת־בְּרִיתִי אִתָּךְ וּבָאתָ אֶל־הַתֵּבָה אַתָּה וּבָנֶיךָ וְאִשְׁתְּךָ וּנְשֵׁי־בָנֶיךָ אִתָּךְ: 19וּמִכָּל־הָחַי מִכָּל־בָּשָׂר שְׁנַיִם מִכֹּל תָּבִיא אֶל־הַתֵּבָה לְהַחֲיֹת אִתָּךְ זָכָר וּנְקֵבָה יִהְיוּ: 20מֵהָעוֹף לְמִינֵהוּ וּמִן־הַבְּהֵמָה לְמִינָהּ מִכֹּל רֶמֶשׂ הָאֲדָמָה לְמִינֵהוּ שְׁנַיִם מִכֹּל יָבֹאוּ אֵלֶיךָ לְהַחֲיוֹת: 21וְאַתָּה קַח־לְךָ מִכָּל־מַאֲכָל אֲשֶׁר יֵאָכֵל וְאָסַפְתָּ אֵלֶיךָ וְהָיָה לְךָ וְלָהֶם לְאָכְלָה: 22וַיַּעַשׂ נֹחַ כְּכֹל אֲשֶׁר צִוָּה אֹתוֹ אֱלֹהִים כֵּן עָשָׂה: ס
7 1וַיֹּאמֶר יְהוָה לְנֹחַ בֹּא־אַתָּה וְכָל־בֵּיתְךָ אֶל־הַתֵּבָה כִּי־אֹתְךָ רָאִיתִי צַדִּיק לְפָנַי בַּדּוֹר הַזֶּה:

6:12. **all flesh had corrupted its way**. All animal life, not just humans.

6:12. **on the earth**. Land animals, not sea creatures. Sadly, in the current era, we are corrupting the sea (and the sky, and space) as well.

6:13. **destroying**. The word in Hebrew, *mašḥîtām*, has the same root meaning as the word for what all flesh have done in the preceding verse: corrupted, Hebrew *hišḥît*. The same pun is used in Moses' description of the golden calf event (Deut 9:12,26). This is not just wordplay for its own sake. It conveys the principle that punishment is meant to be in proportion to the crime. It also shows once again the environment suffering because of human corruption.

2Of all the pure animals, take seven pairs, man and his woman; and of the animals that are not pure, two, man and his woman. 3Also of the birds of the skies seven pairs, male and female, to keep seed alive on the face of the earth. 4Because in seven more days I'll rain on the earth, forty days and forty nights, and I'll wipe out all the substance that I've made from on the face of the earth."

5And Noah did according to all that YHWH had commanded him. 6And Noah was six hundred years old when the flood was, water on the earth. 7And Noah and his sons and his wife and his sons' wives with him came to the ark from before the waters of the flood. 8Of the animals that were pure and of the animals that were not pure, and of the birds and every one that creeps on the ground, 9they came by twos to Noah, to the ark, male and female, as God had commanded Noah. 10And seven days later the waters of the flood were on the earth. 11In the six hundredth year of Noah's life, in the second month, in the seventeenth day of the month, on this day all the fountains of the great deep were split open, and the apertures of the skies were opened. 12And there was rain on the earth, forty days and forty nights. 13In this very day Noah came, and Shem and Ham and Yaphet, Noah's sons, and Noah's wife and his sons' three wives with them to the

2מִכֹּל ׀ הַבְּהֵמָה הַטְּהוֹרָה תִּקַּח־לְךָ שִׁבְעָה שִׁבְעָה אִישׁ וְאִשְׁתּוֹ וּמִן־הַבְּהֵמָה אֲשֶׁר לֹא טְהֹרָה הִוא שְׁנַיִם אִישׁ וְאִשְׁתּוֹ: 3גַּם מֵעוֹף הַשָּׁמַיִם שִׁבְעָה שִׁבְעָה זָכָר וּנְקֵבָה לְחַיּוֹת זֶרַע עַל־פְּנֵי כָל־הָאָרֶץ: 4כִּי לְיָמִים עוֹד שִׁבְעָה אָנֹכִי מַמְטִיר עַל־הָאָרֶץ אַרְבָּעִים יוֹם וְאַרְבָּעִים לָיְלָה וּמָחִיתִי אֶת־כָּל־הַיְקוּם אֲשֶׁר עָשִׂיתִי מֵעַל פְּנֵי הָאֲדָמָה: 5וַיַּעַשׂ נֹחַ כְּכֹל אֲשֶׁר־צִוָּהוּ יְהֹוָה:

6וְנֹחַ בֶּן־שֵׁשׁ מֵאוֹת שָׁנָה וְהַמַּבּוּל הָיָה מַיִם עַל־הָאָרֶץ: 7וַיָּבֹא נֹחַ וּבָנָיו וְאִשְׁתּוֹ וּנְשֵׁי־בָנָיו אִתּוֹ אֶל־הַתֵּבָה מִפְּנֵי מֵי הַמַּבּוּל: 8מִן־הַבְּהֵמָה הַטְּהוֹרָה וּמִן־הַבְּהֵמָה אֲשֶׁר אֵינֶנָּה טְהֹרָה וּמִן־הָעוֹף וְכֹל אֲשֶׁר־רֹמֵשׂ עַל־הָאֲדָמָה: 9שְׁנַיִם שְׁנַיִם בָּאוּ אֶל־נֹחַ אֶל־הַתֵּבָה זָכָר וּנְקֵבָה כַּאֲשֶׁר צִוָּה אֱלֹהִים אֶת־נֹחַ: 10וַיְהִי לְשִׁבְעַת הַיָּמִים וּמֵי הַמַּבּוּל הָיוּ עַל־הָאָרֶץ: 11בִּשְׁנַת שֵׁשׁ־מֵאוֹת שָׁנָה לְחַיֵּי־נֹחַ בַּחֹדֶשׁ הַשֵּׁנִי בְּשִׁבְעָה־עָשָׂר יוֹם לַחֹדֶשׁ בַּיּוֹם הַזֶּה נִבְקְעוּ כָּל־מַעְיְנֹת תְּהוֹם רַבָּה וַאֲרֻבֹּת הַשָּׁמַיִם נִפְתָּחוּ: 12וַיְהִי הַגֶּשֶׁם עַל־הָאָרֶץ אַרְבָּעִים יוֹם וְאַרְבָּעִים לָיְלָה: 13בְּעֶצֶם הַיּוֹם הַזֶּה בָּא נֹחַ וְשֵׁם־וְחָם וָיֶפֶת בְּנֵי־נֹחַ וְאֵשֶׁת נֹחַ וּשְׁלֹשֶׁת נְשֵׁי־בָנָיו אִתָּם אֶל־

7:2. **pure.** This has also been translated as "clean." Neither English word captures the sense of the Hebrew. Here it refers to animals that are fit for sacrifice, which is to say: for humans to eat. Noah takes seven pairs of the "pure" animals and only one pair of the "not pure," because he will offer sacrifices after the flood. If he were to have only two sheep, then his sacrifice would wipe out the species.

7:11. **the fountains of the great deep . . . and the apertures of the skies were opened.** One must have a picture of the structure of the universe that is described in Genesis 1 in order to comprehend the significance of the destruction that is narrated in the flood story. The creation account pictures a clear firmament or space holding back the waters that are above the firmament and those that are below. Now the narrative reports that "all the fountains of the great deep were split open, and the apertures of the skies were opened." The cosmic waters are able to spill in from above and below, filling the habitable bubble, thus:

ark, ¹⁴they and all the wild animals by their kind and all the domestic animals by their kind and all the creeping animals that creep on the earth

הַתֵּבָה: ¹⁴הֵמָּה וְכָל־הַחַיָּה לְמִינָהּ וְכָל־הַבְּהֵמָה לְמִינָהּ וְכָל־הָרֶמֶשׂ הָרֹמֵשׂ עַל־הָאָרֶץ לְמִינֵהוּ וְכָל־

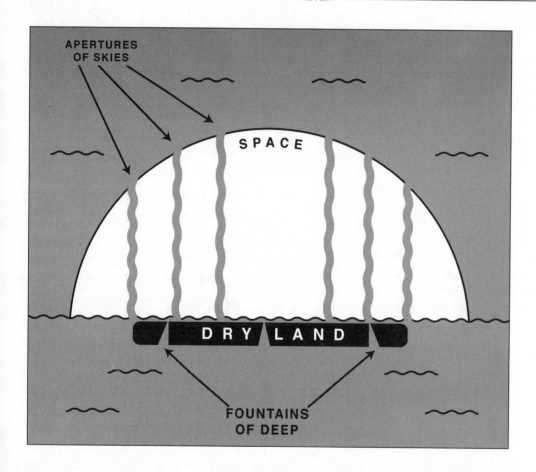

It is far more than an ordinary rain. It is a cosmic crisis, in which the very structure of the universe is endangered.

7:13. **the ark**. At the same time that the threat at the cosmic level is more powerful than is usually pictured, the condition of the humans in the story is more vulnerable. As commonly pictured in art, the "ark" that bears the humans and animals through the floodwaters is a boat. This would be a correct view of the vehicle in the Mesopotamian flood account, now contained in one form in Tablet XI of the epic of Gilgamesh. There the hero, Utnapishtim, takes his family, his possessions, and the animals into a boat to escape a flood brought on by the gods. The parallels to the biblical account are tantalizing: Utnapishtim's boat comes to rest on a mountaintop; he sends out three birds, including a dove and a raven; and he builds an altar and offers a sacrifice. A notable difference, however, is precisely that the biblical flood hero,

38

by their kind and all the birds by their kind, all fowl, all winged things. 15And they came to Noah, to the ark, by twos of all flesh in which was the breath of life, 16and those that came were male and female; some from all flesh came, as God had commanded him. And YHWH closed it for him. 17And the flood was on the earth for forty days, and the waters multiplied and raised the ark, and it was lifted from the earth. 18And the waters grew strong and multiplied very much on the earth, and the ark went on the face of the waters. 19And the waters had grown very, very strong on the earth, so they covered all the high mountains that are under all the skies. 20Fifteen cubits above, the waters grew stronger, and they covered the mountains. 21And all flesh that creep on the earth—of the birds and of the domestic animals and of the wild animals and of all the swarming creatures that swarm on the earth, and all the humans—expired. 22Everything that had the breathing spirit of life in its nostrils, everything that was on the ground, died. 23And He wiped out all the substance that was on the face of the earth, from human to animal to creeping thing and to bird of the skies, and they were wiped out from the earth, and just Noah and those who were with him in the ark were left. 24And the water grew strong on the earth a hundred fifty days.

הָע֖וֹף לְמִינֵ֑הוּ כֹּ֤ל צִפּוֹר֙ כָּל־כָּנָ֔ף׃ 15וַיָּבֹ֥אוּ אֶל־נֹ֖חַ אֶל־הַתֵּבָ֑ה שְׁנַ֤יִם שְׁנַ֙יִם֙ מִכָּל־הַבָּשָׂ֔ר אֲשֶׁר־בּ֖וֹ ר֥וּחַ חַיִּֽים׃ 16וְהַבָּאִ֗ים זָכָ֤ר וּנְקֵבָה֙ מִכָּל־בָּשָׂר֙ בָּ֔אוּ כַּאֲשֶׁ֛ר צִוָּ֥ה אֹת֖וֹ אֱלֹהִ֑ים וַיִּסְגֹּ֥ר יְהוָ֖ה בַּעֲדֽוֹ׃ 17וַֽיְהִ֧י הַמַּבּ֛וּל אַרְבָּעִ֥ים י֖וֹם עַל־הָאָ֑רֶץ וַיִּרְבּ֣וּ הַמַּ֗יִם וַיִּשְׂאוּ֙ אֶת־הַתֵּבָ֔ה וַתָּ֖רָם מֵעַ֥ל הָאָֽרֶץ׃ 18וַיִּגְבְּר֥וּ הַמַּ֛יִם וַיִּרְבּ֥וּ מְאֹ֖ד עַל־הָאָ֑רֶץ וַתֵּ֥לֶךְ הַתֵּבָ֖ה עַל־פְּנֵ֥י הַמָּֽיִם׃ 19וְהַמַּ֗יִם גָּ֥בְר֛וּ מְאֹ֥ד מְאֹ֖ד עַל־הָאָ֑רֶץ וַיְכֻסּ֗וּ כָּל־הֶֽהָרִים֙ הַגְּבֹהִ֔ים אֲשֶׁר־תַּ֖חַת כָּל־הַשָּׁמָֽיִם׃ 20חֲמֵ֨שׁ עֶשְׂרֵ֤ה אַמָּה֙ מִלְמַ֔עְלָה גָּבְר֖וּ הַמָּ֑יִם וַיְכֻסּ֖וּ הֶהָרִֽים׃ 21וַיִּגְוַ֞ע כָּל־בָּשָׂ֣ר ׀ הָרֹמֵ֣שׂ עַל־הָאָ֗רֶץ בָּע֤וֹף וּבַבְּהֵמָה֙ וּבַ֣חַיָּ֔ה וּבְכָל־הַשֶּׁ֖רֶץ הַשֹּׁרֵ֣ץ עַל־הָאָ֑רֶץ וְכֹ֖ל הָאָדָֽם׃ 22כֹּ֡ל אֲשֶׁר֩ נִשְׁמַת־ר֨וּחַ חַיִּ֜ים בְּאַפָּ֗יו מִכֹּ֛ל אֲשֶׁ֥ר בֶּחָֽרָבָ֖ה מֵֽתוּ׃ 23וַיִּ֜מַח אֶֽת־כָּל־הַיְק֣וּם ׀ אֲשֶׁ֣ר ׀ עַל־פְּנֵ֣י הָֽאֲדָמָ֗ה מֵאָדָ֤ם עַד־בְּהֵמָה֙ עַד־רֶ֙מֶשׂ֙ וְעַד־ע֣וֹף הַשָּׁמַ֔יִם וַיִּמָּח֖וּ מִן־הָאָ֑רֶץ וַיִּשָּׁ֧אֶר אַךְ־נֹ֛חַ וַֽאֲשֶׁ֥ר אִתּ֖וֹ בַּתֵּבָֽה׃ 24וַיִּגְבְּר֥וּ הַמַּ֖יִם עַל־הָאָ֑רֶץ חֲמִשִּׁ֥ים וּמְאַ֖ת יֽוֹם׃

Noah, does not build a boat, but rather an ark. An ark is a box. The measurements given for it in the text are rectangular, and there is neither a keel nor a rudder nor a sail. The same applies to the box in which the baby Moses is placed in Exod 2:3. Still, I must admit that it is notable that the two objects called *tēbāh* in the Hebrew Bible both float on water. I have used the word "ark" here reluctantly because it is now so familiar that readers would find any other word jarring. Regardless of the word, though, the important fact is that, in such a vessel, the humans and animals are utterly helpless, cast about in the waters without any control over their fate. To appreciate the image that this narrative sets before us, we must picture this helpless box of life tossed about in a violent universe that is breaking at its seams.

7:16. **YHWH closed it for him.** Note the degree of close contact that is pictured between God and humans at this stage. This will reach a high point in Moses' experience at Sinai in Exodus, and then it will gradually diminish through the rest of the *Tanak*.

8 [1]And God remembered Noah and all the wild animals and all the domestic animals that were with him in the ark, and God passed a wind over the earth, and the water decreased. [2]And the fountains of the deep and the apertures of the skies were shut, and the rain was restrained from the skies. [3]And the waters went back from on the earth, going back continually, and the water receded at the end of a hundred fifty days. [4]And the ark rested in the seventh month, in the seventeenth day of the month, on the mountains of Ararat. [5]And the water went on receding until the tenth month. In the tenth month, in the first of the month, the tops of the mountains appeared. [6]And it was at the end of forty days, and Noah opened the window of the ark that he had made. [7]And he let a raven go, and it went back and forth until the water dried up from the earth. [8]And he let a dove go from him to see whether the waters had eased from the face of the earth. [9]And the dove did not find a resting place for its foot, and it came back to him to the ark, for waters were on the face of the earth, and he put out his hand and took it and brought it to him to the ark. [10]And he waited still another seven days, and he again let a dove go from the ark. [11]And the dove came to him at evening time, and here was an olive leaf torn off in its mouth, and Noah knew that the waters had eased from the earth. [12]And he waited still another seven days, and he let a dove go, and it did not come

8 [1]וַיִּזְכֹּר אֱלֹהִים אֶת־נֹחַ וְאֵת כָּל־הַחַיָּה וְאֶת־כָּל־הַבְּהֵמָה אֲשֶׁר אִתּוֹ בַּתֵּבָה וַיַּעֲבֵר אֱלֹהִים רוּחַ עַל־הָאָרֶץ וַיָּשֹׁכּוּ הַמָּיִם: [2]וַיִּסָּכְרוּ מַעְיְנֹת תְּהוֹם וַאֲרֻבֹּת הַשָּׁמָיִם וַיִּכָּלֵא הַגֶּשֶׁם מִן־הַשָּׁמָיִם: [3]וַיָּשֻׁבוּ הַמַּיִם מֵעַל הָאָרֶץ הָלוֹךְ וָשׁוֹב וַיַּחְסְרוּ הַמַּיִם מִקְצֵה חֲמִשִּׁים וּמְאַת יוֹם: [4]וַתָּנַח הַתֵּבָה בַּחֹדֶשׁ הַשְּׁבִיעִי בְּשִׁבְעָה־עָשָׂר יוֹם לַחֹדֶשׁ עַל הָרֵי אֲרָרָט: [5]וְהַמַּיִם הָיוּ הָלוֹךְ וְחָסוֹר עַד הַחֹדֶשׁ הָעֲשִׂירִי בָּעֲשִׂירִי בְּאֶחָד לַחֹדֶשׁ נִרְאוּ רָאשֵׁי הֶהָרִים: [6]וַיְהִי מִקֵּץ אַרְבָּעִים יוֹם וַיִּפְתַּח נֹחַ אֶת־חַלּוֹן הַתֵּבָה אֲשֶׁר עָשָׂה: [7]וַיְשַׁלַּח אֶת־הָעֹרֵב וַיֵּצֵא יָצוֹא וָשׁוֹב עַד־יְבֹשֶׁת הַמַּיִם מֵעַל הָאָרֶץ: [8]וַיְשַׁלַּח אֶת־הַיּוֹנָה מֵאִתּוֹ לִרְאוֹת הֲקַלּוּ הַמַּיִם מֵעַל פְּנֵי הָאֲדָמָה: [9]וְלֹא־מָצְאָה הַיּוֹנָה מָנוֹחַ לְכַף־רַגְלָהּ וַתָּשָׁב אֵלָיו אֶל־הַתֵּבָה כִּי־מַיִם עַל־פְּנֵי כָל־הָאָרֶץ וַיִּשְׁלַח יָדוֹ וַיִּקָּחֶהָ וַיָּבֵא אֹתָהּ אֵלָיו אֶל־הַתֵּבָה: [10]וַיָּחֶל עוֹד שִׁבְעַת יָמִים אֲחֵרִים וַיֹּסֶף שַׁלַּח אֶת־הַיּוֹנָה מִן־הַתֵּבָה: [11]וַתָּבֹא אֵלָיו הַיּוֹנָה לְעֵת עֶרֶב וְהִנֵּה עֲלֵה־זַיִת טָרָף בְּפִיהָ וַיֵּדַע נֹחַ כִּי־קַלּוּ הַמַּיִם מֵעַל הָאָרֶץ: [12]וַיִּיָּחֶל עוֹד שִׁבְעַת יָמִים אֲחֵרִים וַיְשַׁלַּח אֶת־הַיּוֹנָה וְלֹא־יָסְפָה שׁוּב־אֵלָיו עוֹד:

8:1. **God remembered.** There is an old tradition that when the deity is called God (*'ĕlōhîm*) this refers to the deity's aspect of being *just,* and that when the deity is called YHWH it refers to the divine aspect of being *merciful.* But in this verse the deity is being merciful but is still called *God.* Rashi justifies this by saying that the standard of justice is changed into the standard of compassion by means of the prayers of virtuous people. That is a lovely interpretation, but it has no basis in the text. Noah does not pray. (Noah never speaks in this text until after the flood.) And, earlier, when the deity decides to destroy all flesh, the name YHWH, which is supposed to stand for divine mercy, is used (6:7). The fact is that this traditional distinction in the divine names does not hold up through the biblical text. Rather, the relationship between the justice and mercy of God is far more complex than this.

40

back to him ever again. 13And it was in the six hundred and first year, in the first month, in the first of the month: the water dried from on the earth. And Noah turned back the covering of the ark and looked, and here the face of the earth had dried. 14And in the second month, in the twenty-seventh day of the month, the earth dried up.

15And God spoke to Noah, saying, 16"Go out from the ark, you and your wife and your sons and your sons' wives with you. 17Bring out with you all the living things that are with you, of all flesh, of the birds and of the domestic animals and of all the creeping animals that creep on the earth, and they will swarm in the earth and be fruitful and multiply on the earth."

18And Noah went out, and his sons and his wife and his sons' wives with him. 19All the living things, all the creeping animals and all the birds, all that creep on the earth went out from the ark by their families.

20And Noah built an altar to YHWH, and he took some of each of the pure animals and of each of the pure birds, and he offered sacrifices on the altar. 21And YHWH smelled the pleasant smell, and YHWH said to His heart, "I won't curse the ground on account of humankind again, because the inclination of the human heart is bad from their youth, and I won't strike all the living again as I have done. 22All the rest of the earth's days, seed and harvest, and cold and heat, and summer and winter, and day and night will not cease."

9 1And God blessed Noah and his sons and said to them, "Be fruitful and multiply and fill the earth. 2And fear of you and dread of you will be on every living thing of the earth and on every bird of the skies, in every one that will creep on the earth and in all the fish of the sea. They are given into your hand. 3Every creeping

13וַיְהִי בְּאַחַת וְשֵׁשׁ־מֵאוֹת שָׁנָה בָּרִאשׁוֹן בְּאֶחָד לַחֹדֶשׁ חָרְבוּ הַמַּיִם מֵעַל הָאָרֶץ וַיָּסַר נֹחַ אֶת־מִכְסֵה הַתֵּבָה וַיַּרְא וְהִנֵּה חָרְבוּ פְּנֵי הָאֲדָמָה: 14וּבַחֹדֶשׁ הַשֵּׁנִי בְּשִׁבְעָה וְעֶשְׂרִים יוֹם לַחֹדֶשׁ יָבְשָׁה הָאָרֶץ: ס 15וַיְדַבֵּר אֱלֹהִים אֶל־נֹחַ לֵאמֹר: 16צֵא מִן־הַתֵּבָה אַתָּה וְאִשְׁתְּךָ וּבָנֶיךָ וּנְשֵׁי־בָנֶיךָ אִתָּךְ: 17כָּל־הַחַיָּה אֲשֶׁר־אִתְּךָ מִכָּל־בָּשָׂר בָּעוֹף וּבַבְּהֵמָה וּבְכָל־הָרֶמֶשׂ הָרֹמֵשׂ עַל־הָאָרֶץ הוצֵא אִתָּךְ וְשָׁרְצוּ בָאָרֶץ וּפָרוּ וְרָבוּ עַל־הָאָרֶץ: 18וַיֵּצֵא־נֹחַ וּבָנָיו וְאִשְׁתּוֹ וּנְשֵׁי־בָנָיו אִתּוֹ: 19כָּל־הַחַיָּה כָּל־הָרֶמֶשׂ וְכָל־הָעוֹף כֹּל רוֹמֵשׂ עַל־הָאָרֶץ לְמִשְׁפְּחֹתֵיהֶם יָצְאוּ מִן־הַתֵּבָה: 20וַיִּבֶן נֹחַ מִזְבֵּחַ לַיהוָה וַיִּקַּח מִכֹּל ׀ הַבְּהֵמָה הַטְּהוֹרָה וּמִכֹּל הָעוֹף הַטָּהֹר וַיַּעַל עֹלֹת בַּמִּזְבֵּחַ: 21וַיָּרַח יְהוָה אֶת־רֵיחַ הַנִּיחֹחַ וַיֹּאמֶר יְהוָה אֶל־לִבּוֹ לֹא־אֹסִף לְקַלֵּל עוֹד אֶת־הָאֲדָמָה בַּעֲבוּר הָאָדָם כִּי יֵצֶר לֵב הָאָדָם רַע מִנְּעֻרָיו וְלֹא־אֹסִף עוֹד לְהַכּוֹת אֶת־כָּל־חַי כַּאֲשֶׁר עָשִׂיתִי: 22עֹד כָּל־יְמֵי הָאָרֶץ זֶרַע וְקָצִיר וְקֹר וָחֹם וְקַיִץ וָחֹרֶף וְיוֹם וָלַיְלָה לֹא יִשְׁבֹּתוּ:

9 1וַיְבָרֶךְ אֱלֹהִים אֶת־נֹחַ וְאֶת־בָּנָיו וַיֹּאמֶר לָהֶם פְּרוּ וּרְבוּ וּמִלְאוּ אֶת־הָאָרֶץ: 2וּמוֹרַאֲכֶם וְחִתְּכֶם יִהְיֶה עַל כָּל־חַיַּת הָאָרֶץ וְעַל כָּל־עוֹף הַשָּׁמָיִם בְּכֹל אֲשֶׁר תִּרְמֹשׂ הָאֲדָמָה וּבְכָל־דְּגֵי הַיָּם בְּיֶדְכֶם:

קַ הַיְצֵא 8:17

9:3. **Every creeping animal.** Elsewhere this term refers only to certain animals that crawl on the ground, but here it is understood to refer to all animals: "I've given every

animal that is alive will be yours for food; I've given every one to you like a plant of vegetation, ⁴except you shall not eat flesh in its life, its blood, ⁵and except I shall inquire for your blood, for your lives. I shall inquire for it from the hand of every animal and from the hand of a human. I shall inquire for a human's life from the hand of each man for his brother. ⁶One who sheds a human's blood: by a human his blood will be shed, because He made the human in the image of God. ⁷And you, be fruitful and multiply, swarm in the earth and multiply in it."

⁸And God said to Noah and to his sons with him, saying, ⁹"And I: here, I'm establishing my covenant with you and with your seed after you ¹⁰and with every living being that is with you, of the birds, of the domestic animals, and of all the

נָתַ֣תִּי׃ ³כָּל־רֶ֙מֶשׂ֙ אֲשֶׁ֣ר הוּא־חַ֔י לָכֶ֥ם יִהְיֶ֖ה לְאָכְלָ֑ה כְּיֶ֣רֶק עֵ֔שֶׂב נָתַ֥תִּי לָכֶ֖ם אֶת־כֹּֽל׃ ⁴אַךְ־בָּשָׂ֕ר בְּנַפְשׁ֥וֹ דָמ֖וֹ לֹ֥א תֹאכֵֽלוּ׃ ⁵וְאַ֨ךְ אֶת־דִּמְכֶ֤ם לְנַפְשֹֽׁתֵיכֶם֙ אֶדְרֹ֔שׁ מִיַּ֤ד כָּל־חַיָּה֙ אֶדְרְשֶׁ֔נּוּ וּמִיַּ֣ד הָֽאָדָ֗ם מִיַּד֙ אִ֣ישׁ אָחִ֔יו אֶדְרֹ֖שׁ אֶת־נֶ֥פֶשׁ הָֽאָדָֽם׃

⁶שֹׁפֵךְ֙ דַּ֣ם הָֽאָדָ֔ם בָּֽאָדָ֖ם דָּמ֣וֹ יִשָּׁפֵ֑ךְ
כִּ֚י בְּצֶ֣לֶם אֱלֹהִ֔ים עָשָׂ֖ה אֶת־הָֽאָדָֽם׃

⁷וְאַתֶּ֖ם פְּר֣וּ וּרְב֑וּ שִׁרְצ֥וּ בָאָ֖רֶץ וּרְבוּ־בָֽהּ׃ ס

⁸וַיֹּ֤אמֶר אֱלֹהִים֙ אֶל־נֹ֔חַ וְאֶל־בָּנָ֥יו אִתּ֖וֹ לֵאמֹֽר׃ ⁹וַאֲנִ֕י הִנְנִ֥י מֵקִ֛ים אֶת־בְּרִיתִ֖י אִתְּכֶ֑ם וְאֶֽת־זַרְעֲכֶ֖ם אַחֲרֵיכֶֽם׃ ¹⁰וְאֵ֨ת כָּל־נֶ֤פֶשׁ הַֽחַיָּה֙ אֲשֶׁ֣ר אִתְּכֶ֔ם בָּע֧וֹף בַּבְּהֵמָ֛ה וּֽבְכָל־חַיַּ֥ת הָאָ֖רֶץ אִתְּכֶ֑ם מִכֹּל֙

---

one to you like a plant"—meaning that humans are permitted to eat animals in addition to plants. Do humans eat animals before this? Noah makes burnt offerings (*'ōlōt*) after the flood, but that is a type of sacrifice that is not eaten. Abel brings a different kind of offering (*minḥāh*) to God, which is a type of sacrifice that is understood later in the Torah to be eaten by humans. But, prior to Genesis 9, all statements from the deity to humans concerning eating refer only to plants (1:29; 2:16; 3:18). It is therefore commonly understood that humans are not permitted to eat animals until after the flood. Some say that God now permits it as a concession to human appetites. I see no grounds in the text for this view. A more likely explanation for the change in divine requirements is that humans have saved all animal species by taking them in the ark. All animals now owe their lives to humankind, and this may be why humans are now permitted to take their lives for food.

9:5. **I shall inquire for your blood, for your lives**. This expression means that it is forbidden to take a human life unlawfully. It does not necessarily mean that one may never take a human life; for example, it may not forbid taking a life in self-defense. Rather, God will inquire—that is, require an accounting—and hold the guilty responsible, whether human or animal.

9:9. **covenant**. The flood event concludes with a contract between the deity and humans: a covenant. The Noahic covenant is the first of four major covenants that provide the structure in which nearly all of the Bible is framed. (The exceptions, most notably the book of Job, are relatively few.) The Noahic covenant promises the security of the cosmos. The Abrahamic covenant (Genesis 15 and 17) promises the land to Abraham's descendants and makes YHWH their God. The Israelite (or Sinai, or Mosaic) covenant (Exodus 20; 34; Deuteronomy 5; 7:12–15) promises well-being in the promised land. And the Davidic covenant (2 Samuel 7; Psalms 89; 132) promises kingship over Jerusalem and Judah to David and his descendants.

wild animals of the earth with you, from all those coming out of the ark to every living thing of the earth. 11And I shall establish my covenant with you, and all flesh will not be cut off again by the floodwaters, and there will not be a flood again to destroy the earth." 12And God said, "This is the sign of the covenant that I'm giving between me and you and every living being that is with you for eternal generations: 13I've put my rainbow in the clouds, and it will become a covenant sign between me and the earth. 14And it will be when I bring a cloud over the earth, and the rainbow will appear in the cloud, 15and I'll remember my covenant that is between me and you and every living being of all flesh, and the waters will not become a flood to destroy all flesh again. 16And the rainbow will be in the cloud, and I'll see it, to remember an eternal covenant between God and every living being of all flesh that is on the earth." 17And God said to Noah, "This is the sign of the covenant that I've established between me and all flesh that is on the earth."

18And Noah's sons who went out from the ark were Shem and Ham and Yaphet. And Ham: he was the father of Canaan. 19These three were Noah's sons, and all the earth expanded from these. 20And Noah began to be a man of the ground, and he planted a vineyard. 21And he drank from the wine and was drunk. And he was exposed inside his tent. 22And Ham, the father of Canaan, saw his father's nakedness and told his two brothers outside. 23And Shem and Yaphet took a garment and put it on both their shoulders and went backwards and covered their father's nakedness. And they faced backwards and did not see their father's nakedness. 24And Noah woke up from his wine, and he knew what his youngest son had done to him. 25And he said,

11וַהֲקִמֹתִי אֶת־בְּרִיתִי אִתְּכֶם וְלֹא־יִכָּרֵת כָּל־בָּשָׂר עוֹד מִמֵּי הַמַּבּוּל וְלֹא־יִהְיֶה עוֹד מַבּוּל לְשַׁחֵת הָאָרֶץ: 12וַיֹּאמֶר אֱלֹהִים זֹאת אוֹת־הַבְּרִית אֲשֶׁר־אֲנִי נֹתֵן בֵּינִי וּבֵינֵיכֶם וּבֵין כָּל־נֶפֶשׁ חַיָּה אֲשֶׁר אִתְּכֶם לְדֹרֹת עוֹלָם: 13אֶת־קַשְׁתִּי נָתַתִּי בֶּעָנָן וְהָיְתָה לְאוֹת בְּרִית בֵּינִי וּבֵין הָאָרֶץ: 14וְהָיָה בְּעַנְנִי עָנָן עַל־הָאָרֶץ וְנִרְאֲתָה הַקֶּשֶׁת בֶּעָנָן: 15וְזָכַרְתִּי אֶת־בְּרִיתִי אֲשֶׁר בֵּינִי וּבֵינֵיכֶם וּבֵין כָּל־נֶפֶשׁ חַיָּה בְּכָל־בָּשָׂר וְלֹא־יִהְיֶה עוֹד הַמַּיִם לְמַבּוּל לְשַׁחֵת כָּל־בָּשָׂר: 16וְהָיְתָה הַקֶּשֶׁת בֶּעָנָן וּרְאִיתִיהָ לִזְכֹּר בְּרִית עוֹלָם בֵּין אֱלֹהִים וּבֵין כָּל־נֶפֶשׁ חַיָּה בְּכָל־בָּשָׂר אֲשֶׁר עַל־הָאָרֶץ: 17וַיֹּאמֶר אֱלֹהִים אֶל־נֹחַ זֹאת אוֹת־הַבְּרִית אֲשֶׁר הֲקִמֹתִי בֵּינִי וּבֵין כָּל־בָּשָׂר אֲשֶׁר עַל־הָאָרֶץ: פ

18וַיִּהְיוּ בְנֵי־נֹחַ הַיֹּצְאִים מִן־הַתֵּבָה שֵׁם וְחָם וָיָפֶת וְחָם הוּא אֲבִי כְנָעַן: 19שְׁלֹשָׁה אֵלֶּה בְּנֵי־נֹחַ וּמֵאֵלֶּה נָפְצָה כָל־הָאָרֶץ: 20וַיָּחֶל נֹחַ אִישׁ הָאֲדָמָה וַיִּטַּע כָּרֶם: 21וַיֵּשְׁתְּ מִן־הַיַּיִן וַיִּשְׁכָּר וַיִּתְגַּל בְּתוֹךְ אָהֳלֹה: 22וַיַּרְא חָם אֲבִי כְנַעַן אֵת עֶרְוַת אָבִיו וַיַּגֵּד לִשְׁנֵי־אֶחָיו בַּחוּץ: 23וַיִּקַּח שֵׁם וָיֶפֶת אֶת־הַשִּׂמְלָה וַיָּשִׂימוּ עַל־שְׁכֶם שְׁנֵיהֶם וַיֵּלְכוּ אֲחֹרַנִּית וַיְכַסּוּ אֵת עֶרְוַת אֲבִיהֶם וּפְנֵיהֶם אֲחֹרַנִּית וְעֶרְוַת אֲבִיהֶם לֹא רָאוּ: 24וַיִּיקֶץ נֹחַ מִיֵּינוֹ וַיֵּדַע אֵת אֲשֶׁר־עָשָׂה לוֹ בְּנוֹ הַקָּטָן: 25וַיֹּאמֶר

9:13. **rainbow.** It is called this (in Hebrew and in English) because its shape is like a bow that one uses to shoot arrows. The rainbow is the sign of the covenant that promises that God will not destroy the earth again. I heard Rabbi Martin Lawson say that the rainbow symbolizes this because it is "a bow pointed away from the earth."

"Canaan is cursed. He'll be a servant of servants to his brothers." 26And he said, "Blessed is YHWH, God of Shem, and may Canaan be a servant to them. 27May God enlarge Yaphet, and may he dwell in the tents of Shem, and may Canaan be a servant to them."

28And Noah lived after the flood three hundred years and fifty years, 29and all of Noah's days were nine hundred years and fifty years. And he died.

10 1And these are the records of Noah's sons, Shem, Ham, and Yaphet: And children were born to them after the flood. 2Yaphet's children were Gomer and Magog and Madai and Yawan and Tubal and Meshech and Tiras. 3And Gomer's children were Ashkenaz and Riphath and Togarmah. 4And Yawan's children were Elisha and Tarshish, Kittim and Dodanim. 5The islands of the nations in their lands were dispersed out from these, each by its language, by their families within their nations.

6And Ham's children were Cush and Egypt and Put and Canaan. 7And Cush's children were Seba and Havilah and Sabtah and Raamah and Sabteca. And Raamah's children were Sheba and Dedan. 8And Cush fathered Nimrod. He began being a man of power in the earth. 9He was a powerful hunter before YHWH. On account of this it is said: "A powerful hunter before YHWH like Nimrod!" 10And the beginning of his kingdom was Babylon and Erech and Akkad and Cal-

אָר֣וּר כְּנָ֑עַן עֶ֥בֶד עֲבָדִ֖ים יִֽהְיֶ֥ה לְאֶחָֽיו׃

26וַיֹּ֕אמֶר בָּר֥וּךְ יְהֹוָ֖ה אֱלֹ֣הֵי שֵׁ֑ם וִיהִ֥י כְנַ֖עַן עֶ֥בֶד לָֽמוֹ׃

27יַ֤פְתְּ אֱלֹהִים֙ לְיֶ֔פֶת וְיִשְׁכֹּ֖ן בְּאָֽהֳלֵי־שֵׁ֑ם וִיהִ֥י כְנַ֖עַן עֶ֥בֶד לָֽמוֹ׃

28וַֽיְחִי־נֹ֖חַ אַחַ֣ר הַמַּבּ֑וּל שְׁלֹ֤שׁ מֵאוֹת֙ שָׁנָ֔ה וַחֲמִשִּׁ֖ים שָׁנָֽה׃ 29וַיִּֽהְיוּ֙ כָּל־יְמֵי־נֹ֔חַ תְּשַׁ֤ע מֵאוֹת֙ שָׁנָ֔ה וַחֲמִשִּׁ֖ים שָׁנָ֑ה וַיָּמֹֽת׃ פ

10 1וְאֵ֙לֶּה֙ תּוֹלְדֹ֣ת בְּנֵי־נֹ֔חַ שֵׁ֖ם חָ֣ם וָיָ֑פֶת וַיִּוָּלְד֥וּ לָהֶ֛ם בָּנִ֖ים אַחַ֥ר הַמַּבּֽוּל׃ 2בְּנֵ֣י יֶ֔פֶת גֹּ֣מֶר וּמָג֗וֹג וּמָדַ֛י וְיָוָ֥ן וְתֻבָ֖ל וּמֶ֥שֶׁךְ וְתִירָֽס׃ 3וּבְנֵ֖י גֹּ֑מֶר אַשְׁכֲּנַ֥ז וְרִיפַ֖ת וְתֹגַרְמָֽה׃ 4וּבְנֵ֥י יָוָ֖ן אֱלִישָׁ֣ה וְתַרְשִׁ֑ישׁ כִּתִּ֖ים וְדֹדָנִֽים׃ 5מֵ֠אֵלֶּה נִפְרְד֞וּ אִיֵּ֤י הַגּוֹיִם֙ בְּאַרְצֹתָ֔ם אִ֖ישׁ לִלְשֹׁנ֑וֹ לְמִשְׁפְּחֹתָ֖ם בְּגוֹיֵהֶֽם׃ 6וּבְנֵ֖י חָ֑ם כּ֥וּשׁ וּמִצְרַ֖יִם וּפ֥וּט וּכְנָֽעַן׃ 7וּבְנֵ֣י כ֔וּשׁ סְבָ֙א֙ וַֽחֲוִילָ֔ה וְסַבְתָּ֥ה וְרַעְמָ֖ה וְסַבְתְּכָ֑א וּבְנֵ֥י רַעְמָ֖ה שְׁבָ֥א וּדְדָֽן׃ 8וְכ֖וּשׁ יָלַ֣ד אֶת־נִמְרֹ֑ד ה֣וּא הֵחֵ֔ל לִהְי֥וֹת גִּבֹּ֖ר בָּאָֽרֶץ׃ 9הֽוּא־הָיָ֥ה גִבֹּֽר־צַ֖יִד לִפְנֵ֣י יְהֹוָ֑ה עַל־כֵּן֙ יֵֽאָמַ֔ר כְּנִמְרֹ֛ד גִּבּ֥וֹר צַ֖יִד לִפְנֵ֥י יְהֹוָֽה׃ 10וַתְּהִ֙י רֵאשִׁ֣ית מַמְלַכְתּ֔וֹ בָּבֶ֖ל וְאֶ֣רֶךְ וְאַכַּ֑ד וְכַלְנֵ֖ה בְּאֶ֥רֶץ

10:2. **Yawan**. Greece (Ionia).

10:4. **Tarshish**. Where Jonah tries to sail from the Mediterranean port of Joppa. Perhaps Gibraltar or Sardinia.

10:5. **The islands of the nations**. This has been understood to mean seacoast peoples.

10:7,28. **Sheba**. The Sabeans (of southwest Arabia) whose queen would make a famous journey to meet Israel's King Solomon generations later. The confusing thing is that Sheba is traced to both Ham (10:7) and Shem (v. 28). (And this is further confused by a reference to Sheba as descended from Abraham in Gen 25:3.)

neh in the land of Shinar. 11Asshur came out of that land and built Nineveh and Rehovoth-Ir and Calah, 12and Resen between Nineveh and Calah. It is the big city. 13And Egypt fathered Ludim and Anamim and Lehabim and Naphtuhim 14and Pathrusim and Casluhim, from which the Philistines came out, and Caphtorim. 15And Canaan fathered Sidon, his firstborn, and Heth 16and the Jebusite and the Amorite and the Girgashite 17and the Hivite and the Arkite and the Sinite 18and the Arvadite and the Zemarite and the Hamathite. And later the families of the Canaanites were dispersed. 19And the Canaanite border was from Sidon, as you come to Gerar, up to Gaza, as you come to Sodom and Gomorrah and Admah and Zeboim, up to Lasha. 20These are Ham's children, by their families, by their languages, in their lands, within their nations.

21Children were born to Shem, him as well, father of all of Eber's children, older brother of Yaphet. 22Shem's children were Elam and Asshur and Arpachshad and Lud and Aram. 23And Aram's children were Uz and Hul and Gether and Mash. 24And Arpachshad fathered Shelah, and Shelah fathered Eber. 25And two sons were born to Eber. The name of one was Peleg, because in his days the earth was divided, and his brother's name was Joktan. 26And Joktan fathered Almodad and Sheleph and Hazarmaveth and Jerah 27and Hadoram and Uzal and Diklah 28and Obal and Abimael and Sheba 29and Ophir and Havilah and Jobab. All these are Joktan's children. 30And their home was from Mesha, as you come to Sephar, to the mountain of the east. 31These are Shem's children, by their families, by their languages, in their lands, by their nations.

32These are the families of Noah's children by

שִׁנְעָר: ¹¹מִן־הָאָרֶץ הַהִוא יָצָא אַשּׁוּר וַיִּבֶן אֶת־
נִינְוֵה וְאֶת־רְחֹבֹת עִיר וְאֶת־כָּלַח: ¹²וְאֶת־רֶסֶן בֵּין
נִינְוֵה וּבֵין כָּלַח הִוא הָעִיר הַגְּדֹלָה: ¹³וּמִצְרַיִם
יָלַד אֶת־לוּדִים וְאֶת־עֲנָמִים וְאֶת־לְהָבִים וְאֶת־
נַפְתֻּחִים: ¹⁴וְאֶת־פַּתְרֻסִים וְאֶת־כַּסְלֻחִים אֲשֶׁר יָצְאוּ
מִשָּׁם פְּלִשְׁתִּים וְאֶת־כַּפְתֹּרִים: ס ¹⁵וּכְנַעַן יָלַד
אֶת־צִידֹן בְּכֹרוֹ וְאֶת־חֵת: ¹⁶וְאֶת־הַיְבוּסִי וְאֶת־
הָאֱמֹרִי וְאֵת הַגִּרְגָּשִׁי: ¹⁷וְאֶת־הַחִוִּי וְאֶת־הָעַרְקִי
וְאֶת־הַסִּינִי: ¹⁸וְאֶת־הָאַרְוָדִי וְאֶת־הַצְּמָרִי וְאֶת־
הַחֲמָתִי וְאַחַר נָפֹצוּ מִשְׁפְּחוֹת הַכְּנַעֲנִי: ¹⁹וַיְהִי גְּבוּל
הַכְּנַעֲנִי מִצִּידֹן בֹּאֲכָה גְרָרָה עַד־עַזָּה בֹּאֲכָה
סְדֹמָה וַעֲמֹרָה וְאַדְמָה וּצְבֹיִם עַד־לָשַׁע: ²⁰אֵלֶּה
בְנֵי־חָם לְמִשְׁפְּחֹתָם לִלְשֹׁנֹתָם בְּאַרְצֹתָם בְּגוֹיֵהֶם:
ס ²¹וּלְשֵׁם יֻלַּד גַּם־הוּא אֲבִי כָּל־בְּנֵי־עֵבֶר אֲחִי
יֶפֶת הַגָּדוֹל: ²²בְּנֵי שֵׁם עֵילָם וְאַשּׁוּר וְאַרְפַּכְשַׁד
וְלוּד וַאֲרָם: ²³וּבְנֵי אֲרָם עוּץ וְחוּל וְגֶתֶר וָמַשׁ:
²⁴וְאַרְפַּכְשַׁד יָלַד אֶת־שָׁלַח וְשֶׁלַח יָלַד אֶת־עֵבֶר:
²⁵וּלְעֵבֶר יֻלַּד שְׁנֵי בָנִים שֵׁם הָאֶחָד פֶּלֶג כִּי בְיָמָיו
נִפְלְגָה הָאָרֶץ וְשֵׁם אָחִיו יָקְטָן: ²⁶וְיָקְטָן יָלַד אֶת־
אַלְמוֹדָד וְאֶת־שָׁלֶף וְאֶת־חֲצַרְמָוֶת וְאֶת־יָרַח:
²⁷וְאֶת־הֲדוֹרָם וְאֶת־אוּזָל וְאֶת־דִּקְלָה: ²⁸וְאֶת־עוֹבָל
וְאֶת־אֲבִימָאֵל וְאֶת־שְׁבָא: ²⁹וְאֶת־אוֹפִר וְאֶת־חֲוִילָה
וְאֶת־יוֹבָב כָּל־אֵלֶּה בְּנֵי יָקְטָן: ³⁰וַיְהִי מוֹשָׁבָם
מִמֵּשָׁא בֹּאֲכָה סְפָרָה הַר הַקֶּדֶם:
³¹אֵלֶּה בְנֵי־שֵׁם לְמִשְׁפְּחֹתָם לִלְשֹׁנֹתָם בְּאַרְצֹתָם
לְגוֹיֵהֶם: ³²אֵלֶּה מִשְׁפְּחֹת בְּנֵי־נֹחַ לְתוֹלְדֹתָם

10:14. **Casluhim, from which the Philistines came out, and Caphtorim.** But cf. Amos 9:7, which says that the Philistines come from Caphtor. In any case, this first reference to the Philistines in the Torah already identifies them as—unlike the other residents of Canaan—coming from across the Mediterranean. Still, it separates them from the Greeks.

their records in their nations, and the nations were dispersed from these in the earth after the flood.

11 ¹And it was: all the earth was one language and the same words. ²And it was when they were traveling from the east: and they found a valley in the land of Shinar and lived there. ³And they said to one another, "Come on, let's make bricks and fire them." And they had brick for stone, and they had bitumen for mortar. ⁴And they said, "Come on, let's build ourselves a city and a tower, and its top will be in the skies, and we'll make ourselves a name, or else we'll scatter over the face of all the earth."

⁵And YHWH went down to see the city and the tower that the children of humankind had built. ⁶And YHWH said, "Here, they're one people, and they all have one language, and this is what they've begun to do. And now nothing that they'll scheme to do will be precluded from them. ⁷Come on, let's go down and babble their language there so that one won't understand another's language." ⁸And YHWH scattered them from there over the face of all the earth, and they stopped building the city. ⁹On account of this its

בְּגוֹיֵהֶם וּמֵאֵלֶּה נִפְרְדוּ הַגּוֹיִם בָּאָרֶץ אַחַר
הַמַּבּוּל: פ

11 ¹וַיְהִי כָל־הָאָרֶץ שָׂפָה אֶחָת וּדְבָרִים
אֲחָדִים: ²וַיְהִי בְּנָסְעָם מִקֶּדֶם וַיִּמְצְאוּ בִקְעָה
בְּאֶרֶץ שִׁנְעָר וַיֵּשְׁבוּ שָׁם: ³וַיֹּאמְרוּ אִישׁ אֶל־רֵעֵהוּ
הָבָה נִלְבְּנָה לְבֵנִים וְנִשְׂרְפָה לִשְׂרֵפָה וַתְּהִי לָהֶם
הַלְּבֵנָה לְאָבֶן וְהַחֵמָר הָיָה לָהֶם לַחֹמֶר: ⁴וַיֹּאמְרוּ
הָבָה ׀ נִבְנֶה־לָּנוּ עִיר וּמִגְדָּל וְרֹאשׁוֹ בַשָּׁמַיִם
וְנַעֲשֶׂה־לָּנוּ שֵׁם פֶּן־נָפוּץ עַל־פְּנֵי כָל־הָאָרֶץ: ⁵וַיֵּרֶד
יְהוָה לִרְאֹת אֶת־הָעִיר וְאֶת־הַמִּגְדָּל אֲשֶׁר בָּנוּ בְּנֵי
הָאָדָם: ⁶וַיֹּאמֶר יְהוָה הֵן עַם אֶחָד וְשָׂפָה אֶחָת
לְכֻלָּם וְזֶה הַחִלָּם לַעֲשׂוֹת וְעַתָּה לֹא־יִבָּצֵר מֵהֶם
כֹּל אֲשֶׁר יָזְמוּ לַעֲשׂוֹת: ⁷הָבָה נֵרְדָה וְנָבְלָה שָׁם
שְׂפָתָם אֲשֶׁר לֹא יִשְׁמְעוּ אִישׁ שְׂפַת רֵעֵהוּ: ⁸וַיָּפֶץ
יְהוָה אֹתָם מִשָּׁם עַל־פְּנֵי כָל־הָאָרֶץ וַיַּחְדְּלוּ לִבְנֹת
הָעִיר: ⁹עַל־כֵּן קָרָא שְׁמָהּ בָּבֶל כִּי־שָׁם בָּלַל יְהוָה

11:4. **we'll make ourselves a name**. The story of the tower of Babylon has its ambiguity at its center. It tells of an attempt by humanity to build a tower whose top is in the sky, but it never tells what they will do when they finish the tower, what is meant by "make ourselves a name," or why they fear being scattered if they do not have this tower. When YHWH sees the tower He is described as concerned that "now nothing that they'll scheme to do will be precluded from them." Their actions appear to be an act of rebellion of some sort, and in this sense the episode fits with those of Adam and Eve, Cain, and the flood, i.e., that humans as a species are continuously in conflict with the initial "good" state of creation. And so God disperses them and gives them languages that make them less intelligible to one another and thereby less united. The story thus prepares the way for a shift in the narrative away from dealing with the fate of the species and, instead, dealing with individuals. At the same time, this narrative provides the etiology of languages and of the dispersion of humans all over the earth. It also provides a Hebrew etiology for the name Babylon (Hebrew *bbl*) "because YHWH babbled (Hebrew *bll*) the language of all the earth" (11:9). This would have come as a surprise to the people of Babylon, who understood the name to derive from *bab-ilu*, the "Gate of God."

46

name was called Babylon, because YHWH babbled the language of all the earth there, and YHWH scattered them from there over the face of all the earth.

10These are the records of Shem: Shem was a hundred years old, and he fathered Arpachshad, two years after the flood. 11And Shem lived after his fathering Arpachshad five hundred years, and he fathered sons and daughters. 12And Arpachshad lived thirty-five years, and he fathered Shelah. 13And Arpachshad lived after his fathering Shelah three years and four hundred years, and he fathered sons and daughters. 14And Shelah lived thirty years, and he fathered Eber. 15And Shelah lived after his fathering Eber three years and four hundred years, and he fathered sons and daughters. 16And Eber lived forty-three years, and he fathered Peleg. 17And Eber lived after his fathering Peleg thirty years and four hundred years, and he fathered sons and daughters. 18And Peleg lived thirty years, and he fathered Reu. 19And Peleg lived after his fathering Reu nine years and two hundred years, and he fathered sons and daughters. 20And Reu lived thirty-two years, and he fathered Serug. 21And Reu lived after his fathering Serug seven years and two hundred years, and he fathered sons and daughters. 22And Serug lived thirty years, and he fathered Nahor. 23And Serug lived after his fathering Nahor two hundred years, and he fathered sons and daughters. 24And Nahor lived twenty-nine years, and he fathered Terah. 25And Nahor lived after his fathering Terah nineteen years and a hundred years, and he fathered sons and daughters. 26And Terah lived seventy years, and he fathered Abram, Nahor, and Haran.

27And these are the records of Terah: Terah had fathered Abram, Nahor, and Haran, and Haran had fathered Lot. 28And Haran died in the lifetime of Terah, his father, in the land of his birthplace, in Ur of the Chaldees. 29And Abram and Nahor took wives. Abram's wife's name was Sarai, and Nahor's wife's name was Milcah,

שְׂפַת כָּל־הָאָרֶץ וּמִשָּׁם הֱפִיצָם יְהוָה עַל־פְּנֵי כָּל־הָאָרֶץ: פ 10אֵלֶּה תּוֹלְדֹת שֵׁם שֵׁם בֶּן־מְאַת שָׁנָה וַיּוֹלֶד אֶת־אַרְפַּכְשָׁד שְׁנָתַיִם אַחַר הַמַּבּוּל: 11וַיְחִי־שֵׁם אַחֲרֵי הוֹלִידוֹ אֶת־אַרְפַּכְשָׁד חֲמֵשׁ מֵאוֹת שָׁנָה וַיּוֹלֶד בָּנִים וּבָנוֹת: ס 12וְאַרְפַּכְשַׁד חַי חָמֵשׁ וּשְׁלֹשִׁים שָׁנָה וַיּוֹלֶד אֶת־שָׁלַח: 13וַיְחִי אַרְפַּכְשַׁד אַחֲרֵי הוֹלִידוֹ אֶת־שֶׁלַח שָׁלֹשׁ שָׁנִים וְאַרְבַּע מֵאוֹת שָׁנָה וַיּוֹלֶד בָּנִים וּבָנוֹת: ס 14וְשֶׁלַח חַי שְׁלֹשִׁים שָׁנָה וַיּוֹלֶד אֶת־עֵבֶר: 15וַיְחִי־שֶׁלַח אַחֲרֵי הוֹלִידוֹ אֶת־עֵבֶר שָׁלֹשׁ שָׁנִים וְאַרְבַּע מֵאוֹת שָׁנָה וַיּוֹלֶד בָּנִים וּבָנוֹת: ס 16וַיְחִי־עֵבֶר אַרְבַּע וּשְׁלֹשִׁים שָׁנָה וַיּוֹלֶד אֶת־פָּלֶג: 17וַיְחִי־עֵבֶר אַחֲרֵי הוֹלִידוֹ אֶת־פֶּלֶג שְׁלֹשִׁים שָׁנָה וְאַרְבַּע מֵאוֹת שָׁנָה וַיּוֹלֶד בָּנִים וּבָנוֹת: ס 18וַיְחִי־פֶלֶג שְׁלֹשִׁים שָׁנָה וַיּוֹלֶד אֶת־רְעוּ: 19וַיְחִי־פֶלֶג אַחֲרֵי הוֹלִידוֹ אֶת־רְעוּ תֵּשַׁע שָׁנִים וּמָאתַיִם שָׁנָה וַיּוֹלֶד בָּנִים וּבָנוֹת: ס 20וַיְחִי רְעוּ שְׁתַּיִם וּשְׁלֹשִׁים שָׁנָה וַיּוֹלֶד אֶת־שְׂרוּג: 21וַיְחִי רְעוּ אַחֲרֵי הוֹלִידוֹ אֶת־שְׂרוּג שֶׁבַע שָׁנִים וּמָאתַיִם שָׁנָה וַיּוֹלֶד בָּנִים וּבָנוֹת: ס 22וַיְחִי שְׂרוּג שְׁלֹשִׁים שָׁנָה וַיּוֹלֶד אֶת־נָחוֹר: 23וַיְחִי שְׂרוּג אַחֲרֵי הוֹלִידוֹ אֶת־נָחוֹר מָאתַיִם שָׁנָה וַיּוֹלֶד בָּנִים וּבָנוֹת: ס 24וַיְחִי נָחוֹר תֵּשַׁע וְעֶשְׂרִים שָׁנָה וַיּוֹלֶד אֶת־תָּרַח: 25וַיְחִי נָחוֹר אַחֲרֵי הוֹלִידוֹ אֶת־תֶּרַח תְּשַׁע־עֶשְׂרֵה שָׁנָה וּמְאַת שָׁנָה וַיּוֹלֶד בָּנִים וּבָנוֹת: ס 26וַיְחִי תֶרַח שִׁבְעִים שָׁנָה וַיּוֹלֶד אֶת־אַבְרָם אֶת־נָחוֹר וְאֶת־הָרָן:

27וְאֵלֶּה תּוֹלְדֹת תֶּרַח תֶּרַח הוֹלִיד אֶת־אַבְרָם אֶת־נָחוֹר וְאֶת־הָרָן וְהָרָן הוֹלִיד אֶת־לוֹט: 28וַיָּמָת הָרָן עַל־פְּנֵי תֶּרַח אָבִיו בְּאֶרֶץ מוֹלַדְתּוֹ בְּאוּר כַּשְׂדִּים: 29וַיִּקַּח אַבְרָם וְנָחוֹר לָהֶם נָשִׁים שֵׁם אֵשֶׁת־אַבְרָם שָׂרָי וְשֵׁם אֵשֶׁת־נָחוֹר מִלְכָּה בַּת־הָרָן

daughter of Haran—father of Milcah and father of Iscah. 30And Sarai was infertile. She did not have a child. 31And Terah took Abram, his son, and Lot, son of Haran, his grandson, and Sarai, his daughter-in-law, the wife of Abram, his son; and they went with them from Ur of the Chaldees to go to the land of Canaan. And they came as far as Haran, and they stayed there. 32And Terah's days were five years and two hundred years. And Terah died in Haran.

אֲבִי־מִלְכָּה וַאֲבִי יִסְכָּה: 30וַתְּהִי שָׂרַי עֲקָרָה אֵין לָהּ וָלָד: 31וַיִּקַּח תֶּרַח אֶת־אַבְרָם בְּנוֹ וְאֶת־לוֹט בֶּן־הָרָן בֶּן־בְּנוֹ וְאֵת שָׂרַי כַּלָּתוֹ אֵשֶׁת אַבְרָם בְּנוֹ וַיֵּצְאוּ אִתָּם מֵאוּר כַּשְׂדִּים לָלֶכֶת אַרְצָה כְּנַעַן וַיָּבֹאוּ עַד־חָרָן וַיֵּשְׁבוּ שָׁם: 32וַיִּהְיוּ יְמֵי־תֶרַח חָמֵשׁ שָׁנִים וּמָאתַיִם שָׁנָה וַיָּמָת תֶּרַח בְּחָרָן: ס

Go

לך לך

12 1And YHWH said to Abram, "Go from your land and from your birthplace and from your father's house to the land that I'll

12 1וַיֹּאמֶר יְהוָה אֶל־אַבְרָם לֶךְ־לְךָ מֵאַרְצְךָ וּמִמּוֹלַדְתְּךָ וּמִבֵּית אָבִיךָ אֶל־הָאָרֶץ אֲשֶׁר אַרְאֶךָּ:

12:1. **Go.** Hebrew *lek lĕkā*. Much has been made of the second word in this phrase, *lĕkā*, which means "for you." No translation quite captures the sense of the Hebrew ("Go you," "Get you," "Go for yourself"). The second element, *lĕkā* (or *lākem*), occasionally follows verbs in the *Tanak*. For example, in Lev 26:1 we have *lō' ta'ăśû lākem* (you shall not make for yourselves; you shall make you no . . .), and in Num 14:25 we have *sĕ'û lākem* (travel you; travel for yourselves). I believe it is better to use no English term than to use any of the possible equivalents, all of which are clumsy English and do not convey the Hebrew.

12:1. **your land, your birthplace.** But he is in Haran. He has already left Ur of the Chaldeans, which was his land and birthplace. Rashi tries to solve the problem by saying that this means "Go even farther from your land and birthplace." Ibn Ezra tries to solve it by saying that it means "God *had* said [i.e., earlier, back in Ur], 'Go from your land . . . '" But these stretch the meaning of the Hebrew beyond what is possible. And besides, Abraham later sends his servant to get a wife for Isaac, saying, "Go to my land and my birthplace" (24:4), and the servant goes to *Haran* ("to Aram Naharaim, to the city of Nahor," 24:10; which is identified as Haran, 27:43). On these grounds Ramban rejects Rashi's and Ibn Ezra's solutions. Ramban's own solution, though, falls short as well, requiring that Abraham's land and birthplace are Haran, not Ur. This is further complicated by the fact that the Abrahamic covenant begins with God saying to Abraham, "I brought you out of Ur . . . " (15:7). The truth is that this is a case in which the contradiction is a result of the fact that the Torah was composed from several sources. In this case, one of its sources had Abraham coming from Ur, and another had him coming from Haran. The aim of this commentary is to deal with the Torah in its final, combined form and not to analyze its sources. (I have done that elsewhere: in *Who Wrote the Bible?* and *The Hidden Book in the Bible*.) Usually, the combination of sources has produced a richer, more complex story in the Torah. But this passage is one of a

48

show you. ²And I'll make you into a big nation, and I'll bless you and make your name great. And *be* a blessing! ³And I'll bless those who bless you, and those who affront you I'll curse. And all the families of the earth will be blessed through

וְאֶעֶשְׂךָ לְגוֹי גָּדוֹל וַאֲבָרֶכְךָ וַאֲגַדְּלָה שְׁמֶךָ וֶהְיֵה² בְּרָכָה: ³וַאֲבָרֲכָה מְבָרֲכֶיךָ וּמְקַלֶּלְךָ אָאֹר וְנִבְרְכוּ בְךָ כֹּל מִשְׁפְּחֹת הָאֲדָמָה: ¹⁴וַיֵּלֶךְ אַבְרָם כַּאֲשֶׁר

few instances in which the combination has produced an irreconcilable contradiction. In such cases it is better to acknowledge the problem than to stretch to make forced interpretations.

12:1. **your land, your birthplace, and your father's house.** But if he has left his land, then *of course* he has left his birthplace and his father's house. This is geographically backwards. Therefore, the point of this order is not geographical. It is emotional. The three steps are arranged in ascending order of difficulty for Abraham. It is hard to leave one's land, harder if it is where one was born, and harder still to leave one's family. And where is he to go? To "the land that I'll show you." That is, he must leave his homeland without knowing for what he is giving it up. The wording seems designed to make it hard for Abraham. This pattern of testing will be repeated when he is commanded to sacrifice Isaac, thus: "Take your son, your only one, whom you love, Isaac." And where is he to sacrifice him? "On one of the mountains that I'll say to you." (See the comment on 22:2.)

12:3. **all the families of the earth will be blessed through you.** The *Tanak* is so focused on the people of Israel that one can underestimate the overwhelming significance of its opening section. The first eleven chapters (Parashat Bereshit and Parashat Noah) are about the relationship between God and the entire human community. That relationship does not go well, and after ten generations the deity decides to destroy the mass and start over with a single virtuous man's family. But it turns out that choosing a virtuous individual does not guarantee that this individual's descendants will be virtuous as well. Another ten generations pass, and humans in general are not a planet-full of Noahs. So once again the focus narrows to a single virtuous person, Abraham. We must keep in mind what has happened up to this point when we read this, or else we will lose the significance of what is happening here. Wiping out everyone but a virtuous person did not work. So God leaves the species alive but chooses an individual who will produce a family that will ultimately bring blessing to *all the families of the earth.*

To make sure we get it, it is the final point of God's first revelation to Abraham: Go to the land I'll show you. I'll make you a big nation. I'll bless you. "And all the families of the earth will be blessed through you" (Gen 12:3).

To make sure we do not forget it, it is repeated four times—and always in crucial moments of revelation: during the appearance of the three visitors to Abraham (Gen 18:17–18); in the blessing following the near-sacrifice of Isaac (22:16–18); in God's first appearance to Isaac (26:2–4); and in Jacob's first encounter with God in the dream of the ladder at Beth-El (28:10–14).

It is *important*. In some way, at some time, the result of the divine choice of Abraham is supposed to be some good for all humankind. We are never told what this good is supposed to be. Is it that Abraham's descendants are supposed to bring blessing by being "a light to the nations"—setting an example, showing how a community can live: caring for one another, not cheating one another, not enslaving one another, not lending to each other for profit, and so on and on? Or is it that they are to bring blessing by doing things that benefit the species: inventions, cures, literature, music, learning? It does not say. But at minimum it must mean that the people of Israel do not live alone or apart. Their destiny—our destiny—whatever it is, must be bound up in the destiny of all humankind.

This adds a dimension, an additional layer of significance, to every story that will follow in the Torah. When Abraham travels to Canaan, we might imagine it from a God's-eye view above the earth: the tiny movement of a man and his family along the globe is a first step in a process that is to bring benefit for all the earth. When Abraham travels to Egypt, this is the first in a series of encounters that he and his descendants will have with the peoples of the world. When he and Lot are forced to part, this is a step in distinguishing his destiny from that of the families of his brothers Haran and Nahor, though he and his descendants will continue to interact with them. When he joins in a battle among kings in order to rescue Lot (Genesis 14), he is being drawn into world events, and it is another first step, an anticipation of all the times that his descendants, the people of Israel, will be drawn into contact and interaction with nations. When Abraham covenants with God (Genesis 15 and 17) the ceremony includes specific references to Ur of the Chaldees, the land from which Abraham has come; to Egypt, the land where his descendants will be enslaved; and to ten peoples of the land that Abraham is promised. It also includes the announcement of his coming son Isaac, the key to the fulfillment of the destiny to be a blessing to all the families of the earth—as will be confirmed explicitly following the Aqedah. And in between the two chapters concerning the Abrahamic covenant comes the story of the birth of Abraham's son Ishmael, whose descendants, the Ishmaelites, will be among Israel's related neighbors.

All of these episodes are conveying the formative stages of a development that begins with that narrowing of attention to Abraham. The interpretive point is that we must understand every section of the Torah with awareness of what has preceded it and what will come after it. The social and moral point is that Abraham's descendants are not to live by themselves or only for themselves. Whether dealing with non-Jews who live in Israel or dealing with non-Jews who are their neighbors in the countries in which they reside, the Jews are a community that connects its birth with a prediction (?), a promise (?), an obligation (?), a destiny (?) to be a blessing to them all.

12:3. **will be blessed through you**. Rashi takes the plain meaning of this phrase to mean that non-Israelites will bless their children with words such as "May you be like Abraham." His proof for this reading is the wording of Jacob's blessing of his grandsons Ephraim and Manasseh: "Israel will bless with you, saying: 'May God make you like Ephraim and Manasseh'" (Gen 48:20). But that passage uses an active form of the verb (the *Piel*), whereas all the occurrences of this phrase in terms of the nations being blessed use forms that are passive or reflexive (*Niphal* and *Hitpael*), which is a different matter. If we take the meaning as passive, then it is as I have translated it here: "the

you." 4And Abram went as YHWH had spoken to him, and Lot went with him. And Abram was seventy-five years old when he went out from Haran. 5And Abram took Sarai, his wife, and Lot, his brother's son, and all their property that they had accumulated and the persons whom they had gotten in Haran; and they went out to go to the land of Canaan.

And they came to the land of Canaan. 6And Abram passed through the land as far as the place of Shechem, as far as the oak of Moreh. And the Canaanite was in the land then.

7And YHWH appeared to Abram and said, "I'll give this land to your seed." And he built an altar there to YHWH who had appeared to him. 8And he moved on from there to the hill country east of Beth-El and pitched his tent—Beth-El to

דִּבֶּר אֵלָיו יְהוָה וַיֵּלֶךְ אִתּוֹ לוֹט וְאַבְרָם בֶּן־חָמֵשׁ
שָׁנִים וְשִׁבְעִים שָׁנָה בְּצֵאתוֹ מֵחָרָן: 5וַיִּקַּח אַבְרָם
אֶת־שָׂרַי אִשְׁתּוֹ וְאֶת־לוֹט בֶּן־אָחִיו וְאֶת־כָּל־רְכוּשָׁם
אֲשֶׁר רָכָשׁוּ וְאֶת־הַנֶּפֶשׁ אֲשֶׁר־עָשׂוּ בְחָרָן וַיֵּצְאוּ
לָלֶכֶת אַרְצָה כְּנַעַן וַיָּבֹאוּ אַרְצָה כְּנָעַן: 6וַיַּעֲבֹר
אַבְרָם בָּאָרֶץ עַד מְקוֹם שְׁכֶם עַד אֵלוֹן מוֹרֶה
וְהַכְּנַעֲנִי אָז בָּאָרֶץ: 7וַיֵּרָא יְהוָה אֶל־אַבְרָם וַיֹּאמֶר
לְזַרְעֲךָ אֶתֵּן אֶת־הָאָרֶץ הַזֹּאת וַיִּבֶן שָׁם מִזְבֵּחַ
לַיהוָה הַנִּרְאֶה אֵלָיו: 8וַיַּעְתֵּק מִשָּׁם הָהָרָה מִקֶּדֶם
לְבֵית־אֵל וַיֵּט אָהֳלֹה בֵּית־אֵל מִיָּם וְהָעַי מִקֶּדֶם

---

earth's families *will be blessed* through you." If we take it as reflexive, then it can mean "they *will bless themselves* through you," which is Rashi's understanding; but a reflexive can also mean "they will get blessing through you." Interpreters are split on this. I believe that *context* settles the question. The issue in the story until now has been the course of relations between God and all the families of the earth. Now God makes a special bond with Abraham's family and lets him know that this is for the eventual benefit of all families. (See the preceding comment.)

12:4. Abram went as YHWH had spoken to him. Traditionally the emphasis has been on faith as the mark of Abraham's character. But the narrative conveys far more that the mark of Abraham is obedience. Leave your land: "And Abram went." Sacrifice your son: "And Abram got up early." The tests that Abraham undergoes are not necessarily tests of faith but are certainly tests of obedience. At this stage in relations between God and humans, God appears to single out a human who will do what he is told. This will change gradually in the *Tanak,* as humans grow and mature and God cedes more responsibility for the world to them. But for now, obedience is sought.

12:8. Beth-El to the west and Ai to the east. At this site, Abram invokes the name YHWH for the first time, and he builds an altar there. Later Abraham returns to this site and invokes the divine name again (13:3). No explanation of the significance of this place between the two cities—Beth-El and Ai—is given in the Torah. But we learn in the book of Joshua that, many generations later, God delivers Ai into the Israelites' hands by means of an ambush, and it takes place "between Beth-El and Ai, to the west of Ai" (Josh 8:9,12; cf. 12:9). This appears to be a case of "the merit of the fathers." That is, the pious acts of Abraham, Isaac, and Jacob have consequences for their descendants. In this case, the Israelites are successful in the age of settlement of the land thanks to what Abraham had done on the very spot centuries earlier. There will be enough cases of this phenomenon to establish it as a major theme and message of the

the west and Ai to the east—and he built an altar there to YHWH and invoked the name YHWH. 9And Abram traveled on, going to the Negeb.

10And there was a famine in the land, and Abram went down to Egypt to reside there because the famine was heavy in the land. 11And it was when he was close to coming to Egypt: and he said to Sarai, his wife, "Here, I know that you're a beautiful woman. 12And it will be when the Egyptians see you that they'll say, 'This is his wife,' and they'll kill me and keep you alive. 13Say you're my sister so it will be good for me on your account and I'll stay alive because of you." 14And

וַיִּבֶן־שָׁם מִזְבֵּחַ לַיהוָה וַיִּקְרָא בְּשֵׁם יְהוָה: 9וַיִּסַּע אַבְרָם הָלוֹךְ וְנָסוֹעַ הַנֶּגְבָּה: פ

10וַיְהִי רָעָב בָּאָרֶץ וַיֵּרֶד אַבְרָם מִצְרַיְמָה לָגוּר שָׁם כִּי־כָבֵד הָרָעָב בָּאָרֶץ: 11וַיְהִי כַּאֲשֶׁר הִקְרִיב לָבוֹא מִצְרָיְמָה וַיֹּאמֶר אֶל־שָׂרַי אִשְׁתּוֹ הִנֵּה־נָא יָדַעְתִּי כִּי אִשָּׁה יְפַת־מַרְאֶה אָתְּ: 12וְהָיָה כִּי־יִרְאוּ אֹתָךְ הַמִּצְרִים וְאָמְרוּ אִשְׁתּוֹ זֹאת וְהָרְגוּ אֹתִי וְאֹתָךְ יְחַיּוּ: 13אִמְרִי־נָא אֲחֹתִי אָתְּ לְמַעַן יִיטַב־לִי בַעֲבוּרֵךְ וְחָיְתָה נַפְשִׁי בִּגְלָלֵךְ: 14וַיְהִי

Torah: that the good acts that we do have implications for the lives of our children and many generations thereafter: as an example, as a source of strength, and in subtle ways that are impossible to calculate or foresee. This phenomenon of the merit of the parents also acts as a preparation for and a balance to the opposite phenomenon that will be developed in the Torah later: that our sins are visited on the lives of our children and descendants as well.

12:11–13. **Here, I know**. Abraham's words to Sarah contain the first two occurrences of the Hebrew word *nā'*. It is sometimes rendered "now" in English and sometimes rendered "please." But neither is quite right. It is an untranslatable particle that is a sign of polite speech. Its most striking occurrence is in God's words to Abraham in the story of the binding of Isaac: "Take *nā'* your son . . . and offer him" (Gen 22:2). I do not translate it with any English word, because it is closer to the Hebrew to use *no* word than to use such words as "please" or "now."

12:13. **Say you're my sister . . . and I'll stay alive**. All commentators have agonized over this. Abraham constructs a lie and puts Sarah in a compromising position. This may mean that he thinks that he simply has no real choice: it is either lie or die. Or it may convey that Abraham—like other biblical heroes—is not perfect. We cannot know. In either of these cases, he cannot be faulted for choosing to put Sarah in a compromising position, because, in his understanding, Sarah would be taken either way. The concern is that, without the lie, they would also kill him. (In fact he turns out to be wrong. There is no evidence in the Bible that the Egyptians or anyone else ever did what Abraham fears they would do. Here and in two other cases in which Abraham and his son Isaac claim that their wives are their sisters, the Egyptian and Philistine kings send the couple away when they find out that she is his wife.)

12:13. **my sister**. For a while it was common to cite tablets from Nuzi as evidence that there was a Near Eastern practice of adopting one's wife as a sister. But the Nuzi case involved a single family, and scholars recently have questioned whether it is justified to make so much of it. Abraham's actions here (and in Genesis 20; and Isaac's actions in Genesis 26) are treated as an unusual case. They require no Near Eastern legal precedent.

it was as Abram came to Egypt, and the Egyptians saw the woman, that she was very beautiful. 15And Pharaoh's officers saw her and praised her to Pharaoh, and the woman was taken to Pharaoh's house. 16And he was good to Abram on her account, and he had a flock and oxen and he-asses and servants and maids and she-asses and camels. 17And YHWH plagued Pharaoh and his house, big plagues, over the matter of Sarai, Abram's wife.

18And Pharaoh called Abram and said, "What is this you've done to me? Why didn't you tell me that she was your wife? 19Why did you say, 'She's my sister,' so I took her for a wife for myself! And now, here's your wife. Take her and go." 20And Pharaoh commanded people over him, and they let him and his wife and all he had go.

13 1And Abram went up from Egypt, he and his wife and all he had and Lot with him, to the Negeb. 2And Abram was very heavy with livestock and silver and gold. 3And he went on his travels from the Negeb as far as Beth-El, as far as the place where his tent was at the start, between Beth-El and Ai, 4to the place of the altar that he had made there at the beginning. And Abram invoked the name YHWH there.

5And Lot, who was going with Abram, also had a flock and oxen and tents. 6And the land did not suffice them to live together, because their property was great, and they were not able to live together. 7And there was a quarrel between those who herded Abram's livestock and those who herded Lot's livestock. And the

כְּבוֹא אַבְרָם מִצְרָיְמָה וַיִּרְאוּ הַמִּצְרִים אֶת־הָאִשָּׁה כִּי־יָפָה הִוא מְאֹד: 15וַיִּרְאוּ אֹתָהּ שָׂרֵי פַרְעֹה וַיְהַלְלוּ אֹתָהּ אֶל־פַּרְעֹה וַתֻּקַּח הָאִשָּׁה בֵּית פַּרְעֹה: 16וּלְאַבְרָם הֵיטִיב בַּעֲבוּרָהּ וַיְהִי־לוֹ צֹאן־וּבָקָר וַחֲמֹרִים וַעֲבָדִים וּשְׁפָחֹת וַאֲתֹנֹת וּגְמַלִּים: 17וַיְנַגַּע יְהוָה ׀ אֶת־פַּרְעֹה נְגָעִים גְּדֹלִים וְאֶת־בֵּיתוֹ עַל־דְּבַר שָׂרַי אֵשֶׁת אַבְרָם: 18וַיִּקְרָא פַרְעֹה לְאַבְרָם וַיֹּאמֶר מַה־זֹּאת עָשִׂיתָ לִּי לָמָּה לֹא־הִגַּדְתָּ לִּי כִּי אִשְׁתְּךָ הִוא: 19לָמָה אָמַרְתָּ אֲחֹתִי הִוא וָאֶקַּח אֹתָהּ לִי לְאִשָּׁה וְעַתָּה הִנֵּה אִשְׁתְּךָ קַח וָלֵךְ: 20וַיְצַו עָלָיו פַּרְעֹה אֲנָשִׁים וַיְשַׁלְּחוּ אֹתוֹ וְאֶת־אִשְׁתּוֹ וְאֶת־כָּל־אֲשֶׁר־לוֹ:

13 1וַיַּעַל אַבְרָם מִמִּצְרַיִם הוּא וְאִשְׁתּוֹ וְכָל־אֲשֶׁר־לוֹ וְלוֹט עִמּוֹ הַנֶּגְבָּה: 2וְאַבְרָם כָּבֵד מְאֹד בַּמִּקְנֶה בַּכֶּסֶף וּבַזָּהָב: 3וַיֵּלֶךְ לְמַסָּעָיו מִנֶּגֶב וְעַד־בֵּית־אֵל עַד־הַמָּקוֹם אֲשֶׁר־הָיָה שָׁם אָהֳלֹה בַּתְּחִלָּה בֵּין בֵּית־אֵל וּבֵין הָעָי: 4אֶל־מְקוֹם הַמִּזְבֵּחַ אֲשֶׁר־עָשָׂה שָׁם בָּרִאשֹׁנָה וַיִּקְרָא שָׁם אַבְרָם בְּשֵׁם יְהוָה: 5וְגַם־לְלוֹט הַהֹלֵךְ אֶת־אַבְרָם הָיָה צֹאן־וּבָקָר וְאֹהָלִים: 6וְלֹא־נָשָׂא אֹתָם הָאָרֶץ לָשֶׁבֶת יַחְדָּו כִּי־הָיָה רְכוּשָׁם רָב וְלֹא יָכְלוּ לָשֶׁבֶת יַחְדָּו: 7וַיְהִי־רִיב בֵּין רֹעֵי מִקְנֵה־אַבְרָם וּבֵין רֹעֵי מִקְנֵה־לוֹט

13:3 ק אָהֳלוֹ

13:1. **went up from Egypt . . . to the Negeb.** Abraham's movements prefigure the future fate of the Israelites. As he returns from Egypt, going up into the Negeb, so the Israelites will return from Egypt, and Moses will send the first Israelites (the spies) to reenter the land with the words "Go up there in the Negeb" (Num 13:17). (See the next comment.)

13:3. **he went on his travels.** This expression continues the prefiguring of the fate of Abraham's descendants, who went "on their travels" when they left Egypt (Exod 17:1; Num 10:12).

Canaanite and the Perizzite lived in the land then. 8And Abram said to Lot, "Let there be no quarreling between me and you and between my herders and your herders, because we're brothers. 9Isn't the whole land before you? Separate from me: if left then I'll go right, and if right then I'll go left." 10And Lot raised his eyes and saw all the plain of the Jordan, that all of it was well watered (before YHWH's destroying Sodom and Gomorrah) like YHWH's garden, like the land of Egypt, as you come to Zoar. 11And Lot chose all the plain of the Jordan for himself, and Lot traveled east. And they separated, each from his brother. 12Abram lived in the land of Canaan, and Lot lived in the cities of the plain and tented as far as Sodom. 13And the people of Sodom were very bad and sinful to YHWH.

14And YHWH said to Abram after Lot's separation from him, "Lift your eyes and see from the place where you are to the north and south and east and west. 15For all the land that you see, I'll give it to you and to your seed forever. 16And I'll make your seed like the dust of the earth, so that if a man could count the dust of the earth then your seed also could be counted. 17Get up, go around in the land to its length and its width, because I'm giving it to you." 18And Abram took up his tent and came and lived among the oaks of Mamre which are in Hebron, and he built an altar to YHWH there.

14 1And it was in the days of Amraphel, king of Shinar, Arioch, king of Ellasar, Chedorlaomer, king of Elam, and Tidal, king of Goiim: 2They made war with Bera, king of Sodom, and Birsha, king of Gomorrah, Shinab, king of Admah, and Shemeber, king of Zeboiim, and the king of Bela. (That is Zoar.) 3All these were allied at the Siddim Valley. (That is the Dead Sea.) 4Twelve years they served Chedorlaomer, and the thirteenth year they revolted, 5and in the fourteenth year Chedorlaomer and the kings who were with him came, and they struck the Rephaim in Ashteroth Karnaim and the Zuzum in Ham

וְהַכְּנַעֲנִי וְהַפְּרִזִּי אָז יֹשֵׁב בָּאָרֶץ: 8וַיֹּאמֶר אַבְרָם אֶל־לוֹט אַל־נָא תְהִי מְרִיבָה בֵּינִי וּבֵינֶיךָ וּבֵין רֹעַי וּבֵין רֹעֶיךָ כִּי־אֲנָשִׁים אַחִים אֲנָחְנוּ: 9הֲלֹא כָל־הָאָרֶץ לְפָנֶיךָ הִפָּרֶד נָא מֵעָלָי אִם־הַשְּׂמֹאל וְאֵימִנָה וְאִם־הַיָּמִין וְאַשְׂמְאִילָה: 10וַיִּשָּׂא־לוֹט אֶת־עֵינָיו וַיַּרְא אֶת־כָּל־כִּכַּר הַיַּרְדֵּן כִּי כֻלָּהּ מַשְׁקֶה לִפְנֵי ׀ שַׁחֵת יְהוָה אֶת־סְדֹם וְאֶת־עֲמֹרָה כְּגַן־יְהוָה כְּאֶרֶץ מִצְרַיִם בֹּאֲכָה צֹעַר: 11וַיִּבְחַר־לוֹ לוֹט אֵת כָּל־כִּכַּר הַיַּרְדֵּן וַיִּסַּע לוֹט מִקֶּדֶם וַיִּפָּרְדוּ אִישׁ מֵעַל אָחִיו: 12אַבְרָם יָשַׁב בְּאֶרֶץ־כְּנָעַן וְלוֹט יָשַׁב בְּעָרֵי הַכִּכָּר וַיֶּאֱהַל עַד־סְדֹם: 13וְאַנְשֵׁי סְדֹם רָעִים וְחַטָּאִים לַיהוָה מְאֹד: 14וַיהוָה אָמַר אֶל־אַבְרָם אַחֲרֵי הִפָּרֶד־לוֹט מֵעִמּוֹ שָׂא נָא עֵינֶיךָ וּרְאֵה מִן־הַמָּקוֹם אֲשֶׁר־אַתָּה שָׁם צָפֹנָה וָנֶגְבָּה וָקֵדְמָה וָיָמָּה: 15כִּי אֶת־כָּל־הָאָרֶץ אֲשֶׁר־אַתָּה רֹאֶה לְךָ אֶתְּנֶנָּה וּלְזַרְעֲךָ עַד־עוֹלָם: 16וְשַׂמְתִּי אֶת־זַרְעֲךָ כַּעֲפַר הָאָרֶץ אֲשֶׁר ׀ אִם־יוּכַל אִישׁ לִמְנוֹת אֶת־עֲפַר הָאָרֶץ גַּם־זַרְעֲךָ יִמָּנֶה: 17קוּם הִתְהַלֵּךְ בָּאָרֶץ לְאָרְכָּהּ וּלְרָחְבָּהּ כִּי לְךָ אֶתְּנֶנָּה: 18וַיֶּאֱהַל אַבְרָם וַיָּבֹא וַיֵּשֶׁב בְּאֵלֹנֵי מַמְרֵא אֲשֶׁר בְּחֶבְרוֹן וַיִּבֶן־שָׁם מִזְבֵּחַ לַיהוָה: פ

14 1וַיְהִי בִּימֵי אַמְרָפֶל מֶלֶךְ־שִׁנְעָר אַרְיוֹךְ מֶלֶךְ אֶלָּסָר כְּדָרְלָעֹמֶר מֶלֶךְ עֵילָם וְתִדְעָל מֶלֶךְ גּוֹיִם: 2עָשׂוּ מִלְחָמָה אֶת־בֶּרַע מֶלֶךְ סְדֹם וְאֶת־בִּרְשַׁע מֶלֶךְ עֲמֹרָה שִׁנְאָב ׀ מֶלֶךְ אַדְמָה וְשֶׁמְאֵבֶר מֶלֶךְ צְבוֹיִם וּמֶלֶךְ בֶּלַע הִיא־צֹעַר: 3כָּל־אֵלֶּה חָבְרוּ אֶל־עֵמֶק הַשִּׂדִּים הוּא יָם הַמֶּלַח: 4שְׁתֵּים עֶשְׂרֵה שָׁנָה עָבְדוּ אֶת־כְּדָרְלָעֹמֶר וּשְׁלֹשׁ־עֶשְׂרֵה שָׁנָה מָרָדוּ: 5וּבְאַרְבַּע עֶשְׂרֵה שָׁנָה בָּא כְדָרְלָעֹמֶר וְהַמְּלָכִים אֲשֶׁר אִתּוֹ וַיַּכּוּ אֶת־רְפָאִים בְּעַשְׁתְּרֹת קַרְנַיִם וְאֶת־הַזּוּזִים בְּהֶם וְאֵת הָאֵימִים בְּשָׁוֵה

and the Emim in Shaveh Kiriataim 6and the Horites in their mountain Seir to El Paran, which is by the wilderness. 7And they came back and came to En Mishpat (that is Kadesh) and struck the area of the Amalekites and also the Amorites who live in Hazazon Tamar. 8And the king of Sodom and the king of Gomorrah and the king of Admah and the king of Zeboiim and the king of Bela (that is Zoar) went out and aligned with them for war in the Siddim Valley, 9with Chedorlaomer, king of Elam, and Tidal, king of Goiim, and Amraphel, king of Shinar, and Arioch, king of Ellasar—four kings with five. 10And Siddim Valley was pits, pits of bitumen, and the kings of Sodom and Gomorrah fled, and they fell there; and those who were left fled to the mountain. 11And they took all the property of Sodom and Gomorrah and all their food, and they went. 12And they took Lot, Abram's brother's son, and his property when they went. And he had been living in Sodom. 13And an escapee came and told Abram the Hebrew, and he was tenting among the oaks of Mamre the Amorite, brother of Eshcol and brother of Aner; and they were covenant partners of Abram. 14And Abram heard that his brother had been taken prisoner, and he had his trained men, born in his house, unsheathe: three hundred eighteen. And he pursued as far as Dan. 15And he divided against them by night, he and his servants, and he struck them and pursued them as far as Hobah, which is at the left of Damascus. 16And he brought back all the property, and he also brought back Lot, his brother, and his property, and also the women and the people. 17And the king of Sodom came out to him after he came back from striking Chedorlaomer and the kings who were

קְרִיָתָיִם: ⁶וְאֶת־הַחֹרִי בְּהַרְרָם שֵׂעִיר עַד אֵיל פָּארָן אֲשֶׁר עַל־הַמִּדְבָּר: ⁷וַיָּשֻׁבוּ וַיָּבֹאוּ אֶל־עֵין מִשְׁפָּט הִוא קָדֵשׁ וַיַּכּוּ אֶת־כָּל־שְׂדֵה הָעֲמָלֵקִי וְגַם אֶת־הָאֱמֹרִי הַיֹּשֵׁב בְּחַצְצֹן תָּמָר: ⁸וַיֵּצֵא מֶלֶךְ־סְדֹם וּמֶלֶךְ עֲמֹרָה וּמֶלֶךְ אַדְמָה וּמֶלֶךְ צְבֹיִים וּמֶלֶךְ בֶּלַע הִוא־צֹעַר וַיַּעַרְכוּ אִתָּם מִלְחָמָה בְּעֵמֶק הַשִּׂדִּים: ⁹אֵת כְּדָרְלָעֹמֶר מֶלֶךְ עֵילָם וְתִדְעָל מֶלֶךְ גּוֹיִם וְאַמְרָפֶל מֶלֶךְ שִׁנְעָר וְאַרְיוֹךְ מֶלֶךְ אֶלָּסָר אַרְבָּעָה מְלָכִים אֶת־הַחֲמִשָּׁה: ¹⁰וְעֵמֶק הַשִּׂדִּים בֶּאֱרֹת בֶּאֱרֹת חֵמָר וַיָּנֻסוּ מֶלֶךְ־סְדֹם וַעֲמֹרָה וַיִּפְּלוּ־שָׁמָּה וְהַנִּשְׁאָרִים הֶרָה נָּסוּ: ¹¹וַיִּקְחוּ אֶת־כָּל־רְכֻשׁ סְדֹם וַעֲמֹרָה וְאֶת־כָּל־אָכְלָם וַיֵּלֵכוּ: ¹²וַיִּקְחוּ אֶת־לוֹט וְאֶת־רְכֻשׁוֹ בֶּן־אֲחִי אַבְרָם וַיֵּלֵכוּ וְהוּא יֹשֵׁב בִּסְדֹם: ¹³וַיָּבֹא הַפָּלִיט וַיַּגֵּד לְאַבְרָם הָעִבְרִי וְהוּא שֹׁכֵן בְּאֵלֹנֵי מַמְרֵא הָאֱמֹרִי אֲחִי אֶשְׁכֹּל וַאֲחִי עָנֵר וְהֵם בַּעֲלֵי בְרִית־אַבְרָם: ¹⁴וַיִּשְׁמַע אַבְרָם כִּי נִשְׁבָּה אָחִיו וַיָּרֶק אֶת־חֲנִיכָיו יְלִידֵי בֵיתוֹ שְׁמֹנָה עָשָׂר וּשְׁלֹשׁ מֵאוֹת וַיִּרְדֹּף עַד־דָּן: ¹⁵וַיֵּחָלֵק עֲלֵיהֶם ׀ לַיְלָה הוּא וַעֲבָדָיו וַיַּכֵּם וַיִּרְדְּפֵם עַד־חוֹבָה אֲשֶׁר מִשְּׂמֹאל לְדַמָּשֶׂק: ¹⁶וַיָּשֶׁב אֵת כָּל־הָרְכֻשׁ וְגַם אֶת־לוֹט אָחִיו וּרְכֻשׁוֹ הֵשִׁיב וְגַם אֶת־הַנָּשִׁים וְאֶת־הָעָם: ¹⁷וַיֵּצֵא מֶלֶךְ־סְדֹם לִקְרָאתוֹ אַחֲרֵי שׁוּבוֹ מֵהַכּוֹת אֶת־כְּדָר־לָעֹמֶר וְאֶת־הַמְּלָכִים אֲשֶׁר אִתּוֹ אֶל־עֵמֶק שָׁוֵה הוּא עֵמֶק

קְ צְבוֹיִם 14:8

14:13. **the Hebrew.** This is an unusual use of the word "Hebrew." Elsewhere in biblical stories it is used to identify Israelites only when one is speaking among foreigners. It is not the standard term for the people, which is rather "Israelite" at first and "Jew" later. Perhaps it is used here because there are not yet any other Israelites around, and Abraham himself is the foreigner. (Regarding the term "Hebrew slave," see the comment on Exod 21:2.)

with him at the Shaveh Valley. (That is the valley of the king.)

18And Melchizedek, king of Salem, had brought out bread and wine. And he was a priest of El the Highest. 19And he blessed him and said, "Blessed is Abram to El the Highest, creator of skies and earth. 20And blessed is El the Highest, who delivered your foes into your hand." And he gave him a tithe from everything.

21And the king of Sodom said to Abram, "Give the persons to me, and take the property for you."

22And Abram said to the king of Sodom, "I've lifted my hand to YHWH, El the Highest, creator of skies and earth, 23that, from a thread to a shoelace, I won't take anything that is yours, so you won't say, '*I made Abram rich*.' 24Except only what the boys have eaten and the share of the people who went with me: Aner, Eshcol, and Mamre. *They* shall take their share."

15 1After these things YHWH's word came to Abram in a vision, saying, "Don't fear, Abram. I'm a shield for you. Your reward is very much."

2And Abram said, "My Lord, YHWH, what would you give me when I go childless and my household is an acquired person!" (That is Damascus Eliezer.) 3And Abram said, "Here, you haven't given me seed. And, here, a member of my household is taking possession of what is mine."

הַמֶּלֶךְ: 18וּמַלְכִּי־צֶדֶק מֶלֶךְ שָׁלֵם הוֹצִיא לֶחֶם וָיָיִן
וְהוּא כֹהֵן לְאֵל עֶלְיוֹן: 19וַיְבָרְכֵהוּ וַיֹּאמַר
בָּרוּךְ אַבְרָם לְאֵל עֶלְיוֹן קֹנֵה שָׁמַיִם וָאָרֶץ:
20וּבָרוּךְ אֵל עֶלְיוֹן אֲשֶׁר־מִגֵּן צָרֶיךָ בְּיָדֶךָ
וַיִּתֶּן־לוֹ מַעֲשֵׂר מִכֹּל: 21וַיֹּאמֶר מֶלֶךְ־סְדֹם אֶל־
אַבְרָם תֶּן־לִי הַנֶּפֶשׁ וְהָרְכֻשׁ קַח־לָךְ: 22וַיֹּאמֶר
אַבְרָם אֶל־מֶלֶךְ סְדֹם הֲרִימֹתִי יָדִי אֶל־יְהוָה אֵל
עֶלְיוֹן קֹנֵה שָׁמַיִם וָאָרֶץ: 23אִם־מִחוּט וְעַד שְׂרוֹךְ־
נַעַל וְאִם־אֶקַּח מִכָּל־אֲשֶׁר־לָךְ וְלֹא תֹאמַר אֲנִי
הֶעֱשַׁרְתִּי אֶת־אַבְרָם: 24בִּלְעָדַי רַק אֲשֶׁר אָכְלוּ
הַנְּעָרִים וְחֵלֶק הָאֲנָשִׁים אֲשֶׁר הָלְכוּ אִתִּי עָנֵר
אֶשְׁכֹּל וּמַמְרֵא הֵם יִקְחוּ חֶלְקָם: ס

15 1אַחַר הַדְּבָרִים הָאֵלֶּה הָיָה דְבַר־יְהוָה
אֶל־אַבְרָם בַּמַּחֲזֶה לֵאמֹר אַל־תִּירָא אַבְרָם אָנֹכִי
מָגֵן לָךְ שְׂכָרְךָ הַרְבֵּה מְאֹד: 2וַיֹּאמֶר אַבְרָם אֲדֹנָי
יְהוִה מַה־תִּתֶּן־לִי וְאָנֹכִי הוֹלֵךְ עֲרִירִי וּבֶן־מֶשֶׁק
בֵּיתִי הוּא דַּמֶּשֶׂק אֱלִיעֶזֶר: 3וַיֹּאמֶר אַבְרָם הֵן לִי
לֹא נָתַתָּה זָרַע וְהִנֵּה בֶן־בֵּיתִי יוֹרֵשׁ אֹתִי: 4וְהִנֵּה

14:18. **the Highest**. Hebrew *'elyōn*. This is how God is known at the end of the Torah also (Deut 32:8). There (and in Ps 82:6) this is the epithet that is used for God in connection with the formation of the nations of the earth. That makes it notable that here the priest who is associated with El the Highest is not from Abraham's family but from another group. Abraham is not pictured as the only worshiper of this God on earth.

15:3. **a member of my household is taking possession**. The word for "taking possession" means to inherit or acquire. Why would Nahor or Lot not inherit what is Abraham's? Because they are not there. Abraham's brother Nahor did not make the trip to Canaan with Abraham, and Lot moved away to the east. So, if they were to come to claim Abraham's possessions, who would enforce their claim? There is no

4And, here, YHWH's word came to him, saying, "This one won't take possession from you, but rather one who will come out of your insides: *he* will take possession from you." 5And He brought him outside and said, "Look at the skies and count the stars—if you'll be able to count them." And He said to him, "That is how your seed will be."

6And he trusted in YHWH, and He considered it for him as virtue. 7And He said to him, "I am YHWH, who brought you out of Ur of the Chaldees to give you this land, to possess it."

8And he said, "My Lord YHWH, how will I know that I'll possess it?"

9And He said to him, "Take a three-year-old heifer and a three-year-old she-goat and a three-year-old ram and a dove and a pigeon for me."

10And he took all of these for Him and split them up the middle and set each half opposite its other half, but he did not split the birds. 11And birds of prey came down on the carcasses, and Abram retrieved them. 12And the sun was about to set, and a slumber had come over

דְּבַר־יְהוָה אֵלָיו לֵאמֹר לֹא יִירָשְׁךָ זֶה כִּי־אִם אֲשֶׁר יֵצֵא מִמֵּעֶיךָ הוּא יִירָשֶׁךָ: 5וַיּוֹצֵא אֹתוֹ הַחוּצָה וַיֹּאמֶר הַבֶּט־נָא הַשָּׁמַיְמָה וּסְפֹר הַכּוֹכָבִים אִם־תּוּכַל לִסְפֹּר אֹתָם וַיֹּאמֶר לוֹ כֹּה יִהְיֶה זַרְעֶךָ: 6וְהֶאֱמִן בַּיהוָה וַיַּחְשְׁבֶהָ לּוֹ צְדָקָה: 7וַיֹּאמֶר אֵלָיו אֲנִי יְהֹוָה אֲשֶׁר הוֹצֵאתִיךָ מֵאוּר כַּשְׂדִּים לָתֶת לְךָ אֶת־הָאָרֶץ הַזֹּאת לְרִשְׁתָּהּ: 8וַיֹּאמַר אֲדֹנָי יֱהוִֹה בַּמָּה אֵדַע כִּי אִירָשֶׁנָּה: 9וַיֹּאמֶר אֵלָיו קְחָה לִי עֶגְלָה מְשֻׁלֶּשֶׁת וְעֵז מְשֻׁלֶּשֶׁת וְאַיִל מְשֻׁלָּשׁ וְתֹר וְגוֹזָל: 10וַיִּקַּח־לוֹ אֶת־כָּל־אֵלֶּה וַיְבַתֵּר אֹתָם בַּתָּוֶךְ וַיִּתֵּן אִישׁ־בִּתְרוֹ לִקְרַאת רֵעֵהוּ וְאֶת־הַצִּפֹּר לֹא בָתָר: 11וַיֵּרֶד הָעַיִט עַל־הַפְּגָרִים וַיַּשֵּׁב אֹתָם אַבְרָם: 12וַיְהִי הַשֶּׁמֶשׁ לָבוֹא וְתַרְדֵּמָה נָפְלָה עַל־

---

central government of Canaan. We are told over and over that it is a land of Canaanites, Jebusites, Perizzites, and so on—a variety of communities in separate cities.

15:3–4. **take possession**. This term occurs three times here, emphasizing that Abraham's own offspring will someday take possession of everything that is promised to him. It then occurs over sixty times in Deuteronomy as the Israelites are about to enter the land, leaving no doubt of the point that this promise is to be fulfilled.

15:6. **virtue**. We were not told the reason for God's choosing Abraham. We must derive it from Abraham's later behavior: his virtue, his combination of obedience and willingness to question, humility as well as boldness, trust in his God as well as caring about his fellow human beings.

15:10. **he took all of these for Him and split them**. This is the beginning of a covenant ceremony. Such use of animals is well known in ancient Near Eastern covenant ceremonies. The Abrahamic covenant takes up the rest of this chapter and then is added to in Genesis 17.

15:11. **Abram retrieved them**. This is usually taken to mean that Abram drove the birds of prey away, but the Hebrew plural must refer to the split carcasses, not the birds (which are identified by a singular noun, meaning either a single bird or a group of birds for which a collective noun is used).

Abram; and, here, a big, dark terror was coming over him.

13And He said to Abram, "You shall *know* that your seed will be an alien in a land that is not theirs, and they will serve them, and they will degrade them four hundred years. 14But I'll judge the nation whom they'll serve as well, and after that they'll go out with much property. 15And you: you'll come to your fathers in peace. You'll be buried at a good old age. 16And a fourth generation will come back here, because the Amorite's crime is not yet complete."

17And the sun was setting, and there was darkness, and here was an oven of smoke and a flame of fire that went between these pieces. 18In that day YHWH made a covenant with Abram, saying, "I've given this land to your seed, from the river of Egypt to the big river, the river Euphrates: 19the Cainites and the Kenizzites and the Kadmonites 20and the Hittites and the Perizzites and the Rephaim 21and the Amorites and the Canaanites and the Girgashites and the Jebusites."

16 1And Abram's wife Sarai had not given birth by him. And she had an Egyptian maid, and her name was Hagar. 2And Sarai said to Abram, "Here, YHWH has held me back from giving birth. Come to my maid. Maybe I'll get 'childed' through her." And Abram listened to Sarai's voice. 3And Sarai, Abram's wife, took Hagar, the Egyptian, her maid, at the end of ten

אַבְרָ֑ם וְהִנֵּ֥ה אֵימָ֛ה חֲשֵׁכָ֥ה גְדֹלָ֖ה נֹפֶ֥לֶת עָלָֽיו׃
13וַיֹּ֣אמֶר לְאַבְרָ֗ם יָדֹ֨עַ תֵּדַ֜ע כִּי־גֵ֣ר ׀ יִהְיֶ֣ה זַרְעֲךָ֗ בְּאֶ֨רֶץ֙ לֹ֣א לָהֶ֔ם וַעֲבָד֖וּם וְעִנּ֣וּ אֹתָ֑ם אַרְבַּ֥ע מֵא֖וֹת שָׁנָֽה׃ 14וְגַ֧ם אֶת־הַגּ֛וֹי אֲשֶׁ֥ר יַעֲבֹ֖דוּ דָּ֣ן אָנֹ֑כִי וְאַחֲרֵי־ כֵ֥ן יֵצְא֖וּ בִּרְכֻ֥שׁ גָּדֽוֹל׃ 15וְאַתָּ֛ה תָּב֥וֹא אֶל־אֲבֹתֶ֖יךָ בְּשָׁל֑וֹם תִּקָּבֵ֖ר בְּשֵׂיבָ֥ה טוֹבָֽה׃ 16וְד֥וֹר רְבִיעִ֖י יָשׁ֣וּבוּ הֵ֑נָּה כִּ֧י לֹא־שָׁלֵ֛ם עֲוֹ֥ן הָאֱמֹרִ֖י עַד־הֵֽנָּה׃
17וַיְהִ֤י הַשֶּׁ֙מֶשׁ֙ בָּ֔אָה וַעֲלָטָ֖ה הָיָ֑ה וְהִנֵּ֨ה תַנּ֤וּר עָשָׁן֙ וְלַפִּ֣יד אֵ֔שׁ אֲשֶׁ֣ר עָבַ֔ר בֵּ֖ין הַגְּזָרִ֥ים הָאֵֽלֶּה׃ 18בַּיּ֣וֹם הַה֗וּא כָּרַ֧ת יְהֹוָ֛ה אֶת־אַבְרָ֖ם בְּרִ֣ית לֵאמֹ֑ר לְזַרְעֲךָ֗ נָתַ֙תִּי֙ אֶת־הָאָ֣רֶץ הַזֹּ֔את מִנְּהַ֣ר מִצְרַ֔יִם עַד־הַנָּהָ֥ר הַגָּדֹ֖ל נְהַר־פְּרָֽת׃ 19אֶת־הַקֵּינִי֙ וְאֶת־הַקְּנִזִּ֔י וְאֵ֖ת הַקַּדְמֹנִֽי׃ 20וְאֶת־הַחִתִּ֥י וְאֶת־הַפְּרִזִּ֖י וְאֶת־הָרְפָאִֽים׃ 21וְאֶת־הָֽאֱמֹרִי֙ וְאֶת־הַֽכְּנַעֲנִ֔י וְאֶת־הַגִּרְגָּשִׁ֖י וְאֶת־ הַיְבוּסִֽי׃ ס

16 1וְשָׂרַי֙ אֵ֣שֶׁת אַבְרָ֔ם לֹ֥א יָלְדָ֖ה ל֑וֹ וְלָ֛הּ שִׁפְחָ֥ה מִצְרִ֖ית וּשְׁמָ֥הּ הָגָֽר׃ 2וַתֹּ֨אמֶר שָׂרַ֜י אֶל־ אַבְרָ֗ם הִנֵּה־נָ֞א עֲצָרַ֤נִי יְהֹוָה֙ מִלֶּ֔דֶת בֹּא־נָא֙ אֶל־ שִׁפְחָתִ֔י אוּלַ֥י אִבָּנֶ֖ה מִמֶּ֑נָּה וַיִּשְׁמַ֥ע אַבְרָ֖ם לְק֥וֹל שָׂרָֽי׃ 3וַתִּקַּ֞ח שָׂרַ֣י אֵֽשֶׁת־אַבְרָ֗ם אֶת־הָגָ֤ר הַמִּצְרִית֙ שִׁפְחָתָ֔הּ מִקֵּץ֙ עֶ֣שֶׂר שָׁנִ֔ים לְשֶׁ֥בֶת אַבְרָ֖ם בְּאֶ֣רֶץ

15:13. **alien**. No English term is quite equivalent to the Hebrew *gēr*. The English term "alien" has a variety of connotations, but most commonly it means a person residing in a place where he is not a regular citizen, which is what a *gēr* is. In rabbinic Hebrew, *gēr* is the word for a convert to Judaism, but that is not its meaning in the Torah.

15:17. **a flame of fire**. The presence of God is expressed through fire here in the covenant with Abraham. Fire will be the expression of God's presence many more times, including most notably the miraculous burning bush when Moses first meets God, and the fire on Sinai in the covenant with Israel.

15:18. **river of Egypt**. This is generally understood to refer to the Wadi el-'Arîsh.

years of Abram's living in the land of Canaan, and gave her to Abram, her husband, as a wife to him. 4And he came to Hagar, and she became pregnant. And she saw that she had become pregnant, and her mistress was lowered in her eyes.

5And Sarai said to Abram, "My injury is on you. I, *I*, placed my maid in your bosom, and she saw that she had become pregnant, and I was lowered in her eyes. Let YHWH judge between me and you."

6And Abram said to Sarai, "Here, your maid is in your hand. Do to her whatever is good in your eyes." And Sarai degraded her, and she fled from her.

7And an angel of YHWH found her at a spring of water in the wilderness, by the spring on the way to Shur, 8and said, "Hagar, Sarai's maid, from where have you come, and where will you go?"

And she said, "I'm fleeing from Sarai, my mistress."

9And the angel of YHWH said to her, "Go back to your mistress, and suffer the degradation under her hands." 10And the angel of YHWH said, "I'll *multiply* your seed, and it won't be countable because of its great number." 11And the angel of YHWH said to her, "Here, you're pregnant and will give birth to a son, and you shall call his name Ishmael, for YHWH has listened to your suffering. 12And he'll be a wild ass of a man, his hand against everyone, and everyone's hand against him, and he'll tent among all his brothers."

כְּנַעַן וַתִּתֵּן אֹתָהּ לְאַבְרָם אִישָׁהּ לוֹ לְאִשָּׁה: 4וַיָּבֹא
אֶל־הָגָר וַתַּהַר וַתֵּרֶא כִּי הָרָתָה וַתֵּקַל גְּבִרְתָּהּ
בְּעֵינֶיהָ: 5וַתֹּאמֶר שָׂרַי אֶל־אַבְרָם חֲמָסִי עָלֶיךָ
אָנֹכִי נָתַתִּי שִׁפְחָתִי בְּחֵיקֶךָ וַתֵּרֶא כִּי הָרָתָה וָאֵקַל
בְּעֵינֶיהָ יִשְׁפֹּט יְהוָה בֵּינִי וּבֵינֶיךָ: 6וַיֹּאמֶר אַבְרָם
אֶל־שָׂרַי הִנֵּה שִׁפְחָתֵךְ בְּיָדֵךְ עֲשִׂי־לָהּ הַטּוֹב
בְּעֵינָיִךְ וַתְּעַנֶּהָ שָׂרַי וַתִּבְרַח מִפָּנֶיהָ: 7וַיִּמְצָאָהּ
מַלְאַךְ יְהוָה עַל־עֵין הַמַּיִם בַּמִּדְבָּר עַל־הָעַיִן
בְּדֶרֶךְ שׁוּר: 8וַיֹּאמַר הָגָר שִׁפְחַת שָׂרַי אֵי־מִזֶּה
בָאת וְאָנָה תֵלֵכִי וַתֹּאמֶר מִפְּנֵי שָׂרַי גְּבִרְתִּי אָנֹכִי
בֹּרַחַת: 9וַיֹּאמֶר לָהּ מַלְאַךְ יְהוָה שׁוּבִי אֶל־גְּבִרְתֵּךְ
וְהִתְעַנִּי תַּחַת יָדֶיהָ: 10וַיֹּאמֶר לָהּ מַלְאַךְ יְהוָה
הַרְבָּה אַרְבֶּה אֶת־זַרְעֵךְ וְלֹא יִסָּפֵר מֵרֹב:
11וַיֹּאמֶר לָהּ מַלְאַךְ יְהוָה

הִנָּךְ הָרָה וְיֹלַדְתְּ בֵּן וְקָרָאת שְׁמוֹ יִשְׁמָעֵאל
כִּי־שָׁמַע יְהוָה אֶל־עָנְיֵךְ:
12וְהוּא יִהְיֶה פֶּרֶא אָדָם יָדוֹ בַכֹּל וְיַד כֹּל בּוֹ
וְעַל־פְּנֵי כָל־אֶחָיו יִשְׁכֹּן:

16:6. And Sarai degraded her, and she fled. Sarai's treatment of the Egyptian Hagar foreshadows (or is reversed in, or governs) Israel's experience in Egypt. These exact words recur there: Egypt degraded them (Exod 1:12), and they fled (14:5). And note that, like Israel, Hagar fled to the *wilderness* (v. 7).

16:12. he'll tent. The verb is denominative; that is, the verb "to tent" (Hebrew root *škn*) derives from the word *miškān*, a tent or tabernacle. In the blessing of Noah's son Yaphet, it refers explicitly to dwelling in tents (Gen 9:27). In Moses' blessing of Benjamin (Deut 33:12) it is connected to God's "sheltering" (Hebrew *ḥōpēp*, related to *ḥuppāh*, a canopy). Most important, it will be used (in its *Piel* form) for the way in which God tents the Ark of the Testimony inside the Tabernacle. Occasionally it can refer to "dwelling" in general, not necessarily in tents (e.g., Gen 49:13).

13And she called the name of YHWH who spoke to her "You are El-roi," for she said, "Have I also seen after the one who sees me here?" 14On account of this the well was called "the well Lahai-roi." Here it is between Kadesh and Bered.

15And Hagar gave birth to a son for Abram, and Abram called the name of his son whom Hagar had borne Ishmael. 16And Abram was eighty years and six years old when Hagar gave birth to Ishmael for Abram.

17 1And Abram was ninety years and nine years old, and YHWH appeared to Abram and said to him, "I am El Shadday. Walk before me and be unblemished, 2and let me place my covenant between me and you, and I'll make you very, very numerous." 3And Abram fell on his face, and God spoke with him, saying, 4"I: here, my covenant is with you, and you'll become a father of a mass of nations. 5And your name will not be called Abram anymore, but your name will be Abraham, because I've set you to be a father of a mass of nations. 6And I'll make you very, very fruitful and make you into nations. And kings will come out of you. 7And I'll establish my covenant between me and you and your seed after you for their generations as an eternal covenant, to become God to you and to your seed after you. 8And I'll give you and your seed after you the land where you're residing, all the land of Canaan, as an eternal possession, and I'll become a God to them." 9And God said to Abraham, "And you: you shall observe my covenant, you and your seed after you through their generations. 10This is my covenant that you shall observe between me and you and your seed after you: every male is to be circumcised among you. 11And you shall be circumcised at the flesh of

וַתִּקְרָ֤א שֵׁם־יְהוָה֙ הַדֹּבֵ֣ר אֵלֶ֔יהָ אַתָּ֖ה אֵ֣ל רֳאִ֑י כִּ֣י 13
אָֽמְרָ֗ה הֲגַ֥ם הֲלֹ֛ם רָאִ֖יתִי אַחֲרֵ֥י רֹאִֽי׃ עַל־כֵּן֙ 14
קָרָ֣א לַבְּאֵ֔ר בְּאֵ֥ר לַחַ֖י רֹאִ֑י הִנֵּ֥ה בֵין־קָדֵ֖שׁ וּבֵ֥ין
בָּֽרֶד׃ וַתֵּ֧לֶד הָגָ֛ר לְאַבְרָ֖ם בֵּ֑ן וַיִּקְרָ֨א אַבְרָ֥ם שֶׁם־ 15
בְּנ֛וֹ אֲשֶׁר־יָלְדָ֥ה הָגָ֖ר יִשְׁמָעֵֽאל׃ וְאַבְרָ֕ם בֶּן־ 16
שְׁמֹנִ֥ים שָׁנָ֖ה וְשֵׁ֣שׁ שָׁנִ֑ים בְּלֶֽדֶת־הָגָ֥ר אֶת־יִשְׁמָעֵ֖אל
לְאַבְרָֽם׃ ס

וַיְהִ֣י אַבְרָ֔ם בֶּן־תִּשְׁעִ֥ים שָׁנָ֖ה וְתֵ֣שַׁע שָׁנִ֑ים 17 1
וַיֵּרָ֨א יְהוָ֜ה אֶל־אַבְרָ֗ם וַיֹּ֤אמֶר אֵלָיו֙ אֲנִי־אֵ֣ל שַׁדַּ֔י
הִתְהַלֵּ֥ךְ לְפָנַ֖י וֶהְיֵ֥ה תָמִֽים׃ וְאֶתְּנָ֥ה בְרִיתִ֖י בֵּינִ֣י 2
וּבֵינֶ֑ךָ וְאַרְבֶּ֥ה אוֹתְךָ֖ בִּמְאֹ֥ד מְאֹֽד׃ וַיִּפֹּ֥ל אַבְרָ֖ם 3
עַל־פָּנָ֑יו וַיְדַבֵּ֥ר אִתּ֛וֹ אֱלֹהִ֖ים לֵאמֹֽר׃ אֲנִ֕י הִנֵּ֥ה 4
בְרִיתִ֖י אִתָּ֑ךְ וְהָיִ֕יתָ לְאַ֖ב הֲמ֥וֹן גּוֹיִֽם׃ וְלֹא־יִקָּרֵ֨א 5
ע֥וֹד אֶת־שִׁמְךָ֖ אַבְרָ֑ם וְהָיָ֤ה שִׁמְךָ֙ אַבְרָהָ֔ם כִּ֛י אַב־
הֲמ֥וֹן גּוֹיִ֖ם נְתַתִּֽיךָ׃ וְהִפְרֵתִ֤י אֹֽתְךָ֙ בִּמְאֹ֣ד מְאֹ֔ד 6
וּנְתַתִּ֖יךָ לְגוֹיִ֑ם וּמְלָכִ֖ים מִמְּךָ֥ יֵצֵֽאוּ׃ וַהֲקִמֹתִ֣י אֶת־ 7
בְּרִיתִ֗י בֵּינִ֤י וּבֵינֶ֙ךָ֙ וּבֵ֣ין זַרְעֲךָ֧ אַחֲרֶ֛יךָ לְדֹרֹתָ֖ם
לִבְרִ֣ית עוֹלָ֑ם לִהְי֤וֹת לְךָ֙ לֵֽאלֹהִ֔ים וּֽלְזַרְעֲךָ֖
אַחֲרֶֽיךָ׃ וְנָתַתִּ֣י לְ֠ךָ וּלְזַרְעֲךָ֨ אַחֲרֶ֜יךָ אֵ֣ת ׀ אֶ֣רֶץ 8
מְגֻרֶ֗יךָ אֵ֚ת כָּל־אֶ֣רֶץ כְּנַ֔עַן לַאֲחֻזַּ֖ת עוֹלָ֑ם וְהָיִ֥יתִי
לָהֶ֖ם לֵאלֹהִֽים׃ וַיֹּ֤אמֶר אֱלֹהִים֙ אֶל־אַבְרָהָ֔ם וְאַתָּ֖ה 9
אֶת־בְּרִיתִ֣י תִשְׁמֹ֑ר אַתָּ֛ה וְזַרְעֲךָ֥ אַֽחֲרֶ֖יךָ לְדֹרֹתָֽם׃
זֹ֣את בְּרִיתִ֞י אֲשֶׁ֣ר תִּשְׁמְר֗וּ בֵּינִי֙ וּבֵ֣ינֵיכֶ֔ם וּבֵ֥ין 10
זַרְעֲךָ֖ אַחֲרֶ֑יךָ הִמּ֥וֹל לָכֶ֖ם כָּל־זָכָֽר׃ וּנְמַלְתֶּ֕ם אֵ֖ת 11

17:1. El Shadday. Meaning: El, the One of the Mountain. (The old translation "God Almighty" cannot be justified.) The association of gods in general, and YHWH in particular, with mountains is well known. And there are gods called *šadu rabu* ("big mountains") in Akkadian, and gods called *šdyn* in the Deir 'Alla text (an ancient plaster text found in Jordan in 1967).

your foreskin, and it will become a sign of a covenant between me and you. 12And at eight days old every male shall be circumcised among you through your generations: homeborn or purchased with money from any foreigner who is not from your seed. 13Your homeborn and the one purchased with your money *will be circumcised*. And my covenant will become an eternal covenant in your flesh. 14And an uncircumcised—a male the flesh of whose foreskin will not be circumcised—that person will be cut off from his people. He has broken my covenant."

15And God said to Abraham, "Sarai, your wife: you shall not call her name Sarai, because her name is Sarah. 16And I'll bless her, and I'll also give you a son from her. And I'll bless her, and she'll become nations. Kings of peoples will be from her."

17And Abraham fell on his face and laughed and said in his heart, "Will he be born to someone who's a hundred years old?! And will Sarah, who's ninety years old, give birth?!" 18And Abraham said to God, "If only Ishmael will live before you."

19And God said, "But Sarah, your wife, is giving birth to a son for you. And you shall call his

בְּשַׂר עָרְלַתְכֶם וְהָיָה לְאוֹת בְּרִית בֵּינִי וּבֵינֵיכֶם: 12וּבֶן־שְׁמֹנַת יָמִים יִמּוֹל לָכֶם כָּל־זָכָר לְדֹרֹתֵיכֶם יְלִיד בָּיִת וּמִקְנַת־כֶּסֶף מִכֹּל בֶּן־נֵכָר אֲשֶׁר לֹא מִזַּרְעֲךָ הוּא: 13הִמּוֹל ׀ יִמּוֹל יְלִיד בֵּיתְךָ וּמִקְנַת כַּסְפֶּךָ וְהָיְתָה בְרִיתִי בִּבְשַׂרְכֶם לִבְרִית עוֹלָם: 14וְעָרֵל ׀ זָכָר אֲשֶׁר לֹא־יִמּוֹל אֶת־בְּשַׂר עָרְלָתוֹ וְנִכְרְתָה הַנֶּפֶשׁ הַהִוא מֵעַמֶּיהָ אֶת־בְּרִיתִי הֵפַר: ס 15וַיֹּאמֶר אֱלֹהִים אֶל־אַבְרָהָם שָׂרַי אִשְׁתְּךָ לֹא־תִקְרָא אֶת־שְׁמָהּ שָׂרָי כִּי שָׂרָה שְׁמָהּ: 16וּבֵרַכְתִּי אֹתָהּ וְגַם נָתַתִּי מִמֶּנָּה לְךָ בֵּן וּבֵרַכְתִּיהָ וְהָיְתָה לְגוֹיִם מַלְכֵי עַמִּים מִמֶּנָּה יִהְיוּ: 17וַיִּפֹּל אַבְרָהָם עַל־פָּנָיו וַיִּצְחָק וַיֹּאמֶר בְּלִבּוֹ הַלְּבֶן מֵאָה־שָׁנָה יִוָּלֵד וְאִם־שָׂרָה הֲבַת־תִּשְׁעִים שָׁנָה תֵּלֵד: 18וַיֹּאמֶר אַבְרָהָם אֶל־הָאֱלֹהִים לוּ יִשְׁמָעֵאל יִחְיֶה לְפָנֶיךָ: 19וַיֹּאמֶר אֱלֹהִים אֲבָל שָׂרָה אִשְׁתְּךָ יֹלֶדֶת לְךָ בֵּן

17:12. **purchased with money**. A slave.

17:14. **cut off from his people**. No one is certain what this meant. It refers to some sort of punishment produced by God, not humans. It may mean to die without heirs or perhaps not to be buried in the ancestral tomb. (In Gen 49:29 Jacob on his deathbed says, "I'm being gathered to my people." The next thing is that he asks to be buried in the ancestral tomb!) Or it may mean not to join one's ancestors in an afterlife. Its meaning was already unknown for certain by early rabbinic times.

The word has a double meaning here in the context of circumcision: *krt* is the term for Zipporah's circumcision of Gershom in Exod 4:25.

17:18. **If only Ishmael will live before you**. Abraham is content with Ishmael as his successor, but it is God who decides the succession, and God declares that it will be Isaac. Compare this to the development one generation later, in which it is not God but humans who determine the succession: Rebekah and Jacob manipulate the birthright and blessing so that Jacob and not Esau will be Isaac's successor. That is one of many cases in which humans' control of their own destiny increases through the Torah and through the entire *Tanak*.

name Isaac. And I'll establish my covenant with him as an eternal covenant for his seed after him. [20]And I've listened to you about Ishmael. Here, I've blessed him, and I'll make him fruitful and make him very, very numerous. He'll father twelve chieftains, and I'll make him into a big nation. [21]But I'll establish my covenant with Isaac, whom Sarah will bear for you at this appointed time in the next year." [22]And He finished speaking with him, and God went up from Abraham.

[23]And Abraham took Ishmael, his son, and all his homeborn and everyone purchased with his money, every male among the men of Abraham's house, and he circumcised the flesh of their foreskin in that very day, as God had spoken with him. [24]And Abraham was ninety-nine years old when he was circumcised, the flesh of his foreskin, [25]and Ishmael, his son, was thirteen years old when he was circumcised at the flesh of his foreskin. [26]In that very day Abraham was circumcised, and Ishmael, his son; [27]and all the men of his house, homeborn and purchased with money from a foreigner, were circumcised with him.

וְקָרָאתָ אֶת־שְׁמוֹ יִצְחָק וַהֲקִמֹתִי אֶת־בְּרִיתִי אִתּוֹ לִבְרִית עוֹלָם לְזַרְעוֹ אַחֲרָיו: 20וּלְיִשְׁמָעֵאל שְׁמַעְתִּיךָ הִנֵּה ׀ בֵּרַכְתִּי אֹתוֹ וְהִפְרֵיתִי אֹתוֹ וְהִרְבֵּיתִי אֹתוֹ בִּמְאֹד מְאֹד שְׁנֵים־עָשָׂר נְשִׂיאִם יוֹלִיד וּנְתַתִּיו לְגוֹי גָּדוֹל: 21וְאֶת־בְּרִיתִי אָקִים אֶת־יִצְחָק אֲשֶׁר תֵּלֵד לְךָ שָׂרָה לַמּוֹעֵד הַזֶּה בַּשָּׁנָה הָאַחֶרֶת: 22וַיְכַל לְדַבֵּר אִתּוֹ וַיַּעַל אֱלֹהִים מֵעַל אַבְרָהָם:

23וַיִּקַּח אַבְרָהָם אֶת־יִשְׁמָעֵאל בְּנוֹ וְאֵת כָּל־יְלִידֵי בֵיתוֹ וְאֵת כָּל־מִקְנַת כַּסְפּוֹ כָּל־זָכָר בְּאַנְשֵׁי בֵּית אַבְרָהָם וַיָּמָל אֶת־בְּשַׂר עָרְלָתָם בְּעֶצֶם הַיּוֹם הַזֶּה כַּאֲשֶׁר דִּבֶּר אִתּוֹ אֱלֹהִים: 24וְאַבְרָהָם בֶּן־תִּשְׁעִים וָתֵשַׁע שָׁנָה בְּהִמֹּלוֹ בְּשַׂר עָרְלָתוֹ: 25וְיִשְׁמָעֵאל בְּנוֹ בֶּן־שָׁלֹשׁ עֶשְׂרֵה שָׁנָה בְּהִמֹּלוֹ אֵת בְּשַׂר עָרְלָתוֹ: 26בְּעֶצֶם הַיּוֹם הַזֶּה נִמּוֹל אַבְרָהָם וְיִשְׁמָעֵאל בְּנוֹ: 27וְכָל־אַנְשֵׁי בֵיתוֹ יְלִיד בָּיִת וּמִקְנַת־כֶּסֶף מֵאֵת בֶּן־נֵכָר נִמֹּלוּ אִתּוֹ: פ

17:19. **you shall call his name Isaac.** Isaac's father Abram/Abraham and his son Jacob/Israel have their names changed, but Isaac does not. The reason appears to be that Abraham's and Jacob's names are changed by *God*, but Isaac's name is given here by God in the first place.

17:20. **I'll make him into a big nation.** People sometimes speak of Ishmael as if the Bible were picturing him as the ancestor of the Arabs, but the Bible pictures Ishmael only as the ancestor of the Ishmaelites.

17:24. **ninety-nine years old when he was circumcised.** But God has known Abraham for years, so why does God not command this when Abraham is younger? Why not command it at the beginning of their relationship? Because the issue is not the circumcision. It is the *covenant*, of which circumcision is just the sign. So why not make the covenant right at the beginning? Because Abraham has to go through certain things and *merit* a covenant.

17:23,25,26. **Ishmael, his son.** The triple repetition of "his son" conveys concern for Ishmael and feeling for him as Abraham's son. Thus it teaches us about compassion and acceptance. There is no attempt here to minimize Ishmael or his descendants, the Ishmaelites, or to cast aspersions on them.

AND HE APPEARED

וירא

18 ¹And YHWH appeared to him at the oaks of Mamre. And he was sitting at the tent entrance in the heat of the day, ²and he raised his eyes and saw, and here were three people standing over him. And he saw and ran toward them from the tent entrance and bowed to the ground. ³And he said, "My Lord, if I've found favor in your eyes don't pass on from your servant. ⁴Let a little water be gotten, and wash your feet and relax under a tree, ⁵and let me get a bit of bread, and satisfy your heart. Afterward you'll pass on, for that's why you've passed by your servant."

And they said, "Do that, as you've spoken."

⁶And Abraham hurried to the tent, to Sarah, and said, "Hurry, three measures of fine flour. Knead it and make cakes." ⁷And Abraham ran to the herd and took a calf, tender and good, and he gave it to a servant, and he hurried to prepare it. ⁸And he took curds and milk and the calf that

18 ¹וַיֵּרָ֤א אֵלָיו֙ יְהוָ֔ה בְּאֵלֹנֵ֖י מַמְרֵ֑א וְה֛וּא יֹשֵׁ֥ב פֶּֽתַח־הָאֹ֖הֶל כְּחֹ֥ם הַיּֽוֹם׃ ²וַיִּשָּׂ֤א עֵינָיו֙ וַיַּ֔רְא וְהִנֵּה֙ שְׁלֹשָׁ֣ה אֲנָשִׁ֔ים נִצָּבִ֖ים עָלָ֑יו וַיַּ֗רְא וַיָּ֤רָץ לִקְרָאתָם֙ מִפֶּ֣תַח הָאֹ֔הֶל וַיִּשְׁתַּ֖חוּ אָֽרְצָה׃ ³וַיֹּאמַ֑ר אֲדֹנָ֗י אִם־נָ֨א מָצָ֤אתִי חֵן֙ בְּעֵינֶ֔יךָ אַל־נָ֥א תַעֲבֹ֖ר מֵעַ֥ל עַבְדֶּֽךָ׃ ⁴יֻקַּֽח־נָ֣א מְעַט־מַ֔יִם וְרַחֲצ֖וּ רַגְלֵיכֶ֑ם וְהִֽשָּׁעֲנ֖וּ תַּ֥חַת הָעֵֽץ׃ ⁵וְאֶקְחָ֨ה פַת־לֶ֜חֶם וְסַעֲד֤וּ לִבְּכֶם֙ אַחַ֣ר תַּעֲבֹ֔רוּ כִּֽי־עַל־כֵּ֥ן עֲבַרְתֶּ֖ם עַל־עַבְדְּכֶ֑ם וַיֹּ֣אמְר֔וּ כֵּ֥ן תַּעֲשֶׂ֖ה כַּאֲשֶׁ֥ר דִּבַּֽרְתָּ׃ ⁶וַיְמַהֵ֧ר אַבְרָהָ֛ם הָאֹ֖הֱלָה אֶל־שָׂרָ֑ה וַיֹּ֗אמֶר מַהֲרִ֞י שְׁלֹ֤שׁ סְאִים֙ קֶ֣מַח סֹ֔לֶת ל֖וּשִׁי וַעֲשִׂ֥י עֻגֽוֹת׃ ⁷וְאֶל־הַבָּקָ֖ר רָ֣ץ אַבְרָהָ֑ם וַיִּקַּ֨ח בֶּן־בָּקָ֜ר רַ֤ךְ וָטוֹב֙ וַיִּתֵּ֣ן אֶל־הַנַּ֔עַר וַיְמַהֵ֖ר לַעֲשׂ֥וֹת אֹתֽוֹ׃ ⁸וַיִּקַּ֨ח חֶמְאָ֜ה וְחָלָ֗ב וּבֶן־הַבָּקָר֙ אֲשֶׁ֣ר עָשָׂ֔ה

18:2. **bowed**. The word in Hebrew refers to bowing prostrate, nose to the ground.

18:3. **My Lord**. Why does Abraham run to the three people and bow to them but then speak to God? Is he meeting God, people, or angels? Several of the biblical stories involving angels contain confusions such as this, i.e., confusions between when it is the deity and when it is the angel who is speaking or doing something. But it is confusing only so long as we imagine angels as beings who are independent or separate from God. These texts indicate that angels are rather conceived of here as expressions of God's presence. The consistent biblical conception of God is that God cannot possibly be seen by a human ("A human will not see me and live," Exod 33:20) and cannot possibly be contained in any known space ("The heavens . . . will not contain you," 1 Kings 8:27). God, in this conception, can nonetheless make Himself known to humans by a sort of emanation from the Godhead that is visible to human eyes. It is a hypostasis, a concrete expression of the divine presence, which is otherwise inexpressible to human beings. What the human sees when such a hypostasis is in front of him or her looks like "people," like a "man." And the word for such a thing is "angel." Thus Jacob can encounter an angel and still say "I've seen God face-to-face" (Gen 32:31). And Abraham can face three angels and address "my Lord." And an angel can speak God's words in first person or can speak about God in third person. All this is so because in some ways an angel is an identifiable thing itself, and in some ways it is merely a representation of divine presence in human affairs. (See *The Hidden Face of God*, pp. 10–11.)

he had prepared and placed them in front of them, and he was standing over them under the tree, and they ate.

9And they said to him, "Where is Sarah, your wife?"

And he said, "Here in the tent."

10And He said, "I shall *come back* to you at the time of life, and, here, Sarah, your wife, will have a son."

And Sarah was listening at the tent entrance, which was behind him. 11And Abraham and Sarah were old, well along in days; Sarah had stopped having the way of women. 12And Sarah laughed inside her and said, "After I've become worn out am I to have pleasure?! And my lord is old!"

13And YHWH said to Abraham, "Why is this? Sarah laughed, saying, 'Shall I indeed give birth? And I am old!' Is anything too wondrous for YHWH? 14At the appointed time I'll come back to you, at the time of life, and Sarah will have a son."

15And Sarah lied, saying, "I didn't laugh," because she was afraid.

And He said, "No, but you did laugh."

16And the people got up from there and gazed at the sight of Sodom, and Abraham was going with them to send them off. 17And YHWH had said, "Shall I conceal what I'm doing from Abraham, 18since Abraham *will* become a big and powerful nation, and all the nations of the earth will be blessed through him? 19For I've known him for the purpose that he'll command his children and his house after him, and they'll observe YHWH's way, to do virtue and judgment, and for the purpose of YHWH's bringing upon Abraham what He spoke about him."

20And YHWH said, "The cry of Sodom and Gomorrah: how great it is. And their sin: how very heavy it is. 21Let me go down, and I'll see if they've done, all told, like the cry that has come to me. And if not, let me know." 22And the people turned from there and went to Sodom.

And Abraham was still standing before

וַיִּתֵּן לִפְנֵיהֶם וְהֽוּא־עֹמֵד עֲלֵיהֶם תַּחַת הָעֵץ
וַיֹּאכֵֽלוּ: 9וַיֹּאמְרוּ אֵלָיו אַיֵּה שָׂרָה אִשְׁתֶּךָ וַיֹּאמֶר
הִנֵּה בָאֹֽהֶל: 10וַיֹּאמֶר שׁוֹב אָשׁוּב אֵלֶיךָ כָּעֵת חַיָּה
וְהִנֵּה־בֵן לְשָׂרָה אִשְׁתֶּךָ וְשָׂרָה שֹׁמַעַת פֶּתַח הָאֹהֶל
וְהוּא אַחֲרָֽיו: 11וְאַבְרָהָם וְשָׂרָה זְקֵנִים בָּאִים
בַּיָּמִים חָדַל לִהְיוֹת לְשָׂרָה אֹרַח כַּנָּשִֽׁים: 12וַתִּצְחַק
שָׂרָה בְּקִרְבָּהּ לֵאמֹר אַחֲרֵי בְלֹתִי הָֽיְתָה־לִּי עֶדְנָה
וַֽאדֹנִי זָקֵֽן: 13וַיֹּאמֶר יְהוָה אֶל־אַבְרָהָם לָמָּה זֶּה
צָחֲקָה שָׂרָה לֵאמֹר הַאַף אֻמְנָם אֵלֵד וַאֲנִי זָקַֽנְתִּי:
14הֲיִפָּלֵא מֵיְהוָה דָּבָר לַמּוֹעֵד אָשׁוּב אֵלֶיךָ כָּעֵת
חַיָּה וּלְשָׂרָה בֵֽן: 15וַתְּכַחֵשׁ שָׂרָה ׀ לֵאמֹר לֹא
צָחַקְתִּי כִּי ׀ יָרֵאָה וַיֹּאמֶר ׀ לֹא כִּי צָחָֽקְתְּ:
16וַיָּקֻמוּ מִשָּׁם הָֽאֲנָשִׁים וַיַּשְׁקִפוּ עַל־פְּנֵי סְדֹם
וְאַבְרָהָם הֹלֵךְ עִמָּם לְשַׁלְּחָֽם: 17וַֽיהוָֹה אָמָר
הַֽמְכַסֶּה אֲנִי מֵֽאַבְרָהָם אֲשֶׁר אֲנִי עֹשֶֽׂה: 18וְאַבְרָהָם
הָיוֹ יִֽהְיֶה לְגוֹי גָּדוֹל וְעָצוּם וְנִבְרְכוּ בוֹ כֹּל גּוֹיֵי
הָאָֽרֶץ: 19כִּי יְדַעְתִּיו לְמַעַן אֲשֶׁר יְצַוֶּה אֶת־בָּנָיו
וְאֶת־בֵּיתוֹ אַחֲרָיו וְשָֽׁמְרוּ דֶּרֶךְ יְהוָה לַעֲשׂוֹת
צְדָקָה וּמִשְׁפָּט לְמַעַן הָבִיא יְהוָה עַל־אַבְרָהָם אֵת
אֲשֶׁר־דִּבֶּר עָלָֽיו: 20וַיֹּאמֶר יְהוָה זַעֲקַת סְדֹם
וַעֲמֹרָה כִּי־רָבָּה וְחַטָּאתָם כִּי כָבְדָה מְאֹֽד:
21אֵֽרֲדָה־נָּא וְאֶרְאֶה הַכְּצַעֲקָתָהּ הַבָּאָה אֵלַי ׀ עָשׂוּ ׀
כָּלָה וְאִם־לֹא אֵדָֽעָה: 22וַיִּפְנוּ מִשָּׁם הָֽאֲנָשִׁים וַיֵּלְכוּ
סְדֹמָה וְאַבְרָהָם עוֹדֶנּוּ עֹמֵד לִפְנֵי יְהוָֽה: 23וַיִּגַּשׁ

YHWH, 23and Abraham came over and said, "Will you also annihilate the virtuous with the wicked? 24Maybe there are fifty virtuous people within the city. Will you also annihilate and not sustain the place for the fifty virtuous who are in it? 25Far be it from you to do a thing like this, to kill virtuous with wicked—and it will be the same for the virtuous and the wicked—far be it from you. Will the judge of all the earth not do justice?"

26And YHWH said, "If I find in Sodom fifty virtuous people within the city, then I'll sustain the whole place for their sake."

27And Abraham answered, and he said, "Here I've undertaken to speak to my Lord, and I'm dust and ashes. 28Maybe the fifty virtuous people will be short by five. Will you destroy the whole city for the five?"

And He said, "I won't destroy if I find forty-five there."

29And he went on again to speak to Him and said, "Maybe forty will be found there."

And He said, "I won't do it for the sake of the forty."

30And he said, "May my Lord not be angry, and let me speak. Maybe thirty will be found there."

And He said, "I won't do it if I find thirty there."

31And he said, "Here I've undertaken to speak to my Lord. Maybe twenty will be found there."

And He said, "I won't destroy for the sake of the twenty."

32And he said, "May my Lord not be angry, and let me speak just this one time. Maybe ten will be found there."

And He said there, "I won't destroy for the sake of the ten."

33And YHWH went when He had finished

אַבְרָהָם וַיֹּאמַר הַאַף תִּסְפֶּה צַדִּיק עִם־רָשָׁע: 24אוּלַי יֵשׁ חֲמִשִּׁים צַדִּיקִם בְּתוֹךְ הָעִיר הַאַף תִּסְפֶּה וְלֹא־תִשָּׂא לַמָּקוֹם לְמַעַן חֲמִשִּׁים הַצַּדִּיקִם אֲשֶׁר בְּקִרְבָּהּ: 25חָלִלָה לְּךָ מֵעֲשֹׂת ׀ כַּדָּבָר הַזֶּה לְהָמִית צַדִּיק עִם־רָשָׁע וְהָיָה כַצַּדִּיק כָּרָשָׁע חָלִלָה לָּךְ הֲשֹׁפֵט כָּל־הָאָרֶץ לֹא יַעֲשֶׂה מִשְׁפָּט: 26וַיֹּאמֶר יְהוָה אִם־אֶמְצָא בִסְדֹם חֲמִשִּׁים צַדִּיקִם בְּתוֹךְ הָעִיר וְנָשָׂאתִי לְכָל־הַמָּקוֹם בַּעֲבוּרָם: 27וַיַּעַן אַבְרָהָם וַיֹּאמַר הִנֵּה־נָא הוֹאַלְתִּי לְדַבֵּר אֶל־אֲדֹנָי וְאָנֹכִי עָפָר וָאֵפֶר: 28אוּלַי יַחְסְרוּן חֲמִשִּׁים הַצַּדִּיקִם חֲמִשָּׁה הֲתַשְׁחִית בַּחֲמִשָּׁה אֶת־כָּל־הָעִיר וַיֹּאמֶר לֹא אַשְׁחִית אִם־אֶמְצָא שָׁם אַרְבָּעִים וַחֲמִשָּׁה: 29וַיֹּסֶף עוֹד לְדַבֵּר אֵלָיו וַיֹּאמַר אוּלַי יִמָּצְאוּן שָׁם אַרְבָּעִים וַיֹּאמֶר לֹא אֶעֱשֶׂה בַּעֲבוּר הָאַרְבָּעִים: 30וַיֹּאמֶר אַל־נָא יִחַר לַאדֹנָי וַאֲדַבֵּרָה אוּלַי יִמָּצְאוּן שָׁם שְׁלֹשִׁים וַיֹּאמֶר לֹא אֶעֱשֶׂה אִם־אֶמְצָא שָׁם שְׁלֹשִׁים: 31וַיֹּאמֶר הִנֵּה־נָא הוֹאַלְתִּי לְדַבֵּר אֶל־אֲדֹנָי אוּלַי יִמָּצְאוּן שָׁם עֶשְׂרִים וַיֹּאמֶר לֹא אַשְׁחִית בַּעֲבוּר הָעֶשְׂרִים: 32וַיֹּאמֶר אַל־נָא יִחַר לַאדֹנָי וַאֲדַבְּרָה אַךְ־הַפַּעַם אוּלַי יִמָּצְאוּן שָׁם עֲשָׂרָה וַיֹּאמֶר לֹא אַשְׁחִית בַּעֲבוּר הָעֲשָׂרָה: 33וַיֵּלֶךְ יְהוָה כַּאֲשֶׁר כִּלָּה לְדַבֵּר אֶל־

18:25. Far be it from you to do a thing like this. This is the first time in the Bible that a human questions a divine decision. Moses will take this even farther on at least three occasions. Concerning the exchange between God and Abraham, see the comment on Gen 22:3.

speaking to Abraham, and Abraham went back to his place.

19

¹And the two angels came to Sodom in the evening, and Lot was sitting at Sodom's gate, and Lot saw and got up toward them, and he bowed, nose to the ground. ²And he said, "Here, my lords, turn to your servant's house and spend the night and wash your feet, and you'll get up early and go your way."

And they said, "No, we'll spend the night in the square." ³And he pressed them very much, and they turned to him and came to his house, and he made a feast and baked unleavened bread for them, and they ate.

⁴They had not yet lain down, and the people of the city, the people of Sodom, surrounded the house, from youth to old man, all the people, from the farthest reaches. ⁵And they called to Lot and said to him, "Where are the people who came to you tonight? Bring them out to us, and let's know them!"

⁶And Lot went out to them at the entrance and closed the door behind him, ⁷and he said, "Don't do bad, my brothers. ⁸Here I have two daughters who haven't known a man. Let me bring them out to you, and do to them as is good in your eyes. Only don't do anything to these people, because that is why they came under the shadow of my roof."

אַבְרָהָ֔ם וְאַבְרָהָ֖ם שָׁ֥ב לִמְקֹמֽוֹ׃

19 ¹וַ֠יָּבֹ֠אוּ שְׁנֵ֨י הַמַּלְאָכִ֤ים סְדֹ֙מָה֙ בָּעֶ֔רֶב וְל֖וֹט יֹשֵׁ֣ב בְּשַֽׁעַר־סְדֹ֑ם וַיַּרְא־לוֹט֙ וַיָּ֣קָם לִקְרָאתָ֔ם וַיִּשְׁתַּ֥חוּ אַפַּ֖יִם אָֽרְצָה׃ ²וַיֹּ֜אמֶר הִנֶּ֣ה נָּא־אֲדֹנַ֗י ס֤וּרוּ נָא֙ אֶל־בֵּ֤ית עַבְדְּכֶם֙ וְלִ֔ינוּ וְרַחֲצ֖וּ רַגְלֵיכֶ֑ם וְהִשְׁכַּמְתֶּ֖ם וַהֲלַכְתֶּ֣ם לְדַרְכְּכֶ֑ם וַיֹּאמְר֣וּ לֹּ֔א כִּ֥י בָרְח֖וֹב נָלִֽין׃ ³וַיִּפְצַר־בָּ֣ם מְאֹ֔ד וַיָּסֻ֣רוּ אֵלָ֔יו וַיָּבֹ֖אוּ אֶל־בֵּית֑וֹ וַיַּ֤עַשׂ לָהֶם֙ מִשְׁתֶּ֔ה וּמַצּ֥וֹת אָפָ֖ה וַיֹּאכֵֽלוּ׃ ⁴טֶרֶם֮ יִשְׁכָּבוּ֒ וְאַנְשֵׁ֨י הָעִ֜יר אַנְשֵׁ֤י סְדֹם֙ נָסַ֣בּוּ עַל־הַבַּ֔יִת מִנַּ֖עַר וְעַד־זָקֵ֑ן כָּל־הָעָ֖ם מִקָּצֶֽה׃ ⁵וַיִּקְרְא֤וּ אֶל־לוֹט֙ וַיֹּ֣אמְרוּ ל֔וֹ אַיֵּ֧ה הָאֲנָשִׁ֛ים אֲשֶׁר־בָּ֥אוּ אֵלֶ֖יךָ הַלָּ֑יְלָה הוֹצִיאֵ֣ם אֵלֵ֔ינוּ וְנֵדְעָ֖ה אֹתָֽם׃ ⁶וַיֵּצֵ֧א אֲלֵהֶ֛ם ל֖וֹט הַפֶּ֑תְחָה וְהַדֶּ֖לֶת סָגַ֥ר אַחֲרָֽיו׃ ⁷וַיֹּאמַ֑ר אַל־נָ֥א אַחַ֖י תָּרֵֽעוּ׃ ⁸הִנֵּה־נָ֨א לִ֜י שְׁתֵּ֣י בָנ֗וֹת אֲשֶׁ֤ר לֹא־יָֽדְעוּ֙ אִ֔ישׁ אוֹצִֽיאָה־נָּ֤א אֶתְהֶן֙ אֲלֵיכֶ֔ם וַעֲשׂ֣וּ לָהֶ֔ן כַּטּ֖וֹב בְּעֵינֵיכֶ֑ם רַ֠ק לָֽאֲנָשִׁ֤ים הָאֵל֙ אַל־תַּעֲשׂ֣וּ דָבָ֔ר כִּֽי־עַל־כֵּ֥ן בָּ֖אוּ בְּצֵ֥ל קֹרָתִֽי׃ ⁹וַיֹּאמְר֣וּ ׀ גֶּשׁ־הָ֗לְאָה

19:5. **let's know them.** The word "know" sometimes has the meaning of sexual intimacy, as in the case of "Cain knew his wife, and she became pregnant." That is how it is commonly understood in this passage: the people are threatening sexual abuse of the guests. This is possible, and even likely (in light of a parallel story in Judges 19). But this episode is also commonly understood to be about homosexual rape. I see no basis for this whatever. The text says that two *people* come to Sodom, and that *all* of the *people* of Sodom come and say, "Let's know them." The homosexuality interpretation apparently comes from misunderstanding the Hebrew word *'ănāšîm* to mean "men," instead of "people."

19:8. **I have two daughters. . . . do to them as is good in your eyes.** Some say that this is a matter of ancient Near Eastern hospitality: Lot as the host must do *anything* to protect his guests. Some say that daughters were held in low esteem in that world's values. Ramban and others say that this shows that Lot had an evil heart. It seems to

9And they said, "Come over here," and they said, "This one comes to live, and then he *judges!* Now we'll be worse to you than to them." And they pressed the man, Lot, very much and came over to break down the door. 10And the people reached their hand out and brought Lot in to them in the house, and they closed the door. 11And they struck the people who were at the house's entrance with blindness, from smallest to biggest, and they wearied themselves with finding the entrance.

12And the people said to Lot, "Who else do you have here—son-in-law and your sons and your daughters and all that you have in the city— take them out from the place, 13because we're destroying this place, because its cry has grown big before YHWH's face, and YHWH has sent us to destroy it."

14And Lot went out and spoke to his sons-in-law, who had married his daughters, and said, "Get up, get out of this place, for YHWH is destroying the city." And he was like a joker in his sons-in-law's eyes.

15And as the dawn rose the angels urged Lot, saying, "Get up, take your wife and your two daughters who are present, or else you'll be annihilated for the city's crime." 16And he delayed. And the people took hold of his hand and his

וַיֹּאמְר֣וּ ׀ גֶּשׁ־הָ֗לְאָה וַיֹּֽאמְרוּ֙ הָאֶחָ֤ד בָּֽא־לָגוּר֙ וַיִּשְׁפֹּ֣ט שָׁפ֔וֹט עַתָּ֕ה נָרַ֥ע לְךָ֖ מֵהֶ֑ם וַיִּפְצְר֨וּ בָאִ֤ישׁ בְּלוֹט֙ מְאֹ֔ד וַֽיִּגְּשׁ֖וּ לִשְׁבֹּ֥ר הַדָּֽלֶת׃ 10וַיִּשְׁלְח֤וּ הָֽאֲנָשִׁים֙ אֶת־יָדָ֔ם וַיָּבִ֧יאוּ אֶת־ ל֛וֹט אֲלֵיהֶ֖ם הַבָּ֑יְתָה וְאֶת־הַדֶּ֖לֶת סָגָֽרוּ׃ 11וְאֶת־ הָאֲנָשִׁ֞ים אֲשֶׁר־פֶּ֣תַח הַבַּ֗יִת הִכּוּ֙ בַּסַּנְוֵרִ֔ים מִקָּטֹ֖ן וְעַד־גָּד֑וֹל וַיִּלְא֖וּ לִמְצֹ֥א הַפָּֽתַח׃ 12וַיֹּאמְר֨וּ הָאֲנָשִׁ֜ים אֶל־ל֗וֹט עֹ֚ד מִֽי־לְךָ֣ פֹ֔ה חָתָן֙ וּבָנֶ֣יךָ וּבְנֹתֶ֔יךָ וְכֹ֥ל אֲשֶׁר־לְךָ֖ בָּעִ֑יר הוֹצֵ֖א מִן־הַמָּקֽוֹם׃ 13כִּֽי־מַשְׁחִתִ֣ים אֲנַ֔חְנוּ אֶת־הַמָּק֖וֹם הַזֶּ֑ה כִּֽי־גָדְלָ֤ה צַֽעֲקָתָם֙ אֶת־פְּנֵ֣י יְהוָ֔ה וַיְשַׁלְּחֵ֥נוּ יְהוָ֖ה לְשַׁחֲתָֽהּ׃ 14וַיֵּצֵ֨א ל֜וֹט וַיְדַבֵּ֣ר ׀ אֶל־חֲתָנָ֣יו ׀ לֹקְחֵ֣י בְנֹתָ֗יו וַיֹּ֨אמֶר֙ ק֤וּמוּ צְּאוּ֙ מִן־ הַמָּק֣וֹם הַזֶּ֔ה כִּֽי־מַשְׁחִ֥ית יְהוָ֖ה אֶת־הָעִ֑יר וַיְהִ֥י כִמְצַחֵ֖ק בְּעֵינֵ֥י חֲתָנָֽיו׃ 15וּכְמוֹ֙ הַשַּׁ֣חַר עָלָ֔ה וַיָּאִ֥יצוּ הַמַּלְאָכִ֖ים בְּל֣וֹט לֵאמֹ֑ר קוּם֩ קַ֨ח אֶת־אִשְׁתְּךָ֜ וְאֶת־ שְׁתֵּ֤י בְנֹתֶ֨יךָ֙ הַנִּמְצָאֹ֔ת פֶּן־תִּסָּפֶ֖ה בַּעֲוֺ֥ן הָעִֽיר׃ 16וַֽיִּתְמַהְמָ֓הּ ׀ וַיַּחֲזִ֨קוּ הָאֲנָשִׁ֜ים בְּיָד֣וֹ וּבְיַד־אִשְׁתּ֗וֹ

---

me that it is not the Near Eastern tradition of hospitality but of *bargaining* that accounts for what is going on here. When Abraham goes to buy a tomb for Sarah, the seller says to him, "I've *given* it to you!" (Gen 23:11). But he does *not* give it. Then Abraham says, "I've given the *money*" (23:13). Then the seller says, "Land worth four hundred shekels of silver: what's that between me and you?!" (23:15) as if this were a small sum. But it is a very large sum. And Abraham pays it without another word. Interpreters have frequently noted the traditions of negotiating there: deliberate overstatement, saying things one does not mean: "gracious insincerity." I suggest that they apply here as well. Lot is supposed to make an extraordinary gesture. He offers his own daughters. But no one is supposed to take him up on it. And then, in this horrible town, the gesture does not work anyway. The people only become angry. (In the parallel story in Judges 19, in a similar circumstance a host offers his own daughter and his guest's concubine to the crowd. But the guest gives them the concubine. The host does not give his daughter.) For another example of these Near Eastern conventions, see the comment on Gen 33:9.

wife's hand and his two daughters' hands because of YHWH's compassion for him, and they brought him out and set him outside the city.

17And it was as they were bringing them outside, and He said, "Escape for your life. Don't look behind you and don't stop in all of the plain. Escape to the mountain or else you'll be annihilated."

18And Lot said to them, "Let it not be, my Lord. 19Here, your servant has found favor in your eyes, and you've magnified your kindness that you've done for me, keeping my soul alive, and I'm not able to escape to the mountain, in case the bad thing will cling to me and I'll die. 20Here, this city is close to flee there, and it's small. Let me escape there—isn't it small?—and my soul will live."

21And He said to him, "Here, I've granted you this thing, too, that I won't overturn the city of which you spoke. 22Quickly, escape there, because I can't do a thing until you get there."

On account of this the city's name was called Zoar.

23The sun rose on the earth, and Lot came to Zoar. 24And YHWH rained brimstone and fire on Sodom and on Gomorrah, from YHWH out of the skies. 25And He overturned these cities and all of the plain and all of the residents of the cities and all the growth of the ground. 26And his wife looked behind him, and she was a pillar of salt!

27And Abraham got up early in the morning to the place where he had stood in YHWH's presence, 28and he gazed at the sight of Sodom and Gomorrah and at the sight of all the land of the plain. And he saw: and, here, the smoke of the land went up like the smoke of a furnace.

29And it was, when God destroyed the cities of the plain, that God remembered Abraham and let Lot go from inside the overthrow: at the overthrowing of the cities in which Lot lived.

וּבְיַד֙ שְׁתֵּ֣י בְנֹתָ֔יו בְּחֶמְלַ֥ת יְהוָ֖ה עָלָ֑יו וַיֹּצִאֻ֥הוּ וַיַּנִּחֻ֖הוּ מִח֥וּץ לָעִֽיר: 17וַיְהִ֞י כְהוֹצִיאָ֤ם אֹתָם֙ הַח֔וּצָה וַיֹּ֗אמֶר הִמָּלֵ֣ט עַל־נַפְשֶׁ֔ךָ אַל־תַּבִּ֣יט אַחֲרֶ֔יךָ וְאַֽל־תַּעֲמֹ֖ד בְּכָל־הַכִּכָּ֑ר הָהָ֤רָה הִמָּלֵ֖ט פֶּן־תִּסָּפֶֽה: 18וַיֹּ֥אמֶר ל֖וֹט אֲלֵהֶ֑ם אַל־נָ֖א אֲדֹנָֽי: 19הִנֵּה־נָ֠א מָצָ֨א עַבְדְּךָ֣ חֵן֮ בְּעֵינֶיךָ֒ וַתַּגְדֵּ֣ל חַסְדְּךָ֗ אֲשֶׁ֤ר עָשִׂ֙יתָ֙ עִמָּדִ֔י לְהַחֲי֖וֹת אֶת־נַפְשִׁ֑י וְאָנֹכִ֗י לֹ֤א אוּכַל֙ לְהִמָּלֵ֣ט הָהָ֔רָה פֶּן־תִּדְבָּקַ֥נִי הָרָעָ֖ה וָמַֽתִּי: 20הִנֵּה־נָ֠א הָעִ֨יר הַזֹּ֧את קְרֹבָ֛ה לָנ֥וּס שָׁ֖מָּה וְהִ֣יא מִצְעָ֑ר אִמָּֽלְטָ֨ה נָּ֜א שָׁ֗מָּה הֲלֹ֥א מִצְעָ֛ר הִ֖וא וּתְחִ֥י נַפְשִֽׁי: 21וַיֹּ֣אמֶר אֵלָ֔יו הִנֵּה֙ נָשָׂ֣אתִי פָנֶ֔יךָ גַּ֖ם לַדָּבָ֣ר הַזֶּ֑ה לְבִלְתִּ֛י הָפְכִּ֥י אֶת־הָעִ֖יר אֲשֶׁ֥ר דִּבַּֽרְתָּ: 22מַהֵר֙ הִמָּלֵ֣ט שָׁ֔מָּה כִּ֣י לֹ֤א אוּכַל֙ לַעֲשׂ֣וֹת דָּבָ֔ר עַד־בֹּֽאֲךָ֖ שָׁ֑מָּה עַל־כֵּ֛ן קָרָ֥א שֵׁם־הָעִ֖יר צֽוֹעַר: 23הַשֶּׁ֖מֶשׁ יָצָ֣א עַל־הָאָ֑רֶץ וְל֖וֹט בָּ֥א צֹֽעֲרָה: 24וַֽיהוָ֗ה הִמְטִ֧יר עַל־סְדֹ֛ם וְעַל־עֲמֹרָ֖ה גָּפְרִ֣ית וָאֵ֑שׁ מֵאֵ֥ת יְהוָ֖ה מִן־הַשָּׁמָֽיִם: 25וַֽיַּהֲפֹךְ֙ אֶת־הֶעָרִ֣ים הָאֵ֔ל וְאֵ֖ת כָּל־הַכִּכָּ֑ר וְאֵת֙ כָּל־יֹשְׁבֵ֣י הֶעָרִ֔ים וְצֶ֖מַח הָאֲדָמָֽה: 26וַתַּבֵּ֥ט אִשְׁתּ֖וֹ מֵאַחֲרָ֑יו וַתְּהִ֖י נְצִ֥יב מֶֽלַח: 27וַיַּשְׁכֵּ֥ם אַבְרָהָ֖ם בַּבֹּ֑קֶר אֶל־הַ֨מָּק֔וֹם אֲשֶׁר־עָ֥מַד שָׁ֖ם אֶת־פְּנֵ֥י יְהוָֽה: 28וַיַּשְׁקֵ֗ף עַל־פְּנֵ֤י סְדֹם֙ וַעֲמֹרָ֔ה וְעַֽל־כָּל־פְּנֵ֖י אֶ֣רֶץ הַכִּכָּ֑ר וַיַּ֗רְא וְהִנֵּ֤ה עָלָה֙ קִיטֹ֣ר הָאָ֔רֶץ כְּקִיטֹ֖ר הַכִּבְשָֽׁן: 29וַיְהִ֗י בְּשַׁחֵ֤ת אֱלֹהִים֙ אֶת־עָרֵ֣י הַכִּכָּ֔ר וַיִּזְכֹּ֥ר אֱלֹהִ֖ים אֶת־אַבְרָהָ֑ם וַיְשַׁלַּ֤ח אֶת־לוֹט֙ מִתּ֣וֹךְ הַהֲפֵכָ֔ה בַּהֲפֹךְ֙ אֶת־הֶ֣עָרִ֔ים אֲשֶׁר־יָשַׁ֥ב בָּהֵ֖ן לֽוֹט:

19:22. **Zoar**. This name has the same root as the word "small," which Lot uses twice in his plea to go there (19:20).

30And Lot went up from Zoar and lived in the mountain, and his two daughters with him, because he feared to live in Zoar, and he lived in a cave, he and his two daughters. 31And the first-born said to the younger one, "Our father is old, and there's no man in the earth to come to us in the way of all the earth. 32Come on, let's make our father drink wine, and let's lie with him and make seed live from our father." 33And they made their father drink wine in that night, and the firstborn came and lay with her father. And he did not know of her lying down and her getting up. 34And it was on the next day, and the firstborn said to the younger one, "Here, I lay with my father last night. Let's make him drink wine tonight as well, and you come and lie with him, and we'll make seed live from our father." 35And they made their father drink wine in that night as well, and the younger one got up and lay with him, and he did not know of her lying down and her getting up. 36And Lot's two daughters became pregnant by their father. 37And the firstborn gave birth to a son and called his name Moab. He is the father of Moab to this day. 38And the younger one, she too gave birth to a son and called his name ben-Ammi. He is the father of the children of Ammon to this day.

20 1And Abraham traveled from there to the Negeb country and lived between Kadesh and Shur and resided in Gerar. 2And Abraham said of Sarah, his wife, "She's my sister." And Abimelek, king of Gerar, sent and took Sarah.

3And God came to Abimelek in a night dream and said to him, "Here, you're dead over the woman whom you took, for she's a man's wife!" 4And Abimelek had not come close to her, and he said, "My Lord, will you kill a virtuous nation as well? 5Didn't he say to me, 'She's my sister'? And she—she, too—said, 'He's my brother.' I did this in my heart's innocence and in my hands' cleanness."

6And God said to him in the dream, "I, too,

30וַיַּעַל לוֹט מִצּוֹעַר וַיֵּשֶׁב בָּהָר וּשְׁתֵּי בְנֹתָיו עִמּוֹ כִּי יָרֵא לָשֶׁבֶת בְּצוֹעַר וַיֵּשֶׁב בַּמְּעָרָה הוּא וּשְׁתֵּי בְנֹתָיו: 31וַתֹּאמֶר הַבְּכִירָה אֶל־הַצְּעִירָה אָבִינוּ זָקֵן וְאִישׁ אֵין בָּאָרֶץ לָבוֹא עָלֵינוּ כְּדֶרֶךְ כָּל־הָאָרֶץ: 32לְכָה נַשְׁקֶה אֶת־אָבִינוּ יַיִן וְנִשְׁכְּבָה עִמּוֹ וּנְחַיֶּה מֵאָבִינוּ זָרַע: 33וַתַּשְׁקֶיןָ אֶת־אֲבִיהֶן יַיִן בַּלַּיְלָה הוּא וַתָּבֹא הַבְּכִירָה וַתִּשְׁכַּב אֶת־אָבִיהָ וְלֹא־יָדַע בְּשִׁכְבָהּ וּבְקוּמָהּ: 34וַיְהִי מִמָּחֳרָת וַתֹּאמֶר הַבְּכִירָה אֶל־הַצְּעִירָה הֵן־שָׁכַבְתִּי אֶמֶשׁ אֶת־אָבִי נַשְׁקֶנּוּ יַיִן גַּם־הַלַּיְלָה וּבֹאִי שִׁכְבִי עִמּוֹ וּנְחַיֶּה מֵאָבִינוּ זָרַע: 35וַתַּשְׁקֶיןָ גַּם בַּלַּיְלָה הַהוּא אֶת־אֲבִיהֶן יָיִן וַתָּקָם הַצְּעִירָה וַתִּשְׁכַּב עִמּוֹ וְלֹא־יָדַע בְּשִׁכְבָהּ וּבְקֻמָהּ: 36וַתַּהֲרֶיןָ שְׁתֵּי בְנוֹת־לוֹט מֵאֲבִיהֶן: 37וַתֵּלֶד הַבְּכִירָה בֵּן וַתִּקְרָא שְׁמוֹ מוֹאָב הוּא אֲבִי־מוֹאָב עַד־הַיּוֹם: 38וְהַצְּעִירָה גַם־הִוא יָלְדָה בֵּן וַתִּקְרָא שְׁמוֹ בֶּן־עַמִּי הוּא אֲבִי בְנֵי־עַמּוֹן עַד־הַיּוֹם: ס

20 1וַיִּסַּע מִשָּׁם אַבְרָהָם אַרְצָה הַנֶּגֶב וַיֵּשֶׁב בֵּין־קָדֵשׁ וּבֵין שׁוּר וַיָּגָר בִּגְרָר: 2וַיֹּאמֶר אַבְרָהָם אֶל־שָׂרָה אִשְׁתּוֹ אֲחֹתִי הִוא וַיִּשְׁלַח אֲבִימֶלֶךְ מֶלֶךְ גְּרָר וַיִּקַּח אֶת־שָׂרָה: 3וַיָּבֹא אֱלֹהִים אֶל־אֲבִימֶלֶךְ בַּחֲלוֹם הַלָּיְלָה וַיֹּאמֶר לוֹ הִנְּךָ מֵת עַל־הָאִשָּׁה אֲשֶׁר־לָקַחְתָּ וְהִוא בְּעֻלַת בָּעַל: 4וַאֲבִימֶלֶךְ לֹא קָרַב אֵלֶיהָ וַיֹּאמַר אֲדֹנָי הֲגוֹי גַּם־צַדִּיק תַּהֲרֹג: 5הֲלֹא הוּא אָמַר־לִי אֲחֹתִי הִוא וְהִיא־גַם־הִוא אָמְרָה אָחִי הוּא בְּתָם־לְבָבִי וּבְנִקְיֹן כַּפַּי עָשִׂיתִי זֹאת: 6וַיֹּאמֶר אֵלָיו הָאֱלֹהִים בַּחֲלֹם גַּם אָנֹכִי

knew that you did this in your heart's innocence; and I, too, held you back from sinning against me. On account of this, I didn't let you touch her. 7And now, give the man's wife back, because he's a prophet, and he'll pray for you. And live! And if you don't give back, know that you will *die*, you and all that you have."

8And Abimelek got up in the morning and called to all his servants and spoke all these things in their ears, and the people were very afraid. 9And Abimelek called Abraham and said to him, "What have you done to us, and how did I sin against you, that you brought a big sin over me and over my kingdom? You've done things with me that are not done!" 10And Abimelek said to Abraham, "What did you see, that you did this thing?"

11And Abraham said, "Because I said, 'There just isn't the fear of God in this place, and they'll kill me on account of my wife.' 12And also she is, in fact, my sister, my father's daughter but not my mother's daughter, and she became a wife to me. 13And it was when God had me roam from my father's house, and I said to her, 'This will be your kindness that you'll do with me: to every place where we come, say about me, "He's my brother." ' "

14And Abimelek took sheep and oxen and servants and maids, and he gave them to Abraham, and he gave Sarah, his wife, back to him. 15And Abimelek said, "Here's my land in front of you. Live wherever it's good in your eyes." 16And to Sarah he said, "Here, I've given a thousand weights of silver to your brother. Here, it's a covering of eyes for you with everyone with you, and you're justified with everyone."

יָדַ֫עְתִּי כִּ֤י בְתׇם־לְבָבְךָ֙ עָשִׂ֣יתָ זֹּ֔את וָאֶחְשֹׂ֧ךְ גַּם־
אָנֹכִ֛י אֽוֹתְךָ֖ מֵחֲטוֹ־לִ֑י עַל־כֵּ֥ן לֹֽא־נְתַתִּ֖יךָ לִנְגֹּ֥עַ
אֵלֶֽיהָ: 7וְעַתָּ֗ה הָשֵׁ֤ב אֵֽשֶׁת־הָאִישׁ֙ כִּֽי־נָבִ֣יא ה֔וּא
וְיִתְפַּלֵּ֥ל בַּֽעַדְךָ֖ וֶֽחְיֵ֑ה וְאִם־אֵֽינְךָ֣ מֵשִׁ֗יב דַּ֚ע כִּֽי־מ֣וֹת
תָּמ֔וּת אַתָּ֖ה וְכׇל־אֲשֶׁר־לָֽךְ: 8וַיַּשְׁכֵּ֨ם אֲבִימֶ֜לֶךְ
בַּבֹּ֗קֶר וַיִּקְרָא֙ לְכׇל־עֲבָדָ֔יו וַיְדַבֵּ֛ר אֶת־כׇּל־
הַדְּבָרִ֥ים הָאֵ֖לֶּה בְּאׇזְנֵיהֶ֑ם וַיִּֽירְא֥וּ הָאֲנָשִׁ֖ים מְאֹֽד:
9וַיִּקְרָ֨א אֲבִימֶ֜לֶךְ לְאַבְרָהָ֗ם וַיֹּ֨אמֶר ל֜וֹ מֶֽה־עָשִׂ֤יתָ
לָּ֨נוּ֙ וּמֶֽה־חָטָ֣אתִי לָ֔ךְ כִּֽי־הֵבֵ֧אתָ עָלַ֛י וְעַל־מַמְלַכְתִּ֖י
חֲטָאָ֣ה גְדֹלָ֑ה מַעֲשִׂים֙ אֲשֶׁ֣ר לֹא־יֵֽעָשׂ֔וּ עָשִׂ֖יתָ עִמָּדִֽי:
10וַיֹּ֥אמֶר אֲבִימֶ֖לֶךְ אֶל־אַבְרָהָ֑ם מָ֣ה רָאִ֔יתָ כִּ֥י עָשִׂ֖יתָ
אֶת־הַדָּבָ֥ר הַזֶּֽה: 11וַיֹּ֙אמֶר֙ אַבְרָהָ֔ם כִּ֣י אָמַ֗רְתִּי רַ֚ק
אֵין־יִרְאַ֣ת אֱלֹהִ֔ים בַּמָּק֖וֹם הַזֶּ֑ה וַהֲרָג֖וּנִי עַל־דְּבַ֥ר
אִשְׁתִּֽי: 12וְגַם־אׇמְנָ֗ה אֲחֹתִ֤י בַת־אָבִי֙ הִ֔וא אַ֖ךְ לֹ֣א
בַת־אִמִּ֑י וַתְּהִי־לִ֖י לְאִשָּֽׁה: 13וַיְהִ֞י כַּאֲשֶׁ֧ר הִתְע֣וּ אֹתִ֗י
אֱלֹהִים֮ מִבֵּ֣ית אָבִי֒ וָאֹמַ֣ר לָ֔הּ זֶ֣ה חַסְדֵּ֔ךְ אֲשֶׁ֥ר
תַּעֲשִׂ֖י עִמָּדִ֑י אֶ֤ל כׇּל־הַמָּקוֹם֙ אֲשֶׁ֣ר נָב֣וֹא שָׁ֔מָּה
אִמְרִי־לִ֖י אָחִ֥י הֽוּא: 14וַיִּקַּ֨ח אֲבִימֶ֜לֶךְ צֹ֣אן וּבָקָ֗ר
וַעֲבָדִים֙ וּשְׁפָחֹ֔ת וַיִּתֵּ֖ן לְאַבְרָהָ֑ם וַיָּ֣שֶׁב ל֔וֹ אֵ֖ת שָׂרָ֥ה
אִשְׁתּֽוֹ: 15וַיֹּ֣אמֶר אֲבִימֶ֔לֶךְ הִנֵּ֥ה אַרְצִ֖י לְפָנֶ֑יךָ בַּטּ֥וֹב
בְּעֵינֶ֖יךָ שֵֽׁב: 16וּלְשָׂרָ֣ה אָמַ֗ר הִנֵּ֨ה נָתַ֜תִּי אֶ֤לֶף כֶּ֙סֶף֙
לְאָחִ֔יךְ הִנֵּ֤ה הוּא־לָךְ֙ כְּס֣וּת עֵינַ֔יִם לְכֹ֖ל אֲשֶׁ֣ר אִתָּ֑ךְ

20:7. **prophet.** This is the first and only occurrence of the word "prophet" in Genesis. Prophecy as a formal institution begins in Exodus 20. (See the comment on Exod 20:16.)

20:13. **had me roam.** The Hebrew verb that is used in connection with God here is a plural, which is extremely unusual. Possibly this formulation is attributed to Abraham because he is speaking to a pagan king, and this king has not told him that Abraham's God has appeared to him. (The Samaritan text has the singular verb here.)

17And Abraham prayed to God, and God healed Abimelek and his wife and his maids, and they gave birth, 18because YHWH *had held* back every womb of Abimelek's house on account of Sarah, Abraham's wife!

21 1And YHWH took account of Sarah as He had said, and YHWH did to Sarah as He had spoken. 2And Sarah became pregnant and gave birth to a son for Abraham in his old age at the appointed time that God had spoken. 3And Abraham called the name of his son who was born to him, to whom Sarah had given birth for him: Isaac. 4And Abraham circumcised Isaac, his son, at eight days old, as God had commanded him. 5And Abraham was a hundred years old when Isaac, his son, was born to him.

6And Sarah said, "God has made laughter for me. Everyone who hears will laugh for me." 7And she said, "Who would have said to Abraham, 'Sarah has nursed children'? Yet I've given birth to a son in his old age."

8And the boy grew and was weaned. And Abraham made a big feast in the day that Isaac was weaned. 9And Sarah saw the son of Hagar, the Egyptian, whom she had borne to Abraham, fooling around. 10And she said to Abraham, "Drive this maid out—and her son, because the son of this maid will not inherit with my son, with Isaac."

11And the thing was very bad in Abraham's eyes in regard to his son. 12And God said to Abraham, "Let it not be bad in your eyes about the boy and about your maid. Everything that Sarah tells you: listen to her voice; because seed

17וַיִּתְפַּלֵּל אַבְרָהָם אֶל־הָאֱלֹהִים וְאֶת כָּל־וְנֹכַחַת:
וַיִּרְפָּא אֱלֹהִים אֶת־אֲבִימֶלֶךְ וְאֶת־אִשְׁתּוֹ וְאַמְהֹתָיו
וַיֵּלֵדוּ: 18כִּי־עָצֹר עָצַר יְהוָה בְּעַד כָּל־רֶחֶם לְבֵית
אֲבִימֶלֶךְ עַל־דְּבַר שָׂרָה אֵשֶׁת אַבְרָהָם: ס

21 1וַיהוָה פָּקַד אֶת־שָׂרָה כַּאֲשֶׁר אָמָר וַיַּעַשׂ
יְהוָה לְשָׂרָה כַּאֲשֶׁר דִּבֵּר: 2וַתַּהַר וַתֵּלֶד שָׂרָה
לְאַבְרָהָם בֵּן לִזְקֻנָיו לַמּוֹעֵד אֲשֶׁר־דִּבֶּר אֹתוֹ
אֱלֹהִים: 3וַיִּקְרָא אַבְרָהָם אֶת־שֶׁם־בְּנוֹ הַנּוֹלַד־לוֹ
אֲשֶׁר־יָלְדָה־לּוֹ שָׂרָה יִצְחָק: 4וַיָּמָל אַבְרָהָם אֶת־
יִצְחָק בְּנוֹ בֶּן־שְׁמֹנַת יָמִים כַּאֲשֶׁר צִוָּה אֹתוֹ
אֱלֹהִים: 5וְאַבְרָהָם בֶּן־מְאַת שָׁנָה בְּהִוָּלֶד לוֹ אֵת
יִצְחָק בְּנוֹ: 6וַתֹּאמֶר שָׂרָה צְחֹק עָשָׂה לִי אֱלֹהִים
כָּל־הַשֹּׁמֵעַ יִצְחַק־לִי: 7וַתֹּאמֶר מִי מִלֵּל לְאַבְרָהָם
הֵינִיקָה בָנִים שָׂרָה כִּי־יָלַדְתִּי בֵן לִזְקֻנָיו: 8וַיִּגְדַּל
הַיֶּלֶד וַיִּגָּמַל וַיַּעַשׂ אַבְרָהָם מִשְׁתֶּה גָדוֹל בְּיוֹם
הִגָּמֵל אֶת־יִצְחָק: 9וַתֵּרֶא שָׂרָה אֶת־בֶּן־הָגָר
הַמִּצְרִית אֲשֶׁר־יָלְדָה לְאַבְרָהָם מְצַחֵק: 10וַתֹּאמֶר
לְאַבְרָהָם גָּרֵשׁ הָאָמָה הַזֹּאת וְאֶת־בְּנָהּ כִּי לֹא
יִירַשׁ בֶּן־הָאָמָה הַזֹּאת עִם־בְּנִי עִם־יִצְחָק: 11וַיֵּרַע
הַדָּבָר מְאֹד בְּעֵינֵי אַבְרָהָם עַל אוֹדֹת בְּנוֹ:
12וַיֹּאמֶר אֱלֹהִים אֶל־אַבְרָהָם אַל־יֵרַע בְּעֵינֶיךָ
עַל־הַנַּעַר וְעַל־אֲמָתֶךָ כֹּל אֲשֶׁר תֹּאמַר אֵלֶיךָ שָׂרָה

21:9. fooling around. The Greek text has "fooling around with her son Isaac," which can connote either playing with Isaac or mocking him. The word in Hebrew is מְצַחֵק, which is a pun on the name Isaac. It will occur again in the story of Isaac, Rebekah, and Abimelek (Gen 26:8).

21:11. the thing was very bad in Abraham's eyes in regard to his son. The Israelite who wrote this text—which favors his own ancestor, Isaac—still expressed sympathy for Ishmael. He wrote of Abraham's affection for him and God's promise for him.

for you will be called by Isaac. ¹³And I'll make the maid's son into a nation as well, because he's your seed."

¹⁴And Abraham got up early in the morning and took bread and a bottle of water and gave to Hagar—he put them on her shoulder—and the boy, and he sent her off. And she went and strayed in the Beer-sheba wilderness. ¹⁵And the water was finished from the bottle, and she thrust the boy under one of the shrubs, ¹⁶and she went and sat opposite, going as far as a bow-shot, because she said, "Let me not see the boy's death." And she sat opposite and raised her voice and wept.

¹⁷And God heard the boy's voice. And an angel of God called to Hagar from the heavens and said to her, "What trouble do you have, Hagar? Don't be afraid. Because God has heard the boy's voice where he is. ¹⁸Get up. Carry the boy and hold him up in your hand, because I shall make him into a big nation." ¹⁹And God opened her eyes, and she saw a water well, and she went and filled the bottle with water and had the boy drink.

²⁰And God was with the boy, and he grew, and he lived in the wilderness and was a bowman. ²¹And he lived in the Paran wilderness, and his mother took him a wife from the land of Egypt.

²²And it was at that time, and Abimelek and Phichol, the commander of his army, said to Abraham, saying, "God is with you in everything

שְׁמַע בְּקֹלָהּ כִּי בְיִצְחָק יִקָּרֵא לְךָ זָרַע: ¹³וְגַם אֶת־בֶּן־הָאָמָה לְגוֹי אֲשִׂימֶנּוּ כִּי זַרְעֲךָ הוּא: ¹⁴וַיַּשְׁכֵּם אַבְרָהָם ׀ בַּבֹּקֶר וַיִּקַּח־לֶחֶם וְחֵמַת מַיִם וַיִּתֵּן אֶל־הָגָר שָׂם עַל־שִׁכְמָהּ וְאֶת־הַיֶּלֶד וַיְשַׁלְּחֶהָ וַתֵּלֶךְ וַתֵּתַע בְּמִדְבַּר בְּאֵר שָׁבַע: ¹⁵וַיִּכְלוּ הַמַּיִם מִן־הַחֵמֶת וַתַּשְׁלֵךְ אֶת־הַיֶּלֶד תַּחַת אַחַד הַשִּׂיחִם: ¹⁶וַתֵּלֶךְ וַתֵּשֶׁב לָהּ מִנֶּגֶד הַרְחֵק כִּמְטַחֲוֵי קֶשֶׁת כִּי אָמְרָה אַל־אֶרְאֶה בְּמוֹת הַיָּלֶד וַתֵּשֶׁב מִנֶּגֶד וַתִּשָּׂא אֶת־קֹלָהּ וַתֵּבְךְּ: ¹⁷וַיִּשְׁמַע אֱלֹהִים אֶת־קוֹל הַנַּעַר וַיִּקְרָא מַלְאַךְ אֱלֹהִים ׀ אֶל־הָגָר מִן־הַשָּׁמַיִם וַיֹּאמֶר לָהּ מַה־לָּךְ הָגָר אַל־תִּירְאִי כִּי־שָׁמַע אֱלֹהִים אֶל־קוֹל הַנַּעַר בַּאֲשֶׁר הוּא־שָׁם: ¹⁸קוּמִי שְׂאִי אֶת־הַנַּעַר וְהַחֲזִיקִי אֶת־יָדֵךְ בּוֹ כִּי־לְגוֹי גָּדוֹל אֲשִׂימֶנּוּ: ¹⁹וַיִּפְקַח אֱלֹהִים אֶת־עֵינֶיהָ וַתֵּרֶא בְּאֵר מָיִם וַתֵּלֶךְ וַתְּמַלֵּא אֶת־הַחֵמֶת מַיִם וַתַּשְׁקְ אֶת־הַנָּעַר: ²⁰וַיְהִי אֱלֹהִים אֶת־הַנַּעַר וַיִּגְדָּל וַיֵּשֶׁב בַּמִּדְבָּר וַיְהִי רֹבֶה קַשָּׁת: ²¹וַיֵּשֶׁב בְּמִדְבַּר פָּארָן וַתִּקַּח־לוֹ אִמּוֹ אִשָּׁה מֵאֶרֶץ מִצְרָיִם: פ ²²וַיְהִי בָּעֵת הַהִוא וַיֹּאמֶר אֲבִימֶלֶךְ וּפִיכֹל שַׂר־צְבָאוֹ אֶל־אַבְרָהָם לֵאמֹר אֱלֹהִים עִמְּךָ בְּכֹל אֲשֶׁר־אַתָּה עֹשֶׂה: ²³וְעַתָּה

21:12. **seed for you will be called by Isaac.** Meaning: Abraham's best-known line will later be identified as children of Abraham-Isaac-Jacob, rather than Abraham-Ishmael or Abraham-Midian or Abraham-Zimran.

21:13. **I'll make the maid's son into a nation as well.** Namely, the Ishmaelites. Their genealogy appears in Gen 25:13–18, and they will figure in the Joseph story (37:25–28; 39:1). They do not appear in the Torah after that.

21:18. **I shall make him into a big nation.** These words are spoken by the angel, but they certainly appear to be the words of God, not the angel itself. Angels do not make great nations in the *Tanak*. This is another demonstration that angels are not independent beings in the Hebrew Bible but are rather expressions of God's presence. (See the comment on Gen 18:3.)

that you do. 23And now, swear to me here by God that you won't act falsely to me and to my offspring and to my posterity. Like the kindness that I've done with you, you'll do with me and with the land in which you've resided."

24And Abraham said, "I'll swear," 25and Abraham criticized Abimelek about a water well that Abimelek's servants had seized.

26And Abimelek said, "I don't know who did this thing; and also, you didn't tell me; and also, I didn't hear of it except for today." 27And Abraham took sheep and oxen and gave to Abimelek, and the two of them made a covenant. 28And Abraham stood seven ewes of the sheep by themselves. 29And Abimelek said to Abraham, "What are these seven ewes that you've stood by themselves?"

30And he said, "Because you'll take these seven ewes from my hand so that it will be evidence for me that I dug this well." 31On account of this he called that place Beer-sheba, because the two of them swore there 32and made a covenant in Beer-sheba. And Abimelek and Phichol, the commander of his army, got up and went to the land of the Philistines.

33And he planted a tamarisk in Beer-sheba and he called the name of YHWH El Olam. 34And Abraham resided in the land of the Philistines many days.

22

1And it was after these things, and God tested Abraham.
And He said to him, "Abraham."
And he said, "I'm here."

הַשָּׁבְעָה לִּי בֵאלֹהִים הֵנָּה אִם־תִּשְׁקֹר לִי וּלְנִינִי
וּלְנֶכְדִּי כַּחֶסֶד אֲשֶׁר־עָשִׂיתִי עִמְּךָ תַּעֲשֶׂה עִמָּדִי
וְעִם־הָאָרֶץ אֲשֶׁר־גַּרְתָּה בָּהּ: 24וַיֹּאמֶר אַבְרָהָם
אָנֹכִי אִשָּׁבֵעַ: 25וְהוֹכִחַ אַבְרָהָם אֶת־אֲבִימֶלֶךְ עַל־
אֹדוֹת בְּאֵר הַמַּיִם אֲשֶׁר גָּזְלוּ עַבְדֵי אֲבִימֶלֶךְ:
26וַיֹּאמֶר אֲבִימֶלֶךְ לֹא יָדַעְתִּי מִי עָשָׂה אֶת־הַדָּבָר
הַזֶּה וְגַם־אַתָּה לֹא־הִגַּדְתָּ לִּי וְגַם אָנֹכִי לֹא שָׁמַעְתִּי
בִּלְתִּי הַיּוֹם: 27וַיִּקַּח אַבְרָהָם צֹאן וּבָקָר וַיִּתֵּן
לַאֲבִימֶלֶךְ וַיִּכְרְתוּ שְׁנֵיהֶם בְּרִית: 28וַיַּצֵּב אַבְרָהָם
אֶת־שֶׁבַע כִּבְשֹׂת הַצֹּאן לְבַדְּהֶן: 29וַיֹּאמֶר אֲבִימֶלֶךְ
אֶל־אַבְרָהָם מָה הֵנָּה שֶׁבַע כְּבָשֹׂת הָאֵלֶּה אֲשֶׁר
הִצַּבְתָּ לְבַדָּנָה: 30וַיֹּאמֶר כִּי אֶת־שֶׁבַע כְּבָשֹׂת תִּקַּח
מִיָּדִי בַּעֲבוּר תִּהְיֶה־לִּי לְעֵדָה כִּי חָפַרְתִּי אֶת־
הַבְּאֵר הַזֹּאת: 31עַל־כֵּן קָרָא לַמָּקוֹם הַהוּא בְּאֵר
שָׁבַע כִּי שָׁם נִשְׁבְּעוּ שְׁנֵיהֶם: 32וַיִּכְרְתוּ בְרִית
בִּבְאֵר שָׁבַע וַיָּקָם אֲבִימֶלֶךְ וּפִיכֹל שַׂר־צְבָאוֹ
וַיָּשֻׁבוּ אֶל־אֶרֶץ פְּלִשְׁתִּים: 33וַיִּטַּע אֶשֶׁל בִּבְאֵר
שָׁבַע וַיִּקְרָא־שָׁם בְּשֵׁם יְהוָה אֵל עוֹלָם: 34וַיָּגָר
אַבְרָהָם בְּאֶרֶץ פְּלִשְׁתִּים יָמִים רַבִּים: פ
22 1וַיְהִי אַחַר הַדְּבָרִים הָאֵלֶּה וְהָאֱלֹהִים נִסָּה
אֶת־אַבְרָהָם וַיֹּאמֶר אֵלָיו אַבְרָהָם וַיֹּאמֶר הִנֵּנִי:

22:1. He said to him, "Abraham." The Greek and Samaritan versions have his name called twice here: "Abraham, Abraham." This parallels the call by the angel later (v. 11), by which Abraham is stopped from sacrificing Isaac. Thus the instruction to sacrifice him and the instruction to hold back are given equal weight. This also parallels the repetition of Moses' name in God's first words to him at the burning bush (Exod 3:4) and the repetition of Samuel's name the first time God speaks to him (1 Sam 3:10). This appears to be a mark of divine communication at significant moments in the biblical narrative. What stands out about Abraham is that it comes here

²And He said, "Take your son, your only one, whom you love, Isaac, and go to the land of Moriah and make him a burnt offering there on one of the mountains that I'll say to you."

²וַיֹּ֡אמֶר קַח־נָ֠א אֶת־בִּנְךָ֨ אֶת־יְחִ֤ידְךָ֙ אֲשֶׁר־אָהַ֙בְתָּ֙ אֶת־יִצְחָ֔ק וְלֶךְ־לְךָ֔ אֶל־אֶ֖רֶץ הַמֹּרִיָּ֑ה וְהַעֲלֵ֤הוּ שָׁם֙ לְעֹלָ֔ה עַ֚ל אַחַ֣ד הֶֽהָרִ֔ים אֲשֶׁ֖ר אֹמַ֥ר אֵלֶֽיךָ׃ ³וַיַּשְׁכֵּ֨ם

in the Aqedah rather than the first time that God speaks to him. This marks the near-sacrifice as a defining event in Abraham's life and in the destiny of his descendants.

22:2. **Take your son, your only one, whom you love, Isaac.** If the issue were only a matter of identification, just the name Isaac would have been sufficient; but the issue, we are told explicitly in the first verse of the story, is the test. The fourfold, heartrending identification creates background for all that is to come. Now Abraham's unquestioning obedience is understood against this background: "your son, your only one, whom you love, Isaac." The otherwise minor temporal note that "Abraham got up early in the morning" to do the deed becomes a fact worthy of wonder and interpretation against the background of "your son, your only one, whom you love, Isaac." The notation that he puts the wood for the sacrificial fire on Isaac himself to carry becomes an ironic image. Abraham's words to the servants who accompany them—"I and the boy: we'll go over there, and we'll bow, and we'll come back to you"—become not only enigmatic but emotionally charged. (Does his saying *"we'll come back"* suggest extraordinary faith? one last hope? Or is it constructed so as not to frighten Isaac?) The words of the dialogue between the father and son become charged by this background as well, as Isaac adds the phrase "my father" in his question addressed to Abraham, and Abraham adds "my son" in each sentence in response. (The words "son" and "father" occur twelve times in the story and are, in almost every case, unnecessary for identification.) The dialogue moreover begins and ends with the words "and the two of them went together," another mundane phrase turned into a remarkable one by what has preceded.

Most remarkable of all is the exchange between Abraham and Isaac over the obvious absence of an animal to be sacrificed. Isaac says, "Here are the fire and the wood, but where is the sheep for the burnt offering?" To appreciate the artistry of the wording of Abraham's answer, we must keep in mind that the Hebrew has no punctuation. The text says: "God will see to the sheep for the burnt offering my son"—which can be understood in two ways. The last two words can be read as a touching epithet:

"God will see to the sheep for the burnt offering, my son."

But they can also be read as a fearful irony:

"God will see to the sheep for the burnt offering: *My son.*"

—subtly conveying the truth that Isaac himself is to be the sheep for the sacrifice.

And so the short passage, which like the entire chapter expresses no emotions explicitly, reads like a tightly packed container whose contents may burst in a moment:

And the two of them went together.
And Isaac said to Abraham his father; he said, "My father."

³And Abraham got up early in the morning and harnessed his ass and took his two boys with him and Isaac, his son. And he cut the wood for the burnt offering, and he got up and went to the place that God had said to him. ⁴On the third

אַבְרָהָם בַּבֹּקֶר וַיַּחֲבֹשׁ אֶת־חֲמֹרוֹ וַיִּקַּח אֶת־שְׁנֵי נְעָרָיו אִתּוֹ וְאֵת יִצְחָק בְּנוֹ וַיְבַקַּע עֲצֵי עֹלָה וַיָּקָם וַיֵּלֶךְ אֶל־הַמָּקוֹם אֲשֶׁר־אָמַר־לוֹ הָאֱלֹהִים: ⁴בַּיּוֹם

And he said, "I'm here, my son."
And he said, "Here are the fire and the wood, but where is the sheep for the burnt offering?"
And Abraham said, "God will see to the sheep for the burnt offering my son."
And the two of them went together.

The denouement of the story, in which Isaac is spared, is no less charged by all of this expressed and unexpressed background. Indeed, Abraham's feelings (relief? gratitude? reverence? confusion?) are likewise not a part of the narrative. There is rather a reminiscence of the original wording, as God twice says to Abraham that now all is well because "You didn't hold back *your son, your only one*" (22:12,16; cf. 22:2). As biblical interpreters noted centuries ago, the wording suggests that the reward at the end is in proportion to the difficulty of the test as expressed at the beginning.

22:3. **Abraham got up early in the morning**. Abraham fights for the lives of the people of Sodom and Gomorrah but not for the life of Isaac. That is a strange fact itself, and then these two stories are juxtaposed by being placed in the same parashah so that they are regularly read together, which makes the ironic relationship between them even harder to ignore. When God tells Abraham, "The cry of Sodom and Gomorrah: how great it is. And their sin: how very heavy it is. Let me go down, and I'll see if they've done, all told, like the cry that has come to me. And if not, let me know" (18:20-21), Abraham's response is to be the first human in the Bible's story to challenge a divine decision. But when God tells him, "Take your son, your only one, whom you love, Isaac . . . and offer him as a burnt offering," the report is: And Abraham got up early in the morning!

The text does not tell us what Abraham's motive is for questioning his God about the fate of Sodom. Is it because his nephew, Lot, lives there? Or is it Abraham's sense of justice? Or is it his compassion for people who are facing a divine catastrophe? Two of the above? All of the above? Even if it is mainly his concern for Lot, still, that's a nephew. Isaac is his son! Even if it is his compassion for those morally-challenged people of Sodom, still, there must also be compassion for his son. And if it is his sense of justice, is there less of a case for justice in connection with sacrificing an innocent Isaac than in the matter of the destruction of those very guilty people?

One possible answer: The mark of Abraham's personality is *obedience*. He will obey anything that his God commands him to do. Leave your land. Leave your birthplace. Leave your father's house. Circumcise yourself. Even if he is commanded to sacrifice his child, he will do it. There are no arguments or even questions. There is only immediate compliance. But the case of Sodom and Gomorrah is different because in this

case Abraham is not commanded to do anything. He is not the one who is to execute judgment on the cities. It is even intriguing that the deity chooses to inform Abraham of the divine concern over the cries from Sodom and Gomorrah in the first place. Whatever reason one imagines for God to tell Abraham about this, the fact is that by informing Abraham of the divine intention to look into the situation in Sodom and Gomorrah, God opens the door for Abraham to speak up. Commands, on the other hand, leave no room for discussion.

A second answer (*dābar 'aḥēr*): The reason that Abraham speaks up for the more distant relative and for all the unrelated populace of Sodom and Gomorrah but does not speak up for his own son is precisely *because* it is his own son. He is sufficiently distant from Lot and the populace of Sodom that he is in a position to argue whether their destruction would be just. And so he argues: "Will the judge of all the earth not do justice?!" But in the case of Isaac, he is not what we would call an unbiased observer. He has a personal interest in the case, an intensely personal interest. And, as such, he does not have the same standing to argue the justice or injustice of the case.

A third answer (*dābar 'aḥēr*): Another possible explanation is that the outcome of the Sodom and Gomorrah matter itself is what causes Abraham to stay silent in the matter of Isaac. In the famous dialogue between God and Abraham over the fate of the cities of Sodom and Gomorrah, the exchange is subtle as God responds not merely to what Abraham says but apparently to what is in Abraham's heart. Thus: when Abraham learns that God means to judge these cities, he says, "Maybe there are fifty virtuous people within the city" (18:24). God responds, "If I find in Sodom fifty virtuous people within the city, then I'll sustain the whole place for their sake" (18:26). Abraham's next bargaining position will be the sparing of the place for forty-five righteous, but he articulates his question in such a way as to make it seem a small request. He does not say "forty-five." He says:

> Maybe the fifty virtuous people will be short by five.
> Will you destroy the whole city for the *five?*

To which God replies, "I won't destroy if I find *forty-five* there." Thus God would appear to be conveying to Abraham that there is not much point to being cagey in one's words when one is arguing with someone who is omniscient. After this, Abraham words his positions more straightforwardly: What if there are forty? thirty? etc. Abraham gets the message that he may as well say directly what is on his mind because that is what is going to be responded to in any case.

Even then, Abraham succeeds in getting down to ten. God agrees to sustain the cities for ten virtuous people. But not even ten are to be found, and the cities are destroyed. So even though Abraham's dialogue with God is important in several ways—including: it provides Abraham with an opportunity to articulate the principle of justice for future generations; and it is an important step in the growth of humankind's independence and development of responsibility—the fact remains that nothing is changed for Sodom and Gomorrah by this. Abraham learns that, since God knows what is in one's heart, why argue? Since God knows the situation and its necessary outcome, why speak? After the destruction of Sodom and Gomorrah, Abraham never argues with God again. Moses will argue with God, Jonah will, Jeremiah will, but not Abraham. When the creator tells Abraham to listen to Sarah and send Hagar

day: and Abraham raised his eyes and saw the place from a distance. 5And Abraham said to his boys, "Sit here with the ass; and I and the boy: we'll go over there, and we'll bow, and we'll come back to you." 6And Abraham took the wood for the burnt offering and put it on Isaac, his son, and took the fire and the knife in his hand.

And the two of them went together.

7And Isaac said to Abraham, his father; and he said, "My father."

And he said, "I'm here, my son."

And he said, "Here are the fire and the wood, but where is the sheep for the burnt offering?"

8And Abraham said, "God will see to the sheep for the burnt offering, my son."

And the two of them went together.

9And they came to the place that God had said to him. And Abraham built the altar there and arranged the wood, and he bound Isaac, his son, and put him on the altar on top of the wood. 10And Abraham put out his hand and took the knife to slaughter his son.

11And an angel of YHWH called to him from the skies and said, "Abraham! Abraham!"

And he said, "I'm here."

12And he said, "Don't put your hand out toward the boy, and don't do anything to him, because now I know that you fear God, and you didn't withhold your son, your only one, from me." 13And Abraham raised his eyes and saw, and here was a ram behind, caught in the thicket by its horns. And Abraham went and took the

הַשְּׁלִישִׁי וַיִּשָּׂא אַבְרָהָם אֶת־עֵינָיו וַיַּרְא אֶת־הַמָּקוֹם מֵרָחֹק: ⁵וַיֹּאמֶר אַבְרָהָם אֶל־נְעָרָיו שְׁבוּ־לָכֶם פֹּה עִם־הַחֲמוֹר וַאֲנִי וְהַנַּעַר נֵלְכָה עַד־כֹּה וְנִשְׁתַּחֲוֶה וְנָשׁוּבָה אֲלֵיכֶם: ⁶וַיִּקַּח אַבְרָהָם אֶת־עֲצֵי הָעֹלָה וַיָּשֶׂם עַל־יִצְחָק בְּנוֹ וַיִּקַּח בְּיָדוֹ אֶת־הָאֵשׁ וְאֶת־הַמַּאֲכֶלֶת וַיֵּלְכוּ שְׁנֵיהֶם יַחְדָּו: ⁷וַיֹּאמֶר יִצְחָק אֶל־אַבְרָהָם אָבִיו וַיֹּאמֶר אָבִי וַיֹּאמֶר הִנֶּנִּי בְנִי וַיֹּאמֶר הִנֵּה הָאֵשׁ וְהָעֵצִים וְאַיֵּה הַשֶּׂה לְעֹלָה: ⁸וַיֹּאמֶר אַבְרָהָם אֱלֹהִים יִרְאֶה־לּוֹ הַשֶּׂה לְעֹלָה בְּנִי וַיֵּלְכוּ שְׁנֵיהֶם יַחְדָּו: ⁹וַיָּבֹאוּ אֶל־הַמָּקוֹם אֲשֶׁר אָמַר־לוֹ הָאֱלֹהִים וַיִּבֶן שָׁם אַבְרָהָם אֶת־הַמִּזְבֵּחַ וַיַּעֲרֹךְ אֶת־הָעֵצִים וַיַּעֲקֹד אֶת־יִצְחָק בְּנוֹ וַיָּשֶׂם אֹתוֹ עַל־הַמִּזְבֵּחַ מִמַּעַל לָעֵצִים: ¹⁰וַיִּשְׁלַח אַבְרָהָם אֶת־יָדוֹ וַיִּקַּח אֶת־הַמַּאֲכֶלֶת לִשְׁחֹט אֶת־בְּנוֹ: ¹¹וַיִּקְרָא אֵלָיו מַלְאַךְ יְהוָה מִן־הַשָּׁמַיִם וַיֹּאמֶר אַבְרָהָם ׀ אַבְרָהָם וַיֹּאמֶר הִנֵּנִי: ¹²וַיֹּאמֶר אַל־תִּשְׁלַח יָדְךָ אֶל־הַנַּעַר וְאַל־תַּעַשׂ לוֹ מְאוּמָה כִּי ׀ עַתָּה יָדַעְתִּי כִּי־יְרֵא אֱלֹהִים אַתָּה וְלֹא חָשַׂכְתָּ אֶת־בִּנְךָ אֶת־יְחִידְךָ מִמֶּנִּי: ¹³וַיִּשָּׂא אַבְרָהָם אֶת־עֵינָיו וַיַּרְא וְהִנֵּה־אַיִל אַחַר נֶאֱחַז בַּסְּבַךְ בְּקַרְנָיו וַיֵּלֶךְ אַבְרָהָם וַיִּקַּח

---

and Ishmael away, "Abraham got up early in the morning" (21:14). When the creator tells him to sacrifice his son, "Abraham got up early in the morning" (22:3).

But Abraham's obedience is what saves Isaac in the end. What an irony: Abraham's silence over Isaac is more effective than his argument over Sodom and Gomorrah.

22:13. **behind.** Some manuscripts read "one" ram, i.e., Hebrew אחד, rather than "behind," Hebrew אחר. "One" makes plainer sense, but this may very well be a case that suggests the principle of *lectio difficilior praeferenda est* (the more difficult reading is preferable). That is, scribes tend to simplify an unusual reading more often than they make a change that turns a simple reading into a more difficult one. The matter remains unsolved.

ram and made it a burnt offering instead of his son. 14And Abraham called the name of that place "YHWH Yir'eh," as is said today: "In YHWH's mountain it will be seen."

15And an angel of YHWH called to Abraham a second time from the skies 16and said, "I swear by me—word of YHWH—that because you did this thing and didn't withhold your son, your only one, 17that I'll *bless* you and *multiply* your seed like the stars of the skies and like the sand that's on the seashore, and your seed will possess its enemies' gate. 18And all the nations of the earth will be blessed through your seed because you listened to my voice."

19And Abraham went back to his boys, and they got up and went together to Beer-sheba, and Abraham lived in Beer-sheba.

20And it was after these things, and it was told to Abraham, saying, "Here Milcah has given birth, she also, to sons for your brother Nahor: 21Uz, his firstborn, and Buz his brother, and Kemuel, the father of Aram, 22and Chesed and Hazo and Pildash and Jidlaph and Bethuel. 23And Bethuel fathered Rebekah." Milcah gave birth to these eight for Nahor, Abraham's brother. 24And his concubine, whose name was Reumah, she too gave birth, to Tebah and Gaham and Tahash and Maacah.

אֶת־הָאַ֔יִל וַיַּעֲלֵ֥הוּ לְעֹלָ֖ה תַּ֣חַת בְּנֽוֹ: 14וַיִּקְרָ֧א
אַבְרָהָ֛ם שֵֽׁם־הַמָּק֥וֹם הַה֖וּא יְהוָ֣ה ׀ יִרְאֶ֑ה אֲשֶׁ֙ר
יֵאָמֵ֣ר הַיּ֔וֹם בְּהַ֥ר יְהוָ֖ה יֵרָאֶֽה: 15וַיִּקְרָ֛א
מַלְאַ֥ךְ יְהוָ֖ה אֶל־אַבְרָהָ֑ם שֵׁנִ֖ית מִן־
הַשָּׁמָֽיִם: 16וַיֹּ֕אמֶר בִּ֥י נִשְׁבַּ֖עְתִּי נְאֻם־יְהוָ֑ה כִּ֗י יַ֚עַן
אֲשֶׁ֤ר עָשִׂ֙יתָ֙ אֶת־הַדָּבָ֣ר הַזֶּ֔ה וְלֹ֥א חָשַׂ֖כְתָּ אֶת־בִּנְךָ֥
אֶת־יְחִידֶֽךָ: 17כִּֽי־בָרֵ֣ךְ אֲבָרֶכְךָ֗ וְהַרְבָּ֙ה אַרְבֶּ֤ה
אֶֽת־זַרְעֲךָ֙ כְּכוֹכְבֵ֣י הַשָּׁמַ֔יִם וְכַח֕וֹל אֲשֶׁ֖ר עַל־שְׂפַ֣ת
הַיָּ֑ם וְיִרַ֣שׁ זַרְעֲךָ֔ אֵ֖ת שַׁ֥עַר אֹיְבָֽיו: 18וְהִתְבָּרֲכ֣וּ
בְזַרְעֲךָ֔ כֹּ֖ל גּוֹיֵ֣י הָאָ֑רֶץ עֵ֕קֶב אֲשֶׁ֥ר שָׁמַ֖עְתָּ בְּקֹלִֽי:
19וַיָּ֤שָׁב אַבְרָהָם֙ אֶל־נְעָרָ֔יו וַיָּקֻ֥מוּ וַיֵּלְכ֛וּ יַחְדָּ֖ו אֶל־
בְּאֵ֣ר שָׁ֑בַע וַיֵּ֥שֶׁב אַבְרָהָ֖ם בִּבְאֵ֥ר שָֽׁבַע: פ
20וַיְהִ֗י אַחֲרֵי֙ הַדְּבָרִ֣ים הָאֵ֔לֶּה וַיֻּגַּ֥ד לְאַבְרָהָ֖ם
לֵאמֹ֑ר הִ֠נֵּה יָלְדָ֙ה מִלְכָּ֥ה גַם־הִ֛וא בָּנִ֖ים לְנָח֥וֹר
אָחִֽיךָ: 21אֶת־ע֥וּץ בְּכֹר֖וֹ וְאֶת־בּ֣וּז אָחִ֑יו וְאֶת־
קְמוּאֵ֖ל אֲבִ֥י אֲרָֽם: 22וְאֶת־כֶּ֣שֶׂד וְאֶת־חֲז֔וֹ וְאֶת־
פִּלְדָּ֖שׁ וְאֶת־יִדְלָ֑ף וְאֵ֖ת בְּתוּאֵֽל: 23וּבְתוּאֵ֖ל יָלַ֣ד
אֶת־רִבְקָ֑ה שְׁמֹנָ֥ה אֵ֙לֶּה֙ יָלְדָ֣ה מִלְכָּ֔ה לְנָח֖וֹר אֲחִ֥י
אַבְרָהָֽם: 24וּפִֽילַגְשׁ֖וֹ וּשְׁמָ֣הּ רְאוּמָ֑ה וַתֵּ֤לֶד גַּם־הִוא֙
אֶת־טֶ֣בַח וְאֶת־גַּ֔חַם וְאֶת־תַּ֖חַשׁ וְאֶת־מַעֲכָֽה: ס

22:14. **YHWH Yir'eh**. Meaning "YHWH Will See." (Perhaps it should be pointed as YHWH Yera'eh, "YHWH Will Appear"—which is how it appears later in the same verse.)

22:18. **all the nations of the earth will be blessed through your seed**. This is the third occurrence of this promise. (See the comment on Gen 12:3.)

22:19. **Abraham went back to his boys**. The text does not mention Isaac going back. (And Abraham had specifically told the boys, *"We'll* come back to you.") Both midrash and critical scholarship have dared to raise the possibility that in one version of the story Abraham actually sacrifices Isaac (discussed in *Who Wrote the Bible?* p. 257). But in the present form of the text itself, Isaac clearly is spared. And that makes this verse extraordinarily powerful. Following the Aqedah, Isaac and Abraham do not go back together. Moreover: following the Aqedah, Isaac and Abraham are never quoted as speaking to each other.

SARAH'S LIFE

חיי שרה

23 ¹And Sarah's life was a hundred years and twenty years and seven years: the years of Sarah's life. ²And Sarah died in Kiriath Arba—it is Hebron—in the land of Canaan. And Abraham came to grieve for Sarah and to weep for her. ³And Abraham got up from in front of his dead, and he spoke to the children of Heth, saying, ⁴"I'm an alien and a visitor with you. Give me a possession for a tomb with you so I may bury my dead from in front of me."

⁵And the children of Heth answered Abraham, saying to him, ⁶"Listen to us, my lord. You're a chieftain of God among us. Bury your dead in the choice of our tombs. Not a man of us will hold back his tomb from you, from burying your dead."

⁷And Abraham got up and bowed to the people of the land, to the children of Heth, ⁸and he spoke with them, saying, "If it's acceptable to you to bury my dead from in front of me, listen to me, and intercede for me with Ephron, son of Zohar, ⁹that he'll give me the cave of Machpelah which he has, that is at the edge of his field. For full price let him give it to me among you as a possession for a tomb."

¹⁰And Ephron was sitting among the children of Heth, and Ephron, the Hittite, answered Abraham in the ears of the children of Heth, for all who were coming to his city's gate, saying, ¹¹"No,

23 ¹וַיִּהְיוּ חַיֵּי שָׂרָה מֵאָה שָׁנָה וְעֶשְׂרִים שָׁנָה
וְשֶׁבַע שָׁנִים שְׁנֵי חַיֵּי שָׂרָה: ²וַתָּמָת שָׂרָה בְּקִרְיַת
אַרְבַּע הִוא חֶבְרוֹן בְּאֶרֶץ כְּנָעַן וַיָּבֹא אַבְרָהָם
לִסְפֹּד לְשָׂרָה וְלִבְכֹּתָהּ: ³וַיָּקָם אַבְרָהָם מֵעַל פְּנֵי
מֵתוֹ וַיְדַבֵּר אֶל־בְּנֵי־חֵת לֵאמֹר: ⁴גֵּר־וְתוֹשָׁב אָנֹכִי
עִמָּכֶם תְּנוּ לִי אֲחֻזַּת־קֶבֶר עִמָּכֶם וְאֶקְבְּרָה מֵתִי
מִלְּפָנָי: ⁵וַיַּעֲנוּ בְנֵי־חֵת אֶת־אַבְרָהָם לֵאמֹר לוֹ:
⁶שְׁמָעֵנוּ ׀ אֲדֹנִי נְשִׂיא אֱלֹהִים אַתָּה בְּתוֹכֵנוּ בְּמִבְחַר
קְבָרֵינוּ קְבֹר אֶת־מֵתֶךָ אִישׁ מִמֶּנּוּ אֶת־קִבְרוֹ לֹא־
יִכְלֶה מִמְּךָ מִקְּבֹר מֵתֶךָ: ⁷וַיָּקָם אַבְרָהָם וַיִּשְׁתַּחוּ
לְעַם־הָאָרֶץ לִבְנֵי־חֵת: ⁸וַיְדַבֵּר אִתָּם לֵאמֹר אִם־
יֵשׁ אֶת־נַפְשְׁכֶם לִקְבֹּר אֶת־מֵתִי מִלְּפָנַי שְׁמָעוּנִי
וּפִגְעוּ־לִי בְּעֶפְרוֹן בֶּן־צֹחַר: ⁹וְיִתֶּן־לִי אֶת־מְעָרַת
הַמַּכְפֵּלָה אֲשֶׁר־לוֹ אֲשֶׁר בִּקְצֵה שָׂדֵהוּ בְּכֶסֶף מָלֵא
יִתְּנֶנָּה לִי בְּתוֹכְכֶם לַאֲחֻזַּת־קָבֶר: ¹⁰וְעֶפְרוֹן יֹשֵׁב
בְּתוֹךְ בְּנֵי־חֵת וַיַּעַן עֶפְרוֹן הַחִתִּי אֶת־אַבְרָהָם
בְּאָזְנֵי בְנֵי־חֵת לְכֹל בָּאֵי שַׁעַר־עִירוֹ לֵאמֹר: ¹¹לֹא־

23:4. **alien.** (On the meaning of this term, see the comment on 15:13.) Here it is Abraham who is the alien in the land. This is ironic because one day this land will belong to his descendants, and so they are commanded some fifteen times in the Torah to treat aliens well. That is, the Israelites must be fair to non-Israelites who live in Israel because once *they* were the aliens there, and because they were aliens in Egypt: "You know the alien's *soul*, because you were aliens in the land of Egypt" (Exod 23:9).

23:4. **visitor.** Meaning: a sojourner, a person who is staying in a place temporarily. With the hendiadys of "an alien and a sojourner," Abraham emphasizes to the Hittites that he recognizes that he is an outsider in their territory. Even though the deity has already told Abraham that the land of the Hittites will one day belong to his descendants, Abraham deals with them respectfully and courteously.

sir. Listen to me: I've *given* the field to you, and I've given the cave that's in it to you. I've given it to you before the eyes of the children of my people. Bury your dead."

12And Abraham bowed in front of the people of the land, 13and he spoke to Ephron in the ears of the people of the land, saying, "Just if you'll listen to me: I've given the money for the field. Take it from me so I may bury my dead there."

14And Ephron answered Abraham, saying to him, 15"Sir, listen to me. Land worth four hundred shekels of silver: what's that between me and you?! And bury your dead."

16And Abraham listened to Ephron, and Abraham weighed out to Ephron the money that he had spoken in the ears of the children of Heth: four hundred shekels of silver, at the merchant's current rate. 17And Ephron's field that was in Machpelah, which faces Mamre, the field and the cave that was in it and every tree that was in the field, that was in all of its border all around, was established 18for Abraham as a purchase in the eyes of the children of Heth, among all who were coming to his city's gate.

19And after that Abraham buried Sarah, his wife, at the cave of the field of Machpelah, facing Mamre—it is Hebron—in the land of Canaan. 20And the field and the cave that was in it were established for Abraham as a possession for a tomb from the children of Heth.

אֲדֹנִי שְׁמָעֵנִי הַשָּׂדֶה נָתַתִּי לָךְ וְהַמְּעָרָה אֲשֶׁר־בּוֹ לְךָ נְתַתִּיהָ לְעֵינֵי בְנֵי־עַמִּי נְתַתִּיהָ לָךְ קְבֹר מֵתֶךָ: 12וַיִּשְׁתַּחוּ אַבְרָהָם לִפְנֵי עַם הָאָרֶץ: 13וַיְדַבֵּר אֶל־עֶפְרוֹן בְּאָזְנֵי עַם־הָאָרֶץ לֵאמֹר אַךְ אִם־אַתָּה לוּ שְׁמָעֵנִי נָתַתִּי כֶּסֶף הַשָּׂדֶה קַח מִמֶּנִּי וְאֶקְבְּרָה אֶת־מֵתִי שָׁמָּה: 14וַיַּעַן עֶפְרוֹן אֶת־אַבְרָהָם לֵאמֹר לוֹ: 15אֲדֹנִי שְׁמָעֵנִי אֶרֶץ אַרְבַּע מֵאֹת שֶׁקֶל־כֶּסֶף בֵּינִי וּבֵינְךָ מַה־הִוא וְאֶת־מֵתְךָ קְבֹר: 16וַיִּשְׁמַע אַבְרָהָם אֶל־עֶפְרוֹן וַיִּשְׁקֹל אַבְרָהָם לְעֶפְרֹן אֶת־הַכֶּסֶף אֲשֶׁר דִּבֶּר בְּאָזְנֵי בְנֵי־חֵת אַרְבַּע מֵאוֹת שֶׁקֶל כֶּסֶף עֹבֵר לַסֹּחֵר: 17וַיָּקָם ׀ שְׂדֵה עֶפְרוֹן אֲשֶׁר בַּמַּכְפֵּלָה אֲשֶׁר לִפְנֵי מַמְרֵא הַשָּׂדֶה וְהַמְּעָרָה אֲשֶׁר־בּוֹ וְכָל־הָעֵץ אֲשֶׁר בַּשָּׂדֶה אֲשֶׁר בְּכָל־גְּבֻלוֹ סָבִיב: 18לְאַבְרָהָם לְמִקְנָה לְעֵינֵי בְנֵי־חֵת בְּכֹל בָּאֵי שַׁעַר־עִירוֹ: 19וְאַחֲרֵי־כֵן קָבַר אַבְרָהָם אֶת־שָׂרָה אִשְׁתּוֹ אֶל־מְעָרַת שְׂדֵה הַמַּכְפֵּלָה עַל־פְּנֵי מַמְרֵא הִוא חֶבְרוֹן בְּאֶרֶץ כְּנָעַן: 20וַיָּקָם הַשָּׂדֶה וְהַמְּעָרָה אֲשֶׁר־בּוֹ לְאַבְרָהָם לַאֲחֻזַּת־קָבֶר מֵאֵת בְּנֵי־חֵת: ס

23:11. **I've *given* the field to you.** But he has *not* given it to him. They are bargaining, and Ephron follows the practice of adopting an extraordinarily gracious opening position. But one is not supposed to take him up on it, and Abraham in fact does not. This in turn sheds light on the extraordinary offer that Lot makes, to give his daughters to the people of Sodom for abuse (see the comment on Gen 19:8).

23:15. **four hundred shekels of silver: what's that between me and you?!** He says it as if this were a paltry sum. But it is in fact a great deal.

23:19. **it is Hebron.** Why does the story of Sarah's death and burial begin and end with a notice that it is at Hebron (23:2,19)? Because Abraham's purchase of this land establishes unquestionable title to property at Hebron, and this is a basis of Israel's return to the land after the years of slavery in Egypt. Thus, when Moses sends spies into the land, they go to Hebron, which is singled out among all cities of Canaan with a verse of description (Num 13:22).

24 ¹And Abraham was old, well along in days, and YHWH had blessed Abraham in everything. ²And Abraham said to his servant, the elder of his house, who was in charge of all that he had, "Place your hand under my thigh, ³and I'll have you swear by YHWH, God of the skies and God of the earth, that you won't take a wife for my son from the daughters of the Canaanite among whom I live, ⁴but you'll go to my land and my birthplace and take a wife for my son, for Isaac."

⁵And the servant said to him, "Maybe the woman won't be willing to follow me to this land. Shall I *take back* your son to the land you came from?"

⁶And Abraham said to him, "Watch yourself, that you don't take my son back there. ⁷YHWH, God of the skies, who took me from my father's house and from the land of my birth and who spoke to me and who swore to me, saying, 'I'll give this land to your seed,' He'll send His angel ahead of you, and you shall take a wife for my son from there. ⁸And if the woman won't be willing to go after you, then you'll be freed from this oath of mine. Only you are not to take my son back there."

⁹And the servant placed his hand under his lord Abraham's thigh and swore to him about this thing. ¹⁰And the servant took ten camels of his lord's camels and went, and all of his lord's best things were in his hand. And he got up and went to Aram Naharaim, to the city of Nahor, ¹¹and he had the camels kneel outside the city at the water well at evening time, the time that the women went out to draw water. ¹²And he said, "YHWH, God of my lord Abraham, make something happen in front of me today and show

24 ¹וְאַבְרָהָם זָקֵן בָּא בַּיָּמִים וַיהוָה בֵּרַךְ אֶת־אַבְרָהָם בַּכֹּל: ²וַיֹּאמֶר אַבְרָהָם אֶל־עַבְדּוֹ זְקַן בֵּיתוֹ הַמֹּשֵׁל בְּכָל־אֲשֶׁר־לוֹ שִׂים־נָא יָדְךָ תַּחַת יְרֵכִי: ³וְאַשְׁבִּיעֲךָ בַּיהוָה אֱלֹהֵי הַשָּׁמַיִם וֵאלֹהֵי הָאָרֶץ אֲשֶׁר לֹא־תִקַּח אִשָּׁה לִבְנִי מִבְּנוֹת הַכְּנַעֲנִי אֲשֶׁר אָנֹכִי יוֹשֵׁב בְּקִרְבּוֹ: ⁴כִּי אֶל־אַרְצִי וְאֶל־מוֹלַדְתִּי תֵּלֵךְ וְלָקַחְתָּ אִשָּׁה לִבְנִי לְיִצְחָק: ⁵וַיֹּאמֶר אֵלָיו הָעֶבֶד אוּלַי לֹא־תֹאבֶה הָאִשָּׁה לָלֶכֶת אַחֲרַי אֶל־הָאָרֶץ הַזֹּאת הֶהָשֵׁב אָשִׁיב אֶת־בִּנְךָ אֶל־הָאָרֶץ אֲשֶׁר־יָצָאתָ מִשָּׁם: ⁶וַיֹּאמֶר אֵלָיו אַבְרָהָם הִשָּׁמֶר לְךָ פֶּן־תָּשִׁיב אֶת־בְּנִי שָׁמָּה: ⁷יְהוָה ׀ אֱלֹהֵי הַשָּׁמַיִם אֲשֶׁר לְקָחַנִי מִבֵּית אָבִי וּמֵאֶרֶץ מוֹלַדְתִּי וַאֲשֶׁר דִּבֶּר־לִי וַאֲשֶׁר נִשְׁבַּע־לִי לֵאמֹר לְזַרְעֲךָ אֶתֵּן אֶת־הָאָרֶץ הַזֹּאת הוּא יִשְׁלַח מַלְאָכוֹ לְפָנֶיךָ וְלָקַחְתָּ אִשָּׁה לִבְנִי מִשָּׁם: ⁸וְאִם־לֹא תֹאבֶה הָאִשָּׁה לָלֶכֶת אַחֲרֶיךָ וְנִקִּיתָ מִשְּׁבֻעָתִי זֹאת רַק אֶת־בְּנִי לֹא תָשֵׁב שָׁמָּה: ⁹וַיָּשֶׂם הָעֶבֶד אֶת־יָדוֹ תַּחַת יֶרֶךְ אַבְרָהָם אֲדֹנָיו וַיִּשָּׁבַע לוֹ עַל־הַדָּבָר הַזֶּה: ¹⁰וַיִּקַּח הָעֶבֶד עֲשָׂרָה גְמַלִּים מִגְּמַלֵּי אֲדֹנָיו וַיֵּלֶךְ וְכָל־טוּב אֲדֹנָיו בְּיָדוֹ וַיָּקָם וַיֵּלֶךְ אֶל־אֲרַם נַהֲרַיִם אֶל־עִיר נָחוֹר: ¹¹וַיַּבְרֵךְ הַגְּמַלִּים מִחוּץ לָעִיר אֶל־בְּאֵר הַמָּיִם לְעֵת עֶרֶב לְעֵת צֵאת הַשֹּׁאֲבֹת: ¹²וַיֹּאמַר ׀ יְהוָה אֱלֹהֵי אֲדֹנִי אַבְרָהָם הַקְרֵה־נָא לְפָנַי הַיּוֹם וַעֲשֵׂה־

———————•◦•———————

24:12. **make something happen.** The Hebrew includes the particle *nā'*, conveying that this is a polite request. Even as a request, though, it is remarkable: the servant himself asks for a miraculous sign from God, and he himself names what that sign should be. No human thus far, including Abraham himself, has gone this far. Abraham had told this servant that his God "will send His angel ahead of you," and this is presumably what gives the servant the confidence to do this. Still, it is noteworthy as

kindness to my lord Abraham: 13Here I am, standing over the spring of water, and the daughters of the people of the city are going out to draw water. 14And let it be that the girl to whom I'll say, 'Tip your jar so I may drink,' and she'll say, 'Drink, and I'll water your camels, too,' she'll be the one you've pointed out for your servant, for Isaac, and I'll know by this that you've shown kindness to my lord."

15And he had not even finished speaking, and here was Rebekah—who was born to Bethuel son of Milcah, wife of Nahor, Abraham's brother—coming out, and her jar was on her shoulder. 16And the girl was very good-looking, a virgin, and no man had known her. And she went down to the spring and filled her jar and went up. 17And the servant ran toward her and said, "Give me a little water from your jar."

18And she said, "Drink, my lord," and she hurried and lowered her jar on her arm and let him drink.

19And she finished letting him drink, and she said, "I'll draw water for your camels, too, until they finish drinking." 20And she hurried and emptied her jar into the trough and ran again to the well to draw water, and she drew water for all his camels. 21And the man, astonished at her, was keeping quiet so as to know if YHWH had made his trip successful or not.

22And it was when the camels finished drinking: and the man took a gold ring—its weight was a beqa—and two bracelets for her arms—their weight was ten of gold. 23And he said, "Tell me, whose daughter are you? Is there a place at your father's house for us to spend the night?"

24And she said to him, "I'm a daughter of Bethuel, Milcah's son whom she bore to Nahor." 25And she said to him, "We also have plenty of both straw and fodder, also a place to spend the night."

חֶסֶד עִם־אֲדֹנִי אַבְרָהָם: 13הִנֵּה אָנֹכִי נִצָּב עַל־עֵין הַמָּיִם וּבְנוֹת אַנְשֵׁי הָעִיר יֹצְאֹת לִשְׁאֹב מָיִם: 14וְהָיָה הַנַּעֲרָ אֲשֶׁר אֹמַר אֵלֶיהָ הַטִּי־נָא כַדֵּךְ וְאֶשְׁתֶּה וְאָמְרָה שְׁתֵה וְגַם־גְּמַלֶּיךָ אַשְׁקֶה אֹתָהּ הֹכַחְתָּ לְעַבְדְּךָ לְיִצְחָק וּבָהּ אֵדַע כִּי־עָשִׂיתָ חֶסֶד עִם־אֲדֹנִי: 15וַיְהִי־הוּא טֶרֶם כִּלָּה לְדַבֵּר וְהִנֵּה רִבְקָה יֹצֵאת אֲשֶׁר יֻלְּדָה לִבְתוּאֵל בֶּן־מִלְכָּה אֵשֶׁת נָחוֹר אֲחִי אַבְרָהָם וְכַדָּהּ עַל־שִׁכְמָהּ: 16וְהַנַּעֲרָ טֹבַת מַרְאֶה מְאֹד בְּתוּלָה וְאִישׁ לֹא יְדָעָהּ וַתֵּרֶד הָעַיְנָה וַתְּמַלֵּא כַדָּהּ וַתָּעַל: 17וַיָּרָץ הָעֶבֶד לִקְרָאתָהּ וַיֹּאמֶר הַגְמִיאִינִי נָא מְעַט־מַיִם מִכַּדֵּךְ: 18וַתֹּאמֶר שְׁתֵה אֲדֹנִי וַתְּמַהֵר וַתֹּרֶד כַּדָּהּ עַל־יָדָהּ וַתַּשְׁקֵהוּ: 19וַתְּכַל לְהַשְׁקֹתוֹ וַתֹּאמֶר גַּם לִגְמַלֶּיךָ אֶשְׁאָב עַד אִם־כִּלּוּ לִשְׁתֹּת: 20וַתְּמַהֵר וַתְּעַר כַּדָּהּ אֶל־הַשֹּׁקֶת וַתָּרָץ עוֹד אֶל־הַבְּאֵר לִשְׁאֹב וַתִּשְׁאַב לְכָל־גְּמַלָּיו: 21וְהָאִישׁ מִשְׁתָּאֵה לָהּ מַחֲרִישׁ לָדַעַת הַהִצְלִיחַ יְהוָה דַּרְכּוֹ אִם־לֹא: 22וַיְהִי כַּאֲשֶׁר כִּלּוּ הַגְּמַלִּים לִשְׁתּוֹת וַיִּקַּח הָאִישׁ נֶזֶם זָהָב בֶּקַע מִשְׁקָלוֹ וּשְׁנֵי צְמִידִים עַל־יָדֶיהָ עֲשָׂרָה זָהָב מִשְׁקָלָם: 23וַיֹּאמֶר בַּת־מִי אַתְּ הַגִּידִי נָא לִי הֲיֵשׁ בֵּית־אָבִיךְ מָקוֹם לָנוּ לָלִין: 24וַתֹּאמֶר אֵלָיו בַּת־בְּתוּאֵל אָנֹכִי בֶּן־מִלְכָּה אֲשֶׁר יָלְדָה לְנָחוֹר: 25וַתֹּאמֶר אֵלָיו גַּם־תֶּבֶן גַּם־מִסְפּוֹא רַב עִמָּנוּ גַּם־

---

one of a chain of steps that humans are taking toward increasing control of miracle in the *Tanak*.

24:22. **beqa**. Half a shekel (see Exod 38:26).

26And the man knelt and bowed to YHWH 27and said, "Blessed is YHWH, God of my lord Abraham, whose kindness and faithfulness have not left my lord. I: YHWH has led me to the house of my lord's brother."

28And the girl ran and told her mother's household about these things. 29And Rebekah had a brother, and his name was Laban, and Laban ran outside to the man, at the spring. 30And it was when he saw the ring and the bracelets on his sister's hands and when he heard his sister Rebekah's words, saying, "The man spoke like this to me." And he came to the man, and here he was standing by the camels at the spring. 31And he said, "Come, blessed one of YHWH. Why do you stand outside when I've prepared the house and a place for the camels!" 32And the man came to the house and unloaded the camels and gave straw and fodder to the camels and water to wash his feet and the feet of the people who were with him. 33And [bread] was set in front of him to eat.

And he said, "I won't eat until I've said what I have to say."

And he said, "Speak."

34And he said, "I am Abraham's servant. 35And YHWH has blessed my lord very much, and he has become great. And He has given him a flock and oxen and silver and gold and male and female servants and camels and asses. 36And my lord's wife Sarah gave birth to a son by my lord in her old age, and he has given him everything that he has. 37And my lord had me swear, saying, 'You shall not take a wife for my son from the daughters of the Canaanite in whose land I live, 38but you shall go to my father's house and to my family and take a wife for my son.' 39And I said to my lord, 'Maybe the woman won't follow me.' 40And he said to me, 'YHWH, before whom I have walked, will send His angel with you and make your trip successful, and you shall take a wife for my son from my family and from my father's house. 41Then you'll be freed from my oath: when you'll come to my family, and if they

מָק֖וֹם לָל֑וּן׃ 26וַיִּקֹּ֣ד הָאִ֔ישׁ וַיִּשְׁתַּ֖חוּ לַֽיהוָֽה׃ 27וַיֹּ֗אמֶר בָּר֤וּךְ יְהוָה֙ אֱלֹהֵי֙ אֲדֹנִ֣י אַבְרָהָ֔ם אֲשֶׁ֛ר לֹֽא־עָזַ֥ב חַסְדּ֛וֹ וַאֲמִתּ֖וֹ מֵעִ֣ם אֲדֹנִ֑י אָנֹכִ֗י בַּדֶּ֙רֶךְ֙ נָחַ֣נִי יְהוָ֔ה בֵּ֖ית אֲחֵ֥י אֲדֹנִֽי׃ 28וַתָּ֙רָץ֙ הַֽנַּעֲרָ֔ וַתַּגֵּ֖ד לְבֵ֣ית אִמָּ֑הּ כַּדְּבָרִ֖ים הָאֵֽלֶּה׃ 29וּלְרִבְקָ֥ה אָ֖ח וּשְׁמ֣וֹ לָבָ֑ן וַיָּ֨רָץ לָבָ֧ן אֶל־הָאִ֛ישׁ הַח֖וּצָה אֶל־הָעָֽיִן׃ 30וַיְהִ֣י ׀ כִּרְאֹ֣ת אֶת־הַנֶּ֗זֶם וְאֶת־הַצְּמִדִים֮ עַל־יְדֵ֣י אֲחֹתוֹ֒ וּכְשָׁמְע֗וֹ אֶת־דִּבְרֵ֞י רִבְקָ֤ה אֲחֹתוֹ֙ לֵאמֹ֔ר כֹּֽה־דִבֶּ֥ר אֵלַ֖י הָאִ֑ישׁ וַיָּבֹא֙ אֶל־הָאִ֔ישׁ וְהִנֵּ֛ה עֹמֵ֥ד עַל־הַגְּמַלִּ֖ים עַל־הָעָֽיִן׃ 31וַיֹּ֕אמֶר בּ֖וֹא בְּר֣וּךְ יְהוָ֑ה לָ֤מָּה תַעֲמֹד֙ בַּח֔וּץ וְאָנֹכִי֙ פִּנִּ֣יתִי הַבַּ֔יִת וּמָק֖וֹם לַגְּמַלִּֽים׃ 32וַיָּבֹ֤א הָאִישׁ֙ הַבַּ֔יְתָה וַיְפַתַּ֖ח הַגְּמַלִּ֑ים וַיִּתֵּ֨ן תֶּ֤בֶן וּמִסְפּוֹא֙ לַגְּמַלִּ֔ים וּמַ֕יִם לִרְחֹ֣ץ רַגְלָ֔יו וְרַגְלֵ֥י הָאֲנָשִׁ֖ים אֲשֶׁ֥ר אִתּֽוֹ׃ 33וַיִּישֶׂם֙ לְפָנָיו֙ לֶאֱכֹ֔ל וַיֹּ֙אמֶר֙ לֹ֣א אֹכַ֔ל עַ֥ד אִם־דִּבַּ֖רְתִּי דְּבָרָ֑י וַיֹּ֖אמֶר דַּבֵּֽר׃ 34וַיֹּאמַ֑ר עֶ֥בֶד אַבְרָהָ֖ם אָנֹֽכִי׃ 35וַֽיהוָ֞ה בֵּרַ֧ךְ אֶת־אֲדֹנִ֛י מְאֹ֖ד וַיִּגְדָּ֑ל וַיִּתֶּן־ל֞וֹ צֹ֤אן וּבָקָר֙ וְכֶ֣סֶף וְזָהָ֔ב וַעֲבָדִם֙ וּשְׁפָחֹ֔ת וּגְמַלִּ֖ים וַחֲמֹרִֽים׃ 36וַתֵּ֡לֶד שָׂרָה֩ אֵ֨שֶׁת אֲדֹנִ֥י בֵן֙ לַֽאדֹנִ֔י אַחֲרֵ֖י זִקְנָתָ֑הּ וַיִּתֶּן־ל֖וֹ אֶת־כָּל־אֲשֶׁר־לֽוֹ׃ 37וַיַּשְׁבִּעֵ֥נִי אֲדֹנִ֖י לֵאמֹ֑ר לֹא־תִקַּ֤ח אִשָּׁה֙ לִבְנִ֔י מִבְּנוֹת֙ הַֽכְּנַעֲנִ֔י אֲשֶׁ֥ר אָנֹכִ֖י יֹשֵׁ֥ב בְּאַרְצֽוֹ׃ 38אִם־לֹ֧א אֶל־בֵּית־אָבִ֛י תֵּלֵ֖ךְ וְאֶל־מִשְׁפַּחְתִּ֑י וְלָקַחְתָּ֥ אִשָּׁ֖ה לִבְנִֽי׃ 39וָאֹמַ֖ר אֶל־אֲדֹנִ֑י אֻלַ֛י לֹא־תֵלֵ֥ךְ הָאִשָּׁ֖ה אַחֲרָֽי׃ 40וַיֹּ֖אמֶר אֵלָ֑י יְהוָ֞ה אֲשֶׁר־הִתְהַלַּ֣כְתִּי לְפָנָ֗יו יִשְׁלַ֨ח מַלְאָכ֤וֹ אִתָּךְ֙ וְהִצְלִ֣יחַ דַּרְכֶּ֔ךָ וְלָקַחְתָּ֤ אִשָּׁה֙ לִבְנִ֔י מִמִּשְׁפַּחְתִּ֖י וּמִבֵּ֥ית אָבִֽי׃ 41אָ֤ז תִּנָּקֶה֙ מֵאָ֣לָתִ֔י כִּ֥י תָב֖וֹא אֶל־

83

won't give her to you, then you'll be free from my oath.' 42And I came to the spring today, and I said, 'YHWH, God of my lord Abraham, if you're making my trip on which I'm going successful, 43here I am, standing at the spring of water, and let it be that the young woman who goes to draw water and I say to her, "Let me drink a little water from your jar," 44and she says to me, "Both drink yourself and I'll draw water for your camels, too," she will be the woman whom YHWH has designated for my lord's son.' 45I hadn't even finished speaking in my heart, and here was Rebekah coming out, and her jar was on her shoulder, and she went down to the spring and drew water. And I said to her, 'Give me a drink.' 46And she hurried and lowered her jar from on her and said, 'Drink, and I'll water your camels, too.' And I drank, and she watered the camels, too. 47And I asked her and said, 'Whose daughter are you?' And she said, 'The daughter of Bethuel, son of Nahor, whom Milcah bore for him.' And I put the ring on her nose and the bracelets on her hands, 48and I knelt and bowed to YHWH and blessed YHWH, my lord Abraham's God, who had led me in a faithful way to take a daughter of my lord's brother for his son. 49And now, if you're exercising kindness and faithfulness with my lord, tell me; and if not, tell me; so I'll turn to right or to left."

50And Laban and Bethuel answered, and they said, "The thing has come from YHWH. We can't speak bad or good to you. 51Here is Rebekah before you. Take her and go, and let her be a wife to your lord's son as YHWH has spoken." 52And it was, when Abraham's servant heard their words, that he bowed to the ground to YHWH. 53And the servant brought out silver articles and gold articles and garments and gave them to Rebekah and gave precious things to her brother and to her mother. 54And they ate and drank, he and the people who were with him, and spent the night.

And they got up in the morning, and he said, "Send me back to my lord."

מִשְׁפַּחְתִּ֖י וְאִם־לֹ֣א יִתְּנ֣וּ לָ֔ךְ וְהָיִ֥יתָ נָקִ֖י מֵאָלָתִֽי׃ 42וָאָבֹ֥א הַיּ֖וֹם אֶל־הָעָ֑יִן וָאֹמַ֗ר יְהוָה֙ אֱלֹהֵי֙ אֲדֹנִ֣י אַבְרָהָ֔ם אִם־יֶשְׁךָ־נָּא֙ מַצְלִ֣יחַ דַּרְכִּ֔י אֲשֶׁ֥ר אָנֹכִ֖י הֹלֵ֥ךְ עָלֶֽיהָ׃ 43הִנֵּ֛ה אָנֹכִ֥י נִצָּ֖ב עַל־עֵ֣ין הַמָּ֑יִם וְהָיָ֤ה הָעַלְמָה֙ הַיֹּצֵ֣את לִשְׁאֹ֔ב וְאָמַרְתִּ֣י אֵלֶ֔יהָ הַשְׁקִֽינִי־נָ֥א מְעַט־מַ֖יִם מִכַּדֵּֽךְ׃ 44וְאָמְרָ֣ה אֵלַ֔י גַּם־אַתָּ֣ה שְׁתֵ֔ה וְגַ֥ם לִגְמַלֶּ֖יךָ אֶשְׁאָ֑ב הִ֣וא הָֽאִשָּׁ֔ה אֲשֶׁר־הֹכִ֥יחַ יְהוָ֖ה לְבֶן־אֲדֹנִֽי׃ 45אֲנִי֩ טֶ֨רֶם אֲכַלֶּ֜ה לְדַבֵּ֣ר אֶל־לִבִּ֗י וְהִנֵּ֨ה רִבְקָ֤ה יֹצֵאת֙ וְכַדָּ֣הּ עַל־שִׁכְמָ֔הּ וַתֵּ֥רֶד הָעַ֖יְנָה וַתִּשְׁאָ֑ב וָאֹמַ֥ר אֵלֶ֖יהָ הַשְׁקִ֥ינִי נָֽא׃ 46וַתְּמַהֵ֗ר וַתּ֤וֹרֶד כַּדָּהּ֙ מֵֽעָלֶ֔יהָ וַתֹּ֣אמֶר שְׁתֵ֔ה וְגַם־גְּמַלֶּ֖יךָ אַשְׁקֶ֑ה וָאֵ֕שְׁתְּ וְגַ֥ם הַגְּמַלִּ֖ים הִשְׁקָֽתָה׃ 47וָאֶשְׁאַ֣ל אֹתָ֗הּ וָאֹמַר֮ בַּת־מִ֣י אַתְּ֒ וַתֹּ֗אמֶר בַּת־בְּתוּאֵל֙ בֶּן־נָח֔וֹר אֲשֶׁ֥ר יָֽלְדָה־לּ֖וֹ מִלְכָּ֑ה וָאָשִׂ֤ם הַנֶּ֙זֶם֙ עַל־אַפָּ֔הּ וְהַצְּמִידִ֖ים עַל־יָדֶֽיהָ׃ 48וָאֶקֹּ֥ד וָֽאֶשְׁתַּחֲוֶ֖ה לַיהוָ֑ה וָאֲבָרֵ֗ךְ אֶת־יְהוָה֙ אֱלֹהֵי֙ אֲדֹנִ֣י אַבְרָהָ֔ם אֲשֶׁ֤ר הִנְחַ֙נִי֙ בְּדֶ֣רֶךְ אֱמֶ֔ת לָקַ֛חַת אֶת־בַּת־אֲחִ֥י אֲדֹנִ֖י לִבְנֽוֹ׃ 49וְ֠עַתָּה אִם־יֶשְׁכֶ֨ם עֹשִׂ֜ים חֶ֧סֶד וֶֽאֱמֶ֛ת אֶת־אֲדֹנִ֖י הַגִּ֣ידוּ לִ֑י וְאִם־לֹ֕א הַגִּ֣ידוּ לִ֔י וְאֶפְנֶ֥ה עַל־יָמִ֖ין א֥וֹ עַל־שְׂמֹֽאל׃ 50וַיַּ֨עַן לָבָ֤ן וּבְתוּאֵל֙ וַיֹּ֣אמְר֔וּ מֵיְהוָ֖ה יָצָ֣א הַדָּבָ֑ר לֹ֥א נוּכַ֛ל דַּבֵּ֥ר אֵלֶ֖יךָ רַ֥ע אוֹ־טֽוֹב׃ 51הִנֵּֽה־רִבְקָ֥ה לְפָנֶ֖יךָ קַ֣ח וָלֵ֑ךְ וּתְהִ֤י אִשָּׁה֙ לְבֶן־אֲדֹנֶ֔יךָ כַּאֲשֶׁ֖ר דִּבֶּ֥ר יְהוָֽה׃ 52וַיְהִ֕י כַּאֲשֶׁ֥ר שָׁמַ֛ע עֶ֥בֶד אַבְרָהָ֖ם אֶת־דִּבְרֵיהֶ֑ם וַיִּשְׁתַּ֥חוּ אַ֖רְצָה לַֽיהוָֽה׃ 53וַיּוֹצֵ֨א הָעֶ֜בֶד כְּלֵי־כֶ֗סֶף וּכְלֵ֤י זָהָב֙ וּבְגָדִ֔ים וַיִּתֵּ֖ן לְרִבְקָ֑ה וּמִ֨גְדָּנֹ֔ת נָתַ֥ן לְאָחִ֖יהָ וּלְאִמָּֽהּ׃ 54וַיֹּאכְל֣וּ וַיִּשְׁתּ֗וּ ה֛וּא וְהָאֲנָשִׁ֥ים אֲשֶׁר־עִמּ֖וֹ וַיָּלִ֑ינוּ וַיָּק֣וּמוּ בַבֹּ֔קֶר וַיֹּ֖אמֶר שַׁלְּחֻ֥נִי

55And her brother and her mother said, "Let the girl stay with us a few days—or ten. After that, she'll go."

56And he said to them, "Don't hold me back, since YHWH has made my trip successful. Send me away, so I may go to my lord."

57And they said, "We'll call the girl and ask her from her own mouth." 58And they called Rebekah and said to her, "Will you go with this man?"

And she said, "I'll go."

59And they sent their sister Rebekah and her nurse and Abraham's servant and his people. 60And they blessed Rebekah and said to her, "You're our sister. Become thousands of tenthousands. And may your seed possess the gate of those who hate him." 61And Rebekah and her maids got up and rode on the camels and followed the man, and the servant took Rebekah and went.

62And Isaac was coming from the area of the well Lahai-roi, and he was living in the territory of the Negeb, 63and Isaac went to meditate in a field toward evening, and he raised his eyes and saw, and here were camels coming. 64And Rebekah raised her eyes and saw Isaac, and she fell from the camel. 65And she said to the servant, "Who is that man who's walking in the field toward us?"

And the servant said, "He's my lord." And she took a veil and covered herself.

66And the servant told Isaac all the things that he had done. 67And Isaac brought her to his mother Sarah's tent. And he took Rebekah, and she became his wife, and he loved her.

And Isaac was consoled after his mother.

25 1And Abraham went on and took a wife, and her name was Keturah, 2and she gave birth to Zimran and Jokshan and Medan

וַיֹּאמֶר אָחִיהָ וְאִמָּהּ תֵּשֵׁב הַנַּעֲרָ אִתָּנוּ 55לֵאדֹנִי:
יָמִים אוֹ עָשׂוֹר אַחַר תֵּלֵךְ: 56וַיֹּאמֶר אֲלֵהֶם אַל־
תְּאַחֲרוּ אֹתִי וַיהֹוָה הִצְלִיחַ דַּרְכִּי שַׁלְּחוּנִי וְאֵלְכָה
לֵאדֹנִי: 57וַיֹּאמְרוּ נִקְרָא לַנַּעֲרָ וְנִשְׁאֲלָה אֶת־פִּיהָ:
58וַיִּקְרְאוּ לְרִבְקָה וַיֹּאמְרוּ אֵלֶיהָ הֲתֵלְכִי עִם־
הָאִישׁ הַזֶּה וַתֹּאמֶר אֵלֵךְ: 59וַיְשַׁלְּחוּ אֶת־רִבְקָה
אֲחֹתָם וְאֶת־מֵנִקְתָּהּ וְאֶת־עֶבֶד אַבְרָהָם וְאֶת־אֲנָשָׁיו:
60וַיְבָרֲכוּ אֶת־רִבְקָה וַיֹּאמְרוּ לָהּ

אֲחֹתֵנוּ אַתְּ הֲיִי לְאַלְפֵי רְבָבָה
וְיִירַשׁ זַרְעֵךְ אֵת שַׁעַר שֹׂנְאָיו:

61וַתָּקָם רִבְקָה וְנַעֲרֹתֶיהָ וַתִּרְכַּבְנָה עַל־הַגְּמַלִּים
וַתֵּלַכְנָה אַחֲרֵי הָאִישׁ וַיִּקַּח הָעֶבֶד אֶת־רִבְקָה
וַיֵּלַךְ: 62וְיִצְחָק בָּא מִבּוֹא בְּאֵר לַחַי רֹאִי וְהוּא
יוֹשֵׁב בְּאֶרֶץ הַנֶּגֶב: 63וַיֵּצֵא יִצְחָק לָשׂוּחַ בַּשָּׂדֶה
לִפְנוֹת עָרֶב וַיִּשָּׂא עֵינָיו וַיַּרְא וְהִנֵּה גְמַלִּים בָּאִים:
64וַתִּשָּׂא רִבְקָה אֶת־עֵינֶיהָ וַתֵּרֶא אֶת־יִצְחָק וַתִּפֹּל
מֵעַל הַגָּמָל: 65וַתֹּאמֶר אֶל־הָעֶבֶד מִי־הָאִישׁ הַלָּזֶה
הַהֹלֵךְ בַּשָּׂדֶה לִקְרָאתֵנוּ וַיֹּאמֶר הָעֶבֶד הוּא אֲדֹנִי
וַתִּקַּח הַצָּעִיף וַתִּתְכָּס: 66וַיְסַפֵּר הָעֶבֶד לְיִצְחָק אֵת
כָּל־הַדְּבָרִים אֲשֶׁר עָשָׂה: 67וַיְבִאֶהָ יִצְחָק הָאֹהֱלָה
שָׂרָה אִמּוֹ וַיִּקַּח אֶת־רִבְקָה וַתְּהִי־לוֹ לְאִשָּׁה
וַיֶּאֱהָבֶהָ וַיִּנָּחֵם יִצְחָק אַחֲרֵי אִמּוֹ: פ

25 1וַיֹּסֶף אַבְרָהָם וַיִּקַּח אִשָּׁה וּשְׁמָהּ קְטוּרָה:
2וַתֵּלֶד לוֹ אֶת־זִמְרָן וְאֶת־יָקְשָׁן וְאֶת־מְדָן וְאֶת־מִדְיָן

25:1. **Keturah.** The most ignored significant person in the Torah. Rashi follows an old rabbinic idea that she is Hagar. But there is no basis for this in the text, and other traditional commentators reject it (Ibn Ezra, Ramban, Rashbam). Keturah is the mother of tribes located along the route of incense trade, and her name is related to the

and Midian and Ishbak and Shuah for him. 3And Jokshan fathered Sheba and Dedan. And the children of Dedan were Ashurim and Letushim and Leummim. 4And the children of Midian: Ephah and Epher and Hanoch and Abida and El-daah. All these were children of Keturah. 5And Abraham gave everything that he had to Isaac. 6And Abraham gave gifts to the children of the concubines that Abraham had, and he sent them away from Isaac, his son, while he was still living: east, to the land of the East.

7And these are the days of the years of Abraham's life that he lived: a hundred years and seventy years and five years. 8And he expired. And Abraham died at a good old age, old and full, and was gathered to his people. 9And Isaac and Ishmael, his sons, buried him at the cave of Machpelah at the field of Ephron, son of Zohar, the Hittite, facing Mamre, 10the field that Abraham bought from the children of Heth. Abraham was buried there—and Sarah, his wife.

11And it was after Abraham's death, and God blessed Isaac, his son. And Isaac lived at the well Lahai-roi.

12And these are the records of Ishmael, son of Abraham, to whom Hagar, the Egyptian, Sarah's maid, gave birth for Abraham: 13And these are the names of Ishmael's sons, by their names, according to their records: Ishmael's firstborn was Nebaioth, and Kedar and Adbeel and Mibsam 14and Mishma and Dumah and Massa, 15Hadar and Tema, Jetur, Naphish and Kedmah. 16These

וְאֶת־יִשְׁבָּק וְאֶת־שׁוּחַ: 3וְיָקְשָׁן יָלַד אֶת־שְׁבָא וְאֶת־דְּדָן וּבְנֵי דְדָן הָיוּ אַשּׁוּרִם וּלְטוּשִׁים וּלְאֻמִּים: 4וּבְנֵי מִדְיָן עֵיפָה וָעֵפֶר וַחֲנֹךְ וַאֲבִידָע וְאֶלְדָּעָה כָּל־אֵלֶּה בְּנֵי קְטוּרָה: 5וַיִּתֵּן אַבְרָהָם אֶת־כָּל־אֲשֶׁר־לוֹ לְיִצְחָק: 6וְלִבְנֵי הַפִּילַגְשִׁים אֲשֶׁר לְאַבְרָהָם נָתַן אַבְרָהָם מַתָּנֹת וַיְשַׁלְּחֵם מֵעַל יִצְחָק בְּנוֹ בְּעוֹדֶנּוּ חַי קֵדְמָה אֶל־אֶרֶץ קֶדֶם: 7וְאֵלֶּה יְמֵי שְׁנֵי־חַיֵּי אַבְרָהָם אֲשֶׁר־חָי מְאַת שָׁנָה וְשִׁבְעִים שָׁנָה וְחָמֵשׁ שָׁנִים: 8וַיִּגְוַע וַיָּמָת אַבְרָהָם בְּשֵׂיבָה טוֹבָה זָקֵן וְשָׂבֵעַ וַיֵּאָסֶף אֶל־עַמָּיו: 9וַיִּקְבְּרוּ אֹתוֹ יִצְחָק וְיִשְׁמָעֵאל בָּנָיו אֶל־מְעָרַת הַמַּכְפֵּלָה אֶל־שְׂדֵה עֶפְרֹן בֶּן־צֹחַר הַחִתִּי אֲשֶׁר עַל־פְּנֵי מַמְרֵא: 10הַשָּׂדֶה אֲשֶׁר־קָנָה אַבְרָהָם מֵאֵת בְּנֵי־חֵת שָׁמָּה קֻבַּר אַבְרָהָם וְשָׂרָה אִשְׁתּוֹ: 11וַיְהִי אַחֲרֵי מוֹת אַבְרָהָם וַיְבָרֶךְ אֱלֹהִים אֶת־יִצְחָק בְּנוֹ וַיֵּשֶׁב יִצְחָק עִם־בְּאֵר לַחַי רֹאִי: ס

12וְאֵלֶּה תֹּלְדֹת יִשְׁמָעֵאל בֶּן־אַבְרָהָם אֲשֶׁר יָלְדָה הָגָר הַמִּצְרִית שִׁפְחַת שָׂרָה לְאַבְרָהָם: 13וְאֵלֶּה שְׁמוֹת בְּנֵי יִשְׁמָעֵאל בִּשְׁמֹתָם לְתוֹלְדֹתָם בְּכֹר יִשְׁמָעֵאל נְבָיֹת וְקֵדָר וְאַדְבְּאֵל וּמִבְשָׂם: 14וּמִשְׁמָע וְדוּמָה וּמַשָּׂא: 15חֲדַד וְתֵימָא יְטוּר נָפִישׁ

---

word for incense. Notably, the Midianites are among the children of Abraham and Keturah, and the influence of the Midianite priest Jethro on Moses, his son-in-law, is understood to be substantial. And the line of Levites who are descended from Moses thus—alone among the Israelites—derive from Abraham through both Sarah and Keturah.

25:11. **Isaac lived at the well Lahai-roi.** He lives at the place where Hagar was told by an angel that she would give birth to Ishmael, Isaac's brother (Gen 16:14). Ishmael remains significant in the background. It is as if Isaac recognizes that his miraculous birth and his being spared from sacrifice have given him everything that otherwise would have been Ishmael's. Living at Lahai-roi, he is reminded that Ishmael's life, too, was divinely determined.

are they, Ishmael's sons, and these are their names in their settlements and in their encampments, twelve chieftains by their clans. 17And these are the years of Ishmael's life: a hundred years and thirty years and seven years. And he expired and died and was gathered to his people. 18And they tented from Havilah to Shur, which faces Egypt, as you come toward Asshur. He fell facing all of his brothers.

וְקֵדְמָה: 16אֵלֶּה הֵם בְּנֵי יִשְׁמָעֵאל וְאֵלֶּה שְׁמֹתָם בְּחַצְרֵיהֶם וּבְטִירֹתָם שְׁנֵים־עָשָׂר נְשִׂיאִם לְאֻמֹּתָם: 17וְאֵלֶּה שְׁנֵי חַיֵּי יִשְׁמָעֵאל מְאַת שָׁנָה וּשְׁלֹשִׁים שָׁנָה וְשֶׁבַע שָׁנִים וַיִּגְוַע וַיָּמָת וַיֵּאָסֶף אֶל־עַמָּיו: 18וַיִּשְׁכְּנוּ מֵחֲוִילָה עַד־שׁוּר אֲשֶׁר עַל־פְּנֵי מִצְרַיִם בֹּאֲכָה אַשּׁוּרָה עַל־פְּנֵי כָל־אֶחָיו נָפָל: פ

RECORDS

תולדת

19And these are the records of Isaac, son of Abraham: Abraham had fathered Isaac. 20And Isaac was forty years old when he took Rebekah, daughter of Bethuel, the Aramean, from Paddan Aram, sister of Laban, the Aramean, to him as a wife. 21And Isaac prayed to YHWH for his wife because she was infertile, and YHWH was prevailed upon by him, and his wife Rebekah became pregnant. 22And the children struggled inside her, and she said, "If it's like this, why do I exist?" And she went to inquire of YHWH.

23And YHWH said to her,

19וְאֵלֶּה תּוֹלְדֹת יִצְחָק בֶּן־אַבְרָהָם אַבְרָהָם הוֹלִיד אֶת־יִצְחָק: 20וַיְהִי יִצְחָק בֶּן־אַרְבָּעִים שָׁנָה בְּקַחְתּוֹ אֶת־רִבְקָה בַּת־בְּתוּאֵל הָאֲרַמִּי מִפַּדַּן אֲרָם אֲחוֹת לָבָן הָאֲרַמִּי לוֹ לְאִשָּׁה: 21וַיֶּעְתַּר יִצְחָק לַיהֹוָה לְנֹכַח אִשְׁתּוֹ כִּי עֲקָרָה הִוא וַיֵּעָתֶר לוֹ יְהֹוָה וַתַּהַר רִבְקָה אִשְׁתּוֹ: 22וַיִּתְרֹצֲצוּ הַבָּנִים בְּקִרְבָּהּ וַתֹּאמֶר אִם־כֵּן לָמָּה זֶּה אָנֹכִי וַתֵּלֶךְ לִדְרֹשׁ אֶת־יְהֹוָה: 23וַיֹּאמֶר יְהֹוָה לָהּ

25:18. He fell facing all of his brothers. Meaning: his family's places of residence were located among the territories of all their kindred peoples (presumably Israelites, Moabites, Ammonites, Edomites).

25:19. these are the records of Isaac. Isaac's life is different from his father Abraham's and his son Jacob's. Unlike them: He never leaves the promised land. He never fights. He has only one wife. His name is not changed. He is pictured going to meditate. He lives the longest. There are fewer stories about him. He is a relatively passive figure, acted on by his father and his wife and his son. Why is he different? Presumably because he has once lain on an altar as a sacrifice to God. Even though the sacrifice is not consummated, his life is now consecrated, and his life is distinct after this. The actions that parents take regarding their children impact on their children's lives ever after.

25:23. YHWH said to her. Rebekah hears the voice of God before Isaac does. (God first speaks to Isaac in the next chapter, 26:2.) In matters of revelation, man is not more important than woman. The *message* is what is important. Rebekah hears first because her *need* arises first. She is troubled because of the struggling twins in her womb.

Two nations are in your womb,
and two peoples will be dispersed from
   your insides,
and one people will be mightier than the
   other people,
and the older the younger will serve.

שְׁנֵי גוֹיִם֙ בְּבִטְנֵ֔ךְ וּשְׁנֵ֣י לְאֻמִּ֔ים מִמֵּעַ֖יִךְ יִפָּרֵ֑דוּ
וּלְאֹם֙ מִלְאֹ֣ם יֶֽאֱמָ֔ץ וְרַ֖ב יַעֲבֹ֥ד צָעִֽיר׃
²⁴וַיִּמְלְא֥וּ יָמֶ֛יהָ לָלֶ֖דֶת וְהִנֵּ֥ה תוֹמִ֖ם בְּבִטְנָֽהּ׃ ²⁵וַיֵּצֵ֤א
הָרִאשׁוֹן֙ אַדְמוֹנִ֔י כֻּלּ֖וֹ כְּאַדֶּ֣רֶת שֵׂעָ֑ר וַיִּקְרְא֥וּ שְׁמ֖וֹ
עֵשָֽׂו׃ ²⁶וְאַחֲרֵי־כֵ֞ן יָצָ֣א אָחִ֗יו וְיָד֤וֹ אֹחֶ֙זֶת֙ בַּעֲקֵ֣ב
עֵשָׂ֔ו וַיִּקְרָ֥א שְׁמ֖וֹ יַעֲקֹ֑ב וְיִצְחָ֛ק בֶּן־שִׁשִּׁ֥ים שָׁנָ֖ה
בְּלֶ֥דֶת אֹתָֽם׃ ²⁷וַֽיִּגְדְּלוּ֙ הַנְּעָרִ֔ים וַיְהִ֣י עֵשָׂ֗ו אִ֛ישׁ יֹדֵ֥עַ

ק גוֹיִם֙ 25:23

²⁴And her days to give birth were completed, and here were twins in her womb. ²⁵And the first came out all ruddy, like a hairy robe, and they called his name Esau. ²⁶And after that his brother came out, and his hand was holding Esau's heel, and he called his name Jacob. And Isaac was sixty years old at their birth.

²⁷And the boys grew up, and Esau was a man

25:23. the older the younger will serve. As I explained in *The Hidden Face of God*, people have usually taken this to mean that YHWH tells Rebekah that her younger son, Jacob, will dominate her older one, Esau. Some have thought, therefore, that Rebekah is not really manipulating the succession when she sends Jacob to pose as Esau. Rather, she is simply fulfilling God's will. The decision of who is number-one-son thus is still God's. However, this understanding is based on a misunderstanding of the subtle, exquisitely ambiguous biblical wording. The text does not in fact say that the elder son will serve the younger son. In biblical Hebrew, the subject may either precede or follow the verb, and the object likewise may either precede or follow the verb. What that means is that sometimes it is impossible to tell which word in a biblical verse is the subject and which is the object, especially if the verse is in poetry. That is the case in this oracle to Rebekah, which is in poetry. It can mean:

"the elder will serve the younger"

But it equally can mean:

"the elder, the younger will serve"

Like the Delphic oracles in Greece, this prediction contains two opposite meanings, and thus the person who receives it—Rebekah—can hear whatever she wants (consciously or subconsciously) to hear. It can be understood to mean that Jacob will serve Esau or that Esau will serve Jacob. I learned this from my senior colleague, David Noel Freedman.

25:27. Esau. Numerous attempts have been made to denigrate Esau in midrash and even in current biblical interpretation. It is not justified according to the text. The motive is understandable: Jacob's behavior in the matters of the birthright and the blessing is an embarrassment. Even small children express surprise at what this patriarch does to his brother—and his father. The Torah itself neither denigrates Esau nor justifies Jacob. On the contrary, one of the great qualities of the *Tanak* is precisely that

who knew hunting, a man of the field, and Jacob was a simple man, living in tents. 28And Isaac loved Esau because he put game meat in his mouth, and Rebekah loved Jacob.

29And Jacob made a stew, and Esau came from the field, and he was exhausted. 30And Esau said to Jacob, "Will you feed me some of the red stuff, this red stuff, because I'm exhausted." (On account of this he called his name "Edom.")

31And Jacob said, "Sell your birthright to me, today."

32And Esau said, "Here I'm going to die, and what use is this, that I have a birthright?"

33And Jacob said, "Swear to me, today."

And he swore to him and sold his birthright to Jacob. And Jacob gave bread and lentil stew to Esau. And he ate and drank and got up and went. And Esau disdained the birthright.

26 1And there was a famine in the land (other than the first famine, which was in Abraham's days), and Isaac went to Abimelek, king of the Philistines, at Gerar. 2And YHWH appeared to him and said, "Don't go down to Egypt. Reside in the land that I say to you. 3Stay on in this land, and I'll be with you and bless you, for I'll give all these lands to you and your seed, and I'll uphold the oath that I swore to Abraham your father, 4and I'll multiply your seed like the stars of the skies and give to your seed all these lands, and all the nations of the earth will be blessed through your seed 5because

צַיִד אִישׁ שָׂדֶה וְיַעֲקֹב אִישׁ תָּם יֹשֵׁב אֹהָלִים:
28וַיֶּאֱהַב יִצְחָק אֶת־עֵשָׂו כִּי־צַיִד בְּפִיו וְרִבְקָה
אֹהֶבֶת אֶת־יַעֲקֹב: 29וַיָּזֶד יַעֲקֹב נָזִיד וַיָּבֹא עֵשָׂו
מִן־הַשָּׂדֶה וְהוּא עָיֵף: 30וַיֹּאמֶר עֵשָׂו אֶל־יַעֲקֹב
הַלְעִיטֵנִי נָא מִן־הָאָדֹם הָאָדֹם הַזֶּה כִּי עָיֵף אָנֹכִי
עַל־כֵּן קָרָא־שְׁמוֹ אֱדוֹם: 31וַיֹּאמֶר יַעֲקֹב מִכְרָה
כַיּוֹם אֶת־בְּכֹרָתְךָ לִי: 32וַיֹּאמֶר עֵשָׂו הִנֵּה אָנֹכִי
הוֹלֵךְ לָמוּת וְלָמָּה־זֶּה לִי בְּכֹרָה: 33וַיֹּאמֶר יַעֲקֹב
הִשָּׁבְעָה לִּי כַּיּוֹם וַיִּשָּׁבַע לוֹ וַיִּמְכֹּר אֶת־בְּכֹרָתוֹ
לְיַעֲקֹב: 34וְיַעֲקֹב נָתַן לְעֵשָׂו לֶחֶם וּנְזִיד עֲדָשִׁים
וַיֹּאכַל וַיֵּשְׁתְּ וַיָּקָם וַיֵּלַךְ וַיִּבֶז עֵשָׂו אֶת־
הַבְּכֹרָה: ס

26 1וַיְהִי רָעָב בָּאָרֶץ מִלְּבַד הָרָעָב הָרִאשׁוֹן
אֲשֶׁר הָיָה בִּימֵי אַבְרָהָם וַיֵּלֶךְ יִצְחָק אֶל־אֲבִימֶלֶךְ
מֶלֶךְ־פְּלִשְׁתִּים גְּרָרָה: 2וַיֵּרָא אֵלָיו יְהֹוָה וַיֹּאמֶר
אַל־תֵּרֵד מִצְרָיְמָה שְׁכֹן בָּאָרֶץ אֲשֶׁר אֹמַר אֵלֶיךָ:
3גּוּר בָּאָרֶץ הַזֹּאת וְאֶהְיֶה עִמְּךָ וַאֲבָרֲכֶךָּ כִּי־לְךָ
וּלְזַרְעֲךָ אֶתֵּן אֶת־כָּל־הָאֲרָצֹת הָאֵל וַהֲקִמֹתִי אֶת־
הַשְּׁבֻעָה אֲשֶׁר נִשְׁבַּעְתִּי לְאַבְרָהָם אָבִיךָ: 4וְהִרְבֵּיתִי
אֶת־זַרְעֲךָ כְּכוֹכְבֵי הַשָּׁמַיִם וְנָתַתִּי לְזַרְעֲךָ אֵת כָּל־
הָאֲרָצֹת הָאֵל וְהִתְבָּרֲכוּ בְזַרְעֲךָ כֹּל גּוֹיֵי הָאָרֶץ:

none of its heroes is perfect. Moreover, Jacob suffers some corresponding recompense for every deception he commits, as do Laban, Rachel, Reuben, Simeon, Levi, Judah, and Joseph's other brothers. (See the relevant comments below.) The lesson, therefore, is not only that people are not perfect, but also that acts of deception can fester in a family, and that they have consequences. Those who try to excuse Jacob and turn Esau into a villain are unfortunately hiding these essential lessons of the Torah.

26:4. **all the nations of the earth will be blessed through your seed.** This prediction was made to Abraham in his first communication from God. It was repeated to him in Isaac's presence at the Aqedah. Now God gives the same message to Isaac himself. Now that Isaac has grown up and had children himself, the renewal of the message confirms that it is through his descendants that this is to occur.

Abraham listened to my voice and kept my watch, my commandments, my laws, and my instructions." 6And so Isaac lived in Gerar.

7And the people of the place asked about his wife, and he said, "She's my sister," because he was afraid to say, "My wife," or else "the people of the place will kill me for Rebekah, because she's good-looking." 8And it was when his days extended there: and Abimelek, king of the Philistines, gazed through the window, and he saw: and here was Isaac "fooling around" with Rebekah his wife!

9And Abimelek called Isaac and said, "But, here, she's your wife! And how could you say, 'She's my sister'?"

And Isaac said to him, "Because I said, 'Or else I'll die over her.' "

10And Abimelek said, "What is this you've done to us? One of the people nearly could have lain with your wife, and you would have brought guilt on us." 11And Abimelek commanded all the people saying, "He who touches this man or his wife will be put to *death!*"

12And Isaac planted seed in that land, and he harvested a hundredfold in that year. And YHWH blessed him, 13and the man became great, and he went on getting greater until he was very great 14and had livestock of flocks and livestock of herds and a large number of servants. And the Philistines envied him. 15And the Philistines stopped up all the wells that his father's servants had dug in his father Abraham's days, and they filled them with dirt. 16And Abimelek said to Isaac, "Go from among us, because you've become much mightier than we are." 17And Isaac went from there and camped in the wadi of

עֵ֗קֶב אֲשֶׁר־שָׁמַ֣ע אַבְרָהָ֖ם בְּקֹלִ֑י וַיִּשְׁמֹר֙ מִשְׁמַרְתִּ֔י מִצְוֺתַ֖י חֻקּוֹתַ֥י וְתוֹרֹתָֽי׃ 6וַיֵּ֥שֶׁב יִצְחָ֖ק בִּגְרָֽר׃

7וַֽיִּשְׁאֲל֞וּ אַנְשֵׁ֤י הַמָּקוֹם֙ לְאִשְׁתּ֔וֹ וַיֹּ֖אמֶר אֲחֹ֣תִי הִ֑וא כִּ֤י יָרֵא֙ לֵאמֹ֣ר אִשְׁתִּ֔י פֶּן־יַֽהַרְגֻ֜נִי אַנְשֵׁ֤י הַמָּקוֹם֙ עַל־רִבְקָ֔ה כִּֽי־טוֹבַ֥ת מַרְאֶ֖ה הִֽיא׃ 8וַֽיְהִ֗י כִּ֤י אָֽרְכוּ־ל֥וֹ שָׁם֙ הַיָּמִ֔ים וַיַּשְׁקֵ֗ף אֲבִימֶ֙לֶךְ֙ מֶ֣לֶךְ פְּלִשְׁתִּ֔ים בְּעַ֖ד הַֽחַלּ֑וֹן וַיַּ֗רְא וְהִנֵּ֤ה יִצְחָק֙ מְצַחֵ֔ק אֵ֖ת רִבְקָ֥ה אִשְׁתּֽוֹ׃ 9וַיִּקְרָ֨א אֲבִימֶ֜לֶךְ לְיִצְחָ֗ק וַיֹּ֙אמֶר֙ אַ֣ךְ הִנֵּ֤ה אִשְׁתְּךָ֙ הִ֔וא וְאֵ֥יךְ אָמַ֖רְתָּ אֲחֹ֣תִי הִ֑וא וַיֹּ֤אמֶר אֵלָיו֙ יִצְחָ֔ק כִּ֣י אָמַ֔רְתִּי פֶּן־אָמ֖וּת עָלֶֽיהָ׃ 10וַיֹּ֣אמֶר אֲבִימֶ֔לֶךְ מַה־זֹּ֖את עָשִׂ֣יתָ לָּ֑נוּ כִּ֠מְעַ֠ט שָׁכַ֞ב אַחַ֤ד הָעָם֙ אֶת־אִשְׁתֶּ֔ךָ וְהֵבֵאתָ֥ עָלֵ֖ינוּ אָשָֽׁם׃ 11וַיְצַ֤ו אֲבִימֶ֙לֶךְ֙ אֶת־כׇּל־הָעָ֖ם לֵאמֹ֑ר הַנֹּגֵ֜עַ בָּאִ֥ישׁ הַזֶּ֛ה וּבְאִשְׁתּ֖וֹ מ֥וֹת יוּמָֽת׃ 12וַיִּזְרַ֤ע יִצְחָק֙ בָּאָ֣רֶץ הַהִ֔וא וַיִּמְצָ֛א בַּשָּׁנָ֥ה הַהִ֖וא מֵאָ֣ה שְׁעָרִ֑ים וַֽיְבָרְכֵ֖הוּ יְהֹוָֽה׃ 13וַיִּגְדַּ֖ל הָאִ֑ישׁ וַיֵּ֤לֶךְ הָלוֹךְ֙ וְגָדֵ֔ל עַ֥ד כִּֽי־גָדַ֖ל מְאֹֽד׃ 14וַֽיְהִי־ל֤וֹ מִקְנֵה־צֹאן֙ וּמִקְנֵ֣ה בָקָ֔ר וַעֲבֻדָּ֖ה רַבָּ֑ה וַיְקַנְא֥וּ אֹת֖וֹ פְּלִשְׁתִּֽים׃ 15וְכׇל־הַבְּאֵרֹ֗ת אֲשֶׁ֤ר חָֽפְרוּ֙ עַבְדֵ֣י אָבִ֔יו בִּימֵ֖י אַבְרָהָ֣ם אָבִ֑יו סִתְּמ֣וּם פְּלִשְׁתִּ֔ים וַיְמַלְא֖וּם עָפָֽר׃ 16וַיֹּ֥אמֶר אֲבִימֶ֖לֶךְ אֶל־יִצְחָ֑ק לֵ֚ךְ מֵֽעִמָּ֔נוּ כִּֽי־עָצַ֥מְתָּֽ־מִמֶּ֖נּוּ מְאֹֽד׃ 17וַיֵּ֥לֶךְ מִשָּׁ֖ם יִצְחָ֑ק וַיִּ֥חַן בְּנַֽחַל־גְּרָ֖ר וַיֵּ֥שֶׁב שָֽׁם׃ 18וַיָּ֨שׇׁב

26:8. **fooling around.** Hebrew מצחק, a pun on the name Isaac.

26:12–13. **blessed him, and the man became great.** This should be read as one connected thought even though it has been broken into two verses. Compare Gen 24:34, where the servant says about Isaac's father Abraham, "YHWH has blessed my lord very much, and he has become great." The point appears to be that the becoming great is the expression of divine blessing.

Gerar and lived there. ¹⁸And Isaac went back and dug the water wells that they had dug in the days of his father Abraham and that the Philistines had stopped up after Abraham's death, and he called them by names, like the names that his father had called them. ¹⁹And Isaac's servants dug in the wadi and found a well of fresh water there. ²⁰And the shepherds of Gerar quarreled with Isaac's shepherds, saying, "The water is ours." And he called the name of the well Esek because they tangled with him. ²¹And they dug another well, and they quarreled over it also, and he called its name Sitnah. ²²And he moved on from there and dug another well, and they did not quarrel over it, and he called its name Rehovot and said, "Because now YHWH has widened for us, and we've been fruitful in the land."

²³And he went up from there to Beer-sheba. ²⁴And YHWH appeared to him that night and said, "I'm your father Abraham's God. Don't be afraid, because I'm with you, and I'll bless you and multiply your seed on account of Abraham, my servant." ²⁵And he built an altar there and invoked the name YHWH. And he pitched his tent there, and Isaac's servants dug a well there.

²⁶And Abimelek and Ahuzat, his companion, and Phicol, the commander of his army, went to him from Gerar. ²⁷And Isaac said to them, "Why have you come to me, since you hated me and sent me away from you?"

²⁸And they said, "We've *seen* that YHWH has been with you; and we say, 'Let there be an oath between us, between us and you, and let us make a covenant with you ²⁹that you won't do bad toward us as we haven't touched you and as we've done only good toward you and sent you away in peace. You are now blessed by YHWH.' " ³⁰And he made a feast for them, and they ate and drank. ³¹And they got up early in the morning and swore, each man to his brother, and Isaac sent them away, and they went from him in peace.

³²And it was in that day, and Isaac's servants came and told him about the well that they had

יִצְחָק וַיַּחְפֹּר ׀ אֶת־בְּאֵרֹת הַמַּיִם אֲשֶׁר חָפְרוּ בִּימֵי אַבְרָהָם אָבִיו וַיְסַתְּמוּם פְּלִשְׁתִּים אַחֲרֵי מוֹת אַבְרָהָם וַיִּקְרָא לָהֶן שֵׁמוֹת כַּשֵּׁמֹת אֲשֶׁר־קָרָא לָהֶן אָבִיו: ¹⁹וַיַּחְפְּרוּ עַבְדֵי־יִצְחָק בַּנָּחַל וַיִּמְצְאוּ־שָׁם בְּאֵר מַיִם חַיִּים: ²⁰וַיָּרִיבוּ רֹעֵי גְרָר עִם־רֹעֵי יִצְחָק לֵאמֹר לָנוּ הַמָּיִם וַיִּקְרָא שֵׁם־הַבְּאֵר עֵשֶׂק כִּי הִתְעַשְּׂקוּ עִמּוֹ: ²¹וַיַּחְפְּרוּ בְּאֵר אַחֶרֶת וַיָּרִיבוּ גַּם־עָלֶיהָ וַיִּקְרָא שְׁמָהּ שִׂטְנָה: ²²וַיַּעְתֵּק מִשָּׁם וַיַּחְפֹּר בְּאֵר אַחֶרֶת וְלֹא רָבוּ עָלֶיהָ וַיִּקְרָא שְׁמָהּ רְחֹבוֹת וַיֹּאמֶר כִּי־עַתָּה הִרְחִיב יְהוָה לָנוּ וּפָרִינוּ בָאָרֶץ: ²³וַיַּעַל מִשָּׁם בְּאֵר שָׁבַע: ²⁴וַיֵּרָא אֵלָיו יְהוָה בַּלַּיְלָה הַהוּא וַיֹּאמֶר אָנֹכִי אֱלֹהֵי אַבְרָהָם אָבִיךָ אַל־תִּירָא כִּי־אִתְּךָ אָנֹכִי וּבֵרַכְתִּיךָ וְהִרְבֵּיתִי אֶת־זַרְעֲךָ בַּעֲבוּר אַבְרָהָם עַבְדִּי: ²⁵וַיִּבֶן שָׁם מִזְבֵּחַ וַיִּקְרָא בְּשֵׁם יְהוָה וַיֶּט־שָׁם אָהֳלוֹ וַיִּכְרוּ־שָׁם עַבְדֵי־יִצְחָק בְּאֵר: ²⁶וַאֲבִימֶלֶךְ הָלַךְ אֵלָיו מִגְּרָר וַאֲחֻזַּת מֵרֵעֵהוּ וּפִיכֹל שַׂר־צְבָאוֹ: ²⁷וַיֹּאמֶר אֲלֵהֶם יִצְחָק מַדּוּעַ בָּאתֶם אֵלָי וְאַתֶּם שְׂנֵאתֶם אֹתִי וַתְּשַׁלְּחוּנִי מֵאִתְּכֶם: ²⁸וַיֹּאמְרוּ רָאוֹ רָאִינוּ כִּי־הָיָה יְהוָה ׀ עִמָּךְ וַנֹּאמֶר תְּהִי נָא אָלָה בֵּינוֹתֵינוּ בֵּינֵינוּ וּבֵינֶךָ וְנִכְרְתָה בְרִית עִמָּךְ: ²⁹אִם־תַּעֲשֵׂה עִמָּנוּ רָעָה כַּאֲשֶׁר לֹא נְגַעֲנוּךָ וְכַאֲשֶׁר עָשִׂינוּ עִמְּךָ רַק־טוֹב וַנְּשַׁלֵּחֲךָ בְּשָׁלוֹם אַתָּה עַתָּה בְּרוּךְ יְהוָה: ³⁰וַיַּעַשׂ לָהֶם מִשְׁתֶּה וַיֹּאכְלוּ וַיִּשְׁתּוּ: ³¹וַיַּשְׁכִּימוּ בַבֹּקֶר וַיִּשָּׁבְעוּ אִישׁ לְאָחִיו וַיְשַׁלְּחֵם יִצְחָק וַיֵּלְכוּ מֵאִתּוֹ בְּשָׁלוֹם: ³²וַיְהִי ׀ בַּיּוֹם הַהוּא וַיָּבֹאוּ עַבְדֵי יִצְחָק וַיַּגִּדוּ לוֹ עַל־אֹדוֹת הַבְּאֵר אֲשֶׁר חָפְרוּ

dug and said to him, "We found water." 33And he called it Seven. On account of this the name of the city is Beer-sheba to this day.

34And Esau was forty years old, and he took a wife: Judith, daughter of Beeri, the Hittite, and Basemath, daughter of Elon, the Hittite. 35And they were a bitterness of spirit to Isaac and to Rebekah.

27 1And it was when Isaac was old and his eyes were too dim for seeing: and he called Esau, his older son, and said to him, "My son."

And he said to him, "I'm here."

2And he said, "Here, I've become old. I don't know the day of my death. 3And now, take up your implements: your quiver and your bow, and go out to the field and hunt me some game 4and make me the kind of delicacies that I love and bring them to me and let me eat, so my soul will bless you before I die."

5And Rebekah was listening as Isaac was speaking to Esau, his son. And Esau went to the field to hunt game to bring. 6And Rebekah said to Jacob, her son, saying, "Here I've heard your father speaking to Esau, your brother, saying, 7'Bring me game and make me delicacies so I may eat, and I'll bless you in the presence of YHWH before my death.' 8And now, my son, listen to my voice, to what I'm commanding you. 9Go to the flock and take two good goat kids for me from there, and I'll make them the kind of delicacies that your father loves. 10And bring them to your father, and he'll eat, so he'll bless you before his death."

11And Jacob said to Rebekah, his mother, "Here, Esau, my brother, is a hairy man and I'm a smooth man. 12Maybe my father will feel me,

33וַיִּקְרָא אֹתָהּ שִׁבְעָה עַל־ כֵּן שֵׁם־הָעִיר בְּאֵר שֶׁבַע עַד הַיּוֹם הַזֶּה: ס 34וַיְהִי עֵשָׂו בֶּן־אַרְבָּעִים שָׁנָה וַיִּקַּח אִשָּׁה אֶת־יְהוּדִית בַּת־ בְּאֵרִי הַחִתִּי וְאֶת־בָּשְׂמַת בַּת־אֵילֹן הַחִתִּי: 35וַתִּהְיֶיןָ מֹרַת רוּחַ לְיִצְחָק וּלְרִבְקָה: ס

27 1וַיְהִי כִּי־זָקֵן יִצְחָק וַתִּכְהֶיןָ עֵינָיו מֵרְאֹת וַיִּקְרָא אֶת־עֵשָׂו ׀ בְּנוֹ הַגָּדֹל וַיֹּאמֶר אֵלָיו בְּנִי וַיֹּאמֶר אֵלָיו הִנֵּנִי: 2וַיֹּאמֶר הִנֵּה־נָא זָקַנְתִּי לֹא יָדַעְתִּי יוֹם מוֹתִי: 3וְעַתָּה שָׂא־נָא כֵלֶיךָ תֶּלְיְךָ וְקַשְׁתֶּךָ וְצֵא הַשָּׂדֶה וְצוּדָה לִּי צָיִד: 4וַעֲשֵׂה־לִי מַטְעַמִּים כַּאֲשֶׁר אָהַבְתִּי וְהָבִיאָה לִּי וְאֹכֵלָה בַּעֲבוּר תְּבָרֶכְךָ נַפְשִׁי בְּטֶרֶם אָמוּת: 5וְרִבְקָה שֹׁמַעַת בְּדַבֵּר יִצְחָק אֶל־עֵשָׂו בְּנוֹ וַיֵּלֶךְ עֵשָׂו הַשָּׂדֶה לָצוּד צַיִד לְהָבִיא: 6וְרִבְקָה אָמְרָה אֶל־ יַעֲקֹב בְּנָהּ לֵאמֹר הִנֵּה שָׁמַעְתִּי אֶת־אָבִיךָ מְדַבֵּר אֶל־עֵשָׂו אָחִיךָ לֵאמֹר: 7הָבִיאָה לִּי צַיִד וַעֲשֵׂה־לִי מַטְעַמִּים וְאֹכֵלָה וַאֲבָרֶכְכָה לִפְנֵי יְהוָה לִפְנֵי מוֹתִי: 8וְעַתָּה בְנִי שְׁמַע בְּקֹלִי לַאֲשֶׁר אֲנִי מְצַוָּה אֹתָךְ: 9לֶךְ־נָא אֶל־הַצֹּאן וְקַח־לִי מִשָּׁם שְׁנֵי גְּדָיֵי עִזִּים טֹבִים וְאֶעֱשֶׂה אֹתָם מַטְעַמִּים לְאָבִיךָ כַּאֲשֶׁר אָהֵב: 10וְהֵבֵאתָ לְאָבִיךָ וְאָכָל בַּעֲבֻר אֲשֶׁר יְבָרֶכְךָ לִפְנֵי מוֹתוֹ: 11וַיֹּאמֶר יַעֲקֹב אֶל־רִבְקָה אִמּוֹ הֵן עֵשָׂו אָחִי אִישׁ שָׂעִר וְאָנֹכִי אִישׁ חָלָק: 12אוּלַי יְמֻשֵּׁנִי אָבִי וְהָיִיתִי בְעֵינָיו כִּמְתַעְתֵּעַ וְהֵבֵאתִי עָלַי

27:3 צָיִד קְ:

27:5. **to bring.** The Septuagint reads "to bring *to his father*," translating
להביא לאביו. The second word appears to have been omitted from the Masoretic Text
by the scribe because of its similarity to the preceding word.

and I'll be like a trickster in his eyes, and I'll bring a curse on me and not a blessing."

13And his mother said to him, "Let your curse be on me, my son; just listen to my voice and go take them for me." 14And he went and took and brought them to his mother, and his mother made the kind of delicacies that his father loved. 15And Rebekah took the finest clothes of Esau, her older son, that were with her in the house and put them on Jacob, her younger son, 16and put the skins of the goat kids on his hands and on the smooth part of his neck. 17And she put the delicacies and the bread that she'd made in the hand of Jacob, her son. 18And he came to his father.

And he said, "My father."

And he said, "I'm here. Who are you, my son?"

19And Jacob said to his father, "I'm Esau, your firstborn. I did as you spoke to me. Get up, sit, and eat some of my game so your soul will bless me."

20And Isaac said to his son, "What's this? You were quick to find it, my son."

And he said, "Because YHWH your God made it happen for me."

21And Isaac said to Jacob, "Come over, and I'll feel you, my son: is this you, my son Esau, or not?" 22And Jacob came over to Isaac, his father, and he felt him. And he said, "The voice is the voice of Jacob, and the hands are the hands of Esau." 23And he did not recognize him because his hands were hairy like the hands of Esau, his brother, and he blessed him. 24And he said, "Is this you, my son Esau?"

And he said, "I am."

25And he said, "Bring it over to me and let me eat some of my son's game so that my soul will bless you. And he brought it over to him, and he ate; and he brought him wine, and he drank. 26And Isaac, his father, said to him, "Come over and kiss me, my son." 27And he came over and kissed him, and he smelled the aroma of his clothes and blessed him and said, "See, my son's aroma is like the aroma of a field that YHWH has

13וַתֹּ֤אמֶר לוֹ֙ אִמּ֔וֹ עָלַ֖י קִלְלָתְךָ֣ בְּנִ֑י אַ֛ךְ שְׁמַ֥ע בְּקֹלִ֖י וְלֵ֥ךְ קַֽח־לִֽי׃ 14וַיֵּ֙לֶךְ֙ וַיִּקַּ֔ח וַיָּבֵ֖א לְאִמּ֑וֹ וַתַּ֤עַשׂ אִמּוֹ֙ מַטְעַמִּ֔ים כַּאֲשֶׁ֖ר אָהֵ֥ב אָבִֽיו׃ 15וַתִּקַּ֣ח רִ֠בְקָה אֶת־בִּגְדֵ֨י עֵשָׂ֜ו בְּנָ֤הּ הַגָּדֹל֙ הַחֲמֻדֹ֔ת אֲשֶׁ֥ר אִתָּ֖הּ בַּבָּ֑יִת וַתַּלְבֵּ֥שׁ אֶֽת־יַעֲקֹ֖ב בְּנָ֥הּ הַקָּטָֽן׃ 16וְאֵ֗ת עֹרֹת֙ גְּדָיֵ֣י הָֽעִזִּ֔ים הִלְבִּ֖ישָׁה עַל־יָדָ֑יו וְעַ֖ל חֶלְקַ֥ת צַוָּארָֽיו׃ 17וַתִּתֵּ֧ן אֶת־הַמַּטְעַמִּ֛ים וְאֶת־הַלֶּ֖חֶם אֲשֶׁ֣ר עָשָׂ֑תָה בְּיַ֖ד יַעֲקֹ֥ב בְּנָֽהּ׃ 18וַיָּבֹ֥א אֶל־אָבִ֖יו וַיֹּ֣אמֶר אָבִ֑י וַיֹּ֣אמֶר הִנֶּ֔נִּי מִ֥י אַתָּ֖ה בְּנִֽי׃ 19וַיֹּ֨אמֶר יַעֲקֹ֜ב אֶל־אָבִ֗יו אָנֹכִי֙ עֵשָׂ֣ו בְּכֹרֶ֔ךָ עָשִׂ֕יתִי כַּאֲשֶׁ֥ר דִּבַּ֖רְתָּ אֵלָ֑י קֽוּם־נָ֣א שְׁבָ֗ה וְאָכְלָה֙ מִצֵּידִ֔י בַּעֲב֖וּר תְּבָרֲכַ֥נִּי נַפְשֶֽׁךָ׃ 20וַיֹּ֤אמֶר יִצְחָק֙ אֶל־בְּנ֔וֹ מַה־זֶּ֛ה מִהַ֥רְתָּ לִמְצֹ֖א בְּנִ֑י וַיֹּ֕אמֶר כִּ֥י הִקְרָ֛ה יְהוָ֥ה אֱלֹהֶ֖יךָ לְפָנָֽי׃ 21וַיֹּ֤אמֶר יִצְחָק֙ אֶֽל־יַעֲקֹ֔ב גְּשָׁה־נָּ֥א וַאֲמֻֽשְׁךָ֖ בְּנִ֑י הַֽאַתָּ֥ה זֶ֛ה בְּנִ֥י עֵשָׂ֖ו אִם־לֹֽא׃ 22וַיִּגַּ֧שׁ יַעֲקֹ֛ב אֶל־יִצְחָ֥ק אָבִ֖יו וַיְמֻשֵּׁ֑הוּ וַיֹּ֗אמֶר הַקֹּל֙ ק֣וֹל יַעֲקֹ֔ב וְהַיָּדַ֖יִם יְדֵ֥י עֵשָֽׂו׃ 23וְלֹ֣א הִכִּיר֔וֹ כִּֽי־הָי֣וּ יָדָ֗יו כִּידֵ֛י עֵשָׂ֥ו אָחִ֖יו שְׂעִרֹ֑ת וַֽיְבָרֲכֵֽהוּ׃ 24וַיֹּ֕אמֶר אַתָּ֥ה זֶ֖ה בְּנִ֣י עֵשָׂ֑ו וַיֹּ֖אמֶר אָֽנִי׃ 25וַיֹּ֗אמֶר הַגִּ֤שָׁה לִּי֙ וְאֹֽכְלָה֙ מִצֵּ֣יד בְּנִ֔י לְמַ֥עַן תְּבָֽרֶכְךָ֖ נַפְשִׁ֑י וַיַּגֶּשׁ־לוֹ֙ וַיֹּאכַ֔ל וַיָּ֧בֵא ל֦וֹ יַ֖יִן וַיֵּֽשְׁתְּ׃ 26וַיֹּ֥אמֶר אֵלָ֖יו יִצְחָ֣ק אָבִ֑יו גְּשָׁה־נָּ֥א וּשְׁקָה־לִּ֖י בְּנִֽי׃ 27וַיִּגַּשׁ֙ וַיִּשַּׁק־ל֔וֹ וַיָּ֛רַח אֶת־רֵ֥יחַ בְּגָדָ֖יו וַֽיְבָרֲכֵ֑הוּ וַיֹּ֗אמֶר

רְאֵה֙ רֵ֣יחַ בְּנִ֔י כְּרֵ֣יחַ שָׂדֶ֔ה אֲשֶׁ֥ר בֵּרֲכ֖וֹ יְהוָֽה׃

blessed. 28And may God give you from the dew of the skies and from the fat of the earth and much grain and wine. 29May peoples serve you and nations bow to you. Be your brothers' superior, and may your mother's sons bow to you. May those who curse you be cursed and those who bless you be blessed."

30And it was as Isaac finished blessing Jacob, and it was: Jacob had *just gone out* from the presence of Isaac, his father!—and Esau, his brother, came from his hunting. 31And he, too, had made delicacies and brought them to his father. And he said to his father, "Let my father get up and eat some of his son's game so you yourself will bless me."

32And Isaac, his father, said to him, "Who are you?"

And he said, "I'm your son, your firstborn, Esau."

33And Isaac trembled—a very big trembling. And he said, "Who then is the one who hunted game and brought it to me, and I ate some of it all before you came, and I blessed him? He will in fact be blessed."

34When Esau heard his father's words he cried—a very big and bitter cry. And he said to his father, "Bless me, also me, my father."

35And he said, "Your brother came with deception, and he took your blessing."

36And he said, "Was his name really called

וְיִתֶּן־לְךָ֙ הָאֱלֹהִ֔ים מִטַּל֙ הַשָּׁמַ֔יִם 28
וּמִשְׁמַנֵּ֖י הָאָ֑רֶץ
וְרֹ֥ב דָּגָ֖ן וְתִירֹֽשׁ׃
יַֽעַבְד֣וּךָ עַמִּ֗ים וְיִֽשְׁתַּחֲו֤וּ לְךָ֙ לְאֻמִּ֔ים 29
הֱוֵ֤ה גְבִיר֙ לְאַחֶ֔יךָ וְיִשְׁתַּחֲו֥וּ לְךָ֖ בְּנֵ֣י אִמֶּ֑ךָ
אֹרְרֶ֣יךָ אָר֔וּר וּֽמְבָרֲכֶ֖יךָ בָּרֽוּךְ׃
וַיְהִ֗י כַּֽאֲשֶׁ֨ר כִּלָּ֣ה יִצְחָק֮ לְבָרֵ֣ךְ אֶֽת־יַעֲקֹב֒ וַיְהִ֗י 30
אַ֣ךְ יָצֹ֤א יָצָא֙ יַעֲקֹ֔ב מֵאֵ֥ת פְּנֵ֖י יִצְחָ֣ק אָבִ֑יו וְעֵשָׂ֣ו
אָחִ֔יו בָּ֖א מִצֵּידֽוֹ׃ וַיַּ֤עַשׂ גַּם־הוּא֙ מַטְעַמִּ֔ים וַיָּבֵ֖א 31
לְאָבִ֑יו וַיֹּ֣אמֶר לְאָבִ֗יו יָקֻ֤ם אָבִי֙ וְיֹאכַל֙ מִצֵּ֣יד בְּנ֔וֹ
בַּעֲב֖וּר תְּבָרֲכַ֥נִּי נַפְשֶֽׁךָ׃ וַיֹּ֥אמֶר ל֛וֹ יִצְחָ֥ק אָבִ֖יו 32
מִי־אָ֑תָּה וַיֹּ֕אמֶר אֲנִ֛י בִּנְךָ֥ בְכֹרְךָ֖ עֵשָֽׂו׃ וַיֶּחֱרַ֨ד 33
יִצְחָ֣ק חֲרָדָה֮ גְּדֹלָ֣ה עַד־מְאֹד֒ וַיֹּ֡אמֶר מִֽי־אֵפ֡וֹא
ה֣וּא הַצָּֽד־צַ֩יִד֩ וַיָּ֨בֵא לִ֜י וָאֹכַ֥ל מִכֹּ֛ל בְּטֶ֥רֶם תָּב֖וֹא
וָאֲבָרֲכֵ֑הוּ גַּם־בָּר֖וּךְ יִהְיֶֽה׃ כִּשְׁמֹ֤עַ עֵשָׂו֙ אֶת־דִּבְרֵ֣י 34
אָבִ֔יו וַיִּצְעַ֣ק צְעָקָ֔ה גְּדֹלָ֥ה וּמָרָ֖ה עַד־מְאֹ֑ד וַיֹּ֣אמֶר
לְאָבִ֔יו בָּרֲכֵ֥נִי גַם־אָ֖נִי אָבִֽי׃ וַיֹּ֕אמֶר בָּ֥א אָחִ֖יךָ 35
בְּמִרְמָ֑ה וַיִּקַּ֖ח בִּרְכָתֶֽךָ׃ וַיֹּ֗אמֶר הֲכִי֩ קָרָ֨א שְׁמ֜וֹ 36

27:29 קְ וְיִשְׁתַּחֲווּ

27:28,39. **from.** David Noel Freedman notes that there is play on words here, as the blessings of the two sons hinge on the term *min*. In the blessing given to Jacob he is promised access to and a rich share of the rain and the dew, with *min* being used partitively. In Esau's blessing it is used spatially to mean that Esau will be denied access to fertile lands and the fruits of the soil. So what was a blessing for Jacob becomes in effect a kind of curse for Esau, and the words are practically identical.

27:33–34. **a very big trembling . . . a very big and bitter cry.** The sensitivity that is shown here for the feelings of Isaac and of Esau indicates how wrong it is to try to excuse Jacob and sully Esau in our interpretations. The text reveals that Rebekah's plan and Jacob's actions have caused a deep hurt. Rather than excuse them, the story will show how these things are resolved later through maturing and forgiveness.

Jacob! And he's usurped me two times now. He's taken my birthright, and, here, now he's taken my blessing." And he said, "Haven't you saved a blessing for me?"

37And Isaac answered, and he said to Esau, "Here I've made him your superior, and I've given all his brothers as servants, and I've endowed him with grain and wine. And for you: where, what, will I do, my son?"

38And Esau said to his father, "Is it one blessing that you have, my father? Bless me, also me, my father." And Esau raised his voice and wept.

39And Isaac, his father, answered, and he said to him, "Here, away from the fat of the earth will be your home, and from the dew of the skies from above. 40And you'll live by your sword. And you'll serve your brother. And it will be that when you get dominion you'll break his yoke from your neck."

41And Esau despised Jacob because of the blessing with which his father blessed him, and Esau said in his heart, "The days of mourning for my father will be soon, and then I'll kill Jacob, my brother."

42And the words of Esau, her older son, were told to Rebekah, and she sent and called to Jacob, her younger son, and said to him, "Here, Esau, your brother, consoles himself regarding you with the idea of killing you. 43And now, my son, listen to my voice and get up, flee to Laban, my brother, at Haran 44and live with him for a number of days until your brother's fury will turn back, 45until your brother's anger turns back from you and he forgets what you did to him. And I'll send and take you from there. Why

יַעֲקֹב וַיַּעְקְבֵנִי זֶה פַעֲמַיִם אֶת־בְּכֹרָתִי לָקָח וְהִנֵּה
עַתָּה לָקַח בִּרְכָתִי וַיֹּאמַר הֲלֹא־אָצַלְתָּ לִּי בְּרָכָה:
37וַיַּעַן יִצְחָק וַיֹּאמֶר לְעֵשָׂו הֵן גְּבִיר שַׂמְתִּיו לָךְ
וְאֶת־כָּל־אֶחָיו נָתַתִּי לוֹ לַעֲבָדִים וְדָגָן וְתִירֹשׁ
סְמַכְתִּיו וּלְכָה אֵפוֹא מָה אֶעֱשֶׂה בְּנִי: 38וַיֹּאמֶר
עֵשָׂו אֶל־אָבִיו הַבְרָכָה אַחַת הִוא־לְךָ אָבִי בָּרֲכֵנִי
גַם־אָנִי אָבִי וַיִּשָּׂא עֵשָׂו קֹלוֹ וַיֵּבְךְּ: 39וַיַּעַן יִצְחָק
אָבִיו וַיֹּאמֶר אֵלָיו

הִנֵּה מִשְׁמַנֵּי הָאָרֶץ יִהְיֶה מוֹשָׁבֶךָ וּמִטַּל הַשָּׁמַיִם
מֵעָל:

40וְעַל־חַרְבְּךָ תִחְיֶה וְאֶת־אָחִיךָ תַּעֲבֹד
וְהָיָה כַּאֲשֶׁר תָּרִיד וּפָרַקְתָּ עֻלּוֹ מֵעַל צַוָּארֶךָ:
41וַיִּשְׂטֹם עֵשָׂו אֶת־יַעֲקֹב עַל־הַבְּרָכָה אֲשֶׁר בֵּרְכוֹ
אָבִיו וַיֹּאמֶר עֵשָׂו בְּלִבּוֹ יִקְרְבוּ יְמֵי אֵבֶל אָבִי
וְאַהַרְגָה אֶת־יַעֲקֹב אָחִי: 42וַיֻּגַּד לְרִבְקָה אֶת־דִּבְרֵי
עֵשָׂו בְּנָהּ הַגָּדֹל וַתִּשְׁלַח וַתִּקְרָא לְיַעֲקֹב בְּנָהּ
הַקָּטָן וַתֹּאמֶר אֵלָיו הִנֵּה עֵשָׂו אָחִיךָ מִתְנַחֵם לְךָ
לְהָרְגֶךָ: 43וְעַתָּה בְנִי שְׁמַע בְּקֹלִי וְקוּם בְּרַח־לְךָ
אֶל־לָבָן אָחִי חָרָנָה: 44וְיָשַׁבְתָּ עִמּוֹ יָמִים אֲחָדִים
עַד אֲשֶׁר־תָּשׁוּב חֲמַת אָחִיךָ: 45עַד־שׁוּב אַף־אָחִיךָ
מִמְּךָ וְשָׁכַח אֵת אֲשֶׁר־עָשִׂיתָ לּוֹ וְשָׁלַחְתִּי וּלְקַחְתִּיךָ

27:36. **Jacob! And he's usurped me**. Esau makes a new play on the name Jacob, which was derived previously from the word for "heel" (Gen 25:26). Now he derives it from a word meaning "to usurp" or "to catch."

27:40. **when you get dominion**. This refers to the distant future, when Jacob's descendants, Israel, will dominate Esau's descendants, Edom, for a time, after which Edom will become independent. See Num 24:18–19, which speaks of Israel's dominion over Edom. King David conquers Edom, which remains under Judean control until the reign of Jehoram, when Edom breaks free.

should I be bereaved of the two of you as well in one day?"

46And Rebekah said to Isaac, "I'm disgusted with my life because of the daughters of Heth! If Jacob takes a wife from the daughters of Heth like these daughters of the land, why do I have a life!"

28 1And Isaac called Jacob, and he blessed him and commanded him, and he said to him, "You shall not take a wife from the daughters of Canaan. 2Get up. Go to Paddan Aram, to the house of Bethuel, your mother's father, and take a wife from there, from the daughters of Laban, your mother's brother. 3And may El Shadday bless you and make you fruitful and multiply you, so you'll become a community of peoples, 4and may He give you the blessing of Abraham, to you and to your seed with you, for you to possess the land of your residences, which God gave to Abraham." 5And Isaac sent Jacob, and he went to Paddan Aram, to Laban, son of Bethuel, the Aramean, brother of Rebekah, mother of Jacob and Esau.

6And Esau saw that Isaac had blessed Jacob and sent him to Paddan Aram to take a wife for himself from there when he blessed him, and he had commanded him, saying, "You shall not take a wife from the daughters of Canaan," 7and Jacob had listened to his father and to his mother and had gone to Paddan Aram. 8And Esau saw that the daughters of Canaan were bad in his father Isaac's eyes. 9And Esau went to Ishmael and took Mahalath, daughter of Ishmael, son of Abraham, sister of Nebaioth, in addition to his wives as a wife for him.

AND HE LEFT

10And Jacob left Beer-sheba and went to Haran. 11And he happened upon a place and

מִשָּׁם לָמָה אֶשְׁכַּל גַּם־שְׁנֵיכֶם יוֹם אֶחָד:
46וַתֹּאמֶר רִבְקָה אֶל־יִצְחָק קַצְתִּי בְחַיַּי מִפְּנֵי
בְּנוֹת חֵת אִם־לֹקֵחַ יַעֲקֹב אִשָּׁה מִבְּנוֹת־חֵת כָּאֵלֶּה
מִבְּנוֹת הָאָרֶץ לָמָּה לִּי חַיִּים: 28 1וַיִּקְרָא יִצְחָק
אֶל־יַעֲקֹב וַיְבָרֶךְ אֹתוֹ וַיְצַוֵּהוּ וַיֹּאמֶר לוֹ לֹא־תִקַּח
אִשָּׁה מִבְּנוֹת כְּנָעַן: 2קוּם לֵךְ פַּדֶּנָה אֲרָם בֵּיתָה
בְתוּאֵל אֲבִי אִמֶּךָ וְקַח־לְךָ מִשָּׁם אִשָּׁה מִבְּנוֹת לָבָן
אֲחִי אִמֶּךָ: 3וְאֵל שַׁדַּי יְבָרֵךְ אֹתְךָ וְיַפְרְךָ וְיַרְבֶּךָ
וְהָיִיתָ לִקְהַל עַמִּים: 4וְיִתֶּן־לְךָ אֶת־בִּרְכַּת אַבְרָהָם
לְךָ וּלְזַרְעֲךָ אִתָּךְ לְרִשְׁתְּךָ אֶת־אֶרֶץ מְגֻרֶיךָ אֲשֶׁר־
נָתַן אֱלֹהִים לְאַבְרָהָם: 5וַיִּשְׁלַח יִצְחָק אֶת־יַעֲקֹב
וַיֵּלֶךְ פַּדֶּנָה אֲרָם אֶל־לָבָן בֶּן־בְּתוּאֵל הָאֲרַמִּי אֲחִי
רִבְקָה אֵם יַעֲקֹב וְעֵשָׂו: 6וַיַּרְא עֵשָׂו כִּי־בֵרַךְ
יִצְחָק אֶת־יַעֲקֹב וְשִׁלַּח אֹתוֹ פַּדֶּנָה אֲרָם לָקַחַת־לוֹ
מִשָּׁם אִשָּׁה בְּבָרֲכוֹ אֹתוֹ וַיְצַו עָלָיו לֵאמֹר לֹא־
תִקַּח אִשָּׁה מִבְּנוֹת כְּנָעַן: 7וַיִּשְׁמַע יַעֲקֹב אֶל־אָבִיו
וְאֶל־אִמּוֹ וַיֵּלֶךְ פַּדֶּנָה אֲרָם: 8וַיַּרְא עֵשָׂו כִּי רָעוֹת
בְּנוֹת כְּנָעַן בְּעֵינֵי יִצְחָק אָבִיו: 9וַיֵּלֶךְ עֵשָׂו אֶל־
יִשְׁמָעֵאל וַיִּקַּח אֶת־מָחֲלַת ׀ בַּת־יִשְׁמָעֵאל בֶּן־
אַבְרָהָם אֲחוֹת נְבָיוֹת עַל־נָשָׁיו לוֹ לְאִשָּׁה: ס

וַיֵּצֵא

10וַיֵּצֵא יַעֲקֹב מִבְּאֵר שָׁבַע וַיֵּלֶךְ חָרָנָה: 11וַיִּפְגַּע

28:6. **sent.** Reading the verb as Hebrew *Qal* ("and he sent him") as in v. 5, rather than as *Piel* ("and he let him go") with the MT.

stayed the night there because the sun was setting. And he took from the stones of the place and set it as his headrest and lay down in that place. 12And he dreamed. And here was a ladder, set up on the earth, and its top reaching to the skies. And here were angels of God, going up and going down by it. 13And here was YHWH standing over him, and He said, "I am YHWH, your father Abraham's God and Isaac's God. The land on which you're lying: I'll give it to you and to your seed. 14And your seed will be like the dust of the earth, and you'll expand to the west and east and north and south, and all the families on the earth will be blessed through you and through your seed. 15And here I am with you, and I'll watch over you everywhere that you'll go, and I'll bring you back to this land, for I won't leave you until I've done what I've spoken to you."

16And Jacob woke from his sleep and said, "YHWH is actually in this place, and I didn't know!" 17And he was afraid, and he said, "How awesome this place is! This is none other than God's house, and this is the gate of the skies!" 18And Jacob got up early in the morning and took the stone that he had set as his headrest and set it as a pillar and poured oil on its top. 19And he called that place's name Beth-El, though in fact Luz was the name of the city at first. 20And Jacob made a vow, saying, "If God will be with me and watch over me in this way that I'm going and give me bread to eat and clothing to wear, 21and I come back in peace to my father's house, then YHWH will become my God, 22and this stone that I set as a pillar will be God's house, and everything that you'll give me I'll *tithe* to you."

בַּמָּקוֹם וַיָּלֶן שָׁם כִּי־בָא הַשֶּׁמֶשׁ וַיִּקַּח מֵאַבְנֵי הַמָּקוֹם וַיָּשֶׂם מְרַאֲשֹׁתָיו וַיִּשְׁכַּב בַּמָּקוֹם הַהוּא: 12וַיַּחֲלֹם וְהִנֵּה סֻלָּם מֻצָּב אַרְצָה וְרֹאשׁוֹ מַגִּיעַ הַשָּׁמָיְמָה וְהִנֵּה מַלְאֲכֵי אֱלֹהִים עֹלִים וְיֹרְדִים בּוֹ: 13וְהִנֵּה יְהוָה נִצָּב עָלָיו וַיֹּאמַר אֲנִי יְהוָה אֱלֹהֵי אַבְרָהָם אָבִיךָ וֵאלֹהֵי יִצְחָק הָאָרֶץ אֲשֶׁר אַתָּה שֹׁכֵב עָלֶיהָ לְךָ אֶתְּנֶנָּה וּלְזַרְעֶךָ: 14וְהָיָה זַרְעֲךָ כַּעֲפַר הָאָרֶץ וּפָרַצְתָּ יָמָּה וָקֵדְמָה וְצָפֹנָה וָנֶגְבָּה וְנִבְרְכוּ בְךָ כָּל־מִשְׁפְּחֹת הָאֲדָמָה וּבְזַרְעֶךָ: 15וְהִנֵּה אָנֹכִי עִמָּךְ וּשְׁמַרְתִּיךָ בְּכֹל אֲשֶׁר־תֵּלֵךְ וַהֲשִׁבֹתִיךָ אֶל־הָאֲדָמָה הַזֹּאת כִּי לֹא אֶעֱזָבְךָ עַד אֲשֶׁר אִם־עָשִׂיתִי אֵת אֲשֶׁר־דִּבַּרְתִּי לָךְ: 16וַיִּיקַץ יַעֲקֹב מִשְּׁנָתוֹ וַיֹּאמֶר אָכֵן יֵשׁ יְהוָה בַּמָּקוֹם הַזֶּה וְאָנֹכִי לֹא יָדָעְתִּי: 17וַיִּירָא וַיֹּאמַר מַה־נּוֹרָא הַמָּקוֹם הַזֶּה אֵין זֶה כִּי אִם־בֵּית אֱלֹהִים וְזֶה שַׁעַר הַשָּׁמָיִם: 18וַיַּשְׁכֵּם יַעֲקֹב בַּבֹּקֶר וַיִּקַּח אֶת־הָאֶבֶן אֲשֶׁר־שָׂם מְרַאֲשֹׁתָיו וַיָּשֶׂם אֹתָהּ מַצֵּבָה וַיִּצֹק שֶׁמֶן עַל־רֹאשָׁהּ: 19וַיִּקְרָא אֶת־שֵׁם־הַמָּקוֹם הַהוּא בֵּית־אֵל וְאוּלָם לוּז שֵׁם־הָעִיר לָרִאשֹׁנָה: 20וַיִּדַּר יַעֲקֹב נֶדֶר לֵאמֹר אִם־יִהְיֶה אֱלֹהִים עִמָּדִי וּשְׁמָרַנִי בַּדֶּרֶךְ הַזֶּה אֲשֶׁר אָנֹכִי הוֹלֵךְ וְנָתַן־לִי לֶחֶם לֶאֱכֹל וּבֶגֶד לִלְבֹּשׁ: 21וְשַׁבְתִּי בְשָׁלוֹם אֶל־בֵּית אָבִי וְהָיָה יְהוָה לִי לֵאלֹהִים: 22וְהָאֶבֶן הַזֹּאת אֲשֶׁר־שַׂמְתִּי מַצֵּבָה יִהְיֶה בֵּית אֱלֹהִים וְכֹל אֲשֶׁר תִּתֶּן־לִי עַשֵּׂר אֲעַשְּׂרֶנּוּ לָךְ:

28:14. **all the families on the earth.** The prediction that God made to Abraham and Isaac that all humankind will be blessed through them is now repeated to Jacob as well. The confirmation of this prediction to each of the three patriarchs individually highlights its tremendous importance.

29 ¹And Jacob lifted his feet and went to the land of the people of the east. ²And he looked, and here was a well in the field, and here were three flocks of sheep lying by it, because they watered the flocks from that well, and the stone on the mouth of the well was big, ³and all the flocks would be gathered there, and they would roll the stone from the mouth of the well and would water the sheep and then would put the stone back in its place on the mouth of the well. ⁴And Jacob said to them, "My brothers, where are you from?"

And they said, "We're from Haran."

⁵And he said to them, "Do you know Laban, son of Nahor?"

And they said, "We know."

⁶And he said to them, "Is he well?"

And they said, "Well. And here's Rachel, his daughter, coming with the sheep."

⁷And he said, "Here, it will still be daytime for a long time, not the time for gathering the livestock. Water the sheep and go, pasture them."

⁸And they said, "We can't until all the flocks will be gathered and they'll roll the stone from the mouth of the well, and then we'll water the sheep."

⁹He was still speaking with them, and Rachel came with her father's sheep, because she was a shepherdess. ¹⁰And it was when Jacob saw Rachel, daughter of Laban, his mother's brother, and the sheep of Laban, his mother's brother: and he went over and rolled the stone from the mouth of the well and watered the sheep of Laban, his mother's brother. ¹¹And Jacob kissed Rachel and raised his voice and wept. ¹²And Jacob told Rachel that he was her father's kin and that he was Rebekah's son, and she ran and told her father. ¹³And it was, when Laban heard the news of Jacob, his sister's son, that he ran to him and embraced him and kissed him and brought him to his house. And he told Laban all these things. ¹⁴And Laban said to him, "You are indeed my bone and my flesh." And he stayed with him a month. ¹⁵And Laban said to Jacob, "Is it right

29 ¹וַיִּשָּׂא יַעֲקֹב רַגְלָיו וַיֵּלֶךְ אַרְצָה בְנֵי־קֶדֶם: ²וַיַּרְא וְהִנֵּה בְאֵר בַּשָּׂדֶה וְהִנֵּה־שָׁם שְׁלֹשָׁה עֶדְרֵי־צֹאן רֹבְצִים עָלֶיהָ כִּי מִן־הַבְּאֵר הַהִוא יַשְׁקוּ הָעֲדָרִים וְהָאֶבֶן גְּדֹלָה עַל־פִּי הַבְּאֵר: ³וְנֶאֶסְפוּ־שָׁמָּה כָל־הָעֲדָרִים וְגָלֲלוּ אֶת־הָאֶבֶן מֵעַל פִּי הַבְּאֵר וְהִשְׁקוּ אֶת־הַצֹּאן וְהֵשִׁיבוּ אֶת־הָאֶבֶן עַל־פִּי הַבְּאֵר לִמְקֹמָהּ: ⁴וַיֹּאמֶר לָהֶם יַעֲקֹב אַחַי מֵאַיִן אַתֶּם וַיֹּאמְרוּ מֵחָרָן אֲנָחְנוּ: ⁵וַיֹּאמֶר לָהֶם הַיְדַעְתֶּם אֶת־לָבָן בֶּן־נָחוֹר וַיֹּאמְרוּ יָדָעְנוּ: ⁶וַיֹּאמֶר לָהֶם הֲשָׁלוֹם לוֹ וַיֹּאמְרוּ שָׁלוֹם וְהִנֵּה רָחֵל בִּתּוֹ בָּאָה עִם־הַצֹּאן: ⁷וַיֹּאמֶר הֵן עוֹד הַיּוֹם גָּדוֹל לֹא־עֵת הֵאָסֵף הַמִּקְנֶה הַשְׁקוּ הַצֹּאן וּלְכוּ רְעוּ: ⁸וַיֹּאמְרוּ לֹא נוּכַל עַד אֲשֶׁר יֵאָסְפוּ כָּל־הָעֲדָרִים וְגָלֲלוּ אֶת־הָאֶבֶן מֵעַל פִּי הַבְּאֵר וְהִשְׁקִינוּ הַצֹּאן: ⁹עוֹדֶנּוּ מְדַבֵּר עִמָּם וְרָחֵל ׀ בָּאָה עִם־הַצֹּאן אֲשֶׁר לְאָבִיהָ כִּי רֹעָה הִוא: ¹⁰וַיְהִי כַּאֲשֶׁר רָאָה יַעֲקֹב אֶת־רָחֵל בַּת־לָבָן אֲחִי אִמּוֹ וְאֶת־צֹאן לָבָן אֲחִי אִמּוֹ וַיִּגַּשׁ יַעֲקֹב וַיָּגֶל אֶת־הָאֶבֶן מֵעַל פִּי הַבְּאֵר וַיַּשְׁקְ אֶת־צֹאן לָבָן אֲחִי אִמּוֹ: ¹¹וַיִּשַּׁק יַעֲקֹב לְרָחֵל וַיִּשָּׂא אֶת־קֹלוֹ וַיֵּבְךְּ: ¹²וַיַּגֵּד יַעֲקֹב לְרָחֵל כִּי אֲחִי אָבִיהָ הוּא וְכִי בֶן־רִבְקָה הוּא וַתָּרָץ וַתַּגֵּד לְאָבִיהָ: ¹³וַיְהִי כִשְׁמֹעַ לָבָן אֶת־שֵׁמַע ׀ יַעֲקֹב בֶּן־אֲחֹתוֹ וַיָּרָץ לִקְרָאתוֹ וַיְחַבֶּק־לוֹ וַיְנַשֶּׁק־לוֹ וַיְבִיאֵהוּ אֶל־בֵּיתוֹ וַיְסַפֵּר לְלָבָן אֵת כָּל־הַדְּבָרִים הָאֵלֶּה: ¹⁴וַיֹּאמֶר לוֹ לָבָן אַךְ עַצְמִי וּבְשָׂרִי אָתָּה וַיֵּשֶׁב עִמּוֹ חֹדֶשׁ יָמִים: ¹⁵וַיֹּאמֶר לָבָן לְיַעֲקֹב הֲכִי־אָחִי אַתָּה

because you're my brother that you should work for me for free? Tell me what your pay should be." 16And Laban had two daughters. The older one's name was Leah, and the younger one's name was Rachel. 17And Leah's eyes were tender, and Rachel had an attractive figure and was beautiful. 18And Jacob loved Rachel.

And he said, "I'll work for you seven years for Rachel, your younger daughter."

19And Laban said, "Better for me to give her to you than for me to give her to another man. Live with me."

20And Jacob worked seven years for Rachel, and they were like a few days in his eyes because of his loving her. 21And Jacob said to Laban, "Give me my wife, because my days have been completed, and let me come to her." 22And Laban gathered all the people of the place and made a feast.

23And it was in the evening, and he took Leah, his daughter, and brought her to him. And he came to her.

24And Laban gave her his maid Zilpah—to Leah, his daughter, as a maid.

25And it was in the morning, and here she was: Leah! And he said to Laban, "What is this you've done to me? Didn't I work with you for Rachel? And why have you deceived me?"

26And Laban said, "It's not done like that in our place, to give the younger one before the firstborn. 27Complete this week, and this one will be given to you as well—for the work that you'll do with me: another seven years."

28And Jacob did so; and he completed this week, and he gave him Rachel, his daughter, for a wife. 29And Laban gave his maid Bilhah to Rachel, his daughter—to her as a maid. 30And he also came to Rachel. And he also loved Rachel more than Leah. And he worked with him another seven years.

16וּלְלָבָ֖ן וַעֲבַדְתַּ֑נִי חִנָּ֔ם הַגִּ֣ידָה לִּ֔י מַה־מַּשְׂכֻּרְתֶּֽךָ׃ שְׁתֵּ֣י בָנ֑וֹת שֵׁ֤ם הַגְּדֹלָה֙ לֵאָ֔ה וְשֵׁ֥ם הַקְּטַנָּ֖ה רָחֵֽל׃ 17וְעֵינֵ֥י לֵאָ֖ה רַכּ֑וֹת וְרָחֵל֙ הָֽיְתָ֔ה יְפַת־תֹּ֖אַר וִיפַ֥ת מַרְאֶֽה׃ 18וַיֶּאֱהַ֥ב יַעֲקֹ֖ב אֶת־רָחֵ֑ל וַיֹּ֗אמֶר אֶֽעֱבׇדְךָ֙ שֶׁ֣בַע שָׁנִ֔ים בְּרָחֵ֥ל בִּתְּךָ֖ הַקְּטַנָּֽה׃ 19וַיֹּ֣אמֶר לָבָ֗ן ט֚וֹב תִּתִּ֣י אֹתָ֣הּ לָ֔ךְ מִתִּתִּ֥י אֹתָ֖הּ לְאִ֣ישׁ אַחֵ֑ר שְׁבָ֖ה עִמָּדִֽי׃ 20וַיַּעֲבֹ֧ד יַעֲקֹ֛ב בְּרָחֵ֖ל שֶׁ֣בַע שָׁנִ֑ים וַיִּהְי֤וּ בְעֵינָיו֙ כְּיָמִ֣ים אֲחָדִ֔ים בְּאַהֲבָת֖וֹ אֹתָֽהּ׃ 21וַיֹּ֨אמֶר יַעֲקֹ֤ב אֶל־לָבָן֙ הָבָ֣ה אֶת־אִשְׁתִּ֔י כִּ֥י מָלְא֖וּ יָמָ֑י וְאָב֖וֹאָה אֵלֶֽיהָ׃ 22וַיֶּאֱסֹ֥ף לָבָ֛ן אֶת־כׇּל־אַנְשֵׁ֥י הַמָּק֖וֹם וַיַּ֥עַשׂ מִשְׁתֶּֽה׃ 23וַיְהִ֣י בָעֶ֔רֶב וַיִּקַּח֙ אֶת־לֵאָ֣ה בִתּ֔וֹ וַיָּבֵ֥א אֹתָ֖הּ אֵלָ֑יו וַיָּבֹ֖א אֵלֶֽיהָ׃ 24וַיִּתֵּ֤ן לָבָן֙ לָ֔הּ אֶת־זִלְפָּ֖ה שִׁפְחָת֑וֹ לְלֵאָ֥ה בִתּ֖וֹ שִׁפְחָֽה׃ 25וַיְהִ֣י בַבֹּ֔קֶר וְהִנֵּה־הִ֖וא לֵאָ֑ה וַיֹּ֣אמֶר אֶל־לָבָ֗ן מַה־זֹּאת֙ עָשִׂ֣יתָ לִּ֔י הֲלֹ֤א בְרָחֵל֙ עָבַ֣דְתִּי עִמָּ֔ךְ וְלָ֖מָּה רִמִּיתָֽנִי׃ 26וַיֹּ֣אמֶר לָבָ֔ן לֹא־יֵעָשֶׂ֥ה כֵ֖ן בִּמְקוֹמֵ֑נוּ לָתֵ֥ת הַצְּעִירָ֖ה לִפְנֵ֥י הַבְּכִירָֽה׃ 27מַלֵּ֖א שְׁבֻ֣עַ זֹ֑את וְנִתְּנָ֤ה לְךָ֙ גַּם־אֶת־זֹ֔את בַּעֲבֹדָה֙ אֲשֶׁ֣ר תַּעֲבֹ֣ד עִמָּדִ֔י ע֖וֹד שֶֽׁבַע־שָׁנִ֥ים אֲחֵרֽוֹת׃ 28וַיַּ֤עַשׂ יַעֲקֹב֙ כֵּ֔ן וַיְמַלֵּ֖א שְׁבֻ֣עַ זֹ֑את וַיִּתֶּן־ל֛וֹ אֶת־רָחֵ֥ל בִּתּ֖וֹ ל֥וֹ לְאִשָּֽׁה׃ 29וַיִּתֵּ֤ן לָבָן֙ לְרָחֵ֣ל בִּתּ֔וֹ אֶת־בִּלְהָ֖ה שִׁפְחָת֑וֹ לָ֖הּ לְשִׁפְחָֽה׃ 30וַיָּבֹא֙ גַּ֣ם אֶל־רָחֵ֔ל וַיֶּאֱהַ֥ב גַּֽם־אֶת־רָחֵ֖ל מִלֵּאָ֑ה וַיַּעֲבֹ֣ד עִמּ֔וֹ ע֖וֹד שֶֽׁבַע־שָׁנִ֥ים אֲחֵרֽוֹת׃ 31וַיַּ֤רְא יְהֹוָה֙

29:26. **the firstborn.** Not the younger before the "older" (as many translations mistakenly have it) but the younger before the *firstborn*. Jacob, who appropriated his brother's birthright, now suffers because of the birthright of his beloved's sister!

31And YHWH saw that Leah was hated, and He opened her womb, and Rachel was infertile. 32And Leah became pregnant and gave birth to a son and called his name Reuben because she said, "Because YHWH looked at my suffering, so that now my man will love me." 33And she be-

כִּי־שְׂנוּאָה לֵאָה וַיִּפְתַּח אֶת־רַחְמָהּ וְרָחֵל עֲקָרָה: 32וַתַּהַר לֵאָה וַתֵּלֶד בֵּן וַתִּקְרָא שְׁמוֹ רְאוּבֵן כִּי אָמְרָה כִּי־רָאָה יְהוָה בְּעָנְיִי כִּי עַתָּה יֶאֱהָבַנִי

29:32. **and [she] called his name Reuben.** Jacob's two wives name their own children and those born by their maids. In other cases the fathers name the children. What is the convention, and what are the exceptions? The record of who names whom in Genesis is:

Eve names Cain.

The text does not say who names Abel.

Eve and Adam are both said to have named Seth (4:25; 5:3).

Lamech names Noah.

Lot's elder daughter names Moab.

Lot's younger daughter names Ben-ammi (Ammon).

An angel tells Hagar to name Ishmael, but Abraham names him.

Abraham (obeying God) names Isaac.

"They" (meaning both Isaac and Rebekah?) name Esau.

"He" (meaning Esau himself? or Jacob?) calls Esau Edom.

"He" (meaning Isaac?) names Jacob.

Leah names Reuben, Simeon, Judah, Gad, Asher, Issachar, Zebulun, Dinah.

"He" (meaning Jacob?) names Levi.

Rachel names Dan, Naphtali, Joseph, and Ben-oni, but Jacob names him Benjamin.

Judah names Er, Perez, and Zerah.

Judah's first wife names Onan and Shelah.

Joseph names Ephraim and Manasseh.

Here are two possible explanations of this picture: (1) There is no clear pattern here whatever, and we can learn from this that we do not have to squeeze a great lesson out of every single distribution of wording in the Torah. (2) We can observe that the person who does the naming in each story is the person on whom that particular story is primarily focused. This works in every case except the naming of Levi, Onan, and Shelah (and arguably Cain): not 100 percent, but enough cases to be worth noting. Thus the rivalry between Leah and Rachel is the focus of this story, and so it should not come as a surprise that the naming is ascribed to them.

100

came pregnant again and gave birth to a son and said, "Because YHWH listened because I was hated and gave me this one, too." And she called his name Simeon. 34And she became pregnant again and gave birth to a son, and she said, "Now, this time my man will become bound to me because I've given birth to three sons for him." On account of this his name was called Levi. 35And she became pregnant again and gave birth to a son and said, "This time I'll praise YHWH." On account of this she called his name Judah. And she stopped giving birth.

30 1And Rachel saw that she had not given birth for Jacob, and Rachel was jealous of her sister, and she said to Jacob, "Give me children. And if not I'm dying!"

2And Jacob's anger flared at Rachel, and he said, "Am I in place of God, who has held back the fruit of the womb from you?!"

3And she said, "Here's my maid, Bilhah. Come to her, and she'll give birth on my knees, and I too will get a child through her." 4And she gave him Bilhah, her maid, as a wife, and Jacob came to her. 5And Bilhah became pregnant and gave birth to a son for Jacob. 6And Rachel said, "God has judged me and heard my prayer as well and has given me a son." On account of this she called his name Dan. 7And Bilhah, Rachel's maid, became pregnant again and gave birth to a second son for Jacob. 8And Rachel said, "I've had Godlike struggles with my sister. I've also prevailed." And she called his name Naphtali.

9And Leah saw that she had stopped giving birth, and she took Zilpah, her maid, and gave her to Jacob as a wife. 10And Zilpah, Leah's maid, gave birth to a son for Jacob. 11And Leah said, "With fortune!" and called his name Gad. 12And Zilpah, Leah's maid, gave birth to a second son for Jacob. 13And Leah said, "With my happiness!—because daughters will wish me happiness," and called his name Asher.

14And in the days of wheat harvest Reuben

אִישִׁי: 33וַתַּהַר עוֹד וַתֵּלֶד בֵּן וַתֹּאמֶר כִּי־שָׁמַע יְהוָה כִּי־שְׂנוּאָה אָנֹכִי וַיִּתֶּן־לִי גַּם־אֶת־זֶה וַתִּקְרָא שְׁמוֹ שִׁמְעוֹן: 34וַתַּהַר עוֹד וַתֵּלֶד בֵּן וַתֹּאמֶר עַתָּה הַפַּעַם יִלָּוֶה אִישִׁי אֵלַי כִּי־יָלַדְתִּי לוֹ שְׁלֹשָׁה בָנִים עַל־כֵּן קָרָא־שְׁמוֹ לֵוִי: 35וַתַּהַר עוֹד וַתֵּלֶד בֵּן וַתֹּאמֶר הַפַּעַם אוֹדֶה אֶת־יְהוָה עַל־כֵּן קָרְאָה שְׁמוֹ יְהוּדָה וַתַּעֲמֹד מִלֶּדֶת: 30 1וַתֵּרֶא רָחֵל כִּי לֹא יָלְדָה לְיַעֲקֹב וַתְּקַנֵּא רָחֵל בַּאֲחֹתָהּ וַתֹּאמֶר אֶל־יַעֲקֹב הָבָה־לִּי בָנִים וְאִם־אַיִן מֵתָה אָנֹכִי: 2וַיִּחַר־אַף יַעֲקֹב בְּרָחֵל וַיֹּאמֶר הֲתַחַת אֱלֹהִים אָנֹכִי אֲשֶׁר־מָנַע מִמֵּךְ פְּרִי־בָטֶן: 3וַתֹּאמֶר הִנֵּה אֲמָתִי בִלְהָה בֹּא אֵלֶיהָ וְתֵלֵד עַל־בִּרְכַּי וְאִבָּנֶה גַם־אָנֹכִי מִמֶּנָּה: 4וַתִּתֶּן־לוֹ אֶת־בִּלְהָה שִׁפְחָתָהּ לְאִשָּׁה וַיָּבֹא אֵלֶיהָ יַעֲקֹב: 5וַתַּהַר בִּלְהָה וַתֵּלֶד לְיַעֲקֹב בֵּן: 6וַתֹּאמֶר רָחֵל דָּנַנִּי אֱלֹהִים וְגַם שָׁמַע בְּקֹלִי וַיִּתֶּן־לִי בֵּן עַל־כֵּן קָרְאָה שְׁמוֹ דָּן: 7וַתַּהַר עוֹד וַתֵּלֶד בִּלְהָה שִׁפְחַת רָחֵל בֵּן שֵׁנִי לְיַעֲקֹב: 8וַתֹּאמֶר רָחֵל נַפְתּוּלֵי אֱלֹהִים ׀ נִפְתַּלְתִּי עִם־אֲחֹתִי גַּם־יָכֹלְתִּי וַתִּקְרָא שְׁמוֹ נַפְתָּלִי: 9וַתֵּרֶא לֵאָה כִּי עָמְדָה מִלֶּדֶת וַתִּקַּח אֶת־זִלְפָּה שִׁפְחָתָהּ וַתִּתֵּן אֹתָהּ לְיַעֲקֹב לְאִשָּׁה: 10וַתֵּלֶד זִלְפָּה שִׁפְחַת לֵאָה לְיַעֲקֹב בֵּן: 11וַתֹּאמֶר לֵאָה בְּגָד וַתִּקְרָא אֶת־שְׁמוֹ גָּד: 12וַתֵּלֶד זִלְפָּה שִׁפְחַת לֵאָה בֵּן שֵׁנִי לְיַעֲקֹב: 13וַתֹּאמֶר לֵאָה בְּאָשְׁרִי כִּי אִשְּׁרוּנִי בָּנוֹת וַתִּקְרָא אֶת־שְׁמוֹ אָשֵׁר: 14וַיֵּלֶךְ רְאוּבֵן בִּימֵי קְצִיר־חִטִּים

30:11 בָּא גָד קְ

went and found mandrakes in the field and brought them to Leah, his mother. And Rachel said to Leah, "Give me some of your son's mandrakes."

15And she said to her, "Is your taking my man a small thing? And you're taking my son's mandrakes, too?!"

And Rachel said, "Then let him lie with you tonight in return for your son's mandrakes."

16And Jacob came from the field in the evening, and Leah went out to him and said, "You are to come to me, because I've *hired* you with my son's mandrakes." And he lay with her that night. 17And God listened to Leah, and she became pregnant and gave birth to a fifth son for Jacob. 18And Leah said, "God has given my hire because I gave my maid to my man," and she called his name Issachar. 19And Leah became pregnant again and gave birth to a sixth son for Jacob. 20And Leah said, "God has given me a good gift. This time my man will value me highly, because I've given birth to six sons for him," and she called his name Zebulun. 21And after that she gave birth to a daughter and called her name Dinah.

22And God remembered Rachel, and God listened to her and opened her womb, 23and she became pregnant and gave birth to a son. And she said, "God has taken away my humiliation" 24and called his name Joseph, saying, "May YHWH add another son to me." 25And it was when Rachel had given birth to Joseph: and Jacob said to Laban, "Send me away so I may go to my place and my land. 26Give me my wives and my children for whom I've worked for you and let me go; because *you* know my work that I've done for you."

27And Laban said to him, "If I've found favor in your eyes, I've divined that YHWH has blessed

וַיִּמְצָא דֽוּדָאִים֙ בַּשָּׂדֶ֔ה וַיָּבֵ֣א אֹתָ֔ם אֶל־לֵאָ֖ה אִמּ֑וֹ וַתֹּ֤אמֶר רָחֵל֙ אֶל־לֵאָ֔ה תְּנִי־נָ֣א לִ֔י מִדּֽוּדָאֵ֖י בְּנֵֽךְ׃ 15וַתֹּ֣אמֶר לָ֗הּ הַמְעַט֙ קַחְתֵּ֣ךְ אֶת־אִישִׁ֔י וְלָקַ֕חַת גַּ֥ם אֶת־דּֽוּדָאֵ֖י בְּנִ֑י וַתֹּ֣אמֶר רָחֵ֗ל לָכֵן֙ יִשְׁכַּ֤ב עִמָּךְ֙ הַלַּ֔יְלָה תַּ֖חַת דּֽוּדָאֵ֥י בְנֵֽךְ׃ 16וַיָּבֹ֨א יַעֲקֹ֣ב מִן־הַשָּׂדֶה֮ בָּעֶרֶב֒ וַתֵּצֵ֨א לֵאָ֜ה לִקְרָאת֗וֹ וַתֹּ֙אמֶר֙ אֵלַ֣י תָּב֔וֹא כִּ֣י שָׂכֹ֤ר שְׂכַרְתִּ֙יךָ֙ בְּדֽוּדָאֵ֖י בְּנִ֑י וַיִּשְׁכַּ֥ב עִמָּ֖הּ בַּלַּ֥יְלָה הֽוּא׃ 17וַיִּשְׁמַ֥ע אֱלֹהִ֖ים אֶל־לֵאָ֑ה וַתַּ֙הַר֙ וַתֵּ֣לֶד לְיַעֲקֹ֖ב בֵּ֥ן חֲמִישִֽׁי׃ 18וַתֹּ֣אמֶר לֵאָ֗ה נָתַ֤ן אֱלֹהִים֙ שְׂכָרִ֔י אֲשֶׁר־נָתַ֥תִּי שִׁפְחָתִ֖י לְאִישִׁ֑י וַתִּקְרָ֥א שְׁמ֖וֹ יִשָּׂשכָֽר׃ 19וַתַּ֤הַר עוֹד֙ לֵאָ֔ה וַתֵּ֥לֶד בֵּן־שִׁשִּׁ֖י לְ‍ֽיַעֲקֹֽב׃ 20וַתֹּ֣אמֶר לֵאָה֮ זְבָדַ֨נִי אֱלֹהִ֥ים ׀ אֹתִי֮ זֶ֣בֶד טוֹב֒ הַפַּ֙עַם֙ יִזְבְּלֵ֣נִי אִישִׁ֔י כִּֽי־יָלַ֥דְתִּי ל֖וֹ שִׁשָּׁ֣ה בָנִ֑ים וַתִּקְרָ֥א אֶת־שְׁמ֖וֹ זְבֻלֽוּן׃ 21וְאַחַ֖ר יָ֣לְדָה בַּ֑ת וַתִּקְרָ֥א אֶת־שְׁמָ֖הּ דִּינָֽה׃ 22וַיִּזְכֹּ֥ר אֱלֹהִ֖ים אֶת־רָחֵ֑ל וַיִּשְׁמַ֤ע אֵלֶ֙יהָ֙ אֱלֹהִ֔ים וַיִּפְתַּ֖ח אֶת־רַחְמָֽהּ׃ 23וַתַּ֖הַר וַתֵּ֣לֶד בֵּ֑ן וַתֹּ֕אמֶר אָסַ֥ף אֱלֹהִ֖ים אֶת־חֶרְפָּתִֽי׃ 24וַתִּקְרָ֧א אֶת־שְׁמ֛וֹ יוֹסֵ֖ף לֵאמֹ֑ר יֹסֵ֧ף יְהוָ֛ה לִ֖י בֵּ֥ן אַחֵֽר׃ 25וַיְהִ֕י כַּאֲשֶׁ֛ר יָלְדָ֥ה רָחֵ֖ל אֶת־יוֹסֵ֑ף וַיֹּ֤אמֶר יַעֲקֹב֙ אֶל־לָבָ֔ן שַׁלְּחֵ֙נִי֙ וְאֵ֣לְכָ֔ה אֶל־מְקוֹמִ֖י וּלְאַרְצִֽי׃ 26תְּנָ֞ה אֶת־נָשַׁ֣י וְאֶת־יְלָדַ֗י אֲשֶׁ֨ר עָבַ֧דְתִּי אֹֽתְךָ֛ בָּהֵ֖ן וְאֵלֵ֑כָה כִּ֚י אַתָּ֣ה יָדַ֔עְתָּ אֶת־עֲבֹדָתִ֖י אֲשֶׁ֥ר עֲבַדְתִּֽיךָ׃ 27וַיֹּ֤אמֶר אֵלָיו֙ לָבָ֔ן אִם־נָ֛א מָצָ֥אתִי חֵ֖ן בְּעֵינֶ֑יךָ נִחַ֕שְׁתִּי וַיְבָרֲכֵ֥נִי יְהוָ֖ה בִּגְלָלֶֽךָ׃ 28וַיֹּאמַ֑ר נָקְבָ֠ה

30:14. **mandrakes**. This flowering plant has been believed to have medicinal or magical properties. It is supposed to look like a small human being, with exaggerated sexual features, and to serve as an aphrodisiac, with magical powers to produce conception.

me because of you," 28and he said, "Designate your pay for me, and I'll give it."

29And he said to him, "*You* know how I've worked for you and how your cattle have become with me, 30that a little that you had before me expanded into a lot, and YHWH blessed you wherever I set foot. And now, when shall *I* also take care of *my* house?"

31And he said, "What shall I give you?"

And Jacob said, "You won't *give* me anything—if you'll do this thing for me: Let me go back; I'll tend and watch over your flock. 32I'll pass among all your flock today removing from there every speckled and spotted lamb and every brown lamb among the sheep and every spotted and speckled one among the goats—and that will be my pay. 33And my virtue will answer for me in a future day: when you'll come upon my pay, it will be in front of you. Any one that isn't speckled and spotted among the goats and brown among the sheep, it's stolen with me."

34And Laban said, "Here, let it be according to your word." 35And in that day he removed the he-goats that were streaked and spotted and the she-goats that were speckled and spotted, every one that had white in it, and every brown one among the sheep, and set them in his sons' hand 36and put three days' distance between him and Jacob. And Jacob was tending Laban's remaining sheep.

37And Jacob took a rod of fresh poplar and one of almond tree and one of plane tree, and he peeled white stripes in them, exposing the white that was on the rods. 38And he set up the rods that he had peeled in the channels in the watering troughs at which the flock came to drink, facing the flock. And they copulated when they came to drink. 39And the flock mated at the rods, and the flock gave birth to streaked, speckled,

שְׂכָרֶךָ עָלַי וְאֶתֵּנָה: 29וַיֹּאמֶר אֵלָיו אַתָּה יָדַעְתָּ אֵת אֲשֶׁר עֲבַדְתִּיךָ וְאֵת אֲשֶׁר־הָיָה מִקְנְךָ אִתִּי: 30כִּי מְעַט אֲשֶׁר־הָיָה לְךָ לְפָנַי וַיִּפְרֹץ לָרֹב וַיְבָרֶךְ יְהוָה אֹתְךָ לְרַגְלִי וְעַתָּה מָתַי אֶעֱשֶׂה גַם־אָנֹכִי לְבֵיתִי: 31וַיֹּאמֶר מָה אֶתֶּן־לָךְ וַיֹּאמֶר יַעֲקֹב לֹא־תִתֶּן־לִי מְאוּמָה אִם־תַּעֲשֶׂה־לִּי הַדָּבָר הַזֶּה אָשׁוּבָה אֶרְעֶה צֹאנְךָ אֶשְׁמֹר: 32אֶעֱבֹר בְּכָל־צֹאנְךָ הַיּוֹם הָסֵר מִשָּׁם כָּל־שֶׂה ׀ נָקֹד וְטָלוּא וְכָל־שֶׂה־חוּם בַּכְּשָׂבִים וְטָלוּא וְנָקֹד בָּעִזִּים וְהָיָה שְׂכָרִי: 33וְעָנְתָה־בִּי צִדְקָתִי בְּיוֹם מָחָר כִּי־תָבוֹא עַל־שְׂכָרִי לְפָנֶיךָ כֹּל אֲשֶׁר־אֵינֶנּוּ נָקֹד וְטָלוּא בָּעִזִּים וְחוּם בַּכְּשָׂבִים גָּנוּב הוּא אִתִּי: 34וַיֹּאמֶר לָבָן הֵן לוּ יְהִי כִדְבָרֶךָ: 35וַיָּסַר בַּיּוֹם הַהוּא אֶת־הַתְּיָשִׁים הָעֲקֻדִּים וְהַטְּלֻאִים וְאֵת כָּל־הָעִזִּים הַנְּקֻדּוֹת וְהַטְּלֻאֹת כֹּל אֲשֶׁר־לָבָן בּוֹ וְכָל־חוּם בַּכְּשָׂבִים וַיִּתֵּן בְּיַד־בָּנָיו: 36וַיָּשֶׂם דֶּרֶךְ שְׁלֹשֶׁת יָמִים בֵּינוֹ וּבֵין יַעֲקֹב וְיַעֲקֹב רֹעֶה אֶת־צֹאן לָבָן הַנּוֹתָרֹת: 37וַיִּקַּח־לוֹ יַעֲקֹב מַקַּל לִבְנֶה לַח וְלוּז וְעַרְמוֹן וַיְפַצֵּל בָּהֵן פְּצָלוֹת לְבָנוֹת מַחְשֹׂף הַלָּבָן אֲשֶׁר עַל־הַמַּקְלוֹת: 38וַיַּצֵּג אֶת־הַמַּקְלוֹת אֲשֶׁר פִּצֵּל בָּרֳהָטִים בְּשִׁקֲתוֹת הַמָּיִם אֲשֶׁר תָּבֹאןָ הַצֹּאן לִשְׁתּוֹת לְנֹכַח הַצֹּאן וַיֵּחַמְנָה בְּבֹאָן לִשְׁתּוֹת: 39וַיֶּחֱמוּ הַצֹּאן אֶל־הַמַּקְלוֹת וַתֵּלַדְןָ הַצֹּאן עֲקֻדִּים

30:39. the flock mated at the rods and . . . gave birth to streaked, speckled, and spotted ones. Jacob sets up the peeled (phallic?) sticks where the animals mate. When they mate in front of the sticks, they have offspring that have patterns like those on the peeled sticks. It is unclear if this was believed to work genetically, or was thought

and spotted ones. 40And Jacob separated the sheep and had the flock face the streaked and every brown one among Laban's flock, and he set his own droves apart and did not set them by Laban's flock. 41And it was that whenever the fittest sheep would copulate Jacob would put the rods in the channels before the sheep's eyes so that they would copulate by the rods, 42and when the sheep were feebler he would not put them, so the feeble ones became Laban's and the fitter ones became Jacob's. 43And the man expanded very, very much, and he had many sheep and female and male servants and camels and asses.

31 1And he heard Laban's sons' words, saying, "Jacob has taken everything that was our father's, and he has made all this wealth from what was our father's." 2And Jacob saw Laban's face; and, here, he was not like the day before yesterday with him. 3And YHWH said to Jacob, "Go back to your fathers' land and to your birthplace, and I'll be with you." 4And Jacob sent and called Rachel and Leah to the field, to his flock, 5and said to them, "I see your father's face, that he's not like the day before yesterday to me. And my father's God has been with me, 6and you know that I served your father with all my might, 7and your father has toyed with me and changed my pay ten times, and God hasn't let him do bad with me. 8If he would say this: 'The speckled will be your pay,' then all the flock gave birth to speckled. And if he would say this: 'The streaked will be your pay,' then all the flock gave birth to

נְקֻדִּים וּטְלֻאִים: 40וְהַכְּשָׂבִים הִפְרִיד יַעֲקֹב וַיִּתֵּן פְּנֵי הַצֹּאן אֶל־עָקֹד וְכָל־חוּם בְּצֹאן לָבָן וַיָּשֶׁת־לוֹ עֲדָרִים לְבַדּוֹ וְלֹא שָׁתָם עַל־צֹאן לָבָן: 41וְהָיָה בְּכָל־יַחֵם הַצֹּאן הַמְקֻשָּׁרוֹת וְשָׂם יַעֲקֹב אֶת־הַמַּקְלוֹת לְעֵינֵי הַצֹּאן בָּרְהָטִים לְיַחְמֵנָּה בַּמַּקְלוֹת: 42וּבְהַעֲטִיף הַצֹּאן לֹא יָשִׂים וְהָיָה הָעֲטֻפִים לְלָבָן וְהַקְּשֻׁרִים לְיַעֲקֹב: 43וַיִּפְרֹץ הָאִישׁ מְאֹד מְאֹד וַיְהִי־לוֹ צֹאן רַבּוֹת וּשְׁפָחוֹת וַעֲבָדִים וּגְמַלִּים וַחֲמֹרִים:

31 1וַיִּשְׁמַע אֶת־דִּבְרֵי בְנֵי־לָבָן לֵאמֹר לָקַח יַעֲקֹב אֵת כָּל־אֲשֶׁר לְאָבִינוּ וּמֵאֲשֶׁר לְאָבִינוּ עָשָׂה אֵת כָּל־הַכָּבֹד הַזֶּה: 2וַיַּרְא יַעֲקֹב אֶת־פְּנֵי לָבָן וְהִנֵּה אֵינֶנּוּ עִמּוֹ כִּתְמוֹל שִׁלְשׁוֹם: 3וַיֹּאמֶר יְהוָה אֶל־יַעֲקֹב שׁוּב אֶל־אֶרֶץ אֲבוֹתֶיךָ וּלְמוֹלַדְתֶּךָ וְאֶהְיֶה עִמָּךְ: 4וַיִּשְׁלַח יַעֲקֹב וַיִּקְרָא לְרָחֵל וּלְלֵאָה הַשָּׂדֶה אֶל־צֹאנוֹ: 5וַיֹּאמֶר לָהֶן רֹאֶה אָנֹכִי אֶת־פְּנֵי אֲבִיכֶן כִּי־אֵינֶנּוּ אֵלַי כִּתְמֹל שִׁלְשֹׁם וֵאלֹהֵי אָבִי הָיָה עִמָּדִי: 6וְאַתֵּנָה יְדַעְתֶּן כִּי בְּכָל־כֹּחִי עָבַדְתִּי אֶת־אֲבִיכֶן: 7וַאֲבִיכֶן הֵתֶל בִּי וְהֶחֱלִף אֶת־מַשְׂכֻּרְתִּי עֲשֶׂרֶת מֹנִים וְלֹא־נְתָנוֹ אֱלֹהִים לְהָרַע עִמָּדִי: 8אִם־כֹּה יֹאמַר נְקֻדִּים יִהְיֶה שְׂכָרֶךָ וְיָלְדוּ כָל־הַצֹּאן נְקֻדִּים וְאִם־כֹּה יֹאמַר עֲקֻדִּים יִהְיֶה שְׂכָרֶךָ וְיָלְדוּ

---

to be a practice of sympathetic magic, or was thought to be miraculous. Jacob later claims to his wives that it happened through God's power, but it is unclear from his wording if he is supposed to be modifying what has happened as he presents it to them.

30:42. **the feeble ones became Laban's and the fitter ones became Jacob's.** By thus manipulating Laban's flock, Jacob pays Laban back for the Rachel-Leah deception. The sign of the connection between Jacob's deception and Laban's is when Jacob later speaks to Laban about his "ewes" and "rams"—which plays on the names of Rachel and Leah. (See the comment on 31:38.)

streaked. 9And God has delivered your father's livestock and given them to me. 10And it was at the time of the flock's being in heat, and I raised my eyes and saw in a dream: and here were the he-goats that were going up on the flock: streaked, speckled, and spotted.

11"And an angel of God said to me in the dream, 'Jacob.'

"And I said, 'I'm here.'

12"And he said, 'Raise your eyes and see all the he-goats that are going up on the flock: streaked, speckled, and spotted. Because I've seen everything that Laban is doing to you. 13I am the God at Beth-El, where you anointed a pillar, where you made a vow to me. Now get up, go from this land, and go back to the land of your birth.' "

14And Rachel and Leah answered, and they said to him, "Do we still have a portion and legacy in our father's house? 15Aren't we thought of as foreigners by him, because he sold us and has *eaten up* our money as well?! 16Because all the wealth that God has delivered from our father: it's ours and our children's. And now, do everything that that God has said to you." 17And Jacob got up and carried his children and his wives on the camels. 18And he drove all his cattle and all his property that he had acquired, the cattle that were in his possession that he had acquired in Paddan Aram, to come to Isaac, his father, at the land of Canaan.

19And Laban had gone to shear his flock. And Rachel stole the teraphim that her father had. 20And Jacob stole the heart of Laban, the Arame-

כָּל־הַצֹּאן עֲקֻדִּים: 9וַיַּצֵּל אֱלֹהִים אֶת־מִקְנֵה אֲבִיכֶם וַיִּתֶּן־לִי: 10וַיְהִי בְּעֵת יַחֵם הַצֹּאן וָאֶשָּׂא עֵינַי וָאֵרֶא בַּחֲלוֹם וְהִנֵּה הָעַתֻּדִים הָעֹלִים עַל־הַצֹּאן עֲקֻדִּים נְקֻדִּים וּבְרֻדִּים: 11וַיֹּאמֶר אֵלַי מַלְאַךְ הָאֱלֹהִים בַּחֲלוֹם יַעֲקֹב וָאֹמַר הִנֵּנִי: 12וַיֹּאמֶר שָׂא־נָא עֵינֶיךָ וּרְאֵה כָּל־הָעַתֻּדִים הָעֹלִים עַל־הַצֹּאן עֲקֻדִּים נְקֻדִּים וּבְרֻדִּים כִּי רָאִיתִי אֵת כָּל־אֲשֶׁר לָבָן עֹשֶׂה לָּךְ: 13אָנֹכִי הָאֵל בֵּית־אֵל אֲשֶׁר מָשַׁחְתָּ שָּׁם מַצֵּבָה אֲשֶׁר נָדַרְתָּ לִּי שָׁם נֶדֶר עַתָּה קוּם צֵא מִן־הָאָרֶץ הַזֹּאת וְשׁוּב אֶל־אֶרֶץ מוֹלַדְתֶּךָ: 14וַתַּעַן רָחֵל וְלֵאָה וַתֹּאמַרְנָה לוֹ הַעוֹד לָנוּ חֵלֶק וְנַחֲלָה בְּבֵית אָבִינוּ: 15הֲלוֹא נָכְרִיּוֹת נֶחְשַׁבְנוּ לוֹ כִּי מְכָרָנוּ וַיֹּאכַל גַּם־אָכוֹל אֶת־כַּסְפֵּנוּ: 16כִּי כָל־הָעֹשֶׁר אֲשֶׁר הִצִּיל אֱלֹהִים מֵאָבִינוּ לָנוּ הוּא וּלְבָנֵינוּ וְעַתָּה כֹּל אֲשֶׁר אָמַר אֱלֹהִים אֵלֶיךָ עֲשֵׂה: 17וַיָּקָם יַעֲקֹב וַיִּשָּׂא אֶת־בָּנָיו וְאֶת־נָשָׁיו עַל־הַגְּמַלִּים: 18וַיִּנְהַג אֶת־כָּל־מִקְנֵהוּ וְאֶת־כָּל־רְכֻשׁוֹ אֲשֶׁר רָכָשׁ מִקְנֵה קִנְיָנוֹ אֲשֶׁר רָכַשׁ בְּפַדַּן אֲרָם לָבוֹא אֶל־יִצְחָק אָבִיו אַרְצָה כְּנָעַן: 19וְלָבָן הָלַךְ לִגְזֹז אֶת־צֹאנוֹ וַתִּגְנֹב רָחֵל אֶת־הַתְּרָפִים אֲשֶׁר לְאָבִיהָ: 20וַיִּגְנֹב יַעֲקֹב אֶת־לֵב לָבָן הָאֲרַמִּי עַל־

31:13. **the God at Beth-El.** The Hebrew construction is unclear. The Septuagint reads: "I am the God who appeared to you at Beth-El," which is presumably what the Hebrew means.

31:19,34. **teraphim.** These are icons (Septuagint has *eidolon*, meaning "image"), which may relate to ancestor worship. Ancestor veneration was common in Israel at least until the reign of King Hezekiah (c. 700 B.C.E.). King Josiah burns teraphim along with other items related to communicating with the dead (אובות and ידעונים) in 2 Kings 23:24.

31:20. **stole the heart of Laban . . . by not telling him.** Note the pun, a string of plays on the consonants of the name Laban: ויגנב את לב לבן על בלי. Some puns in

an, by not telling him that he was fleeing. 21And he fled, he and everyone he had, and he got up and crossed the river and set his face toward the mountain of Gilead. 22And it was told to Laban on the third day that Jacob had fled. 23And he took his brothers with him and pursued him seven days' journey and caught up to him in the mountain of Gilead. 24And God came to Laban, the Aramean, in a night dream and said to him, "Watch yourself in case you speak with Jacob: from good to bad."

25And Laban caught up to Jacob, and Jacob had set up his tent in the mountain, and Laban set up with his brothers in the mountain of Gilead. 26And Laban said to Jacob, "What have you done, that you've stolen my heart and driven off my daughters like prisoners by the sword? 27Why did you hide so as to flee, and you stole from me, and you didn't tell me? And I would have sent you off with happiness and with songs and with a drum and with a lyre. 28And you didn't permit me to kiss my sons and my daughters. Now you've been foolish to do this. 29The god at my hand has the means to do bad to you. But your father's God said to me yesterday, saying, 'Watch

בְּלִי הִגִּיד לוֹ כִּי בֹרֵחַ הוּא: 21וַיִּבְרַח הוּא וְכָל־אֲשֶׁר־לוֹ וַיָּקָם וַיַּעֲבֹר אֶת־הַנָּהָר וַיָּשֶׂם אֶת־פָּנָיו הַר הַגִּלְעָד: 22וַיֻּגַּד לְלָבָן בַּיּוֹם הַשְּׁלִישִׁי כִּי בָרַח יַעֲקֹב: 23וַיִּקַּח אֶת־אֶחָיו עִמּוֹ וַיִּרְדֹּף אַחֲרָיו דֶּרֶךְ שִׁבְעַת יָמִים וַיַּדְבֵּק אֹתוֹ בְּהַר הַגִּלְעָד: 24וַיָּבֹא אֱלֹהִים אֶל־לָבָן הָאֲרַמִּי בַּחֲלֹם הַלָּיְלָה וַיֹּאמֶר לוֹ הִשָּׁמֶר לְךָ פֶּן־תְּדַבֵּר עִם־יַעֲקֹב מִטּוֹב עַד־רָע: 25וַיַּשֵּׂג לָבָן אֶת־יַעֲקֹב וְיַעֲקֹב תָּקַע אֶת־אָהֳלוֹ בָּהָר וְלָבָן תָּקַע אֶת־אֶחָיו בְּהַר הַגִּלְעָד: 26וַיֹּאמֶר לָבָן לְיַעֲקֹב מֶה עָשִׂיתָ וַתִּגְנֹב אֶת־לְבָבִי וַתְּנַהֵג אֶת־בְּנֹתַי כִּשְׁבֻיוֹת חָרֶב: 27לָמָּה נַחְבֵּאתָ לִבְרֹחַ וַתִּגְנֹב אֹתִי וְלֹא־הִגַּדְתָּ לִּי וָאֲשַׁלֵּחֲךָ בְּשִׂמְחָה וּבְשִׁרִים בְּתֹף וּבְכִנּוֹר: 28וְלֹא נְטַשְׁתַּנִי לְנַשֵּׁק לְבָנַי וְלִבְנֹתָי עַתָּה הִסְכַּלְתָּ עֲשׂוֹ: 29יֶשׁ־לְאֵל יָדִי לַעֲשׂוֹת עִמָּכֶם רָע וֵאלֹהֵי אֲבִיכֶם אֶמֶשׁ אָמַר אֵלַי לֵאמֹר

---

the Torah convey subtle or ironic messages. This pun may have no purpose other than the artistry for its own sake, or it may suggest a comeuppance: the play on language here describes a deception of Laban, a person who uses language to deceive others.

31:22–23,25. **And it was told to Laban . . . that Jacob had fled. And he took . . . and pursued . . . and caught up**. Compare the words describing Egypt's pursuit of Israel to the Red Sea: "And it was told to the king of Egypt that the people had fled . . . and he took . . . and he pursued. . . . And they caught up" (Exod 14:5–9). The Laban episode prefigures the flight from Egypt, and it hints once again that the merit of the patriarchs lies in the background when Israel is saved from dangers.

31:28. **to do this**. The Hebrew עשׂו puns on the name of Esau (עשׂו), who returns to the story in the next chapter (32:4).

31:29. **your father's God**. Hebrew אביכם. "Your" is a plural here, and "father" is singular. The text as it is does not appear to make sense. To whom would the plural "your" refer? Is it Jacob and his wives? But then "your father" would be Laban himself. Is it Jacob and his sons? But then "your father" would be Isaac. But why would Laban formulate it this way, since he has the same relationship as Isaac with Jacob's sons? We would rather have expected Hebrew אבותך, "the God of your fathers." This

yourself from speaking with Jacob: from good to bad.' 30And now, you *went*, because you *longed* for your father's house. Why did you steal my gods?"

31And Jacob answered, and he said to Laban, "Because I was afraid. Because I said, 'In case you'll seize your daughters from me.' 32Let the one with whom you'll find your gods not live. In front of our brothers, recognize and take what of yours is with me." And Jacob did not know that Rachel had stolen them.

33And Laban came in Jacob's tent and Leah's tent and the two maids' tent, and he did not find them. And he came out from Leah's tent and came in Rachel's tent. 34And Rachel had taken the teraphim and put them in the camel's saddle and sat on them. And Laban felt around the whole tent and did not find them. 35And she said to her father, "Let it not offend in my lord's eyes that I'm not able to get up before you, because I have the way of women." And he searched and did not find the teraphim.

36And Jacob was angered, and he quarreled with Laban, and Jacob answered, and he said to Laban, "What is my offense? What is my sin, that

הִשָּׁ֧מֶר לְךָ֛ מִדַּבֵּ֥ר עִֽם־יַעֲקֹ֖ב מִטּ֥וֹב עַד־רָֽע׃ 30וְעַתָּה֙ הָלֹ֣ךְ הָלַ֔כְתָּ כִּֽי־נִכְסֹ֥ף נִכְסַ֖פְתָּה לְבֵ֣ית אָבִ֑יךָ לָ֥מָּה גָנַ֖בְתָּ אֶת־אֱלֹהָֽי׃ 31וַיַּ֥עַן יַעֲקֹ֖ב וַיֹּ֣אמֶר לְלָבָ֑ן כִּ֣י יָרֵ֔אתִי כִּ֣י אָמַ֔רְתִּי פֶּן־תִּגְזֹ֥ל אֶת־בְּנוֹתֶ֖יךָ מֵעִמִּֽי׃ 32עִ֠ם אֲשֶׁ֨ר תִּמְצָ֣א אֶת־אֱלֹהֶיךָ֮ לֹ֣א יִֽחְיֶה֒ נֶ֣גֶד אַחֵ֧ינוּ הַֽכֶּר־לְךָ֛ מָ֥ה עִמָּדִ֖י וְקַֽח־לָ֑ךְ וְלֹֽא־יָדַ֣ע יַעֲקֹ֔ב כִּ֥י רָחֵ֖ל גְּנָבָֽתַם׃ 33וַיָּבֹ֨א לָבָ֜ן בְּאֹ֥הֶל יַעֲקֹ֣ב ׀ וּבְאֹ֣הֶל לֵאָ֗ה וּבְאֹ֛הֶל שְׁתֵּ֥י הָאֲמָהֹ֖ת וְלֹ֣א מָצָ֑א וַיֵּצֵא֙ מֵאֹ֣הֶל לֵאָ֔ה וַיָּבֹ֖א בְּאֹ֥הֶל רָחֵֽל׃ 34וְרָחֵ֞ל לָקְחָ֣ה אֶת־הַתְּרָפִ֗ים וַתְּשִׂמֵ֛ם בְּכַ֥ר הַגָּמָ֖ל וַתֵּ֣שֶׁב עֲלֵיהֶ֑ם וַיְמַשֵּׁ֥שׁ לָבָ֛ן אֶת־כָּל־הָאֹ֖הֶל וְלֹ֥א מָצָֽא׃ 35וַתֹּ֣אמֶר אֶל־אָבִ֗יהָ אַל־יִ֙חַר֙ בְּעֵינֵ֣י אֲדֹנִ֔י כִּ֣י ל֤וֹא אוּכַל֙ לָק֣וּם מִפָּנֶ֔יךָ כִּי־דֶ֥רֶךְ נָשִׁ֖ים לִ֑י וַיְחַפֵּ֕שׂ וְלֹ֥א מָצָ֖א אֶת־הַתְּרָפִֽים׃ 36וַיִּ֥חַר לְיַעֲקֹ֖ב וַיָּ֣רֶב בְּלָבָ֑ן וַיַּ֤עַן יַעֲקֹב֙ וַיֹּ֣אמֶר לְלָבָ֔ן מַה־פִּשְׁעִי֙ מַ֣ה חַטָּאתִ֔י כִּ֥י

---

may possibly be one of the very few grammatical errors to be transmitted in the biblical text. Presumably, the wrong element of the word has been pluralized. Or: Perhaps the error should be understood to be *Laban's!* As he tries to make a dignified speech, claiming the moral high ground in this matter, calling Jacob the foolish one, he undermines his pretensions by making a clumsy mistake in the middle of his sentence.

31:32. **Let the one with whom you'll find your gods not live.** By saying this, Jacob unwittingly puts a curse on Rachel, who has the teraphim.

31:34,37. **felt around.** This is the same verb that Jacob used in the context of deceiving his father in order to get Esau's blessing: "Maybe my father will *feel* me." The treatment he receives from his wives' father here is the first hint that his deception of his own father still remains unsettled. Recompense for that deception is coming (Genesis 37).

31:35. **I have the way of women.** Rachel tells her father that she is menstruating, which keeps him away, so he does not search where she is sitting. But she is deceiving him. She cannot in fact be menstruating, because we find out below that she must be pregnant at this time. Her deception is a recompense for Laban's having substituted Leah for her and made her share her husband with her sister.

you *blazed* after me, 37that you *felt around* all my belongings? What did you find out of all of your house's belongings? Set it here, in front of my brothers and your brothers, and let them judge between the two of us. 38This twenty years I've been with you, your ewes and your she-goats haven't lost their offspring, and I haven't eaten your flock's rams. 39I haven't brought you one torn up. I would miss it: you would ask it from my hand, be it stolen by day or stolen by night. 40I was . . . In the daytime heat ate me up, and ice in the night. And my sleep fled from my eyes. 41This twenty years I've had in your house: I worked for you fourteen years for your two daughters and six years for your flock, and you changed my pay ten times. 42If I hadn't had my father's God, the God of Abraham and Awe of Isaac, by now you would have sent me away empty-handed. God saw my degradation and my hands' exhaustion, and He pointed it out last night."

43And Laban answered, and he said to Jacob, "The daughters are my daughters, and the sons are my sons, and the flock is my flock, and everything that you see: it's mine. But what shall I do to my daughters, to these, today, or to their children to whom they've given birth? 44So now,

דָּלַקְתָּ אַחֲרָי: 37כִּי־מִשַּׁשְׁתָּ אֶת־כָּל־כֵּלַי מַה־מָּצָאתָ מִכֹּל כְּלֵי־בֵיתֶךָ שִׂים כֹּה נֶגֶד אַחַי וְאַחֶיךָ וְיוֹכִיחוּ בֵּין שְׁנֵינוּ: 38זֶה עֶשְׂרִים שָׁנָה אָנֹכִי עִמָּךְ רְחֵלֶיךָ וְעִזֶּיךָ לֹא שִׁכֵּלוּ וְאֵילֵי צֹאנְךָ לֹא אָכָלְתִּי: 39טְרֵפָה לֹא־הֵבֵאתִי אֵלֶיךָ אָנֹכִי אֲחַטֶּנָּה מִיָּדִי תְּבַקְשֶׁנָּה גְּנֻבְתִי יוֹם וּגְנֻבְתִי לָיְלָה: 40הָיִיתִי בַיּוֹם אֲכָלַנִי חֹרֶב וְקֶרַח בַּלָּיְלָה וַתִּדַּד שְׁנָתִי מֵעֵינָי: 41זֶה־לִּי עֶשְׂרִים שָׁנָה בְּבֵיתֶךָ עֲבַדְתִּיךָ אַרְבַּע־עֶשְׂרֵה שָׁנָה בִּשְׁתֵּי בְנֹתֶיךָ וְשֵׁשׁ שָׁנִים בְּצֹאנֶךָ וַתַּחֲלֵף אֶת־מַשְׂכֻּרְתִּי עֲשֶׂרֶת מֹנִים: 42לוּלֵי אֱלֹהֵי אָבִי אֱלֹהֵי אַבְרָהָם וּפַחַד יִצְחָק הָיָה לִי כִּי עַתָּה רֵיקָם שִׁלַּחְתָּנִי אֶת־עָנְיִי וְאֶת־יְגִיעַ כַּפַּי רָאָה אֱלֹהִים וַיּוֹכַח אָמֶשׁ: 43וַיַּעַן לָבָן וַיֹּאמֶר אֶל־יַעֲקֹב הַבָּנוֹת בְּנֹתַי וְהַבָּנִים בָּנַי וְהַצֹּאן צֹאנִי וְכֹל אֲשֶׁר־אַתָּה רֹאֶה לִי־הוּא וְלִבְנֹתַי מָה־אֶעֱשֶׂה לָאֵלֶּה הַיּוֹם אוֹ לִבְנֵיהֶן אֲשֶׁר יָלָדוּ: 44וְעַתָּה לְכָה נִכְרְתָה

31:38. **ewes, rams**. In Hebrew, a ewe is a *rākēl*, i.e., a "Rachel." And a ram is an *'ayil*, which is a play on "Leah." Jacob's words to Laban thus have a double meaning. He has protected Laban's animals and has done right by his daughters as well. Moreover, they give Laban a hint that Jacob has paid him back for the Rachel-Leah deception— just as Laban's words to Jacob ("We don't give the younger before the *firstborn*") once gave Jacob a hint that he was being paid back for getting his brother's birthright.

31:40. **I was . . . In the daytime heat**. The first words of the verse, "I was," have no referent or continuation in the rest of the sentence. Commentators and translators have taken it to mean "Thus I was: in the daytime heat ate me up," etc. But perhaps the confusion that results from this break in the sentence is precisely the point. Jacob is speaking up after twenty years. He is rattling off a list of his complaints as fast and as strongly as he can. And, as people often do in such bursts of anger, he starts a point and then interrupts himself and says something else that occurs to him. Indeed, it is at this juncture that Jacob changes directions. He has been listing his merits; now he suddenly switches and points out the abuses that he has been suffering.

come and let's make a covenant, I and you, and let it be a witness between me and you."

45And Jacob took a stone and set it up as a pillar, 46and Jacob said to his brothers, "Collect stones." And they took stones and made a pile and ate there at the pile. 47And Laban called it *yĕgar sāhădûta'*, and Jacob called it *gal-'ēd*.

48And Laban said, "This pile is a witness between me and you today." On account of this he called its name Gal-Ed. (49And Mizpah, because he said, "May YHWH observe between me and you when one is hidden from the other.") 50"If you degrade my daughters and if you take wives in addition to my daughters, no *man* is with us. See: *God* is witness between me and you." 51And Laban said to Jacob, "Here is this pile, and here is the pillar that I've cast between me and you. 52This pile is a witness, and the pillar is a witness that I won't cross this pile to you and you won't cross this pile and this pillar to me for bad. 53Let Abraham's God and Nahor's gods, their father's gods, judge between us."

And Jacob swore by the Awe of his father, Isaac. 54And Jacob made a sacrifice in the mountain and called his brothers to eat bread, and they ate bread and spent the night in the mountain.

32 1And Laban got up early in the morning and kissed his sons and his daughters and blessed them and went. And Laban went back to his place, 2and Jacob went his way. And angels of God came upon him. 3And Jacob said when he saw them, "This is a camp of God," and he called that place's name Mahanaim.

AND HE SENT

4And Jacob sent messengers ahead of him to Esau, his brother, to the land of Seir, the territo-

בְּרִית אֲנִי וָאָתָּה וְהָיָה לְעֵד בֵּינִי וּבֵינֶךָ: 45וַיִּקַּח
יַעֲקֹב אָבֶן וַיְרִימֶהָ מַצֵּבָה: 46וַיֹּאמֶר יַעֲקֹב לְאֶחָיו
לִקְטוּ אֲבָנִים וַיִּקְחוּ אֲבָנִים וַיַּעֲשׂוּ־גָל וַיֹּאכְלוּ שָׁם
עַל־הַגָּל: 47וַיִּקְרָא־לוֹ לָבָן יְגַר שָׂהֲדוּתָא וְיַעֲקֹב
קָרָא לוֹ גַּלְעֵד: 48וַיֹּאמֶר לָבָן הַגַּל הַזֶּה עֵד בֵּינִי
וּבֵינֶךָ הַיּוֹם עַל־כֵּן קָרָא־שְׁמוֹ גַּלְעֵד: 49וְהַמִּצְפָּה
אֲשֶׁר אָמַר יִצֶף יְהוָה בֵּינִי וּבֵינֶךָ כִּי נִסָּתֵר אִישׁ
מֵרֵעֵהוּ: 50אִם־תְּעַנֶּה אֶת־בְּנֹתַי וְאִם־תִּקַּח נָשִׁים
עַל־בְּנֹתַי אֵין אִישׁ עִמָּנוּ רְאֵה אֱלֹהִים עֵד בֵּינִי
וּבֵינֶךָ: 51וַיֹּאמֶר לָבָן לְיַעֲקֹב הִנֵּה ׀ הַגַּל הַזֶּה וְהִנֵּה
הַמַּצֵּבָה אֲשֶׁר יָרִיתִי בֵּינִי וּבֵינֶךָ: 52עֵד הַגַּל הַזֶּה
וְעֵדָה הַמַּצֵּבָה אִם־אָנִי לֹא־אֶעֱבֹר אֵלֶיךָ אֶת־הַגַּל
הַזֶּה וְאִם־אַתָּה לֹא־תַעֲבֹר אֵלַי אֶת־הַגַּל הַזֶּה וְאֶת־
הַמַּצֵּבָה הַזֹּאת לְרָעָה: 53אֱלֹהֵי אַבְרָהָם וֵאלֹהֵי
נָחוֹר יִשְׁפְּטוּ בֵינֵינוּ אֱלֹהֵי אֲבִיהֶם וַיִּשָּׁבַע יַעֲקֹב
בְּפַחַד אָבִיו יִצְחָק: 54וַיִּזְבַּח יַעֲקֹב זֶבַח בָּהָר
וַיִּקְרָא לְאֶחָיו לֶאֱכָל־לָחֶם וַיֹּאכְלוּ לֶחֶם וַיָּלִינוּ
בָּהָר: 32 1וַיַּשְׁכֵּם לָבָן בַּבֹּקֶר וַיְנַשֵּׁק לְבָנָיו
וְלִבְנוֹתָיו וַיְבָרֶךְ אֶתְהֶם וַיֵּלֶךְ וַיָּשָׁב לָבָן לִמְקֹמוֹ:
2וְיַעֲקֹב הָלַךְ לְדַרְכּוֹ וַיִּפְגְּעוּ־בוֹ מַלְאֲכֵי אֱלֹהִים:
3וַיֹּאמֶר יַעֲקֹב כַּאֲשֶׁר רָאָם מַחֲנֵה אֱלֹהִים זֶה
וַיִּקְרָא שֵׁם־הַמָּקוֹם הַהוּא מַחֲנָיִם: פ

וישלח

4וַיִּשְׁלַח יַעֲקֹב מַלְאָכִים לְפָנָיו אֶל־עֵשָׂו אָחִיו

31:53. Abraham's God and Nahor's gods, their father's gods. Since the Hebrew word for God, *'ĕlōhîm*, can be singular or plural, and since there is no capitalization to distinguish between references to the God of the patriarchs and the pagan gods, Laban's meaning is uncertain.

ry of Edom, 5and commanded them saying, "You shall say this: 'To my lord, to Esau, your servant Jacob said this, "I've stayed with Laban and delayed until now, 6and ox and ass and sheep and male and female servant have become mine. And I'm sending to tell my lord so as to find favor in your eyes." ' "

7And the messengers came back to Jacob saying, "We came to your brother, to Esau, and also he's coming to you—and four hundred men with him." 8And Jacob was very afraid, and he had anguish. And he divided the people who were with him and the sheep and the oxen and the camels into two camps. 9And he said, "If Esau will come to one camp and strike it, then the camp that is left will survive."

10And Jacob said, "God of my father Abraham and God of my father Isaac, YHWH, who said to me, 'Go back to your land and to your birthplace, and I'll deal well with you,' 11I'm not worthy of all the kindnesses and all the faithfulness that you've done with your servant, because I crossed this Jordan with just my rod, and now I've become two camps. 12Save me from my brother's hand, from Esau's hand, because I fear him, in case he'll come and strike me, mother with children. 13And *you've* said, 'I'll do *well* with you, and I'll make your seed like the sand of the sea, that it won't be countable because of its great number.' "

14And he spent that night there.

And he took an offering for Esau, his brother, from what had come into his hand: 15two hundred she-goats and twenty he-goats, two hundred ewes and twenty rams, 16thirty nursing camels and their offspring, forty cows and ten bulls, twenty she-asses and ten he-asses. 17And

אַ֫רְצָה שֵׂעִ֖יר שְׂדֵ֥ה אֱדֽוֹם: 5וַיְצַ֣ו אֹתָם֮ לֵאמֹר֒ כֹּ֣ה תֹאמְר֔וּן לַֽאדֹנִ֖י לְעֵשָׂ֑ו כֹּ֤ה אָמַר֙ עַבְדְּךָ֣ יַֽעֲקֹ֔ב עִם־לָבָ֣ן גַּ֔רְתִּי וָאֵחַ֖ר עַד־עָֽתָּה: 6וַֽיְהִי־לִי֙ שׁ֣וֹר וַֽחֲמ֔וֹר צֹ֖אן וְעֶ֣בֶד וְשִׁפְחָ֑ה וָֽאֶשְׁלְחָה֙ לְהַגִּ֣יד לַֽאדֹנִ֔י לִמְצֹא־חֵ֖ן בְּעֵינֶֽיךָ: 7וַיָּשֻׁ֨בוּ֙ הַמַּלְאָכִ֔ים אֶל־יַֽעֲקֹ֖ב לֵאמֹ֑ר בָּ֤אנוּ אֶל־אָחִ֨יךָ֙ אֶל־עֵשָׂ֔ו וְגַם֙ הֹלֵ֣ךְ לִקְרָֽאתְךָ֔ וְאַרְבַּע־מֵא֥וֹת אִ֖ישׁ עִמּֽוֹ: 8וַיִּירָ֧א יַֽעֲקֹ֛ב מְאֹ֖ד וַיֵּ֣צֶר ל֑וֹ וַיַּ֜חַץ אֶת־הָעָ֣ם אֲשֶׁר־אִתּ֗וֹ וְאֶת־הַצֹּ֧אן וְאֶת־הַבָּקָ֛ר וְהַגְּמַלִּ֖ים לִשְׁנֵ֥י מַֽחֲנֽוֹת: 9וַיֹּ֕אמֶר אִם־יָב֥וֹא עֵשָׂ֛ו אֶל־הַמַּֽחֲנֶ֥ה הָֽאַחַ֖ת וְהִכָּ֑הוּ וְהָיָ֛ה הַמַּֽחֲנֶ֥ה הַנִּשְׁאָ֖ר לִפְלֵיטָֽה: 10וַיֹּאמֶר֮ יַֽעֲקֹב֒ אֱלֹהֵי֙ אָבִ֣י אַבְרָהָ֔ם וֵֽאלֹהֵ֖י אָבִ֣י יִצְחָ֑ק יְהֹוָ֞ה הָֽאֹמֵ֣ר אֵלַ֗י שׁ֧וּב לְאַרְצְךָ֛ וּלְמֽוֹלַדְתְּךָ֖ וְאֵיטִ֥יבָה עִמָּֽךְ: 11קָטֹ֜נְתִּי מִכֹּ֤ל הַֽחֲסָדִים֙ וּמִכָּל־הָ֣אֱמֶ֔ת אֲשֶׁ֥ר עָשִׂ֖יתָ אֶת־עַבְדֶּ֑ךָ כִּ֣י בְמַקְלִ֗י עָבַ֨רְתִּי֙ אֶת־הַיַּרְדֵּ֣ן הַזֶּ֔ה וְעַתָּ֥ה הָיִ֖יתִי לִשְׁנֵ֥י מַֽחֲנֽוֹת: 12הַצִּילֵ֥נִי נָ֛א מִיַּ֥ד אָחִ֖י מִיַּ֣ד עֵשָׂ֑ו כִּֽי־יָרֵ֤א אָֽנֹכִי֙ אֹת֔וֹ פֶּן־יָב֣וֹא וְהִכַּ֔נִי אֵ֖ם עַל־בָּנִֽים: 13וְאַתָּ֣ה אָמַ֔רְתָּ הֵיטֵ֥ב אֵיטִ֖יב עִמָּ֑ךְ וְשַׂמְתִּ֣י אֶֽת־זַרְעֲךָ֗ כְּח֣וֹל הַיָּ֔ם אֲשֶׁ֥ר לֹֽא־יִסָּפֵ֖ר מֵרֹֽב: 14וַיָּ֥לֶן שָׁ֖ם בַּלַּ֣יְלָה הַה֑וּא וַיִּקַּ֞ח מִן־הַבָּ֧א בְיָד֛וֹ מִנְחָ֖ה לְעֵשָׂ֥ו אָחִֽיו: 15עִזִּ֣ים מָאתַ֗יִם וּתְיָשִׁים֙ עֶשְׂרִ֔ים רְחֵלִ֥ים מָאתַ֖יִם וְאֵילִ֥ים עֶשְׂרִֽים: 16גְּמַלִּ֧ים מֵֽינִיק֛וֹת וּבְנֵיהֶ֖ם שְׁלֹשִׁ֑ים פָּר֤וֹת אַרְבָּעִים֙ וּפָרִ֣ים עֲשָׂרָ֔ה אֲתֹנֹ֣ת עֶשְׂרִ֔ים וַעְיָרִ֖ם עֲשָׂרָֽה: 17וַיִּתֵּן֙ בְּיַד־עֲבָדָ֔יו עֵ֖דֶר עֵ֑דֶר

32:5. **I've stayed with Laban.** Rashi conveys a tradition that this means: "I lived temporarily with him, but I learned nothing from his bad ways." But Jacob does in fact learn from Laban. The deceiver meets a deceiver. He learns how it feels to *receive* an injustice, not just how it feels to dish it out. He learns that it hurts. It is a step in his development as a man. And it apparently brings about the honorable way in which he behaves toward Esau when he returns.

he placed them in his servants' hands, each herd by itself, and he said to his servants, "Pass on in front of me, and keep a distance between each herd and the next." 18And he commanded the first, saying, "When my brother, Esau, meets you and asks you, saying, 'To whom do you belong, and where are you going, and to whom do these in front of you belong?' 19then you'll say, 'To your servant, to Jacob. It's an offering sent to my lord, to Esau. And here he is behind us as well.' " 20And he also commanded the second, also the third, also all of those who were going behind the herds, saying, "You'll speak this way to Esau when you find him, 21and you'll say, 'Here is your servant, Jacob, behind us as well.' " Because he said, "Let me appease his face with the offering that's going in front of me, and after that I'll see his face; maybe he'll raise my face." 22And the offering passed ahead of him. And he spent that night in the camp.

23And he got up in that night and took his two wives and his two maids and his eleven boys and crossed the Jabbok ford. 24And he took them and had them cross the wadi, and he had everything that was his cross. 25And Jacob was left by himself.

לְבַדּוֹ וַיֹּאמֶר אֶל־עֲבָדָיו עִבְרוּ לְפָנַי וְרֶוַח תָּשִׂימוּ בֵּין עֵדֶר וּבֵין עֵדֶר: 18וַיְצַו אֶת־הָרִאשׁוֹן לֵאמֹר כִּי יִפְגָּשְׁךָ עֵשָׂו אָחִי וִשְׁאֵלְךָ לֵאמֹר לְמִי־אַתָּה וְאָנָה תֵלֵךְ וּלְמִי אֵלֶּה לְפָנֶיךָ: 19וְאָמַרְתָּ לְעַבְדְּךָ לְיַעֲקֹב מִנְחָה הִוא שְׁלוּחָה לַאדֹנִי לְעֵשָׂו וְהִנֵּה גַם־הוּא אַחֲרֵינוּ: 20וַיְצַו גַּם אֶת־הַשֵּׁנִי גַּם אֶת־הַשְּׁלִישִׁי גַּם אֶת־כָּל־הַהֹלְכִים אַחֲרֵי הָעֲדָרִים לֵאמֹר כַּדָּבָר הַזֶּה תְּדַבְּרוּן אֶל־עֵשָׂו בְּמֹצַאֲכֶם אֹתוֹ: 21וַאֲמַרְתֶּם גַּם הִנֵּה עַבְדְּךָ יַעֲקֹב אַחֲרֵינוּ כִּי־אָמַר אֲכַפְּרָה פָנָיו בַּמִּנְחָה הַהֹלֶכֶת לְפָנָי וְאַחֲרֵי־כֵן אֶרְאֶה פָנָיו אוּלַי יִשָּׂא פָנָי: 22וַתַּעֲבֹר הַמִּנְחָה עַל־פָּנָיו וְהוּא לָן בַּלַּיְלָה־הַהוּא בַּמַּחֲנֶה:
23וַיָּקָם | בַּלַּיְלָה הוּא וַיִּקַּח אֶת־שְׁתֵּי נָשָׁיו וְאֶת־שְׁתֵּי שִׁפְחֹתָיו וְאֶת־אַחַד עָשָׂר יְלָדָיו וַיַּעֲבֹר אֵת מַעֲבַר יַבֹּק: 24וַיִּקָּחֵם וַיַּעֲבִרֵם אֶת־הַנָּחַל וַיַּעֲבֵר אֶת־אֲשֶׁר־לוֹ: 25וַיִּוָּתֵר יַעֲקֹב לְבַדּוֹ וַיֵּאָבֵק

32:21–22. **his face . . . in front of me . . . I'll see his face . . . my face . . . ahead of him**. The word "face" recurs five times in this line and all through these two chapters (as does the word "raise"). It also is part of the term that is translated as the preposition "in front of" or "ahead of" (in Hebrew, *lĕpānāy*). The repetition conveys the force of this juncture in Jacob's life. He must face his past. He must face his brother, whom he wronged. And in the middle of the account of his facing his brother will come the account of his most immediate contact with God in his life, his struggle after which he will say, "I've seen God face-to-face." And the two encounters, first with his God and then with his brother, will then be brought together as he says to Esau, "I've seen your face—like seeing God's face!" (33:10).

This is also ironic because Jacob left twenty years earlier in the wake of his deception, which worked because his weak-eyed father could not see his face!

32:23. **his eleven boys**. His daughter, Dinah, is not mentioned.

And a man wrestled with him until the dawn's rising. 26And he saw that he was not able against him, and he touched the inside of his thigh, and the inside of Jacob's thigh was dislocated during his wrestling with him.

27And he said, "Let me go, because the dawn has risen."

And he said, "I won't let you go unless you bless me."

28And he said to him, "What is your name?"

And he said, "Jacob."

29And he said, "Your name won't be said 'Jacob' anymore but 'Israel,' because you've struggled with God and with people and were able."

אִישׁ עִמּוֹ עַד עֲלוֹת הַשָּׁחַר: 26וַיַּרְא כִּי לֹא יָכֹל לוֹ וַיִּגַּע בְּכַף־יְרֵכוֹ וַתֵּקַע כַּף־יֶרֶךְ יַעֲקֹב בְּהֵאָבְקוֹ עִמּוֹ: 27וַיֹּאמֶר שַׁלְּחֵנִי כִּי עָלָה הַשָּׁחַר וַיֹּאמֶר לֹא אֲשַׁלֵּחֲךָ כִּי אִם־בֵּרַכְתָּנִי: 28וַיֹּאמֶר אֵלָיו מַה־שְּׁמֶךָ וַיֹּאמֶר יַעֲקֹב: 29וַיֹּאמֶר לֹא יַעֲקֹב יֵאָמֵר עוֹד שִׁמְךָ כִּי אִם־יִשְׂרָאֵל כִּי־שָׂרִיתָ עִם־אֱלֹהִים וְעִם־אֲנָשִׁים

32:25. **a man wrestled with him**. With whom does he wrestle? It says "a man." But he is able against the man, and later the man names him *yiśrā-'ēl*, which is interpreted to mean "struggles with God," and says to him, "You've struggled with God and with people and were able." And Jacob names the place Peni-El, meaning "face of God," and says, "I've seen God face-to-face." This all indicates that he has wrestled with God in human form. But the prophet Hosea refers to this moment and says, "He fought with God, and he fought with an angel and was able" (Hos 12:5–6). This is consistent with the description of angels that I gave in the matter of the three people who visit Abraham (18:3). Angels are material expressions of God's presence (emanations from the Godhead, hypostases). When they are in front of a human, they look like a "man," like "people." That is why Hosea can say "He fought with God" and then say in poetic parallel about the same event "he fought with an angel."

32:26. **dislocated**. This is the term that is used in Num 25:4 for a punishment that is inflicted on the Israelites following a heresy at Baal Peor. Its meaning is uncertain both there and here. There it may mean to hang or impale, in which case here it might mean that the thigh bone is hanging out of joint.

32:27. **I won't let you go unless you bless me**. Jacob *demands* a blessing. Is it usual to demand a blessing from someone with whom we have been fighting?! The struggle with God takes such an exertion of one's strength, and takes such a toll, that the human who does it has to live with the wounds thereafter (Jacob limps after this struggle). And so he is in need of blessing—and has earned it.

32:29. **Israel**. There is little character development in Adam, Eve, Noah, Abraham, Sarah, Isaac, or Rebekah, all of whom remain basically constant figures through the stories about them. But Jacob changes, and the matter of deception is intimately related to that development. As Esau points out, Jacob's very name connotes deception: to catch. And Jacob starts out as a manipulator. But Jacob is changed after his experiences in Mesopotamia. He has been the deceiver and the deceived. He has hurt and been hurt. He is now a husband and a father, a man who has struggled and prospered.

30And Jacob asked, and he said, "Tell your name."

And he said, "Why is this that you ask my name?" And he blessed him there.

31And Jacob called the place's name Peni-El, "because I've seen God face-to-face, and my life has been delivered."

32And the sun rose on him as he passed Penuel, and he was faltering on his thigh. 33On account of this the children of Israel to this day will not eat the tendon of the vein that is on the inside of the thigh, because he touched the inside of Jacob's thigh, the tendon of the vein.

33

1And Jacob raised his eyes and looked, and here was Esau coming, and four hundred men with him. And he divided the children among Leah and Rachel and the two maids; 2and he placed the maids and their children first, and Leah and her children following, and Rachel and Joseph following, 3and he passed in front of them. And he bowed to the ground seven times until he came up to his brother. 4And Esau ran to him and embraced him and fell on his neck and kissed him. And they wept. 5And he raised his

וַתּוֹכָל: 30וַיִּשְׁאַל יַעֲקֹב וַיֹּאמֶר הַגִּידָה־נָּא שְׁמֶךָ וַיֹּאמֶר לָמָּה זֶּה תִּשְׁאַל לִשְׁמִי וַיְבָרֶךְ אֹתוֹ שָׁם: 31וַיִּקְרָא יַעֲקֹב שֵׁם הַמָּקוֹם פְּנִיאֵל כִּי־רָאִיתִי אֱלֹהִים פָּנִים אֶל־פָּנִים וַתִּנָּצֵל נַפְשִׁי: 32וַיִּזְרַח־לוֹ הַשֶּׁמֶשׁ כַּאֲשֶׁר עָבַר אֶת־פְּנוּאֵל וְהוּא צֹלֵעַ עַל־יְרֵכוֹ: 33עַל־כֵּן לֹא־יֹאכְלוּ בְנֵי־יִשְׂרָאֵל אֶת־גִּיד הַנָּשֶׁה אֲשֶׁר עַל־כַּף הַיָּרֵךְ עַד הַיּוֹם הַזֶּה כִּי נָגַע בְּכַף־יֶרֶךְ יַעֲקֹב בְּגִיד הַנָּשֶׁה:

33 1וַיִּשָּׂא יַעֲקֹב עֵינָיו וַיַּרְא וְהִנֵּה עֵשָׂו בָּא וְעִמּוֹ אַרְבַּע מֵאוֹת אִישׁ וַיַּחַץ אֶת־הַיְלָדִים עַל־לֵאָה וְעַל־רָחֵל וְעַל שְׁתֵּי הַשְּׁפָחוֹת: 2וַיָּשֶׂם אֶת־הַשְּׁפָחוֹת וְאֶת־יַלְדֵיהֶן רִאשֹׁנָה וְאֶת־לֵאָה וִילָדֶיהָ אַחֲרֹנִים וְאֶת־רָחֵל וְאֶת־יוֹסֵף אַחֲרֹנִים: 3וְהוּא עָבַר לִפְנֵיהֶם וַיִּשְׁתַּחוּ אַרְצָה שֶׁבַע פְּעָמִים עַד־גִּשְׁתּוֹ עַד־אָחִיו: 4וַיָּרָץ עֵשָׂו לִקְרָאתוֹ וַיְחַבְּקֵהוּ וַיִּפֹּל עַל־צַוָּארָו וַיִּשָּׁקֵהוּ וַיִּבְכּוּ: 5וַיִּשָּׂא אֶת־עֵינָיו

For the rest of the story he is no longer pictured as a man of action but, more often, as a relatively passive man, like his father Isaac, seeking to appease his brother, avoiding strife and risk. And precisely at the juncture that marks this change in Jacob's character he has his encounter with God at Penuel. God blesses him in a remarkable etiology/etymology: "Your name shall no longer be called Jacob, but Israel [*yiśrā-'ēl*, understood here to mean 'he struggles with God'], because you've struggled with God and with people and were able. Is this divine encounter the signpost of the change in Jacob's character, or the cause? Either way, as his character changes, and he ceases to be the deceiver, just then he sheds the name Jacob (the one who catches) and becomes instead Israel (the one who struggles with God).

33:1. **Jacob.** Abraham and Sarah have their names changed permanently, but Jacob is still called Jacob many times after his name is changed to Israel. Rabbi Simcha Weiser teaches that this shows that "Israel" (struggle with God) is something to be attained. It is a long process in one's life.

33:4. **fell on his neck.** Jacob deceived his father and displaced Esau by putting skins "on the smooth part of his *neck*" (27:16). Then there was a hint that Esau would be compensated for his loss one day by the use of the metaphor that "you'll break his

eyes and saw the women and the children, and he said, "Who are these whom you have?"

And he said, "The children with whom God has graced your servant."

⁶And the maids came over, they and their children, and bowed. ⁷And Leah and her children, too, came over, and they bowed. And then Joseph and Rachel came over, and they bowed.

⁸And he said, "Who is all this camp of yours that I met?"

And he said, "To find favor in my lord's eyes."

⁹And Esau said, "I have a great deal, my brother. Let what's yours be yours."

¹⁰And Jacob said, "Don't. If I've found favor in your eyes, then you'll take my offering from my hand, because on account of this I've seen your face—like seeing God's face!—and you've accepted me. ¹¹Take my blessing that's been brought to

וַיַּרְא אֶת־הַנָּשִׁים וְאֶת־הַיְלָדִים וַיֹּאמֶר מִי־אֵלֶּה לָּךְ וַיֹּאמַר הַיְלָדִים אֲשֶׁר־חָנַן אֱלֹהִים אֶת־עַבְדֶּךָ: ⁶וַתִּגַּשְׁןָ הַשְּׁפָחוֹת הֵנָּה וְיַלְדֵיהֶן וַתִּשְׁתַּחֲוֶיןָ: ⁷וַתִּגַּשׁ גַּם־לֵאָה וִילָדֶיהָ וַיִּשְׁתַּחֲווּ וְאַחַר נִגַּשׁ יוֹסֵף וְרָחֵל וַיִּשְׁתַּחֲווּ: ⁸וַיֹּאמֶר מִי לְךָ כָּל־הַמַּחֲנֶה הַזֶּה אֲשֶׁר פָּגָשְׁתִּי וַיֹּאמֶר לִמְצֹא־חֵן בְּעֵינֵי אֲדֹנִי: ⁹וַיֹּאמֶר עֵשָׂו יֶשׁ־לִי רָב אָחִי יְהִי לְךָ אֲשֶׁר־לָךְ: ¹⁰וַיֹּאמֶר יַעֲקֹב אַל־נָא אִם־נָא מָצָאתִי חֵן בְּעֵינֶיךָ וְלָקַחְתָּ מִנְחָתִי מִיָּדִי כִּי עַל־כֵּן רָאִיתִי פָנֶיךָ כִּרְאֹת פְּנֵי אֱלֹהִים וַתִּרְצֵנִי: ¹¹קַח־נָא אֶת־בִּרְכָתִי אֲשֶׁר הֻבָאת לָךְ

---

yoke from your *neck*" (27:40). And now, the reconciliation between the twins is conveyed as Esau runs and embraces Jacob and "fell on his *neck.*"

33:7. **Joseph and Rachel came over**. Leah, Bilhah, and Zilpah are mentioned before their children, but Joseph is mentioned before Rachel, yielding a picture of him approaching ahead of her. In his favor, we might take this as a protective gesture toward his mother. Alternatively, we might take this as consistent with the next picture we shall have of his early years: seeing himself in a special status relative to his family.

33:9. **Let what's yours be yours**. Esau graciously refuses Jacob's gift. Then Jacob presses him to accept it. Then Esau takes it. As in the episode of Abraham's purchase of the tomb for Sarah, and Lot's offering his daughters to the people of Sodom, Jacob and Esau are going through the classic Near Eastern conventions, which continue to this day.

33:10. **I've seen your face—like seeing God's face**. Esau has no idea just how literally this is meant. Jacob had prayed for help because he was afraid of Esau. Then he had the encounter after which he said, "I've seen God face-to-face." And this, presumably, enabled him to face his brother. Esau may take Jacob's words as a great compliment, but they actually convey that, after facing God, one is certainly able to face any human.

33:11. **Take my blessing**. It was Jacob's taking of Esau's blessing that led to the brothers' separation. His description now of what he is offering as "my blessing" suggests that it is an act of compensation for what he did to Esau twenty years earlier. Unlike biblical interpreters who try to defend Jacob's earlier actions, Jacob himself is pictured as (1) not trying to make any excuses, and (2) trying to make amends.

you, because God has been gracious to me and because I have everything." And he pressed him, and he took it.

12And he said, "Let's travel, and let's go. And let me go alongside you."

13And he said to him, "My lord knows that the children are weak and the nursing sheep and oxen are with me, and they'll drive them one day and all the sheep will die. 14Let my lord pass on in front of his servant; and I, let me move along at my pace required by the task that's before me and required by the children until I come to my lord at Seir."

15And Esau said, "Let me set with you some of the people who are with me."

And he said, "Why have I found favor in my lord's eyes?"

16And Esau went back on his way to Seir that day, 17and Jacob traveled to Sukkot. And he built a house for himself and made booths for his cattle. On account of this he called the place's name Sukkot. 18And Jacob came, safe, to the city of Shechem, which was in the land of Canaan, when he was coming from Paddan Aram, and camped in front of the city. 19And he bought the section of field in which he pitched his tent from the hand of the sons of Hamor, father of Shechem, for a hundred qesita. 20And he set up an altar there and called it "El, God of Israel."

34

1And Dinah, Leah's daughter, whom she had borne to Jacob, went out to see the daughters of the land. 2And Shechem, son of Hamor, the Hivite, the chieftain of the land, saw her. And he took her and lay with her and de-

כִּי־חַנַּנִי אֱלֹהִים וְכִי יֶשׁ־לִי־כֹל וַיִּפְצַר־בּוֹ וַיִּקָּח: 12וַיֹּאמֶר נִסְעָה וְנֵלֵכָה וְאֵלְכָה לְנֶגְדֶּךָ: 13וַיֹּאמֶר אֵלָיו אֲדֹנִי יֹדֵעַ כִּי־הַיְלָדִים רַכִּים וְהַצֹּאן וְהַבָּקָר עָלוֹת עָלָי וּדְפָקוּם יוֹם אֶחָד וָמֵתוּ כָּל־הַצֹּאן: 14יַעֲבָר־נָא אֲדֹנִי לִפְנֵי עַבְדּוֹ וַאֲנִי אֶתְנָהֲלָה לְאִטִּי לְרֶגֶל הַמְּלָאכָה אֲשֶׁר־לְפָנַי וּלְרֶגֶל הַיְלָדִים עַד אֲשֶׁר־אָבֹא אֶל־אֲדֹנִי שֵׂעִירָה: 15וַיֹּאמֶר עֵשָׂו אַצִּיגָה־נָּא עִמְּךָ מִן־הָעָם אֲשֶׁר אִתִּי וַיֹּאמֶר לָמָּה זֶּה אֶמְצָא־חֵן בְּעֵינֵי אֲדֹנִי: 16וַיָּשָׁב בַּיּוֹם הַהוּא עֵשָׂו לְדַרְכּוֹ שֵׂעִירָה: 17וְיַעֲקֹב נָסַע סֻכֹּתָה וַיִּבֶן לוֹ בָּיִת וּלְמִקְנֵהוּ עָשָׂה סֻכֹּת עַל־כֵּן קָרָא שֵׁם־הַמָּקוֹם סֻכּוֹת: ס 18וַיָּבֹא יַעֲקֹב שָׁלֵם עִיר שְׁכֶם אֲשֶׁר בְּאֶרֶץ כְּנַעַן בְּבֹאוֹ מִפַּדַּן אֲרָם וַיִּחַן אֶת־פְּנֵי הָעִיר: 19וַיִּקֶן אֶת־חֶלְקַת הַשָּׂדֶה אֲשֶׁר נָטָה־שָׁם אָהֳלוֹ מִיַּד בְּנֵי־חֲמוֹר אֲבִי שְׁכֶם בְּמֵאָה קְשִׂיטָה: 20וַיַּצֶּב־שָׁם מִזְבֵּחַ וַיִּקְרָא־לוֹ אֵל אֱלֹהֵי יִשְׂרָאֵל:

ס

34 1וַתֵּצֵא דִינָה בַּת־לֵאָה אֲשֶׁר יָלְדָה לְיַעֲקֹב לִרְאוֹת בִּבְנוֹת הָאָרֶץ: 2וַיַּרְא אֹתָהּ שְׁכֶם בֶּן־חֲמוֹר הַחִוִּי נְשִׂיא הָאָרֶץ וַיִּקַּח אֹתָהּ וַיִּשְׁכַּב אֹתָהּ וַיְעַנֶּהָ:

33:15. Why have I found favor in my lord's eyes? Jacob seems to be saying, "No, no, I don't deserve this kindness from you," which appears to be an extremely polite way of declining Esau's offer. Understandably, this offer to post some men with Jacob is not attractive to him: Jacob has just told Esau that he will meet him in Seir, but in fact the next two verses report that Esau goes back to Seir but Jacob goes to Sukkot!

34:2. he took her and lay with her and degraded her. This is commonly treated as a story of a rape. Some Bibles even put a heading over it: "The Rape of Dinah." But,

graded her. 3And his soul clung to Dinah, Jacob's daughter, and he loved the girl and spoke on the girl's heart. 4And Shechem said to Hamor, his father, "Get me this girl for a wife."

5And Jacob heard that he had defiled Dinah, his daughter; and his sons were with his cattle in the field, and Jacob kept quiet until they came. 6And Hamor, Shechem's father, went out to Jacob to speak with him. 7And Jacob's sons came from the field when they heard, and the men were pained, and they were very furious, for he had done a foolhardy thing among Israel, to lie with Jacob's daughter, and such a thing is not done. 8And Hamor spoke with them, saying, "Shechem—my son—his soul longs for your daughter. Give her to him as a wife, 9and marry with us; give your daughters to us and take our daughters to you, 10and live with us; and the land will be before you: live and go around in it and take possession in it."

11And Shechem said to her father and to her brothers, "Let me find favor in your eyes, and I'll give whatever you say to me. 12Make a bride-price and gift on me very great, and let me give whatever you say to me, and give me the girl as a wife."

13And Jacob's sons answered Shechem and

3וַתִּדְבַּק נַפְשׁוֹ בְּדִינָה בַּת־יַעֲקֹב וַיֶּאֱהַב אֶת־הַנַּעֲרָ וַיְדַבֵּר עַל־לֵב הַנַּעֲרָ: 4וַיֹּאמֶר שְׁכֶם אֶל־חֲמוֹר אָבִיו לֵאמֹר קַח־לִי אֶת־הַיַּלְדָּה הַזֹּאת לְאִשָּׁה: 5וְיַעֲקֹב שָׁמַע כִּי טִמֵּא אֶת־דִּינָה בִתּוֹ וּבָנָיו הָיוּ אֶת־מִקְנֵהוּ בַּשָּׂדֶה וְהֶחֱרִשׁ יַעֲקֹב עַד־בֹּאָם: 6וַיֵּצֵא חֲמוֹר אֲבִי־שְׁכֶם אֶל־יַעֲקֹב לְדַבֵּר אִתּוֹ: 7וּבְנֵי יַעֲקֹב בָּאוּ מִן־הַשָּׂדֶה כְּשָׁמְעָם וַיִּתְעַצְּבוּ הָאֲנָשִׁים וַיִּחַר לָהֶם מְאֹד כִּי־נְבָלָה עָשָׂה בְיִשְׂרָאֵל לִשְׁכַּב אֶת־בַּת־יַעֲקֹב וְכֵן לֹא יֵעָשֶׂה: 8וַיְדַבֵּר חֲמוֹר אִתָּם לֵאמֹר שְׁכֶם בְּנִי חָשְׁקָה נַפְשׁוֹ בְּבִתְּכֶם תְּנוּ נָא אֹתָהּ לוֹ לְאִשָּׁה: 9וְהִתְחַתְּנוּ אֹתָנוּ בְּנֹתֵיכֶם תִּתְּנוּ־לָנוּ וְאֶת־בְּנֹתֵינוּ תִּקְחוּ לָכֶם: 10וְאִתָּנוּ תֵּשֵׁבוּ וְהָאָרֶץ תִּהְיֶה לִפְנֵיכֶם שְׁבוּ וּסְחָרוּהָ וְהֵאָחֲזוּ בָּהּ: 11וַיֹּאמֶר שְׁכֶם אֶל־אָבִיהָ וְאֶל־אַחֶיהָ אֶמְצָא־חֵן בְּעֵינֵיכֶם וַאֲשֶׁר תֹּאמְרוּ אֵלַי אֶתֵּן: 12הַרְבּוּ עָלַי מְאֹד מֹהַר וּמַתָּן וְאֶתְּנָה כַּאֲשֶׁר תֹּאמְרוּ אֵלָי וּתְנוּ־לִי אֶת־הַנַּעֲרָ לְאִשָּׁה: 13וַיַּעֲנוּ בְנֵי־יַעֲקֹב אֶת־שְׁכֶם

the nature of the act is not in fact clear from this wording. The three key terms here (took, lay, degraded) appear to suggest force, but all three are used without such a meaning in the Torah's laws concerning marriage and rape. To "take" (*lāqaḥ*) a woman is used even to mean marriage (Deut 22:13); and to "lie with" (*šākab*) and to "degrade" (*'innāh*) are both used in a case that is specifically ruled *not* to be a rape (Deut 22:23–24). The following case there adds the words "he took hold of her" (22:25), and that case is ruled to be a rape. Also the story of Amnon and Tamar (2 Samuel 13) is comparable to the Dinah story in a notable number of details and terms. In that story there is unquestionably a rape, and it uses the terms "lay with her" and "degraded her," but it also adds "he took hold of her" (13:11–12,14). That determining verb in Deuteronomy and in the Tamar story is not present here in the Dinah story. It may be a rape, but we cannot be sure. What we can say, at minimum, is that whether it is a rape, a seduction, or even consensual intercourse, Shechem's act, taking place before the request for marriage, is regarded as disgraceful by Dinah's family. This leads to Simeon's and Levi's violent deception, and this in turn has consequences ultimately for the destiny of the family (see the next comment).

Hamor, his father, with deception as they spoke because he had defiled Dinah, their sister. 14And they said to them, "We aren't able to do this thing, to give our sister to a man who has a foreskin, because that's a disgrace to us. 15Only this way will we consent to you: if you'll be like us, every male among you to be circumcised. 16And we'll give our daughters to you and take your daughters to us, and we'll live with you, and we'll become one people. 17And if you won't listen to us, to be circumcised, then we'll take our daughter and go."

18And their words were good in Hamor's eyes and in Hamor's son Shechem's eyes. 19And the boy did not delay to do the thing, for he desired Jacob's daughter. And he was more respected than all his father's house. 20And Hamor and his son Shechem came to the gate of their city and spoke to the people of their city, saying, 21"These people are peaceable with us, and they'll live in the land and go around in it, and the land, here, has enough breadth for them. Let's take their daughters for us as wives and give our daughters to them. 22Only in this way will these people consent to us to live with us, to be one people: if every male among us is circumcised as they are circumcised. 23Their cattle and possessions and all their animals: won't they be ours? Only let's consent to them, and they'll live with us." 24And everyone who went out of the gate of his city listened to Hamor and to his son Shechem; and every male, everyone who went out of the gate of his city, was circumcised.

25And it was on the third day, when they were hurting, and two of Jacob's sons, Simeon and Levi, Dinah's brothers, each took his sword, and they came upon the city stealthily, and they killed every male. 26And they killed Hamor and his son Shechem by the sword and took Dinah from Shechem's house and went out. 27Jacob's sons had come upon the corpses and despoiled the city because they had defiled their sister. 28They took their sheep and their oxen and their asses and what was in the city and what was in

וְאֶת־חֲמוֹר אָבִיו בְּמִרְמָה וַיְדַבֵּרוּ אֲשֶׁר טִמֵּא אֵת דִּינָה אֲחֹתָם: 14וַיֹּאמְרוּ אֲלֵיהֶם לֹא נוּכַל לַעֲשׂוֹת הַדָּבָר הַזֶּה לָתֵת אֶת־אֲחֹתֵנוּ לְאִישׁ אֲשֶׁר־לוֹ עָרְלָה כִּי־חֶרְפָּה הִוא לָנוּ: 15אַךְ־בְּזֹאת נֵאוֹת לָכֶם אִם תִּהְיוּ כָמֹנוּ לְהִמֹּל לָכֶם כָּל־זָכָר: 16וְנָתַנּוּ אֶת־בְּנֹתֵינוּ לָכֶם וְאֶת־בְּנֹתֵיכֶם נִקַּח־לָנוּ וְיָשַׁבְנוּ אִתְּכֶם וְהָיִינוּ לְעַם אֶחָד: 17וְאִם־לֹא תִשְׁמְעוּ אֵלֵינוּ לְהִמּוֹל וְלָקַחְנוּ אֶת־בִּתֵּנוּ וְהָלָכְנוּ: 18וַיִּיטְבוּ דִבְרֵיהֶם בְּעֵינֵי חֲמוֹר וּבְעֵינֵי שְׁכֶם בֶּן־חֲמוֹר: 19וְלֹא־אֵחַר הַנַּעַר לַעֲשׂוֹת הַדָּבָר כִּי חָפֵץ בְּבַת־יַעֲקֹב וְהוּא נִכְבָּד מִכֹּל בֵּית אָבִיו: 20וַיָּבֹא חֲמוֹר וּשְׁכֶם בְּנוֹ אֶל־שַׁעַר עִירָם וַיְדַבְּרוּ אֶל־אַנְשֵׁי עִירָם לֵאמֹר: 21הָאֲנָשִׁים הָאֵלֶּה שְׁלֵמִים הֵם אִתָּנוּ וְיֵשְׁבוּ בָאָרֶץ וְיִסְחֲרוּ אֹתָהּ וְהָאָרֶץ הִנֵּה רַחֲבַת־יָדַיִם לִפְנֵיהֶם אֶת־בְּנֹתָם נִקַּח־לָנוּ לְנָשִׁים וְאֶת־בְּנֹתֵינוּ נִתֵּן לָהֶם: 22אַךְ־בְּזֹאת יֵאֹתוּ לָנוּ הָאֲנָשִׁים לָשֶׁבֶת אִתָּנוּ לִהְיוֹת לְעַם אֶחָד בְּהִמּוֹל לָנוּ כָּל־זָכָר כַּאֲשֶׁר הֵם נִמֹּלִים: 23מִקְנֵהֶם וְקִנְיָנָם וְכָל־בְּהֶמְתָּם הֲלוֹא לָנוּ הֵם אַךְ נֵאוֹתָה לָהֶם וְיֵשְׁבוּ אִתָּנוּ: 24וַיִּשְׁמְעוּ אֶל־חֲמוֹר וְאֶל־שְׁכֶם בְּנוֹ כָּל־יֹצְאֵי שַׁעַר עִירוֹ וַיִּמֹּלוּ כָּל־זָכָר כָּל־יֹצְאֵי שַׁעַר עִירוֹ: 25וַיְהִי בַיּוֹם הַשְּׁלִישִׁי בִּהְיוֹתָם כֹּאֲבִים וַיִּקְחוּ שְׁנֵי־בְנֵי־יַעֲקֹב שִׁמְעוֹן וְלֵוִי אֲחֵי דִינָה אִישׁ חַרְבּוֹ וַיָּבֹאוּ עַל־הָעִיר בֶּטַח וַיַּהַרְגוּ כָּל־זָכָר: 26וְאֶת־חֲמוֹר וְאֶת־שְׁכֶם בְּנוֹ הָרְגוּ לְפִי־חָרֶב וַיִּקְחוּ אֶת־דִּינָה מִבֵּית שְׁכֶם וַיֵּצֵאוּ: 27בְּנֵי יַעֲקֹב בָּאוּ עַל־הַחֲלָלִים וַיָּבֹזּוּ הָעִיר אֲשֶׁר טִמְּאוּ אֲחוֹתָם: 28אֶת־צֹאנָם וְאֶת־בְּקָרָם וְאֶת־חֲמֹרֵיהֶם וְאֵת אֲשֶׁר־בָּעִיר וְאֶת־אֲשֶׁר

the field. 29And they captured and despoiled all their wealth and all their infants and their wives and everything that was in the house. 30And Jacob said to Simeon and to Levi, "You've caused me anguish, making me odious to those who live in the land, to the Canaanite and to the Perizzite, and I'm few in number, and they'll be gathered against me and strike me, and I'll be destroyed, I and my house."

31And they said, "Shall he treat our sister like a prostitute?"

35 1And God said to Jacob, "Get up. Go up to Beth-El and live there and make an altar there to God, who appeared to you when you were fleeing from Esau, your brother."

2And Jacob said to his house and to everyone who was with him, "Put away the foreign gods that are among you and be purified and change your clothes; 3and let's get up and go up to Beth-El, and I'll make an altar there to God, who answered me in a day of my trouble, and He was with me in the way that I went." 4And they gave all the foreign gods that were in their hand and the rings that were in their ears to Jacob, and Jacob stashed them under the oak that was by Shechem. 5And they traveled, and God's terror was on the cities that were around them, and they did not pursue the children of Jacob. 6And Jacob came to Luz, which is in the land of Canaan—it is Beth-El—he and all the people who were with him. 7And he built an altar there and called the place El of Beth-El because God was revealed to him there when he was fleeing from his brother.

8And Deborah, Rebekah's nurse, died and was buried beneath Beth-El, beneath an oak, and he called its name Oak of Weeping.

בַּשָּׂדֶה לָקָחוּ: 29וְאֶת־כָּל־חֵילָם וְאֶת־כָּל־טַפָּם וְאֶת־נְשֵׁיהֶם שָׁבוּ וַיָּבֹזּוּ וְאֵת כָּל־אֲשֶׁר בַּבָּיִת: 30וַיֹּאמֶר יַעֲקֹב אֶל־שִׁמְעוֹן וְאֶל־לֵוִי עֲכַרְתֶּם אֹתִי לְהַבְאִישֵׁנִי בְּיֹשֵׁב הָאָרֶץ בַּכְּנַעֲנִי וּבַפְּרִזִּי וַאֲנִי מְתֵי מִסְפָּר וְנֶאֶסְפוּ עָלַי וְהִכּוּנִי וְנִשְׁמַדְתִּי אֲנִי וּבֵיתִי: 31וַיֹּאמְרוּ הַכְזוֹנָה יַעֲשֶׂה אֶת־אֲחוֹתֵנוּ: פ

35 1וַיֹּאמֶר אֱלֹהִים אֶל־יַעֲקֹב קוּם עֲלֵה בֵית־אֵל וְשֶׁב־שָׁם וַעֲשֵׂה־שָׁם מִזְבֵּחַ לָאֵל הַנִּרְאֶה אֵלֶיךָ בְּבָרְחֲךָ מִפְּנֵי עֵשָׂו אָחִיךָ: 2וַיֹּאמֶר יַעֲקֹב אֶל־בֵּיתוֹ וְאֶל כָּל־אֲשֶׁר עִמּוֹ הָסִרוּ אֶת־אֱלֹהֵי הַנֵּכָר אֲשֶׁר בְּתֹכְכֶם וְהִטַּהֲרוּ וְהַחֲלִיפוּ שִׂמְלֹתֵיכֶם: 3וְנָקוּמָה וְנַעֲלֶה בֵּית־אֵל וְאֶעֱשֶׂה־שָּׁם מִזְבֵּחַ לָאֵל הָעֹנֶה אֹתִי בְּיוֹם צָרָתִי וַיְהִי עִמָּדִי בַּדֶּרֶךְ אֲשֶׁר הָלָכְתִּי: 4וַיִּתְּנוּ אֶל־יַעֲקֹב אֵת כָּל־אֱלֹהֵי הַנֵּכָר אֲשֶׁר בְּיָדָם וְאֶת־הַנְּזָמִים אֲשֶׁר בְּאָזְנֵיהֶם וַיִּטְמֹן אֹתָם יַעֲקֹב תַּחַת הָאֵלָה אֲשֶׁר עִם־שְׁכֶם: 5וַיִּסָּעוּ וַיְהִי ׀ חִתַּת אֱלֹהִים עַל־הֶעָרִים אֲשֶׁר סְבִיבֹתֵיהֶם וְלֹא רָדְפוּ אַחֲרֵי בְּנֵי יַעֲקֹב: 6וַיָּבֹא יַעֲקֹב לוּזָה אֲשֶׁר בְּאֶרֶץ כְּנַעַן הִוא בֵּית־אֵל הוּא וְכָל־הָעָם אֲשֶׁר־עִמּוֹ: 7וַיִּבֶן שָׁם מִזְבֵּחַ וַיִּקְרָא לַמָּקוֹם אֵל בֵּית־אֵל כִּי שָׁם נִגְלוּ אֵלָיו הָאֱלֹהִים בְּבָרְחוֹ מִפְּנֵי אָחִיו: 8וַתָּמָת דְּבֹרָה מֵינֶקֶת רִבְקָה וַתִּקָּבֵר מִתַּחַת לְבֵית־אֵל תַּחַת הָאַלּוֹן וַיִּקְרָא שְׁמוֹ אַלּוֹן בָּכוּת:

34:31. **Shall he treat our sister like a prostitute?** Simeon and Levi seem to have the last word here, but the recompense for their violence comes many years later. In his deathbed blessing of his sons, Jacob criticizes them, demotes them from the order of birthright, and condemns them to being scattered (Gen 49:5–7). This comes true, as the tribes of Levi and Simeon became landless.

9And God appeared to Jacob again when he was coming from Paddan Aram, and He blessed him. 10And God said to him, "Your name is Jacob. Your name will not be called Jacob anymore, but rather Israel will be your name." And He called his name Israel. 11And God said to him, "I am El Shadday. Be fruitful and multiply. A nation and a community of nations will be from you, and kings will come out from your hips. 12And the land that I gave to Abraham and to Isaac: I'll give it to you, and I'll give the land to your seed after you." 13And God went up from on him in the place where He had spoken with him. 14And Jacob set up a pillar in the place where He had spoken with him, a stone pillar, and he poured a libation on it and spilled oil on it. 15And Jacob called the name of the place where God had spoken to him there Beth-El.

16And they traveled from Beth-El, and there was still the span of the land to come to Ephrat, and Rachel gave birth, and she had difficulty in her labor. 17And it was when she was having difficulty in her labor, and the midwife said to her, "Don't be afraid, because this, too, is a son for you." 18And it was as her soul was going out—because she died—and she called his name Ben-oni. And his father called him Benjamin. 19And Rachel died. And she was buried on the road to Ephrat. It is Bethlehem. 20And Jacob set up a pillar on her grave. It is the pillar of Rachel's grave to this day.

21And Israel traveled and pitched his tent past Migdal-Eder. 22And it was when Israel was tenting in that land: and Reuben went and lay with Bilhah, his father's concubine. And Israel heard.

פ 9וַיֵּרָא אֱלֹהִים אֶל־יַעֲקֹב עוֹד בְּבֹאוֹ מִפַּדַּן אֲרָם וַיְבָרֶךְ אֹתוֹ: 10וַיֹּאמֶר־לוֹ אֱלֹהִים שִׁמְךָ יַעֲקֹב לֹא־יִקָּרֵא שִׁמְךָ עוֹד יַעֲקֹב כִּי אִם־יִשְׂרָאֵל יִהְיֶה שְׁמֶךָ וַיִּקְרָא אֶת־שְׁמוֹ יִשְׂרָאֵל: 11וַיֹּאמֶר לוֹ אֱלֹהִים אֲנִי אֵל שַׁדַּי פְּרֵה וּרְבֵה גּוֹי וּקְהַל גּוֹיִם יִהְיֶה מִמֶּךָּ וּמְלָכִים מֵחֲלָצֶיךָ יֵצֵאוּ: 12וְאֶת־הָאָרֶץ אֲשֶׁר נָתַתִּי לְאַבְרָהָם וּלְיִצְחָק לְךָ אֶתְּנֶנָּה וּלְזַרְעֲךָ אַחֲרֶיךָ אֶתֵּן אֶת־הָאָרֶץ: 13וַיַּעַל מֵעָלָיו אֱלֹהִים בַּמָּקוֹם אֲשֶׁר־דִּבֶּר אִתּוֹ: 14וַיַּצֵּב יַעֲקֹב מַצֵּבָה בַּמָּקוֹם אֲשֶׁר־דִּבֶּר אִתּוֹ מַצֶּבֶת אָבֶן וַיַּסֵּךְ עָלֶיהָ נֶסֶךְ וַיִּצֹק עָלֶיהָ שָׁמֶן: 15וַיִּקְרָא יַעֲקֹב אֶת־שֵׁם הַמָּקוֹם אֲשֶׁר דִּבֶּר אִתּוֹ שָׁם אֱלֹהִים בֵּית־אֵל: 16וַיִּסְעוּ מִבֵּית אֵל וַיְהִי־עוֹד כִּבְרַת־הָאָרֶץ לָבוֹא אֶפְרָתָה וַתֵּלֶד רָחֵל וַתְּקַשׁ בְּלִדְתָּהּ: 17וַיְהִי בְהַקְשֹׁתָהּ בְּלִדְתָּהּ וַתֹּאמֶר לָהּ הַמְיַלֶּדֶת אַל־תִּירְאִי כִּי־גַם־זֶה לָךְ בֵּן: 18וַיְהִי בְּצֵאת נַפְשָׁהּ כִּי מֵתָה וַתִּקְרָא שְׁמוֹ בֶּן־אוֹנִי וְאָבִיו קָרָא־לוֹ בִנְיָמִין: 19וַתָּמָת רָחֵל וַתִּקָּבֵר בְּדֶרֶךְ אֶפְרָתָה הִוא בֵּית לָחֶם: 20וַיַּצֵּב יַעֲקֹב מַצֵּבָה עַל־קְבֻרָתָהּ הִוא מַצֶּבֶת קְבֻרַת־רָחֵל עַד־הַיּוֹם: 21וַיִּסַּע יִשְׂרָאֵל וַיֵּט אָהֳלֹה מֵהָלְאָה לְמִגְדַּל־עֵדֶר: 22וַיְהִי בִּשְׁכֹּן יִשְׂרָאֵל בָּאָרֶץ הַהִוא וַיֵּלֶךְ רְאוּבֵן וַיִּשְׁכַּב אֶת־בִּלְהָה פִּילֶגֶשׁ אָבִיו וַיִּשְׁמַע יִשְׂרָאֵל פ וַיִּהְיוּ בְנֵי־יַעֲקֹב

35:19. **Rachel died.** This is the saddest and most ironic consequence of all the deceptions in this narrative. Jacob had unwittingly put a curse on her by telling Laban, "Let the one with whom you'll find your gods not live" (31:32). Rachel had told her father that she was menstruating so as to keep him from searching her (31:35). Now she dies in childbirth, which both reveals her deception—that she could not have been menstruating—and is the horrible fulfillment of Jacob's words.

35:22. **Israel heard.** The story seems to end unfinished, with Reuben suffering no

And Jacob's sons were twelve. 23The sons of Leah were Jacob's firstborn, Reuben, and Simeon and Levi and Judah and Issachar and Zebulun. 24The sons of Rachel were Joseph and Benjamin. 25And the sons of Bilhah, Rachel's maid, were Dan and Naphtali. 26And the sons of Zilpah, Leah's maid, were Gad and Asher. These were Jacob's sons, who were born to him in Paddan Aram.

27And Jacob came to Isaac, his father, at Mamre, at Kiriath Arba—it is Hebron—where Abraham and Isaac had resided.

28And Isaac's days were a hundred years and eighty years, 29and Isaac expired. And he died and was gathered to his people, old and full of days. And Esau and Jacob, his sons, buried him.

36 1And these are the records of Esau: He is Edom. 2Esau had taken his wives from the daughters of Canaan: Adah, daughter of

23בְּנֵי לֵאָה בְּכוֹר יַעֲקֹב רְאוּבֵן שְׁנֵים עָשָׂר:
וְשִׁמְעוֹן וְלֵוִי וִיהוּדָה וְיִשָּׂשכָר וּזְבוּלֻן: 24בְּנֵי רָחֵל
יוֹסֵף וּבִנְיָמִן: 25וּבְנֵי בִלְהָה שִׁפְחַת רָחֵל דָּן
וְנַפְתָּלִי: 26וּבְנֵי זִלְפָּה שִׁפְחַת לֵאָה גָּד וְאָשֵׁר אֵלֶּה
בְּנֵי יַעֲקֹב אֲשֶׁר יֻלַּד־לוֹ בְּפַדַּן אֲרָם: 27וַיָּבֹא
יַעֲקֹב אֶל־יִצְחָק אָבִיו מַמְרֵא קִרְיַת הָאַרְבַּע הִוא
חֶבְרוֹן אֲשֶׁר־גָּר־שָׁם אַבְרָהָם וְיִצְחָק: 28וַיִּהְיוּ יְמֵי
יִצְחָק מְאַת שָׁנָה וּשְׁמֹנִים שָׁנָה: 29וַיִּגְוַע יִצְחָק וַיָּמָת
וַיֵּאָסֶף אֶל־עַמָּיו זָקֵן וּשְׂבַע יָמִים וַיִּקְבְּרוּ אֹתוֹ עֵשָׂו
וְיַעֲקֹב בָּנָיו: פ

36 1וְאֵלֶּה תֹּלְדוֹת עֵשָׂו הוּא אֱדוֹם: 2עֵשָׂו לָקַח
אֶת־נָשָׁיו מִבְּנוֹת כְּנָעַן אֶת־עָדָה בַּת־אֵילוֹן הַחִתִּי

---

consequence for taking his father's concubine. But, as with Simeon and Levi (see the comment on Gen 34:31), Reuben pays dearly in his father's deathbed blessing of his sons. Jacob criticizes Reuben and demotes him from his birthright, "for you ascended your father's bed" (Gen 49:3–4).

35:29. **Isaac expired**. Isaac's life is markedly different from the lives of his father Abraham and his son Jacob. They both spend time in the two great centers of civilization at that time, Mesopotamia and Egypt, but Isaac never leaves the land of the covenant. They both have multiple wives and concubines, but Isaac has only Rebekah. They both have their names changed, but Isaac does not (see the comment on Gen 17:19). They both fight, but Isaac does not. There are fewer stories about Isaac, and he is a fairly passive figure in them. Regarding the two most famous stories of Isaac: in the story of his near-sacrifice he is acted upon by his father, and in the story of Jacob's appropriation of Esau's blessing he is acted upon by his son. Perhaps the explanation for his being different is that he once lay on the altar as a sacrifice, and so his life is consecrated in a singular way.

35:29. **Esau and Jacob, his sons**. It is hard to miss the order here: Esau before Jacob. It is not simply a matter of birth order, because Isaac is listed before Ishmael in the corresponding passage (25:9). This seems rather to be a sign of recognition, compassion, and compensation to Esau for his displacement by Jacob.

36:2–3. **Adah, daughter of Elon ... Aholibamah, daughter of Anah ... Basemath, daughter of Ishmael**. These names are in conflict with the names of Esau's wives given earlier (26:34; 28:9). Rashi gives midrashic explanations for this confu-

120

Elon, the Hittite, and Aholibamah, daughter of Anah, daughter of Zibeon, the Hivite, 3and Basemath, daughter of Ishmael, sister of Nebaioth. 4And Adah gave birth for Esau to Eliphaz, and Basemath gave birth to Reuel, 5and Aholibamah gave birth to Jeush and Jalam and Korah. These are Esau's sons, who were born to him in the land of Canaan. 6And Esau took his wives and his sons and his daughters and all the persons of his household and his cattle and all of his animals and all of his possessions that he had acquired in the land of Canaan, and he went to a land, from the presence of Jacob, his brother, 7because their property was too great for them to live together, and the land of their residences was not able to suffice them because of their cattle. 8And Esau lived in Mount Seir. Esau: he is Edom.

9And these are the records of Esau, father of Edom, in Mount Seir. 10These are the names of Esau's sons: Eliphaz, son of Adah, Esau's wife; Reuel, son of Basemath, Esau's wife. 11And Eliphaz's sons were Teman, Omar, Zepho, and Gatam and Kenaz. 12And Timna had been a concubine of Eliphaz, son of Esau, and she gave birth to Amalek for Eliphaz. These are the sons of Adah, Esau's wife. 13And these are the sons of Reuel: Nahath and Zerah, Shammah and Mizzeh. These were the sons of Basemath, Esau's wife. 14And these were the sons of Aholibamah, daughter of Anah, daughter of Zibeon, Esau's wife: and she gave birth for Esau to Jeush and Jalam and Korah.

3וְאֶת־אָהֳלִיבָמָה֙ בַּת־עֲנָ֔ה בַּת־צִבְע֖וֹן הַֽחִוִּ֑י׃ וְאֶת־
בָּשְׂמַ֥ת בַּת־יִשְׁמָעֵ֖אל אֲח֥וֹת נְבָיֽוֹת׃ 4וַתֵּ֧לֶד עָדָ֛ה
לְעֵשָׂ֖ו אֶת־אֱלִיפָ֑ז וּבָ֣שְׂמַ֔ת יָלְדָ֖ה אֶת־רְעוּאֵֽל׃
5וְאָהֳלִֽיבָמָה֙ יָֽלְדָ֔ה אֶת־יעיש וְאֶת־יַעְלָ֖ם וְאֶת־קֹ֑רַח
אֵ֚לֶּה בְּנֵ֣י עֵשָׂ֔ו אֲשֶׁ֥ר יֻלְּדוּ־ל֖וֹ בְּאֶ֥רֶץ כְּנָֽעַן׃ 6וַיִּקַּ֣ח
עֵשָׂ֡ו אֶת־נָ֠שָׁיו וְאֶת־בָּנָ֣יו וְאֶת־בְּנֹתָיו֮ וְאֶת־כָּל־נַפְשׁ֣וֹת
בֵּיתוֹ֒ וְאֶת־מִקְנֵ֣הוּ וְאֶת־כָּל־בְּהֶמְתּ֗וֹ וְאֵת֙ כָּל־קִנְיָנ֔וֹ
אֲשֶׁ֥ר רָכַ֖שׁ בְּאֶ֣רֶץ כְּנָ֑עַן וַיֵּ֣לֶךְ אֶל־אֶ֔רֶץ מִפְּנֵ֖י
יַעֲקֹ֥ב אָחִֽיו׃ 7כִּֽי־הָיָ֧ה רְכוּשָׁ֛ם רָ֖ב מִשֶּׁ֣בֶת יַחְדָּ֑ו
וְלֹ֨א יָֽכְלָ֜ה אֶ֤רֶץ מְגֽוּרֵיהֶם֙ לָשֵׂ֣את אֹתָ֔ם מִפְּנֵ֖י
מִקְנֵיהֶֽם׃ 8וַיֵּ֤שֶׁב עֵשָׂו֙ בְּהַ֣ר שֵׂעִ֔יר עֵשָׂ֖ו ה֥וּא אֱדֽוֹם׃
9וְאֵ֣לֶּה תֹּלְד֧וֹת עֵשָׂ֛ו אֲבִ֥י אֱד֖וֹם בְּהַ֥ר שֵׂעִֽיר׃
10אֵ֖לֶּה שְׁמ֣וֹת בְּנֵֽי־עֵשָׂ֑ו אֱלִיפַ֗ז בֶּן־עָדָה֙ אֵ֣שֶׁת עֵשָׂ֔ו
רְעוּאֵ֕ל בֶּן־בָּשְׂמַ֖ת אֵ֥שֶׁת עֵשָֽׂו׃ 11וַיִּהְי֖וּ בְּנֵ֣י אֱלִיפָ֑ז
תֵּימָ֣ן אוֹמָ֔ר צְפ֥וֹ וְגַעְתָּ֖ם וּקְנַֽז׃ 12וְתִמְנַ֣ע ׀ הָיְתָ֣ה
פִילֶ֗גֶשׁ לֶֽאֱלִיפַז֙ בֶּן־עֵשָׂ֔ו וַתֵּ֥לֶד לֶאֱלִיפַ֖ז אֶת־עֲמָלֵ֑ק
אֵ֕לֶּה בְּנֵ֥י עָדָ֖ה אֵ֥שֶׁת עֵשָֽׂו׃ 13וְאֵ֙לֶּה֙ בְּנֵ֣י רְעוּאֵ֔ל
נַ֥חַת וָזֶ֖רַח שַׁמָּ֣ה וּמִזָּ֑ה אֵ֣לֶּה הָי֔וּ בְּנֵ֥י בָשְׂמַ֖ת אֵ֥שֶׁת
עֵשָֽׂו׃ 14וְאֵ֣לֶּה הָי֗וּ בְּנֵ֞י אָהֳלִיבָמָ֛ה בַת־עֲנָ֥ה בַּת־
צִבְע֖וֹן אֵ֣שֶׁת עֵשָׂ֑ו וַתֵּ֣לֶד לְעֵשָׂו֙ אֶת־יעיש וְאֶת־
יַעְלָ֖ם וְאֶת־קֹֽרַח׃

יְע֖וּשׁ קׄ 36:5
יְע֖וּשׁ קׄ 36:14

sion, Ibn Ezra suggests that they each had two names, and Ramban says that it is possible that Esau's first two wives died, he married two others, and he renamed his third wife. The character and variety of their solutions indicate that they did not know what the reason was for this confusion in the text. Critical scholars have not solved it in terms of standard source divisions either. It may be a combination of scribal and source reasons. It remains a classic puzzle to be solved.

36:6. **a land.** The name of the land is not given. It may have been omitted due to a scribal error. Or: some understand the verse to mean that he went to a land that was away from Jacob. The Septuagint reads, "he went out of the land of Canaan," which makes sense.

15These are the chiefs of the children of Esau: the sons of Eliphaz, Esau's firstborn: chief Teman, chief Omar, chief Zepho, chief Kenaz, 16chief Korah, chief Gatam, chief Amalek. These are the chiefs of Eliphaz in the land of Edom. These are the sons of Adah. 17And these are the sons of Reuel, son of Esau: chief Nahath, chief Zerah, chief Shammah, chief Mizzah. These are the chiefs of Reuel in the land of Edom. These are the sons of Basemath, Esau's wife. 18And these are the sons of Aholibamah, Esau's wife: chief Jeush, chief Jalam, chief Korah. These were the chiefs of Aholibamah, daughter of Anah, Esau's wife. 19These are the sons of Esau, and these are their chiefs. That is Edom.

20These are the sons of Seir the Horite, who live in the land: Lotan and Shobal and Zibeon and Anah 21and Dishon and Ezer and Dishan. These are the chiefs of the Horites, the children of Seir, in the land of Edom. 22And the children of Lotan are Hori and Hemam, and Lotan's sister is Timna. 23And these are the children of Shobal: Alvan and Manahath and Ebal, Shepho and Onam. 24And these are the children of Zibeon: Ajah and Anah—that is Anah who found the water in the wilderness when he tended the asses of Zibeon, his father. 25And these are the children of Anah: Dishon and Aholibamah, daughter of Anah. 26And these are the children of Dishon: Hemdan and Eshban and Ithran and Cheran. 27These are the children of Ezer: Bilhan and Zaavan and Akan. 28These are the children of Dishan: Uz and Aran. 29These are the chiefs of the Horites: chief Lotan, chief Shobal, chief Zibeon, chief Anah, 30chief Dishon, chief Ezer, chief Dishan. These are the chiefs of the Horites by their chiefdoms in the land of Seir.

31And these are the kings who ruled in the land of Edom before a king ruled the children of Israel. 32And Bela son of Beor ruled in Edom, and the name of his city was Dinhabah. 33And Bela died, and Jobab son of Zerah from Bozrah ruled in his place. 34And Jobab died, and Husham of the land of Temani ruled in his place.

15אֵ֣לֶּה אַלּוּפֵ֣י בְנֵֽי־עֵשָׂ֗ו בְּנֵ֤י אֱלִיפַז֙ בְּכ֣וֹר עֵשָׂ֔ו אַלּ֤וּף תֵּימָן֙ אַלּ֣וּף אוֹמָ֔ר אַלּ֥וּף צְפ֖וֹ אַלּ֥וּף קְנַֽז׃ 16אַלּֽוּף־קֹ֥רַח אַלּ֥וּף גַּעְתָּ֖ם אַלּ֣וּף עֲמָלֵ֑ק אֵ֣לֶּה אַלּוּפֵ֤י אֱלִיפַז֙ בְּאֶ֣רֶץ אֱד֔וֹם אֵ֖לֶּה בְּנֵ֥י עָדָֽה׃ 17וְאֵ֗לֶּה בְּנֵ֤י רְעוּאֵל֙ בֶּן־עֵשָׂ֔ו אַלּ֥וּף נַ֙חַת֙ אַלּ֣וּף זֶ֔רַח אַלּ֥וּף שַׁמָּ֖ה אַלּ֣וּף מִזָּ֑ה אֵ֣לֶּה אַלּוּפֵ֤י רְעוּאֵל֙ בְּאֶ֣רֶץ אֱד֔וֹם אֵ֣לֶּה בְּנֵ֥י בָשְׂמַ֖ת אֵ֥שֶׁת עֵשָֽׂו׃ 18וְאֵ֗לֶּה בְּנֵ֤י אָהֳלִֽיבָמָה֙ אֵ֣שֶׁת עֵשָׂ֔ו אַלּ֥וּף יְע֛וּשׁ אַלּ֥וּף יַעְלָ֖ם אַלּ֣וּף קֹ֑רַח אֵ֣לֶּה אַלּוּפֵ֞י אָהֳלִֽיבָמָ֛ה בַּת־עֲנָ֖ה אֵ֥שֶׁת עֵשָֽׂו׃ 19אֵ֧לֶּה בְנֵי־עֵשָׂ֛ו וְאֵ֥לֶּה אַלּוּפֵיהֶ֖ם ה֥וּא אֱדֽוֹם׃ ס

20אֵ֤לֶּה בְנֵֽי־שֵׂעִיר֙ הַחֹרִ֔י יֹשְׁבֵ֖י הָאָ֑רֶץ לוֹטָ֥ן וְשׁוֹבָ֖ל וְצִבְע֥וֹן וַעֲנָֽה׃ 21וְדִשׁ֥וֹן וְאֵ֖צֶר וְדִישָׁ֑ן אֵ֣לֶּה אַלּוּפֵ֧י הַחֹרִ֛י בְּנֵ֥י שֵׂעִ֖יר בְּאֶ֥רֶץ אֱדֽוֹם׃ 22וַיִּהְי֥וּ בְנֵֽי־לוֹטָ֖ן חֹרִ֣י וְהֵימָ֑ם וַאֲח֥וֹת לוֹטָ֖ן תִּמְנָֽע׃ 23וְאֵ֙לֶּה֙ בְּנֵ֣י שׁוֹבָ֔ל עַלְוָ֥ן וּמָנַ֖חַת וְעֵיבָ֑ל שְׁפ֖וֹ וְאוֹנָֽם׃ 24וְאֵ֥לֶּה בְנֵֽי־צִבְע֖וֹן וְאַיָּ֣ה וַעֲנָ֑ה ה֣וּא עֲנָ֗ה אֲשֶׁ֨ר מָצָ֤א אֶת־הַיֵּמִם֙ בַּמִּדְבָּ֔ר בִּרְעֹת֥וֹ אֶת־הַחֲמֹרִ֖ים לְצִבְע֥וֹן אָבִֽיו׃ 25וְאֵ֥לֶּה בְנֵֽי־עֲנָ֖ה דִּשֹׁ֑ן וְאָהֳלִֽיבָמָ֖ה בַּת־עֲנָֽה׃ 26וְאֵ֖לֶּה בְּנֵ֣י דִישָׁ֑ן חֶמְדָּ֥ן וְאֶשְׁבָּ֖ן וְיִתְרָ֥ן וּכְרָֽן׃ 27אֵ֖לֶּה בְּנֵי־אֵ֑צֶר בִּלְהָ֥ן וְזַעֲוָ֖ן וַעֲקָֽן׃ 28אֵ֥לֶּה בְנֵֽי־דִישָׁ֖ן ע֥וּץ וַאֲרָֽן׃ 29אֵ֖לֶּה אַלּוּפֵ֣י הַחֹרִ֑י אַלּ֤וּף לוֹטָן֙ אַלּ֣וּף שׁוֹבָ֔ל אַלּ֥וּף צִבְע֖וֹן אַלּ֥וּף עֲנָֽה׃ 30אַלּ֥וּף דִּשֹׁ֛ן אַלּ֥וּף אֵ֖צֶר אַלּ֣וּף דִּישָׁ֑ן אֵ֣לֶּה אַלּוּפֵ֧י הַחֹרִ֛י לְאַלֻּפֵיהֶ֖ם בְּאֶ֥רֶץ שֵׂעִֽיר׃ פ 31וְאֵ֙לֶּה֙ הַמְּלָכִ֔ים אֲשֶׁ֥ר מָלְכ֖וּ בְּאֶ֣רֶץ אֱד֑וֹם לִפְנֵ֥י מְלָךְ־מֶ֖לֶךְ לִבְנֵ֥י יִשְׂרָאֵֽל׃ 32וַיִּמְלֹ֣ךְ בֶּֽאֱד֔וֹם בֶּ֖לַע בֶּן־בְּע֑וֹר וְשֵׁ֥ם עִיר֖וֹ דִּנְהָֽבָה׃ 33וַיָּ֖מָת בָּ֑לַע וַיִּמְלֹ֣ךְ תַּחְתָּ֗יו יוֹבָ֛ב בֶּן־זֶ֖רַח מִבָּצְרָֽה׃ 34וַיָּ֖מָת יוֹבָ֑ב וַיִּמְלֹ֣ךְ תַּחְתָּ֔יו חֻשָׁ֖ם

122

35And Husham died, and Hadad son of Bedad, who struck Midian in the field of Moab, ruled in his place, and the name of his city was Avith. 36And Hadad died, and Samlah of Masrekah ruled in his place. 37And Samlah died, and Saul of Rehoboth on the river ruled in his place. 38And Saul died, and Baal-hanan son of Achbor ruled in his place. 39And Baal-hanan son of Achbor died, and Hadar ruled in his place, and the name of his city was Pau; and his wife's name was Mehetabel daughter of Matred daughter of Mezahab.

40And these are the names of the chiefs of Esau by their families, by their places, by their names: chief Timnah, chief Alvah, chief Jetheth, 41chief Aholibamah, chief Elah, chief Pinon, 42chief Kenaz, chief Teman, chief Mibzar, 43chief Magdiel, chief Iram.

These are the chiefs of Edom by their homes in the land of their possession. That is Esau, father of Edom.

AND HE LIVED

37 1And Jacob lived in the land of his father's residences, in the land of Canaan. 2These are the records of Jacob: Joseph, at seventeen years old, had been tending the sheep with his brothers, and he was a boy with the sons of Bilhah and the sons of Zilpah, his father's wives; and Joseph brought a bad report of them to their father. 3And Israel had loved Joseph the most of all his children because he was a son of old age to him. And he made him a coat of many colors.

Hebrew column

וַיָּמָת חֻשָׁם וַיִּמְלֹךְ תַּחְתָּיו הֲדַד 35מֵאֶרֶץ הַתֵּימָנִי:
בֶּן־בְּדַד הַמַּכֶּה אֶת־מִדְיָן בִּשְׂדֵה מוֹאָב וְשֵׁם עִירוֹ
עֲוִית: 36וַיָּמָת הֲדָד וַיִּמְלֹךְ תַּחְתָּיו שַׂמְלָה
מִמַּשְׂרֵקָה: 37וַיָּמָת שַׂמְלָה וַיִּמְלֹךְ תַּחְתָּיו שָׁאוּל
מֵרְחֹבוֹת הַנָּהָר: 38וַיָּמָת שָׁאוּל וַיִּמְלֹךְ תַּחְתָּיו בַּעַל
חָנָן בֶּן־עַכְבּוֹר: 39וַיָּמָת בַּעַל חָנָן בֶּן־עַכְבּוֹר
וַיִּמְלֹךְ תַּחְתָּיו הֲדַר וְשֵׁם עִירוֹ פָּעוּ וְשֵׁם אִשְׁתּוֹ
מְהֵיטַבְאֵל בַּת־מַטְרֵד בַּת מֵי זָהָב: 40וְאֵלֶּה שְׁמוֹת
אַלּוּפֵי עֵשָׂו לְמִשְׁפְּחֹתָם לִמְקֹמֹתָם בִּשְׁמֹתָם אַלּוּף
תִּמְנָע אַלּוּף עַלְוָה אַלּוּף יְתֵת: 41אַלּוּף אָהֳלִיבָמָה
אַלּוּף אֵלָה אַלּוּף פִּינֹן: 42אַלּוּף קְנַז אַלּוּף תֵּימָן
אַלּוּף מִבְצָר: 43אַלּוּף מַגְדִּיאֵל אַלּוּף עִירָם אֵלֶּה ׀
אַלּוּפֵי אֱדוֹם לְמֹשְׁבֹתָם בְּאֶרֶץ אֲחֻזָּתָם הוּא עֵשָׂו
אֲבִי אֱדוֹם: פ

וישב

37 1וַיֵּשֶׁב יַעֲקֹב בְּאֶרֶץ מְגוּרֵי אָבִיו בְּאֶרֶץ
כְּנָעַן: 2אֵלֶּה ׀ תֹּלְדוֹת יַעֲקֹב יוֹסֵף בֶּן־שְׁבַע־עֶשְׂרֵה
שָׁנָה הָיָה רֹעֶה אֶת־אֶחָיו בַּצֹּאן וְהוּא נַעַר אֶת־בְּנֵי
בִלְהָה וְאֶת־בְּנֵי זִלְפָּה נְשֵׁי אָבִיו וַיָּבֵא יוֹסֵף אֶת־
דִּבָּתָם רָעָה אֶל־אֲבִיהֶם: 3וְיִשְׂרָאֵל אָהַב אֶת־יוֹסֵף
מִכָּל־בָּנָיו כִּי־בֶן־זְקֻנִים הוּא לוֹ וְעָשָׂה לוֹ כְּתֹנֶת

37:3. **coat of many colors.** We have no idea what the Hebrew means, so I have retained the traditional "many colors." Some have tried to derive something about its meaning from the story of Tamar, who is wearing one when her brother Amnon rapes her (2 Samuel 13). But this is difficult because these two stories appear to be intentionally connected. (I brought evidence that they come from the same source in *The Hidden Book in the Bible.*) It is hardly coincidental that the two people who wear a coat of many colors in the Bible are both victims of violence by their brothers, and that both coats are torn. The significance of the coat, therefore, is as a symbol of injustice

4And his brothers saw that their father loved him the most of all his brothers. And they hated him. And they were not able to speak a greeting to him.

5And Joseph had a dream and told it to his brothers, and they went on to hate him more. 6And he said to them, "Listen to this dream that I had: 7and here we were binding sheaves in the field; and here was my sheaf rising and standing up, too; and, here, your sheaves surrounded and bowed to my sheaf."

8And his brothers said to him, "Will you *rule* over us?! Will you *dominate* us?!" And they went on to hate him more because of his dreams and because of his words.

9And he had yet another dream and told it to his brothers. And he said, "Here, I've had another dream, and here were the sun and the moon and eleven stars bowing to me." 10And he told it to his father and to his brothers.

And his father was annoyed at him and said to him, "What is this dream that you've had? Shall *we* come, I and your mother and your brothers, to bow to you to the ground?!" 11And his brothers were jealous of him, and his father took note of the thing.

פַּסִּים: 4וַיִּרְא֣וּ אֶחָ֗יו כִּֽי־אֹת֞וֹ אָהַ֤ב אֲבִיהֶם֙ מִכָּל־
אֶחָ֔יו וַֽיִּשְׂנְא֖וּ אֹת֑וֹ וְלֹ֥א יָכְל֖וּ דַּבְּר֥וֹ לְשָׁלֹֽם: 5וַיַּחֲלֹ֤ם
יוֹסֵף֙ חֲל֔וֹם וַיַּגֵּ֖ד לְאֶחָ֑יו וַיּוֹסִ֥פוּ ע֖וֹד שְׂנֹ֥א אֹתֽוֹ:
6וַיֹּ֖אמֶר אֲלֵיהֶ֑ם שִׁמְעוּ־נָ֕א הַחֲל֥וֹם הַזֶּ֖ה אֲשֶׁ֥ר
חָלָֽמְתִּי: 7וְ֠הִנֵּה אֲנַ֜חְנוּ מְאַלְּמִ֤ים אֲלֻמִּים֙ בְּת֣וֹךְ
הַשָּׂדֶ֔ה וְהִנֵּ֛ה קָ֥מָה אֲלֻמָּתִ֖י וְגַם־נִצָּ֑בָה וְהִנֵּ֤ה תְסֻבֶּ֙ינָה֙
אֲלֻמֹּ֣תֵיכֶ֔ם וַתִּֽשְׁתַּחֲוֶ֖יןָ לַאֲלֻמָּתִֽי: 8וַיֹּ֤אמְרוּ לוֹ֙ אֶחָ֔יו
הֲמָלֹ֤ךְ תִּמְלֹךְ֙ עָלֵ֔ינוּ אִם־מָשׁ֥וֹל תִּמְשֹׁ֖ל בָּ֑נוּ וַיּוֹסִ֤פוּ
ע֙וֹד שְׂנֹ֣א אֹת֔וֹ עַל־חֲלֹמֹתָ֖יו וְעַל־דְּבָרָֽיו: 9וַיַּחֲלֹ֨ם
ע֜וֹד חֲל֣וֹם אַחֵ֗ר וַיְסַפֵּ֤ר אֹתוֹ֙ לְאֶחָ֔יו וַיֹּ֗אמֶר הִנֵּ֨ה
חָלַ֤מְתִּֽי חֲלוֹם֙ ע֔וֹד וְהִנֵּ֧ה הַשֶּׁ֣מֶשׁ וְהַיָּרֵ֗חַ וְאַחַ֤ד עָשָׂר֙
כּֽוֹכָבִ֔ים מִֽשְׁתַּחֲוִ֖ים לִֽי: 10וַיְסַפֵּ֣ר אֶל־אָבִיו֮ וְאֶל־
אֶחָיו֒ וַיִּגְעַר־בּ֣וֹ אָבִ֔יו וַיֹּ֣אמֶר ל֔וֹ מָ֛ה הַחֲל֥וֹם הַזֶּ֖ה
אֲשֶׁ֣ר חָלָ֑מְתָּ הֲב֣וֹא נָב֗וֹא אֲנִי֙ וְאִמְּךָ֣ וְאַחֶ֔יךָ
לְהִשְׁתַּחֲוֺ֥ת לְךָ֖ אָֽרְצָה: 11וַיְקַנְאוּ־ב֖וֹ אֶחָ֑יו וְאָבִ֖יו

---

among siblings. This significance is doubled when we see the fate of the coat. See the comment on 37:31.

37:4. **to speak a greeting to him.** Literally "to speak to him of peace," it appears to refer to the standard Hebrew greetings: one says *šālôm* (peace/well-being) for hello; and one says *hăšālôm lô* (does he have peace?) for "How is he?" (Gen 29:6). That is, the brothers cannot even bid him "hello" or ask how he is. This is rendered ironic by the fact that Joseph's father will soon send him to check on his brothers, telling him, "See how your brothers are [*šālôm*]." It is rendered doubly ironic later when Joseph tells the Pharaoh that it is possible to interpret Pharaoh's dream because "God will answer regarding Pharaoh's well-being [*šālôm*]," suggesting that God shows even more care for the Pharaoh than Joseph's brothers are able to show him. (And see the comment on 43:27.)

37:10. **What is this dream that you've had?** No one seems to know that the dreams are prophetic: not the brothers, not Jacob, not even Joseph himself. Joseph will be able to interpret other people's dreams—but not his own. Like many of us, he will learn what every psychoanalyst knows: that seeing the meaning of one's own dreams is the hardest.

12And his brothers went to feed their father's sheep in Shechem. 13And Israel said to Joseph, "Aren't your brothers feeding in Shechem? Come on and I'll send you to them."

And he said to him, "I'm here."

14And he said to him, "Go, see how your brothers are and how the sheep are and bring me back word." And he sent him from the valley of Hebron.

And he came to Shechem. 15And a man found him, and here he was straying in a field. And the man asked him, saying, "What are you looking for?"

16And he said, "I'm looking for my brothers. Tell me, where are they feeding?"

17And the man said, "They traveled on from here. Because I heard them saying, 'Let's go to Dothan.'"

And Joseph went after his brothers and found them in Dothan. 18And they saw him from a distance, and before he came close to them they conspired against him: to kill him. 19And the brothers said to one another, "Here comes the dream-master, that one there! 20And now, come on and let's kill him and throw him in one of the pits, and we'll say a wild animal ate him, and we'll see what his dreams will be!" 21And Reuben heard, and he saved him from their hand. And he said, "Let's not take his life." 22And Reuben said to them, "Don't spill blood. Throw him into this pit that's in the wilderness, and don't put out a hand against him"—in order to save him from their hand, to bring him back to his father. 23And it was when Joseph came to his brothers: and they took off Joseph's coat, the coat of many colors, which he had on. 24And they took him and

שָׁמַר אֶת־הַדָּבָר: 12וַיֵּלְכוּ אֶחָיו לִרְעוֹת אֶת־צֹאן אֲבִיהֶם בִּשְׁכֶם: 13וַיֹּאמֶר יִשְׂרָאֵל אֶל־יוֹסֵף הֲלוֹא אַחֶיךָ רֹעִים בִּשְׁכֶם לְכָה וְאֶשְׁלָחֲךָ אֲלֵיהֶם וַיֹּאמֶר לוֹ הִנֵּנִי: 14וַיֹּאמֶר לוֹ לֶךְ־נָא רְאֵה אֶת־שְׁלוֹם אַחֶיךָ וְאֶת־שְׁלוֹם הַצֹּאן וַהֲשִׁבֵנִי דָּבָר וַיִּשְׁלָחֵהוּ מֵעֵמֶק חֶבְרוֹן וַיָּבֹא שְׁכֶמָה: 15וַיִּמְצָאֵהוּ אִישׁ וְהִנֵּה תֹעֶה בַּשָּׂדֶה וַיִּשְׁאָלֵהוּ הָאִישׁ לֵאמֹר מַה־תְּבַקֵּשׁ: 16וַיֹּאמֶר אֶת־אַחַי אָנֹכִי מְבַקֵּשׁ הַגִּידָה־נָּא לִי אֵיפֹה הֵם רֹעִים: 17וַיֹּאמֶר הָאִישׁ נָסְעוּ מִזֶּה כִּי שָׁמַעְתִּי אֹמְרִים נֵלְכָה דֹּתָיְנָה וַיֵּלֶךְ יוֹסֵף אַחַר אֶחָיו וַיִּמְצָאֵם בְּדֹתָן: 18וַיִּרְאוּ אֹתוֹ מֵרָחֹק וּבְטֶרֶם יִקְרַב אֲלֵיהֶם וַיִּתְנַכְּלוּ אֹתוֹ לַהֲמִיתוֹ: 19וַיֹּאמְרוּ אִישׁ אֶל־אָחִיו הִנֵּה בַּעַל הַחֲלֹמוֹת הַלָּזֶה בָּא: 20וְעַתָּה | לְכוּ וְנַהַרְגֵהוּ וְנַשְׁלִכֵהוּ בְּאַחַד הַבֹּרוֹת וְאָמַרְנוּ חַיָּה רָעָה אֲכָלָתְהוּ וְנִרְאֶה מַה־יִּהְיוּ חֲלֹמֹתָיו: 21וַיִּשְׁמַע רְאוּבֵן וַיַּצִּלֵהוּ מִיָּדָם וַיֹּאמֶר לֹא נַכֶּנּוּ נָפֶשׁ: 22וַיֹּאמֶר אֲלֵהֶם | רְאוּבֵן אַל־תִּשְׁפְּכוּ־דָם הַשְׁלִיכוּ אֹתוֹ אֶל־הַבּוֹר הַזֶּה אֲשֶׁר בַּמִּדְבָּר וְיָד אַל־תִּשְׁלְחוּ־בוֹ לְמַעַן הַצִּיל אֹתוֹ מִיָּדָם לַהֲשִׁיבוֹ אֶל־אָבִיו: 23וַיְהִי כַּאֲשֶׁר־בָּא יוֹסֵף אֶל־אֶחָיו וַיַּפְשִׁיטוּ אֶת־יוֹסֵף אֶת־כֻּתָּנְתּוֹ אֶת־כְּתֹנֶת הַפַּסִּים אֲשֶׁר

37:20,33. **wild animal.** Literally, a *bad* animal—not just any wild animal. This expression will occur one more time in the Torah: the blessings of the covenant at Sinai will include a divine promise to eliminate wild (bad) animals from the land. The value of that blessing is rendered more visible by the recollection of Jacob's pain when he believes that such a creature has taken the life of his child.

threw him into the pit. And the pit was empty; there was no water in it. 25And they sat down to eat bread.

And they raised their eyes and saw, and here was a caravan of Ishmaelites coming from Gilead, and their camels were carrying spices and balsam and myrrh, going to bring them down to Egypt. 26And Judah said to his brothers, "What profit is there if we kill our brother and cover his blood? 27Come on and let's sell him to the Ishmaelites, and let our hand not be on him, because he's our brother, our flesh." And his brothers listened. 28And Midianite people, merchants, passed, and they pulled and lifted Joseph from the pit. And they sold Joseph to the Ishmaelites for twenty weights of silver. And they brought Joseph to Egypt. 29And Reuben came back to the pit, and here: Joseph was not in the pit. And he tore his clothes. 30And he went back to his brothers and said, "The boy's gone! And I, where can I go?"

31And they took Joseph's coat and slaughtered a he-goat and dipped the coat in the blood.

עָלָֽיו: 24וַיִּ֨קָּחֻ֔הוּ וַיַּשְׁלִ֥כוּ אֹת֖וֹ הַבֹּ֑רָה וְהַבּ֣וֹר רֵ֔ק אֵ֥ין בּ֖וֹ מָֽיִם: 25וַיֵּשְׁבוּ֮ לֶֽאֱכָל־לֶחֶם֒ וַיִּשְׂא֤וּ עֵֽינֵיהֶם֙ וַיִּרְא֔וּ וְהִנֵּה֙ אֹֽרְחַ֣ת יִשְׁמְעֵאלִ֔ים בָּאָ֖ה מִגִּלְעָ֑ד וּגְמַלֵּיהֶ֣ם נֹֽשְׂאִ֗ים נְכֹאת֙ וּצְרִ֣י וָלֹ֔ט הֽוֹלְכִ֖ים לְהוֹרִ֥יד מִצְרָֽיְמָה: 26וַיֹּ֥אמֶר יְהוּדָ֖ה אֶל־אֶחָ֑יו מַה־בֶּ֗צַע כִּ֤י נַֽהֲרֹג֙ אֶת־אָחִ֔ינוּ וְכִסִּ֖ינוּ אֶת־דָּמֽוֹ: 27לְכ֞וּ וְנִמְכְּרֶ֣נּוּ לַיִּשְׁמְעֵאלִ֗ים וְיָדֵ֨נוּ֙ אַל־תְּהִי־ב֔וֹ כִּֽי־אָחִ֥ינוּ בְשָׂרֵ֖נוּ ה֑וּא וַֽיִּשְׁמְע֖וּ אֶחָֽיו: 28וַיַּֽעַבְרוּ֩ אֲנָשִׁ֨ים מִדְיָנִ֜ים סֹֽחֲרִ֗ים וַֽיִּמְשְׁכוּ֙ וַיַּֽעֲל֤וּ אֶת־יוֹסֵף֙ מִן־הַבּ֔וֹר וַיִּמְכְּר֧וּ אֶת־יוֹסֵ֛ף לַיִּשְׁמְעֵאלִ֖ים בְּעֶשְׂרִ֣ים כָּ֑סֶף וַיָּבִ֥יאוּ אֶת־יוֹסֵ֖ף מִצְרָֽיְמָה: 29וַיָּ֤שָׁב רְאוּבֵן֙ אֶל־הַבּ֔וֹר וְהִנֵּ֥ה אֵין־יוֹסֵ֖ף בַּבּ֑וֹר וַיִּקְרַ֖ע אֶת־בְּגָדָֽיו: 30וַיָּ֥שָׁב אֶל־אֶחָ֖יו וַיֹּאמַ֑ר הַיֶּ֣לֶד אֵינֶ֔נּוּ וַֽאֲנִ֖י אָ֥נָה אֲנִי־בָֽא: 31וַיִּקְח֖וּ אֶת־כְּתֹ֣נֶת יוֹסֵ֑ף וַֽיִּשְׁחֲטוּ֙ שְׂעִ֣יר עִזִּ֔ים וַיִּטְבְּל֥וּ אֶת־הַכֻּתֹּ֖נֶת בַּדָּֽם: 32וַֽיְשַׁלְּח֞וּ אֶת־כְּתֹ֣נֶת

37:24. the pit was empty; there was no water in it. Rashi takes this to be redundant: if it is empty, of course there is no water in it. He concludes that there are snakes and scorpions in it. But it is not redundant. Rather, two things are conveyed: It is empty. This conveys that he is alone and helpless. There is no water in it. This conveys that his survival is in danger.

37:26. What profit is there. Judah's motives are a mystery. Is he really concerned with money ("let's sell him to the Ishmaelites") and avoiding performing fratricide ("let our hand not be on him, because he's our brother")? Or is his motive to save Joseph's life? Judah's later behavior toward Benjamin and his great reward at the end (see the comment on 49:8) suggest that his behavior here is positive. Reuben's failed plan leads Joseph to the pit; Judah's plan leads him to Egypt. And Abraham's unions with Hagar and Keturah produced the Ishmaelites and the Midianites, who are now crucial to Joseph's going from the pit to Egypt! Perhaps the point is how complex and fragile our fate is.

37:31. they took Joseph's coat and slaughtered a he-goat. Jacob was ironically paid back for appropriating his brother's birthright: he had to work an additional seven years for Rachel on account of her sister's birthright (see the comment on Gen 29:26). Now he is likewise paid back for appropriating his brother's blessing: He deceived his father using his brother's clothing and the meat and skins of a goat. Now his own sons deceive him using their brother's clothing and the blood of a goat. The

³²And they sent the coat of many colors and brought it to their father and said, "We found this. Recognize: is it your son's coat or not?"

³³And he recognized it and said, "My son's coat. A wild animal ate him. Joseph is *torn up!*" ³⁴And Jacob ripped his clothes and wore sackcloth on his hips and mourned over his son many days. ³⁵And all his sons and all his daughters got up to console him, and he refused to be consoled, and he said, "Because I'll go down mourning to my son at Sheol," and his father wept for him.

³⁶And the Medanites sold him to Egypt, to Potiphar, an official of Pharaoh, chief of the guards.

38 ¹And it was at that time, and Judah went down from his brothers and turned to an Adullamite man, and his name was Hirah. ²And Judah saw a daughter of a Canaanite man there, and his name was Shua. And he took her and came to her. ³And she became pregnant and gave birth to a son, and he called his name Er. ⁴And she became pregnant again and gave birth to a son, and she called his name Onan. ⁵And she proceeded again to give birth to a son, and she called his name Shelah. (And he was at Chezib when she gave birth to him.) ⁶And Judah took a wife for Er, his firstborn, and her name was Tamar. ⁷And Er, Judah's firstborn, was bad in YHWH's eyes, and YHWH killed him. ⁸And Judah said to Onan, "Come to your brother's wife and couple as a brother-in-law with her and

הַפַּסִּים וַיָּבִיאוּ אֶל־אֲבִיהֶם וַיֹּאמְרוּ זֹאת מָצָאנוּ הַכֶּר־נָא הַכְּתֹנֶת בִּנְךָ הִוא אִם־לֹא: ³³וַיַּכִּירָהּ וַיֹּאמֶר כְּתֹנֶת בְּנִי חַיָּה רָעָה אֲכָלָתְהוּ טָרֹף טֹרַף יוֹסֵף: ³⁴וַיִּקְרַע יַעֲקֹב שִׂמְלֹתָיו וַיָּשֶׂם שַׂק בְּמָתְנָיו וַיִּתְאַבֵּל עַל־בְּנוֹ יָמִים רַבִּים: ³⁵וַיָּקֻמוּ כָל־בָּנָיו וְכָל־בְּנֹתָיו לְנַחֲמוֹ וַיְמָאֵן לְהִתְנַחֵם וַיֹּאמֶר כִּי־אֵרֵד אֶל־בְּנִי אָבֵל שְׁאֹלָה וַיֵּבְךְּ אֹתוֹ אָבִיו: ³⁶וְהַמְּדָנִים מָכְרוּ אֹתוֹ אֶל־מִצְרָיִם לְפוֹטִיפַר סְרִיס פַּרְעֹה שַׂר הַטַּבָּחִים: פ

38 ¹וַיְהִי בָּעֵת הַהִוא וַיֵּרֶד יְהוּדָה מֵאֵת אֶחָיו וַיֵּט עַד־אִישׁ עֲדֻלָּמִי וּשְׁמוֹ חִירָה: ²וַיַּרְא־שָׁם יְהוּדָה בַּת־אִישׁ כְּנַעֲנִי וּשְׁמוֹ שׁוּעַ וַיִּקָּחֶהָ וַיָּבֹא אֵלֶיהָ: ³וַתַּהַר וַתֵּלֶד בֵּן וַיִּקְרָא אֶת־שְׁמוֹ עֵר: ⁴וַתַּהַר עוֹד וַתֵּלֶד בֵּן וַתִּקְרָא אֶת־שְׁמוֹ אוֹנָן: ⁵וַתֹּסֶף עוֹד וַתֵּלֶד בֵּן וַתִּקְרָא אֶת־שְׁמוֹ שֵׁלָה וְהָיָה בִכְזִיב בְּלִדְתָּהּ אֹתוֹ: ⁶וַיִּקַּח יְהוּדָה אִשָּׁה לְעֵר בְּכוֹרוֹ וּשְׁמָהּ תָּמָר: ⁷וַיְהִי עֵר בְּכוֹר יְהוּדָה רַע בְּעֵינֵי יְהוָה וַיְמִתֵהוּ יְהוָה: ⁸וַיֹּאמֶר יְהוּדָה לְאוֹנָן בֹּא אֶל־אֵשֶׁת אָחִיךָ וְיַבֵּם אֹתָהּ וְהָקֵם זֶרַע

Torah does not excuse Jacob's behavior. It rather teaches that such acts have consequences.

38:1. **Judah**. The eponymous ancestor of the Jews, Judah is the most prominent of the brothers in the Joseph stories, and here he is the only one of Jacob's sons besides Joseph to have a separate story about him. Some say that the word יהודה means "to be thankful." Its derivation is unknown.

38:1. **Judah went down.** The next chapter begins with "Joseph had been brought down." The contrast is blatant (even more so in the Hebrew) between Judah's independence and Joseph's weakness: Judah *went* down, and Joseph *was brought* down.

raise seed for your brother." 9And Onan knew that the seed would not be his. And it was when he came to his brother's wife: and he spent on the ground so as not to give seed for his brother. 10And what he did was bad in YHWH's eyes, and He killed him, too.

11And Judah said to Tamar, his daughter-in-law, "Live as a widow at your father's house until my son Shelah grows up" (because he said, "Or else he, too, will die like his brothers"). And Tamar went and lived at her father's house.

12And the days were many, and Judah's wife, the daughter of Shua, died. And Judah was consoled. And he went up to his sheepshearers, he and his friend Hirah, the Adullamite, to Timnah.

13And it was told to Tamar, saying, "Here, your father-in-law is going up to Timnah to shear his sheep." 14And she took off her widowhood clothes from on her and covered herself with a veil and wrapped herself and sat in a visible place that was on the road to Timnah, because she saw that Shelah had grown up and she had not been given to him as a wife. 15And Judah saw her and thought her to be a prostitute because she had covered her face. 16And he turned to her by the road.

And he said, "Come on. Let me come to you," because he did not know that she was his daughter-in-law.

And she said, "What will you give me when you come to me?"

17And he said, "I'll have a goat kid sent from the flock."

And she said, "If you'll give a pledge until you send it."

18And he said, "What is the pledge that I'll give you?"

And she said, "Your seal and your cord and your staff that's in your hand." And he gave them

לְאָחִֽיךָ: 9וַיֵּ֣דַע אוֹנָ֔ן כִּ֛י לֹ֥א ל֖וֹ יִהְיֶ֣ה הַזָּ֑רַע וְהָיָ֞ה אִם־בָּ֨א אֶל־אֵ֤שֶׁת אָחִיו֙ וְשִׁחֵ֣ת אַ֔רְצָה לְבִלְתִּ֥י נְתָן־זֶ֖רַע לְאָחִֽיו: 10וַיֵּ֛רַע בְּעֵינֵ֥י יְהֹוָ֖ה אֲשֶׁ֣ר עָשָׂ֑ה וַיָּ֖מֶת גַּם־אֹתֽוֹ: 11וַיֹּ֣אמֶר יְהוּדָה֩ לְתָמָ֨ר כַּלָּת֜וֹ שְׁבִ֧י אַלְמָנָ֣ה בֵית־אָבִ֗יךְ עַד־יִגְדַּל֙ שֵׁלָ֣ה בְנִ֔י כִּ֣י אָמַ֔ר פֶּן־יָמ֥וּת גַּם־ה֖וּא כְּאֶחָ֑יו וַתֵּ֣לֶךְ תָּמָ֔ר וַתֵּ֖שֶׁב בֵּ֥ית אָבִֽיהָ: 12וַיִּרְבּוּ֙ הַיָּמִ֔ים וַתָּ֖מָת בַּת־שׁ֣וּעַ אֵֽשֶׁת־יְהוּדָ֑ה וַיִּנָּ֣חֶם יְהוּדָ֗ה וַיַּ֜עַל עַל־גֹּֽזְזֵ֤י צֹאנוֹ֙ ה֣וּא וְחִירָ֣ה רֵעֵ֥הוּ הָעֲדֻלָּמִ֖י תִּמְנָֽתָה: 13וַיֻּגַּ֥ד לְתָמָ֖ר לֵאמֹ֑ר הִנֵּ֥ה חָמִ֛יךְ עֹלֶ֥ה תִמְנָ֖תָה לָגֹ֥ז צֹאנֽוֹ: 14וַתָּ֩סַר֩ בִּגְדֵ֨י אַלְמְנוּתָ֜הּ מֵֽעָלֶ֗יהָ וַתְּכַ֤ס בַּצָּעִיף֙ וַתִּתְעַלָּ֔ף וַתֵּ֙שֶׁב֙ בְּפֶ֣תַח עֵינַ֔יִם אֲשֶׁ֖ר עַל־דֶּ֣רֶךְ תִּמְנָ֑תָה כִּ֤י רָֽאֲתָה֙ כִּֽי־גָדַ֣ל שֵׁלָ֔ה וְה֕וּא לֹֽא־נִתְּנָ֥ה ל֖וֹ לְאִשָּֽׁה: 15וַיִּרְאֶ֣הָ יְהוּדָ֔ה וַֽיַּחְשְׁבֶ֖הָ לְזוֹנָ֑ה כִּ֥י כִסְּתָ֖ה פָּנֶֽיהָ: 16וַיֵּ֨ט אֵלֶ֜יהָ אֶל־הַדֶּ֗רֶךְ וַיֹּ֙אמֶר֙ הָֽבָה־נָּא֙ אָב֣וֹא אֵלַ֔יִךְ כִּ֚י לֹ֣א יָדַ֔ע כִּ֥י כַלָּת֖וֹ הִ֑וא וַתֹּ֙אמֶר֙ מַה־תִּתֶּן־לִּ֔י כִּ֥י תָב֖וֹא אֵלָֽי: 17וַיֹּ֕אמֶר אָֽנֹכִ֛י אֲשַׁלַּ֥ח גְּדִֽי־עִזִּ֖ים מִן־הַצֹּ֑אן וַתֹּ֕אמֶר אִם־תִּתֵּ֥ן עֵֽרָב֖וֹן עַ֥ד שָׁלְחֶֽךָ: 18וַיֹּ֗אמֶר מָ֣ה הָֽעֵֽרָבוֹן֮ אֲשֶׁ֣ר אֶתֶּן־לָךְ֒ וַתֹּ֗אמֶר חֹתָֽמְךָ֙ וּפְתִילֶ֔ךָ וּמַטְּךָ֖ אֲשֶׁ֣ר בְּיָדֶ֑ךָ וַיִּתֶּן־לָּ֥הּ וַיָּבֹ֖א

38:8. **raise seed for your brother**. This is known as the law of levirate marriage, from the Latin *levir*, meaning brother-in-law. See Deuteronomy 25 and the comments on it.

to her, and he came to her, and she became pregnant by him.

19And she got up and went and took off her veil from on her and put on her widowhood clothes. 20And Judah sent the goat kid by the hand of his friend the Adullamite to take back the pledge from the woman's hand, and he did not find her. 21And he asked the people of her place, saying, "Where is the sacred prostitute? She was visibly by the road."

And they said, "There was no sacred prostitute here."

22And he came back to Judah and said, "I didn't find her, and also the people of the place said 'There was no sacred prostitute here.'"

23And Judah said, "Let her take them or else we'll be a disgrace. Here, I've sent this goat kid, and you didn't find her."

24And it was about three months, and it was told to Judah, saying, "Your daughter-in-law Tamar has whored, and, here, she's pregnant by whoring as well."

And Judah said, "Bring her out and let her be burned."

25She was brought out. And she sent to her father-in-law, saying, "I'm pregnant by the man to whom these belong," and she said, "Recognize: to whom do these seal and cords and staff belong?"

26And Judah recognized and said, "She's more right than I am, because of the fact that I didn't

אֵלֶיהָ וַתַּהַר לֹו: 19וַתָּקָם וַתֵּלֶךְ וַתָּסַר צְעִיפָהּ
מֵעָלֶיהָ וַתִּלְבַּשׁ בִּגְדֵי אַלְמְנוּתָהּ: 20וַיִּשְׁלַח יְהוּדָה
אֶת־גְּדִי הָעִזִּים בְּיַד רֵעֵהוּ הָעֲדֻלָּמִי לָקַחַת
הָעֵרָבֹון מִיַּד הָאִשָּׁה וְלֹא מְצָאָהּ: 21וַיִּשְׁאַל אֶת־
אַנְשֵׁי מְקֹמָהּ לֵאמֹר אַיֵּה הַקְּדֵשָׁה הִוא בָעֵינַיִם
עַל־הַדָּרֶךְ וַיֹּאמְרוּ לֹא־הָיְתָה בָזֶה קְדֵשָׁה: 22וַיָּשָׁב
אֶל־יְהוּדָה וַיֹּאמֶר לֹא מְצָאתִיהָ וְגַם אַנְשֵׁי הַמָּקֹום
אָמְרוּ לֹא־הָיְתָה בָזֶה קְדֵשָׁה: 23וַיֹּאמֶר יְהוּדָה
תִּקַּח־לָהּ פֶּן נִהְיֶה לָבוּז הִנֵּה שָׁלַחְתִּי הַגְּדִי הַזֶּה
וְאַתָּה לֹא מְצָאתָהּ: 24וַיְהִי ׀ כְּמִשְׁלֹשׁ חֳדָשִׁים וַיֻּגַּד
לִיהוּדָה לֵאמֹר זָנְתָה תָּמָר כַּלָּתֶךָ וְגַם הִנֵּה הָרָה
לִזְנוּנִים וַיֹּאמֶר יְהוּדָה הֹוצִיאוּהָ וְתִשָּׂרֵף: 25הִוא
מוּצֵאת וְהִיא שָׁלְחָה אֶל־חָמִיהָ לֵאמֹר לְאִישׁ
אֲשֶׁר־אֵלֶּה לֹּו אָנֹכִי הָרָה וַתֹּאמֶר הַכֶּר־נָא לְמִי
הַחֹתֶמֶת וְהַפְּתִילִים וְהַמַּטֶּה הָאֵלֶּה: 26וַיַּכֵּר יְהוּדָה
וַיֹּאמֶר צָדְקָה מִמֶּנִּי כִּי־עַל־כֵּן לֹא־נְתַתִּיהָ לְשֵׁלָה

38:21. **sacred prostitute**. On sacred prostitution, see the comment on Deut 23:18. The immediate point in this episode is that Judah is described as thinking that Tamar is a prostitute (*zōnāh*) (38:15), but now his friend uses what is seemingly a more refined word, "sacred prostitute" (*qĕdēšāh*)—which may also denote a higher level of prostitute—when he discreetly inquires about her.

38:25. **Recognize**. Tamar lays down the evidence and uses the same word that Joseph's brothers used when they laid down the evidence of Joseph's demise (the bloodstained coat of many colors) in front of Jacob. Like father, like son: Judah might well feel a chill down his back when he hears the word and knows that he was a guilty party on both occasions. We might even imagine that this double sense of his own errors is what moves him to declare: "She's more right than I am."

give her to my son Shelah." And he did not go on to know her again.

27And it was at the time that she was giving birth, and here were twins in her womb. 28And it was as she was giving birth, and one put out his hand, and the midwife took a scarlet thread and tied it on his hand, saying, "This one came out first." 29And it was as he pulled his hand back, and here his brother came out. And she said, "What a breach you've made for yourself!" And he called his name Perez. 30And his brother who had the scarlet thread on his hand came out after. And he called his name Zerah.

39 1And Joseph had been brought down to Egypt. And an Egyptian man, Potiphar, an official of Pharaoh, chief of the guards, bought him from the hand of the Ishmaelites who had brought him down there. 2And YHWH was with Joseph, and he was a successful man, and he was in his Egyptian lord's house. 3And his lord saw that YHWH was with him, and YHWH made everything he was doing successful in his hand. 4And Joseph found favor in his eyes, and he attended him, and he appointed him over his house and put everything he had in his hand. 5And it was from the time that he appointed him in his house and over all that he had that YHWH blessed the Egyptian's house because of Joseph, and YHWH's blessing was in everything that he had, in the house and in the field. 6And he left everything that he had in Joseph's hand and did not know a thing about what he had except the bread that he was eating.

And Joseph had an attractive figure and was handsome. 7And it was after these things, and his lord's wife raised her eyes to Joseph and said, "Lie with me."

8And he refused, and he said to his lord's wife, "Here, my lord doesn't know what he has with me in the house, and he's put everything that he has in my hand. 9No one is bigger than I am in this house, and he hasn't held back a thing from me except you because you're his wife, and how

בְּנִי וְלֹא־יָסַף עוֹד לְדַעְתָּהּ: 27וַיְהִי בְּעֵת לִדְתָּהּ וְהִנֵּה תְאוֹמִים בְּבִטְנָהּ: 28וַיְהִי בְלִדְתָּהּ וַיִּתֶּן־יָד וַתִּקַּח הַמְיַלֶּדֶת וַתִּקְשֹׁר עַל־יָדוֹ שָׁנִי לֵאמֹר זֶה יָצָא רִאשֹׁנָה: 29וַיְהִי ׀ כְּמֵשִׁיב יָדוֹ וְהִנֵּה יָצָא אָחִיו וַתֹּאמֶר מַה־פָּרַצְתָּ עָלֶיךָ פָּרֶץ וַיִּקְרָא שְׁמוֹ פָּרֶץ: 30וְאַחַר יָצָא אָחִיו אֲשֶׁר עַל־יָדוֹ הַשָּׁנִי וַיִּקְרָא שְׁמוֹ זָרַח: ס

39 1וְיוֹסֵף הוּרַד מִצְרָיְמָה וַיִּקְנֵהוּ פּוֹטִיפַר סְרִיס פַּרְעֹה שַׂר הַטַּבָּחִים אִישׁ מִצְרִי מִיַּד הַיִּשְׁמְעֵאלִים אֲשֶׁר הוֹרִדֻהוּ שָׁמָּה: 2וַיְהִי יְהוָה אֶת־יוֹסֵף וַיְהִי אִישׁ מַצְלִיחַ וַיְהִי בְּבֵית אֲדֹנָיו הַמִּצְרִי: 3וַיַּרְא אֲדֹנָיו כִּי יְהוָה אִתּוֹ וְכֹל אֲשֶׁר־הוּא עֹשֶׂה יְהוָה מַצְלִיחַ בְּיָדוֹ: 4וַיִּמְצָא יוֹסֵף חֵן בְּעֵינָיו וַיְשָׁרֶת אֹתוֹ וַיַּפְקִדֵהוּ עַל־בֵּיתוֹ וְכָל־יֶשׁ־לוֹ נָתַן בְּיָדוֹ: 5וַיְהִי מֵאָז הִפְקִיד אֹתוֹ בְּבֵיתוֹ וְעַל כָּל־אֲשֶׁר יֶשׁ־לוֹ וַיְבָרֶךְ יְהוָה אֶת־בֵּית הַמִּצְרִי בִּגְלַל יוֹסֵף וַיְהִי בִּרְכַּת יְהוָה בְּכָל־אֲשֶׁר יֶשׁ־לוֹ בַּבַּיִת וּבַשָּׂדֶה: 6וַיַּעֲזֹב כָּל־אֲשֶׁר־לוֹ בְּיַד־יוֹסֵף וְלֹא־יָדַע אִתּוֹ מְאוּמָה כִּי אִם־הַלֶּחֶם אֲשֶׁר־הוּא אוֹכֵל וַיְהִי יוֹסֵף יְפֵה־תֹאַר וִיפֵה מַרְאֶה: 7וַיְהִי אַחַר הַדְּבָרִים הָאֵלֶּה וַתִּשָּׂא אֵשֶׁת־אֲדֹנָיו אֶת־עֵינֶיהָ אֶל־יוֹסֵף וַתֹּאמֶר שִׁכְבָה עִמִּי: 8וַיְמָאֵן ׀ וַיֹּאמֶר אֶל־אֵשֶׁת אֲדֹנָיו הֵן אֲדֹנִי לֹא־יָדַע אִתִּי מַה־בַּבָּיִת וְכֹל אֲשֶׁר־יֶשׁ־לוֹ נָתַן בְּיָדִי: 9אֵינֶנּוּ גָדוֹל בַּבַּיִת הַזֶּה מִמֶּנִּי וְלֹא־חָשַׂךְ מִמֶּנִּי מְאוּמָה כִּי אִם־אוֹתָךְ בַּאֲשֶׁר אַתְּ־

could I do this great wrong? And I would sin against God." 10And it was, when she spoke to Joseph day after day, that he didn't listen to her, to lie by her, to be with her. 11And it was on a day like this, and he came to the house to do his work, and not one of the people of the house was there in the house.

12And she grasped him by his garment, saying, "Lie with me!" And he left his garment in her hand and fled and went outside. 13And it was, when she saw that he had left his garment in her hand and run off outside, 14that she called to the people of her house and said to them, saying, "See, he brought us a Hebrew man to fool with us. He came to me, to lie with me, and I called in a loud voice. 15And it was when he heard that I raised my voice and called that he left his garment by me and fled and went outside." 16And she laid his garment down by her until his lord came to his house. 17And she spoke things like these to him, saying, "The Hebrew slave, whom you brought us, came to me, to fool with me. 18And it was when I raised my voice and called that he left his garment by me and fled outside." 19And it was, when his lord heard his wife's words that she spoke to him, saying, "Your servant did things like these to me," that his anger flared. 20And Joseph's lord took him and put him in prison, a place where the king's prisoners were kept.

And he was there in the prison, 21and YHWH was with Joseph and extended kindness to him and gave him favor in the eyes of the warden. 22And the warden put all the prisoners who were in the prison into Joseph's hand, and he was

אִשְׁתּוֹ וְאֵיךְ אֶעֱשֶׂה הָרָעָה הַגְּדֹלָה הַזֹּאת וְחָטָאתִי לֵאלֹהִים: 10וַיְהִי כְּדַבְּרָהּ אֶל־יוֹסֵף יוֹם ׀ יוֹם וְלֹא־שָׁמַע אֵלֶיהָ לִשְׁכַּב אֶצְלָהּ לִהְיוֹת עִמָּהּ: 11וַיְהִי כְּהַיּוֹם הַזֶּה וַיָּבֹא הַבַּיְתָה לַעֲשׂוֹת מְלַאכְתּוֹ וְאֵין אִישׁ מֵאַנְשֵׁי הַבַּיִת שָׁם בַּבָּיִת: 12וַתִּתְפְּשֵׂהוּ בְּבִגְדוֹ לֵאמֹר שִׁכְבָה עִמִּי וַיַּעֲזֹב בִּגְדוֹ בְּיָדָהּ וַיָּנָס וַיֵּצֵא הַחוּצָה: 13וַיְהִי כִּרְאוֹתָהּ כִּי־עָזַב בִּגְדוֹ בְּיָדָהּ וַיָּנָס הַחוּצָה: 14וַתִּקְרָא לְאַנְשֵׁי בֵיתָהּ וַתֹּאמֶר לָהֶם לֵאמֹר רְאוּ הֵבִיא לָנוּ אִישׁ עִבְרִי לְצַחֶק בָּנוּ בָּא אֵלַי לִשְׁכַּב עִמִּי וָאֶקְרָא בְּקוֹל גָּדוֹל: 15וַיְהִי כְשָׁמְעוֹ כִּי־הֲרִימֹתִי קוֹלִי וָאֶקְרָא וַיַּעֲזֹב בִּגְדוֹ אֶצְלִי וַיָּנָס וַיֵּצֵא הַחוּצָה: 16וַתַּנַּח בִּגְדוֹ אֶצְלָהּ עַד־בּוֹא אֲדֹנָיו אֶל־בֵּיתוֹ: 17וַתְּדַבֵּר אֵלָיו כַּדְּבָרִים הָאֵלֶּה לֵאמֹר בָּא־אֵלַי הָעֶבֶד הָעִבְרִי אֲשֶׁר־הֵבֵאתָ לָּנוּ לְצַחֶק בִּי: 18וַיְהִי כַּהֲרִימִי קוֹלִי וָאֶקְרָא וַיַּעֲזֹב בִּגְדוֹ אֶצְלִי וַיָּנָס הַחוּצָה: 19וַיְהִי כִשְׁמֹעַ אֲדֹנָיו אֶת־דִּבְרֵי אִשְׁתּוֹ אֲשֶׁר דִּבְּרָה אֵלָיו לֵאמֹר כַּדְּבָרִים הָאֵלֶּה עָשָׂה לִי עַבְדֶּךָ וַיִּחַר אַפּוֹ: 20וַיִּקַּח אֲדֹנֵי יוֹסֵף אֹתוֹ וַיִּתְּנֵהוּ אֶל־בֵּית הַסֹּהַר מְקוֹם אֲשֶׁר־אֲסוּרֵי הַמֶּלֶךְ אֲסוּרִים וַיְהִי־שָׁם בְּבֵית הַסֹּהַר: 21וַיְהִי יְהוָה אֶת־יוֹסֵף וַיֵּט אֵלָיו חָסֶד וַיִּתֵּן חִנּוֹ בְּעֵינֵי שַׂר בֵּית־הַסֹּהַר: 22וַיִּתֵּן שַׂר בֵּית־הַסֹּהַר בְּיַד־יוֹסֵף אֵת כָּל־הָאֲסִירִם אֲשֶׁר בְּבֵית הַסֹּהַר

39:20 קֿ אֲסִירֵי

39:14,17. **to fool with us . . . to fool with me.** She says "to fool with *us*" when she tells the household, but she says "to fool with *me*" when she tells her husband. Deceivers formulate their words carefully to persuade their particular audience.

39:17. **whom you brought us.** She uses the same device that Adam had used when trying to exonerate himself in Eden when he said, "The woman, whom *you* placed with me . . ." It is an attempt to help one's position by putting part of the blame on one's judge. It works better for Potiphar's wife, using it on a human authority, than it did for Adam, who tried to use it on God.

doing all the things that they do there. 23The warden was not seeing anything in his hand because YHWH was with him, and YHWH would make whatever he did successful.

40 1And it was, after these things, the drink-steward of the king of Egypt and the baker sinned against their lord, against the king of Egypt. 2And Pharaoh was angry at his two officers, at the chief of the drink-stewards and at the chief of the bakers, 3and he put them under watch at the house of the chief of the guards, into prison, the place where Joseph was held. 4And the chief of the guards assigned Joseph with them, and he attended them.

And they were under watch for days. 5And the two of them had a dream, each his own dream, in one night, each with his own dream's meaning, the drink-steward and the baker whom the king of Egypt had, who were held in the prison. 6And Joseph came to them in the morning and saw them, and here they were upset. 7And he asked Pharaoh's officers who were with him under watch at his lord's house, saying, "Why are your faces bad today?"

8And they said to him, "We had a dream, and there's no one who can tell the meaning of it."

And Joseph said to them, "Don't meanings belong to God? Tell me."

9And the chief of the drink-stewards told his dream to Joseph, and he said to him, "In my dream: And here was a vine in front of me, 10and in the vine were three branches, and it was like it was blooming: its blossom came up; its clusters produced grapes. 11And Pharaoh's cup was in my hand. And I took the grapes and pressed them into Pharaoh's cup and set the cup on Pharaoh's hand."

12And Joseph said to him, "This is its meaning: The three branches, they're three days. 13In

וְאֵת כָּל־אֲשֶׁר עֹשִׂים שָׁם הוּא הָיָה עֹשֶׂה: 23אֵין | שַׂר בֵּית־הַסֹּהַר רֹאֶה אֶת־כָּל־מְא֫וּמָה בְּיָד֫וֹ בַּאֲשֶׁר יְהוָה אִתּ֑וֹ וַאֲשֶׁר־הוּא עֹשֶׂה יְהוָה מַצְלִיחַ: ס

40 1וַיְהִי אַחַר הַדְּבָרִים הָאֵלֶּה חָטְא֫וּ מַשְׁקֵה מֶלֶךְ־מִצְרַיִם וְהָאֹפֶה לַאֲדֹנֵיהֶם לְמֶלֶךְ מִצְרָיִם: 2וַיִּקְצֹף פַּרְעֹה עַל שְׁנֵי סָרִיסָיו עַל שַׂר הַמַּשְׁקִים וְעַל שַׂר הָאוֹפִים: 3וַיִּתֵּן אֹתָם בְּמִשְׁמַר בֵּית שַׂר הַטַּבָּחִים אֶל־בֵּית הַסֹּהַר מְק֫וֹם אֲשֶׁר יוֹסֵף אָס֫וּר שָׁם: 4וַיִּפְקֹד שַׂר הַטַּבָּחִים אֶת־יוֹסֵף אִתָּם וַיְשָׁרֶת אֹתָם וַיִּהְיוּ יָמִים בְּמִשְׁמָר: 5וַיַּחַלְמוּ חֲלוֹם שְׁנֵיהֶם אִישׁ חֲלֹמוֹ בְּלַיְלָה אֶחָד אִישׁ כְּפִתְרוֹן חֲלֹמ֑וֹ הַמַּשְׁקֶה וְהָאֹפֶה אֲשֶׁר לְמֶלֶךְ מִצְרַיִם אֲשֶׁר אֲסוּרִים בְּבֵית הַסֹּהַר: 6וַיָּבֹא אֲלֵיהֶם יוֹסֵף בַּבֹּקֶר וַיַּרְא אֹתָם וְהִנָּם זֹעֲפִים: 7וַיִּשְׁאַל אֶת־סְרִיסֵי פַרְעֹה אֲשֶׁר אִתּוֹ בְמִשְׁמַר בֵּית אֲדֹנָיו לֵאמֹר מַדּוּעַ פְּנֵיכֶם רָעִים הַיּוֹם: 8וַיֹּאמְרוּ אֵלָיו חֲלוֹם חָלַמְנוּ וּפֹתֵר אֵין אֹת֑וֹ וַיֹּאמֶר אֲלֵהֶם יוֹסֵף הֲלוֹא לֵאלֹהִים פִּתְרֹנִים סַפְּרוּ־נָא לִי: 9וַיְסַפֵּר שַׂר־הַמַּשְׁקִים אֶת־חֲלֹמוֹ לְיוֹסֵף וַיֹּאמֶר לוֹ בַּחֲלוֹמִי וְהִנֵּה־גֶפֶן לְפָנָי: 10וּבַגֶּפֶן שְׁלֹשָׁה שָׂרִיגִם וְהִיא כְפֹרַחַת עָלְתָה נִצָּהּ הִבְשִׁילוּ אַשְׁכְּלֹתֶיהָ עֲנָבִים: 11וְכוֹס פַּרְעֹה בְּיָדִי וָאֶקַּח אֶת־הָעֲנָבִים וָאֶשְׂחַט אֹתָם אֶל־כּוֹס פַּרְעֹה וָאֶתֵּן אֶת־הַכּוֹס עַל־כַּף פַּרְעֹה: 12וַיֹּאמֶר לוֹ יוֹסֵף זֶה פִּתְרֹנ֑וֹ שְׁלֹשֶׁת הַשָּׂרִגִים שְׁלֹשֶׁת יָמִים הֵם:

40:12. **This is its meaning.** Joseph's ability to interpret dreams is the first time in the Torah that a human possesses a divine power. (The only preceding case is Jacob's manipulation of the coloring of Laban's flocks, but we cannot be certain if that was

three more days Pharaoh will lift your head up, and he'll put you back at your station, and you'll set Pharaoh's cup in his hand—like the original manner when you were his drink-steward. 14So if you'll remember me with you when it will be good for you, and you'll practice kindness with me, then you'll bring up the memory of me to Pharaoh, and you'll bring me out of this house. 15Because I was *stolen* from the land of the Hebrews; and here, too, I haven't done anything that they should have put me in the pit."

16And the chief of the bakers saw that he told a good meaning, and he said to Joseph, "Me, too. In my dream: And here were three baskets of white bread on my head, 17and in the highest basket were some of all of Pharaoh's foods, baked goods. And the birds were eating them from the basket, from on my head."

18And Joseph answered, and he said, "This is its meaning: The three baskets, they're three days. 19In three more days Pharaoh will lift your head up from you, and he'll hang you on a tree, and the birds will eat your flesh from you."

20And it was in the third day, Pharaoh's birthday, and Pharaoh made a feast for all his servants. And he held up the head of the chief of the drink-stewards and the head of the chief of the bakers among his servants. 21And he put the

בְּעוֹד ׀ שְׁלֹשֶׁת יָמִים יִשָּׂא פַרְעֹה אֶת־רֹאשֶׁךָ 13
וַהֲשִׁיבְךָ עַל־כַּנֶּךָ וְנָתַתָּ כוֹס־פַּרְעֹה בְּיָדוֹ כַּמִּשְׁפָּט
הָרִאשׁוֹן אֲשֶׁר הָיִיתָ מַשְׁקֵהוּ: 14כִּי אִם־זְכַרְתַּנִי
אִתְּךָ כַּאֲשֶׁר יִיטַב לָךְ וְעָשִׂיתָ־נָּא עִמָּדִי חָסֶד
וְהִזְכַּרְתַּנִי אֶל־פַּרְעֹה וְהוֹצֵאתַנִי מִן־הַבַּיִת הַזֶּה:
15כִּי־גֻנֹּב גֻּנַּבְתִּי מֵאֶרֶץ הָעִבְרִים וְגַם־פֹּה לֹא־
עָשִׂיתִי מְאוּמָה כִּי־שָׂמוּ אֹתִי בַּבּוֹר: 16וַיַּרְא שַׂר־
הָאֹפִים כִּי טוֹב פָּתָר וַיֹּאמֶר אֶל־יוֹסֵף אַף־אֲנִי
בַּחֲלוֹמִי וְהִנֵּה שְׁלֹשָׁה סַלֵּי חֹרִי עַל־רֹאשִׁי: 17וּבַסַּל
הָעֶלְיוֹן מִכֹּל מַאֲכַל פַּרְעֹה מַעֲשֵׂה אֹפֶה וְהָעוֹף
אֹכֵל אֹתָם מִן־הַסַּל מֵעַל רֹאשִׁי: 18וַיַּעַן יוֹסֵף
וַיֹּאמֶר זֶה פִּתְרֹנוֹ שְׁלֹשֶׁת הַסַּלִּים שְׁלֹשֶׁת יָמִים הֵם:
19בְּעוֹד ׀ שְׁלֹשֶׁת יָמִים יִשָּׂא פַרְעֹה אֶת־רֹאשְׁךָ
מֵעָלֶיךָ וְתָלָה אוֹתְךָ עַל־עֵץ וְאָכַל הָעוֹף אֶת־
בְּשָׂרְךָ מֵעָלֶיךָ: 20וַיְהִי ׀ בַּיּוֹם הַשְּׁלִישִׁי יוֹם הֻלֶּדֶת
אֶת־פַּרְעֹה וַיַּעַשׂ מִשְׁתֶּה לְכָל־עֲבָדָיו וַיִּשָּׂא אֶת־
רֹאשׁ ׀ שַׂר הַמַּשְׁקִים וְאֶת־רֹאשׁ שַׂר הָאֹפִים בְּתוֹךְ

---

understood to be a miraculous power or rather a case of wisdom or cleverness, because we do not know what notions of heredity and miracle are presumed there.) The significance of dreams in human experience—and the significance of dream *interpretation* especially—is reflected by this fact: the first divine power possessed by a human in the *Tanak* is the interpretation of dreams.

We should also note that something has changed in Joseph. At the beginning of his story he appeared not to be aware of the prophetic import of his own dreams, but now he is able to interpret the dreams of others, and next he will be able to interpret the dreams of Pharaoh, affecting the destiny of countries and of his own family. We shall see other changes in Joseph as he grows older.

40:14. **bring me out of this house.** Joseph's words to describe his liberation from his enslavement in Egypt prefigure the description of the children of Israel's liberation from enslavement in Egypt in the opening words of the Ten Commandments: "who *brought you out* from the land of Egypt, *from a house* of slaves."

chief of the drink-stewards back over his stewardship, and he set the cup on Pharaoh's hand; [22]and he hanged the chief of the bakers—as Joseph had told the meaning for them. [23]And the chief of the drink-stewards did not remember Joseph. And he forgot him.

AT THE END

41 [1]And it was at the end of two years' time, and Pharaoh was dreaming: and here he was standing by the Nile. [2]And here, coming up from the Nile, were seven cows, beautiful-looking and fat-fleshed, and they fed in the reeds. [3]And here were seven other cows coming up after them from the Nile, bad-looking and thin-fleshed, and they stood by the cows that were by the bank of the Nile. [4]And the bad-looking and thin-fleshed cows ate the seven beautiful-looking and fat cows—and Pharaoh woke up.

[5]And he slept and dreamed a second time, and here were seven ears of grain coming up on one stalk, fat and good. [6]And here were seven ears of grain, thin and scorched by the east wind, growing after them. [7]And the thin ears of grain swallowed the seven fat and full ears of grain—and Pharaoh woke up, and here it was a dream.

[8]And it was in the morning, and his spirit was moved, and he sent and called all of Egypt's magicians and all its wise men. And Pharaoh told them his dream, and there was no one who could tell the meaning of them to Pharaoh.

[9]And the chief of the drink-stewards spoke to Pharaoh, saying, "I'm recalling my sins today: [10]Pharaoh had been angry at his servants, and he put me under watch at the house of the chief of the guards, me and the chief of the bakers. [11]And we had a dream in one night, I and he; we each dreamed with his own dream's meaning. [12]And there, with us, was a Hebrew boy, a slave of the chief of the guards; and we told him, and he told us the meaning of our dreams. He told the meaning according to each one's dream. [13]And it

עֲבָדָיו: 21וַיָּשֶׁב אֶת־שַׂר הַמַּשְׁקִים עַל־מַשְׁקֵהוּ וַיִּתֵּן הַכּוֹס עַל־כַּף פַּרְעֹה: 22וְאֵת שַׂר הָאֹפִים תָּלָה כַּאֲשֶׁר פָּתַר לָהֶם יוֹסֵף: 23וְלֹא־זָכַר שַׂר־הַמַּשְׁקִים אֶת־יוֹסֵף וַיִּשְׁכָּחֵהוּ: פ

מקץ

41 1וַיְהִי מִקֵּץ שְׁנָתַיִם יָמִים וּפַרְעֹה חֹלֵם וְהִנֵּה עֹמֵד עַל־הַיְאֹר: 2וְהִנֵּה מִן־הַיְאֹר עֹלֹת שֶׁבַע פָּרוֹת יְפוֹת מַרְאֶה וּבְרִיאֹת בָּשָׂר וַתִּרְעֶינָה בָּאָחוּ: 3וְהִנֵּה שֶׁבַע פָּרוֹת אֲחֵרוֹת עֹלוֹת אַחֲרֵיהֶן מִן־הַיְאֹר רָעוֹת מַרְאֶה וְדַקּוֹת בָּשָׂר וַתַּעֲמֹדְנָה אֵצֶל הַפָּרוֹת עַל־שְׂפַת הַיְאֹר: 4וַתֹּאכַלְנָה הַפָּרוֹת רָעוֹת הַמַּרְאֶה וְדַקֹּת הַבָּשָׂר אֵת שֶׁבַע הַפָּרוֹת יְפֹת הַמַּרְאֶה וְהַבְּרִיאֹת וַיִּיקַץ פַּרְעֹה: 5וַיִּישָׁן וַיַּחֲלֹם שֵׁנִית וְהִנֵּה ׀ שֶׁבַע שִׁבֳּלִים עֹלוֹת בְּקָנֶה אֶחָד בְּרִיאוֹת וְטֹבוֹת: 6וְהִנֵּה שֶׁבַע שִׁבֳּלִים דַּקּוֹת וּשְׁדוּפֹת קָדִים צֹמְחוֹת אַחֲרֵיהֶן: 7וַתִּבְלַעְנָה הַשִּׁבֳּלִים הַדַּקּוֹת אֵת שֶׁבַע הַשִּׁבֳּלִים הַבְּרִיאוֹת וְהַמְּלֵאוֹת וַיִּיקַץ פַּרְעֹה וְהִנֵּה חֲלוֹם: 8וַיְהִי בַבֹּקֶר וַתִּפָּעֶם רוּחוֹ וַיִּשְׁלַח וַיִּקְרָא אֶת־כָּל־חַרְטֻמֵּי מִצְרַיִם וְאֶת־כָּל־חֲכָמֶיהָ וַיְסַפֵּר פַּרְעֹה לָהֶם אֶת־חֲלֹמוֹ וְאֵין־פּוֹתֵר אוֹתָם לְפַרְעֹה: 9וַיְדַבֵּר שַׂר הַמַּשְׁקִים אֶת־פַּרְעֹה לֵאמֹר אֶת־חֲטָאַי אֲנִי מַזְכִּיר הַיּוֹם: 10פַּרְעֹה קָצַף עַל־עֲבָדָיו וַיִּתֵּן אֹתִי בְּמִשְׁמַר בֵּית שַׂר הַטַּבָּחִים אֹתִי וְאֵת שַׂר הָאֹפִים: 11וַנַּחַלְמָה חֲלוֹם בְּלַיְלָה אֶחָד אֲנִי וָהוּא אִישׁ כְּפִתְרוֹן חֲלֹמוֹ חָלָמְנוּ: 12וְשָׁם אִתָּנוּ נַעַר עִבְרִי עֶבֶד לְשַׂר הַטַּבָּחִים וַנְּסַפֶּר־לוֹ וַיִּפְתָּר־לָנוּ אֶת־חֲלֹמֹתֵינוּ אִישׁ כַּחֲלֹמוֹ פָּתָר: 13וַיְהִי כַּאֲשֶׁר

was—as he told the meaning for us, so it was: me he put back at my station, and him he hanged."

14And Pharaoh sent and called Joseph, and they rushed him from the pit, and he shaved and changed his clothing and came to Pharaoh. 15And Pharaoh said to Joseph, "I've had a dream, and there's no one who can tell the meaning of it, and I've heard about you, saying you hear a dream so as to tell the meaning of it."

16And Joseph answered Pharaoh, saying, "Not I. God will answer regarding Pharaoh's well-being."

17And Pharaoh spoke to Joseph, "In my dream, here I was standing by the bank of the Nile. 18And here, coming up from the Nile, were seven cows, fat-fleshed and beautiful-figured, and they fed in the reeds. 19And here were seven other cows coming up after them, weak and very bad-figured and scrawny-fleshed. I haven't seen any like these in all the land of Egypt for bad! 20And the cows that were scrawny and bad ate the first seven cows that were fat, 21and they came inside, and it wasn't known that they had come inside! And their appearance was bad, as at first. And I woke up.

22"And I saw in my dream, and here were seven ears of grain coming up on one stalk, full and good. 23And here were seven ears of grain, dried up, thin, scorched by the east wind, growing after them. 24And the thin ears of grain swallowed the seven good ears of grain.

"And I said it to the magicians, and there's no one who can tell me."

פֹּתַר־לָ֖נוּ כֵּ֣ן הָיָ֑ה אֹתִ֛י הֵשִׁ֥יב עַל־כַּנִּ֖י וְאֹת֥וֹ תָלָֽה׃
14וַיִּשְׁלַ֤ח פַּרְעֹה֙ וַיִּקְרָ֣א אֶת־יוֹסֵ֔ף וַיְרִיצֻ֖הוּ מִן־הַבּ֑וֹר וַיְגַלַּח֙ וַיְחַלֵּ֣ף שִׂמְלֹתָ֔יו וַיָּבֹ֖א אֶל־פַּרְעֹֽה׃
15וַיֹּ֤אמֶר פַּרְעֹה֙ אֶל־יוֹסֵ֔ף חֲל֣וֹם חָלַ֔מְתִּי וּפֹתֵ֖ר אֵ֣ין אֹת֑וֹ וַאֲנִ֗י שָׁמַ֤עְתִּי עָלֶ֨יךָ֙ לֵאמֹ֔ר תִּשְׁמַ֥ע חֲל֖וֹם לִפְתֹּ֥ר אֹתֽוֹ׃
16וַיַּ֨עַן יוֹסֵ֧ף אֶת־פַּרְעֹ֛ה לֵאמֹ֖ר בִּלְעָדָ֑י אֱלֹהִ֕ים יַעֲנֶ֖ה אֶת־שְׁל֥וֹם פַּרְעֹֽה׃
17וַיְדַבֵּ֥ר פַּרְעֹ֖ה אֶל־יוֹסֵ֑ף בַּחֲלֹמִ֕י הִנְנִ֥י עֹמֵ֖ד עַל־שְׂפַ֥ת הַיְאֹֽר׃
18וְהִנֵּ֣ה מִן־הַיְאֹ֗ר עֹלֹת֙ שֶׁ֣בַע פָּר֔וֹת בְּרִיא֥וֹת בָּשָׂ֖ר וִיפֹ֣ת תֹּ֑אַר וַתִּרְעֶ֖ינָה בָּאָֽחוּ׃
19וְהִנֵּ֞ה שֶֽׁבַע־פָּר֤וֹת אֲחֵרוֹת֙ עֹל֣וֹת אַחֲרֵיהֶ֔ן דַּלּ֨וֹת וְרָע֥וֹת תֹּ֛אַר מְאֹ֖ד וְרַקּ֣וֹת בָּשָׂ֑ר לֹֽא־רָאִ֧יתִי כָהֵ֛נָּה בְּכָל־אֶ֥רֶץ מִצְרַ֖יִם לָרֹֽעַ׃
20וַתֹּאכַ֨לְנָה֙ הַפָּר֔וֹת הָרַקּ֖וֹת וְהָרָע֑וֹת אֵ֣ת שֶׁ֧בַע הַפָּר֛וֹת הָרִאשֹׁנ֖וֹת הַבְּרִיאֹֽת׃
21וַתָּבֹ֣אנָה אֶל־קִרְבֶּ֗נָה וְלֹ֤א נוֹדַע֙ כִּי־בָ֣אוּ אֶל־קִרְבֶּ֔נָה וּמַרְאֵיהֶ֣ן רַ֔ע כַּאֲשֶׁ֖ר בַּתְּחִלָּ֑ה וָאִיקָֽץ׃
22וָאֵ֖רֶא בַּחֲלֹמִ֑י וְהִנֵּ֣ה ׀ שֶׁ֣בַע שִׁבֳּלִ֗ים עֹלֹ֛ת בְּקָנֶ֥ה אֶחָ֖ד מְלֵאֹ֥ת וְטֹבֽוֹת׃
23וְהִנֵּה֙ שֶׁ֣בַע שִׁבֳּלִ֔ים צְנֻמ֥וֹת דַּקּ֖וֹת שְׁדֻפ֣וֹת קָדִ֑ים צֹמְח֖וֹת אַחֲרֵיהֶֽם׃
24וַתִּבְלַ֨עְןָ֙ הַשִּׁבֳּלִ֣ים הַדַּקֹּ֔ת אֵ֛ת שֶׁ֥בַע הַשִּׁבֳּלִ֖ים הַטֹּב֑וֹת וָאֹמַר֙ אֶל־הַֽחַרְטֻמִּ֔ים וְאֵ֥ין מַגִּ֖יד לִֽי׃
25וַיֹּ֥אמֶר יוֹסֵ֖ף אֶל־

41:19. scrawny. There is confusion in the wording in regard to both the ears of grain and the cows, going back and forth between the word "thin" and the word "scrawny" (see 41:3,4,19,20,27). This minor point is instructive because it is a good example of a well-known scribal phenomenon, the confusion of the letters *dalet* and *resh*, which looked similar in many periods. The two words in Hebrew are דקות (thin) and רקות (scrawny). An error is easily made. And the chance of error is increased because the word is sometimes followed by רעות (bad), and this alliteration further draws a scribe's eye to see a *resh* in place of a *dalet*.

25And Joseph said to Pharaoh, "Pharaoh's dream: it is *one*. It has told to Pharaoh what God is doing. 26The seven good cows: they're seven years. And the seven good ears of grain: they're seven years. It's one dream. 27And the seven cows that were scrawny and bad that were coming up after them: they're seven years. And the seven ears of grain that were scrawny, scorched by the east wind, will be seven years of famine. 28That is the thing that I spoke to Pharaoh: it has shown Pharaoh what God is doing. 29Here, seven years are coming: big bountifulness in all the land of Egypt. 30And seven years of famine will rise after them, and all the bountifulness in the land of Egypt will be forgotten, and the famine will finish off the land. 31And the bountifulness won't be known in the land on account of that famine afterwards because it will be very heavy. 32And about the recurrence of the dream to Pharaoh two times: because the thing is right from God, and God is hurrying to do it. 33And now, let Pharaoh look out for an understanding and wise man and set him over the land of Egypt. 34Let Pharaoh do it and appoint overseers over the land and five-out the land of Egypt in the seven years of bountifulness. 35And let them gather all the food of these coming good years and pile up grain under Pharaoh's hand, food in the cities, and watch over it. 36And the food will become a

חֲלוֹם פַּרְעֹה אֶחָד הוּא אֵת אֲשֶׁר הָאֱלֹהִים פַּרְעֹה
עֹשֶׂה הִגִּיד לְפַרְעֹה: 26שֶׁבַע פָּרֹת הַטֹּבֹת שֶׁבַע
שָׁנִים הֵנָּה וְשֶׁבַע הַשִּׁבֳּלִים הַטֹּבֹת שֶׁבַע שָׁנִים הֵנָּה
חֲלוֹם אֶחָד הוּא: 27וְשֶׁבַע הַפָּרוֹת הָרַקּוֹת וְהָרָעֹת
הָעֹלֹת אַחֲרֵיהֶן שֶׁבַע שָׁנִים הֵנָּה וְשֶׁבַע הַשִּׁבֳּלִים
הָרֵקוֹת שְׁדֻפוֹת הַקָּדִים יִהְיוּ שֶׁבַע שְׁנֵי רָעָב:
28הוּא הַדָּבָר אֲשֶׁר דִּבַּרְתִּי אֶל־פַּרְעֹה אֲשֶׁר
הָאֱלֹהִים עֹשֶׂה הֶרְאָה אֶת־פַּרְעֹה: 29הִנֵּה שֶׁבַע
שָׁנִים בָּאוֹת שָׂבָע גָּדוֹל בְּכָל־אֶרֶץ מִצְרָיִם: 30וְקָמוּ
שֶׁבַע שְׁנֵי רָעָב אַחֲרֵיהֶן וְנִשְׁכַּח כָּל־הַשָּׂבָע בְּאֶרֶץ
מִצְרָיִם וְכִלָּה הָרָעָב אֶת־הָאָרֶץ: 31וְלֹא־יִוָּדַע
הַשָּׂבָע בָּאָרֶץ מִפְּנֵי הָרָעָב הַהוּא אַחֲרֵי־כֵן כִּי־
כָבֵד הוּא מְאֹד: 32וְעַל הִשָּׁנוֹת הַחֲלוֹם אֶל־פַּרְעֹה
פַּעֲמָיִם כִּי־נָכוֹן הַדָּבָר מֵעִם הָאֱלֹהִים וּמְמַהֵר
הָאֱלֹהִים לַעֲשֹׂתוֹ: 33וְעַתָּה יֵרֶא פַרְעֹה אִישׁ נָבוֹן
וְחָכָם וִישִׁיתֵהוּ עַל־אֶרֶץ מִצְרָיִם: 34יַעֲשֶׂה פַרְעֹה
וְיַפְקֵד פְּקִדִים עַל־הָאָרֶץ וְחִמֵּשׁ אֶת־אֶרֶץ מִצְרַיִם
בְּשֶׁבַע שְׁנֵי הַשָּׂבָע: 35וְיִקְבְּצוּ אֶת־כָּל־אֹכֶל הַשָּׁנִים
הַטֹּבֹת הַבָּאֹת הָאֵלֶּה וְיִצְבְּרוּ־בָר תַּחַת יַד־פַּרְעֹה
אֹכֶל בֶּעָרִים וְשָׁמָרוּ: 36וְהָיָה הָאֹכֶל לְפִקָּדוֹן

41:25. Pharaoh's dream: it is *one*. It has told to Pharaoh what God is doing. The pronoun is unclear. The verse could mean that *God* has told Pharaoh what He is doing or that the *dream* has told Pharaoh what God is doing. Even on the latter meaning, Joseph has already said that "meanings belong to God" and that "God will answer regarding Pharaoh's well-being." But the question is still whether God has provided both the dream and the interpretation of it—or just the interpretation, while the dream itself may derive from elsewhere. This question remains unanswered in the text! (The same applies to 41:28, "It has shown Pharaoh what God is doing.")

41:32. right from God. This term for "right" (Hebrew *nakôn*) will be recalled to play an important part in the story of the exodus (Exod 8:22; see the text and comment there).

41:34. five-out. This perhaps means to divide the land into portions of five and save one-fifth for the bad years, but the meaning is uncertain because this is the only occurrence of this verb in the Hebrew Bible.

deposit for the land for the seven years of famine that will be in the land of Egypt so the land won't be cut off in the famine."

37And the thing was good in Pharaoh's eyes and in all his servants' eyes. 38And Pharaoh said to his servants, "Will we find such a man as this, that God's spirit is in him?" 39And Pharaoh said to Joseph, "Since God has made you know all this, there's no one as understanding and wise as you. 40You shall be over my house, and at your mouth all my people shall conform. I shall be greater than you only in the throne." 41And Pharaoh said to Joseph, "See, I've put you over all the land of Egypt." 42And Pharaoh took off his ring

לָאָרֶץ לְשֶׁבַע שְׁנֵי הָרָעָב אֲשֶׁר תִּהְיֶיןָ בְּאֶרֶץ מִצְרָיִם וְלֹא־תִכָּרֵת הָאָרֶץ בָּרָעָב: 37וַיִּיטַב הַדָּבָר בְּעֵינֵי פַרְעֹה וּבְעֵינֵי כָּל־עֲבָדָיו: 38וַיֹּאמֶר פַּרְעֹה אֶל־עֲבָדָיו הֲנִמְצָא כָזֶה אִישׁ אֲשֶׁר רוּחַ אֱלֹהִים בּוֹ: 39וַיֹּאמֶר פַּרְעֹה אֶל־יוֹסֵף אַחֲרֵי הוֹדִיעַ אֱלֹהִים אוֹתְךָ אֶת־כָּל־זֹאת אֵין־נָבוֹן וְחָכָם כָּמוֹךָ: 40אַתָּה תִּהְיֶה עַל־בֵּיתִי וְעַל־פִּיךָ יִשַּׁק כָּל־עַמִּי רַק הַכִּסֵּא אֶגְדַּל מִמֶּךָּ: 41וַיֹּאמֶר פַּרְעֹה אֶל־יוֹסֵף רְאֵה נָתַתִּי אֹתְךָ עַל כָּל־אֶרֶץ מִצְרָיִם: 42וַיָּסַר

41:39. **understanding and wise.** Some interpreters identify the Joseph story as a wisdom tale. It is treated as comparable to wisdom tales from numerous cultures about a wise young man who is successful in a royal court because of his cleverness. The story of Mordecai in the book of Esther and the story of Daniel are compared in this context as well. I would caution that there is a danger here of overdefining the word "wisdom." The term was commonly used to refer to the books of Proverbs, Job, and Ecclesiastes, works similar to philosophy; composed, like the pre-Socratics, in poetry; sometimes set in very loose story contexts (Job, Ecclesiastes), but basically dealing with issues outright, not developing them through a prose narrative fabric. Now, in the first place, if we redefine wisdom to include the Joseph cycle, and thus the books of Daniel and Esther, we shall be forced to include a number of other comparable sections of the Hebrew Bible under this heading as well. We shall be left with a category of works with more elements of variety than commonality (Ecclesiastes and Esther?), and the term "wisdom" will be rendered less descriptive and useful. Second, the facts of the Joseph story do not really fit this model in any case. Joseph is not successful initially because of his cleverness or his sage advice. He succeeds because he can interpret dreams, apparently by revelation rather than by his own insight, since even the most brilliant Freudian analyst would be unlikely to guess that a dream of cows eating cows means that there will be prosperity followed by famine in the Near East. Joseph is described as stating that it is God and not he who directs events and sheds light on dreams (40:8; 41:16,25; 50:20). One might suggest that this story is still based on the wisdom tale model but has been adapted to fit the biblical author's literary and theological requirements. That would be an interesting phenomenon to pursue, but it would be a study of adaptation, not of wisdom. To understand biblical wisdom, we are better advised to study wisdom literature as it has classically been understood: Proverbs, Job, and Ecclesiastes.

41:40. **conform.** The verb here, which usually means "to kiss," is a problem for all translators. It may reflect a scribal problem or an idiom that is no longer familiar to us.

from his hand and put it on Joseph's hand, and he had him dressed in linen garments, and he set a gold chain on his neck, [43]and he had him driven in the chariot of the second-in-command whom he had, and they called in front of him, "Kneel," so putting him over all the land of Egypt. [44]And Pharaoh said to Joseph, "I am Pharaoh, and without you a man won't lift his hand and his foot in all the land of Egypt."

[45]And Pharaoh called Joseph's name Zaphenath-paneah. And he gave him Asenath, daughter of Poti-phera, priest of On, as a wife. And Joseph went out over the land of Egypt. [46]And Joseph was thirty years old when he stood in front of Pharaoh, king of Egypt. And Joseph went out from in front of Pharaoh and passed through all the land of Egypt.

[47]And the land produced in the seven years of bountifulness by fistfuls. [48]And he gathered all the food of the seven years, which were in the land of Egypt, and he put food in cities; he put the food of the city's fields that were around it inside of it. [49]And Joseph piled up grain like the sand of the sea, very much, until he stopped counting, because it was without number.

[50]And two sons were born to Joseph before the year of famine came—to whom Asenath, daughter of Poti-phera, priest of On, gave birth for him. [51]And Joseph called the firstborn's name Manasseh, "because God has made me forget all of my trouble and all of my father's house." [52]And he called the second one's name Ephraim, "because God has made me fruitful in the land of my degradation."

פַּרְעֹה אֶת־טַבַּעְתּוֹ מֵעַל יָדוֹ וַיִּתֵּן אֹתָהּ עַל־יַד יוֹסֵף וַיַּלְבֵּשׁ אֹתוֹ בִּגְדֵי־שֵׁשׁ וַיָּשֶׂם רְבִד הַזָּהָב עַל־צַוָּארוֹ: [43]וַיַּרְכֵּב אֹתוֹ בְּמִרְכֶּבֶת הַמִּשְׁנֶה אֲשֶׁר־לוֹ וַיִּקְרְאוּ לְפָנָיו אַבְרֵךְ וְנָתוֹן אֹתוֹ עַל כָּל־אֶרֶץ מִצְרָיִם: [44]וַיֹּאמֶר פַּרְעֹה אֶל־יוֹסֵף אֲנִי פַרְעֹה וּבִלְעָדֶיךָ לֹא־יָרִים אִישׁ אֶת־יָדוֹ וְאֶת־רַגְלוֹ בְּכָל־אֶרֶץ מִצְרָיִם: [45]וַיִּקְרָא פַרְעֹה שֵׁם־יוֹסֵף צָפְנַת פַּעְנֵחַ וַיִּתֶּן־לוֹ אֶת־אָסְנַת בַּת־פּוֹטִי פֶרַע כֹּהֵן אֹן לְאִשָּׁה וַיֵּצֵא יוֹסֵף עַל־אֶרֶץ מִצְרָיִם: [46]וְיוֹסֵף בֶּן־שְׁלֹשִׁים שָׁנָה בְּעָמְדוֹ לִפְנֵי פַּרְעֹה מֶלֶךְ־מִצְרָיִם וַיֵּצֵא יוֹסֵף מִלִּפְנֵי פַרְעֹה וַיַּעֲבֹר בְּכָל־אֶרֶץ מִצְרָיִם: [47]וַתַּעַשׂ הָאָרֶץ בְּשֶׁבַע שְׁנֵי הַשָּׂבָע לִקְמָצִים: [48]וַיִּקְבֹּץ אֶת־כָּל־אֹכֶל ׀ שֶׁבַע שָׁנִים אֲשֶׁר הָיוּ בְּאֶרֶץ מִצְרַיִם וַיִּתֶּן־אֹכֶל בֶּעָרִים אֹכֶל שְׂדֵה־הָעִיר אֲשֶׁר סְבִיבֹתֶיהָ נָתַן בְּתוֹכָהּ: [49]וַיִּצְבֹּר יוֹסֵף בָּר כְּחוֹל הַיָּם הַרְבֵּה מְאֹד עַד כִּי־חָדַל לִסְפֹּר כִּי־אֵין מִסְפָּר: [50]וּלְיוֹסֵף יֻלַּד שְׁנֵי בָנִים בְּטֶרֶם תָּבוֹא שְׁנַת הָרָעָב אֲשֶׁר יָלְדָה־לּוֹ אָסְנַת בַּת־פּוֹטִי פֶרַע כֹּהֵן אֹן: [51]וַיִּקְרָא יוֹסֵף אֶת־שֵׁם הַבְּכוֹר מְנַשֶּׁה כִּי־נַשַּׁנִי אֱלֹהִים אֶת־כָּל־עֲמָלִי וְאֵת כָּל־בֵּית אָבִי: [52]וְאֵת שֵׁם הַשֵּׁנִי קָרָא אֶפְרָיִם כִּי־הִפְרַנִי אֱלֹהִים בְּאֶרֶץ עָנְיִי: [53]וַתִּכְלֶינָה שֶׁבַע שְׁנֵי

41:43. **Kneel.** Hebrew *'abrēk.* Its meaning is unknown. Some see a derivation from an Egyptian term. One rabbinic interpretation takes it to mean "Bend the knee."

41:45. **Asenath, daughter of Poti-phera, priest of On.** Like Moses, Joseph marries the daughter of a priest. The Pharaoh would naturally provide Joseph with a prestigious marriage, but he would be disinclined to let Joseph, a foreigner, marry anyone from the royal house. Marriage to a woman from a distinguished priestly family would be the next best thing.

53And the seven years of the bountifulness that was in the land of Egypt finished, 54and the seven years of famine started to come, as Joseph had said. And there was famine in all the lands, and in all the land of Egypt there was bread. 55And all the land of Egypt hungered, and the people cried to Pharaoh for the bread, and Pharaoh said to all Egypt, "Go to Joseph. Do what he'll tell you." 56And the famine was on all the face of the earth. And Joseph opened everything that was in them and sold to Egypt. And the famine was strong in the land of Egypt. 57And all the earth came to Egypt to buy, to Joseph, because the famine was strong in all the earth.

42 1And Jacob saw that there was grain in Egypt, and Jacob said to his sons, "Why do you look at each other?" 2And he said, "Here I've heard that there's grain in Egypt. Go down there and buy grain for us from there, and we'll live and not die." 3And ten of Joseph's brothers went down to buy grain from Egypt, 4and Jacob did not send Joseph's brother Benjamin with his brothers because, he said, "In case some harm will happen to him."

5And the sons of Israel came to buy among those who were coming, because the famine was in the land of Canaan. 6And Joseph was the one

הַשֶּׁבַע אֲשֶׁר הָיָה בְּאֶרֶץ מִצְרָיִם: 54וַתְּחִלֶּינָה שֶׁבַע שְׁנֵי הָרָעָב לָבוֹא כַּאֲשֶׁר אָמַר יוֹסֵף וַיְהִי רָעָב בְּכָל־הָאֲרָצוֹת וּבְכָל־אֶרֶץ מִצְרַיִם הָיָה לָחֶם: 55וַתִּרְעַב כָּל־אֶרֶץ מִצְרַיִם וַיִּצְעַק הָעָם אֶל־פַּרְעֹה לַלָּחֶם וַיֹּאמֶר פַּרְעֹה לְכָל־מִצְרַיִם לְכוּ אֶל־יוֹסֵף אֲשֶׁר־יֹאמַר לָכֶם תַּעֲשׂוּ: 56וְהָרָעָב הָיָה עַל כָּל־פְּנֵי הָאָרֶץ וַיִּפְתַּח יוֹסֵף אֶת־כָּל־אֲשֶׁר בָּהֶם וַיִּשְׁבֹּר לְמִצְרַיִם וַיֶּחֱזַק הָרָעָב בְּאֶרֶץ מִצְרָיִם: 57וְכָל־הָאָרֶץ בָּאוּ מִצְרַיְמָה לִשְׁבֹּר אֶל־יוֹסֵף כִּי־חָזַק הָרָעָב בְּכָל־הָאָרֶץ:

42 1וַיַּרְא יַעֲקֹב כִּי יֶשׁ־שֶׁבֶר בְּמִצְרָיִם וַיֹּאמֶר יַעֲקֹב לְבָנָיו לָמָּה תִּתְרָאוּ: 2וַיֹּאמֶר הִנֵּה שָׁמַעְתִּי כִּי יֶשׁ־שֶׁבֶר בְּמִצְרָיִם רְדוּ־שָׁמָּה וְשִׁבְרוּ־לָנוּ מִשָּׁם וְנִחְיֶה וְלֹא נָמוּת: 3וַיֵּרְדוּ אֲחֵי־יוֹסֵף עֲשָׂרָה לִשְׁבֹּר בָּר מִמִּצְרָיִם: 4וְאֶת־בִּנְיָמִין אֲחִי יוֹסֵף לֹא־שָׁלַח יַעֲקֹב אֶת־אֶחָיו כִּי אָמַר פֶּן־יִקְרָאֶנּוּ אָסוֹן: 5וַיָּבֹאוּ בְּנֵי יִשְׂרָאֵל לִשְׁבֹּר בְּתוֹךְ הַבָּאִים כִּי־הָיָה הָרָעָב בְּאֶרֶץ כְּנָעַן: 6וְיוֹסֵף הוּא הַשַּׁלִּיט עַל־הָאָרֶץ הוּא

41:56. **everything that was in them**. In what? The Septuagint reads, "Joseph opened all the grain storehouses" (אצרות בר), which is consistent with 41:49.

42:1. **Jacob saw**. The text says that "Jacob *saw* that there was grain in Egypt. . . . And he said, "I've *heard* that there's grain in Egypt." How could he have *seen* it? Rashi says that he had a vision. This rather reflects the metaphor of *seeing* as meaning to know, to learn, to find out, to comprehend. It shows the high value we place on sight over the other senses. The Torah will convey this in many ways, including a progression: Isaac cannot see on his deathbed, and so he is deceived. Jacob cannot see on his deathbed, but he has more insight than he did when he was young and could see. (He sees his grandsons' destinies, when earlier he could not see what was going on among his sons.) And then Moses' "eye was not dim" up to the time of his death at the age of 120.

42:5. **sons of Israel**. Until now they have been called "sons of Jacob." Now they are called "sons of Israel" for the first time just as they come to Egypt. One explanation is that it is in Egypt that they will grow and become the nation that will be known as

in charge over the land; he was the one who sold grain to all the people of the land. And Joseph's brothers came and bowed to him, noses to the ground. 7And Joseph saw his brothers and recognized them, but he made himself unrecognizable to them, and he spoke with them in hard tones. And he said to them, "From where have you come?"

And they said, "From the land of Canaan, to buy food."

8And Joseph recognized his brothers, but they did not recognize him, 9and Joseph remembered the dreams that he had had about them. And he said to them, "You're spies. You came to see the land exposed."

10And they said to him, "No, my lord, your servants came to buy food. 11We're all sons of one man. We're honest men. Your servants weren't spying."

12And he said to them, "No, but you've come to see the land exposed."

13And they said, "Your servants are twelve brothers. We're sons of one man in the land of Canaan, and, here, the youngest is with our father today, and one is no more."

14And Joseph said to them, "It's as I spoke to you, saying: you're spies. 15By this you'll be tested: by Pharaoh's life, you won't go out of here except by your youngest brother's coming here. 16Send one from among you, and let him get your brother, and you remain in prison, and your words will be tested: is the truth with you? And if not, then by Pharaoh's life you're spies." 17And he gathered them under watch for three days. 18And Joseph said to them on the third day,

הַמַּשְׁבִּיר לְכָל־עַם הָאָרֶץ וַיָּבֹאוּ אֲחֵי יוֹסֵף וַיִּשְׁתַּחֲווּ־לוֹ אַפַּיִם אָרְצָה: 7וַיַּרְא יוֹסֵף אֶת־אֶחָיו וַיַּכִּרֵם וַיִּתְנַכֵּר אֲלֵיהֶם וַיְדַבֵּר אִתָּם קָשׁוֹת וַיֹּאמֶר אֲלֵהֶם מֵאַיִן בָּאתֶם וַיֹּאמְרוּ מֵאֶרֶץ כְּנַעַן לִשְׁבָּר־אֹכֶל: 8וַיַּכֵּר יוֹסֵף אֶת־אֶחָיו וְהֵם לֹא הִכִּרֻהוּ: 9וַיִּזְכֹּר יוֹסֵף אֵת הַחֲלֹמוֹת אֲשֶׁר חָלַם לָהֶם וַיֹּאמֶר אֲלֵהֶם מְרַגְּלִים אַתֶּם לִרְאוֹת אֶת־עֶרְוַת הָאָרֶץ בָּאתֶם: 10וַיֹּאמְרוּ אֵלָיו לֹא אֲדֹנִי וַעֲבָדֶיךָ בָּאוּ לִשְׁבָּר־אֹכֶל: 11כֻּלָּנוּ בְּנֵי אִישׁ־אֶחָד נָחְנוּ כֵּנִים אֲנַחְנוּ לֹא־הָיוּ עֲבָדֶיךָ מְרַגְּלִים: 12וַיֹּאמֶר אֲלֵהֶם לֹא כִּי־עֶרְוַת הָאָרֶץ בָּאתֶם לִרְאוֹת: 13וַיֹּאמְרוּ שְׁנֵים עָשָׂר עֲבָדֶיךָ אַחִים אֲנַחְנוּ בְּנֵי אִישׁ־אֶחָד בְּאֶרֶץ כְּנָעַן וְהִנֵּה הַקָּטֹן אֶת־אָבִינוּ הַיּוֹם וְהָאֶחָד אֵינֶנּוּ: 14וַיֹּאמֶר אֲלֵהֶם יוֹסֵף הוּא אֲשֶׁר דִּבַּרְתִּי אֲלֵכֶם לֵאמֹר מְרַגְּלִים אַתֶּם: 15בְּזֹאת תִּבָּחֵנוּ חֵי פַרְעֹה אִם־תֵּצְאוּ מִזֶּה כִּי אִם־בְּבוֹא אֲחִיכֶם הַקָּטֹן הֵנָּה: 16שִׁלְחוּ מִכֶּם אֶחָד וְיִקַּח אֶת־אֲחִיכֶם וְאַתֶּם הֵאָסְרוּ וְיִבָּחֲנוּ דִּבְרֵיכֶם הַאֱמֶת אִתְּכֶם וְאִם־לֹא חֵי פַרְעֹה כִּי מְרַגְּלִים אַתֶּם: 17וַיֶּאֱסֹף אֹתָם אֶל־מִשְׁמָר שְׁלֹשֶׁת יָמִים: 18וַיֹּאמֶר אֲלֵהֶם יוֹסֵף בַּיּוֹם

Israel. (The nation is called "children of Israel" 350 times in the Torah but never called "children of Jacob.") Another explanation: it is now, as they enter Egypt, that they will themselves have a struggle with God (yiśrā-'ēl). They will unknowingly confront Joseph, who has risen in Egypt through the divine power of interpreting dreams (41:16). And in the end Joseph will tell them that, although they thought they were struggling with Joseph, God had been in control all along (45:8; 50:20).

42:13. **one is no more.** We must keep in mind that the brothers do not *know* what happened to Joseph.

"Do this and live, as I fear God: ¹⁹If you're honest, one brother from among you will be held at the place where you're under watch; and you, go, bring grain for the famine in your houses. ²⁰And you will bring your youngest brother to me, and your words will be confirmed, and you won't die." And they did so.

²¹And they said, each to his brother, "But we're guilty over our brother, because we saw his soul's distress when he implored us and we didn't listen. On account of that this distress has come to us!"

²²And Reuben answered them, saying, "Didn't I say to you, saying, 'Don't sin against the boy'? And you didn't listen. And his blood, too, is required here!"

²³And they did not know that Joseph was listening, because an interpreter was between them. ²⁴And he turned from them and wept. And he came back to them and spoke to them and took Simeon from them and shackled him before their eyes. ²⁵And Joseph commanded that they fill their containers with grain and to put their silver back in each man's sack and to give them provisions for the road. And he did that for them. ²⁶And they loaded their grain on their asses and went from there.

²⁷And one opened his sack to give fodder to his ass at a lodging place, and he saw his silver, and here it was in the mouth of his bag. ²⁸And he said to his brothers, "My silver's been put back, and here it is in my bag, too."

And their heart went out, and the brothers trembled to one another, saying, "What is this that God has done to us?"

²⁹And they came to Jacob, their father, to the

הַשְּׁלִישִׁי זֹאת עֲשׂוּ וִחְיוּ אֶת־הָאֱלֹהִים אֲנִי יָרֵא: ¹⁹אִם־כֵּנִים אַתֶּם אֲחִיכֶם אֶחָד יֵאָסֵר בְּבֵית מִשְׁמַרְכֶם וְאַתֶּם לְכוּ הָבִיאוּ שֶׁבֶר רַעֲבוֹן בָּתֵּיכֶם: ²⁰וְאֶת־אֲחִיכֶם הַקָּטֹן תָּבִיאוּ אֵלַי וְיֵאָמְנוּ דִבְרֵיכֶם וְלֹא תָמוּתוּ וַיַּעֲשׂוּ־כֵן: ²¹וַיֹּאמְרוּ אִישׁ אֶל־אָחִיו אֲבָל אֲשֵׁמִים ׀ אֲנַחְנוּ עַל־אָחִינוּ אֲשֶׁר רָאִינוּ צָרַת נַפְשׁוֹ בְּהִתְחַנְנוֹ אֵלֵינוּ וְלֹא שָׁמָעְנוּ עַל־כֵּן בָּאָה אֵלֵינוּ הַצָּרָה הַזֹּאת: ²²וַיַּעַן רְאוּבֵן אֹתָם לֵאמֹר הֲלוֹא אָמַרְתִּי אֲלֵיכֶם ׀ לֵאמֹר אַל־תֶּחֶטְאוּ בַיֶּלֶד וְלֹא שְׁמַעְתֶּם וְגַם־דָּמוֹ הִנֵּה נִדְרָשׁ: ²³וְהֵם לֹא יָדְעוּ כִּי שֹׁמֵעַ יוֹסֵף כִּי הַמֵּלִיץ בֵּינֹתָם: ²⁴וַיִּסֹּב מֵעֲלֵיהֶם וַיֵּבְךְּ וַיָּשָׁב אֲלֵהֶם וַיְדַבֵּר אֲלֵהֶם וַיִּקַּח מֵאִתָּם אֶת־שִׁמְעוֹן וַיֶּאֱסֹר אֹתוֹ לְעֵינֵיהֶם: ²⁵וַיְצַו יוֹסֵף וַיְמַלְאוּ אֶת־כְּלֵיהֶם בָּר וּלְהָשִׁיב כַּסְפֵּיהֶם אִישׁ אֶל־שַׂקּוֹ וְלָתֵת לָהֶם צֵדָה לַדָּרֶךְ וַיַּעַשׂ לָהֶם כֵּן: ²⁶וַיִּשְׂאוּ אֶת־שִׁבְרָם עַל־חֲמֹרֵיהֶם וַיֵּלְכוּ מִשָּׁם: ²⁷וַיִּפְתַּח הָאֶחָד אֶת־שַׂקּוֹ לָתֵת מִסְפּוֹא לַחֲמֹרוֹ בַּמָּלוֹן וַיַּרְא אֶת־כַּסְפּוֹ וְהִנֵּה־הוּא בְּפִי אַמְתַּחְתּוֹ: ²⁸וַיֹּאמֶר אֶל־אֶחָיו הוּשַׁב כַּסְפִּי וְגַם הִנֵּה בְאַמְתַּחְתִּי וַיֵּצֵא לִבָּם וַיֶּחֶרְדוּ אִישׁ אֶל־אָחִיו לֵאמֹר מַה־זֹּאת עָשָׂה אֱלֹהִים לָנוּ: ²⁹וַיָּבֹאוּ אֶל־יַעֲקֹב אֲבִיהֶם אַרְצָה

42:21,35. **his soul's distress . . . this distress has come to us . . . and here was each man's bundle**. Note the pun on *ṣrh* (trouble) and *ṣrr* (bundle), which conveys the irony of the recompense that is happening to them though they do not yet know it.

42:24. **Simeon**. Since Reuben, the oldest, had originally opposed selling Joseph and had not been present at the time of the deed, it was *Simeon*, the second oldest, who was responsible, so his imprisonment is a hidden recompense.

land of Canaan, and told him all the things that happened to them, saying, ³⁰"The man, the lord of the land, spoke with us hard and accused us of spying on the land. ³¹And we said to him, 'We're honest. We weren't spying. ³²We're twelve brothers, our father's sons; one is no more, and the youngest is with our father in the land of Canaan today.' ³³And the man, the lord of the land, said to us, 'By this I'll know that you're honest: leave one brother from among you with me, and take for the famine in your houses and go, ³⁴and bring your youngest brother to me, so I may know that you aren't spies, that you're honest. I'll give you your brother, and you'll go around in the land.' "

³⁵And it was: they were emptying their sacks, and here was each man's bundle of silver in his sack, and they saw the bundles of their silver, they and their father, and they were afraid. ³⁶And their father, Jacob, said to them, "You've bereaved me! Joseph is gone, and Simeon's gone, and you'll take Benjamin. All these have happened to me!"

³⁷And Reuben said to his father, saying, "Kill my two sons if I don't bring him back to you. Put him in my hand, and I'll bring him back to you."

³⁸And he said, "My son will not go down with you. Because his brother's dead, and he's left by himself, and if some harm would happen to him on the way in which you're going then you'll bring down my gray hair in anguish to Sheol."

43 ¹And the famine was heavy in the land. ²And it was when they had finished eating the grain that they had brought from Egypt: and their father said to them, "Go back. Buy us a little food."

³And Judah said to him, saying, "The man *certified* to us, saying, 'You won't see my face unless your brother is with you.' ⁴If you're sending our brother with us, we'll go down and buy food for you, ⁵and if you're not sending, we won't go down, because the man said to us, 'You won't see my face unless your brother is with you.' "

⁶And Israel said, "Why have you done me

כְּנַעַן וַיַּגִּידוּ לוֹ אֵת כָּל־הַקֹּרֹת אֹתָם לֵאמֹר:
³⁰דִּבֶּר הָאִישׁ אֲדֹנֵי הָאָרֶץ אִתָּנוּ קָשׁוֹת וַיִּתֵּן אֹתָנוּ
כִּמְרַגְּלִים אֶת־הָאָרֶץ: ³¹וַנֹּאמֶר אֵלָיו כֵּנִים אֲנָחְנוּ
לֹא הָיִינוּ מְרַגְּלִים: ³²שְׁנֵים־עָשָׂר אֲנַחְנוּ אַחִים בְּנֵי
אָבִינוּ הָאֶחָד אֵינֶנּוּ וְהַקָּטֹן הַיּוֹם אֶת־אָבִינוּ בְּאֶרֶץ
כְּנָעַן: ³³וַיֹּאמֶר אֵלֵינוּ הָאִישׁ אֲדֹנֵי הָאָרֶץ בְּזֹאת
אֵדַע כִּי כֵנִים אַתֶּם אֲחִיכֶם הָאֶחָד הַנִּיחוּ אִתִּי
וְאֶת־רַעֲבוֹן בָּתֵּיכֶם קְחוּ וָלֵכוּ: ³⁴וְהָבִיאוּ אֶת־
אֲחִיכֶם הַקָּטֹן אֵלַי וְאֵדְעָה כִּי לֹא מְרַגְּלִים אַתֶּם
כִּי כֵנִים אַתֶּם אֶת־אֲחִיכֶם אֶתֵּן לָכֶם וְאֶת־הָאָרֶץ
תִּסְחָרוּ: ³⁵וַיְהִי הֵם מְרִיקִים שַׂקֵּיהֶם וְהִנֵּה־אִישׁ
צְרוֹר־כַּסְפּוֹ בְּשַׂקּוֹ וַיִּרְאוּ אֶת־צְרֹרוֹת כַּסְפֵּיהֶם
הֵמָּה וַאֲבִיהֶם וַיִּירָאוּ: ³⁶וַיֹּאמֶר אֲלֵהֶם יַעֲקֹב
אֲבִיהֶם אֹתִי שִׁכַּלְתֶּם יוֹסֵף אֵינֶנּוּ וְשִׁמְעוֹן אֵינֶנּוּ
וְאֶת־בִּנְיָמִן תִּקָּחוּ עָלַי הָיוּ כֻלָּנָה: ³⁷וַיֹּאמֶר רְאוּבֵן
אֶל־אָבִיו לֵאמֹר אֶת־שְׁנֵי בָנַי תָּמִית אִם־לֹא
אֲבִיאֶנּוּ אֵלֶיךָ תְּנָה אֹתוֹ עַל־יָדִי וַאֲנִי אֲשִׁיבֶנּוּ
אֵלֶיךָ: ³⁸וַיֹּאמֶר לֹא־יֵרֵד בְּנִי עִמָּכֶם כִּי־אָחִיו מֵת
וְהוּא לְבַדּוֹ נִשְׁאָר וּקְרָאָהוּ אָסוֹן בַּדֶּרֶךְ אֲשֶׁר
תֵּלְכוּ־בָהּ וְהוֹרַדְתֶּם אֶת־שֵׂיבָתִי בְּיָגוֹן שְׁאוֹלָה:
43 ¹וְהָרָעָב כָּבֵד בָּאָרֶץ: ²וַיְהִי כַּאֲשֶׁר כִּלּוּ
לֶאֱכֹל אֶת־הַשֶּׁבֶר אֲשֶׁר הֵבִיאוּ מִמִּצְרָיִם וַיֹּאמֶר
אֲלֵיהֶם אֲבִיהֶם שֻׁבוּ שִׁבְרוּ־לָנוּ מְעַט־אֹכֶל:
³וַיֹּאמֶר אֵלָיו יְהוּדָה לֵאמֹר הָעֵד הֵעִד בָּנוּ הָאִישׁ
לֵאמֹר לֹא־תִרְאוּ פָנַי בִּלְתִּי אֲחִיכֶם אִתְּכֶם: ⁴אִם־
יֶשְׁךָ מְשַׁלֵּחַ אֶת־אָחִינוּ אִתָּנוּ נֵרְדָה וְנִשְׁבְּרָה לְךָ
אֹכֶל: ⁵וְאִם־אֵינְךָ מְשַׁלֵּחַ לֹא נֵרֵד כִּי־הָאִישׁ אָמַר
אֵלֵינוּ לֹא־תִרְאוּ פָנַי בִּלְתִּי אֲחִיכֶם אִתְּכֶם: ⁶וַיֹּאמֶר

wrong, to tell the man that you have another brother?"

7And they said, "The man *asked* about us and about our birthplace, saying, 'Is your father still alive? Do you have a brother?' And we told him about these things. Could we have *known* that he would say, 'Bring your brother down'?"

8And Judah said to Israel, his father, "Send the boy with me, so we may get up and go, and we'll live and not die, we and you and our infants as well. 9I'll be security for him. You'll seek him from my hand. If I don't bring him to you and set him before you, then I'll have sinned against you for all time. 10For, if we hadn't delayed, by now we would have come back twice."

11And Israel, their father, said to them, "If that's how it is, then do this: Take some of the best fruit of the land in your containers and take a gift down to the man, a little balm and a little honey, gum and myrrh, pistachios and almonds. 12And take double the silver in your hand, and take back in your hand the silver that was put back in the mouth of your bags. Maybe it was a mistake. 13And take your brother. And get up, go back to the man. 14And may El Shadday give you mercy before the man, so he'll send your other brother and Benjamin to you. And I: if I'm bereaved I'm bereaved!"

15And the men took this gift and took double the silver in their hand and Benjamin and got up and went down to Egypt and stood before Joseph. 16And Joseph saw Benjamin with them and said to the one who was over his house, "Bring the men to the house, and slaughter and prepare an animal, because the men will eat with me at noon." 17And the man did as Joseph said, and the man brought the men to Joseph's house.

18And the men were afraid because they were brought to Joseph's house, and they said, "We're being brought on account of the silver that came back in our bags the first time, in order to roll over us and to fall upon us and to take us as slaves—and our asses." 19And they went over to the man who was over Joseph's house and spoke

יִשְׂרָאֵל לָמָה הֲרֵעֹתֶם לִי לְהַגִּיד לָאִישׁ הַעוֹד לָכֶם אָח: 7וַיֹּאמְרוּ שָׁאוֹל שָׁאַל־הָאִישׁ לָנוּ וּלְמוֹלַדְתֵּנוּ לֵאמֹר הַעוֹד אֲבִיכֶם חַי הֲיֵשׁ לָכֶם אָח וַנַּגֶּד־לוֹ עַל־פִּי הַדְּבָרִים הָאֵלֶּה הֲיָדוֹעַ נֵדַע כִּי יֹאמַר הוֹרִידוּ אֶת־אֲחִיכֶם: 8וַיֹּאמֶר יְהוּדָה אֶל־יִשְׂרָאֵל אָבִיו שִׁלְחָה הַנַּעַר אִתִּי וְנָקוּמָה וְנֵלֵכָה וְנִחְיֶה וְלֹא נָמוּת גַּם־אֲנַחְנוּ גַם־אַתָּה גַּם־טַפֵּנוּ: 9אָנֹכִי אֶעֶרְבֶנּוּ מִיָּדִי תְּבַקְשֶׁנּוּ אִם־לֹא הֲבִיאֹתִיו אֵלֶיךָ וְהִצַּגְתִּיו לְפָנֶיךָ וְחָטָאתִי לְךָ כָּל־הַיָּמִים: 10כִּי לוּלֵא הִתְמַהְמָהְנוּ כִּי־עַתָּה שַׁבְנוּ זֶה פַעֲמָיִם: 11וַיֹּאמֶר אֲלֵהֶם יִשְׂרָאֵל אֲבִיהֶם אִם־כֵּן אֵפוֹא זֹאת עֲשׂוּ קְחוּ מִזִּמְרַת הָאָרֶץ בִּכְלֵיכֶם וְהוֹרִידוּ לָאִישׁ מִנְחָה מְעַט צֳרִי וּמְעַט דְּבַשׁ נְכֹאת וָלֹט בָּטְנִים וּשְׁקֵדִים: 12וְכֶסֶף מִשְׁנֶה קְחוּ בְיֶדְכֶם וְאֶת־הַכֶּסֶף הַמּוּשָׁב בְּפִי אַמְתְּחֹתֵיכֶם תָּשִׁיבוּ בְיֶדְכֶם אוּלַי מִשְׁגֶּה הוּא: 13וְאֶת־אֲחִיכֶם קָחוּ וְקוּמוּ שׁוּבוּ אֶל־הָאִישׁ: 14וְאֵל שַׁדַּי יִתֵּן לָכֶם רַחֲמִים לִפְנֵי הָאִישׁ וְשִׁלַּח לָכֶם אֶת־אֲחִיכֶם אַחֵר וְאֶת־בִּנְיָמִין וַאֲנִי כַּאֲשֶׁר שָׁכֹלְתִּי שָׁכָלְתִּי:

15וַיִּקְחוּ הָאֲנָשִׁים אֶת־הַמִּנְחָה הַזֹּאת וּמִשְׁנֶה־כֶּסֶף לָקְחוּ בְיָדָם וְאֶת־בִּנְיָמִן וַיָּקֻמוּ וַיֵּרְדוּ מִצְרַיִם וַיַּעַמְדוּ לִפְנֵי יוֹסֵף: 16וַיַּרְא יוֹסֵף אִתָּם אֶת־בִּנְיָמִין וַיֹּאמֶר לַאֲשֶׁר עַל־בֵּיתוֹ הָבֵא אֶת־הָאֲנָשִׁים הַבָּיְתָה וּטְבֹחַ טֶבַח וְהָכֵן כִּי אִתִּי יֹאכְלוּ הָאֲנָשִׁים בַּצָּהֳרָיִם: 17וַיַּעַשׂ הָאִישׁ כַּאֲשֶׁר אָמַר יוֹסֵף וַיָּבֵא הָאִישׁ אֶת־הָאֲנָשִׁים בֵּיתָה יוֹסֵף: 18וַיִּירְאוּ הָאֲנָשִׁים כִּי הוּבְאוּ בֵּית יוֹסֵף וַיֹּאמְרוּ עַל־דְּבַר הַכֶּסֶף הַשָּׁב בְּאַמְתְּחֹתֵינוּ בַּתְּחִלָּה אֲנַחְנוּ מוּבָאִים לְהִתְגֹּלֵל עָלֵינוּ וּלְהִתְנַפֵּל עָלֵינוּ וְלָקַחַת אֹתָנוּ לַעֲבָדִים וְאֶת־חֲמֹרֵינוּ: 19וַיִּגְּשׁוּ אֶל־הָאִישׁ אֲשֶׁר עַל־בֵּית

to him at the entrance of the house ²⁰and said, "Please, my lord, we *came down* the first time to buy food, ²¹and it was when we came to the lodging place, and we opened our bags, and here was each man's silver in the mouth of his bag, our money in its full weight. And we've brought it in our hand, ²²and we've brought down additional silver in our hand to buy food. We don't know who put our silver in our bags."

²³And he said, "Peace to you. Don't be afraid. Your God and your father's God put treasure in your bags for you. Your silver came to me." And he brought Simeon out to them.

²⁴And the man brought the men to Joseph's house, and he gave water, and they washed their feet, and he gave fodder for their asses. ²⁵And they prepared the gift until Joseph's arrival at noon because they heard that they would eat bread there. ²⁶And Joseph came to the house, and they brought the gift for him that was in their hand to the house, and they bowed to him to the ground.

²⁷And he asked if they were well, and he said, "Is your old father whom you mentioned well? Is he still alive?"

²⁸And they said, "Your servant, our father, is well. He's still alive." And they knelt and bowed.

יוֹסֵף וַיְדַבְּרוּ אֵלָיו פֶּתַח הַבָּיִת: ²⁰וַיֹּאמְרוּ בִּי אֲדֹנִי יָרֹד יָרַדְנוּ בַּתְּחִלָּה לִשְׁבָּר־אֹכֶל: ²¹וַיְהִי כִּי־בָאנוּ אֶל־הַמָּלוֹן וַנִּפְתְּחָה אֶת־אַמְתְּחֹתֵינוּ וְהִנֵּה כֶסֶף־אִישׁ בְּפִי אַמְתַּחְתּוֹ כַּסְפֵּנוּ בְּמִשְׁקָלוֹ וַנָּשֶׁב אֹתוֹ בְּיָדֵנוּ: ²²וְכֶסֶף אַחֵר הוֹרַדְנוּ בְיָדֵנוּ לִשְׁבָּר־אֹכֶל לֹא יָדַעְנוּ מִי־שָׂם כַּסְפֵּנוּ בְּאַמְתְּחֹתֵינוּ: ²³וַיֹּאמֶר שָׁלוֹם לָכֶם אַל־תִּירָאוּ אֱלֹהֵיכֶם וֵאלֹהֵי אֲבִיכֶם נָתַן לָכֶם מַטְמוֹן בְּאַמְתְּחֹתֵיכֶם כַּסְפְּכֶם בָּא אֵלָי וַיּוֹצֵא אֲלֵהֶם אֶת־שִׁמְעוֹן: ²⁴וַיָּבֵא הָאִישׁ אֶת־הָאֲנָשִׁים בֵּיתָה יוֹסֵף וַיִּתֶּן־מַיִם וַיִּרְחֲצוּ רַגְלֵיהֶם וַיִּתֵּן מִסְפּוֹא לַחֲמֹרֵיהֶם: ²⁵וַיָּכִינוּ אֶת־הַמִּנְחָה עַד־בּוֹא יוֹסֵף בַּצָּהֳרָיִם כִּי שָׁמְעוּ כִּי־שָׁם יֹאכְלוּ לָחֶם: ²⁶וַיָּבֹא יוֹסֵף הַבַּיְתָה וַיָּבִיאּוּ לוֹ אֶת־הַמִּנְחָה אֲשֶׁר־בְּיָדָם הַבָּיְתָה וַיִּשְׁתַּחֲווּ־לוֹ אָרְצָה: ²⁷וַיִּשְׁאַל לָהֶם לְשָׁלוֹם וַיֹּאמֶר הֲשָׁלוֹם אֲבִיכֶם הַזָּקֵן אֲשֶׁר אֲמַרְתֶּם הַעוֹדֶנּוּ חָי: ²⁸וַיֹּאמְרוּ שָׁלוֹם לְעַבְדְּךָ לְאָבִינוּ עוֹדֶנּוּ חָי וַיִּקְּדוּ וַיִּשְׁתַּחֲו: ²⁹וַיִּשָּׂא עֵינָיו וַיַּרְא אֶת־

43:28 וַיִּשְׁתַּחֲווּ קְ

43:27. he asked if they were well. Recall that the brothers were described earlier as being unable to speak to Joseph of *šālôm*, that is, to say "hello" or "how are you?" (see the comment on 37:4). Now they and Joseph finally speak of *šālôm* (vv. 23,27–28). Even though it is unwitting, it is the beginning of their reconciliation with their brother.

43:27. Is he still alive? Here is an exceptional example of the emotional power that looms in the background in the Torah's stories. From the point of view of the brothers and the Egyptians who are present, Joseph is just making polite conversation, graciously asking about "your old father whom you mentioned." But, inside, Joseph is about to find out—with anticipation, dread, even guilt?—whether his own father, who loved him the most, is alive or dead.

43:28. He's still alive. In the Septuagint and Samaritan, Joseph responds to this news about Jacob. They read: "And he said, 'Blessed of God is that man.'" This line presumably was lost from the Masoretic Text as a result of haplography when a scribe's eye jumped from the *wy* at the beginning of *wayy'ōmer* to the beginning of *wayyiqqĕdû*.

144

29And he raised his eyes and saw Benjamin, his brother, his mother's son, and said, "Is this your youngest brother whom you mentioned to me?" And he said, "May God be gracious to you, my son." 30And Joseph hurried because his feelings for his brother were boiling, and he looked for a place to weep and came to his room and wept there. 31And he washed his face and went out and restrained himself and said, "Put out bread." 32And they put it out for him by himself and for them by themselves and for the Egyptians who were eating with him by themselves, because the Egyptians could not eat bread with the Hebrews because that is an offensive thing to Egypt. 33And they sat before him, the firstborn according to his birthright and the youngest according to his youth. And the men looked amazed at one another. 34And he conveyed portions from before him to them, and he made Benjamin's portion five times more than the portions of all of them, and they drank and were drunk with him.

44 1And he commanded the one who was over his house, saying, "Fill the men's bags with as much food as they can carry and put each man's silver in the mouth of his bag, 2and put my cup, the silver cup, in the mouth of the youngest one's bag, and the silver for his grain." And he did according to Joseph's word that he spoke.

3The morning was light: and the men had been sent away, they and their asses. 4They had gone out of the city. They had not gone far, and Joseph had said to the one who was over his house, "Get up. Pursue the men, and you'll catch up with them and say to them, 'Why did you pay back bad for good? 5Isn't this the thing from

בִּנְיָמִין אָחִיו בֶּן־אִמּוֹ וַיֹּאמֶר הֲזֶה אֲחִיכֶם הַקָּטֹן אֲשֶׁר אֲמַרְתֶּם אֵלָי וַיֹּאמַר אֱלֹהִים יָחְנְךָ בְּנִי: 30וַיְמַהֵר יוֹסֵף כִּי־נִכְמְרוּ רַחֲמָיו אֶל־אָחִיו וַיְבַקֵּשׁ לִבְכּוֹת וַיָּבֹא הַחַדְרָה וַיֵּבְךְ שָׁמָּה: 31וַיִּרְחַץ פָּנָיו וַיֵּצֵא וַיִּתְאַפַּק וַיֹּאמֶר שִׂימוּ לָחֶם: 32וַיָּשִׂימוּ לוֹ לְבַדּוֹ וְלָהֶם לְבַדָּם וְלַמִּצְרִים הָאֹכְלִים אִתּוֹ לְבַדָּם כִּי לֹא יוּכְלוּן הַמִּצְרִים לֶאֱכֹל אֶת־הָעִבְרִים לֶחֶם כִּי־תוֹעֵבָה הִוא לְמִצְרָיִם: 33וַיֵּשְׁבוּ לְפָנָיו הַבְּכֹר כִּבְכֹרָתוֹ וְהַצָּעִיר כִּצְעִרָתוֹ וַיִּתְמְהוּ הָאֲנָשִׁים אִישׁ אֶל־רֵעֵהוּ: 34וַיִּשָּׂא מַשְׂאֹת מֵאֵת פָּנָיו אֲלֵהֶם וַתֵּרֶב מַשְׂאַת בִּנְיָמִן מִמַּשְׂאֹת כֻּלָּם חָמֵשׁ יָדוֹת וַיִּשְׁתּוּ וַיִּשְׁכְּרוּ עִמּוֹ:

44 1וַיְצַו אֶת־אֲשֶׁר עַל־בֵּיתוֹ לֵאמֹר מַלֵּא אֶת־ אַמְתְּחֹת הָאֲנָשִׁים אֹכֶל כַּאֲשֶׁר יוּכְלוּן שְׂאֵת וְשִׂים כֶּסֶף־אִישׁ בְּפִי אַמְתַּחְתּוֹ: 2וְאֶת־גְּבִיעִי גְּבִיעַ הַכֶּסֶף תָּשִׂים בְּפִי אַמְתַּחַת הַקָּטֹן וְאֵת כֶּסֶף שִׁבְרוֹ וַיַּעַשׂ כִּדְבַר יוֹסֵף אֲשֶׁר דִּבֵּר: 3הַבֹּקֶר אוֹר וְהָאֲנָשִׁים שֻׁלְּחוּ הֵמָּה וַחֲמֹרֵיהֶם: 4הֵם יָצְאוּ אֶת־הָעִיר לֹא הִרְחִיקוּ וְיוֹסֵף אָמַר לַאֲשֶׁר עַל־בֵּיתוֹ קוּם רְדֹף אַחֲרֵי הָאֲנָשִׁים וְהִשַּׂגְתָּם וְאָמַרְתָּ אֲלֵהֶם לָמָּה שִׁלַּמְתֶּם רָעָה תַּחַת טוֹבָה: 5הֲלוֹא זֶה אֲשֶׁר יִשְׁתֶּה

44:1. **each man's silver.** The first time, when ten brothers come to Egypt, Joseph imprisons Simeon, and he has their silver placed back in their *nine* sacks. The second time, when they return with Benjamin, Joseph releases Simeon, and he has their silver placed back in their *eleven* sacks. The total number of portions of silver returned is *twenty*, corresponding to the price that was paid for Joseph (37:28). It is yet another case of a hidden link between acts of deception and their payback in later events.

which my lord drinks? And he *divines* by it! You've done bad, this thing that you've done.' " 6And he caught up with them and spoke these things to them.

7And they said to him, "Why would my lord speak things like these? Far be it from your servants to do a thing like this. 8Here, we brought the silver that we found in the mouth of our bags back to you from the land of Canaan, so how would we steal silver or gold from your lord's house?! 9The one among your servants with whom it's found, let him die, and also we'll become my lord's servants."

10And he said, "Now, also, it will be so according to your words: the one with whom it's found will become my servant. And you will be free."

11And they hurried, and each man lowered his bag to the ground, and each man opened his bag. 12And he searched. With the oldest he began, and with the youngest he finished. And the cup was found in Benjamin's bag. 13And they ripped their clothes, and each man loaded his ass, and they went back to the city. 14And Judah and his brothers came to Joseph's house, and he was still there, and they fell to the ground before him.

15And Joseph said to them, "What is this thing that you've done? Didn't you know that a man like me would *divine?*"

16And Judah said, "What shall we say to my lord? What shall we speak? By what shall we justify ourselves? God has found your servants' crime. Here we're my lord's servants, both we and the one in whose hand the cup was found."

17And he said, "Far be it from me to do this. The man in whose hand the cup was found: he will be my servant; and you, go up in peace to your father."

AND HE WENT OVER

18And Judah went over to him and said, "Please, my lord, let your servant speak something in my lord's ears, and let your anger not

אֲדֹנִי֙ בּ֔וֹ וְה֕וּא נַחֵ֥שׁ יְנַחֵ֖שׁ בּ֑וֹ הֲרֵעֹתֶ֖ם אֲשֶׁ֥ר עֲשִׂיתֶֽם: ⁶וַֽיַּשִּׂגֵ֑ם וַיְדַבֵּ֣ר אֲלֵהֶ֔ם אֶת־הַדְּבָרִ֖ים הָאֵֽלֶּה: ⁷וַיֹּאמְר֣וּ אֵלָ֔יו לָ֥מָּה יְדַבֵּ֛ר אֲדֹנִ֖י כַּדְּבָרִ֣ים הָאֵ֑לֶּה חָלִ֙ילָה֙ לַעֲבָדֶ֔יךָ מֵעֲשׂ֖וֹת כַּדָּבָ֥ר הַזֶּֽה: ⁸הֵ֣ן כֶּ֗סֶף אֲשֶׁ֤ר מָצָ֙אנוּ֙ בְּפִ֣י אַמְתְּחֹתֵ֔ינוּ הֱשִׁיבֹ֥נוּ אֵלֶ֖יךָ מֵאֶ֣רֶץ כְּנָ֑עַן וְאֵ֗יךְ נִגְנֹב֙ מִבֵּ֣ית אֲדֹנֶ֔יךָ כֶּ֖סֶף א֥וֹ זָהָֽב: ⁹אֲשֶׁ֙ר יִמָּצֵ֥א אִתּ֛וֹ מֵעֲבָדֶ֖יךָ וָמֵ֑ת וְגַם־אֲנַ֕חְנוּ נִהְיֶ֥ה לַֽאדֹנִ֖י לַעֲבָדִֽים: ¹⁰וַיֹּ֕אמֶר גַּם־עַתָּ֥ה כְדִבְרֵיכֶ֖ם כֶּן־ה֑וּא אֲשֶׁ֙ר יִמָּצֵ֤א אִתּוֹ֙ יִהְיֶה־לִּ֣י עָ֔בֶד וְאַתֶּ֖ם תִּהְי֥וּ נְקִיִּֽם: ¹¹וַֽיְמַהֲר֗וּ וַיּוֹרִ֛דוּ אִ֥ישׁ אֶת־אַמְתַּחְתּ֖וֹ אָ֑רְצָה וַֽיִּפְתְּח֖וּ אִ֥ישׁ אַמְתַּחְתּֽוֹ: ¹²וַיְחַפֵּ֕שׂ בַּגָּד֣וֹל הֵחֵ֔ל וּבַקָּטֹ֖ן כִּלָּ֑ה וַיִּמָּצֵא֙ הַגָּבִ֔יעַ בְּאַמְתַּ֖חַת בִּנְיָמִֽן: ¹³וַֽיִּקְרְע֖וּ שִׂמְלֹתָ֑ם וַֽיַּעֲמֹס֙ אִ֣ישׁ עַל־חֲמֹר֔וֹ וַיָּשֻׁ֖בוּ הָעִֽירָה: ¹⁴וַיָּבֹ֙א יְהוּדָ֤ה וְאֶחָיו֙ בֵּ֣יתָה יוֹסֵ֔ף וְה֖וּא עוֹדֶ֣נּוּ שָׁ֑ם וַיִּפְּל֥וּ לְפָנָ֖יו אָֽרְצָה: ¹⁵וַיֹּ֤אמֶר לָהֶם֙ יוֹסֵ֔ף מָֽה־הַמַּעֲשֶׂ֥ה הַזֶּ֖ה אֲשֶׁ֣ר עֲשִׂיתֶ֑ם הֲל֣וֹא יְדַעְתֶּ֔ם כִּֽי־נַחֵ֥שׁ יְנַחֵ֖שׁ אִ֥ישׁ אֲשֶׁ֥ר כָּמֹֽנִי: ¹⁶וַיֹּ֣אמֶר יְהוּדָ֗ה מַה־נֹּאמַר֙ לַֽאדֹנִ֔י מַה־נְּדַבֵּ֖ר וּמַה־נִּצְטַדָּ֑ק הָאֱלֹהִ֗ים מָצָא֙ אֶת־עֲוֺ֣ן עֲבָדֶ֔יךָ הִנֶּנּ֤וּ עֲבָדִים֙ לַֽאדֹנִ֔י גַּם־אֲנַ֕חְנוּ גַּ֕ם אֲשֶׁר־נִמְצָ֥א הַגָּבִ֖יעַ בְּיָדֽוֹ: ¹⁷וַיֹּ֕אמֶר חָלִ֣ילָה לִּ֔י מֵעֲשׂ֖וֹת זֹ֑את הָאִ֡ישׁ אֲשֶׁר֩ נִמְצָ֙א הַגָּבִ֜יעַ בְּיָד֗וֹ ה֚וּא יִהְיֶה־לִּ֣י עָ֔בֶד וְאַתֶּ֕ם עֲל֥וּ לְשָׁל֖וֹם אֶל־אֲבִיכֶֽם: פ

וַיִּגַּשׁ

¹⁸וַיִּגַּ֙שׁ אֵלָ֜יו יְהוּדָ֗ה וַיֹּאמֶר֘ בִּ֣י אֲדֹנִי֒ יְדַבֶּר־נָ֙א עַבְדְּךָ֜ דָבָ֗ר בְּאׇזְנֵ֣י אֲדֹנִ֔י וְאַל־יִ֥חַר אַפְּךָ֖

flare at your servant, because you're like Pharaoh himself. ¹⁹My lord asked his servants, saying, 'Do you have a father or brother?' ²⁰and we said to my lord, 'We have an old father and a young son of his old age, and his brother's dead, and he's left alone of his mother, and his father loves him.' ²¹And you said to your servants, 'Bring him down to me, so I may set my eye on him.' ²²And we said to my lord, 'The boy can't leave his father; if he left his father he'd die.' ²³And you said to your servants, 'If your youngest brother doesn't come down with you, you won't see my face again.' ²⁴And it was, when we went up to your servant, my father, and told him my lord's words, ²⁵that our father said, 'Go back. Buy us a little food.' ²⁶And we said, 'We can't go down. If our youngest brother is with us then we'll go down, because we can't see the man's face if our youngest brother isn't with us.' ²⁷And your servant, my father, said to us, 'You know that my wife gave birth to two for me, ²⁸and one went away from me, and I said he's surely *torn up*, and I haven't seen him since. ²⁹And if you take this one from me as well and some harm happens to him, then you'll bring down my gray hair in wretchedness to Sheol.' ³⁰And now, when I come to your servant, my father, and the boy isn't with us, and he's bound to him soul to soul, ³¹it will be, when he sees that the boy isn't there, that he'll die. And your servants will have brought down your servant our father's gray hair in anguish to Sheol, ³²because your servant offered security for the boy to my father, saying, 'If I don't bring him to you, then I'll have sinned against my father for all time.' ³³And now, let your servant stay as my lord's servant in place of the boy, and let the boy go up with his brothers— ³⁴for how could I go up to my father and the boy isn't with me—or else I'll see the wretchedness that will find my father."

בְּעַבְדְּךָ כִּי כָמוֹךָ כְּפַרְעֹה: ¹⁹אֲדֹנִי שָׁאַל אֶת־עֲבָדָיו לֵאמֹר הֲיֵשׁ־לָכֶם אָב אוֹ־אָח: ²⁰וַנֹּאמֶר אֶל־אֲדֹנִי יֶשׁ־לָנוּ אָב זָקֵן וְיֶלֶד זְקֻנִים קָטָן וְאָחִיו מֵת וַיִּוָּתֵר הוּא לְבַדּוֹ לְאִמּוֹ וְאָבִיו אֲהֵבוֹ: ²¹וַתֹּאמֶר אֶל־עֲבָדֶיךָ הוֹרִדֻהוּ אֵלָי וְאָשִׂימָה עֵינִי עָלָיו: ²²וַנֹּאמֶר אֶל־אֲדֹנִי לֹא־יוּכַל הַנַּעַר לַעֲזֹב אֶת־אָבִיו וְעָזַב אֶת־אָבִיו וָמֵת: ²³וַתֹּאמֶר אֶל־עֲבָדֶיךָ אִם־לֹא יֵרֵד אֲחִיכֶם הַקָּטֹן אִתְּכֶם לֹא תֹסִפוּן לִרְאוֹת פָּנָי: ²⁴וַיְהִי כִּי עָלִינוּ אֶל־עַבְדְּךָ אָבִי וַנַּגֶּד־לוֹ אֵת דִּבְרֵי אֲדֹנִי: ²⁵וַיֹּאמֶר אָבִינוּ שֻׁבוּ שִׁבְרוּ־לָנוּ מְעַט־אֹכֶל: ²⁶וַנֹּאמֶר לֹא נוּכַל לָרֶדֶת אִם־יֵשׁ אָחִינוּ הַקָּטֹן אִתָּנוּ וְיָרַדְנוּ כִּי־לֹא נוּכַל לִרְאוֹת פְּנֵי הָאִישׁ וְאָחִינוּ הַקָּטֹן אֵינֶנּוּ אִתָּנוּ: ²⁷וַיֹּאמֶר עַבְדְּךָ אָבִי אֵלֵינוּ אַתֶּם יְדַעְתֶּם כִּי שְׁנַיִם יָלְדָה־לִּי אִשְׁתִּי: ²⁸וַיֵּצֵא הָאֶחָד מֵאִתִּי וָאֹמַר אַךְ טָרֹף טֹרָף וְלֹא רְאִיתִיו עַד־הֵנָּה: ²⁹וּלְקַחְתֶּם גַּם־אֶת־זֶה מֵעִם פָּנַי וְקָרָהוּ אָסוֹן וְהוֹרַדְתֶּם אֶת־שֵׂיבָתִי בְּרָעָה שְׁאֹלָה: ³⁰וְעַתָּה כְּבֹאִי אֶל־עַבְדְּךָ אָבִי וְהַנַּעַר אֵינֶנּוּ אִתָּנוּ וְנַפְשׁוֹ קְשׁוּרָה בְנַפְשׁוֹ: ³¹וְהָיָה כִּרְאוֹתוֹ כִּי־אֵין הַנַּעַר וָמֵת וְהוֹרִידוּ עֲבָדֶיךָ אֶת־שֵׂיבַת עַבְדְּךָ אָבִינוּ בְּיָגוֹן שְׁאֹלָה: ³²כִּי עַבְדְּךָ עָרַב אֶת־הַנַּעַר מֵעִם אָבִי לֵאמֹר אִם־לֹא אֲבִיאֶנּוּ אֵלֶיךָ וְחָטָאתִי לְאָבִי כָּל־הַיָּמִים: ³³וְעַתָּה יֵשֶׁב־נָא עַבְדְּךָ תַּחַת הַנַּעַר עֶבֶד לַאדֹנִי וְהַנַּעַר יַעַל עִם־אֶחָיו: ³⁴כִּי־אֵיךְ אֶעֱלֶה אֶל־אָבִי וְהַנַּעַר אֵינֶנּוּ אִתִּי פֶּן אֶרְאֶה

44:28; 45:8. **since.** It is hard to convey the irony in the wording in English translation. Jacob says, "I haven't seen him since" (literally, "up to here," עד הנה), and later Joseph says, "You didn't send me here" (הנה).

45 ¹And Joseph was not able to restrain himself in front of everyone who was standing by him, and he called, "Take everyone out from my presence." And not a man stood with him when Joseph made himself known to his brothers. ²And he wept out loud. And Egypt heard, and Pharaoh's house heard. ³And Joseph said to his brothers, "I'm Joseph. Is my father still alive?" And his brothers were not able to answer him, because they were terrified in front of him. ⁴And Joseph said to his brothers, "Come over to me." And they went over. And he said, "I'm Joseph, your brother, whom you sold to Egypt. ⁵And now, don't be sad and let there be no anger in your eyes because you sold me here, because God sent me before you to preserve life. ⁶For it's two years that the famine is in the land, and for five more years there'll be no plowing and harvest. ⁷And God sent me ahead of you to provide a remnant for you in the earth and to keep you alive as a big, surviving community. ⁸And now, it wasn't you who sent me here, but God, and he

וְלֹא־יָכֹל יוֹסֵף 45 :בְּרַע אֲשֶׁר יִמְצָא אֶת־אָבִי
לְהִתְאַפֵּק לְכֹל הַנִּצָּבִים עָלָיו וַיִּקְרָא הוֹצִיאוּ כָל־
אִישׁ מֵעָלָי וְלֹא־עָמַד אִישׁ אִתּוֹ בְּהִתְוַדַּע יוֹסֵף
אֶל־אֶחָיו: ²וַיִּתֵּן אֶת־קֹלוֹ בִּבְכִי וַיִּשְׁמְעוּ מִצְרַיִם
וַיִּשְׁמַע בֵּית פַּרְעֹה: ³וַיֹּאמֶר יוֹסֵף אֶל־אֶחָיו אֲנִי
יוֹסֵף הַעוֹד אָבִי חָי וְלֹא־יָכְלוּ אֶחָיו לַעֲנוֹת אֹתוֹ
כִּי נִבְהֲלוּ מִפָּנָיו: ⁴וַיֹּאמֶר יוֹסֵף אֶל־אֶחָיו גְּשׁוּ־נָא
אֵלַי וַיִּגָּשׁוּ וַיֹּאמֶר אֲנִי יוֹסֵף אֲחִיכֶם אֲשֶׁר־מְכַרְתֶּם
אֹתִי מִצְרָיְמָה: ⁵וְעַתָּה | אַל־תֵּעָצְבוּ וְאַל־יִחַר
בְּעֵינֵיכֶם כִּי־מְכַרְתֶּם אֹתִי הֵנָּה כִּי לְמִחְיָה שְׁלָחַנִי
אֱלֹהִים לִפְנֵיכֶם: ⁶כִּי־זֶה שְׁנָתַיִם הָרָעָב בְּקֶרֶב
הָאָרֶץ וְעוֹד חָמֵשׁ שָׁנִים אֲשֶׁר אֵין־חָרִישׁ וְקָצִיר:
⁷וַיִּשְׁלָחֵנִי אֱלֹהִים לִפְנֵיכֶם לָשׂוּם לָכֶם שְׁאֵרִית
בָּאָרֶץ וּלְהַחֲיוֹת לָכֶם לִפְלֵיטָה גְּדֹלָה: ⁸וְעַתָּה לֹא־
אַתֶּם שְׁלַחְתֶּם אֹתִי הֵנָּה כִּי הָאֱלֹהִים וַיְשִׂימֵנִי לְאָב

45:1. not able to restrain himself. He has toyed with his brothers long enough. Judah's words, "the wretchedness that will find my father," are more than Joseph can bear, and so at last he reveals himself to them.

45:3. Is my father still alive? But he *knows* that his father is still alive. He already asked his brothers this (43:27). Even the major traditional commentators do not address this. In critical scholarship it is understood that these two seemingly conflicting passages come from two different sources. But even if this is so, how shall we understand Joseph's question in the context of the narrative as it stands? It seems to me that the key is that when he asks them the first time, it is in the role that he is playing as an Egyptian official, with his real identity hidden from them. But now he puts together his revelation of who he really is with his question about Jacob: "I'm Joseph. Is my father still alive?" For all he knows, his brothers were lying to him as the Egyptian official, but now he asks them: tell me, your brother, Joseph, is he really alive?

45:8. it wasn't you who sent me here, but God. Is this the same Joseph who spoke so naively to his brothers about his dreams at the beginning of these events? Like the character of his father Jacob, Joseph's character develops through the events of his life. Here, immediately after revealing himself to them, he goes into a chain of assurances, responding to every fear they would have: come close to me; don't be sad or angry or afraid of me; it wasn't your fault; I'll provide for you during the famine; your families will be safe; bring our father. He has become a wise, sensitive man. And, like his fa-

made me into a father to Pharaoh and a lord to all his house and a ruler in all the land of Egypt. [9]Hurry, and go up to my father and say to him: 'Your son Joseph said this: God has made me a lord to all Egypt. Come down to me. Don't stand back. [10]And you'll live in the land of Goshen, and you'll be close to me, you and your children and your children's children and your flock and your oxen and everything you have. [11]And I'll provide for you there, because there are five more years of famine, or else you and your house and everything you have will be impoverished.' [12]And here your eyes see, and the eyes of my brother Benjamin, that it's my mouth that speaks to you. [13]And you'll tell my father of all my glory in Egypt and of all that you've seen, and hurry and bring my father down here." [14]And he fell on his brother Benjamin's neck and wept, and Benjamin wept on his neck. [15]And he kissed all his brothers and wept over them. And after that his brothers spoke with him.

[16]And the report was heard at Pharaoh's house, saying, "Joseph's brothers have come." And it was good in Pharaoh's eyes and in his servants' eyes. [17]And Pharaoh said to Joseph, "Say to your brothers, 'Do this: load your beasts and go; come to the land of Canaan, [18]and take your father and your households and come to me, and I'll give you the best of the land of Egypt; and eat the fat of the land.' [19]And you are commanded, 'Do this: Take wagons from the land of Egypt for your infants and for your wives, and carry your father and come. [20]And let your eye not care about your possessions, for the best of all the land of Egypt is yours.' "

[21]And the children of Israel did so. And Joseph gave them wagons by order of Pharaoh and gave them provisions for the road. [22]For all of them he gave each man changes of clothes, and he gave Benjamin three hundred weights of silver and five changes of clothes. [23]And to his father

לְפַרְעֹה וּלְאָדוֹן לְכָל־בֵּיתוֹ וּמֹשֵׁל בְּכָל־אֶרֶץ מִצְרָיִם: [9]מַהֲרוּ וַעֲלוּ אֶל־אָבִי וַאֲמַרְתֶּם אֵלָיו כֹּה אָמַר בִּנְךָ יוֹסֵף שָׂמַנִי אֱלֹהִים לְאָדוֹן לְכָל־מִצְרָיִם רְדָה אֵלַי אַל־תַּעֲמֹד: [10]וְיָשַׁבְתָּ בְאֶרֶץ־גֹּשֶׁן וְהָיִיתָ קָרוֹב אֵלַי אַתָּה וּבָנֶיךָ וּבְנֵי בָנֶיךָ וְצֹאנְךָ וּבְקָרְךָ וְכָל־אֲשֶׁר־לָךְ: [11]וְכִלְכַּלְתִּי אֹתְךָ שָׁם כִּי־עוֹד חָמֵשׁ שָׁנִים רָעָב פֶּן־תִּוָּרֵשׁ אַתָּה וּבֵיתְךָ וְכָל־אֲשֶׁר־לָךְ: [12]וְהִנֵּה עֵינֵיכֶם רֹאוֹת וְעֵינֵי אָחִי בִנְיָמִין כִּי־פִי הַמְדַבֵּר אֲלֵיכֶם: [13]וְהִגַּדְתֶּם לְאָבִי אֶת־כָּל־כְּבוֹדִי בְּמִצְרַיִם וְאֵת כָּל־אֲשֶׁר רְאִיתֶם וּמִהַרְתֶּם וְהוֹרַדְתֶּם אֶת־אָבִי הֵנָּה: [14]וַיִּפֹּל עַל־צַוְּארֵי בִנְיָמִן אָחִיו וַיֵּבְךְּ וּבִנְיָמִן בָּכָה עַל־צַוָּארָיו: [15]וַיְנַשֵּׁק לְכָל־אֶחָיו וַיֵּבְךְּ עֲלֵיהֶם וְאַחֲרֵי כֵן דִּבְּרוּ אֶחָיו אִתּוֹ: [16]וְהַקֹּל נִשְׁמַע בֵּית פַּרְעֹה לֵאמֹר בָּאוּ אֲחֵי יוֹסֵף וַיִּיטַב בְּעֵינֵי פַרְעֹה וּבְעֵינֵי עֲבָדָיו: [17]וַיֹּאמֶר פַּרְעֹה אֶל־יוֹסֵף אֱמֹר אֶל־אַחֶיךָ זֹאת עֲשׂוּ טַעֲנוּ אֶת־בְּעִירְכֶם וּלְכוּ־בֹאוּ אַרְצָה כְּנָעַן: [18]וּקְחוּ אֶת־אֲבִיכֶם וְאֶת־בָּתֵּיכֶם וּבֹאוּ אֵלָי וְאֶתְּנָה לָכֶם אֶת־טוּב אֶרֶץ מִצְרַיִם וְאִכְלוּ אֶת־חֵלֶב הָאָרֶץ: [19]וְאַתָּה צֻוֵּיתָה זֹאת עֲשׂוּ קְחוּ־לָכֶם מֵאֶרֶץ מִצְרַיִם עֲגָלוֹת לְטַפְּכֶם וְלִנְשֵׁיכֶם וּנְשָׂאתֶם אֶת־אֲבִיכֶם וּבָאתֶם: [20]וְעֵינְכֶם אַל־תָּחֹס עַל־כְּלֵיכֶם כִּי־טוּב כָּל־אֶרֶץ מִצְרַיִם לָכֶם הוּא: [21]וַיַּעֲשׂוּ־כֵן בְּנֵי יִשְׂרָאֵל וַיִּתֵּן לָהֶם יוֹסֵף עֲגָלוֹת עַל־פִּי פַרְעֹה וַיִּתֵּן לָהֶם צֵדָה לַדָּרֶךְ: [22]לְכֻלָּם נָתַן לָאִישׁ חֲלִפוֹת שְׂמָלֹת וּלְבִנְיָמִן נָתַן שְׁלֹשׁ מֵאוֹת כֶּסֶף וְחָמֵשׁ חֲלִפֹת שְׂמָלֹת:

ther, the change in him came during the period in which he had contact with the divine, when he was given the divine power to interpret dreams.

he sent as follows: ten asses bearing Egypt's best, and ten she-asses bearing grain, bread, and food supply for his father for the road. 24And he sent his brothers off, and they went, and he said to them, "Don't quarrel on the road."

25And they went up from Egypt and came to the land of Canaan, to Jacob, their father, 26and told him, saying, "Joseph is still alive! And he rules all the land of Egypt!" And his heart grew numb because he did not believe them. 27And they spoke to him all of Joseph's words that he had spoken to them, and he saw the wagons that Joseph had sent to carry him, and their father Jacob's spirit came alive.

28And Israel said, "So much! Joseph, my son, is still alive. Let me go and see him before I die."

46 1And Israel and everyone he had traveled and came to Beer-sheba, and he offered sacrifices to the God of his father, Isaac. 2And God said to Israel in night visions, and He said, "Jacob, Jacob."

And he said, "I'm here."

3And He said, "I am God, your father's God. Don't be afraid of going down to Egypt, because I'll make you into a big nation there. 4I shall go down with you to Egypt, and I shall also bring you up. And Joseph will set his hand on your eyes."

5And Jacob got up from Beer-sheba. And the children of Israel carried Jacob, their father, and their infants and their wives in the wagons that Pharaoh had sent to carry him. 6And they took their cattle and their property that they had acquired in the land of Canaan, and they came to

²³וּלְאָבִ֞יו שָׁלַ֤ח כְּזֹאת֙ עֲשָׂרָ֣ה חֲמֹרִ֔ים נֹשְׂאִ֖ים מִטּ֣וּב מִצְרָ֑יִם וְעֶ֣שֶׂר אֲתֹנֹ֡ת נֹֽשְׂאֹת֩ בָּ֨ר וָלֶ֧חֶם וּמָז֛וֹן לְאָבִ֖יו לַדָּֽרֶךְ׃ ²⁴וַיְשַׁלַּ֥ח אֶת־אֶחָ֖יו וַיֵּלֵ֑כוּ וַיֹּ֣אמֶר אֲלֵהֶ֔ם אַֽל־תִּרְגְּז֖וּ בַּדָּֽרֶךְ׃ ²⁵וַֽיַּעֲל֖וּ מִמִּצְרָ֑יִם וַיָּבֹ֙אוּ֙ אֶ֣רֶץ כְּנַ֔עַן אֶֽל־יַעֲקֹ֖ב אֲבִיהֶֽם׃ ²⁶וַיַּגִּ֨דוּ ל֜וֹ לֵאמֹ֗ר ע֚וֹד יוֹסֵ֣ף חַ֔י וְכִֽי־ה֥וּא מֹשֵׁ֖ל בְּכָל־אֶ֣רֶץ מִצְרָ֑יִם וַיָּ֣פָג לִבּ֔וֹ כִּ֥י לֹא־הֶאֱמִ֖ין לָהֶֽם׃ ²⁷וַיְדַבְּר֣וּ אֵלָ֗יו אֵ֣ת כָּל־דִּבְרֵ֤י יוֹסֵף֙ אֲשֶׁ֣ר דִּבֶּ֣ר אֲלֵהֶ֔ם וַיַּרְא֙ אֶת־הָ֣עֲגָל֔וֹת אֲשֶׁר־שָׁלַ֥ח יוֹסֵ֖ף לָשֵׂ֣את אֹת֑וֹ וַתְּחִ֕י ר֖וּחַ יַעֲקֹ֥ב אֲבִיהֶֽם׃ ²⁸וַיֹּ֙אמֶר֙ יִשְׂרָאֵ֔ל רַ֛ב עֽוֹד־יוֹסֵ֥ף בְּנִ֖י חָ֑י אֵֽלְכָ֥ה וְאֶרְאֶ֖נּוּ בְּטֶ֥רֶם אָמֽוּת׃

46 ¹וַיִּסַּ֤ע יִשְׂרָאֵל֙ וְכָל־אֲשֶׁר־ל֔וֹ וַיָּבֹ֖א בְּאֵ֣רָה שָּׁ֑בַע וַיִּזְבַּ֣ח זְבָחִ֔ים לֵאלֹהֵ֖י אָבִ֥יו יִצְחָֽק׃ ²וַיֹּ֨אמֶר אֱלֹהִ֤ים ׀ לְיִשְׂרָאֵל֙ בְּמַרְאֹ֣ת הַלַּ֔יְלָה וַיֹּ֖אמֶר יַעֲקֹ֣ב ׀ יַעֲקֹ֑ב וַיֹּ֖אמֶר הִנֵּֽנִי׃ ³וַיֹּ֕אמֶר אָנֹכִ֥י הָאֵ֖ל אֱלֹהֵ֣י אָבִ֑יךָ אַל־תִּירָא֙ מֵרְדָ֣ה מִצְרַ֔יְמָה כִּֽי־לְג֥וֹי גָּד֖וֹל אֲשִֽׂימְךָ֥ שָֽׁם׃ ⁴אָנֹכִ֗י אֵרֵ֤ד עִמְּךָ֙ מִצְרַ֔יְמָה וְאָנֹכִ֖י אַעַלְךָ֣ גַם־עָלֹ֑ה וְיוֹסֵ֕ף יָשִׁ֥ית יָד֖וֹ עַל־עֵינֶֽיךָ׃ ⁵וַיָּ֥קָם יַעֲקֹ֖ב מִבְּאֵ֣ר שָׁ֑בַע וַיִּשְׂא֨וּ בְנֵֽי־יִשְׂרָאֵ֜ל אֶת־יַעֲקֹ֣ב אֲבִיהֶ֗ם וְאֶת־טַפָּם֙ וְאֶת־נְשֵׁיהֶ֔ם בָּעֲגָל֕וֹת אֲשֶׁר־שָׁלַ֥ח פַּרְעֹ֖ה לָשֵׂ֥את אֹתֽוֹ׃ ⁶וַיִּקְח֣וּ אֶת־מִקְנֵיהֶ֗ם וְאֶת־רְכוּשָׁם֙ אֲשֶׁ֤ר רָֽכְשׁוּ֙ בְּאֶ֣רֶץ כְּנַ֔עַן וַיָּבֹ֖אוּ מִצְרָֽיְמָה

46:2. **"Jacob, Jacob." And he said, "I'm here."** This is the second of three times that this pattern occurs. When Abraham is about to sacrifice Isaac, an angel calls, "Abraham! Abraham!" And he said, "I'm here" (22:11). There it is to save a life. Here it is to assure Jacob that he has nothing to fear in Egypt. Both cases are about reunions of patriarchs with their sons. And this forms the background to the third time the pattern will occur. When Moses comes to the burning bush, God says, "Moses, Moses." And he said, "I'm here" (Exod 3:4). Like Abraham, Moses is told that Abraham's children are to be saved. Like Jacob, he is taught not to be afraid. Like both, this is about reunion of the people with the land where the patriarchs are (see comment on Gen. 22:1).

Egypt, Jacob and all his seed with him. 7He brought his sons and his grandsons with him, his daughters and his granddaughters and all his seed with him to Egypt.

8And these are the names of the children of Israel who came to Egypt, Jacob and his sons: Jacob's firstborn was Reuben. 9And Reuben's sons were Hanoch and Pallu and Hezron and Carmi. 10And Simeon's sons were Jemuel and Jamin and Ohad and Jachin and Zohar and Saul, the son of a Canaanite woman. 11And Levi's sons were Gershon, Kohath, and Merari. 12And Judah's sons were Er and Onan and Shelah and Perez and Zerah. And Er and Onan died in the land of Canaan, and Perez's sons were Hezron and Hamul. 13And Issachar's sons were Tola and Puvah and Job and Shimron. 14And Zebulun's sons were Sered and Elon and Jahleel. 15These were the sons of Leah, to whom she gave birth for Jacob in Paddan Aram, and Dinah, his daughter, every person of his sons and his daughters, thirty-three. 16And Gad's sons were Ziphion and Haggai and Shuni and Ezbon, Eri and Arodi and Areli. 17And Asher's sons were Imnah and Ishvah and Ishvi and Beriah, and Serah was their sister. And Beriah's sons were Hever and Malchiel. 18These were the sons of Zilpah, whom Laban gave to Leah, his daughter, and she gave birth to these for Jacob, sixteen persons. 19The sons of Rachel, Jacob's wife, were Joseph and Benjamin. 20And Manasseh and Ephraim were born to Joseph in the land of Egypt, to whom Asenath, daughter of Poti-phera, priest of On, gave birth for him. 21And Benjamin's sons were Bela and Becher and Ashbel, Gera and Naaman, Ehi and Rosh, Muppim and Huppim and Ard. 22These were Rachel's sons, who were born to Jacob. All the persons were fourteen. 23And Dan's sons: Hushim. 24And Naphtali's sons were Jahzeel and Guni and Jezer and Shillem. 25These were the sons of Bilhah, whom Laban gave to Rachel, his daughter, and she gave birth to these for Jacob. All the persons were seven. 26All the persons of Jacob's who came to Egypt, who came

יַעֲקֹב וְכָל־זַרְעוֹ אִתּוֹ: 7בָּנָיו וּבְנֵי בָנָיו אִתּוֹ בְּנֹתָיו וּבְנוֹת בָּנָיו וְכָל־זַרְעוֹ הֵבִיא אִתּוֹ מִצְרָיְמָה: ס 8וְאֵלֶּה שְׁמוֹת בְּנֵי־יִשְׂרָאֵל הַבָּאִים מִצְרַיְמָה יַעֲקֹב וּבָנָיו בְּכֹר יַעֲקֹב רְאוּבֵן: 9וּבְנֵי רְאוּבֵן חֲנוֹךְ וּפַלּוּא וְחֶצְרוֹן וְכַרְמִי: 10וּבְנֵי שִׁמְעוֹן יְמוּאֵל וְיָמִין וְאֹהַד וְיָכִין וְצֹחַר וְשָׁאוּל בֶּן־הַכְּנַעֲנִית: 11וּבְנֵי לֵוִי גֵּרְשׁוֹן קְהָת וּמְרָרִי: 12וּבְנֵי יְהוּדָה עֵר וְאוֹנָן וְשֵׁלָה וָפֶרֶץ וָזָרַח וַיָּמָת עֵר וְאוֹנָן בְּאֶרֶץ כְּנַעַן וַיִּהְיוּ בְנֵי־פֶרֶץ חֶצְרוֹן וְחָמוּל: 13וּבְנֵי יִשָּׂשכָר תּוֹלָע וּפֻוָה וְיוֹב וְשִׁמְרוֹן: 14וּבְנֵי זְבוּלֻן סֶרֶד וְאֵלוֹן וְיַחְלְאֵל: 15אֵלֶּה בְּנֵי לֵאָה אֲשֶׁר יָלְדָה לְיַעֲקֹב בְּפַדַּן אֲרָם וְאֵת דִּינָה בִתּוֹ כָּל־נֶפֶשׁ בָּנָיו וּבְנוֹתָיו שְׁלֹשִׁים וְשָׁלֹשׁ: 16וּבְנֵי גָד צִפְיוֹן וְחַגִּי שׁוּנִי וְאֶצְבֹּן עֵרִי וַאֲרוֹדִי וְאַרְאֵלִי: 17וּבְנֵי אָשֵׁר יִמְנָה וְיִשְׁוָה וְיִשְׁוִי וּבְרִיעָה וְשֶׂרַח אֲחֹתָם וּבְנֵי בְרִיעָה חֶבֶר וּמַלְכִּיאֵל: 18אֵלֶּה בְּנֵי זִלְפָּה אֲשֶׁר־נָתַן לָבָן לְלֵאָה בִתּוֹ וַתֵּלֶד אֶת־אֵלֶּה לְיַעֲקֹב שֵׁשׁ עֶשְׂרֵה נָפֶשׁ: 19בְּנֵי רָחֵל אֵשֶׁת יַעֲקֹב יוֹסֵף וּבִנְיָמִן: 20וַיִּוָּלֵד לְיוֹסֵף בְּאֶרֶץ מִצְרַיִם אֲשֶׁר יָלְדָה־לּוֹ אָסְנַת בַּת־פּוֹטִי פֶרַע כֹּהֵן אֹן אֶת־מְנַשֶּׁה וְאֶת־אֶפְרָיִם: 21וּבְנֵי בִנְיָמִן בֶּלַע וָבֶכֶר וְאַשְׁבֵּל גֵּרָא וְנַעֲמָן אֵחִי וָרֹאשׁ מֻפִּים וְחֻפִּים וָאָרְדְּ: 22אֵלֶּה בְּנֵי רָחֵל אֲשֶׁר יֻלַּד לְיַעֲקֹב כָּל־נֶפֶשׁ אַרְבָּעָה עָשָׂר: 23וּבְנֵי־דָן חֻשִׁים: 24וּבְנֵי נַפְתָּלִי יַחְצְאֵל וְגוּנִי וְיֵצֶר וְשִׁלֵּם: 25אֵלֶּה בְּנֵי בִלְהָה אֲשֶׁר־נָתַן לָבָן לְרָחֵל בִּתּוֹ וַתֵּלֶד אֶת־אֵלֶּה לְיַעֲקֹב כָּל־נֶפֶשׁ שִׁבְעָה: 26כָּל־הַנֶּפֶשׁ הַבָּאָה

151

out from his thigh, outside of Jacob's sons' wives, all the persons were sixty-six. 27And Joseph's sons who were born to him in Egypt were two persons. All the persons of Jacob's house who came to Egypt were seventy.

28And he sent Judah ahead of him to Joseph to direct him in advance to Goshen. And they came to the land of Goshen. 29And Joseph hitched his chariot and went up to Israel, his father, at Goshen. And he appeared to him and fell on his neck and wept on his neck a long time. 30And Israel said to Joseph, "Let me die now after I've seen your face, that you're still alive."

31And Joseph said to his brothers and to his father's house, "Let me go up and tell Pharaoh and say to him, 'My brothers and my father's house that were in the land of Canaan have come to me. 32And the people are shepherds, because they were livestock people, and they've brought their flock and their oxen and all they have.' 33And it will be, when Pharaoh will call you and say, 'What is your occupation?' 34that you'll say, 'Your servants were livestock people from our youth until now, both we and our fathers,' so that you'll live in the land of Goshen, because any shepherd is an offensive thing to Egypt."

47 1And Joseph came and told Pharaoh and said, "My father and my brothers and their flock and their oxen and all that they own have come from the land of Canaan, and here they are in the land of Goshen." 2And he took several of his brothers, five men, and set them before Pharaoh.

3And Pharaoh said to his brothers, "What is your work?"

And they said to Pharaoh, "Your servants are shepherds, both we and our fathers," 4and they

לְיַעֲקֹב מִצְרַיְמָה יֹצְאֵי יְרֵכוֹ מִלְּבַד נְשֵׁי בְנֵי־יַעֲקֹב כָּל־נֶפֶשׁ שִׁשִּׁים וָשֵׁשׁ: 27וּבְנֵי יוֹסֵף אֲשֶׁר־יֻלַּד־לוֹ בְמִצְרַיִם נֶפֶשׁ שְׁנָיִם כָּל־הַנֶּפֶשׁ לְבֵית־יַעֲקֹב הַבָּאָה מִצְרַיְמָה שִׁבְעִים: פ 28וְאֶת־יְהוּדָה שָׁלַח לְפָנָיו אֶל־יוֹסֵף לְהוֹרֹת לְפָנָיו גֹּשְׁנָה וַיָּבֹאוּ אַרְצָה גֹּשֶׁן: 29וַיֶּאְסֹר יוֹסֵף מֶרְכַּבְתּוֹ וַיַּעַל לִקְרַאת־יִשְׂרָאֵל אָבִיו גֹּשְׁנָה וַיֵּרָא אֵלָיו וַיִּפֹּל עַל־צַוָּארָיו וַיֵּבְךְּ עַל־צַוָּארָיו עוֹד: 30וַיֹּאמֶר יִשְׂרָאֵל אֶל־יוֹסֵף אָמוּתָה הַפָּעַם אַחֲרֵי רְאוֹתִי אֶת־פָּנֶיךָ כִּי עוֹדְךָ חָי: 31וַיֹּאמֶר יוֹסֵף אֶל־אֶחָיו וְאֶל־בֵּית אָבִיו אֶעֱלֶה וְאַגִּידָה לְפַרְעֹה וְאֹמְרָה אֵלָיו אַחַי וּבֵית־אָבִי אֲשֶׁר בְּאֶרֶץ־כְּנַעַן בָּאוּ אֵלָי: 32וְהָאֲנָשִׁים רֹעֵי צֹאן כִּי־ אַנְשֵׁי מִקְנֶה הָיוּ וְצֹאנָם וּבְקָרָם וְכָל־אֲשֶׁר לָהֶם הֵבִיאוּ: 33וְהָיָה כִּי־יִקְרָא לָכֶם פַּרְעֹה וְאָמַר מַה־ מַעֲשֵׂיכֶם: 34וַאֲמַרְתֶּם אַנְשֵׁי מִקְנֶה הָיוּ עֲבָדֶיךָ מִנְּעוּרֵינוּ וְעַד־עַתָּה גַּם־אֲנַחְנוּ גַּם־אֲבֹתֵינוּ בַּעֲבוּר תֵּשְׁבוּ בְּאֶרֶץ גֹּשֶׁן כִּי־תוֹעֲבַת מִצְרַיִם כָּל־רֹעֵה צֹאן: 47 1וַיָּבֹא יוֹסֵף וַיַּגֵּד לְפַרְעֹה וַיֹּאמֶר אָבִי וְאַחַי וְצֹאנָם וּבְקָרָם וְכָל־אֲשֶׁר לָהֶם בָּאוּ מֵאֶרֶץ כְּנָעַן וְהִנָּם בְּאֶרֶץ גֹּשֶׁן: 2וּמִקְצֵה אֶחָיו לָקַח חֲמִשָּׁה אֲנָשִׁים וַיַּצִּגֵם לִפְנֵי פַרְעֹה: 3וַיֹּאמֶר פַּרְעֹה אֶל־ אֶחָיו מַה־מַּעֲשֵׂיכֶם וַיֹּאמְרוּ אֶל־פַּרְעֹה רֹעֵה צֹאן עֲבָדֶיךָ גַּם־אֲנַחְנוּ גַּם־אֲבוֹתֵינוּ: 4וַיֹּאמְרוּ אֶל־פַּרְעֹה

47:3. Your servants are shepherds. Joseph had just told them not to answer Pharaoh that they are shepherds (46:33–34), yet they go ahead and say it! Some might surmise that this seeming contradiction is the result of the combination of two sources into one story. But that is not correct. This has nothing to do with the sources that are identified in critical biblical scholarship. This is one continuous passage (all

said to Pharaoh, "We came to reside in the land because there's no pasture for your servants' flock because the famine is heavy in the land of Canaan. And now may your servants live in the land of Goshen."

⁵And Pharaoh said to Joseph, saying, "Your father and your brothers have come to you. ⁶The land of Egypt is before you. Settle your father and your brothers in the best of the land. Let them live in the land of Goshen. And if you know—and if there are among them—worthy men, then you shall make them livestock officers over those that I have."

⁷And Joseph brought Jacob, his father, and stood him in front of Pharaoh. And Jacob blessed Pharaoh. ⁸And Pharaoh said to Jacob, "How many are the days of the years of your life?"

⁹And Jacob said to Pharaoh, "The days of the years of my residences are a hundred thirty years. The days of the years of my life have been few and bad, and they haven't attained the days of

לָגוּר בָּאָרֶץ בָּאנוּ כִּי־אֵין מִרְעֶה לַצֹּאן אֲשֶׁר
לַעֲבָדֶיךָ כִּי־כָבֵד הָרָעָב בְּאֶרֶץ כְּנָעַן וְעַתָּה יֵשְׁבוּ־
נָא עֲבָדֶיךָ בְּאֶרֶץ גֹּשֶׁן: ⁵וַיֹּאמֶר פַּרְעֹה אֶל־יוֹסֵף
לֵאמֹר אָבִיךָ וְאַחֶיךָ בָּאוּ אֵלֶיךָ: ⁶אֶרֶץ מִצְרַיִם
לְפָנֶיךָ הִוא בְּמֵיטַב הָאָרֶץ הוֹשֵׁב אֶת־אָבִיךָ וְאֶת־
אַחֶיךָ יֵשְׁבוּ בְּאֶרֶץ גֹּשֶׁן וְאִם־יָדַעְתָּ וְיֶשׁ־בָּם אַנְשֵׁי־
חַיִל וְשַׂמְתָּם שָׂרֵי מִקְנֶה עַל־אֲשֶׁר־לִי: ⁷וַיָּבֵא יוֹסֵף
אֶת־יַעֲקֹב אָבִיו וַיַּעֲמִדֵהוּ לִפְנֵי פַרְעֹה וַיְבָרֶךְ
יַעֲקֹב אֶת־פַּרְעֹה: ⁸וַיֹּאמֶר פַּרְעֹה אֶל־יַעֲקֹב כַּמָּה
יְמֵי שְׁנֵי חַיֶּיךָ: ⁹וַיֹּאמֶר יַעֲקֹב אֶל־פַּרְעֹה יְמֵי שְׁנֵי
מְגוּרַי שְׁלֹשִׁים וּמְאַת שָׁנָה מְעַט וְרָעִים הָיוּ יְמֵי שְׁנֵי
חַיַּי וְלֹא הִשִּׂיגוּ אֶת־יְמֵי שְׁנֵי חַיֵּי אֲבֹתַי בִּימֵי

---

from the source known in scholarship as J). The difficulty in the brothers' words must therefore be understood as being a part of the story itself. The brothers simply do not follow Joseph's instructions. He has told them to say that they are cowherds, not shepherds, because Egyptians disdain shepherds; but they are not willing to misrepresent themselves in this way. Are they right? On one hand, Pharaoh does permit them to settle and offers them the best of Egypt's land. But, on the other hand, Pharaoh stops speaking directly to them. He switches to speaking about them in the third person to Joseph. And he offers to have some of them serve as officers over his *cattle* even though they have just said they are shepherds, not cattlemen.

47:9. **few and bad, and . . . haven't attained**. Jacob is critical of his life, in itself and in comparison with Abraham's and Isaac's lives. This is consistent with the telling of the story until now, which has not excused or sanitized Jacob the way some Sunday schools, early commentaries, and modern interpreters do. The biblical writers seem to have been quite content to leave their heroes imperfect. Why? Why even conceive of such a story? Perhaps the author thus pointed to deception in the world and said, "It comes back." Or perhaps the author conceived it in literary protest against the ancient Near Eastern practice of glorifying national heroes. As has frequently been observed, to read the ancient reports one would think that no Near Eastern king ever lost a battle. A clear majority of the biblical authors, however, show their heroes with weaknesses and imperfections, making errors and committing offenses. For whatever purpose the author of the Jacob cycle conceived this story, the fact is that this author

the years of my fathers' lives, in the days of their residences." 10And Jacob blessed Pharaoh and went out from in front of Pharaoh.

11And Joseph settled his father and his brothers and gave them a possession in the land of Egypt, in the best of the land, in the land of Rameses, as Pharaoh had commanded. 12And Joseph supported his father and his brothers and all of his father's household, bread by the number of infants.

13And there was no bread in all the land of Egypt, because the famine was very heavy, and the land of Egypt and the land of Canaan languished because of the famine. 14And Joseph collected all the silver that was found in the land of Egypt and in the land of Canaan for the grain that they were buying, and Joseph brought the silver to Pharaoh's house. 15And the silver came to an end from the land of Egypt and from the land of Canaan. And all of Egypt came to Joseph, saying, "Give us bread! And why should we die in front of you? Because there's no more silver!"

16And Joseph said, "Give your livestock, and I'll give it to you for your livestock if there's no more silver."

17And they brought their livestock to Joseph, and Joseph gave them bread for the horses and for the livestock of the flocks and for the livestock of the oxen and for the asses, and he sustained them with bread for all their livestock in that year. 18And that year came to an end, and they came to him in the second year and said to him, "We won't conceal from my lord that the silver has come to an end and the cattle livestock have gone to my lord. Nothing is left in front of my lord except our body and our land. 19Why should we die before your eyes, both we and our

מְגוּרֵיהֶם: 10וַיְבָ֣רֶךְ יַעֲקֹ֖ב אֶת־פַּרְעֹ֑ה וַיֵּצֵ֖א מִלִּפְנֵ֥י פַרְעֹֽה: 11וַיּוֹשֵׁ֣ב יוֹסֵף֮ אֶת־אָבִ֣יו וְאֶת־אֶחָיו֒ וַיִּתֵּ֨ן לָהֶ֤ם אֲחֻזָּה֙ בְּאֶ֣רֶץ מִצְרַ֔יִם בְּמֵיטַ֥ב הָאָ֖רֶץ בְּאֶ֣רֶץ רַעְמְסֵ֑ס כַּאֲשֶׁ֖ר צִוָּ֥ה פַרְעֹֽה: 12וַיְכַלְכֵּ֤ל יוֹסֵף֙ אֶת־אָבִ֣יו וְאֶת־אֶחָ֔יו וְאֵ֖ת כָּל־בֵּ֣ית אָבִ֑יו לֶ֖חֶם לְפִ֥י הַטָּֽף:

13וְלֶ֤חֶם אֵין֙ בְּכָל־הָאָ֔רֶץ כִּֽי־כָבֵ֥ד הָרָעָ֖ב מְאֹ֑ד וַתֵּ֜לַהּ אֶ֤רֶץ מִצְרַ֙יִם֙ וְאֶ֣רֶץ כְּנַ֔עַן מִפְּנֵ֖י הָרָעָֽב: 14וַיְלַקֵּ֣ט יוֹסֵ֗ף אֶת־כָּל־הַכֶּ֙סֶף֙ הַנִּמְצָ֣א בְאֶֽרֶץ־מִצְרַ֙יִם֙ וּבְאֶ֣רֶץ כְּנַ֔עַן בַּשֶּׁ֖בֶר אֲשֶׁר־הֵ֣ם שֹׁבְרִ֑ים וַיָּבֵ֥א יוֹסֵ֛ף אֶת־הַכֶּ֖סֶף בֵּ֥יתָה פַרְעֹֽה: 15וַיִּתֹּ֣ם הַכֶּ֗סֶף מֵאֶ֤רֶץ מִצְרַ֙יִם֙ וּמֵאֶ֣רֶץ כְּנַ֔עַן וַיָּבֹאוּ֩ כָל־מִצְרַ֨יִם אֶל־יוֹסֵ֤ף לֵאמֹר֙ הָֽבָה־לָּ֣נוּ לֶ֔חֶם וְלָ֥מָּה נָמ֖וּת נֶגְדֶּ֑ךָ כִּ֥י אָפֵ֖ס כָּֽסֶף: 16וַיֹּ֤אמֶר יוֹסֵף֙ הָב֣וּ מִקְנֵיכֶ֔ם וְאֶתְּנָ֥ה לָכֶ֖ם בְּמִקְנֵיכֶ֑ם אִם־אָפֵ֖ס כָּֽסֶף: 17וַיָּבִ֣יאוּ אֶת־מִקְנֵיהֶם֮ אֶל־יוֹסֵף֒ וַיִּתֵּ֣ן לָהֶ֩ם יוֹסֵ֨ף לֶ֜חֶם בַּסּוּסִ֗ים וּבְמִקְנֵ֤ה הַצֹּאן֙ וּבְמִקְנֵ֣ה הַבָּקָ֔ר וּבַחֲמֹרִ֑ים וַיְנַהֲלֵ֤ם בַּלֶּ֙חֶם֙ בְּכָל־מִקְנֵהֶ֔ם בַּשָּׁנָ֖ה הַהִֽוא: 18וַתִּתֹּם֮ הַשָּׁנָ֣ה הַהִוא֒ וַיָּבֹ֨אוּ אֵלָ֜יו בַּשָּׁנָ֣ה הַשֵּׁנִ֗ית וַיֹּ֤אמְרוּ לוֹ֙ לֹֽא־נְכַחֵ֣ד מֵֽאֲדֹנִ֔י כִּ֚י אִם־תַּ֣ם הַכֶּ֔סֶף וּמִקְנֵ֥ה הַבְּהֵמָ֖ה אֶל־אֲדֹנִ֑י לֹ֤א נִשְׁאַר֙ לִפְנֵ֣י אֲדֹנִ֔י בִּלְתִּ֥י אִם־גְּוִיָּתֵ֖נוּ וְאַדְמָתֵֽנוּ: 19לָ֧מָּה נָמ֣וּת

---

exhibited an historical, realistic impulse, a sense of the psychological complexity of families: sibling rivalry, fathers and sons in conflict, mothers finding channels of influence in male family structures, women torn between fathers and husbands. Further, it may be said that by not glorifying its human heroes the text glorifies its other central figure, the deity. The message here may well be that God can work through anyone: through an all-obedient man, a passive, dim-eyed patriarch, or a deceiver.

land? Buy us and our land for bread, and we and our land will be servants to Pharaoh; and give seed so we'll live and not die, and the land won't be devastated." 20And Joseph bought all the land of Egypt for Pharaoh, because Egypt, each man, sold his field, because the famine was strong on them. And the land became Pharaoh's. 21And the people: he moved them to cities, from one edge of Egypt's border to its other edge. 22Only the priests' land he did not buy, because it was a law for the priests from Pharaoh, and they ate their statutory share that Pharaoh had given them. On account of this they did not sell their land.

23And Joseph said to the people, "Here, I've bought you and your land for Pharaoh today. Look: seed for you. And you'll sow the land; 24and it will be, at the harvests, that you'll give a fifth to Pharaoh, and the four parts will be yours for field seed and for you to eat and for whoever is in your households and for your infants to eat."

25And they said, "You've kept us alive! Let us find favor in my lord's eyes, and we'll be servants to Pharaoh."

26And Joseph set it as a law to this day on Egypt's land: to Pharaoh the fifth. Only the land of the priests alone was not Pharaoh's.

27And Israel lived in Egypt in the land of Goshen, and they held property in it. And they were fruitful and multiplied very much.

AND HE LIVED

28And Jacob lived in the land of Egypt seventeen years. And Jacob's days, the years of his life, were seven years and a hundred forty years.

29And Israel's days to die drew close. And he called his son, Joseph, and said to him, "If I've found favor in your eyes, place your hand under my thigh and practice kindness and faithfulness with me: don't bury me in Egypt. 30And I'll lie with my fathers, and you'll carry me out of Egypt and bury me in their burial place."

לְעֵינֶ֔יךָ גַּם־אֲנַ֙חְנוּ֙ גַּ֣ם אַדְמָתֵ֔נוּ קְנֵה־אֹתָ֥נוּ וְאֶת־אַדְמָתֵ֖נוּ בַּלָּ֑חֶם וְנִֽהְיֶ֣ה אֲנַ֣חְנוּ וְאַדְמָתֵ֗נוּ עֲבָדִ֣ים לְפַרְעֹ֔ה וְתֶן־זֶ֗רַע וְנִֽחְיֶה֙ וְלֹ֣א נָמ֔וּת וְהָאֲדָמָ֖ה לֹ֥א תֵשָֽׁם: 20וַיִּ֨קֶן יוֹסֵ֜ף אֶת־כָּל־אַדְמַ֤ת מִצְרַ֙יִם֙ לְפַרְעֹ֔ה כִּֽי־מָכְר֤וּ מִצְרַ֙יִם֙ אִ֣ישׁ שָׂדֵ֔הוּ כִּֽי־חָזַ֥ק עֲלֵהֶ֖ם הָרָעָ֑ב וַתְּהִ֥י הָאָ֖רֶץ לְפַרְעֹֽה: 21וְאֶ֨ת־הָעָ֔ם הֶעֱבִ֥יר אֹת֖וֹ לֶעָרִ֑ים מִקְצֵ֥ה גְבֽוּל־מִצְרַ֖יִם וְעַד־קָצֵֽהוּ: 22רַ֛ק אַדְמַ֥ת הַכֹּהֲנִ֖ים לֹ֣א קָנָ֑ה כִּי֩ חֹ֨ק לַכֹּהֲנִ֜ים מֵאֵ֣ת פַּרְעֹ֗ה וְאָֽכְל֤וּ אֶת־חֻקָּם֙ אֲשֶׁ֨ר נָתַ֤ן לָהֶם֙ פַּרְעֹ֔ה עַל־כֵּ֕ן לֹ֥א מָכְר֖וּ אֶת־אַדְמָתָֽם: 23וַיֹּ֥אמֶר יוֹסֵ֖ף אֶל־הָעָ֑ם הֵן֩ קָנִ֨יתִי אֶתְכֶ֤ם הַיּוֹם֙ וְאֶת־אַדְמַתְכֶ֖ם לְפַרְעֹ֑ה הֵֽא־לָכֶ֣ם זֶ֔רַע וּזְרַעְתֶּ֖ם אֶת־הָאֲדָמָֽה: 24וְהָיָה֙ בַּתְּבוּאֹ֔ת וּנְתַתֶּ֥ם חֲמִישִׁ֖ית לְפַרְעֹ֑ה וְאַרְבַּ֣ע הַיָּדֹ֡ת יִהְיֶ֣ה לָכֶם֩ לְזֶ֨רַע הַשָּׂדֶ֧ה וּֽלְאָכְלְכֶ֛ם וְלַאֲשֶׁ֥ר בְּבָתֵּיכֶ֖ם וְלֶאֱכֹ֥ל לְטַפְּכֶֽם: 25וַיֹּאמְר֖וּ הֶחֱיִתָ֑נוּ נִמְצָא־חֵן֙ בְּעֵינֵ֣י אֲדֹנִ֔י וְהָיִ֥ינוּ עֲבָדִ֖ים לְפַרְעֹֽה: 26וַיָּ֣שֶׂם אֹתָ֣הּ יוֹסֵ֡ף לְחֹק֩ עַד־הַיּ֨וֹם הַזֶּ֜ה עַל־אַדְמַ֤ת מִצְרַ֙יִם֙ לְפַרְעֹ֖ה לַחֹ֑מֶשׁ רַ֞ק אַדְמַ֤ת הַכֹּֽהֲנִים֙ לְבַדָּ֔ם לֹ֥א הָיְתָ֖ה לְפַרְעֹֽה: 27וַיֵּ֧שֶׁב יִשְׂרָאֵ֛ל בְּאֶ֥רֶץ מִצְרַ֖יִם בְּאֶ֣רֶץ גֹּ֑שֶׁן וַיֵּאָחֲז֣וּ בָ֔הּ וַיִּפְר֥וּ וַיִּרְבּ֖וּ מְאֹֽד:

וַיְחִי

28וַיְחִ֤י יַעֲקֹב֙ בְּאֶ֣רֶץ מִצְרַ֔יִם שְׁבַ֥ע עֶשְׂרֵ֖ה שָׁנָ֑ה וַיְהִ֤י יְמֵֽי־יַעֲקֹב֙ שְׁנֵ֣י חַיָּ֔יו שֶׁ֣בַע שָׁנִ֔ים וְאַרְבָּעִ֥ים וּמְאַ֖ת שָׁנָֽה: 29וַיִּקְרְב֣וּ יְמֵֽי־יִשְׂרָאֵל֘ לָמוּת֒ וַיִּקְרָ֣א ׀ לִבְנ֣וֹ לְיוֹסֵ֗ף וַיֹּ֤אמֶר לוֹ֙ אִם־נָ֨א מָצָ֤אתִי חֵן֙ בְּעֵינֶ֔יךָ שִֽׂים־נָ֥א יָדְךָ֖ תַּ֣חַת יְרֵכִ֑י וְעָשִׂ֤יתָ עִמָּדִי֙ חֶ֣סֶד וֶאֱמֶ֔ת אַל־נָ֥א תִקְבְּרֵ֖נִי בְּמִצְרָֽיִם: 30וְשָֽׁכַבְתִּי֙ עִם־אֲבֹתַ֔י וּנְשָׂאתַ֙נִי֙ מִמִּצְרַ֔יִם וּקְבַרְתַּ֖נִי בִּקְבֻרָתָ֑ם

And he said, "I'll do according to your word." And he said, "Swear to me."

And he swore to him. And Israel bowed at the head of the bed.

48 ¹And it was after these things, and one said to Joseph, "Here, your father is sick." And he took his two sons with him, Manasseh and Ephraim. ²And one told Jacob and said, "Here, your son Joseph is coming to you." And Israel fortified himself and sat up on the bed.

³And Jacob said to Joseph, "El Shadday appeared to me in Luz in the land of Canaan, and He blessed me ⁴and said to me, 'Here, I'm making you fruitful and multiplying you, and I'll make you into a community of peoples, and I'll give this land to your seed after you, an eternal possession.' ⁵And now, your two sons who were born to you in the land of Egypt by my arrival to you at Egypt: they're mine. Ephraim and Manasseh will be like Reuben and Simeon to me. ⁶And your offspring that you'll have after them will be yours. They shall be called by their brothers' names with regard to their inheritance. ⁷And I: when I was coming from Paddan Aram, Rachel died by me in the land of Canaan on the way, when there was still a span of land to come to Ephrat, and I buried her there on the Ephrat road. That's Bethlehem."

⁸And Israel saw Joseph's sons and said, "Who are these?"

⁹And Joseph said to his father, "They're my sons, whom God has given me here."

And he said, "Bring them to me, and I'll bless

31וַיֹּאמֶר הִשָּׁבְעָה לִי וַיֹּאמֶר אָנֹכִי אֶעֱשֶׂה כִדְבָרֶךָ: וַיִּשָּׁבַע לֹו וַיִּשְׁתַּחוּ יִשְׂרָאֵל עַל־רֹאשׁ הַמִּטָּה: פ

48 ¹וַיְהִי אַחֲרֵי הַדְּבָרִים הָאֵלֶּה וַיֹּאמֶר לְיוֹסֵף הִנֵּה אָבִיךָ חֹלֶה וַיִּקַּח אֶת־שְׁנֵי בָנָיו עִמֹּו אֶת־מְנַשֶּׁה וְאֶת־אֶפְרָיִם: ²וַיַּגֵּד לְיַעֲקֹב וַיֹּאמֶר הִנֵּה בִּנְךָ יוֹסֵף בָּא אֵלֶיךָ וַיִּתְחַזֵּק יִשְׂרָאֵל וַיֵּשֶׁב עַל־הַמִּטָּה: ³וַיֹּאמֶר יַעֲקֹב אֶל־יוֹסֵף אֵל שַׁדַּי נִרְאָה־אֵלַי בְּלוּז בְּאֶרֶץ כְּנָעַן וַיְבָרֶךְ אֹתִי: ⁴וַיֹּאמֶר אֵלַי הִנְנִי מַפְרְךָ וְהִרְבִּיתִךָ וּנְתַתִּיךָ לִקְהַל עַמִּים וְנָתַתִּי אֶת־הָאָרֶץ הַזֹּאת לְזַרְעֲךָ אַחֲרֶיךָ אֲחֻזַּת עוֹלָם: ⁵וְעַתָּה שְׁנֵי־בָנֶיךָ הַנּוֹלָדִים לְךָ בְּאֶרֶץ מִצְרַיִם עַד־בֹּאִי אֵלֶיךָ מִצְרַיְמָה לִי־הֵם אֶפְרַיִם וּמְנַשֶּׁה כִּרְאוּבֵן וְשִׁמְעוֹן יִהְיוּ־לִי: ⁶וּמוֹלַדְתְּךָ אֲשֶׁר־הוֹלַדְתָּ אַחֲרֵיהֶם לְךָ יִהְיוּ עַל שֵׁם אֲחֵיהֶם יִקָּרְאוּ בְּנַחֲלָתָם: ⁷וַאֲנִי בְּבֹאִי מִפַּדָּן מֵתָה עָלַי רָחֵל בְּאֶרֶץ כְּנַעַן בַּדֶּרֶךְ בְּעוֹד כִּבְרַת־אֶרֶץ לָבֹא אֶפְרָתָה וָאֶקְבְּרֶהָ שָּׁם בְּדֶרֶךְ אֶפְרָת הִוא בֵּית לָחֶם: ⁸וַיַּרְא יִשְׂרָאֵל אֶת־בְּנֵי יוֹסֵף וַיֹּאמֶר מִי־אֵלֶּה: ⁹וַיֹּאמֶר יוֹסֵף אֶל־אָבִיו בָּנַי הֵם אֲשֶׁר־נָתַן־לִי אֱלֹהִים בָּזֶה וַיֹּאמַר קָחֶם־נָא

48:4. **I'm making you fruitful and multiplying you, and I'll make you** . . . But God did not say, "*I'll make you* fruitful . . ." God said, "*Be* fruitful . . ." (35:11). Why does Jacob tell Joseph that God promised to do it when God actually told *him* to do it? Perhaps it is because Jacob has only one more son (Benjamin) after God tells him this, and so the becoming fruitful must refer to the births of his grandchildren and great-grandchildren. Jacob would not see this as in his power but rather as God's doing, and so he understands God's words not as a command but as a promise and a blessing.

them." 10And Israel's eyes were heavy from old age. He was not able to see. And he brought them close to him, and he kissed them and embraced them. 11And Israel said to Joseph, "I didn't expect to see your face; and, here, God has shown me your seed as well." 12And Joseph brought them out from between his knees, and he bowed, his nose to the ground. 13And Joseph took the two of them, Ephraim in his right hand, at Israel's left; and Manasseh in his left hand, at Israel's right; and he brought them over to him. 14And Israel put out his right hand and placed it on Ephraim's head—and he was the younger—and his left hand on Manasseh's head. He crossed his hands—because Manasseh was the firstborn. 15And he blessed Joseph and said, "The God before whom my fathers, Abraham and Isaac, walked, who shepherded me from my start to this day, 16the angel who redeemed me from all bad, may He bless the boys. And may my name be called on them, and the name of my fathers, Abraham and Isaac. And may they spawn into a great number within the earth."

17And Joseph saw that his father had placed his right hand on Ephraim's head, and it was bad in his eyes, and he held up his father's hand to turn it from on Ephraim's head onto Manasseh's head, 18and Joseph said to his father, "Not like that, my father, because this is the firstborn. Set your right hand on his head."

19And his father refused and said, "I know, my son, I know. He, too, will become a people; and he, too, will be great. But in fact his little brother will be greater than he, and his seed will be

אֵלָי וַאֲבָרֲכֵם: 10וְעֵינֵי יִשְׂרָאֵל כָּבְדוּ מִזֹּקֶן לֹא
יוּכַל לִרְאוֹת וַיַּגֵּשׁ אֹתָם אֵלָיו וַיִּשַּׁק לָהֶם וַיְחַבֵּק
לָהֶם: 11וַיֹּאמֶר יִשְׂרָאֵל אֶל־יוֹסֵף רְאֹה פָנֶיךָ לֹא
פִלָּלְתִּי וְהִנֵּה הֶרְאָה אֹתִי אֱלֹהִים גַּם אֶת־זַרְעֶךָ:
12וַיּוֹצֵא יוֹסֵף אֹתָם מֵעִם בִּרְכָּיו וַיִּשְׁתַּחוּ לְאַפָּיו
אָרְצָה: 13וַיִּקַּח יוֹסֵף אֶת־שְׁנֵיהֶם אֶת־אֶפְרַיִם
בִּימִינוֹ מִשְּׂמֹאל יִשְׂרָאֵל וְאֶת־מְנַשֶּׁה בִשְׂמֹאלוֹ מִימִין
יִשְׂרָאֵל וַיַּגֵּשׁ אֵלָיו: 14וַיִּשְׁלַח יִשְׂרָאֵל אֶת־יְמִינוֹ
וַיָּשֶׁת עַל־רֹאשׁ אֶפְרַיִם וְהוּא הַצָּעִיר וְאֶת־שְׂמֹאלוֹ
עַל־רֹאשׁ מְנַשֶּׁה שִׂכֵּל אֶת־יָדָיו כִּי מְנַשֶּׁה הַבְּכוֹר:
15וַיְבָרֶךְ אֶת־יוֹסֵף וַיֹּאמַר
הָאֱלֹהִים אֲשֶׁר הִתְהַלְּכוּ אֲבֹתַי
לְפָנָיו אַבְרָהָם וְיִצְחָק
הָאֱלֹהִים הָרֹעֶה אֹתִי מֵעוֹדִי עַד־הַיּוֹם הַזֶּה:
16הַמַּלְאָךְ הַגֹּאֵל אֹתִי מִכָּל־רָע
יְבָרֵךְ אֶת־הַנְּעָרִים
וְיִקָּרֵא בָהֶם שְׁמִי וְשֵׁם אֲבֹתַי אַבְרָהָם וְיִצְחָק
וְיִדְגּוּ לָרֹב בְּקֶרֶב הָאָרֶץ:
17וַיַּרְא יוֹסֵף כִּי־יָשִׁית אָבִיו יַד־יְמִינוֹ עַל־רֹאשׁ
אֶפְרַיִם וַיֵּרַע בְּעֵינָיו וַיִּתְמֹךְ יַד־אָבִיו לְהָסִיר אֹתָהּ
מֵעַל רֹאשׁ־אֶפְרַיִם עַל־רֹאשׁ מְנַשֶּׁה: 18וַיֹּאמֶר יוֹסֵף
אֶל־אָבִיו לֹא־כֵן אָבִי כִּי־זֶה הַבְּכֹר שִׂים יְמִינְךָ
עַל־רֹאשׁוֹ: 19וַיְמָאֵן אָבִיו וַיֹּאמֶר יָדַעְתִּי בְנִי יָדַעְתִּי
גַּם־הוּא יִהְיֶה־לְעָם וְגַם־הוּא יִגְדָּל וְאוּלָם אָחִיו
הַקָּטֹן יִגְדַּל מִמֶּנּוּ וְזַרְעוֹ יִהְיֶה מְלֹא־הַגּוֹיִם:

48:10. **Israel's eyes were heavy from old age.** The analogy to his father is obvious. When Isaac had been old, on his deathbed, unable to see, Jacob had come and appropriated his brother Esau's blessing. Now Jacob himself is old, on his deathbed, unable to see, and he favors the younger son, Ephraim, in his blessing.

48:15. **before whom my fathers walked.** Note here and in Gen 6:9 and 17:1 that this is technical covenant terminology known from ancient Near Eastern documents to mean loyalty to one's partner in a covenant.

full-fledged of nations." ²⁰And he blessed them in that day, saying, "Israel will bless with you, saying: 'May God make you like Ephraim and like Manasseh.' " And he set Ephraim before Manasseh.

²¹And Israel said to Joseph, "Here, I'm dying. And God will be with you and will bring you back to your fathers' land. And I've given you one shoulder over your brothers, which I took from the Amorite's hand with my sword and my bow."

49

¹And Jacob called to his sons and said:

Gather, and I'll tell you what will happen
    to you in the future days.
2   Assemble and listen, sons of Jacob,
    and listen to Israel, your father.
3   Reuben, you're my firstborn,
    my power, and the beginning of my
      might,
    preeminent in bearing and preeminent
      in strength.
4   Unstable as water, you'll not be
      preeminent,
    for you ascended your father's bed;
    then you defiled, going up to my
      couch.
5   Simeon and Levi are brothers:
    Implements of violence are their tools
      of trade.
6   Let my soul not come in their council;

²⁰וַיְבָרֲכֵם בַּיּוֹם הַהוּא לֵאמוֹר
בְּךָ יְבָרֵךְ יִשְׂרָאֵל לֵאמֹר
יְשִׂמְךָ אֱלֹהִים כְּאֶפְרַיִם וְכִמְנַשֶּׁה
וַיָּשֶׂם אֶת־אֶפְרַיִם לִפְנֵי מְנַשֶּׁה: ²¹וַיֹּאמֶר יִשְׂרָאֵל
אֶל־יוֹסֵף הִנֵּה אָנֹכִי מֵת וְהָיָה אֱלֹהִים עִמָּכֶם
וְהֵשִׁיב אֶתְכֶם אֶל־אֶרֶץ אֲבֹתֵיכֶם: ²²וַאֲנִי נָתַתִּי לְךָ
שְׁכֶם אַחַד עַל־אַחֶיךָ אֲשֶׁר לָקַחְתִּי מִיַּד הָאֱמֹרִי
בְּחַרְבִּי וּבְקַשְׁתִּי: פ

49 ¹וַיִּקְרָא יַעֲקֹב אֶל־בָּנָיו וַיֹּאמֶר
הֵאָסְפוּ וְאַגִּידָה לָכֶם אֵת אֲשֶׁר־יִקְרָא אֶתְכֶם
בְּאַחֲרִית הַיָּמִים:
²הִקָּבְצוּ וְשִׁמְעוּ בְּנֵי יַעֲקֹב
וְשִׁמְעוּ אֶל־יִשְׂרָאֵל אֲבִיכֶם:
³רְאוּבֵן בְּכֹרִי אַתָּה כֹּחִי וְרֵאשִׁית אוֹנִי
יֶתֶר שְׂאֵת וְיֶתֶר עָז:
⁴פַּחַז כַּמַּיִם אַל־תּוֹתַר כִּי עָלִיתָ מִשְׁכְּבֵי אָבִיךָ
אָז חִלַּלְתָּ יְצוּעִי עָלָה: פ
⁵שִׁמְעוֹן וְלֵוִי אַחִים כְּלֵי חָמָס מְכֵרֹתֵיהֶם:
⁶בְּסֹדָם אַל־תָּבֹא נַפְשִׁי בִּקְהָלָם אַל־תֵּחַד כְּבֹדִי

48:19. **full-fledged of nations**. The unusual phrase *mĕlō'-haggōyim* is usually taken to mean a multitude of nations, but that makes no particular sense in terms of the fate of the single tribe of Ephraim. Elsewhere *mĕlō'* can mean a full unit among a group (as in 2 Sam 8:2). It may mean here that Ephraim will be thought of as a nation, for Ephraim later comes to dominate the kingdom of Israel, and the name Ephraim is sometimes used to refer to the entire Israelite kingdom (Isa 7:2–17; Hos 5:3; 6:10; 7:1).

48:21. **one shoulder over your brothers**. This expression appears to refer to Joseph's getting two tribes while each of his brothers gets only one. But it also puns on the word for shoulder, Hebrew *šĕkem* (Shechem). Shechem is the name of the city that will one day be the capital of the kingdom of Israel, and it is located in one of the Joseph tribes (Manasseh).

let my glory not be united in their
    society.
For in their anger they killed a man,
    and by their will they crippled an ox.

7   Cursed is their anger, for it's strong,
    and their wrath, for it's hard.
    I'll divide them in Jacob,
    and I'll scatter them in Israel.

8   Judah: You, your brothers will praise you.
    Your hand on your enemies' neck,
    your father's sons will bow to you.

9   A lion's whelp is Judah;
    from prey, my son, you've risen.
    He bent, crouched, like a lion;
    and, like a feline, who will rouse him?

10   The scepter won't depart from Judah
    or a ruler from between his legs
    until he comes to Shiloh,
    and peoples' obedience is his.

11   Tying his ass to the vine
    and his she-ass's foal to the choice
      vine,
    he washed in wine his clothing
    and in blood of grapes his garment,

12   eyes darker than wine
    and teeth whiter than milk.

13   Zebulun will dwell by seashores:
    and he'll be a shore for boats,
    and his border at Sidon.

14   Issachar is a strong ass
    crouching between the saddle-packs:

15   and he saw rest, that it was good,
    and the land, that it was pleasant,

כִּי בְאַפָּם הָרְגוּ אִישׁ וּבִרְצֹנָם עִקְּרוּ־שֽׁוֹר:
7 אָרוּר אַפָּם כִּי עָז וְעֶבְרָתָם כִּי קָשָׁתָה
אֲחַלְּקֵם בְּיַעֲקֹב וַאֲפִיצֵם בְּיִשְׂרָאֵֽל: ס
8 יְהוּדָה אַתָּה יוֹדוּךָ אַחֶיךָ יָדְךָ בְּעֹרֶף אֹיְבֶיךָ
יִשְׁתַּחֲווּ לְךָ בְּנֵי אָבִֽיךָ:
9 גּוּר אַרְיֵה יְהוּדָה מִטֶּרֶף בְּנִי עָלִיתָ
כָּרַע רָבַץ כְּאַרְיֵה וּכְלָבִיא מִי יְקִימֶֽנּוּ:
10 לֹא־יָסוּר שֵׁבֶט מִיהוּדָה וּמְחֹקֵק מִבֵּין רַגְלָיו
עַד כִּי־יָבֹא שִׁילֹה וְלוֹ יִקְּהַת עַמִּֽים:
11 אֹסְרִי לַגֶּפֶן עִירֹה וְלַשֹּׂרֵקָה בְּנִי אֲתֹנוֹ
כִּבֵּס בַּיַּיִן לְבֻשׁוֹ וּבְדַם־עֲנָבִים סוּתֹֽה:
12 חַכְלִילִי עֵינַיִם מִיָּיִן וּלְבֶן־שִׁנַּיִם מֵחָלָֽב: פ
13 זְבוּלֻן לְחוֹף יַמִּים יִשְׁכֹּן וְהוּא לְחוֹף אֳנִיֹּת
וְיַרְכָתוֹ עַל־צִידֹֽן: ס
14 יִשָּׂשכָר חֲמֹר גָּרֶם רֹבֵץ בֵּין הַמִּשְׁפְּתָֽיִם:
15 וַיַּרְא מְנֻחָה כִּי טוֹב וְאֶת־הָאָרֶץ כִּי נָעֵמָה

49:10   קְ שִׁילוֹ
49:11   קְ עִירוֹ
49:11   קְ סוּתוֹ:

    49:8. Judah. Reuben is demoted from firstborn preeminence (49:4); Simeon and
Levi are condemned to be scattered (49:7). The fourth-born Judah is the one to receive
praise, success, and dominion. The fulfillment will come when Judah becomes the
largest of the tribes, and its royal family, the kings descended from David, rule for centuries and hold the messianic promise. Judah was the brother who saved Joseph's life,
who promised to be the protector of Benjamin, whose relationship with Tamar resulted in the birth of the clan of the future kings of Israel. The patriarchs will all be
buried in Hebron, the capital city of the tribe of Judah. Here at the end of Genesis we
find the denouement of the stories of the brothers, and we are made aware of their significance for the future.

and he leaned his shoulder to bear
and became a work-company servant.

וַיֵּ֤ט שִׁכְמוֹ֙ לִסְבֹּ֔ל וַיְהִ֖י לְמַס־עֹבֵֽד: ס

16 Dan will judge his people
as one of the tribes of Israel:

16 דָּ֖ן יָדִ֣ין עַמּ֑וֹ כְּאַחַ֖ד שִׁבְטֵ֥י יִשְׂרָאֵֽל:

17 Dan will be a snake on a road,
a venomous snake on a path,
that bites a horse's heels,
and its rider falls backward.

17 יְהִי־דָן֙ נָחָ֣שׁ עֲלֵי־דֶ֔רֶךְ שְׁפִיפֹ֖ן עֲלֵי־אֹ֑רַח
הַנֹּשֵׁךְ֙ עִקְּבֵי־ס֔וּס וַיִּפֹּ֥ל רֹכְב֖וֹ אָחֽוֹר:

18 I wait for your salvation, YHWH.

18 לִישׁוּעָתְךָ֖ קִוִּ֥יתִי יְהוָֽה:

19 Gad: a troop will trap him,
and he'll trap their heel.

19 גָּ֖ד גְּד֣וּד יְגוּדֶ֑נּוּ וְה֖וּא יָגֻ֥ד עָקֵֽב: ס

20 Asher: his bread will be rich,
and he'll provide a king's delights.

20 מֵאָשֵׁ֖ר שְׁמֵנָ֣ה לַחְמ֑וֹ וְה֥וּא יִתֵּ֖ן מַֽעֲדַנֵּי־מֶֽלֶךְ: ס

21 Naphtali: a hind let loose,
who gives lovely words.

21 נַפְתָּלִ֖י אַיָּלָ֣ה שְׁלֻחָ֑ה הַנֹּתֵ֖ן אִמְרֵי־שָֽׁפֶר: ס

22 A fruitful bough is Joseph,
a fruitful bough over a spring,
branches running over a wall:

22 בֵּ֤ן פֹּרָת֙ יוֹסֵ֔ף בֵּ֥ן פֹּרָ֖ת עֲלֵי־עָ֑יִן
בָּנ֕וֹת צָעֲדָ֖ה עֲלֵי־שֽׁוּר:

23 And archers bitterly attacked him,
shot at him, and despised him.

23 וַֽיְמָרֲרֻ֖הוּ וָרֹ֑בּוּ וַֽיִּשְׂטְמֻ֖הוּ בַּעֲלֵ֥י חִצִּֽים:

24 And his bow stayed strong,
and his forearms were nimble,
from the hands of the Mighty One of
Jacob,
from there, the shepherd, the rock of
Israel,

24 וַתֵּ֤שֶׁב בְּאֵיתָן֙ קַשְׁתּ֔וֹ וַיָּפֹ֖זּוּ זְרֹעֵ֣י יָדָ֑יו
מִידֵי֙ אֲבִ֣יר יַעֲקֹ֔ב מִשָּׁ֥ם רֹעֶ֖ה אֶ֥בֶן יִשְׂרָאֵֽל:

25 from your father's God, and He'll
strengthen you,
and Shadday, and He'll bless you,
blessings of skies from above,
blessings of deep, crouching below,
blessings of breast and womb.

25 מֵאֵ֨ל אָבִ֜יךָ וְיַעְזְרֶ֗ךָ וְאֵ֤ת שַׁדַּי֙ וִיבָרְכֶ֔ךָ
בִּרְכֹ֤ת שָׁמַ֙יִם֙ מֵעָ֔ל בִּרְכֹ֥ת תְּה֖וֹם רֹבֶ֣צֶת תָּ֑חַת
בִּרְכֹ֥ת שָׁדַ֖יִם וָרָֽחַם:

49:16. as one of the tribes of Israel. David Noel Freedman says: "as one of the tribes of Israel" is too banal to merit utterance. '*ḥd* must mean "first" as in the opening chapter of Genesis. Now why should Dan be first among the tribes? Because it is always mentioned first, when anyone describes the territory of Israel: from Dan to Beer-sheba.

49:20. Asher. The MT says "*from* Asher," but that is a scribal mistake. The Hebrew letter *mem* (meaning "from") has been displaced from the end of the preceding word, '*āqēbām* (where it means "their" heel).

49:25. Shadday. The MT reads just Shadday, but evidence from other versions indicates that the line should read El Shadday. (The MT reads '*et* where it should read '*ēl*.)

26   blessings of your father, the mighty
        and most high,
     blessings of the mountains of old
     desired object of the hills of antiquity.
     They'll be on Joseph's head,
        on the top of the head of the one
        separate from his brothers.
27   Benjamin is a tearing wolf:
        in the morning eating prey,
        and at evening dividing booty.

28All these are the tribes of Israel, twelve, and this is what their father spoke to them, and he blessed them. He blessed them each according to his blessing. 29And he commanded them and said to them, "I'm being gathered to my people. Bury me: to my fathers, to the cave that's in the field of Ephron, the Hittite, 30in the cave that's in the field of Machpelah, which faces Mamre in the land of Canaan, as Abraham bought the field from Ephron, the Hittite, as a possession for a tomb. 31There they buried Abraham and Sarah, his wife. There they buried Isaac and Rebekah, his wife. And there I buried Leah. 32The field and the cave that's in it were a purchase from the children of Heth." 33And Jacob finished commanding his sons, and he gathered his feet into the bed, and he expired, and he was gathered to his people.

50 1And Joseph fell upon his father's face and wept over him and kissed him. 2And Joseph commanded his servants, the physicians, to embalm his father. And the physicians embalmed Israel, 3and they spent forty days on him, because that is the number of days they spent on the embalming, and Egypt mourned him seventy

26בִּרְכֹת אָבִיךָ גָּבְרוּ עַל־בִּרְכֹת הוֹרַי עַד־
תַּאֲוַת גִּבְעֹת עוֹלָם
תִּהְיֶיןָ לְרֹאשׁ יוֹסֵף וּלְקָדְקֹד נְזִיר אֶחָיו: פ
27בִּנְיָמִין זְאֵב יִטְרָף בַּבֹּקֶר יֹאכַל עַד
וְלָעֶרֶב יְחַלֵּק שָׁלָל:
28כָּל־אֵלֶּה שִׁבְטֵי יִשְׂרָאֵל שְׁנֵים עָשָׂר וְזֹאת אֲשֶׁר־
דִּבֶּר לָהֶם אֲבִיהֶם וַיְבָרֶךְ אוֹתָם אִישׁ אֲשֶׁר
כְּבִרְכָתוֹ בֵּרַךְ אֹתָם: 29וַיְצַו אוֹתָם וַיֹּאמֶר אֲלֵהֶם
אֲנִי נֶאֱסָף אֶל־עַמִּי קִבְרוּ אֹתִי אֶל־אֲבֹתָי אֶל־
הַמְּעָרָה אֲשֶׁר בִּשְׂדֵה עֶפְרוֹן הַחִתִּי: 30בַּמְּעָרָה
אֲשֶׁר בִּשְׂדֵה הַמַּכְפֵּלָה אֲשֶׁר עַל־פְּנֵי־מַמְרֵא בְּאֶרֶץ
כְּנַעַן אֲשֶׁר קָנָה אַבְרָהָם אֶת־הַשָּׂדֶה מֵאֵת עֶפְרֹן
הַחִתִּי לַאֲחֻזַּת־קָבֶר: 31שָׁמָּה קָבְרוּ אֶת־אַבְרָהָם
וְאֵת שָׂרָה אִשְׁתּוֹ שָׁמָּה קָבְרוּ אֶת־יִצְחָק וְאֵת
רִבְקָה אִשְׁתּוֹ וְשָׁמָּה קָבַרְתִּי אֶת־לֵאָה: 32מִקְנֵה
הַשָּׂדֶה וְהַמְּעָרָה אֲשֶׁר־בּוֹ מֵאֵת בְּנֵי־חֵת: 33וַיְכַל
יַעֲקֹב לְצַוֹּת אֶת־בָּנָיו וַיֶּאֱסֹף רַגְלָיו אֶל־הַמִּטָּה
וַיִּגְוַע וַיֵּאָסֶף אֶל־עַמָּיו:
50 1וַיִּפֹּל יוֹסֵף עַל־פְּנֵי אָבִיו וַיֵּבְךְּ עָלָיו וַיִּשַּׁק־לוֹ:
2וַיְצַו יוֹסֵף אֶת־עֲבָדָיו אֶת־הָרֹפְאִים לַחֲנֹט אֶת־
אָבִיו וַיַּחַנְטוּ הָרֹפְאִים אֶת־יִשְׂרָאֵל: 3וַיִּמְלְאוּ־לוֹ
אַרְבָּעִים יוֹם כִּי כֵּן יִמְלְאוּ יְמֵי הַחֲנֻטִים וַיִּבְכּוּ
אֹתוֹ מִצְרַיִם שִׁבְעִים יוֹם: 4וַיַּעַבְרוּ יְמֵי בְכִיתוֹ

49:26. **the mighty and most high**. This is based on a reconstruction proposed by David Noel Freedman, reading גבר ועל instead of גברו על.

49:26. **mountains of old**. This understanding involves an emendation of the text based on the parallel with "hills of antiquity" in the next line and on comparison with Moses' blessing of Joseph: "from the top of the ancient mountains, and from the most precious of the hills of antiquity" (Deut 33:15).

days. 4And his mourning days passed, and Joseph spoke to Pharaoh's house, saying, "If I've found favor in your eyes, speak in Pharaoh's ears, saying, 5'My father had me swear, saying, "Here I'm dying. In my tomb, which I dug for me in the land of Canaan: you shall bury me there." And now, let me go up so I may bury my father and come back.' "

6And Pharaoh said, "Go up and bury your father as he had you swear."

7And Joseph went up to bury his father, and all of Pharaoh's servants, the elders of his house, and all the elders of the land of Egypt, 8and all of Joseph's house and his brothers and his father's house. Only their infants and their flock and their oxen they left in the land of Goshen. 9And both chariots and horsemen went up with him. It was a very heavy camp. 10And they came to the threshing floor of Atad, which is across the Jordan, and they had a very big and heavy funeral, and he made a mourning for his father for seven days. 11And the Canaanite residents of the land saw the mourning at the threshing floor of Atad and said, "This is a heavy mourning to Egypt." On account of this its name was called Abel of Egypt, which is beyond the Jordan. 12And his sons did so for him, as he had commanded them. 13And his sons carried him to the land of Canaan and buried him in the cave of the field of Machpelah, as Abraham had bought the field as a possession for a tomb from Ephron, the Hittite, facing Mamre.

14And, after his burial of his father, Joseph came back to Egypt, he and his brothers and all those who went up with him to bury his father.

15And Joseph's brothers saw that their father was dead, and they said, "If Joseph will despise us he'll *pay us back* all the bad that we dealt to him." 16And they commanded to Joseph, saying,

וַיְדַבֵּ֣ר יוֹסֵ֗ף אֶל־בֵּ֤ית פַּרְעֹה֙ לֵאמֹ֔ר אִם־נָ֨א מָצָ֤אתִי חֵן֙ בְּעֵ֣ינֵיכֶ֔ם דַּבְּרוּ־נָ֕א בְּאָזְנֵ֥י פַרְעֹ֖ה לֵאמֹֽר: 5אָבִ֞י הִשְׁבִּיעַ֣נִי לֵאמֹ֗ר הִנֵּ֣ה אָנֹכִי֮ מֵת֒ בְּקִבְרִ֗י אֲשֶׁ֨ר כָּרִ֤יתִי לִי֙ בְּאֶ֣רֶץ כְּנַ֔עַן שָׁ֖מָּה תִּקְבְּרֵ֑נִי וְעַתָּ֗ה אֶעֱלֶה־נָּ֛א וְאֶקְבְּרָ֥ה אֶת־אָבִ֖י וְאָשֽׁוּבָה: 6וַיֹּ֖אמֶר פַּרְעֹ֑ה עֲלֵ֛ה וּקְבֹ֥ר אֶת־אָבִ֖יךָ כַּאֲשֶׁ֥ר הִשְׁבִּיעֶֽךָ: 7וַיַּ֥עַל יוֹסֵ֖ף לִקְבֹּ֣ר אֶת־אָבִ֑יו וַיַּֽעֲל֨וּ אִתּ֜וֹ כָּל־עַבְדֵ֤י פַרְעֹה֙ זִקְנֵ֣י בֵית֔וֹ וְכֹ֖ל זִקְנֵ֥י אֶֽרֶץ־מִצְרָֽיִם: 8וְכֹל֙ בֵּ֣ית יוֹסֵ֔ף וְאֶחָ֖יו וּבֵ֣ית אָבִ֑יו רַ֗ק טַפָּם֙ וְצֹאנָ֣ם וּבְקָרָ֔ם עָזְב֖וּ בְּאֶ֥רֶץ גֹּֽשֶׁן: 9וַיַּ֣עַל עִמּ֔וֹ גַּם־רֶ֖כֶב גַּם־פָּרָשִׁ֑ים וַיְהִ֥י הַֽמַּחֲנֶ֖ה כָּבֵ֥ד מְאֹֽד: 10וַיָּבֹ֜אוּ עַד־גֹּ֣רֶן הָאָטָ֗ד אֲשֶׁר֙ בְּעֵ֣בֶר הַיַּרְדֵּ֔ן וַיִּ֨סְפְּדוּ־שָׁ֔ם מִסְפֵּ֛ד גָּד֥וֹל וְכָבֵ֖ד מְאֹ֑ד וַיַּ֧עַשׂ לְאָבִ֛יו אֵ֖בֶל שִׁבְעַ֥ת יָמִֽים: 11וַיַּ֡רְא יוֹשֵׁב֩ הָאָ֨רֶץ הַֽכְּנַעֲנִ֜י אֶת־הָאֵ֗בֶל בְּגֹ֙רֶן֙ הָֽאָטָ֔ד וַיֹּ֣אמְר֔וּ אֵֽבֶל־כָּבֵ֥ד זֶ֖ה לְמִצְרָ֑יִם עַל־כֵּ֞ן קָרָ֤א שְׁמָהּ֙ אָבֵ֣ל מִצְרַ֔יִם אֲשֶׁ֖ר בְּעֵ֥בֶר הַיַּרְדֵּֽן: 12וַיַּעֲשׂ֥וּ בָנָ֖יו ל֑וֹ כֵּ֖ן כַּאֲשֶׁ֥ר צִוָּֽם: 13וַיִּשְׂא֨וּ אֹת֤וֹ בָנָיו֙ אַ֣רְצָה כְּנַ֔עַן וַיִּקְבְּר֣וּ אֹת֔וֹ בִּמְעָרַ֖ת שְׂדֵ֣ה הַמַּכְפֵּלָ֑ה אֲשֶׁ֣ר קָנָ֣ה אַבְרָהָ֠ם אֶת־הַשָּׂדֶ֜ה לַאֲחֻזַּת־קֶ֗בֶר מֵאֵ֛ת עֶפְרֹ֥ן הַחִתִּ֖י עַל־פְּנֵ֥י מַמְרֵֽא: 14וַיָּ֨שָׁב יוֹסֵ֤ף מִצְרַ֙יְמָה֙ ה֣וּא וְאֶחָ֔יו וְכָל־הָעֹלִ֥ים אִתּ֖וֹ לִקְבֹּ֣ר אֶת־אָבִ֑יו אַחֲרֵ֖י קָבְר֥וֹ אֶת־אָבִֽיו: 15וַיִּרְא֤וּ אֲחֵֽי־יוֹסֵף֙ כִּי־מֵ֣ת אֲבִיהֶ֔ם וַיֹּ֣אמְר֔וּ ל֚וּ יִשְׂטְמֵ֣נוּ יוֹסֵ֔ף וְהָשֵׁ֥ב יָשִׁיב֙ לָ֔נוּ אֵ֚ת כָּל־הָ֣רָעָ֔ה אֲשֶׁ֥ר גָּמַ֖לְנוּ אֹתֽוֹ: 16וַיְצַוּ֕וּ

50:16. **they commanded**. Why would they *command*? The problem appears to be scribal. The Septuagint appears to be translating Hebrew ויגשו, meaning "they approached," instead of the MT ויצו, meaning "they commanded." A scribe apparently

"Your father had commanded before his death, saying, 17'You shall say this to Joseph: Please, bear your brothers' offense and their sin, because they dealt you bad.' And now bear the offense of the servants of your father's God."

And Joseph wept when they spoke to him.

18And his brothers also went and fell in front of him and said, "Here, we're yours as slaves."

19And Joseph said to them, "Don't be afraid, because am I in God's place? 20And *you* thought bad against me. *God* thought for good: in order to do as it is today, to keep alive a numerous people. 21And now, don't be afraid. I'll provide for you and your infants." And he consoled them. And he spoke on their heart.

22And Joseph lived in Egypt, he and his father's house. And Joseph lived a hundred ten years, 23and Joseph saw children of Ephraim's of the third generation. Also children of Machir, son of Manasseh, were born on Joseph's knees.

אֶל־יוֹסֵף לֵאמֹר אָבִיךָ צִוָּה לִפְנֵי מוֹתוֹ לֵאמֹר: 17כֹּה־תֹאמְרוּ לְיוֹסֵף אָנָּא שָׂא נָא פֶּשַׁע אַחֶיךָ וְחַטָּאתָם כִּי־רָעָה גְמָלוּךָ וְעַתָּה שָׂא נָא לְפֶשַׁע עַבְדֵי אֱלֹהֵי אָבִיךָ וַיֵּבְךְּ יוֹסֵף בְּדַבְּרָם אֵלָיו: 18וַיֵּלְכוּ גַּם־אֶחָיו וַיִּפְּלוּ לְפָנָיו וַיֹּאמְרוּ הִנֶּנּוּ לְךָ לַעֲבָדִים: 19וַיֹּאמֶר אֲלֵהֶם יוֹסֵף אַל־תִּירָאוּ כִּי הֲתַחַת אֱלֹהִים אָנִי: 20וְאַתֶּם חֲשַׁבְתֶּם עָלַי רָעָה אֱלֹהִים חֲשָׁבָהּ לְטֹבָה לְמַעַן עֲשֹׂה כַּיּוֹם הַזֶּה לְהַחֲיֹת עַם־רָב: 21וְעַתָּה אַל־תִּירָאוּ אָנֹכִי אֲכַלְכֵּל אֶתְכֶם וְאֶת־טַפְּכֶם וַיְנַחֵם אוֹתָם וַיְדַבֵּר עַל־לִבָּם: 22וַיֵּשֶׁב יוֹסֵף בְּמִצְרַיִם הוּא וּבֵית אָבִיו וַיְחִי יוֹסֵף מֵאָה וָעֶשֶׂר שָׁנִים: 23וַיַּרְא יוֹסֵף לְאֶפְרַיִם בְּנֵי שִׁלֵּשִׁים גַּם בְּנֵי מָכִיר בֶּן־מְנַשֶּׁה יֻלְּדוּ עַל־בִּרְכֵּי

---

changed the word under the influence of the word "command" which comes up later in the verse.

50:16. **Your father had commanded before his death**. We never find out whether Joseph—or his brothers—ever told Jacob what his brothers did to him. The brothers *claim* that Jacob commanded that Joseph should forgive them, but we do not know if they are making this up or not. Either way, it is the right message: after a parent's death, the children should try to heal any old wounds and draw close.

50:18. **we're yours as slaves**. This is the final ironic recompense in the chain of deceptions in this family. The brothers who once sold Joseph as a slave now say that they will be *his* slaves.

50:21. **he spoke on their heart**. We have seen that each act of deception since Jacob led to another deception that came as a recompense. Thus deceptions and hurts within a family can go on in a perpetual cycle. In order to bring it to an end, one member of the family who is entitled to retribution must stop the cycle and forgive instead. That is what Joseph does here.

This beautiful end of the story of deceptions and retributions completes an intricately embroidered narrative. Many interpreters have treated the Joseph cycle as if it were a separate entity, referring to it as a "novella." Insofar as that term connotes an independent work, it is misleading, cutting off what is an integral part of this connected narrative. Symbols, ironies, and relationships of characters and events are lost when one performs this surgery and separates the Joseph cycle from the rest of the story.

24And Joseph said to his brothers, "I'm dying. And God *will* take account of you and will bring you up from this land to the land that He swore to Abraham, to Isaac, and to Jacob." 25And Joseph had the children of Israel swear, saying, "God *will* take account of you, and you'll bring up my bones from here."

26And Joseph died, a hundred ten years old, and they embalmed him and set him in a coffin in Egypt.

יוֹסֵף: 24וַיֹּאמֶר יוֹסֵף אֶל־אֶחָיו אָנֹכִי מֵת וֵאלֹהִים פָּקֹד יִפְקֹד אֶתְכֶם וְהֶעֱלָה אֶתְכֶם מִן־הָאָרֶץ הַזֹּאת אֶל־הָאָרֶץ אֲשֶׁר נִשְׁבַּע לְאַבְרָהָם לְיִצְחָק וּלְיַעֲקֹב: 25וַיַּשְׁבַּע יוֹסֵף אֶת־בְּנֵי יִשְׂרָאֵל לֵאמֹר פָּקֹד יִפְקֹד אֱלֹהִים אֶתְכֶם וְהַעֲלִתֶם אֶת־עַצְמֹתַי מִזֶּה: 26וַיָּמָת יוֹסֵף בֶּן־מֵאָה וָעֶשֶׂר שָׁנִים וַיַּחַנְטוּ אֹתוֹ וַיִּישֶׂם בָּאָרוֹן בְּמִצְרָיִם:

EXODUS

—

שמות

*T*he book of Exodus tells the story of the birth of a nation in slavery and ends with the nation's establishment of its own center, leaders, and symbols in freedom. Genesis involves a continuous narrowing of attention from the universe to the earth to humanity to a particular family; Exodus begins to broaden the circumference of attention again as the family grows into a nation—and comes into conflict with another nation. Whereas Genesis sets the rest of the books of the Bible in context, Exodus does not set them in context so much as introduce fundamental components that will function centrally in almost all the coming books of the Bible. Exodus introduces the nation of Israel. It introduces prophecy. It introduces law. Arguably most important of all, it introduces the theme of YHWH's becoming known to the world.

NAMES

שמות

1 ¹And these are the names of the children of Israel who came to Egypt. With Jacob, each and his household had come: ²Reuben, Simeon, Levi, and Judah, ³Issachar, Zebulun, and Benjamin, ⁴Dan and Naphtali, Gad and Asher. ⁵And all the persons coming out from Jacob's thigh were seventy persons. And Joseph had been in Egypt.

⁶And Joseph and all of his brothers and all of that generation died. ⁷And the children of Israel were fruitful and teemed and multiplied and became very, very powerful, and the land was filled with them.

⁸And a new king rose over Egypt—who did

1 ¹וְאֵ֗לֶּה שְׁמוֹת֙ בְּנֵ֣י יִשְׂרָאֵ֔ל הַבָּאִ֖ים מִצְרָ֑יְמָה אֵ֣ת יַעֲקֹ֔ב אִ֥ישׁ וּבֵית֖וֹ בָּֽאוּ׃ ²רְאוּבֵ֣ן שִׁמְע֔וֹן לֵוִ֖י וִֽיהוּדָֽה׃ ³יִשָּׂשכָ֥ר זְבוּלֻ֖ן וּבִנְיָמִֽן׃ ⁴דָּ֥ן וְנַפְתָּלִ֖י גָּ֥ד וְאָשֵֽׁר׃ ⁵וַֽיְהִ֗י כָּל־נֶ֛פֶשׁ יֹצְאֵ֥י יֶֽרֶךְ־יַעֲקֹ֖ב שִׁבְעִ֣ים נָ֑פֶשׁ וְיוֹסֵ֖ף הָיָ֥ה בְמִצְרָֽיִם׃ ⁶וַיָּ֤מָת יוֹסֵף֙ וְכָל־אֶחָ֔יו וְכֹ֖ל הַדּ֥וֹר הַהֽוּא׃ ⁷וּבְנֵ֣י יִשְׂרָאֵ֗ל פָּר֧וּ וַיִּשְׁרְצ֛וּ וַיִּרְבּ֥וּ וַיַּֽעַצְמ֖וּ בִּמְאֹ֣ד מְאֹ֑ד וַתִּמָּלֵ֥א הָאָ֖רֶץ אֹתָֽם׃ פ

⁸וַיָּ֥קָם מֶֽלֶךְ־חָדָ֖שׁ עַל־מִצְרָ֑יִם אֲשֶׁ֥ר לֹֽא־יָדַ֖ע

1:5. **seventy**. Septuagint and Qumran texts read "seventy-five." The difference of five reflects Joseph's sons Ephraim and Manasseh plus Manasseh's son and Ephraim's two sons. These are named in Gen 46:20 in the Septuagint but not in the Masoretic Text. The problem is that the children of Israel are identified here in v. 1 as those "who came to Egypt," which would exclude Joseph's children and grandchildren because they do not *come* to Egypt; they are born there. But the people are identified in v. 5 as "all the persons coming out from Jacob's thigh," which would include Joseph's offspring no matter where they were born. It appears that each scribe used the number that fit what he understood to be the logic of the text.

(Small differences of a few letters in the text such as this occur throughout the Torah. They show that schemes that count the letters of the Bible in order to uncover hidden "codes" are nonsense. Such codes became popular recently but were carried out by persons who were unqualified to do this serious study of the text of the Torah in all its versions. Examination of their misuse of statistical analysis further undermined their claims, which unfortunately misled sincere people. Let us hope that the repudiation of such popular schemes will serve to remind people anew that what is great in the Torah is in what it says, not in secret patterns in its letters.)

1:8. **a new king**. There are five Pharaohs in the Torah: the Pharaoh who thought Sarah was Abraham's sister, the Pharaoh who knew Joseph, the Pharaoh who did not know Joseph, the Pharaoh who sought to kill Moses (who may or may not be the same Pharaoh who did not know Joseph), and the Pharaoh of the exodus. Why are none of their names given? Names of Pharaohs (Shishak, Neco) are given in later books. Their absence in the Torah gives the narrative a nonhistorical quality, which is contrary to the manifest aim of the Torah to present history. One might argue that this is evidence that the stories are not true, that they were made up by writers who could not name these kings because they had no idea of the names of ancient Pharaohs. In the case of the two Pharaohs in Genesis, we have hardly any evidence to argue for or

not know Joseph. ⁹And he said to his people, "Here, the people of the children of Israel is more numerous and powerful than we. ¹⁰Come on, let's be wise toward it or else it will increase; and it will be, when war will happen, that it, too, will be added to our enemies and will war against us and go up from the land."

¹¹And they set commanders of work-companies over it in order to degrade it with their burdens. And they built storage cities for Pharaoh: Pithom and Rameses. ¹²And the more they degraded it, the more it increased, and the more it expanded; and they felt a disgust at the children of Israel. ¹³And Egypt made the children of Israel serve with harshness; ¹⁴and they made their lives bitter with hard work, with mortar and with

9וַיֹּאמֶר אֶל־עַמּוֹ הִנֵּה עַם בְּנֵי יִשְׂרָאֵל רַב וְעָצוּם מִמֶּנּוּ: 10הָבָה נִתְחַכְּמָה לוֹ פֶּן־יִרְבֶּה וְהָיָה כִּי־תִקְרֶאנָה מִלְחָמָה וְנוֹסַף גַּם־הוּא עַל־שֹׂנְאֵינוּ וְנִלְחַם־בָּנוּ וְעָלָה מִן־הָאָרֶץ: 11וַיָּשִׂימוּ עָלָיו שָׂרֵי מִסִּים לְמַעַן עַנֹּתוֹ בְּסִבְלֹתָם וַיִּבֶן עָרֵי מִסְכְּנוֹת לְפַרְעֹה אֶת־פִּתֹם וְאֶת־רַעַמְסֵס: 12וְכַאֲשֶׁר יְעַנּוּ אֹתוֹ כֵּן יִרְבֶּה וְכֵן יִפְרֹץ וַיָּקֻצוּ מִפְּנֵי בְּנֵי יִשְׂרָאֵל: 13וַיַּעֲבִדוּ מִצְרַיִם אֶת־בְּנֵי יִשְׂרָאֵל בְּפָרֶךְ: 14וַיְמָרְרוּ אֶת־חַיֵּיהֶם בַּעֲבֹדָה קָשָׁה בְּחֹמֶר

---

against this. But in the case of the Exodus Pharaohs, I think that there is sufficient likelihood that the oppression and exodus are historical, so there must be some other reason why the Pharaohs are not named. My friend Jonathan Saville suggests that perhaps the reason, consciously or not, is to downgrade the Pharaoh, as when people sometimes avoid saying the name of someone toward whom they feel hostile. Or perhaps the names of the Pharaohs were no longer preserved in the tradition by the time the stories came to be written.

1:10. **will be added.** The Hebrew (נוֹסַף) is punning on the name Joseph (יוֹסֵף), meaning "may He add." The Pharaoh does not know Joseph, but when he is pictured as worrying that the people "will be added" this summons Joseph back to mind. This pun is not merely wordplay for its own sake. The notation that this is a Pharaoh who does not know Joseph makes a strong break at the beginning of Exodus from what has come before this in Genesis. The reminder of Joseph's presence reconnects this phase of the story to everything that has come before it. Even stronger connections are coming.

1:11. **work-companies.** The Hebrew term, *missîm*, refers not to individually owned household slaves but to a policy of forced labor imposed on an entire community (a corvée). The Israelites build whole cities, and they all live in a particular region of Egypt (Goshen), separate from the Egyptian population (Exod 8:18; 9:26).

Centuries later, King Solomon imposes *missîm* on Israel, requiring, in addition to monetary taxes, a period of labor on national projects. This so infuriates the Israelites that they stone to death the king's minister of *missîm* (1 Kings 5:27–28; 12:18). Israelites will bear taxation, but the requirement of forced labor implies control over people's bodies by the government. This is appalling to a people whose recollection of having been slaves is a central doctrine to their understanding of themselves and their history.

bricks and with all work in the field—all their work that they did for them—with harshness.

¹⁵And the king of Egypt said to the Hebrew midwives—of whom the name of one was Shiphrah and the name of the second was Puah— ¹⁶and he said, "When you deliver the Hebrew women, and you look at the two stones, if it's a boy then kill him, and if it's a girl then she'll live." ¹⁷And the midwives feared God and did not do what the king of Egypt had spoken to them, and they kept the boys alive. ¹⁸And the king of Egypt called the midwives and said to them, "Why have you done this thing and kept the boys alive?"

¹⁹And the midwives said to Pharaoh, "Because the Hebrews aren't like the Egyptian women, because they're animals! Before the midwife comes to them, they've given birth!"

²⁰And God was good to the midwives. And the people increased, and they became very powerful, ²¹and it was because the midwives feared God, and He made them households.

²²And Pharaoh commanded all of his people, saying, "Every son who is born: you shall throw him into the Nile. And every daughter you shall keep alive."

וּבִלְבֵנִים וּבְכָל־עֲבֹדָה בַּשָּׂדֶה אֵת כָּל־עֲבֹדָתָ֔ם
אֲשֶׁר־עָבְד֥וּ בָהֶ֖ם בְּפָֽרֶךְ: ¹⁵וַיֹּ֙אמֶר֙ מֶ֣לֶךְ מִצְרַ֔יִם
לַֽמְיַלְּדֹ֖ת הָֽעִבְרִיֹּ֑ת אֲשֶׁ֨ר שֵׁ֤ם הָֽאַחַת֙ שִׁפְרָ֔ה וְשֵׁ֥ם
הַשֵּׁנִ֖ית פּוּעָֽה: ¹⁶וַיֹּ֗אמֶר בְּיַלֶּדְכֶן֙ אֶת־הָֽעִבְרִיּ֔וֹת
וּרְאִיתֶ֖ן עַל־הָאָבְנָ֑יִם אִם־בֵּ֥ן הוּא֙ וַהֲמִתֶּ֣ן אֹת֔וֹ וְאִם־
בַּ֥ת הִ֖יא וָחָֽיָה: ¹⁷וַתִּירֶ֤אןָ הַֽמְיַלְּדֹת֙ אֶת־הָ֣אֱלֹהִ֔ים
וְלֹ֣א עָשׂ֔וּ כַּֽאֲשֶׁ֛ר דִּבֶּ֥ר אֲלֵיהֶ֖ן מֶ֣לֶךְ מִצְרָ֑יִם וַתְּחַיֶּ֖יןָ
אֶת־הַיְלָדִֽים: ¹⁸וַיִּקְרָ֤א מֶֽלֶךְ־מִצְרַ֨יִם֙ לַֽמְיַלְּדֹ֔ת
וַיֹּ֣אמֶר לָהֶ֔ן מַדּ֥וּעַ עֲשִׂיתֶ֖ן הַדָּבָ֣ר הַזֶּ֑ה וַתְּחַיֶּ֖יןָ אֶת־
הַיְלָדִֽים: ¹⁹וַתֹּאמַ֤רְןָ הַֽמְיַלְּדֹת֙ אֶל־פַּרְעֹ֔ה כִּ֣י לֹ֧א
כַנָּשִׁ֛ים הַמִּצְרִיֹּ֖ת הָֽעִבְרִיֹּ֑ת כִּֽי־חָי֣וֹת הֵ֔נָּה בְּטֶ֧רֶם
תָּב֛וֹא אֲלֵהֶ֥ן הַֽמְיַלֶּ֖דֶת וְיָלָֽדוּ: ²⁰וַיֵּ֥יטֶב אֱלֹהִ֖ים
לַֽמְיַלְּדֹ֑ת וַיִּ֧רֶב הָעָ֛ם וַיַּֽעַצְמ֖וּ מְאֹֽד: ²¹וַיְהִ֕י כִּֽי־יָֽרְא֥וּ
הַֽמְיַלְּדֹ֖ת אֶת־הָֽאֱלֹהִ֑ים וַיַּ֥עַשׂ לָהֶ֖ם בָּתִּֽים: ²²וַיְצַ֣ו
פַּרְעֹ֔ה לְכָל־עַמּ֖וֹ לֵאמֹ֑ר כָּל־הַבֵּ֣ן הַיִּלּ֗וֹד הַיְאֹ֨רָה֙
תַּשְׁלִיכֻ֔הוּ וְכָל־הַבַּ֖ת תְּחַיּֽוּן: ס

1:15. **Hebrew midwives.** The Hebrew may be read as "Hebrew midwives," meaning that these two women are Israelites; or it may be "midwives of the Hebrews," in which case one cannot know whether or not they themselves are Israelites. "Hebrew midwives" is more likely because the Israelites are never referred to as "the Hebrews" by the narrator in the Torah. It is a term used in quotation when speaking to foreigners (Gen 40:15; Exod 5:3; see the comment on Gen 14:13) or as an adjective in the fixed phrase "Hebrew slave" (see the comment on Exod 21:2). Here, too, it may be such an adjectival usage. This is supported by the fact that these names are much more likely to be Semitic than Egyptian, implying that the midwives are Israelites.

1:16. **the two stones.** This is often understood to mean some sort of birthing stool made of two stones, but the more natural understanding here in the context of identifying boys is that the two stones refer to the testicles.

1:19. **they're animals!** The vowels inserted in the Masoretic Text would make this an adjective ("they're lively"), but that form of the word does not occur anywhere else in the Bible. I think that it is more likely that the midwives are meant to be speaking in this negative way about the Israelite women in order to hide their own violation of the king's order.

2 ¹And a man from the house of Levi went and took a daughter of Levi. ²And the woman became pregnant and gave birth to a son. And she saw him, that he was good, and she concealed him for three months. ³And she was not able to conceal him anymore, and she took an ark made of bulrushes for him and smeared it with bitumen and with pitch and put the boy in it and put it in the reeds by the bank of the Nile. ⁴And his sister stood still at a distance to know what would be done to him. ⁵And the Pharaoh's daughter went down to bathe at the Nile, and her girls were going alongside the Nile, and she saw the ark among the reeds and sent her maid, and she took it. ⁶And she opened it and saw him, the child: and here was a boy crying, and she had compassion on him, and she said, "This is one of the Hebrews' children."

⁷And his sister said to Pharaoh's daughter, "Shall I go and call a nursing woman from the Hebrews for you, and she'll nurse the child for you?"

⁸And Pharaoh's daughter said to her, "Go." And the girl went and called the child's mother. ⁹And Pharaoh's daughter said to her, "Take this

2 ¹וַיֵּ֥לֶךְ אִ֖ישׁ מִבֵּ֣ית לֵוִ֑י וַיִּקַּ֖ח אֶת־בַּת־לֵוִֽי׃ ²וַתַּ֥הַר הָאִשָּׁ֖ה וַתֵּ֣לֶד בֵּ֑ן וַתֵּ֤רֶא אֹתוֹ֙ כִּי־ט֣וֹב ה֔וּא וַתִּצְפְּנֵ֖הוּ שְׁלֹשָׁ֥ה יְרָחִֽים׃ ³וְלֹא־יָכְלָ֣ה עוֹד֮ הַצְּפִינוֹ֒ וַתִּֽקַּֽח־לוֹ֙ תֵּ֣בַת גֹּ֔מֶא וַתַּחְמְרָ֥ה בַחֵמָ֖ר וּבַזָּ֑פֶת וַתָּ֤שֶׂם בָּהּ֙ אֶת־הַיֶּ֔לֶד וַתָּ֥שֶׂם בַּסּ֖וּף עַל־שְׂפַ֥ת הַיְאֹֽר׃ ⁴וַתֵּתַצַּ֥ב אֲחֹת֖וֹ מֵרָחֹ֑ק לְדֵעָ֕ה מַה־יֵּעָשֶׂ֖ה לֽוֹ׃ ⁵וַתֵּ֤רֶד בַּת־פַּרְעֹה֙ לִרְחֹ֣ץ עַל־הַיְאֹ֔ר וְנַעֲרֹתֶ֥יהָ הֹלְכֹ֖ת עַל־יַ֣ד הַיְאֹ֑ר וַתֵּ֤רֶא אֶת־הַתֵּבָה֙ בְּת֣וֹךְ הַסּ֔וּף וַתִּשְׁלַ֥ח אֶת־אֲמָתָ֖הּ וַתִּקָּחֶֽהָ׃ ⁶וַתִּפְתַּח֙ וַתִּרְאֵ֣הוּ אֶת־הַיֶּ֔לֶד וְהִנֵּה־נַ֖עַר בֹּכֶ֑ה וַתַּחְמֹ֣ל עָלָ֔יו וַתֹּ֕אמֶר מִיַּלְדֵ֥י הָֽעִבְרִ֖ים זֶֽה׃ ⁷וַתֹּ֣אמֶר אֲחֹתוֹ֮ אֶל־בַּת־פַּרְעֹה֒ הַאֵלֵ֗ךְ וְקָרָ֤אתִי לָךְ֙ אִשָּׁ֣ה מֵינֶ֔קֶת מִ֖ן הָעִבְרִיֹּ֑ת וְתֵינִ֥ק לָ֖ךְ אֶת־הַיָּֽלֶד׃ ⁸וַתֹּֽאמֶר־לָ֥הּ בַּת־פַּרְעֹ֖ה לֵ֑כִי וַתֵּ֨לֶךְ֙ הָֽעַלְמָ֔ה וַתִּקְרָ֖א אֶת־אֵ֥ם הַיָּֽלֶד׃ ⁹וַתֹּ֧אמֶר לָ֣הּ בַּת־

2:2. **gave birth to a son.** Moses is profoundly a lone figure. Although he has a family, Exodus is not about family relations and does not develop them in Moses' case. Coming on the heels of Genesis, with its long stories of families, this is striking. We learn little of Moses' mother and less of his father. The most central family relationship is between Moses and his brother Aaron, yet it plays no role in the story. Aaron need not be Moses' brother for the sake of the development of the story; their interactions usually do not depend on it at all. And Miriam, when she is first identified by name, is identified as "the sister of Aaron," rather than of Moses (15:20), and she and Moses are never pictured exchanging any words. Family members play a part in the birth story of Moses, but the account establishes, after all, not a relationship but the distance between Moses and his family; it is about his being raised by others, from another people. Moses has a family of which he is husband and father, but this just further demonstrates the point, because the text merely *reports* that he has a wife and sons. They play no role. There is no story about them except the strange story of Zipporah's circumcising their son, and it is only three verses long (4:24–26), and it is incomprehensible. (See the comment on 4:24.)

2:3. **the Nile.** The same river that means death for all the other male newborns means life for Moses.

child and nurse him for me, and I'll give your pay." And the woman took the boy and nursed him. ¹⁰And the boy grew older, and she brought him to Pharaoh's daughter, and he became her son. And she called his name Moses, and she said, "Because I drew him from the water."

פַּרְעֹה הֵילִיכִי אֶת־הַיֶּלֶד הַזֶּה וְהֵינִקִהוּ לִי וַאֲנִי אֶתֵּן אֶת־שְׂכָרֵךְ וַתִּקַּח הָאִשָּׁה הַיֶּלֶד וַתְּנִיקֵהוּ: ¹⁰וַיִּגְדַּל הַיֶּלֶד וַתְּבִאֵהוּ לְבַת־פַּרְעֹה וַיְהִי־לָהּ לְבֵן וַתִּקְרָא שְׁמוֹ מֹשֶׁה וַתֹּאמֶר כִּי מִן־הַמַּיִם מְשִׁיתִהוּ:

2:10. **Pharaoh's daughter, and he became her son**. The story is intriguingly similar to the legend of the Mesopotamian king Sargon, found in Assyrian and Babylonian texts, in which a priestess places her infant son in a basket of rushes with pitch on its exterior and casts him into the river, and a water-drawer retrieves the baby and rears him as his son. This and other literary parallels to the birth account of Moses suggest how enigmatic the biblical story is. Freud observed that such stories generally involve three steps: (1) a child is born of noble or royal lineage, (2) the child comes to be brought up as a commoner, and (3) the child grows up and eventually arrives back at his rightful place in a royal house. Freud noted that such stories were conceived etiologically, composed as justifications of cases in which commoners rose to thrones. The historical truth in such cases lay in the second step: the king really came from commoner roots. The story was composed to legitimize his kingship, as an answer to those who would deny his royal blood. Freud considered the birth story of Moses against this background and suggested the possibility that here, too, the truth behind the etiology lay in the second step, that Moses was an Egyptian, and that the birth story was composed to explain how an Egyptian had come to be the leader of the Israelites. Freud's interest (on this particular point of his larger study) was primarily historical, and his hypothesis has never been proved or disproved; but it is also important because it indicates what the Torah and its audience valued. In the Israelite story, the values are reversed. The royal house is step two, the aberration, rather than the prized position. Moses' royal placement simply is not what is important. There is no information about his early life in the Egyptian court. We are informed that he is nursed by his own mother, but we are not certain what this report is supposed to establish. We cannot even be certain that it means that Moses thus knows that he is Israelite. Later the text says that he "went out to his brothers and saw their burdens" (2:11), but this wording, too, is not definitive as to whether he knows that the Israelites are his kin. There is even ambiguity in his killing of an Egyptian taskmaster whom he sees striking a slave: is it because of his bond with the Israelites or his sense of justice? In a curious parallel to the deity Himself, Moses' background and motives are mysterious.

2:10. **she called his name Moses**. Even learned people often recall this story out of order, imagining the Pharaoh's daughter naming Moses as she draws him from the water, but she does not in fact name him until after he has grown and his mother brings him to her. What was he called until that time? Classical and recent commentators have not addressed this. Since the text does not tell us, we must assume that the concern is to explain the origin of the name Moses and that there is no interest in pursuing whether there was any prior name given by his parents. Presumably the only name known in tradition and history was Moses, and so the author was not free to

11And it was in those days, and Moses grew older, and he went out to his brothers and saw their burdens, and he saw an Egyptian man striking a Hebrew man, one of his brothers. 12And he turned this way and that way and saw that there

וַיְהִי ׀ בַּיָּמִים הָהֵם וַיִּגְדַּל מֹשֶׁה וַיֵּצֵא אֶל־אֶחָיו 11 וַיַּרְא בְּסִבְלֹתָם וַיַּרְא אִישׁ מִצְרִי מַכֶּה אִישׁ־עִבְרִי מֵאֶחָיו: 12 וַיִּפֶן כֹּה וָכֹה וַיַּרְא כִּי אֵין אִישׁ וַיַּךְ אֶת־

---

make up any other. And the story had to ascribe the naming to the Pharaoh's daughter because she was the one in power, the one who would present him to the Egyptian society, and so on. Still, we can hardly resist wondering why the parents would not be pictured as giving their son a name. If he is with them until he is weaned, that may be several years, and we can hardly resist imagining what the parents would call him. I imagine—this is my midrash—that they do not give him a name. They call him "the child" (Hebrew *hayyeled*). When they talk to him they call him "my child" (*yaldî*). And this gives those years a mysterious, portentous quality. They know that his naming simply is not in their power. And so his fate is not in their hands either. Count how many times you call your child by his or her name in a day, and you will know how many times these parents are reminded of their unique situation: thankful that their son alone is spared from death but sad and frightened that he will be raised by others, from the very household that is their enemy, and worried that he will not know who his real people and family are. From the perspective of Jewish history, this is not a singular experience. In the twentieth century Jewish parents in Europe gave their children to non-Jewish families to save them during the holocaust.

2:10. **Because I drew him**. The naming of Moses argues both for and against the story's historicity. On one hand, there is the unlikelihood of the idea that the princess would know Hebrew, let alone choose to derive the baby's name from a Hebrew etymology. And in fact the name Moses is not Hebrew. It is Egyptian, meaning "is born," as in the name Ramesses, meaning "Ra (the sun god) bore him." On the other hand, the fact that the great leader of the Israelites has an Egyptian name (as do other early priests: Phinehas, Hophni) is evidence that Israelites did indeed live for some time in Egypt. Names are valuable evidence in tracing a community's origins and history. One might suggest that the Egyptian name Moses was just made up to make the story sound authentic. But we can be fairly certain that the Israelites did not make it up, precisely because they told the story about the princess calling him Moses "because I drew him"—which shows that the Israelites were not *conscious* of the name's Egyptian meaning!

2:11. **Moses**. Although Exodus is ultimately about God, Israel, and Egypt, the narrative attention is focused on Moses from its second chapter to the end. Thus, although Exodus is about nations and extraordinary divine interventions into the course of human affairs, it directs its readers to this dynamic through the lens of an individual man. Notably, even though Exodus is not about individuals in the way that Genesis is, it introduces a figure in whom character development reaches a new level, equaled by no other figure in the Hebrew Bible except possibly David. Moses is pictured at various stages in his life, expressing a variety of moods and emotions, changing, especially in the way in which he relates and speaks to God.

was no man, and he struck the Egyptian and hid him in the sand. 13And he went out on the second day, and here were two Hebrew men fighting. And he said to the one who was in the wrong, "Why do you strike your companion?"

14And he said, "Who made you a commander and judge over us? Are you saying you'd kill me—the way you killed the Egyptian?!"

And Moses was afraid and said, "The thing is known for sure." 15And Pharaoh heard this thing and sought to kill Moses, and Moses fled from Pharaoh's presence and lived in the land of Midian.

And he sat by a well. 16And a priest of Midian had seven daughters, and they came and drew water and filled the troughs to water their father's flock, 17and the shepherds came and drove them away. And Moses got up and saved them and watered their flock. 18And they came to Reuel, their father, and he said, "Why were you so quick to come today?"

19And they said, "An Egyptian man rescued us from the shepherds' hand, and he *drew water* for us and watered the flock, too."

20And he said to his daughters, "And where is he? Why is this that you've left the man? Call him, and let him eat bread."

21And Moses was content to live with the man. And he gave Zipporah, his daughter, to Moses, 22and she gave birth to a son, and he called his name Gershom, "because," he said, "I was an alien in a foreign land."

23And it was after those many days, and the king of Egypt died.

And the children of Israel groaned from the work, and they cried out, and their wail went up to God from the work. 24And God heard their moaning, and God remembered His covenant with Abraham, with Isaac, and with Jacob. 25And God saw the children of Israel. And God knew!

הַמִּצְרִי וַיִּטְמְנֵהוּ בַּחְוֹל: 13וַיֵּצֵא בַּיּוֹם הַשֵּׁנִי וְהִנֵּה שְׁנֵי־אֲנָשִׁים עִבְרִים נִצִּים וַיֹּאמֶר לָרָשָׁע לָמָּה תַכֶּה רֵעֶךָ: 14וַיֹּאמֶר מִי שָׂמְךָ לְאִישׁ שַׂר וְשֹׁפֵט עָלֵינוּ הַלְהָרְגֵנִי אַתָּה אֹמֵר כַּאֲשֶׁר הָרַגְתָּ אֶת־הַמִּצְרִי וַיִּירָא מֹשֶׁה וַיֹּאמַר אָכֵן נוֹדַע הַדָּבָר: 15וַיִּשְׁמַע פַּרְעֹה אֶת־הַדָּבָר הַזֶּה וַיְבַקֵּשׁ לַהֲרֹג אֶת־מֹשֶׁה וַיִּבְרַח מֹשֶׁה מִפְּנֵי פַרְעֹה וַיֵּשֶׁב בְּאֶרֶץ־מִדְיָן וַיֵּשֶׁב עַל־הַבְּאֵר: 16וּלְכֹהֵן מִדְיָן שֶׁבַע בָּנוֹת וַתָּבֹאנָה וַתִּדְלֶנָה וַתְּמַלֶּאנָה אֶת־הָרְהָטִים לְהַשְׁקוֹת צֹאן אֲבִיהֶן: 17וַיָּבֹאוּ הָרֹעִים וַיְגָרְשׁוּם וַיָּקָם מֹשֶׁה וַיּוֹשִׁעָן וַיַּשְׁקְ אֶת־צֹאנָם: 18וַתָּבֹאנָה אֶל־רְעוּאֵל אֲבִיהֶן וַיֹּאמֶר מַדּוּעַ מִהַרְתֶּן בֹּא הַיּוֹם: 19וַתֹּאמַרְןָ אִישׁ מִצְרִי הִצִּילָנוּ מִיַּד הָרֹעִים וְגַם־דָּלֹה דָלָה לָנוּ וַיַּשְׁקְ אֶת־הַצֹּאן: 20וַיֹּאמֶר אֶל־בְּנֹתָיו וְאַיּוֹ לָמָּה זֶּה עֲזַבְתֶּן אֶת־הָאִישׁ קִרְאֶן לוֹ וְיֹאכַל לָחֶם: 21וַיּוֹאֶל מֹשֶׁה לָשֶׁבֶת אֶת־הָאִישׁ וַיִּתֵּן אֶת־צִפֹּרָה בִתּוֹ לְמֹשֶׁה: 22וַתֵּלֶד בֵּן וַיִּקְרָא אֶת־שְׁמוֹ גֵּרְשֹׁם כִּי אָמַר גֵּר הָיִיתִי בְּאֶרֶץ נָכְרִיָּה: פ 23וַיְהִי בַיָּמִים הָרַבִּים הָהֵם וַיָּמָת מֶלֶךְ מִצְרַיִם וַיֵּאָנְחוּ בְנֵי־יִשְׂרָאֵל מִן־הָעֲבֹדָה וַיִּזְעָקוּ וַתַּעַל שַׁוְעָתָם אֶל־הָאֱלֹהִים מִן־הָעֲבֹדָה: 24וַיִּשְׁמַע אֱלֹהִים אֶת־נַאֲקָתָם וַיִּזְכֹּר אֱלֹהִים אֶת־בְּרִיתוֹ אֶת־אַבְרָהָם אֶת־יִצְחָק וְאֶת־יַעֲקֹב: 25וַיַּרְא אֱלֹהִים אֶת־בְּנֵי יִשְׂרָאֵל וַיֵּדַע אֱלֹהִים: ס

2:23–24. **groan, cry, wail, moan.** Four different words are used in the Hebrew to describe their crying. This conveys that their agony is intense, continuous, and pervasive.

3 ¹And Moses had been shepherding the flock of Jethro, his father-in-law, priest of Midian. And he drove the flock at the far side of the wilderness, and he came to the Mountain of God, to Horeb. ²And an angel of YHWH appeared to him in a fire's flame from inside a bush. And he looked, and here: the bush was burning in the fire, and the bush was not consumed! ³And Moses said, "Let me turn and see this great sight. Why doesn't the bush burn?"

⁴And YHWH saw that he turned to see. And God called to him from inside the bush, and He said, "Moses, Moses."

And he said, "I'm here."

⁵And He said, "Don't come close here. Take off your shoes from your feet, because the place on which you're standing: it's holy ground." ⁶And He said, "I'm your father's God, Abraham's God, Isaac's God, and Jacob's God." And Moses hid his face, because he was afraid of looking at God. ⁷And YHWH said, "I've *seen* the degradation of my people who are in Egypt, and I've heard their wail on account of their taskmasters, because I know their pains. ⁸And I've come down to rescue them from Egypt's hand and to bring

ומֹשֶׁה הָיָה רֹעֶה אֶת־צֹאן יִתְרוֹ חֹתְנוֹ כֹּהֵן 3 מִדְיָן וַיִּנְהַג אֶת־הַצֹּאן אַחַר הַמִּדְבָּר וַיָּבֹא אֶל־הַר הָאֱלֹהִים חֹרֵבָה: ²וַיֵּרָא מַלְאַךְ יְהוָה אֵלָיו בְּלַבַּת־ אֵשׁ מִתּוֹךְ הַסְּנֶה וַיַּרְא וְהִנֵּה הַסְּנֶה בֹּעֵר בָּאֵשׁ וְהַסְּנֶה אֵינֶנּוּ אֻכָּל: ³וַיֹּאמֶר מֹשֶׁה אָסֻרָה־נָּא וְאֶרְאֶה אֶת־הַמַּרְאֶה הַגָּדֹל הַזֶּה מַדּוּעַ לֹא־יִבְעַר הַסְּנֶה: ⁴וַיַּרְא יְהוָה כִּי סָר לִרְאוֹת וַיִּקְרָא אֵלָיו אֱלֹהִים מִתּוֹךְ הַסְּנֶה וַיֹּאמֶר מֹשֶׁה מֹשֶׁה וַיֹּאמֶר הִנֵּנִי: ⁵וַיֹּאמֶר אַל־תִּקְרַב הֲלֹם שַׁל־נְעָלֶיךָ מֵעַל רַגְלֶיךָ כִּי הַמָּקוֹם אֲשֶׁר אַתָּה עוֹמֵד עָלָיו אַדְמַת־ קֹדֶשׁ הוּא: ⁶וַיֹּאמֶר אָנֹכִי אֱלֹהֵי אָבִיךָ אֱלֹהֵי אַבְרָהָם אֱלֹהֵי יִצְחָק וֵאלֹהֵי יַעֲקֹב וַיַּסְתֵּר מֹשֶׁה פָּנָיו כִּי יָרֵא מֵהַבִּיט אֶל־הָאֱלֹהִים: ⁷וַיֹּאמֶר יְהוָה רָאֹה רָאִיתִי אֶת־עֳנִי עַמִּי אֲשֶׁר בְּמִצְרָיִם וְאֶת־ צַעֲקָתָם שָׁמַעְתִּי מִפְּנֵי נֹגְשָׂיו כִּי יָדַעְתִּי אֶת־ מַכְאֹבָיו: ⁸וָאֵרֵד לְהַצִּילוֹ ׀ מִיַּד מִצְרַיִם וּלְהַעֲלֹתוֹ

3:1. **to the Mountain of God, to Horeb**. Horeb and Sinai are understood to be two names of the same place.

3:2. **the bush was not consumed**. Insofar as this phenomenon does not conform to the natural course of cause and effect, YHWH is understood, once again, not as a force in nature but as outside nature, manipulating it. Unlike the pagan gods, YHWH causes being. The name YHWH, which is revealed to Moses in this first meeting, means "He causes to be." That is, it is a third-person masculine singular causative form of the verb "to be." This fits with the biblical picture of the deity as the quintessential creator God, who creates light *ex nihilo*—and thus can cause burning without consumption—and who is not *in* the natural realm of existence, but rather transcends it.

3:4. **God called to him**. The text does not say why Moses is selected to bring Israel out of Egypt. As we observed in Genesis, it rarely does state the reasons that particular persons are chosen. We only know that, once Moses is chosen and commissioned, virtually the entire narrative is developed through him.

3:6. **I'm your father's God**. God's acquaintance with Moses is personal from the start. God does not introduce Himself as "I am the creator of the universe" or "I am the God of Israel," but: "I'm your *father's* God."

them up from that land to a good and wide-spread land, to a land flowing with milk and honey, to the place of the Canaanite and the Hittite and the Amorite and the Perizzite and the Hivite and the Jebusite.

9"And now, here, the cry of the children of Israel has come to me, and also I've seen the oppression that Egypt is causing them. 10And now go, and I'll send you to Pharaoh, and bring out my people, the children of Israel, from Egypt."

11And Moses said to God, "Who am I that I should go to Pharaoh and that I should bring out the children of Israel from Egypt?"

12And He said, "Because I'll be with you. And this is the sign for you that I have sent you. When you bring out the people from Egypt you shall serve God on this mountain."

מִן־הָאָ֫רֶץ הַהִוא֙ אֶל־אֶ֣רֶץ טוֹבָה֙ וּרְחָבָ֔ה אֶל־אֶ֗רֶץ זָבַ֥ת חָלָ֖ב וּדְבָ֑שׁ אֶל־מְק֤וֹם הַֽכְּנַעֲנִי֙ וְהַ֣חִתִּ֔י וְהָ֣אֱמֹרִי֙ וְהַ֣פְּרִזִּ֔י וְהַֽחִוִּ֖י וְהַיְבוּסִֽי: 9וְעַתָּ֕ה הִנֵּ֛ה צַעֲקַ֥ת בְּנֵֽי־ יִשְׂרָאֵ֖ל בָּ֣אָה אֵלָ֑י וְגַם־רָאִ֨יתִי֙ אֶת־הַלַּ֔חַץ אֲשֶׁ֥ר מִצְרַ֖יִם לֹחֲצִ֥ים אֹתָֽם: 10וְעַתָּ֣ה לְכָ֔ה וְאֶ֨שְׁלָחֲךָ֖ אֶל־ פַּרְעֹ֑ה וְהוֹצֵ֛א אֶת־עַמִּ֥י בְנֵֽי־יִשְׂרָאֵ֖ל מִמִּצְרָֽיִם: 11וַיֹּ֤אמֶר מֹשֶׁה֙ אֶל־הָ֣אֱלֹהִ֔ים מִ֣י אָנֹ֔כִי כִּ֥י אֵלֵ֖ךְ אֶל־ פַּרְעֹ֑ה וְכִ֥י אוֹצִ֛יא אֶת־בְּנֵ֥י יִשְׂרָאֵ֖ל מִמִּצְרָֽיִם: 12וַיֹּ֨אמֶר֙ כִּֽי־אֶֽהְיֶ֣ה עִמָּ֔ךְ וְזֶה־לְּךָ֣ הָא֔וֹת כִּ֥י אָנֹכִ֖י שְׁלַחְתִּ֑יךָ בְּהוֹצִֽיאֲךָ֤ אֶת־הָעָם֙ מִמִּצְרַ֔יִם תַּֽעַבְדוּן֙ אֶת־הָ֣אֱלֹהִ֔ים עַ֖ל הָהָ֥ר הַזֶּֽה: 13וַיֹּ֤אמֶר מֹשֶׁה֙ אֶל־

3:8. **the place of the Canaanite . . .** We would expect the list of the seven groups (as in Deut 7:1). Why are the Girgashites left out here (and in v. 17)? It is simply a scribal error. The Girgashites are in fact included in the Qumran, Septuagint, and Samaritan versions of this text. We should accept the fact that not every question has a deep literary or moral answer to it. Sometimes the explanation is simple, mundane, and human.

3:10. **And now *go*, and I'll send you to Pharaoh**. Until now, it has all been good news to Moses: God is aware of Israel's problems back in Egypt and is going to do something about them. But Moses still has no knowledge of why God is revealing this to *him*. Then these words come: "Go!" "I'll send *you!*" And then comes the command: "And [*you*] bring out my people!" Moses might well ask, "Who am *I*, that *I* should go?" And so he does.

3:11–12. **"Who am I?" "Because I'll be with you."** Some say that Moses' first response shows his extreme humility. But in that case, God's answer is strange: "Because I'll be with you" is not an answer to the question "Who am I?" Rather, as in the case of the exchange with Abraham over Sodom and Gomorrah, God apparently answers what is in the person's heart rather than what he says with his mouth. "Because I shall be with you" is a response to someone who is saying in his heart: "I'm afraid." Moses has just been told that *he* must do this. Now God assures him that "I'll be with you."

3:12. **this is the sign**. *What* is the sign? Is it the bush itself? Is it the fact that he hears the divine voice from the bush? Is it that he will successfully "bring the people from Egypt to serve God on this mountain"? Or is it the very fact that "I'll be with you"? We get a clue near the end of the Torah, in Deuteronomy (4:11). There Moses says that Mount Horeb "was burning"—using the same word that is used here for the burning of the bush. This suggests that the burning bush that Moses experienced was already

13And Moses said to God, "Here, I'm coming to the children of Israel, and I'll say to them, 'Your fathers' God sent me to you.' And they'll say to me, 'What is His name?' What shall I say to them?"

14And God said to Moses, "I am who I am." And He said, "You shall say this to the children of Israel: 'I Am' has sent me to you." 15And God said further to Moses, "You shall say this to the children of Israel: YHWH, your fathers' God, Abraham's God, Isaac's God, and Jacob's God has sent me to you. This is my name forever, and this is how I am to be remembered for generation after generation.

16"Go and gather Israel's elders and say to them, 'YHWH, your fathers' God, has appeared to me—the God of Abraham, Isaac, and Jacob—saying: I *have taken account* of you and what has been done to you in Egypt, 17and I say I shall

הָאֱלֹהִים הִנֵּה אָנֹכִי בָא אֶל־בְּנֵי יִשְׂרָאֵל וְאָמַרְתִּי לָהֶם אֱלֹהֵי אֲבוֹתֵיכֶם שְׁלָחַנִי אֲלֵיכֶם וְאָמְרוּ־לִי מַה־שְּׁמוֹ מָה אֹמַר אֲלֵהֶם: 14וַיֹּאמֶר אֱלֹהִים אֶל־מֹשֶׁה אֶהְיֶה אֲשֶׁר אֶהְיֶה וַיֹּאמֶר כֹּה תֹאמַר לִבְנֵי יִשְׂרָאֵל אֶהְיֶה שְׁלָחַנִי אֲלֵיכֶם: 15וַיֹּאמֶר עוֹד אֱלֹהִים אֶל־מֹשֶׁה כֹּה־תֹאמַר אֶל־בְּנֵי יִשְׂרָאֵל יְהֹוָה אֱלֹהֵי אֲבֹתֵיכֶם אֱלֹהֵי אַבְרָהָם אֱלֹהֵי יִצְחָק וֵאלֹהֵי יַעֲקֹב שְׁלָחַנִי אֲלֵיכֶם זֶה־שְּׁמִי לְעֹלָם וְזֶה זִכְרִי לְדֹר דֹּר: 16לֵךְ וְאָסַפְתָּ אֶת־זִקְנֵי יִשְׂרָאֵל וְאָמַרְתָּ אֲלֵהֶם יְהֹוָה אֱלֹהֵי אֲבֹתֵיכֶם נִרְאָה אֵלַי אֱלֹהֵי אַבְרָהָם יִצְחָק וְיַעֲקֹב לֵאמֹר פָּקֹד פָּקַדְתִּי אֶתְכֶם וְאֶת־הֶעָשׂוּי לָכֶם בְּמִצְרָיִם: 17וָאֹמַר אַעֲלֶה אֶתְכֶם

---

a sign of what was to come. And this in turn suggests that the sign to which God refers here is the miraculous burning bush itself. And it prefigures what will happen when the people come back to that mountain. This point is supported later in that same chapter in Deuteronomy when Moses reminds the people that at Horeb "you heard His voice from inside the fire" (4:36)—which recalls how Moses himself hears God call "from inside the bush" that is on fire (Exod 3:4).

3:14. **I am who I am.** (Or: "I shall be who I shall be." The imperfect verb here is not limited to present or future time.) This answer to Moses' second response is the first formal presentation of the divine name, revealed first in the first person, 'HYH, and thereafter in the third person, YHWH. It has long been uncertain why this double identification occurs here. In v. 14 God tells Moses to say "'HYH sent me," and in v. 15 God tells him to say "YHWH sent me." It appears most likely to me that the former is expressed in the first person because it is the deity's own first articulation of His identity in the world. And the second is the deity's informing Moses of the name in the form in which humans will know it forever after, naturally in the third person.

3:15. **YHWH.** The name of God is now revealed. It is a verb. It is third person. It is singular. And it is masculine. Its root meaning is "to be." It is generally understood to be a causative form. Its tense is the imperfect, and it cannot be limited to a past, present, or future time. Its nearest translation would be: He Causes To Be.

Regarding its masculine gender, we must acknowledge that all the signs indicate that biblical Israel conceived of God as male. The terms for the deity are all masculine words. The word that became most associated with a feminine aspect of deity in later Judaism, "Shechinah," does not occur in the *Tanak*.

bring you up from the degradation of Egypt to the land of the Canaanite and the Hittite and the Amorite and the Perizzite and the Hivite and the Jebusite, to a land flowing with milk and honey. [18]And they'll listen to your voice, and you'll come, you and Israel's elders, to the king of Egypt, and you'll say to him, 'YHWH, God of the Hebrews, has communicated with us. And now, let us go on a trip of three days in the wilderness so we may sacrifice to YHWH, our God.' [19]And I know that the king of Egypt won't allow you to go, and not by a strong hand, [20]and I'll put out my hand and strike Egypt with all my wonders that I'll do among them, and after that he'll let you go. [21]And I'll put this people's favor in Egypt's eyes; and it will be, when you go, you won't go empty-handed. [22]And each woman will ask for silver articles and gold articles and clothes from her neighbor and from anyone staying in her house, and you'll put them on your sons and on your daughters, and you'll despoil Egypt."

4 [1]And Moses answered, and he said, "And here, they won't believe me and won't listen to my voice, because they'll say, 'YHWH hasn't appeared to you!'"

[2]And YHWH said to him, "What's this in your hand?"

מֵעֲנִי מִצְרַיִם אֶל־אֶרֶץ הַכְּנַעֲנִי וְהַחִתִּי וְהָאֱמֹרִי וְהַפְּרִזִּי וְהַחִוִּי וְהַיְבוּסִי אֶל־אֶרֶץ זָבַת חָלָב וּדְבָשׁ: [18]וְשָׁמְעוּ לְקֹלֶךָ וּבָאתָ אַתָּה וְזִקְנֵי יִשְׂרָאֵל אֶל־ מֶלֶךְ מִצְרַיִם וַאֲמַרְתֶּם אֵלָיו יְהוָה אֱלֹהֵי הָעִבְרִיִּים נִקְרָה עָלֵינוּ וְעַתָּה נֵלֲכָה־נָּא דֶּרֶךְ שְׁלֹשֶׁת יָמִים בַּמִּדְבָּר וְנִזְבְּחָה לַיהוָה אֱלֹהֵינוּ: [19]וַאֲנִי יָדַעְתִּי כִּי לֹא־יִתֵּן אֶתְכֶם מֶלֶךְ מִצְרַיִם לַהֲלֹךְ וְלֹא בְּיָד חֲזָקָה: [20]וְשָׁלַחְתִּי אֶת־יָדִי וְהִכֵּיתִי אֶת־מִצְרַיִם בְּכֹל נִפְלְאֹתַי אֲשֶׁר אֶעֱשֶׂה בְּקִרְבּוֹ וְאַחֲרֵי־כֵן יְשַׁלַּח אֶתְכֶם: [21]וְנָתַתִּי אֶת־חֵן הָעָם־הַזֶּה בְּעֵינֵי מִצְרַיִם וְהָיָה כִּי תֵלֵכוּן לֹא תֵלְכוּ רֵיקָם: [22]וְשָׁאֲלָה אִשָּׁה מִשְּׁכֶנְתָּהּ וּמִגָּרַת בֵּיתָהּ כְּלֵי־כֶסֶף וּכְלֵי זָהָב וּשְׂמָלֹת וְשַׂמְתֶּם עַל־בְּנֵיכֶם וְעַל־בְּנֹתֵיכֶם וְנִצַּלְתֶּם אֶת־מִצְרַיִם:

4 [1]וַיַּעַן מֹשֶׁה וַיֹּאמֶר וְהֵן לֹא־יַאֲמִינוּ לִי וְלֹא יִשְׁמְעוּ בְּקֹלִי כִּי יֹאמְרוּ לֹא־נִרְאָה אֵלֶיךָ יְהוָה: [2]וַיֹּאמֶר אֵלָיו יְהוָה מַזֶּה בְיָדֶךָ וַיֹּאמֶר מַטֶּה:

ק מַה־זֶּה 4:2

4:1. **they won't listen to my voice.** Moses' third response is surprising because he appears to doubt, even to contradict, what God has already told him explicitly. YHWH instructs him to gather the elders of Israel and tell them that their ancestors' God has appeared to him and is going to take them out of Egypt, and YHWH informs him directly that *"They'll listen to your voice"* (3:18). God then goes on for five verses with details of what Moses should say to the king of Egypt, what the king's response will be, what YHWH will do in return, and how Israel will leave and despoil Egypt. But Moses, appearing to have missed the content of these last five verses, questions the earlier point, the last point that directly referred to him himself. He says, "And here, they won't believe me and won't listen to my voice" (4:1). This can also be understood to mean "And *what if* they will not believe me and will not listen to my voice." Even on this understanding, it is remarkable. Either way, it is depicting Moses as questioning what God has just told him. When God Himself tells a human, "They'll listen to you," we do not normally expect the human to say, "But what if they don't?" Again YHWH does not answer the question but instead responds directly to the problem at hand. That is, instead of telling Moses what to do if they do not listen, God gives Moses three miraculous signs, which will guarantee that they *will* listen.

And he said, "A staff."

³And He said, "Throw it to the ground."

And he threw it to the ground. And it became a snake! And Moses fled from it.

⁴And YHWH said to Moses, "Put out your hand and take hold of its tail."

And he put out his hand and held onto it, and it became a staff in his hand.

⁵"So that they will believe that YHWH, their fathers' God, Abraham's God, Isaac's God, and Jacob's God, has appeared to you!"

⁶And YHWH said to him further, "Bring your hand into your bosom."

And he brought his hand into his bosom. And he brought it out; and, here, his hand was leprous like snow!

⁷And He said, "Put your hand back to your bosom."

And he put his hand back to his bosom. And he brought it out from his bosom; and, here, it had gone back like its flesh.

⁸"And it will be, if they won't believe you and won't listen to the voice of the first sign, then they'll believe the voice of the latter one. ⁹And it will be, if they also won't believe in these two signs and won't listen to your voice, then you'll take some of the water of the Nile and spill it on the dry ground. And it will be water that you'll take from the Nile, and it will become blood on the dry ground."

¹⁰And Moses said to YHWH, "Please, my Lord, I'm not a man of words. Neither yesterday nor the day before—nor since you spoke to your servant! Because I'm heavy of mouth and heavy of tongue."

וַיֹּאמֶר֩ הַשְׁלִיכֵ֨הוּ אַ֜רְצָה וַיַּשְׁלִיכֵ֤הוּ אַ֙רְצָה֙ וַיְהִ֣י ³
לְנָחָ֔שׁ וַיָּ֥נׇס מֹשֶׁ֖ה מִפָּנָֽיו׃ ⁴וַיֹּ֤אמֶר יְהֹוָה֙ אֶל־מֹשֶׁ֔ה
שְׁלַח֙ יָ֣דְךָ֔ וֶאֱחֹ֖ז בִּזְנָב֑וֹ וַיִּשְׁלַ֤ח יָדוֹ֙ וַיַּ֣חֲזֶק בּ֔וֹ וַיְהִ֥י
לְמַטֶּ֖ה בְּכַפּֽוֹ׃ ⁵לְמַ֣עַן יַאֲמִ֔ינוּ כִּֽי־נִרְאָ֥ה אֵלֶ֖יךָ יְהֹוָ֑ה
אֱלֹהֵ֣י אֲבֹתָ֑ם אֱלֹהֵ֧י אַבְרָהָ֛ם אֱלֹהֵ֥י יִצְחָ֖ק וֵאלֹהֵ֥י
יַעֲקֹֽב׃ ⁶וַיֹּ֩אמֶר֩ יְהֹוָ֨ה ל֜וֹ ע֗וֹד הָֽבֵא־נָ֤א יָֽדְךָ֙ בְּחֵיקֶ֔ךָ
וַיָּבֵ֥א יָד֖וֹ בְּחֵיק֑וֹ וַיּ֣וֹצִאָ֔הּ וְהִנֵּ֥ה יָד֖וֹ מְצֹרַ֥עַת כַּשָּֽׁלֶג׃
⁷וַיֹּ֗אמֶר הָשֵׁ֤ב יָֽדְךָ֙ אֶל־חֵיקֶ֔ךָ וַיָּ֥שֶׁב יָד֖וֹ אֶל־חֵיק֑וֹ
וַיּֽוֹצִאָהּ֙ מֵֽחֵיק֔וֹ וְהִנֵּה־שָׁ֖בָה כִּבְשָׂרֽוֹ׃ ⁸וְהָיָה֙ אִם־לֹ֣א
יַאֲמִ֣ינוּ לָ֔ךְ וְלֹ֣א יִשְׁמְע֔וּ לְקֹ֖ל הָאֹ֣ת הָרִאשׁ֑וֹן
וְהֶֽאֱמִ֔ינוּ לְקֹ֖ל הָאֹ֥ת הָאַחֲרֽוֹן׃ ⁹וְהָיָ֡ה אִם־לֹ֣א
יַאֲמִ֡ינוּ גַּם֩ לִשְׁנֵ֨י הָאֹת֜וֹת הָאֵ֗לֶּה וְלֹ֤א יִשְׁמְעוּן֙
לְקֹלֶ֔ךָ וְלָקַחְתָּ֙ מִמֵּימֵ֣י הַיְאֹ֔ר וְשָׁפַכְתָּ֖ הַיַּבָּשָׁ֑ה וְהָי֤וּ
הַמַּ֙יִם֙ אֲשֶׁ֣ר תִּקַּ֣ח מִן־הַיְאֹ֔ר וְהָי֥וּ לְדָ֖ם בַּיַּבָּֽשֶׁת׃
¹⁰וַיֹּ֨אמֶר מֹשֶׁ֣ה אֶל־יְהֹוָה֮ בִּ֣י אֲדֹנָי֒ לֹא֩ אִ֨ישׁ דְּבָרִ֜ים
אָנֹ֗כִי גַּ֤ם מִתְּמוֹל֙ גַּ֣ם מִשִּׁלְשֹׁ֔ם גַּ֛ם מֵאָ֥ז דַּבֶּרְךָ֖ אֶל־
עַבְדֶּ֑ךָ כִּ֧י כְבַד־פֶּ֛ה וּכְבַ֥ד לָשׁ֖וֹן אָנֹֽכִי׃ ¹¹וַיֹּ֨אמֶר

4:9. **two signs.** The two signs are that the staff becomes a snake and his hand becomes leprous as snow. Why these two things? They foreshadow coming events: the snake on a pole (Num 21:5–9) and Miriam's being leprous as snow (Num 12:10).

4:10. **I'm not a man of words.** These words, Moses' fourth response, will reverberate at the beginning of Moses' last speech. (See the comment on Deut 1:1.)

4:10. **heavy of mouth and heavy of tongue.** This is frequently taken to mean some sort of speech defect. It is frequently translated as "slow of speech"; and a famous

11And YHWH said to him, "Who set a mouth for humans? Or who will set a mute or deaf or seeing or blind? Is it not I, YHWH? 12And now go, and *I'll* be with your mouth, and I'll instruct you what you shall speak."

יְהֹוָה אֵלָיו מִי שָׂם פֶּה לָאָדָם אוֹ מִי־יָשׂוּם אִלֵּם אוֹ חֵרֵשׁ אוֹ פִקֵּחַ אוֹ עִוֵּר הֲלֹא אָנֹכִי יְהֹוָה: 12וְעַתָּה לֵךְ וְאָנֹכִי אֶהְיֶה עִם־פִּיךָ וְהוֹרֵיתִיךָ אֲשֶׁר תְּדַבֵּר:

---

midrash goes so far as to recount the origin of Moses' speech impediment in a story that pictures him burning his tongue in his infancy in the Egyptian palace. More cautiously, we are best advised to seek the meaning of a biblical idiom by, first of all, observing where else it occurs in Scripture. "Heavy of tongue" occurs in one other place, Ezek 3:5–7. There YHWH tells Ezekiel that he is not being sent to peoples who are "deep of lip and heavy of tongue," whose words Ezekiel cannot understand. YHWH says, ironically, that such peoples would listen, but the house of Israel will not listen! In that context, "heavy of tongue" refers to nations who speak foreign languages. It has therefore been suggested that Moses' protest here in Exodus is that he does not speak Egyptian. This is difficult to defend, though, given the explicit report in Exodus 2 that Moses has been raised in the Egyptian court. Still, the meaning of "heavy of tongue" as referring to speaking a foreign language fits our context in Exodus 4, I believe, because YHWH has told Moses to gather and speak to *the elders of Israel*. Moses' protest may perhaps be best understood, then, as being on the grounds that he does not yet speak *Hebrew!* God's response in fact confirms that the problem for Moses is speaking "to the people," not to the Egyptians (4:16). And the final confirmation is that in the first meeting with the people's elders "*Aaron* spoke all the words that YHWH had spoken to Moses" (4:30); but in the first meeting with *Pharaoh*, both Moses and Aaron speak (5:1,3).

4:10. **nor since you spoke to your servant**. Another understanding of "I'm not a man of words" and "heavy of mouth and heavy of tongue" is that Moses is saying that he is not eloquent. And this is a wonderful irony, because his humble wording here is in fact an eloquent formulation ("Neither yesterday nor the day before—nor since you spoke to your servant!"). Moses, as it were, undermines his own denial.

Whether "heavy of mouth and heavy of tongue" means a speech defect, a foreign language, or a lack of eloquence, a question remains: why choose a man who has a speaking problem for a task that requires speaking?! The lesson may be (as with Jacob) that God can work through anyone. Or it may be that it takes divine insight to comprehend what would make someone the best person for a task. Perhaps it is precisely Moses' heaviness of mouth that makes his acts most impressive in Egypt, rather than their being performed by a person who heralds each of the miraculous plagues with a grand speech. And perhaps such a greater speaker would shift the focus too much from God to the human himself. Also, one can learn from the divine choice that one should not judge a person's ability to do a task too hastily or by the most obvious characteristics. Even an individual who has a disadvantage may be the best suited to be successful.

4:12. **I'll be**. Hebrew 'HYH. Note the significance of the first recurrence of the word here. It also came in 3:12, before the revelation of the divine name. It will come again

13And he said, "Please, my Lord, send by the hand you'll send."

14And YHWH's anger flared at Moses, and He said, "Isn't Aaron your Levite brother? I knew that *he* will *speak!* And also here he is, coming out toward you! And he'll see you and be happy in his heart. 15And you'll speak to him and set

13וַיֹּאמֶר בִּי אֲדֹנָי שְׁלַח־נָא בְּיַד־תִּשְׁלָח: 14וַיִּחַר־אַף יְהוָה בְּמֹשֶׁה וַיֹּאמֶר הֲלֹא אַהֲרֹן אָחִיךָ הַלֵּוִי יָדַעְתִּי כִּי־דַבֵּר יְדַבֵּר הוּא וְגַם הִנֵּה־הוּא יֹצֵא לִקְרָאתֶךָ וְרָאֲךָ וְשָׂמַח בְּלִבּוֹ: 15וְדִבַּרְתָּ אֵלָיו

---

in 4:15. So the answer to Moses' first, second, third, and fourth responses is, in essence, the same: 'HYH. I Am. I'll Be with you.

4:13. send by the hand you'll send. There are two opposite meanings that this strange clause may have. It may mean: send whoever—which is to say, anyone but me. Or it may mean that Moses now acquiesces to the divine will, in the sense of "Very well, then, send the one you want." The fact that God is angry at Moses in the next verse fits more naturally with the former meaning. In either case, the one common element of the two meanings is: they both denote that Moses is out of excuses. God has nullified each of his four attempts to avoid this task. He can only acquiesce or beg off. He cannot raise problems or objections. This is also further evidence that fear of the task is what has motivated Moses all along. He is forced now to the essential point. It is not "Who am I" or "What shall I tell them?" or "They won't believe me." It is Moses' reluctance about the hand whom God has chosen to send.

Through all five responses, Moses' reluctance stands out and perhaps comes as a surprise to many who find it difficult to imagine someone's receiving a prophetic commission directly from God and trying to avoid it. Yet this image of the reluctant prophet recurs in several other places in the Bible (Elijah, Jonah, Jeremiah). It does not appear to me to be simply a recurring literary motif in the way that some understand, for example, the "wise courtier" theme. It seems rather to reflect a shared conviction, by a number of the biblical authors, that it is not necessarily an honor or a joy to be a prophet. It is a burden, almost beyond human endurance. Here, in the book that introduces the role of the prophet as the individual who brings a revelation to a community, we learn from the beginning that this is not attractive. To hear the voice of God is frightening. To experience the divine power is terrifying. To deliver a divine message to the community is thankless, frustrating, and occasionally even dangerous.

4:14. your Levite brother. This means a fellow Levite. The text does not yet identify Aaron as Moses' actual brother. That is not stated explicitly until Exod 6:20. After that, Aaron is referred to as "your brother" (7:1,2) and never again as "your Levite brother."

4:14. I knew that *he* will *speak!* This has usually been taken to mean only that God is aware that Aaron is a capable speaker. But the tenses and context possibly indicate that it is much stronger: that God is informing Moses that He knew all along that Aaron would have to do the talking for Moses. This would only be a case of divine foreknowledge (knowing something in advance), not of God preordaining or manipulating human affairs. This in turn opens the question of why God would be angry at

the words in his mouth, and I, I shall be with your mouth and with his mouth, and I shall instruct you what you shall do. ¹⁶And *he* will speak for you to the people. And it will be: he will become a mouth for you, and you will become a god for him! ¹⁷And you shall take this staff in your hand, by which you'll do the signs."

¹⁸And Moses went.

And he went back to Jether, his father-in-law, and said to him, "Let me go so I may go back to my brothers who are in Egypt and see if they're still living."

And Jethro said to Moses, "Go in peace."

¹⁹And YHWH said to Moses in Midian, "Go. Go back to Egypt, because all the people who sought your life have died." ²⁰And Moses took his wife and his sons and rode them on an ass, and he went back to the land of Egypt. And Moses took the staff of God in his hand. ²¹And YHWH said to Moses, "When you're going to go back to Egypt, see all the wonders that I've set in your hand, and you shall do them in front of Pharaoh. And I: I'll strengthen his heart, and he won't let the people go. ²²And you shall say to Pharaoh, 'YHWH said this: My child, my firstborn, is Israel. ²³And I've said to you: Let my

וְשַׂמְתָּ אֶת־הַדְּבָרִים בְּפִיו וְאָנֹכִי אֶהְיֶה עִם־פִּיךָ
וְעִם־פִּיהוּ וְהוֹרֵיתִי אֶתְכֶם אֵת אֲשֶׁר תַּעֲשׂוּן:
¹⁶וְדִבֶּר־הוּא לְךָ אֶל־הָעָם וְהָיָה הוּא יִהְיֶה־לְּךָ
לְפֶה וְאַתָּה תִּהְיֶה־לּוֹ לֵאלֹהִים: ¹⁷וְאֶת־הַמַּטֶּה הַזֶּה
תִּקַּח בְּיָדֶךָ אֲשֶׁר תַּעֲשֶׂה־בּוֹ אֶת־הָאֹתֹת: פ
¹⁸וַיֵּלֶךְ מֹשֶׁה וַיָּשָׁב ׀ אֶל־יֶתֶר חֹתְנוֹ וַיֹּאמֶר לוֹ
אֵלְכָה נָּא וְאָשׁוּבָה אֶל־אַחַי אֲשֶׁר־בְּמִצְרַיִם וְאֶרְאֶה
הַעוֹדָם חַיִּים וַיֹּאמֶר יִתְרוֹ לְמֹשֶׁה לֵךְ לְשָׁלוֹם:
¹⁹וַיֹּאמֶר יְהוָה אֶל־מֹשֶׁה בְּמִדְיָן לֵךְ שֻׁב מִצְרָיִם
כִּי־מֵתוּ כָּל־הָאֲנָשִׁים הַמְבַקְשִׁים אֶת־נַפְשֶׁךָ: ²⁰וַיִּקַּח
מֹשֶׁה אֶת־אִשְׁתּוֹ וְאֶת־בָּנָיו וַיַּרְכִּבֵם עַל־הַחֲמֹר
וַיָּשָׁב אַרְצָה מִצְרָיִם וַיִּקַּח מֹשֶׁה אֶת־מַטֵּה הָאֱלֹהִים
בְּיָדוֹ: ²¹וַיֹּאמֶר יְהוָה אֶל־מֹשֶׁה בְּלֶכְתְּךָ לָשׁוּב
מִצְרַיְמָה רְאֵה כָּל־הַמֹּפְתִים אֲשֶׁר־שַׂמְתִּי בְיָדֶךָ
וַעֲשִׂיתָם לִפְנֵי פַרְעֹה וַאֲנִי אֲחַזֵּק אֶת־לִבּוֹ וְלֹא
יְשַׁלַּח אֶת־הָעָם: ²²וְאָמַרְתָּ אֶל־פַּרְעֹה כֹּה אָמַר
יְהוָה בְּנִי בְכֹרִי יִשְׂרָאֵל: ²³וָאֹמַר אֵלֶיךָ שַׁלַּח אֶת־

Moses' protest. The ambiguity here is tied to the complexity of Hebrew verb tenses (which are not simply past, present, and future, as they are often taught), and so the meaning of this verse remains uncertain.

4:16. **you will become a god for him**. No matter how figuratively we take this image, it is extraordinary. To speak of a human, Moses, in terms of the divine is awesome, and it will recur later when God tells Moses, "I've made you a *god* to Pharaoh!" (7:1). The idea that Moses will in any way be godlike in other humans' perceptions sets up a theme that will continue after the exodus: Moses must repeatedly insist to the people that their complaints are against God and not against *him*. This in turn recalls Joseph's insistence to the wine steward, the baker, and Pharaoh that "Not I. *God* will answer . . . " (Gen 41:16).

4:18. **Jether**. His name is Jethro. The change to *yeter* here may be part of a wordplay to come later (10:5; see the comment there).

4:22. **My child, my firstborn, is Israel**. God tells Moses to say this to Pharaoh, but Moses is never reported as saying it. He also is never reported as saying the rest of this message: "Should you refuse to let it go, here: I'm killing your child, your firstborn!"

child go and serve me. And should you refuse to let it go, here: I'm killing your child, your first-born!'"

24And he was on the way, at a lodging place, and YHWH met him, and he asked to kill him. 25And Zipporah took a flint and cut her son's foreskin and touched his feet, and she said, "Because you're a bridegroom of blood to me."

בְּנִי וַיְעַבְדֵנִי וַתְּמָאֵן לְשַׁלְּחוֹ הִנֵּה אָנֹכִי הֹרֵג אֶת־בִּנְךָ בְּכֹרֶךָ: 24וַיְהִי בַדֶּרֶךְ בַּמָּלוֹן וַיִּפְגְּשֵׁהוּ יְהֹוָה וַיְבַקֵּשׁ הֲמִיתוֹ: 25וַתִּקַּח צִפֹּרָה צֹר וַתִּכְרֹת אֶת־עָרְלַת בְּנָהּ וַתַּגַּע לְרַגְלָיו וַתֹּאמֶר כִּי חֲתַן־דָּמִים אַתָּה לִי: 26וַיִּרֶף

Why does he not say this to Pharaoh? It is apparently because his first words to Pharaoh do not work. Moses begins by speaking strongly to Pharaoh: "YHWH said, 'Let my people go.'" But Pharaoh, unmoved, replies, "I don't know YHWH, and I won't let Israel go." Moses then changes his approach dramatically. He starts over and this time does not use the commanding wording (the imperative), but rather the polite particle of request (Hebrew *nā'*) and the gentler form: "please that we might go" (the cohortative). Moses has backed off somewhat and taken a more conciliatory approach rather than taking the even tougher approach of threatening Pharaoh with the death of his own son. This conciliatory wording is given to Moses at the burning bush as well (3:18), so it appears that God is giving Moses both the tough and the gentle options. In any negotiation—in law, business, or any human relationship, including marriage—one must use wisdom to know when to exercise each approach.

4:24. **he asked to kill him**. No one knows what the episode at the lodging place means. The explanation that accounts for more of the connections than any other is that of my colleague William Propp: The reason that God seeks to put Moses to death is because Moses still bears the bloodguilt for having killed an Egyptian. The blood of the circumcision serves to expiate the guilt, making it possible for Moses to live and return to Egypt. The word for "blood" in this story is the plural *dāmîm*, which is usually associated with bloodguilt. The word for "bridegroom" also means "circumcision" in Arabic (and in some cultures circumcision is performed just before marriage). Propp suggests that the original bridegroom/circumcision connection had been lost by the time this story was composed, and so it was created to explain an old expression: *ḥătan dāmîm*, "bridegroom of blood." Also, this use of blood to avert death is a foreshadowing of the tenth plague in Egypt.

Still, like all explanations I have seen, this leaves the question of why God would choose Moses, make a miraculous appearance to him, insist on his going to Egypt despite his five attempts to avoid it, and then seek to kill him. I therefore understand the confused use of the pronoun "he" in this story in a different way. All commentators recognize that it is unclear when it refers to God, to Moses, or to Moses' son. But they all take the *first* "he" to refer to God: He (God) sought to kill Moses. I am raising the possibility (reflected in my translation: "he asked to kill him") that it means that Moses is asking God to take his life (rather than send him to Egypt). This is consistent with another time in Moses' life when he will ask God to kill him (Num 11:15, where he says emphatically: "*Kill* me!"). And it fits with a model of prophets who ask God to take their lives—Elijah (1 Kings 19:4) and Jonah (4:4)—or say that they prefer

184

26And he held back from Him. Then she said, "A bridegroom of blood for circumcisions."

27And YHWH said to Aaron, "Go toward Moses, to the wilderness." And he went, and he met him in the Mountain of God, and he kissed him. 28And Moses told Aaron all YHWH's words that He had sent him and all the signs that He had commanded him. 29And Moses went, and Aaron, and they gathered all the elders of the children of Israel, 30and Aaron spoke all the words that YHWH had spoken to Moses. And he did the signs before the people's eyes. 31And the people believed, and they heard that YHWH had taken account of the children of Israel and that He had seen their degradation. And they knelt and bowed.

5 1And after that Moses and Aaron came and said to Pharaoh, "YHWH, God of Israel, said

מִמֶּנּוּ אָז אָמְרָה חֲתַן דָּמִים לַמּוּלֹת: פ

27וַיֹּאמֶר יְהוָה אֶל־אַהֲרֹן לֵךְ לִקְרַאת מֹשֶׁה הַמִּדְבָּרָה וַיֵּלֶךְ וַיִּפְגְּשֵׁהוּ בְּהַר הָאֱלֹהִים וַיִּשַּׁק־לוֹ: 28וַיַּגֵּד מֹשֶׁה לְאַהֲרֹן אֵת כָּל־דִּבְרֵי יְהוָה אֲשֶׁר שְׁלָחוֹ וְאֵת כָּל־הָאֹתֹת אֲשֶׁר צִוָּהוּ: 29וַיֵּלֶךְ מֹשֶׁה וְאַהֲרֹן וַיַּאַסְפוּ אֶת־כָּל־זִקְנֵי בְּנֵי יִשְׂרָאֵל: 30וַיְדַבֵּר אַהֲרֹן אֵת כָּל־הַדְּבָרִים אֲשֶׁר־דִּבֶּר יְהוָה אֶל־מֹשֶׁה וַיַּעַשׂ הָאֹתֹת לְעֵינֵי הָעָם: 31וַיַּאֲמֵן הָעָם וַיִּשְׁמְעוּ כִּי־פָקַד יְהוָה אֶת־בְּנֵי יִשְׂרָאֵל וְכִי רָאָה אֶת־עָנְיָם וַיִּקְּדוּ וַיִּשְׁתַּחֲווּ:

5 1וְאַחַר בָּאוּ מֹשֶׁה וְאַהֲרֹן וַיֹּאמְרוּ אֶל־פַּרְעֹה כֹּה־אָמַר יְהוָה אֱלֹהֵי יִשְׂרָאֵל שַׁלַּח אֶת־עַמִּי וְיָחֹגּוּ

---

death to being prophets—Jeremiah (20:14–18). (Note that these are the same three prophets who, like Moses, are famous for being reluctant; see the comment on 4:13.)

If Moses is seeking his own death here, then Zipporah's action might be understood as her passionate response to her husband's wish to die: You have a wife! You have a son, who should live to marry and be a part of the covenant!

4:26. **And he held back from Him.** Meaning that Moses stopped asking God to kill him.

5:1. **Moses and Aaron came and said to Pharaoh.** It is against the background of the confrontation between Moses and God at the bush that we must picture the confrontation between Moses and the Pharaoh. The narrative that precedes the burning-bush scene gives us relatively little background of the sort that would add depth and understanding of the character of Moses at the point of his meeting God. Moses' meeting with the Pharaoh, on the other hand, comes after we have seen him in conversation with the deity. That scene has revealed facets of his character, both strengths and weaknesses, that are now a part of the figure of Moses as he arrives on the scene of human affairs. Moreover, the encounter with God can hardly be disregarded itself as having impacted upon Moses' personality. He has received more than the three miracles with which to impress the Israelites and the Pharaoh. He has spoken with God. Presumably, setting foot on the floor of the palace is different after one has set foot on holy ground, and conversing with a king is different after one has conversed with the creator. Exodus leads us through a series of dynamics as Moses confronts, first, the deity, then a king, and then a community, with each dynamic growing more complicated as it becomes richer in background.

this: 'Let my people go, so they will celebrate a festival for me in the wilderness.'"

²And Pharaoh said, "Who is YHWH that I should listen to His voice, to let Israel go?! I don't know YHWH, and also I won't let Israel go."

³And they said, "The God of the Hebrews has communicated with us. Let us go on a trip of three days in the wilderness so we may sacrifice to YHWH, our God, or else He'll strike us with an epidemic or with the sword."

⁴And the king of Egypt said to them, "Why, Moses and Aaron, do you turn the people loose from its work? Go to your burdens!" ⁵And Pha-

לִי בַּמִּדְבָּר: ²וַיֹּאמֶר פַּרְעֹה מִי יְהֹוָה אֲשֶׁר אֶשְׁמַע
בְּקֹלוֹ לְשַׁלַּח אֶת־יִשְׂרָאֵל לֹא יָדַעְתִּי אֶת־יְהֹוָה וְגַם
אֶת־יִשְׂרָאֵל לֹא אֲשַׁלֵּחַ: ³וַיֹּאמְרוּ אֱלֹהֵי הָעִבְרִים
נִקְרָא עָלֵינוּ נֵלֲכָה נָּא דֶּרֶךְ שְׁלֹשֶׁת יָמִים בַּמִּדְבָּר
וְנִזְבְּחָה לַיהֹוָה אֱלֹהֵינוּ פֶּן־יִפְגָּעֵנוּ בַּדֶּבֶר אוֹ
בֶחָרֶב: ⁴וַיֹּאמֶר אֲלֵהֶם מֶלֶךְ מִצְרַיִם לָמָּה
מֹשֶׁה וְאַהֲרֹן תַּפְרִיעוּ אֶת־הָעָם מִמַּעֲשָׂיו לְכוּ

5:2. **Who is YHWH.** The issue of YHWH's becoming known, which is to become a major component of subsequent books, begins in Exodus. In Genesis, YHWH is known personally only to a few individuals and to no nations. God's actions in the world are not *identifiably* God's. That is, the narrator informs the reader that it is YHWH who brings the flood, but the masses of humans in the narrative are not portrayed as being aware of the source of their catastrophe. There is likewise no suggestion that the generation of the tower of Babylon know whose force is confounding and scattering them. The same is true of the victims of the destruction of Sodom and Gomorrah, and the only eyewitness turns to salt. Joseph informs the Pharaoh that it is God who brings his dream, who makes its interpretation known, and who is the cause of the events that it reveals; but Joseph refers to the deity only generically, as "God." He is never pictured as revealing to the Egyptians the name of the deity who is at work (Gen 41:16,25,28,32). In Exodus, however, YHWH makes His presence known to Israel, to Egypt, and to other inhabitants of the region (Exod 15:14–15). The Egyptian king's first words to Moses are, "Who is YHWH . . . ? I don't know YHWH" (5:2). By the end of the story he knows.

5:3. **Let us go on a trip of three days**. Moses and Aaron do not ask for the Israelites' liberation from Egypt. They ask only to make a three-day sacrificial pilgrimage. They just do not mention the fact that they do not plan to return!

5:3. **strike**. The word here (Hebrew *pg'*) is the same as the word for the Israelites' "meeting" Moses later in v. 20. The range of meanings of this root makes a wordplay that is enhanced by clustering with the blatant pun in the next verse.

5:3. **strike us**. Moses and Aaron say that God may strike "us," the Israelites, if they don't go to sacrifice to Him, but the Hebrew suffix has a subtle double meaning: it can also mean "strike him"—which could apply to Pharaoh himself or to a nonspecific person, that is, to the Egyptians who will in fact suffer the plagues. The double meaning here is not merely playful but meaningful to the context.

5:4. **turn loose**. With the Hebrew root *pr'*, this is a pun on "Pharaoh." An even

raoh said, "Here, the people of the land are now many, and you've made them cease from their burdens." 6And Pharaoh commanded the taskmasters among the people and its officers in that day, saying, 7"You shall not continue to give straw to the people to make bricks as yesterday and the day before. *They* shall go and collect straw for themselves. 8And you shall impose on them the quota of the bricks that they were making yesterday and the day before. You shall not subtract from it. Because they're lazy. On account of this they're crying, saying, 'Let us go and sacrifice to our God.' 9Let the work be heavy on the people, and let them do it, and let them not pay attention to words that are a lie!"

10And the people's taskmasters and its officers went out and said to the people, saying, "Pharaoh said this: 'I am not giving you straw. 11You, go, take straw for yourselves from wherever you'll find it, because not a thing is subtracted from your work.'"

לְסַבְלֹתֵיכֶם: 5וַיֹּאמֶר פַּרְעֹה הֵן־רַבִּים עַתָּה עַם הָאָרֶץ וְהִשְׁבַּתֶּם אֹתָם מִסִּבְלֹתָם: 6וַיְצַו פַּרְעֹה בַּיּוֹם הַהוּא אֶת־הַנֹּגְשִׂים בָּעָם וְאֶת־שֹׁטְרָיו לֵאמֹר: 7לֹא תֹאסִפוּן לָתֵת תֶּבֶן לָעָם לִלְבֹּן הַלְּבֵנִים כִּתְמוֹל שִׁלְשֹׁם הֵם יֵלְכוּ וְקֹשְׁשׁוּ לָהֶם תֶּבֶן: 8וְאֶת־מַתְכֹּנֶת הַלְּבֵנִים אֲשֶׁר הֵם עֹשִׂים תְּמוֹל שִׁלְשֹׁם תָּשִׂימוּ עֲלֵיהֶם לֹא תִגְרְעוּ מִמֶּנּוּ כִּי־נִרְפִּים הֵם עַל־כֵּן הֵם צֹעֲקִים לֵאמֹר נֵלְכָה נִזְבְּחָה לֵאלֹהֵינוּ: 9תִּכְבַּד הָעֲבֹדָה עַל־הָאֲנָשִׁים וְיַעֲשׂוּ־בָהּ וְאַל־יִשְׁעוּ בְּדִבְרֵי־שָׁקֶר: 10וַיֵּצְאוּ נֹגְשֵׂי הָעָם וְשֹׁטְרָיו וַיֹּאמְרוּ אֶל־הָעָם לֵאמֹר כֹּה אָמַר פַּרְעֹה אֵינֶנִּי נֹתֵן לָכֶם תֶּבֶן: 11אַתֶּם לְכוּ קְחוּ לָכֶם תֶּבֶן מֵאֲשֶׁר תִּמְצָאוּ כִּי אֵין נִגְרָע מֵעֲבֹדַתְכֶם דָּבָר: 12וַיָּפֶץ הָעָם בְּכָל־

---

stronger play on this word will occur later, in the middle of the golden calf episode (Exod 32:25).

5:4. **Go to your burdens!** He talks down to Moses and Aaron, telling them to get back to work, and thus conveying to them that they are just slaves like everyone else.

5:5. **cease.** This is the term that describes God's ceasing on the seventh day of creation, Hebrew *šbt*, cognate to the word "Sabbath."

5:9. **Let the work be heavy**. The idiom of Moses' "heavy mouth and heavy tongue" initiates a chain of puns on the various shades of meaning of the word "heavy" (Hebrew *kbd*, meaning weighty, difficult, or substantial). Here Pharaoh orders that the work of the Israelites be made heavy. The hardening of the Pharaoh's heart is expressed several times through this term (7:14; 8:11,28; 9:7,34; 10:1). Four of the plagues on Egypt are described as heavy: insects (8:20), pestilence (9:3), hail (9:18,24), and locusts (10:14). The Israelites leave with a heavy supply of livestock (12:38). As Moses holds up his arms in support of the Israelites while they battle the Amalekites, his arms become heavy (17:12). Moses' father-in-law warns him that his efforts to manage the entire nation on his own are foolish, "because the thing is too heavy for you" (18:18). The chain of puns culminates at Sinai, as a heavy cloud is on the mountain while the people hear the voice of God (19:16). It is not that the narrator's vocabulary is too limited to produce other adjectives. Rather, the construction of such chains of wordplay is a technique of biblical narrative, deployed in other biblical books as well. Here the chain contributes to the narrative's unity, rather than the narrative's appearing to be a series of loosely bound episodes.

12And the people scattered through all the land of Egypt to collect stubble for straw. 13And the taskmasters were prodding, saying, "Finish your work, the day's thing in that very day, as when there was the straw." 14And the officers of the children of Israel whom Pharaoh's taskmasters had set over them were beaten—saying, "Why haven't you finished your requirement to make brick like the day before yesterday, also yesterday, also today?"

15And the officers of the children of Israel came and cried to Pharaoh, saying, "Why do you do a thing like this to your servants? 16Straw isn't given to your servants, and they say to us: Make bricks. And here, your servants are beaten, and it's your people's sin."

17And he said, "You're lazy, lazy! On account of this you're saying, 'Let us go and sacrifice to YHWH.' 18And now go, work! And straw will not be given to you, and you shall give the quota of bricks!"

19And the officers of the children of Israel saw themselves in a bad state—saying, "You shall not subtract from your bricks, the day's thing in that very day." 20And they met Moses and Aaron, standing opposite them when they came out from Pharaoh, 21and they said to them, "May YHWH look on you and judge, that you've made our smell odious in Pharaoh's eyes and in his servants' eyes, to give a sword in their hand to kill us!"

22And Moses went back to YHWH and said, "My Lord, why have you done bad to this people? Why did you send me here? 23And since I came to Pharaoh to speak in your name he has done bad to this people, and you *haven't* rescued your people!"

6 1And YHWH said to Moses, "Now you'll see what I shall do to Pharaoh, because with a

אֶרֶץ מִצְרָיִם לְקֹשֵׁשׁ קַשׁ לַתֶּבֶן: 13וְהַנֹּגְשִׂים אָצִים לֵאמֹר כַּלּוּ מַעֲשֵׂיכֶם דְּבַר־יוֹם בְּיוֹמוֹ כַּאֲשֶׁר בִּהְיוֹת הַתֶּבֶן: 14וַיֻּכּוּ שֹׁטְרֵי בְּנֵי יִשְׂרָאֵל אֲשֶׁר־שָׂמוּ עֲלֵהֶם נֹגְשֵׂי פַרְעֹה לֵאמֹר מַדּוּעַ לֹא כִלִּיתֶם חָקְכֶם לִלְבֹּן כִּתְמוֹל שִׁלְשֹׁם גַּם־תְּמוֹל גַּם־הַיּוֹם: 15וַיָּבֹאוּ שֹׁטְרֵי בְּנֵי יִשְׂרָאֵל וַיִּצְעֲקוּ אֶל־פַּרְעֹה לֵאמֹר לָמָּה תַעֲשֶׂה כֹה לַעֲבָדֶיךָ: 16תֶּבֶן אֵין נִתָּן לַעֲבָדֶיךָ וּלְבֵנִים אֹמְרִים לָנוּ עֲשׂוּ וְהִנֵּה עֲבָדֶיךָ מֻכִּים וְחָטָאת עַמֶּךָ: 17וַיֹּאמֶר נִרְפִּים אַתֶּם נִרְפִּים עַל־כֵּן אַתֶּם אֹמְרִים נֵלְכָה נִזְבְּחָה לַיהוָה: 18וְעַתָּה לְכוּ עִבְדוּ וְתֶבֶן לֹא־יִנָּתֵן לָכֶם וְתֹכֶן לְבֵנִים תִּתֵּנוּ: 19וַיִּרְאוּ שֹׁטְרֵי בְנֵי־יִשְׂרָאֵל אֹתָם בְּרָע לֵאמֹר לֹא־תִגְרְעוּ מִלִּבְנֵיכֶם דְּבַר־יוֹם בְּיוֹמוֹ: 20וַיִּפְגְּעוּ אֶת־מֹשֶׁה וְאֶת־אַהֲרֹן נִצָּבִים לִקְרָאתָם בְּצֵאתָם מֵאֵת פַּרְעֹה: 21וַיֹּאמְרוּ אֲלֵהֶם יֵרֶא יְהוָה עֲלֵיכֶם וְיִשְׁפֹּט אֲשֶׁר הִבְאַשְׁתֶּם אֶת־רֵיחֵנוּ בְּעֵינֵי פַרְעֹה וּבְעֵינֵי עֲבָדָיו לָתֶת־חֶרֶב בְּיָדָם לְהָרְגֵנוּ: 22וַיָּשָׁב מֹשֶׁה אֶל־יְהוָה וַיֹּאמַר אֲדֹנָי לָמָה הֲרֵעֹתָה לָעָם הַזֶּה לָמָּה זֶּה שְׁלַחְתָּנִי: 23וּמֵאָז בָּאתִי אֶל־פַּרְעֹה לְדַבֵּר בִּשְׁמֶךָ הֵרַע לָעָם הַזֶּה וְהַצֵּל לֹא־הִצַּלְתָּ אֶת־עַמֶּךָ: 6 1וַיֹּאמֶר יְהוָה אֶל־מֹשֶׁה עַתָּה תִרְאֶה אֲשֶׁר

5:21. **our smell odious in Pharaoh's eyes.** People smell with their noses, not their eyes! This may be just an expression or even the author's oversight, but I rather think that the contradiction is purposeful: the people's officers misspeak because they are upset. We *frequently* do that.

strong hand he'll let them go, and with a strong hand he'll drive them from his land."

אֶעֱשֶׂה לְפַרְעֹה כִּי בְיָד חֲזָקָה יְשַׁלְּחֵם וּבְיָד חֲזָקָה
יְגָרְשֵׁם מֵאַרְצֽוֹ׃ ס

AND I APPEARED

וארא

²And God spoke to Moses and said to him, "I am YHWH. ³And I appeared to Abraham, to Isaac, and to Jacob as El Shadday, and I was not known to them by my name, YHWH. ⁴And I also established my covenant with them, to give them the land of Canaan, the land of their residences, in which they resided. ⁵And also: I've heard the cry of the children of Israel as Egypt is enslaving them, and I've remembered my covenant. ⁶Therefore, say to the children of Israel: 'I am YHWH, and I shall bring you out from under Egypt's burdens, and I shall rescue you from their toil, and I shall redeem you with an outstretched arm and with tremendous judgments, ⁷and I shall take you to me as a people, and I shall become your God, and you'll know that I am YHWH, your God, who is bringing you out from under Egypt's burdens. ⁸And I shall bring you to the land that I raised my hand to give to Abra-

²וַיְדַבֵּר אֱלֹהִים אֶל־מֹשֶׁה וַיֹּאמֶר אֵלָיו אֲנִי
יְהוָֽה׃ ³וָאֵרָא אֶל־אַבְרָהָם אֶל־יִצְחָק וְאֶֽל־יַעֲקֹב
בְּאֵל שַׁדָּי וּשְׁמִי יְהוָה לֹא נוֹדַעְתִּי לָהֶֽם׃ ⁴וְגַם
הֲקִמֹתִי אֶת־בְּרִיתִי אִתָּם לָתֵת לָהֶם אֶת־אֶרֶץ כְּנָעַן
אֵת אֶרֶץ מְגֻרֵיהֶם אֲשֶׁר־גָּרוּ בָֽהּ׃ ⁵וְגַם ׀ אֲנִי
שָׁמַעְתִּי אֶת־נַאֲקַת בְּנֵי יִשְׂרָאֵל אֲשֶׁר מִצְרַיִם
מַעֲבִדִים אֹתָם וָאֶזְכֹּר אֶת־בְּרִיתִֽי׃ ⁶לָכֵן אֱמֹר
לִבְנֵֽי־יִשְׂרָאֵל אֲנִי יְהוָה וְהוֹצֵאתִי אֶתְכֶם מִתַּחַת
סִבְלֹת מִצְרַיִם וְהִצַּלְתִּי אֶתְכֶם מֵעֲבֹדָתָם וְגָאַלְתִּי
אֶתְכֶם בִּזְרוֹעַ נְטוּיָה וּבִשְׁפָטִים גְּדֹלִֽים׃ ⁷וְלָקַחְתִּי
אֶתְכֶם לִי לְעָם וְהָיִיתִי לָכֶם לֵאלֹהִים וִידַעְתֶּם כִּי
אֲנִי יְהוָה אֱלֹהֵיכֶם הַמּוֹצִיא אֶתְכֶם מִתַּחַת סִבְלוֹת
מִצְרָֽיִם׃ ⁸וְהֵבֵאתִי אֶתְכֶם אֶל־הָאָרֶץ אֲשֶׁר נָשָׂאתִי
אֶת־יָדִי לָתֵת אֹתָהּ לְאַבְרָהָם לְיִצְחָק וּֽלְיַעֲקֹב

6:1. **with a strong hand he'll let them go**. But with *whose* strong hand? God's or Moses' own? The probable meaning is: God's. But the ambiguity is rich because either meaning is instructive.

6:3. **I was not known to them by my name, YHWH**. But God *was* known to them by this name (Gen 13:4; 15:2; 22:14,16; 26:22,25; 28:13). I have discussed the significance of the understanding of this problem in critical scholarship elsewhere (*Who Wrote the Bible?*). It has to do with the case for multiple sources from which the Torah was composed. But in terms of the final composition, the full Torah as we know it, how shall we understand this verse? Perhaps covenantally: In the Noahic covenant (Gen 9:8–9), God is called *ʾĕlōhîm*. In the Abrahamic covenant, God is known as El Shadday (Gen 17:1–2). But the covenant that will be made with this generation at Sinai will be with the use of the name YHWH (Exod 20:2). In support of this understanding: the very next words here are "And I also established my *covenant* with them."

6:7. **you'll know that I am YHWH, your God, who is bringing you out**. The dominant theme of Exodus, YHWH's becoming known, is connected explicitly here to the rescue from slavery and to the "judgments" that will occur in Egypt. It will continue to be stated, several times, as a reason for the miraculous plagues.

ham, to Isaac, and to Jacob, and I shall give it to you as a possession. I am YHWH.'"

9And Moses spoke this to the children of Israel, and they did not listen to Moses because of shortage of spirit and because of hard work.

10And YHWH spoke to Moses, saying, 11"Come, speak to Pharaoh, king of Egypt, that he should let the children of Israel go from his land."

12And Moses spoke in front of YHWH, saying, "Here, the children of Israel didn't listen to me, and how will *Pharaoh* listen to me?! And I'm uncircumcised of lips!"

13And YHWH spoke to Moses and to Aaron and commanded them regarding the children of Israel and regarding Pharaoh, king of Egypt, to bring out the children of Israel from the land of Egypt. 14These are the heads of their fathers' houses:

The sons of Reuben, Israel's firstborn: Hanoch and Pallu, Hezron, and Carmi. These are the families of Reuben. 15And the sons of Simeon: Jemuel and Jamin and Ohad and Jachin and Zohar and Saul, son of a Canaanite woman. These are the families of Simeon. 16And these are the names of the sons of Levi by their records: Gershon and Kohath and Merari. And the years of Levi's life were a hundred thirty-seven years. 17The sons of Gershon: Libni and Shimei, by their families. 18And the sons of Kohath: Amram and Izhar and Hebron and Uzziel. And the years of Kohath's life were a hundred thirty-three

וְנָתַתִּ֨י אֹתָ֤הּ לָכֶם֙ מוֹרָשָׁ֔ה אֲנִ֖י יְהוָֽה׃ 9וַיְדַבֵּ֥ר מֹשֶׁ֛ה כֵּ֖ן אֶל־בְּנֵ֣י יִשְׂרָאֵ֑ל וְלֹ֤א שָֽׁמְעוּ֙ אֶל־מֹשֶׁ֔ה מִקֹּ֣צֶר ר֔וּחַ וּמֵעֲבֹדָ֖ה קָשָֽׁה׃ פ 10וַיְדַבֵּ֥ר יְהוָ֖ה אֶל־מֹשֶׁ֥ה לֵּאמֹֽר׃ 11בֹּ֣א דַבֵּ֔ר אֶל־פַּרְעֹ֖ה מֶ֣לֶךְ מִצְרָ֑יִם וִֽישַׁלַּ֥ח אֶת־בְּנֵֽי־יִשְׂרָאֵ֖ל מֵאַרְצֽוֹ׃ 12וַיְדַבֵּ֣ר מֹשֶׁ֔ה לִפְנֵ֥י יְהוָ֖ה לֵאמֹ֑ר הֵ֤ן בְּנֵֽי־יִשְׂרָאֵל֙ לֹֽא־שָׁמְע֣וּ אֵלַ֔י וְאֵיךְ֙ יִשְׁמָעֵ֣נִי פַרְעֹ֔ה וַאֲנִ֖י עֲרַ֥ל שְׂפָתָֽיִם׃ פ 13וַיְדַבֵּ֣ר יְהוָה֮ אֶל־מֹשֶׁ֣ה וְאֶֽל־אַהֲרֹן֒ וַיְצַוֵּם֙ אֶל־בְּנֵ֣י יִשְׂרָאֵ֔ל וְאֶל־פַּרְעֹ֖ה מֶ֣לֶךְ מִצְרָ֑יִם לְהוֹצִ֥יא אֶת־בְּנֵֽי־יִשְׂרָאֵ֖ל מֵאֶ֥רֶץ מִצְרָֽיִם׃ ס

14אֵ֖לֶּה רָאשֵׁ֣י בֵית־אֲבֹתָ֑ם בְּנֵ֨י רְאוּבֵ֜ן בְּכֹ֣ר יִשְׂרָאֵ֗ל חֲנ֤וֹךְ וּפַלּוּא֙ חֶצְרֹ֣ן וְכַרְמִ֔י אֵ֖לֶּה מִשְׁפְּחֹ֥ת רְאוּבֵֽן׃ 15וּבְנֵ֣י שִׁמְע֗וֹן יְמוּאֵ֨ל וְיָמִ֤ין וְאֹ֙הַד֙ וְיָכִ֣ין וְצֹ֔חַר וְשָׁא֖וּל בֶּן־הַֽכְּנַעֲנִ֑ית אֵ֖לֶּה מִשְׁפְּחֹ֥ת שִׁמְעֽוֹן׃ 16וְאֵ֨לֶּה שְׁמ֤וֹת בְּנֵֽי־לֵוִי֙ לְתֹ֣לְדֹתָ֔ם גֵּרְשׁ֕וֹן וּקְהָ֖ת וּמְרָרִ֑י וּשְׁנֵי֙ חַיֵּ֣י לֵוִ֔י שֶׁ֧בַע וּשְׁלֹשִׁ֛ים וּמְאַ֖ת שָׁנָֽה׃ 17בְּנֵ֥י גֵרְשׁ֛וֹן לִבְנִ֥י וְשִׁמְעִ֖י לְמִשְׁפְּחֹתָֽם׃ 18וּבְנֵ֣י קְהָ֔ת עַמְרָ֣ם וְיִצְהָ֔ר וְחֶבְר֖וֹן וְעֻזִּיאֵ֑ל וּשְׁנֵי֙ חַיֵּ֣י קְהָ֔ת שָׁלֹ֥שׁ

6:12,30. **uncircumcised of lips**. Does this shed light on the meaning of "heavy of tongue and heavy of mouth"? It seems rather to be even harder to interpret. Uncircumcision is used elsewhere in the Torah as a metaphor as well. Lev 26:41 and Deut 10:16 refer to the people's uncircumcised heart. (The prophets Jeremiah and Ezekiel use this image also.) There it is a strong image, criticizing the people who understand that their covenant requires circumcision of the skin that covers the penis, but who do not appreciate that they must likewise remove the impediment to their hearts. But the meaning of the image here is less clear. We still do not know what the impediment is. All we can say is that Moses is again pictured as unconfident, feeling inadequate to the task. The repeated emphasis on this point will make the eventual success of the exodus that much more dramatic.

years. ¹⁹And the sons of Merari: Mahli and Mushi. These are the families of Levi by their records. ²⁰And Amram took Jochebed, his aunt, as a wife; and she gave birth to Aaron and Moses for him. And the years of Amram's life were a hundred thirty-seven years. ²¹And the sons of Izhar: Korah and Nepheg and Zichri. ²²And the sons of Uzziel: Mishael and Elzaphan and Sithri. ²³And Aaron took Elisheba, daughter of Amminadab, sister of Nahshon as a wife; and she gave birth to Nadab and Abihu, Eleazar, and Ithamar for him. ²⁴And the sons of Korah: Assir and Elkanah and Abiasaph. These are the families of the Korahites. ²⁵And Eleazar son of Aaron had taken one of the daughters of Putiel as a wife, and she gave birth for him to Phinehas. These are the heads of the fathers of the Levites according to their families.

²⁶That is Aaron and Moses, to whom YHWH

וּשְׁלֹשִׁים וּמְאַת שָׁנָה: ¹⁹וּבְנֵי מְרָרִי מַחְלִי וּמוּשִׁי אֵלֶּה מִשְׁפְּחֹת הַלֵּוִי לְתֹלְדֹתָם: ²⁰וַיִּקַּח עַמְרָם אֶת־יוֹכֶבֶד דֹּדָתוֹ לוֹ לְאִשָּׁה וַתֵּלֶד לוֹ אֶת־אַהֲרֹן וְאֶת־מֹשֶׁה וּשְׁנֵי חַיֵּי עַמְרָם שֶׁבַע וּשְׁלֹשִׁים וּמְאַת שָׁנָה: ²¹וּבְנֵי יִצְהָר קֹרַח וָנֶפֶג וְזִכְרִי: ²²וּבְנֵי עֻזִּיאֵל מִישָׁאֵל וְאֶלְצָפָן וְסִתְרִי: ²³וַיִּקַּח אַהֲרֹן אֶת־אֱלִישֶׁבַע בַּת־עַמִּינָדָב אֲחוֹת נַחְשׁוֹן לוֹ לְאִשָּׁה וַתֵּלֶד לוֹ אֶת־נָדָב וְאֶת־אֲבִיהוּא אֶת־אֶלְעָזָר וְאֶת־אִיתָמָר: ²⁴וּבְנֵי קֹרַח אַסִּיר וְאֶלְקָנָה וַאֲבִיאָסָף אֵלֶּה מִשְׁפְּחֹת הַקָּרְחִי: ²⁵וְאֶלְעָזָר בֶּן־אַהֲרֹן לָקַח־לוֹ מִבְּנוֹת פּוּטִיאֵל לוֹ לְאִשָּׁה וַתֵּלֶד לוֹ אֶת־פִּינְחָס אֵלֶּה רָאשֵׁי אֲבוֹת הַלְוִיִּם לְמִשְׁפְּחֹתָם: ²⁶הוּא אַהֲרֹן

6:20. **she gave birth to Aaron and Moses**. Until now, it has not been clear that Moses and Aaron are brothers. There is no reference to a brother in the story of Moses' birth, and at the bush Aaron is referred to as "your Levite brother," which sounds like a fellow Levite, not an actual brother. The list in which this appears (6:13–25) seems strange: it comes in the middle of a conversation between God and Moses, and it covers only Reuben, Simeon, and Levi, and then leaves out the rest of the tribes. But it appears that the point of the list was to get to Aaron: to identify him as Moses' brother, to state that he is married to the sister of the chieftain of the tribe of Judah, and to name his son and grandson who will be his successors. The order also indicates that Aaron is the firstborn; this is confirmed in Exod 7:7.

6:20. **Aaron and Moses**. And what about Miriam? One Hebrew manuscript and the Septuagint and Samaritan texts have the words "and their sister Miriam." The scribe appears to have accidentally omitted these words here.

6:23. **daughter of Amminadab, sister of Nahshon**. Aaron marries the sister of the chieftain of the tribe of Judah. It is noteworthy that the priestly and political elite marry (and this suggests that such marriages occured later between the royal and high priestly families of Israel).

6:26–27. **Aaron and Moses . . . Moses and Aaron**. Both word orders are given: Aaron first, then Moses first, suggesting that each is important in a different way. The recognition of Aaron here is especially significant because it is natural to think of Moses first, but this notice follows a genealogy that has listed Aaron as the firstborn and identified his wife and children. (The Septuagint and Qumran texts have the order in v. 27 reversed, which unfortunately loses this point.)

said, "Bring out the children of Israel from the land of Egypt by their masses." 27They were the ones speaking to Pharaoh, king of Egypt, to bring out the children of Israel from Egypt. That is Moses and Aaron.

28And it was in the day that YHWH spoke to Moses in the land of Egypt, 29and YHWH spoke to Moses, saying, "I am YHWH. Speak to Pharaoh, king of Egypt, everything that I speak to you."

30And Moses said in front of YHWH, "Here, I'm uncircumcised of lips, and how will Pharaoh listen to me?!"

7 1And YHWH said to Moses, "See, I've made you a god to Pharaoh, and Aaron, your brother, will be your prophet. 2You shall speak everything that I'll command you; and Aaron, your brother, shall speak to Pharaoh, that he let the children of Israel go from his land. 3And I, I'll harden Pharaoh's heart, and I'll multiply my signs and my wonders in the land of Egypt. 4And Pharaoh won't listen to you, and I'll set my hand in Egypt and bring out my masses, my people, the children of Israel, from the land of Egypt with great judgments. 5And Egypt will know that I am YHWH when I reach out my hand on Egypt, and I'll bring out the children of Israel from among them."

6And Moses and Aaron did as YHWH had commanded them. They did so. 7And Moses was eighty years old, and Aaron was eighty-three years old when they spoke to Pharaoh.

8And YHWH said to Moses and to Aaron, saying, 9"When Pharaoh will speak to you, saying, 'Produce a wonder!' then say to Aaron, 'Take your staff and throw it in front of Pharaoh. Let it become a serpent.'" 10And Moses and Aaron

וּמֹשֶׁה אֲשֶׁר אָמַ֨ר יְהוָה֙ לָהֶ֔ם הוֹצִ֨יאוּ אֶת־בְּנֵ֧י יִשְׂרָאֵ֛ל מֵאֶ֥רֶץ מִצְרַ֖יִם עַל־צִבְאֹתָֽם׃ 27הֵ֣ם הַֽמְדַבְּרִ֗ים אֶל־פַּרְעֹה֙ מֶֽלֶךְ־מִצְרַ֔יִם לְהוֹצִ֥יא אֶת־בְּנֵֽי־יִשְׂרָאֵ֖ל מִמִּצְרָ֑יִם ה֥וּא מֹשֶׁ֖ה וְאַהֲרֹֽן׃ 28וַיְהִ֗י בְּי֨וֹם דִּבֶּ֧ר יְהוָ֛ה אֶל־מֹשֶׁ֖ה בְּאֶ֥רֶץ מִצְרָֽיִם׃ פ 29וַיְדַבֵּ֧ר יְהוָ֛ה אֶל־מֹשֶׁ֖ה לֵּאמֹ֑ר אֲנִ֣י יְהוָ֑ה דַּבֵּ֗ר אֶל־פַּרְעֹה֙ מֶ֣לֶךְ מִצְרַ֔יִם אֵ֛ת כָּל־אֲשֶׁ֥ר אֲנִ֖י דֹּבֵ֥ר אֵלֶֽיךָ׃ 30וַיֹּ֥אמֶר מֹשֶׁ֖ה לִפְנֵ֣י יְהוָ֑ה הֵ֤ן אֲנִי֙ עֲרַ֣ל שְׂפָתַ֔יִם וְאֵ֕יךְ יִשְׁמַ֥ע אֵלַ֖י פַּרְעֹֽה׃ פ

7 1וַיֹּ֤אמֶר יְהוָה֙ אֶל־מֹשֶׁ֔ה רְאֵ֛ה נְתַתִּ֥יךָ אֱלֹהִ֖ים לְפַרְעֹ֑ה וְאַהֲרֹ֥ן אָחִ֖יךָ יִהְיֶ֥ה נְבִיאֶֽךָ׃ 2אַתָּ֣ה תְדַבֵּ֔ר אֵ֖ת כָּל־אֲשֶׁ֣ר אֲצַוֶּ֑ךָּ וְאַהֲרֹ֤ן אָחִ֨יךָ֙ יְדַבֵּ֣ר אֶל־פַּרְעֹ֔ה וְשִׁלַּ֥ח אֶת־בְּנֵֽי־יִשְׂרָאֵ֖ל מֵאַרְצֽוֹ׃ 3וַאֲנִ֥י אַקְשֶׁ֖ה אֶת־לֵ֣ב פַּרְעֹ֑ה וְהִרְבֵּיתִ֧י אֶת־אֹתֹתַ֛י וְאֶת־מוֹפְתַ֖י בְּאֶ֥רֶץ מִצְרָֽיִם׃ 4וְלֹֽא־יִשְׁמַ֤ע אֲלֵכֶם֙ פַּרְעֹ֔ה וְנָתַתִּ֥י אֶת־יָדִ֖י בְּמִצְרָ֑יִם וְהוֹצֵאתִ֨י אֶת־צִבְאֹתַ֜י אֶת־עַמִּ֤י בְנֵֽי־יִשְׂרָאֵל֙ מֵאֶ֣רֶץ מִצְרַ֔יִם בִּשְׁפָטִ֖ים גְּדֹלִֽים׃ 5וְיָדְע֤וּ מִצְרַ֨יִם֙ כִּֽי־אֲנִ֣י יְהוָ֔ה בִּנְטֹתִ֥י אֶת־יָדִ֖י עַל־מִצְרָ֑יִם וְהוֹצֵאתִ֥י אֶת־בְּנֵֽי־יִשְׂרָאֵ֖ל מִתּוֹכָֽם׃ 6וַיַּ֥עַשׂ מֹשֶׁ֖ה וְאַהֲרֹ֑ן כַּאֲשֶׁ֨ר צִוָּ֧ה יְהוָ֛ה אֹתָ֖ם כֵּ֥ן עָשֽׂוּ׃ 7וּמֹשֶׁה֙ בֶּן־שְׁמֹנִ֣ים שָׁנָ֔ה וְאַֽהֲרֹ֔ן בֶּן־שָׁלֹ֥שׁ וּשְׁמֹנִ֖ים שָׁנָ֑ה בְּדַבְּרָ֖ם אֶל־פַּרְעֹֽה׃ פ 8וַיֹּ֣אמֶר יְהוָ֔ה אֶל־מֹשֶׁ֥ה וְאֶֽל־אַהֲרֹ֖ן לֵאמֹֽר׃ 9כִּי֩ יְדַבֵּ֨ר אֲלֵכֶ֤ם פַּרְעֹה֙ לֵאמֹ֔ר תְּנ֥וּ לָכֶ֖ם מוֹפֵ֑ת וְאָמַרְתָּ֣ אֶֽל־אַהֲרֹ֗ן קַ֧ח אֶֽת־מַטְּךָ֛ וְהַשְׁלֵ֥ךְ לִפְנֵֽי־פַרְעֹ֖ה יְהִ֥י לְתַנִּֽין׃ 10וַיָּבֹ֨א מֹשֶׁ֤ה

7:9. **a serpent**. Not a snake. This is different from the *snake* (Hebrew *nāḥāš*) that *Moses'* staff became in Exod 4:3. Moses performed that miracle for the Israelite elders (4:30). Now, in front of Pharaoh, *Aaron's* staff becomes a *tannîn*. This is the term that is used for the big sea serpents that God makes on the fifth day of creation (Gen 1:21). They are not merely snakes, as people have often pictured them. They are extraordinary creatures from a seemingly unearthly realm.

came to Pharaoh and did so, as YHWH had commanded, and Aaron threw his staff in front of Pharaoh and in front of his servants, and it became a serpent. ¹¹And Pharaoh, too, called the wise men and the sorcerers; and they, too, Egypt's magicians, did so with their charms: ¹²and they each threw his staff, and they became serpents. And Aaron's staff swallowed their staffs!

¹³And Pharaoh's heart was strong, and he did not listen to them—as YHWH had spoken.

¹⁴And YHWH said to Moses, "Pharaoh's heart is heavy. He has refused to let the people go. ¹⁵Go to Pharaoh in the morning—here, he'll be going out to the water—and you'll stand opposite him on the bank of the Nile, and you shall take in your hand the staff that was changed into a snake. ¹⁶And you'll say to him, 'YHWH, the God of the Hebrews, sent me to you, saying: "Let my people go so they may serve me in the wilderness." And here, you haven't listened so far. ¹⁷YHWH said this: "By this you'll know that I am YHWH." Here, I'm striking with the staff that's in my hand on the waters that are in the Nile, and they'll be changed into blood. ¹⁸And the fish that are in the Nile will die, and the Nile will stink, and Egypt will weary themselves to drink water from the Nile.'"

¹⁹And YHWH said to Moses, "Say to Aaron,

וְאַהֲרֹן אֶל־פַּרְעֹה וַיַּעֲשׂוּ כֵן כַּאֲשֶׁר צִוָּה יְהוָה וַיַּשְׁלֵךְ אַהֲרֹן אֶת־מַטֵּהוּ לִפְנֵי פַרְעֹה וְלִפְנֵי עֲבָדָיו וַיְהִי לְתַנִּין: ¹¹וַיִּקְרָא גַּם־פַּרְעֹה לַחֲכָמִים וְלַמְכַשְּׁפִים וַיַּעֲשׂוּ גַם־הֵם חַרְטֻמֵּי מִצְרַיִם בְּלַהֲטֵיהֶם כֵּן: ¹²וַיַּשְׁלִיכוּ אִישׁ מַטֵּהוּ וַיִּהְיוּ לְתַנִּינִם וַיִּבְלַע מַטֵּה־אַהֲרֹן אֶת־מַטֹּתָם: ¹³וַיֶּחֱזַק לֵב פַּרְעֹה וְלֹא שָׁמַע אֲלֵהֶם כַּאֲשֶׁר דִּבֶּר יְהוָה: פ

¹⁴וַיֹּאמֶר יְהוָה אֶל־מֹשֶׁה כָּבֵד לֵב פַּרְעֹה מֵאֵן לְשַׁלַּח הָעָם: ¹⁵לֵךְ אֶל־פַּרְעֹה בַּבֹּקֶר הִנֵּה יֹצֵא הַמַּיְמָה וְנִצַּבְתָּ לִקְרָאתוֹ עַל־שְׂפַת הַיְאֹר וְהַמַּטֶּה אֲשֶׁר־נֶהְפַּךְ לְנָחָשׁ תִּקַּח בְּיָדֶךָ: ¹⁶וְאָמַרְתָּ אֵלָיו יְהוָה אֱלֹהֵי הָעִבְרִים שְׁלָחַנִי אֵלֶיךָ לֵאמֹר שַׁלַּח אֶת־עַמִּי וְיַעַבְדֻנִי בַּמִּדְבָּר וְהִנֵּה לֹא־שָׁמַעְתָּ עַד־כֹּה: ¹⁷כֹּה אָמַר יְהוָה בְּזֹאת תֵּדַע כִּי אֲנִי יְהוָה הִנֵּה אָנֹכִי מַכֶּה בַּמַּטֶּה אֲשֶׁר־בְּיָדִי עַל־הַמַּיִם אֲשֶׁר בַּיְאֹר וְנֶהֶפְכוּ לְדָם: ¹⁸וְהַדָּגָה אֲשֶׁר־בַּיְאֹר תָּמוּת וּבָאַשׁ הַיְאֹר וְנִלְאוּ מִצְרַיִם לִשְׁתּוֹת מַיִם מִן הַיְאֹר: ס ¹⁹וַיֹּאמֶר יְהוָה אֶל־מֹשֶׁה אֱמֹר אֶל־אַהֲרֹן

7:14. **Pharaoh's heart is heavy.** The stream of descriptions of elements as "heavy" that began in Exod 4:10 with Moses' heavy mouth and heavy tongue continues to flow here and in what follows.

7:17. **By this you'll know that I am YHWH.** This is the story of the introduction of the deity *by name* to the world, so this statement can be understood not only as establishing the existence of the named deity to Pharaoh, but also as establishing what the name *conveys*. Thus: By this (a miracle involving a change in nature) you'll know that I am *the one who causes being*.

7:18. **will stink.** Hebrew באשׁ (*bā'ēš*). This is the same word that the people used metaphorically in their complaint to Moses earlier: "You've made our smell odious in Pharaoh's eyes" (5:21). They now see the divine power giving the Egyptians something *literally* odious to smell. This in turn demonstrates how mistaken they were when they judged the situation so early in the process.

'Take your staff and reach your hand over Egypt's waters, over their rivers, over their canals, and over their pools, and over every concentration of their waters.' And they will be blood! And blood will be in all the land of Egypt—and in the trees and in the stones!" 20And Moses and Aaron did so, as YHWH had commanded. And he raised the staff and struck the waters that were in the Nile before Pharaoh's eyes and before his servants' eyes, and all the waters that were in the Nile were changed into blood. 21And the fish in the Nile died, and the Nile had an odor, and Egypt was not able to drink water from the Nile. And the blood was in all the land of Egypt. 22And Egypt's magicians did so with their charms. And Pharaoh's heart was strong, and he did not listen to them—as YHWH had spoken. 23And Pharaoh turned and came into his house and did not pay heed to this as well. 24And all Egypt dug around the Nile for water to drink, because they were not able to drink from the Nile's waters. 25And seven days were filled after YHWH's striking the Nile.

26And YHWH said to Moses, "Come to Pharaoh, and you'll say to him, 'YHWH said this: Let my people go, so they may serve me. 27And if you refuse to let go, here, I'm plaguing all your border with frogs, 28and the Nile will teem with frogs, and they'll go up and come in your house and in your bedroom and on your bed and in your servants' house and among your people and in your ovens and in your bowls, 29and the frogs will go up on you and on your people and on all your servants.'"

8 1And YHWH said to Moses, "Say to Aaron, 'Reach out your hand with your staff over the rivers, over the canals, and over the pools, and bring up the frogs on the land of Egypt.'" 2And Aaron reached out his hand over Egypt's waters, and the frogs came up and covered the land of Egypt. 3And the magicians did so with their charms. And they brought up the frogs on the land of Egypt.

קַח מַטְּךָ וּנְטֵה־יָדְךָ עַל־מֵימֵי מִצְרַיִם עַל־נַהֲרֹתָם ׀ עַל־יְאֹרֵיהֶם וְעַל־אַגְמֵיהֶם וְעַל כָּל־מִקְוֵה מֵימֵיהֶם וְיִהְיוּ־דָם וְהָיָה דָם בְּכָל־אֶרֶץ מִצְרַיִם וּבָעֵצִים וּבָאֲבָנִים: 20וַיַּעֲשׂוּ־כֵן מֹשֶׁה וְאַהֲרֹן ׀ כַּאֲשֶׁר ׀ צִוָּה יְהֹוָה וַיָּרֶם בַּמַּטֶּה וַיַּךְ אֶת־הַמַּיִם אֲשֶׁר בַּיְאֹר לְעֵינֵי פַרְעֹה וּלְעֵינֵי עֲבָדָיו וַיֵּהָפְכוּ כָּל־הַמַּיִם אֲשֶׁר־בַּיְאֹר לְדָם: 21וְהַדָּגָה אֲשֶׁר־בַּיְאֹר מֵתָה וַיִּבְאַשׁ הַיְאֹר וְלֹא־יָכְלוּ מִצְרַיִם לִשְׁתּוֹת מַיִם מִן־הַיְאֹר וַיְהִי הַדָּם בְּכָל־אֶרֶץ מִצְרָיִם: 22וַיַּעֲשׂוּ־כֵן חַרְטֻמֵּי מִצְרַיִם בְּלָטֵיהֶם וַיֶּחֱזַק לֵב־פַּרְעֹה וְלֹא־שָׁמַע אֲלֵהֶם כַּאֲשֶׁר דִּבֶּר יְהֹוָה: 23וַיִּפֶן פַּרְעֹה וַיָּבֹא אֶל־בֵּיתוֹ וְלֹא־שָׁת לִבּוֹ גַּם־לָזֹאת: 24וַיַּחְפְּרוּ כָל־מִצְרַיִם סְבִיבֹת הַיְאֹר מַיִם לִשְׁתּוֹת כִּי לֹא יָכְלוּ לִשְׁתֹּת מִמֵּימֵי הַיְאֹר: 25וַיִּמָּלֵא שִׁבְעַת יָמִים אַחֲרֵי הַכּוֹת־יְהֹוָה אֶת־הַיְאֹר: פ

26וַיֹּאמֶר יְהֹוָה אֶל־מֹשֶׁה בֹּא אֶל־פַּרְעֹה וְאָמַרְתָּ אֵלָיו כֹּה אָמַר יְהֹוָה שַׁלַּח אֶת־עַמִּי וְיַעַבְדֻנִי: 27וְאִם־מָאֵן אַתָּה לְשַׁלֵּחַ הִנֵּה אָנֹכִי נֹגֵף אֶת־כָּל־גְּבוּלְךָ בַּצְפַרְדְּעִים: 28וְשָׁרַץ הַיְאֹר צְפַרְדְּעִים וְעָלוּ וּבָאוּ בְּבֵיתֶךָ וּבַחֲדַר מִשְׁכָּבְךָ וְעַל־מִטָּתֶךָ וּבְבֵית עֲבָדֶיךָ וּבְעַמֶּךָ וּבְתַנּוּרֶיךָ וּבְמִשְׁאֲרוֹתֶיךָ: 29וּבְכָה וּבְעַמְּךָ וּבְכָל־עֲבָדֶיךָ יַעֲלוּ הַצְפַרְדְּעִים: 8וַיֹּאמֶר יְהֹוָה אֶל־מֹשֶׁה אֱמֹר אֶל־אַהֲרֹן נְטֵה אֶת־יָדְךָ בְּמַטֶּךָ עַל־הַנְּהָרֹת עַל־הַיְאֹרִים וְעַל־הָאֲגַמִּים וְהַעַל אֶת־הַצְפַרְדְּעִים עַל־אֶרֶץ מִצְרָיִם: 2וַיֵּט אַהֲרֹן אֶת־יָדוֹ עַל מֵימֵי מִצְרָיִם וַתַּעַל הַצְפַרְדֵּעַ וַתְּכַס אֶת־אֶרֶץ מִצְרָיִם: 3וַיַּעֲשׂוּ־כֵן הַחֲרְטֻמִּים בְּלָטֵיהֶם וַיַּעֲלוּ אֶת־הַצְפַרְדְּעִים עַל־אֶרֶץ מִצְרָיִם: 4וַיִּקְרָא פַרְעֹה

4And Pharaoh called Moses and Aaron and said, "Pray to YHWH that He will take away the frogs from me and from my people so I may let the people go, and they'll sacrifice to YHWH."

5And Moses said to Pharaoh, "Be honored over me as to when I'll pray for you and for your servants and for your people to cut off the frogs from you and from your houses—they'll be left only in the river."

6And he said, "As of tomorrow."

And he said, "According to your word: so that you'll know that there's none like YHWH, our God. 7And the frogs will turn away from you and from your houses and from your servants and from your people—they'll be left only in the river." 8And Moses and Aaron went out from Pharaoh. And Moses cried to YHWH over the matter of the frogs that he had set upon Pharaoh. 9And YHWH did according to Moses' word, and the frogs died from the houses, from the yards, and from the fields. 10And they piled them up, heaps and heaps, and the land smelled. 11And Pharaoh saw that there was a break, and he made his heart heavy, and he did not listen to them— as YHWH had spoken.

12And YHWH said to Moses, "Say to Aaron, 'Reach out your staff and strike the dust of the earth, and it will become lice in all the land of Egypt.'" 13And they did so, and Aaron reached out his hand with his staff and struck the dust of the earth, and the lice were in the humans and in the animals. All the dust of the earth was lice in all the land of Egypt.

14And the magicians did so with their charms, to bring out the lice, and they were not able. And the lice were in the humans and in the animals.

לְמֹשֶׁה וּלְאַהֲרֹן וַיֹּאמֶר הַעְתִּירוּ אֶל־יְהוָה וְיָסֵר הַצְפַרְדְּעִים מִמֶּנִּי וּמֵעַמִּי וַאֲשַׁלְּחָה אֶת־הָעָם וְיִזְבְּחוּ לַיהוָה: 5וַיֹּאמֶר מֹשֶׁה לְפַרְעֹה הִתְפָּאֵר עָלַי לְמָתַי ׀ אַעְתִּיר לְךָ וְלַעֲבָדֶיךָ וּלְעַמְּךָ לְהַכְרִית הַצְפַרְדְּעִים מִמְּךָ וּמִבָּתֶּיךָ רַק בַּיְאֹר תִּשָּׁאַרְנָה: 6וַיֹּאמֶר לְמָחָר וַיֹּאמֶר כִּדְבָרְךָ לְמַעַן תֵּדַע כִּי־אֵין כַּיהוָה אֱלֹהֵינוּ: 7וְסָרוּ הַצְפַרְדְּעִים מִמְּךָ וּמִבָּתֶּיךָ וּמֵעֲבָדֶיךָ וּמֵעַמֶּךָ רַק בַּיְאֹר תִּשָּׁאַרְנָה: 8וַיֵּצֵא מֹשֶׁה וְאַהֲרֹן מֵעִם פַּרְעֹה וַיִּצְעַק מֹשֶׁה אֶל־יְהוָה עַל־דְּבַר הַצְפַרְדְּעִים אֲשֶׁר־שָׂם לְפַרְעֹה: 9וַיַּעַשׂ יְהוָה כִּדְבַר מֹשֶׁה וַיָּמֻתוּ הַצְפַרְדְּעִים מִן־הַבָּתִּים מִן־הַחֲצֵרֹת וּמִן־הַשָּׂדֹת: 10וַיִּצְבְּרוּ אֹתָם חֳמָרִם חֳמָרִם וַתִּבְאַשׁ הָאָרֶץ: 11וַיַּרְא פַּרְעֹה כִּי הָיְתָה הָרְוָחָה וְהַכְבֵּד אֶת־לִבּוֹ וְלֹא שָׁמַע אֲלֵהֶם כַּאֲשֶׁר דִּבֶּר יְהוָה: ס

12וַיֹּאמֶר יְהוָה אֶל־מֹשֶׁה אֱמֹר אֶל־אַהֲרֹן נְטֵה אֶת־מַטְּךָ וְהַךְ אֶת־עֲפַר הָאָרֶץ וְהָיָה לְכִנִּם בְּכָל־אֶרֶץ מִצְרָיִם: 13וַיַּעֲשׂוּ־כֵן וַיֵּט אַהֲרֹן אֶת־יָדוֹ בְמַטֵּהוּ וַיַּךְ אֶת־עֲפַר הָאָרֶץ וַתְּהִי הַכִּנָּם בָּאָדָם וּבַבְּהֵמָה כָּל־עֲפַר הָאָרֶץ הָיָה כִנִּים בְּכָל־אֶרֶץ מִצְרָיִם: 14וַיַּעֲשׂוּ־כֵן הַחַרְטֻמִּים בְּלָטֵיהֶם לְהוֹצִיא אֶת־הַכִּנִּים וְלֹא יָכֹלוּ וַתְּהִי הַכִּנָּם בָּאָדָם וּבַבְּהֵמָה:

8:10. **they piled them up.** This term was used twice for Joseph's piling up the grain (Gen 41:35,49), and these are its only occurrences in biblical prose. The wordplay appears to make the point that the good that Joseph did for Egypt was repaid with bad by the subsequent Pharaohs, and this makes the current plague more clearly a punishment to suit the crime. Also, the term for "were left" in 8:5,7 plays on the "bowls" (both have root *š'r*) in 7:28. And this whole paragraph is filled with words using the Hebrew letter *ṣadeh*, perhaps playing on *šĕpardēʿa* (frogs).

15And the magicians said to Pharaoh, "It's the finger of God!" And Pharaoh's heart was strong, and he did not listen to them—as YHWH had spoken.

16And YHWH said to Moses, "Get up early in the morning and stand up in front of Pharaoh. Here, he's going out to the water. And you'll say to him, 'YHWH said this: Let my people go so they may serve me. 17Because if you're not letting my people go, here, I'm causing an insect swarm to be let go on you and on your servants and on your people and on your houses. And the houses of Egypt will be filled with the insect swarm, and also the ground that they're on. 18And I shall distinguish in that day the land of Goshen, on which my people is standing, for no insect swarm to be there, so that you will know that I, YHWH, am within the land. 19And I shall set a distinction between my people and your people. This sign will be tomorrow.'"

20And YHWH did so. And a heavy insect swarm came to Pharaoh's house and his servants' house, and in all the land of Egypt the land was corrupted because of the insect swarm. 21And Pharaoh called Moses and Aaron. And he said, "Go. Sacrifice to your God *in the land*."

22And Moses said, "It's not right to do so, be-

15וַיֹּאמְר֤וּ הַֽחַרְטֻמִּים֙ אֶל־פַּרְעֹ֔ה אֶצְבַּ֥ע אֱלֹהִ֖ים ה֑וּא וַיֶּחֱזַ֤ק לֵב־פַּרְעֹה֙ וְלֹֽא־שָׁמַ֣ע אֲלֵהֶ֔ם כַּאֲשֶׁ֖ר דִּבֶּ֥ר יְהוָֽה: ס

16וַיֹּ֨אמֶר יְהוָ֜ה אֶל־מֹשֶׁ֗ה הַשְׁכֵּ֤ם בַּבֹּ֙קֶר֙ וְהִתְיַצֵּב֙ לִפְנֵ֣י פַרְעֹ֔ה הִנֵּ֖ה יוֹצֵ֣א הַמָּ֑יְמָה וְאָמַרְתָּ֣ אֵלָ֗יו כֹּ֚ה אָמַ֣ר יְהוָ֔ה שַׁלַּ֥ח עַמִּ֖י וְיַֽעַבְדֻֽנִי: 17כִּ֣י אִם־אֵֽינְךָ֮ מְשַׁלֵּ֣חַ אֶת־עַמִּי֒ הִנְנִי֩ מַשְׁלִ֨יחַ בְּךָ֜ וּבַעֲבָדֶ֤יךָ וּֽבְעַמְּךָ֙ וּבְבָתֶּ֔יךָ אֶת־הֶֽעָרֹ֑ב וּמָ֨לְא֜וּ בָּתֵּ֤י מִצְרַ֙יִם֙ אֶת־הֶ֣עָרֹ֔ב וְגַ֥ם הָאֲדָמָ֖ה אֲשֶׁר־הֵ֥ם עָלֶֽיהָ: 18וְהִפְלֵיתִי֩ בַיּ֨וֹם הַה֜וּא אֶת־אֶ֣רֶץ גֹּ֗שֶׁן אֲשֶׁ֤ר עַמִּי֙ עֹמֵ֣ד עָלֶ֔יהָ לְבִלְתִּ֥י הֱיֽוֹת־שָׁ֖ם עָרֹ֑ב לְמַ֣עַן תֵּדַ֔ע כִּ֛י אֲנִ֥י יְהוָ֖ה בְּקֶ֥רֶב הָאָֽרֶץ: 19וְשַׂמְתִּ֣י פְדֻ֔ת בֵּ֥ין עַמִּ֖י וּבֵ֣ין עַמֶּ֑ךָ לְמָחָ֥ר יִהְיֶ֖ה הָאֹ֥ת הַזֶּֽה: 20וַיַּ֤עַשׂ יְהוָה֙ כֵּ֔ן וַיָּבֹא֙ עָרֹ֣ב כָּבֵ֔ד בֵּ֥יתָה פַרְעֹ֖ה וּבֵ֣ית עֲבָדָ֑יו וּבְכָל־אֶ֧רֶץ מִצְרַ֛יִם תִּשָּׁחֵ֥ת הָאָ֖רֶץ מִפְּנֵ֥י הֶעָרֹֽב: 21וַיִּקְרָ֣א פַרְעֹ֔ה אֶל־מֹשֶׁ֖ה וּֽלְאַהֲרֹ֑ן וַיֹּ֕אמֶר לְכ֛וּ זִבְח֥וּ לֵאלֹֽהֵיכֶ֖ם בָּאָֽרֶץ: 22וַיֹּ֣אמֶר מֹשֶׁ֗ה לֹ֤א נָכוֹן֙ לַעֲשׂ֣וֹת

8:18. **I, YHWH, am within the land**. As earlier (7:17), this can also be understood in terms of the *meaning* of the divine name, thus meaning "So that you will know that *I am the one who causes being* in the land."

8:19. **distinction**. The Hebrew reads *pĕdūt*, "ransom?" The Greek and the Vulgate read "distinction," which makes more apparent sense and relates to the distinguishing that is predicted in the preceding verse.

8:20. **heavy**. Starting with the insect swarm, several plagues now join the stream of elements in the narrative that are described as "heavy."

8:21. **Sacrifice to your God *in the land***. Pharaoh is not fooled by the request for a "trip of three days." He takes a step back from his tough stance, and he turns to negotiation: You can sacrifice to your God, but do it here in Egypt, not out in the wilderness. A process of bargaining will follow, but note that, really, all the bargaining is on Pharaoh's part. Moses' position never changes, and in the end Pharaoh must capitulate completely.

8:22. **It's not right**. "Right" (*nākôn*) is the word Joseph used to tell Pharaoh that the

196

cause we'll be sacrificing to YHWH, our God, an offensive thing to Egypt. Here, we'll be sacrificing an offensive thing to Egypt before their eyes; and will they not stone us?! 23We'll go on a trip of three days in the wilderness, and we'll sacrifice to YHWH, our God, whatever He'll say to us."

24And Pharaoh said, "I'll let you go, and you'll sacrifice to YHWH, your God, in the wilderness. Only you shall not go *far.* Pray for me."

25And Moses said, "Here, I'm going out from you, and I'll pray to YHWH, and the insect swarm will turn away from Pharaoh and from his servants and from his people tomorrow. Only let Pharaoh not continue to toy so as not to let the people go to sacrifice to YHWH."

26And Moses went out from Pharaoh, and he prayed to YHWH. 27And YHWH did according to Moses' word, and the insect swarm turned away from Pharaoh and from his servants and from his people. Not one was left. 28And Pharaoh made his heart heavy this time as well, and he did not let the people go.

9 1And YHWH said to Moses, "Come to Pharaoh and speak to him: 'YHWH, God of the Hebrews, said this: Let my people go, so they may serve me. 2Because if you refuse to let go and you are still holding on to them, 3here, YHWH's hand is on your livestock that are in the field, on the horses, on the asses, on the camels, on the oxen, and on the flock—a very heavy epidemic.

כֵּן כִּי תּוֹעֲבַת מִצְרַיִם נִזְבַּח לַיהוָה אֱלֹהֵינוּ הֵן נִזְבַּח אֶת־תּוֹעֲבַת מִצְרַיִם לְעֵינֵיהֶם וְלֹא יִסְקְלֻנוּ׃ 23דֶּרֶךְ שְׁלֹשֶׁת יָמִים נֵלֵךְ בַּמִּדְבָּר וְזָבַחְנוּ לַיהוָה אֱלֹהֵינוּ כַּאֲשֶׁר יֹאמַר אֵלֵינוּ׃ 24וַיֹּאמֶר פַּרְעֹה אָנֹכִי אֲשַׁלַּח אֶתְכֶם וּזְבַחְתֶּם לַיהוָה אֱלֹהֵיכֶם בַּמִּדְבָּר רַק הַרְחֵק לֹא־תַרְחִיקוּ לָלֶכֶת הַעְתִּירוּ בַּעֲדִי׃ 25וַיֹּאמֶר מֹשֶׁה הִנֵּה אָנֹכִי יוֹצֵא מֵעִמָּךְ וְהַעְתַּרְתִּי אֶל־יְהוָה וְסָר הֶעָרֹב מִפַּרְעֹה מֵעֲבָדָיו וּמֵעַמּוֹ מָחָר רַק אַל־יֹסֵף פַּרְעֹה הָתֵל לְבִלְתִּי שַׁלַּח אֶת־הָעָם לִזְבֹּחַ לַיהוָה׃ 26וַיֵּצֵא מֹשֶׁה מֵעִם פַּרְעֹה וַיֶּעְתַּר אֶל־יְהוָה׃ 27וַיַּעַשׂ יְהוָה כִּדְבַר מֹשֶׁה וַיָּסַר הֶעָרֹב מִפַּרְעֹה מֵעֲבָדָיו וּמֵעַמּוֹ לֹא נִשְׁאַר אֶחָד׃ 28וַיַּכְבֵּד פַּרְעֹה אֶת־לִבּוֹ גַּם בַּפַּעַם הַזֹּאת וְלֹא שִׁלַּח אֶת־הָעָם׃ פ

9 1וַיֹּאמֶר יְהוָה אֶל־מֹשֶׁה בֹּא אֶל־פַּרְעֹה וְדִבַּרְתָּ אֵלָיו כֹּה־אָמַר יְהוָה אֱלֹהֵי הָעִבְרִים שַׁלַּח אֶת־עַמִּי וְיַעַבְדֻנִי׃ 2כִּי אִם־מָאֵן אַתָּה לְשַׁלֵּחַ וְעוֹדְךָ מַחֲזִיק בָּם׃ 3הִנֵּה יַד־יְהוָה הוֹיָה בְּמִקְנְךָ אֲשֶׁר בַּשָּׂדֶה בַּסּוּסִים בַּחֲמֹרִים בַּגְּמַלִּים בַּבָּקָר וּבַצֹּאן דֶּבֶר כָּבֵד מְאֹד׃ 4וְהִפְלָה יְהוָה בֵּין מִקְנֵה

---

repetition of his dream meant that the seven good and seven bad years were certainly coming (Gen 41:32). In that same speech, Joseph used the word "heavy" for the famine (41:31). As with the "piling up" in Exod 8:10, the cluster of language from the Joseph story suggests that the good that Joseph did for Egypt was repaid with bad by the subsequent Pharaohs, and this, again, suggests that the current plague suits the crime.

8:22. **an offensive thing to Egypt.** As we have seen in the Joseph story, there are matters relating to the Israelites' food that are pictured as being "an offensive thing to Egypt." There the Egyptians will not eat with Israelites (Gen 43:32), and they disdain the Israelite consumption of sheep. Now Moses uses this fact—which worked against the Israelites in Joseph's day—in the Israelites' favor.

8:25. **let Pharaoh not continue.** The Hebrew word for "continue" here is *yōsēp*— Joseph—thus culminating the string of connections of this story to the Joseph story.

4And YHWH will distinguish between Israel's livestock and Egypt's livestock, and not a thing out of all that Israel has will die. 5And YHWH has set an appointed time, saying: Tomorrow YHWH will do this thing in the land.'"

6And YHWH did this thing on the next day, and all Egypt's livestock died, and of all the livestock of the children of Israel not one died. 7And Pharaoh sent; and, here, not even one of Israel's livestock had died. And Pharaoh's heart was heavy, and he did not let the people go.

8And YHWH said to Moses and to Aaron, "Take handfuls of furnace ash, and let Moses fling it to the skies before Pharaoh's eyes. 9And it will become a powder on all the land of Egypt, and it will become a boil breaking out in sores on the humans and on the animals in all the land of Egypt." 10And they took the furnace ash and stood in front of Pharaoh, and Moses flung it to the skies, and it was a boil breaking out in sores in the humans and in the animals. 11And the magicians were not able to stand in front of Moses on account of the boil, because the boil was in the magicians and in all Egypt.

12And YHWH strengthened Pharaoh's heart, and he did not listen to them—as YHWH had spoken to Moses.

13And YHWH said to Moses, "Get up early in the morning and stand in front of Pharaoh, and you'll say to him, 'YHWH, God of the Hebrews,

יִשְׂרָאֵל וּבֵין מִקְנֵה מִצְרָיִם וְלֹא יָמוּת מִכָּל־לִבְנֵי יִשְׂרָאֵל דָּבָר: 5וַיָּשֶׂם יְהוָה מוֹעֵד לֵאמֹר מָחָר יַעֲשֶׂה יְהוָה הַדָּבָר הַזֶּה בָּאָרֶץ: 6וַיַּעַשׂ יְהוָה אֶת־הַדָּבָר הַזֶּה מִמָּחֳרָת וַיָּמָת כֹּל מִקְנֵה מִצְרָיִם וּמִמִּקְנֵה בְנֵי־יִשְׂרָאֵל לֹא־מֵת אֶחָד: 7וַיִּשְׁלַח פַּרְעֹה וְהִנֵּה לֹא־מֵת מִמִּקְנֵה יִשְׂרָאֵל עַד־אֶחָד וַיִּכְבַּד לֵב פַּרְעֹה וְלֹא שִׁלַּח אֶת־הָעָם: פ

8וַיֹּאמֶר יְהוָה אֶל־מֹשֶׁה וְאֶל־אַהֲרֹן קְחוּ לָכֶם מְלֹא חָפְנֵיכֶם פִּיחַ כִּבְשָׁן וּזְרָקוֹ מֹשֶׁה הַשָּׁמַיְמָה לְעֵינֵי פַרְעֹה: 9וְהָיָה לְאָבָק עַל כָּל־אֶרֶץ מִצְרָיִם וְהָיָה עַל־הָאָדָם וְעַל־הַבְּהֵמָה לִשְׁחִין פֹּרֵחַ אֲבַעְבֻּעֹת בְּכָל־אֶרֶץ מִצְרָיִם: 10וַיִּקְחוּ אֶת־פִּיחַ הַכִּבְשָׁן וַיַּעַמְדוּ לִפְנֵי פַרְעֹה וַיִּזְרֹק אֹתוֹ מֹשֶׁה הַשָּׁמַיְמָה וַיְהִי שְׁחִין אֲבַעְבֻּעֹת פֹּרֵחַ בָּאָדָם וּבַבְּהֵמָה: 11וְלֹא־יָכְלוּ הַחַרְטֻמִּים לַעֲמֹד לִפְנֵי מֹשֶׁה מִפְּנֵי הַשְּׁחִין כִּי־הָיָה הַשְּׁחִין בַּחַרְטֻמִּם וּבְכָל־מִצְרָיִם: 12וַיְחַזֵּק יְהוָה אֶת־לֵב פַּרְעֹה וְלֹא שָׁמַע אֲלֵהֶם כַּאֲשֶׁר דִּבֶּר יְהוָה אֶל־מֹשֶׁה: ס

13וַיֹּאמֶר יְהוָה אֶל־מֹשֶׁה הַשְׁכֵּם בַּבֹּקֶר וְהִתְיַצֵּב לִפְנֵי פַרְעֹה וְאָמַרְתָּ אֵלָיו כֹּה־אָמַר יְהוָה אֱלֹהֵי

9:8. **furnace.** The mention of a furnace is ominous because the only use of the word until now was to describe the smoke of the destruction of Sodom and Gomorrah (Gen 19:28). Now it comes again as a harbinger of something awful. But the next time it will be mentioned will be in connection with God's descent onto Mount Sinai (Exod 19:18). Then it will still be frightening, but it will be transformed from something ominous into something reflecting the closest that God ever comes to a human community in the Bible. And then the word will never occur again in the Bible. The point: humans must overcome their fear in order to come close to the divine.

9:12. **YHWH strengthened.** Until this point the text has said "Pharaoh's heart was strong." But now that a plague has struck even the magicians themselves, one might expect that Pharaoh would begin to weaken, and so God bolsters Pharaoh's resolve so as to achieve a particular outcome. See the comment on Exod 10:1. (For more on the meaning of this expression, see the comment on Deut 5:26.)

said this: Let my people go so they may serve me. [14]Because this time I am sending all my plagues at your heart and at your servants and at your people, so that you'll know that there is none like me in all the land. [15]Because by now I could have put out my hand and struck you and your people with an epidemic, and you would have been obliterated from the land. [16]And in fact I established you for this purpose, for the purpose of showing you my power—and in order to tell my name in all the earth. [17]You are still elevating yourself against my people by not letting them go. [18]Here, I'll be showering at this time tomorrow a very heavy hail, that there hasn't been one like it in Egypt from the day of its founding until now. [19]And now send, protect your livestock and everything that you have in the field. Every human and animal that will be found in the field and will not be gathered to the house: the hail will come down on them, and they'll die.'"

[20]Whoever feared YHWH's word among Pharaoh's servants had his servants and his livestock flee to the houses. [21]And whoever did not pay heed to YHWH's word left his servants and his livestock in the field.

[22]And YHWH said to Moses, "Reach out your hand at the skies, and let there be hail in all the land of Egypt: on human and on animal and on all vegetation of the field in the land of Egypt." [23]And Moses reached out his staff at the skies, and YHWH gave out thunders and hail, and lightning went to the ground. And YHWH showered hail on the land of Egypt. [24]And it was hail with lightning flashing in the hail, very heavy, that there had not been anything like it in all the land of Egypt since the time it became a nation. [25]And the hail struck in all the land of Egypt

הָעִבְרִים שַׁלַּח אֶת־עַמִּי וְיַעַבְדֻנִי: ‏14כִּי ׀ בַּפַּעַם הַזֹּאת אֲנִי שֹׁלֵחַ אֶת־כָּל־מַגֵּפֹתַי אֶל־לִבְּךָ וּבַעֲבָדֶיךָ וּבְעַמֶּךָ בַּעֲבוּר תֵּדַע כִּי אֵין כָּמֹנִי בְּכָל־הָאָרֶץ: ‏15כִּי עַתָּה שָׁלַחְתִּי אֶת־יָדִי וָאַךְ אוֹתְךָ וְאֶת־עַמְּךָ בַּדָּבֶר וַתִּכָּחֵד מִן־הָאָרֶץ: ‏16וְאוּלָם בַּעֲבוּר זֹאת הֶעֱמַדְתִּיךָ בַּעֲבוּר הַרְאֹתְךָ אֶת־כֹּחִי וּלְמַעַן סַפֵּר שְׁמִי בְּכָל־הָאָרֶץ: ‏17עוֹדְךָ מִסְתּוֹלֵל בְּעַמִּי לְבִלְתִּי שַׁלְּחָם: ‏18הִנְנִי מַמְטִיר כָּעֵת מָחָר בָּרָד כָּבֵד מְאֹד אֲשֶׁר לֹא־הָיָה כָמֹהוּ בְּמִצְרַיִם לְמִן־הַיּוֹם הִוָּסְדָה וְעַד־עָתָּה: ‏19וְעַתָּה שְׁלַח הָעֵז אֶת־מִקְנְךָ וְאֵת כָּל־אֲשֶׁר לְךָ בַּשָּׂדֶה כָּל־הָאָדָם וְהַבְּהֵמָה אֲשֶׁר־יִמָּצֵא בַשָּׂדֶה וְלֹא יֵאָסֵף הַבַּיְתָה וְיָרַד עֲלֵהֶם הַבָּרָד וָמֵתוּ: ‏20הַיָּרֵא אֶת־דְּבַר יְהוָה מֵעַבְדֵי פַּרְעֹה הֵנִיס אֶת־עֲבָדָיו וְאֶת־מִקְנֵהוּ אֶל־הַבָּתִּים: ‏21וַאֲשֶׁר לֹא־שָׂם לִבּוֹ אֶל־דְּבַר יְהוָה וַיַּעֲזֹב אֶת־עֲבָדָיו וְאֶת־מִקְנֵהוּ בַּשָּׂדֶה: פ ‏22וַיֹּאמֶר יְהוָה אֶל־מֹשֶׁה נְטֵה אֶת־יָדְךָ עַל־הַשָּׁמַיִם וִיהִי בָרָד בְּכָל־אֶרֶץ מִצְרָיִם עַל־הָאָדָם וְעַל־הַבְּהֵמָה וְעַל כָּל־עֵשֶׂב הַשָּׂדֶה בְּאֶרֶץ מִצְרָיִם: ‏23וַיֵּט מֹשֶׁה אֶת־מַטֵּהוּ עַל־הַשָּׁמַיִם וַיהוָה נָתַן קֹלֹת וּבָרָד וַתִּהֲלַךְ אֵשׁ אָרְצָה וַיַּמְטֵר יְהוָה בָּרָד עַל־אֶרֶץ מִצְרָיִם: ‏24וַיְהִי בָרָד וְאֵשׁ מִתְלַקַּחַת בְּתוֹךְ הַבָּרָד כָּבֵד מְאֹד אֲשֶׁר לֹא־הָיָה כָמֹהוּ בְּכָל־אֶרֶץ מִצְרַיִם מֵאָז הָיְתָה לְגוֹי: ‏25וַיַּךְ הַבָּרָד בְּכָל־אֶרֶץ מִצְרַיִם

9:23. **his staff.** Plagues are initiated with Aaron's staff, Moses' staff, and Moses' hand, or directly by God—four different ways—showing that it is not the staff or the hand that is doing it. They only usher in the miracles.

9:23. **thunders.** Literally, "sounds."

9:23. **lightning.** Literally, "fire."

everything that was in the field, from human to animal, and the hail struck all the vegetation of the field and shattered every tree of the field. ²⁶Only in the land of Goshen, where the children of Israel were, there was no hail.

²⁷And Pharaoh sent and called Moses and Aaron and said to them, "I sinned this time. YHWH is the virtuous one, and I and my people are the wicked ones. ²⁸Pray to YHWH, and enough of there being God's thunders and hail, so I may let you go, and you won't continue to stay."

²⁹And Moses said to him, "As I go out of the city I'll spread my hands to YHWH, the thunders will stop, and the hail won't be anymore, so that you'll know that the earth is YHWH's. ³⁰And you and your servants: I know that you don't yet fear in front of YHWH, God." (³¹And the flax and the barley were struck, because the barley was fresh and the flax was in bud. ³²And the wheat and the spelt were not struck, because they were late crops.) ³³And Moses went out from Pharaoh, from the city, and spread his hands to YHWH, and the thunders and the hail stopped, and a shower did not pour to the earth. ³⁴And Pharaoh saw that the shower and the hail and the thunder stopped, and he continued to sin, and he made his heart heavy, he and his servants. ³⁵And Pharaoh's heart was strong, and he did not let the children of Israel go—as YHWH had spoken by Moses' hand.

אֶת כָּל־אֲשֶׁר בַּשָּׂדֶה מֵאָדָם וְעַד־בְּהֵמָה וְאֵת כָּל־
עֵשֶׂב הַשָּׂדֶה הִכָּה הַבָּרָד וְאֶת־כָּל־עֵץ הַשָּׂדֶה
שִׁבֵּר: ²⁶רַק בְּאֶרֶץ גֹּשֶׁן אֲשֶׁר־שָׁם בְּנֵי יִשְׂרָאֵל לֹא
הָיָה בָּרָד: ²⁷וַיִּשְׁלַח פַּרְעֹה וַיִּקְרָא לְמֹשֶׁה וּלְאַהֲרֹן
וַיֹּאמֶר אֲלֵהֶם חָטָאתִי הַפָּעַם יְהוָה הַצַּדִּיק וַאֲנִי
וְעַמִּי הָרְשָׁעִים: ²⁸הַעְתִּירוּ אֶל־יְהוָה וְרַב מִהְיֹת
קֹלֹת אֱלֹהִים וּבָרָד וַאֲשַׁלְּחָה אֶתְכֶם וְלֹא תֹסִפוּן
לַעֲמֹד: ²⁹וַיֹּאמֶר אֵלָיו מֹשֶׁה כְּצֵאתִי אֶת־הָעִיר
אֶפְרֹשׂ אֶת־כַּפַּי אֶל־יְהוָה הַקֹּלוֹת יֶחְדָּלוּן וְהַבָּרָד
לֹא יִהְיֶה־עוֹד לְמַעַן תֵּדַע כִּי לַיהוָה הָאָרֶץ:
³⁰וְאַתָּה וַעֲבָדֶיךָ יָדַעְתִּי כִּי טֶרֶם תִּירְאוּן מִפְּנֵי
יְהוָה אֱלֹהִים: ³¹וְהַפִּשְׁתָּה וְהַשְּׂעֹרָה נֻכָּתָה כִּי
הַשְּׂעֹרָה אָבִיב וְהַפִּשְׁתָּה גִּבְעֹל: ³²וְהַחִטָּה וְהַכֻּסֶּמֶת
לֹא נֻכּוּ כִּי אֲפִילֹת הֵנָּה: ³³וַיֵּצֵא מֹשֶׁה מֵעִם פַּרְעֹה
אֶת־הָעִיר וַיִּפְרֹשׂ כַּפָּיו אֶל־יְהוָה וַיַּחְדְּלוּ הַקֹּלוֹת
וְהַבָּרָד וּמָטָר לֹא־נִתַּךְ אָרְצָה: ³⁴וַיַּרְא פַּרְעֹה כִּי־
חָדַל הַמָּטָר וְהַבָּרָד וְהַקֹּלֹת וַיֹּסֶף לַחֲטֹא וַיַּכְבֵּד
לִבּוֹ הוּא וַעֲבָדָיו: ³⁵וַיֶּחֱזַק לֵב פַּרְעֹה וְלֹא שִׁלַּח
אֶת־בְּנֵי יִשְׂרָאֵל כַּאֲשֶׁר דִּבֶּר יְהוָה בְּיַד־מֹשֶׁה: פ

COME

10

¹And YHWH said to Moses, "Come to Pharaoh, because I have made his heart and his servants' heart heavy for the purpose of

בא

10 ¹וַיֹּאמֶר יְהוָה אֶל־מֹשֶׁה בֹּא אֶל־פַּרְעֹה כִּי־
אֲנִי הִכְבַּדְתִּי אֶת־לִבּוֹ וְאֶת־לֵב עֲבָדָיו לְמַעַן שִׁתִי

9:29. **the earth is YHWH's.** Hebrew 'ereṣ can mean the "earth" or the "land." It is usually apparent which it means in context. But here either is possible. It may mean that all the world belongs to God. Or it may be a direct message to Pharaoh that the land of Egypt belongs to God and not to him.

10:1. **I have made his heart heavy.** Earlier the text says that *Pharaoh* made his heart heavy. Now it says that God claims to have done it. This verse may refer only to the

my setting these signs of mine among them ²and for the purpose that you will tell in the ears of your son and your son's son about how I abused Egypt and about my signs that I set among them, and you will know that I am YHWH."

³And Moses and Aaron came to Pharaoh and said to him, "YHWH, God of the Hebrews, said this: 'How long do you refuse to be humbled in front of me? Let my people go, so they may serve me. ⁴Because if you refuse to let my people go, here, I'm bringing a locust swarm in your border tomorrow, ⁵and it will cover the eye of the land, and one won't be able to see the land! And it will eat the remains of what has survived that is left to you from the hail, and it will eat every tree that is growing for you from the field. ⁶And

אֹתֹתַ֥י אֵ֖לֶּה בְּקִרְבּֽוֹ׃ ²וּלְמַ֡עַן תְּסַפֵּר֩ בְּאָזְנֵ֨י בִנְךָ֜ וּבֶן־בִּנְךָ֗ אֵ֣ת אֲשֶׁ֤ר הִתְעַלַּ֙לְתִּי֙ בְּמִצְרַ֔יִם וְאֶת־אֹתֹתַ֖י אֲשֶׁר־שַׂ֣מְתִּי בָ֑ם וִידַעְתֶּ֖ם כִּי־אֲנִ֥י יְהוָֽה׃ ³וַיָּבֹ֨א מֹשֶׁ֣ה וְאַהֲרֹן֮ אֶל־פַּרְעֹה֒ וַיֹּאמְר֣וּ אֵלָ֗יו כֹּֽה־אָמַ֤ר יְהוָה֙ אֱלֹהֵ֣י הָֽעִבְרִ֔ים עַד־מָתַ֣י מֵאַ֔נְתָּ לֵעָנֹ֖ת מִפָּנָ֑י שַׁלַּ֥ח עַמִּ֖י וְיַֽעַבְדֻֽנִי׃ ⁴כִּ֛י אִם־מָאֵ֥ן אַתָּ֖ה לְשַׁלֵּ֣חַ אֶת־עַמִּ֑י הִנְנִ֨י מֵבִ֥יא מָחָ֛ר אַרְבֶּ֖ה בִּגְבֻלֶֽךָ׃ ⁵וְכִסָּה֙ אֶת־עֵ֣ין הָאָ֔רֶץ וְלֹ֥א יוּכַ֖ל לִרְאֹ֣ת אֶת־הָאָ֑רֶץ וְאָכַ֣ל ׀ אֶת־יֶ֣תֶר הַפְּלֵטָ֗ה הַנִּשְׁאֶ֤רֶת לָכֶם֙ מִן־הַבָּרָ֔ד וְאָכַל֙ אֶת־כָּל־הָעֵ֔ץ הַצֹּמֵ֥חַ לָכֶ֖ם מִן־הַשָּׂדֶֽה׃ ⁶וּמָלְא֨וּ בָתֶּ֜יךָ

immediate condition; that is, that Pharaoh hardened his own heart before, but now it is God doing it. Or it may suggest dual causation; that is, even when the human (Pharaoh) decides himself, it is still God who is causing this decision. It is in the theme of YHWH's becoming known that we may find the explanation of the contradiction that has occurred even to little children: why does God harden Pharaoh's heart against releasing Israel and then plague Egypt for not letting them go?! The fact is that the Torah does not present the plagues as punishment of the Egyptians for enslaving the Israelites, but rather as signs by which YHWH will become known. Thus it pictures God stating unambiguously here:

> I have made his heart and his servants' heart heavy *for the purpose of* my setting these signs of mine among them and for the purpose that you will tell in the ears of your son and your son's son about how I abused Egypt and about my signs that I set among them, *and you will know that I am YHWH.*

Even more dramatically, YHWH tells Moses to inform the Pharaoh that "And in fact I established you for this purpose, for the purpose of showing you my power—and in order to tell my name in all the earth" (9:16). Dispersed through the account are frequent reminders that this is the purpose of the hardening of Pharaoh's heart (7:3–5; 11:9–10; 14:4,17–18) and that this is the purpose of the plagues (7:17; 8:6,18; 9:14,29). The Egyptians' suffering in the plagues may be understood to be justified, a consequence of their cruelty; but, still, the *purpose* of the plagues is not punishment but rather to make YHWH known.

10:5. **cover the eye of the land.** Meaning: the locust swarm will be so thick as to make the land invisible.

10:5. **the remains of what has survived that is left.** The phrase is a triple redundancy: *yeter happĕlētāh hanniš'eret.* Its purpose may be to develop the pun on the name of Jether, Moses' father-in-law (Exod 4:18).

they'll fill your houses and the houses of all your servants and the houses of all Egypt, which your fathers and your fathers' fathers did not see, from the day they were on the land until this day!" And he turned and went out from Pharaoh.

⁷And Pharaoh's servants said to him, "How long will this be a trap for us? Let the people go, so they may serve YHWH, their God. Don't you know yet that Egypt has perished?!"

⁸And Moses and Aaron were brought back to Pharaoh. And he said to them, "Go. Serve YHWH, your God. Who are the ones who are going?"

⁹And Moses said, "We'll go with our young and with our old, we'll go with our sons and with our daughters, with our sheep and with our oxen, because we have a festival of YHWH."

¹⁰And he said to them, "YHWH *would* be with you like that, when I would let you *and your infants* go, see, because bad is in front of your faces. ¹¹It is *not* like that. Go—the men!—and serve YHWH, because that is what you're asking." And he drove them out from Pharaoh's face.

¹²And YHWH said to Moses, "Reach out your hand at the land of Egypt for the locust, and it will come up on the land of Egypt and eat all the land's vegetation, everything that the hail has

וּבָתֶּיךָ כָל־עֲבָדֶיךָ וּבָתֵּי כָל־מִצְרַיִם אֲשֶׁר לֹא־רָאוּ אֲבֹתֶיךָ וַאֲבוֹת אֲבֹתֶיךָ מִיּוֹם הֱיוֹתָם עַל־הָאֲדָמָה עַד הַיּוֹם הַזֶּה וַיִּפֶן וַיֵּצֵא מֵעִם פַּרְעֹה: ⁷וַיֹּאמְרוּ עַבְדֵי פַרְעֹה אֵלָיו עַד־מָתַי יִהְיֶה זֶה לָנוּ לְמוֹקֵשׁ שַׁלַּח אֶת־הָאֲנָשִׁים וְיַעַבְדוּ אֶת־יְהוָה אֱלֹהֵיהֶם הֲטֶרֶם תֵּדַע כִּי אָבְדָה מִצְרָיִם: ⁸וַיּוּשַׁב אֶת־מֹשֶׁה וְאֶת־אַהֲרֹן אֶל־פַּרְעֹה וַיֹּאמֶר אֲלֵהֶם לְכוּ עִבְדוּ אֶת־יְהוָה אֱלֹהֵיכֶם מִי וָמִי הַהֹלְכִים: ⁹וַיֹּאמֶר מֹשֶׁה בִּנְעָרֵינוּ וּבִזְקֵנֵינוּ נֵלֵךְ בְּבָנֵינוּ וּבִבְנוֹתֵנוּ בְּצֹאנֵנוּ וּבִבְקָרֵנוּ נֵלֵךְ כִּי חַג־יְהוָה לָנוּ: ¹⁰וַיֹּאמֶר אֲלֵהֶם יְהִי כֵן יְהוָה עִמָּכֶם כַּאֲשֶׁר אֲשַׁלַּח אֶתְכֶם וְאֶת־טַפְּכֶם רְאוּ כִּי רָעָה נֶגֶד פְּנֵיכֶם: ¹¹לֹא כֵן לְכוּ־נָא הַגְּבָרִים וְעִבְדוּ אֶת־יְהוָה כִּי אֹתָהּ אַתֶּם מְבַקְשִׁים וַיְגָרֶשׁ אֹתָם מֵאֵת פְּנֵי פַרְעֹה: פ ¹²וַיֹּאמֶר יְהוָה אֶל־מֹשֶׁה נְטֵה יָדְךָ עַל־אֶרֶץ מִצְרַיִם בָּאַרְבֶּה וְיַעַל עַל־אֶרֶץ מִצְרָיִם וְיֹאכַל אֶת־כָּל־עֵשֶׂב הָאָרֶץ אֵת כָּל־אֲשֶׁר הִשְׁאִיר הַבָּרָד: ¹³וַיֵּט מֹשֶׁה אֶת־מַטֵּהוּ

10:7. **Egypt has perished**. They speak as if the country is already destroyed. Interpreters and translators have tried to make their statement more logical by understanding it to mean "Egypt is lost" or "ruined." But I think that Pharaoh's servants are pictured here as speaking with deliberate hyperbole. The Israelites themselves will use this very same hyperbole later: following the Korah rebellion, they say, "We have expired. We have perished" (Num 17:27).

10:10. **YHWH *would* be with you like that**. It is difficult to convey the Pharaoh's cynicism that is expressed in the Hebrew jussive. He says "Let it be so" in the sense that there is no chance at all that it could be so.

10:10. **and your infants**. Pharaoh is still negotiating, trying to give the minimum. First he refused to let the people have their religious festival. His second position was that they could have it in the land rather than leave Egypt. Now he says that they may leave, but their children must stay—thus guaranteeing that the people will return.

10:11. **the men**. The women must stay as well.

10:11. **he drove them out from Pharaoh's face**. Meaning: from Pharaoh's presence.

left." 13And Moses reached out his staff at the land of Egypt, and YHWH drove an east wind through the land all that day and all the night. It was the morning: and the east wind had carried the locust swarm. 14And the locust swarm came up over all the land of Egypt and lingered in all of Egypt's border, very heavy: before it there was no such locust swarm like it, and after it there will not be such. 15And it covered the eye of all the land, and the land was dark; and it ate all the land's vegetation and the fruit of every tree that the hail had left, and not any plant was left, in the tree and in the field's vegetation, in all the land of Egypt.

16And Pharaoh hurried to call Moses and Aaron, and he said, "I've sinned against YHWH, your God, and against you. 17And now, bear my sin just this one time and pray to YHWH, your God, that He'll turn just this death away from me." 18And he went out from Pharaoh and prayed to YHWH, 19and YHWH turned back a very strong west wind, and it picked up the locust swarm and blew it to the Red Sea. Not one locust was left in all of Egypt's border. 20And YHWH strengthened Pharaoh's heart, and he did not let the children of Israel go.

21And YHWH said to Moses, "Reach out your hand at the skies, and let there be darkness on the land of Egypt, and one will *feel* darkness." 22And Moses reached out his hand at the skies, and there was dismal darkness in all the land of Egypt—three days. 23Each man did not see his

עַל־אֶרֶץ מִצְרַיִם וַיהוָה נִהַג רוּחַ קָדִים בָּאָרֶץ כָּל־הַיּוֹם הַהוּא וְכָל־הַלָּיְלָה הַבֹּקֶר הָיָה וְרוּחַ הַקָּדִים נָשָׂא אֶת־הָאַרְבֶּה: 14וַיַּעַל הָאַרְבֶּה עַל כָּל־אֶרֶץ מִצְרַיִם וַיָּנַח בְּכֹל גְּבוּל מִצְרָיִם כָּבֵד מְאֹד לְפָנָיו לֹא־הָיָה כֵן אַרְבֶּה כָּמֹהוּ וְאַחֲרָיו לֹא יִהְיֶה־כֵּן: 15וַיְכַס אֶת־עֵין כָּל־הָאָרֶץ וַתֶּחְשַׁךְ הָאָרֶץ וַיֹּאכַל אֶת־כָּל־עֵשֶׂב הָאָרֶץ וְאֵת כָּל־פְּרִי הָעֵץ אֲשֶׁר הוֹתִיר הַבָּרָד וְלֹא־נוֹתַר כָּל־יֶרֶק בָּעֵץ וּבְעֵשֶׂב הַשָּׂדֶה בְּכָל־אֶרֶץ מִצְרָיִם: 16וַיְמַהֵר פַּרְעֹה לִקְרֹא לְמֹשֶׁה וּלְאַהֲרֹן וַיֹּאמֶר חָטָאתִי לַיהוָה אֱלֹהֵיכֶם וְלָכֶם: 17וְעַתָּה שָׂא נָא חַטָּאתִי אַךְ הַפַּעַם וְהַעְתִּירוּ לַיהוָה אֱלֹהֵיכֶם וְיָסֵר מֵעָלַי רַק אֶת־הַמָּוֶת הַזֶּה: 18וַיֵּצֵא מֵעִם פַּרְעֹה וַיֶּעְתַּר אֶל־יְהוָה: 19וַיַּהֲפֹךְ יְהוָה רוּחַ־יָם חָזָק מְאֹד וַיִּשָּׂא אֶת־הָאַרְבֶּה וַיִּתְקָעֵהוּ יָמָּה סּוּף לֹא נִשְׁאַר אַרְבֶּה אֶחָד בְּכֹל גְּבוּל מִצְרָיִם: 20וַיְחַזֵּק יְהוָה אֶת־לֵב פַּרְעֹה וְלֹא שִׁלַּח אֶת־בְּנֵי יִשְׂרָאֵל: פ

21וַיֹּאמֶר יְהוָה אֶל־מֹשֶׁה נְטֵה יָדְךָ עַל־הַשָּׁמַיִם וִיהִי חֹשֶׁךְ עַל־אֶרֶץ מִצְרַיִם וְיָמֵשׁ חֹשֶׁךְ: 22וַיֵּט מֹשֶׁה אֶת־יָדוֹ עַל־הַשָּׁמָיִם וַיְהִי חֹשֶׁךְ־אֲפֵלָה בְּכָל־אֶרֶץ מִצְרַיִם שְׁלֹשֶׁת יָמִים: 23לֹא־רָאוּ אִישׁ אֶת־

10:19. **Red Sea**. Not the so-called "Reed" Sea. See the comment on Exod 13:18.

10:21. **one will *feel* darkness**. Like the other plagues, this one is explicitly identified as different from what is found in nature at other times. The hail and locusts are unlike anything that has ever happened in Egypt. The darkness can be *felt*. There is no chance whatever that the Egyptians—or any interpreter of this text—can understand these as being chance occurrences of nature.

Note also that the word for "felt," Hebrew *yāmēš*, plays on the name Moses, *mōšeh*.

10:22. **three days**. This is further indication that no natural occurrence, such as an eclipse, is intended here; no eclipse lasts three days.

brother, and each man did not get up from under it—three days. And for all the children of Israel there was light in their homes.

24And Pharaoh called Moses, and he said, "Go. Serve YHWH. Only your sheep and your oxen will stay put. Your infants will go with you as well."

25And Moses said, "*You* shall put sacrifices and offerings in our hand as well, so we'll do them for YHWH, our God. 26And our livestock will go with us as well. Not a hoof will be left. Because we'll take from it to serve YHWH, our God, and we won't know how we'll serve YHWH until we come there."

27And YHWH strengthened Pharaoh's heart, and he was not willing to let them go.

28And Pharaoh said to him, "Go away from me! Watch yourself! Don't continue to see my face. Because in the day you see my face you'll die!"

29And Moses said, "So you've spoken: I won't continue to see your face anymore."

11 1And YHWH said to Moses, "I'll bring one more plague on Pharaoh and on Egypt. After that he'll let you go from here. When he lets go completely he'll *drive you out* from here! 2Speak in the people's ears that each man will ask of his neighbor and each woman of her neighbor items of silver and items of gold." 3And

אָחִ֔יו וְלֹא־קָ֛מוּ אִ֥ישׁ מִתַּחְתָּ֖יו שְׁלֹ֣שֶׁת יָמִ֑ים וּֽלְכָל־
בְּנֵ֧י יִשְׂרָאֵ֛ל הָ֥יָה א֖וֹר בְּמוֹשְׁבֹתָֽם: 24וַיִּקְרָ֨א פַרְעֹ֜ה
אֶל־מֹשֶׁ֗ה וַיֹּ֨אמֶר֙ לְכוּ֙ עִבְד֣וּ אֶת־יְהוָ֔ה רַ֛ק צֹאנְכֶ֥ם
וּבְקַרְכֶ֖ם יֻצָּ֑ג גַּֽם־טַפְּכֶ֖ם יֵלֵ֥ךְ עִמָּכֶֽם: 25וַיֹּ֣אמֶר
מֹשֶׁ֔ה גַּם־אַתָּ֛ה תִּתֵּ֥ן בְּיָדֵ֖נוּ זְבָחִ֣ים וְעֹלֹ֑ת וְעָשִׂ֖ינוּ
לַיהוָ֥ה אֱלֹהֵֽינוּ: 26וְגַם־מִקְנֵ֜נוּ יֵלֵ֣ךְ עִמָּ֗נוּ לֹ֤א תִשָּׁאֵר֙
פַּרְסָ֔ה כִּ֚י מִמֶּ֣נּוּ נִקַּ֔ח לַעֲבֹ֖ד אֶת־יְהוָ֣ה אֱלֹהֵ֑ינוּ
וַאֲנַ֣חְנוּ לֹֽא־נֵדַ֗ע מַֽה־נַּעֲבֹד֙ אֶת־יְהוָ֔ה עַד־בֹּאֵ֖נוּ
שָֽׁמָּה: 27וַיְחַזֵּ֣ק יְהוָ֔ה אֶת־לֵ֖ב פַּרְעֹ֑ה וְלֹ֥א אָבָ֖ה
לְשַׁלְּחָֽם: 28וַיֹּֽאמֶר־ל֤וֹ פַרְעֹה֙ לֵ֣ךְ מֵעָלָ֔י הִשָּׁ֣מֶר לְךָ֗
אַל־תֹּ֨סֶף֙ רְא֣וֹת פָּנַ֔י כִּ֗י בְּי֛וֹם רְאֹתְךָ֥ פָנַ֖י תָּמֽוּת:
29וַיֹּ֥אמֶר מֹשֶׁ֖ה כֵּ֣ן דִּבַּ֑רְתָּ לֹא־אֹסִ֥ף ע֖וֹד רְא֥וֹת
פָּנֶֽיךָ: פ

11 1וַיֹּ֨אמֶר יְהוָ֜ה אֶל־מֹשֶׁ֗ה ע֣וֹד נֶ֤גַע אֶחָד֙
אָבִ֤יא עַל־פַּרְעֹה֙ וְעַל־מִצְרַ֔יִם אַֽחֲרֵי־כֵ֕ן יְשַׁלַּ֥ח
אֶתְכֶ֖ם מִזֶּ֑ה כְּשַׁ֨לְּח֔וֹ כָּלָ֕ה גָּרֵ֛שׁ יְגָרֵ֥שׁ אֶתְכֶ֖ם מִזֶּֽה:
2דַּבֶּר־נָ֖א בְּאָזְנֵ֣י הָעָ֑ם וְיִשְׁאֲל֞וּ אִ֣ישׁ ׀ מֵאֵ֣ת רֵעֵ֗הוּ
וְאִשָּׁה֙ מֵאֵ֣ת רְעוּתָ֔הּ כְּלֵי־כֶ֖סֶף וּכְלֵ֥י זָהָֽב: 3וַיִּתֵּ֨ן

10:23. **from under it.** The Hebrew (מתחתיו) can mean "from under it" or "from his place." Everyone else makes it "from his place" or some equivalent, but I think that the meaning "from under it" is possible, even preferable. It conveys a much more vivid picture: of a thick darkness settling like a blanket on Egypt so that no one would even dare to move beneath it.

10:24. **your sheep and your oxen will stay put.** Still negotiating, Pharaoh now agrees to let the children go but wants the livestock to stay. It is not as strong a guarantee to force Israel to return as holding the children was, but it would mean that the Israelites would not have sufficient food to make a long journey, or at least it would mean that the Egyptians would get the livestock.

10:28,29; 11:6. **continue.** The word—Hebrew root *ysp*, meaning to do again, add, continue—occurs three times in succession, a final reminder of Joseph (*yôsēp*), whom the oppressing Pharaohs did not know.

YHWH put the people's favor in the Egyptians' eyes. Also, the man Moses was very big in the land of Egypt in the eyes of Pharaoh's servants and in the people's eyes.

4And Moses said, "YHWH said this: In the middle of the night I am going out through Egypt, 5and every firstborn in the land of Egypt will die, from the firstborn of Pharaoh who is sitting on his throne to the firstborn of the maid who is behind the mill and every firstborn of an animal. 6And there will be a big cry in all the land of Egypt, that there has been none like it and there won't continue to be like it. 7But not a dog will move its tongue at any of the children of Israel, from man to animal, so that you'll know that YHWH will distinguish between Egypt and Israel. 8And all these servants of yours will come down to *me*, and they'll bow to *me*, saying: 'Go out, you and all the people who are at your feet.' And after that I'll go out!" And he went out from Pharaoh in a flaring of anger.

יְהוָה אֶת־חֵן הָעָם בְּעֵינֵי מִצְרָיִם גַּם ׀ הָאִישׁ מֹשֶׁה גָּדוֹל מְאֹד בְּאֶרֶץ מִצְרַיִם בְּעֵינֵי עַבְדֵי־פַרְעֹה וּבְעֵינֵי הָעָם: ס 4וַיֹּאמֶר מֹשֶׁה כֹּה אָמַר יְהוָה כַּחֲצֹת הַלַּיְלָה אֲנִי יוֹצֵא בְּתוֹךְ מִצְרָיִם: 5וּמֵת כָּל־בְּכוֹר בְּאֶרֶץ מִצְרַיִם מִבְּכוֹר פַּרְעֹה הַיֹּשֵׁב עַל־כִּסְאוֹ עַד בְּכוֹר הַשִּׁפְחָה אֲשֶׁר אַחַר הָרֵחָיִם וְכֹל בְּכוֹר בְּהֵמָה: 6וְהָיְתָה צְעָקָה גְדֹלָה בְּכָל־אֶרֶץ מִצְרָיִם אֲשֶׁר כָּמֹהוּ לֹא נִהְיָתָה וְכָמֹהוּ לֹא תֹסִף: 7וּלְכֹל ׀ בְּנֵי יִשְׂרָאֵל לֹא יֶחֱרַץ־כֶּלֶב לְשֹׁנוֹ לְמֵאִישׁ וְעַד־בְּהֵמָה לְמַעַן תֵּדְעוּן אֲשֶׁר יַפְלֶה יְהוָה בֵּין מִצְרַיִם וּבֵין יִשְׂרָאֵל: 8וְיָרְדוּ כָל־עֲבָדֶיךָ אֵלֶּה אֵלַי וְהִשְׁתַּחֲווּ־לִי לֵאמֹר צֵא אַתָּה וְכָל־הָעָם אֲשֶׁר־בְּרַגְלֶיךָ וְאַחֲרֵי־כֵן אֵצֵא וַיֵּצֵא מֵעִם־פַּרְעֹה

11:4. **I am going out through Egypt.** YHWH Himself. Later Jewish tradition, presumably unable to bear the thought of God personally passing through Egypt and causing the deaths, introduced the horrible concept of the "Angel of Death." But there is no such thing as an Angel of Death in the Bible. The text is explicit that God personally passes through Egypt. The subtlety comes in the question of the relationship between the deity and the agent of the destruction: on one hand, God says, "I strike Egypt" (12:13), and, on the other hand, it appears that God halts at the door and prevents this destroyer (*mašḥît*) from coming into the house. Is the *mašḥît* a sickness? a force? or a personified being? The wording of 12:13 ("a plague among you as a destroyer") indicates that the destroyer is the plague itself and not some person or angel. In any case, God clearly is responsible for the creation of it and can therefore say "*I* strike."

11:8. **they'll bow to *me*.** Read this speech carefully. At the beginning, when Moses uses the first person he is quoting God: "*I* am going out through Egypt . . ." But here at the end, the first person refers to himself: "will come down to *me*, and they'll bow to *me*. . . . And after that *I*'ll go out!" It is hard to say where in the text he stops quoting God and starts referring to himself. This is tremendously important, a turning point in Moses' life. His fear of Pharaoh and his lack of confidence are gone. And he has shifted Pharaoh's attention from God to himself. He has not stepped over the line and failed to credit God, but he will do that years later in his sin at Meribah (Numbers 20). This moment in the Pharaoh's court is thus a step in the long process of Moses' evolving relationship with his God and his people, which will have a tragic aspect in the end.

9And YHWH said to Moses, "Pharaoh won't listen to you—in order to multiply my wonders in the land of Egypt." 10And Moses and Aaron had done all these wonders in front of Pharaoh, and YHWH strengthened Pharaoh's heart, and he did not let the children of Israel go from his land.

12 1And YHWH said to Moses and to Aaron in the land of Egypt, saying, 2"This month is the beginning of months for you. It is first of the months of the year for you. 3Speak to all of the congregation of Israel, saying: On the tenth of this month, let them each take a lamb for the fathers' houses, a lamb per house. 4And if the household will be too few for a lamb, then he and his neighbor who is close to his house will take it according to the count of persons; you shall count each person according to what he eats for the lamb. 5You shall have an unblemished, male, year-old lamb; you shall take it from the sheep or from the goats. 6And it will be for you to watch over until the fourteenth day of this month. And all the community of the congregation of Israel will slaughter it 'between the two evenings.' 7And they will take some of the blood and place it on the two doorposts and on the lintel on the houses in which they will eat it. 8And they will eat the meat in this night; they will eat it fire-roasted and with unleavened bread on bitter herbs. 9Do not eat any of it raw or *cooked* in water, but fire-roasted: its head with its legs and with its innards. 10And do not leave any of it

וַיֹּאמֶר יְהוָה אֶל־מֹשֶׁה לֹא־יִשְׁמַע 9 ס בַּחֲרִי־אָף:
אֲלֵיכֶם פַּרְעֹה לְמַעַן רְבוֹת מוֹפְתַי בְּאֶרֶץ מִצְרָיִם:
10וּמֹשֶׁה וְאַהֲרֹן עָשׂוּ אֶת־כָּל־הַמֹּפְתִים הָאֵלֶּה לִפְנֵי
פַרְעֹה וַיְחַזֵּק יְהוָה אֶת־לֵב פַּרְעֹה וְלֹא־שִׁלַּח אֶת־
בְּנֵי־יִשְׂרָאֵל מֵאַרְצוֹ: פ

12 1וַיֹּאמֶר יְהוָה אֶל־מֹשֶׁה וְאֶל־אַהֲרֹן בְּאֶרֶץ
מִצְרַיִם לֵאמֹר: 2הַחֹדֶשׁ הַזֶּה לָכֶם רֹאשׁ חֳדָשִׁים
רִאשׁוֹן הוּא לָכֶם לְחָדְשֵׁי הַשָּׁנָה: 3דַּבְּרוּ אֶל־כָּל־
עֲדַת יִשְׂרָאֵל לֵאמֹר בֶּעָשֹׂר לַחֹדֶשׁ הַזֶּה וְיִקְחוּ
לָהֶם אִישׁ שֶׂה לְבֵית־אָבֹת שֶׂה לַבָּיִת: 4וְאִם־יִמְעַט
הַבַּיִת מִהְיֹת מִשֶּׂה וְלָקַח הוּא וּשְׁכֵנוֹ הַקָּרֹב אֶל־
בֵּיתוֹ בְּמִכְסַת נְפָשֹׁת אִישׁ לְפִי אָכְלוֹ תָּכֹסּוּ עַל־
הַשֶּׂה: 5שֶׂה תָמִים זָכָר בֶּן־שָׁנָה יִהְיֶה לָכֶם מִן־
הַכְּבָשִׂים וּמִן־הָעִזִּים תִּקָּחוּ: 6וְהָיָה לָכֶם לְמִשְׁמֶרֶת
עַד אַרְבָּעָה עָשָׂר יוֹם לַחֹדֶשׁ הַזֶּה וְשָׁחֲטוּ אֹתוֹ כֹּל
קְהַל עֲדַת־יִשְׂרָאֵל בֵּין הָעַרְבָּיִם: 7וְלָקְחוּ מִן־הַדָּם
וְנָתְנוּ עַל־שְׁתֵּי הַמְּזוּזֹת וְעַל־הַמַּשְׁקוֹף עַל הַבָּתִּים
אֲשֶׁר־יֹאכְלוּ אֹתוֹ בָּהֶם: 8וְאָכְלוּ אֶת־הַבָּשָׂר בַּלַּיְלָה
הַזֶּה צְלִי־אֵשׁ וּמַצּוֹת עַל־מְרֹרִים יֹאכְלֻהוּ: 9אַל־
תֹּאכְלוּ מִמֶּנּוּ נָא וּבָשֵׁל מְבֻשָּׁל בַּמָּיִם כִּי אִם־צְלִי־
אֵשׁ רֹאשׁוֹ עַל־כְּרָעָיו וְעַל־קִרְבּוֹ: 10וְלֹא־תוֹתִירוּ

12:2. **first of the months of the year**. According to the Torah, the new year begins in spring, not in the fall as Jews celebrate it now. The holiday that comes on the first day of fall is never referred to in the Torah as Rosh Hashanah (Lev 23:23–25).

12:2–11. **This month . . .** This is sometimes thought to be the instruction for the annual observance of Passover for all time. But the wording and context seem rather to apply only to the night before the actual exodus from Egypt. The Passover instructions for future generations come later, starting at 12:14.

12:6. **between the two evenings**. Understood to mean the early evening hours: "dusk" or "twilight."

until morning; and you shall burn what is left of it until morning in fire. [11]And you shall eat it like this: your hips clothed, your shoes on your feet, and your staff in your hand; and you shall eat it in haste. It is YHWH's Passover.

[12]"And I shall pass through the land of Egypt in this night, and I shall strike every firstborn in the land of Egypt, from human to animal, and I shall make judgments on all the gods of Egypt. I am YHWH. [13]And the blood will be as a sign for you on the houses in which you are, and I shall see the blood, and I shall halt at you, and there won't be a plague among you as a destroyer when I strike in the land of Egypt.

[14]"And this day will become a commemoration for you, and you shall celebrate it, a festival to YHWH; you shall celebrate it through your generations, an eternal law: [15]Seven days you shall eat unleavened bread. Indeed, on the first

מִמֶּנּוּ עַד־בֹּקֶר וְהַנֹּתָר מִמֶּנּוּ עַד־בֹּקֶר בָּאֵשׁ תִּשְׂרֹפוּ: 11וְכָכָה תֹּאכְלוּ אֹתוֹ מָתְנֵיכֶם חֲגֻרִים נַעֲלֵיכֶם בְּרַגְלֵיכֶם וּמַקֶּלְכֶם בְּיֶדְכֶם וַאֲכַלְתֶּם אֹתוֹ בְּחִפָּזוֹן פֶּסַח הוּא לַיהוָה: 12וְעָבַרְתִּי בְאֶרֶץ־ מִצְרַיִם בַּלַּיְלָה הַזֶּה וְהִכֵּיתִי כָל־בְּכוֹר בְּאֶרֶץ מִצְרַיִם מֵאָדָם וְעַד־בְּהֵמָה וּבְכָל־אֱלֹהֵי מִצְרַיִם אֶעֱשֶׂה שְׁפָטִים אֲנִי יְהוָה: 13וְהָיָה הַדָּם לָכֶם לְאֹת עַל הַבָּתִּים אֲשֶׁר אַתֶּם שָׁם וְרָאִיתִי אֶת־הַדָּם וּפָסַחְתִּי עֲלֵכֶם וְלֹא־יִהְיֶה בָכֶם נֶגֶף לְמַשְׁחִית בְּהַכֹּתִי בְּאֶרֶץ מִצְרַיִם: 14וְהָיָה הַיּוֹם הַזֶּה לָכֶם לְזִכָּרוֹן וְחַגֹּתֶם אֹתוֹ חַג לַיהוָה לְדֹרֹתֵיכֶם חֻקַּת עוֹלָם תְּחָגֻּהוּ: 15שִׁבְעַת יָמִים מַצּוֹת תֹּאכֵלוּ אַךְ

12:12. **judgments on all the gods of Egypt.** The best-known deity of Egyptian religion is the sun, and Egyptian religion was profoundly concerned with death. The plagues culminate with "judgments" on these. In the ninth plague there is darkness for three days. And in the final plague death itself is shown to be in YHWH's control, as only firstborn humans and animals die. (The first plague turns Egypt's waters to blood, and this too undermines Egyptian deities.) Some readers may see in this an implicit recognition of the existence of the pagan deities, who must be thought to exist in order to be thus defeated. The text, however, does not present these "judgments" as a *defeat* of the gods. The plagues are rather a show of where power resides, namely, outside the gods (which is to say, outside of nature), beyond them. The forces of nature are not personified in the plagues narrative, and they do not confront or challenge the God of Israel. They are merely manipulated in the course of events.

12:13,23,27. **halt.** Hebrew *pāsaḥ* does not mean "to pass over." That wording has led people to images of the deity floating over houses. The verb means "to halt" or "to walk in a halting manner"; it can refer to limping (2 Sam 4:4). The noun form *pissēaḥ* means a cripple (2 Sam 9:13). Admittedly, this verb occurs in Isaiah in a verse that pictures God defending Jerusalem "like birds flying" (31:5). Still, "halting" fits with the context here in Exodus, especially in 12:23, where it suggests a conception of the deity moving along through Egypt, spotting the blood on the doorposts, and coming to an abrupt stop. God "halts on the threshold" and does not allow the destroying force to enter the house. "Passing over" the threshold does not really fit with this picture of blocking or preventing the destroyer.

12:13,23. **destroyer.** The Hebrew pun conveys the message: the Israelites are to slaughter (root שׁחט) the lamb so as to keep out the destroyer (root שׁחת).

day you shall make leaven *cease* from your houses. Because anyone who eats leavened bread: that person will be cut off from Israel— from the first day to the seventh day. 16And you will have a holy assembly on the first day and a holy assembly on the seventh day. Not any work will be done on them. Just what will be eaten by each person: that alone will be done for you. 17And you shall observe the unleavened bread, because in this very day I brought out your masses from the land of Egypt, and you shall observe this day through your generations, an eternal law. 18In the first month, on the fourteenth day of the month, in the evening, you shall eat unleavened bread, until the twenty-first day of the month, in the evening. 19Seven days leaven shall not be found in your houses, because anyone who eats something leavened: that person will be cut off from the congregation of Israel, whether the alien or the citizen of the land. 20You shall not eat anything leavened; in all your homes you shall eat unleavened bread."

21And Moses called all Israel's elders, and he said to them, "Pull out and take a sheep for your families and slaughter the Passover. 22And you'll take a bunch of hyssop and dip in the blood that is in a basin and touch some of the blood that is in the basin to the lintel and to the two door-posts. And you shall not go out, each one, from

בַּיּוֹם הָרִאשׁוֹן תַּשְׁבִּיתוּ שְּׂאֹר מִבָּתֵּיכֶם כִּי ׀ כָּל־
אֹכֵל חָמֵץ וְנִכְרְתָה הַנֶּפֶשׁ הַהִוא מִיִּשְׂרָאֵל מִיּוֹם
הָרִאשֹׁן עַד־יוֹם הַשְּׁבִעִי: 16וּבַיּוֹם הָרִאשׁוֹן מִקְרָא־
קֹדֶשׁ וּבַיּוֹם הַשְּׁבִיעִי מִקְרָא־קֹדֶשׁ יִהְיֶה לָכֶם כָּל־
מְלָאכָה לֹא־יֵעָשֶׂה בָהֶם אַךְ אֲשֶׁר יֵאָכֵל לְכָל־נֶפֶשׁ
הוּא לְבַדּוֹ יֵעָשֶׂה לָכֶם: 17וּשְׁמַרְתֶּם אֶת־הַמַּצּוֹת כִּי
בְּעֶצֶם הַיּוֹם הַזֶּה הוֹצֵאתִי אֶת־צִבְאוֹתֵיכֶם מֵאֶרֶץ
מִצְרָיִם וּשְׁמַרְתֶּם אֶת־הַיּוֹם הַזֶּה לְדֹרֹתֵיכֶם חֻקַּת
עוֹלָם: 18בָּרִאשֹׁן בְּאַרְבָּעָה עָשָׂר יוֹם לַחֹדֶשׁ בָּעֶרֶב
תֹּאכְלוּ מַצֹּת עַד יוֹם הָאֶחָד וְעֶשְׂרִים לַחֹדֶשׁ
בָּעָרֶב: 19שִׁבְעַת יָמִים שְׂאֹר לֹא יִמָּצֵא בְּבָתֵּיכֶם
כִּי ׀ כָּל־אֹכֵל מַחְמֶצֶת וְנִכְרְתָה הַנֶּפֶשׁ הַהִוא
מֵעֲדַת יִשְׂרָאֵל בַּגֵּר וּבְאֶזְרַח הָאָרֶץ: 20כָּל־מַחְמֶצֶת
לֹא תֹאכֵלוּ בְּכֹל מוֹשְׁבֹתֵיכֶם תֹּאכְלוּ מַצּוֹת: פ
21וַיִּקְרָא מֹשֶׁה לְכָל־זִקְנֵי יִשְׂרָאֵל וַיֹּאמֶר
אֲלֵהֶם מִשְׁכוּ וּקְחוּ לָכֶם צֹאן לְמִשְׁפְּחֹתֵיכֶם וְשַׁחֲטוּ
הַפָּסַח: 22וּלְקַחְתֶּם אֲגֻדַּת אֵזוֹב וּטְבַלְתֶּם בַּדָּם
אֲשֶׁר־בַּסַּף וְהִגַּעְתֶּם אֶל־הַמַּשְׁקוֹף וְאֶל־שְׁתֵּי
הַמְּזוּזֹת מִן־הַדָּם אֲשֶׁר בַּסָּף וְאַתֶּם לֹא תֵצְאוּ אִישׁ

12:15. make leaven *cease*. In the preceding verse it is said that the Passover festival is to be celebrated as a commemoration of what happened in Egypt. The wording now conveys this: The command to "make leaven cease" recalls Pharaoh's first meeting with Moses, in which he says, "You've *made them cease* from their burdens" (Exod 5:5).

12:17. observe the unleavened bread. Meaning: observe the commandment concerning the unleavened bread. The Septuagint and the Samaritan have "the commandment." The confusion may owe to the fact that the words "unleavened bread" and "commandment" look the same in Hebrew consonants: מצות.

12:21. Passover. I have retained the English translation "Passover" rather than using some form of the word "halt." Although the latter would preserve the connection between this word and the story of God's halting, the fact remains that Passover is now the established, famous name of the holiday, and there is no point in ignoring this in a translation.

his house's entrance until morning. 23And YHWH will pass to strike Egypt, and He'll see the blood on the lintel and on the two doorposts, and YHWH will halt at the entrance and will not allow the destroyer to come to your houses to strike. 24And you shall observe this thing as a law for you and your children forever. 25And it will be, when you will come to the land that YHWH will give to you as He has spoken, that you shall observe this service. 26And it will be, when your children will say to you, 'What is this service to you?' 27that you shall say, 'It is the Passover sacrifice to YHWH, because He halted at the houses of the children of Israel in Egypt when He struck Egypt, and He saved our houses.'"

And the people knelt and bowed. 28And the children of Israel went and did as YHWH had commanded Moses and Aaron. They did so.

29And it was in the middle of the night, and YHWH struck every firstborn in the land of Egypt, from the firstborn of Pharaoh who was sitting on his throne to the firstborn of the prisoner who was in the prison house and every firstborn of an animal. 30And Pharaoh got up at night, he and all his servants and all Egypt, and there was a big cry in Egypt, because there was not a house in which there was not one dead. 31And he called Moses and Aaron at night, and he said, "Get up. Go out from among my people, both you and the children of Israel, and go, serve YHWH as you spoke. 32Take your sheep also,

מִפֶּתַח־בֵּיתֹו עַד־בֹּקֶר: 23וְעָבַר יְהוָה לִנְגֹּף אֶת־מִצְרַיִם וְרָאָה אֶת־הַדָּם עַל־הַמַּשְׁקֹוף וְעַל שְׁתֵּי הַמְּזוּזֹת וּפָסַח יְהוָה עַל־הַפֶּתַח וְלֹא יִתֵּן הַמַּשְׁחִית לָבֹא אֶל־בָּתֵּיכֶם לִנְגֹּף: 24וּשְׁמַרְתֶּם אֶת־הַדָּבָר הַזֶּה לְחָק־לְךָ וּלְבָנֶיךָ עַד־עֹולָם: 25וְהָיָה כִּי־תָבֹאוּ אֶל־הָאָרֶץ אֲשֶׁר יִתֵּן יְהוָה לָכֶם כַּאֲשֶׁר דִּבֵּר וּשְׁמַרְתֶּם אֶת־הָעֲבֹדָה הַזֹּאת: 26וְהָיָה כִּי־יֹאמְרוּ אֲלֵיכֶם בְּנֵיכֶם מָה הָעֲבֹדָה הַזֹּאת לָכֶם: 27וַאֲמַרְתֶּם זֶבַח־פֶּסַח הוּא לַיהוָה אֲשֶׁר פָּסַח עַל־בָּתֵּי בְנֵי־יִשְׂרָאֵל בְּמִצְרַיִם בְּנָגְפֹּו אֶת־מִצְרַיִם וְאֶת־בָּתֵּינוּ הִצִּיל וַיִּקֹּד הָעָם וַיִּשְׁתַּחֲווּ: 28וַיֵּלְכוּ וַיַּעֲשׂוּ בְּנֵי יִשְׂרָאֵל כַּאֲשֶׁר צִוָּה יְהוָה אֶת־מֹשֶׁה וְאַהֲרֹן כֵּן עָשׂוּ: ס 29וַיְהִי | בַּחֲצִי הַלַּיְלָה וַיהוָה הִכָּה כָל־בְּכֹור בְּאֶרֶץ מִצְרַיִם מִבְּכֹר פַּרְעֹה הַיֹּשֵׁב עַל־כִּסְאֹו עַד בְּכֹור הַשְּׁבִי אֲשֶׁר בְּבֵית הַבֹּור וְכֹל בְּכֹור בְּהֵמָה: 30וַיָּקָם פַּרְעֹה לַיְלָה הוּא וְכָל־עֲבָדָיו וְכָל־מִצְרַיִם וַתְּהִי צְעָקָה גְדֹלָה בְּמִצְרָיִם כִּי־אֵין בַּיִת אֲשֶׁר אֵין־שָׁם מֵת: 31וַיִּקְרָא לְמֹשֶׁה וּלְאַהֲרֹן לַיְלָה וַיֹּאמֶר קוּמוּ צְּאוּ מִתֹּוךְ עַמִּי גַּם־אַתֶּם גַּם־בְּנֵי יִשְׂרָאֵל וּלְכוּ עִבְדוּ אֶת־יְהוָה כְּדַבֶּרְכֶם: 32גַּם־צֹאנְכֶם גַּם־בְּקַרְכֶם קְחוּ כַּאֲשֶׁר

12:31. **he called Moses and Aaron.** It is not clear whether this means that they go back to him or that they just receive a message from him. The issue is that Pharaoh had said, "Don't continue to see my face. Because in the day you see my face you'll die!" And Moses had answered, "So you've spoken: I won't continue to see your face anymore" (10:28–29). So if Pharaoh sees Moses now, it means that his threat has proved empty; and Moses' answer to him must be cynical: "So *you've* spoken!" Or, if Pharaoh and Moses do not see each other now, then Moses' answer must be understood to be ironic: "You're right, I won't see you again, because we'll be gone!"

12:31. **as you spoke.** What we have seen here is a gradual overwhelming of the power of Egypt through twists of events and personalities, stymieing the Pharaoh's initial confidence and leading him to surrender unconditionally. In the first meeting he is unbending. In the second meeting and through the first two plagues, he stands firm

your oxen also, as you spoke, and go. And you'll bless me as well!"

33And Egypt was forceful on the people to hurry to let them go from the land, because they said, "We're all dead!" 34And the people carried off its dough before it leavened, their bowls being wrapped in their garments on their shoulder. 35And the children of Israel had done according to Moses' word, and they asked items of silver and items of gold and garments from Egypt. 36And YHWH had put the people's favor in the Egyptians' eyes, and they lent to them, and they despoiled Egypt.

37And the children of Israel traveled from Rameses to Succoth, about six hundred thousand on foot—men, apart from infants. 38And also a great mixture had gone up with them, and

33וַתֶּחֱזַק מִצְרַיִם דִּבַּרְתֶּם וְלֵכוּ וּבֵרַכְתֶּם גַּם־אֹתִי: עַל־הָעָם לְמַהֵר לְשַׁלְּחָם מִן־הָאָרֶץ כִּי אָמְרוּ כֻּלָּנוּ מֵתִים: 34וַיִּשָּׂא הָעָם אֶת־בְּצֵקוֹ טֶרֶם יֶחְמָץ מִשְׁאֲרֹתָם צְרֻרֹת בְּשִׂמְלֹתָם עַל־שִׁכְמָם: 35וּבְנֵי־ יִשְׂרָאֵל עָשׂוּ כִּדְבַר מֹשֶׁה וַיִּשְׁאֲלוּ מִמִּצְרַיִם כְּלֵי־ כֶסֶף וּכְלֵי זָהָב וּשְׂמָלֹת: 36וַיהֹוָה נָתַן אֶת־חֵן הָעָם בְּעֵינֵי מִצְרַיִם וַיַּשְׁאִלוּם וַיְנַצְּלוּ אֶת־מִצְרָיִם: פ 37וַיִּסְעוּ בְנֵי־יִשְׂרָאֵל מֵרַעְמְסֵס סֻכֹּתָה כְּשֵׁשׁ־מֵאוֹת אֶלֶף רַגְלִי הַגְּבָרִים לְבַד מִטָּף: 38וְגַם־עֵרֶב רַב

---

as his magicians perform the wonders as well. The magicians cannot perform the third plague, and so the Pharaoh, no longer commanding cosmic forces himself, negotiates on the fourth ("Only don't go too far"). He gets away with his reneging on the negotiation, and so he stands firm again through the fifth plague. His magicians themselves suffer the sixth plague, and, following this indication that the opposing power can even encroach on his forces, the Pharaoh talks to Moses again on the seventh, generously sharing the blame with his subjects ("I *and my people* are wrong . . . "). When he reneges yet again, and an eighth plague strikes, his own servants urge him to give up resisting ("Don't you know yet that Egypt has perished?"). He then negotiates again ("just the men"). When this only leads to a ninth plague, darkening Egypt's divine sun, he negotiates again, allowing the children, but not the livestock, to go. When Moses insists on the livestock as well, the Pharaoh returns to his original position, refusing to let the people go and harshly telling Moses to get out and never return. The horror of the tenth plague then comes, and the Pharaoh capitulates utterly. It becomes clear that this had never been a matter of negotiation at all, but rather an agonizing, gradual drawing of the Pharaoh to a decision that had been inescapable from the start.

12:34. before it leavened. My colleague William Propp asks: Is the bread on the night of the exodus leavened or unleavened? He answers that it is leavened. The reason it does not rise is that the people carry off the dough before it has time to rise. The ban on eating leaven on Passover forever after this is a commemoration of this occurrence: "You shall eat unleavened bread . . . because you went out from the land of Egypt in haste" (Deut 16:3). He may be right, or perhaps we should understand this verse to mean that the people carry off the dough before they have time to put in the leaven, or that they deliberately do not leaven the dough because they anticipate leaving in a hurry. In any case, the historical origin of not eating leaven on Passover has associations beyond this etiological story. See the comment on Exod 29:2.

sheep and oxen, a very heavy livestock. ³⁹And they baked the dough that they brought out of Egypt: cakes of unleavened bread, because it had not leavened, because they were driven from Egypt and were not able to delay, and they also had not made provisions for themselves.

⁴⁰And the duration of the children of Israel that they lived in Egypt was thirty years and four hundred years. ⁴¹And it was at the end of thirty years and four hundred years, and it was in that very day: all of YHWH's masses went out from the land of Egypt. ⁴²It is a night to be observed for YHWH for bringing them out from the land of Egypt. It is this night, to be observed for YHWH for all the children of Israel through their generations.

⁴³And YHWH said to Moses and Aaron, "This is the law of the Passover: any foreigner shall not eat from it. ⁴⁴And every slave of a man, purchased with money: you shall circumcise him; then he shall eat from it. ⁴⁵A visitor and an employee shall not eat from it. ⁴⁶It shall be eaten in one house; you shall not take any of the meat from the house outside. And you shall not break a bone from it. ⁴⁷All of the congregation of Israel shall do it. ⁴⁸And if an alien will reside with you and will make a Passover to YHWH, let him be circumcised, every male, and then he may

עָלָה אִתָּם וְצֹאן וּבָקָר מִקְנֶה כָּבֵד מְאֹד: ³⁹וַיֹּאפוּ אֶת־הַבָּצֵק אֲשֶׁר הוֹצִיאוּ מִמִּצְרַיִם עֻגֹת מַצּוֹת כִּי לֹא חָמֵץ כִּי־גֹרְשׁוּ מִמִּצְרַיִם וְלֹא יָכְלוּ לְהִתְמַהְמֵהַּ וְגַם־צֵדָה לֹא־עָשׂוּ לָהֶם: ⁴⁰וּמוֹשַׁב בְּנֵי יִשְׂרָאֵל אֲשֶׁר יָשְׁבוּ בְּמִצְרָיִם שְׁלֹשִׁים שָׁנָה וְאַרְבַּע מֵאוֹת שָׁנָה: ⁴¹וַיְהִי מִקֵּץ שְׁלֹשִׁים שָׁנָה וְאַרְבַּע מֵאוֹת שָׁנָה וַיְהִי בְּעֶצֶם הַיּוֹם הַזֶּה יָצְאוּ כָּל־צִבְאוֹת יְהוָה מֵאֶרֶץ מִצְרָיִם: ⁴²לֵיל שִׁמֻּרִים הוּא לַיהוָה לְהוֹצִיאָם מֵאֶרֶץ מִצְרָיִם הוּא־הַלַּיְלָה הַזֶּה לַיהוָה שִׁמֻּרִים לְכָל־בְּנֵי יִשְׂרָאֵל לְדֹרֹתָם: פ

⁴³וַיֹּאמֶר יְהוָה אֶל־מֹשֶׁה וְאַהֲרֹן זֹאת חֻקַּת הַפָּסַח כָּל־בֶּן־נֵכָר לֹא־יֹאכַל בּוֹ: ⁴⁴וְכָל־עֶבֶד אִישׁ מִקְנַת־כָּסֶף וּמַלְתָּה אֹתוֹ אָז יֹאכַל בּוֹ: ⁴⁵תּוֹשָׁב וְשָׂכִיר לֹא־יֹאכַל־בּוֹ: ⁴⁶בְּבַיִת אֶחָד יֵאָכֵל לֹא־תוֹצִיא מִן־הַבַּיִת מִן־הַבָּשָׂר חוּצָה וְעֶצֶם לֹא תִשְׁבְּרוּ־בוֹ: ⁴⁷כָּל־עֲדַת יִשְׂרָאֵל יַעֲשׂוּ אֹתוֹ: ⁴⁸וְכִי־יָגוּר אִתְּךָ גֵּר וְעָשָׂה פֶסַח לַיהוָה הִמּוֹל לוֹ כָל־

12:38. **heavy.** The word that described the Pharaoh's oppression and the force of the plagues now recurs to describe, for the first time, something good: the substantial quantity of possessions that the people are able to take with them. It is as if this good is in proportion to the bad that they have experienced.

12:44. **slave.** It is extraordinary that, just two verses after reporting that Israel went free from Egypt, there is a reference to the possibility of an Israelite having a slave! The Torah does not forbid slavery. Nor does it criticize the Egyptians for having slaves, but rather for *maltreating* their slaves. The Torah rather initiates a process that eventually is to bring about an end to all slavery on earth, for Israelites and for everyone else. See the comments on Lev 25:43.

12:45. **A visitor and an employee shall not eat from it.** These are non-Israelites, who do not partake of the Passover sacrificial meal. This does not apply to the Seder meal, which has been celebrated in place of the sacrificial meal ever since the destruction of the Temple in 70 C.E. brought an end to all sacrifices in Judaism.

come forward to do it, and he will be like a citizen of the land, but everyone who is uncircumcised shall not eat from it. 49There shall be one instruction for the citizen and for the alien who resides among you."

50And all the children of Israel did as YHWH had commanded Moses and Aaron. They did so. 51And it was in this very day: YHWH brought out the children of Israel from the land of Egypt by their masses.

13 1And YHWH spoke to Moses, saying, 2"Consecrate every firstborn for me. The first birth of every womb of the children of Israel, of a human and of an animal: it is mine."

3And Moses said to the people, "Remember this day in which you went out from Egypt, from a house of slaves, because YHWH brought you out of here by strength of hand: And no leavened bread shall be eaten. 4Today you are going out, in the month of Abib. 5And it will be, when YHWH will bring you to the land of the Canaanite and the Hittite and the Amorite and the Hivite and the Jebusite, which He swore to your fathers to give you, a land flowing with milk and honey, that you will perform this service in this month. 6You shall eat unleavened bread seven days, and on the seventh day is a festival to YHWH. 7Unleavened bread will be eaten for the seven days, and leavened bread shall not be seen for you, and leaven shall not be seen for you within all your borders. 8And you shall tell your child in that day, saying, 'Because of that which YHWH did for me when I went out from Egypt.'

זָכָ֗ר וְאָ֤ז יִקְרַב֙ לַעֲשֹׂת֔וֹ וְהָיָ֖ה כְּאֶזְרַ֣ח הָאָ֑רֶץ וְכָל־
עָרֵ֖ל לֹא־יֹ֥אכַל בּֽוֹ׃ 49תּוֹרָ֣ה אַחַ֔ת יִהְיֶ֖ה לָֽאֶזְרָ֑ח
וְלַגֵּ֖ר הַגָּ֣ר בְּתוֹכְכֶֽם׃ 50וַֽיַּעֲשׂ֖וּ כָּל־בְּנֵ֣י יִשְׂרָאֵ֑ל
כַּאֲשֶׁ֨ר צִוָּ֤ה יְהוָה֙ אֶת־מֹשֶׁ֣ה וְאֶֽת־אַהֲרֹ֔ן כֵּ֖ן עָשֽׂוּ׃
ס 51וַיְהִ֕י בְּעֶ֖צֶם הַיּ֣וֹם הַזֶּ֑ה הוֹצִ֨יא יְהוָ֜ה אֶת־בְּנֵ֧י
יִשְׂרָאֵ֛ל מֵאֶ֥רֶץ מִצְרַ֖יִם עַל־צִבְאֹתָֽם׃ פ

13 1וַיְדַבֵּ֥ר יְהוָ֖ה אֶל־מֹשֶׁ֥ה לֵּאמֹֽר׃ 2קַדֶּשׁ־לִ֨י
כָל־בְּכ֜וֹר פֶּ֤טֶר כָּל־רֶ֙חֶם֙ בִּבְנֵ֣י יִשְׂרָאֵ֔ל בָּֽאָדָ֖ם
וּבַבְּהֵמָ֑ה לִ֖י הֽוּא׃

3וַיֹּ֨אמֶר מֹשֶׁ֜ה אֶל־הָעָ֗ם זָכ֞וֹר אֶת־הַיּ֤וֹם הַזֶּה֙
אֲשֶׁ֨ר יְצָאתֶ֤ם מִמִּצְרַ֙יִם֙ מִבֵּ֣ית עֲבָדִ֔ים כִּ֚י בְּחֹ֣זֶק יָ֔ד
הוֹצִ֧יא יְהוָ֛ה אֶתְכֶ֖ם מִזֶּ֑ה וְלֹ֥א יֵאָכֵ֖ל חָמֵֽץ׃ 4הַיּ֖וֹם
אַתֶּ֣ם יֹצְאִ֑ים בְּחֹ֖דֶשׁ הָאָבִֽיב׃ 5וְהָיָ֣ה כִֽי־יְבִֽיאֲךָ֣
יְהוָ֡ה אֶל־אֶ֣רֶץ הַֽכְּנַעֲנִ֣י וְהַֽחִתִּ֡י וְהָֽאֱמֹרִי֩ וְהַֽחִוִּ֨י
וְהַיְבוּסִ֜י אֲשֶׁ֨ר נִשְׁבַּ֤ע לַֽאֲבֹתֶ֙יךָ֙ לָ֣תֶת לָ֔ךְ אֶ֛רֶץ זָבַ֥ת
חָלָ֖ב וּדְבָ֑שׁ וְעָֽבַדְתָּ֛ אֶת־הָעֲבֹדָ֥ה הַזֹּ֖את בַּחֹ֥דֶשׁ
הַזֶּֽה׃ 6שִׁבְעַ֥ת יָמִ֖ים תֹּאכַ֣ל מַצֹּ֑ת וּבַיּוֹם֙ הַשְּׁבִיעִ֔י חַ֖ג
לַֽיהוָֽה׃ 7מַצּוֹת֙ יֵֽאָכֵ֔ל אֵ֖ת שִׁבְעַ֣ת הַיָּמִ֑ים וְלֹֽא־יֵרָאֶ֨ה
לְךָ֜ חָמֵ֗ץ וְלֹֽא־יֵרָאֶ֥ה לְךָ֛ שְׂאֹ֖ר בְּכָל־גְּבֻלֶֽךָ׃
8וְהִגַּדְתָּ֣ לְבִנְךָ֔ בַּיּ֥וֹם הַה֖וּא לֵאמֹ֑ר בַּעֲב֣וּר זֶ֗ה עָשָׂ֤ה
יְהוָה֙ לִ֔י בְּצֵאתִ֖י מִמִּצְרָֽיִם׃ 9וְהָיָה֩ לְךָ֨ לְא֜וֹת עַל־

12:49. **one instruction for the citizen and for the alien.** "Instruction" is the translation of Hebrew *Tôrāh* because it denotes both "teaching" and "law." This is the first occurrence of the word "Torah" in the Torah. It is impressive beyond description that its first appearance is in a verse declaring that a foreigner residing among the people of Israel has the same legal status as an Israelite. The context here concerns the Passover statute, but this principle of treating a resident alien the same as any citizen will be repeated many (about fifteen) times in the Torah.

13:4. **the month of Abib.** This is the name of the first month of the year in the Torah, the month in which spring begins. Later, the name Nisan is used instead.

9And it will become a sign on your hand and a reminder between your eyes for you so that YHWH's instruction will be in your mouth, because YHWH brought you out from Egypt with a strong hand. 10And you shall observe this law at its appointed time, regularly. 11And it will be, when YHWH will bring you to the land of the Canaanite as He swore to you and to your fathers and will give it to you, 12that you will pass every first birth of a womb to YHWH; and every first birth, offspring of an animal, that you will have—the males—is YHWH's. 13And you shall redeem every first birth of an ass with a lamb, and if you will not redeem, then you shall break its neck. And you shall redeem every human firstborn among your sons. 14And it will be, when your child will ask you tomorrow, saying, 'What is this?' that you'll say to him, 'With strength of hand YHWH brought us out from Egypt, from a house of slaves. 15And it was when Pharaoh hardened against letting us go, and YHWH killed every firstborn in the land of Egypt, from firstborn of a human to firstborn of

יָדְךָ וּלְזִכָּרוֹן בֵּין עֵינֶיךָ לְמַעַן תִּהְיֶה תּוֹרַת יְהוָה בְּפִיךָ כִּי בְּיָד חֲזָקָה הוֹצִאֲךָ יְהוָה מִמִּצְרָיִם: 10וְשָׁמַרְתָּ אֶת־הַחֻקָּה הַזֹּאת לְמוֹעֲדָהּ מִיָּמִים יָמִימָה: ס 11וְהָיָה כִּי־יְבִאֲךָ יְהוָה אֶל־אֶרֶץ הַכְּנַעֲנִי כַּאֲשֶׁר נִשְׁבַּע לְךָ וְלַאֲבֹתֶיךָ וּנְתָנָהּ לָךְ: 12וְהַעֲבַרְתָּ כָל־פֶּטֶר־רֶחֶם לַיהוָה וְכָל־פֶּטֶר ׀ שֶׁגֶר בְּהֵמָה אֲשֶׁר יִהְיֶה לְךָ הַזְּכָרִים לַיהוָה: 13וְכָל־פֶּטֶר חֲמֹר תִּפְדֶּה בְשֶׂה וְאִם־לֹא תִפְדֶּה וַעֲרַפְתּוֹ וְכֹל בְּכוֹר אָדָם בְּבָנֶיךָ תִּפְדֶּה: 14וְהָיָה כִּי־יִשְׁאָלְךָ בִנְךָ מָחָר לֵאמֹר מַה־זֹּאת וְאָמַרְתָּ אֵלָיו בְּחֹזֶק יָד הוֹצִיאָנוּ יְהוָה מִמִּצְרַיִם מִבֵּית עֲבָדִים: 15וַיְהִי כִּי־הִקְשָׁה פַרְעֹה לְשַׁלְּחֵנוּ וַיַּהֲרֹג יְהוָה כָּל־בְּכוֹר בְּאֶרֶץ מִצְרַיִם מִבְּכֹר אָדָם וְעַד־בְּכוֹר בְּהֵמָה עַל־

13:10. regularly. Literally, "from days to days," an expression meaning "from year to year."

13:11. He swore to you. But God did not swear it to them. Could it mean *for* you? Probably not. Rashi, citing the Mechilta, says He swore when He said, "And I'll bring you to the land that I raised my hand . . . " (Exod 6:8). But there is no swearing of an oath to the people there. Ramban suggests that the word of God itself may constitute an oath, but that is not correct. The *Tanak* definitely distinguishes the cases in which a divine oath is sworn. Ramban also takes the earlier words "He swore to your fathers to give to you" (13:5) to constitute an oath to the people. If an oath to the ancestors is in fact the explanation of this, then I believe we should focus on the words that God says to Abraham in the middle of their covenant ceremony. There the fire that expresses the presence of God passes between the parts of animals, which constitutes an oath ceremony; and the stated purpose of this ceremony is to confirm that Abraham will possess the land. God states that after a period of slavery "a fourth generation will come back here" (Gen 15:7–16). Or, more generally, we may say that the promise to Abraham is repeated to his descendants, the later patriarchs, showing that the oath carries through the lineage to the descendants. Since the whole people of Israel is a descendant of Abraham, the oath may be regarded as made to them as well. I am not certain of the answer to this problem. I point it out in order to make it known and in the hope that someone else may solve it.

an animal. On account of this I am sacrificing to YHWH every first birth of a womb—the males—and I shall redeem every firstborn of my sons." ¹⁶And it will become a sign on your hand and bands between your eyes, because with strength of hand YHWH brought us out from Egypt."

כֵּ֣ן אֲנִ֣י זֹבֵ֩חַ֩ לַֽיהוָ֨ה כָּל־פֶּ֤טֶר רֶ֙חֶם֙ הַזְּכָרִ֔ים וְכָל־בְּכ֥וֹר בָּנַ֖י אֶפְדֶּֽה: ¹⁶וְהָיָ֤ה לְאוֹת֙ עַל־יָ֣דְכָ֔ה וּלְטוֹטָפֹ֖ת בֵּ֣ין עֵינֶ֑יךָ כִּ֚י בְּחֹ֣זֶק יָ֔ד הוֹצִיאָ֥נוּ יְהוָ֖ה מִמִּצְרָֽיִם: ס

WHEN HE LET GO

בשלח

¹⁷And it was, when Pharaoh let the people go, that God did not lead them by way of the Philistines' land—because it was close—because God said, "In case the people will be dissuaded when they see war, and they'll go back to Egypt." ¹⁸And God turned the people by way of the wilderness of the Red Sea. And the children of Israel went up

¹⁷וַיְהִ֗י בְּשַׁלַּ֣ח פַּרְעֹה֘ אֶת־הָעָם֒ וְלֹא־נָחָ֣ם אֱלֹהִ֗ים דֶּ֚רֶךְ אֶ֣רֶץ פְּלִשְׁתִּ֔ים כִּ֥י קָר֖וֹב ה֑וּא כִּ֣י ׀ אָמַ֣ר אֱלֹהִ֗ים פֶּֽן־יִנָּחֵ֥ם הָעָ֛ם בִּרְאֹתָ֥ם מִלְחָמָ֖ה וְשָׁ֥בוּ מִצְרָֽיְמָה: ¹⁸וַיַּסֵּ֨ב אֱלֹהִ֧ים ׀ אֶת־הָעָ֛ם דֶּ֥רֶךְ הַמִּדְבָּ֖ר יַם־ס֑וּף וַחֲמֻשִׁ֛ים עָל֥וּ בְנֵֽי־יִשְׂרָאֵ֖ל מֵאֶ֥רֶץ מִצְרָֽיִם:

13:16. a sign on your hand and bands between your eyes. The context of this and the similar expression in v. 9 indicates clearly that this is a metaphor, meaning that the Passover observance is to become a vivid, conscious concern of the people of Israel. The occurrence of the similar expression in Deut 6:8 came to be taken literally, referring to the practice of wrapping one's hand and forehead in phylacteries (*tephillin*).

13:17. Philistines. Philistines are present along the coast by the time of Ramesses III, who mentions them in "The War against the Sea Peoples" (c. 1188 B.C.E.).

13:18. by way of the wilderness of the Red Sea. They are not sent through Philistine territory because they might be afraid and turn back. But then they are sent to the Red Sea! Is that better? And, in fact, at the Red Sea they *will* be afraid and wish they were back in Egypt! (14:10–12). The difference is psychological. They have been slaves for generations. Decision making, willpower, and responsibility have not been part of their lives. One does not acquire responsibility instantly when one becomes free. Facing opponents and having to take arms and fight would terrify them, and their natural reaction would be to turn and flee. But the Red Sea situation is different. With the Egyptian army behind them and an opened sea in front of them, they do not need to make a decision, exert willpower, or take responsibility. They have no choice but to go forward.

13:18. Red Sea. Recent commentators and translators have called this the "Sea of Reeds," a different body of water from the Red Sea; but there is no such body of water. They say this because (1) the sea is called *yam sûp* in the Hebrew, and *sûp* elsewhere means a reed (Exod 2:3); (2) reeds do not grow by the Red Sea; and (3) they conceive of a smaller body of water than the Red Sea being subject to some sort of drying or splitting, as opposed to the larger, deeper Red Sea. But none of these considerations outweighs the simple fact that the *Tanak* refers to the *eastern* arm of the sea—the body

214

armed from the land of Egypt. ¹⁹And Moses took Joseph's bones with him, because he had had the children of Israel *swear*, saying, "God *will take account* of you, and you'll bring up my bones from here with you."

²⁰And they traveled from Succoth and camped in Etham at the edge of the wilderness. ²¹And YHWH was going in front of them by day in a column of cloud to show them the way, and by night in a column of fire to shed light for them, so as to go by day and by night. ²²The column of cloud by day and the column of fire by night did not depart in front of the people.

14 ¹And YHWH spoke to Moses, saying, ²"Speak to the children of Israel that they should go back and camp in front of Pi-Hahiroth, between Migdol and the sea, in front of Baal-Zephon. You shall camp facing it, by the sea. ³And Pharaoh will say about the children of

19וַיִּקַּ֥ח מֹשֶׁ֛ה אֶת־עַצְמ֥וֹת יוֹסֵ֖ף עִמּ֑וֹ כִּי֩ הַשְׁבֵּ֨עַ הִשְׁבִּ֜יעַ אֶת־בְּנֵ֤י יִשְׂרָאֵל֙ לֵאמֹ֔ר פָּקֹ֨ד יִפְקֹ֤ד אֱלֹהִים֙ אֶתְכֶ֔ם וְהַעֲלִיתֶ֧ם אֶת־עַצְמֹתַ֛י מִזֶּ֖ה אִתְּכֶֽם: 20וַיִּסְע֖וּ מִסֻּכֹּ֑ת וַיַּחֲנ֣וּ בְאֵתָ֔ם בִּקְצֵ֖ה הַמִּדְבָּֽר: 21וַֽיהוָ֡ה הֹלֵךְ֩ לִפְנֵיהֶ֨ם יוֹמָ֜ם בְּעַמּ֤וּד עָנָן֙ לַנְחֹתָ֣ם הַדֶּ֔רֶךְ וְלַ֛יְלָה בְּעַמּ֥וּד אֵ֖שׁ לְהָאִ֣יר לָהֶ֑ם לָלֶ֖כֶת יוֹמָ֥ם וָלָֽיְלָה: 22לֹֽא־יָמִ֞ישׁ עַמּ֤וּד הֶֽעָנָן֙ יוֹמָ֔ם וְעַמּ֥וּד הָאֵ֖שׁ לָ֑יְלָה לִפְנֵ֖י הָעָֽם: פ

14 1וַיְדַבֵּ֥ר יְהוָ֖ה אֶל־מֹשֶׁ֥ה לֵּאמֹֽר: 2דַּבֵּר֮ אֶל־בְּנֵ֣י יִשְׂרָאֵל֒ וְיָשֻׁ֗בוּ וְיַחֲנוּ֙ לִפְנֵי֙ פִּ֣י הַחִירֹ֔ת בֵּ֥ין מִגְדֹּ֖ל וּבֵ֣ין הַיָּ֑ם לִפְנֵי֙ בַּ֣עַל צְפֹ֔ן נִכְח֥וֹ תַחֲנ֖וּ עַל־הַיָּֽם: 3וְאָמַ֤ר פַּרְעֹה֙ לִבְנֵ֣י יִשְׂרָאֵ֔ל נְבֻכִ֥ים הֵ֖ם

of water now known as the Gulf of Eilat or the Gulf of Aqaba—as *yam sûp* as well (Num 14:25; 21:4; Deut 1:40; 2:1; Judg 11:16; 1 Kings 9:26; Jer 49:21). There is therefore no doubt that the body of water that is pictured in the story of the splitting of the sea in the Torah is the body of water that is known in English as the Red Sea. I have returned to this traditional English translation so it will be clear what body of water is meant. I have no objection to translations that use "Reed Sea" or "Sea of Suph" as long as it is clear that it is this body of water. (As for its Hebrew name, *yam sûp*, we just do not know how that came to be its name.)

13:18. **armed.** Or prepared to fight, or resolute (Propp). But the text has just said that God does not want them to have to face a fight with the Philistines. So why note that they are armed at this point? Answer: (1) because they will fight the Amalekites a short time later (see the comment on 17:9); and (2) in recognition of the fact that one day they will have to fight for the promised land.

13:21. **a column of cloud and a column of fire.** The cloud and fire have a two-sided function, both conveying God's presence and reflecting God's mysteriousness. The narrative reports that YHWH Himself goes in front of the Israelites in the wilderness, but they do not see the deity because He travels in the daytime in the column of cloud and by night in the column of fire. Exodus must be read with a consciousness that the cloud or the fire is present at all times, a constant miracle, an introduction of the cosmic in history. One must have a sense of the awe involved in this phenomenon, particularly expressed in fire. It is a miraculously burning bush that first draws Moses. Now the people experience a similar phenomenon: a continuous, miraculous fire.

Israel: 'They're muddled in the land! The wilderness has closed them in.' 4And I'll strengthen Pharaoh's heart, and he'll pursue them, and I'll be glorified against Pharaoh and against all of his army, and Egypt will know that I am YHWH." And they did so.

5And it was told to the king of Egypt that the people had fled, and the heart of Pharaoh and his servants was changed toward the people. And they said, "What is this that we've done, that we let Israel go from serving us?!" 6And he hitched his chariot and took his people with him. 7And he took six hundred chosen chariots—and all the chariotry of Egypt—and officers over all of it. 8And YHWH strengthened the heart of Pharaoh, king of Egypt, and he pursued the children of Israel. And the children of Israel were going out with a high hand. 9And Egypt pursued them, and they caught up to them, camping by the sea—every chariot horse of Pharaoh and his horsemen and his army—at Pi-Hahiroth, in front of Baal-Zephon. 10And Pharaoh came close! And the children of Israel raised their eyes, and here was Egypt coming after them, and they were very afraid. And the children of Israel cried out to YHWH.

11And they said to Moses, "Was it because of an absence—none!—of graves in Egypt that you took us to die in the wilderness?! What is this that you've done to us to bring us out of Egypt?

בָּאָרֶץ סָגַר עֲלֵיהֶם הַמִּדְבָּר: 4וְחִזַּקְתִּי אֶת־לֵב־פַּרְעֹה וְרָדַף אַחֲרֵיהֶם וְאִכָּבְדָה בְּפַרְעֹה וּבְכָל־חֵילוֹ וְיָדְעוּ מִצְרַיִם כִּי־אֲנִי יְהוָה וַיַּעֲשׂוּ־כֵן: 5וַיֻּגַּד לְמֶלֶךְ מִצְרַיִם כִּי בָרַח הָעָם וַיֵּהָפֵךְ לְבַב פַּרְעֹה וַעֲבָדָיו אֶל־הָעָם וַיֹּאמְרוּ מַה־זֹּאת עָשִׂינוּ כִּי־שִׁלַּחְנוּ אֶת־יִשְׂרָאֵל מֵעָבְדֵנוּ: 6וַיֶּאְסֹר אֶת־רִכְבּוֹ וְאֶת־עַמּוֹ לָקַח עִמּוֹ: 7וַיִּקַּח שֵׁשׁ־מֵאוֹת רֶכֶב בָּחוּר וְכֹל רֶכֶב מִצְרָיִם וְשָׁלִשִׁם עַל־כֻּלּוֹ: 8וַיְחַזֵּק יְהוָֹה אֶת־לֵב פַּרְעֹה מֶלֶךְ מִצְרַיִם וַיִּרְדֹּף אַחֲרֵי בְּנֵי יִשְׂרָאֵל וּבְנֵי יִשְׂרָאֵל יֹצְאִים בְּיָד רָמָה: 9וַיִּרְדְּפוּ מִצְרַיִם אַחֲרֵיהֶם וַיַּשִּׂיגוּ אוֹתָם חֹנִים עַל־הַיָּם כָּל־סוּס רֶכֶב פַּרְעֹה וּפָרָשָׁיו וְחֵילוֹ עַל־פִּי הַחִירֹת לִפְנֵי בַּעַל צְפֹן: 10וּפַרְעֹה הִקְרִיב וַיִּשְׂאוּ בְנֵי־יִשְׂרָאֵל אֶת־עֵינֵיהֶם וְהִנֵּה מִצְרַיִם ׀ נֹסֵעַ אַחֲרֵיהֶם וַיִּירְאוּ מְאֹד וַיִּצְעֲקוּ בְנֵי־יִשְׂרָאֵל אֶל־יְהוָה: 11וַיֹּאמְרוּ אֶל־מֹשֶׁה הֲמִבְּלִי אֵין־קְבָרִים בְּמִצְרַיִם לְקַחְתָּנוּ לָמוּת בַּמִּדְבָּר מַה־זֹּאת עָשִׂיתָ לָּנוּ

14:5. **and the heart of Pharaoh . . . was changed.** The word that was used for the stick's changing into a snake and the water's changing into blood and the changing of the wind that carried away the locusts is now used to describe Pharaoh's change of heart. Those past cases, plus the passive (*Niphal*) form of the verb here, indicate that it is not Pharaoh himself but God who causes the change.

14:11. **an absence—none!—of graves.** Their words are redundant. The prophet Elijah uses the same expression: "Is it because of an absence—none!—of a God in Israel that you go to inquire of Baal?!" (2 Kings 1:3,6,16). The redundancy dramatizes the question in each case, as if to say, "Was it because of a complete and utter lack . . . "—the way people speak when accusing someone of doing something completely senseless.

14:11. *you've* **done to us.** As with Joseph, people focus on the human, Moses, as if he and not God were the one who brought this about.

216

12Isn't this the thing that we spoke to you in Egypt, saying: Stop from us! And let's serve Egypt. Because serving Egypt is better for us than our dying in the wilderness!"

13And Moses said to the people, "Don't be afraid. Stand still and see YHWH's salvation that He'll do for you today. For, as you've seen Egypt today, you'll never see them again, ever. 14*YHWH* will fight for you, and *you'll* keep quiet!"

15And YHWH said to Moses, "Why do you cry out to me? Speak to the children of Israel that they should move! 16And you, lift your staff and reach your hand out over the sea—and split it! And the children of Israel will come through the sea on the dry ground. 17And I, here, I'm strengthening Egypt's heart, and they'll come after them, and I'll be glorified against Pharaoh and against all of his army, against his chariots and against his horsemen. 18And Egypt will know that I am YHWH when I'm glorified against Pharaoh, against his chariots and against his horsemen."

19And the angel of God who was going in front of the camp of Israel moved and went behind them, and the column of cloud went from in front of them and stood behind them. 20And it came between the camp of Egypt and the camp of Israel. And there was the cloud and darkness [for the Egyptians], while it [the column of fire] lit the night [for the Israelites], and one did not come near the other all night. 21And Moses reached his hand out over the sea, and YHWH drove back the sea with a strong east wind all night and turned the sea into dry ground, and the sea was split. 22And the children of Israel came through the sea on the dry ground. And the water was a wall to them at their right and at their left. 23And Egypt pursued and came after them, every horse of Pharaoh, his chariots and his horsemen, through the sea. 24And it was in the morning watch, and YHWH gazed at Egypt's camp through a column of fire and cloud and threw Egypt's camp into tumult, 25and He turned

לְהוֹצִיאָ֖נוּ מִמִּצְרָֽיִם׃ 12הֲלֹא־זֶ֣ה הַדָּבָ֗ר אֲשֶׁר֩ דִּבַּ֨רְנוּ אֵלֶ֤יךָ בְמִצְרַ֙יִם֙ לֵאמֹ֔ר חֲדַ֥ל מִמֶּ֖נּוּ וְנַֽעַבְדָ֣ה אֶת־מִצְרָ֑יִם כִּ֣י ט֥וֹב לָ֙נוּ֙ עֲבֹ֣ד אֶת־מִצְרַ֔יִם מִמֻּתֵ֖נוּ בַּמִּדְבָּֽר׃ 13וַיֹּ֨אמֶר מֹשֶׁ֣ה אֶל־הָעָם֮ אַל־תִּירָאוּ֒ הִֽתְיַצְּב֗וּ וּרְאוּ֙ אֶת־יְשׁוּעַ֣ת יְהוָ֔ה אֲשֶׁר־יַעֲשֶׂ֥ה לָכֶ֖ם הַיּ֑וֹם כִּ֗י אֲשֶׁ֨ר רְאִיתֶ֤ם אֶת־מִצְרַ֙יִם֙ הַיּ֔וֹם לֹ֥א תֹסִ֛פוּ לִרְאֹתָ֥ם ע֖וֹד עַד־עוֹלָֽם׃ 14יְהוָ֖ה יִלָּחֵ֣ם לָכֶ֑ם וְאַתֶּ֖ם תַּחֲרִישֽׁוּן׃ פ

15וַיֹּ֤אמֶר יְהוָה֙ אֶל־מֹשֶׁ֔ה מַה־תִּצְעַ֖ק אֵלָ֑י דַּבֵּ֥ר אֶל־בְּנֵי־יִשְׂרָאֵ֖ל וְיִסָּֽעוּ׃ 16וְאַתָּ֞ה הָרֵ֣ם אֶֽת־מַטְּךָ֗ וּנְטֵ֧ה אֶת־יָדְךָ֛ עַל־הַיָּ֖ם וּבְקָעֵ֑הוּ וְיָבֹ֧אוּ בְנֵֽי־יִשְׂרָאֵ֛ל בְּת֥וֹךְ הַיָּ֖ם בַּיַּבָּשָֽׁה׃ 17וַאֲנִ֗י הִנְנִ֤י מְחַזֵּק֙ אֶת־לֵ֣ב מִצְרַ֔יִם וְיָבֹ֖אוּ אַחֲרֵיהֶ֑ם וְאִכָּבְדָ֤ה בְּפַרְעֹה֙ וּבְכָל־חֵיל֔וֹ בְּרִכְבּ֖וֹ וּבְפָרָשָֽׁיו׃ 18וְיָדְע֥וּ מִצְרַ֖יִם כִּֽי־אֲנִ֣י יְהוָ֑ה בְּהִכָּבְדִ֣י בְּפַרְעֹ֔ה בְּרִכְבּ֖וֹ וּבְפָרָשָֽׁיו׃ 19וַיִּסַּ֞ע מַלְאַ֣ךְ הָאֱלֹהִ֗ים הַהֹלֵךְ֙ לִפְנֵי֙ מַחֲנֵ֣ה יִשְׂרָאֵ֔ל וַיֵּ֖לֶךְ מֵאַחֲרֵיהֶ֑ם וַיִּסַּ֞ע עַמּ֤וּד הֶֽעָנָן֙ מִפְּנֵיהֶ֔ם וַיַּֽעֲמֹ֖ד מֵאַחֲרֵיהֶֽם׃ 20וַיָּבֹ֞א בֵּ֣ין ׀ מַחֲנֵ֣ה מִצְרַ֗יִם וּבֵין֙ מַחֲנֵ֣ה יִשְׂרָאֵ֔ל וַיְהִ֤י הֶֽעָנָן֙ וְהַחֹ֔שֶׁךְ וַיָּ֖אֶר אֶת־הַלָּ֑יְלָה וְלֹא־קָרַ֥ב זֶ֛ה אֶל־זֶ֖ה כָּל־הַלָּֽיְלָה׃ 21וַיֵּ֨ט מֹשֶׁ֣ה אֶת־יָדוֹ֮ עַל־הַיָּם֒ וַיּ֣וֹלֶךְ יְהוָ֣ה ׀ אֶת־הַ֠יָּם בְּר֨וּחַ קָדִ֤ים עַזָּה֙ כָּל־הַלַּ֔יְלָה וַיָּ֥שֶׂם אֶת־הַיָּ֖ם לֶחָרָבָ֑ה וַיִּבָּקְע֖וּ הַמָּֽיִם׃ 22וַיָּבֹ֧אוּ בְנֵֽי־יִשְׂרָאֵ֛ל בְּת֥וֹךְ הַיָּ֖ם בַּיַּבָּשָׁ֑ה וְהַמַּ֤יִם לָהֶם֙ חֹמָ֔ה מִֽימִינָ֖ם וּמִשְּׂמֹאלָֽם׃ 23וַיִּרְדְּפ֤וּ מִצְרַ֙יִם֙ וַיָּבֹ֣אוּ אַחֲרֵיהֶ֔ם כֹּ֚ל ס֣וּס פַּרְעֹ֔ה רִכְבּ֖וֹ וּפָרָשָׁ֑יו אֶל־תּ֖וֹךְ הַיָּֽם׃ 24וַֽיְהִי֙ בְּאַשְׁמֹ֣רֶת הַבֹּ֔קֶר וַיַּשְׁקֵ֤ף יְהוָה֙ אֶל־מַחֲנֵ֣ה מִצְרַ֔יִם בְּעַמּ֥וּד אֵ֖שׁ וְעָנָ֑ן וַיָּ֕הָם אֵ֖ת מַחֲנֵ֥ה מִצְרָֽיִם׃ 25וַיָּ֗סַר אֵ֚ת אֹפַ֣ן מַרְכְּבֹתָ֔יו וַיְנַהֲגֵ֖הוּ

its chariots' wheel so that it drove it with heaviness.

And Egypt said, "Let me flee from Israel, because YHWH is fighting for them against Egypt!"

26And YHWH said to Moses, "Reach your hand out over the sea, and the water will go back over Egypt, over his chariots and over his horsemen."

27And Moses reached his hand out over the sea, and the sea went back to its strong flow toward morning, and Egypt was fleeing toward it. And YHWH tossed the Egyptians into the sea. 28And the waters went back and covered the chariots and the horsemen—all of Pharaoh's army who were coming after them in the sea. Not even one of them was left. 29And the children of Israel had gone on the dry ground through the sea, and the water had been a wall to them at their right and at their left.

30And YHWH saved Israel from Egypt's hand that day. And Israel saw Egypt dead on the seashore, 31and Israel saw the big hand that YHWH had used against Egypt, and the people feared YHWH, and they trusted in YHWH and in Moses His servant.

בְּכְבֵדֻת וַיֹּאמֶר מִצְרַיִם אָנוּסָה מִפְּנֵי יִשְׂרָאֵל כִּי יְהֹוָה נִלְחָם לָהֶם בְּמִצְרָיִם: פ 26וַיֹּאמֶר יְהֹוָה אֶל־מֹשֶׁה נְטֵה אֶת־יָדְךָ עַל־הַיָּם וְיָשֻׁבוּ הַמַּיִם עַל־מִצְרַיִם עַל־רִכְבּוֹ וְעַל־פָּרָשָׁיו: 27וַיֵּט מֹשֶׁה אֶת־יָדוֹ עַל־הַיָּם וַיָּשָׁב הַיָּם לִפְנוֹת בֹּקֶר לְאֵיתָנוֹ וּמִצְרַיִם נָסִים לִקְרָאתוֹ וַיְנַעֵר יְהֹוָה אֶת־מִצְרַיִם בְּתוֹךְ הַיָּם: 28וַיָּשֻׁבוּ הַמַּיִם וַיְכַסּוּ אֶת־הָרֶכֶב וְאֶת־הַפָּרָשִׁים לְכֹל חֵיל פַּרְעֹה הַבָּאִים אַחֲרֵיהֶם בַּיָּם לֹא־נִשְׁאַר בָּהֶם עַד־אֶחָד: 29וּבְנֵי יִשְׂרָאֵל הָלְכוּ בַיַּבָּשָׁה בְּתוֹךְ הַיָּם וְהַמַּיִם לָהֶם חֹמָה מִימִינָם וּמִשְּׂמֹאלָם: 30וַיּוֹשַׁע יְהֹוָה בַּיּוֹם הַהוּא אֶת־יִשְׂרָאֵל מִיַּד מִצְרָיִם וַיַּרְא יִשְׂרָאֵל אֶת־מִצְרַיִם מֵת עַל־שְׂפַת הַיָּם: 31וַיַּרְא יִשְׂרָאֵל אֶת־הַיָּד הַגְּדֹלָה אֲשֶׁר עָשָׂה יְהֹוָה בְּמִצְרַיִם וַיִּירְאוּ הָעָם אֶת־יְהֹוָה וַיַּאֲמִינוּ בַּיהֹוָה וּבְמֹשֶׁה עַבְדּוֹ: פ

14:25. **heaviness.** The recurrence of the word "heavy" to describe yet another event conveys that the plagues section of the story and the Red Sea section are united. The event at the sea is not just one more episode; it is a climax to what has been happening.

14:31. **they trusted.** This word is also translated often as "believed" (Hebrew *wayya'ămînû*). It does not have the meaning here that it has in later religious concepts. That is, it does not function in the sense of believing that a God exists. This notion of belief *in* does not occur in Biblical Hebrew (nor in other ancient Near Eastern languages). In pagan religion the gods, being observable forces in nature (e.g., the sun, the sky, the storm wind), are not a matter of belief but of knowledge. So in the conception of YHWH in Exodus, God becomes *known*; God's existence and power are a matter of knowledge, not belief. When one has seen ten plagues and a sea split and has a column of cloud and fire visible at all times, one does not ask, "Do you believe in God?" As the term is used in the Hebrew Bible, it means not belief *in*, but belief *that*; that is, it means that if YHWH says He will do something one can *trust* that He will do it.

218

15

¹Then Moses and the children of Israel sang this song to YHWH. And they said, saying:

Let me sing to YHWH, for He *triumphed!*
Horse and its rider He cast in the sea.

2   My strength and song are Yah,
and He became a salvation for me.
This is my God, and I'll praise Him,
my father's God, and I'll hail Him.

3   YHWH is a warrior.
YHWH is His name.

4   Pharaoh's chariots and his army He
plunged in the sea
and the choice of his troops drowned in
the Red Sea.

5   The deeps covered them.
They sank in the depths like a stone.

6   Your right hand, YHWH, awesome in
power,
your right hand, YHWH, crushed the foe.

7   And in your triumph's greatness you
threw down your adversaries.
You let go your fury: it consumed them
like straw.

8   And by wind from your nostrils water
was massed,
surf piled up like a heap,
the deeps congealed in the heart of the
sea.

9   The enemy said, "I'll pursue!
I'll catch up!
I'll divide spoil!
My soul will be sated!
I'll unsheathe my sword!
My hand will deprive them!"

10   You blew with your wind. Sea covered
them.
They sank like lead in the awesome
water.

15 ¹אָ֣ז יָשִֽׁיר־מֹשֶׁה֩ וּבְנֵ֨י יִשְׂרָאֵ֜ל אֶת־הַשִּׁירָ֤ה
הַזֹּאת֙ לַֽיהֹוָ֔ה וַיֹּאמְר֖וּ לֵאמֹ֑ר
אָשִׁ֤ירָה לַֽיהֹוָה֙ כִּֽי־גָאֹ֣ה גָּאָ֔ה
ס֥וּס וְרֹכְב֖וֹ רָמָ֥ה בַיָּֽם׃
²עׇזִּ֤י וְזִמְרָת֙ יָ֔הּ וַֽיְהִי־לִ֖י לִֽישׁוּעָ֑ה
זֶ֤ה אֵלִי֙ וְאַנְוֵ֔הוּ אֱלֹהֵ֥י אָבִ֖י וַאֲרֹֽמְמֶֽנְהוּ׃
³יְהֹוָ֖ה אִ֣ישׁ מִלְחָמָ֑ה יְהֹוָ֖ה שְׁמֽוֹ׃
⁴מַרְכְּבֹ֥ת פַּרְעֹ֛ה וְחֵיל֖וֹ יָרָ֣ה בַיָּ֑ם וּמִבְחַ֥ר
שָֽׁלִשָׁ֖יו טֻבְּע֥וּ בְיַם־סֽוּף׃
⁵תְּהֹמֹ֖ת יְכַסְיֻ֑מוּ יָרְד֥וּ בִמְצוֹלֹ֖ת כְּמוֹ־אָֽבֶן׃
⁶יְמִֽינְךָ֣ יְהֹוָ֔ה נֶאְדָּרִ֖י בַּכֹּ֑חַ
יְמִֽינְךָ֥ יְהֹוָ֖ה תִּרְעַ֥ץ אוֹיֵֽב׃
⁷וּבְרֹ֥ב גְּאֽוֹנְךָ֖ תַּהֲרֹ֣ס קָמֶ֑יךָ
תְּשַׁלַּח֙ חֲרֹ֣נְךָ֔ יֹאכְלֵ֖מוֹ כַּקַּֽשׁ׃
⁸וּבְר֤וּחַ אַפֶּ֙יךָ֙ נֶ֣עֶרְמוּ מַ֔יִם נִצְּב֥וּ כְמוֹ־נֵ֖ד נֹזְלִ֑ים
קָֽפְא֥וּ תְהֹמֹ֖ת בְּלֶב־יָֽם׃
⁹אָמַ֥ר אוֹיֵ֛ב אֶרְדֹּ֥ף אַשִּׂ֖יג אֲחַלֵּ֣ק שָׁלָ֑ל
תִּמְלָאֵ֣מוֹ נַפְשִׁ֔י
אָרִ֣יק חַרְבִּ֔י תּֽוֹרִישֵׁ֖מוֹ יָדִֽי׃
¹⁰נָשַׁ֥פְתָּ בְרֽוּחֲךָ֖ כִּסָּ֣מוֹ יָ֑ם
צָֽלְלוּ֙ כַּֽעוֹפֶ֔רֶת בְּמַ֖יִם אַדִּירִֽים׃

15:1. **rider.** This refers to those who are riding in the chariots. Cavalry was not used in Egypt in this period.

11 Who is like you among the gods, YHWH!
Who is like you:
awesome in holiness!
fearsome with splendors!
making miracles!

12 You reached your right hand: earth
swallowed them.

13 You led, in your kindness, the people you
redeemed;
you ushered, in your strength, to your
holy abode.

14 Peoples heard—they shuddered.
Shaking seized Philistia's residents.

15 Then Edom's chiefs were terrified.
Moab's chieftains: trembling seized them.
All Canaan's residents melted.

16 Terror and fear came over them.
At the power of your arm they're silent
like stone.
'Til your people passed, YHWH,
'til the people you created passed.

17 You'll bring them and plant them in your
legacy's mountain,
your throne's platform, that you made,
YHWH;
a holy place, Lord, that your hands
reared.

18 YHWH will reign forever and ever!

19Because Pharaoh's horses with his chariots and
with his horsemen came in the sea, and YHWH
brought back the water of the sea over them, and
the children of Israel had gone on the dry ground
through the sea.

20And Miriam, the prophetess, Aaron's sister,
took a drum in her hand, and all the women

מִי־כָמֹכָה בָּאֵלִם יְהוָה¹¹
מִי כָּמֹכָה נֶאְדָּר בַּקֹּדֶשׁ
נוֹרָא תְהִלֹּת עֹשֵׂה פֶלֶא: ¹²נָטִיתָ יְמִינְךָ
תִּבְלָעֵמוֹ אָרֶץ:
נָחִיתָ בְחַסְדְּךָ עַם־זוּ גָּאָלְתָּ¹³
נֵהַלְתָּ בְעָזְּךָ אֶל־נְוֵה קָדְשֶׁךָ:
שָׁמְעוּ עַמִּים יִרְגָּזוּן חִיל אָחַז יֹשְׁבֵי פְּלָשֶׁת:¹⁴
אָז נִבְהֲלוּ אַלּוּפֵי אֱדוֹם אֵילֵי מוֹאָב¹⁵
יֹאחֲזֵמוֹ רָעַד
נָמֹגוּ כֹּל יֹשְׁבֵי כְנָעַן:
תִּפֹּל עֲלֵיהֶם אֵימָתָה וָפַחַד בִּגְדֹל זְרוֹעֲךָ¹⁶
יִדְּמוּ כָּאָבֶן
עַד־יַעֲבֹר עַמְּךָ יְהוָה עַד־יַעֲבֹר עַם־זוּ קָנִיתָ:
תְּבִאֵמוֹ וְתִטָּעֵמוֹ בְּהַר נַחֲלָתְךָ מָכוֹן לְשִׁבְתְּךָ¹⁷
פָּעַלְתָּ יְהוָה
מִקְּדָשׁ אֲדֹנָי כּוֹנְנוּ יָדֶיךָ: ¹⁸יְהוָה ׀ יִמְלֹךְ
לְעֹלָם וָעֶד:
כִּי בָא סוּס פַּרְעֹה בְּרִכְבּוֹ וּבְפָרָשָׁיו בַּיָּם וַיָּשֶׁב¹⁹
יְהוָה עֲלֵהֶם אֶת־מֵי הַיָּם וּבְנֵי יִשְׂרָאֵל הָלְכוּ
בַיַּבָּשָׁה בְּתוֹךְ הַיָּם: פ
וַתִּקַּח מִרְיָם הַנְּבִיאָה אֲחוֹת אַהֲרֹן אֶת־הַתֹּף²⁰

15:14. **Peoples heard**. This is not just about Egypt. As in the matter of the plagues,
the object is not only to defeat or punish the Egyptians. It is to make YHWH known
in the world. So the Song of the Sea declares that others hear of this event: Philistia,
Edom, Moab, *all* of Canaan's residents.

15:20. **Miriam, the prophetess**. Here we are informed that she is a prophetess. This
will be crucial later, when she and Aaron will speak against Moses, saying, "Has YHWH
only just spoken through Moses? Hasn't He also spoken through us?" (Num 12:2).

went out behind her with drums and with dances. 21And Miriam sang to them:

> Sing to YHWH for He *triumphed!*
> Horse and its rider He cast in the sea.

22And Moses had Israel travel from the Red Sea, and they went out to the wilderness of Shur. And they went three days in the wilderness. And they did not find water. 23And they came to Marah, and they were not able to drink water from Marah because it was bitter. On account of this he called its name Marah. 24And the people complained at Moses, saying, "What shall we drink?" 25And he cried to YHWH, and YHWH showed him a tree, and he threw it into the water, and the water sweetened.

He set law and judgment for them there, and He tested them there. 26And He said, "If you'll *listen* to the voice of YHWH, your God, and you'll do what is right in His eyes and turn your ear to His commandments and observe all His laws, I won't set on you any of the sickness that I set on Egypt, because I, YHWH, am your healer."

בְּיָדָהּ וַתֵּצֶאןָ כָל־הַנָּשִׁים אַחֲרֶיהָ בְּתֻפִּים וּבִמְחֹלֹת:

21וַתַּעַן לָהֶם מִרְיָם
שִׁירוּ לַיהוָה כִּי־גָאֹה גָּאָה
סוּס וְרֹכְבוֹ רָמָה בַיָּם: ס

22וַיַּסַּע מֹשֶׁה אֶת־יִשְׂרָאֵל מִיַּם־סוּף וַיֵּצְאוּ אֶל־מִדְבַּר־שׁוּר וַיֵּלְכוּ שְׁלֹשֶׁת־יָמִים בַּמִּדְבָּר וְלֹא־מָצְאוּ מָיִם: 23וַיָּבֹאוּ מָרָתָה וְלֹא יָכְלוּ לִשְׁתֹּת מַיִם מִמָּרָה כִּי מָרִים הֵם עַל־כֵּן קָרָא־שְׁמָהּ מָרָה: 24וַיִּלֹּנוּ הָעָם עַל־מֹשֶׁה לֵּאמֹר מַה־נִּשְׁתֶּה: 25וַיִּצְעַק אֶל־יְהוָה וַיּוֹרֵהוּ יְהוָה עֵץ וַיַּשְׁלֵךְ אֶל־הַמַּיִם וַיִּמְתְּקוּ הַמָּיִם שָׁם שָׂם לוֹ חֹק וּמִשְׁפָּט וְשָׁם נִסָּהוּ: 26וַיֹּאמֶר אִם־שָׁמוֹעַ תִּשְׁמַע לְקוֹל ׀ יְהוָה אֱלֹהֶיךָ וְהַיָּשָׁר בְּעֵינָיו תַּעֲשֶׂה וְהַאֲזַנְתָּ לְמִצְוֹתָיו וְשָׁמַרְתָּ כָּל־חֻקָּיו כָּל־הַמַּחֲלָה אֲשֶׁר־שַׂמְתִּי בְמִצְרַיִם לֹא־אָשִׂים עָלֶיךָ כִּי אֲנִי יְהוָה רֹפְאֶךָ: ס 27וַיָּבֹאוּ אֵילִמָה וְשָׁם

15:21. **Miriam sang**. This song is therefore known both as the Song of the Sea and as the Song of Miriam. My teacher Frank Moore Cross and my senior colleague David Noel Freedman demonstrated together that this is one of the oldest—if not the oldest—passages in the Bible. The Red Sea episode was thus an early and decisive element of Israel's story.

15:22. **they went three days in the wilderness**. The original request they made of Pharaoh—a three-day trip in the wilderness—is now fulfilled. And they are not returning!

15:24. **the people complained at Moses**. The narrative has proceeded from the confrontation between Moses and the deity to that between Moses and the Pharaoh, and now to the ongoing confrontation between Moses and the people. And, as I indicated earlier, each new stage of confrontation carries with it the background of what has come before, so that Moses' experiences with the people—involving sometimes wisdom, sometimes rage, and sometimes affection—must be read with some appreciation of the growth that has taken place in his personality through his earlier encounters with divinity and royalty. Having defeated the leader of Egypt, Moses now finds himself to be the leader of a people, a people who never chose him to lead them. Through a series of crises, the people doubt his competence and rebel against his authority.

27And they came to Elim. And twelve springs of water and seventy palm trees were there. And they camped there by the water.

16 1And they traveled from Elim, and all of the congregation of the children of Israel came to the wilderness of Sîn, which is between Elim and Sinai, on the fifteenth day of the second month after their exodus from the land of Egypt. 2And all of the congregation of the children of Israel complained at Moses and at Aaron in the wilderness. 3And the children of Israel said to them, "Who would make it so that we had died by YHWH's hand in the land of Egypt, when we sat by a pot of meat, when we ate bread to the full! Because you brought us out to this wilderness to kill this whole community with starvation!"

4And YHWH said to Moses, "Here, I'm raining bread from the skies for you, and let the people go out and gather the daily ration in its day in order that I can test them: will they go by my instruction or not. 5And it will be that on the sixth day they'll prepare what they bring in, and it will be twice as much as they'll gather on regular days."

6And Moses and Aaron said to all the children of Israel, "At evening you'll know that *YHWH* brought you out from the land of Egypt, 7and in the morning you'll see YHWH's glory, because

שְׁתֵּים עֶשְׂרֵה עֵינֹת מַיִם וְשִׁבְעִים תְּמָרִים וַיַּחֲנוּ־שָׁם עַל־הַמָּיִם:

16 1וַיִּסְעוּ מֵאֵילִם וַיָּבֹאוּ כָּל־עֲדַת בְּנֵי־יִשְׂרָאֵל אֶל־מִדְבַּר־סִין אֲשֶׁר בֵּין־אֵילִם וּבֵין סִינָי בַּחֲמִשָּׁה עָשָׂר יוֹם לַחֹדֶשׁ הַשֵּׁנִי לְצֵאתָם מֵאֶרֶץ מִצְרָיִם: 2וַיִּלּוֹנוּ כָּל־עֲדַת בְּנֵי־יִשְׂרָאֵל עַל־מֹשֶׁה וְעַל־אַהֲרֹן בַּמִּדְבָּר: 3וַיֹּאמְרוּ אֲלֵהֶם בְּנֵי יִשְׂרָאֵל מִי־יִתֵּן מוּתֵנוּ בְיַד־יְהוָה בְּאֶרֶץ מִצְרַיִם בְּשִׁבְתֵּנוּ עַל־סִיר הַבָּשָׂר בְּאָכְלֵנוּ לֶחֶם לָשֹׂבַע כִּי־הוֹצֵאתֶם אֹתָנוּ אֶל־הַמִּדְבָּר הַזֶּה לְהָמִית אֶת־כָּל־הַקָּהָל הַזֶּה בָּרָעָב: ס 4וַיֹּאמֶר יְהוָה אֶל־מֹשֶׁה הִנְנִי מַמְטִיר לָכֶם לֶחֶם מִן־הַשָּׁמָיִם וְיָצָא הָעָם וְלָקְטוּ דְּבַר־יוֹם בְּיוֹמוֹ לְמַעַן אֲנַסֶּנּוּ הֲיֵלֵךְ בְּתוֹרָתִי אִם־לֹא: 5וְהָיָה בַּיּוֹם הַשִּׁשִּׁי וְהֵכִינוּ אֵת אֲשֶׁר־יָבִיאוּ וְהָיָה מִשְׁנֶה עַל אֲשֶׁר־יִלְקְטוּ יוֹם | יוֹם: ס 6וַיֹּאמֶר מֹשֶׁה וְאַהֲרֹן אֶל־כָּל־בְּנֵי יִשְׂרָאֵל עֶרֶב וִידַעְתֶּם כִּי יְהוָה הוֹצִיא אֶתְכֶם מֵאֶרֶץ מִצְרָיִם: 7וּבֹקֶר וּרְאִיתֶם אֶת־

16:2 קְ וַיִּלּוֹנוּ

16:2. **at Moses and at Aaron**. This is one of the most explicit cases in the Bible of the way humans focus on the visible human figure rather than on God. They complain at Moses and Aaron. They say, "*You* brought us out" (16:3). Moses answers that they will soon see that "*YHWH* brought you out" (16:6). And he tells them that their complaints are "at *YHWH*," and he adds, "What are *we*, that you complain at *us*?!" (16:8). The miracle of manna follows, confirming the message that Moses has just told them in three different ways. But by the very next chapter: "the people complained at *Moses* and said, 'Why did *you* bring us up?'" (17:3). They continue to resist the fact that they are experiencing divine power, that they are actually encountering God.

16:5. **on regular days**. Hebrew *yôm yôm;* meaning that the sixth day's yield will be double what is gathered on an ordinary day of the week (Sunday through Thursday).

16:7. **YHWH's glory**. The glory surrounds God when in the presence of humans. It

He has heard your complaints about *YHWH*. And what are *we*, that you complain at *us?!*" [8]And Moses said, "When YHWH gives you meat to eat in the evening and bread to the full in the morning, because YHWH has heard your complaints that you're making at *Him!* And what are *we?* Your complaints are not at us but at YHWH!" [9]And Moses said to Aaron, "Say to all of the congregation of the children of Israel, 'Come close in front of YHWH, because He has heard your complaints.'"

[10]And it was as Aaron was speaking to all of the congregation of the children of Israel: and they turned to the wilderness, and here was YHWH's glory appearing in a cloud.

[11]And YHWH spoke to Moses, saying, [12]"I've heard the complaints of the children of Israel. Speak to them, saying, 'Between the two evenings you shall eat meat, and in the morning you shall be filled with bread, and you will know that I am YHWH, your God.'"

[13]And it was in the evening, and quail went up and covered the camp. And in the morning there was a layer of dew around the camp. [14]And the layer of dew went up, and here, on the face of the wilderness: scaly thin, thin as frost on the ground. [15]And the children of Israel saw, and each said to his brother, "What is it?"—because they did not know what it was.

כְּב֤וֹד יְהוָה֙ בְּשָׁמְע֔וֹ אֶת־תְּלֻנֹּ֣תֵיכֶ֔ם עַל־יְהוָ֑ה וְנַ֣חְנוּ מָ֔ה כִּ֥י תַלִּ֖ינוּ עָלֵֽינוּ: [8]וַיֹּ֣אמֶר מֹשֶׁ֗ה בְּתֵ֣ת יְהוָה֩ לָכֶ֨ם בָּעֶ֜רֶב בָּשָׂ֣ר לֶאֱכֹ֗ל וְלֶ֤חֶם בַּבֹּ֙קֶר֙ לִשְׂבֹּ֔עַ בִּשְׁמֹ֤עַ יְהוָה֙ אֶת־תְּלֻנֹּ֣תֵיכֶ֔ם אֲשֶׁר־אַתֶּ֥ם מַלִּינִ֖ם עָלָ֑יו וְנַ֣חְנוּ מָ֔ה לֹא־עָלֵ֥ינוּ תְלֻנֹּתֵיכֶ֖ם כִּ֥י עַל־יְהוָֽה: [9]וַיֹּ֤אמֶר מֹשֶׁה֙ אֶֽל־אַהֲרֹ֔ן אֱמֹ֗ר אֶֽל־כָּל־עֲדַת֙ בְּנֵ֣י יִשְׂרָאֵ֔ל קִרְב֖וּ לִפְנֵ֣י יְהוָ֑ה כִּ֣י שָׁמַ֔ע אֵ֖ת תְּלֻנֹּתֵיכֶֽם: [10]וַיְהִ֗י כְּדַבֵּ֤ר אַהֲרֹן֙ אֶל־כָּל־עֲדַ֣ת בְּנֵֽי־יִשְׂרָאֵ֔ל וַיִּפְנ֖וּ אֶל־הַמִּדְבָּ֑ר וְהִנֵּה֙ כְּב֣וֹד יְהוָ֔ה נִרְאָ֖ה בֶּעָנָֽן: פ [11]וַיְדַבֵּ֥ר יְהוָ֖ה אֶל־מֹשֶׁ֥ה לֵּאמֹֽר: [12]שָׁמַ֞עְתִּי אֶת־תְּלוּנֹּת֮ בְּנֵ֣י יִשְׂרָאֵל֒ דַּבֵּ֨ר אֲלֵהֶ֜ם לֵאמֹ֗ר בֵּ֤ין הָֽעַרְבַּ֙יִם֙ תֹּאכְל֣וּ בָשָׂ֔ר וּבַבֹּ֖קֶר תִּשְׂבְּעוּ־לָ֑חֶם וִֽידַעְתֶּ֕ם כִּ֛י אֲנִ֥י יְהוָ֖ה אֱלֹהֵיכֶֽם: [13]וַיְהִ֣י בָעֶ֔רֶב וַתַּ֣עַל הַשְּׂלָ֔ו וַתְּכַ֖ס אֶת־הַֽמַּחֲנֶ֑ה וּבַבֹּ֗קֶר הָֽיְתָה֙ שִׁכְבַ֣ת הַטַּ֔ל סָבִ֖יב לַֽמַּחֲנֶֽה: [14]וַתַּ֖עַל שִׁכְבַ֣ת הַטָּ֑ל וְהִנֵּ֞ה עַל־פְּנֵ֤י הַמִּדְבָּר֙ דַּ֣ק מְחֻסְפָּ֔ס דַּ֥ק כַּכְּפֹ֖ר עַל־הָאָֽרֶץ: [15]וַיִּרְא֣וּ בְנֵֽי־יִשְׂרָאֵ֗ל וַיֹּ֨אמְר֜וּ אִ֤ישׁ אֶל־אָחִיו֙ מָ֣ן ה֔וּא כִּ֛י לֹ֥א יָדְע֖וּ מַה־ה֑וּא וַיֹּ֤אמֶר מֹשֶׁה֙

16:7 קְ תַלִּֽינוּ

---

is some sort of indescribable substance that veils or masks the deity, who cannot be seen. "A human will not see me and live." Even the glory itself is seen through a cloud.

This is the first mention of the divine glory, and a few verses later it is seen for the first time. It then does not occur again until the revelation at Sinai. It is impressive, but also sad, that its first appearance comes in response to the people's complaints over food rather than as the surrounding of the Sinai event. It suggests the extreme seriousness of what is taking place in this first period following the exodus. The people are unprepared, vulnerable, and frightened; and they are apparently in need of manifest evidence that the power that brought them out of Egypt is still present, that the exodus was just the beginning, that what comes next is the acquaintance and continuing relationship with God.

16:15. **What is it?** Hebrew *mān hû'*. This is a play on words, because these words can also mean "It is manna." It thus explains the origin of the word "manna" as coming from their not having a name for something new. The famous comedy routine of

And Moses said to them, "That is the bread that YHWH has given you for food. ¹⁶This is the thing that YHWH has commanded: Collect some of it, each according to what he eats; you shall take an omer per head, the number of your persons, each for whoever is in his tent." ¹⁷And the children of Israel did so. And they collected—the one who took the most and the one who took the least. ¹⁸And they measured by the omer, and the one who took the most had not exceeded, and the one who took the least had not fallen short. Each had collected according to what he eats. ¹⁹And Moses said to them, "Let no one leave any of it over until morning." ²⁰And they did not listen to Moses, and people left some of it over until morning, and it yielded worms and stank. And Moses was angry at them. ²¹And they collected it morning by morning, each by what he eats, and when the sun was hot it melted. ²²And it was: on the sixth day they collected double bread, two times the omer for each one, and all the chiefs of the congregation came and told Moses. ²³And he said to them, "That is what YHWH spoke. Tomorrow is a ceasing, a holy Sabbath to YHWH. Bake what you'll bake, and cook what you'll cook, and leave what is left over for keeping until the morning." ²⁴And they left it until the morning, as Moses had commanded, and it did not stink, and there was not a worm in it. ²⁵And Moses said, "Eat it today, because today is a Sabbath to YHWH. Today you won't find it in the field. ²⁶Six days you shall collect it. And on the seventh day is a Sabbath; there will not be any in it." ²⁷And it was: on the seventh day some

אֲלֵהֶם הוּא הַלֶּחֶם אֲשֶׁר נָתַן יְהוָה לָכֶם לְאָכְלָה: ¹⁶זֶה הַדָּבָר אֲשֶׁר צִוָּה יְהוָה לִקְטוּ מִמֶּנּוּ אִישׁ לְפִי אָכְלוֹ עֹמֶר לַגֻּלְגֹּלֶת מִסְפַּר נַפְשֹׁתֵיכֶם אִישׁ לַאֲשֶׁר בְּאָהֳלוֹ תִּקָּחוּ: ¹⁷וַיַּעֲשׂוּ־כֵן בְּנֵי יִשְׂרָאֵל וַיִּלְקְטוּ הַמַּרְבֶּה וְהַמַּמְעִיט: ¹⁸וַיָּמֹדּוּ בָעֹמֶר וְלֹא הֶעְדִּיף הַמַּרְבֶּה וְהַמַּמְעִיט לֹא הֶחְסִיר אִישׁ לְפִי־אָכְלוֹ לָקָטוּ: ¹⁹וַיֹּאמֶר מֹשֶׁה אֲלֵהֶם אִישׁ אַל־יוֹתֵר מִמֶּנּוּ עַד־בֹּקֶר: ²⁰וְלֹא־שָׁמְעוּ אֶל־מֹשֶׁה וַיּוֹתִרוּ אֲנָשִׁים מִמֶּנּוּ עַד־בֹּקֶר וַיָּרֻם תּוֹלָעִים וַיִּבְאַשׁ וַיִּקְצֹף עֲלֵהֶם מֹשֶׁה: ²¹וַיִּלְקְטוּ אֹתוֹ בַּבֹּקֶר בַּבֹּקֶר אִישׁ כְּפִי אָכְלוֹ וְחַם הַשֶּׁמֶשׁ וְנָמָס: ²²וַיְהִי בַּיּוֹם הַשִּׁשִּׁי לָקְטוּ לֶחֶם מִשְׁנֶה שְׁנֵי הָעֹמֶר לָאֶחָד וַיָּבֹאוּ כָּל־נְשִׂיאֵי הָעֵדָה וַיַּגִּידוּ לְמֹשֶׁה: ²³וַיֹּאמֶר אֲלֵהֶם הוּא אֲשֶׁר דִּבֶּר יְהוָה שַׁבָּתוֹן שַׁבַּת־קֹדֶשׁ לַיהוָה מָחָר אֵת אֲשֶׁר־תֹּאפוּ אֵפוּ וְאֵת אֲשֶׁר־תְּבַשְּׁלוּ בַּשֵּׁלוּ וְאֵת כָּל־הָעֹדֵף הַנִּיחוּ לָכֶם לְמִשְׁמֶרֶת עַד־הַבֹּקֶר: ²⁴וַיַּנִּיחוּ אֹתוֹ עַד־הַבֹּקֶר כַּאֲשֶׁר צִוָּה מֹשֶׁה וְלֹא הִבְאִישׁ וְרִמָּה לֹא־הָיְתָה בּוֹ: ²⁵וַיֹּאמֶר מֹשֶׁה אִכְלֻהוּ הַיּוֹם כִּי־שַׁבָּת הַיּוֹם לַיהוָה הַיּוֹם לֹא תִמְצָאֻהוּ בַּשָּׂדֶה: ²⁶שֵׁשֶׁת יָמִים תִּלְקְטֻהוּ וּבַיּוֹם הַשְּׁבִיעִי שַׁבָּת לֹא יִהְיֶה־בּוֹ: ²⁷וַיְהִי בַּיּוֹם הַשְּׁבִיעִי

"Who's on first" in English is actually an equivalent that conveys what is happening here. They say, "It's what?" And people then take this not as a *question* but as a *statement*: "It's 'What'!" And it is known thereafter as "What."

16:24. **as Moses had commanded.** Until now, the text has always said "as YHWH had commanded" or "as God had commanded." Here, for the first time, it attributes the commanding to Moses—even though Moses has said explicitly in the preceding verse that this is what YHWH has spoken. Moses still acts only by God's direction, but the wording participates in the gradual impression through the *Tanak* that humans' share in the responsibility for their fate is growing.

224

of the people went out to collect, and they did not find any.

28And YHWH said to Moses, "How long do you refuse to observe my commandments and my instructions? 29See that YHWH has given you the Sabbath. On account of this He is giving you two days' bread on the sixth day. Stay, each in his place. Let no man go out from his place in the seventh day." 30And the people ceased in the seventh day.

31And the house of Israel called its name "manna." And it was like a coriander seed, white, and its taste was like a wafer in honey.

32And Moses said, "This is the thing that YHWH has commanded: 'an omer-ful of it is for watching over through your generations so that they will see the bread that I fed you in the wilderness when I brought you out from the land of Egypt.'" 33And Moses said to Aaron, "Take one jar and place an omer-ful of manna there and lay it in front of YHWH for watching over through your generations," 34as YHWH had commanded Moses. And Aaron laid it in front of the Testimony for watching over. 35And the children of Israel ate the manna forty years until they came to settled land. They ate the manna until they came to the edge of the land of Canaan. 36(And an omer is a tenth of an ephah.)

28וַיֹּאמֶר ס יָצְא֛וּ מִן־הָעָ֖ם לִלְקֹ֑ט וְלֹ֖א מָצָֽאוּ׃
יְהוָ֖ה אֶל־מֹשֶׁ֑ה עַד־אָ֙נָה֙ מֵאַנְתֶּ֔ם לִשְׁמֹ֥ר מִצְוֺתַ֖י
וְתוֹרֹתָֽי׃ 29רְא֗וּ כִּֽי־יְהוָה֮ נָתַ֣ן לָכֶ֣ם הַשַּׁבָּת֒ עַל־כֵּ֠ן
ה֣וּא נֹתֵ֥ן לָכֶ֛ם בַּיּ֥וֹם הַשִּׁשִּׁ֖י לֶ֣חֶם יוֹמָ֑יִם שְׁב֣וּ ׀ אִ֣ישׁ
תַּחְתָּ֗יו אַל־יֵ֥צֵא אִ֛ישׁ מִמְּקֹמ֖וֹ בַּיּ֥וֹם הַשְּׁבִיעִֽי׃
30וַיִּשְׁבְּת֥וּ הָעָ֖ם בַּיּ֥וֹם הַשְּׁבִעִֽי׃ 31וַיִּקְרְא֧וּ בֵית־
יִשְׂרָאֵ֛ל אֶת־שְׁמ֖וֹ מָ֑ן וְה֗וּא כְּזֶ֤רַע גַּד֙ לָבָ֔ן וְטַעְמ֖וֹ
כְּצַפִּיחִ֥ת בִּדְבָֽשׁ׃ 32וַיֹּ֣אמֶר מֹשֶׁ֗ה זֶ֤ה הַדָּבָר֙ אֲשֶׁ֣ר
צִוָּ֣ה יְהוָ֔ה מְלֹ֤א הָעֹ֙מֶר֙ מִמֶּ֔נּוּ לְמִשְׁמֶ֖רֶת לְדֹרֹתֵיכֶ֑ם
לְמַ֣עַן ׀ יִרְא֣וּ אֶת־הַלֶּ֗חֶם אֲשֶׁ֨ר הֶאֱכַ֤לְתִּי אֶתְכֶם֙
בַּמִּדְבָּ֔ר בְּהוֹצִיאִ֥י אֶתְכֶ֖ם מֵאֶ֥רֶץ מִצְרָֽיִם׃ 33וַיֹּ֨אמֶר
מֹשֶׁ֜ה אֶֽל־אַהֲרֹ֗ן קַ֚ח צִנְצֶ֣נֶת אַחַ֔ת וְתֶן־שָׁ֥מָּה מְלֹֽא־
הָעֹ֖מֶר מָ֑ן וְהַנַּ֤ח אֹתוֹ֙ לִפְנֵ֣י יְהוָ֔ה לְמִשְׁמֶ֖רֶת
לְדֹרֹתֵיכֶֽם׃ 34כַּאֲשֶׁ֛ר צִוָּ֥ה יְהוָ֖ה אֶל־מֹשֶׁ֑ה וַיַּנִּיחֵ֧הוּ
אַהֲרֹ֛ן לִפְנֵ֥י הָעֵדֻ֖ת לְמִשְׁמָֽרֶת׃ 35וּבְנֵ֣י יִשְׂרָאֵ֗ל אָֽכְל֤וּ
אֶת־הַמָּן֙ אַרְבָּעִ֣ים שָׁנָ֔ה עַד־בֹּאָ֖ם אֶל־אֶ֣רֶץ נוֹשָׁ֑בֶת
אֶת־הַמָּן֙ אָֽכְל֔וּ עַד־בֹּאָ֕ם אֶל־קְצֵ֖ה אֶ֥רֶץ כְּנָֽעַן׃
36וְהָעֹ֕מֶר עֲשִׂרִ֥ית הָאֵיפָ֖ה הֽוּא׃ פ

16:34. **the Testimony**. This term is introduced later as referring to the words of the Ten Commandments on the "tablets of the Testimony" (Exod 31:18), which are kept in the "Ark of the Testimony" (25:22), which is in turn housed in the "Tabernacle of the Testimony" (38:21). It seems chronologically out of place to report here that Aaron placed the manna there, when the tablets, ark, and Tabernacle have not yet been made. This problem has nothing to do with questions of authorship in critical biblical scholarship. Nor is it to be explained by the traditional rabbinic principle of "There is no early or late in the Torah." Rather, there is a series of items that are reported to have been placed by the Testimony in the Tabernacle: the manna, the incense, Aaron's staff. The placement of each is reported in the context of the story or law that relates to it. Since the story of the manna is told here, the report that Aaron placed it at the Testimony is included here as well. To have saved this report for a later, more chronologically appropriate, point in the Torah would have meant cutting it off from the rest of the manna story. The report in the next verse that they ate the manna for forty years likewise goes chronologically past the present moment in the story. It thus further confirms that the purpose of the present context is to cover the entire matter of the manna in one place.

17 ¹And all of the congregation of the children of Israel traveled from the wilderness of Sîn on their travels by YHWH's word, and they camped in Rephidim. And there was no water for the people to drink. ²And the people quarreled with Moses. And they said, "Give us water, and let us drink."

And Moses said to them, "Why do you quarrel with me? Why do you test YHWH?!"

³And the people thirsted for water there, and the people complained at Moses and said, "Why is this that you brought us up from Egypt: to kill me and my children and my cattle with thirst?!"

⁴And Moses cried to YHWH, saying, "What shall I do to this people? A little more and they'll stone me!"

⁵And YHWH said to Moses, "Pass in front of the people and take some of Israel's elders with you, and take your staff with which you struck the Nile in your hand, and you'll go. ⁶Here, I'll be standing in front of you there on a rock at Horeb. And you'll strike the rock, and water will

17 ¹וַיִּסְעוּ כָּל־עֲדַת בְּנֵי־יִשְׂרָאֵל מִמִּדְבַּר־סִין לְמַסְעֵיהֶם עַל־פִּי יְהוָה וַיַּחֲנוּ בִּרְפִידִים וְאֵין מַיִם לִשְׁתֹּת הָעָם: ²וַיָּרֶב הָעָם עִם־מֹשֶׁה וַיֹּאמְרוּ תְּנוּ־לָנוּ מַיִם וְנִשְׁתֶּה וַיֹּאמֶר לָהֶם מֹשֶׁה מַה־תְּרִיבוּן עִמָּדִי מַה־תְּנַסּוּן אֶת־יְהוָה: ³וַיִּצְמָא שָׁם הָעָם לַמַּיִם וַיִּלֶּן הָעָם עַל־מֹשֶׁה וַיֹּאמֶר לָמָּה זֶּה הֶעֱלִיתָנוּ מִמִּצְרַיִם לְהָמִית אֹתִי וְאֶת־בָּנַי וְאֶת־מִקְנַי בַּצָּמָא: ⁴וַיִּצְעַק מֹשֶׁה אֶל־יְהוָה לֵאמֹר מָה אֶעֱשֶׂה לָעָם הַזֶּה עוֹד מְעַט וּסְקָלֻנִי: ⁵וַיֹּאמֶר יְהוָה אֶל־מֹשֶׁה עֲבֹר לִפְנֵי הָעָם וְקַח אִתְּךָ מִזִּקְנֵי יִשְׂרָאֵל וּמַטְּךָ אֲשֶׁר הִכִּיתָ בּוֹ אֶת־הַיְאֹר קַח בְּיָדְךָ וְהָלָכְתָּ: ⁶הִנְנִי עֹמֵד לְפָנֶיךָ שָּׁם ׀ עַל־הַצּוּר בְּחֹרֵב

17:2. **test**. In each of the two chapters that precede this, God is described as testing the people (15:25; 16:4). (It is the same word that is used for God's testing Abraham in ordering him to sacrifice Isaac—Gen 22:1.) Now the people dare to test God, and Moses asks them why they do that. It is a rhetorical question: the point is that there is no reason to test God. It is presumptuous, because God can be counted upon. This is significant enough that at the end of the episode the place is named Massah, meaning "Test," because of what the people dared to do there.

17:6. **on a rock at Horeb**. The word "rock" refers not to a small stone but to a crag of the mountain. God stands at a crag of Mount Horeb/Sinai.

17:6. **at Horeb**. Here is the story's geography: Moses and the elders are to go on ahead of the people to Mount Horeb (Sinai). The miracle of the water will occur *there*, not at the site of the quarrel and testing. Only the elders see it, not the people (17:6). The people receive the water somewhere near Horeb, and then they return to the camp in the region of Rephidim (or perhaps the water flows all the way to where the people are). The site of their quarrel there is named Massah and Meribah. Amalek attacks and fights them there (17:8). Then Jethro goes to meet Moses at Horeb, where Moses is now encamped (18:5). Moses comes out to meet him and Moses' wife and children there (18:7). Then Aaron and the elders join them for a sacred meal there. The people come there later from Rephidim (19:2). The important thing, often overlooked, is that the miracle of the water from the rock takes place at Mount Sinai. I learned this from William Propp.

come out of it, and the people will drink." And Moses did so before the eyes of Israel's elders. 7And he called the place's name Massah and Meribah because of the quarrel of the children of Israel and because of their testing YHWH, saying, "Is YHWH among us or not?"

8And Amalek came and fought with Israel in Rephidim. 9And Moses said to Joshua, "Choose men for us and go, fight against Amalek. Tomorrow I'll be standing up on the hilltop, and the staff of God in my hand." 10And Joshua did as Moses said to him, to fight against Amalek; and Moses, Aaron, and Hur went up to the hilltop. 11And it was: when Moses would lift his hand, then Israel would predominate; and when he would rest his hand, then Amalek would predominate. 12And Moses' hands were heavy. And they took a stone and set it under him, and he sat on it, and Aaron and Hur held up his hands, one from this side and one from this side, and his hands were supported until the sunset. 13And Joshua defeated Amalek and his people by the sword.

וְהִכִּ֣יתָ בַצּ֗וּר וְיָצְא֥וּ מִמֶּ֛נּוּ מַ֖יִם וְשָׁתָ֣ה הָעָ֑ם וַיַּ֤עַשׂ כֵּן֙ מֹשֶׁ֔ה לְעֵינֵ֖י זִקְנֵ֥י יִשְׂרָאֵֽל׃ 7וַיִּקְרָא֙ שֵׁ֣ם הַמָּק֔וֹם מַסָּ֖ה וּמְרִיבָ֑ה עַל־רִ֣יב ׀ בְּנֵ֣י יִשְׂרָאֵ֗ל וְעַ֤ל נַסֹּתָם֙ אֶת־יְהוָה֙ לֵאמֹ֔ר הֲיֵ֧שׁ יְהוָ֛ה בְּקִרְבֵּ֖נוּ אִם־אָֽיִן׃ פ 8וַיָּבֹ֖א עֲמָלֵ֑ק וַיִּלָּ֥חֶם עִם־יִשְׂרָאֵ֖ל בִּרְפִידִֽם׃ 9וַיֹּ֨אמֶר מֹשֶׁ֤ה אֶל־יְהוֹשֻׁ֙עַ֙ בְּחַר־לָ֣נוּ אֲנָשִׁ֔ים וְצֵ֖א הִלָּחֵ֣ם בַּֽעֲמָלֵ֑ק מָחָ֗ר אָֽנֹכִ֤י נִצָּב֙ עַל־רֹ֣אשׁ הַגִּבְעָ֔ה וּמַטֵּ֥ה הָאֱלֹהִ֖ים בְּיָדִֽי׃ 10וַיַּ֣עַשׂ יְהוֹשֻׁ֗עַ כַּֽאֲשֶׁ֤ר אָֽמַר־לוֹ֙ מֹשֶׁ֔ה לְהִלָּחֵ֖ם בַּֽעֲמָלֵ֑ק וּמֹשֶׁה֙ אַהֲרֹ֣ן וְח֔וּר עָל֖וּ רֹ֥אשׁ הַגִּבְעָֽה׃ 11וְהָיָ֗ה כַּֽאֲשֶׁ֨ר יָרִ֥ים מֹשֶׁ֛ה יָד֖וֹ וְגָבַ֣ר יִשְׂרָאֵ֑ל וְכַֽאֲשֶׁ֥ר יָנִ֛יחַ יָד֖וֹ וְגָבַ֥ר עֲמָלֵֽק׃ 12וִידֵ֤י מֹשֶׁה֙ כְּבֵדִ֔ים וַיִּקְחוּ־אֶ֛בֶן וַיָּשִׂ֥ימוּ תַחְתָּ֖יו וַיֵּ֣שֶׁב עָלֶ֑יהָ וְאַהֲרֹ֨ן וְח֜וּר תָּֽמְכ֣וּ בְיָדָ֗יו מִזֶּ֤ה אֶחָד֙ וּמִזֶּ֣ה אֶחָ֔ד וַיְהִ֥י יָדָ֛יו אֱמוּנָ֖ה עַד־בֹּ֥א הַשָּֽׁמֶשׁ׃ 13וַיַּֽחֲלֹ֧שׁ יְהוֹשֻׁ֛עַ אֶת־עֲמָלֵ֥ק וְאֶת־עַמּ֖וֹ לְפִי־חָֽרֶב׃ פ

17:6. **you'll strike the rock, and water will come out of it**. Moses, who was drawn from water, and whose name stands for drawing from water, now draws water from the rock. He also met his wife by defending her right to draw water; the first plague he introduced involved turning the waters (from which he had once been drawn) to blood; he initiated the splitting of the sea; and he acted to sweeten the bitter water at Marah. There will be several more incidents involving water in Moses' life. It seems to be a key element in his destiny, which will culminate in his tragic act when he strikes a rock to get water again at a second Meribah (Numbers 20). For this act he will be forbidden to enter the promised land. His life will end, as it began, at a river, the Jordan, which he will not be permitted to cross.

17:7. **he called the place's name Massah and Meribah**. That is, he named it Testing and Quarrel.

17:9. **fight against Amalek**. Israel was not sent by way of the Philistines' land because they would be afraid of war (13:17), but now, just a few chapters later, they are sent to war against the Amalek! And Israel prevails! How do we explain this? Apparently the intervening events have made a change in the Israelites so that now they have the confidence and fortitude to fight. What are the intervening events: Red Sea, Marah, manna, Meribah. They have received four miraculous signs that their God is still with them even after they have left Egypt.

14And YHWH said to Moses, "Write this—a memorial—in a scroll and set it in Joshua's ears, because I shall *wipe out* the memory of Amalek from under the skies!" 15And Moses built an altar and called its name "YHWH is my standard." 16And he said, "Because—hand on YH's throne—YHWH has war against Amalek from generation to generation."

JETHRO

18 1And Jethro, priest of Midian, Moses' father-in-law, heard everything that God had done for Moses and for Israel, His people, that YHWH had brought Israel out from Egypt. 2And Jethro, Moses' father-in-law, took Zipporah, Moses' wife, after her being sent off, 3and her two sons, of whom one's name was Gershom, because he said, "I was an alien in a foreign land," 4and one's name was Eliezer, "because my father's God was my help and rescued me from Pharaoh's sword." 5And Jethro, Moses' father-in-law, and his sons and his wife came to Moses, to the wilderness in which he was camping, at the Mountain of God. 6And he said to Moses, "I, your father-in-law, Jethro, have come to you, and your wife and her two sons with her." 7And Moses went out to his father-in-law, and he

14וַיֹּאמֶר יְהוָה אֶל־מֹשֶׁה כְּתֹב זֹאת זִכָּרוֹן בַּסֵּפֶר וְשִׂים בְּאָזְנֵי יְהוֹשֻׁעַ כִּי־מָחֹה אֶמְחֶה אֶת־זֵכֶר עֲמָלֵק מִתַּחַת הַשָּׁמָיִם: 15וַיִּבֶן מֹשֶׁה מִזְבֵּחַ וַיִּקְרָא שְׁמוֹ יְהוָה ׀ נִסִּי: 16וַיֹּאמֶר כִּי־יָד עַל־כֵּס יָהּ מִלְחָמָה לַיהוָה בַּעֲמָלֵק מִדֹּר דֹּר: פ

יתרו

1וַיִּשְׁמַע יִתְרוֹ כֹהֵן מִדְיָן חֹתֵן מֹשֶׁה אֵת 18 כָּל־אֲשֶׁר עָשָׂה אֱלֹהִים לְמֹשֶׁה וּלְיִשְׂרָאֵל עַמּוֹ כִּי־הוֹצִיא יְהוָה אֶת־יִשְׂרָאֵל מִמִּצְרָיִם: 2וַיִּקַּח יִתְרוֹ חֹתֵן מֹשֶׁה אֶת־צִפֹּרָה אֵשֶׁת מֹשֶׁה אַחַר שִׁלּוּחֶיהָ: 3וְאֵת שְׁנֵי בָנֶיהָ אֲשֶׁר שֵׁם הָאֶחָד גֵּרְשֹׁם כִּי אָמַר גֵּר הָיִיתִי בְּאֶרֶץ נָכְרִיָּה: 4וְשֵׁם הָאֶחָד אֱלִיעֶזֶר כִּי־אֱלֹהֵי אָבִי בְּעֶזְרִי וַיַּצִּלֵנִי מֵחֶרֶב פַּרְעֹה: 5וַיָּבֹא יִתְרוֹ חֹתֵן מֹשֶׁה וּבָנָיו וְאִשְׁתּוֹ אֶל־מֹשֶׁה אֶל־הַמִּדְבָּר אֲשֶׁר־הוּא חֹנֶה שָׁם הַר הָאֱלֹהִים: 6וַיֹּאמֶר אֶל־מֹשֶׁה אֲנִי חֹתֶנְךָ יִתְרוֹ בָּא אֵלֶיךָ וְאִשְׁתְּךָ וּשְׁנֵי בָנֶיהָ עִמָּהּ: 7וַיֵּצֵא מֹשֶׁה לִקְרַאת חֹתְנוֹ וַיִּשְׁתַּחוּ

17:16. **hand on YH's throne.** No one is sure what this means. It may be an oath formula. The word for "throne," Hebrew *kēs*, may be a form of *kissē'*, as some versions have understood it.

18:7. **Moses went out to his father-in-law.** Jethro arrives with Moses' wife and sons, but only Moses' meeting with Jethro is described. There is nothing about his reunion with his family. The Bible's silences are frustrating (where did Cain find his wife? how did Sarah feel about her son's being sacrificed?), but I think that we should learn to live with them. Often they are very loud silences—which is to say: very powerful. Why does the Torah announce the arrival of Moses' wife and children but not describe a personal meeting scene between them and Moses? Presumably, this is because it was important to let us know that his wife and children were present with the Israelites during the wilderness period, but it was not deemed important to describe their family relations. Family relations are described in the age of the patriarchs and in the age of the kings because, there, they play a role in the destiny of the people.

bowed, and he kissed him, and they asked each other how they were, and they came to the tent. 8And Moses told his father-in-law everything that YHWH had done to Pharaoh and to Egypt with regard to Israel, all the hardship that had found them on the way, and YHWH rescued them. 9And Jethro rejoiced over all the good that YHWH had done for Israel, that He had rescued it from Egypt's hand. 10And Jethro said, "Blessed is YHWH, who rescued you from Egypt's hand and from Pharaoh's hand, who rescued the people from under Egypt's hand: 11now I know that YHWH is bigger than all the gods, because of the thing that they plotted against them." 12And Jethro, Moses' father-in-law, took a burnt offering and sacrifices to God. And Aaron and all of Israel's elders came to eat bread with Moses' father-in-law before God.

13And it was the next day, and Moses sat to judge the people. And the people stood by Moses from the morning to the evening. 14And Moses'

וַיִּשַּׁק־לוֹ וַיִּשְׁאֲלוּ אִישׁ־לְרֵעֵהוּ לְשָׁלוֹם וַיָּבֹאוּ הָאֹהֱלָה: 8וַיְסַפֵּר מֹשֶׁה לְחֹתְנוֹ אֵת כָּל־אֲשֶׁר עָשָׂה יְהוָה לְפַרְעֹה וּלְמִצְרַיִם עַל אוֹדֹת יִשְׂרָאֵל אֵת כָּל־הַתְּלָאָה אֲשֶׁר מְצָאָתַם בַּדֶּרֶךְ וַיַּצִּלֵם יְהוָה: 9וַיִּחַדְּ יִתְרוֹ עַל כָּל־הַטּוֹבָה אֲשֶׁר־עָשָׂה יְהוָה לְיִשְׂרָאֵל אֲשֶׁר הִצִּילוֹ מִיַּד מִצְרָיִם: 10וַיֹּאמֶר יִתְרוֹ בָּרוּךְ יְהוָה אֲשֶׁר הִצִּיל אֶתְכֶם מִיַּד מִצְרַיִם וּמִיַּד פַּרְעֹה אֲשֶׁר הִצִּיל אֶת־הָעָם מִתַּחַת יַד־מִצְרָיִם: 11עַתָּה יָדַעְתִּי כִּי־גָדוֹל יְהוָה מִכָּל־הָאֱלֹהִים כִּי בַדָּבָר אֲשֶׁר זָדוּ עֲלֵיהֶם: 12וַיִּקַּח יִתְרוֹ חֹתֵן מֹשֶׁה עֹלָה וּזְבָחִים לֵאלֹהִים וַיָּבֹא אַהֲרֹן וְכֹל ׀ זִקְנֵי יִשְׂרָאֵל לֶאֱכָל־לֶחֶם עִם־חֹתֵן מֹשֶׁה לִפְנֵי הָאֱלֹהִים: 13וַיְהִי מִמָּחֳרָת וַיֵּשֶׁב מֹשֶׁה לִשְׁפֹּט אֶת־הָעָם וַיַּעֲמֹד הָעָם עַל־מֹשֶׁה מִן־הַבֹּקֶר עַד־הָעָרֶב: 14וַיַּרְא חֹתֵן

They are described in the cases of Jephthah and Samson because they propel the life events of those persons. But in Moses' case the family episodes are few: his mother and sister protect him as a baby, his wife has a confrontation with him at the inn on the way to Egypt, Aaron and Miriam criticize his Cushite wife and are rebuked by God. The rest of Moses' family life is personal. His wife speaks three sentences in the Torah. His sons speak none. That tells us, at the very least, that his particular life mission is primarily about him and God, on the one hand, and him and the people, on the other. And the nature of that mission is such that his family situation is not permitted to impinge upon it. The missions of Abraham, David, and the rest of us are not like that.

It is our frustration with the silences and our hunger for more Torah that give birth to midrash. So I was once asked to make a midrash on what might have happened between Moses and his wife and sons. I suggested: He told them everything—the confrontations with Pharaoh, the snakes, the plagues, the splitting of the sea. And his sons asked him why he had sent them away and thus kept them from seeing all that. And he told them that it was dangerous, and he was protecting them. Did that show insufficient faith on his part that things would go well in Egypt? Of course, he says. But he was just starting out and did not yet know the divine power—or the divine character. And so a father's love was his first motive. But now, he assured them, they would stay with him and get to see an even greater event: Sinai.

18:11. **the thing that they plotted against them**. Meaning: Egypt's plot to control the Israelites by enslaving them.

father-in-law saw all that he was doing for the people, and he said, "What's this thing that you're doing for the people? Why are you sitting by yourself, and the entire people is standing up by you from morning until evening?"

15And Moses said to his father-in-law, "Because the people come to me to inquire of God. 16When they have a matter, it comes to me, and I judge between each one and his companion, and I make known God's laws and His instructions."

17And Moses' father-in-law said to him, "The thing that you're doing isn't good. 18You'll be *worn out*, both you and this people who are with you, because the thing is too heavy for you. You won't be able to do it by yourself. 19Now listen to my voice, and I'll advise you, and may God be with you. *You* be for the people toward God, and *you* will bring the matters to God. 20And you'll enlighten them with the laws and the instructions, and you'll make known to them the way in which they'll go and the thing that they'll do. 21And *you* will envision, out of all the people, worthy men, who fear God, men of truth, who hate bribery, and you'll set chiefs of thousands, chiefs of hundreds, chiefs of fifties, and chiefs of tens over them. 22And they'll judge the people at all times. And it will be: they'll bring every matter that is big to you, and *they* will judge every matter that is small. And make it lighter on you, and they'll bear it with you. 23If you'll do this thing, and YHWH will command you, then you'll be able to stand, and also this entire people will come to its place in peace."

מֹשֶׁה אֵת כָּל־אֲשֶׁר־הוּא עֹשֶׂה לָעָם וַיֹּאמֶר מָה־
הַדָּבָר הַזֶּה אֲשֶׁר אַתָּה עֹשֶׂה לָעָם מַדּוּעַ אַתָּה
יוֹשֵׁב לְבַדֶּךָ וְכָל־הָעָם נִצָּב עָלֶיךָ מִן־בֹּקֶר עַד־
עָרֶב: 15וַיֹּאמֶר מֹשֶׁה לְחֹתְנוֹ כִּי־יָבֹא אֵלַי הָעָם
לִדְרֹשׁ אֱלֹהִים: 16כִּי־יִהְיֶה לָהֶם דָּבָר בָּא אֵלַי
וְשָׁפַטְתִּי בֵּין אִישׁ וּבֵין רֵעֵהוּ וְהוֹדַעְתִּי אֶת־חֻקֵּי
הָאֱלֹהִים וְאֶת־תּוֹרֹתָיו: 17וַיֹּאמֶר חֹתֵן מֹשֶׁה אֵלָיו
לֹא־טוֹב הַדָּבָר אֲשֶׁר אַתָּה עֹשֶׂה: 18נָבֹל תִּבֹּל גַּם־
אַתָּה גַּם־הָעָם הַזֶּה אֲשֶׁר עִמָּךְ כִּי־כָבֵד מִמְּךָ
הַדָּבָר לֹא־תוּכַל עֲשֹׂהוּ לְבַדֶּךָ: 19עַתָּה שְׁמַע
בְּקֹלִי אִיעָצְךָ וִיהִי אֱלֹהִים עִמָּךְ הֱיֵה אַתָּה לָעָם
מוּל הָאֱלֹהִים וְהֵבֵאתָ אַתָּה אֶת־הַדְּבָרִים אֶל־
הָאֱלֹהִים: 20וְהִזְהַרְתָּה אֶתְהֶם אֶת־הַחֻקִּים וְאֶת־
הַתּוֹרֹת וְהוֹדַעְתָּ לָהֶם אֶת־הַדֶּרֶךְ יֵלְכוּ בָהּ וְאֶת־
הַמַּעֲשֶׂה אֲשֶׁר יַעֲשׂוּן: 21וְאַתָּה תֶחֱזֶה מִכָּל־הָעָם
אַנְשֵׁי־חַיִל יִרְאֵי אֱלֹהִים אַנְשֵׁי אֱמֶת שֹׂנְאֵי בָצַע
וְשַׂמְתָּ עֲלֵהֶם שָׂרֵי אֲלָפִים שָׂרֵי מֵאוֹת שָׂרֵי חֲמִשִּׁים
וְשָׂרֵי עֲשָׂרֹת: 22וְשָׁפְטוּ אֶת־הָעָם בְּכָל־עֵת וְהָיָה
כָּל־הַדָּבָר הַגָּדֹל יָבִיאוּ אֵלֶיךָ וְכָל־הַדָּבָר הַקָּטֹן
יִשְׁפְּטוּ־הֵם וְהָקֵל מֵעָלֶיךָ וְנָשְׂאוּ אִתָּךְ: 23אִם אֶת־
הַדָּבָר הַזֶּה תַּעֲשֶׂה וְצִוְּךָ אֱלֹהִים וְיָכָלְתָּ עֲמֹד וְגַם
כָּל־הָעָם הַזֶּה עַל־מְקֹמוֹ יָבֹא בְשָׁלוֹם: 24וַיִּשְׁמַע

18:18. **too heavy for you.** "Heavy" again. See the comment on Exod 5:9. And see Num 11:14.

18:18. **able to do it by yourself.** The convergence of the terms for "to be by oneself" and "to be able" (twice: vv. 18 and 23) in this passage is striking because they both appear in the story of Jacob wrestling with God (Gen 32:24–33), which begins with the notice that "he was left by himself" and later notes (twice) that Jacob "was able" in the struggle. It is remarkable that Jacob was pictured as able to struggle with God by himself but Moses is pictured as not being able to manage the people by himself. Does a person stand a better chance of being successful in a personal struggle with God than in taking on a community of humans?

24And Moses listened to his father-in-law's voice and did everything that he had said. 25And Moses chose worthy men out of all of Israel and made them heads over the people: chiefs of thousands, chiefs of hundreds, chiefs of fifties, and chiefs of tens. 26And they judged the people at all times. They would bring the matter that was hard to Moses, and *they* would judge every matter that was small.

27And Moses let his father-in-law go, and he went to his land.

19 ¹In the third month after the exodus of the children of Israel from the land of Egypt, on this day, they came to the wilderness of Sinai. ²And they traveled from Rephidim and came to the wilderness of Sinai and camped in the wilderness. And Israel camped there opposite the mountain.

³And Moses had gone up to God. And YHWH called to him from the mountain, saying, "This is what you shall say to the house of Jacob and tell to the children of Israel: ⁴'You've seen what I did to Egypt, and I carried you on eagles' wings and brought you to me. ⁵And now, if you'll *listen* to my voice and observe my covenant, then you'll be a treasure to me out of all the peoples, be-

מֹשֶׁה לְק֣וֹל חֹתְנ֑וֹ וַיַּ֕עַשׂ כֹּ֖ל אֲשֶׁ֥ר אָמָֽר׃ 25וַיִּבְחַ֨ר מֹשֶׁ֤ה אַנְשֵׁי־חַ֨יִל֙ מִכָּל־יִשְׂרָאֵ֔ל וַיִּתֵּ֥ן אֹתָ֛ם רָאשִׁ֖ים עַל־הָעָ֑ם שָׂרֵ֤י אֲלָפִים֙ שָׂרֵ֣י מֵא֔וֹת שָׂרֵ֥י חֲמִשִּׁ֖ים וְשָׂרֵ֥י עֲשָׂרֹֽת׃ 26וְשָׁפְט֥וּ אֶת־הָעָ֖ם בְּכָל־עֵ֑ת אֶת־הַדָּבָ֤ר הַקָּשֶׁה֙ יְבִיא֣וּן אֶל־מֹשֶׁ֔ה וְכָל־הַדָּבָ֥ר הַקָּטֹ֖ן יִשְׁפּוּט֥וּ הֵֽם׃ 27וַיְשַׁלַּ֥ח מֹשֶׁ֖ה אֶת־חֹתְנ֑וֹ וַיֵּ֥לֶךְ ל֖וֹ אֶל־אַרְצֽוֹ׃ פ

19 ¹בַּחֹ֙דֶשׁ֙ הַשְּׁלִישִׁ֔י לְצֵ֥את בְּנֵֽי־יִשְׂרָאֵ֖ל מֵאֶ֣רֶץ מִצְרָ֑יִם בַּיּ֣וֹם הַזֶּ֔ה בָּ֖אוּ מִדְבַּ֥ר סִינָֽי׃ ²וַיִּסְע֣וּ מֵרְפִידִ֗ים וַיָּבֹ֙אוּ֙ מִדְבַּ֣ר סִינַ֔י וַֽיַּחֲנ֖וּ בַּמִּדְבָּ֑ר וַיִּֽחַן־שָׁ֥ם יִשְׂרָאֵ֖ל נֶ֥גֶד הָהָֽר׃ ³וּמֹשֶׁ֥ה עָלָ֖ה אֶל־הָאֱלֹהִ֑ים וַיִּקְרָ֨א אֵלָ֤יו יְהוָה֙ מִן־הָהָ֣ר לֵאמֹ֔ר כֹּ֤ה תֹאמַר֙ לְבֵ֣ית יַעֲקֹ֔ב וְתַגֵּ֖יד לִבְנֵ֥י יִשְׂרָאֵֽל׃ ⁴אַתֶּ֣ם רְאִיתֶ֔ם אֲשֶׁ֥ר עָשִׂ֖יתִי לְמִצְרָ֑יִם וָאֶשָּׂ֤א אֶתְכֶם֙ עַל־כַּנְפֵ֣י נְשָׁרִ֔ים וָאָבִ֥א אֶתְכֶ֖ם אֵלָֽי׃ ⁵וְעַתָּ֗ה אִם־שָׁמ֤וֹעַ תִּשְׁמְעוּ֙ בְּקֹלִ֔י וּשְׁמַרְתֶּ֖ם אֶת־בְּרִיתִ֑י וִהְיִ֨יתֶם לִ֤י סְגֻלָּה֙ מִכָּל־הָ֣עַמִּ֔ים כִּי־לִ֖י כָּל־הָאָֽרֶץ׃ ⁶וְאַתֶּ֧ם

19:3. **Moses had gone up to God**. While "going up to God" is an intriguing image, the Septuagint text is more probably correct. It reads "up to *the mountain of* God," which fits better with the words that follow: "And YHWH called to him from the mountain."

19:4. **on eagles' wings**. The eagle is the highest-flying bird, so there is no threat from above. Eagles fly with their young on their backs.

19:5. **if**. This first occurrence of the word *segullah* (treasure) is not ambiguous in context: The people of Israel will be a treasured possession of God *only if* they listen and fulfill their covenant. Their status is not based on some intrinsic quality but on their behavior. God is about to make a covenant with them. If they keep their part of it, then they will be *segullah*. (For more on the matter of being chosen and a treasured people, see the comment on Deut 7:6.)

19:5. **a treasure to me out of all the peoples**. Since the verse says explicitly that this treasured status is based on their behavior, and not on their being superior to any-one else, what then is the purpose of their being chosen to observe this covenant? The

cause all the earth is mine. 6And you'll be a kingdom of priests and a holy nation to me.' These are the words that you shall speak to the children of Israel."

7And Moses came and called the people's elders and set before them all these words that YHWH had commanded him. 8And all the people responded together, and they said, "We'll do everything that YHWH has spoken." And Moses brought back the people's words to YHWH.

9And YHWH said to Moses, "Here, I am coming to you in a mass of cloud for the purpose that the people will hear when I am speaking with you, and they will believe in you as well forever." And Moses told the people's words to YHWH. 10And YHWH said to Moses, "Go to the people and consecrate them today and tomorrow; and they shall wash their clothes 11and be ready for the third day, because on the third day YHWH will come down on Mount Sinai before the eyes of all the people. 12And you shall limit the people all around, saying, 'Watch yourselves about going up in the mountain and touching its edge. Anyone who touches the mountain shall be *put to death*. 13A hand shall not touch him, but he shall be *stoned* or *shot*. Whether animal or man, he will not live.' At the blowing of the horn they shall go up the mountain."

14And Moses went down from the mountain to the people. And he consecrated the people,

תִּהְיוּ־לִי מַמְלֶכֶת כֹּהֲנִים וְגוֹי קָדוֹשׁ אֵלֶּה הַדְּבָרִים אֲשֶׁר תְּדַבֵּר אֶל־בְּנֵי יִשְׂרָאֵל: 7וַיָּבֹא מֹשֶׁה וַיִּקְרָא לְזִקְנֵי הָעָם וַיָּשֶׂם לִפְנֵיהֶם אֵת כָּל־הַדְּבָרִים הָאֵלֶּה אֲשֶׁר צִוָּהוּ יְהוָה: 8וַיַּעֲנוּ כָל־הָעָם יַחְדָּו וַיֹּאמְרוּ כֹּל אֲשֶׁר־דִּבֶּר יְהוָה נַעֲשֶׂה וַיָּשֶׁב מֹשֶׁה אֶת־דִּבְרֵי הָעָם אֶל־יְהוָה: 9וַיֹּאמֶר יְהוָה אֶל־מֹשֶׁה הִנֵּה אָנֹכִי בָּא אֵלֶיךָ בְּעַב הֶעָנָן בַּעֲבוּר יִשְׁמַע הָעָם בְּדַבְּרִי עִמָּךְ וְגַם־בְּךָ יַאֲמִינוּ לְעוֹלָם וַיַּגֵּד מֹשֶׁה אֶת־דִּבְרֵי הָעָם אֶל־יְהוָה: 10וַיֹּאמֶר יְהוָה אֶל־מֹשֶׁה לֵךְ אֶל־הָעָם וְקִדַּשְׁתָּם הַיּוֹם וּמָחָר וְכִבְּסוּ שִׂמְלֹתָם: 11וְהָיוּ נְכֹנִים לַיּוֹם הַשְּׁלִישִׁי כִּי ׀ בַּיּוֹם הַשְּׁלִשִׁי יֵרֵד יְהוָה לְעֵינֵי כָל־הָעָם עַל־הַר סִינָי: 12וְהִגְבַּלְתָּ אֶת־הָעָם סָבִיב לֵאמֹר הִשָּׁמְרוּ לָכֶם עֲלוֹת בָּהָר וּנְגֹעַ בְּקָצֵהוּ כָּל־הַנֹּגֵעַ בָּהָר מוֹת יוּמָת: 13לֹא־תִגַּע בּוֹ יָד כִּי־סָקוֹל יִסָּקֵל אוֹ־יָרֹה יִיָּרֶה אִם־בְּהֵמָה אִם־אִישׁ לֹא יִחְיֶה בִּמְשֹׁךְ הַיֹּבֵל הֵמָּה יַעֲלוּ בָהָר: 14וַיֵּרֶד מֹשֶׁה מִן־הָהָר אֶל־הָעָם וַיְקַדֵּשׁ אֶת־הָעָם

---

reason was stated, no less explicitly, to their ancestor Abraham: to be a blessing to all the families of the earth.

19:6. **holy**. For a long time we have taught that this word, Hebrew *qādōš*, does not refer to some sacred, elevated condition but rather that it denotes being separate, set aside for some particular purpose. But, really, it does in fact refer to a special consecrated state. When God tells Moses at the bush, "Take off your shoes from your feet, because the place on which you're standing: it's holy ground," this means more than that the ground is "set aside." It means "holy" in just the way that people naturally understand it on first reading. The ground has a special quality deriving from the realm of the divine which makes shoes inappropriate there. And in the present context, "holy nation" does not mean that Israel will be separate from other nations. It means that Israel will be *consecrated* if the people will live the life that their divine covenant requires of them. (See also the comment on Exod 29:37.)

and they washed their clothes. 15And he said to the people, "Be ready for three days. Don't come close to a woman."

16And it was on the third day, when it was morning, and it was: thunders and lightning and a heavy cloud on the mountain, and a sound of a horn, very strong. And the entire people that was in the camp trembled. 17And Moses brought out the people toward God from the camp, and they stood up at the bottom of the mountain. 18And Mount Sinai was all smoke because YHWH came down on it in fire, and its smoke went up like the smoke of a furnace, and the whole mountain trembled greatly. 19And the sound of the horn was getting much stronger. Moses would speak, and God would answer him in a voice. 20And YHWH came down on Mount Sinai, at the top of the mountain, and YHWH called to Moses at the top of the mountain, and Moses went up. 21And YHWH said to Moses, "Go down. Warn the people in case they break through to YHWH, to see, and many of them fall. 22And also let the priests who approach YHWH consecrate themselves, or else YHWH will break out against them."

23And Moses said to YHWH, "The people is not able to go up to Mount Sinai, because you warned us, saying, 'Limit the mountain and consecrate it.'"

15וַיֹּאמֶר אֶל־הָעָם הֱיוּ נְכֹנִים לִשְׁלֹשֶׁת יָמִים אַל־תִּגְּשׁוּ אֶל־אִשָּׁה: 16וַיְהִי בַיֹּום הַשְּׁלִישִׁי בִּהְיֹת הַבֹּקֶר וַיְהִי קֹלֹת וּבְרָקִים וְעָנָן כָּבֵד עַל־הָהָר וְקֹל שֹׁפָר חָזָק מְאֹד וַיֶּחֱרַד כָּל־הָעָם אֲשֶׁר בַּמַּחֲנֶה: 17וַיֹּוצֵא מֹשֶׁה אֶת־הָעָם לִקְרַאת הָאֱלֹהִים מִן־הַמַּחֲנֶה וַיִּתְיַצְּבוּ בְּתַחְתִּית הָהָר: 18וְהַר סִינַי עָשַׁן כֻּלֹּו מִפְּנֵי אֲשֶׁר יָרַד עָלָיו יְהוָה בָּאֵשׁ וַיַּעַל עֲשָׁנֹו כְּעֶשֶׁן הַכִּבְשָׁן וַיֶּחֱרַד כָּל־הָהָר מְאֹד: 19וַיְהִי קֹול הַשֹּׁופָר הֹולֵךְ וְחָזֵק מְאֹד מֹשֶׁה יְדַבֵּר וְהָאֱלֹהִים יַעֲנֶנּוּ בְקֹול: 20וַיֵּרֶד יְהוָה עַל־הַר סִינַי אֶל־רֹאשׁ הָהָר וַיִּקְרָא יְהוָה לְמֹשֶׁה אֶל־רֹאשׁ הָהָר וַיַּעַל מֹשֶׁה: 21וַיֹּאמֶר יְהוָה אֶל־מֹשֶׁה רֵד הָעֵד בָּעָם פֶּן־יֶהֶרְסוּ אֶל־יְהוָה לִרְאֹות וְנָפַל מִמֶּנּוּ רָב: 22וְגַם הַכֹּהֲנִים הַנִּגָּשִׁים אֶל־יְהוָה יִתְקַדָּשׁוּ פֶּן־יִפְרֹץ בָּהֶם יְהוָה: 23וַיֹּאמֶר מֹשֶׁה אֶל־יְהוָה לֹא־יוּכַל הָעָם לַעֲלֹת אֶל־הַר סִינַי כִּי־אַתָּה הַעֵדֹתָה בָּנוּ לֵאמֹר הַגְבֵּל אֶת־הָהָר וְקִדַּשְׁתֹּו:

19:15. **he said to the people, "Don't come close to a woman."** If he is speaking to "the people," which includes both men and women, why does he say, "Don't come close to a woman"? Like many passages, this may have two opposite interpretations. It may be a case of male chauvinism in language, in which an address to "the people" means *the men*. Or it may reflect a perception that a command to abstain from sex for three days needs to be particularly directed to men because men are more likely than women to violate the instruction.

19:16. **a heavy cloud.** The word "heavy" recurs, but this time it refers to something divine.

19:19. **in a voice.** Here, Hebrew *bĕqôl* can mean "in a voice" or "with sound" (i.e., aloud) or "with thunder." In v. 16 the word refers first to thunder sounds and then to the sound of a horn. But the divine statement in v. 9 that "the people will hear when I am speaking with you" suggests that the people will hear spoken words between God and Moses, and that is what now happens in v. 19.

²⁴And YHWH said to him, "Go. Go down. Then you'll come up, you and Aaron with you. And let the priests and the people not break through to come up to YHWH, or else He'll break out against them." ²⁵And Moses went down to the people, and he said it to them.

24וַיֹּ֨אמֶר אֵלָ֤יו יְהוָה֙ לֶךְ־רֵ֔ד וְעָלִ֥יתָ אַתָּ֖ה וְאַהֲרֹ֣ן עִמָּ֑ךְ וְהַכֹּהֲנִ֣ים וְהָעָ֗ם אַל־יֶהֶרְס֛וּ לַעֲלֹ֥ת אֶל־יְהוָ֖ה פֶּן־יִפְרָץ־בָּֽם׃ 25וַיֵּ֥רֶד מֹשֶׁ֖ה אֶל־הָעָ֑ם וַיֹּ֖אמֶר אֲלֵהֶֽם׃ ס

20 1וַיְדַבֵּ֣ר אֱלֹהִ֔ים אֵ֛ת כָּל־הַדְּבָרִ֥ים הָאֵ֖לֶּה

20 ¹And God spoke all these words, saying:

20:1. **God spoke all these words**. God speaks the words of the Ten Commandments aloud directly to the people. The Ten Commandments are the text of the covenant between God and Israel. One of the most fruitful discoveries of biblical research was the independent recognition by three scholars (E. Bickermann, G. Mendenhall, and K. Baltzer) in the 1950s that there is a formal similarity between the Israelite covenant and international legal documents of the ancient Near Eastern countries. The treaty documents, dictated by regional kings (suzerains) to the local city kings (vassals) who were subject to them, formalized the relationship between the two. They regularly included a specific group of formal elements:

1. The suzerain's introduction of himself by name.

2. An historical prologue, giving the history of the relations between the parties, generally showing what the suzerain had done for his vassal, and thus establishing that the vassal was in the suzerain's debt.

3. The prime stipulation of the treaty, namely that the vassal was to have allegiance to this suzerain and to no other.

4. The rest of the stipulations, e.g., the vassal's obligation to pay tribute, to come when summoned to the suzerain's court, and to provide troops for the suzerain's military defense.

The Sinai covenant here exhibits striking parallels to this legal structure, containing the key elements:

1. Introduction:	I am YHWH your God
2. Historical Prologue:	who brought you out from the land of Egypt, from a house of slaves
3. Prime Stipulation:	You shall not have other gods
4. Other Stipulations:	You shall not make a statue
	You shall not bring up the name of YHWH, your God, for a falsehood
	Remember the Sabbath . . .
	Honor your father and your mother . . .

²I am YHWH, your God, who brought you out from the land of Egypt, from a house of slaves.

לֵאמֹֽר׃ ס ²אָֽנֹכִי֙ יְהוָ֣ה אֱלֹהֶ֔יךָ אֲשֶׁ֧ר הוֹצֵאתִ֛יךָ מֵאֶ֥רֶץ מִצְרַ֖יִם מִבֵּ֣ית עֲבָדִ֑ים׃ ³לֹ֣א יִהְיֶֽה־לְךָ֥

The Near Eastern suzerainty treaties also include other features that appear here in the covenant. They included an oath sworn by the vassal pledging fidelity to the suzerain and to the requirements of the treaty, and they included provision for the treaty document, requiring that it be deposited in a sacred place. In Exodus the people pledge their obedience (24:3,7), and the covenant text is deposited in the ark in the Tabernacle (25:16,21; 40:20).

Thus Israel's relations with its God are conceived in the legal terms of that world. The words of the Ten Commandments and of the Covenant Code are not only orders that must be obeyed. They are legal corpora, concluded contractually between the creator and a human community.

20:2. **I am YHWH, your God**. People question whether this first verse of the covenant is a commandment or a statement, and they argue over what, exactly, it commands. The evidence from the ancient Near Eastern documents makes clear that this is not to be counted as one of the commandments. Introductory statements such as this one are common and fundamental to these documents: stating the name of the one who is dictating the terms and stating the history of what this one has done for the recipient of these terms. They leave no doubt that the first commandment is not "I am YHWH . . ." but rather "You shall have no other gods. . . ." This is confirmed by the fact that when one counts "I am YHWH . . ." as a commandment, one comes out with eleven commandments. Those who have thought this to be a commandment have had to combine two of the later commandments into one.

In any case, the question of what the opening words command arises in part because in English we call this text by the name "the Ten Commandments." That misleads us, though, because in the Torah itself (Exod 34:28; Deut 10:4), this text is called simply the Ten Things (or Ten Words, or Ten Statements; Hebrew *'ăśeret haddĕbārîm*).

20:2. **who brought you out from the land of Egypt**. In the relationship between the covenant and the ancient Near Eastern legal texts, the historical prologue has special importance: In the Torah, *law is set in history*. Law is *never* given in the *Tanak* in the abstract, apart from a historical context. There is always an understanding that the commandments are to be followed because God did something for the humans who are being commanded. There are more than sixty chapters of Torah before the first law to Israel occurs (Exodus 12). Indeed, as I said in my first comment (Gen 1:1), Rashi began his commentary with the question of why the Torah starts with creation and subsequent history rather than being strictly a law code and starting with the first law in Exodus 12. I would now add another answer: that biblical Israel understood this law to require historical context. The law was conceived to have been born at a turning point in history.

³You shall not have other gods before my face.

⁴You shall not make a statue or any form that is in the skies above or that is in the

אֱלֹהִים אֲחֵרִים עַל־פָּנָיַ: ⁴לֹא תַעֲשֶׂה־לְךָ פֶסֶל ׀
וְכָל־תְּמוּנָה אֲשֶׁר בַּשָּׁמַיִם ׀ מִמַּעַל וַאֲשֶׁר בָּאָרֶץ

20:3. You shall not have other gods. Various groups have counted the Ten Commandments differently because of the matter of the historical prologue. Some identify the first commandment as "I am YHWH, your God, who brought you out from the land of Egypt, from a house of slaves." Others list "You shall have no other gods before me" as the first commandment. The evidence from the Near Eastern treaties indicates that the latter way is correct. The first line is not a commandment. It is the historical prologue. (See the comment on 20:2.)

20:3. before my face. Hebrew *'al pānāy* has no good English equivalent. The point is that *everywhere* is *'al pānāy*, i.e., before God's face, so the commandment means that one simply cannot have any other gods. Monotheism has become so successful in Western civilization and much of Eastern civilization that it is difficult now for us to recapture the original force of this commandment. The profound has become the norm, so people forget that it is profound.

Some argue that the wording of the first commandment is not properly monotheistic. They say the commandment "You shall not have other gods before my face (or: in my presence, or: before me)" suggests a recognition that other gods exist. They therefore argue that the commandment only prohibits the *worship* of other deities but does not deny their reality. This appears to be a too-careful reading of these words. The fact is that it is difficult to word a command of monotheism without referring to other deities. This is simply a fact of language. (I frequently suggest to my students that they try to compose a number of formulations of a command of monotheism, and we regularly find that a substantial number of the possible formulations will contain reference to other gods.) Those who hold the view that monotheism came late in Israel cannot build a case on the wording of the first commandment. The issue here is linguistic, not theological.

20:4. statue. Pagan religion in the ancient Near East, as in Greece, was not idol worship. The statues of the gods and goddesses were icons, symbols that represented the deities' presence. They provided a direction for prayer, a feeling of awe, a sense of one's god's closeness. But pagans did not believe that the statue was the god. The god was a force, known through its particular power in the universe: sky, earth, sun, wind, grain, fertility. So, if the statues were not themselves worshiped, why are Israelites forbidden to have them? One reason may be that they were inconsistent with monotheism: If Israel was not permitted to have other gods, of course they could not have statues of them. And the issue then was not making statues of the pagan gods but making statues of *YHWH*. In the first place, YHWH was not to be identified with any single force in nature. Likewise, a statue would limit what YHWH was, identifying God with something visible in this world. Moreover, multiple statues of YHWH in multiple places would not be felt to be consistent with God's oneness. In the Torah, only one Temple is permitted, only one sacrificial altar. Sacrifice to YHWH is not permitted anywhere

earth below or that is in the water below the earth. ⁵You shall not bow to them, and you shall not serve them. Because I, YHWH, your God, am a jealous God, counting parents' crime on children, on the third generation, and on the fourth generation of those who hate me, ⁶but practicing kindness to thousands for those who love me and for those who observe my commandments.

⁷You shall not bring up the name of YHWH, your God, for a falsehood, because YHWH will not make one innocent who will bring up His name for a falsehood.

מִתַּ֫חַת וַאֲשֶׁ֣ר בַּמַּ֣יִם ׀ מִתַּ֖חַת לָאָֽרֶץ׃ ⁵לֹֽא־תִשְׁתַּחֲוֶ֥ה לָהֶ֖ם וְלֹ֣א תָֽעָבְדֵ֑ם כִּ֣י אָֽנֹכִ֞י יְהוָ֤ה אֱלֹהֶ֨יךָ֙ אֵ֣ל קַנָּ֔א פֹּ֠קֵד עֲוֺ֨ן אָבֹ֧ת עַל־בָּנִ֛ים עַל־שִׁלֵּשִׁ֥ים וְעַל־רִבֵּעִ֖ים לְשֹׂנְאָֽי׃ ⁶וְעֹ֤שֶׂה חֶ֨סֶד֙ לַאֲלָפִ֔ים לְאֹהֲבַ֖י וּלְשֹׁמְרֵ֥י מִצְוֺתָֽי׃ ס ⁷לֹ֥א תִשָּׂ֛א אֶת־שֵֽׁם־יְהוָ֥ה אֱלֹהֶ֖יךָ לַשָּׁ֑וְא כִּ֣י לֹ֤א יְנַקֶּה֙ יְהוָ֔ה אֵ֛ת אֲשֶׁר־יִשָּׂ֥א אֶת־שְׁמ֖וֹ לַשָּֽׁוְא׃

---

else on earth (Leviticus 17; Deuteronomy 12). Confirmation of the fact that the issue is making statues of YHWH comes from archaeological evidence: small figures of females are extremely common finds, but in all the excavations in Israel so far only two male figures have ever been found. (And one of them, which my friend Yigal Shiloh uncovered in the City of David excavations of biblical Jerusalem, was clearly not Israelite.) That is, female figures often escaped the ban on statues, but male figures did not—not because they were Baal or Dagon figures, but because they could be YHWH.

20:5. **a jealous God.** What could it mean for a god to be jealous? A pagan deity might be thought to be jealous of another deity's powers or possessions but would not be jealous of another god's *existence*. Jealousy is a profoundly monotheistic quality in a god. The God of Israel does not tolerate making a statue of another god, bowing to another god, or serving another god, of any form.

20:6. **thousands.** Of generations.

20:7. **bring up His name for a falsehood.** (Traditionally translated "take His name in vain.") This does not mean that one cannot say the divine name in an exclamation—much less does it mean saying the words "God" or "Lord" in an exclamation. It refers to falsehood. The term refers to a false report (Exod 23:1) and a false witness (Deut 5:17; which corresponds to the term "lying witness" here in Exod 20:13). This commandment means that one cannot make an oath in God's name and not fulfill it. To appreciate the seriousness of this commandment, note the case of Joshua, who is deceived by the Gibeonites into making an oath of nonaggression. When Joshua learns that the Gibeonites are among the Canaanite residents whom he was commanded by God to destroy, he lets them live, disobeying a direct command from God rather than violate one of the Ten Commandments (Joshua 9). And note the case of Jephthah, who makes an oath to sacrifice the first thing to come out of his gate, which turns out to be his daughter. He sacrifices her rather than violate this commandment (Judges 11). (It is not reckoned legally as murder. Human sacrifice is forbidden, but it is legally distinguished from murder, which involves malice.) As horrible as this is (especially in light of the Aqedah), it conveys the seriousness of this commandment and of the principle that the Ten Commandments outweigh other laws.

8Remember the Sabbath day, to make it holy. 9Six days you shall labor and do all your work, 10and the seventh day is a Sabbath to YHWH, your God. You shall not do any work: you and your son and your daughter, your servant and your maid and your animal and your alien who is in your gates. 11Because for six days YHWH made the skies and the earth, the sea, and everything that is in them, and He rested on the seventh day. On account of this, YHWH blessed the Sabbath day and made it holy.

12Honor your father and your mother, so that your days will be extended on the land that YHWH, your God, is giving you.

13You shall not murder.

זָכוֹר֩ אֶת־י֨וֹם הַשַּׁבָּ֜ת לְקַדְּשׁ֗וֹ 9שֵׁ֣שֶׁת יָמִ֣ים תַּֽעֲבֹד֮ וְעָשִׂ֣יתָ כָּל־מְלַאכְתֶּ֒ךָ֒ 10וְי֙וֹם הַשְּׁבִיעִ֔י שַׁבָּ֖ת ׀ לַיהוָ֣ה אֱלֹהֶ֑יךָ לֹֽא־תַעֲשֶׂ֣ה כָל־מְלָאכָ֡ה אַתָּ֣ה ׀ וּבִנְךָֽ־וּ֠בִתֶּךָ עַבְדְּךָ֙ וַאֲמָֽתְךָ֜ וּבְהֶמְתֶּ֗ךָ וְגֵרְךָ֙ אֲשֶׁ֣ר בִּשְׁעָרֶ֔יךָ 11כִּ֣י שֵֽׁשֶׁת־יָמִים֩ עָשָׂ֨ה יְהוָ֜ה אֶת־הַשָּׁמַ֣יִם וְאֶת־הָאָ֗רֶץ אֶת־הַיָּם֙ וְאֶת־כָּל־אֲשֶׁר־בָּ֔ם וַיָּ֖נַח בַּי֣וֹם הַשְּׁבִיעִ֑י עַל־כֵּ֗ן בֵּרַ֧ךְ יְהוָ֛ה אֶת־י֥וֹם הַשַּׁבָּ֖ת וַֽיְקַדְּשֵֽׁהוּ׃ ס 12כַּבֵּ֣ד אֶת־אָבִ֖יךָ וְאֶת־אִמֶּ֑ךָ לְמַ֙עַן֙ יַאֲרִכ֣וּן יָמֶ֔יךָ עַ֚ל הָֽאֲדָמָ֔ה אֲשֶׁר־יְהוָ֥ה אֱלֹהֶ֖יךָ נֹתֵ֥ן לָֽךְ׃ ס 13לֹ֥א תִרְצָ֖ח׃ ס 14לֹ֖א תִּנְאָֽף׃

20:8. **the Sabbath**. On the significance of the Sabbath, see the comments on Gen 2:2 and 2:3.

20:12. **your days will be extended on the land**. My father taught me that the commandment to honor one's parents is the only commandment that offers a reward.

People have sometimes understood these words to mean that the reward is that if one honors one's parents one will have a long life. That is not a correct understanding. The commandment speaks of duration of days *on the land*. It means that if the people of Israel is composed of individuals who honor their parents then they will endure in their land. This suggests the enormous importance of the fifth commandment relative to the other nine. Those who honor their parents are likely to be people who will not murder, steal, or violate the other commandments. In thus preserving the terms of the covenant, they would be deserving of the covenant promise of the homeland. At the same time, this is a commandment on the father and mother as well: to be worthy of honor, and to convey the value of the commandments themselves in such a way that their children, in honoring the parents, will be moved to keep the commandments.

This pivotal importance of the commandment to honor one's parents may account for its position in the order of the commandments: The first four commandments concern the relationship between humans and God. The last five concern the relationship between humans and other humans. And the commandment that comes between—and connects?—these two groups is: Honor your father and your mother!

20:13. **murder**. Hebrew, like English, distinguishes between "murder" and "killing." "Murder" refers only to the taking of *human* life, and it is subject to the death penalty only when committed with malicious intent. The cases of manslaughter, killing through negligence, killing in war, execution for crimes, killing animals, animals killing humans, and human sacrifice are all treated separately from this in the

238

14You shall not commit adultery.

15You shall not steal.

16You shall not testify against your neighbor as a lying witness.

17You shall not covet your neighbor's house. You shall not covet your neighbor's wife or his servant or his maid or his ox or his ass or anything that your neighbor has.

18And all the people were seeing the thunders

ס 15לֹא תִּגְנֹב׃ ס 16לֹא־תַעֲנֶה בְרֵעֲךָ עֵד שָׁקֶר׃

ס 17לֹא תַחְמֹד בֵּית רֵעֶךָ לֹא־תַחְמֹד אֵשֶׁת רֵעֶךָ

וְעַבְדּוֹ וַאֲמָתוֹ וְשׁוֹרוֹ וַחֲמֹרוֹ וְכֹל אֲשֶׁר לְרֵעֶךָ׃ פ

18וְכָל־הָעָם רֹאִים אֶת־הַקּוֹלֹת וְאֶת־הַלַּפִּידִם

Torah, and terms other than "murder" are used. (On the special circumstance of the one who murders without malice, see Deut 4:41–42.) At the time that I am writing this, technology has raised new cases, including abortion and assisted suicide. Whatever one's view of these matters, one cannot simply claim that they are prohibited by the commandment against murder. One must argue whether they are consistent with the other cases that constitute murder or if they belong among the cases that involve taking life but still are not murder.

20:14. **adultery.** It is commonly said that adultery in the Torah is defined as sex between a man and a married woman—but not between a single woman and a married man. The reason for this definition is that ancient Israel was polygamous, and it was acceptable for a man to have several wives or concubines (as long as none of them was married to another man). But now, for those who live in monogamous societies, the issue for either spouse is the same: violation of their marriage commitment to each other. Sex with someone other than one's spouse is equally prohibited for husbands and wives by this commandment.

20:16. **neighbor.** See the explanation of this term on Lev 19:18.

20:16. **lying witness.** Is false testimony not already forbidden by the command against taking God's name in vain by lying in an oath sworn to God? This question assumes that testimony in court was in fact taken under oath in biblical times. But: (1) The Torah does not say that oaths are required—except for the case of the suspected adulteress in Numbers 5. (2) The case of the suspected adulteress may well be the exception that proves that the rule was *not* to take oaths. (3) The inclusion in the Decalogue of this commandment against being a false witness appears to me to be itself the evidence that testimony was not taken under oath, because, if it were, this commandment would indeed be unnecessary.

20:17. **covet.** This comes at the end of the Ten Commandments, and it is different: it commands regarding an emotional state. This seems like an extra burden, but it comes as a help. It is saying: Do you want some help to avoid breaking the other commandments? Very well, don't covet!

20:18. **the people saw.** The Masoretic Text reads "saw," but the Greek, Samaritan, and other versions of the text read "were afraid." The consonants of the Hebrew words for "saw" and for "were afraid" are the same (ירא). "Were afraid" is probably correct,

and the flashes and the sound of the horn and the mountain smoking. And the people saw, and they moved and stood at a distance, [19]and they said to Moses, "*You* speak with us so we may listen, but let God not speak with us or else we'll die."

[20]And Moses said to the people, "Don't be afraid, because God is coming for the purpose of testing you and for the purpose that his fear will be on your faces so that you won't sin."

[21]And the people stood at a distance, and Moses went over to the nimbus where God was. [22]And YHWH said to Moses, "You shall say this to the children of Israel: You have seen that I have spoken with you from the skies. [23]You shall not make gods of silver with me, and you shall not make gods of gold for yourselves. [24]You shall make an altar of earth for me, and you shall sacrifice on it your burnt offerings and your peace offerings, your sheep and your oxen. In every place where I'll have my name commemorated I'll come to you, and I'll bless you. [25]And if you'll make an altar of stones for me, you shall not make them cut. When you have elevated your sword over it, then you have desecrated it. [26]And you shall not go up by stairs on my altar, so that your nudity will not be exposed over it."

וְאֵת֙ ק֣וֹל הַשֹּׁפָ֔ר וְאֶת־הָהָ֖ר עָשֵׁ֑ן וַיַּ֤רְא הָעָם֙ וַיָּנֻ֔עוּ וַיַּעַמְד֖וּ מֵֽרָחֹֽק׃ 19וַיֹּֽאמְרוּ֙ אֶל־מֹשֶׁ֔ה דַּבֵּר־אַתָּ֥ה עִמָּ֖נוּ וְנִשְׁמָ֑עָה וְאַל־יְדַבֵּ֥ר עִמָּ֛נוּ אֱלֹהִ֖ים פֶּן־נָמֽוּת׃ 20וַיֹּ֨אמֶר מֹשֶׁ֣ה אֶל־הָעָם֮ אַל־תִּירָאוּ֒ כִּ֗י לְבַֽעֲבוּר֙ נַסּ֣וֹת אֶתְכֶ֔ם בָּ֖א הָאֱלֹהִ֑ים וּבַעֲב֗וּר תִּהְיֶ֧ה יִרְאָת֛וֹ עַל־פְּנֵיכֶ֖ם לְבִלְתִּ֥י תֶחֱטָֽאוּ׃ 21וַיַּעֲמֹ֥ד הָעָ֖ם מֵֽרָחֹ֑ק וּמֹשֶׁה֙ נִגַּ֣שׁ אֶל־הָ֣עֲרָפֶ֔ל אֲשֶׁר־שָׁ֖ם הָאֱלֹהִֽים׃ פ 22וַיֹּ֤אמֶר יְהוָה֙ אֶל־מֹשֶׁ֔ה כֹּ֥ה תֹאמַ֖ר אֶל־בְּנֵ֣י יִשְׂרָאֵ֑ל אַתֶּ֣ם רְאִיתֶ֔ם כִּ֚י מִן־הַשָּׁמַ֔יִם דִּבַּ֖רְתִּי עִמָּכֶֽם׃ 23לֹ֥א תַעֲשׂ֖וּן אִתִּ֑י אֱלֹ֤הֵי כֶ֙סֶף֙ וֵאלֹהֵ֣י זָהָ֔ב לֹ֥א תַעֲשׂ֖וּ לָכֶֽם׃ 24מִזְבַּ֣ח אֲדָמָה֮ תַּעֲשֶׂה־לִּי֒ וְזָבַחְתָּ֣ עָלָ֗יו אֶת־עֹלֹתֶ֙יךָ֙ וְאֶת־שְׁלָמֶ֔יךָ אֶת־צֹֽאנְךָ֖ וְאֶת־בְּקָרֶ֑ךָ בְּכָל־הַמָּקוֹם֙ אֲשֶׁ֣ר אַזְכִּ֣יר אֶת־שְׁמִ֔י אָב֥וֹא אֵלֶ֖יךָ וּבֵרַכְתִּֽיךָ׃ 25וְאִם־מִזְבַּ֤ח אֲבָנִים֙ תַּעֲשֶׂה־לִּ֔י לֹֽא־תִבְנֶ֥ה אֶתְהֶ֖ן גָּזִ֑ית כִּ֧י חַרְבְּךָ֛ הֵנַ֥פְתָּ עָלֶ֖יהָ וַתְּחַֽלְלֶֽהָ׃ 26וְלֹֽא־תַעֲלֶ֥ה בְמַעֲלֹ֖ת עַל־מִזְבְּחִ֑י אֲשֶׁ֛ר לֹֽא־תִגָּלֶ֥ה עֶרְוָתְךָ֖ עָלָֽיו׃ פ

---

because Moses tells the people, "Don't be afraid," two verses later. This technical point of Hebrew consonants is important because it establishes the people's state of mind: hearing the voice of God terrifies them, and that is why they tell Moses, "Let God not speak with us or else we'll die."

20:19. **You speak with us**. The absence of prophecy in Genesis—in the way that it is usually meant in the rest of the Hebrew Bible—is not extraordinary, for prophecy by its very essence relates to a community; and Genesis, as we have already observed, is primarily about individuals, not communities. The birth of prophecy in Exodus is related to the birth of the Israelite community in this book. In Exodus, YHWH initially sends Moses with His words to the Israelites and to the Egyptians. That is already a straightforward depiction of prophecy, but, more crucially, the book proceeds to formalize the prophetic role. When the Israelites come to Sinai, YHWH personally speaks directly to the entire nation, pronouncing the Ten Commandments aloud from the sky. The Israelites' response here is to tell Moses: "You speak with us so we may listen, but let God not speak with us or else we'll die." From this moment on, all revelation to Israel is mediated by a prophet. God never speaks directly to the people again in any book of the *Tanak*.

JUDGMENTS

משפטים

21 [1]"And these are the judgments that you shall set before them:

[2]"When you will buy a Hebrew slave, he shall work six years, and in the seventh he shall go out liberated for free. [3]If he will come by himself, he shall go out by himself. If he is a woman's husband, then his wife shall go out with him. [4]If his master will give him a wife, and she will give birth to sons or daughters for him, the wife and her children will be her master's, and he shall go out by himself. [5]And if the slave will *say:* 'I love my master, my wife, and my children; I won't go out liberated!' [6]then his master shall bring him over to God and bring him over to the door or to the doorpost, and his master shall pierce his ear with an awl, and he shall serve him forever.

[7]"And if a man will sell his daughter as a maid, she shall not go out as the slaves go out. [8]If she is bad in the eyes of her master who has designated her for himself, then he shall let her be redeemed. He shall not dominate so as to sell her to a foreign people in his betrayal of her. [9]And if he will designate her for his son, he shall treat her according to the manner of daughters.

מִשְׁפָּטִים אֲשֶׁר תָּשִׂים לִפְנֵיהֶם: 21 [1]וְאֵ֫לֶּה הַמִּשְׁפָּטִ֗ים אֲשֶׁר תָּשִׂים לִפְנֵיהֶם: [2]כִּי תִקְנֶה֙ עֶ֣בֶד עִבְרִ֔י שֵׁ֥שׁ שָׁנִ֖ים יַעֲבֹ֑ד וּבַ֨שְּׁבִעִ֔ת יֵצֵ֥א לַֽחָפְשִׁ֖י חִנָּֽם: [3]אִם־בְּגַפּ֣וֹ יָבֹ֔א בְּגַפּ֖וֹ יֵצֵ֑א אִם־בַּ֤עַל אִשָּׁה֙ ה֔וּא וְיָצְאָ֥ה אִשְׁתּ֖וֹ עִמּֽוֹ: [4]אִם־אֲדֹנָ֤יו יִתֶּן־לוֹ֙ אִשָּׁ֔ה וְיָֽלְדָה־ל֥וֹ בָנִ֖ים א֣וֹ בָנ֑וֹת הָֽאִשָּׁ֣ה וִֽילָדֶ֗יהָ תִּהְיֶה֙ לַֽאדֹנֶ֔יהָ וְה֖וּא יֵצֵ֥א בְגַפּֽוֹ: [5]וְאִם־אָמֹ֤ר יֹאמַר֙ הָעֶ֔בֶד אָהַ֨בְתִּי֙ אֶת־אֲדֹנִ֔י אֶת־אִשְׁתִּ֖י וְאֶת־בָּנָ֑י לֹ֥א אֵצֵ֖א חָפְשִֽׁי: [6]וְהִגִּישׁ֤וֹ אֲדֹנָיו֙ אֶל־הָ֣אֱלֹהִ֔ים וְהִגִּישׁוֹ֙ אֶל־הַדֶּ֔לֶת א֖וֹ אֶל־הַמְּזוּזָ֑ה וְרָצַ֨ע אֲדֹנָ֤יו אֶת־אָזְנוֹ֙ בַּמַּרְצֵ֔עַ וַעֲבָד֖וֹ לְעֹלָֽם: ס [7]וְכִֽי־יִמְכֹּ֥ר אִ֛ישׁ אֶת־בִּתּ֖וֹ לְאָמָ֑ה לֹ֥א תֵצֵ֖א כְּצֵ֥את הָעֲבָדִֽים: [8]אִם־רָעָ֞ה בְּעֵינֵ֧י אֲדֹנֶ֛יהָ אֲשֶׁר־ל֥וֹ יְעָדָ֖הּ וְהֶפְדָּ֑הּ לְעַ֥ם נָכְרִ֛י לֹא־יִמְשֹׁ֥ל לְמָכְרָ֖הּ בְּבִגְדוֹ־בָֽהּ: [9]וְאִם־לִבְנ֖וֹ יִֽיעָדֶ֑נָּה כְּמִשְׁפַּ֥ט הַבָּנ֖וֹת יַעֲשֶׂה־לָּֽהּ:

21:8 קְ לוֹ

21:1. **these are the judgments that you shall set**. These three chapters, Exodus 21–23, are a corpus of law known as the Covenant Code.

21:2. **Hebrew slave**. In biblical narrative the term "Hebrew" is used to identify Israelites only when speaking among foreigners. It is not the standard term for the people, which is rather "Israelite" at first, and "Jew" later. Its use here in biblical law, where we would have expected "Israelite slave," probably occurs because this had become a fixed phrase through assonance: the two words, "slave" (עבד, *'ebed*) and "Hebrew" (עברי, *'ibrî*), begin with the same two letters.

21:8. **He shall not dominate**. Recall that part of the curse on woman in Eden was that "he'll dominate you" (Gen 3:16). But here we are told of a case in which a man is explicitly not free to dominate a woman. Even in that worldview that recognized male control of women, there was an understanding that this control is not unlimited. This point of respect for women and recognition of a legal right that they possessed was a first small step in the breakdown of that worldview. And this passage teaches that a commandment can change or become limited even within the Torah itself.

10If he will take another for himself, he shall not subtract from her food, her apparel, and her hygiene. 11And if he will not do these three for her, then she shall go out free. There is no money.

12"One who strikes a man, and he dies, he shall be *put to death*. 13And one who did not scheme, but God conveyed it to his hand, I shall set a place for you, that he shall flee there. 14But if a man will plot against his neighbor, to kill him with treachery, you shall take him from my altar to die.

15"And one who strikes his father and his mother shall be *put to death*.

16"And one who steals a man and has sold him, or he was found in his hand, *will be put to death*.

17"And one who curses his father and his mother shall be *put to death*.

18"And if people will quarrel, and a man strikes his neighbor with a stone or with a fist, and he does not die, and he falls to bed, 19if he will get up and walk himself outside on his staff, then the one who struck will be innocent. Only he shall compensate for his staying home and shall *have him healed*.

20"And if a man will strike his slave or his maid with a rod, and he dies by his hand, he shall be *avenged*. 21Just: if he will stand for a day

10אִם־אַחֶרֶת יִקַּֽח־לֹ֑ו שְׁאֵרָ֛הּ כְּסוּתָ֥הּ וְעֹנָתָ֖הּ לֹ֥א יִגְרָֽע׃ 11וְאִם־שְׁלָשׁ־אֵ֔לֶּה לֹ֥א יַעֲשֶׂ֖ה לָ֑הּ וְיָצְאָ֥ה חִנָּ֖ם אֵ֥ין כָּֽסֶף׃ ס 12מַכֵּ֥ה אִ֛ישׁ וָמֵ֖ת מֹ֥ות יוּמָֽת׃ 13וַאֲשֶׁר֙ לֹ֣א צָדָ֔ה וְהָאֱלֹהִ֖ים אִנָּ֣ה לְיָד֑וֹ וְשַׂמְתִּ֤י לְךָ֙ מָקֹ֔ום אֲשֶׁ֥ר יָנ֖וּס שָֽׁמָּה׃ ס 14וְכִֽי־יָזִ֥ד אִ֛ישׁ עַל־רֵעֵ֖הוּ לְהָרְג֣וֹ בְעָרְמָ֑ה מֵעִ֣ם מִזְבְּחִ֔י תִּקָּחֶ֖נּוּ לָמֽוּת׃ ס 15וּמַכֵּ֥ה אָבִ֛יו וְאִמֹּ֖ו מֹ֥ות יוּמָֽת׃ 16וְגֹנֵ֨ב אִ֧ישׁ וּמְכָר֛וֹ וְנִמְצָ֥א בְיָד֖וֹ מֹ֥ות יוּמָֽת׃ ס 17וּמְקַלֵּ֥ל אָבִ֛יו וְאִמֹּ֖ו מֹ֥ות יוּמָֽת׃ ס 18וְכִֽי־יְרִיבֻ֣ן אֲנָשִׁ֗ים וְהִכָּה־אִישׁ֙ אֶת־רֵעֵ֔הוּ בְּאֶ֖בֶן אֹ֣ו בְאֶגְרֹ֑ף וְלֹ֥א יָמ֖וּת וְנָפַ֥ל לְמִשְׁכָּֽב׃ 19אִם־יָק֞וּם וְהִתְהַלֵּ֥ךְ בַּח֛וּץ עַל־מִשְׁעַנְתֹּ֖ו וְנִקָּ֣ה הַמַּכֶּ֑ה רַ֥ק שִׁבְתֹּ֛ו יִתֵּ֖ן וְרַפֹּ֥א יְרַפֵּֽא׃ ס 20וְכִֽי־יַכֶּה֩ אִ֨ישׁ אֶת־עַבְדֹּ֜ו אֹ֤ו אֶת־אֲמָתֹו֙ בַּשֵּׁ֔בֶט וּמֵ֖ת תַּ֣חַת יָדֹ֑ו נָקֹ֖ם יִנָּקֵֽם׃ 21אַ֥ךְ אִם־יֹ֛ום אֹ֥ו יֹומַ֖יִם יַעֲמֹ֑ד לֹ֥א יֻקַּ֖ם

21:10. **hygiene**. Shalom Paul has shown parallels from ancient Near Eastern texts that indicate that, beside providing food and clothing, the husband must provide the necessary cosmetics for his wife's cleanliness and appearance. A second possibility is that the word here, *'ōnātāh*, is cognate to Hebrew *mā'ôn*, meaning a dwelling, in which case the text means that the husband provides food, clothing, and shelter. A third possibility is the traditional view that this refers to sex, but there is no evidence in support of this.

21:14. **plot**. The verb *zyd* elsewhere refers to cooking (e.g., Jacob's cooking the stew in Gen 25:29). Here it refers to someone's committing murder with intent, rather than manslaughter. (It also refers to the Egyptians' scheme to enslave the Israelites in Exod 18:11.) Like the English expression "to cook up," the Hebrew word has the range of both cooking and plotting.

21:21. **stand**. If he will not die immediately but will live for a day or two after being struck.

or two days, he shall not be avenged, because he is his money.

22"And if people will fight, and they strike a pregnant woman, and her children go out, and there will not be an injury, he shall be *penalized* according to what the woman's husband will impose on him, and he will give it by the judges. 23And if there will be an injury, then you shall give a life for a life, 24an eye for an eye, a tooth for a tooth, a hand for a hand, a foot for a foot, 25a burn for a burn, a wound for a wound, a hurt for a hurt.

26"And if a man will strike his slave's eye or his maid's eye and destroy it, he shall let him go, liberated, for his eye. 27And if he will knock out his

כִּי כַסְפּוֹ הוּא: ס ‎22וְכִי־יִנָּצוּ אֲנָשִׁים וְנָגְפוּ אִשָּׁה הָרָה וְיָצְאוּ יְלָדֶיהָ וְלֹא יִהְיֶה אָסוֹן עָנוֹשׁ יֵעָנֵשׁ כַּאֲשֶׁר יָשִׁית עָלָיו בַּעַל הָאִשָּׁה וְנָתַן בִּפְלִלִים: ‎23וְאִם־אָסוֹן יִהְיֶה וְנָתַתָּה נֶפֶשׁ תַּחַת נָפֶשׁ: ‎24עַיִן תַּחַת עַיִן שֵׁן תַּחַת שֵׁן יָד תַּחַת יָד רֶגֶל תַּחַת רָגֶל: ‎25כְּוִיָּה תַּחַת כְּוִיָּה פֶּצַע תַּחַת פָּצַע חַבּוּרָה תַּחַת חַבּוּרָה: ס ‎26וְכִי־יַכֶּה אִישׁ אֶת־עֵין עַבְדּוֹ אוֹ־אֶת־עֵין אֲמָתוֹ וְשִׁחֲתָהּ לַחָפְשִׁי יְשַׁלְּחֶנּוּ תַּחַת עֵינוֹ: ס

21:21. **he is his money**. The slave is the master's property. This indicates that the master is empowered to strike his slave, but he is not free to be the immediate cause of the slave's death.

21:22. **her children go out, and there will not be an injury**. This can mean: if the woman has a miscarriage, but there is no other physical damage to the woman herself. Or it can mean: if the woman goes into labor, and the child is born without any physical damage. Scholars generally understand it to be the former.

This passage has been cited in debates over abortion. However, the issues in this case are different, and the wording is so complex, and its meaning is so uncertain, that one should be extremely hesitant to use this case for either side of that debate.

21:22. **he will give it by the judges**. The meaning is uncertain, but the penalty is determined and enforced in some way involving both the husband and the judges.

21:23-24. **a life for a life, an eye for an eye** . . . The inclusion of "a burn for a burn" here—in a case in which "burn" has no apparent relevance—indicates that this list comes to apply a *fundamental principle* to this case. Concerning the eye-for-an-eye principle, see the comment on Lev 24:20.

21:26. **liberated, for his eye**. Even in a system that allows slavery, a master does not own the slave's body. The master can require work from a slave, but damaging the slave's eye or tooth steps over the line, and the master no longer owns the slave. This reminds us also of the Egyptian enslavement of Israel. The Egyptians are not criticized for having slaves, but rather for the way they *treat* the slaves: "They degraded them. . . . They made them serve with harshness . . . they made their lives bitter with hard work . . ." They killed the male infants. The Torah did not bring about the end of slavery by abolishing it. It established principles regarding slaves' dignity, rights, and treatment. And these gradually contributed to humans' own rejection of slavery in much (though not yet all) of the world. This is a crucial point itself: that some of the laws of the Torah command things outright, while others lead humans to grow and change themselves.

slave's tooth or his maid's tooth, he shall let him go liberated for his tooth.

28"And if an ox will gore a man or a woman and they die, the ox shall be *stoned*, and its meat shall not be eaten—and the ox's owner is innocent. 29And if it was a goring ox from the day before yesterday, and it had been so testified to its owner, and he did not watch it, and it killed a man or a woman, the ox will be stoned, and its owner will be put to death as well. 30If a ransom will be set on him, then he shall give everything that will be set on him for the redemption of his life. 31Whether it will gore a son or it will gore a daughter, according to this judgment shall be done to it. 32If the ox will gore a slave or a maid, he shall pay thirty silver shekels to his owner, and the ox shall be stoned.

33"And if a man will open a pit, or if a man will dig a pit, and he will not cover it, and an ox or an ass will fall there, 34the owner of the pit shall pay; he shall pay back money to its owner, and the dead one will be his. 35And if a man's ox will strike his neighbor's ox, and it dies, then they shall sell the live ox and split the money for it, and they shall split the dead one as well. 36Or: if it was known that it was a goring ox from the day before yesterday, and its owner did not watch it, he shall *pay* an ox for the ox, and the dead one shall be his.

37"If a man will steal an ox or a sheep and slaughter it or sell it, he shall pay five oxen for the ox and four sheep for the sheep.

22 1"If the thief will be found while breaking in and will be struck, and he dies, there is no blood for him. 2If the sun has risen

כז וְאִם־שֵׁן עַבְדּוֹ אוֹ־שֵׁן אֲמָתוֹ יַפִּיל לַחָפְשִׁי יְשַׁלְּחֶנּוּ תַּחַת שִׁנּוֹ: פ

כח וְכִי־יִגַּח שׁוֹר אֶת־אִישׁ אוֹ אֶת־אִשָּׁה וָמֵת סָקוֹל יִסָּקֵל הַשּׁוֹר וְלֹא יֵאָכֵל אֶת־בְּשָׂרוֹ וּבַעַל הַשּׁוֹר נָקִי: כט וְאִם שׁוֹר נַגָּח הוּא מִתְּמֹל שִׁלְשֹׁם וְהוּעַד בִּבְעָלָיו וְלֹא יִשְׁמְרֶנּוּ וְהֵמִית אִישׁ אוֹ אִשָּׁה הַשּׁוֹר יִסָּקֵל וְגַם־בְּעָלָיו יוּמָת: ל אִם־כֹּפֶר יוּשַׁת עָלָיו וְנָתַן פִּדְיֹן נַפְשׁוֹ כְּכֹל אֲשֶׁר־יוּשַׁת עָלָיו: לא אוֹ־בֵן יִגָּח אוֹ־בַת יִגָּח כַּמִּשְׁפָּט הַזֶּה יֵעָשֶׂה לּוֹ: לב אִם־עֶבֶד יִגַּח הַשּׁוֹר אוֹ אָמָה כֶּסֶף שְׁלֹשִׁים שְׁקָלִים יִתֵּן לַאדֹנָיו וְהַשּׁוֹר יִסָּקֵל: ס לג וְכִי־יִפְתַּח אִישׁ בּוֹר אוֹ כִּי־יִכְרֶה אִישׁ בֹּר וְלֹא יְכַסֶּנּוּ וְנָפַל־שָׁמָּה שּׁוֹר אוֹ חֲמוֹר: לד בַּעַל הַבּוֹר יְשַׁלֵּם כֶּסֶף יָשִׁיב לִבְעָלָיו וְהַמֵּת יִהְיֶה־לּוֹ: ס לה וְכִי־יִגֹּף שׁוֹר־אִישׁ אֶת־שׁוֹר רֵעֵהוּ וָמֵת וּמָכְרוּ אֶת־הַשּׁוֹר הַחַי וְחָצוּ אֶת־כַּסְפּוֹ וְגַם אֶת־הַמֵּת יֶחֱצוּן: לו אוֹ נוֹדַע כִּי שׁוֹר נַגָּח הוּא מִתְּמוֹל שִׁלְשֹׁם וְלֹא יִשְׁמְרֶנּוּ בְּעָלָיו שַׁלֵּם יְשַׁלֵּם שׁוֹר תַּחַת הַשּׁוֹר וְהַמֵּת יִהְיֶה־לּוֹ: ס לז כִּי יִגְנֹב־אִישׁ שׁוֹר אוֹ־שֶׂה וּטְבָחוֹ אוֹ מְכָרוֹ חֲמִשָּׁה בָקָר יְשַׁלֵּם תַּחַת הַשּׁוֹר וְאַרְבַּע־צֹאן תַּחַת הַשֶּׂה: 22 א אִם־בַּמַּחְתֶּרֶת יִמָּצֵא הַגַּנָּב וְהֻכָּה וָמֵת אֵין לוֹ דָּמִים: ב אִם־זָרְחָה הַשֶּׁמֶשׁ עָלָיו דָּמִים

21:29. **from the day before yesterday.** Meaning: this ox had gored before.

21:31–32. **a son or . . . a daughter . . . a slave or a maid.** No distinction is made on the basis of sex; a distinction is made on the basis of class: free versus slave.

22:1. **no blood for him.** Meaning: there is no bloodguilt for killing him. The person who killed the thief who was in the act of breaking in (at night) cannot be held legally responsible for the death.

22.2. **If the sun has risen on him there is blood for him.** If the theft was in the

on him there is blood for him. He shall *pay.* If he does not have it, then he shall be sold for his theft. [3]If the theft will be *found* in his hand—from ox to ass to sheep—alive, he shall pay two.

[4]"If a man will have a field or a vineyard grazed, and he will let his beast go and graze in another person's field, he shall pay the best of his field and the best of his vineyard.

[5]"If fire will break out and find thorns and stacked grain or standing grain or a field is consumed, the one who set the blaze shall *pay.*

[6]"If a man will give his neighbor money or items to watch, and it will be stolen from the man's house, if the thief will be found he shall pay two. [7]If the thief will not be found, then the owner of the house shall be brought near to God: that he has not put out his hand into his neighbor's property.

[8]"Over every case of an offense, over an ox, over an ass, over a sheep, over clothing, over every loss about which one will say that 'This is it,' the word of the two of them shall come to God. The one whom God will implicate shall pay two to his neighbor.

[9]"If a man will give an ass or an ox or a sheep or any animal to his neighbor to watch, and it dies or is injured or is seized—no one seeing—[10]an oath of YHWH shall be between the two of them: that he has not put out his hand into his neighbor's property; and its owner shall take it,

לֹ֥ו שַׁלֵּ֖ם אִם־אֵ֣ין ל֑וֹ וְנִמְכַּ֖ר בִּגְנֵבָתֽוֹ׃ [3]אִֽם־הִמָּצֵא֩ תִמָּצֵ֨א בְיָד֜וֹ הַגְּנֵבָ֗ה מִשּׁ֧וֹר עַד־חֲמ֛וֹר עַד־שֶׂ֖ה חַיִּ֣ים שְׁנָ֥יִם יְשַׁלֵּֽם׃ ס [4]כִּ֤י יַבְעֶר־אִישׁ֙ שָׂדֶ֣ה אֽוֹ־כֶ֔רֶם וְשִׁלַּח֙ אֶת־בְּעִירֹ֔ה וּבִעֵ֖ר בִּשְׂדֵ֣ה אַחֵ֑ר מֵיטַ֥ב שָׂדֵ֛הוּ וּמֵיטַ֥ב כַּרְמ֖וֹ יְשַׁלֵּֽם׃ ס [5]כִּֽי־תֵצֵ֨א אֵ֜שׁ וּמָצְאָ֣ה קֹצִים֮ וְנֶאֱכַ֣ל גָּדִ֔ישׁ א֥וֹ הַקָּמָ֖ה א֣וֹ הַשָּׂדֶ֑ה שַׁלֵּ֣ם יְשַׁלֵּ֔ם הַמַּבְעִ֖ר אֶת־הַבְּעֵרָֽה׃ ס [6]כִּֽי־יִתֵּן֩ אִ֨ישׁ אֶל־רֵעֵ֜הוּ כֶּ֤סֶף אֽוֹ־כֵלִים֙ לִשְׁמֹ֔ר וְגֻנַּ֖ב מִבֵּ֣ית הָאִ֑ישׁ אִם־יִמָּצֵ֥א הַגַּנָּ֖ב יְשַׁלֵּ֥ם שְׁנָֽיִם׃ [7]אִם־לֹ֤א יִמָּצֵא֙ הַגַּנָּ֔ב וְנִקְרַ֥ב בַּֽעַל־הַבַּ֖יִת אֶל־הָֽאֱלֹהִ֑ים אִם־לֹ֥א שָׁלַ֛ח יָד֖וֹ בִּמְלֶ֥אכֶת רֵעֵֽהוּ׃ [8]עַֽל־כָּל־דְּבַר־פֶּ֡שַׁע עַל־שׁ֡וֹר עַל־חֲ֠מוֹר עַל־שֶׂ֨ה עַל־שַׂלְמָ֜ה עַל־כָּל־אֲבֵדָ֗ה אֲשֶׁ֤ר יֹאמַר֙ כִּי־ה֣וּא זֶ֔ה עַ֚ד הָֽאֱלֹהִ֔ים יָבֹ֖א דְּבַר־שְׁנֵיהֶ֑ם אֲשֶׁ֤ר יַרְשִׁיעֻן֙ אֱלֹהִ֔ים יְשַׁלֵּ֥ם שְׁנַ֖יִם לְרֵעֵֽהוּ׃ ס [9]כִּֽי־יִתֵּן֩ אִ֨ישׁ אֶל־רֵעֵ֜הוּ חֲמ֨וֹר אוֹ־שׁ֥וֹר אוֹ־שֶׂ֛ה וְכָל־בְּהֵמָ֖ה לִשְׁמֹ֑ר וּמֵ֛ת אוֹ־נִשְׁבַּ֥ר אוֹ־נִשְׁבָּ֖ה אֵ֥ין רֹאֶֽה׃ [10]שְׁבֻעַ֣ת יְהוָ֗ה תִּהְיֶה֙ בֵּ֣ין שְׁנֵיהֶ֔ם אִם־לֹ֥א שָׁלַ֛ח יָד֖וֹ בִּמְלֶ֣אכֶת רֵעֵ֑הוּ וְלָקַ֥ח בְּעָלָ֖יו וְלֹ֥א

22:4 ק בְּעִירֽוֹ

daytime—which is less frightening and when escape, help, and witnesses are more possible—then one is legally responsible if one kills the thief.

22:2. **He shall *pay.*** If the thief is caught, not killed, he must pay for his theft.

22:2. **If he does not have it, then he shall be sold for his theft.** If the thief does not have the money to pay for his theft, then he is sold into servitude.

22:7. **brought near to God: that he has not put out his hand.** The wording (starting with *'im*) plus the notice of being brought "near to God" indicate that he is to take an oath that he has not taken the missing property for which he was responsible. The wording occurs again in 22:10 with an explicit reference to an oath.

22:8. **implicate.** The verb here is plural. Some therefore take its subject, *'ĕlōhîm,* not to refer to God here and in the preceding verse. (See Rashi and Ibn Ezra.) Rather, it is understood to refer to the judges before whom the case is brought.

and he shall not pay. ¹¹And if it will be *stolen* from him, he shall pay its owner. ¹²If it will be *torn*, he shall bring it in witness; he shall not pay for the torn one. ¹³And if a man will ask it of his neighbor, and it is injured or dies, its owner not being with it, he shall *pay*. ¹⁴If its owner is with it, he shall not pay. If it was hired, he has its hire coming to him.

¹⁵"And if a man will deceive a virgin who is not betrothed, and he lies with her, he shall *espouse her by a bride-price* to him as a wife. ¹⁶If her father will *refuse* to give her to him, he shall weigh out money corresponding to the bride-price of virgins.

¹⁷"You shall not let a witch live.

¹⁸"Anyone who lies with an animal shall be *put to death.*

¹⁹"One who sacrifices to gods shall be completely destroyed—except to YHWH alone.

²⁰"And you shall not persecute an alien, and you shall not oppress him, because you were aliens in the land of Egypt.

²¹"You shall not degrade any widow or orphan. ²²If you will *degrade* them, when they will *cry out* to me I'll *hear* their cry, ²³and my anger

יְשַׁלֵּם: ¹¹וְאִם־גָּנֹב יִגָּנֵב מֵעִמּוֹ יְשַׁלֵּם לִבְעָלָיו:
¹²אִם־טָרֹף יִטָּרֵף יְבִאֵהוּ עֵד הַטְּרֵפָה לֹא יְשַׁלֵּם:
פ ¹³וְכִי־יִשְׁאַל אִישׁ מֵעִם רֵעֵהוּ וְנִשְׁבַּר אוֹ־מֵת בְּעָלָיו אֵין־עִמּוֹ שַׁלֵּם יְשַׁלֵּם: ¹⁴אִם־בְּעָלָיו עִמּוֹ לֹא יְשַׁלֵּם אִם־שָׂכִיר הוּא בָּא בִּשְׂכָרוֹ: ס ¹⁵וְכִי־יְפַתֶּה אִישׁ בְּתוּלָה אֲשֶׁר לֹא־אֹרָשָׂה וְשָׁכַב עִמָּהּ מָהֹר יִמְהָרֶנָּה לּוֹ לְאִשָּׁה: ¹⁶אִם־מָאֵן יְמָאֵן אָבִיהָ לְתִתָּהּ לוֹ כֶּסֶף יִשְׁקֹל כְּמֹהַר הַבְּתוּלֹת: ס ¹⁷מְכַשֵּׁפָה לֹא תְחַיֶּה: ס ¹⁸כָּל־שֹׁכֵב עִם־בְּהֵמָה מוֹת יוּמָת: ס ¹⁹זֹבֵחַ לָאֱלֹהִים יָחֳרָם בִּלְתִּי לַיהוָה לְבַדּוֹ: ²⁰וְגֵר לֹא־תוֹנֶה וְלֹא תִלְחָצֶנּוּ כִּי־גֵרִים הֱיִיתֶם בְּאֶרֶץ מִצְרָיִם: ²¹כָּל־אַלְמָנָה וְיָתוֹם לֹא תְעַנּוּן: ²²אִם־עַנֵּה תְעַנֶּה אֹתוֹ כִּי אִם־צָעֹק יִצְעַק אֵלַי שָׁמֹעַ אֶשְׁמַע צַעֲקָתוֹ: ²³וְחָרָה אַפִּי וְהָרַגְתִּי אֶתְכֶם

22:10. **he shall not pay.** The person who was watching the animal does not pay anything to the animal's owner.

22:12. **witness.** Rashi understands this to mean that he brings witnesses. Ibn Ezra suggests that it means that he brings a portion of the torn animal as evidence. The latter is the understanding of most contemporary translators.

22:13. **ask.** That is, borrow.

22:17. **a witch.** Why does the text condemn only women and not male sorcerers? Males are identified as practicing magic as well, as in the case of the Egyptian magicians (Exod 7:11). The feminine form of this word occurs only here out of the entire *Tanak.* And the Septuagint has the masculine plural (which is used to include both men and women) here instead of the Masoretic Text's feminine singular. This suggests that the original text forbids the practice of magic by either men or women (sorcerers or witches). Note also: the text does not deny that magic *works.* (On the contrary, the Egyptian magicians can turn staffs into snakes.) It forbids the *practice* of magic.

22:19. **completely destroyed.** Hebrew *ḥerem* refers to the rule of destroying an individual or community along with all his family, animals, and possessions and thus dedicating them to the deity rather than profiting in any way from them.

will flare, and I'll kill you with a sword, and *your* wives will be widows and *your* children orphans! ²⁴"If you will lend money to my people, to the poor who is with you, you shall not be like a creditor to him; you shall not impose interest on him. ²⁵If you *take* your neighbor's clothing as *security*, you shall give it back to him by the sunset, ²⁶because it is his only apparel; it is his clothing for his skin. In what will he sleep? And it will be, when he will cry out to me, that I shall listen, because I am gracious.

²⁷"You shall not blaspheme God, and you shall not curse a chieftain among your people.

²⁸"You shall not delay your fulfillment and your flowing.

"You shall give me the firstborn of your sons.

²⁹"You shall do this to your ox and to your sheep: Seven days it will be with its mother. On the eighth day you shall give it to me.

³⁰"And you shall be holy people to me.

"And you shall not eat meat in the field that is torn. You shall throw it to the dog.

23 ¹"You shall not bring up a false report. Do not join your hand with a wicked person to be a malevolent witness. ²You shall not be following many to do bad. And you shall not

בְּחָ֑רֶב וְהָי֤וּ נְשֵׁיכֶם֙ אַלְמָנ֔וֹת וּבְנֵיכֶ֖ם יְתֹמִֽים׃ פ
²⁴אִם־כֶּ֣סֶף ׀ תַּלְוֶ֣ה אֶת־עַמִּ֗י אֶת־הֶֽעָנִי֙ עִמָּ֔ךְ לֹא־תִהְיֶ֥ה ל֖וֹ כְּנֹשֶׁ֑ה לֹֽא־תְשִׂימ֥וּן עָלָ֖יו נֶֽשֶׁךְ׃ ²⁵אִם־חָבֹ֥ל תַּחְבֹּ֖ל שַׂלְמַ֣ת רֵעֶ֑ךָ עַד־בֹּ֥א הַשֶּׁ֖מֶשׁ תְּשִׁיבֶ֥נּוּ לֽוֹ׃ ²⁶כִּ֣י הִ֤וא כְסוּתֹה֙ לְבַדָּ֔הּ הִ֥וא שִׂמְלָת֖וֹ לְעֹר֑וֹ בַּמֶּ֣ה יִשְׁכָּ֔ב וְהָיָה֙ כִּֽי־יִצְעַ֣ק אֵלַ֔י וְשָׁמַעְתִּ֖י כִּֽי־חַנּ֥וּן אָֽנִי׃ ס ²⁷אֱלֹהִ֖ים לֹ֣א תְקַלֵּ֑ל וְנָשִׂ֥יא בְעַמְּךָ֖ לֹ֥א תָאֹֽר׃ ²⁸מְלֵאָתְךָ֥ וְדִמְעֲךָ֖ לֹ֣א תְאַחֵ֑ר בְּכ֥וֹר בָּנֶ֖יךָ תִּתֶּן־לִֽי׃ ²⁹כֵּֽן־תַּעֲשֶׂ֥ה לְשֹׁרְךָ֖ לְצֹאנֶ֑ךָ שִׁבְעַ֤ת יָמִים֙ יִהְיֶ֣ה עִם־אִמּ֔וֹ בַּיּ֥וֹם הַשְּׁמִינִ֖י תִּתְּנוֹ־לִֽי׃ ³⁰וְאַנְשֵׁי־קֹ֖דֶשׁ תִּהְי֣וּן לִ֑י וּבָשָׂ֨ר בַּשָּׂדֶ֤ה טְרֵפָה֙ לֹ֣א תֹאכֵ֔לוּ לַכֶּ֖לֶב תַּשְׁלִכ֥וּן אֹתֽוֹ׃ ס

²³ ¹לֹ֥א תִשָּׂ֖א שֵׁ֣מַע שָׁ֑וְא אַל־תָּ֤שֶׁת יָֽדְךָ֙ עִם־רָשָׁ֔ע לִהְיֹ֖ת עֵ֥ד חָמָֽס׃ ס ²לֹֽא־תִהְיֶ֥ה אַחֲרֵֽי־רַבִּ֖ים

22:26 קְ כְּסוּתוֹ

22:27. **chieftain.** Hebrew *nāśî'*. Elsewhere in the Torah the text refers to the chieftain of a tribe (Num 2:3–29) or of a priestly family (Num 3:24–35) or of a city (Gen 34:2). Here it may allude to a king of Israel, "a chieftain among your people" (as in 1 Kings 11:34; Ezek 34:24), or it may mean any of these leaders.

22:28. **fulfillment and your flowing.** Everyone is unsure of what this means.

22:30. **meat that is torn.** This refers to the meat of an animal that was killed by another animal rather than having been killed in the sacred manner prescribed by the law. The word for "torn" (Hebrew *tĕrēpāh*) later came to be used for any prohibited foods.

23:2. **not be following many to do bad.** Do not follow a group, a crowd, a majority if what they are doing is wrong. Do not do it for acceptance, for the secure feeling of being in a group, or for the sadistic pleasure of being able to exclude someone. It is easy to be hurtful in a group. And it is easy to keep silent when one's group does harm—or when its leaders do harm from their position, which derives its power from the group. All of this is forbidden. It is utterly inconsistent with the Torah's conceptions of what a human should be and how one should behave toward other human beings. This comment should be unnecessary.

testify about a dispute to bend following many, to bend it. ³And you shall not favor a weak person in his dispute.

⁴"If you will happen upon your enemy's ox or his ass straying, you shall *bring it back* to him. ⁵If you will see the ass of someone who hates you sagging under its burden, and you would hold back from helping him: you shall *help* with him.

⁶"You shall not bend the judgment of your poor in his dispute.

⁷"You shall keep far from a word of a lie, and do not kill an innocent and a virtuous person, because I shall not vindicate a wicked person.

⁸"And you shall not take a bribe, because bribery will blind those who can see and will undermine the words of the virtuous.

⁹"And you shall not oppress an alien—since you know the alien's *soul*, because you were aliens in the land of Egypt.

לְרָעֹת וְלֹא־תַעֲנֶה עַל־רִב לִנְטֹת אַחֲרֵי רַבִּים לְהַטֹּת: ³וְדָל לֹא תֶהְדַּר בְּרִיבוֹ: ס ⁴כִּי תִפְגַּע שׁוֹר אֹיִבְךָ אוֹ חֲמֹרוֹ תֹעֶה הָשֵׁב תְּשִׁיבֶנּוּ לוֹ: ס ⁵כִּי־תִרְאֶה חֲמוֹר שֹׂנַאֲךָ רֹבֵץ תַּחַת מַשָּׂאוֹ וְחָדַלְתָּ מֵעֲזֹב לוֹ עָזֹב תַּעֲזֹב עִמּוֹ: ס ⁶לֹא תַטֶּה מִשְׁפַּט אֶבְיֹנְךָ בְּרִיבוֹ: ⁷מִדְּבַר־שֶׁקֶר תִּרְחָק וְנָקִי וְצַדִּיק אַל־תַּהֲרֹג כִּי לֹא־אַצְדִּיק רָשָׁע: ⁸וְשֹׁחַד לֹא תִקָּח כִּי הַשֹּׁחַד יְעַוֵּר פִּקְחִים וִיסַלֵּף דִּבְרֵי צַדִּיקִים: ⁹וְגֵר לֹא תִלְחָץ וְאַתֶּם יְדַעְתֶּם אֶת־נֶפֶשׁ הַגֵּר כִּי־גֵרִים הֱיִיתֶם בְּאֶרֶץ מִצְרָיִם: ¹⁰וְשֵׁשׁ שָׁנִים תִּזְרָע

23:2. **to bend following many, to bend it**. When giving testimony or when sitting in judgment, do not incline toward the majority of those involved in the case or toward the majority of the public. To "bend" toward them is to "bend" justice.

23:3. **you shall not favor a weak person**. *Of course* one should not favor the majority, or the rich, or the famous, or the powerful. *Of course* we should not bend the law for bad motives. We are reminded that we also must not bend the law or the truth even for good motives, such as feelings of compassion for the poor. Compare Lev 19:15.

23:5. **you would hold back from helping him**. That is, you would hold back from helping your adversary.

23:5. **help**. The Hebrew *'zb* (to leave) is difficult. One possibility, suggested here, is to read the word as *'zr* (to help). Alternatively, it may mean: "If you will see the ass of someone who hates you sagging under its burden, then you shall hold back from leaving it for him; you shall leave it *with* him." That is, do not leave it for him to handle himself; do what is necessary to assist and leave it back with him. By any reading, though, the main point is that one must be of help, even to someone who bears one ill will—perhaps *especially* to someone who bears ill will.

23:6. **your poor**. It is natural to use the phrase *"your* enemy," as in the preceding verses, but we would not readily expect *"your* poor" linguistically. But the issue is not linguistic. It is moral. The poor are not neutral as a group. They are *your* poor, your responsibility.

23:9. **you know the alien's *soul***. This verse, commanding not to oppress an alien residing among Israel, repeats a commandment that has already been given just a lit-

10"And six years you shall sow your land and gather its produce; 11and the seventh: you shall let it lie fallow and leave it, and your people's indigent will eat, and what they leave the animal of the field will eat. You shall do this to your vineyard, to your olives.

12"Six days you shall do the things you do, and on the seventh day you shall cease, so that your ox and your ass will rest, and your maid's son and the alien will be refreshed.

13"And you shall be watchful in everything that I have said to you. And you shall not commemorate the name of other gods. Let it not be heard on your mouth.

14"You shall celebrate three pilgrimages for me in the year:

15"You shall observe the Festival of Unleavened Bread. Seven days you shall eat unleavened bread, as I commanded you, at the appointed time of the month of Abib, because you went out of Egypt in it. And none shall appear before me empty.

16"And the Festival of Harvest, the first fruits of what you do, of what you will sow in the field.

"And the Festival of Gathering, at the end of the year, when you gather what you have done from the field.

17"Three times in the year every male of yours shall appear in front of the Lord YHWH.

אֶת־אַרְצֶ֔ךָ וְאָסַפְתָּ֖ אֶת־תְּבוּאָתָֽהּ׃ 11וְהַשְּׁבִיעִ֞ת תִּשְׁמְטֶ֣נָּה וּנְטַשְׁתָּ֗הּ וְאָֽכְלוּ֙ אֶבְיֹנֵ֣י עַמֶּ֔ךָ וְיִתְרָ֕ם תֹּאכַ֖ל חַיַּ֣ת הַשָּׂדֶ֑ה כֵּֽן־תַּעֲשֶׂ֥ה לְכַרְמְךָ֖ לְזֵיתֶֽךָ׃ 12שֵׁ֤שֶׁת יָמִים֙ תַּעֲשֶׂ֣ה מַעֲשֶׂ֔יךָ וּבַיּ֥וֹם הַשְּׁבִיעִ֖י תִּשְׁבֹּ֑ת לְמַ֣עַן יָנ֗וּחַ שֽׁוֹרְךָ֙ וַחֲמֹרֶ֔ךָ וְיִנָּפֵ֥שׁ בֶּן־אֲמָתְךָ֖ וְהַגֵּֽר׃ 13וּבְכֹ֛ל אֲשֶׁר־אָמַ֥רְתִּי אֲלֵיכֶ֖ם תִּשָּׁמֵ֑רוּ וְשֵׁ֨ם אֱלֹהִ֤ים אֲחֵרִים֙ לֹ֣א תַזְכִּ֔ירוּ לֹ֥א יִשָּׁמַ֖ע עַל־פִּֽיךָ׃ 14שָׁלֹ֣שׁ רְגָלִ֔ים תָּחֹ֥ג לִ֖י בַּשָּׁנָֽה׃ 15אֶת־חַ֣ג הַמַּצּוֹת֮ תִּשְׁמֹר֒ שִׁבְעַ֣ת יָמִים֩ תֹּאכַ֨ל מַצּ֜וֹת כַּֽאֲשֶׁ֣ר צִוִּיתִ֗ךָ לְמוֹעֵד֙ חֹ֣דֶשׁ הָֽאָבִ֔יב כִּי־ב֖וֹ יָצָ֣אתָ מִמִּצְרָ֑יִם וְלֹא־יֵרָא֥וּ פָנַ֖י רֵיקָֽם׃ 16וְחַ֤ג הַקָּצִיר֙ בִּכּוּרֵ֣י מַעֲשֶׂ֔יךָ אֲשֶׁ֥ר תִּזְרַ֖ע בַּשָּׂדֶ֑ה וְחַ֤ג הָֽאָסִף֙ בְּצֵ֣את הַשָּׁנָ֔ה בְּאָסְפְּךָ֥ אֶֽת־מַעֲשֶׂ֖יךָ מִן־הַשָּׂדֶֽה׃ 17שָׁלֹ֥שׁ פְּעָמִ֖ים בַּשָּׁנָ֑ה יֵרָאֶה֙ כָּל־זְכ֣וּרְךָ֔ אֶל־פְּנֵ֖י הָֽאָדֹ֥ן ׀

───────────────

tle earlier, in 22:20. But it says it even more eloquently. You have been aliens, so you *know* the alien. You know how he or she *feels* oppression inside.

Few of the laws in this code have an extra line of explanation like this. Notably, another law protecting aliens in the preceding chapter also adds a line of explanation (22:20). Again, the treatment of a non-Israelite who is within Israel's power is singled out in a special way.

23:13. **commemorate.** Other translations take this to mean "mention," i.e., that one cannot even say the name of another god—but compare Exod 20:21, where this same word appears to refer to mentioning YHWH's name *institutionally*. I therefore understand this verse to mean that one is commanded not to say another god's name in a setting of worship.

23:15. **empty.** Meaning: empty-handed. One must go to the designated place and bring a sacrifice.

18"You shall not offer the blood of my sacrifice on leavened bread. And the fat of my festival shall not remain until morning.

19"You shall bring the first of the firstfruits of your land to the house of YHWH, your God.

"You shall not cook a kid in its mother's milk.

20"Here, I'm sending an angel ahead of you to watch over you on the way and to bring you to the place that I've prepared. 21Be watchful in front of him and listen to his voice. Don't rebel against him, because he will not bear your offense, because my name is within him. 22But if

יְהוָֹה: 18לֹא־תִזְבַּח עַל־חָמֵץ דַּם־זִבְחִי וְלֹא־יָלִין
חֵלֶב־חַגִּי עַד־בֹּקֶר: 19רֵאשִׁית בִּכּוּרֵי אַדְמָתְךָ
תָּבִיא בֵּית יְהוָה אֱלֹהֶיךָ לֹא־תְבַשֵּׁל גְּדִי בַּחֲלֵב
אִמּוֹ: ס

20הִנֵּה אָנֹכִי שֹׁלֵחַ מַלְאָךְ לְפָנֶיךָ לִשְׁמָרְךָ
בַּדָּרֶךְ וְלַהֲבִיאֲךָ אֶל־הַמָּקוֹם אֲשֶׁר הֲכִנֹתִי:
21הִשָּׁמֶר מִפָּנָיו וּשְׁמַע בְּקֹלוֹ אַל־תַּמֵּר בּוֹ כִּי לֹא
יִשָּׂא לְפִשְׁעֲכֶם כִּי שְׁמִי בְּקִרְבּוֹ: 22כִּי אִם־שָׁמֹעַ

23:19. **the house of YHWH.** This is a reference to the Temple, the building that will one day be the only sanctioned place of sacrifice and the central place of worship. The first house of YHWH will be located at Shiloh. The second and third will be located at Jerusalem.

23:19. **a kid in its mother's milk.** A Canaanite (Ugaritic) text may picture the chief god, El, having kid cooked in milk. This biblical law may thus be a prohibition against eating something that was regarded as a food for a deity. This explanation is uncertain because the Canaanite text does not specify *mother's* milk, and the word there that is read as "kid" is partly effaced. Alternatively, the biblical law may be a moral one, consistent with other biblical law, which prohibits sacrificing an ox or sheep on the same day as its offspring (Lev 22:28) or taking a mother bird along with her eggs in the wild (Deut 22:6–7).

This law came to be taken in later Jewish practice to amount to a complete separation of meat and dairy consumption. This practice is not commanded in the Torah but is rather based on postbiblical rabbinic rulings.

23:20. **I'm sending an angel ahead of you.** This will be repeated twice (32:34; 33:2). It is another recurrence of language from the accounts of the patriarchs: Abraham told his servant that God will send "His angel ahead of you," which would lead to the success of his mission to get a wife for Isaac (Gen 24:7; see also 32:4). That is now a reminder that the preceding angel on a journey is an assurance and protection.

23:21. **rebel.** The Hebrew, *tammēr*, here in the Masoretic Text has the form of a *Hiphil* of the root *mrr*, meaning "to make bitter." But these vowel points are generally understood to be incorrect. The word should rather be read as *temer*, a form of the root *mrh*, meaning "to rebel," which is how the Greek reads. The theme of rebellion will figure strongly in the events to come. Alternatively, one might argue that it is an allusion to the story of the bitter waters at Marah, which was the people's first rebellion after crossing the Red Sea.

23:21. **my name is within him.** This fits with my understanding of what angels are (see the comment on Gen 18:3) and with my understanding of the divine name (see the comment on Deut 12:5). Both are hypostases: tangible expressions of the intangi-

you will *listen* to his voice and do everything that I speak, then I'll be an enemy to your enemies and an opponent to your opponents. 23When my angel will go ahead of you and will bring you to the Amorite and the Hittite and the Perizzite and the Canaanite, the Hivite, and the Jebusite, and I obliterate them, 24you shall not bow to their gods, and you shall not serve them, and you shall not do like the things they do; but you shall *tear* them down and *shatter* their pillars. 25And you will serve YHWH, your God, and He will bless your bread and your water, and I shall turn sickness away from within you. 26There won't be a bereaved woman and an infertile woman in your land. I shall fulfill the number of your days. 27I shall have my terror go ahead of you, and I shall throw all the people against whom you come into tumult, and I shall give all your enemies to you by the back. 28And I shall send the hornet ahead of you, and it will drive out the Hivite, the Canaanite, and the Hittite from in front of you. 29I won't drive them out from in front of you in one year, or else the land will be a devastation, and the animal of the field will be many at you. 30Little by little I shall drive them out from in front of you, until you will be fruitful, and you will have a legacy of the land. 31And I shall set your border from the Red Sea to the sea of the Philistines and from the wilderness to the

תִּשְׁמַע בְּקֹלוֹ וְעָשִׂיתָ כֹּל אֲשֶׁר אֲדַבֵּר וְאָיַבְתִּי אֶת־אֹיְבֶיךָ וְצַרְתִּי אֶת־צֹרְרֶיךָ: 23כִּי־יֵלֵךְ מַלְאָכִי לְפָנֶיךָ וֶהֱבִיאֲךָ אֶל־הָאֱמֹרִי וְהַחִתִּי וְהַפְּרִזִּי וְהַכְּנַעֲנִי הַחִוִּי וְהַיְבוּסִי וְהִכְחַדְתִּיו: 24לֹא־תִשְׁתַּחֲוֶה לֵאלֹהֵיהֶם וְלֹא תָעָבְדֵם וְלֹא תַעֲשֶׂה כְּמַעֲשֵׂיהֶם כִּי הָרֵס תְּהָרְסֵם וְשַׁבֵּר תְּשַׁבֵּר מַצֵּבֹתֵיהֶם: 25וַעֲבַדְתֶּם אֵת יְהוָה אֱלֹהֵיכֶם וּבֵרַךְ אֶת־לַחְמְךָ וְאֶת־מֵימֶיךָ וַהֲסִרֹתִי מַחֲלָה מִקִּרְבֶּךָ: 26לֹא תִהְיֶה מְשַׁכֵּלָה וַעֲקָרָה בְּאַרְצֶךָ אֶת־מִסְפַּר יָמֶיךָ אֲמַלֵּא:

27אֶת־אֵימָתִי אֲשַׁלַּח לְפָנֶיךָ וְהַמֹּתִי אֶת־כָּל־הָעָם אֲשֶׁר תָּבֹא בָּהֶם וְנָתַתִּי אֶת־כָּל־אֹיְבֶיךָ אֵלֶיךָ עֹרֶף: 28וְשָׁלַחְתִּי אֶת־הַצִּרְעָה לְפָנֶיךָ וְגֵרְשָׁה אֶת־הַחִוִּי אֶת־הַכְּנַעֲנִי וְאֶת־הַחִתִּי מִלְּפָנֶיךָ: 29לֹא אֲגָרְשֶׁנּוּ מִפָּנֶיךָ בְּשָׁנָה אֶחָת פֶּן־תִּהְיֶה הָאָרֶץ שְׁמָמָה וְרַבָּה עָלֶיךָ חַיַּת הַשָּׂדֶה: 30מְעַט מְעַט אֲגָרְשֶׁנּוּ מִפָּנֶיךָ עַד אֲשֶׁר תִּפְרֶה וְנָחַלְתָּ אֶת־הָאָרֶץ: 31וְשַׁתִּי אֶת־גְּבֻלְךָ מִיַּם־סוּף וְעַד־יָם פְּלִשְׁתִּים וּמִמִּדְבָּר

---

ble presence of God, finite expressions of the infinite, forms of the divine that humans are able to experience.

23:27. **by the back.** The enemies will turn their backs and flee. This image of Israel's enemies occurs in 2 Sam 22:41 and Ps 18:41. As a terrifying lesson, it is reversed in a case of a serious violation by an Israelite of a divine command, and then it is Israel that turns its back to its enemies (Josh 7:8,12).

23:31. **the Red Sea.** This refers to the *eastern* arm of the Red Sea, presently the site of Eilat. The promised territory of Israel is never conceived of in the Torah as extending all the way across the Sinai Peninsula to the western arm of the Red Sea. It stops at the "river of Egypt," the Wadi el-'Arîsh, which is north of the eastern arm of the Red Sea.

23:31. **the sea of the Philistines.** The Mediterranean Sea. The Philistines came across the Mediterranean from the Greek islands. They lived in cities near the Mediterranean coast (Ashdod, Ashkelon, Ekron, Gath, and Gaza).

river, because I shall put the residents of the land in your hand, and you'll drive them out from in front of you. ³²You shall not make a covenant with them and with their gods. ³³They shall not live in your land, in case they will make you sin against me when you'll serve their gods, because it will be a trap for you."

עַד־הַנָּהָר כִּי ׀ אֶתֵּן בְּיֶדְכֶם אֵת יֹשְׁבֵי הָאָרֶץ וְגֵרַשְׁתָּמוֹ מִפָּנֶיךָ: ³²לֹא־תִכְרֹת לָהֶם וְלֵאלֹהֵיהֶם בְּרִית: ³³לֹא יֵשְׁבוּ בְּאַרְצְךָ פֶּן־יַחֲטִיאוּ אֹתְךָ לִי כִּי תַעֲבֹד אֶת־אֱלֹהֵיהֶם כִּי־יִהְיֶה לְךָ לְמוֹקֵשׁ: פ

24 ¹And He said to Moses, "Come up to YHWH: you and Aaron, Nadab and Abihu, and seventy of Israel's elders, and bow from a distance. ²And Moses will come over

24 ¹וְאֶל־מֹשֶׁה אָמַר עֲלֵה אֶל־יְהוָה אַתָּה וְאַהֲרֹן נָדָב וַאֲבִיהוּא וְשִׁבְעִים מִזִּקְנֵי יִשְׂרָאֵל וְהִשְׁתַּחֲוִיתֶם מֵרָחֹק: ²וְנִגַּשׁ מֹשֶׁה לְבַדּוֹ אֶל־יְהוָה

23:31. the river. This is commonly understood to refer to the Euphrates.

24:1. from a distance. This account has a multitude of parallels to the account of the binding of Isaac (Genesis 22): Moses says the same words to the elders that Abraham says to the servant boys: "Sit here . . . we'll come back to you." The Exodus account has servant boys (*nă'ārîm*) as well. Both accounts use the term "from a distance" (*mērāḥōq*). Both use the term "to bow" (*hištaḥăwôt*). Both Moses and Abraham come up a mountain. Both have a burnt offering (*ha'ălôt 'ōlāh*). The two accounts share a chain of ten verbs: "and he said," "and he took . . . and he set," "and he got up early," "and he built an altar," "and he put out his hand," "and he/it was," "and he/they got up," "and he/they came," "and he/they saw." All these parallels alert us to the fact that some important connection exists here. The culminating parallels indicate what that connection is: Abraham is rewarded at the end "because you did this thing"; and the people in Exodus promise that "We'll do all the things." Abraham is rewarded because "you listened to my voice"; and Exodus reports that "they said with one voice," and they say, "we'll listen." So (1) this is a reminder that the merit of Abraham remains the basis on which all of this now happens. (2) This is a fulfillment of promises made following Abraham's acts of extraordinary obedience. And (3) Abraham's obedience is an example for the people to emulate.

The contrast is striking as well. Abraham's obedience is the centerpiece of the first story. In this second story, the people will soon commit their worst act of *dis*obedience, the golden calf event.

Note also: The first story is at "the mountain of YHWH." The second is at "the mountain of God." And both *state* that they are about divine appearances. The divine appearances mark the sacredness of the two mountain locations. The "mountain of God" is Horeb/Sinai. The identity of the "mountain of YHWH" is uncertain, although elsewhere it refers to the location of the Temple in Jerusalem. The parallels of these two stories connect the mountain where the greatest revelation takes place to the mountain where the divine promise was confirmed in the past—and where the Temple will stand in the future. (The location of the Temple is identified with the place of the binding of Isaac—Moriah—in 2 Chr 3:1.) The two sacred mountains are connect-

alone to YHWH, and they shall not come over, and the people shall not come up with him."

3And Moses came and told the people all of YHWH's words and all the judgments. And all the people answered, one voice, and they said, "We'll do all the things that YHWH has spoken." 4And Moses wrote all of YHWH's words. And he got up early in the morning and built an altar below the mountain and twelve pillars for twelve tribes of Israel. 5And he sent young men of the children of Israel, and they made burnt offerings, and they made peace-offering sacrifices to YHWH: bulls. 6And Moses took half of the blood and set it in basins and threw half of the blood on the altar. 7And he took the scroll of the covenant and read in the people's ears. And they said, "We'll do everything that YHWH has spoken, and we'll listen."

8And Moses took the blood and threw it on the people, and he said, "Here is the blood of the covenant that YHWH has made with you regarding all these things."

9And Moses and Aaron, Nadab and Abihu, and seventy of Israel's elders went up. 10And they saw the God of Israel. And below His feet it was

וְהֵם֙ לֹ֣א יִגָּ֔שׁוּ וְהָעָ֖ם לֹ֥א יַעֲל֖וּ עִמּֽוֹ: 3וַיָּבֹ֣א מֹשֶׁ֗ה וַיְסַפֵּ֤ר לָעָם֙ אֵ֣ת כָּל־דִּבְרֵ֣י יְהֹוָ֔ה וְאֵ֖ת כָּל־הַמִּשְׁפָּטִ֑ים וַיַּ֨עַן כָּל־הָעָ֜ם ק֤וֹל אֶחָד֙ וַיֹּ֣אמְר֔וּ כָּל־הַדְּבָרִ֛ים אֲשֶׁר־דִּבֶּ֥ר יְהֹוָ֖ה נַעֲשֶֽׂה: 4וַיִּכְתֹּ֣ב מֹשֶׁ֗ה אֵ֚ת כָּל־דִּבְרֵ֣י יְהֹוָ֔ה וַיַּשְׁכֵּ֣ם בַּבֹּ֔קֶר וַיִּ֥בֶן מִזְבֵּ֖חַ תַּ֣חַת הָהָ֑ר וּשְׁתֵּ֤ים עֶשְׂרֵה֙ מַצֵּבָ֔ה לִשְׁנֵ֥ים עָשָׂ֖ר שִׁבְטֵ֥י יִשְׂרָאֵֽל: 5וַיִּשְׁלַ֗ח אֶֽת־נַעֲרֵי֙ בְּנֵ֣י יִשְׂרָאֵ֔ל וַיַּֽעֲל֖וּ עֹלֹ֑ת וַיִּזְבְּח֞וּ זְבָחִ֧ים שְׁלָמִ֛ים לַיהֹוָ֖ה פָּרִֽים: 6וַיִּקַּ֤ח מֹשֶׁה֙ חֲצִ֣י הַדָּ֔ם וַיָּ֖שֶׂם בָּאַגָּנֹ֑ת וַחֲצִ֣י הַדָּ֔ם זָרַ֖ק עַל־הַמִּזְבֵּֽחַ: 7וַיִּקַּח֙ סֵ֣פֶר הַבְּרִ֔ית וַיִּקְרָ֖א בְּאָזְנֵ֣י הָעָ֑ם וַיֹּ֣אמְר֔וּ כֹּ֛ל אֲשֶׁר־דִּבֶּ֥ר יְהֹוָ֖ה נַעֲשֶׂ֥ה וְנִשְׁמָֽע: 8וַיִּקַּ֤ח מֹשֶׁה֙ אֶת־הַדָּ֔ם וַיִּזְרֹ֖ק עַל־הָעָ֑ם וַיֹּ֕אמֶר הִנֵּ֤ה דַֽם־הַבְּרִית֙ אֲשֶׁ֨ר כָּרַ֤ת יְהֹוָה֙ עִמָּכֶ֔ם עַ֥ל כָּל־הַדְּבָרִ֖ים הָאֵֽלֶּה: 9וַיַּ֥עַל מֹשֶׁ֖ה וְאַהֲרֹ֑ן נָדָב֙ וַאֲבִיה֔וּא וְשִׁבְעִ֖ים מִזִּקְנֵ֥י יִשְׂרָאֵֽל: 10וַיִּרְא֕וּ אֵ֖ת אֱלֹהֵ֣י יִשְׂרָאֵ֑ל וְתַ֣חַת רַגְלָ֗יו כְּמַעֲשֵׂה֙ לִבְנַ֣ת הַסַּפִּ֔יר

---

ed; the patriarch and his descendants are connected; past, present, and future are connected—all in the embroidery of the Torah's wording.

24:7. **We'll do . . . and we'll listen.** It has been noted that the word order here seems backward: doesn't one have to listen to the command before one can do it?! The promises to do and to listen come together in the order of this sentence in the Hebrew, so it may be that they were a known formula, constituting an oath of absolute obedience. But I understand them to be separate: The people's promise *to do* the commandments is a repetition of what they had said before in v. 3. They repeat it formally now because Moses has just read them the written document. The people's promise *to listen* is, as Rashbam wrote, a further promise, a commitment to follow the things that their God will say to them in the future. In Hebrew as in English, words for "listening" also imply obeying, as in: "Listen to your mother!" "Do you hear me?!" (As an alternative and more banal explanation of the seemingly backward order: the Septuagint has the two words in reverse order.)

24:10–11. **And they saw God. . . . And they envisioned God.** Some have taken this to mean that they literally, physically see God. But, as Ibn Ezra properly observed, the verb for "they saw" (Hebrew *r'h*) is also used to refer to seeing *in a vision,* as when Isaiah says, "I saw the Lord sitting on a throne" (Isa 6:1). This meaning of "they saw" here

like a structure of sapphire brick and like the essence of the skies for clarity. 11And He did not put out His hand to the chiefs of the children of Israel. And they envisioned God. And they ate and drank.

12And YHWH said to Moses, "Come up to me, to the mountain, and be there, and I'll give you stone tablets and the instruction and the commandment that I've written to instruct them."

13And Moses and Joshua, his attendant, got up, and Moses went up to the Mountain of God. 14And he said to the elders, "Sit for us here until we'll come back to you. And here, Aaron and Hur are with you. Let whoever has any matters go over to them." 15And Moses went up to the mountain. And the cloud covered the mountain. 16And YHWH's glory settled on Mount Sinai, and the cloud covered it six days. And He called to Moses on the seventh day from inside the cloud. 17And the appearance of YHWH's glory was like a consuming fire in the mountaintop before the eyes of the children of Israel. 18And Moses came inside the cloud and went up into the mountain. And Moses was in the mountain forty days and forty nights.

וּכְעֶצֶם הַשָּׁמַיִם לָטֹהַר: 11וְאֶל־אֲצִילֵי בְּנֵי יִשְׂרָאֵל לֹא שָׁלַח יָדוֹ וַיֶּחֱזוּ אֶת־הָאֱלֹהִים וַיֹּאכְלוּ וַיִּשְׁתּוּ: ס 12וַיֹּאמֶר יְהוָה אֶל־מֹשֶׁה עֲלֵה אֵלַי הָהָרָה וֶהְיֵה־שָׁם וְאֶתְּנָה לְךָ אֶת־לֻחֹת הָאֶבֶן וְהַתּוֹרָה וְהַמִּצְוָה אֲשֶׁר כָּתַבְתִּי לְהוֹרֹתָם: 13וַיָּקָם מֹשֶׁה וִיהוֹשֻׁעַ מְשָׁרְתוֹ וַיַּעַל מֹשֶׁה אֶל־הַר הָאֱלֹהִים: 14וְאֶל־הַזְּקֵנִים אָמַר שְׁבוּ־לָנוּ בָזֶה עַד אֲשֶׁר־נָשׁוּב אֲלֵיכֶם וְהִנֵּה אַהֲרֹן וְחוּר עִמָּכֶם מִי־בַעַל דְּבָרִים יִגַּשׁ אֲלֵהֶם: 15וַיַּעַל מֹשֶׁה אֶל־הָהָר וַיְכַס הֶעָנָן אֶת־הָהָר: 16וַיִּשְׁכֹּן כְּבוֹד־יְהוָה עַל־הַר סִינַי וַיְכַסֵּהוּ הֶעָנָן שֵׁשֶׁת יָמִים וַיִּקְרָא אֶל־מֹשֶׁה בַּיּוֹם הַשְּׁבִיעִי מִתּוֹךְ הֶעָנָן: 17וּמַרְאֵה כְּבוֹד יְהוָה כְּאֵשׁ אֹכֶלֶת בְּרֹאשׁ הָהָר לְעֵינֵי בְּנֵי יִשְׂרָאֵל: 18וַיָּבֹא מֹשֶׁה בְּתוֹךְ הֶעָנָן וַיַּעַל אֶל־הָהָר וַיְהִי מֹשֶׁה בָּהָר אַרְבָּעִים יוֹם וְאַרְבָּעִים לָיְלָה: פ

---

is confirmed by the parallel use in v. 11 of the word "envisioned" (Hebrew *ḥzh*), which regularly means to have a vision (as, for example in Isa 1:1). Also, this is consistent with the idea that no one ever sees the actual form of God except Moses on a single occasion. This idea is understood throughout the *Tanak*, without exception. (On the distinction between vision and regular experience, see *The Hidden Face of God*, pp. 17–18, 62–63.)

24:11. **He did not put out His hand**. Those who take the passage to mean that this group actually sees God understand "He did not put out His hand" to mean that God does not kill them for seeing God. But the text says "He did not put out His hand *to the chiefs . . .*" The phrase "to put out one's hand" followed by the preposition "to" (Hebrew *'el*) never refers to killing in the *Tanak*. (When referring to killing, the phrase occurs with the preposition *bĕ*.) And, in any case, there are other cases of the expression of God putting out a hand to humans that are meant positively. In Ps 144:7, this refers to God *saving* someone. And there is an even closer parallel in Jer 1:9, where it takes place in a *vision* and refers to God reaching out to touch Jeremiah's mouth to enable him to speak. Here in Exodus, perhaps it means that in their vision they see but are not touched by God.

254

DONATION

תרומה

25 ¹And YHWH spoke to Moses, saying, ²"Speak to the children of Israel that they shall take a donation for me. You shall take my donation from every man whose heart will move him. ³And this is the donation that you shall take from them: gold and silver and bronze ⁴and blue and purple and scarlet and linen and goats' hair ⁵and rams' skins dyed red and leather skins and acacia wood, ⁶oil for lighting, spices for the anointing oil and for the incense fragrances, ⁷onyx stones and stones to be set for the ephod and for the breastplate. ⁸And they shall make me a holy place, and I shall tent among them. ⁹According to everything that I show you: the design of the Tabernacle and the design of all its equipment. And you shall do so.

25 ¹וַיְדַבֵּר יְהוָה אֶל־מֹשֶׁה לֵּאמֹר: ²דַּבֵּר אֶל־
בְּנֵי יִשְׂרָאֵל וְיִקְחוּ־לִי תְּרוּמָה מֵאֵת כָּל־אִישׁ אֲשֶׁר
יִדְּבֶנּוּ לִבּוֹ תִּקְחוּ אֶת־תְּרוּמָתִי: ³וְזֹאת הַתְּרוּמָה
אֲשֶׁר תִּקְחוּ מֵאִתָּם זָהָב וָכֶסֶף וּנְחֹשֶׁת: ⁴וּתְכֵלֶת
וְאַרְגָּמָן וְתוֹלַעַת שָׁנִי וְשֵׁשׁ וְעִזִּים: ⁵וְעֹרֹת אֵילִם
מְאָדָּמִים וְעֹרֹת תְּחָשִׁים וַעֲצֵי שִׁטִּים: ⁶שֶׁמֶן לַמָּאֹר
בְּשָׂמִים לְשֶׁמֶן הַמִּשְׁחָה וְלִקְטֹרֶת הַסַּמִּים: ⁷אַבְנֵי־
שֹׁהַם וְאַבְנֵי מִלֻּאִים לָאֵפֹד וְלַחֹשֶׁן: ⁸וְעָשׂוּ לִי
מִקְדָּשׁ וְשָׁכַנְתִּי בְּתוֹכָם: ⁹כְּכֹל אֲשֶׁר אֲנִי מַרְאֶה
אוֹתְךָ אֵת תַּבְנִית הַמִּשְׁכָּן וְאֵת תַּבְנִית כָּל־כֵּלָיו
וְכֵן תַּעֲשׂוּ: ס

25:2. Speak to the children of Israel that they shall take a donation for me. You shall take my donation from every man whose heart will move him. The command is to all the people—to take from individuals, who are themselves part of the people. It is strange linguistically. The whole people is not commanded to give. People only have to give if they are individually moved to do so. But the whole people is commanded to collect it. It is like when someone says that he gave a gift to his congregation when he himself is a member of the congregation.

25:5. leather. Hebrew: skins that are *tĕḥāšîm*. No one knows what this means. It has been understood to be dolphin skins, badger skins, goatskins, and skins of a particular color. It is cognate to an Arabic word meaning dolphin; but, since this word does not occur in the list of sea or land animals that are forbidden or permitted for food in Leviticus 11, it may not refer to a particular species of animal at all. It may just mean skins that have been tanned; that is: leather.

25:8. I shall tent among them. Forms of this Hebrew verb (*šākantî*) are frequently taken to mean "to dwell"; but when it refers to God, this verb is a denominative from the noun *miškān*: Tabernacle. As God explains to David, "I haven't lived in a house from the day I brought the children of Israel up from Egypt to this day, but I've been going about in a tent and in a Tabernacle" (2 Sam 7:6). The creator cannot be pictured as *residing* on the earth but rather is understood to *tent* among humans, that is, to be present in association with a non permanent, movable structure. Even after the Temple is built, God is associated with the Tabernacle, which is housed there (1 Kings 8:4; Babylonian Talmud Tractate Soṭa 9a) and represented by the space under the wings of the cherubs in the Holy of Holies (Ps 61:5).

25:9. Tabernacle. There is more about the Tabernacle and its contents than any

10"And they shall make an ark of acacia wood, its length two and a half cubits and its width a cubit and a half and its height a cubit and a half. 11And you shall plate it with pure gold. You shall plate it inside and outside. And you shall make a border of gold all around on it. 12And you shall cast four rings of gold for it and place them on its four bases: and two rings on its one side and two rings on its second side. 13And you shall make poles of acacia wood and plate them with gold, 14and bring the poles through the rings on the ark's sides, in order to carry the ark with them. 15The poles shall be in the ark's rings; they shall not depart from it. 16And you shall place in the ark the Testimony that I shall give you. 17And you shall make an atonement dais of pure gold, its length two and a half cubits and its width a cubit and a half. 18And you shall make two cherubs of gold—you shall make them of hammered work—at the two ends of the atonement dais. 19And make one cherub at this end and one cherub at that end. You shall make the cherubs from the atonement dais on its two sides. 20And the two cherubs will be spreading wings above, covering over the atonement dais with their wings, and their faces each toward its brother: the cherubs' faces shall be toward the atonement dais. 21And you shall place the atonement dais on the ark, from above, and you shall place in the ark the Testimony that I shall give you. 22And I shall meet with you there and speak with you from above the atonement dais, from between the two cherubs that are on the Ark of the Testimony, everything that I shall command you to the children of Israel.

וְעָשׂוּ אֲרוֹן עֲצֵי שִׁטִּים אַמָּתַיִם וָחֵצִי אָרְכּוֹ¹⁰
וְאַמָּה וָחֵצִי רָחְבּוֹ וְאַמָּה וָחֵצִי קֹמָתוֹ: ¹¹וְצִפִּיתָ
אֹתוֹ זָהָב טָהוֹר מִבַּיִת וּמִחוּץ תְּצַפֶּנּוּ וְעָשִׂיתָ עָלָיו
זֵר זָהָב סָבִיב: ¹²וְיָצַקְתָּ לּוֹ אַרְבַּע טַבְּעֹת זָהָב
וְנָתַתָּה עַל אַרְבַּע פַּעֲמֹתָיו וּשְׁתֵּי טַבָּעֹת עַל־צַלְעוֹ
הָאֶחָת וּשְׁתֵּי טַבָּעֹת עַל־צַלְעוֹ הַשֵּׁנִית: ¹³וְעָשִׂיתָ
בַדֵּי עֲצֵי שִׁטִּים וְצִפִּיתָ אֹתָם זָהָב: ¹⁴וְהֵבֵאתָ אֶת־
הַבַּדִּים בַּטַּבָּעֹת עַל צַלְעֹת הָאָרֹן לָשֵׂאת אֶת־
הָאָרֹן בָּהֶם: ¹⁵בְּטַבְּעֹת הָאָרֹן יִהְיוּ הַבַּדִּים לֹא
יָסֻרוּ מִמֶּנּוּ: ¹⁶וְנָתַתָּ אֶל־הָאָרֹן אֵת הָעֵדֻת אֲשֶׁר
אֶתֵּן אֵלֶיךָ: ¹⁷וְעָשִׂיתָ כַפֹּרֶת זָהָב טָהוֹר אַמָּתַיִם
וָחֵצִי אָרְכָּהּ וְאַמָּה וָחֵצִי רָחְבָּהּ: ¹⁸וְעָשִׂיתָ שְׁנַיִם
כְּרֻבִים זָהָב מִקְשָׁה תַּעֲשֶׂה אֹתָם מִשְּׁנֵי קְצוֹת
הַכַּפֹּרֶת: ¹⁹וַעֲשֵׂה כְּרוּב אֶחָד מִקָּצָה מִזֶּה וּכְרוּב־
אֶחָד מִקָּצָה מִזֶּה מִן־הַכַּפֹּרֶת תַּעֲשׂוּ אֶת־הַכְּרֻבִים
עַל־שְׁנֵי קְצוֹתָיו: ²⁰וְהָיוּ הַכְּרֻבִים פֹּרְשֵׂי כְנָפַיִם
לְמַעְלָה סֹכְכִים בְּכַנְפֵיהֶם עַל־הַכַּפֹּרֶת וּפְנֵיהֶם
אִישׁ אֶל־אָחִיו אֶל־הַכַּפֹּרֶת יִהְיוּ פְּנֵי הַכְּרֻבִים:
²¹וְנָתַתָּ אֶת־הַכַּפֹּרֶת עַל־הָאָרֹן מִלְמָעְלָה וְאֶל־
הָאָרֹן תִּתֵּן אֶת־הָעֵדֻת אֲשֶׁר אֶתֵּן אֵלֶיךָ: ²²וְנוֹעַדְתִּי
לְךָ שָׁם וְדִבַּרְתִּי אִתְּךָ מֵעַל הַכַּפֹּרֶת מִבֵּין שְׁנֵי
הַכְּרֻבִים אֲשֶׁר עַל־אֲרֹן הָעֵדֻת אֵת כָּל־אֲשֶׁר אֲצַוֶּה
אוֹתְךָ אֶל־בְּנֵי יִשְׂרָאֵל: פ

---

other subject in the Torah. There are long chapters dealing with the building of the Tabernacle, filled with details of materials and measurements in cubits. Tedious reading though it may be for most readers, it conveys the significance of the Tabernacle as the channel to YHWH. Exodus notes explicitly that the function of the Tabernacle is: "I shall meet there with the children of Israel . . . " (29:43; 25:22). The book of Exodus culminates in the Tabernacle's consecration (Exodus 40).

25:22. **meet**. The term denotes meeting at an appointed place or at an appointed time. Thus the Tabernacle itself is known as the Tent of Meeting.

23"And you shall make a table of acacia wood, its length two cubits and its width a cubit and its height a cubit and a half. 24And you shall plate it with pure gold and make a border of gold all around for it 25and make a rim of a handbreadth for it all around and make a border of gold for its rim all around. 26And you shall make four rings of gold for it and put the rings on the four corners that its four legs have. 27The rings shall be in juxtaposition to the rim as housings for the poles in order to carry the table. 28And you shall make the poles of acacia wood and plate them with gold, and the table will be carried with them. 29And you shall make its dishes and its pans and its jars and its bowls with which libations will be poured. You shall make them of pure gold. 30And you shall place show bread on the table in front of me always.

31"And you shall make a menorah of pure gold. The menorah shall be made of hammered work—its shaft and its branch, its cups, its ornaments, and its flowers shall be part of it— 32and six branches coming out from its sides, three of the menorah's branches from its one side and three of the menorah's branches from its second side, 33three almond-shaped cups in the one branch, with ornament and flower, and three almond-shaped cups in the other branch, with ornament and flower. So it is for the six branches that come out from the menorah, 34and four almond-shaped cups within the menorah, with its ornaments and its flowers, 35and an ornament under the two branches from it, and an ornament under the two branches from it, and an ornament under the two branches from it, for the six branches that come out from the menorah. 36Their ornaments and their branches shall be part of it, all of it one hammered work of pure gold. 37And you shall make its lamps seven, and it will hold up its lamps and light the area in front of it. 38And its tongs and its fire-holders of pure gold. 39He shall make it—all of these items—of a talent of pure gold. 40And see and

כג וְעָשִׂיתָ שֻׁלְחָן עֲצֵי שִׁטִּים אַמָּתַיִם אָרְכּוֹ וְאַמָּה רָחְבּוֹ וְאַמָּה וָחֵצִי קֹמָתוֹ: כד וְצִפִּיתָ אֹתוֹ זָהָב טָהוֹר וְעָשִׂיתָ לּוֹ זֵר זָהָב סָבִיב: כה וְעָשִׂיתָ לּוֹ מִסְגֶּרֶת טֹפַח סָבִיב וְעָשִׂיתָ זֵר־זָהָב לְמִסְגַּרְתּוֹ סָבִיב: כו וְעָשִׂיתָ לּוֹ אַרְבַּע טַבְּעֹת זָהָב וְנָתַתָּ אֶת־הַטַּבָּעֹת עַל אַרְבַּע הַפֵּאֹת אֲשֶׁר לְאַרְבַּע רַגְלָיו: כז לְעֻמַּת הַמִּסְגֶּרֶת תִּהְיֶיןָ הַטַּבָּעֹת לְבָתִּים לְבַדִּים לָשֵׂאת אֶת־הַשֻּׁלְחָן: כח וְעָשִׂיתָ אֶת־הַבַּדִּים עֲצֵי שִׁטִּים וְצִפִּיתָ אֹתָם זָהָב וְנִשָּׂא־בָם אֶת־הַשֻּׁלְחָן: כט וְעָשִׂיתָ קְּעָרֹתָיו וְכַפֹּתָיו וּקְשׂוֹתָיו וּמְנַקִּיֹּתָיו אֲשֶׁר יֻסַּךְ בָּהֵן זָהָב טָהוֹר תַּעֲשֶׂה אֹתָם: ל וְנָתַתָּ עַל־הַשֻּׁלְחָן לֶחֶם פָּנִים לְפָנַי תָּמִיד: פ

לא וְעָשִׂיתָ מְנֹרַת זָהָב טָהוֹר מִקְשָׁה תֵּעָשֶׂה הַמְּנוֹרָה יְרֵכָהּ וְקָנָהּ גְּבִיעֶיהָ כַּפְתֹּרֶיהָ וּפְרָחֶיהָ מִמֶּנָּה יִהְיוּ: לב וְשִׁשָּׁה קָנִים יֹצְאִים מִצִּדֶּיהָ שְׁלֹשָׁה ׀ קְנֵי מְנֹרָה מִצִּדָּהּ הָאֶחָד וּשְׁלֹשָׁה קְנֵי מְנֹרָה מִצִּדָּהּ הַשֵּׁנִי: לג שְׁלֹשָׁה גְבִעִים מְשֻׁקָּדִים בַּקָּנֶה הָאֶחָד כַּפְתֹּר וָפֶרַח וּשְׁלֹשָׁה גְבִעִים מְשֻׁקָּדִים בַּקָּנֶה הָאֶחָד כַּפְתֹּר וָפָרַח כֵּן לְשֵׁשֶׁת הַקָּנִים הַיֹּצְאִים מִן־הַמְּנֹרָה: לד וּבַמְּנֹרָה אַרְבָּעָה גְבִעִים מְשֻׁקָּדִים כַּפְתֹּרֶיהָ וּפְרָחֶיהָ: לה וְכַפְתֹּר תַּחַת שְׁנֵי הַקָּנִים מִמֶּנָּה וְכַפְתֹּר תַּחַת שְׁנֵי הַקָּנִים מִמֶּנָּה וְכַפְתֹּר תַּחַת־שְׁנֵי הַקָּנִים מִמֶּנָּה לְשֵׁשֶׁת הַקָּנִים הַיֹּצְאִים מִן־הַמְּנֹרָה: לו כַּפְתֹּרֵיהֶם וּקְנֹתָם מִמֶּנָּה יִהְיוּ כֻּלָּהּ מִקְשָׁה אַחַת זָהָב טָהוֹר: לז וְעָשִׂיתָ אֶת־נֵרֹתֶיהָ שִׁבְעָה וְהֶעֱלָה אֶת־נֵרֹתֶיהָ וְהֵאִיר עַל־עֵבֶר פָּנֶיהָ: לח וּמַלְקָחֶיהָ וּמַחְתֹּתֶיהָ זָהָב טָהוֹר: לט כִּכָּר זָהָב טָהוֹר יַעֲשֶׂה אֹתָהּ אֵת כָּל־הַכֵּלִים הָאֵלֶּה: מ וּרְאֵה

make them by their design that you are shown in the mountain.

26 1"And you shall make the Tabernacle with ten curtains of woven linen and blue and purple and scarlet, with cherubs—you

וְעֲשֵׂה בְּתַבְנִיתָם אֲשֶׁר־אַתָּה מָרְאֶה בָּהָר: ס

26 ‏¹וְאֶת־הַמִּשְׁכָּן תַּעֲשֶׂה עֶשֶׂר יְרִיעֹת שֵׁשׁ מָשְׁזָר וּתְכֵלֶת וְאַרְגָּמָן וְתֹלַעַת שָׁנִי כְּרֻבִים מַעֲשֵׂה

26:1. make the Tabernacle. No one has ever figured out how the Tabernacle is put together. The components are given here, but the text does not say how they are put together. Twenty frames are used for each side wall and six for the rear wall (plus two more for supporting the rear corners). The frames are ten cubits tall and "a cubit and a half cubit" wide. People have therefore assumed that the Tabernacle is thirty cubits long by ten cubits wide, and ten cubits high. Curtains fit over these frames, and the curtains are made of two giant fabrics. Each fabric is made of five pieces sewn together; the pieces are four cubits by twenty-eight cubits wide. So the two fabrics are each twenty by twenty-eight. They are attached together with gold clasps, making a double fabric that is forty by twenty-eight. When this forty-cubit piece is placed over the thirty-cubit-long structure of frames, it covers the top and has ten cubits left over to cover the ten-cubit-high rear wall. In support of this, people have noted that Solomon's Temple is sixty cubits long by twenty wide, so the Temple and Tabernacle are in two-to-one proportion.

But there are many things wrong with this. (1) The Temple is thirty cubits high, so the proportion there is three-to-one, not two-to-one. (2) The ten-cubit width is wrong, because six frames of a cubit and a half each make only a nine-cubit width. (3) The twenty-eight-cubits-wide curtains do not fit this structure. Its two sidewalls are each ten cubits high, and its ceiling is ten cubits across, which requires a cover that is thirty cubits wide. The twenty-eight-cubits-wide curtain leaves a whole cubit (eighteen inches) uncovered on each side. (4) A second set of curtains is made into two large fabrics like the first set, but this second set (made of goats' hair) is made of curtains that are four cubits by thirty, instead of four by twenty-eight, and there is an extra, eleventh curtain at one end. The extra curtain has no purpose, and the thirty-cubits-length hangs down past the bottom of the inner fabric. (5) The gold clasps cannot be seen in this arrangement.

Also, this arrangement leaves questions: (6) Why would the frames be a cubit and a half wide instead of just one cubit or two cubits? And why does it say "a cubit and a half cubit" instead of the normal wording, "a cubit and a half"? (7) Why are the curtains in groups of five, which are each four cubits wide? What is significant about four cubits?

All of these problems and questions point to a different way that the Tabernacle is put together. I propose that the reason that the frames are "a cubit and a half cubit" is because they overlap each other by the extra half-cubit. This is more stable and better for ventilation than if they stood side by side (Figures 1 and 2). The twenty-frame length by six-frame width means a structure that is twenty cubits by six cubits on the inside. If the frames are a half-cubit wide, then it is twenty by eight on the outside (Figure 3). Now, if we take the two large fabrics that are twenty by twenty-eight cubits, and

shall make them designer's work. ²The length of one curtain shall be twenty-eight in cubits, and the width of one curtain four in cubits: one size to all the curtains. ³Five curtains will be connected, each to its sister-piece, and five curtains connected, each to its sister-piece. ⁴And you shall make loops of blue on the side of the one curtain at the end of the connected group, and you shall

חֹשֵׁב תַּעֲשֶׂה אֹתָם: ²אֹרֶךְ | הַיְרִיעָה הָאַחַת שְׁמֹנֶה וְעֶשְׂרִים֙ בָּֽאַמָּ֔ה וְרֹ֙חַב֙ אַרְבַּ֣ע בָּֽאַמָּ֔ה הַיְרִיעָ֖ה הָאֶחָ֑ת מִדָּ֥ה אַחַ֖ת לְכָל־הַיְרִיעֹֽת: ³חֲמֵ֣שׁ הַיְרִיעֹ֗ת תִּֽהְיֶ֙יןָ֙ חֹֽבְרֹ֔ת אִשָּׁ֖ה אֶל־אֲחֹתָ֑הּ וְחָמֵ֤שׁ יְרִיעֹת֙ חֹֽבְרֹ֔ת אִשָּׁ֖ה אֶל־אֲחֹתָֽהּ: ⁴וְעָשִׂ֜יתָ לֻֽלְאֹ֣ת תְּכֵ֗לֶת עַ֣ל שְׂפַ֤ת הַיְרִיעָה֙ הָֽאֶחָ֔ת מִקָּצָ֖ה בַּחֹבָ֑רֶת וְכֵ֤ן תַּעֲשֶׂה֙ בִּשְׂפַ֣ת

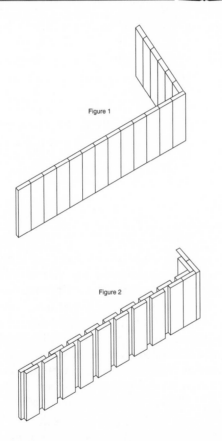

Figure 1

Figure 2

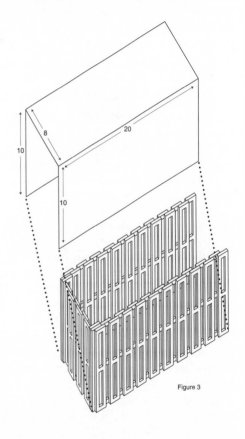

Figure 3

we connect them with the clasps, and then we fold it in half along the clasps, it fits this structure. The gold clasps now are visible: they surround the entrance to the Tabernacle. The twenty-cubit width of the fabric matches the twenty-cubit length of the Tabernacle. And the twenty-eight-cubit length of the fabric goes up one side of the Tabernacle (ten cubits high), across the ceiling (eight cubits), and down the other side (ten cubits).

A temple has been excavated in Israel at Arad. Its measurements are twenty cubits by six cubits, the same as the (inside dimensions of the) Tabernacle.

On the significance of these dimensions, see the comment on 26:30.

do so in the side of the end curtain in the second connected group. ⁵You shall make fifty loops in the one curtain, and you shall make fifty loops in the end of the curtain that is in the second connected group, with the loops parallel: each to its sister-piece. ⁶And you shall make fifty clasps of gold and connect the curtains, each to its sister-piece, with the clasps. And the Tabernacle will be one.

⁷"And you shall make curtains of goats' hair for a tent over the Tabernacle. You shall make them eleven curtains. ⁸The length of one curtain shall be thirty in cubits, and the width of one curtain four in cubits: one size for eleven curtains. ⁹And you shall connect five of the curtains by themselves and six of the curtains by themselves. And you shall double-fold the sixth curtain opposite the front of the tent. ¹⁰And you shall make fifty loops on the side of the one end curtain in the connected group and fifty loops on the side of the curtain of the second connected group. ¹¹And you shall make fifty clasps of

הַיְרִיעָה הַקִּיצוֹנָה בַּמַּחְבֶּרֶת הַשֵּׁנִית: ⁵חֲמִשִּׁים לֻלָאֹת תַּעֲשֶׂה בַּיְרִיעָה הָאֶחָת וַחֲמִשִּׁים לֻלָאֹת תַּעֲשֶׂה בִּקְצֵה הַיְרִיעָה אֲשֶׁר בַּמַּחְבֶּרֶת הַשֵּׁנִית מַקְבִּילֹת הַלֻּלָאֹת אִשָּׁה אֶל־אֲחֹתָהּ: ⁶וְעָשִׂיתָ חֲמִשִּׁים קַרְסֵי זָהָב וְחִבַּרְתָּ אֶת־הַיְרִיעֹת אִשָּׁה אֶל־אֲחֹתָהּ בַּקְּרָסִים וְהָיָה הַמִּשְׁכָּן אֶחָד: פ ⁷וְעָשִׂיתָ יְרִיעֹת עִזִּים לְאֹהֶל עַל־הַמִּשְׁכָּן עַשְׁתֵּי־עֶשְׂרֵה יְרִיעֹת תַּעֲשֶׂה אֹתָם: ⁸אֹרֶךְ ׀ הַיְרִיעָה הָאַחַת שְׁלֹשִׁים בָּאַמָּה וְרֹחַב אַרְבַּע בָּאַמָּה הַיְרִיעָה הָאֶחָת מִדָּה אַחַת לְעַשְׁתֵּי עֶשְׂרֵה יְרִיעֹת: ⁹וְחִבַּרְתָּ אֶת־חֲמֵשׁ הַיְרִיעֹת לְבָד וְאֶת־שֵׁשׁ הַיְרִיעֹת לְבָד וְכָפַלְתָּ אֶת־הַיְרִיעָה הַשִּׁשִּׁית אֶל־מוּל פְּנֵי הָאֹהֶל: ¹⁰וְעָשִׂיתָ חֲמִשִּׁים לֻלָאֹת עַל שְׂפַת הַיְרִיעָה הָאֶחָת הַקִּיצֹנָה בַּחֹבָרֶת וַחֲמִשִּׁים לֻלָאֹת עַל שְׂפַת הַיְרִיעָה הַחֹבֶרֶת הַשֵּׁנִית: ¹¹וְעָשִׂיתָ קַרְסֵי נְחֹשֶׁת

26:6. **the Tabernacle will be one**. In the simplest sense, this means that once they sew all the curtains together and connect all the loops and clasps, the Tabernacle will be one whole piece. But the wording—"the Tabernacle will be one"—also fits with the centrality of the Tabernacle to Israel's monotheism. One God, one Tabernacle, one altar, only one place of worship. Later it will be confirmed by divine commandment that Israel may have only one place of sacrifice, and that this one place is in front of the Tabernacle (Leviticus 17). There cannot be more than one place to worship God, because that might suggest that there is more than one God. Or, to put it more essentially: it is inconceivable in the first place in this new religion of a single deity that there could possibly be more than a single sanctuary. Those who claim that Israel's religion was not a real monotheism until a very late stage (Second Temple) have not appreciated the significance of the commandment of centralization of worship at a single location.

26:9. **double-fold the sixth curtain**. The extra, eleventh curtain of the tent is four cubits wide. When folded, each half of it covers half of the eight-cubits-wide back of the Tabernacle (Figure 4). This also answers the question of why the curtains are four cubits wide. And it further confirms that the Tabernacle is eight cubits wide.

26:9. **opposite the front of the tent**. Meaning: it falls along the *back* wall, *facing* the front. Thus v. 12 refers to "the hanging one that is left over among the tent's curtains" and instructs that "you shall hang half of the leftover curtain on the back parts of the Tabernacle."

bronze and bring the clasps into the loops and connect the tent. And it will be one. 12And the hanging one that is left over among the tent's curtains: you shall hang half of the leftover curtain on the back parts of the Tabernacle. 13And the cubit on this side and the cubit on that side in the leftover in the length of the tent's curtains shall be hung on the sides of the Tabernacle, on this side and on that side, to cover it. 14And you shall make a covering for the tent of rams' skins dyed red and a covering of leather skins above.

15"And you shall make the frames for the Tabernacle of acacia wood, standing. 16The frame's length shall be ten cubits, and the width of one frame a cubit and a half cubit. 17One frame has two projections, each aligned with its sister-piece: so you shall make for all the Tabernacle's frames. 18And you shall make the frames for the Tabernacle: twenty frames for the south side—to the south. 19And you shall make forty

חֲמִשִּׁים וְהֵבֵאתָ אֶת־הַקְּרָסִים בַּלֻּלָאֹת וְחִבַּרְתָּ אֶת־הָאֹהֶל וְהָיָה אֶחָד: 12וְסֶרַח הָעֹדֵף בִּירִיעֹת הָאֹהֶל חֲצִי הַיְרִיעָה הָעֹדֶפֶת תִּסְרַח עַל אֲחֹרֵי הַמִּשְׁכָּן: 13וְהָאַמָּה מִזֶּה וְהָאַמָּה מִזֶּה בָּעֹדֵף בְּאֹרֶךְ יְרִיעֹת הָאֹהֶל יִהְיֶה סָרוּחַ עַל־צִדֵּי הַמִּשְׁכָּן מִזֶּה וּמִזֶּה לְכַסֹּתוֹ: 14וְעָשִׂיתָ מִכְסֶה לָאֹהֶל עֹרֹת אֵילִם מְאָדָּמִים וּמִכְסֵה עֹרֹת תְּחָשִׁים מִלְמָעְלָה: פ
15וְעָשִׂיתָ אֶת־הַקְּרָשִׁים לַמִּשְׁכָּן עֲצֵי שִׁטִּים עֹמְדִים: 16עֶשֶׂר אַמּוֹת אֹרֶךְ הַקָּרֶשׁ וְאַמָּה וַחֲצִי הָאַמָּה רֹחַב הַקֶּרֶשׁ הָאֶחָד: 17שְׁתֵּי יָדוֹת לַקֶּרֶשׁ הָאֶחָד מְשֻׁלָּבֹת אִשָּׁה אֶל־אֲחֹתָהּ כֵּן תַּעֲשֶׂה לְכֹל קַרְשֵׁי הַמִּשְׁכָּן: 18וְעָשִׂיתָ אֶת־הַקְּרָשִׁים לַמִּשְׁכָּן עֶשְׂרִים קֶרֶשׁ לִפְאַת נֶגְבָּה תֵימָנָה: 19וְאַרְבָּעִים

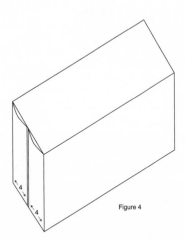

Figure 4

26:13. **the cubit on this side and the cubit on that side in the leftover in the length**. This second set of curtains is thirty cubits long. When it is spread over the inside set of curtains, which is only twenty-eight cubits, there is thus a cubit left over on each side. It "shall be hung on the sides of the Tabernacle, on this side and on that side, to cover it." That is, it is folded under the inside linen fabric so as to protect it from touching the ground.

26:15. **frames**. Trellises—not solid boards or planks. If they were solid, then the linen curtains would be sandwiched between the boards on the inside and the goats' hair and leather coverings on the outside and could never be seen.

bases of silver under the twenty frames: two bases under one frame for its two projections and two bases under each other frame for its two projections. 20And for the Tabernacle's second side, for the north side: twenty frames 21and their forty bases of silver, two bases under one frame and two bases under each other frame. 22And for the rear of the Tabernacle, to the west, you shall make six frames. 23And you shall make two frames for the Tabernacle's corners in the rear, 24and they shall be doubles from below, and together they shall be integrated on its top to one ring. It shall be so for the two of them; they will be for the two corners. 25And they shall be eight frames and their bases of silver, sixteen bases, two bases under one frame and two bases under each other frame. 26And you shall make bars of acacia wood: five for the frames of one side of the Tabernacle 27and five bars for the frames of the second side of the Tabernacle and five bars for the frames of the side of the Tabernacle at the rear, to the west, 28and the middle bar through the frames extending from end to end. 29And you shall plate the frames with gold, and you shall make their rings gold, housings for the bars, and you shall plate the bars with gold. 30And you shall set up the Tabernacle according

אַדְנֵי־כֶסֶף תַּעֲשֶׂה תַּחַת עֶשְׂרִים הַקֶּרֶשׁ שְׁנֵי אֲדָנִים תַּחַת־הַקֶּרֶשׁ הָאֶחָד לִשְׁתֵּי יְדֹתָיו וּשְׁנֵי אֲדָנִים תַּחַת־הַקֶּרֶשׁ הָאֶחָד לִשְׁתֵּי יְדֹתָיו: 20וּלְצֶלַע הַמִּשְׁכָּן הַשֵּׁנִית לִפְאַת צָפוֹן עֶשְׂרִים קָרֶשׁ: 21וְאַרְבָּעִים אַדְנֵיהֶם כָּסֶף שְׁנֵי אֲדָנִים תַּחַת הַקֶּרֶשׁ הָאֶחָד וּשְׁנֵי אֲדָנִים תַּחַת הַקֶּרֶשׁ הָאֶחָד: 22וּלְיַרְכְּתֵי הַמִּשְׁכָּן יָמָּה תַּעֲשֶׂה שִׁשָּׁה קְרָשִׁים: 23וּשְׁנֵי קְרָשִׁים תַּעֲשֶׂה לִמְקֻצְעֹת הַמִּשְׁכָּן בַּיַּרְכָתָיִם: 24וְיִהְיוּ תֹאֲמִים מִלְּמַטָּה וְיַחְדָּו יִהְיוּ תַמִּים עַל־רֹאשׁוֹ אֶל־הַטַּבַּעַת הָאֶחָת כֵּן יִהְיֶה לִשְׁנֵיהֶם לִשְׁנֵי הַמִּקְצֹעֹת יִהְיוּ: 25וְהָיוּ שְׁמֹנָה קְרָשִׁים וְאַדְנֵיהֶם כֶּסֶף שִׁשָּׁה עָשָׂר אֲדָנִים שְׁנֵי אֲדָנִים תַּחַת הַקֶּרֶשׁ הָאֶחָד וּשְׁנֵי אֲדָנִים תַּחַת הַקֶּרֶשׁ הָאֶחָד: 26וְעָשִׂיתָ בְרִיחִם עֲצֵי שִׁטִּים חֲמִשָּׁה לְקַרְשֵׁי צֶלַע־הַמִּשְׁכָּן הָאֶחָד: 27וַחֲמִשָּׁה בְרִיחִם לְקַרְשֵׁי צֶלַע־הַמִּשְׁכָּן הַשֵּׁנִית וַחֲמִשָּׁה בְרִיחִם לְקַרְשֵׁי צֶלַע הַמִּשְׁכָּן לַיַּרְכָתַיִם יָמָּה: 28וְהַבְּרִיחַ הַתִּיכֹן בְּתוֹךְ הַקְּרָשִׁים מַבְרִחַ מִן־הַקָּצֶה אֶל־הַקָּצֶה: 29וְאֶת־הַקְּרָשִׁים תְּצַפֶּה זָהָב וְאֶת־טַבְּעֹתֵיהֶם תַּעֲשֶׂה זָהָב בָּתִּים לַבְּרִיחִם וְצִפִּיתָ אֶת־הַבְּרִיחִם זָהָב: 30וַהֲקֵמֹתָ אֶת־הַמִּשְׁכָּן כְּמִשְׁפָּטוֹ

26:30. **set up the Tabernacle**. What difference do these cubits make? Why does it matter whether the Tabernacle is eight by twenty cubits or ten by thirty? Because eight by twenty cubits, and ten cubits high, is *the size of the space under the wings of the cherubs inside the Holy of Holies in the Temple in Jerusalem.* Either the Tabernacle really stood in that space, or the space represented it symbolically while the Tabernacle itself was stored away somewhere inside the building. The *Tanak* reports that the Tabernacle is in fact brought to the Temple on the day of its dedication (1 Kings 8:4; 2 Chr 5:5). The Talmud reports that it was in fact thus stored beneath the Temple (Soṭa 9a). The ancient historian Josephus says that the effect of the cherubs' wings in the Temple was to appear like a tent (*Ant.* 8.103). A psalm says: "I'll reside in your tent forever, I'll conceal myself in the hidden place of your wings" (Ps 61:5). The book of 1 Chronicles (9:23) refers to the Temple as "the House of the Tent" (*bêt hā'ōhel*). It also speaks of the "Tabernacle of the House of God" (6:33; see also 1 Chr 23:22; 2 Chr 29:6-7; 24:6). What this means is that the Temple was not just the *successor* to the Tabernacle. The Tabernacle, revered as the ancient channel to God, was actually located *inside* the Temple. So all the laws in the Torah that command that something be done at the Tabernacle applied as long as the first Temple stood in Jerusalem. By the time of the

to the model of it that you were shown in the mountain.

31"And you shall make a pavilion of blue and purple and scarlet and woven linen; he shall make them designer's work with cherubs. 32And you shall place it on four acacia columns plated with gold, their hooks of gold, on four bases of silver. 33And you shall place the pavilion under the clasps. And you shall bring the Ark of the

וְעָשִׂיתָ פָרֹכֶת תְּכֵלֶת ס 31 אֲשֶׁר הָרְאֵיתָ בָּהָר: וְאַרְגָּמָן וְתוֹלַעַת שָׁנִי וְשֵׁשׁ מָשְׁזָר מַעֲשֵׂה חֹשֵׁב יַעֲשֶׂה אֹתָהּ כְּרֻבִים: 32וְנָתַתָּה אֹתָהּ עַל־אַרְבָּעָה עַמּוּדֵי שִׁטִּים מְצֻפִּים זָהָב וָוֵיהֶם זָהָב עַל־אַרְבָּעָה אַדְנֵי־כָסֶף: 33וְנָתַתָּה אֶת־הַפָּרֹכֶת תַּחַת הַקְּרָסִים וְהֵבֵאתָ שָׁמָּה מִבֵּית לַפָּרֹכֶת אֵת אֲרוֹן הָעֵדוּת

Temple's destruction (587 B.C.E.), the Tabernacle and its contents—the ark, the tablets—disappear from the Bible. The rabbinic tradition is that the presence of God (Shechinah; which, by the way, has the same root as the word for the Tabernacle: *miškān*) was in the first Temple but not in the second (Yoma 21b; Rashi on Gen 9:27). This contributes to an impression of growing distance from the original feeling of a direct connection with God in the Hebrew Bible.

This construction of the Tabernacle also goes against the dominant view of biblical scholars for the past century: that the Tabernacle was not real, that it was simply a fiction, invented to stand for the second Temple in Jerusalem. That view was based on the two-to-one correspondence of the measurements of the Tabernacle and the Temple. In the first place, we have seen that the correspondence is not correct. (See point number one in the comment on 26:1 above.) Second, those measurements were based on the *first* Temple, not the second, in any case. And, third, this chapter is part of a text that is written in Classical Hebrew, which comes from a period long before the second Temple.

26:31. **pavilion.** Hebrew *pārōket*. In the second Temple this came to be a curtain, veiling the Holy of Holies. Subsequently in synagogues it likewise has been a curtain, veiling the ark. But in the Tabernacle it is a pavilion, a tent within the tent, not a veil. It hangs on four posts, it provides a cover over the ark (*wĕsakkōtā 'al hā'ārōn*; Exod 40:3), it is *over* the Testimony (Exod 27:21), and it is referred to as "the covering pavilion," *pārōket hammāsāk* (Exod 40:21; Num 4:5). (It is the same root word that is used earlier to describe how the cherubs' wings "cover over" the atonement dais; 25:20.) Such a *sukkāh* is referred to in Ps 27:5 and in Lam 2:6 as well. Made of fabric identical to that of the Tabernacle, it provides the Tabernacle's necessary rear fabric wall. In the Talmudic age, when the *pārōket* had come to be a curtain, the sages assumed that it had always been a curtain, and so they were puzzled that in the Torah it is pictured as a *sukkāh* and that it is described as being "over" the ark (Sukkah 7b; cf. Soṭa 37a; Menahot 62a, 98a).

26:33. **under the clasps.** The Greek text says "upon the frames," meaning up against them, or near them. In Hebrew, the frames are *qĕrāšîm*, and the clasps are *qĕrāšîm*. The similarity of the two words led to the scribal confusion here. The Greek fits with the understanding that the *pārōket* is a pavilion, not a veil. The Masoretic Text makes little sense if it is a pavilion. (If it were a veil, and if the Tabernacle were thirty cubits long, then the Masoretic Text would mean that the veil hangs down under the

Testimony there, inside the pavilion, and the pavilion will distinguish for you between the Holy and the Holy of Holies. ³⁴And you shall place the *atonement dais* on the Ark of the Testimony in the Holy of Holies. ³⁵And you shall place the table outside the pavilion, and the menorah opposite the table on the south side of the Tabernacle, and you shall place the table on the north side.

³⁶"And you shall make a cover for the entrance of the tent: blue and purple and scarlet and woven linen—embroiderer's work. ³⁷And you shall make five acacia columns for the cover and plate them with gold, their hooks of gold, and cast five bases of bronze for them.

27 ¹"And you shall make the altar of acacia wood. Five cubits long and five cubits wide, the altar shall be square—and its height three cubits. ²And you shall make its horns on its four corners. Its horns shall be part of it. And you shall plate it with bronze. ³And you shall make its pots to remove ashes from it, and its shovels

וְהִבְדִּ֣ילָה הַפָּרֹ֨כֶת֙ לָכֶ֔ם בֵּ֥ין הַקֹּ֖דֶשׁ וּבֵ֥ין קֹ֥דֶשׁ הַקֳּדָשִֽׁים׃ ³⁴וְנָֽתַתָּ֙ אֶת־הַכַּפֹּ֔רֶת עַ֖ל אֲר֣וֹן הָעֵדֻ֑ת בְּקֹ֖דֶשׁ הַקֳּדָשִֽׁים׃ ³⁵וְשַׂמְתָּ֤ אֶת־הַשֻּׁלְחָן֙ מִח֣וּץ לַפָּרֹ֔כֶת וְאֶת־הַמְּנֹרָה֙ נֹ֣כַח הַשֻּׁלְחָ֔ן עַ֛ל צֶ֥לַע הַמִּשְׁכָּ֖ן תֵּימָ֑נָה וְהַ֨שֻּׁלְחָ֔ן תִּתֵּ֖ן עַל־צֶ֥לַע צָפֽוֹן׃ ³⁶וְעָשִׂ֤יתָ מָסָךְ֙ לְפֶ֣תַח הָאֹ֔הֶל תְּכֵ֧לֶת וְאַרְגָּמָ֛ן וְתוֹלַ֥עַת שָׁנִ֖י וְשֵׁ֣שׁ מָשְׁזָ֑ר מַעֲשֵׂ֖ה רֹקֵֽם׃ ³⁷וְעָשִׂ֣יתָ לַמָּסָ֗ךְ חֲמִשָּׁה֙ עַמּוּדֵ֣י שִׁטִּ֔ים וְצִפִּיתָ֤ אֹתָם֙ זָהָ֔ב וָֽוֵיהֶ֖ם זָהָ֑ב וְיָצַקְתָּ֣ לָהֶ֔ם חֲמִשָּׁ֖ה אַדְנֵ֥י נְחֹֽשֶׁת׃ ס ²⁷וְעָשִׂ֥יתָ אֶת־הַמִּזְבֵּ֖חַ עֲצֵ֣י שִׁטִּ֑ים חָמֵשׁ֩ אַמּ֨וֹת אֹ֜רֶךְ וְחָמֵ֧שׁ אַמּ֣וֹת רֹ֗חַב רָב֤וּעַ יִהְיֶה֙ הַמִּזְבֵּ֔חַ וְשָׁלֹ֥שׁ אַמּ֖וֹת קֹמָתֽוֹ׃ ²וְעָשִׂ֣יתָ קַרְנֹתָ֗יו עַ֚ל אַרְבַּ֣ע פִּנֹּתָ֔יו מִמֶּ֖נּוּ תִּהְיֶ֣יןָ קַרְנֹתָ֑יו וְצִפִּיתָ֥ אֹת֖וֹ נְחֹֽשֶׁת׃ ³וְעָשִׂ֤יתָ סִּֽירֹתָיו֙ לְדַשְּׁנ֔וֹ וְיָעָ֕יו וּמִזְרְקֹתָ֖יו וּמִזְלְגֹתָ֣יו וּמַחְתֹּתָ֑יו

---

clasps, which come at the point of separation between the Holy place and the Holy of Holies.)

26:33. bring the Ark of the Testimony there, inside the pavilion. The ark is surrounded by a series of layers: first the pavilion (the *pārōket*), then the Tabernacle (the linen tent), then the tent (the goats' hair tent), then the covering (the tent of rams' skins dyed red), then the covering of leather skins, then a courtyard surrounded by linen hangings. The Israelites are thus given to understand that there is a sequence of holiness, ever increasing, as one comes closer to the sacred object in the center. Anyone who pursues holiness must be aware that he or she must pass through a progression of levels, with increasing awe and increasing danger as one comes closer to the sacred.

26:33. the Holy. The space from the entrance up to the *pārōket* is referred to as the Holy.

26:33. the Holy of Holies. The space inside the *pārōket* is the Holy of Holies, meaning the holiest of all holy places.

27:1. And you shall make. The quantity of detail in these chapters is an indication that these are authentic descriptions of the Tabernacle and its accouterments. What motive would there be to make all of this up? The dominant view in critical biblical scholarship for over a hundred years has been that the Tabernacle is a fiction. The character of the text, however, argues against that view as much as the content does.

264

and its basins and its forks and its fire-holders. You shall make all of its equipment bronze. 4And you shall make a grate for it, a network of bronze, and on the net you shall make four rings of bronze on its four ends. 5And you shall place it under the altar's ledge below so that the net will be up to the middle of the altar. 6And you shall make poles for the altar, poles of acacia wood, and plate them with bronze. 7And its poles shall be brought through rings so that the poles shall be on the altar's two sides when carrying it. 8You shall make it hollow of boards, as it was shown to you in the mountain. They shall do it so.

9"And you shall make the Tabernacle's courtyard: for the south side—to the south, hangings for the courtyard of woven linen, one side having a hundred in cubits, 10and its columns twenty, and their bases twenty of bronze, and the columns' hooks and their rods of silver. 11And so for the north side: in length, hangings of a hundred long, and its columns twenty, and their bases twenty of bronze, and the columns' hooks and their bands of silver. 12And the courtyard's width for the west side: hangings of fifty cubits, their columns ten and their bases ten. 13And the courtyard's width for the east side—to the east— fifty cubits. 14And the panel shall have fifteen cubits of hangings, their columns three and their bases three; 15and the second panel shall have fifteen of hangings, their columns three and their bases three. 16And the courtyard's gate shall have a cover of twenty cubits: blue and purple and scarlet and woven linen, embroiderer's work, their columns four and their bases four. 17All of the courtyard's columns all around shall be banded with silver, their hooks of silver and their bases bronze. 18The courtyard's length a hundred in cubits, and width consistently fifty, and height five cubits of woven linen, and their bases of bronze. 19For all of the Tabernacle's equipment in all of the service of it, and all of its pegs and all of the courtyard's pegs: bronze.

לְכָל־כֵּלָיו תַּעֲשֶׂה נְחֹשֶׁת: ⁴וְעָשִׂיתָ לּוֹ מִכְבָּר
מַעֲשֵׂה רֶשֶׁת נְחֹשֶׁת וְעָשִׂיתָ עַל־הָרֶשֶׁת אַרְבַּע
טַבְּעֹת נְחֹשֶׁת עַל אַרְבַּע קְצוֹתָיו: ⁵וְנָתַתָּה אֹתָהּ
תַּחַת כַּרְכֹּב הַמִּזְבֵּחַ מִלְּמָטָּה וְהָיְתָה הָרֶשֶׁת עַד
חֲצִי הַמִּזְבֵּחַ: ⁶וְעָשִׂיתָ בַדִּים לַמִּזְבֵּחַ בַּדֵּי עֲצֵי
שִׁטִּים וְצִפִּיתָ אֹתָם נְחֹשֶׁת: ⁷וְהוּבָא אֶת־בַּדָּיו
בַּטַּבָּעֹת וְהָיוּ הַבַּדִּים עַל־שְׁתֵּי צַלְעֹת הַמִּזְבֵּחַ
בִּשְׂאֵת אֹתוֹ: ⁸נְבוּב לֻחֹת תַּעֲשֶׂה אֹתוֹ כַּאֲשֶׁר הֶרְאָה
אֹתְךָ בָּהָר כֵּן יַעֲשׂוּ: ס ⁹וְעָשִׂיתָ אֵת חֲצַר הַמִּשְׁכָּן
לִפְאַת נֶגֶב־תֵּימָנָה קְלָעִים לֶחָצֵר שֵׁשׁ מָשְׁזָר מֵאָה
בָאַמָּה אֹרֶךְ לַפֵּאָה הָאֶחָת: ¹⁰וְעַמֻּדָיו עֶשְׂרִים
וְאַדְנֵיהֶם עֶשְׂרִים נְחֹשֶׁת וָוֵי הָעַמֻּדִים וַחֲשֻׁקֵיהֶם
כָּסֶף: ¹¹וְכֵן לִפְאַת צָפוֹן בָּאֹרֶךְ קְלָעִים מֵאָה
אֹרֶךְ וְעַמֻּדוֹ עֶשְׂרִים וְאַדְנֵיהֶם עֶשְׂרִים נְחֹשֶׁת וָוֵי
הָעַמֻּדִים וַחֲשֻׁקֵיהֶם כָּסֶף: ¹²וְרֹחַב הֶחָצֵר לִפְאַת־
יָם קְלָעִים חֲמִשִּׁים אַמָּה עַמֻּדֵיהֶם עֲשָׂרָה וְאַדְנֵיהֶם
עֲשָׂרָה: ¹³וְרֹחַב הֶחָצֵר לִפְאַת קֵדְמָה מִזְרָחָה
חֲמִשִּׁים אַמָּה: ¹⁴וַחֲמֵשׁ עֶשְׂרֵה אַמָּה קְלָעִים לַכָּתֵף
עַמֻּדֵיהֶם שְׁלֹשָׁה וְאַדְנֵיהֶם שְׁלֹשָׁה: ¹⁵וְלַכָּתֵף הַשֵּׁנִית
חֲמֵשׁ עֶשְׂרֵה קְלָעִים עַמֻּדֵיהֶם שְׁלֹשָׁה וְאַדְנֵיהֶם
שְׁלֹשָׁה: ¹⁶וּלְשַׁעַר הֶחָצֵר מָסָךְ | עֶשְׂרִים אַמָּה
תְּכֵלֶת וְאַרְגָּמָן וְתוֹלַעַת שָׁנִי וְשֵׁשׁ מָשְׁזָר מַעֲשֵׂה
רֹקֵם עַמֻּדֵיהֶם אַרְבָּעָה וְאַדְנֵיהֶם אַרְבָּעָה: ¹⁷כָּל־
עַמּוּדֵי הֶחָצֵר סָבִיב מְחֻשָּׁקִים כֶּסֶף וָוֵיהֶם כָּסֶף
וְאַדְנֵיהֶם נְחֹשֶׁת: ¹⁸אֹרֶךְ הֶחָצֵר מֵאָה בָאַמָּה
וְרֹחַב | חֲמִשִּׁים בַּחֲמִשִּׁים וְקֹמָה חָמֵשׁ אַמּוֹת שֵׁשׁ
מָשְׁזָר וְאַדְנֵיהֶם נְחֹשֶׁת: ¹⁹לְכֹל כְּלֵי הַמִּשְׁכָּן בְּכֹל
עֲבֹדָתוֹ וְכָל־יְתֵדֹתָיו וְכָל־יִתְדֹת הֶחָצֵר נְחֹשֶׁת: ס

קְ וְעַמּוּדָיו 27:11

COMMAND

תצוה

20"And you: you shall command the children of Israel that they shall bring clear pressed olive oil to you for the light, to keep up a lamp always. 21In the Tent of Meeting, outside the pavilion that is over the Testimony, Aaron and his sons shall arrange it from evening until morning in front of YHWH, an eternal law through their generations from the children of Israel.

28 1"And you, bring Aaron, your brother, forward to you, and his sons with him, from among the children of Israel, for him to function as a priest for me: Aaron, Nadab and Abihu, Eleazar and Ithamar, Aaron's sons. 2And you shall make holy clothes for Aaron, your brother, for glory and for beauty. 3And you shall speak to all the wise of heart whom I have filled with a spirit of wisdom, that they shall make Aaron's clothes, to sanctify him for him to function as a priest for me. 4And these are the clothes that they shall make: breastplate and ephod and robe and patterned coat, a headdress and a sash. And they shall make holy clothes for Aaron, your brother, and for his sons, for him to function as a priest for me. 5And *they* shall take the gold and the blue and the purple and the scarlet and the linen.

6"And they shall make the ephod: gold, blue, and purple, scarlet, and woven linen, designer's work. 7It shall have two connected shoulder-pieces at its two ends, and it will be connected. 8And the ephod's designed belt that is on it shall be like its work and be a part of it: gold, blue, and purple, and scarlet and woven linen. 9And you shall take two onyx stones and inscribe the names of the children of Israel on them: 10six of their names on one stone and the names of the

20וְאַתָּה תְּצַוֶּה ׀ אֶת־בְּנֵי יִשְׂרָאֵל וְיִקְחוּ אֵלֶיךָ שֶׁמֶן זַיִת זָךְ כָּתִית לַמָּאוֹר לְהַעֲלֹת נֵר תָּמִיד: 21בְּאֹהֶל מוֹעֵד מִחוּץ לַפָּרֹכֶת אֲשֶׁר עַל־הָעֵדֻת יַעֲרֹךְ אֹתוֹ אַהֲרֹן וּבָנָיו מֵעֶרֶב עַד־בֹּקֶר לִפְנֵי יְהֹוָה חֻקַּת עוֹלָם לְדֹרֹתָם מֵאֵת בְּנֵי יִשְׂרָאֵל: ס

28 1וְאַתָּה הַקְרֵב אֵלֶיךָ אֶת־אַהֲרֹן אָחִיךָ וְאֶת־בָּנָיו אִתּוֹ מִתּוֹךְ בְּנֵי יִשְׂרָאֵל לְכַהֲנוֹ־לִי אַהֲרֹן נָדָב וַאֲבִיהוּא אֶלְעָזָר וְאִיתָמָר בְּנֵי אַהֲרֹן: 2וְעָשִׂיתָ בִגְדֵי־קֹדֶשׁ לְאַהֲרֹן אָחִיךָ לְכָבוֹד וּלְתִפְאָרֶת: 3וְאַתָּה תְּדַבֵּר אֶל־כָּל־חַכְמֵי־לֵב אֲשֶׁר מִלֵּאתִיו רוּחַ חָכְמָה וְעָשׂוּ אֶת־בִּגְדֵי אַהֲרֹן לְקַדְּשׁוֹ לְכַהֲנוֹ־לִי: 4וְאֵלֶּה הַבְּגָדִים אֲשֶׁר יַעֲשׂוּ חֹשֶׁן וְאֵפוֹד וּמְעִיל וּכְתֹנֶת תַּשְׁבֵּץ מִצְנֶפֶת וְאַבְנֵט וְעָשׂוּ בִגְדֵי־קֹדֶשׁ לְאַהֲרֹן אָחִיךָ וּלְבָנָיו לְכַהֲנוֹ־לִי: 5וְהֵם יִקְחוּ אֶת־הַזָּהָב וְאֶת־הַתְּכֵלֶת וְאֶת־הָאַרְגָּמָן וְאֶת־תּוֹלַעַת הַשָּׁנִי וְאֶת־הַשֵּׁשׁ: פ 6וְעָשׂוּ אֶת־הָאֵפֹד זָהָב תְּכֵלֶת וְאַרְגָּמָן תּוֹלַעַת שָׁנִי וְשֵׁשׁ מָשְׁזָר מַעֲשֵׂה חֹשֵׁב: 7שְׁתֵּי כְתֵפֹת חֹבְרֹת יִהְיֶה־לּוֹ אֶל־שְׁנֵי קְצוֹתָיו וְחֻבָּר: 8וְחֵשֶׁב אֲפֻדָּתוֹ אֲשֶׁר עָלָיו כְּמַעֲשֵׂהוּ מִמֶּנּוּ יִהְיֶה זָהָב תְּכֵלֶת וְאַרְגָּמָן וְתוֹלַעַת שָׁנִי וְשֵׁשׁ מָשְׁזָר: 9וְלָקַחְתָּ אֶת־שְׁתֵּי אַבְנֵי־שֹׁהַם וּפִתַּחְתָּ עֲלֵיהֶם שְׁמוֹת בְּנֵי יִשְׂרָאֵל: 10שִׁשָּׁה מִשְּׁמֹתָם עַל הָאֶבֶן הָאֶחָת וְאֶת־שְׁמוֹת הַשִּׁשָּׁה הַנּוֹתָרִים עַל־הָאֶבֶן

28:2. **for glory and for beauty.** Beauty inspires. Building beautiful places for the practice of religion is a valuable thing. *Of course* this does not mean building great edifices at the expense of the starving masses, nor does it mean focusing on the outer trappings and missing the content and spirit that they serve. There must be balance—wisdom. But we must recognize the value of art and beauty: the building, the priests' clothing, the music, the smells, the tastes. Religion is not the enemy of the senses.

remaining six on the second stone, according to their birth orders. [11]By a stone engraver's work you shall inscribe the two stones with signet inscriptions according to the names of the children of Israel. You shall make them surrounded by settings of gold. [12]And you shall set the two stones on the ephod's shoulder-pieces, commemorative stones for the children of Israel, and Aaron shall carry their names in front of YHWH on his two shoulders as a commemoration.

[13]"And you shall make settings of gold [14]and two chains of pure gold. You shall make them twisted, rope work, and put the rope chains on the settings.

[15]"And you shall make a breastplate of judgment, designer's work. You shall make it like the work of the ephod. You shall make it gold, blue, and purple and scarlet and woven linen. [16]It shall be square when doubled, its length a span and its width a span. [17]And you shall put a mounting of stones in it: four rows of stone. A row of a carnelian, a topaz, and an emerald: the one row. [18]And the second row: a ruby, a sapphire, and a diamond. [19]And the third row: a jacinth, an agate, and an amethyst. [20]And the fourth row: a beryl and an onyx and a jasper. They shall be set in gold in their mountings. [21]And the stones shall be with the names of the children of Israel, twelve with their names; they shall be signet engravings, each with its name, for twelve tribes. [22]And you shall make twisted chains, rope work, of pure gold, on the breastplate. [23]And you shall make two rings of gold on the breastplate and put the two rings on the two ends of the breastplate [24]and put the two ropes of gold on the two rings at the ends of the breastplate. [25]And you shall put the two ends of the two ropes on the two settings, and you shall put them on the ephod's shoulder-pieces opposite the front of it. [26]And you shall make two rings of gold and set them on the breastplate's two ends on its side that is adjacent to the ephod, inward. [27]And you shall make two rings of gold and put them on the ephod's two shoulder-pieces below,

הַשֵּׁנִית כְּתוֹלְדֹתָם: [11]מַעֲשֵׂה חָרַשׁ אֶבֶן פִּתּוּחֵי חֹתָם תְּפַתַּח אֶת־שְׁתֵּי הָאֲבָנִים עַל־שְׁמֹת בְּנֵי יִשְׂרָאֵל מֻסַבֹּת מִשְׁבְּצוֹת זָהָב תַּעֲשֶׂה אֹתָם: [12]וְשַׂמְתָּ אֶת־שְׁתֵּי הָאֲבָנִים עַל כִּתְפֹת הָאֵפֹד אַבְנֵי זִכָּרֹן לִבְנֵי יִשְׂרָאֵל וְנָשָׂא אַהֲרֹן אֶת־שְׁמוֹתָם לִפְנֵי יְהוָה עַל־שְׁתֵּי כְתֵפָיו לְזִכָּרֹן: ס [13]וְעָשִׂיתָ מִשְׁבְּצֹת זָהָב: [14]וּשְׁתֵּי שַׁרְשְׁרֹת זָהָב טָהוֹר מִגְבָּלֹת תַּעֲשֶׂה אֹתָם מַעֲשֵׂה עֲבֹת וְנָתַתָּה אֶת־שַׁרְשְׁרֹת הָעֲבֹתֹת עַל־הַמִּשְׁבְּצֹת: ס [15]וְעָשִׂיתָ חֹשֶׁן מִשְׁפָּט מַעֲשֵׂה חֹשֵׁב כְּמַעֲשֵׂה אֵפֹד תַּעֲשֶׂנּוּ זָהָב תְּכֵלֶת וְאַרְגָּמָן וְתוֹלַעַת שָׁנִי וְשֵׁשׁ מָשְׁזָר תַּעֲשֶׂה אֹתוֹ: [16]רָבוּעַ יִהְיֶה כָּפוּל זֶרֶת אָרְכּוֹ וְזֶרֶת רָחְבּוֹ: [17]וּמִלֵּאתָ בוֹ מִלֻּאַת אֶבֶן אַרְבָּעָה טוּרִים אָבֶן טוּר אֹדֶם פִּטְדָה וּבָרֶקֶת הַטּוּר הָאֶחָד: [18]וְהַטּוּר הַשֵּׁנִי נֹפֶךְ סַפִּיר וְיָהֲלֹם: [19]וְהַטּוּר הַשְּׁלִישִׁי לֶשֶׁם שְׁבוֹ וְאַחְלָמָה: [20]וְהַטּוּר הָרְבִיעִי תַּרְשִׁישׁ וְשֹׁהַם וְיָשְׁפֵה מְשֻׁבָּצִים זָהָב יִהְיוּ בְּמִלּוּאֹתָם: [21]וְהָאֲבָנִים תִּהְיֶיןָ עַל־שְׁמֹת בְּנֵי־יִשְׂרָאֵל שְׁתֵּים עֶשְׂרֵה עַל־שְׁמֹתָם פִּתּוּחֵי חוֹתָם אִישׁ עַל־שְׁמוֹ תִּהְיֶיןָ לִשְׁנֵי עָשָׂר שָׁבֶט: [22]וְעָשִׂיתָ עַל־הַחֹשֶׁן שַׁרְשֹׁת גַּבְלֻת מַעֲשֵׂה עֲבֹת זָהָב טָהוֹר: [23]וְעָשִׂיתָ עַל־הַחֹשֶׁן שְׁתֵּי טַבְּעוֹת זָהָב וְנָתַתָּ אֶת־שְׁתֵּי הַטַּבָּעוֹת עַל־שְׁנֵי קְצוֹת הַחֹשֶׁן: [24]וְנָתַתָּה אֶת־שְׁתֵּי עֲבֹתֹת הַזָּהָב עַל־שְׁתֵּי הַטַּבָּעֹת אֶל־קְצוֹת הַחֹשֶׁן: [25]וְאֵת שְׁתֵּי קְצוֹת שְׁתֵּי הָעֲבֹתֹת תִּתֵּן עַל־שְׁתֵּי הַמִּשְׁבְּצוֹת וְנָתַתָּה עַל־כִּתְפוֹת הָאֵפֹד אֶל־מוּל פָּנָיו: [26]וְעָשִׂיתָ שְׁתֵּי טַבְּעוֹת זָהָב וְשַׂמְתָּ אֹתָם עַל־שְׁנֵי קְצוֹת הַחֹשֶׁן עַל־שְׂפָתוֹ אֲשֶׁר אֶל־עֵבֶר הָאֵפֹד בָּיְתָה: [27]וְעָשִׂיתָ שְׁתֵּי טַבְּעוֹת זָהָב וְנָתַתָּה אֹתָם עַל־שְׁתֵּי כִתְפוֹת הָאֵפוֹד מִלְּמַטָּה מִמּוּל פָּנָיו

opposite the front of it, by its connection, above the ephod's designed belt. 28And they shall attach the breastplate from its rings to the ephod's rings with a blue string so it will be on the ephod's designed belt and the breastplate will not be detached from the ephod. 29And Aaron shall carry the names of the children of Israel in the breastplate of judgment on his heart when he comes into the Holy, as a commemorative in front of YHWH always. 30And you shall put the Urim and Tummim in the breastplate of judgment, and they shall be on Aaron's heart when he comes in front of YHWH, and Aaron shall carry the judgment of the children of Israel on his heart in front of YHWH always.

31"And you shall make the robe of the ephod all of blue. 32And its head-opening shall be within it. It shall have a binding for its opening all around, weaver's work. It shall be like the opening of a coat of mail for him; it will not be torn. 33And you shall make on its skirts pomegranates of blue and purple and scarlet, on its skirts all around, and bells of gold within them all around: 34a golden bell and a pomegranate, a golden bell and a pomegranate, on the robe's skirts all around. 35And it shall be on Aaron for ministering: and the sound of it will be heard when he comes to the Holy in front of YHWH and when he goes out, so he will not die.

36"And you shall make a plate of pure gold and make signet inscriptions on it: 'Holiness to

לְעֻמַּת מֶחְבַּרְתּוֹ מִמַּעַל לְחֵשֶׁב הָאֵפוֹד: 28וְיִרְכְּסוּ אֶת־הַחֹשֶׁן מִטַּבְּעֹתָו אֶל־טַבְּעֹת הָאֵפֹד בִּפְתִיל תְּכֵלֶת לִהְיוֹת עַל־חֵשֶׁב הָאֵפוֹד וְלֹא־יִזַּח הַחֹשֶׁן מֵעַל הָאֵפוֹד: 29וְנָשָׂא אַהֲרֹן אֶת־שְׁמוֹת בְּנֵי־יִשְׂרָאֵל בְּחֹשֶׁן הַמִּשְׁפָּט עַל־לִבּוֹ בְּבֹאוֹ אֶל־הַקֹּדֶשׁ לְזִכָּרֹן לִפְנֵי־יהוה תָּמִיד: 30וְנָתַתָּ אֶל־חֹשֶׁן הַמִּשְׁפָּט אֶת־הָאוּרִים וְאֶת־הַתֻּמִּים וְהָיוּ עַל־לֵב אַהֲרֹן בְּבֹאוֹ לִפְנֵי יהוה וְנָשָׂא אַהֲרֹן אֶת־מִשְׁפַּט בְּנֵי־יִשְׂרָאֵל עַל־לִבּוֹ לִפְנֵי יהוה תָּמִיד: ס 31וְעָשִׂיתָ אֶת־מְעִיל הָאֵפוֹד כְּלִיל תְּכֵלֶת: 32וְהָיָה פִי־רֹאשׁוֹ בְּתוֹכוֹ שָׂפָה יִהְיֶה לְפִיו סָבִיב מַעֲשֵׂה אֹרֵג כְּפִי תַחְרָא יִהְיֶה־לּוֹ לֹא יִקָּרֵעַ: 33וְעָשִׂיתָ עַל־שׁוּלָיו רִמֹּנֵי תְּכֵלֶת וְאַרְגָּמָן וְתוֹלַעַת שָׁנִי עַל־שׁוּלָיו סָבִיב וּפַעֲמֹנֵי זָהָב בְּתוֹכָם סָבִיב: 34פַּעֲמֹן זָהָב וְרִמּוֹן פַּעֲמֹן זָהָב וְרִמּוֹן עַל־שׁוּלֵי הַמְּעִיל סָבִיב: 35וְהָיָה עַל־אַהֲרֹן לְשָׁרֵת וְנִשְׁמַע קוֹלוֹ בְּבֹאוֹ אֶל־הַקֹּדֶשׁ לִפְנֵי יהוה וּבְצֵאתוֹ וְלֹא יָמוּת: ס 36וְעָשִׂיתָ צִּיץ זָהָב טָהוֹר וּפִתַּחְתָּ עָלָיו פִּתּוּחֵי חֹתָם קֹדֶשׁ לַיהוה:

28:28 קְ מִטַּבְּעֹתָיו

28:30. Urim and Tummim. We have pondered for centuries what these are. They have something to do with inquiring of God for an answer to a question. They may contain letters that can spell out long answers, or they may provide only a "yes" or "no," or they may also provide a third option of "no response." They are mentioned four times in the Torah, twice in 1 Samuel (14:41, where the Greek text differs from the Masoretic Text by a full line; and 25:6), and then never again in Israel's history until the narrative of Ezra and Nehemiah, where it is noted that answers through the Urim and Tummim are not available (Ezra 2:63; Neh 7:65). We must admit it: we just do not know what they are. What is important is that several different biblical sources indicate that there was a belief that it was possible to ask questions of God and get an answer, and that this was done through a priest, not a prophet. It was a mechanism other than prophecy to learn the will of God. And it is known as a practice only in Israel's earliest era.

YHWH.' 37And you shall set it on a blue string, and it shall be on the headdress. It shall be opposite the front of the headdress. 38And it shall be on Aaron's forehead, and Aaron shall bear the crime of the holy things that the children of Israel will sanctify, for all their holy gifts. And it shall be on his forehead always for acceptance for them in front of YHWH. 39And you shall weave the coat in a pattern of linen and make a headdress of linen. And you shall make a sash, embroiderer's work, 40and you shall make coats for Aaron's sons, and you shall make sashes for them, and you shall make hats for them—for glory and for beauty. 41And you shall dress them—Aaron, your brother, and his sons with him—and you shall anoint them and fill their hand and sanctify them, and they shall function as priests for me. 42And make shorts of linen for them, to cover naked flesh; they shall be from hips to thighs. 43And they shall be on Aaron and on his sons when they come to the Tent of Meeting or when they come close to the altar to minister in the Holy, so they will not bear a crime

37וְשַׂמְתָּ אֹתוֹ עַל־פְּתִיל תְּכֵלֶת וְהָיָה עַל־הַמִּצְנָפֶת אֶל־מוּל פְּנֵי־הַמִּצְנֶפֶת יִהְיֶה: 38וְהָיָה עַל־מֵצַח אַהֲרֹן וְנָשָׂא אַהֲרֹן אֶת־עֲוֹן הַקֳּדָשִׁים אֲשֶׁר יַקְדִּישׁוּ בְּנֵי יִשְׂרָאֵל לְכָל־מַתְּנֹת קָדְשֵׁיהֶם וְהָיָה עַל־מִצְחוֹ תָּמִיד לְרָצוֹן לָהֶם לִפְנֵי יְהוָה: 39וְשִׁבַּצְתָּ הַכְּתֹנֶת שֵׁשׁ וְעָשִׂיתָ מִצְנֶפֶת שֵׁשׁ וְאַבְנֵט תַּעֲשֶׂה מַעֲשֵׂה רֹקֵם: 40וְלִבְנֵי אַהֲרֹן תַּעֲשֶׂה כֻתֳּנֹת וְעָשִׂיתָ לָהֶם אַבְנֵטִים וּמִגְבָּעוֹת תַּעֲשֶׂה לָהֶם לְכָבוֹד וּלְתִפְאָרֶת: 41וְהִלְבַּשְׁתָּ אֹתָם אֶת־אַהֲרֹן אָחִיךָ וְאֶת־בָּנָיו אִתּוֹ וּמָשַׁחְתָּ אֹתָם וּמִלֵּאתָ אֶת־יָדָם וְקִדַּשְׁתָּ אֹתָם וְכִהֲנוּ לִי: 42וַעֲשֵׂה לָהֶם מִכְנְסֵי־בָד לְכַסּוֹת בְּשַׂר עֶרְוָה מִמָּתְנַיִם וְעַד־יְרֵכַיִם יִהְיוּ: 43וְהָיוּ עַל־אַהֲרֹן וְעַל־בָּנָיו בְּבֹאָם ׀ אֶל־אֹהֶל מוֹעֵד אוֹ בְגִשְׁתָּם אֶל־הַמִּזְבֵּחַ לְשָׁרֵת בַּקֹּדֶשׁ וְלֹא־יִשְׂאוּ עָוֹן וָמֵתוּ חֻקַּת

28:38,43. bear a crime. This difficult expression is thought to have a range of meanings. In these passages it conveys that the priests bear an enormous responsibility on account of their closeness to the holy. Coming close to the holy objects or to the altar, they risk violation of the sacred if they act incorrectly. The seriousness of this matter will become manifest when two of Aaron's sons violate the holy and die (Leviticus 10). After the destruction of the first Temple in Jerusalem and the loss of the ark, tablets, Tabernacle, and Urim and Tummim, much of the feeling for the sacred must have been lost. And since the destruction of the second Temple, our sense of the sacred has diminished even more. So it has become ever harder to comprehend this aspect of the biblical world and to appreciate the power and awe that were associated with sacred objects, sacred places, and the priesthood.

28:41. anoint them. The Hebrew word for anointing is *mšḥ*. Its English form is messiah. Later it is used for kings. Kings Saul and David are each referred to as the messiah (1 Sam 12:3; 24:7; 2 Sam 19:22). And, later still, Jewish ideas of a coming messiah (Hebrew *māšîaḥ*) developed out of this royal role of anointing. But here in its first occurrence in the Torah, it is understood that the original use of anointing is for ordaining the high priests.

28:41; 29:9. fill their hand. In the Torah and elsewhere in the Bible, this expression, "to fill one's hand," means to take on the role of priest (Lev 8:33; 16:32; 21:10; Num 3:3; 1 Kings 13:33). In Leviticus it is usually related to donning the priestly garments.

and die. It is an eternal law for him and for his seed after him.

29

¹"And this is the thing that you shall do to them to sanctify them to function as priests for me: Take one bull of the cattle and two unblemished rams ²and unleavened bread and unleavened cakes mixed with oil and unleavened wafers with oil poured on them—you shall make them of fine flour of wheat. ³And you shall put them on one basket and bring them forward in the basket—and the bull and the two rams. ⁴And you shall bring Aaron and his sons forward to the Tent of Meeting and wash them with water. ⁵And you shall take the clothes and dress Aaron with the coat and with the ephod's robe and with the ephod and with the breastplate, and you shall put on the ephod for him with the ephod's designed belt. ⁶And you shall set the headdress on his head and put the crown of Holiness on the headdress. ⁷And you shall take the anointing oil and pour it on his head and anoint him. ⁸And you shall bring his sons forward, and you shall dress them in coats ⁹and you shall belt them with a sash, Aaron and his sons, and put hats on for them. And they shall have priesthood as an eternal law. And you shall fill Aaron's hand and his sons' hand. ¹⁰And you shall bring the bull forward in front of the Tent of Meeting, and Aaron and his sons shall lay their hands on the bull's head. ¹¹And you shall slaughter the bull in front of YHWH at the entrance of the Tent of Meeting. ¹²And you shall take some of the bull's

עוֹלָ֖ם ל֣וֹ וּלְזַרְע֣וֹ אַחֲרָֽיו׃ ס

29 ¹וְזֶ֣ה הַדָּבָ֞ר אֲשֶֽׁר־תַּעֲשֶׂ֤ה לָהֶם֙ לְקַדֵּ֣שׁ אֹתָ֔ם לְכַהֵ֖ן לִ֑י לְ֠קַח פַּ֣ר אֶחָ֧ד בֶּן־בָּקָ֛ר וְאֵילִ֥ם שְׁנַ֖יִם תְּמִימִֽם׃ ²וְלֶ֣חֶם מַצּ֗וֹת וְחַלֹּ֤ת מַצֹּת֙ בְּלוּלֹ֣ת בַּשֶּׁ֔מֶן וּרְקִיקֵ֥י מַצּ֖וֹת מְשֻׁחִ֣ים בַּשָּׁ֑מֶן סֹ֥לֶת חִטִּ֖ים תַּעֲשֶׂ֥ה אֹתָֽם׃ ³וְנָתַתָּ֤ אוֹתָם֙ עַל־סַ֣ל אֶחָ֔ד וְהִקְרַבְתָּ֥ אֹתָ֖ם בַּסָּ֑ל וְאֶ֨ת־הַפָּ֔ר וְאֵ֖ת שְׁנֵ֥י הָאֵילִֽם׃ ⁴וְאֶת־אַהֲרֹ֤ן וְאֶת־בָּנָיו֙ תַּקְרִ֔יב אֶל־פֶּ֖תַח אֹ֣הֶל מוֹעֵ֑ד וְרָחַצְתָּ֥ אֹתָ֖ם בַּמָּֽיִם׃ ⁵וְלָקַחְתָּ֣ אֶת־הַבְּגָדִ֗ים וְהִלְבַּשְׁתָּ֤ אֶֽת־אַהֲרֹן֙ אֶת־הַכֻּתֹּ֔נֶת וְאֵת֙ מְעִ֣יל הָאֵפֹ֔ד וְאֶת־הָ֣אֵפֹ֔ד וְאֶת־הַחֹ֑שֶׁן וְאָפַדְתָּ֣ ל֔וֹ בְּחֵ֖שֶׁב הָאֵפֹֽד׃ ⁶וְשַׂמְתָּ֥ הַמִּצְנֶ֖פֶת עַל־רֹאשׁ֑וֹ וְנָתַתָּ֛ אֶת־נֵ֥זֶר הַקֹּ֖דֶשׁ עַל־הַמִּצְנָֽפֶת׃ ⁷וְלָקַחְתָּ֙ אֶת־שֶׁ֣מֶן הַמִּשְׁחָ֔ה וְיָצַקְתָּ֖ עַל־רֹאשׁ֑וֹ וּמָשַׁחְתָּ֖ אֹתֽוֹ׃ ⁸וְאֶת־בָּנָ֖יו תַּקְרִ֑יב וְהִלְבַּשְׁתָּ֖ם כֻּתֳּנֹֽת׃ ⁹וְחָגַרְתָּ֩ אֹתָ֨ם אַבְנֵ֜ט אַהֲרֹ֣ן וּבָנָ֗יו וְחָבַשְׁתָּ֤ לָהֶם֙ מִגְבָּעֹ֔ת וְהָיְתָ֥ה לָהֶ֛ם כְּהֻנָּ֖ה לְחֻקַּ֣ת עוֹלָ֑ם וּמִלֵּאתָ֥ יַֽד־אַהֲרֹ֖ן וְיַד־בָּנָֽיו׃ ¹⁰וְהִקְרַבְתָּ֙ אֶת־הַפָּ֔ר לִפְנֵ֖י אֹ֣הֶל מוֹעֵ֑ד וְסָמַ֨ךְ אַהֲרֹ֤ן וּבָנָיו֙ אֶת־יְדֵיהֶ֔ם עַל־רֹ֖אשׁ הַפָּֽר׃ ¹¹וְשָׁחַטְתָּ֥ אֶת־הַפָּ֖ר לִפְנֵ֣י יְהוָ֑ה פֶּ֖תַח אֹ֥הֶל מוֹעֵֽד׃ ¹²וְלָקַחְתָּ֙ מִדַּ֣ם הַפָּ֔ר וְנָתַתָּ֛ה

29:2. **unleavened bread.** Unleavened bread is the food of the priests. It is eaten with the meat of the sacrifices. Leaven is seen as something inappropriate for the holy realm, perhaps because its power in the process of making bread rise is seen as something mysterious. Biologically, yeast is classified as distinct, not belonging to either the plant or the animal kingdom. This singular status of yeast presumably has to do with the origin of the prohibition of leaven on Passover as well. On Passover, all Israelites behave like priests, eating no leaven.

29:6. **crown of Holiness.** It is clarified later (Exod 39:30; Lev 8:9) that this is the golden plate that has the words "Holiness to YHWH" inscribed on it, as described in Exod 28:36. Like a king (2 Sam 1:10; 2 Kings 11:12), the high priest wears a crown.

blood and put it on the horns of the altar with your finger, and you shall spill all of the blood at the base of the altar. 13And you shall take all of the fat that covers the inside and the appendage on the liver and the two kidneys and the fat that is on them, and you shall burn them into smoke at the altar. 14And you shall burn the meat of the bull and its skin and its dung in fire outside the camp. It is a sin offering. 15And you shall take the one ram, and Aaron and his sons shall lay their hands on the ram's head. 16And you shall slaughter the ram and take its blood and fling it on the altar all around. 17And you shall cut up the ram into its parts, and you shall wash its inside and its legs and put them on its parts and on its head. 18And you shall burn all of the ram to smoke at the altar. It is a burnt offering to YHWH. It is a pleasant smell, an offering by fire to YHWH. 19And you shall take the second ram, and Aaron and his sons shall lay their hands on the ram's head. 20And you shall slaughter the ram and take some of its blood and put it on Aaron's earlobe and on his sons' earlobe, the right one, and on the thumb of their right hand and on the big toe of their right foot. And you shall fling the blood on the altar all around. 21And you shall take some of the blood that is on the altar and some of the anointing oil and sprinkle it on Aaron and on his clothes and on his sons and on his sons' clothes with him. And he and his clothes and his sons and his sons' clothes with him will be holy. 22And you shall take the fat from the ram and the *fat tail* and the fat that covers the inside and the appendage of the liver and the two kidneys and the fat that is on them and the right thigh—because it is a ram of ordination— 23and one loaf of bread and one cake of bread with oil and one wafer from the basket of unleavened bread that is in front of YHWH. 24And you shall put it all on Aaron's

עַל־קַרְנֹ֤ת הַמִּזְבֵּ֙חַ֙ בְּאֶצְבָּעֶ֔ךָ וְאֶת־כָּל־הַדָּ֖ם תִּשְׁפֹּ֑ךְ אֶל־יְס֖וֹד הַמִּזְבֵּֽחַ׃ 13וְלָ֣קַחְתָּ֔ אֶֽת־כָּל־הַחֵ֗לֶב הַֽמְכַסֶּה֙ אֶת־הַקֶּ֔רֶב וְאֵ֤ת הַיֹּתֶ֙רֶת֙ עַל־הַכָּבֵ֔ד וְאֵת֙ שְׁתֵּ֣י הַכְּלָיֹ֔ת וְאֶת־הַחֵ֖לֶב אֲשֶׁ֣ר עֲלֵיהֶ֑ן וְהִקְטַרְתָּ֖ הַמִּזְבֵּֽחָה׃ 14וְאֶת־בְּשַׂ֤ר הַפָּר֙ וְאֶת־עֹר֣וֹ וְאֶת־פִּרְשׁ֔וֹ תִּשְׂרֹ֣ף בָּאֵ֔שׁ מִח֖וּץ לַֽמַּחֲנֶ֑ה חַטָּ֖את הֽוּא׃ 15וְאֶת־הָאַ֥יִל הָאֶחָ֖ד תִּקָּ֑ח וְסָ֨מְכ֜וּ אַהֲרֹ֧ן וּבָנָ֛יו אֶת־יְדֵיהֶ֖ם עַל־רֹ֥אשׁ הָאָֽיִל׃ 16וְשָׁחַטְתָּ֖ אֶת־הָאָ֑יִל וְלָ֣קַחְתָּ֙ אֶת־דָּמ֔וֹ וְזָרַקְתָּ֥ עַל־הַמִּזְבֵּ֖חַ סָבִֽיב׃ 17וְאֶ֨ת־הָאַ֔יִל תְּנַתֵּ֖חַ לִנְתָחָ֑יו וְרָחַצְתָּ֤ קִרְבּוֹ֙ וּכְרָעָ֔יו וְנָתַתָּ֥ עַל־נְתָחָ֖יו וְעַל־רֹאשֽׁוֹ׃ 18וְהִקְטַרְתָּ֤ אֶת־כָּל־הָאַ֙יִל֙ הַמִּזְבֵּ֔חָה עֹלָ֥ה ה֖וּא לַֽיהֹוָ֑ה רֵ֣יחַ נִיח֗וֹחַ אִשֶּׁ֛ה לַֽיהֹוָ֖ה הֽוּא׃ 19וְלָ֣קַחְתָּ֔ אֵ֖ת הָאַ֣יִל הַשֵּׁנִ֑י וְסָמַ֨ךְ אַהֲרֹ֧ן וּבָנָ֛יו אֶת־יְדֵיהֶ֖ם עַל־רֹ֥אשׁ הָאָֽיִל׃ 20וְשָׁחַטְתָּ֣ אֶת־הָאַ֗יִל וְלָקַחְתָּ֤ מִדָּמוֹ֙ וְנָתַתָּ֡ה עַל־תְּנוּךְ֩ אֹ֨זֶן אַהֲרֹ֜ן וְעַל־תְּנ֨וּךְ אֹ֤זֶן בָּנָיו֙ הַיְמָנִ֔ית וְעַל־בֹּ֤הֶן יָדָם֙ הַיְמָנִ֔ית וְעַל־בֹּ֖הֶן רַגְלָ֣ם הַיְמָנִ֑ית וְזָרַקְתָּ֧ אֶת־הַדָּ֛ם עַל־הַמִּזְבֵּ֖חַ סָבִֽיב׃ 21וְלָקַחְתָּ֞ מִן־הַדָּ֨ם אֲשֶׁ֥ר עַל־הַמִּזְבֵּ֘חַ֮ וּמִשֶּׁ֣מֶן הַמִּשְׁחָה֒ וְהִזֵּיתָ֤ עַֽל־אַהֲרֹן֙ וְעַל־בְּגָדָ֔יו וְעַל־בָּנָ֛יו וְעַל־בִּגְדֵ֥י בָנָ֖יו אִתּ֑וֹ וְקָדַ֥שׁ הוּא֙ וּבְגָדָ֔יו וּבָנָ֥יו וּבִגְדֵ֥י בָנָ֖יו אִתּֽוֹ׃ 22וְלָקַחְתָּ֣ מִן־הָ֠אַ֠יִל הַחֵ֨לֶב וְהָֽאַלְיָ֜ה וְאֶת־הַחֵ֣לֶב ׀ הַֽמְכַסֶּ֣ה אֶת־הַקֶּ֗רֶב וְאֵ֨ת יֹתֶ֤רֶת הַכָּבֵד֙ וְאֵ֣ת ׀ שְׁתֵּ֣י הַכְּלָיֹ֗ת וְאֶת־הַחֵ֙לֶב֙ אֲשֶׁ֣ר עֲלֵהֶ֔ן וְאֵ֖ת שׁ֣וֹק הַיָּמִ֑ין כִּ֛י אֵ֥יל מִלֻּאִ֖ים הֽוּא׃ 23וְכִכַּ֨ר לֶ֜חֶם אַחַ֗ת וְֽחַלַּ֨ת לֶ֥חֶם שֶׁ֛מֶן אַחַ֖ת וְרָקִ֣יק אֶחָ֑ד מִסַּל֙ הַמַּצּ֔וֹת אֲשֶׁ֖ר לִפְנֵ֥י יְהֹוָֽה׃ 24וְשַׂמְתָּ֣ הַכֹּ֔ל

29:22. **ordination.** The root meaning of "filling" relates back to the term "to fill the hand," further conveying that this term means to assume the role of priest (as in 28:41; 29:9).

hands and on his sons' hands and *elevate* them as an elevation offering in front of YHWH. 25And you shall take them from their hand and burn them to smoke at the altar in addition to the burnt offering as a pleasant smell in front of YHWH. It is an offering by fire to YHWH. 26And you shall take the breast from the ram of ordination that is Aaron's and elevate it as an elevation offering in front of YHWH, and it shall be a portion for you. 27And you shall sanctify the breast that is an elevation offering and the thigh that is a donation, that is elevated and that is donated, from the ram of ordination, from Aaron's and from his sons'. 28And it shall be Aaron's and his sons' as an eternal law from the children of Israel, because it *is* a donation, and it *will be* a donation from the children of Israel from the sacrifices of their peace offerings, their donation to YHWH. 29And the holy clothes that are Aaron's shall be his sons' after him, to be anointed in them and to fill their hand in them. 30The priest in his place from among his sons, who will come to the Tent of Meeting to minister in the Holy, shall wear them for seven days. 31And you shall take the ram of ordination and cook its meat in a holy place, 32and Aaron and his sons shall eat the meat of the ram and the bread that is in the basket at the entrance of the Tent of Meeting. 33And those who have acquired atonement by them shall eat them, to fill their hand, to make them holy; and an outsider shall not eat, because they are holy. 34And if some of the meat of the ordination or some of the bread will be left until the morning, then you shall burn what is left in fire. It shall not be eaten, because it is holy.

35"And you shall do thus to Aaron and to his sons, according to all that I have commanded you. You shall fill their hand for seven days. 36And you shall do a bull sin offering per day for

עַל כַּפֵּי אַהֲרֹן וְעַל כַּפֵּי בָנָיו וְהֵנַפְתָּ אֹתָם תְּנוּפָה לִפְנֵי יְהוָה: 25וְלָקַחְתָּ אֹתָם מִיָּדָם וְהִקְטַרְתָּ הַמִּזְבֵּחָה עַל־הָעֹלָה לְרֵיחַ נִיחוֹחַ לִפְנֵי יְהוָה אִשֶּׁה הוּא לַיהוָה: 26וְלָקַחְתָּ אֶת־הֶחָזֶה מֵאֵיל הַמִּלֻּאִים אֲשֶׁר לְאַהֲרֹן וְהֵנַפְתָּ אֹתוֹ תְּנוּפָה לִפְנֵי יְהוָה וְהָיָה לְךָ לְמָנָה: 27וְקִדַּשְׁתָּ אֵת ׀ חֲזֵה הַתְּנוּפָה וְאֵת שׁוֹק הַתְּרוּמָה אֲשֶׁר הוּנַף וַאֲשֶׁר הוּרָם מֵאֵיל הַמִּלֻּאִים מֵאֲשֶׁר לְאַהֲרֹן וּמֵאֲשֶׁר לְבָנָיו: 28וְהָיָה לְאַהֲרֹן וּלְבָנָיו לְחָק־עוֹלָם מֵאֵת בְּנֵי יִשְׂרָאֵל כִּי תְרוּמָה הוּא וּתְרוּמָה יִהְיֶה מֵאֵת בְּנֵי־יִשְׂרָאֵל מִזִּבְחֵי שַׁלְמֵיהֶם תְּרוּמָתָם לַיהוָה: 29וּבִגְדֵי הַקֹּדֶשׁ אֲשֶׁר לְאַהֲרֹן יִהְיוּ לְבָנָיו אַחֲרָיו לְמָשְׁחָה בָהֶם וּלְמַלֵּא־בָם אֶת־יָדָם: 30שִׁבְעַת יָמִים יִלְבָּשָׁם הַכֹּהֵן תַּחְתָּיו מִבָּנָיו אֲשֶׁר יָבֹא אֶל־אֹהֶל מוֹעֵד לְשָׁרֵת בַּקֹּדֶשׁ: 31וְאֵת אֵיל הַמִּלֻּאִים תִּקָּח וּבִשַּׁלְתָּ אֶת־בְּשָׂרוֹ בְּמָקֹם קָדֹשׁ: 32וְאָכַל אַהֲרֹן וּבָנָיו אֶת־בְּשַׂר הָאַיִל וְאֶת־הַלֶּחֶם אֲשֶׁר בַּסָּל פֶּתַח אֹהֶל מוֹעֵד: 33וְאָכְלוּ אֹתָם אֲשֶׁר כֻּפַּר בָּהֶם לְמַלֵּא אֶת־יָדָם לְקַדֵּשׁ אֹתָם וְזָר לֹא־יֹאכַל כִּי־קֹדֶשׁ הֵם: 34וְאִם־יִוָּתֵר מִבְּשַׂר הַמִּלֻּאִים וּמִן־הַלֶּחֶם עַד־הַבֹּקֶר וְשָׂרַפְתָּ אֶת־הַנּוֹתָר בָּאֵשׁ לֹא יֵאָכֵל כִּי־קֹדֶשׁ הוּא: 35וְעָשִׂיתָ לְאַהֲרֹן וּלְבָנָיו כָּכָה כְּכֹל אֲשֶׁר־צִוִּיתִי אֹתָכָה שִׁבְעַת יָמִים תְּמַלֵּא יָדָם: 36וּפַר חַטָּאת תַּעֲשֶׂה לַיּוֹם עַל־

29:33. **outsider**. The word, Hebrew *zār*, refers to a person who is not a member of the group that is covered by a law. If the law applies to priests, the term refers to laypersons. If it applies to brothers, the term refers to anyone who is outside their family (Deut 25:5).

atonement, and you shall make a sin offering on the altar when you make atonement for it, and you shall anoint it to make it holy. ³⁷Seven days you shall make atonement on the altar and make it holy, and the altar shall be holy of holies. Anyone who touches the altar will be holy.

³⁸"And this is what you shall do on the altar: year-old lambs, two per day, always. ³⁹You shall do the one sheep in the morning and do the second sheep between the two evenings. ⁴⁰And a tenth of a measure of fine flour mixed with a fourth of a hin of pressed oil and a libation of a fourth of a hin of wine for the first lamb. ⁴¹And you shall do the second lamb between the two evenings. You shall do it like the morning grain offering and like its libation for a pleasant smell, an offering by fire to YHWH, ⁴²a continual burnt offering through your generations at the entrance of the Tent of Meeting in front of YHWH, where I shall meet with you to speak to you there. ⁴³And I shall meet there with the children of Israel, and it will be made holy through my glory. ⁴⁴And I shall make the Tent of Meeting and the altar holy, and I shall make Aaron and his sons holy to function as priests for me. ⁴⁵And I shall tent among the children of Israel, and I

הַכִּפֻּרִים וְחִטֵּאתָ֙ עַל־הַמִּזְבֵּ֔חַ בְּכַפֶּרְךָ֖ עָלָ֑יו וּמָשַׁחְתָּ֥ אֹת֖וֹ לְקַדְּשׁ֑וֹ: ³⁷שִׁבְעַ֣ת יָמִ֗ים תְּכַפֵּר֙ עַל־הַמִּזְבֵּ֔חַ וְקִדַּשְׁתָּ֖ אֹת֑וֹ וְהָיָ֤ה הַמִּזְבֵּ֙חַ֙ קֹ֣דֶשׁ קָֽדָשִׁ֔ים כָּל־הַנֹּגֵ֥עַ בַּמִּזְבֵּ֖חַ יִקְדָּֽשׁ: ס

³⁸וְזֶ֕ה אֲשֶׁ֥ר תַּעֲשֶׂ֖ה עַל־הַמִּזְבֵּ֑חַ כְּבָשִׂ֧ים בְּנֵֽי־שָׁנָ֛ה שְׁנַ֥יִם לַיּ֖וֹם תָּמִֽיד: ³⁹אֶת־הַכֶּ֥בֶשׂ הָאֶחָ֖ד תַּעֲשֶׂ֣ה בַבֹּ֑קֶר וְאֵת֙ הַכֶּ֣בֶשׂ הַשֵּׁנִ֔י תַּעֲשֶׂ֖ה בֵּ֥ין הָעַרְבָּֽיִם: ⁴⁰וְעִשָּׂרֹ֨ן סֹ֜לֶת בָּל֨וּל בְּשֶׁ֤מֶן כָּתִית֙ רֶ֣בַע הַהִ֔ין וְנֵ֕סֶךְ רְבִיעִ֥ת הַהִ֖ין יָ֑יִן לַכֶּ֖בֶשׂ הָאֶחָֽד: ⁴¹וְאֵת֙ הַכֶּ֣בֶשׂ הַשֵּׁנִ֔י תַּעֲשֶׂ֖ה בֵּ֣ין הָעַרְבָּ֑יִם כְּמִנְחַ֨ת הַבֹּ֤קֶר וּכְנִסְכָּהּ֙ תַּֽעֲשֶׂה־לָּ֔הּ לְרֵ֣יחַ נִיחֹ֔חַ אִשֶּׁ֖ה לַֽיהוָֽה: ⁴²עֹלַ֤ת תָּמִיד֙ לְדֹרֹ֣תֵיכֶ֔ם פֶּ֥תַח אֹֽהֶל־מוֹעֵ֖ד לִפְנֵ֣י יְהוָ֑ה אֲשֶׁ֨ר אִוָּעֵ֤ד לָכֶם֙ שָׁ֔מָּה לְדַבֵּ֥ר אֵלֶ֖יךָ שָֽׁם: ⁴³וְנֹעַדְתִּ֥י שָׁ֖מָּה לִבְנֵ֣י יִשְׂרָאֵ֑ל וְנִקְדַּ֖שׁ בִּכְבֹדִֽי: ⁴⁴וְקִדַּשְׁתִּ֛י אֶת־אֹ֥הֶל מוֹעֵ֖ד וְאֶת־הַמִּזְבֵּ֑חַ וְאֶת־אַהֲרֹ֧ן וְאֶת־בָּנָ֛יו אֲקַדֵּ֖שׁ לְכַהֵ֥ן לִֽי: ⁴⁵וְשָׁכַנְתִּ֕י בְּת֖וֹךְ בְּנֵ֥י יִשְׂרָאֵ֑ל

29:37. holy of holies. Like the Holy of Holies in the Tabernacle, this phrase means that this altar is the holiest of all.

29:37. Anyone who touches the altar will be holy. The quality of being holy can spread. Coming into contact with the ark, which is in a state of holiness, renders one holy as well. The condition of impurity may spread by contact, too. (This will be a concern in Leviticus.) The Torah involves a belief that there are certain conditions which are invisible but which have an effect on persons and objects. The spreading of holiness by contact also confirms that the word "holy" does not refer to just being "apart" or "separate," as we have often taught in the past. Holiness is a powerful condition related to closeness to the divine. (See the comment on Exod 19:6.)

29:45–46. I shall tent. . . . And they will know. In case anyone might get lost in all the details of these many chapters on the Tabernacle and the priesthood, this powerful statement comes in the middle of the section. Once these things are established, then: YHWH will meet with Moses and the people there, YHWH will be present among the people, YHWH will be their God, and they will know that YHWH is their God. It is one of the most crucial passages in the Torah. It is the basis of all of the law and most of the episodes that will come in Leviticus, Numbers, and Deuteronomy.

shall be God to them. 46And they will know that I am YHWH, their God, who brought them out from the land of Egypt for me to tent among them. I am YHWH, their God.

30 1"And you shall make an altar for burning incense. You shall make it of acacia wood. 2Its length a cubit and its width a cubit, it shall be square, and its height two cubits, its horns a part of it. 3And you shall plate it with pure gold, its roof and its walls all around and its horns. And you shall make a border of gold for it all around. 4And you shall make two rings of gold for it below its rim on its two sides; you shall make it on its two sidewalls, and it will be for housings for poles with which to carry it. 5And you shall make the poles of acacia wood and plate them with gold. 6And you shall put it in front of the pavilion that is over the Ark of the Testimony, in front of the atonement dais that is over the Testimony, where I shall meet with you. 7And Aaron shall burn incense of fragrances on it. Morning by morning, when he attends to the lamps, he shall burn it, 8and when Aaron puts up the lamps between the two evenings he shall burn it: a continual incense in front of YHWH through your generations. 9You shall not offer unfitting incense or a burnt offering or a grain offering on it, and you shall not pour a libation on it. 10And Aaron shall make atonement on its horns once per year; he shall make atonement on it with the blood of the sin offering of atone-

וְהָיִ֥יתִי לָהֶ֖ם לֵאלֹהִֽים: 46וְיָדְע֗וּ כִּ֣י אֲנִ֤י יְהוָה֙ אֱלֹ֣הֵיהֶ֔ם אֲשֶׁ֨ר הוֹצֵ֧אתִי אֹתָ֛ם מֵאֶ֥רֶץ מִצְרַ֖יִם לְשָׁכְנִ֣י בְתוֹכָ֑ם אֲנִ֖י יְהוָ֥ה אֱלֹהֵיהֶֽם: פ

30 1וְעָשִׂ֥יתָ מִזְבֵּ֖חַ מִקְטַ֣ר קְטֹ֑רֶת עֲצֵ֥י שִׁטִּ֖ים תַּעֲשֶׂ֥ה אֹתֽוֹ: 2אַמָּ֨ה אָרְכּ֜וֹ וְאַמָּ֤ה רָחְבּוֹ֙ רָב֣וּעַ יִהְיֶ֔ה וְאַמָּתַ֖יִם קֹמָת֑וֹ מִמֶּ֖נּוּ קַרְנֹתָֽיו: 3וְצִפִּיתָ֨ אֹת֜וֹ זָהָ֣ב טָה֗וֹר אֶת־גַּגּ֧וֹ וְאֶת־קִירֹתָ֛יו סָבִ֖יב וְאֶת־קַרְנֹתָ֑יו וְעָשִׂ֥יתָ לּ֛וֹ זֵ֥ר זָהָ֖ב סָבִֽיב: 4וּשְׁתֵּי֩ טַבְּעֹ֨ת זָהָ֜ב תַּֽעֲשֶׂה־לּ֣וֹ ׀ מִתַּ֣חַת לְזֵר֗וֹ עַ֚ל שְׁתֵּ֣י צַלְעֹתָ֔יו תַּעֲשֶׂ֖ה עַל־שְׁנֵ֣י צִדָּ֑יו וְהָיָה֙ לְבָתִּ֣ים לְבַדִּ֔ים לָשֵׂ֥את אֹת֖וֹ בָּהֵֽמָּה: 5וְעָשִׂ֥יתָ אֶת־הַבַּדִּ֖ים עֲצֵ֣י שִׁטִּ֑ים וְצִפִּיתָ֥ אֹתָ֖ם זָהָֽב: 6וְנָתַתָּ֤ה אֹתוֹ֙ לִפְנֵ֣י הַפָּרֹ֔כֶת אֲשֶׁ֖ר עַל־אֲרֹ֣ן הָעֵדֻ֑ת לִפְנֵ֣י הַכַּפֹּ֗רֶת אֲשֶׁר֙ עַל־הָ֣עֵדֻ֔ת אֲשֶׁ֛ר אִוָּעֵ֥ד לְךָ֖ שָֽׁמָּה: 7וְהִקְטִ֥יר עָלָ֛יו אַהֲרֹ֖ן קְטֹ֣רֶת סַמִּ֑ים בַּבֹּ֣קֶר בַּבֹּ֗קֶר בְּהֵיטִיב֛וֹ אֶת־הַנֵּרֹ֖ת יַקְטִירֶֽנָּה: 8וּֽבְהַעֲלֹ֨ת אַהֲרֹ֧ן אֶת־הַנֵּרֹ֛ת בֵּ֥ין הָעַרְבַּ֖יִם יַקְטִירֶ֑נָּה קְטֹ֧רֶת תָּמִ֛יד לִפְנֵ֥י יְהוָ֖ה לְדֹרֹתֵיכֶֽם: 9לֹא־תַעֲל֥וּ עָלָ֛יו קְטֹ֥רֶת זָרָ֖ה וְעֹלָ֣ה וּמִנְחָ֑ה וְנֵ֕סֶךְ לֹ֥א תִסְּכ֖וּ עָלָֽיו: 10וְכִפֶּ֤ר אַהֲרֹן֙ עַל־קַרְנֹתָ֔יו אַחַ֖ת בַּשָּׁנָ֑ה מִדַּ֞ם

30:1. **an altar for burning incense**. The incense altar goes in the Holy, so why is it not treated with the ark, table, and menorah? Elsewhere it is in fact listed together with them (Exod 31:7–8; 35:11–15; 39:36–38). So why is it separated here by other matters for four chapters? The reason that it comes out of order here appears to be connected with the fact that it now follows the section concerning the inauguration of Aaron and his sons as priests. The burning of the incense is now listed first among their priestly functions. And they are commanded not to offer "unfitting incense." But that is exactly what Aaron's sons Nadab and Abihu will do in the frightful story of the events on the day of their inauguration (Lev 10:1). The order of the commands concerning the incense altar here sets the stage for those coming events. And it establishes the extreme importance of precise obedience to the ritual commandments, especially by those who are closest to the realm of the holy: the priests.

ment once per year through your generations. It is holy of holies to YHWH."

חַטַּאת הַכִּפֻּרִים אַחַת בַּשָּׁנָה יְכַפֵּר עָלָיו לְדֹרֹתֵיכֶם קֹדֶשׁ־קָדָשִׁים הוּא לַיהוָה: פ

WHEN YOU ADD

כִּי תִשָּׂא

11 וַיְדַבֵּר יְהוָה אֶל־מֹשֶׁה לֵּאמֹר: 12 כִּי תִשָּׂא אֶת־רֹאשׁ בְּנֵי־יִשְׂרָאֵל לִפְקֻדֵיהֶם וְנָתְנוּ אִישׁ כֹּפֶר נַפְשׁוֹ לַיהוָה בִּפְקֹד אֹתָם וְלֹא־יִהְיֶה בָהֶם נֶגֶף בִּפְקֹד אֹתָם: 13 זֶה ׀ יִתְּנוּ כָּל־הָעֹבֵר עַל־הַפְּקֻדִים מַחֲצִית הַשֶּׁקֶל בְּשֶׁקֶל הַקֹּדֶשׁ עֶשְׂרִים גֵּרָה הַשֶּׁקֶל מַחֲצִית הַשֶּׁקֶל תְּרוּמָה לַיהוָה: 14 כֹּל הָעֹבֵר עַל־הַפְּקֻדִים מִבֶּן עֶשְׂרִים שָׁנָה וָמָעְלָה יִתֵּן תְּרוּמַת יְהוָה: 15 הֶעָשִׁיר לֹא־יַרְבֶּה וְהַדַּל לֹא יַמְעִיט מִמַּחֲצִית הַשָּׁקֶל לָתֵת אֶת־תְּרוּמַת יְהוָה לְכַפֵּר עַל־נַפְשֹׁתֵיכֶם: 16 וְלָקַחְתָּ אֶת־כֶּסֶף הַכִּפֻּרִים מֵאֵת בְּנֵי יִשְׂרָאֵל וְנָתַתָּ אֹתוֹ עַל־עֲבֹדַת אֹהֶל מוֹעֵד וְהָיָה לִבְנֵי יִשְׂרָאֵל לְזִכָּרוֹן לִפְנֵי יְהוָה לְכַפֵּר עַל־נַפְשֹׁתֵיכֶם: פ

17 וַיְדַבֵּר יְהוָה אֶל־מֹשֶׁה לֵּאמֹר: 18 וְעָשִׂיתָ כִּיּוֹר נְחֹשֶׁת וְכַנּוֹ נְחֹשֶׁת לְרָחְצָה וְנָתַתָּ אֹתוֹ בֵּין־אֹהֶל מוֹעֵד וּבֵין הַמִּזְבֵּחַ וְנָתַתָּ שָׁמָּה מָיִם: 19 וְרָחֲצוּ אַהֲרֹן וּבָנָיו מִמֶּנּוּ אֶת־יְדֵיהֶם וְאֶת־רַגְלֵיהֶם: 20 בְּבֹאָם אֶל־אֹהֶל מוֹעֵד יִרְחֲצוּ־מַיִם וְלֹא יָמֻתוּ אוֹ בְגִשְׁתָּם אֶל־הַמִּזְבֵּחַ לְשָׁרֵת לְהַקְטִיר אִשֶּׁה לַיהוָה:

11And YHWH spoke to Moses, saying, 12"When you add up the heads of the children of Israel by their counts, each of them shall give a ransom for his life to YHWH when counting them, so there will not be a plague among them when counting them. 13Everyone who passes through the counts shall give this: half of a shekel, by the shekel of the Holy (the shekel is twenty gerah); half of a shekel as a donation to YHWH. 14Everyone who passes through the counts, from twenty years old and up, shall give YHWH's donation. 15The rich one shall not multiply, and the poor one shall not diminish from the half of a shekel, to give YHWH's donation, to make atonement for your lives. 16And you shall take the atonement money from the children of Israel and give it for the service of the Tent of Meeting, and it shall become a commemorative for the children of Israel in front of YHWH, to make atonement for your lives."

17And YHWH spoke to Moses, saying, 18"And you shall make a basin of bronze and its stand of bronze for washing, and you shall put it between the Tent of Meeting and the altar and put water there. 19And Aaron and his sons will wash their hands and their feet from it. 20When they come to the Tent of Meeting they shall wash with water, and they will not die—or when they come near to the altar to minister, to burn an offering by fire to YHWH to smoke. 21And they shall

---

30:12. **add up the heads**. Meaning: when you take a census.

30:12. **so there will not be a plague among them when counting them**. Why would there be a plague when the Israelites are being counted? In biblical Israel a census is regarded as a negative thing. It gives a central leader control: for conscription, corvée (forced labor), and taxation. When King David takes a census, the result is a plague (2 Samuel 24). And so here a ransom must be taken for everyone counted in the census so there will not be a plague.

wash their hands and their feet, and they will not die. And it will be an eternal law for them—for him and for his seed through their generations."

22And YHWH spoke to Moses, saying, 23"And you, take spices, choice: flowing myrrh, five hundred; and aromatic cinnamon, half as much, two hundred fifty; and aromatic reed, two hundred fifty; 24and cassia, five hundred—by the shekel of the Holy—and olive oil, a hin. 25And you shall make it oil of holy anointing, an ointment mixture, the work of an ointment-maker. It shall be oil of holy anointing. 26And you shall anoint the Tent of Meeting and the Ark of the Testimony with it, 27and the table and all its equipment and the menorah and its equipment and the incense altar 28and the altar of burnt offering and all its equipment and the basin and its stand. 29And you shall make them holy, and they shall be holy of holies. Anyone who touches them will be holy. 30And you shall anoint Aaron and his sons and make them holy to function as priests for me. 31And you shall speak to the children of Israel, saying, 'This shall be oil of holy anointing for me through your generations. 32It shall not be poured on human flesh, and you shall not make anything else like it in its quantities. It is a holy thing. It shall be a holy thing to you. 33Anyone who will make a compound like it and who will give some of it to an outsider: he will be cut off from his people.'"

34And YHWH said to Moses, "Take fragrances—stacte and onycha and galbanum—fragrances and clear frankincense; it shall be part for part. 35And you shall make it ointment incense, the work of an ointment-maker: salted,

---

30:29. **Anyone who touches them will be holy**. As in 29:37 above, the quality of being holy can spread. Coming into contact with something that is in a state of holiness renders one holy as well.

30:33. **cut off from his people**. The meaning of this phrase is not known for certain. See the comment on Gen 17:14.

30:34. **part for part**. Meaning: there are to be equal portions of each of the ingredients in the compound.

pure, holy. ³⁶And you shall pound some of it, making it thin, and put some of it in front of the Testimony in the Tent of Meeting where I shall meet with you. It shall be holy of holies to you. ³⁷And the incense that you will make: you shall not make for yourselves in its quantities. It shall be a holy thing to you for YHWH. ³⁸Anyone who will make anything like it to make a fragrance with it will be cut off from his people."

31 ¹And YHWH spoke to Moses, saying, ²"See, I've called by name Bezalel, son of Uri, son of Hur, of the tribe of Judah. ³And I've filled him with the spirit of God in wisdom and in understanding and in knowledge and in every kind of work, ⁴to form conceptions to make in gold and in silver and in bronze ⁵and in cutting stone for setting and in cutting wood—for making things in every kind of work. ⁶And I: here, I've put Oholiab, son of Ahisamach, of the tribe of Dan, with him. And in the heart of every wise-hearted person I've put wisdom. And they'll make everything that I've commanded you: ⁷the Tent of Meeting and the Ark of the Testimony

³⁶וְשָׁחַקְתָּ מִמֶּנָּה הָדֵק וְנָתַתָּה מִמֶּנָּה לִפְנֵי הָעֵדֻת בְּאֹהֶל מוֹעֵד אֲשֶׁר אִוָּעֵד לְךָ שָׁמָּה קֹדֶשׁ קָדָשִׁים תִּהְיֶה לָכֶם: ³⁷וְהַקְּטֹרֶת אֲשֶׁר תַּעֲשֶׂה בְּמַתְכֻּנְתָּהּ לֹא תַעֲשׂוּ לָכֶם קֹדֶשׁ תִּהְיֶה לְךָ לַיהֹוָה: ³⁸אִישׁ אֲשֶׁר־יַעֲשֶׂה כָמוֹהָ לְהָרִיחַ בָּהּ וְנִכְרַת מֵעַמָּיו: ס

31 ¹וַיְדַבֵּר יְהֹוָה אֶל־מֹשֶׁה לֵּאמֹר: ²רְאֵה קָרָאתִי בְשֵׁם בְּצַלְאֵל בֶּן־אוּרִי בֶן־חוּר לְמַטֵּה יְהוּדָה: ³וָאֲמַלֵּא אֹתוֹ רוּחַ אֱלֹהִים בְּחָכְמָה וּבִתְבוּנָה וּבְדַעַת וּבְכָל־מְלָאכָה: ⁴לַחְשֹׁב מַחֲשָׁבֹת לַעֲשׂוֹת בַּזָּהָב וּבַכֶּסֶף וּבַנְּחֹשֶׁת: ⁵וּבַחֲרֹשֶׁת אֶבֶן לְמַלֹּאת וּבַחֲרֹשֶׁת עֵץ לַעֲשׂוֹת בְּכָל־מְלָאכָה: ⁶וַאֲנִי הִנֵּה נָתַתִּי אִתּוֹ אֵת אָהֳלִיאָב בֶּן־אֲחִיסָמָךְ לְמַטֵּה־דָן וּבְלֵב כָּל־חֲכַם־לֵב נָתַתִּי חָכְמָה וְעָשׂוּ אֵת כָּל־אֲשֶׁר צִוִּיתִךָ: ⁷אֵת | אֹהֶל מוֹעֵד וְאֶת־הָאָרֹן לָעֵדֻת

30:37. **you shall not make for yourselves in its quantities**. One cannot make ordinary incense to burn in one's home out of the same substances and same proportions as the Tabernacle incense.

31:1. **Bezalel**. Bezalel is the first artist, and he is summoned by name. The irony is that immediately after this a work of art, the golden calf, is made! The special importance of the artist and his or her relationship to the work of art is conveyed as Aaron makes the calf (32:4) but then, when he has to explain it to Moses, speaks as if it somehow came to exist by itself: "I threw it into the fire, and this calf came out!"

Some have taken the name Bezalel to mean "in the shadow of God" (*běṣēl ʾēl*). To me it also intimates "in the image of God" (*běṣelem ʾělōhîm*) from the creation story (Gen 1:27). (On the absence of the letter *mem*, compare the name Noah being related to the root *nḥm*, and the name Samuel being related to the root *š'l*. See the comment on Gen 5:29.) And Bezalel is filled with the "spirit of God," which also comes from the creation story (1:2). The allusions to creation are attractive because Bezalel, after all, as the great artist of the Torah, is the creative one, who fashions the Tabernacle and its contents, including the ark. Being creative is the ultimate *imitatio Dei*. And the conclusion of the account of the construction of the Tabernacle uses some of the same language as the conclusion of the creation account. (See the comment on Exod 39:32.)

and the atonement dais that is on it and all the equipment of the tent [8]and the table and its equipment and the pure menorah and all its equipment and the incense altar [9]and the burnt offering altar and all its equipment and the basin and its stand [10]and the fabric clothes and the holy clothes for Aaron, the priest, and his sons' clothes for functioning as priests [11]and the anointing oil and the incense of fragrances for the Holy. According to everything that I've commanded you, they shall do."

[12]And YHWH said to Moses, saying, [13]"And you, speak to the children of Israel, saying, 'Just: you shall observe my Sabbaths, because it is a sign between me and you through your generations: to know that I, YHWH, make you holy. [14]And you shall observe the Sabbath, because it is a holy thing to you. One who desecrates it shall be *put to death*. Because anyone who does work in it: that person will be cut off from

וְאֶת־הַכַּפֹּ֫רֶת אֲשֶׁ֣ר עָלָ֔יו וְאֵ֖ת כָּל־כְּלֵ֥י הָאֹֽהֶל׃
[8]וְאֶת־הַשֻּׁלְחָן֙ וְאֶת־כֵּלָ֔יו וְאֶת־הַמְּנֹרָ֥ה הַטְּהֹרָ֖ה וְאֶת־כָּל־כֵּלֶ֑יהָ וְאֵ֖ת מִזְבַּ֥ח הַקְּטֹֽרֶת׃ [9]וְאֶת־מִזְבַּ֥ח הָעֹלָ֖ה וְאֶת־כָּל־כֵּלָ֑יו וְאֶת־הַכִּיּ֖וֹר וְאֶת־כַּנּֽוֹ׃ [10]וְאֵ֖ת בִּגְדֵ֣י הַשְּׂרָ֑ד וְאֶת־בִּגְדֵ֤י הַקֹּ֙דֶשׁ֙ לְאַהֲרֹ֣ן הַכֹּהֵ֔ן וְאֶת־בִּגְדֵ֥י בָנָ֖יו לְכַהֵֽן׃ [11]וְאֵ֨ת שֶׁ֤מֶן הַמִּשְׁחָה֙ וְאֶת־קְטֹ֣רֶת הַסַּמִּ֖ים לַקֹּ֑דֶשׁ כְּכֹ֥ל אֲשֶׁר־צִוִּיתִ֖ךָ יַעֲשֽׂוּ׃ פ

[12]וַיֹּ֥אמֶר יְהוָ֖ה אֶל־מֹשֶׁ֥ה לֵּאמֹֽר׃ [13]וְאַתָּ֞ה דַּבֵּ֨ר אֶל־בְּנֵ֤י יִשְׂרָאֵל֙ לֵאמֹ֔ר אַ֥ךְ אֶת־שַׁבְּתֹתַ֖י תִּשְׁמֹ֑רוּ כִּ֣י א֗וֹת הִ֞וא בֵּינִ֤י וּבֵֽינֵיכֶם֙ לְדֹרֹ֣תֵיכֶ֔ם לָדַ֕עַת כִּ֛י אֲנִ֥י יְהוָ֖ה מְקַדִּשְׁכֶֽם׃ [14]וּשְׁמַרְתֶּם֙ אֶת־הַשַּׁבָּ֔ת כִּ֛י קֹ֥דֶשׁ הִ֖וא לָכֶ֑ם מְחַֽלְלֶ֙יהָ֙ מ֣וֹת יוּמָ֔ת כִּ֗י כָּל־הָעֹשֶׂ֥ה בָהּ֙ מְלָאכָ֔ה וְנִכְרְתָ֛ה הַנֶּ֥פֶשׁ הַהִ֖וא מִקֶּ֥רֶב עַמֶּֽיהָ׃

31:13. Just. The force of this word here seems to be to say that the section preceding this tells what the skilled craftsmen will do, and what God will do, to produce the holy place and all the holy objects; and now it will be specified what the people must do to become holy themselves. Why just the Sabbath out of all the commandments? Because "it is a sign between me and you." As the sign of the Noahic covenant is the rainbow and the sign of the Abrahamic covenant is circumcision, so the sign of the Israelite covenant is the Sabbath. *A sign participates in the thing that it symbolizes.* (Thus, at first a flag is just a country's symbol, but later people will say, "I'd die for the flag!") And so its fulfillment is of exceptional importance. The rainbow sign is provided by God, and so it is certain. The signs of the other two covenants must be performed by humans, and so they are commanded with extreme emphasis and strictness. Both declare that failure to perform the sign will result in "cutting off" (Gen 17:14; Exod 31:14).

31:14,15. *put to death.* The extreme punishment of execution for violation of the Sabbath must be understood in the context of the singular importance of the Sabbath: as sign of the covenant and as *imitatio Dei*—see the previous comment. Also, as I discussed in my comments on Genesis 1, the special place of the Sabbath in the creation of the universe marks it as having cosmic significance as well as historical significance. Combining the cosmic with history, it sets the history of human events that begins with Genesis 1 in the context of the very nature of the universe. And it makes time holy. Thus this long list of holy *objects* concludes with this reminder that periods of *time* are holy as well. The Sabbath is thus so phenomenally important that a violation of the Sabbath bears an extraordinary punishment.

among his people. 15Six days work shall be done, and in the seventh day is a Sabbath, a ceasing, a holy thing to YHWH. Anyone who does work in the Sabbath day shall be *put to death.* 16And the children of Israel shall observe the Sabbath, to make the Sabbath through their generations, an eternal covenant. 17Between me and the children of Israel it is a sign forever, because for six days YHWH made the skies and the earth, and in the seventh day He ceased and was *refreshed.'"*

18And when He finished speaking with him in Mount Sinai, He gave the two tablets of the Testimony to Moses, tablets of stone, written by the finger of God.

32 1And the people saw that Moses was delaying to come down from the mountain, and the people assembled at Aaron and said to him, "Get up. Make gods for us who will go in front of us, because this Moses, the man who brought us up from the land of Egypt: we don't know what has become of him!"

2And Aaron said to them, "Take off the gold

15שֵׁשֶׁת יָמִים יֵעָשֶׂה מְלָאכָה וּבַיּוֹם הַשְּׁבִיעִי שַׁבַּת שַׁבָּתוֹן קֹדֶשׁ לַיהוָה כָּל־הָעֹשֶׂה מְלָאכָה בְּיוֹם הַשַּׁבָּת מוֹת יוּמָת: 16וְשָׁמְרוּ בְנֵי־יִשְׂרָאֵל אֶת־הַשַּׁבָּת לַעֲשׂוֹת אֶת־הַשַּׁבָּת לְדֹרֹתָם בְּרִית עוֹלָם: 17בֵּינִי וּבֵין בְּנֵי יִשְׂרָאֵל אוֹת הִוא לְעֹלָם כִּי־שֵׁשֶׁת יָמִים עָשָׂה יְהוָה אֶת־הַשָּׁמַיִם וְאֶת־הָאָרֶץ וּבַיּוֹם הַשְּׁבִיעִי שָׁבַת וַיִּנָּפַשׁ: ס

18וַיִּתֵּן אֶל־מֹשֶׁה כְּכַלֹּתוֹ לְדַבֵּר אִתּוֹ בְּהַר סִינַי שְׁנֵי לֻחֹת הָעֵדֻת לֻחֹת אֶבֶן כְּתֻבִים בְּאֶצְבַּע אֱלֹהִים:

32 1וַיַּרְא הָעָם כִּי־בֹשֵׁשׁ מֹשֶׁה לָרֶדֶת מִן־הָהָר וַיִּקָּהֵל הָעָם עַל־אַהֲרֹן וַיֹּאמְרוּ אֵלָיו קוּם ׀ עֲשֵׂה־לָנוּ אֱלֹהִים אֲשֶׁר יֵלְכוּ לְפָנֵינוּ כִּי־זֶה ׀ מֹשֶׁה הָאִישׁ אֲשֶׁר הֶעֱלָנוּ מֵאֶרֶץ מִצְרַיִם לֹא יָדַעְנוּ מֶה־הָיָה לוֹ: 2וַיֹּאמֶר אֲלֵהֶם אַהֲרֹן פָּרְקוּ נִזְמֵי הַזָּהָב אֲשֶׁר

31:17. **refreshed.** This verb occurs only twice in the Torah: here, referring to God's Sabbath rest; and in Exod 23:12, where it refers to the Sabbath rest of "your maid's son and the alien." It is remarkable that the parallel cases are the son of a slave and an alien. And this comes in the middle of one of the most blatant cases of *imitatio Dei* in the Torah: humans are to cease on the Sabbath because God ceased creating on the Sabbath. This now conveys that every human participates in this divine phenomenon. One cannot rest but still require his or her slave to work. One cannot rest but still count on non-Israelites in the community to do the work.

31:18. **two tablets of the Testimony.** There are two tablets of testimony/witness, and there must always be at least two witnesses to give testimony in law. And Moses names two witnesses, heaven and earth, concerning the people's future at the end of the Torah (Deut 31:28; 32:1).

32:1. **this Moses, the man who brought us up from the land of Egypt.** They talk about Moses as if it is necessary to identify who he is. That is, they minimize him and push him into the past tense, to make the case to Aaron that he should act.

32:1. **the man who brought us up from the land of Egypt.** Less than forty days earlier they heard the divine voice itself say that *God* brought them out of Egypt, but, like the wine steward and Joseph's Pharaoh, they still focus on the human rather than on the deity.

rings that are in your wives', your sons', and your daughters' ears, and bring them to me." ³And all the people took off the gold rings that were in their ears and brought them to Aaron. ⁴And he took them from their hand and fashioned it with a stylus and made it a molten calf.

And they said, "These are your gods, Israel, who brought you up from the land of Egypt!"

⁵And Aaron saw, and he built an altar in front of it, and Aaron called, and he said, "A festival to YHWH tomorrow!" ⁶And they got up early the next day, and they made burnt offerings and brought over peace offerings, and the people sat

בְּאָזְנֵי נְשֵׁיכֶם בְּנֵיכֶם וּבְנֹתֵיכֶם וְהָבִיאוּ אֵלָי: ³וַיִּתְפָּרְקוּ כָּל־הָעָם אֶת־נִזְמֵי הַזָּהָב אֲשֶׁר בְּאָזְנֵיהֶם וַיָּבִיאוּ אֶל־אַהֲרֹן: ⁴וַיִּקַּח מִיָּדָם וַיָּצַר אֹתוֹ בַּחֶרֶט וַיַּעֲשֵׂהוּ עֵגֶל מַסֵּכָה וַיֹּאמְרוּ אֵלֶּה אֱלֹהֶיךָ יִשְׂרָאֵל אֲשֶׁר הֶעֱלוּךָ מֵאֶרֶץ מִצְרָיִם: ⁵וַיַּרְא אַהֲרֹן וַיִּבֶן מִזְבֵּחַ לְפָנָיו וַיִּקְרָא אַהֲרֹן וַיֹּאמַר חַג לַיהוָה מָחָר: ⁶וַיַּשְׁכִּימוּ מִמָּחֳרָת וַיַּעֲלוּ עֹלֹת וַיַּגִּשׁוּ שְׁלָמִים וַיֵּשֶׁב

32:4. calf. "Calf" is a bit misleading. It is a young bull. I retained the word "calf" in the translation because the episode is now famous as the "golden calf" story.

32:4–5. These are your gods. . . . And Aaron saw . . . A festival to YHWH tomorrow. So many questions: Why do they use the plural, "These are your gods," when there is only one calf? What did Aaron see? Why does he proclaim a festival to *YHWH* in the middle of a pagan heresy? I gave the critical explanation of these problems elsewhere (see *Who Wrote the Bible?*). Here I want to give a *pĕšaṭ* explanation of them as they appear in the text. The plural "gods" does not appear to refer to the calf. In the pagan religions of the ancient Near East, people did not worship animals, and they did not worship idols. They worshiped gods who were represented or honored by statues. The gods were sometimes pictured as enthroned on a platform, and the platform was commonly composed of figures of cherubs or of young bulls. Since there is only one young bull here, together with plural "gods," we must understand the people to be perceiving the bull as a throne platform for gods whom they will worship. Note that the calf itself is not referred to as an idol.

What Aaron sees is this behavior on the people's part. The text does not reveal what Aaron has in mind when he makes the golden calf: does he mean it as a throne platform for such pagan deities, or as a throne platform for YHWH?! All we know is that, after he sees the people associating it with gods and claiming that these gods brought them out of Egypt, he declares that the worship that is to take place is "A festival to *YHWH*!" (Indeed, the word for "And Aaron *saw*" is Hebrew וירא. In the original Hebrew text, before the vowels were added, it can also have meant "And Aaron *was afraid*"! That would make it even clearer why he would redirect the worship back to YHWH.) Aaron is not completely innocent in the matter of the golden calf, as we can see from the defense he offers to Moses afterward (32:24); but it may be that he is to be credited as a person who recognizes that he has made a dangerous mistake and tries to turn it to something good. In recognizing his own error, and in trying to steer a people who have gone wrong onto a different course, Aaron becomes an extraordinarily valuable model—and the story teaches an extraordinarily valuable lesson.

down to eat and drink, and they got up to fool around.

⁷And YHWH spoke to Moses: "Go. Go down. Because your people, whom you brought up from the land of Egypt, has corrupted. ⁸They've turned quickly from the way that I commanded them. They've made themselves a molten calf, and they've bowed to it and sacrificed to it and said, 'These are your gods, Israel, who brought you up from the land of Egypt!'" ⁹And YHWH said to Moses, "I've seen this people; and, here, it's a hard-necked people. ¹⁰And now, leave off from me, and my anger will flare at them, and I'll finish them, and I'll make you into a big nation!"

הָעָם֙ לֶאֱכֹ֣ל וְשָׁת֔וֹ וַיָּקֻ֖מוּ לְצַחֵֽק: פ ⁷וַיְדַבֵּ֥ר יְהוָ֖ה אֶל־מֹשֶׁ֑ה לֶךְ־רֵ֕ד כִּ֚י שִׁחֵ֣ת עַמְּךָ֔ אֲשֶׁ֥ר הֶעֱלֵ֖יתָ מֵאֶ֥רֶץ מִצְרָֽיִם: ⁸סָ֣רוּ מַהֵ֗ר מִן־הַדֶּ֙רֶךְ֙ אֲשֶׁ֣ר צִוִּיתִ֔ם עָשׂ֣וּ לָהֶ֔ם עֵ֖גֶל מַסֵּכָ֑ה וַיִּשְׁתַּֽחֲווּ־לוֹ֙ וַיִּזְבְּחוּ־ל֔וֹ וַיֹּ֣אמְר֔וּ אֵ֤לֶּה אֱלֹהֶ֙יךָ֙ יִשְׂרָאֵ֔ל אֲשֶׁ֥ר הֶעֱל֖וּךָ מֵאֶ֥רֶץ מִצְרָֽיִם: ⁹וַיֹּ֥אמֶר יְהוָ֖ה אֶל־מֹשֶׁ֑ה רָאִ֙יתִי֙ אֶת־הָעָ֣ם הַזֶּ֔ה וְהִנֵּ֥ה עַם־קְשֵׁה־עֹ֖רֶף הֽוּא: ¹⁰וְעַתָּה֙ הַנִּ֣יחָה לִּ֔י וְיִֽחַר־אַפִּ֥י בָהֶ֖ם וַאֲכַלֵּ֑ם וְאֶֽעֱשֶׂ֥ה אוֹתְךָ֖ לְג֥וֹי גָּדֽוֹל:

32:6. **fool around.** Some of the occurrences of this word involve sex (Gen 26:8; 39:14,17), and some do not (Gen 19:14; 21:9; Judg 16:25). It is not justified, therefore, to assume that sexual play is implied here.

32:7. *your* **people, whom** *you* **brought up from the land of Egypt.** The issue of who brought the people out, which came up in v. 1, now has an extraordinary twist. Like a parent who says to one's spouse about a naughty child, "Guess what *your* child did today!"—so God now says to Moses, "*Your* people, whom *you* brought up from the land of Egypt, has corrupted!" But look at Moses' words in response. He seeks to appeal to God's compassion and feelings for the people, and so he turns the pronoun around, saying, "Why should your anger flare at *your* people, whom *you* brought out from the land of Egypt? . . . Relent about the bad to *your* people." And the text conveys that Moses' case is successful, because it concludes: "YHWH relented about the bad that He had spoken, to do to *His* people"!

32:8. **They've turned quickly.** How could they have committed the golden calf sin so soon after the revelation—within forty days after actually hearing God speak from the sky? It is when God is *closest* that humans commit the greatest sin. Similarly in the story of Eden, where God walks among humans, they violate a direct command. Similarly through the wilderness period to come, in which the people see miracles *daily* (manna, column of cloud and fire), they are repeatedly rebellious. It appears that close proximity to divinity—to an all-seeing, all-knowing divine parent who is always watching, commanding, and judging—is barely tolerable for human beings. Like adolescents who love and need their parents but who long for independence, humankind is pictured as longing to be out of the divine shadow. Note that at the end of the *Tanak*, in the books of Ezra, Nehemiah, and Esther, there are no miracles, angels, or appearances of God. The words "And God spoke to" never occur. And in these books, where God is the *least* visible, humans are pictured as relatively good, listening to their leaders, changing their ways when criticized, and observing the commandments.

11And Moses conciliated in front of YHWH, his God, and said, "Why, YHWH, should your anger flare at your people whom you brought out from the land of Egypt with big power and with a strong hand? 12Why should Egypt say, saying, 'He brought them out for bad, to kill them in the mountains, and to finish them from on the face of the earth'? Turn back from your flaring anger, and relent about the bad to your people. 13Remember Abraham, Isaac, and Israel, your servants, that you swore to them by yourself, and you spoke to them: 'I'll multiply your seed like the stars of the skies, and I'll give to your seed all this land that I've said, and they'll possess it forever.'" 14And YHWH relented about the bad that He had spoken, to do to His people.

15And Moses turned and went down from the mountain. And the two tablets of witness were in his hand, tablets written from their two sides: from this side and from this side they were written. 16And the tablets: they were God's doing. And the writing: it was God's writing, inscribed on the tablets.

17And Joshua heard the sound of the people in its shouting, and he said to Moses, "A sound of war is in the camp."

11וַיְחַל מֹשֶׁה אֶת־פְּנֵי יְהוָה אֱלֹהָיו וַיֹּאמֶר לָמָה יְהוָה יֶחֱרֶה אַפְּךָ בְּעַמֶּךָ אֲשֶׁר הוֹצֵאתָ מֵאֶרֶץ מִצְרַיִם בְּכֹחַ גָּדוֹל וּבְיָד חֲזָקָה: 12לָמָּה יֹאמְרוּ מִצְרַיִם לֵאמֹר בְּרָעָה הוֹצִיאָם לַהֲרֹג אֹתָם בֶּהָרִים וּלְכַלֹּתָם מֵעַל פְּנֵי הָאֲדָמָה שׁוּב מֵחֲרוֹן אַפֶּךָ וְהִנָּחֵם עַל־הָרָעָה לְעַמֶּךָ: 13זְכֹר לְאַבְרָהָם לְיִצְחָק וּלְיִשְׂרָאֵל עֲבָדֶיךָ אֲשֶׁר נִשְׁבַּעְתָּ לָהֶם בָּךְ וַתְּדַבֵּר אֲלֵהֶם אַרְבֶּה אֶת־זַרְעֲכֶם כְּכוֹכְבֵי הַשָּׁמָיִם וְכָל־הָאָרֶץ הַזֹּאת אֲשֶׁר אָמַרְתִּי אֶתֵּן לְזַרְעֲכֶם וְנָחֲלוּ לְעֹלָם: 14וַיִּנָּחֶם יְהוָה עַל־הָרָעָה אֲשֶׁר דִּבֶּר לַעֲשׂוֹת לְעַמּוֹ: פ

15וַיִּפֶן וַיֵּרֶד מֹשֶׁה מִן־הָהָר וּשְׁנֵי לֻחֹת הָעֵדֻת בְּיָדוֹ לֻחֹת כְּתֻבִים מִשְּׁנֵי עֶבְרֵיהֶם מִזֶּה וּמִזֶּה הֵם כְּתֻבִים: 16וְהַלֻּחֹת מַעֲשֵׂה אֱלֹהִים הֵמָּה וְהַמִּכְתָּב מִכְתַּב אֱלֹהִים הוּא חָרוּת עַל־הַלֻּחֹת: 17וַיִּשְׁמַע יְהוֹשֻׁעַ אֶת־קוֹל הָעָם בְּרֵעֹה וַיֹּאמֶר אֶל־מֹשֶׁה קוֹל

32:15. **tablets of witness.** It is a crucial concept here and in Deuteronomy (and Kings) that there is written witness/testimony confirming what God has said, so subsequent generations can never say, "We didn't know." Even though the people have actually heard it from the voice of God, the Sinai covenant is a legal procedure and requires a formal, written document. The Noahic and Abrahamic covenants are sealed with a divine oath; and, since God's violating His own promise is unthinkable, no document is required. But the Sinai covenant is sealed by the *people's* promise that "We'll do it, and we'll listen"; and human commitments require written witness. That is why there are tablets, and that is why they are called the tablets of witness.

32:15. **written from their two sides.** Does this mean: written on both tablets? or written on both the front and the back of each tablet? The former seems too obvious to require this mention: of course it is written on both tablets; otherwise, why have two tablets? So the point here is precisely that they are written on both sides of each tablet. For pictorial purposes (in art and film), it is preferable to put the commandments all on the same side of each tablet, but the text suggests otherwise. And we know of numerous ancient royal inscriptions and statues that were written on both sides, front and back.

282

18And he said, "It's not a sound of singing of victory, and it's not a sound of singing of defeat. It's just the sound of singing I hear!"

19And it was when he came close to the camp, and he saw the calf and dancing: and Moses' anger flared, and he threw the tablets from his hands and shattered them below the mountain. 20And he took the calf that they had made, and he burned it in fire and ground it until it was thin, and he scattered it on the face of the water, and he made the children of Israel drink!

21And Moses said to Aaron, "What did this people do to you, that you've brought a big sin on it?!"

מִלְחָמָ֖ה בַּֽמַּחֲנֶֽה׃ 18וַיֹּ֗אמֶר אֵ֥ין קוֹל֙ עֲנ֣וֹת גְּבוּרָ֔ה
וְאֵ֥ין ק֖וֹל עֲנ֣וֹת חֲלוּשָׁ֑ה
ק֣וֹל עַנּ֔וֹת אָנֹכִ֖י שֹׁמֵֽעַ׃
19וַֽיְהִ֗י כַּאֲשֶׁ֤ר קָרַב֙ אֶל־הַֽמַּחֲנֶ֔ה וַיַּ֥רְא אֶת־
הָעֵ֖גֶל וּמְחֹלֹ֑ת וַיִּֽחַר־אַ֣ף מֹשֶׁ֗ה וַיַּשְׁלֵ֤ךְ מִיָּדָו֙ אֶת־
הַלֻּחֹ֔ת וַיְשַׁבֵּ֥ר אֹתָ֖ם תַּ֥חַת הָהָֽר׃ 20וַיִּקַּ֞ח אֶת־הָעֵ֣גֶל
אֲשֶׁ֣ר עָשׂ֗וּ וַיִּשְׂרֹ֤ף בָּאֵשׁ֙ וַיִּטְחַ֣ן עַ֣ד אֲשֶׁר־דָּ֔ק וַיִּ֙זֶר֙
עַל־פְּנֵ֣י הַמַּ֔יִם וַיַּ֖שְׁקְ אֶת־בְּנֵ֥י יִשְׂרָאֵֽל׃ 21וַיֹּ֤אמֶר
מֹשֶׁה֙ אֶֽל־אַהֲרֹ֔ן מֶֽה־עָשָׂ֥ה לְךָ֖ הָעָ֣ם הַזֶּ֑ה כִּֽי־הֵבֵ֥אתָ

32:19 ק֣ מִיָּדָֽיו

32:19. **Moses' anger flared**. God had said, "My anger will flare at them," but Moses dissuaded God, saying, "Why should your anger flare at your people?" But when Moses himself returns to the people and sees the bull, the text reports that "his anger flared," the very words for what he persuaded God not to do! He smashes the tablets that he was bringing back to the people, and he calls for a bloody purge of thousands among the people. Quintessentially among prophets, Moses comes to God as a human, pleading the human case; and he comes to the people as a confidant of God, feeling the divine disappointment and anger with humans (albeit apparently still lacking the divine restraint and capacity to relent). It is the curse of the prophet: to God he represents humans, and to humans he represents God.

32:20. **thin**. In Deut 9:21, Moses elaborates that this means "thin as dust." Many English translations say "ground it to powder."

32:20. **he scattered it on the face of the water**. What water? It is natural to find streams at the bases of mountains, but in fact the last water mentioned is the water that came out of the crag of Horeb/Sinai. That would add irony: that the water that ended one rebellion now carries off the product of the next rebellion. And, as the people now see the dust of the golden calf on the water, they may be reminded that this water came to them from God and through Moses, whom they have been quick to forget.

32:20. **he made the children of Israel drink**. Classical and recent commentators have compared this to the law of a woman suspected of adultery (*sōṭāh*), who must drink a mixture of dust and water (Num 5:11–31). Indeed, both cases use the unusual word *prʿ* (see comment on 32:25 below). And the issue in both is betrayal. The prophets, most notably Hosea, compare the people's turning to other gods with adultery. Still, I urge great caution in interpreting the connection. The people in Exodus are guilty! The *sōṭāh* case is a process designed to *determine* whether someone is guilty or innocent. And the dust there comes from the Tabernacle, which is something positive, while the dust of the calf here is the opposite. The similarities between the two matters may reflect only very general common concerns.

22And Aaron said, "Let my lord's anger not flare. You know the people, that it's in a bad state. 23And they said to me, 'Make gods for us who will go in front of us, because this Moses, the man who brought us up from the land of Egypt: we don't know what has become of him!' 24And I said to them, 'Whoever has gold: take it off.' And they gave it to me, and I threw it into the fire, and this calf came out!"

25And Moses saw the people, that it was turned loose, because Aaron had turned it loose—to denigration among their adversaries! 26And Moses stood in the gate of the camp and said, "Whoever is for YHWH: to me!" And all the children of Levi were gathered to him. 27And he said to them, "YHWH, God of Israel, said this: 'Set, each man, his sword on his thigh; cross over and come back from gate to gate in the camp; and kill, each man, his brother and, each man, his neighbor and, each man, his relative.'" 28And

22וַיֹּאמֶר אַהֲרֹן אַל־יִחַר אַף אֲדֹנִי עָלָיו חָטָאָה גְדֹלָה: אַתָּה יָדַעְתָּ אֶת־הָעָם כִּי בְרָע הוּא: 23וַיֹּאמְרוּ לִי עֲשֵׂה־לָנוּ אֱלֹהִים אֲשֶׁר יֵלְכוּ לְפָנֵינוּ כִּי־זֶה ׀ מֹשֶׁה הָאִישׁ אֲשֶׁר הֶעֱלָנוּ מֵאֶרֶץ מִצְרַיִם לֹא יָדַעְנוּ מֶה־הָיָה לוֹ: 24וָאֹמַר לָהֶם לְמִי זָהָב הִתְפָּרָקוּ וַיִּתְּנוּ־לִי וָאַשְׁלִכֵהוּ בָאֵשׁ וַיֵּצֵא הָעֵגֶל הַזֶּה: 25וַיַּרְא מֹשֶׁה אֶת־הָעָם כִּי פָרֻעַ הוּא כִּי־פְרָעֹה אַהֲרֹן לְשִׁמְצָה בְּקָמֵיהֶם: 26וַיַּעֲמֹד מֹשֶׁה בְּשַׁעַר הַמַּחֲנֶה וַיֹּאמֶר מִי לַיהוָה אֵלָי וַיֵּאָסְפוּ אֵלָיו כָּל־בְּנֵי לֵוִי: 27וַיֹּאמֶר לָהֶם כֹּה־אָמַר יְהוָה אֱלֹהֵי יִשְׂרָאֵל שִׂימוּ אִישׁ־חַרְבּוֹ עַל־יְרֵכוֹ עִבְרוּ וָשׁוּבוּ מִשַּׁעַר לָשַׁעַר בַּמַּחֲנֶה וְהִרְגוּ אִישׁ־אֶת־אָחִיו וְאִישׁ אֶת־רֵעֵהוּ וְאִישׁ אֶת־קְרֹבוֹ: 28וַיַּעֲשׂוּ בְנֵי־לֵוִי

32:22. in a bad state. In the sense of "in for trouble," "up to no good," or "in a sorry state."

32:24. and this calf came out. A strong lie uses as much of the truth as possible. Aaron quotes the people exactly. Then he quotes his own words with slight changes. And then he transforms the production of the calf from his own fashioning to "and this calf came out!" He also addresses Moses as "my lord," and he emphasizes the people's bad state. Thus, in a very brief response he does a great deal to minimize any culpability of his own.

Why is there no consequence for Aaron? Some say that the consequence is the deaths of his sons Nadab and Abihu (Leviticus 10). Alternatively, the answer may be that just prior to the making of the calf God has designated Aaron as the people's high priest. In that position he cannot suffer any direct punishment from God, which would both disqualify him and demean the office of high priest. And so what is left is for Aaron to make amends through personal atonement. (The same would apply to the case in which he and Miriam criticize Moses about his wife. Miriam becomes leprous, but Aaron does not suffer any consequence. See the comment on Num 12:11.)

32:25. turned it loose. The word in Hebrew consonants is *pr'h*, a pun on the word "Pharaoh." Aaron has "Pharaohed" the people; he has done something to them that Pharaohs had done: made them ignoble in the eyes of those who oppose them. Or one could say that he has brought them back to the condition in which they were before the Sinai revelation: in disarray, without the law.

32:25. denigration. Scornful whispering.

the children of Levi did according to Moses' word, and about three thousand men fell from the people in that day. 29And Moses said, "Fill your hand to YHWH today—because each man was at his son and at his brother—and to put a blessing on you today."

30And it was on the next day, and Moses said to the people, "You've committed a big sin. And now I'll go up to YHWH. Perhaps I may make atonement for your sin." 31And Moses went back to YHWH and said, "Please, this people has committed a big sin and made gods of gold for them-

כִּדְבַ֣ר מֹשֶׁ֑ה וַיִּפֹּ֤ל מִן־הָעָם֙ בַּיֹּ֣ום הַה֔וּא כִּשְׁלֹ֖שֶׁת אַלְפֵ֥י אִֽישׁ: 29וַיֹּ֣אמֶר מֹשֶׁ֗ה מִלְא֨וּ יֶדְכֶ֤ם הַיֹּום֙ לַֽיהֹוָ֔ה כִּ֣י אִ֥ישׁ בִּבְנֹ֖ו וּבְאָחִ֑יו וְלָתֵ֧ת עֲלֵיכֶ֛ם הַיֹּ֖ום בְּרָכָֽה: 30וַֽיְהִי֙ מִֽמָּחֳרָ֔ת וַיֹּ֤אמֶר מֹשֶׁה֙ אֶל־הָעָ֔ם אַתֶּ֥ם חֲטָאתֶ֖ם חֲטָאָ֣ה גְדֹלָ֑ה וְעַתָּה֙ אֶֽעֱלֶ֣ה אֶל־יְהֹוָ֔ה אוּלַ֥י אֲכַפְּרָ֖ה בְּעַ֥ד חַטַּאתְכֶֽם: 31וַיָּ֧שָׁב מֹשֶׁ֛ה אֶל־יְהֹוָ֖ה וַיֹּאמַ֑ר אָ֣נָּ֗א חָטָ֞א הָעָ֤ם הַזֶּה֙ חֲטָאָ֣ה גְדֹלָ֔ה וַיַּֽעֲשׂ֥וּ לָהֶ֖ם אֱלֹהֵ֥י זָהָֽב: 32וְעַתָּ֖ה אִם־תִּשָּׂ֣א חַטָּאתָם֒

32:29. **Fill your hand**. This phrase refers to volunteering for divine service. See the comment on 28:41.

32:29. **to YHWH today—because each man was at his son and at his brother—and to put a blessing on you today**. The grammar of this verse is difficult in the Hebrew and more so in translation. It appears to mean that, because of the Levites' violent zeal, they are now chosen to consecrate themselves as Israel's priesthood and are to receive divine blessing. It is ironic that Levi is criticized in Jacob's deathbed blessing for his violent slaughter in Shechem (Gen 34:25; 49:5–7), but Levi's descendants are rewarded for a violent slaughter here. The lesson may be that an act is not judged, in the Torah, apart from its circumstances. What the Levites do in response to a heresy of destiny-changing proportions is not comparable to Levi's (and Simeon's) massacre of a city in response to the offense committed by their ruler's son.

32:31. **Please**. This word, Hebrew *'ānnâ*, occurs only twice in the Torah, here and in Gen 50:17; and in both instances it is used in the context of asking someone to "bear a sin." In both cases it is a tremendous sin, and in both cases there are no grounds for defense. It is thus a particle that expresses emotional entreaty. Interestingly, the case in Genesis 50 is the plea by Joseph's brothers to forgive them for what they did to him, and Joseph does in fact forgive them. Again the story of Moses and the Israelites contains an allusion to a story from the era of the patriarchs, hinting to the reader that there is reason for hope; for if a great man can forgive, certainly God can as well.

32:31. **gods of gold**. Or "a god of gold." It is uncertain whether Moses refers here to the calf statue as a god or if he refers to gods for whom the calf is a throne dais.

32:31. **made gods of gold for themselves**. Moses does not describe what they have done in the language of the Ten Commandments ("You shall not make a statue or any form . . . "); he rather uses the wording of one of the commands that come later: "You shall not make gods of gold for yourselves" (Exod 20:20). Breaking one of the Ten Commandments is far more serious than a violation of the other commandments of the Torah, because the Ten Commandments form the text of the Sinai covenant, and to violate them is to breach the covenant itself. There are cases in the *Tanak* in which

selves. 32And now, if you will bear their sin—and if not, wipe me out from your scroll that you've written."

33And YHWH said to Moses, "The one who has sinned against me, I'll wipe him out from my scroll. 34And now, go. Lead the people to where I spoke to you. Here, my angel will go ahead of you. And, in the day that I take account, I'll account their sin on them." 35And YHWH struck the people because they had made the calf, which Aaron had made.

וְאִם־אַ֔יִן מְחֵ֣נִי נָ֔א מִֽסִּפְרְךָ֖ אֲשֶׁ֥ר כָּתָֽבְתָּ׃ 33וַיֹּ֥אמֶר יְהוָ֖ה אֶל־מֹשֶׁ֑ה מִ֚י אֲשֶׁ֣ר חָֽטָא־לִ֔י אֶמְחֶ֖נּוּ מִסִּפְרִֽי׃ 34וְעַתָּ֞ה לֵ֣ךְ ׀ נְחֵ֣ה אֶת־הָעָ֗ם אֶ֤ל אֲשֶׁר־דִּבַּ֙רְתִּי֙ לָ֔ךְ הִנֵּ֥ה מַלְאָכִ֖י יֵלֵ֣ךְ לְפָנֶ֑יךָ וּבְי֣וֹם פָּקְדִ֔י וּפָקַדְתִּ֥י עֲלֵיהֶ֖ם חַטָּאתָֽם׃ 35וַיִּגֹּ֥ף יְהוָ֖ה אֶת־הָעָ֑ם עַ֚ל אֲשֶׁ֣ר עָשׂ֣וּ אֶת־הָעֵ֔גֶל אֲשֶׁ֥ר עָשָׂ֖ה אַהֲרֹֽן׃ ס

---

individuals or the nation are faced with a choice of breaking one of the Ten Commandments or else one of the other laws. They choose to break the other laws, even though there are terrible consequences, rather than break one of the Ten.

32:32. if you will bear their sin—and if not . . . Moses seems to break his sentence in the middle and jump to the other side of the coin: "If you will bear their sin"—then what? Perhaps there is nothing to say. He is not in a position to offer God a reward if He *does* bear their sin. He can only turn to the alternative: "If you *won't* bear their sin, then wipe me out from your scroll . . . "

32:32. your scroll that you've written. The reference is either to the scroll of the Covenant Code (Exod 24:7) or to the scroll concerning Amalek (17:14). In the account of the Amalek scroll, the same word that is used here for "to wipe out" occurs twice. Moses may be implying, "Please do this, or else erase me from history the way you said you would erase Amalek."

32:33-34. The one who has sinned against me, I'll wipe him out. . . . And now, go. Moses' gesture is both selfless and audacious at the same time. He takes a great risk to himself for the sake of winning forgiveness for his people, but at the same time he is speaking more boldly to God than he has dared to do before—and he is ascribing much importance to himself in assuming that "wipe me out of your scroll" carries enough weight to affect a divine decision. But God's answer seems to brush aside Moses' gesture, as if to say, "Don't tell me whom to write in my scroll. I'll do whatever I'll do. Now, go."

32:35. they had made the calf, which Aaron had made. Some have taken this wording to be a scribal error because it says both that the people made it and that Aaron made it. (And some of the versions say: "they had *served* the calf which Aaron had made.") But both *did* make it, and both are culpable. The community produced the calf: initiating the event, asking for gods to be made, contributing the gold, responding to the finished product. And Aaron was responsible in two ways: as the leader of the community and as the one who fashioned the calf. A group and an individual who acts as the group's agent share in the responsibility for the things they do.

33 ¹And YHWH spoke to Moses: "Go. Go up from here, you and the people whom you brought up from the land of Egypt, to the land that I swore to Abraham, to Isaac, and to Jacob, saying, 'I'll give it to your seed.' ²And I'll send an angel ahead of you—and I'll drive out the Canaanite, the Amorite, and the Hittite and the Perizzite and the Hivite and the Jebusite— ³to a land flowing with milk and honey, because I won't go up among you, because you're a hard-necked people, or else I'll finish you on the way." ⁴And the people heard this bad thing, and they mourned, and not a man put his jewelry on him. ⁵And YHWH said to Moses, "Say to the children of Israel: 'You're a hard-necked people. If I would go up among you for one moment, I would finish you! And now, put your jewelry down from on you, so I may know what I'll do with you.'" ⁶And the children of Israel divested their jewelry from Mount Horeb.

⁷And Moses would take the tent and pitch it outside of the camp, going far from the camp, and he called it the Tent of Meeting. And it

33 ¹וַיְדַבֵּר יְהוָה אֶל־מֹשֶׁה לֵךְ עֲלֵה מִזֶּה אַתָּה וְהָעָם אֲשֶׁר הֶעֱלִיתָ מֵאֶרֶץ מִצְרָיִם אֶל־הָאָרֶץ אֲשֶׁר נִשְׁבַּעְתִּי לְאַבְרָהָם לְיִצְחָק וּלְיַעֲקֹב לֵאמֹר לְזַרְעֲךָ אֶתְּנֶנָּה: ²וְשָׁלַחְתִּי לְפָנֶיךָ מַלְאָךְ וְגֵרַשְׁתִּי אֶת־הַכְּנַעֲנִי הָאֱמֹרִי וְהַחִתִּי וְהַפְּרִזִּי הַחִוִּי וְהַיְבוּסִי: ³אֶל־אֶרֶץ זָבַת חָלָב וּדְבָשׁ כִּי לֹא אֶעֱלֶה בְּקִרְבְּךָ כִּי עַם־קְשֵׁה־עֹרֶף אַתָּה פֶּן־אֲכֶלְךָ בַּדָּרֶךְ: ⁴וַיִּשְׁמַע הָעָם אֶת־הַדָּבָר הָרָע הַזֶּה וַיִּתְאַבָּלוּ וְלֹא־שָׁתוּ אִישׁ עֶדְיוֹ עָלָיו: ⁵וַיֹּאמֶר יְהוָה אֶל־מֹשֶׁה אֱמֹר אֶל־בְּנֵי־יִשְׂרָאֵל אַתֶּם עַם־קְשֵׁה־עֹרֶף רֶגַע אֶחָד אֶעֱלֶה בְקִרְבְּךָ וְכִלִּיתִיךָ וְעַתָּה הוֹרֵד עֶדְיְךָ מֵעָלֶיךָ וְאֵדְעָה מָה אֶעֱשֶׂה־לָּךְ: ⁶וַיִּתְנַצְּלוּ בְנֵי־יִשְׂרָאֵל אֶת־עֶדְיָם מֵהַר חוֹרֵב: ⁷וּמֹשֶׁה יִקַּח אֶת־הָאֹהֶל וְנָטָה־לוֹ ׀ מִחוּץ לַמַּחֲנֶה הַרְחֵק מִן־הַמַּחֲנֶה וְקָרָא לוֹ אֹהֶל מוֹעֵד

33:5. put your jewelry down. Did they not already take it off (v. 4)?! But here the text appears to refer to permanent removal. Thus in v. 6 we learn that they "divested their jewelry from Mount Horeb"—meaning: from Mount Horeb on.

33:7. the Tent of Meeting This is the first mention of the tent where God will communicate with Israel. It will be the central place of worship, the only place where sacrifice is allowed, for all the years that they will spend in the wilderness and for centuries after that in the promised land, until its disappearance at the time of the destruction of the Temple of Solomon.

The problem is that the Tent of Meeting is not yet built at this point. It is not set up until Exodus 40. Rashi and Ibn Ezra therefore identified the tent in this verse as Moses' own tent (which has been mentioned already in 18:7). Ibn Ezra also says that there are those who say that it is *ʾōhel hammiškān*, the Tent of the Tabernacle. From the point of view of critical scholarship, the problem is the result of the combining of two of the sources of the Torah: the report of the moving and naming of the Tent is identified as coming from E; the later report of the setting up of the Tent is identified as coming from P. That is an explanation of how the text was composed, but in understanding the text as it stands, I believe that Rashi's and Ibn Ezra's explanation fits the text best. It appears that Moses' tent serves as the Tent of Meeting until the Tabernacle is set up. The Tabernacle then replaces Moses' tent as the Tent of Meeting. This is significant because the transition of the sacred place of revelation away from Moses' per-

would be: everyone seeking YHWH would go out to the Tent of Meeting, which was outside of the camp. 8And it would be, when Moses would go out to the Tent, all the people would get up, and they would stand up, each one at the entrance of his tent, and they would look after Moses until he came to the Tent. 9And it would be, when Moses came to the Tent, the column of cloud would come down, and it would stand at the entrance of the Tent, and He would speak with Moses. 10And all the people would see the column of cloud standing at the entrance of the Tent, and all the people would get up and bow, each at the entrance of his tent. 11And YHWH would speak to Moses face-to-face, the way a man speaks to his fellow man. And he would come back to the camp. And his attendant, Joshua, son of Nun, a young man, would not depart from inside the Tent.

12And Moses said to YHWH, "See, you say to me, 'Bring this people up,' and you haven't made known to me whom you will send with me. And you've said, 'I've known you by name,' and also 'You've found favor in my eyes.' 13And now, if I've found favor in your eyes, make your way known to me, so I may know you, so that I'll find favor

וְהָיָה כָּל־מְבַקֵּשׁ יְהוָה יֵצֵא אֶל־אֹהֶל מוֹעֵד אֲשֶׁר מִחוּץ לַמַּחֲנֶה: 8וְהָיָה כְּצֵאת מֹשֶׁה אֶל־הָאֹהֶל יָקוּמוּ כָּל־הָעָם וְנִצְּבוּ אִישׁ פֶּתַח אָהֳלוֹ וְהִבִּיטוּ אַחֲרֵי מֹשֶׁה עַד־בֹּאוֹ הָאֹהֱלָה: 9וְהָיָה כְּבֹא מֹשֶׁה הָאֹהֱלָה יֵרֵד עַמּוּד הֶעָנָן וְעָמַד פֶּתַח הָאֹהֶל וְדִבֶּר עִם־מֹשֶׁה: 10וְרָאָה כָל־הָעָם אֶת־עַמּוּד הֶעָנָן עֹמֵד פֶּתַח הָאֹהֶל וְקָם כָּל־הָעָם וְהִשְׁתַּחֲווּ אִישׁ פֶּתַח אָהֳלוֹ: 11וְדִבֶּר יְהוָה אֶל־מֹשֶׁה פָּנִים אֶל־פָּנִים כַּאֲשֶׁר יְדַבֵּר אִישׁ אֶל־רֵעֵהוּ וְשָׁב אֶל־הַמַּחֲנֶה וּמְשָׁרְתוֹ יְהוֹשֻׁעַ בִּן־נוּן נַעַר לֹא יָמִישׁ מִתּוֹךְ הָאֹהֶל: ס

12וַיֹּאמֶר מֹשֶׁה אֶל־יְהוָה רְאֵה אַתָּה אֹמֵר אֵלַי הַעַל אֶת־הָעָם הַזֶּה וְאַתָּה לֹא הוֹדַעְתַּנִי אֵת אֲשֶׁר־תִּשְׁלַח עִמִּי וְאַתָּה אָמַרְתָּ יְדַעְתִּיךָ בְשֵׁם וְגַם־מָצָאתָ חֵן בְּעֵינָי: 13וְעַתָּה אִם־נָא מָצָאתִי חֵן בְּעֵינֶיךָ הוֹדִעֵנִי נָא אֶת־דְּרָכֶךָ וְאֵדָעֲךָ לְמַעַן אֶמְצָא־חֵן

sonal residence reduces the impression of Moses' own proprietary role. There is a continuing issue of the people's focusing on Moses rather than on the deity, and the use of Moses' residence as the sacred place would contribute to their impression.

33:11. **face-to-face**. This does not mean that Moses has seen God's face. He has not seen it up to this point, and a few verses later God will tell him explicitly that he will see God from behind, and "my face won't be seen" (33:23). For further evidence that this expression does not mean literally seeing a face, see the comment on its occurrence in Deut 5:4. Another occurrence of this expression in the Torah is when Jacob says "I've seen God face-to-face" (Gen 32:31) after he has struggled with "a man," which refers to an angel (see the comments on Genesis 32).

33:13. **so I may know you, so that I'll find favor in your eyes**. Moses' words in this passage seem unclear and even self-contradictory, but they are not. Moses is asking God to tell him how He will help him lead the people to the land. Moses quotes God as saying "I've known you" and "You've found favor in my eyes," but he indicates that he cannot really know God and find favor with God unless God informs him what His *way* will be.

288

in your eyes. And see that this nation is your people."

14And He said, "My face will go, and I'll let you rest."

15And he said to Him, "If your face isn't going, don't take us up from here. 16And by what then will it be known that I've found favor in your eyes, I and your people? Is it not by your going with us? And we'll be distinguished, I and your people, from every people that is on the face of the earth."

17And YHWH said to Moses, "I'll do this thing that you've spoken as well, because you've found favor in my eyes, and I've known you by name."

18And he said, "Show me your glory!"

19And He said, "I shall have all my good pass in front of you, and I shall invoke the name YHWH in front of you. And I shall show grace to whomever I shall show grace, and I shall show mercy to whomever I shall show mercy." 20And He said, "You won't be able to see my face, because a human will not see me and live." 21And YHWH said, "Here is a place with me, and you'll stand up on a rock; 22and it will be, when my

בְּעֵינֶיךָ וּרְאֵה כִּי עַמְּךָ הַגּוֹי הַזֶּה: 14וַיֹּאמַר פָּנַי
יֵלֵכוּ וַהֲנִחֹתִי לָךְ: 15וַיֹּאמֶר אֵלָיו אִם־אֵין פָּנֶיךָ
הֹלְכִים אַל־תַּעֲלֵנוּ מִזֶּה: 16וּבַמֶּה ׀ יִוָּדַע אֵפוֹא כִּי־
מָצָאתִי חֵן בְּעֵינֶיךָ אֲנִי וְעַמֶּךָ הֲלוֹא בְּלֶכְתְּךָ עִמָּנוּ
וְנִפְלֵינוּ אֲנִי וְעַמְּךָ מִכָּל־הָעָם אֲשֶׁר עַל־פְּנֵי
הָאֲדָמָה: פ 17וַיֹּאמֶר יְהוָה אֶל־מֹשֶׁה גַּם אֶת־
הַדָּבָר הַזֶּה אֲשֶׁר דִּבַּרְתָּ אֶעֱשֶׂה כִּי־מָצָאתָ חֵן
בְּעֵינַי וָאֵדָעֲךָ בְּשֵׁם: 18וַיֹּאמַר הַרְאֵנִי נָא אֶת־
כְּבֹדֶךָ: 19וַיֹּאמֶר אֲנִי אַעֲבִיר כָּל־טוּבִי עַל־פָּנֶיךָ
וְקָרָאתִי בְשֵׁם יְהוָה לְפָנֶיךָ וְחַנֹּתִי אֶת־אֲשֶׁר אָחֹן
וְרִחַמְתִּי אֶת־אֲשֶׁר אֲרַחֵם: 20וַיֹּאמֶר לֹא תוּכַל
לִרְאֹת אֶת־פָּנָי כִּי לֹא־יִרְאַנִי הָאָדָם וָחָי: 21וַיֹּאמֶר
יְהוָה הִנֵּה מָקוֹם אִתִּי וְנִצַּבְתָּ עַל־הַצּוּר: 22וְהָיָה

33:13. And see that this nation is your people. Moses ends his plea with an expression of caring for his people as well. In God's words (33:1) and in Moses' quotation of those words (33:12), God speaks of "*the* people," but Moses continues the battle of the pronouns (see my comment on 32:7) and pleads: "See that they're *your* people."

33:16. distinguished. This refers to being different from the other peoples in this one respect: that God's presence is among them. It does not necessarily imply distinction in the sense of being superior in any way.

33:17. you've found favor in my eyes, and I've known you by name. God repeats the exact phrases that Moses used as the basis of his case, thus confirming His acceptance of Moses' point.

33:18. Show me your glory. Using the Hebrew *nā'* particle of polite request, Moses boldly dares to ask to be allowed to see God. And see how far Moses has come: at the burning bush "Moses hid his face, because he was afraid of looking at God" (Exod 3:6), but now, after a time of acquaintance with God and after seeing and sometimes wielding divine power, he has grown in intimacy with God and has grown in his own confidence enough to ask God to see the divine form.

33:21. a place with me, and you'll stand up on a rock. Earlier, in the episode of

glory passes, that I'll set you in a cleft of the rock, and I'll cover my hand over you until I've passed, ²³and I'll turn my hand away, and you'll see my back, but my face won't be seen."

34 ¹And YHWH said to Moses, "Carve two tablets of stones like the first ones, and I'll write on the tablets the words that were on the first tablets, which you shattered. ²And be ready for the morning, and you shall go up in the morning to Mount Sinai and present yourself to me there on the top of the mountain. ³And no man shall go up with you, and also let no man be seen in all of the mountain. Also let the flock and the oxen not feed opposite that mountain." ⁴And he carved two tablets of stones like the first ones, and Moses got up early in the morning and went up to Mount Sinai as YHWH had commanded him, and he took in his hand two tablets of stones. ⁵And YHWH came down in a cloud and stood with him there, and he invoked the name YHWH. ⁶And YHWH passed in front of him and called,

YHWH, YHWH, merciful and gracious God, slow to anger and abounding in kindness and faithfulness, ⁷keeping kindness for thousands, bearing crime and offense and sin; though not making one *innocent:* reck-

בַּעֲבֹר כְּבֹדִי וְשַׂמְתִּיךָ בְּנִקְרַת הַצּוּר וְשַׂכֹּתִי כַפִּי עָלֶיךָ עַד־עָבְרִי: ²³וַהֲסִרֹתִי אֶת־כַּפִּי וְרָאִיתָ אֶת־אֲחֹרָי וּפָנַי לֹא יֵרָאוּ: ס

34 ¹וַיֹּאמֶר יְהוָה אֶל־מֹשֶׁה פְּסָל־לְךָ שְׁנֵי־לֻחֹת אֲבָנִים כָּרִאשֹׁנִים וְכָתַבְתִּי עַל־הַלֻּחֹת אֶת־הַדְּבָרִים אֲשֶׁר הָיוּ עַל־הַלֻּחֹת הָרִאשֹׁנִים אֲשֶׁר שִׁבַּרְתָּ: ²וֶהְיֵה נָכוֹן לַבֹּקֶר וְעָלִיתָ בַבֹּקֶר אֶל־הַר סִינַי וְנִצַּבְתָּ לִי שָׁם עַל־רֹאשׁ הָהָר: ³וְאִישׁ לֹא־יַעֲלֶה עִמָּךְ וְגַם־אִישׁ אַל־יֵרָא בְּכָל־הָהָר גַּם־הַצֹּאן וְהַבָּקָר אַל־יִרְעוּ אֶל־מוּל הָהָר הַהוּא: ⁴וַיִּפְסֹל שְׁנֵי־לֻחֹת אֲבָנִים כָּרִאשֹׁנִים וַיַּשְׁכֵּם מֹשֶׁה בַבֹּקֶר וַיַּעַל אֶל־הַר סִינַי כַּאֲשֶׁר צִוָּה יְהוָה אֹתוֹ וַיִּקַּח בְּיָדוֹ שְׁנֵי לֻחֹת אֲבָנִים: ⁵וַיֵּרֶד יְהוָה בֶּעָנָן וַיִּתְיַצֵּב עִמּוֹ שָׁם וַיִּקְרָא בְשֵׁם יְהוָה: ⁶וַיַּעֲבֹר יְהוָה ׀ עַל־פָּנָיו וַיִּקְרָא יְהוָה ׀ יְהוָה אֵל רַחוּם וְחַנּוּן אֶרֶךְ אַפַּיִם וְרַב־חֶסֶד וֶאֱמֶת: ⁷נֹצֵר חֶסֶד לָאֲלָפִים נֹשֵׂא עָוֹן וָפֶשַׁע וְחַטָּאָה וְנַקֵּה לֹא יְנַקֶּה פֹּקֵד ׀ עֲוֹן

---

the water from the rock, God stands on the crag of Horeb, while Moses stands opposite (Exod 17:6). But now Moses stands on the crag *with* God. Whatever this means physically, it shows Moses moving closer to God. His intimacy with the deity grows through the course of his life. (A student of mine, Brian Kelly, observed this. Ramban saw a connection between these two episodes as well.)

34:6. **and called, YHWH, YHWH.** This is the traditional understanding: that the name of God is repeated. But the verse may also be read thus: "and YHWH called, 'YHWH, merciful and gracious God . . .'"

34:6–7. **merciful, gracious, slow to anger, kindness, faithfulness, bearing crime and offense and sin.** This is possibly the most repeated and quoted formula in the *Tanak* (Num 14:18–19; Jon 4:2; Joel 2:13; Mic 7:18; Pss 86:15; 103:8; 145:8; 2 Chr 30:9; Neh 9:17,31). The Torah never says what the essence of God is, in contrast to the pagan gods. Baal is the storm wind, Dagon is grain, Shamash is the sun. But what *is* YHWH? This formula, expressed in the moment of the closest revelation any human has of God in the Bible, is the closest the Torah comes to describing the nature of God.

oning fathers' crime on children and on children's children, on third generations and on fourth generations.

8And Moses hurried and knelt to the ground and bowed, 9and he said, "If I've found favor in your eyes, my Lord, may my Lord go among us, because it is a stiff-necked people, and forgive our crime and our sin, and make us your legacy."

10And He said, "Here, I'm making a covenant. Before all your people I'll do wonders that haven't been created in all the earth and among all the nations; and all the people whom you're among will see YHWH's deeds, because that which I'm doing with you is awesome. 11Watch yourself regarding what I command you today. Here, I'm driving out from before you the Amorite and the Canaanite and the Hittite and the Perizzite and the Hivite and the Jebusite. 12Be watchful of yourself that you don't make a covenant with the resident of the land onto which you're coming, that he doesn't become a trap among you. 13But you

אָבוֹת עַל־בָּנִים וְעַל־בְּנֵי בָנִים עַל־שִׁלֵּשִׁים וְעַל־רִבֵּעִים: 8וַיְמַהֵר מֹשֶׁה וַיִּקֹּד אַרְצָה וַיִּשְׁתָּחוּ: 9וַיֹּאמֶר אִם־נָא מָצָאתִי חֵן בְּעֵינֶיךָ אֲדֹנָי יֵלֶךְ־נָא אֲדֹנָי בְּקִרְבֵּנוּ כִּי עַם־קְשֵׁה־עֹרֶף הוּא וְסָלַחְתָּ לַעֲוֹנֵנוּ וּלְחַטָּאתֵנוּ וּנְחַלְתָּנוּ: 10וַיֹּאמֶר הִנֵּה אָנֹכִי כֹּרֵת בְּרִית נֶגֶד כָּל־עַמְּךָ אֶעֱשֶׂה נִפְלָאֹת אֲשֶׁר לֹא־נִבְרְאוּ בְכָל־הָאָרֶץ וּבְכָל־הַגּוֹיִם וְרָאָה כָל־הָעָם אֲשֶׁר־אַתָּה בְקִרְבּוֹ אֶת־מַעֲשֵׂה יְהוָה כִּי־נוֹרָא הוּא אֲשֶׁר אֲנִי עֹשֶׂה עִמָּךְ: 11שְׁמָר־לְךָ אֵת אֲשֶׁר אָנֹכִי מְצַוְּךָ הַיּוֹם הִנְנִי גֹרֵשׁ מִפָּנֶיךָ אֶת־הָאֱמֹרִי וְהַכְּנַעֲנִי וְהַחִתִּי וְהַפְּרִזִּי וְהַחִוִּי וְהַיְבוּסִי: 12הִשָּׁמֶר לְךָ פֶּן־תִּכְרֹת בְּרִית לְיוֹשֵׁב הָאָרֶץ אֲשֶׁר אַתָּה בָּא עָלֶיהָ פֶּן־יִהְיֶה לְמוֹקֵשׁ בְּקִרְבֶּךָ: 13כִּי אֶת־

Although humans are not to know what the essence is, they can know what are the marks of the divine personality: mercy, grace. In eight (or nine) different ways we are told of God's *compassion*. The last line of the formula ("though not making one innocent") conveys that this does not mean that one can just get away with anything; there is still justice. But the formula clearly places the weight on divine mercy over divine justice, and it never mentions divine anger. Those who speak of the "Old Testament God of wrath" focus disproportionately on the episodes of anger in the Bible and somehow lose this crucial passage and the hundreds of times that the divine mercy functions in the Hebrew Bible.

34:7. **on fourth generations.** The list covers five generations: from parents to the fourth generation of their offspring (great-great-grandchildren). Why? First, five generations constitutes the likely maximum of living acquaintance. People occasionally live to see their great-great-grandchildren, but great-great-great is practically unheard of. Second, Israelite rock-cut tombs prior to the seventh century were multi chambered, with room for at least four generations of offspring. The ancestral bond was thus thought to go at least that far back. Third, psychologically one can observe traits persevering through that many generations. I have personally observed ongoing dynamics within my family through four generations. This does not mean that an individual's bad deed will be duplicated by his or her children and grandchildren. But it may recognize that such deeds have consequences, for better or worse (pride or embarrassment, stigmas, reactions, conscious or unconscious imitation), that persist through generations.

shall demolish their altars and shatter their pillars and cut down their Asherahs.

14For you shall not bow to another god—because YHWH: His name is Jealous, He is a jealous God— 15that you not make a covenant with the resident of the land, and they will prostitute themselves after their gods and sacrifice to their gods, and he will call to you, and you will eat from his sacrifice. 16And you will take some of his daughters for your sons, and his daughters will prostitute themselves after their gods and cause your sons to prostitute themselves after their gods.

17You shall not make molten gods for yourself.

18You shall observe the Festival of Unleavened Bread. Seven days you shall eat unleavened bread, which I commanded you, at the appointed time, the month of Abib; because in the month of Abib you went out of Egypt.

19Every first birth of a womb is mine, and all your animals that have a male first birth, ox or sheep. 20And you shall redeem an ass's first birth with a sheep, and if you do not redeem it then you shall break its neck. You shall redeem every firstborn of

מִזְבְּחֹתָם֙ תִּתֹּצ֔וּן וְאֶת־מַצֵּבֹתָ֖ם תְּשַׁבֵּר֑וּן וְאֶת־אֲשֵׁרָ֖יו תִּכְרֹת֑וּן: 14כִּ֛י לֹ֥א תִֽשְׁתַּחֲוֶ֖ה לְאֵ֣ל אַחֵ֑ר כִּ֤י יְהוָה֙ קַנָּ֣א שְׁמ֔וֹ אֵ֥ל קַנָּ֖א הֽוּא: 15פֶּן־תִּכְרֹ֤ת בְּרִית֙ לְיוֹשֵׁ֣ב הָאָ֔רֶץ וְזָנ֣וּ ׀ אַחֲרֵ֣י אֱלֹֽהֵיהֶ֗ם וְזָבְחוּ֙ לֵֽאלֹ֣הֵיהֶ֔ם וְקָרָ֣א לְךָ֔ וְאָכַלְתָּ֖ מִזִּבְחֽוֹ: 16וְלָקַחְתָּ֥ מִבְּנֹתָ֖יו לְבָנֶ֑יךָ וְזָנ֣וּ בְנֹתָ֗יו אַחֲרֵי֙ אֱלֹ֣הֵיהֶ֔ן וְהִזְנוּ֙ אֶת־בָּנֶ֔יךָ אַחֲרֵ֖י אֱלֹהֵיהֶֽן: 17אֱלֹהֵ֥י מַסֵּכָ֖ה לֹ֥א תַעֲשֶׂה־לָּֽךְ: 18אֶת־חַ֣ג הַמַּצּוֹת֮ תִּשְׁמֹר֒ שִׁבְעַ֨ת יָמִ֜ים תֹּאכַ֤ל מַצּוֹת֙ אֲשֶׁ֣ר צִוִּיתִ֔ךָ לְמוֹעֵ֖ד חֹ֣דֶשׁ הָאָבִ֑יב כִּ֚י בְּחֹ֣דֶשׁ הָֽאָבִ֔יב יָצָ֖אתָ מִמִּצְרָֽיִם: 19כָּל־פֶּ֥טֶר רֶ֖חֶם לִ֑י וְכָֽל־מִקְנְךָ֙ תִּזָּכָ֔ר פֶּ֖טֶר שׁ֥וֹר וָשֶֽׂה: 20וּפֶ֤טֶר חֲמוֹר֙ תִּפְדֶּ֣ה בְשֶׂ֔ה וְאִם־לֹ֥א תִפְדֶּ֖ה וַעֲרַפְתּ֑וֹ כֹּ֣ל בְּכ֤וֹר בָּנֶ֙יךָ֙

34:14. a jealous God. See the comment on Exod 20:5.

34:16. you will take some of his daughters for your sons. The Septuagint adds, "and you will give some of your daughters to their sons," which was probably lost in the Masoretic Text because a scribe's eye jumped from one occurrence of the word "sons" to the next. Marrying persons from other groups happens with both sexes.

34:17. molten gods. Only *after* the golden calf incident is the commandment added: Don't make molten gods (*massēkāh*)! If there was any doubt about their permissibility before, there is none now. In the wake of that event, no such statue is ever to be made again. This is notable in connection with the point I made above, that the golden calf is a throne dais for deities, because there will be two golden cherubs in the Temple of Solomon. The cherubs are the throne dais of YHWH, but they are not molten; they are rather made of wood and then gold-plated (1 Kings 6:23,28). They are therefore not criticized. But when the northern kingdom of Israel establishes two molten golden calves (1 Kings 12), the kings of Israel are condemned for having them (2 Kings 10:29; 17:22–23).

your sons. And none shall appear before me empty-handed.

21Six days you shall work, and in the seventh day you shall cease. In plowing time and in harvest, you shall cease.

22And you shall make a Festival of Weeks, of the firstfruits of the wheat harvest, and the Festival of Gathering at the end of the year. 23Three times in the year every one of your males shall appear before the Lord YHWH, God of Israel. 24For I shall dispossess nations before you and widen your border, and no man will covet your land while you are going up to appear before YHWH, your God, three times in the year.

25You shall not offer the blood of my sacrifice on leavened bread.

And the sacrifice of the Festival of Passover shall not remain until the morning.

26You shall bring the first of the firstfruits of your land to the house of YHWH, your God.

You shall not cook a kid in its mother's milk.

27And YHWH said to Moses, "Write these words for yourself, because I've made a covenant with you and with Israel based on these words." 28And he was there with YHWH forty days and forty nights. He did not eat bread, and he did not drink water. And he wrote on the tablets the words of the covenant, the Ten Commandments.

29And it was when Moses was coming down

תִּפְדֶּה וְלֹא־יֵרָאוּ פָנַי רֵיקָם: 21שֵׁשֶׁת יָמִים תַּעֲבֹד וּבַיּוֹם הַשְּׁבִיעִי תִּשְׁבֹּת בֶּחָרִישׁ וּבַקָּצִיר תִּשְׁבֹּת: 22וְחַג שָׁבֻעֹת תַּעֲשֶׂה לְךָ בִּכּוּרֵי קְצִיר חִטִּים וְחַג הָאָסִיף תְּקוּפַת הַשָּׁנָה: 23שָׁלֹשׁ פְּעָמִים בַּשָּׁנָה יֵרָאֶה כָּל־זְכוּרְךָ אֶת־פְּנֵי הָאָדֹן | יְהוָה אֱלֹהֵי יִשְׂרָאֵל: 24כִּי־אוֹרִישׁ גּוֹיִם מִפָּנֶיךָ וְהִרְחַבְתִּי אֶת־גְּבֻלֶךָ וְלֹא־יַחְמֹד אִישׁ אֶת־אַרְצְךָ בַּעֲלֹתְךָ לֵרָאוֹת אֶת־פְּנֵי יְהוָה אֱלֹהֶיךָ שָׁלֹשׁ פְּעָמִים בַּשָּׁנָה: 25לֹא־תִשְׁחַט עַל־חָמֵץ דַּם־זִבְחִי וְלֹא־יָלִין לַבֹּקֶר זֶבַח חַג הַפָּסַח: 26רֵאשִׁית בִּכּוּרֵי אַדְמָתְךָ תָּבִיא בֵּית יְהוָה אֱלֹהֶיךָ לֹא־תְבַשֵּׁל גְּדִי בַּחֲלֵב אִמּוֹ: פ 27וַיֹּאמֶר יְהוָה אֶל־מֹשֶׁה כְּתָב־לְךָ אֶת־הַדְּבָרִים הָאֵלֶּה כִּי עַל־פִּי | הַדְּבָרִים הָאֵלֶּה כָּרַתִּי אִתְּךָ בְּרִית וְאֶת־יִשְׂרָאֵל: 28וַיְהִי־שָׁם עִם־יְהוָה אַרְבָּעִים יוֹם וְאַרְבָּעִים לַיְלָה לֶחֶם לֹא אָכַל וּמַיִם לֹא שָׁתָה וַיִּכְתֹּב עַל־הַלֻּחֹת אֵת דִּבְרֵי הַבְּרִית עֲשֶׂרֶת הַדְּבָרִים: 29וַיְהִי בְּרֶדֶת מֹשֶׁה מֵהַר

34:25. **You shall not offer the blood of my sacrifice on leavened bread**. Leaven is considered inappropriate for sacrifices. See the comment on Exod 29:2.

34:28. **the Ten Commandments**. Hebrew 'ăseret haddĕbārîm, literally, "the ten things." This is what the Ten Commandments are called in Hebrew.

34:28. **the Ten Commandments**. The second set of the commandments appears here in vv. 14–26. Three of them are similar to the commandments that appear in Exodus 20: the commandment against bowing to other gods (34:14–16), the commandment against molten gods (v. 17), and the commandment to cease work on the seventh day (v. 21). The other seven are different from the Ten Commandments that God speaks aloud over Sinai. In critical biblical scholarship we understand these two versions of the Decalogue to come from two different ancient sources. But how are we

from Mount Sinai, and the two tablets of the Testimony were in Moses' hand when he was coming down from the mountain. And Moses had
not known that the skin of his face was transformed when He was speaking with him. 30And

סִינַי וּשְׁנֵי לֻחֹת הָעֵדֻת בְּיַד־מֹשֶׁה בְּרִדְתּוֹ מִן־הָהָר
וּמֹשֶׁה לֹא־יָדַע כִּי קָרַן עוֹר פָּנָיו בְּדַבְּרוֹ אִתּוֹ:

---

to understand them in the final form of the Torah? The answer may lie in a second
contradiction: In the first verse of this chapter God tells Moses that "*I'll* write on the
tablets the words that were on the first tablets." But now God tells Moses, "Write these
words for *yourself*" (34:27). Perhaps we should understand this to mean that God
writes the words on one side of the tablets, and Moses writes the words of the second
set of commandments on the other side. As is commonly noted, the majority of the
first set are *ethical* commandments, involving relations between humans and other
humans: don't murder, don't steal . . . The second set are mainly ritual commandments: observe the holidays, redeem the firstborn, don't sacrifice with leaven . . . The
two sets are thus complementary, involving the two essential kinds of commandments: relations between humans and humans, and relations between humans and
God.

Another explanation: We may understand this to mean that God writes the words
of the Ten Commandments on both the first and the second set of tablets, while
Moses writes these other matters on another document.

34:29. **transformed**. Coming out of the fiery top of the mountain, and back from
his once-in-human-history encounter with God, Moses is transformed in some way
that is unfortunately obscured in a difficult Hebrew passage (34:30,35). It has often
been understood to mean that Moses' face beams light, and it has been erroneously
visualized in numerous artistic depictions as a horned Moses, the most famous of
which is Michelangelo's Moses. William Propp has argued persuasively that it more
probably means that Moses' face is in some way disfigured (from the fire? from the
experience of encountering the deity?). Whatever it is about Moses' skin, though, it is
a marker, from this point on in the narrative, of Moses' exceptional position. After
having beheld God, he has himself become fearful for other humans to behold. For
the rest of the narrative in Exodus (and in the next three books of the Hebrew Bible),
he is to be pictured wearing a veil. He removes it only when speaking with the deity
and when revealing the divine commandments to the people. Moses' continuing communication with God, moreover, is to take place inside the precincts of the Tabernacle, a place that is forbidden to the lay population. That is, the book of Exodus introduces a series of layers in a channel to God: Moses' veil, then the Tabernacle, which is
a series of tents within tents (the *pārōket*, the *miškān*, the *'ōhel*, the leather cover; see
the comment on 26:33) into which Moses enters and from which he returns with the
word of God. Interestingly, the layers do not appear to function as barriers between
the people and their God in this narrative, but, quite the contrary, there is more of a
feeling of connection to the deity via this channel. The veil that hides Moses' face is,
at the same time, a visible indicator of the proximity of deity. The Tabernacle is the visible shrine, confirmed by the appearance of YHWH's cloud and glory, that marks
God's presence among the people. The fabrics of the veil and the tents give a tangibil-

Aaron and all the children of Israel saw Moses; and, here, the skin of his face was transformed, and they were afraid of going over to him. 31And Moses called to them. And Aaron and all the chiefs in the congregation came back to him, and he spoke to them. 32And after that all the children of Israel went over. And he commanded them everything that YHWH had spoken with him in Mount Sinai. 33And Moses finished speaking with them, and he put a veil on his face. 34And when Moses would come in front of YHWH to speak with Him, he would turn away the veil until he would go out; and he would go out and speak to the children of Israel what he had been commanded. 35And the children of Israel would see Moses' face, that the skin of Moses' face was transformed, and Moses would put back the veil on his face until he would come to speak with Him.

AND HE ASSEMBLED

35 1And Moses assembled all of the congregation of the children of Israel and said to them, "These are the things that YHWH commanded, to do them: 2Six days work shall be done, and in the seventh day you shall have a holy thing, a Sabbath, a ceasing to YHWH. Any-

וַיַּרְא אַהֲרֹן וְכָל־בְּנֵי יִשְׂרָאֵל אֶת־מֹשֶׁה וְהִנֵּה קָרַן 30
עוֹר פָּנָיו וַיִּירְאוּ מִגֶּשֶׁת אֵלָיו: 31וַיִּקְרָא אֲלֵהֶם
מֹשֶׁה וַיָּשֻׁבוּ אֵלָיו אַהֲרֹן וְכָל־הַנְּשִׂאִים בָּעֵדָה
וַיְדַבֵּר מֹשֶׁה אֲלֵהֶם: 32וְאַחֲרֵי־כֵן נִגְּשׁוּ כָּל־בְּנֵי
יִשְׂרָאֵל וַיְצַוֵּם אֵת כָּל־אֲשֶׁר דִּבֶּר יְהוָה אִתּוֹ בְּהַר
סִינָי: 33וַיְכַל מֹשֶׁה מִדַּבֵּר אִתָּם וַיִּתֵּן עַל־פָּנָיו
מַסְוֶה: 34וּבְבֹא מֹשֶׁה לִפְנֵי יְהוָה לְדַבֵּר אִתּוֹ יָסִיר
אֶת־הַמַּסְוֶה עַד־צֵאתוֹ וְיָצָא וְדִבֶּר אֶל־בְּנֵי יִשְׂרָאֵל
אֵת אֲשֶׁר יְצֻוֶּה: 35וְרָאוּ בְנֵי־יִשְׂרָאֵל אֶת־פְּנֵי מֹשֶׁה
כִּי קָרַן עוֹר פְּנֵי מֹשֶׁה וְהֵשִׁיב מֹשֶׁה אֶת־הַמַּסְוֶה
עַל־פָּנָיו עַד־בֹּאוֹ לְדַבֵּר אִתּוֹ: ס

ויקהל

35 1וַיַּקְהֵל מֹשֶׁה אֶת־כָּל־עֲדַת בְּנֵי יִשְׂרָאֵל
וַיֹּאמֶר אֲלֵהֶם אֵלֶּה הַדְּבָרִים אֲשֶׁר־צִוָּה יְהוָה
לַעֲשֹׂת אֹתָם: 2שֵׁשֶׁת יָמִים תֵּעָשֶׂה מְלָאכָה וּבַיּוֹם
הַשְּׁבִיעִי יִהְיֶה לָכֶם קֹדֶשׁ שַׁבַּת שַׁבָּתוֹן לַיהוָה כָּל־

---

ity to the channel of communication with the divine, and at the same time they preserve the quality of mystery that we have seen to surround the knowledge of YHWH.

34:32. after that. First, everyone is afraid when they see Moses. Then, Aaron and the leaders approach Moses. And, after that, the entire people approach him. This indicates the role and importance of leaders. And it indicates that it is natural to be fearful, and that some people (leaders) are needed to be bold, to give others assurance.

35:2. Sabbath. The Tabernacle commands end with the Sabbath (Exod 31:12–17), and Moses' repetition of them here begins with the Sabbath. What is the connection between the Sabbath and the Tabernacle? Recall that the creation of the world in Genesis 1 also ends with the Sabbath. There I discussed the role of the Sabbath as a sanctification of *time*, as opposed to the creation of things in space. Now again, as Israel begins to construct the Tabernacle, the most holy space on earth, they are reminded of the importance of the sanctification of time as well.

one who does work in it shall be put to death. ³You shall not burn a fire in all of your homes on the Sabbath day."

⁴And Moses said to all of the congregation of the children of Israel, saying, "This is the thing that YHWH commanded, saying, ⁵'Take a donation for YHWH from among you. Everyone whose heart is moved shall bring it, YHWH's donation: gold and silver and bronze ⁶and blue and purple and crimson and linen and goats' hair ⁷and rams' skins dyed red and leather skins and acacia wood ⁸and oil for lighting and spices for the anointing oil and for the incense fragrances ⁹and onyx stones and stones to be set for the ephod and for the breastplate. ¹⁰And let everyone wise of heart among you come and make everything that YHWH has commanded: ¹¹the Taber-

הָעֹשֶׂה בוֹ מְלָאכָה יוּמָת: ³לֹא־תְבַעֲרוּ אֵשׁ בְּכֹל מֹשְׁבֹתֵיכֶם בְּיוֹם הַשַּׁבָּת: פ

⁴וַיֹּאמֶר מֹשֶׁה אֶל־כָּל־עֲדַת בְּנֵי־יִשְׂרָאֵל לֵאמֹר זֶה הַדָּבָר אֲשֶׁר־צִוָּה יְהוָה לֵאמֹר: ⁵קְחוּ מֵאִתְּכֶם תְּרוּמָה לַיהוָה כֹּל נְדִיב לִבּוֹ יְבִיאֶהָ אֵת תְּרוּמַת יְהוָה זָהָב וָכֶסֶף וּנְחֹשֶׁת: ⁶וּתְכֵלֶת וְאַרְגָּמָן וְתוֹלַעַת שָׁנִי וְשֵׁשׁ וְעִזִּים: ⁷וְעֹרֹת אֵילִם מְאָדָּמִים וְעֹרֹת תְּחָשִׁים וַעֲצֵי שִׁטִּים: ⁸וְשֶׁמֶן לַמָּאוֹר וּבְשָׂמִים לְשֶׁמֶן הַמִּשְׁחָה וְלִקְטֹרֶת הַסַּמִּים: ⁹וְאַבְנֵי־שֹׁהַם וְאַבְנֵי מִלֻּאִים לָאֵפוֹד וְלַחֹשֶׁן: ¹⁰וְכָל־חֲכַם־לֵב בָּכֶם יָבֹאוּ וְיַעֲשׂוּ אֵת כָּל־אֲשֶׁר צִוָּה יְהוָה: ¹¹אֶת־הַמִּשְׁכָּן אֶת־

35:2. put to death. When God tells Moses to give this commandment to the people, He commands him to say that anyone who works on the Sabbath shall be *"put to death"*—using the Hebrew emphatic form *môt yûmāt* (31:14,15). But Moses just says "put to death" (*yûmāt*)—leaving out the emphatic particle *môt*. That is, Moses softens the wording of the commandment. The convicted person might not feel any different to know that he is just being put to death, and not being *put to death!* But it is as if Moses cannot bring himself to pronounce the powerful, fearful condemnation.

35:3. You shall not burn a fire. The classical commentators ask why fire is singled out from all the things forbidden on the Sabbath. But, even more essentially, we may ask how Moses comes to be mentioning fire at all. He appears to be giving the people the commandment that God had instructed him to give regarding working six days and ceasing on the seventh (31:15) almost verbatim. But then he adds the part about fire, which was not in God's instruction. Fire has not been associated with the Sabbath until now. Why does Moses add it? What has happened between the instruction and Moses' fulfillment of it? Fire has been mentioned twice since then: Aaron has claimed that the golden calf came out of a fire, and Moses has destroyed the calf with fire (32:20,24). The prohibition of fire on the Sabbath may thus be understood as a reminder of the golden calf rebellion. (An interesting comparison is the prohibition of playing musical instruments on the Sabbath, which was instituted as a memorial of the destruction of the Temple.) Moreover, it is a reminder that the Sabbath is not just about work and rest. There are things that one does not do on the Sabbath even if one can do them without the effort associated with work, such as lighting a fire. And there are things that one *does* do on the Sabbath, not just because it is permitted but because it is a spiritual joy, such as singing Sabbath songs. The Sabbath is about separation and sanctification of time. It is about peace and respite, about family, and about community.

nacle, its tent and its cover and its clasps and its frames, its bars, its columns and its bases, 12the ark and its poles, the atonement dais and the covering pavilion, 13the table and its poles and all of its equipment and the show bread 14and the menorah for lighting and its equipment and its lamps and the oil for lighting 15and the incense altar and its poles and the anointing oil and the incense fragrances and the entrance cover for the Tabernacle's entrance, 16the altar of burnt offering and the bronze grate that it has, its poles and all of its equipment, the basin and its stand, 17the courtyard's hangings, its columns and its bases and the cover of the courtyard's gate, 18the Tabernacle's pegs and the courtyard's pegs and their cords, 19the fabric clothes for ministering in the Holy, the holy clothes for Aaron the priest, and his sons' clothes for functioning as priests.'"

20And all of the congregation of the children of Israel went out from in front of Moses. 21And everyone whose heart inspired him came, and everyone whose spirit moved him brought a contribution for YHWH for the work of the Tent of Meeting and for all of its construction and for the holy clothes. 22And the men came together with the women. All whose hearts moved them had brought brooches and earrings and rings

אָהֳלוֹ וְאֶת־מִכְסֵהוּ אֶת־קְרָסָיו וְאֶת־קְרָשָׁיו אֶת־
בְּרִיחָו אֶת־עַמֻּדָיו וְאֶת־אֲדָנָיו: 12אֶת־הָאָרֹן וְאֶת־
בַּדָּיו אֶת־הַכַּפֹּרֶת וְאֵת פָּרֹכֶת הַמָּסָךְ: 13אֶת־
הַשֻּׁלְחָן וְאֶת־בַּדָּיו וְאֶת־כָּל־כֵּלָיו וְאֵת לֶחֶם
הַפָּנִים: 14וְאֶת־מְנֹרַת הַמָּאוֹר וְאֶת־כֵּלֶיהָ וְאֶת־
נֵרֹתֶיהָ וְאֵת שֶׁמֶן הַמָּאוֹר: 15וְאֶת־מִזְבַּח הַקְּטֹרֶת
וְאֶת־בַּדָּיו וְאֵת שֶׁמֶן הַמִּשְׁחָה וְאֵת קְטֹרֶת הַסַּמִּים
וְאֶת־מָסַךְ הַפֶּתַח לְפֶתַח הַמִּשְׁכָּן: 16אֵת ׀ מִזְבַּח
הָעֹלָה וְאֶת־מִכְבַּר הַנְּחֹשֶׁת אֲשֶׁר־לוֹ אֶת־בַּדָּיו
וְאֶת־כָּל־כֵּלָיו אֶת־הַכִּיֹּר וְאֶת־כַּנּוֹ: 17אֵת קַלְעֵי
הֶחָצֵר אֶת־עַמֻּדָיו וְאֶת־אֲדָנֶיהָ וְאֵת מָסַךְ שַׁעַר
הֶחָצֵר: 18אֶת־יִתְדֹת הַמִּשְׁכָּן וְאֶת־יִתְדֹת הֶחָצֵר
וְאֶת־מֵיתְרֵיהֶם: 19אֶת־בִּגְדֵי הַשְּׂרָד לְשָׁרֵת בַּקֹּדֶשׁ
אֶת־בִּגְדֵי הַקֹּדֶשׁ לְאַהֲרֹן הַכֹּהֵן וְאֶת־בִּגְדֵי בָנָיו
לְכַהֵן: 20וַיֵּצְאוּ כָּל־עֲדַת בְּנֵי־יִשְׂרָאֵל מִלִּפְנֵי מֹשֶׁה:
21וַיָּבֹאוּ כָּל־אִישׁ אֲשֶׁר־נְשָׂאוֹ לִבּוֹ וְכֹל אֲשֶׁר נָדְבָה
רוּחוֹ אֹתוֹ הֵבִיאוּ אֶת־תְּרוּמַת יְהוָה לִמְלֶאכֶת אֹהֶל
מוֹעֵד וּלְכָל־עֲבֹדָתוֹ וּלְבִגְדֵי הַקֹּדֶשׁ: 22וַיָּבֹאוּ
הָאֲנָשִׁים עַל־הַנָּשִׁים כֹּל ׀ נְדִיב לֵב הֵבִיאוּ חָח

35:22. **the men came together with the women.** Given that the Torah usually either focuses on men alone or else uses the masculine plural to refer to all Israelites as a group, this passage stands out for referring repeatedly to both females and males (35:29; 36:6). The Hebrew uses an atypical term: literally, "the men came *upon* the women." The variety of reactions to this is revealing. Ibn Ezra treats it entirely as an issue of grammar, pointing out that the word for "upon" (Hebrew 'al) often means "with." Rashi interprets it in women's favor: he derives the implication that "the men came *upon* the women" means that the men came right after the women. Sforno's view is less favorable regarding women's status: he interprets the phrase to mean that the women's husbands had to accompany them and agree to their donations or else they would not be accepted. Ramban, similarly to Rashi, understands the donation of jewelry to apply more to women than to men, and so the women come first, and then they brought those men who happened to have some jewelry. In the commentary *kĕlî yāqār*, the atypical term is tied back to the fact that the women did not give their jewelry for making the golden calf while the men did. But, on any of these readings, the central point is that the women and men are equally enthusiastic in support of the sacred place, they make their gifts together, and their donations are equally welcome.

and ornaments, every kind of gold item. And every man who brought an elevation offering of gold to YHWH 23and every man with whom was found blue and purple and scarlet and linen and goats' hair and rams' skins dyed red and leather skins had brought them. 24Everyone making a donation of silver and bronze had brought YHWH's donation. And everyone with whom was found acacia wood for all the work of the construction had brought it. 25And every woman who was wise of heart with her hands had spun, and they brought yarn, the blue and the purple, the scarlet and the linen. 26And all the women whose hearts inspired them with wisdom had spun the goats' hair. 27And the chieftains had brought onyx stones and stones to be set for the ephod and for the breastplate 28and the spice and the oil for lighting and for the anointing oil and for the incense fragrances. 29Every man and woman whose heart moved them to bring for all the work that YHWH had commanded to do by the hand of Moses: the children of Israel brought a contribution for YHWH.

30And Moses said to the children of Israel, "See, YHWH has called Bezalel, son of Uri, son of Hur, of the tribe of Judah by name, 31and He has filled him with the spirit of God in wisdom, in understanding and in knowledge and in every kind of work 32and to form conceptions to make in gold and in silver and in bronze 33and in cutting stone for setting and in cutting wood, for making every kind of conceived work. 34And He has put it in his heart to instruct: he and Oholiab, son of Ahisamach, of the tribe of Dan. 35He has filled them with wisdom of heart to do all the work of the cutter and the designer and the embroiderer in the blue and in the purple, in the scarlet and in the linen and the weaver: those who do every kind of work and form conceptions. 36 1And Bezalel and Oholiab and every

וָנֶ֨זֶם וְטַבַּ֜עַת וְכוּמָ֗ז כָּל־כְּלִ֥י זָהָ֛ב וְכָל־אִ֕ישׁ אֲשֶׁ֥ר הֵנִ֛יף תְּנוּפַ֥ת זָהָ֖ב לַֽיהוָֽה׃ 23וְכָל־אִ֞ישׁ אֲשֶׁר־נִמְצָ֣א אִתּ֡וֹ תְּכֵ֨לֶת וְאַרְגָּמָ֜ן וְתוֹלַ֧עַת שָׁנִ֛י וְשֵׁ֥שׁ וְעִזִּ֖ים וְעֹרֹ֨ת אֵילִ֧ם מְאָדָּמִ֛ים וְעֹרֹ֥ת תְּחָשִׁ֖ים הֵבִֽיאוּ׃ 24כָּל־מֵרִ֗ים תְּרוּמַ֤ת כֶּ֨סֶף֙ וּנְחֹ֔שֶׁת הֵבִ֕יאוּ אֵ֖ת תְּרוּמַ֣ת יְהוָ֑ה וְכֹ֡ל אֲשֶׁר֩ נִמְצָ֨א אִתּ֜וֹ עֲצֵ֥י שִׁטִּ֛ים לְכָל־מְלֶ֥אכֶת הָעֲבֹדָ֖ה הֵבִֽיאוּ׃ 25וְכָל־אִשָּׁ֥ה חַכְמַת־לֵ֖ב בְּיָדֶ֣יהָ טָו֑וּ וַיָּבִ֣יאוּ מַטְוֶ֗ה אֶֽת־הַתְּכֵ֨לֶת֙ וְאֶת־הָ֣אַרְגָּמָ֔ן אֶת־תּוֹלַ֥עַת הַשָּׁנִ֖י וְאֶת־הַשֵּֽׁשׁ׃ 26וְכָל־הַ֨נָּשִׁ֔ים אֲשֶׁ֨ר נָשָׂ֥א לִבָּ֛ן אֹתָ֖נָה בְּחָכְמָ֑ה טָו֖וּ אֶת־הָעִזִּֽים׃ 27וְהַנְּשִׂאִ֣ם הֵבִ֔יאוּ אֵ֚ת אַבְנֵ֣י הַשֹּׁ֔הַם וְאֵ֖ת אַבְנֵ֣י הַמִּלֻּאִ֑ים לָאֵפ֖וֹד וְלַחֹֽשֶׁן׃ 28וְאֶת־הַבֹּ֖שֶׂם וְאֶת־הַשָּׁ֑מֶן לְמָא֕וֹר וּלְשֶׁ֨מֶן֙ הַמִּשְׁחָ֔ה וְלִקְטֹ֖רֶת הַסַּמִּֽים׃ 29כָּל־אִ֣ישׁ וְאִשָּׁ֗ה אֲשֶׁ֨ר נָדַ֣ב לִבָּם֮ אֹתָם֒ לְהָבִיא֙ לְכָל־הַמְּלָאכָ֔ה אֲשֶׁ֨ר צִוָּ֧ה יְהוָ֛ה לַעֲשׂ֖וֹת בְּיַד־מֹשֶׁ֑ה הֵבִ֧יאוּ בְנֵֽי־יִשְׂרָאֵ֛ל נְדָבָ֖ה לַֽיהוָֽה׃ פ

30וַיֹּ֤אמֶר מֹשֶׁה֙ אֶל־בְּנֵ֣י יִשְׂרָאֵ֔ל רְא֛וּ קָרָ֥א יְהוָ֖ה בְּשֵׁ֑ם בְּצַלְאֵ֛ל בֶּן־אוּרִ֥י בֶן־ח֖וּר לְמַטֵּ֥ה יְהוּדָֽה׃ 31וַיְמַלֵּ֥א אֹת֖וֹ ר֣וּחַ אֱלֹהִ֑ים בְּחָכְמָ֛ה בִּתְבוּנָ֥ה וּבְדַ֖עַת וּבְכָל־מְלָאכָֽה׃ 32וְלַחְשֹׁ֖ב מַֽחֲשָׁבֹ֑ת לַעֲשֹׂ֛ת בַּזָּהָ֥ב וּבַכֶּ֖סֶף וּבַנְּחֹֽשֶׁת׃ 33וּבַחֲרֹ֧שֶׁת אֶ֛בֶן לְמַלֹּ֖את וּבַחֲרֹ֣שֶׁת עֵ֑ץ לַעֲשׂ֖וֹת בְּכָל־מְלֶ֥אכֶת מַחֲשָֽׁבֶת׃ 34וּלְהוֹרֹ֖ת נָתַ֣ן בְּלִבּ֑וֹ ה֕וּא וְאָֽהֳלִיאָ֥ב בֶּן־אֲחִיסָמָ֖ךְ לְמַטֵּה־דָֽן׃ 35מִלֵּ֨א אֹתָ֜ם חָכְמַת־לֵ֗ב לַעֲשׂוֹת֮ כָּל־מְלֶ֣אכֶת חָרָ֣שׁ ׀ וְחֹשֵׁב֒ וְרֹקֵ֞ם בַּתְּכֵ֣לֶת וּבָֽאַרְגָּמָ֗ן בְּתוֹלַ֧עַת הַשָּׁנִ֛י וּבַשֵּׁ֖שׁ וְאֹרֵ֑ג עֹשֵׂי֙ כָּל־מְלָאכָ֔ה וְחֹשְׁבֵ֖י מַחֲשָׁבֹֽת׃ 36 1וְעָשָׂה֩ בְצַלְאֵ֨ל וְאָהֳלִיאָ֜ב

35:29. **whose heart moved them to bring**. This puns (twice) on the names of Aaron's sons Nadab and Abihu: נדב . . . להביא (*nādab . . . lĕhābî'*) and נדבה . . . הביאו (*hēbî'û . . . nĕdābāh*). (See also 35:21,23; 36:3.)

man who is wise of heart, in whom YHWH has put wisdom and understanding to know how to do all the work of the service of the Holy shall do it, for everything that YHWH has commanded."

2And Moses called Bezalel and Oholiab and every man who was wise of heart, in whose heart YHWH had put wisdom, everyone whose heart inspired him to come forward for the work, to do it. 3And they took from in front of Moses all of the donation that the children of Israel had brought for the work of the construction of the Holy, to do it. And they had brought him more contribution, morning by morning. 4And all the wise persons who were doing all the work of the Holy came, each from his kind of work that they were doing, 5and they said to Moses, saying, "The people are bringing more than enough for the construction, for the work that YHWH has commanded, to do it!"

6And Moses commanded, and they passed an announcement through the camp saying, "Man and woman: let them not do any more work for the donation for the Holy." And the people were held back from bringing. 7And the work had been enough for them, for all the work, to do it and more. 8And all those who were wise of heart among those who were doing the work made the

וְכֹל ׀ אִישׁ חֲכַם־לֵב אֲשֶׁר נָתַן יְהֹוָה חׇכְמָה וּתְבוּנָה בָּהֵמָּה לָדַעַת לַעֲשֹׂת אֶת־כׇּל־מְלֶאכֶת עֲבֹדַת הַקֹּדֶשׁ לְכֹל אֲשֶׁר־צִוָּה יְהֹוָה:
2וַיִּקְרָא מֹשֶׁה אֶל־בְּצַלְאֵל וְאֶל־אׇהֳלִיאָב וְאֶל כׇּל־אִישׁ חֲכַם־לֵב אֲשֶׁר נָתַן יְהֹוָה חׇכְמָה בְּלִבּוֹ כֹּל אֲשֶׁר נְשָׂאוֹ לִבּוֹ לְקׇרְבָה אֶל־הַמְּלָאכָה לַעֲשֹׂת אֹתָהּ: 3וַיִּקְחוּ מִלִּפְנֵי מֹשֶׁה אֵת כׇּל־הַתְּרוּמָה אֲשֶׁר הֵבִיאוּ בְּנֵי יִשְׂרָאֵל לִמְלֶאכֶת עֲבֹדַת הַקֹּדֶשׁ לַעֲשֹׂת אֹתָהּ וְהֵם הֵבִיאוּ אֵלָיו עוֹד נְדָבָה בַּבֹּקֶר בַּבֹּקֶר: 4וַיָּבֹאוּ כׇּל־הַחֲכָמִים הָעֹשִׂים אֵת כׇּל־מְלֶאכֶת הַקֹּדֶשׁ אִישׁ־אִישׁ מִמְּלַאכְתּוֹ אֲשֶׁר־הֵמָּה עֹשִׂים: 5וַיֹּאמְרוּ אֶל־מֹשֶׁה לֵּאמֹר מַרְבִּים הָעָם לְהָבִיא מִדֵּי הָעֲבֹדָה לַמְּלָאכָה אֲשֶׁר־צִוָּה יְהֹוָה לַעֲשֹׂת אֹתָהּ: 6וַיְצַו מֹשֶׁה וַיַּעֲבִירוּ קוֹל בַּמַּחֲנֶה לֵאמֹר אִישׁ וְאִשָּׁה אַל־יַעֲשׂוּ־עוֹד מְלָאכָה לִתְרוּמַת הַקֹּדֶשׁ וַיִּכָּלֵא הָעָם מֵהָבִיא: 7וְהַמְּלָאכָה הָיְתָה דַיָּם לְכׇל־הַמְּלָאכָה לַעֲשׂוֹת אֹתָהּ וְהוֹתֵר: ס
8וַיַּעֲשׂוּ כׇל־חֲכַם־לֵב בְּעֹשֵׂי הַמְּלָאכָה אֶת־

36:1. **all the work of the service of the Holy.** Chapters 36–39 contain a repetition of nearly all the Tabernacle details, now reporting that the work was all carried out. It doubles the message that the Tabernacle is supremely important: the channel through which divine and human communicate.

36:5. **The people are bringing more than enough.** My teacher Yohanan Muffs pointed out a paradox about sacrifice: people are commanded to do it, yet sacrifices are regarded as a freewill offering. The same applies here at the point of the establishment of Israel's entire ritual structure. The people are *commanded* to bring donations (Exod 25:1–9), yet they act with a kind of zeal that reflects more than just obedience to a commandment. They bring far more than what was required of them. This is an essential concept ultimately for the entire notion of law and commandment in Judaism. The law is not regarded as a burden. It is mandatory, yet one fulfills it out of choice and with joy. Thus the word for commandment, *miṣwāh* (popularly spelled and pronounced mitzvah), has two meanings to this day: it means a law that must be obeyed, but Jews also commonly understand it to mean a good deed, freely performed.

Tabernacle with ten curtains of woven linen and blue and purple and scarlet, with cherubs. They made them designer's work. 9The length of one curtain was twenty-eight in cubits, and the width of one curtain four in cubits: one size to all the curtains. 10And he connected five of the curtains, one to one; and he connected five curtains, one to one. 11And he made loops of blue on the side of one curtain at the end of the connected group. He did so in the side of the end curtain in the second connected group. 12He made fifty loops in the one curtain and made fifty loops in the end of the curtain that was in the second connected group with the loops parallel: one to one. 13And he made fifty clasps of gold and connected the curtains, one to one, with the clasps. And the Tabernacle was one.

14And he made curtains of goats' hair for the tent over the Tabernacle. He made them eleven curtains. 15The length of one curtain was thirty in cubits, and the width of one curtain was four cubits: one size for eleven curtains. 16And he connected five of the curtains by themselves and six of the curtains by themselves. 17And he made fifty loops on the side of the end curtain in the connected group and made fifty loops on the side of the curtain of the second connected group. 18And he made fifty bronze clasps to connect the tent, to be one. 19And he made a covering for the tent of rams' skins dyed red and a covering of leather skins above.

20And he made the frames for the Tabernacle of acacia wood, standing. 21The frame's length was ten cubits, and the width of one frame was a cubit and a half cubit. 22One frame had two projections, aligned one to one: so he made for all of the Tabernacle's frames. 23And he made the frames for the Tabernacle: twenty frames for the south side—to the south. 24And he made forty bases of silver under the twenty frames: two bases under one frame for its two projections and two bases under each other frame for its two projections. 25And for the Tabernacle's second side, for the north side, he made twenty frames

הַמִּשְׁכָּן עָשָׂה עֶשֶׂר יְרִיעֹת שֵׁשׁ מָשְׁזָר וּתְכֵלֶת וְאַרְגָּמָן וְתוֹלַעַת שָׁנִי כְּרֻבִים מַעֲשֵׂה חֹשֵׁב עָשָׂה אֹתָם: 9אֹרֶךְ הַיְרִיעָה הָאַחַת שְׁמֹנֶה וְעֶשְׂרִים בָּאַמָּה וְרֹחַב אַרְבַּע בָּאַמָּה הַיְרִיעָה הָאֶחָת מִדָּה אַחַת לְכָל־ הַיְרִיעֹת: 10וַיְחַבֵּר אֶת־חֲמֵשׁ הַיְרִיעֹת אַחַת אֶל־ אֶחָת וְחָמֵשׁ יְרִיעֹת חִבַּר אַחַת אֶל־אֶחָת: 11וַיַּעַשׂ לֻלְאֹת תְּכֵלֶת עַל שְׂפַת הַיְרִיעָה הָאֶחָת מִקָּצָה בַּמַּחְבָּרֶת כֵּן עָשָׂה בִּשְׂפַת הַיְרִיעָה הַקִּיצוֹנָה בַּמַּחְבֶּרֶת הַשֵּׁנִית: 12חֲמִשִּׁים לֻלָאֹת עָשָׂה בַּיְרִיעָה הָאֶחָת וַחֲמִשִּׁים לֻלָאֹת עָשָׂה בִּקְצֵה הַיְרִיעָה אֲשֶׁר בַּמַּחְבֶּרֶת הַשֵּׁנִית מַקְבִּילֹת הַלֻּלָאֹת אַחַת אֶל־ אֶחָת: 13וַיַּעַשׂ חֲמִשִּׁים קַרְסֵי זָהָב וַיְחַבֵּר אֶת־ הַיְרִיעֹת אַחַת אֶל־אַחַת בַּקְּרָסִים וַיְהִי הַמִּשְׁכָּן אֶחָד: ס 14וַיַּעַשׂ יְרִיעֹת עִזִּים לְאֹהֶל עַל־הַמִּשְׁכָּן עַשְׁתֵּי־עֶשְׂרֵה יְרִיעֹת עָשָׂה אֹתָם: 15אֹרֶךְ הַיְרִיעָה הָאַחַת שְׁלֹשִׁים בָּאַמָּה וְאַרְבַּע אַמּוֹת רֹחַב הַיְרִיעָה הָאֶחָת מִדָּה אַחַת לְעַשְׁתֵּי עֶשְׂרֵה יְרִיעֹת: 16וַיְחַבֵּר אֶת־חֲמֵשׁ הַיְרִיעֹת לְבָד וְאֶת־שֵׁשׁ הַיְרִיעֹת לְבָד: 17וַיַּעַשׂ לֻלָאֹת חֲמִשִּׁים עַל שְׂפַת הַיְרִיעָה הַקִּיצֹנָה בַּמַּחְבָּרֶת וַחֲמִשִּׁים לֻלָאֹת עָשָׂה עַל־שְׂפַת הַיְרִיעָה הַחֹבֶרֶת הַשֵּׁנִית: 18וַיַּעַשׂ קַרְסֵי נְחֹשֶׁת חֲמִשִּׁים לְחַבֵּר אֶת־הָאֹהֶל לִהְיֹת אֶחָד: 19וַיַּעַשׂ מִכְסֶה לָאֹהֶל עֹרֹת אֵלִים מְאָדָּמִים וּמִכְסֵה עֹרֹת תְּחָשִׁים מִלְמָעְלָה: ס 20וַיַּעַשׂ אֶת־הַקְּרָשִׁים לַמִּשְׁכָּן עֲצֵי שִׁטִּים עֹמְדִים: 21עֶשֶׂר אַמֹּת אֹרֶךְ הַקָּרֶשׁ וְאַמָּה וַחֲצִי הָאַמָּה רֹחַב הַקֶּרֶשׁ הָאֶחָד: 22שְׁתֵּי יָדֹת לַקֶּרֶשׁ הָאֶחָד מְשֻׁלָּבֹת אַחַת אֶל־אֶחָת כֵּן עָשָׂה לְכֹל קַרְשֵׁי הַמִּשְׁכָּן: 23וַיַּעַשׂ אֶת־הַקְּרָשִׁים לַמִּשְׁכָּן עֶשְׂרִים קְרָשִׁים לִפְאַת נֶגֶב תֵּימָנָה: 24וְאַרְבָּעִים אַדְנֵי־כֶסֶף עָשָׂה תַּחַת עֶשְׂרִים הַקְּרָשִׁים שְׁנֵי אֲדָנִים תַּחַת־הַקֶּרֶשׁ הָאֶחָד לִשְׁתֵּי יְדֹתָיו וּשְׁנֵי אֲדָנִים תַּחַת־הַקֶּרֶשׁ הָאֶחָד לִשְׁתֵּי יְדֹתָיו: 25וּלְצֶלַע הַמִּשְׁכָּן הַשֵּׁנִית לִפְאַת צָפוֹן עָשָׂה עֶשְׂרִים קְרָשִׁים:

26and their forty bases of silver, two bases under one frame and two bases under each other frame. 27And for the rear of the Tabernacle, to the west, he made six frames. 28And he made two frames for the Tabernacle's corners in the rear, 29and they were *doubles* from below, and together they were *integrated* on its top to one ring. He made it so for the two of them, for the two corners. 30And they were eight frames and their bases of silver, sixteen bases, two bases and two bases under each one frame. 31And he made bars of acacia wood: five for the frames of one side of the Tabernacle 32and five bars for the frames of the second side of the Tabernacle and five bars for the frames of the side of the Tabernacle at the rear, to the west. 33And he made the middle bar to extend through the frames from end to end. 34And he plated the frames with gold, and he made their rings gold, housings for the bars, and he plated the bars with gold.

35And he made the pavilion of blue and purple and scarlet and woven linen; he made it designer's work with cherubs. 36And he made four acacia columns for it and plated them with gold, their hooks of gold, and he cast four bases of silver for them. 37And he made a cover for the entrance of the tent: blue and purple and scarlet and woven linen—embroiderer's work— 38and its five columns and their hooks, and he plated their tops and their bands with gold, and their five bases were bronze.

37 1And Bezalel made the ark of acacia wood, its length two and a half cubits and its width a cubit and a half and its height a cubit and a half. 2And he plated it with pure gold inside and outside. And he made a border of gold all around for it. 3And he cast four rings of gold for it on its four bottoms: and two rings on its one side and two rings on its second side. 4And he made poles of acacia wood and plated them with gold 5and brought the poles through the rings on the ark's sides, in order to carry the ark. 6And he made an atonement dais of pure gold, its length two and a half cubits and its

26וְאַרְבָּעִים אַדְנֵיהֶם כָּסֶף שְׁנֵי אֲדָנִים תַּחַת הַקֶּרֶשׁ הָאֶחָד וּשְׁנֵי אֲדָנִים תַּחַת הַקֶּרֶשׁ הָאֶחָד: 27וּלְיַרְכְּתֵי הַמִּשְׁכָּן יָמָּה עָשָׂה שִׁשָּׁה קְרָשִׁים: 28וּשְׁנֵי קְרָשִׁים עָשָׂה לִמְקֻצְעֹת הַמִּשְׁכָּן בַּיַּרְכָתָיִם: 29וְהָיוּ תוֹאֲמִם מִלְּמַטָּה וְיַחְדָּו יִהְיוּ תַמִּים אֶל־רֹאשׁוֹ אֶל־הַטַּבַּעַת הָאֶחָת כֵּן עָשָׂה לִשְׁנֵיהֶם לִשְׁנֵי הַמִּקְצֹעֹת: 30וְהָיוּ שְׁמֹנָה קְרָשִׁים וְאַדְנֵיהֶם כֶּסֶף שִׁשָּׁה עָשָׂר אֲדָנִים שְׁנֵי אֲדָנִים שְׁנֵי אֲדָנִים תַּחַת הַקֶּרֶשׁ הָאֶחָד: 31וַיַּעַשׂ בְּרִיחֵי עֲצֵי שִׁטִּים חֲמִשָּׁה לְקַרְשֵׁי צֶלַע־הַמִּשְׁכָּן הָאֶחָת: 32וַחֲמִשָּׁה בְרִיחִם לְקַרְשֵׁי צֶלַע־הַמִּשְׁכָּן הַשֵּׁנִית וַחֲמִשָּׁה בְרִיחִם לְקַרְשֵׁי הַמִּשְׁכָּן לַיַּרְכָתַיִם יָמָּה: 33וַיַּעַשׂ אֶת־הַבְּרִיחַ הַתִּיכֹן לִבְרֹחַ בְּתוֹךְ הַקְּרָשִׁים מִן־הַקָּצֶה אֶל־הַקָּצֶה: 34וְאֶת־הַקְּרָשִׁים צִפָּה זָהָב וְאֶת־טַבְּעֹתָם עָשָׂה זָהָב בָּתִּים לַבְּרִיחִם וַיְצַף אֶת־הַבְּרִיחִם זָהָב: 35וַיַּעַשׂ אֶת־הַפָּרֹכֶת תְּכֵלֶת וְאַרְגָּמָן וְתוֹלַעַת שָׁנִי וְשֵׁשׁ מָשְׁזָר מַעֲשֵׂה חֹשֵׁב עָשָׂה אֹתָהּ כְּרֻבִים: 36וַיַּעַשׂ לָהּ אַרְבָּעָה עַמּוּדֵי שִׁטִּים וַיְצַפֵּם זָהָב וָוֵיהֶם זָהָב וַיִּצֹק לָהֶם אַרְבָּעָה אַדְנֵי־כָסֶף: 37וַיַּעַשׂ מָסָךְ לְפֶתַח הָאֹהֶל תְּכֵלֶת וְאַרְגָּמָן וְתוֹלַעַת שָׁנִי וְשֵׁשׁ מָשְׁזָר מַעֲשֵׂה רֹקֵם: 38וְאֶת־עַמּוּדָיו חֲמִשָּׁה וְאֶת־וָוֵיהֶם וְצִפָּה רָאשֵׁיהֶם וַחֲשֻׁקֵיהֶם זָהָב וְאַדְנֵיהֶם חֲמִשָּׁה נְחֹשֶׁת: פ

37 1וַיַּעַשׂ בְּצַלְאֵל אֶת־הָאָרֹן עֲצֵי שִׁטִּים אַמָּתַיִם וָחֵצִי אָרְכּוֹ וְאַמָּה וָחֵצִי רָחְבּוֹ וְאַמָּה וָחֵצִי קֹמָתוֹ: 2וַיְצַפֵּהוּ זָהָב טָהוֹר מִבַּיִת וּמִחוּץ וַיַּעַשׂ לוֹ זֵר זָהָב סָבִיב: 3וַיִּצֹק לוֹ אַרְבַּע טַבְּעֹת זָהָב עַל אַרְבַּע פַּעֲמֹתָיו וּשְׁתֵּי טַבָּעֹת עַל־צַלְעוֹ הָאֶחָת וּשְׁתֵּי טַבָּעוֹת עַל־צַלְעוֹ הַשֵּׁנִית: 4וַיַּעַשׂ בַּדֵּי עֲצֵי שִׁטִּים וַיְצַף אֹתָם זָהָב: 5וַיָּבֵא אֶת־הַבַּדִּים בַּטַּבָּעֹת עַל צַלְעֹת הָאָרֹן לָשֵׂאת אֶת־הָאָרֹן: 6וַיַּעַשׂ כַּפֹּרֶת זָהָב טָהוֹר אַמָּתַיִם וָחֵצִי אָרְכָּהּ וְאַמָּה וָחֵצִי

width a cubit and a half. 7And he made two cherubs of gold—he made them of hammered work—at the two ends of the atonement dais, 8one cherub at this end and one cherub at that end. He made the cherubs from the atonement dais at its two sides. 9And the two cherubs were spreading wings above, covering over the atonement dais with their wings, and their faces each toward its brother: the cherubs' faces were toward the atonement dais.

10And he made the table of acacia wood, its length two cubits and its width a cubit and its height a cubit and a half. 11And he plated it with pure gold and made a border of gold all around for it 12and made a rim of a handbreadth for it all around and made a border of gold for its rim all around. 13And he cast four rings of gold for it and put the rings on the four corners that its four legs had. 14The rings were in juxtaposition to the rim, housings for the poles in order to carry the table. 15And he made the poles of acacia wood and plated them with gold in order to carry the table. 16And he made the items that were on the table—its dishes and its pans and its bowls and its jars with which libations would be poured—of pure gold.

17And he made the menorah of pure gold. He made the menorah of hammered work—its shaft and its branch, its cups, its ornaments, and its flowers were part of it— 18and six branches coming out from its sides, three of the menorah's branches from its one side and three of the menorah's branches from its second side, 19three almond-shaped cups in the one branch, with ornament and flower, and three almond-shaped cups in the other branch, with ornament and flower. So it was for the six branches that came out from the menorah, 20and four almond-shaped cups within the menorah, with its ornaments and its flowers, 21and an ornament under the two branches from it, and an ornament under the two branches from it, and an ornament under the two branches from it, for the six branches that came out from it. 22Their orna-

רְחָבָּה: 7וַיַּעַשׂ שְׁנֵי כְרֻבִים זָהָב מִקְשָׁה עָשָׂה אֹתָם מִשְּׁנֵי קְצוֹת הַכַּפֹּרֶת: 8כְּרוּב־אֶחָד מִקָּצָה מִזֶּה וּכְרוּב־אֶחָד מִקָּצָה מִזֶּה מִן־הַכַּפֹּרֶת עָשָׂה אֶת־הַכְּרֻבִים מִשְּׁנֵי קצוותו קְצוֹתָיו: 9וַיִּהְיוּ הַכְּרֻבִים פֹּרְשֵׂי כְנָפַיִם לְמַעְלָה סֹכְכִים בְּכַנְפֵיהֶם עַל־הַכַּפֹּרֶת וּפְנֵיהֶם אִישׁ אֶל־אָחִיו אֶל־הַכַּפֹּרֶת הָיוּ פְּנֵי הַכְּרֻבִים: פ 10וַיַּעַשׂ אֶת־הַשֻּׁלְחָן עֲצֵי שִׁטִּים אַמָּתַיִם אָרְכּוֹ וְאַמָּה רָחְבּוֹ וְאַמָּה וָחֵצִי קֹמָתוֹ: 11וַיְצַף אֹתוֹ זָהָב טָהוֹר וַיַּעַשׂ לוֹ זֵר זָהָב סָבִיב: 12וַיַּעַשׂ לוֹ מִסְגֶּרֶת טֹפַח סָבִיב וַיַּעַשׂ זֵר־זָהָב לְמִסְגַּרְתּוֹ סָבִיב: 13וַיִּצֹק לוֹ אַרְבַּע טַבְּעֹת זָהָב וַיִּתֵּן אֶת־הַטַּבָּעֹת עַל אַרְבַּע הַפֵּאֹת אֲשֶׁר לְאַרְבַּע רַגְלָיו: 14לְעֻמַּת הַמִּסְגֶּרֶת הָיוּ הַטַּבָּעֹת בָּתִּים לַבַּדִּים לָשֵׂאת אֶת־הַשֻּׁלְחָן: 15וַיַּעַשׂ אֶת־הַבַּדִּים עֲצֵי שִׁטִּים וַיְצַף אֹתָם זָהָב לָשֵׂאת אֶת־הַשֻּׁלְחָן: 16וַיַּעַשׂ אֶת־הַכֵּלִים ׀ אֲשֶׁר עַל־הַשֻּׁלְחָן אֶת־קְעָרֹתָיו וְאֶת־כַּפֹּתָיו וְאֵת מְנַקִּיֹּתָיו וְאֶת־הַקְּשָׂוֹת אֲשֶׁר יֻסַּךְ בָּהֵן זָהָב טָהוֹר: פ 17וַיַּעַשׂ אֶת־הַמְּנֹרָה זָהָב טָהוֹר מִקְשָׁה עָשָׂה אֶת־הַמְּנֹרָה יְרֵכָהּ וְקָנָהּ גְּבִיעֶיהָ כַּפְתֹּרֶיהָ וּפְרָחֶיהָ מִמֶּנָּה הָיוּ: 18וְשִׁשָּׁה קָנִים יֹצְאִים מִצִּדֶּיהָ שְׁלֹשָׁה ׀ קְנֵי מְנֹרָה מִצִּדָּהּ הָאֶחָד וּשְׁלֹשָׁה קְנֵי מְנֹרָה מִצִּדָּהּ הַשֵּׁנִי: 19שְׁלֹשָׁה גְבִעִים מְשֻׁקָּדִים בַּקָּנֶה הָאֶחָד כַּפְתֹּר וָפֶרַח וּשְׁלֹשָׁה גְבִעִים מְשֻׁקָּדִים בְּקָנֶה אֶחָד כַּפְתֹּר וָפָרַח כֵּן לְשֵׁשֶׁת הַקָּנִים הַיֹּצְאִים מִן־הַמְּנֹרָה: 20וּבַמְּנֹרָה אַרְבָּעָה גְבִעִים מְשֻׁקָּדִים כַּפְתֹּרֶיהָ וּפְרָחֶיהָ: 21וְכַפְתֹּר תַּחַת שְׁנֵי הַקָּנִים מִמֶּנָּה וְכַפְתֹּר תַּחַת שְׁנֵי הַקָּנִים מִמֶּנָּה וְכַפְתֹּר תַּחַת־שְׁנֵי הַקָּנִים מִמֶּנָּה לְשֵׁשֶׁת הַקָּנִים הַיֹּצְאִים מִמֶּנָּה: 22כַּפְתֹּרֵיהֶם וּקְנֹתָם

37:8 קְצוֹתָיו ק

ments and their branches were part of it, all of it one hammered work of pure gold. 23And he made its lamps, seven, and its tongs and its fire-holders of pure gold. 24He made it and all of its equipment out of a talent of pure gold.

25And he made the incense altar of acacia wood: its length a cubit and its width a cubit, square, and its height two cubits; its horns were a part of it. 26And he plated it with pure gold, its roof and its walls all around and its horns. And he made a border of gold for it all around. 27And he made two rings of gold for it below its rim on its two sides, on its two sidewalls, for housings for poles with which to carry it. 28And he made the poles of acacia wood and plated them with gold. 29And he made the holy anointing oil and the pure incense fragrances, the work of an oint-ment-maker.

38 1And he made the altar of burnt offering of acacia wood, its length five cubits and its width five cubits, square, and its height three cubits. 2And he made its horns on its four cor-ners. Its horns were part of it. And he plated it with bronze. 3And he made all the altar's equip-ment: the pots, the shovels and the basins, the forks and the fire-holders. He made all of its equipment bronze. 4And he made a grate for the altar, a network of bronze, under its ledge up to the middle of it. 5And he cast four rings in the bronze grate's four ends: housings for the poles. 6And he made the poles of acacia wood and plat-ed them with bronze 7and brought the poles through the rings on the altar's sides in order to carry it with them. He made it hollow of boards.

8And he made the basin of bronze and its stand of bronze with the mirrors of the women who served at the entrance of the Tent of Meeting.

מִמֶּנָּה הָיוּ כֻּלָּהּ מִקְשָׁה אַחַת זָהָב טָהוֹר: 23וַיַּעַשׂ
אֶת־נֵרֹתֶיהָ שִׁבְעָה וּמַלְקָחֶיהָ וּמַחְתֹּתֶיהָ זָהָב טָהוֹר:
24כִּכָּר זָהָב טָהוֹר עָשָׂה אֹתָהּ וְאֵת כָּל־כֵּלֶיהָ: פ
25וַיַּעַשׂ אֶת־מִזְבַּח הַקְּטֹרֶת עֲצֵי שִׁטִּים אַמָּה אָרְכּוֹ
וְאַמָּה רָחְבּוֹ רָבוּעַ וְאַמָּתַיִם קֹמָתוֹ מִמֶּנּוּ הָיוּ
קַרְנֹתָיו: 26וַיְצַף אֹתוֹ זָהָב טָהוֹר אֶת־גַּגּוֹ וְאֶת־
קִירֹתָיו סָבִיב וְאֶת־קַרְנֹתָיו וַיַּעַשׂ לוֹ זֵר זָהָב
סָבִיב: 27וּשְׁתֵּי טַבְּעֹת זָהָב עָשָׂה־לוֹ ׀ מִתַּחַת לְזֵרוֹ
עַל שְׁתֵּי צַלְעֹתָיו עַל שְׁנֵי צִדָּיו לְבָתִּים לְבַדִּים
לָשֵׂאת אֹתוֹ בָּהֶם: 28וַיַּעַשׂ אֶת־הַבַּדִּים עֲצֵי שִׁטִּים
וַיְצַף אֹתָם זָהָב: 29וַיַּעַשׂ אֶת־שֶׁמֶן הַמִּשְׁחָה קֹדֶשׁ
וְאֶת־קְטֹרֶת הַסַּמִּים טָהוֹר מַעֲשֵׂה רֹקֵחַ: פ

38 1וַיַּעַשׂ אֶת־מִזְבַּח הָעֹלָה עֲצֵי שִׁטִּים חָמֵשׁ
אַמּוֹת אָרְכּוֹ וְחָמֵשׁ־אַמּוֹת רָחְבּוֹ רָבוּעַ וְשָׁלֹשׁ אַמּוֹת
קֹמָתוֹ: 2וַיַּעַשׂ קַרְנֹתָיו עַל אַרְבַּע פִּנֹּתָיו מִמֶּנּוּ הָיוּ
קַרְנֹתָיו וַיְצַף אֹתוֹ נְחֹשֶׁת: 3וַיַּעַשׂ אֶת־כָּל־כְּלֵי
הַמִּזְבֵּחַ אֶת־הַסִּירֹת וְאֶת־הַיָּעִים וְאֶת־הַמִּזְרָקֹת אֶת־
הַמִּזְלָגֹת וְאֶת־הַמַּחְתֹּת כָּל־כֵּלָיו עָשָׂה נְחֹשֶׁת:
4וַיַּעַשׂ לַמִּזְבֵּחַ מִכְבָּר מַעֲשֵׂה רֶשֶׁת נְחֹשֶׁת תַּחַת
כַּרְכֻּבּוֹ מִלְמַטָּה עַד־חֶצְיוֹ: 5וַיִּצֹק אַרְבַּע טַבָּעֹת
בְּאַרְבַּע הַקְּצָוֹת לְמִכְבַּר הַנְּחֹשֶׁת בָּתִּים לַבַּדִּים:
6וַיַּעַשׂ אֶת־הַבַּדִּים עֲצֵי שִׁטִּים וַיְצַף אֹתָם נְחֹשֶׁת:
7וַיָּבֵא אֶת־הַבַּדִּים בַּטַּבָּעֹת עַל צַלְעֹת הַמִּזְבֵּחַ
לָשֵׂאת אֹתוֹ בָּהֶם נְבוּב לֻחֹת עָשָׂה אֹתוֹ: ס 8וַיַּעַשׂ
אֵת הַכִּיּוֹר נְחֹשֶׁת וְאֵת כַּנּוֹ נְחֹשֶׁת בְּמַרְאֹת הַצֹּבְאֹת
אֲשֶׁר צָבְאוּ פֶּתַח אֹהֶל מוֹעֵד: ס 9וַיַּעַשׂ אֶת־

38:8. women who served at the entrance of the Tent of Meeting. This is the first mention of the female workers at the Tabernacle. They are mentioned one time out-side the Torah: a few generations after Moses, the priest Eli's sons have illicit sex with them at Shiloh. The temptation of males in power to take advantage of their high po-sition in the eyes of women who work under them has persisted for centuries. It is crit-icized in the *Tanak*. In the case of the Shiloh priests, it is one of the acts that leads to the downfall of that priestly house and its replacement by Samuel (1 Sam 2:22–26).

9And he made the courtyard: for the south side—to the south, the courtyard's hangings of woven linen, a hundred in cubits, 10their columns twenty, and their bases twenty of bronze, and the columns' hooks and their rods of silver. 11And for the north side: a hundred in cubits, their columns twenty, and their bases twenty of bronze, and the columns' hooks and their bands of silver. 12And for the west side: hangings of fifty in cubits, their columns ten, and their bases ten, the columns' hooks and their bands of silver. 13And the courtyard's width for the east side—to the east—fifty cubits. 14Fifteen cubits of hangings to the panel, their columns three and their bases three; 15and the second panel—on this side and that side of the courtyard's gate—hangings of fifteen cubits, their columns three and their bases three. 16All of the courtyard's hangings, all around, were woven linen. 17And the column's bases were bronze, the columns' hooks and their bands were silver, and the plating of their tops was silver, and they were banded with silver: all of the courtyard's columns. 18And the cover of the courtyard's gate was embroiderer's work, blue and purple and scarlet and woven linen, and twenty cubits in length, and five cubits in height in the width, in juxtaposition to the courtyard's hangings. 19And their columns were four and their bases four of bronze, their hooks silver, and the plating of their tops and their bands silver. 20And all of the pegs of the Tabernacle and the courtyard all around were bronze.

הֶחָצֵר לִפְאַת ׀ נֶגֶב תֵּימָנָה קַלְעֵי הֶחָצֵר שֵׁשׁ מָשְׁזָר מֵאָה בָּאַמָּה: 10עַמּוּדֵיהֶם עֶשְׂרִים וְאַדְנֵיהֶם עֶשְׂרִים נְחֹשֶׁת וָוֵי הָעַמֻּדִים וַחֲשֻׁקֵיהֶם כָּסֶף: 11וְלִפְאַת צָפוֹן מֵאָה בָאַמָּה עַמּוּדֵיהֶם עֶשְׂרִים וְאַדְנֵיהֶם עֶשְׂרִים נְחֹשֶׁת וָוֵי הָעַמּוּדִים וַחֲשֻׁקֵיהֶם כָּסֶף: 12וְלִפְאַת־יָם קְלָעִים חֲמִשִּׁים בָּאַמָּה עַמּוּדֵיהֶם עֲשָׂרָה וְאַדְנֵיהֶם עֲשָׂרָה וָוֵי הָעַמֻּדִים וַחֲשׁוּקֵיהֶם כָּסֶף: 13וְלִפְאַת קֵדְמָה מִזְרָחָה חֲמִשִּׁים אַמָּה: 14קְלָעִים חֲמֵשׁ־עֶשְׂרֵה אַמָּה אֶל־הַכָּתֵף עַמּוּדֵיהֶם שְׁלֹשָׁה וְאַדְנֵיהֶם שְׁלֹשָׁה: 15וְלַכָּתֵף הַשֵּׁנִית מִזֶּה וּמִזֶּה לְשַׁעַר הֶחָצֵר קְלָעִים חֲמֵשׁ עֶשְׂרֵה אַמָּה עַמֻּדֵיהֶם שְׁלֹשָׁה וְאַדְנֵיהֶם שְׁלֹשָׁה: 16כָּל־קַלְעֵי הֶחָצֵר סָבִיב שֵׁשׁ מָשְׁזָר: 17וְהָאֲדָנִים לָעַמֻּדִים נְחֹשֶׁת וָוֵי הָעַמּוּדִים וַחֲשׁוּקֵיהֶם כֶּסֶף וְצִפּוּי רָאשֵׁיהֶם כָּסֶף וְהֵם מְחֻשָּׁקִים כֶּסֶף כֹּל עַמֻּדֵי הֶחָצֵר: 18וּמָסַךְ שַׁעַר הֶחָצֵר מַעֲשֵׂה רֹקֵם תְּכֵלֶת וְאַרְגָּמָן וְתוֹלַעַת שָׁנִי וְשֵׁשׁ מָשְׁזָר וְעֶשְׂרִים אַמָּה אֹרֶךְ וְקוֹמָה בְרֹחַב חָמֵשׁ אַמּוֹת לְעֻמַּת קַלְעֵי הֶחָצֵר: 19וְעַמֻּדֵיהֶם אַרְבָּעָה וְאַדְנֵיהֶם אַרְבָּעָה נְחֹשֶׁת וָוֵיהֶם כֶּסֶף וְצִפּוּי רָאשֵׁיהֶם וַחֲשֻׁקֵיהֶם כָּסֶף: 20וְכָל־הַיְתֵדֹת לַמִּשְׁכָּן וְלֶחָצֵר סָבִיב נְחֹשֶׁת: ס

38:18. five cubits in height in the width. I understand the cover to be a canopy above the entrance (as opposed to a screen or curtain hanging). The Hebrew (*māsāk*) denotes a thing that covers *over* something else (Exod 40:3; 2 Sam 17:19; Ps 105:39). So the phrase in this verse means that the entire width of the courtyard's cover, from front to back, is suspended five cubits above the ground, or that both its width and its height above the ground are five cubits.

ACCOUNTS

פְקוּדֵי

21These are the accounts of the Tabernacle, the Tabernacle of the Testimony, that were made by Moses' word, the work of the Levites by the hand of Ithamar, son of Aaron, the priest. 22And Bezalel, son of Uri, son of Hur, of the tribe of Judah, made everything that YHWH had commanded Moses. 23And with him was Oholiab, son of Ahisamach, of the tribe of Dan, an engraver and designer and embroiderer in blue and in purple and in scarlet and in linen. 24All the gold that was used for the work, in all the work of the Holy: and the gold of the elevation offering was twenty-nine talents and seven hundred thirty shekels by the shekel of the Holy.

25And the silver of the congregation's accounts was a hundred talents and a thousand seven hundred seventy-five shekels by the shekel of the Holy: 26a beqa per head, half of a shekel by the shekel of the Holy, for everyone who passed through the counts, from twenty years old and up, for six hundred thousand and three thousand five hundred fifty. 27And the hundred talents of silver were for casting the bases of the Holy and the bases of the pavilion, a hundred bases to the hundred talents, a talent per base. 28And he made the thousand seven hundred seventy-five into hooks for the columns, and he plated their tops and banded them.

29And the bronze of the elevation offering was seventy talents and two thousand four hundred shekels. 30And with it he made the bases of the entrance of the Tent of Meeting and the bronze altar and the bronze network that it had and all of the altar's equipment 31and the bases of the courtyard all around and the bases of the courtyard's gate and all of the Tabernacle's pegs and all of the courtyard's pegs all around.

21אֵלֶּה פְקוּדֵי הַמִּשְׁכָּן מִשְׁכַּן הָעֵדֻת אֲשֶׁר פֻּקַּד עַל־פִּי מֹשֶׁה עֲבֹדַת הַלְוִיִּם בְּיַד אִיתָמָר בֶּן־אַהֲרֹן הַכֹּהֵן: 22וּבְצַלְאֵל בֶּן־אוּרִי בֶן־חוּר לְמַטֵּה יְהוּדָה עָשָׂה אֵת כָּל־אֲשֶׁר־צִוָּה יְהוָה אֶת־מֹשֶׁה: 23וְאִתּוֹ אָהֳלִיאָב בֶּן־אֲחִיסָמָךְ לְמַטֵּה־דָן חָרָשׁ וְחֹשֵׁב וְרֹקֵם בַּתְּכֵלֶת וּבָאַרְגָּמָן וּבְתוֹלַעַת הַשָּׁנִי וּבַשֵּׁשׁ: ס 24כָּל־הַזָּהָב הֶעָשׂוּי לַמְּלָאכָה בְּכֹל מְלֶאכֶת הַקֹּדֶשׁ וַיְהִי זְהַב הַתְּנוּפָה תֵּשַׁע וְעֶשְׂרִים כִּכָּר וּשְׁבַע מֵאוֹת וּשְׁלֹשִׁים שֶׁקֶל בְּשֶׁקֶל הַקֹּדֶשׁ: 25וְכֶסֶף פְּקוּדֵי הָעֵדָה מְאַת כִּכָּר וְאֶלֶף וּשְׁבַע מֵאוֹת וַחֲמִשָּׁה וְשִׁבְעִים שֶׁקֶל בְּשֶׁקֶל הַקֹּדֶשׁ: 26בֶּקַע לַגֻּלְגֹּלֶת מַחֲצִית הַשֶּׁקֶל בְּשֶׁקֶל הַקֹּדֶשׁ לְכֹל הָעֹבֵר עַל־הַפְּקֻדִים מִבֶּן עֶשְׂרִים שָׁנָה וָמַעְלָה לְשֵׁשׁ־מֵאוֹת אֶלֶף וּשְׁלֹשֶׁת אֲלָפִים וַחֲמֵשׁ מֵאוֹת וַחֲמִשִּׁים: 27וַיְהִי מְאַת כִּכַּר הַכֶּסֶף לָצֶקֶת אֵת אַדְנֵי הַקֹּדֶשׁ וְאֵת אַדְנֵי הַפָּרֹכֶת מְאַת אֲדָנִים לִמְאַת הַכִּכָּר כִּכָּר לָאָדֶן: 28וְאֶת־הָאֶלֶף וּשְׁבַע הַמֵּאוֹת וַחֲמִשָּׁה וְשִׁבְעִים עָשָׂה וָוִים לָעַמּוּדִים וְצִפָּה רָאשֵׁיהֶם וְחִשַּׁק אֹתָם: 29וּנְחֹשֶׁת הַתְּנוּפָה שִׁבְעִים כִּכָּר וְאַלְפַּיִם וְאַרְבַּע־מֵאוֹת שָׁקֶל: 30וַיַּעַשׂ בָּהּ אֶת־אַדְנֵי פֶּתַח אֹהֶל מוֹעֵד וְאֵת מִזְבַּח הַנְּחֹשֶׁת וְאֶת־מִכְבַּר הַנְּחֹשֶׁת אֲשֶׁר־לוֹ וְאֵת כָּל־כְּלֵי הַמִּזְבֵּחַ: 31וְאֶת־אַדְנֵי הֶחָצֵר סָבִיב וְאֶת־אַדְנֵי שַׁעַר הֶחָצֵר וְאֵת כָּל־יִתְדֹת הַמִּשְׁכָּן וְאֶת־כָּל־יִתְדֹת הֶחָצֵר סָבִיב:

38:21. by the hand of Ithamar. Meaning: under the direction of Ithamar.

39

¹And from the blue and the purple and the scarlet they made fabric clothes for ministering in the Holy, and they made the holy clothes that were Aaron's, as YHWH had commanded Moses.

²And he made the ephod: gold, blue, and purple and scarlet and woven linen. ³And they hammered out foil sheets of the gold, and he cut threads to use among the blue and among the purple and among the scarlet and among the linen—designer's work. ⁴They made shoulder-pieces for it, connected: on its two ends it was connected. ⁵And its ephod designed belt that was on it was a part of it, like its work, gold, blue, and purple and scarlet and woven linen, as YHWH had commanded Moses. ⁶And they made the onyx stones surrounded by settings of gold, inscribed with signet inscriptions with the names of the children of Israel. ⁷And he set them on the ephod's shoulder-pieces, commemorative stones for the children of Israel, as YHWH had commanded Moses.

⁸And he made the breastplate, designer's work, like the work of the ephod: gold, blue, and purple and scarlet and woven linen. ⁹It was square. They made the breastplate doubled, its length a span and its width a span, doubled. ¹⁰And they mounted four rows of stones in it: a row of a carnelian, a topaz, and an emerald: the one row; ¹¹and the second row: a ruby, a sapphire, and a diamond; ¹²and the third row: a *jacinth*, an agate, and an amethyst; ¹³and the fourth row: a beryl, an onyx, and a jasper—set in gold in their mountings. ¹⁴And the stones: they were with the names of the children of Israel, twelve with their names, signet engravings, each with its name, for twelve tribes. ¹⁵And they made twisted chains, rope work, of pure gold, on the breastplate. ¹⁶And they made two settings of gold and two rings of gold and put the two rings on the two ends of the breastplate ¹⁷and put the two ropes of gold on the two rings at the ends of the breastplate. ¹⁸And they put the two ends of the two ropes on the two settings and put them

39 ¹וּמִן־הַתְּכֵ֤לֶת וְהָֽאַרְגָּמָן֙ וְתוֹלַ֣עַת הַשָּׁנִ֔י עָשׂ֥וּ בִגְדֵי־שְׂרָ֖ד לְשָׁרֵ֣ת בַּקֹּ֑דֶשׁ וַֽיַּעֲשׂ֞וּ אֶת־בִּגְדֵ֤י הַקֹּ֨דֶשׁ֙ אֲשֶׁ֣ר לְאַהֲרֹ֔ן כַּאֲשֶׁ֛ר צִוָּ֥ה יְהוָ֖ה אֶת־מֹשֶֽׁה׃ פ ²וַיַּ֖עַשׂ אֶת־הָאֵפֹ֑ד זָהָ֗ב תְּכֵ֧לֶת וְאַרְגָּמָ֛ן וְתוֹלַ֥עַת שָׁנִ֖י וְשֵׁ֥שׁ מָשְׁזָֽר׃ ³וַֽיְרַקְּע֞וּ אֶת־פַּחֵ֣י הַזָּהָב֮ וְקִצֵּ֣ץ פְּתִילִם֒ לַעֲשׂ֗וֹת בְּת֤וֹךְ הַתְּכֵ֨לֶת֙ וּבְת֣וֹךְ הָֽאַרְגָּמָ֔ן וּבְת֛וֹךְ תּוֹלַ֥עַת הַשָּׁנִ֖י וּבְת֣וֹךְ הַשֵּׁ֑שׁ מַעֲשֵׂ֖ה חֹשֵֽׁב׃ ⁴כְּתֵפֹ֥ת עָֽשׂוּ־ל֖וֹ חֹבְרֹ֑ת עַל־שְׁנֵ֥י קצוותו[קְצוֹתָ֖יו] חֻבָּֽר׃ ⁵וְחֵ֨שֶׁב אֲפֻדָּת֜וֹ אֲשֶׁ֣ר עָלָ֗יו מִמֶּ֤נּוּ הוּא֙ כְּמַעֲשֵׂ֔הוּ זָהָ֗ב תְּכֵ֧לֶת וְאַרְגָּמָ֛ן וְתוֹלַ֥עַת שָׁנִ֖י וְשֵׁ֣שׁ מָשְׁזָ֑ר כַּאֲשֶׁ֛ר צִוָּ֥ה יְהוָ֖ה אֶת־מֹשֶֽׁה׃ ⁶וַֽיַּעֲשׂוּ֙ אֶת־אַבְנֵ֣י הַשֹּׁ֔הַם מֻֽסַבֹּ֖ת מִשְׁבְּצֹ֣ת זָהָ֑ב מְפֻתָּחֹת֙ פִּתּוּחֵ֣י חוֹתָ֔ם עַל־שְׁמ֖וֹת בְּנֵ֥י יִשְׂרָאֵֽל׃ ⁷וַיָּ֣שֶׂם אֹתָ֗ם עַ֚ל כִּתְפֹ֣ת הָאֵפֹ֔ד אַבְנֵ֥י זִכָּר֖וֹן לִבְנֵ֣י יִשְׂרָאֵ֑ל כַּאֲשֶׁ֛ר צִוָּ֥ה יְהוָ֖ה אֶת־מֹשֶֽׁה׃ פ ⁸וַיַּ֧עַשׂ אֶת־הַחֹ֛שֶׁן מַעֲשֵׂ֥ה חֹשֵׁ֖ב כְּמַעֲשֵׂ֣ה אֵפֹ֑ד זָהָ֗ב תְּכֵ֧לֶת וְאַרְגָּמָ֛ן וְתוֹלַ֥עַת שָׁנִ֖י וְשֵׁ֥שׁ מָשְׁזָֽר׃ ⁹רָב֧וּעַ הָיָ֛ה כָּפ֖וּל עָשׂ֣וּ אֶת־הַחֹ֑שֶׁן זֶ֧רֶת אָרְכּ֛וֹ וְזֶ֥רֶת רָחְבּ֖וֹ כָּפֽוּל׃ ¹⁰וַיְמַלְאוּ־ב֔וֹ אַרְבָּעָ֖ה ט֣וּרֵי אָ֑בֶן ט֗וּר אֹ֤דֶם פִּטְדָה֙ וּבָרֶ֔קֶת הַטּ֖וּר הָאֶחָֽד׃ ¹¹וְהַטּ֖וּר הַשֵּׁנִ֑י נֹ֥פֶךְ סַפִּ֖יר וְיָהֲלֹֽם׃ ¹²וְהַטּ֖וּר הַשְּׁלִישִׁ֑י לֶ֥שֶׁם שְׁב֖וֹ וְאַחְלָֽמָה׃ ¹³וְהַטּוּר֙ הָֽרְבִיעִ֔י תַּרְשִׁ֥ישׁ שֹׁ֖הַם וְיָשְׁפֵ֑ה מֽוּסַבֹּ֛ת מִשְׁבְּצֹ֥ת זָהָ֖ב בְּמִלֻּאֹתָֽם׃ ¹⁴וְ֠הָאֲבָנִים עַל־שְׁמֹ֨ת בְּנֵֽי־יִשְׂרָאֵ֥ל הֵ֛נָּה שְׁתֵּ֥ים עֶשְׂרֵ֖ה עַל־שְׁמֹתָ֑ם פִּתּוּחֵ֤י חֹתָם֙ אִ֣ישׁ עַל־שְׁמ֔וֹ לִשְׁנֵ֥ים עָשָׂ֖ר שָֽׁבֶט׃ ¹⁵וַיַּעֲשׂ֧וּ עַל־הַחֹ֛שֶׁן שַׁרְשְׁרֹ֥ת גַּבְלֻ֖ת מַעֲשֵׂ֣ה עֲבֹ֑ת זָהָ֖ב טָהֽוֹר׃ ¹⁶וַֽיַּעֲשׂ֗וּ שְׁתֵּי֙ מִשְׁבְּצֹ֣ת זָהָ֔ב וּשְׁתֵּ֖י טַבְּעֹ֣ת זָהָ֑ב וַֽיִּתְּנ֗וּ אֶת־שְׁתֵּי֙ הַטַּבָּעֹ֔ת עַל־שְׁנֵ֖י קְצ֥וֹת הַחֹֽשֶׁן׃ ¹⁷וַֽיִּתְּנ֗וּ שְׁתֵּי֙ הָעֲבֹתֹ֣ת הַזָּהָ֔ב עַל־שְׁתֵּ֖י הַטַּבָּעֹ֑ת עַל־קְצ֖וֹת הַחֹֽשֶׁן׃ ¹⁸וְאֵ֨ת שְׁתֵּ֤י קְצוֹת֙ שְׁתֵּ֣י הָעֲבֹתֹ֔ת נָתְנ֖וּ עַל־שְׁתֵּ֣י הַֽמִּשְׁבְּצֹ֑ת וַֽיִּתְּנֻ֛ם עַל־כִּתְפֹ֥ת

39:4 ק קְצוֹתָֽיו

on the ephod's shoulder-pieces opposite the front of it. 19And they made two rings of gold and put them on the breastplate's two ends on its side that is adjacent to the ephod, inward. 20And they made two rings of gold and put them on the ephod's two shoulder-pieces below, opposite the front of it, by its connection, above the ephod's designed belt. 21And they attached the breastplate from its rings to the ephod's rings with a blue string so it would be on the ephod's designed belt and the breastplate would not be detached from the ephod, as YHWH had commanded Moses.

22And he made the robe of the ephod, weaver's work, all of blue, 23and the robe's opening within it like the opening of a coat of mail, a binding for its opening all around so it would not be torn. 24And they made on the robe's skirts pomegranates of blue and purple and scarlet, woven. 25And they made bells of pure gold and put the bells among the pomegranates on the robe's skirts all around among the pomegranates: 26bell and pomegranate, bell and pomegranate, on the robe's skirts all around, for ministering, as YHWH had commanded Moses.

27And they made the coats of linen, weaver's work, for Aaron and for his sons, 28and the headdress of linen and the beautiful hats of linen and the shorts of linen, woven linen, 29and the sash of woven linen and blue and purple and scarlet, embroiderer's work, as YHWH had commanded Moses.

30And they made the plate of the crown of Holiness of pure gold, and they wrote on it a text of signet inscriptions: "Holiness to YHWH." 31And

הָאֵפֹד אֶל־מוּל פָּנָיו: 19וַיַּעֲשׂוּ שְׁתֵּי טַבְּעֹת זָהָב וַיָּשִׂימוּ עַל־שְׁנֵי קְצוֹת הַחֹשֶׁן עַל־שְׂפָתוֹ אֲשֶׁר אֶל־עֵבֶר הָאֵפֹד בָּיְתָה: 20וַיַּעֲשׂוּ שְׁתֵּי טַבְּעֹת זָהָב וַיִּתְּנֻם עַל־שְׁתֵּי כִתְפֹת הָאֵפֹד מִלְמַטָּה מִמּוּל פָּנָיו לְעֻמַּת מֶחְבַּרְתּוֹ מִמַּעַל לְחֵשֶׁב הָאֵפֹד: 21וַיִּרְכְּסוּ אֶת־הַחֹשֶׁן מִטַּבְּעֹתָיו אֶל־טַבְּעֹת הָאֵפֹד בִּפְתִיל תְּכֵלֶת לִהְיֹת עַל־חֵשֶׁב הָאֵפֹד וְלֹא־יִזַּח הַחֹשֶׁן מֵעַל הָאֵפֹד כַּאֲשֶׁר צִוָּה יְהוָה אֶת־מֹשֶׁה: 22וַיַּעַשׂ אֶת־מְעִיל הָאֵפֹד מַעֲשֵׂה אֹרֵג כְּלִיל תְּכֵלֶת: 23וּפִי־הַמְּעִיל בְּתוֹכוֹ כְּפִי תַחְרָא שָׂפָה לְפִיו סָבִיב לֹא יִקָּרֵעַ: 24וַיַּעֲשׂוּ עַל־שׁוּלֵי הַמְּעִיל רִמּוֹנֵי תְּכֵלֶת וְאַרְגָּמָן וְתוֹלַעַת שָׁנִי מָשְׁזָר: 25וַיַּעֲשׂוּ פַעֲמֹנֵי זָהָב טָהוֹר וַיִּתְּנוּ אֶת־הַפַּעֲמֹנִים בְּתוֹךְ הָרִמֹּנִים עַל־שׁוּלֵי הַמְּעִיל סָבִיב בְּתוֹךְ הָרִמֹּנִים: 26פַּעֲמֹן וְרִמֹּן פַּעֲמֹן וְרִמֹּן עַל־שׁוּלֵי הַמְּעִיל סָבִיב לְשָׁרֵת כַּאֲשֶׁר צִוָּה יְהוָה אֶת־מֹשֶׁה: ס 27וַיַּעֲשׂוּ אֶת־הַכָּתְנֹת שֵׁשׁ מַעֲשֵׂה אֹרֵג לְאַהֲרֹן וּלְבָנָיו: 28וְאֵת הַמִּצְנֶפֶת שֵׁשׁ וְאֶת־פַּאֲרֵי הַמִּגְבָּעֹת שֵׁשׁ וְאֶת־מִכְנְסֵי הַבָּד שֵׁשׁ מָשְׁזָר: 29וְאֶת־הָאַבְנֵט שֵׁשׁ מָשְׁזָר וּתְכֵלֶת וְאַרְגָּמָן וְתוֹלַעַת שָׁנִי מַעֲשֵׂה רֹקֵם כַּאֲשֶׁר צִוָּה יְהוָה אֶת־מֹשֶׁה: ס 30וַיַּעֲשׂוּ אֶת־צִיץ נֵזֶר־הַקֹּדֶשׁ זָהָב טָהוֹר וַיִּכְתְּבוּ עָלָיו מִכְתַּב פִּתּוּחֵי חוֹתָם קֹדֶשׁ לַיהוָה:

39:21. **as YHWH had commanded Moses.** A major sentence is missing from the Masoretic Text (and the Septuagint) here. A Dead Sea scroll and the Samaritan text add it: "And they made the Urim and Tummim, as YHWH had commanded Moses." Presumably it was omitted from the MT because the scribe's eye jumped from the first occurrence of the phrase "as YHWH had commanded Moses" to the second. This is another case of the scribal phenomenon known as haplography, and it shows that even important matters can be lost by scribal errors of copying. (For other implications of scribal changes, see the comment on Exod 1:5.)

they put a blue string on it for putting it on the headdress above, as YHWH had commanded Moses.

³²And all of the construction of the Tabernacle of the Tent of Meeting was finished. And the children of Israel did according to everything that YHWH had commanded Moses. They did so. ³³And they brought the Tabernacle to Moses: the tent and all of its equipment, its clasps, its frames, its bars, and its columns and its bases, ³⁴and the covering of rams' skins dyed red and the covering of leather skins, and the covering pavilion, ³⁵the Ark of the Testimony and its poles and the atonement dais, ³⁶the table and all of its equipment and the show bread, ³⁷the pure menorah, its lamps, lamps for the row, and all of its equipment, and the oil for lighting, ³⁸and the golden altar and the anointing oil and the incense of fragrances and the cover of the entrance of the Tent, ³⁹the bronze altar and the bronze grate that it had, its poles and all of its equipment, the basin and its stand, ⁴⁰the courtyard's hangings, its columns and its bases and the cover for the courtyard's gate, its cords and its pegs, and all the equipment for the service of the Tabernacle of the Tent of Meeting, ⁴¹the fabric clothes for ministering in the Holy, the holy clothes for Aaron, the priest, and his sons' clothes for functioning as priests. ⁴²According to everything that YHWH had commanded Moses: so the children of Israel did all of the construction. ⁴³And Moses saw all of the work; and, here, they had done it as YHWH had commanded. They did so. And Moses blessed them.

40 ¹And YHWH spoke to Moses, saying, ²"On the day of the first month, on the

---

³¹וַיִּתְּנ֤וּ עָלָיו֙ פְּתִ֣יל תְּכֵ֔לֶת לָתֵ֥ת עַל־הַמִּצְנֶ֖פֶת מִלְמָ֑עְלָה כַּאֲשֶׁ֛ר צִוָּ֥ה יְהוָ֖ה אֶת־מֹשֶֽׁה׃ ס

³²וַתֵּ֕כֶל כָּל־עֲבֹדַ֕ת מִשְׁכַּ֖ן אֹ֣הֶל מוֹעֵ֑ד וַֽיַּעֲשׂוּ֙ בְּנֵ֣י יִשְׂרָאֵ֔ל כְּ֠כֹל אֲשֶׁ֨ר צִוָּ֧ה יְהוָ֛ה אֶת־מֹשֶׁ֖ה כֵּ֥ן עָשֽׂוּ׃ פ ³³וַיָּבִ֤יאוּ אֶת־הַמִּשְׁכָּן֙ אֶל־מֹשֶׁ֔ה אֶת־הָאֹ֖הֶל וְאֶת־כָּל־כֵּלָ֑יו קְרָסָ֣יו קְרָשָׁ֔יו בְּרִיחָ֖ו וְעַמֻּדָ֥יו וַאֲדָנָֽיו׃ ³⁴וְאֶת־מִכְסֵ֞ה עוֹרֹ֤ת הָֽאֵילִם֙ הַמְאָדָּמִ֔ים וְאֶת־מִכְסֵ֖ה עֹרֹ֣ת הַתְּחָשִׁ֑ים וְאֵ֖ת פָּרֹ֥כֶת הַמָּסָֽךְ׃ ³⁵אֶת־אֲרֹ֥ן הָעֵדֻ֖ת וְאֶת־בַּדָּ֑יו וְאֵ֖ת הַכַּפֹּֽרֶת׃ ³⁶אֶת־הַשֻּׁלְחָן֙ אֶת־כָּל־כֵּלָ֔יו וְאֵ֖ת לֶ֥חֶם הַפָּנִֽים׃ ³⁷אֶת־הַמְּנֹרָ֨ה הַטְּהֹרָ֜ה אֶת־נֵרֹתֶ֗יהָ נֵרֹ֛ת הַמַּֽעֲרָכָ֖ה וְאֶת־כָּל־כֵּלֶ֑יהָ וְאֵ֖ת שֶׁ֥מֶן הַמָּאֽוֹר׃ ³⁸וְאֵת֙ מִזְבַּ֣ח הַזָּהָ֔ב וְאֵת֙ שֶׁ֣מֶן הַמִּשְׁחָ֔ה וְאֵ֖ת קְטֹ֣רֶת הַסַּמִּ֑ים וְאֵ֕ת מָסַ֖ךְ פֶּ֥תַח הָאֹֽהֶל׃ ³⁹אֵ֣ת ׀ מִזְבַּ֣ח הַנְּחֹ֗שֶׁת וְאֶת־מִכְבַּ֤ר הַנְּחֹ֙שֶׁת֙ אֲשֶׁר־ל֔וֹ אֶת־בַּדָּ֖יו וְאֶת־כָּל־כֵּלָ֑יו אֶת־הַכִּיֹּ֖ר וְאֶת־כַּנּֽוֹ׃ ⁴⁰אֵת֩ קַלְעֵ֨י הֶחָצֵ֜ר אֶת־עַמֻּדֶ֣יהָ וְאֶת־אֲדָנֶ֗יהָ וְאֶת־הַמָּסָךְ֙ לְשַׁ֣עַר הֶֽחָצֵ֔ר אֶת־מֵיתָרָ֖יו וִיתֵדֹתֶ֑יהָ וְאֵ֗ת כָּל־כְּלֵ֛י עֲבֹדַ֥ת הַמִּשְׁכָּ֖ן לְאֹ֥הֶל מוֹעֵֽד׃ ⁴¹אֶת־בִּגְדֵ֥י הַשְּׂרָ֖ד לְשָׁרֵ֣ת בַּקֹּ֑דֶשׁ אֶת־בִּגְדֵ֤י הַקֹּ֙דֶשׁ֙ לְאַהֲרֹ֣ן הַכֹּהֵ֔ן וְאֶת־בִּגְדֵ֥י בָנָ֖יו לְכַהֵֽן׃ ⁴²כְּכֹ֛ל אֲשֶׁר־צִוָּ֥ה יְהוָ֖ה אֶת־מֹשֶׁ֑ה כֵּ֤ן עָשׂוּ֙ בְּנֵ֣י יִשְׂרָאֵ֔ל אֵ֖ת כָּל־הָעֲבֹדָֽה׃ ⁴³וַיַּ֨רְא מֹשֶׁ֜ה אֶת־כָּל־הַמְּלָאכָ֗ה וְהִנֵּה֙ עָשׂ֣וּ אֹתָ֔הּ כַּאֲשֶׁ֛ר צִוָּ֥ה יְהוָ֖ה כֵּ֣ן עָשׂ֑וּ וַיְבָ֥רֶךְ אֹתָ֖ם מֹשֶֽׁה׃ פ

40 ¹וַיְדַבֵּ֥ר יְהוָ֖ה אֶל־מֹשֶׁ֥ה לֵּאמֹֽר׃ ²בְּיוֹם־הַחֹ֥דֶשׁ הָרִאשׁ֖וֹן בְּאֶחָ֣ד לַחֹ֑דֶשׁ תָּקִ֕ים אֶת־מִשְׁכַּ֖ן

קְ בְּרִיחָיו 39:33

39:32,43; 40:9. finished, saw, work, did, blessed, made holy. The conclusion of the account of the people's construction of the Tabernacle mirrors the language of the conclusion of the account of God's creation of the universe (Gen 1:31–2:3). This further reminds us of the role of the Tabernacle as the channel through which divine and human communicate. And it indicates that, after the first revelation at Sinai, such communication requires action by humans in order to receive it.

first of the month, you shall set up the Tabernacle of the Tent of Meeting. 3And you shall set the Ark of the Testimony there and have the pavilion cover over the ark. 4And you shall bring the table and make its arrangement, and bring the menorah and put up its lamps. 5And you shall put the golden altar for incense in front of the Ark of the Testimony, and you shall set the cover of the entrance of the Tabernacle. 6And you shall put the altar of burnt offering in front of the entrance of the Tabernacle of the Tent of Meeting. 7And you shall put the basin between the Tent of Meeting and the altar and put water there. 8And you shall set the courtyard all around and put on the cover of the courtyard's gate. 9And you shall take the anointing oil and anoint the Tabernacle and everything that is in it, and you shall make it and all of its equipment holy, and it will be holiness. 10And you shall anoint the altar of burnt offering and all of its equipment, and you shall make the altar holy: and the altar will be holy of holies. 11And you shall anoint the basin and its stand and make it holy.

12"And you shall bring Aaron and his sons forward to the entrance of the Tent of Meeting and wash them with water. 13And you shall dress Aaron with the holy clothes and anoint him and make him holy, and he shall function as a priest for me. 14And you shall bring his sons forward and dress them with coats 15and anoint them as you anointed their father, and they shall function as priests for me. And it will be for their anointing to be theirs as an eternal priesthood

אֹהֶל מוֹעֵד: 3וְשַׂמְתָּ שָׁם אֵת אֲרוֹן הָעֵדֻת וְסַכֹּתָ עַל־הָאָרֹן אֶת־הַפָּרֹכֶת: 4וְהֵבֵאתָ אֶת־הַשֻּׁלְחָן וְעָרַכְתָּ אֶת־עֶרְכּוֹ וְהֵבֵאתָ אֶת־הַמְּנֹרָה וְהַעֲלֵיתָ אֶת־נֵרֹתֶיהָ: 5וְנָתַתָּה אֶת־מִזְבַּח הַזָּהָב לִקְטֹרֶת לִפְנֵי אֲרוֹן הָעֵדֻת וְשַׂמְתָּ אֶת־מָסַךְ הַפֶּתַח לַמִּשְׁכָּן: 6וְנָתַתָּה אֵת מִזְבַּח הָעֹלָה לִפְנֵי פֶּתַח מִשְׁכַּן אֹהֶל־מוֹעֵד: 7וְנָתַתָּ אֶת־הַכִּיֹּר בֵּין־אֹהֶל מוֹעֵד וּבֵין הַמִּזְבֵּחַ וְנָתַתָּ שָׁם מָיִם: 8וְשַׂמְתָּ אֶת־הֶחָצֵר סָבִיב וְנָתַתָּ אֶת־מָסַךְ שַׁעַר הֶחָצֵר: 9וְלָקַחְתָּ אֶת־שֶׁמֶן הַמִּשְׁחָה וּמָשַׁחְתָּ אֶת־הַמִּשְׁכָּן וְאֶת־כָּל־אֲשֶׁר־בּוֹ וְקִדַּשְׁתָּ אֹתוֹ וְאֶת־כָּל־כֵּלָיו וְהָיָה קֹדֶשׁ: 10וּמָשַׁחְתָּ אֶת־מִזְבַּח הָעֹלָה וְאֶת־כָּל־כֵּלָיו וְקִדַּשְׁתָּ אֶת־הַמִּזְבֵּחַ וְהָיָה הַמִּזְבֵּחַ קֹדֶשׁ קָדָשִׁים: 11וּמָשַׁחְתָּ אֶת־הַכִּיֹּר וְאֶת־כַּנּוֹ וְקִדַּשְׁתָּ אֹתוֹ: 12וְהִקְרַבְתָּ אֶת־אַהֲרֹן וְאֶת־בָּנָיו אֶל־פֶּתַח אֹהֶל מוֹעֵד וְרָחַצְתָּ אֹתָם בַּמָּיִם: 13וְהִלְבַּשְׁתָּ אֶת־אַהֲרֹן אֵת בִּגְדֵי הַקֹּדֶשׁ וּמָשַׁחְתָּ אֹתוֹ וְקִדַּשְׁתָּ אֹתוֹ וְכִהֵן לִי: 14וְאֶת־בָּנָיו תַּקְרִיב וְהִלְבַּשְׁתָּ אֹתָם כֻּתֳּנֹת: 15וּמָשַׁחְתָּ אֹתָם כַּאֲשֶׁר מָשַׁחְתָּ אֶת־אֲבִיהֶם וְכִהֲנוּ לִי וְהָיְתָה לִהְיֹת לָהֶם מָשְׁחָתָם לִכְהֻנַּת עוֹלָם לְדֹרֹתָם:

40:3. **have the pavilion cover over the ark**. The *pārōket* is clearly a pavilion, not a curtain. It is mounted so as to *cover over* the ark. The word is *sakkōtā*, meaning to make a covering: a sukkah. Thus a psalm about the Tent and the Temple says: "He'll conceal me in His *sukkah* in a day of trouble; He'll hide me in His tent's hidden place" (Ps 27:5; cf. Lam 2:6). The *pārōket* later became a curtain (presumably in the second Temple) when there was no longer an ark to place under it, and then people mistakenly understood it retroactively to have been a curtain in the Tabernacle and first Temple as well. (See the comment on 26:31.)

through their generations." 16And Moses did it. According to everything that YHWH commanded him, he did so.

17And it was: in the first month, in the second year, on the first of the month, the Tabernacle was set up. 18And Moses set up the Tabernacle and put on its bases and set its frames and put on its bars and set up its columns. 19And he spread the Tent over the Tabernacle and set the Tent's covering on it above, as YHWH had commanded Moses. 20And he took the Testimony and put it into the ark, and he set the poles on the ark, and he put the atonement dais on the ark above. 21And he brought the ark into the Tabernacle and set the covering pavilion and covered over the Ark of the Testimony, as YHWH had commanded Moses.

22And he put the table in the Tent of Meeting on the northward side of the Tabernacle, outside of the pavilion. 23And he made the arrangement of bread on it in front of YHWH, as YHWH had commanded Moses.

24And he set the menorah in the Tent of Meeting opposite the table, on the southward side of the Tabernacle, 25and he put up the lamps in front of YHWH, as YHWH had commanded Moses.

16וַיַּעַשׂ מֹשֶׁה כְּכֹל אֲשֶׁר צִוָּה יְהוָה אֹתוֹ כֵּן
עָשָׂה: ס 17וַיְהִי בַּחֹדֶשׁ הָרִאשׁוֹן בַּשָּׁנָה הַשֵּׁנִית
בְּאֶחָד לַחֹדֶשׁ הוּקַם הַמִּשְׁכָּן: 18וַיָּקֶם מֹשֶׁה אֶת־
הַמִּשְׁכָּן וַיִּתֵּן אֶת־אֲדָנָיו וַיָּשֶׂם אֶת־קְרָשָׁיו וַיִּתֵּן אֶת־
בְּרִיחָיו וַיָּקֶם אֶת־עַמּוּדָיו: 19וַיִּפְרֹשׂ אֶת־הָאֹהֶל
עַל־הַמִּשְׁכָּן וַיָּשֶׂם אֶת־מִכְסֵה הָאֹהֶל עָלָיו
מִלְמָעְלָה כַּאֲשֶׁר צִוָּה יְהוָה אֶת־מֹשֶׁה: ס 20וַיִּקַּח
וַיִּתֵּן אֶת־הָעֵדֻת אֶל־הָאָרֹן וַיָּשֶׂם אֶת־הַבַּדִּים עַל־
הָאָרֹן וַיִּתֵּן אֶת־הַכַּפֹּרֶת עַל־הָאָרֹן מִלְמָעְלָה:
21וַיָּבֵא אֶת־הָאָרֹן אֶל־הַמִּשְׁכָּן וַיָּשֶׂם אֵת פָּרֹכֶת
הַמָּסָךְ וַיָּסֶךְ עַל אֲרוֹן הָעֵדוּת כַּאֲשֶׁר צִוָּה יְהוָה
אֶת־מֹשֶׁה: ס 22וַיִּתֵּן אֶת־הַשֻּׁלְחָן בְּאֹהֶל מוֹעֵד עַל
יֶרֶךְ הַמִּשְׁכָּן צָפֹנָה מִחוּץ לַפָּרֹכֶת: 23וַיַּעֲרֹךְ עָלָיו
עֵרֶךְ לֶחֶם לִפְנֵי יְהוָה כַּאֲשֶׁר צִוָּה יְהוָה אֶת־מֹשֶׁה:
ס 24וַיָּשֶׂם אֶת־הַמְּנֹרָה בְּאֹהֶל מוֹעֵד נֹכַח הַשֻּׁלְחָן
עַל יֶרֶךְ הַמִּשְׁכָּן נֶגְבָּה: 25וַיַּעַל הַנֵּרֹת לִפְנֵי יְהוָה
כַּאֲשֶׁר צִוָּה יְהוָה אֶת־מֹשֶׁה: ס 26וַיָּשֶׂם אֶת־מִזְבַּח

40:16. **And Moses did it. According to everything that YHWH commanded him, he did so.** These are the exact words that are used to describe Noah's obedience (except for the mention of the name of God here). There are several parallels between Noah and Moses. They are the two biblical persons associated with floating in arks (Gen 6:14; Exod 2:3)! But the most explicit, verbatim, parallel is focused on their obedience to divine commands. Especially for those who hear the divine commands directly, precise obedience is the primary concern.

40:16. **He did so.** Exodus concludes with silence on Moses' part. In the final chapter of the book, Moses does not speak. (He is last said to have spoken in the last verse of Exodus 39.) He sets up the ark and Tabernacle as commanded. He anoints Aaron and his sons as priests. The cloud and glory fill the Tabernacle so that Moses cannot enter. And it is reported that the people's travels are to depend on the movements of the cloud and glory. Thus the book of Exodus ends as it began, with the attention on the people—and their relationship with their God. The person of Moses is the focus of the story in the intervening chapters, but the nature of the opening and concluding chapters would suggest that he is just that: a tangible focus of a larger dynamic, between God and a human community.

26And he set the golden altar in the Tent of Meeting in front of the pavilion, 27and he burned the incense of fragrances on it, as YHWH had commanded Moses.

28And he set the cover of the entrance of the Tabernacle. 29And he set the altar of burnt offering at the entrance of Tabernacle of the Tent of Meeting, and he offered up the burnt offering and the grain offering on it, as YHWH had commanded Moses.

30And he set the basin between the Tent of Meeting and the altar, and he put water for washing there. 31And Moses and Aaron and his sons washed their hands and their feet from it. 32When they came to the Tent of Meeting and when they came forward to the altar they would wash, as YHWH had commanded Moses.

33And he set up the courtyard all around the Tabernacle and the altar, and he put on the cover of the courtyard's gate.

And Moses finished the work.

34And the cloud covered the Tent of Meeting, and YHWH's glory filled the Tabernacle. 35And Moses was not able to come into the Tent of Meeting, because the cloud had settled on it and YHWH's glory filled the Tabernacle. 36And when the cloud was lifted from on the Tabernacle, the children of Israel would travel—in all their travels— 37and if the cloud would not be lifted, then they would not travel until the day that it would be lifted. 38Because YHWH's cloud was on the Tabernacle by day, and fire would be in it at night, before the eyes of all the house of Israel in all their travels.

הַזָּהָב בְּאֹהֶל מוֹעֵד לִפְנֵי הַפָּרֹכֶת: 27וַיַּקְטֵר עָלָיו קְטֹרֶת סַמִּים כַּאֲשֶׁר צִוָּה יְהוָה אֶת־מֹשֶׁה: פ 28וַיָּשֶׂם אֶת־מָסַךְ הַפֶּתַח לַמִּשְׁכָּן: 29וְאֵת מִזְבַּח הָעֹלָה שָׂם פֶּתַח מִשְׁכַּן אֹהֶל־מוֹעֵד וַיַּעַל עָלָיו אֶת־הָעֹלָה וְאֶת־הַמִּנְחָה כַּאֲשֶׁר צִוָּה יְהוָה אֶת־מֹשֶׁה: ס 30וַיָּשֶׂם אֶת־הַכִּיֹּר בֵּין־אֹהֶל מוֹעֵד וּבֵין הַמִּזְבֵּחַ וַיִּתֵּן שָׁמָּה מַיִם לְרָחְצָה: 31וְרָחֲצוּ מִמֶּנּוּ מֹשֶׁה וְאַהֲרֹן וּבָנָיו אֶת־יְדֵיהֶם וְאֶת־רַגְלֵיהֶם: 32בְּבֹאָם אֶל־אֹהֶל מוֹעֵד וּבְקָרְבָתָם אֶל־הַמִּזְבֵּחַ יִרְחָצוּ כַּאֲשֶׁר צִוָּה יְהוָה אֶת־מֹשֶׁה: ס 33וַיָּקֶם אֶת־הֶחָצֵר סָבִיב לַמִּשְׁכָּן וְלַמִּזְבֵּחַ וַיִּתֵּן אֶת־מָסַךְ שַׁעַר הֶחָצֵר

וַיְכַל מֹשֶׁה אֶת־הַמְּלָאכָה: פ 34וַיְכַס הֶעָנָן אֶת־אֹהֶל מוֹעֵד וּכְבוֹד יְהוָה מָלֵא אֶת־הַמִּשְׁכָּן: 35וְלֹא־יָכֹל מֹשֶׁה לָבוֹא אֶל־אֹהֶל מוֹעֵד כִּי־שָׁכַן עָלָיו הֶעָנָן וּכְבוֹד יְהוָה מָלֵא אֶת־הַמִּשְׁכָּן: 36וּבְהֵעָלוֹת הֶעָנָן מֵעַל הַמִּשְׁכָּן יִסְעוּ בְּנֵי יִשְׂרָאֵל בְּכֹל מַסְעֵיהֶם: 37וְאִם־לֹא יֵעָלֶה הֶעָנָן וְלֹא יִסְעוּ עַד־יוֹם הֵעָלֹתוֹ: 38כִּי עֲנַן יְהוָה עַל־הַמִּשְׁכָּן יוֹמָם וְאֵשׁ תִּהְיֶה לַיְלָה בּוֹ לְעֵינֵי כָל־בֵּית־יִשְׂרָאֵל בְּכָל־מַסְעֵיהֶם:

LEVITICUS

*A*fter the rush of forces in Exodus, Leviticus is a rather tranquil book. Following the mighty *acts* of God in Exodus, Leviticus is disproportionately the *words* of God. There is very little narrative—barely three chapters out of twenty-seven in the book—and no poetry (with the possible exception of a few isolated verses). More than the other four of the Five Books of Moses, Leviticus pictures the deity speaking. Consistent with this is the absence of movement in Leviticus. Unlike Genesis and Exodus, the entire book of Leviticus is set in one place: at the foot of Mount Sinai. In Exodus, the universe—the land, waters, and sky—is in disarray. Following that, Leviticus is concerned with orderliness, arrangement.

Leviticus pictures the beginning of the solidification—the formation of an identity—of a people through law. The law is significant as a subject of study in itself and in context of the study of history as well. But, also in narrative terms, it is important to see the place of the law in the development of the story of the people: laws of how to behave toward other human beings, laws that bring identity (what to eat, religious ceremonies, holidays). The laws are not merely listed. They are narrated as words of YHWH to Moses (and Aaron) and thus are presented as an integrated component of the account.

In Leviticus the knowledge of God, which is an explicit, continuing component in Exodus, likewise resides in the background. The term "to know" (Hebrew *yd'*) never occurs in Leviticus in the sense of knowledge of God. YHWH now *is* known to Israel. This is assumed.

Impressively, the story stops being about Moses in Leviticus. The laws are conveyed through him, certainly, but the book is *about* the laws themselves and the fact of their being revealed to the people. The only stories are primarily about Aaron and his sons. More broadly, Leviticus does not develop personalities. It is about institutions, not individuals. And this, too, contributes to the reduction of tension in Leviticus following the great confrontations of Exodus.

All of this contributes to the change of feeling of this book. Leviticus is both integral to the context of the books that precede and follow it and, at the same time, anomalous in character.

Unlike in Exodus, there are few miracles portrayed in Leviticus, yet the book, rich in background like the two books that precede it, is pervaded with the presence of the divine. The continuing scene has already been set in Exodus: A column of cloud or fire is visible at all times. A Tent of Meeting, the Tabernacle, stands outside the camp. Moses goes in and out of the tent, his face veiled and then unveiled, bringing laws from God. The book begins with God speaking from the Tabernacle, thus establishing the Tabernacle from the outset as the visible, present entity among the people through which the divine word enters the world. The cosmic/miraculous thus looms, and a channel between it and the earthly operates.

AND HE CALLED

ויקרא

1 ¹And He called to Moses, and YHWH spoke to him from the Tent of Meeting, saying, ²"Speak to the children of Israel. And you shall say to them: A human from you who will make an offering to YHWH—you shall make your offering from the domestic animals: from the herd and from the flock.

³"If his offering is a burnt offering from the herd, he shall make it an unblemished male. He shall bring it forward to the entrance of the Tent of Meeting for his acceptance in front of YHWH. ⁴And he shall lay his hand on the head of the burnt offering, and it will be accepted for him, to

1 ¹וַיִּקְרָא אֶל־מֹשֶׁה וַיְדַבֵּר יְהוָה אֵלָיו מֵאֹהֶל מוֹעֵד לֵאמֹר: ²דַּבֵּר אֶל־בְּנֵי יִשְׂרָאֵל וְאָמַרְתָּ אֲלֵהֶם אָדָם כִּי־יַקְרִיב מִכֶּם קָרְבָּן לַיהוָה מִן־הַבְּהֵמָה מִן־הַבָּקָר וּמִן־הַצֹּאן תַּקְרִיבוּ אֶת־קָרְבַּנְכֶם: ³אִם־עֹלָה קָרְבָּנוֹ מִן־הַבָּקָר זָכָר תָּמִים יַקְרִיבֶנּוּ אֶל־פֶּתַח אֹהֶל מוֹעֵד יַקְרִיב אֹתוֹ לִרְצֹנוֹ לִפְנֵי יְהוָה: ⁴וְסָמַךְ יָדוֹ עַל רֹאשׁ הָעֹלָה וְנִרְצָה לוֹ

1:2. **A human.** The laws of sacrifice begin by referring to the offerer by the species term "a human" (Hebrew *'ādām*). Rashi gives a midrashic explanation for this. But we should note that the text next refers to the offerer as "a person" (Hebrew *nepeš*, Lev 2:1) and then as "a man" (Hebrew *'îš*, Lev 7:8), and this is the same order in which these terms are used to refer to human beings in the book of Genesis (*'ādām* in Gen 1:26; *nepeš* in 2:7; *'îš* in 2:23). This makes a link between the books of the Torah, and it makes a link between God's creation of humans on the one hand and humans' sacrifices to their creator on the other. Creation and sacrifice are linked. Creation produces life. Sacrifice takes life. And so the word order here subtly reminds us that, when we take animals' lives in order to support our own, we should remember that both their lives and ours are part of a common creation, and that both are treated in the Torah as sacred.

1:3. **to the entrance of the Tent of Meeting.** From this time on, there is only one place on earth where an Israelite may perform a sacrifice: at the altar at the entrance of the Tent of Meeting. This applies here to a burnt offering. Later in this section we learn that it also applies to the peace offering (3:2), the sin offering (4:3), the guilt offering (7:2), and the grain offering (6:7–9). This applies to the period of Israel's travels through the wilderness. Then the tent is set up at Shiloh (Josh 18:1), then at Gibeah (2 Chr 1:3), and then finally it is brought to the Temple that King Solomon builds in Jerusalem (1 Kings 8:4; 1 Chr 5:5). One exception: the prophet Elijah makes a sacrifice at Mount Carmel in a duel with the priests of Baal; but it is presented as an extraordinary occurrence, led by a prophet, involving a miracle, the last miracle in the *Tanak* that is said to be performed in front of the entire people of Israel (1 Kings 18). All other sacrifice is to take place at the Tent of Meeting. This *centralization* of worship in Israel's religion is crucially important. It is a powerful corollary of Israelite monotheism: one God, one altar.

atone for him. 5And he shall slaughter the herd animal in front of YHWH, and the sons of Aaron, the priests, shall bring the blood forward and fling the blood on the altar, all around, which is at the entrance of the Tent of Meeting. 6And he shall flay the burnt offering and cut it into its parts. 7And the sons of Aaron, the priest, shall put fire on the altar and arrange wood on the fire. 8And the sons of Aaron, the priests, shall arrange the parts, the head, and the suet on the wood that is on the fire that is on the altar. 9And he shall wash its innards and its legs with water. And the priest shall burn it all to smoke at the altar, a burnt offering, an offering by fire of a pleasant smell to YHWH.

10"And if his offering is from the flock—from the sheep or from the goats—for a burnt offering, he shall make it an unblemished male. 11And he shall slaughter it on the northward side of the altar in front of YHWH. And the sons of Aaron, the priests, shall fling its blood on the altar, all around. 12And he shall cut it into its parts and its head and its suet. And the priest

לְכַפֵּ֥ר עָלָ֖יו: 5וְשָׁחַ֛ט אֶת־בֶּ֥ן הַבָּקָ֖ר לִפְנֵ֣י יְהוָ֑ה
וְהִקְרִ֩יבוּ֩ בְּנֵ֨י אַהֲרֹ֤ן הַכֹּֽהֲנִים֙ אֶת־הַדָּ֔ם וְזָרְק֨וּ אֶת־
הַדָּ֤ם עַל־הַמִּזְבֵּ֙חַ֙ סָבִ֔יב אֲשֶׁר־פֶּ֖תַח אֹ֥הֶל מוֹעֵֽד:
6וְהִפְשִׁ֖יט אֶת־הָעֹלָ֑ה וְנִתַּ֥ח אֹתָ֖הּ לִנְתָחֶֽיהָ: 7וְנָתְנ֡וּ
בְּנֵי֩ אַהֲרֹ֨ן הַכֹּהֵ֥ן אֵ֖שׁ עַל־הַמִּזְבֵּ֑חַ וְעָרְכ֥וּ עֵצִ֖ים
עַל־הָאֵֽשׁ: 8וְעָרְכ֗וּ בְּנֵ֤י אַהֲרֹן֙ הַכֹּ֣הֲנִ֔ים אֵ֖ת הַנְּתָחִ֑ים
אֶת־הָרֹ֖אשׁ וְאֶת־הַפָּ֑דֶר עַל־הָ֣עֵצִ֔ים אֲשֶׁ֥ר עַל־הָאֵ֖שׁ
אֲשֶׁ֥ר עַל־הַמִּזְבֵּֽחַ: 9וְקִרְבּ֥וֹ וּכְרָעָ֖יו יִרְחַ֣ץ בַּמָּ֑יִם
וְהִקְטִ֨יר הַכֹּהֵ֤ן אֶת־הַכֹּל֙ הַמִּזְבֵּ֔חָה עֹלָ֛ה אִשֵּׁ֥ה רֵֽיחַ־
נִיחֹ֖חַ לַֽיהוָֽה: ס 10וְאִם־מִן־הַצֹּ֨אן קָרְבָּנ֜וֹ מִן־
הַכְּשָׂבִ֛ים א֥וֹ מִן־הָעִזִּ֖ים לְעֹלָ֑ה זָכָ֥ר תָּמִ֖ים
יַקְרִיבֶֽנּוּ: 11וְשָׁחַ֣ט אֹת֗וֹ עַ֛ל יֶ֥רֶךְ הַמִּזְבֵּ֖חַ צָפֹ֑נָה
לִפְנֵ֣י יְהוָ֑ה וְזָרְק֡וּ בְּנֵי֩ אַהֲרֹ֨ן הַכֹּהֲנִ֧ים אֶת־דָּמ֛וֹ עַל־
הַמִּזְבֵּ֖חַ סָבִֽיב: 12וְנִתַּ֤ח אֹתוֹ֙ לִנְתָחָ֔יו וְאֶת־רֹאשׁ֖וֹ

1:5. **he shall slaughter . . . and the priests shall bring the blood forward**. The *individual* slaughters the animal; the *priests* handle the blood. This is consistent with the conception found elsewhere in the Torah that blood is sacred. It can contaminate, it can protect, and it "is the life."

1:7. **the sons of Aaron, the priest**. Leviticus's laws, as well as its narrative, are fundamentally concerned with priesthood, and thus with leadership, authority—human authority, but sanctioned by God—transforming the Israelites from a ragtag mass of ex-slaves into an organized society. The priests are installed and anointed, their sacrificial function is institutionalized, and they are commissioned to teach (10:10–11), a commission that implies authority. The installation of the priesthood—Aaron and his sons—is divinely stamped by the only appearance of the divine glory (the *kěbôd YHWH*) in Leviticus, at the end of eight days of inaugural ceremonies of the priesthood and the sacrificial system. And it is emphasized that the priestly laws applying to Aaron and his sons are eternal (10:9,15). The consecration of the priesthood had been announced in summary in Exodus 40. Now it is narrated. The priests' ritual and ethical activity is tied to sacrifice, and so the narrative's first concern is the new priesthood's first sacrificial offering. But sacrifice cannot be performed in any way one wishes. One must perform it in a prescribed manner. And so first there are seven chapters of prescription. This is consistent with a theme of prescription that pervades the book. There is a way to behave: in morality, in ethics, and in ritual.

318

shall arrange them on the wood that is on the fire that is on the altar. ¹³And he shall wash the innards and the legs with water. And the priest shall bring it all forward and burn it to smoke at the altar. It is a burnt offering, an offering by fire of a pleasant smell to YHWH.

¹⁴"And if his offering to YHWH is a burnt offering from birds, then he shall make his offering from turtledoves or from pigeons. ¹⁵And the priest shall bring it forward to the altar and wring its head and burn it to smoke at the altar, and its blood shall be drained on the wall of the altar. ¹⁶And he shall take away its crop with its feathers and throw it beside the altar eastward to the place of the ashes. ¹⁷And he shall tear it open by its wings—he shall not divide it—and the priest shall burn it to smoke at the altar on the wood that is on the fire. It is a burnt offering, an offering by fire of a pleasant smell to YHWH.

2 ¹"And a person who will make an offering of a grain offering to YHWH, his offering shall be of fine flour, and he shall pour oil on it and put frankincense on it. ²And he shall bring it to the sons of Aaron, the priests. And he shall take the fill of his fist from there: from its fine flour and from its oil in addition to all of its frankincense. And the priest shall burn a representative portion of it to smoke at the altar, an offering by fire of a pleasant smell to YHWH. ³And the remainder from the grain offering is Aaron's and his sons', the holy of holies from YHWH's offerings by fire.

⁴"And if he will make an offering of an oven-baked grain offering: fine flour, unleavened cakes

וְאֶת־פִּדְרֹ֔ו וְעָרַ֤ךְ הַכֹּהֵן֙ אֹתָ֔ם עַל־הָעֵצִים֙ אֲשֶׁ֣ר עַל־הָאֵ֔שׁ אֲשֶׁ֖ר עַל־הַמִּזְבֵּֽחַ׃ ¹³וְהַקֶּ֥רֶב וְהַכְּרָעַ֖יִם יִרְחַ֣ץ בַּמָּ֑יִם וְהִקְרִ֨יב הַכֹּהֵ֤ן אֶת־הַכֹּל֙ וְהִקְטִ֣יר הַמִּזְבֵּ֔חָה עֹלָ֣ה ה֗וּא אִשֵּׁ֛ה רֵ֥יחַ נִיחֹ֖חַ לַיהוָֽה׃ פ

¹⁴וְאִ֧ם מִן־הָעֹ֛וף עֹלָ֥ה קָרְבָּנֹ֖ו לַֽיהוָ֑ה וְהִקְרִ֣יב מִן־הַתֹּרִ֗ים אֹ֤ו מִן־בְּנֵ֣י הַיֹּונָ֔ה אֶת־קָרְבָּנֹֽו׃ ¹⁵וְהִקְרִיבֹ֤ו הַכֹּהֵן֙ אֶל־הַמִּזְבֵּ֔חַ וּמָלַק֙ אֶת־רֹאשֹׁ֔ו וְהִקְטִ֖יר הַמִּזְבֵּ֑חָה וְנִמְצָ֣ה דָמֹ֔ו עַ֖ל קִ֥יר הַמִּזְבֵּֽחַ׃ ¹⁶וְהֵסִ֥יר אֶת־מֻרְאָתֹ֖ו בְּנֹצָתָ֑הּ וְהִשְׁלִ֨יךְ אֹתָ֜הּ אֵ֤צֶל הַמִּזְבֵּ֙חַ֙ קֵ֔דְמָה אֶל־מְקֹ֖ום הַדָּֽשֶׁן׃ ¹⁷וְשִׁסַּ֨ע אֹתֹ֣ו בִכְנָפָיו֮ לֹ֣א יַבְדִּיל֒ וְהִקְטִ֨יר אֹתֹ֤ו הַכֹּהֵן֙ הַמִּזְבֵּ֔חָה עַל־הָעֵצִ֖ים אֲשֶׁ֣ר עַל־הָאֵ֑שׁ עֹלָ֣ה ה֗וּא אִשֵּׁ֛ה רֵ֥יחַ נִיחֹ֖חַ לַיהוָֽה׃ ס

2 ¹וְנֶ֗פֶשׁ כִּֽי־תַקְרִ֞יב קָרְבַּ֤ן מִנְחָה֙ לַֽיהוָ֔ה סֹ֖לֶת יִהְיֶ֣ה קָרְבָּנֹ֑ו וְיָצַ֤ק עָלֶ֙יהָ֙ שֶׁ֔מֶן וְנָתַ֥ן עָלֶ֖יהָ לְבֹנָֽה׃ ²וֶהֱבִיאָ֗הּ אֶל־בְּנֵ֣י אַהֲרֹן֮ הַכֹּהֲנִים֒ וְקָמַ֨ץ מִשָּׁ֜ם מְלֹ֣א קֻמְצֹ֗ו מִסָּלְתָּהּ֙ וּמִשַּׁמְנָ֔הּ עַ֖ל כָּל־לְבֹנָתָ֑הּ וְהִקְטִ֨יר הַכֹּהֵ֜ן אֶת־אַזְכָּרָתָהּ֙ הַמִּזְבֵּ֔חָה אִשֵּׁ֛ה רֵ֥יחַ נִיחֹ֖חַ לַֽיהוָֽה׃ ³וְהַנֹּותֶ֙רֶת֙ מִן־הַמִּנְחָ֔ה לְאַהֲרֹ֖ן וּלְבָנָ֑יו קֹ֥דֶשׁ קָֽדָשִׁ֖ים מֵאִשֵּׁ֥י יְהוָֽה׃ ס ⁴וְכִ֥י תַקְרִ֛ב קָרְבַּ֥ן מִנְחָ֖ה מַאֲפֵ֣ה תַנּ֑וּר סֹ֣לֶת חַלֹּ֤ות מַצֹּת֙ בְּלוּלֹ֣ת בַּשֶּׁ֔מֶן

1:17. **he shall not divide it.** One cuts up herd and flock animals during a sacrifice, but one does not divide birds this way. This summons to mind the original sacrifice that sealed the covenant between God and Abraham, in which Abraham cuts all the animals in half but leaves the birds whole (Gen 15:10), and a fire representing God's presence passes between the parts of the animals. Thus Israel's manner of sacrifice now memorializes the fact that God bound Himself to Israel through a ceremony of animal sacrifice.

mixed with oil and unleavened wafers with oil poured on them.

5"And if your offering is a grain offering on a griddle, it shall be fine flour, mixed with oil, unleavened. 6Break it into pieces and pour oil on it. It is a grain offering.

7"And if your offering is a grain offering from a pan, it shall be made of fine flour in oil.

8"And you shall bring the grain offering that one will make from these things to YHWH, and one shall bring it forward to the priest, and he shall bring it over to the altar. 9And the priest shall lift from the grain offering a representative portion of it and burn it to smoke at the altar, an offering by fire of a pleasant smell to YHWH. 10And the remainder from the grain offering is Aaron's and his sons', the holy of holies from YHWH's offerings by fire. 11Every grain offering that you will bring forward to YHWH shall not be made with leavening, because all leaven and all honey: you shall not burn any of it to smoke as an offering by fire to YHWH. 12You shall bring them forward to YHWH as an offering of a first thing, but they shall not go up to the altar as a pleasant smell. 13And you shall sprinkle every offering of a grain offering with salt. And you shall not let the salt of your God's covenant cease from on your grain offering; you shall bring salt on all your offerings.

14"And if you will bring a grain offering of firstfruits to YHWH, you shall bring the grain offering of your firstfruits *ripe*, parched with fire, groats of fresh grain. 15And you shall put oil on it and set frankincense on it. It is a grain offering. 16And the priest shall burn a representative portion of it to smoke, from its groats and from its oil, in addition to all of its frankincense, an offering by fire to YHWH.

וּרְקִיקֵי מַצּוֹת מְשֻׁחִים בַּשָּׁמֶן: ס 5וְאִם־מִנְחָה עַל־ הַמַּחֲבַת קָרְבָּנֶךָ סֹלֶת בְּלוּלָה בַשֶּׁמֶן מַצָּה תִהְיֶה: 6פָּתוֹת אֹתָהּ פִּתִּים וְיָצַקְתָּ עָלֶיהָ שָׁמֶן מִנְחָה הִוא: ס 7וְאִם־מִנְחַת מַרְחֶשֶׁת קָרְבָּנֶךָ סֹלֶת בַּשֶּׁמֶן תֵּעָשֶׂה: 8וְהֵבֵאתָ אֶת־הַמִּנְחָה אֲשֶׁר יֵעָשֶׂה מֵאֵלֶּה לַיהוָה וְהִקְרִיבָהּ אֶל־הַכֹּהֵן וְהִגִּישָׁהּ אֶל־הַמִּזְבֵּחַ: 9וְהֵרִים הַכֹּהֵן מִן־הַמִּנְחָה אֶת־אַזְכָּרָתָהּ וְהִקְטִיר הַמִּזְבֵּחָה אִשֵּׁה רֵיחַ נִיחֹחַ לַיהוָה: 10וְהַנּוֹתֶרֶת מִן־ הַמִּנְחָה לְאַהֲרֹן וּלְבָנָיו קֹדֶשׁ קָדָשִׁים מֵאִשֵּׁי יְהוָה: 11כָּל־הַמִּנְחָה אֲשֶׁר תַּקְרִיבוּ לַיהוָה לֹא תֵעָשֶׂה חָמֵץ כִּי כָל־שְׂאֹר וְכָל־דְּבַשׁ לֹא־תַקְטִירוּ מִמֶּנּוּ אִשֶּׁה לַיהוָה: 12קָרְבַּן רֵאשִׁית תַּקְרִיבוּ אֹתָם לַיהוָה וְאֶל־הַמִּזְבֵּחַ לֹא־יַעֲלוּ לְרֵיחַ נִיחֹחַ: 13וְכָל־ קָרְבַּן מִנְחָתְךָ בַּמֶּלַח תִּמְלָח וְלֹא תַשְׁבִּית מֶלַח בְּרִית אֱלֹהֶיךָ מֵעַל מִנְחָתֶךָ עַל כָּל־קָרְבָּנְךָ תַּקְרִיב מֶלַח: ס 14וְאִם־תַּקְרִיב מִנְחַת בִּכּוּרִים לַיהוָה אָבִיב קָלוּי בָּאֵשׁ גֶּרֶשׂ כַּרְמֶל תַּקְרִיב אֵת מִנְחַת בִּכּוּרֶיךָ: 15וְנָתַתָּ עָלֶיהָ שֶׁמֶן וְשַׂמְתָּ עָלֶיהָ לְבֹנָה מִנְחָה הִוא: 16וְהִקְטִיר הַכֹּהֵן אֶת־אַזְכָּרָתָהּ מִגִּרְשָׂהּ וּמִשַּׁמְנָהּ עַל כָּל־לְבֹנָתָהּ אִשֶּׁה לַיהוָה: פ

2:11. **Every grain offering . . . shall not be made with leavening.** That is, *no* grain offering shall be made with leaven. See the comment on Exod 29:2.

2:13. **sprinkle every offering of a grain offering with salt.** The requirement to use salt with these offerings is now memorialized by the custom of putting salt on bread when one says the blessing over bread (*hammōṣî'*) at the beginning of a meal.

3 [1]"And if his offering is a peace-offering sacrifice, if he is offering from the herd, whether male or female, he shall make it unblemished in front of YHWH. [2]And he shall lay his hand on the head of his offering and slaughter it at the entrance of the Tent of Meeting. And the sons of Aaron, the priests, shall fling the blood on the altar all around. [3]And he shall bring forward from the peace-offering sacrifice an offering by fire to YHWH: the fat that covers the innards and all the fat that is on the innards [4]and the two kidneys and the fat that is on them, that is on the loins; and the lobe on the liver: he shall take it away with the kidneys. [5]And the sons of Aaron shall burn it to smoke at the altar upon the burnt offering that is on the wood that is on the fire, an offering by fire of a pleasant smell to YHWH.

[6]"And if his offering as a peace-offering sacrifice to YHWH is from the flock, male or female, he shall make it unblemished. [7]If he is making his offering a sheep, then he shall bring it forward in front of YHWH [8]and lay his hand on the head of his offering and slaughter it in front of the Tent of Meeting. And the sons of Aaron shall fling its blood on the altar all around. [9]And he shall bring forward from the peace-offering sacrifice an offering by fire to YHWH: its fat, the entire fat tail—he shall take it away from the backbone—and the fat that covers the innards and all the fat that is on the innards [10]and the two kidneys and the fat that is on them, that is on the loins; and the lobe on the liver: he shall take it away with the kidneys. [11]And the priest shall burn it to smoke at the altar: food, an offering by fire to YHWH.

[12]"And if his offering is a goat, then he shall bring it forward in front of YHWH [13]and lay his hand on its head and slaughter it in front of the Tent of Meeting. And the sons of Aaron shall fling its blood on the altar all around. [14]And he shall make his offering from it, an offering by fire to YHWH: the fat that covers the innards and all the fat that is on the innards [15]and the two kid-

3 [1]וְאִם־זֶ֥בַח שְׁלָמִ֖ים קָרְבָּנֹ֑ו אִ֤ם מִן־הַבָּקָר֙ ה֣וּא מַקְרִ֔יב אִם־זָכָר֙ אִם־נְקֵבָ֔ה תָּמִ֥ים יַקְרִיבֶ֖נּוּ לִפְנֵ֥י יְהוָֽה׃ [2]וְסָמַ֤ךְ יָדֹו֙ עַל־רֹ֣אשׁ קָרְבָּנֹ֔ו וּשְׁחָטֹ֕ו פֶּ֖תַח אֹ֣הֶל מֹועֵ֑ד וְזָרְק֡וּ בְּנֵי֩ אַהֲרֹ֨ן הַכֹּהֲנִ֧ים אֶת־הַדָּ֛ם עַל־הַמִּזְבֵּ֖חַ סָבִֽיב׃ [3]וְהִקְרִיב֙ מִזֶּ֣בַח הַשְּׁלָמִ֔ים אִשֶּׁ֖ה לַֽיהוָ֑ה אֶת־הַחֵ֙לֶב֙ הַֽמְכַסֶּ֣ה אֶת־הַקֶּ֔רֶב וְאֵת֙ כָּל־הַחֵ֔לֶב אֲשֶׁ֖ר עַל־הַקֶּֽרֶב׃ [4]וְאֵת֙ שְׁתֵּ֣י הַכְּלָיֹ֔ת וְאֶת־הַחֵ֙לֶב֙ אֲשֶׁ֣ר עֲלֵהֶ֔ן אֲשֶׁ֖ר עַל־הַכְּסָלִ֑ים וְאֶת־הַיֹּתֶ֙רֶת֙ עַל־הַכָּבֵ֔ד עַל־הַכְּלָיֹ֖ות יְסִירֶֽנָּה׃ [5]וְהִקְטִ֨ירוּ אֹתֹ֤ו בְנֵֽי־אַהֲרֹן֙ הַמִּזְבֵּ֔חָה עַל־הָ֣עֹלָ֔ה אֲשֶׁ֥ר עַל־הָעֵצִ֖ים אֲשֶׁ֣ר עַל־הָאֵ֑שׁ אִשֵּׁ֛ה רֵ֥יחַ נִיחֹ֖חַ לַֽיהוָֽה׃ פ

[6]וְאִם־מִן־הַצֹּ֧אן קָרְבָּנֹ֛ו לְזֶ֥בַח שְׁלָמִ֖ים לַיהוָ֑ה זָכָר֙ אֹ֣ו נְקֵבָ֔ה תָּמִ֖ים יַקְרִיבֶֽנּוּ׃ [7]אִם־כֶּ֥שֶׂב הֽוּא־מַקְרִ֖יב אֶת־קָרְבָּנֹ֑ו וְהִקְרִ֥יב אֹתֹ֖ו לִפְנֵ֥י יְהוָֽה׃ [8]וְסָמַ֤ךְ אֶת־יָדֹו֙ עַל־רֹ֣אשׁ קָרְבָּנֹ֔ו וְשָׁחַ֣ט אֹתֹ֔ו לִפְנֵ֖י אֹ֣הֶל מֹועֵ֑ד וְ֠זָרְקוּ בְּנֵ֨י אַהֲרֹ֧ן אֶת־דָּמֹ֛ו עַל־הַמִּזְבֵּ֖חַ סָבִֽיב׃ [9]וְהִקְרִ֨יב מִזֶּ֣בַח הַשְּׁלָמִים֮ אִשֶּׁ֣ה לַיהוָה֒ חֶלְבֹּו֙ הָאַלְיָ֣ה תְמִימָ֔ה לְעֻמַּ֥ת הֶעָצֶ֖ה יְסִירֶ֑נָּה וְאֶת־הַחֵ֙לֶב֙ הַֽמְכַסֶּ֣ה אֶת־הַקֶּ֔רֶב וְאֵת֙ כָּל־הַחֵ֔לֶב אֲשֶׁ֖ר עַל־הַקֶּֽרֶב׃ [10]וְאֵת֙ שְׁתֵּ֣י הַכְּלָיֹ֔ת וְאֶת־הַחֵ֙לֶב֙ אֲשֶׁ֣ר עֲלֵהֶ֔ן אֲשֶׁ֖ר עַל־הַכְּסָלִ֑ים וְאֶת־הַיֹּתֶ֙רֶת֙ עַל־הַכָּבֵ֔ד עַל־הַכְּלָיֹ֖ת יְסִירֶֽנָּה׃ [11]וְהִקְטִירֹ֥ו הַכֹּהֵ֖ן הַמִּזְבֵּ֑חָה לֶ֥חֶם אִשֶּׁ֖ה לַיהוָֽה׃ פ [12]וְאִ֥ם עֵ֖ז קָרְבָּנֹ֑ו וְהִקְרִיבֹ֖ו לִפְנֵ֥י יְהוָֽה׃ [13]וְסָמַ֤ךְ אֶת־יָדֹו֙ עַל־רֹאשֹׁ֔ו וְשָׁחַ֣ט אֹתֹ֔ו לִפְנֵ֖י אֹ֣הֶל מֹועֵ֑ד וְ֠זָרְקוּ בְּנֵ֨י אַהֲרֹ֧ן אֶת־דָּמֹ֛ו עַל־הַמִּזְבֵּ֖חַ סָבִֽיב׃ [14]וְהִקְרִ֤יב מִמֶּ֙נּוּ֙ קָרְבָּנֹ֔ו אִשֶּׁ֖ה לַֽיהוָ֑ה אֶת־הַחֵ֙לֶב֙ הַֽמְכַסֶּ֣ה אֶת־הַקֶּ֔רֶב וְאֵת֙ כָּל־הַחֵ֔לֶב אֲשֶׁ֖ר עַל־הַקֶּֽרֶב׃ [15]וְאֵת֙ שְׁתֵּ֣י הַכְּלָיֹ֔ת וְאֶת־

neys and the fat that is on them, that is on the loins; and the lobe on the liver: he shall take it away with the kidneys. [16]And the priest shall burn them to smoke at the altar: food, an offering by fire as a pleasant smell. All fat is YHWH's. [17]It is an eternal law, through your generations, in all your homes: you shall not eat any fat and any blood."

4 [1]And YHWH spoke to Moses, saying, [2]"Speak to the children of Israel, saying: A

הַחֵ֙לֶב֙ אֲשֶׁ֣ר עֲלֵהֶ֔ן אֲשֶׁר֙ עַל־הַכְּסָלִ֔ים וְאֶת־הַיֹּתֶ֙רֶת֙ עַל־הַכָּבֵ֔ד עַל־הַכְּלָי֖וֹת יְסִירֶֽנָּה׃ [16]וְהִקְטִירָ֥ם הַכֹּהֵ֖ן הַמִּזְבֵּ֑חָה לֶ֤חֶם אִשֶּׁה֙ לְרֵ֣יחַ נִיחֹ֔חַ כָּל־חֵ֖לֶב לַיהוָֽה׃ [17]חֻקַּ֤ת עוֹלָם֙ לְדֹרֹ֣תֵיכֶ֔ם בְּכֹ֖ל מוֹשְׁבֹתֵיכֶ֑ם כָּל־חֵ֥לֶב וְכָל־דָּ֖ם לֹ֥א תֹאכֵֽלוּ׃ פ

4 [1]וַיְדַבֵּ֥ר יְהוָ֖ה אֶל־מֹשֶׁ֥ה לֵּאמֹֽר׃ [2]דַּבֵּ֞ר אֶל־

4:2. **A person who sins**. At the time that I am writing this, it has been almost two thousand years since the second Jerusalem Temple was destroyed and sacrifices ended in Judaism. The two largest religions, Christianity and Islam, also do not perform sacrifices, and so it has been so long since we have seen or done this practice that all but a few people are unclear about what sacrifice was. Frequently they imagine that it meant that people regularly destroyed much of their livestock for no reason. This is wrong.

The purpose of sacrifice was to recognize that an animal's life was sacred.

The order of the book of Leviticus itself may have contributed to the misunderstanding of sacrifice. It deals with the sacrifices that go to the priests first (in Leviticus 1–7) and does not get to the "food" sacrifices until Leviticus 17.

Most sacrificed animals are eaten by the persons who bring the animals to the altar. There is also a second group of sacrifices, which involve the ritual slaughter of an animal that is not for consumption by the person who brings the sacrifice. Rather, the meat is eaten by the priests or is entirely burnt. Such sacrifices relate to guilt and expiation. The introduction of law means the introduction of violations of the law. Besides addressing matters of punishment (compensation, execution), the system requires some means of dealing with individuals' feelings of guilt—and with public condemnation. This is achieved through the sacrificial system, including sacrifices for unwitting violations, by individuals or the community (Leviticus 4 and 5), and sacrifices for various other feelings on the part of the offerer (Leviticus 1–3). The system that provides grounds for guilt also provides a mechanism for expiation and forgiveness.

Sacrifice is the only mechanism for forgiveness in the book of Leviticus. There is no suggestion in Leviticus that repentance alone can bring forgiveness for violations of the laws, no indication that one can appeal to YHWH's mercy, His grace, or His kindness for atonement. Indeed, the words "repentance" (*šûb*), "mercy" (*raḥămîm*), "grace" (*ḥēn*), and "kindness" (*ḥesed*) do not occur in Leviticus. Thus the psychological and spiritual state of the community is linked powerfully to this visible, tangible act. And this psychological and spiritual focus, together with the very physical focus of the consumption of meat, places sacrifice in a critical and pervasive role in the community's life. And it places the priests who alone can perform sacrifice in a correspondingly critical role. And, no less significantly, it concentrates the community's at-

person who sins by mistake—of any of YHWH's commandments that are not to be done—and does any one of them:

³"If the anointed priest will sin, causing the people's guilt, then he shall bring forward for his sin that he committed: a bull of the cattle, unblemished, for YHWH as a sin offering. ⁴And he shall bring the bull to the entrance of the Tent of Meeting in front of YHWH. And he shall lay his hand on the bull's head and slaughter the bull in front of YHWH. ⁵And the anointed priest shall take some of the bull's blood and bring it to the Tent of Meeting. ⁶And the priest shall dip his finger in the blood and sprinkle some of the blood seven times in front of YHWH before the pavilion of the Holy. ⁷And the priest shall put some of the blood on the horns of the altar of the incense of fragrances, in front of YHWH, which is in the Tent of Meeting. And he shall spill all of the

בְּנֵי יִשְׂרָאֵל לֵאמֹר נֶפֶשׁ כִּי־תֶחֱטָא בִשְׁגָגָה מִכֹּל מִצְוֹת יְהוָה אֲשֶׁר לֹא תֵעָשֶׂינָה וְעָשָׂה מֵאַחַת מֵהֵנָּה: ³אִם הַכֹּהֵן הַמָּשִׁיחַ יֶחֱטָא לְאַשְׁמַת הָעָם וְהִקְרִיב עַל חַטָּאתוֹ אֲשֶׁר חָטָא פַּר בֶּן־בָּקָר תָּמִים לַיהוָה לְחַטָּאת: ⁴וְהֵבִיא אֶת־הַפָּר אֶל־פֶּתַח אֹהֶל מוֹעֵד לִפְנֵי יְהוָה וְסָמַךְ אֶת־יָדוֹ עַל־רֹאשׁ הַפָּר וְשָׁחַט אֶת־הַפָּר לִפְנֵי יְהוָה: ⁵וְלָקַח הַכֹּהֵן הַמָּשִׁיחַ מִדַּם הַפָּר וְהֵבִיא אֹתוֹ אֶל־אֹהֶל מוֹעֵד: ⁶וְטָבַל הַכֹּהֵן אֶת־אֶצְבָּעוֹ בַּדָּם וְהִזָּה מִן־הַדָּם שֶׁבַע פְּעָמִים לִפְנֵי יְהוָה אֶת־פְּנֵי פָּרֹכֶת הַקֹּדֶשׁ: ⁷וְנָתַן הַכֹּהֵן מִן־הַדָּם עַל־קַרְנוֹת מִזְבַּח קְטֹרֶת הַסַּמִּים לִפְנֵי יְהוָה אֲשֶׁר בְּאֹהֶל מוֹעֵד וְאֵת ׀ כָּל־דַּם הַפָּר יִשְׁפֹּךְ אֶל־יְסוֹד

---

tention on the single place where sacrifice can be performed: the Tabernacle, or Tent of Meeting.

4:2. **by mistake.** This begins a lengthy section on what to do when people sin by mistake: a priest, the entire community, a leader, or an individual. Humans make mistakes. But even a sin that is committed by mistake requires some act of atonement. People still feel guilty when they do harm, even if they meant no harm, and so this provides a mechanism for purging the guilt and putting the act in the past. Now, in the absence of sacrifice, other means of atonement have risen in importance. Notably, the Day of Atonement (Yom Kippur) has become the most sacred and widely observed holiday; whereas, in the Torah, Passover stands out as the first and foremost of the holidays.

4:3. **the anointed priest.** Hebrew *hakkōhēn hammāšîaḥ*. This is the first occurrence of the word *māšîaḥ*, meaning "anointed" and commonly translated elsewhere in the *Tanak* as "Messiah." In the Torah *māšîaḥ* always refers to the high priest and not, as it later came to mean, the king. The relationship between priest and king was always a complex one in the *Tanak* and in the postbiblical world as well. The judge Gideon declines to be made Israel's first king, but he acts as a priest, which may well have involved greater power, distinction, and income (Judg 8:22–27). David makes some of his sons priests (2 Sam 8:18). The Hasmoneans (Maccabees) were initially high priests but later were simultaneously priests and kings.

4:6. **the pavilion of the Holy.** The pavilion (*pārōket*) is over the Holy of Holies, the inner part of the Tabernacle, not over the Holy, the outer part. So why is it called "the pavilion of the Holy" here? As in Lev 16:2, "the Holy" can refer generally to the holiness that is inside the Holiest of Holies.

bull's blood at the base of the altar of burnt offering, which is at the entrance of the Tent of Meeting. [8]And he shall take off all the fat of the bull of the sin offering from it: the fat that covers the innards and all the fat that is on the innards [9]and the two kidneys and the fat that is on them, that is on the loins; and the lobe on the liver: he shall take it away with the kidneys [10]when it will be taken off from the ox of the peace-offering sacrifice. And the priest shall burn them to smoke on the altar of burnt offering. [11]And the bull's skin and all of its meat with its head and with its legs and its innards and its dung: [12]and he shall bring all of the bull outside the camp, to a pure place, to the place where ash is spilled, and burn it on wood in fire. It shall be burned at the place where ash is spilled.

[13]"And if all the congregation of Israel will make a mistake, and something will be hidden from the community's eyes, and they do one of any of YHWH's commandments that are not to be done, and they are guilty, [14]and the sin over which they have sinned will become known, then the community shall bring forward a bull of the cattle as a sin offering, and they shall bring it in front of the Tent of Meeting. [15]And the community's elders shall lay their hands on the bull's head in front of YHWH, and he shall slaughter the bull in front of YHWH. [16]And the anointed priest shall bring some of the bull's blood to the Tent of Meeting. [17]And the priest shall dip his finger from the blood and sprinkle seven times in front of YHWH before the pavilion. [18]And he shall put some of the blood on the horns of the altar that is in front of YHWH, that is in the Tent of Meeting, and he shall spill all of the blood at the base of the altar of burnt offering, which is at the entrance of the Tent of Meeting. [19]And he shall take off all of its fat from it and burn it to smoke at the altar. [20]And he shall do to the bull as he did to the bull of the sin offering. So he shall do to it. And the priest shall make atonement over them, and it will be forgiven for them. [21]And he shall bring the bull outside the camp

מִזְבַּח הָעֹלָה אֲשֶׁר־פֶּתַח אֹהֶל מוֹעֵד: [8]וְאֶת־כָּל־חֵלֶב פַּר הַחַטָּאת יָרִים מִמֶּנּוּ אֶת־הַחֵלֶב הַמְכַסֶּה עַל־הַקֶּרֶב וְאֵת כָּל־הַחֵלֶב אֲשֶׁר עַל־הַקֶּרֶב: [9]וְאֵת שְׁתֵּי הַכְּלָיֹת וְאֶת־הַחֵלֶב אֲשֶׁר עֲלֵיהֶן אֲשֶׁר עַל־הַכְּסָלִים וְאֶת־הַיֹּתֶרֶת עַל־הַכָּבֵד עַל־הַכְּלָיוֹת יְסִירֶנָּה: [10]כַּאֲשֶׁר יוּרַם מִשּׁוֹר זֶבַח הַשְּׁלָמִים וְהִקְטִירָם הַכֹּהֵן עַל מִזְבַּח הָעֹלָה: [11]וְאֶת־עוֹר הַפָּר וְאֶת־כָּל־בְּשָׂרוֹ עַל־רֹאשׁוֹ וְעַל־כְּרָעָיו וְקִרְבּוֹ וּפִרְשׁוֹ: [12]וְהוֹצִיא אֶת־כָּל־הַפָּר אֶל־מִחוּץ לַמַּחֲנֶה אֶל־מָקוֹם טָהוֹר אֶל־שֶׁפֶךְ הַדֶּשֶׁן וְשָׂרַף אֹתוֹ עַל־עֵצִים בָּאֵשׁ עַל־שֶׁפֶךְ הַדֶּשֶׁן יִשָּׂרֵף: פ [13]וְאִם כָּל־עֲדַת יִשְׂרָאֵל יִשְׁגּוּ וְנֶעְלַם דָּבָר מֵעֵינֵי הַקָּהָל וְעָשׂוּ אַחַת מִכָּל־מִצְוֹת יְהוָה אֲשֶׁר לֹא־תֵעָשֶׂינָה וְאָשֵׁמוּ: [14]וְנוֹדְעָה הַחַטָּאת אֲשֶׁר חָטְאוּ עָלֶיהָ וְהִקְרִיבוּ הַקָּהָל פַּר בֶּן־בָּקָר לְחַטָּאת וְהֵבִיאוּ אֹתוֹ לִפְנֵי אֹהֶל מוֹעֵד: [15]וְסָמְכוּ זִקְנֵי הָעֵדָה אֶת־יְדֵיהֶם עַל־רֹאשׁ הַפָּר לִפְנֵי יְהוָה וְשָׁחַט אֶת־הַפָּר לִפְנֵי יְהוָה: [16]וְהֵבִיא הַכֹּהֵן הַמָּשִׁיחַ מִדַּם הַפָּר אֶל־אֹהֶל מוֹעֵד: [17]וְטָבַל הַכֹּהֵן אֶצְבָּעוֹ מִן־הַדָּם וְהִזָּה שֶׁבַע פְּעָמִים לִפְנֵי יְהוָה אֵת פְּנֵי הַפָּרֹכֶת: [18]וּמִן־הַדָּם יִתֵּן ׀ עַל־קַרְנֹת הַמִּזְבֵּחַ אֲשֶׁר לִפְנֵי יְהוָה אֲשֶׁר בְּאֹהֶל מוֹעֵד וְאֵת כָּל־הַדָּם יִשְׁפֹּךְ אֶל־יְסוֹד מִזְבַּח הָעֹלָה אֲשֶׁר־פֶּתַח אֹהֶל מוֹעֵד: [19]וְאֵת כָּל־חֶלְבּוֹ יָרִים מִמֶּנּוּ וְהִקְטִיר הַמִּזְבֵּחָה: [20]וְעָשָׂה לַפָּר כַּאֲשֶׁר עָשָׂה לְפַר הַחַטָּאת כֵּן יַעֲשֶׂה־לּוֹ וְכִפֶּר עֲלֵהֶם הַכֹּהֵן וְנִסְלַח לָהֶם: [21]וְהוֹצִיא אֶת־הַפָּר אֶל־מִחוּץ לַמַּחֲנֶה

and burn it as he burned the first bull. It is the community's sin offering.

22"When a chieftain will sin and do one of any of the commandments of YHWH, his God, that are not to be done, by mistake, and he is guilty, 23or his sin by which he has sinned has been made known to him, then he shall bring his offering, a goat, male, unblemished. 24And he shall lay his hand on the goat's head and slaughter it at the place where he would slaughter a burnt offering in front of YHWH. It is a sin offering. 25And the priest shall take some of the blood of the sin offering with his finger and put it on the horns of the altar of burnt offering, and he shall spill its blood at the base of the altar of burnt offering. 26And he shall burn all its fat to smoke at the altar like the fat of the peace-offering sacrifice. And the priest shall make atonement over him from his sin, and it will be forgiven for him.

27"And if one person from the people of the land will sin by mistake by doing one of YHWH's commandments that are not to be done and is guilty, 28or his sin that he has committed has been made known to him, then he shall bring his offering, a goat, unblemished, female, for his sin that he committed. 29And he shall lay his hand on the head of the sin offering and slaughter the sin offering at the place of burnt offering. 30And the priest shall take some of its blood with his finger and put it on the horns of the altar of burnt offering, and he shall spill all its blood at the base of the altar. 31And he shall take away all of its fat as the fat was taken away from on the peace-offering sacrifice, and the priest shall burn it to smoke at the altar as a pleasant smell to YHWH, and the priest shall make atonement over him, and it will be forgiven for him.

32"And if he will bring a lamb as his offering for a sin offering, he shall bring a female, un-

וְשָׂרַף אֹתֹו כַּאֲשֶׁר שָׂרַף אֵת הַפָּר הָרִאשֹׁון חַטַּאת הַקָּהָל הוּא: פ

22אֲשֶׁר נָשִׂיא יֶחֱטָא וְעָשָׂה אַחַת מִכָּל־מִצְוֺת יְהוָה אֱלֹהָיו אֲשֶׁר לֹא־תֵעָשֶׂינָה בִּשְׁגָגָה וְאָשֵׁם: 23אֹו־הֹודַע אֵלָיו חַטָּאתֹו אֲשֶׁר חָטָא בָּהּ וְהֵבִיא אֶת־קָרְבָּנֹו שְׂעִיר עִזִּים זָכָר תָּמִים: 24וְסָמַךְ יָדֹו עַל־רֹאשׁ הַשָּׂעִיר וְשָׁחַט אֹתֹו בִּמְקֹום אֲשֶׁר־יִשְׁחַט אֶת־הָעֹלָה לִפְנֵי יְהוָה חַטָּאת הוּא: 25וְלָקַח הַכֹּהֵן מִדַּם הַחַטָּאת בְּאֶצְבָּעֹו וְנָתַן עַל־קַרְנֹת מִזְבַּח הָעֹלָה וְאֶת־דָּמֹו יִשְׁפֹּךְ אֶל־יְסֹוד מִזְבַּח הָעֹלָה: 26וְאֶת־כָּל־חֶלְבֹּו יַקְטִיר הַמִּזְבֵּחָה כְּחֵלֶב זֶבַח הַשְּׁלָמִים וְכִפֶּר עָלָיו הַכֹּהֵן מֵחַטָּאתֹו וְנִסְלַח לֹו: פ

27וְאִם־נֶפֶשׁ אַחַת תֶּחֱטָא בִשְׁגָגָה מֵעַם הָאָרֶץ בַּעֲשֹׂתָהּ אַחַת מִמִּצְוֺת יְהוָה אֲשֶׁר לֹא־תֵעָשֶׂינָה וְאָשֵׁם: 28אֹו הֹודַע אֵלָיו חַטָּאתֹו אֲשֶׁר חָטָא וְהֵבִיא קָרְבָּנֹו שְׂעִירַת עִזִּים תְּמִימָה נְקֵבָה עַל־חַטָּאתֹו אֲשֶׁר חָטָא: 29וְסָמַךְ אֶת־יָדֹו עַל רֹאשׁ הַחַטָּאת וְשָׁחַט אֶת־הַחַטָּאת בִּמְקֹום הָעֹלָה: 30וְלָקַח הַכֹּהֵן מִדָּמָהּ בְּאֶצְבָּעֹו וְנָתַן עַל־קַרְנֹת מִזְבַּח הָעֹלָה וְאֶת־כָּל־דָּמָהּ יִשְׁפֹּךְ אֶל־יְסֹוד הַמִּזְבֵּחַ: 31וְאֶת־כָּל־חֶלְבָּהּ יָסִיר כַּאֲשֶׁר הוּסַר חֵלֶב מֵעַל זֶבַח הַשְּׁלָמִים וְהִקְטִיר הַכֹּהֵן הַמִּזְבֵּחָה לְרֵיחַ נִיחֹחַ לַיהוָה וְכִפֶּר עָלָיו הַכֹּהֵן וְנִסְלַח לֹו: פ 32וְאִם־כֶּבֶשׂ יָבִיא קָרְבָּנֹו לְחַטָּאת נְקֵבָה תְמִימָה יְבִיאֶנָּה:

4:22. **chieftain.** Hebrew *nāśī'*. Elsewhere in the Torah the word refers to the chieftain of a tribe (Num 2:3–29) or of a priestly family (Num 3:24–35) or of a city (Gen 34:2). Here it may allude to a king of Israel, "a chieftain among your people" (as in 1 Kings 11:34; Ezek 34:24), or it may mean any of these leaders.

blemished. 33And he shall lay his hand on the head of the sin offering and slaughter it as a sin offering at the place where he would slaughter a burnt offering. 34And the priest shall take some of the blood of the sin offering with his finger and put it on the horns of the altar of burnt offering, and he shall spill all its blood at the base of the altar. 35And he shall take away all of its fat as the sheep's fat was taken away from the peace-offering sacrifice, and the priest shall burn them to smoke at the altar with YHWH's offerings by fire, and the priest shall make atonement over him, over his sin that he committed, and it will be forgiven for him.

5 1"And a person who will sin in that he has heard a pronouncement of an oath, and he was a witness—whether he saw or he knew: if he will not tell, then he shall bear his crime.

2"Or a person who will touch any impure thing or the carcass of an impure wild animal or the carcass of an impure domestic animal or the carcass of an impure swarming creature, and it was hidden from him, so he had become impure and had become guilty; 3or when he will touch a human's impurity—for any impurity of his through which he will become impure—and it was hidden from him, and then he had come to know and had become guilty; 4or a person who will swear so as to let out of his lips to do bad or to do good—for anything that a human would let out in an oath—and it was hidden from him, and then he had come to know and had become guilty by one of these: 5And it will be that when he becomes guilty by one of these he shall con-

33וְסָמַךְ אֶת־יָדוֹ עַל רֹאשׁ הַחַטָּאת וְשָׁחַט אֹתָהּ לְחַטָּאת בִּמְקוֹם אֲשֶׁר יִשְׁחַט אֶת־הָעֹלָה: 34וְלָקַח הַכֹּהֵן מִדַּם הַחַטָּאת בְּאֶצְבָּעוֹ וְנָתַן עַל־קַרְנֹת מִזְבַּח הָעֹלָה וְאֶת־כָּל־דָּמָהּ יִשְׁפֹּךְ אֶל־יְסוֹד הַמִּזְבֵּחַ: 35וְאֶת־כָּל־חֶלְבָּהּ יָסִיר כַּאֲשֶׁר יוּסַר חֵלֶב־הַכֶּשֶׂב מִזֶּבַח הַשְּׁלָמִים וְהִקְטִיר הַכֹּהֵן אֹתָם הַמִּזְבֵּחָה עַל אִשֵּׁי יְהוָה וְכִפֶּר עָלָיו הַכֹּהֵן עַל־חַטָּאתוֹ אֲשֶׁר־חָטָא וְנִסְלַח לוֹ: פ

5 1וְנֶפֶשׁ כִּי־תֶחֱטָא וְשָׁמְעָה קוֹל אָלָה וְהוּא עֵד אוֹ רָאָה אוֹ יָדָע אִם־לוֹא יַגִּיד וְנָשָׂא עֲוֹנוֹ: 2אוֹ נֶפֶשׁ אֲשֶׁר תִּגַּע בְּכָל־דָּבָר טָמֵא אוֹ בְנִבְלַת חַיָּה טְמֵאָה אוֹ בְּנִבְלַת בְּהֵמָה טְמֵאָה אוֹ בְּנִבְלַת שֶׁרֶץ טָמֵא וְנֶעְלַם מִמֶּנּוּ וְהוּא טָמֵא וְאָשֵׁם: 3אוֹ כִי יִגַּע בְּטֻמְאַת אָדָם לְכֹל טֻמְאָתוֹ אֲשֶׁר יִטְמָא בָּהּ וְנֶעְלַם מִמֶּנּוּ וְהוּא יָדַע וְאָשֵׁם: 4אוֹ נֶפֶשׁ כִּי תִשָּׁבַע לְבַטֵּא בִשְׂפָתַיִם לְהָרַע אוֹ לְהֵיטִיב לְכֹל אֲשֶׁר יְבַטֵּא הָאָדָם בִּשְׁבֻעָה וְנֶעְלַם מִמֶּנּוּ וְהוּא־יָדַע וְאָשֵׁם לְאַחַת מֵאֵלֶּה: 5וְהָיָה כִי־יֶאְשַׁם לְאַחַת מֵאֵלֶּה

5:1. **bear his crime**. This expression means that the person is not punished by a court. It is between the individual and God. After all, in this case, it may be that no one but the person himself is even aware that he did the sin. The reverse expression occurs in the great formula of God's compassion in Exod 34:7, where it says that *God bears crime* (nōsē' 'āwōn) for humans. That very emphasis on the usual divine mercy makes cases like the current one so frightening: here it is the human who must bear the crime himself. This expression will be used in a number of cases in Leviticus and Numbers. By saying that a case is beyond the jurisdiction of any court or ruler, the Torah recognizes that some things are beyond humans' ability and humans' right to judge or punish.

fess that he has sinned over it, 6and he shall bring his guilt offering to YHWH over his sin that he has committed: a female from the flock, a sheep or a goat, as a sin offering, and the priest shall make atonement over him from his sin.

7"And if his hand will not attain enough for a sheep, then he shall bring as his guilt offering for having sinned two turtledoves or two pigeons to YHWH: one for a sin offering and one for a burnt offering. 8And he shall bring them to the priest, and he shall bring forward the one that is for the sin offering first and will wring but not separate its head at the point opposite its neck. 9And he shall sprinkle some of the blood of the sin offering on the wall of the altar, and what remains of the blood shall be drained at the base of the altar. It is a sin offering. 10And he shall make the second one a burnt offering according to the required manner. And the priest shall make atonement over him from his sin that he committed, and it shall be forgiven for him.

11"And if his hand cannot attain enough for two turtledoves or two pigeons, then he shall bring as his offering for having sinned a tenth of an ephah of fine flour for a sin offering. He shall not set oil on it, and he shall not put frankincense on it, because it is a sin offering. 12And he shall bring it to the priest, and the priest shall take the fill of his fist from it, a representative portion of it, and he shall burn it to smoke at the altar with YHWH's offerings by fire. It is a sin offering. 13And the priest shall make atonement over him, over his sin that he committed, from one of these, and it shall be forgiven for him. And it shall be the priest's, like the grain offering."

14And YHWH spoke to Moses, saying, 15"A person who will make a breach and sin by mistake among YHWH's holy things: he shall bring

וְהִתְוַדָּה אֲשֶׁר חָטָא עָלֶיהָ: 6וְהֵבִיא אֶת־אֲשָׁמוֹ לַיהֹוָה עַל חַטָּאתוֹ אֲשֶׁר חָטָא נְקֵבָה מִן־הַצֹּאן כִּשְׂבָּה אוֹ־שְׂעִירַת עִזִּים לְחַטָּאת וְכִפֶּר עָלָיו הַכֹּהֵן מֵחַטָּאתוֹ: 7וְאִם־לֹא תַגִּיעַ יָדוֹ דֵּי שֶׂה וְהֵבִיא אֶת־אֲשָׁמוֹ אֲשֶׁר חָטָא שְׁתֵּי תֹרִים אוֹ־שְׁנֵי בְנֵי־יוֹנָה לַיהֹוָה אֶחָד לְחַטָּאת וְאֶחָד לְעֹלָה: 8וְהֵבִיא אֹתָם אֶל־הַכֹּהֵן וְהִקְרִיב אֶת־אֲשֶׁר לַחַטָּאת רִאשׁוֹנָה וּמָלַק אֶת־רֹאשׁוֹ מִמּוּל עָרְפּוֹ וְלֹא יַבְדִּיל: 9וְהִזָּה מִדַּם הַחַטָּאת עַל־קִיר הַמִּזְבֵּחַ וְהַנִּשְׁאָר בַּדָּם יִמָּצֵה אֶל־יְסוֹד הַמִּזְבֵּחַ חַטָּאת הוּא: 10וְאֶת־הַשֵּׁנִי יַעֲשֶׂה עֹלָה כַּמִּשְׁפָּט וְכִפֶּר עָלָיו הַכֹּהֵן מֵחַטָּאתוֹ אֲשֶׁר־חָטָא וְנִסְלַח לוֹ: ס 11וְאִם־לֹא תַשִּׂיג יָדוֹ לִשְׁתֵּי תֹרִים אוֹ לִשְׁנֵי בְנֵי־יוֹנָה וְהֵבִיא אֶת־קָרְבָּנוֹ אֲשֶׁר חָטָא עֲשִׂירִת הָאֵפָה סֹלֶת לְחַטָּאת לֹא־יָשִׂים עָלֶיהָ שֶׁמֶן וְלֹא־יִתֵּן עָלֶיהָ לְבֹנָה כִּי חַטָּאת הִיא: 12וֶהֱבִיאָהּ אֶל־הַכֹּהֵן וְקָמַץ הַכֹּהֵן מִמֶּנָּה מְלוֹא קֻמְצוֹ אֶת־אַזְכָּרָתָהּ וְהִקְטִיר הַמִּזְבֵּחָה עַל אִשֵּׁי יְהֹוָה חַטָּאת הִוא: 13וְכִפֶּר עָלָיו הַכֹּהֵן עַל־חַטָּאתוֹ אֲשֶׁר־חָטָא מֵאַחַת מֵאֵלֶּה וְנִסְלַח לוֹ וְהָיְתָה לַכֹּהֵן כַּמִּנְחָה: ס

14וַיְדַבֵּר יְהֹוָה אֶל־מֹשֶׁה לֵּאמֹר: 15נֶפֶשׁ כִּי־תִמְעֹל מַעַל וְחָטְאָה בִּשְׁגָגָה מִקָּדְשֵׁי יְהֹוָה וְהֵבִיא

5:7,11. **if his hand will not attain enough**. Meaning: if he will not be able to afford it. A person is not to be prevented from getting atonement because of lack of money.

5:15. **make a breach**. The term, Hebrew ma'al, refers to trespassing into a zone that is forbidden. Here it refers to a layperson's mistakenly taking some of the holy objects,

his guilt offering to YHWH, an unblemished ram from the flock by your evaluation of silver by shekels, by the shekel of the Holy, as a guilt offering. 16And for what he sinned from the Holy he shall pay and add to it a fifth of it and give it to the priest, and the priest shall make atonement over him with the ram of the guilt offering, and it shall be forgiven for him.

17"And if a person who will sin and commit one of any of YHWH's commandments that are not to be done and did not know and became guilty, then he shall bear his crime. 18And he shall bring an unblemished ram from the flock by your evaluation as a guilt offering to the priest, and the priest shall make atonement over him, over his mistake that he made and had not known, and it shall be forgiven for him. 19It is a guilt offering. He *is* guilty to YHWH."

20And YHWH spoke to Moses, saying, 21"A person who will sin and make a breach against YHWH and tell a lie against his fellow in a matter of a deposit or something set in hand or by robbery, or has exploited his fellow 22or has found something that was lost and has lied about it or sworn to a falsehood—for one of any of these that a human will do to sin: 23it will be, when he sins and is guilty, that he shall bring back the thing that he robbed or the thing that he coerced or the thing that was deposited with him or the lost thing that he found 24or anything about which he swore as a falsehood, and he shall pay it in its worth and add to it a fifth of it. He shall give it to the one whose it is on the day of his being guilty, 25and he shall bring his guilt

אֶת־אֲשָׁמ֣וֹ לַיהוָ֗ה אַ֧יִל תָּמִ֛ים מִן־הַצֹּ֖אן בְּעֶרְכְּךָ֥ כֶּֽסֶף־שְׁקָלִ֛ים בְּשֶֽׁקֶל־הַקֹּ֖דֶשׁ לְאָשָֽׁם: 16וְאֵ֣ת אֲשֶׁ֣ר חָטָ֗א מִן־הַקֹּ֙דֶשׁ֙ יְשַׁלֵּ֔ם וְאֶת־חֲמִֽישִׁתוֹ֙ יוֹסֵ֣ף עָלָ֔יו וְנָתַ֥ן אֹת֖וֹ לַכֹּהֵ֑ן וְהַכֹּהֵ֗ן יְכַפֵּ֥ר עָלָ֛יו בְּאֵ֥יל הָאָשָׁ֖ם וְנִסְלַ֥ח לֽוֹ: פ 17וְאִם־נֶ֙פֶשׁ֙ כִּ֣י תֶֽחֱטָ֔א וְעָֽשְׂתָ֗ה אַחַת֙ מִכָּל־מִצְוֺ֣ת יְהוָ֔ה אֲשֶׁ֖ר לֹ֣א תֵעָשֶׂ֑ינָה וְלֹֽא־יָדַ֥ע וְאָשֵׁ֖ם וְנָשָׂ֥א עֲוֺנֽוֹ: 18וְ֠הֵבִיא אַ֣יִל תָּמִ֧ים מִן־הַצֹּ֛אן בְּעֶרְכְּךָ֥ לְאָשָׁ֖ם אֶל־הַכֹּהֵ֑ן וְכִפֶּר֩ עָלָ֨יו הַכֹּהֵ֜ן עַ֣ל שִׁגְגָת֧וֹ אֲשֶׁר־שָׁגָ֛ג וְה֥וּא לֹֽא־יָדַ֖ע וְנִסְלַ֥ח לֽוֹ: 19אָשָׁ֖ם ה֑וּא אָשֹׁ֥ם אָשַׁ֖ם לַיהוָֽה: פ 20וַיְדַבֵּ֥ר יְהוָ֖ה אֶל־מֹשֶׁ֥ה לֵּאמֹֽר: 21נֶ֗פֶשׁ כִּ֣י תֶחֱטָ֔א וּמָעֲלָ֥ה מַ֖עַל בַּֽיהוָ֑ה וְכִחֵ֨שׁ בַּעֲמִית֜וֹ בְּפִקָּד֗וֹן אֽוֹ־בִתְשׂ֤וּמֶת יָד֙ א֣וֹ בְגָזֵ֔ל א֖וֹ עָשַׁ֥ק אֶת־עֲמִיתֽוֹ: 22אֽוֹ־מָצָ֧א אֲבֵדָ֛ה וְכִ֥חֶשׁ בָּ֖הּ וְנִשְׁבַּ֣ע עַל־שָׁ֑קֶר עַל־אַחַ֗ת מִכֹּ֛ל אֲשֶׁר־יַעֲשֶׂ֥ה הָאָדָ֖ם לַחֲטֹ֥א בָהֵֽנָּה: 23וְהָיָה֮ כִּֽי־יֶחֱטָ֣א וְאָשֵׁם֒ וְהֵשִׁ֨יב אֶת־הַגְּזֵלָ֜ה אֲשֶׁ֣ר גָּזָ֗ל א֤וֹ אֶת־הָעֹ֙שֶׁק֙ אֲשֶׁ֣ר עָשָׁ֔ק א֚וֹ אֶת־הַפִּקָּד֔וֹן אֲשֶׁ֥ר הָפְקַ֖ד אִתּ֑וֹ א֥וֹ אֶת־הָאֲבֵדָ֖ה אֲשֶׁ֥ר מָצָֽא: 24א֠וֹ מִכֹּ֞ל אֲשֶׁר־יִשָּׁבַ֣ע עָלָיו֮ לַשֶּׁקֶר֒ וְשִׁלַּ֤ם אֹתוֹ֙ בְּרֹאשׁ֔וֹ וַחֲמִשִׁתָ֖יו יֹסֵ֣ף עָלָ֑יו לַאֲשֶׁ֨ר ה֥וּא ל֛וֹ יִתְּנֶ֖נּוּ בְּי֥וֹם אַשְׁמָתֽוֹ: 25וְאֶת־אֲשָׁמ֥וֹ

---

something that is no longer available, which would in most cases mean food that was meant for the priests. (Lev 22:14–16 refers explicitly to a layperson mistakenly eating the holy things, and the penalty is the same: add a fifth.) In Joshua 7:1, this term, "breach," refers to Achan's taking some of the spoils of Jericho, which the Israelites had been forbidden to take under the law of *ḥerem* (complete destruction in wars commanded by God; see, e.g., Deut 13:18). In Num 5:6, it refers to unlawful acquisition of another person's property. In Num 5:12, a woman's adultery is referred to as a *ma'al* against her husband. In Lev 26:40, it refers generally to a breach of faith toward God by the community.

offering to YHWH: an unblemished ram from the flock by your evaluation as a guilt offering, to the priest. 26And the priest shall atone over him in front of YHWH, and it will be forgiven for him, for any one out of all that he will do to become guilty through it."

COMMAND

צו

6 1And YHWH spoke to Moses, saying, 2"Command Aaron and his sons, saying: This is the instruction for the burnt offering. It is the one that goes up on its place of burning on the altar all night until morning, and the altar's fire shall be kept burning through it. 3And the priest shall wear his linen garment and shall wear linen drawers on his flesh. And he shall lift the ashes to which the fire will consume the burnt offering on the altar, and he shall set them beside the altar. 4And he shall take off his clothes and wear other clothes, and he shall take the ashes outside the camp, to a pure place. 5And the fire on the altar shall be kept burning through it. It shall not go out. And the priest shall burn wood on it morning by morning, and he shall arrange the burnt offering on it, and he shall burn the fat of the peace offerings to smoke on it. 6Fire always shall be kept burning on the altar. It shall not go out.

יָבִיא לַיהוָה אַיִל תָּמִים מִן־הַצֹּאן בְּעֶרְכְּךָ לְאָשָׁם אֶל־הַכֹּהֵן: 26וְכִפֶּר עָלָיו הַכֹּהֵן לִפְנֵי יְהוָה וְנִסְלַח לוֹ עַל־אַחַת מִכֹּל אֲשֶׁר־יַעֲשֶׂה לְאַשְׁמָה בָהּ: פ

6 1וַיְדַבֵּר יְהוָה אֶל־מֹשֶׁה לֵּאמֹר: 2צַו אֶת־אַהֲרֹן וְאֶת־בָּנָיו לֵאמֹר זֹאת תּוֹרַת הָעֹלָה הִוא הָעֹלָה עַל מוֹקְדָה עַל־הַמִּזְבֵּחַ כָּל־הַלַּיְלָה עַד־הַבֹּקֶר וְאֵשׁ הַמִּזְבֵּחַ תּוּקַד בּוֹ: 3וְלָבַשׁ הַכֹּהֵן מִדּוֹ בַד וּמִכְנְסֵי־בַד יִלְבַּשׁ עַל־בְּשָׂרוֹ וְהֵרִים אֶת־הַדֶּשֶׁן אֲשֶׁר תֹּאכַל הָאֵשׁ אֶת־הָעֹלָה עַל־הַמִּזְבֵּחַ וְשָׂמוֹ אֵצֶל הַמִּזְבֵּחַ: 4וּפָשַׁט אֶת־בְּגָדָיו וְלָבַשׁ בְּגָדִים אֲחֵרִים וְהוֹצִיא אֶת־הַדֶּשֶׁן אֶל־מִחוּץ לַמַּחֲנֶה אֶל־מָקוֹם טָהוֹר: 5וְהָאֵשׁ עַל־הַמִּזְבֵּחַ תּוּקַד־בּוֹ לֹא תִכְבֶּה וּבִעֵר עָלֶיהָ הַכֹּהֵן עֵצִים בַּבֹּקֶר בַּבֹּקֶר וְעָרַךְ עָלֶיהָ הָעֹלָה וְהִקְטִיר עָלֶיהָ חֶלְבֵי הַשְּׁלָמִים: 6אֵשׁ תָּמִיד תּוּקַד עַל־הַמִּזְבֵּחַ לֹא

6:2. **the one that goes up on its place of burning.** Unlike the sacrifices that are eaten, the "burnt offering"—literally "the one that goes up"—is completely burned.

6:4. **he shall take off his clothes and wear other clothes.** The priest wears the special priestly garments when he gathers the ashes in the Tabernacle courtyard, but he changes to other clothes when he carries the ashes out of the camp. Why? Because the sacred garments can be worn only in the sacred place. This is another case of zones of holiness.

6:6. **Fire always shall be kept burning on the altar. It shall not go out.** If it will always be kept burning, of course it will not go out. This is redundant, and this makes it emphatic: this ritual law has special significance because it brings together space and time. YHWH tells Moses to command Aaron and his sons to keep an eternal fire burning at the altar. This law thus provides for a visual expression of the idea that the ritual structure that is starting here is to prevail for all time to come. This fire that is not

7"And this is the instruction for the grain offering. The sons of Aaron shall bring it forward in front of YHWH to the front of the altar. 8And he shall lift some of it in his fist, some of the fine flour of the grain offering and some of its oil and all of the frankincense that is on the grain offering, and he shall burn a representative portion of it to smoke at the altar as a pleasant smell to YHWH. 9And Aaron and his sons shall eat the remainder of it. It shall be eaten as unleavened bread, in a holy place. They shall eat it in the courtyard of the Tent of Meeting. 10It shall not be baked with leaven. I have given it as their portion from my offerings by fire. It is the holy of holies, like the sin offering and like the guilt offering. 11Every male among the sons of Aaron shall eat it—an eternal law through your generations—from YHWH's offerings by fire. Anything that will touch them will become holy."

12And YHWH spoke to Moses, saying, 13"This is the offering of Aaron and his sons that they shall bring to YHWH in the day of his being anointed: a tenth of an ephah of fine flour as a continual grain offering, half of it in the morning and half of it in the evening. 14It shall be made on a griddle in oil. You shall bring it well mixed. You shall offer it as cakes of a grain offering of pieces, a pleasant smell to YHWH. 15And the anointed priest in his place from among his sons shall do it, an eternal law, for YHWH: it shall be burned to smoke entirely. 16And every grain offering of a priest shall be done entirely. It shall not be eaten."

17And YHWH spoke to Moses, saying, 18"Speak to Aaron and to his sons, saying: This is the instruction for the sin offering. In the place

תְּכֻבָּה: ס 7וְזֹאת תּוֹרַת הַמִּנְחָה הַקְרֵב אֹתָהּ בְּנֵי־
אַהֲרֹן לִפְנֵי יְהוָה אֶל־פְּנֵי הַמִּזְבֵּחַ: 8וְהֵרִים מִמֶּנּוּ
בְּקֻמְצוֹ מִסֹּלֶת הַמִּנְחָה וּמִשַּׁמְנָהּ וְאֵת כָּל־הַלְּבֹנָה
אֲשֶׁר עַל־הַמִּנְחָה וְהִקְטִיר הַמִּזְבֵּחַ רֵיחַ נִיחֹחַ
אַזְכָּרָתָהּ לַיהוָה: 9וְהַנּוֹתֶרֶת מִמֶּנָּה יֹאכְלוּ אַהֲרֹן
וּבָנָיו מַצּוֹת תֵּאָכֵל בְּמָקוֹם קָדֹשׁ בַּחֲצַר אֹהֶל
מוֹעֵד יֹאכְלוּהָ: 10לֹא תֵאָפֶה חָמֵץ חֶלְקָם נָתַתִּי
אֹתָהּ מֵאִשָּׁי קֹדֶשׁ קָדָשִׁים הִוא כַּחַטָּאת וְכָאָשָׁם:
11כָּל־זָכָר בִּבְנֵי אַהֲרֹן יֹאכְלֶנָּה חָק־עוֹלָם
לְדֹרֹתֵיכֶם מֵאִשֵּׁי יְהוָה כֹּל אֲשֶׁר־יִגַּע בָּהֶם יִקְדָּשׁ:
פ 12וַיְדַבֵּר יְהוָה אֶל־מֹשֶׁה לֵּאמֹר: 13זֶה קָרְבַּן
אַהֲרֹן וּבָנָיו אֲשֶׁר־יַקְרִיבוּ לַיהוָה בְּיוֹם הִמָּשַׁח אֹתוֹ
עֲשִׂירִת הָאֵפָה סֹלֶת מִנְחָה תָּמִיד מַחֲצִיתָהּ בַּבֹּקֶר
וּמַחֲצִיתָהּ בָּעָרֶב: 14עַל־מַחֲבַת בַּשֶּׁמֶן תֵּעָשֶׂה
מֻרְבֶּכֶת תְּבִיאֶנָּה תֻּפִינֵי מִנְחַת פִּתִּים תַּקְרִיב רֵיחַ־
נִיחֹחַ לַיהוָה: 15וְהַכֹּהֵן הַמָּשִׁיחַ תַּחְתָּיו מִבָּנָיו יַעֲשֶׂה
אֹתָהּ חָק־עוֹלָם לַיהוָה כָּלִיל תָּקְטָר: 16וְכָל־מִנְחַת
כֹּהֵן כָּלִיל תִּהְיֶה לֹא תֵאָכֵל: פ 17וַיְדַבֵּר יְהוָה
אֶל־מֹשֶׁה לֵּאמֹר: 18דַּבֵּר אֶל־אַהֲרֹן וְאֶל־בָּנָיו
לֵאמֹר זֹאת תּוֹרַת הַחַטָּאת בִּמְקוֹם אֲשֶׁר תִּשָּׁחֵט

---

to be quenched is also reminiscent of the account in Exodus of Moses' encounter with YHWH at a bush that burns without being consumed. Like the laws of distinction that are reminiscent of the creation in Genesis 1 (see the comment on Lev 10:10), this passage serves to connect the law and the Torah's story. In both cases, the priests are required by the law to perform an act that is imitative of something that God has done in the narrative—which further points to the bond between law and history in the Torah.

where the burnt offering will be slaughtered, the sin offering shall be slaughtered, in front of YHWH. It is the holy of holies. 19The priest who makes it a sin offering shall eat it. It shall be eaten in a holy place, in the courtyard of the Tent of Meeting. 20Anything that will touch the meat of it will become holy. And if some of its blood will spatter on clothing, you shall wash the thing on which it will spatter in a holy place. 21And a clay container in which it will be boiled shall be broken. And if it was boiled in a brass container then it shall be scoured and rinsed with water. 22Every male among the priests shall eat it. It is the holy of holies. 23And every sin offering some of whose blood will be brought to the Tent of Meeting for atoning in the Holy shall not be eaten. It shall be burned in fire.

7 1"And this is the instruction for the guilt of-fering. It is the holy of holies. 2They shall slaughter the guilt offering in the place where they slaughter the burnt offering. And he shall fling its blood on the altar all around. 3And he shall bring forward from it all its fat, the fat tail and the fat that covers the innards, 4and the two kidneys and the fat that is on them, that is on the loins; and the lobe on the liver: he shall take it away with the kidneys. 5And the priest shall burn them to smoke at the altar, an offering by fire to YHWH. It is a guilt offering. 6Every male among the priests shall eat it. It shall be eaten in a holy place. It is the holy of holies. 7As with the sin of-fering, so with the guilt offering: they have one instruction. The priest who will make atonement with it: it shall be his. 8And the priest who brings forward a man's burnt offering: the skin of the burnt offering that he brought forward is for the priest; it shall be his. 9And every grain offering that will be baked in an oven and every one made in a pan and on a griddle shall be for the priest who brings it; it shall be his. 10And every grain offering mixed with oil or dry shall be for all the sons of Aaron, each like his brother.

11"And this is the instruction of the peace-offering sacrifice that one shall bring forward to

הָעֹלָ֑ה תִּשָּׁחֵ֣ט הַֽחַטָּ֗את לִפְנֵ֣י יְהוָ֔ה קֹ֥דֶשׁ קָֽדָשִׁ֖ים ה֑וּא: 19הַכֹּהֵ֛ן הַֽמְחַטֵּ֥א אֹתָ֖הּ יֹאכְלֶ֑נָּה בְּמָק֤וֹם קָדֹשׁ֙ תֵּֽאָכֵ֔ל בַּֽחֲצַ֖ר אֹ֥הֶל מוֹעֵֽד: 20כֹּ֛ל אֲשֶׁר־יִגַּ֥ע בִּבְשָׂרָ֖הּ יִקְדָּ֑שׁ וַֽאֲשֶׁ֨ר יִזֶּ֤ה מִדָּמָהּ֙ עַל־הַבֶּ֔גֶד אֲשֶׁר֙ יִזֶּ֣ה עָלֶ֔יהָ תְּכַבֵּ֖ס בְּמָק֥וֹם קָדֹֽשׁ: 21וּכְלִי־חֶ֛רֶשׂ אֲשֶׁ֥ר תְּבֻשַּׁל־בּ֖וֹ יִשָּׁבֵ֑ר וְאִם־בִּכְלִ֤י נְחֹ֨שֶׁת֙ בֻּשָּׁ֔לָה וּמֹרַ֥ק וְשֻׁטַּ֖ף בַּמָּֽיִם: 22כָּל־זָכָ֥ר בַּכֹּֽהֲנִ֖ים יֹאכַ֣ל אֹתָ֑הּ קֹ֥דֶשׁ קָֽדָשִׁ֖ים הֽוּא: 23וְכָל־חַטָּ֡את אֲשֶׁר֩ יוּבָ֨א מִדָּמָ֜הּ אֶל־אֹ֧הֶל מוֹעֵ֛ד לְכַפֵּ֥ר בַּקֹּ֖דֶשׁ לֹ֣א תֵֽאָכֵ֑ל בָּאֵ֖שׁ תִּשָּׂרֵֽף: פ

7 1וְזֹ֥את תּוֹרַ֖ת הָֽאָשָׁ֑ם קֹ֥דֶשׁ קָֽדָשִׁ֖ים הֽוּא: 2בִּמְק֗וֹם אֲשֶׁ֤ר יִשְׁחֲטוּ֙ אֶת־הָ֣עֹלָ֔ה יִשְׁחֲט֖וּ אֶת־הָֽאָשָׁ֑ם וְאֶת־דָּמ֛וֹ יִזְרֹ֥ק עַל־הַמִּזְבֵּ֖חַ סָבִֽיב: 3וְאֵ֥ת כָּל־חֶלְבּ֖וֹ יַקְרִ֣יב מִמֶּ֑נּוּ אֵ֚ת הָֽאַלְיָ֔ה וְאֶת־הַחֵ֖לֶב הַֽמְכַסֶּ֥ה אֶת־הַקֶּֽרֶב: 4וְאֵת֙ שְׁתֵּ֣י הַכְּלָיֹ֔ת וְאֶת־הַחֵ֨לֶב֙ אֲשֶׁ֣ר עֲלֵיהֶ֔ן אֲשֶׁ֖ר עַל־הַכְּסָלִ֑ים וְאֶת־הַיֹּתֶ֨רֶת֙ עַל־הַכָּבֵ֔ד עַל־הַכְּלָיֹ֖ת יְסִירֶֽנָּה: 5וְהִקְטִ֨יר אֹתָ֤ם הַכֹּהֵן֙ הַמִּזְבֵּ֔חָה אִשֶּׁ֖ה לַֽיהוָ֑ה אָשָׁ֖ם הֽוּא: 6כָּל־זָכָ֥ר בַּכֹּֽהֲנִ֖ים יֹֽאכְלֶ֑נּוּ בְּמָק֤וֹם קָדוֹשׁ֙ יֵֽאָכֵ֔ל קֹ֥דֶשׁ קָֽדָשִׁ֖ים הֽוּא: 7כַּֽחַטָּאת֙ כָּֽאָשָׁ֔ם תּוֹרָ֥ה אַחַ֖ת לָהֶ֑ם הַכֹּהֵ֛ן אֲשֶׁ֥ר יְכַפֶּר־בּ֖וֹ ל֥וֹ יִֽהְיֶֽה: 8וְהַ֨כֹּהֵ֔ן הַמַּקְרִ֖יב אֶת־עֹ֣לַת אִ֑ישׁ ע֤וֹר הָֽעֹלָה֙ אֲשֶׁ֣ר הִקְרִ֔יב לַכֹּהֵ֖ן ל֥וֹ יִֽהְיֶֽה: 9וְכָל־מִנְחָ֗ה אֲשֶׁ֤ר תֵּֽאָפֶה֙ בַּתַּנּ֔וּר וְכָל־נַֽעֲשָׂ֥ה בַמַּרְחֶ֖שֶׁת וְעַל־מַֽחֲבַ֑ת לַכֹּהֵ֛ן הַמַּקְרִ֥יב אֹתָ֖הּ ל֥וֹ תִֽהְיֶֽה: 10וְכָל־מִנְחָ֥ה בְלוּלָֽה־בַשֶּׁ֖מֶן וַֽחֲרֵבָ֑ה לְכָל־בְּנֵ֧י אַֽהֲרֹ֛ן תִּֽהְיֶ֖ה אִ֥ישׁ כְּאָחִֽיו: פ

11וְזֹ֥את תּוֹרַ֖ת זֶ֣בַח הַשְּׁלָמִ֑ים אֲשֶׁ֥ר יַקְרִ֖יב

YHWH. 12If he will bring it forward out of thanks then he shall bring forward with the sacrifice of thanks unleavened cakes mixed with oil and unleavened wafers with oil poured on them and fine flour well mixed, cakes, mixed with oil. 13He shall make his offering with cakes of leavened bread, with his peace-offering sacrifice of thanks. 14And he shall bring forward from it one of each offering as a donation for YHWH. For the priest who flings the blood of the peace offerings: it shall be his. 15And the meat of his peace-offering sacrifice shall be eaten on the day of his offering. He shall not leave any of it until morning. 16And if his sacrificial offering is a vow or a contribution, it shall be eaten on the day that he brings forward his sacrifice, and on the next day what is left of it may be eaten. 17And what is left of the meat of the sacrifice on the third day shall be burned in fire. 18And if any of the meat of his peace-offering sacrifice *will* be eaten on the third day, it shall not be acceptable. The one who brings it forward: it shall not be counted for him. It shall be a repugnant thing. And the person who eats any of it shall bear his crime. 19And meat that will touch any impure thing shall not be eaten. It shall be burned in fire. And meat: everyone who is pure may eat meat, 20but the person who will eat meat from the peace-offering sacrifice that is YHWH's while his impurity is on him, that person will be cut off from his people. 21And a person who will touch any impure thing, human impurity or an impure animal or any impure detestable thing, and will eat some of the meat of the peace-offering sacrifice that is YHWH's: that person will be cut off from his people."

22And YHWH spoke to Moses, saying, 23"Speak to the children of Israel, saying: You shall not eat any fat of an ox or sheep or goat. 24And fat of a carcass and fat of a torn animal may be used for any work, but you shall not *eat* it. 25Because anyone who eats fat from an animal

לַיהוָה: 12אִם עַל־תּוֹדָה יַקְרִיבֶנּוּ וְהִקְרִיב ׀ עַל־זֶבַח הַתּוֹדָה חַלּוֹת מַצּוֹת בְּלוּלֹת בַּשֶּׁמֶן וּרְקִיקֵי מַצּוֹת מְשֻׁחִים בַּשָּׁמֶן וְסֹלֶת מֻרְבֶּכֶת חַלֹּת בְּלוּלֹת בַּשֶּׁמֶן: 13עַל־חַלֹּת לֶחֶם חָמֵץ יַקְרִיב קָרְבָּנוֹ עַל־זֶבַח תּוֹדַת שְׁלָמָיו: 14וְהִקְרִיב מִמֶּנּוּ אֶחָד מִכָּל־קָרְבָּן תְּרוּמָה לַיהוָה לַכֹּהֵן הַזֹּרֵק אֶת־דַּם הַשְּׁלָמִים לוֹ יִהְיֶה: 15וּבְשַׂר זֶבַח תּוֹדַת שְׁלָמָיו בְּיוֹם קָרְבָּנוֹ יֵאָכֵל לֹא־יַנִּיחַ מִמֶּנּוּ עַד־בֹּקֶר: 16וְאִם־נֶדֶר ׀ אוֹ נְדָבָה זֶבַח קָרְבָּנוֹ בְּיוֹם הַקְרִיבוֹ אֶת־זִבְחוֹ יֵאָכֵל וּמִמָּחֳרָת וְהַנּוֹתָר מִמֶּנּוּ יֵאָכֵל: 17וְהַנּוֹתָר מִבְּשַׂר הַזָּבַח בַּיּוֹם הַשְּׁלִישִׁי בָּאֵשׁ יִשָּׂרֵף: 18וְאִם הֵאָכֹל יֵאָכֵל מִבְּשַׂר־זֶבַח שְׁלָמָיו בַּיּוֹם הַשְּׁלִישִׁי לֹא יֵרָצֶה הַמַּקְרִיב אֹתוֹ לֹא יֵחָשֵׁב לוֹ פִּגּוּל יִהְיֶה וְהַנֶּפֶשׁ הָאֹכֶלֶת מִמֶּנּוּ עֲוֺנָהּ תִּשָּׂא: 19וְהַבָּשָׂר אֲשֶׁר־יִגַּע בְּכָל־טָמֵא לֹא יֵאָכֵל בָּאֵשׁ יִשָּׂרֵף וְהַבָּשָׂר כָּל־טָהוֹר יֹאכַל בָּשָׂר: 20וְהַנֶּפֶשׁ אֲשֶׁר־תֹּאכַל בָּשָׂר מִזֶּבַח הַשְּׁלָמִים אֲשֶׁר לַיהוָה וְטֻמְאָתוֹ עָלָיו וְנִכְרְתָה הַנֶּפֶשׁ הַהִוא מֵעַמֶּיהָ: 21וְנֶפֶשׁ כִּי־תִגַּע בְּכָל־טָמֵא בְּטֻמְאַת אָדָם אוֹ ׀ בִּבְהֵמָה טְמֵאָה אוֹ בְּכָל־שֶׁקֶץ טָמֵא וְאָכַל מִבְּשַׂר־זֶבַח הַשְּׁלָמִים אֲשֶׁר לַיהוָה וְנִכְרְתָה הַנֶּפֶשׁ הַהִוא מֵעַמֶּיהָ: פ

22וַיְדַבֵּר יְהוָה אֶל־מֹשֶׁה לֵּאמֹר: 23דַּבֵּר אֶל־בְּנֵי יִשְׂרָאֵל לֵאמֹר כָּל־חֵלֶב שׁוֹר וְכֶשֶׂב וָעֵז לֹא תֹאכֵלוּ: 24וְחֵלֶב נְבֵלָה וְחֵלֶב טְרֵפָה יֵעָשֶׂה לְכָל־מְלָאכָה וְאָכֹל לֹא תֹאכְלֻהוּ: 25כִּי כָּל־אֹכֵל חֵלֶב

7:24. **carcass**. The body of an animal that died on its own.

7:24. **torn animal**. The body of an animal that was killed by another animal.

from which one would bring forward an offering by fire to YHWH, the person who eats it will be cut off from his people. 26And you shall not eat any blood in all of your homes, a bird's or an animal's. 27Any person who will eat any blood, that person will be cut off from his people."

28And YHWH spoke to Moses, saying, 29"Speak to the children of Israel, saying: The one who brings forward his peace-offering sacrifice to YHWH shall bring his offering to YHWH from his peace-offering sacrifice: 30his hands shall bring YHWH's offerings by fire. He shall bring it, the fat with the breast: the breast so as to elevate it, an elevation offering in front of YHWH. 31And the priest shall burn the fat to smoke at the altar, and the breast shall be Aaron's and his sons'. 32And you shall give the right thigh as a donation to the priest from your peace-offering sacrifices. 33The one from the sons of Aaron who brings forward the blood of the peace offerings and the fat: the right thigh shall be his as a portion. 34Because I have taken the breast of the elevation offering and the thigh of the donation from the children of Israel, from their peace-offering sacrifices, and I have given them to Aaron the priest and to his sons as an eternal law from the children of Israel."

35This is the anointing of Aaron and the anointing of his sons from YHWH's offerings by fire in the day He brought them forward to function as priests for YHWH, 36which YHWH commanded to give to them in the day of His anointing them from among the children of Israel, an eternal law through their generations.

37This is the instruction of the burnt offering, of the grain offering, and of the sin offering and

מִן־הַבְּהֵמָה אֲשֶׁר יַקְרִיב מִמֶּנָּה אִשֶּׁה לַיהוָה וְנִכְרְתָה הַנֶּפֶשׁ הָאֹכֶלֶת מֵעַמֶּיהָ: 26וְכָל־דָּם לֹא תֹאכְלוּ בְּכֹל מוֹשְׁבֹתֵיכֶם לָעוֹף וְלַבְּהֵמָה: 27כָּל־נֶפֶשׁ אֲשֶׁר־תֹּאכַל כָּל־דָּם וְנִכְרְתָה הַנֶּפֶשׁ הַהִוא מֵעַמֶּיהָ: פ

28וַיְדַבֵּר יְהוָה אֶל־מֹשֶׁה לֵּאמֹר: 29דַּבֵּר אֶל־בְּנֵי יִשְׂרָאֵל לֵאמֹר הַמַּקְרִיב אֶת־זֶבַח שְׁלָמָיו לַיהוָה יָבִיא אֶת־קָרְבָּנוֹ לַיהוָה מִזֶּבַח שְׁלָמָיו: 30יָדָיו תְּבִיאֶינָה אֵת אִשֵּׁי יְהוָה אֶת־הַחֵלֶב עַל־הֶחָזֶה יְבִיאֶנּוּ אֵת הֶחָזֶה לְהָנִיף אֹתוֹ תְּנוּפָה לִפְנֵי יְהוָה: 31וְהִקְטִיר הַכֹּהֵן אֶת־הַחֵלֶב הַמִּזְבֵּחָה וְהָיָה הֶחָזֶה לְאַהֲרֹן וּלְבָנָיו: 32וְאֵת שׁוֹק הַיָּמִין תִּתְּנוּ תְרוּמָה לַכֹּהֵן מִזִּבְחֵי שַׁלְמֵיכֶם: 33הַמַּקְרִיב אֶת־דַּם הַשְּׁלָמִים וְאֶת־הַחֵלֶב מִבְּנֵי אַהֲרֹן לוֹ תִהְיֶה שׁוֹק הַיָּמִין לְמָנָה: 34כִּי אֶת־חֲזֵה הַתְּנוּפָה וְאֵת ׀ שׁוֹק הַתְּרוּמָה לָקַחְתִּי מֵאֵת בְּנֵי־יִשְׂרָאֵל מִזִּבְחֵי שַׁלְמֵיהֶם וָאֶתֵּן אֹתָם לְאַהֲרֹן הַכֹּהֵן וּלְבָנָיו לְחָק־עוֹלָם מֵאֵת בְּנֵי יִשְׂרָאֵל: 35זֹאת מִשְׁחַת אַהֲרֹן וּמִשְׁחַת בָּנָיו מֵאִשֵּׁי יְהוָה בְּיוֹם הִקְרִיב אֹתָם לְכַהֵן לַיהוָה: 36אֲשֶׁר צִוָּה יְהוָה לָתֵת לָהֶם בְּיוֹם מָשְׁחוֹ אֹתָם מֵאֵת בְּנֵי יִשְׂרָאֵל חֻקַּת עוֹלָם לְדֹרֹתָם: 37זֹאת הַתּוֹרָה לָעֹלָה לַמִּנְחָה וְלַחַטָּאת וְלָאָשָׁם

7:35. **the anointing**. Meaning: the share of the sacrificial offerings that they acquire by virtue of being anointed as Israel's priests.

7:37. **This is the instruction of the burnt offering** . . . This concludes seven chapters of laws about sacrifices. Because it has been nearly two millennia since the Temple sacrifices ended, what can substitute for sacrifice as something that can give people some of the things that sacrifices provided: a feeling of fulfillment, closeness to God, sacredness of life, a link to Israel's history? My friend Rabbi Lawson says: charity.

of the guilt offering and of the ordination and of the peace-offering sacrifice, 38which YHWH commanded Moses in Mount Sinai in the day that He commanded the children of Israel to make their offerings to YHWH in the wilderness of Sinai.

8 1And YHWH spoke to Moses, saying, 2"Take Aaron and his sons with him and the clothes and the anointing oil and the bull for the sin offering and the two rams and the basket of unleavened bread, 3and assemble all of the congregation to the entrance of the Tent of Meeting." 4And Moses did as YHWH commanded him.

וְלַמִּלּוּאִים וּלְזֶבַח הַשְּׁלָמִים: 38אֲשֶׁר צִוָּה יְהוָה אֶת־מֹשֶׁה בְּהַר סִינָי בְּיוֹם צַוֺּתוֹ אֶת־בְּנֵי יִשְׂרָאֵל לְהַקְרִיב אֶת־קָרְבְּנֵיהֶם לַיהוָה בְּמִדְבַּר סִינָי: פ

8 1וַיְדַבֵּר יְהוָה אֶל־מֹשֶׁה לֵּאמֹר: 2קַח אֶת־אַהֲרֹן וְאֶת־בָּנָיו אִתּוֹ וְאֵת הַבְּגָדִים וְאֵת שֶׁמֶן הַמִּשְׁחָה וְאֵת ׀ פַּר הַחַטָּאת וְאֵת שְׁנֵי הָאֵילִים וְאֵת סַל הַמַּצּוֹת: 3וְאֵת כָּל־הָעֵדָה הַקְהֵל אֶל־פֶּתַח אֹהֶל מוֹעֵד: 4וַיַּעַשׂ מֹשֶׁה כַּאֲשֶׁר צִוָּה יְהוָה אֹתוֹ

A parallel question: what can substitute for ancestor veneration, which was well known in the biblical world? Lawson says: charity in memory of persons who have died. Many would say that we have prayer as well as charity to compensate for the lack of sacrifice. And we have other acts of atonement, such as fasting. All of this may be true, but I note that people had prayer and charity and fasting in biblical times, too. So these are not replacements for sacrifice. They existed beside sacrifice all along. My question is: what do we have now that they did *not* have? Answer: *study*. What we have that no one in the biblical world (until Ezra) had is: the Torah. What we have that no one at all in biblical times had is the full *Tanak*. Our task is to study it, to shine our own new light on it, and to shine its light on us. This is our task individually, in groups, and as a community.

8:2. **Take Aaron and his sons**. Leviticus has only two narrative accounts. The first is the story of the consecration of Aaron and his sons to the priesthood of Israel (Leviticus 8–10). It is a lengthy and detailed account. Most of the ceremonies that it describes have already been presented in Exodus 29 as commands that YHWH gives to Moses, and now the fulfillment of these commands is narrated. The details of the rituals are impressive, picturing Moses placing the priestly garments one by one on Aaron, then picturing him anointing, first, the Tabernacle and its contents, then the altar, then Aaron. Next he has Aaron's sons clothed. Then the inaugural sacrifices of the priesthood are described, with details of Moses' slaughtering of a bull and two rams and his dabbing of their blood on the altar and on the right ears, thumbs, and big toes of Aaron and his sons. Moses directs Aaron and his sons to eat the sacrificial meat at the entrance of the Tent of Meeting, from which they are not permitted to depart for seven days. On the eighth day, another series of sacrifices is pictured, but it is no longer Moses who performs them, but rather Aaron and his sons. Then Aaron blesses the people and, for the first time, enters the Tent of Meeting alongside Moses. When they come out, they bless the people together, the glory of YHWH appears to the people, divine fire comes and consumes the offering, and the people shout and fall to the ground.

And the congregation was gathered to the entrance of the Tent of Meeting. 5And Moses said to the congregation, "This is the thing that YHWH has commanded to do."

6And Moses brought Aaron and his sons forward, and he washed them with water. 7And he put the coat on him and belted him with the sash and dressed him with the robe and put the ephod on him and belted him with the ephod's designed belt and put on the ephod for him with it. 8And he set the breastplate on him and put the Urim and Tummim into the breastplate. 9And he set the headdress on his head and set the gold plate, the crown of Holiness, on the headdress opposite the front of it, as YHWH had commanded Moses.

10And Moses took the anointing oil, and he anointed the Tabernacle and everything that was in it, so he consecrated them. 11And he sprinkled some of it on the altar seven times and anointed the altar and all of its equipment and the basin and its stand to consecrate them. 12And he poured some of the anointing oil on Aaron's head and anointed him to consecrate him. 13And Moses brought forward Aaron's sons and dressed them in coats and belted them with a sash and put on hats for them, as YHWH had commanded Moses.

14And he brought up the bull for the sin offering. And Aaron and his sons laid their hands on the head of the bull for the sin offering. 15And Moses slaughtered it and took the blood and put it on the altar's horns all around with his finger and purified the altar from sin, and he poured the blood at the base of the altar, and he consecrated it to make atonement on it. 16And he took all the fat that was on the innards and the lobe of the liver and the two kidneys and their fat, and Moses burned them to smoke at the altar. 17And he burned the bull and its skin and

וַתִּקָּהֵל֙ הָעֵדָ֔ה אֶל־פֶּ֖תַח אֹ֣הֶל מוֹעֵֽד׃ 5וַיֹּ֖אמֶר מֹשֶׁ֑ה אֶל־הָעֵדָ֑ה זֶ֣ה הַדָּבָ֔ר אֲשֶׁר־צִוָּ֥ה יְהוָ֖ה לַעֲשֽׂוֹת׃ 6וַיַּקְרֵ֣ב מֹשֶׁ֔ה אֶֽת־אַהֲרֹ֖ן וְאֶת־בָּנָ֑יו וַיִּרְחַ֥ץ אֹתָ֖ם בַּמָּֽיִם׃ 7וַיִּתֵּ֨ן עָלָ֜יו אֶת־הַכֻּתֹּ֗נֶת וַיַּחְגֹּ֤ר אֹתוֹ֙ בָּֽאַבְנֵ֔ט וַיַּלְבֵּ֤שׁ אֹתוֹ֙ אֶֽת־הַמְּעִ֔יל וַיִּתֵּ֥ן עָלָ֖יו אֶת־הָאֵפֹ֑ד וַיַּחְגֹּ֣ר אֹת֗וֹ בְּחֵ֙שֶׁב֙ הָֽאֵפֹ֔ד וַיֶּאְפֹּ֥ד ל֖וֹ בּֽוֹ׃ 8וַיָּ֥שֶׂם עָלָ֖יו אֶת־הַחֹ֑שֶׁן וַיִּתֵּן֙ אֶל־הַחֹ֔שֶׁן אֶת־הָאוּרִ֖ים וְאֶת־הַתֻּמִּֽים׃ 9וַיָּ֥שֶׂם אֶת־הַמִּצְנֶ֖פֶת עַל־רֹאשׁ֑וֹ וַיָּ֣שֶׂם עַֽל־הַמִּצְנֶ֗פֶת אֶל־מ֣וּל פָּנָ֔יו אֵ֣ת צִ֤יץ הַזָּהָב֙ נֵ֣זֶר הַקֹּ֔דֶשׁ כַּאֲשֶׁ֛ר צִוָּ֥ה יְהוָ֖ה אֶת־מֹשֶֽׁה׃ 10וַיִּקַּ֤ח מֹשֶׁה֙ אֶת־שֶׁ֣מֶן הַמִּשְׁחָ֔ה וַיִּמְשַׁ֥ח אֶת־הַמִּשְׁכָּ֖ן וְאֶת־כָּל־אֲשֶׁר־בּ֑וֹ וַיְקַדֵּ֖שׁ אֹתָֽם׃ 11וַיַּ֥ז מִמֶּ֛נּוּ עַל־הַמִּזְבֵּ֖חַ שֶׁ֣בַע פְּעָמִ֑ים וַיִּמְשַׁ֨ח אֶת־הַמִּזְבֵּ֜חַ וְאֶת־כָּל־כֵּלָ֗יו וְאֶת־הַכִּיֹּ֛ר וְאֶת־כַּנּ֖וֹ לְקַדְּשָֽׁם׃ 12וַיִּצֹ֛ק מִשֶּׁ֥מֶן הַמִּשְׁחָ֖ה עַ֣ל רֹ֣אשׁ אַהֲרֹ֑ן וַיִּמְשַׁ֥ח אֹת֖וֹ לְקַדְּשֽׁוֹ׃ 13וַיַּקְרֵ֨ב מֹשֶׁ֜ה אֶת־בְּנֵ֣י אַהֲרֹ֗ן וַיַּלְבִּשֵׁ֤ם כֻּתֳּנֹת֙ וַיַּחְגֹּ֤ר אֹתָם֙ אַבְנֵ֔ט וַיַּחֲבֹ֤שׁ לָהֶם֙ מִגְבָּע֔וֹת כַּאֲשֶׁ֛ר צִוָּ֥ה יְהוָ֖ה אֶת־מֹשֶֽׁה׃ 14וַיַּגֵּ֕שׁ אֵ֖ת פַּ֣ר הַֽחַטָּ֑את וַיִּסְמֹ֨ךְ אַהֲרֹ֤ן וּבָנָיו֙ אֶת־יְדֵיהֶ֔ם עַל־רֹ֖אשׁ פַּ֥ר הַֽחַטָּֽאת׃ 15וַיִּשְׁחָ֗ט וַיִּקַּ֤ח מֹשֶׁה֙ אֶת־הַדָּ֔ם וַ֠יִּתֵּן עַל־קַרְנ֨וֹת הַמִּזְבֵּ֤חַ סָבִיב֙ בְּאֶצְבָּע֔וֹ וַֽיְחַטֵּ֖א אֶת־הַמִּזְבֵּ֑חַ וְאֶת־הַדָּ֗ם יָצַק֙ אֶל־יְס֣וֹד הַמִּזְבֵּ֔חַ וַֽיְקַדְּשֵׁ֖הוּ לְכַפֵּ֥ר עָלָֽיו׃ 16וַיִּקַּ֗ח אֶת־כָּל־הַחֵלֶב֮ אֲשֶׁ֣ר עַל־הַקֶּרֶב֒ וְאֵת֙ יֹתֶ֣רֶת הַכָּבֵ֔ד וְאֶת־שְׁתֵּ֥י הַכְּלָיֹ֖ת וְאֶֽת־חֶלְבְּהֶ֑ן וַיַּקְטֵ֥ר מֹשֶׁ֖ה הַמִּזְבֵּֽחָה׃ 17וְאֶת־הַפָּ֤ר וְאֶת־עֹרוֹ֙ וְאֶת־בְּשָׂר֣וֹ וְאֶת־פִּרְשׁ֔וֹ שָׂרַ֣ף

8:15. **Moses slaughtered it.** Moses personally performs all the sacrifices in this ceremony of ordaining Aaron and his sons as priests. After this day, all sacrifices will be performed by Aaron and his sons, never again by Moses.

its meat and its dung in fire outside the camp, as YHWH had commanded Moses.

18And he brought forward the ram for the burnt offering. And Aaron and his sons laid their hands on the ram's head. 19And he slaughtered it, and Moses flung the blood on the altar all around. 20And he cut the ram into its parts, and Moses burned the head and the parts and the suet to smoke. 21And he washed the innards and the legs with water. And Moses burned all of the ram to smoke at the altar. It was a burnt offering as a pleasant smell. It was an offering by fire to YHWH, as YHWH had commanded Moses.

22And he brought forward the second ram, the ram of ordination. And Aaron and his sons laid their hands on the ram's head. 23And he slaughtered it, and Moses took some of its blood and put it on Aaron's right earlobe and on the thumb of his right hand and on the big toe of his right foot. 24And he brought Aaron's sons forward, and Moses put some of the blood on their right earlobe and on the thumb of their right hand and on the big toe of their right foot. And Moses flung the blood on the altar all around. 25And he took the fat and the fat tail and all the fat that was on the innards and the lobe of the liver and the two kidneys and their fat and the right thigh. 26And from the basket of unleavened bread that was in front of YHWH he took one cake of unleavened bread and one cake of bread with oil and one wafer, and he set them on the fats and on the right thigh. 27And he put it all on Aaron's hands and on his sons' hands and elevated them, an elevation offering in front of YHWH. 28And Moses took them from on their hands and burned them to smoke at the altar with the burnt offering. They were an ordination offering as a pleasant smell. It was an offering by fire to YHWH. 29And Moses took the breast and elevated it, an elevation offering in front of YHWH from the ram of ordination. It was Moses' for a portion, as YHWH had commanded Moses.

30And Moses took some of the anointing oil and some of the blood that was on the altar and

בָאֵשׁ מִחוּץ לַמַּחֲנֶה כַּאֲשֶׁר צִוָּה יְהוָה אֶת־מֹשֶׁה: 18וַיַּקְרֵב אֵת אֵיל הָעֹלָה וַיִּסְמְכוּ אַהֲרֹן וּבָנָיו אֶת־יְדֵיהֶם עַל־רֹאשׁ הָאָיִל: 19וַיִּשְׁחָט וַיִּזְרֹק מֹשֶׁה אֶת־הַדָּם עַל־הַמִּזְבֵּחַ סָבִיב: 20וְאֶת־הָאַיִל נִתַּח לִנְתָחָיו וַיַּקְטֵר מֹשֶׁה אֶת־הָרֹאשׁ וְאֶת־הַנְּתָחִים וְאֶת־הַפָּדֶר: 21וְאֶת־הַקֶּרֶב וְאֶת־הַכְּרָעַיִם רָחַץ בַּמָּיִם וַיַּקְטֵר מֹשֶׁה אֶת־כָּל־הָאַיִל הַמִּזְבֵּחָה עֹלָה הוּא לְרֵיחַ־נִיחֹחַ אִשֶּׁה הוּא לַיהוָה כַּאֲשֶׁר צִוָּה יְהוָה אֶת־מֹשֶׁה: 22וַיַּקְרֵב אֶת־הָאַיִל הַשֵּׁנִי אֵיל הַמִּלֻּאִים וַיִּסְמְכוּ אַהֲרֹן וּבָנָיו אֶת־יְדֵיהֶם עַל־רֹאשׁ הָאָיִל: 23וַיִּשְׁחָט ׀ וַיִּקַּח מֹשֶׁה מִדָּמוֹ וַיִּתֵּן עַל־תְּנוּךְ אֹזֶן אַהֲרֹן הַיְמָנִית וְעַל־בֹּהֶן יָדוֹ הַיְמָנִית וְעַל־בֹּהֶן רַגְלוֹ הַיְמָנִית: 24וַיַּקְרֵב אֶת־בְּנֵי אַהֲרֹן וַיִּתֵּן מֹשֶׁה מִן־הַדָּם עַל־תְּנוּךְ אָזְנָם הַיְמָנִית וְעַל־בֹּהֶן יָדָם הַיְמָנִית וְעַל־בֹּהֶן רַגְלָם הַיְמָנִית וַיִּזְרֹק מֹשֶׁה אֶת־הַדָּם עַל־הַמִּזְבֵּחַ סָבִיב: 25וַיִּקַּח אֶת־הַחֵלֶב וְאֶת־הָאַלְיָה וְאֶת־כָּל־הַחֵלֶב אֲשֶׁר עַל־הַקֶּרֶב וְאֵת יֹתֶרֶת הַכָּבֵד וְאֶת־שְׁתֵּי הַכְּלָיֹת וְאֶת־חֶלְבְּהֶן וְאֵת שׁוֹק הַיָּמִין: 26וּמִסַּל הַמַּצּוֹת אֲשֶׁר ׀ לִפְנֵי יְהוָה לָקַח חַלַּת מַצָּה אַחַת וְחַלַּת לֶחֶם שֶׁמֶן אַחַת וְרָקִיק אֶחָד וַיָּשֶׂם עַל־הַחֲלָבִים וְעַל שׁוֹק הַיָּמִין: 27וַיִּתֵּן אֶת־הַכֹּל עַל כַּפֵּי אַהֲרֹן וְעַל כַּפֵּי בָנָיו וַיָּנֶף אֹתָם תְּנוּפָה לִפְנֵי יְהוָה: 28וַיִּקַּח מֹשֶׁה אֹתָם מֵעַל כַּפֵּיהֶם וַיַּקְטֵר הַמִּזְבֵּחָה עַל־הָעֹלָה מִלֻּאִים הֵם לְרֵיחַ נִיחֹחַ אִשֶּׁה הוּא לַיהוָה: 29וַיִּקַּח מֹשֶׁה אֶת־הֶחָזֶה וַיְנִיפֵהוּ תְנוּפָה לִפְנֵי יְהוָה מֵאֵיל הַמִּלֻּאִים לְמֹשֶׁה הָיָה לְמָנָה כַּאֲשֶׁר צִוָּה יְהוָה אֶת־מֹשֶׁה: 30וַיִּקַּח מֹשֶׁה מִשֶּׁמֶן הַמִּשְׁחָה וּמִן־הַדָּם אֲשֶׁר עַל־

sprinkled them on Aaron, on his clothes, and on his sons and on his sons' clothes with him, and he consecrated Aaron, his clothes, and his sons and his sons' clothes with him.

31And Moses said to Aaron and to his sons, "Cook the meat at the entrance of the Tent of Meeting and eat it and the bread that's in the basket of ordination there, as I commanded, saying, 'Aaron and his sons shall eat it.' 32And you shall burn what is left of the meat and of the bread in fire. 33And you shall not go out from the Tent of Meeting for seven days, until the day of completion of the days of your ordination, because He will fill your hand for seven days. 34What has been done on this day YHWH commanded to do, to make atonement over you. 35And you shall sit at the entrance of the Tent of Meeting day and night, seven days, and you shall keep

הַמִּזְבֵּחַ וַיַּז עַל־אַהֲרֹן עַל־בְּגָדָיו וְעַל־
בָּנָיו וְעַל־בִּגְדֵי בָנָיו אִתּוֹ וַיְקַדֵּשׁ אֶת־אַהֲרֹן אֶת־בְּגָדָיו וְאֶת־
בָּנָיו וְאֶת־בִּגְדֵי בָנָיו אִתּוֹ: 31וַיֹּאמֶר מֹשֶׁה אֶל־אַהֲרֹן
וְאֶל־בָּנָיו בַּשְּׁלוּ אֶת־הַבָּשָׂר פֶּתַח אֹהֶל מוֹעֵד וְשָׁם
תֹּאכְלוּ אֹתוֹ וְאֶת־הַלֶּחֶם אֲשֶׁר בְּסַל הַמִּלֻּאִים
כַּאֲשֶׁר צִוֵּיתִי לֵאמֹר אַהֲרֹן וּבָנָיו יֹאכְלֻהוּ:
32וְהַנּוֹתָר בַּבָּשָׂר וּבַלָּחֶם בָּאֵשׁ תִּשְׂרֹפוּ: 33וּמִפֶּתַח
אֹהֶל מוֹעֵד לֹא תֵצְאוּ שִׁבְעַת יָמִים עַד יוֹם מְלֹאת
יְמֵי מִלֻּאֵיכֶם כִּי שִׁבְעַת יָמִים יְמַלֵּא אֶת־יֶדְכֶם:
34כַּאֲשֶׁר עָשָׂה בַּיּוֹם הַזֶּה צִוָּה יְהוָה לַעֲשֹׂת לְכַפֵּר
עֲלֵיכֶם: 35וּפֶתַח אֹהֶל מוֹעֵד תֵּשְׁבוּ יוֹמָם וָלַיְלָה
שִׁבְעַת יָמִים וּשְׁמַרְתֶּם אֶת־מִשְׁמֶרֶת יְהוָה וְלֹא

8:31. **as I commanded**. But it was God, not Moses, who commanded this (Exod 29:31–32). Therefore, this should be read as the Hebrew passive (*Pual*) as in Lev 8:35 and 10:13 rather than as the active (*Piel*)—the two look the same in the Hebrew text without the vowel points—and it should be understood to mean "as I was commanded."

Another explanation: Twice Moses says "as *I* commanded" when we would have expected him to say "as *God* commanded"—here and in Lev 10:18 (cf. 10:13)—and in both cases he is speaking to his brother, Aaron. This therefore may be related back to two occasions on which God states that there is to be a special relationship between Moses and Aaron: in Exod 4:16, "he will become a mouth for you, and you will become a god for him!" and in Exod 7:1, "I've made you a god to Pharaoh, and Aaron, your brother, will be your prophet." The relationship between Moses and Aaron is like no other in the Bible. And this, too, is part of the preparation for the climactic moment of their lives when Moses strikes the rock at Meribah (Numbers 20). Although Moses says the words and performs the deed while Aaron does not speak a word, Aaron shares the same fate as Moses: death before entering the promised land. Aaron's life is inseparably bound to the path of his younger brother, whose words and acts have authority and consequences for him.

8:33. **fill your hand**. See the comment on Exod 29:29.

8:35. **seven days**. This parashah (צו, Command) ends with Aaron and his sons sitting for seven days at the Tabernacle's entrance, preparing for the climax that is coming in the next week, building anticipation for the inauguration of the priesthood. And so, if we follow the weekly cycle of readings of the Torah, we emulate what is happening in the text: we wait for seven days! To be sure that we get the connection, the next parashah is titled *šĕmînî*, Eighth. If we pay proper attention to this, we come to

YHWH's charge, and you will not die, because that is what I was commanded."

36And Aaron and his sons did all the things that YHWH commanded by Moses' hand.

EIGHTH

9 1And it was, on the eighth day, Moses called to Aaron and to his sons and to Israel's elders. 2And he said to Aaron, "Take a calf of the cattle for a sin offering and a ram for a burnt offering—unblemished—and bring them forward in front of YHWH. 3And you shall speak to the children of Israel, saying, 'Take a goat for a sin offering and a calf and a lamb, unblemished one-year-olds, for a burnt offering 4and an ox and a ram for peace offerings to sacrifice in front of YHWH, and a grain offering mixed with oil, because today YHWH is appearing to you.'"

5And they took what Moses had commanded to the front of the Tent of Meeting, and they brought forward all of the congregation, and they stood in front of YHWH.

6And Moses said, "This is the thing that YHWH has commanded that you shall do, and YHWH's glory will appear to you." 7And Moses said to Aaron, "Come forward to the altar and make your sin offering and your burnt offering and make atonement for yourself and for the people, and make the people's offering and make atonement for them as YHWH commanded."

8And Aaron came forward to the altar and slaughtered the calf for the sin offering that he had. 9And Aaron's sons brought forward the blood to him, and he dipped his finger in the blood and put it on the altar's horns, and he poured the blood to the base of the altar. 10And he burned the fat and the kidneys and the lobe from the liver from the sin offering to smoke at

תְּמֻתוּ כִּי־כֵן צֻוֵּיתִי: 36וַיַּעַשׂ אַהֲרֹן וּבָנָיו אֵת כָּל־הַדְּבָרִים אֲשֶׁר־צִוָּה יְהוָה בְּיַד־מֹשֶׁה: ס

שְׁמִינִי

9 1וַיְהִי בַּיּוֹם הַשְּׁמִינִי קָרָא מֹשֶׁה לְאַהֲרֹן וּלְבָנָיו וּלְזִקְנֵי יִשְׂרָאֵל: 2וַיֹּאמֶר אֶל־אַהֲרֹן קַח־לְךָ עֵגֶל בֶּן־בָּקָר לְחַטָּאת וְאַיִל לְעֹלָה תְּמִימִם וְהַקְרֵב לִפְנֵי יְהוָה: 3וְאֶל־בְּנֵי יִשְׂרָאֵל תְּדַבֵּר לֵאמֹר קְחוּ שְׂעִיר־עִזִּים לְחַטָּאת וְעֵגֶל וָכֶבֶשׂ בְּנֵי־שָׁנָה תְּמִימִם לְעֹלָה: 4וְשׁוֹר וָאַיִל לִשְׁלָמִים לִזְבֹּחַ לִפְנֵי יְהוָה וּמִנְחָה בְלוּלָה בַשָּׁמֶן כִּי הַיּוֹם יְהוָה נִרְאָה אֲלֵיכֶם: 5וַיִּקְחוּ אֵת אֲשֶׁר צִוָּה מֹשֶׁה אֶל־פְּנֵי אֹהֶל מוֹעֵד וַיִּקְרְבוּ כָּל־הָעֵדָה וַיַּעַמְדוּ לִפְנֵי יְהוָה: 6וַיֹּאמֶר מֹשֶׁה זֶה הַדָּבָר אֲשֶׁר־צִוָּה יְהוָה תַּעֲשׂוּ וְיֵרָא אֲלֵיכֶם כְּבוֹד יְהוָה: 7וַיֹּאמֶר מֹשֶׁה אֶל־אַהֲרֹן קְרַב אֶל־הַמִּזְבֵּחַ וַעֲשֵׂה אֶת־חַטָּאתְךָ וְאֶת־עֹלָתֶךָ וְכַפֵּר בַּעַדְךָ וּבְעַד הָעָם וַעֲשֵׂה אֶת־קָרְבַּן הָעָם וְכַפֵּר בַּעֲדָם כַּאֲשֶׁר צִוָּה יְהוָה: 8וַיִּקְרַב אַהֲרֹן אֶל־הַמִּזְבֵּחַ וַיִּשְׁחַט אֶת־עֵגֶל הַחַטָּאת אֲשֶׁר־לוֹ: 9וַיַּקְרִבוּ בְּנֵי אַהֲרֹן אֶת־הַדָּם אֵלָיו וַיִּטְבֹּל אֶצְבָּעוֹ בַּדָּם וַיִּתֵּן עַל־קַרְנוֹת הַמִּזְבֵּחַ וְאֶת־הַדָּם יָצַק אֶל־יְסוֹד הַמִּזְבֵּחַ: 10וְאֶת־הַחֵלֶב וְאֶת־הַכְּלָיֹת וְאֶת־הַיֹּתֶרֶת מִן־הַכָּבֵד מִן־הַחַטָּאת הִקְטִיר הַמִּזְבֵּחָה

---

the story of the inauguration with anticipation, so we appreciate the story, and we appreciate the power of what goes wrong in the story: the catastrophe of Nadab and Abihu.

the altar, as YHWH had commanded Moses. [11]And he burned the meat and the skin in fire outside the camp. [12]And he slaughtered the burnt offering. And Aaron's sons presented the blood to him, and he flung it on the altar all around. [13]And they presented the burnt offering to him in its parts and the head, and he burned it to smoke on the altar. [14]And he washed the innards and the legs and burned them to smoke with the burnt offering at the altar.

[15]And he made the people's offering: and he took the goat for the sin offering that was the people's, and he slaughtered it and made a sin offering with it like the first one. [16]And he brought forward the burnt offering and made it according to the required manner. [17]And he brought forward the grain offering and filled his hand from it and burned it to smoke on the altar—apart from the morning's burnt offering. [18]And he slaughtered the ox and the ram, the peace-offering sacrifice that was the people's. And Aaron's sons presented the blood to him, and he flung it on the altar all around, [19]and the fats from the ox and from the ram, the fat tail and the covering and the kidneys and the lobe of the liver. [20]And they set the fats on the breasts, and he burned the fats to smoke at the altar. [21]And Aaron elevated the breasts and the right thigh, an elevation offering in front of YHWH, as Moses had commanded. [22]And Aaron raised his hands to the people and blessed them. And he went down from making the sin offering and the burnt offering and the peace offering.

[23]And Moses and Aaron came to the Tent of Meeting, and they went out and blessed the

כַּאֲשֶׁר צִוָּה יְהוָה אֶת־מֹשֶׁה: [11]וְאֶת־הַבָּשָׂר וְאֶת־הָעוֹר שָׂרַף בָּאֵשׁ מִחוּץ לַמַּחֲנֶה: [12]וַיִּשְׁחַט אֶת־הָעֹלָה וַיַּמְצִאוּ בְּנֵי אַהֲרֹן אֵלָיו אֶת־הַדָּם וַיִּזְרְקֵהוּ עַל־הַמִּזְבֵּחַ סָבִיב: [13]וְאֶת־הָעֹלָה הִמְצִיאוּ אֵלָיו לִנְתָחֶיהָ וְאֶת־הָרֹאשׁ וַיַּקְטֵר עַל־הַמִּזְבֵּחַ: [14]וַיִּרְחַץ אֶת־הַקֶּרֶב וְאֶת־הַכְּרָעַיִם וַיַּקְטֵר עַל־הָעֹלָה הַמִּזְבֵּחָה: [15]וַיַּקְרֵב אֵת קָרְבַּן הָעָם וַיִּקַּח אֶת־שְׂעִיר הַחַטָּאת אֲשֶׁר לָעָם וַיִּשְׁחָטֵהוּ וַיְחַטְּאֵהוּ כָּרִאשׁוֹן: [16]וַיַּקְרֵב אֶת־הָעֹלָה וַיַּעֲשֶׂהָ כַּמִּשְׁפָּט: [17]וַיַּקְרֵב אֶת־הַמִּנְחָה וַיְמַלֵּא כַפּוֹ מִמֶּנָּה וַיַּקְטֵר עַל־הַמִּזְבֵּחַ מִלְּבַד עֹלַת הַבֹּקֶר: [18]וַיִּשְׁחַט אֶת־הַשּׁוֹר וְאֶת־הָאַיִל זֶבַח הַשְּׁלָמִים אֲשֶׁר לָעָם וַיַּמְצִאוּ בְּנֵי אַהֲרֹן אֶת־הַדָּם אֵלָיו וַיִּזְרְקֵהוּ עַל־הַמִּזְבֵּחַ סָבִיב: [19]וְאֶת־הַחֲלָבִים מִן־הַשּׁוֹר וּמִן־הָאַיִל הָאַלְיָה וְהַמְכַסֶּה וְהַכְּלָיֹת וְיֹתֶרֶת הַכָּבֵד: [20]וַיָּשִׂימוּ אֶת־הַחֲלָבִים עַל־הֶחָזוֹת וַיַּקְטֵר הַחֲלָבִים הַמִּזְבֵּחָה: [21]וְאֵת הֶחָזוֹת וְאֵת שׁוֹק הַיָּמִין הֵנִיף אַהֲרֹן תְּנוּפָה לִפְנֵי יְהוָה כַּאֲשֶׁר צִוָּה מֹשֶׁה: [22]וַיִּשָּׂא אַהֲרֹן אֶת־יָדָו אֶל־הָעָם וַיְבָרְכֵם וַיֵּרֶד מֵעֲשֹׂת הַחַטָּאת וְהָעֹלָה וְהַשְּׁלָמִים: [23]וַיָּבֹא מֹשֶׁה וְאַהֲרֹן אֶל־אֹהֶל מוֹעֵד וַיֵּצְאוּ וַיְבָרְכוּ אֶת־הָעָם וַיֵּרָא

9:22 קׄ יָדָיו

9:15. **like the first one.** That is, he prepares the sin offering for the people in the same place as the burnt offering that immediately preceded it (9:12–14). This is in fulfillment of the commandment in 6:18.

9:21. **as Moses had commanded.** It is unusual (though certainly not unknown) for Moses to give commands. The Septuagint and Samaritan texts read "as YHWH had commanded Moses," which is likely (though not certain) to be the original reading. See the comment on Lev 8:31.

people. And YHWH's glory appeared to all the people. 24And fire came out from in front of YHWH and consumed the burnt offering and the fats on the altar! And all the people saw, and they shouted, and they fell on their faces!

10 1And Aaron's sons, Nadab and Abihu, each took his fire-holder, and they put fire in them and set incense on it. And they brought forward unfitting fire, which He had not commanded them, in front of YHWH. 2And fire

כְּבוֹד־יְהוָה אֶל־כָּל־הָעָם: 24וַתֵּצֵא אֵשׁ מִלִּפְנֵי יְהוָה וַתֹּאכַל עַל־הַמִּזְבֵּחַ אֶת־הָעֹלָה וְאֶת־הַחֲלָבִים וַיַּרְא כָּל־הָעָם וַיָּרֹנּוּ וַיִּפְּלוּ עַל־פְּנֵיהֶם:

10 1וַיִּקְחוּ בְנֵי־אַהֲרֹן נָדָב וַאֲבִיהוּא אִישׁ מַחְתָּתוֹ וַיִּתְּנוּ בָהֵן אֵשׁ וַיָּשִׂימוּ עָלֶיהָ קְטֹרֶת וַיַּקְרִבוּ לִפְנֵי יְהוָה אֵשׁ זָרָה אֲשֶׁר לֹא צִוָּה אֹתָם:

9:24. fire came out from in front of YHWH and consumed. The sacrifice that inaugurates Israel's priesthood is ignited by a miraculous fire that comes from God, not humans. This is the first of several stories in which miracles occur to confirm that Aaron and his descendants are the only true priests.

10:1. Nadab and Abihu. These are parallel to the names Nadab and Abiyah, the sons of Jeroboam I, the first king of the northern kingdom of Israel (1 Kings 14:1; 15:25). King Jeroboam erects golden calves at sanctuaries at Dan and Beth-El. The similarity of the names of the sons of the two men who make golden calves is striking (Exodus 32; 1 Kings 12:28).

10:1. unfitting fire, which He had not commanded them. It is not clear just what Nadab's and Abihu's offense is. The text says that they bring fire that is *zārāh*, that YHWH had not commanded them. Some have taken this to mean "foreign" fire and therefore have related Nadab's and Abihu's act to foreign worship, i.e., to another god. The term *zārāh*, however, never has the meaning of "foreign" in any other occurrence in the Torah's law or narrative. It rather denotes a person or thing that is outside a particular group. In any context dealing with priests, for example, it refers to a layperson. In the only other context referring to incense burning (Exod 30:9), "unfitting" incense is listed along with sacrifices and libations as things that should not be brought on the special incense altar located inside the Tent of Meeting. That is, there is no suggestion that it means anything foreign, but simply something that is outside the realm of what is permitted, or, as our text says explicitly, "that YHWH had not commanded." Nadab and Abihu might thus be thought of as having had positive intentions—to bring an incense offering to God—but as unfortunately having acted incorrectly. Or, alternatively, we might imagine a variety of less commendable motives in them. The point is that the text does not deal with their motives because that is not the issue. In the realm of the ritual, they have failed to observe a boundary, and so their fate is settled. This is one of several biblical stories that indicate that on the highest levels of the ritual realm, intention does not matter. In the ethical realm it does. The killing of a man, for example, may be found to be murder or to be manslaughter, depending in part on the intention of the person who killed him. In the ritual category, however, there are cases in which innocent motives still do not make one innocent. Only a priest, for example, can enter the Tent of Meeting. If a layperson enters, that person must die, and the law does not provide for taking the motives for the trespass into account. And in the famous case of the ark in 2 Samuel 6, Uzzah touches the ark to steady it because it is

came out from in front of YHWH and consumed them! And they died in front of YHWH.

³And Moses said to Aaron, "That is what YHWH spoke, saying, 'I shall be made holy through those who are close to me, and I shall be honored in front of all the people.'"

וַתֵּצֵא אֵשׁ מִלִּפְנֵי יְהוָה וַתֹּאכַל אוֹתָם וַיָּמֻתוּ לִפְנֵי יְהוָה: ³וַיֹּאמֶר מֹשֶׁה אֶל־אַהֲרֹן הוּא אֲשֶׁר־דִּבֶּר יְהוָה ׀ לֵאמֹר בִּקְרֹבַי אֶקָּדֵשׁ וְעַל־פְּנֵי כָל־הָעָם אֶכָּבֵד

---

rocking on the backs of oxen. His motive is good. But he dies because, like Nadab and Abihu, he has violated the boundary of the holy.

10:2. fire came out from in front of YHWH and consumed. Aaron's inaugural day of priestly sacrifice is thus to have been a glorious day of pomp and ceremony, miraculously sanctioned by the divine glory and fire; but then this extraordinary thing happens. The two eldest of his four sons bring this offering that YHWH had not told them to make, and the divine fire comes and consumes them. After seven chapters of laws of sacrifices and two chapters describing the ordination rituals, the sudden account of this horrible event in the middle of the ceremonies comes as a shock. It is even more powerful because the exact same words that describe the miraculous consumption of the ordination sacrifice two verses earlier (9:24) now describe the miraculous killing of Nadab and Abihu. It is possible that this account of the deaths of Nadab and Abihu should be regarded as a separate story from the account of the consecration. It is frequently understood that way, especially since it occurs here at the beginning of a new chapter. Still, the division of the biblical books into chapters was made centuries after composition of the books, and there is no break in the flow of the story from the consecration of the priesthood to the death of Aaron's sons in the manuscripts of Leviticus. Moreover, the last verses of the story of the consecration picture the events as happening in the presence of the entire people, who are assembled (9:22–24); and Moses explicitly refers to the presence of the people in his first words to Aaron after his sons' deaths. He says, "That is what YHWH spoke, saying, 'I shall be made holy through those who are close to me, and I shall be honored in front of all the people'" (10:3). The story of Nadab and Abihu is therefore most probably to be understood as a horror that occurs during the inauguration of the priesthood.

10:3. That is what YHWH spoke. The meaning of Moses' remark to Aaron is another provocative case of ambiguity in the Torah's narrative. Is Moses to be viewed as saying these words in horrified recognition of a truth? or as a stinging reprimand to Aaron concerning his sons' behavior? or as an explanation? The text here specifically notes that Aaron makes no response ("And Aaron was silent"), which is understandable but not helpful and is itself open to a gamut of interpretations.

10:3. I shall be made holy through those who are close to me. The text goes on conveying that there is a burden on "those who are close to me," as it describes the removal of Aaron's sons' bodies by their cousins, and as Moses instructs Aaron and his remaining sons, Eleazar and Ithamar, that they must not mourn for Nadab and Abihu. There follows an account that further conveys the pain within the priestly family. Moses finds that Aaron and his remaining sons have not eaten the sacrifices of the day as commanded, and he reprimands Eleazar and Ithamar angrily. Aaron replies that,

And Aaron was silent.

4And Moses called to Mishael and to Elzaphan, sons of Uzziel, Aaron's uncle, and said to them, "Come forward. Carry your brothers from in front of the Holy to the outside of the camp."

5And they came forward and carried them by their coats to the outside of the camp as Moses had spoken.

6And Moses said to Aaron and to Eleazar and to Ithamar, his sons, "Don't let loose the hair of your heads and don't tear your clothes, so you won't die and He'll be angry at all the congregation. And your brothers, all the house of Israel, will weep for the burning that YHWH has made. 7And you shall not go out from the entrance of the Tent of Meeting, or else you'll die, because YHWH's anointing oil is on you."

And they did according to Moses' word.

8And YHWH spoke to Aaron, saying, 9"You shall not drink wine and beer, you and your sons

וַיִּדֹּם אַהֲרֹן: 4וַיִּקְרָא מֹשֶׁה אֶל־מִישָׁאֵל וְאֶל אֶלְצָפָן בְּנֵי עֻזִּיאֵל דֹּד אַהֲרֹן וַיֹּאמֶר אֲלֵהֶם קִרְבוּ שְׂאוּ אֶת־אֲחֵיכֶם מֵאֵת פְּנֵי־הַקֹּדֶשׁ אֶל־מִחוּץ לַמַּחֲנֶה: 5וַיִּקְרְבוּ וַיִּשָּׂאֻם בְּכֻתֳּנֹתָם אֶל־מִחוּץ לַמַּחֲנֶה כַּאֲשֶׁר דִּבֶּר מֹשֶׁה: 6וַיֹּאמֶר מֹשֶׁה אֶל־ אַהֲרֹן וּלְאֶלְעָזָר וּלְאִיתָמָר ׀ בָּנָיו רָאשֵׁיכֶם אַל־ תִּפְרָעוּ ׀ וּבִגְדֵיכֶם לֹא־תִפְרֹמוּ וְלֹא תָמֻתוּ וְעַל כָּל־הָעֵדָה יִקְצֹף וַאֲחֵיכֶם כָּל־בֵּית יִשְׂרָאֵל יִבְכּוּ אֶת־הַשְּׂרֵפָה אֲשֶׁר שָׂרַף יְהוָה: 7וּמִפֶּתַח אֹהֶל מוֹעֵד לֹא תֵצְאוּ פֶּן־תָּמֻתוּ כִּי־שֶׁמֶן מִשְׁחַת יְהוָה עֲלֵיכֶם וַיַּעֲשׂוּ כִּדְבַר מֹשֶׁה: פ

8וַיְדַבֵּר יְהוָה אֶל־אַהֲרֹן לֵאמֹר: 9יַיִן וְשֵׁכָר

---

after all that has happened on this day, "If I had eaten a sin offering today would it be good in YHWH's eyes?" And the story concludes with a play on this last wording, noting that Aaron's answer "was good in Moses' eyes" (10:19–20). Their pain is a reminder that the standard for leaders is *tougher* than for others. According to the Torah, leaders do not get away with more because of their positions. Priests, prophets, kings, rabbis, presidents: they suffer *harder* consequences.

This in turn sets up what will happen to Moses and to Aaron themselves later. Moses quotes God here as saying, "I shall be made holy through those who are close to me." For those of us who know what is coming later in the story, this is a shivering preparation for the episode of Moses' own sin. When Moses will strike the rock at Meribah, God will impose a frightful consequence for him and for Aaron. And the reason that God will give to Moses and Aaron will be: "Because you did not trust in me, *to make me holy* before the eyes of the children of Israel" (Num 20:12). Moses' own words to Aaron here will come to testify against him there. And as Aaron is silent here, Moses makes no answer there.

10:8. YHWH spoke to Aaron. This is the first time that God speaks directly to Aaron alone since He first sent him to meet Moses (Exod 4:27), and it is right after the death of his sons! It may be that the significance of what Nadab and Abihu have done is the reason that the deity now addresses Aaron directly concerning the limitations and responsibilities of his family. Or perhaps we should understand this as an act of comfort from God to Aaron after his frightful loss.

10:9. You shall not drink wine and beer. Some have suggested on the basis of this verse that Nadab and Abihu had been drunk and that this is what caused them to

with you, when you come to the Tent of Meeting, so you won't die. It is an eternal law through your generations, ¹⁰and to distinguish between the holy and the secular, and between the impure and the pure, ¹¹and to instruct the children

אַל־תֵּשְׁתְּ ׀ אַתָּה ׀ וּבָנֶיךָ אִתָּךְ בְּבֹאֲכֶם אֶל־אֹהֶל מוֹעֵד וְלֹא תָמֻתוּ חֻקַּת עוֹלָם לְדֹרֹתֵיכֶם: ¹⁰וּלֲהַבְדִּיל בֵּין הַקֹּדֶשׁ וּבֵין הַחֹל וּבֵין הַטָּמֵא וּבֵין הַטָּהוֹר: ¹¹וּלְהוֹרֹת אֶת־בְּנֵי יִשְׂרָאֵל אֵת כָּל־

commit the offense. Admittedly, this prohibition of alcohol for the priests when they enter the Tabernacle seems otherwise unrelated to the context, but that is not sufficient grounds to denigrate these priests. Whether one believes them to be historical persons or literary characters, one must be circumspect in judging biblical figures. It is good practice for being circumspect when we judge living persons.

10:10. **to distinguish.** Leviticus is concerned with orderliness. This orderliness is reminiscent of the creation account in Genesis 1. There are key parallels of wording, especially the term for distinction (*lĕhabdîl*). As God creates by making distinctions, expressed in divine speech, in Genesis ("God distinguished between the light and the darkness"), so the function of the priesthood is described in Leviticus as "to distinguish (*lĕhabdîl*) between the holy and the secular, and between the impure and the pure." Here law is conceived as a reflection in the human realm of the order that was originally pictured in the cosmic realm.

10:10. **to distinguish between the holy and the secular.** Rabbi Simcha Weiser quoted an expression to me: The problem with American Jews today is that they know how to make kiddush (the blessing over wine), but they don't know how to make habdalah (the ceremony ending the Sabbath and beginning the secular week). That is, they do not know how to distinguish between the holy and the secular. James Kugel sent me something he wrote: "One of the crucial concepts of biblical religion is almost altogether absent from modern life. The whole of the biblical world was divided into two great domains, the holy and the profane." In *The Hidden Face of God*, I hinted at a path through discoveries of the last century about the origin of the universe that may lead us back to appreciation of the holy, the awesome, the wonder of the universe.

10:10. **between the impure and the pure.** The Hebrew terms here are also frequently translated as the "unclean" and the "clean." Neither pair of terms quite conveys the sense of the Hebrew, which, first of all, employs terms, *ṭāmē'* and *ṭāhôr*, having two different roots, thus perhaps conveying more clearly that these terms refer to two distinct conditions, each of which has a particular legal status. That is, being *ṭāmē'* is more than merely being un-*ṭāhôr*. To be *ṭāmē'* is to be in a particular condition, the qualities of which are invisible but which can be transmitted to other persons or objects by contact. Therefore, physical separation and various prescribed acts are required to remove this condition. One comes to be in a condition of being *ṭāmē'* as a result of specific occurrences: from menstruation, from other flows of matter from the body's sexual organs, from a woman's giving birth (for a week if it is a male baby, two weeks if it is a female), from contact with a corpse (of a human, of a forbidden animal, or of a permitted animal if it died of disease or was killed by another animal), from certain forms of leprosy, or from contact with persons or objects that are *ṭāmē'*. (One may also become *ṭāmē'* from a forbidden sexual relationship, although the term

343

may possibly be understood differently in the relevant passage, 18:24–30, and is in fact usually rendered differently in translations; cf. also the case of human sacrifice, 20:3.) When one performs certain acts to restrict and remove this condition (separation, bathing, and, in some circumstances, sacrifice), one returns to a condition of being *ṭāhōr*.

The common element appears to be that all these cases that make an individual *ṭāmē'* involve some sort of visible change in body fluids and/or skin, although here, as with the forbidden animals (see the next chapter), there may be a convergence of factors that are operative.

It is sometimes suggested that all these cases are related to death. But this is not correct. One must account for the inclusion of menstruation and childbirth, which relate to the start of life, not to its end. We may extend the explanation, then, and say that all these cases relate to the start or the end of life. But even this does not really account for the inclusion of leprosy among the *ṭāmē'* conditions. My colleague Jacob Milgrom has suggested that the leprous conditions all involve the wasting of a body in some way that resembles the wasting of a corpse. This is possible but hard to prove in the absence of evidence that people in biblical times made this connection in their minds. The evidence that Milgrom gives is the case in which Miriam is stricken with leprosy, and Aaron pleads with Moses, "Let her not be like the dead who, when he comes out of his mother's womb, half of his flesh is eaten up!" But this is a unique case: Miriam is stricken by God with a kind of leprosy so that she is rendered utterly pale ("leprous as snow"). This singular colorless condition of her skin may be what makes her comparable to a corpse. And Aaron is comparing her not just to any corpse but to a stillbirth. His exclamation in that story is not adequate evidence to make a general connection between leprosy and death.

The essential common point, it seems to me, is that these are all things that most people in most societies instinctively do not want to touch: blood, semen, diseased skin, corpses. It may be that ancient Israelites came to give all these things that they found repugnant to touch a common name: *ṭāmē'*. And then, in a second stage, people came to think of *ṭāmē'* as a category and felt the need to find a common underlying factor.

Was being *ṭāmē'* understood to be a condition in which one was covered with some sort of microscopic creatures like a spreading bacterium that had to be washed away (as some have believed to this day), or was it conceived as comparable to an infectious illness, or was it strictly a status that was conceived in legal definition? Biblical law, like biblical narrative, has its share of ambiguities, albeit of a different sort from narrative ambiguity. These gaps in the information that the text provides exist, first, because the laws are pictured as coming directly from God, who is not bound to explain or justify His commandments to those whom He commands. Second, the law codes, like constitutional law, are statements of the primary principles and cases, leaving the details and variations to be worked out by priests or judges as they arise (Lev 10:10–11). Third, much of the law was practiced in the daily life of the people of Israel over centuries, and so what appear as gaps to us may have been common knowledge in the community in which the text was composed.

344

of Israel all the laws that YHWH has spoken to them by the hand of Moses."

12And Moses said to Aaron and to Eleazar and to Ithamar, his sons who were left, "Take the grain offering that is left from YHWH's offerings by fire and eat it as unleavened bread beside the altar, because it is the holy of holies. 13And you shall eat it in a holy place, because it is your statutory share, and it is your sons' statutory share from YHWH's offerings by fire, because that is what I was commanded. 14And you shall eat the breast of the elevation offering and the thigh of the donation in a pure place—you and your sons and your daughters with you—because they have been given as your statutory share and your sons' statutory share from the peace-offering sacrifices of the children of Israel. 15They shall bring the thigh of the donation and the breast of the elevation offering with the offerings by fire of the fats to elevate, an elevation offering in front of YHWH; and it will be yours and your sons' with you as an eternal law, as YHWH commanded."

16And Moses *inquired* about the goat of the sin offering, and here it was burnt! And he was angry at Eleazar and at Ithamar, Aaron's sons who were left, saying, 17"Why didn't you eat the sin offering in the place of the Holy—because it's the holy of holies, and He gave it to you for bearing the congregation's crime, for making atonement over them in front of YHWH! 18Here, its blood hasn't been brought to the Holy, inside. You should have *eaten* it in the Holy as I commanded!"

19And Aaron spoke to Moses: "Here, today

הַחֻקִּים אֲשֶׁר דִּבֶּר יְהוָה אֲלֵיהֶם בְּיַד־מֹשֶׁה: פ
12וַיְדַבֵּר מֹשֶׁה אֶל־אַהֲרֹן וְאֶל אֶלְעָזָר וְאֶל־
אִיתָמָר ׀ בָּנָיו הַנּוֹתָרִים קְחוּ אֶת־הַמִּנְחָה הַנּוֹתֶרֶת
מֵאִשֵּׁי יְהוָה וְאִכְלוּהָ מַצּוֹת אֵצֶל הַמִּזְבֵּחַ כִּי קֹדֶשׁ
קָדָשִׁים הִוא: 13וַאֲכַלְתֶּם אֹתָהּ בְּמָקוֹם קָדֹשׁ כִּי
חָקְךָ וְחָק־בָּנֶיךָ הִוא מֵאִשֵּׁי יְהוָה כִּי־כֵן צֻוֵּיתִי:
14וְאֵת חֲזֵה הַתְּנוּפָה וְאֵת ׀ שׁוֹק הַתְּרוּמָה תֹּאכְלוּ
בְּמָקוֹם טָהוֹר אַתָּה וּבָנֶיךָ וּבְנֹתֶיךָ אִתָּךְ כִּי־חָקְךָ
וְחָק־בָּנֶיךָ נִתְּנוּ מִזִּבְחֵי שַׁלְמֵי בְּנֵי יִשְׂרָאֵל: 15שׁוֹק
הַתְּרוּמָה וַחֲזֵה הַתְּנוּפָה עַל אִשֵּׁי הַחֲלָבִים יָבִיאוּ
לְהָנִיף תְּנוּפָה לִפְנֵי יְהוָה וְהָיָה לְךָ וּלְבָנֶיךָ אִתְּךָ
לְחָק־עוֹלָם כַּאֲשֶׁר צִוָּה יְהוָה: 16וְאֵת ׀ שְׂעִיר
הַחַטָּאת דָּרֹשׁ דָּרַשׁ מֹשֶׁה וְהִנֵּה שֹׂרָף וַיִּקְצֹף עַל־
אֶלְעָזָר וְעַל־אִיתָמָר בְּנֵי אַהֲרֹן הַנּוֹתָרִם לֵאמֹר:
17מַדּוּעַ לֹא־אֲכַלְתֶּם אֶת־הַחַטָּאת בִּמְקוֹם הַקֹּדֶשׁ
כִּי קֹדֶשׁ קָדָשִׁים הִוא וְאֹתָהּ ׀ נָתַן לָכֶם לָשֵׂאת
אֶת־עֲוֹן הָעֵדָה לְכַפֵּר עֲלֵיהֶם לִפְנֵי יְהוָה: 18הֵן
לֹא־הוּבָא אֶת־דָּמָהּ אֶל־הַקֹּדֶשׁ פְּנִימָה אָכוֹל
תֹּאכְלוּ אֹתָהּ בַּקֹּדֶשׁ כַּאֲשֶׁר צִוֵּיתִי: 19וַיְדַבֵּר אַהֲרֹן

10:16. **inquired**. This is the middle of the Torah in terms of words, and, appropriately, it is the word "to inquire" (Hebrew דרש), the word that later comes to mean exegesis of the Torah. (See the comment on 11:42.)

10:18. **as I commanded**. See the comment on Lev 8:31. Here again Moses speaks of himself as commanding something concerning Aaron. And here again there is uncertainty about the text, since other versions differ from this reading in the Masoretic Text; they read that it is God who commands Moses. The uncertainty in the technical matter of the differences in the manuscripts underlines the larger issue: the growth in the stature and authority of Moses.

they brought forward their sin offering and their burnt offering in front of YHWH. When things like these have happened to me, if I had eaten a sin offering today would it be good in YHWH's eyes?"

20And Moses listened, and it was good in his eyes.

11 1And YHWH spoke to Moses and to Aaron, saying to them, 2"Speak to the children of Israel, saying: This is the animal that you shall eat out of all the domestic animals that are

אֶל־מֹשֶׁה הֵן הַיּוֹם הִקְרִיבוּ אֶת־חַטָּאתָם וְאֶת־
עֹלָתָם לִפְנֵי יְהוָה וַתִּקְרֶאנָה אֹתִי כָּאֵלֶּה וְאָכַלְתִּי
חַטָּאת הַיּוֹם הַיִּיטַב בְּעֵינֵי יְהוָה: 20וַיִּשְׁמַע מֹשֶׁה
וַיִּיטַב בְּעֵינָיו: פ

11 1וַיְדַבֵּר יְהוָה אֶל־מֹשֶׁה וְאֶל־אַהֲרֹן לֵאמֹר
אֲלֵהֶם: 2דַּבְּרוּ אֶל־בְּנֵי יִשְׂרָאֵל לֵאמֹר זֹאת הַחַיָּה
אֲשֶׁר תֹּאכְלוּ מִכָּל־הַבְּהֵמָה אֲשֶׁר עַל־הָאָרֶץ:

11:1. **YHWH spoke to Moses and to Aaron, saying**. This is only the second report of laws being addressed to Aaron along with Moses. The first law given to the people, the Passover command, is pronounced to both Moses and Aaron (Exod 12:1), but then the laws are stated only to Moses. Indeed, the only other time that YHWH has *spoken* to both Moses and Aaron until now was at the beginning of their mission in Egypt (and there the text does not report the words that God says to them). The inclusion of Aaron at this point may be more of the divine response to Aaron's loss of his sons (see comment on 10:8). Or it may be because God has just told Aaron that he and his sons are to instruct the people and distinguish between holy and secular and between impure and clean (10:10–11), and so now God begins to inform Aaron of the laws that he needs to know.

11:2. **This is the animal that you shall eat**. The laws of permitted and forbidden animals add further restrictions to the sacrificial laws. God requires not only ritual slaughter, priestly performance, and location at the Tent of Meeting; God delineates to Moses and Aaron which animals may be eaten as well. Among land animals: those that have split hooves and chew their cud. In water: those with scales and fins. (Redundant? All scaled fish have fins.) In the air: the forbidden birds are named one by one, and all flying creatures that have four legs are forbidden. Also forbidden are creatures that have numerous legs, those that crawl on their bellies, and any animals at all that have died on their own or that have been killed by other animals. The reasons for these particular inclusions and exclusions have never been worked out persuasively. Explanations based on health and hygiene are difficult to defend, both because the text never states this and because such explanations cannot be consistently applied to the cases. Popular claims about the unhealthy habits of pigs, for example, apply equally to various fowl that are permitted. Some suggest that the Israelites may have observed empirically that people who ate pork suffered more illness than others, but this is without any textual or historical evidence; nor does it explain how this fact was apparent to Israelites but unobserved by the rest of the world for thousands of years. Popular claims that the forbidden animals were objects of worship are simply wrong. Suggestions that the system is ultimately about matters of ethics and not food—that is, that it teaches discipline, self-denial, and so on—are not supported in the text. The text rather relates various food laws to issues of impurity (see below) and "abomina-

346

tion," which fall in the realm of ritual, not ethical, categories. Observance of ritual laws may have an ethical dimension, such as discipline, but this may be said of all ritual laws. It sheds no special light on this particular group of commandments.

The anthropologist Mary Douglas has suggested what is perhaps the most-cited treatment at present (*Purity and Danger*), which she and I have discussed: that the issue is one of defined classes of animals: Split-hoofed, cud-chewing animals are "the model of the proper kind of food for a pastoralist" (p. 54), and so this became the model of what was appropriate to eat. Wild goats and antelope share these two characteristics and therefore were acceptable. Pigs, which have a split hoof but do not chew their cud, were excluded originally for the sole reason that they did not fit this class as defined. Similarly with the forbidden water creatures: they did not fit the class that had the "right" kind of locomotion, namely fins and scales. Similarly with animals that have two hands and two legs (weasels, mice, lizards) but walk on all fours like a quadruped: they "perversely" use hands for walking. Not having the right form of locomotion, they are forbidden.

Douglas's explanation appears to me to be a self-defining system. Whatever is permitted she identifies as what the Israelites perceived to be "right." Whatever is forbidden, she concludes, came to be forbidden because it did not fit the category. This is mere definitional description unless it can shed some light on the underlying reasons for these perceptions of what was proper. Where Douglas tries to identify the reasons she errs, in my judgment. The assertion that the split hoof and the chewing of cud were "the model of the proper kind of food for a pastoralist" is unhelpful without proof that Israel was in fact primarily a pastoral society. It was not. (And Leviticus 11 certainly does not appear to come from a pastoral circle. It comes from an urban priesthood.) Nor does this explain why the non-Israelite residents of the land, who alternately (and sometimes simultaneously) lived on the same sites, conceived of these same animals so differently. Excavations uncover pig bones in a Canaanite layer of a site, then no pig bones in an Israelite layer of the same site, then pig bones again in the site's next Canaanite layer. There is likewise no reason to associate the presence of scales on a fish with a concept of a proper form of locomotion. And Douglas's notion of a "perverse" form of locomotion by animals whose front limbs are handlike is simply a misunderstanding of the Hebrew term (*kap*), which does not mean "hand." It refers elsewhere to both the hands and the feet (Gen 8:9; Deut 2:5; 11:24; 28:35,56; Josh 1:3; 2 Sam 14:25) and is correctly translated "paws" (a translation that Douglas appears to eschew). In its context here it follows a verse that refers to the matter of split hooves (11:26), and it is simply forbidding all animals that have soft paws rather than hooves. Douglas's treatment may add some helpful perspectives to the discussion, but the essential mystery remains unsolved.

I have tried here to exclude some of the common explanations that appear to me to be looking in the wrong directions, and I mean to identify some elements that should be taken into account. The first is: similarity to humans. The fact that the text elsewhere has conceived of animals, but not plants, as having the quality of life (*nepeš*) in common with humans, even though plants do in fact live and die, already means that the degree of similarity to humans figured in the distinctions, whether consciously or not. Plants were so different from humans as not to be thought of as a life-form in the same sense and therefore not even considered as having to be

on the earth: 3every one that has a hoof and that has a split of hooves, that regurgitates cud among animals, you shall eat it. 4Except you shall not eat this out of those that regurgitate the cud and out of those that have a hoof: The camel, because it regurgitates cud and does not have a hoof; it is impure to you. 5And the rock-badger, because it regurgitates cud and does not have a hoof; it is impure to you. 6And the hare, because it regurgitates cud and does not have a hoof; it is impure to you. 7And the pig, because it has a hoof and

3כֹּל ׀ מַפְרֶסֶת פַּרְסָה וְשֹׁסַעַת שֶׁסַע פְּרָסֹת מַעֲלַת גֵּרָה בַּבְּהֵמָה אֹתָהּ תֹּאכֵלוּ: 4אַךְ אֶת־זֶה לֹא תֹאכְלוּ מִמַּעֲלֵי הַגֵּרָה וּמִמַּפְרִיסֵי הַפַּרְסָה אֶת־הַגָּמָל כִּי־מַעֲלֵה גֵרָה הוּא וּפַרְסָה אֵינֶנּוּ מַפְרִיס טָמֵא הוּא לָכֶם: 5וְאֶת־הַשָּׁפָן כִּי־מַעֲלֵה גֵרָה הוּא וּפַרְסָה לֹא יַפְרִיס טָמֵא הוּא לָכֶם: 6וְאֶת־הָאַרְנֶבֶת כִּי־מַעֲלַת גֵּרָה הִוא וּפַרְסָה לֹא הִפְרִיסָה טְמֵאָה הִוא לָכֶם: 7וְאֶת־הַחֲזִיר כִּי־מַפְרִיס פַּרְסָה הוּא

---

permitted or forbidden. In the animal kingdom, meanwhile, on a continuum of likeness to humans, at one extreme would be cannibalism, which is so extreme as not even to be considered (unless the law against human sacrifice is understood necessarily to prevent it). Next would be the ape family, which is forbidden, having soft hands and feet; then all fellow creatures having soft hands and feet or paws (*kap*) like humans rather than hooves. Next might be all animals that, like humans, are carnivorous (thus including numerous land animals, all birds of prey, and various reptiles). The permissible animals would then be those that are twice-distinguished from humans, both having a split hoof and chewing their cud. Animals that have only one of these are especially singled out by species, such as pigs (which have a split hoof but do not chew the cud) and camels (which chew the cud but do not have a split hoof). This does not explain all of the permissions and prohibitions of Leviticus 11. Notably, it does not account for water creatures (few creatures are as unlike humans as lobsters) or insects (why are locusts permitted?). It does, however, relate to enough of the distinctions that it should be taken into account in any attempt to explain this list. Ultimately, since no single underlying principle has been discovered that accounts for all the distinctions, it appears likely that there is a convergence of two or probably more factors. It could be a combination of a principle (such as likeness to humans) and completely idiosyncratic factors (a distaste, phobia, or even allergy on the part of some individual in an authoritative position).

For the larger purpose of coming to an understanding of Leviticus, it is important for now to note the fact of *distinction* and how seriously and pervasively it is developed here in regard to a basic function of life. The list confirms this explicitly by concluding:

This is the instruction [*tôrāh*] for animal and bird and every living being that moves in the water and for every being that swarms on the earth, *to distinguish* [*lĕhabdîl*] between the impure and the pure, and between the living thing that is eaten and the living thing that shall not be eaten. (11:46–47)

11:3. **a split of hooves.** Each of its hooves is split, e.g., cows; as opposed to those that have a single hoof, e.g., horses.

11:6. **the hare, because it regurgitates cud.** Hares do not regurgitate cud.

has a split of hooves, and it does not chew cud; it is impure to you. 8You shall not eat from their meat, and you shall not touch their carcass. They are impure to you.

9"You shall eat this out of all that are in the water: every one that has fins and scales in the water—in the seas and in the streams—you shall eat them. 10And any one that does not have fins and scales in the seas and in the streams—out of every swarming thing of the water and out of every living being that is in the water—they *are* a detestable thing to you, 11and they *shall be* a detestable thing to you. You shall not eat from their meat, and you shall detest their carcass. 12Every one that does not have scales and fins in the water, it is a detestable thing to you.

13"And you shall detest these out of the flying creatures. They shall not be eaten. They are a detestable thing: the eagle and the vulture and the black vulture 14and the kite and the falcon by its kind, 15every raven by its kind 16and the eagle owl and the nighthawk and the seagull and the hawk by its kind 17and the little owl and the cormorant and the great owl 18and the white owl and the pelican and the fish hawk 19and the stork and the heron by its kind and the hoopoe and the bat. 20Every swarming thing of flying creatures that goes on four—it is a detestable

וְשֹׁסַע שֶׁסַע פַּרְסָה וְהוּא גֵּרָה לֹא־יִגָּר טָמֵא הוּא לָכֶם: 8מִבְּשָׂרָם לֹא תֹאכֵלוּ וּבְנִבְלָתָם לֹא תִגָּעוּ טְמֵאִים הֵם לָכֶם: 9אֶת־זֶה תֹּאכְלוּ מִכֹּל אֲשֶׁר בַּמָּיִם כֹּל אֲשֶׁר־לֹו סְנַפִּיר וְקַשְׂקֶשֶׂת בַּמַּיִם בַּיַּמִּים וּבַנְּחָלִים אֹתָם תֹּאכֵלוּ: 10וְכֹל אֲשֶׁר אֵין־לֹו סְנַפִּיר וְקַשְׂקֶשֶׂת בַּיַּמִּים וּבַנְּחָלִים מִכֹּל שֶׁרֶץ הַמַּיִם וּמִכֹּל נֶפֶשׁ הַחַיָּה אֲשֶׁר בַּמָּיִם שֶׁקֶץ הֵם לָכֶם: 11וְשֶׁקֶץ יִהְיוּ לָכֶם מִבְּשָׂרָם לֹא תֹאכֵלוּ וְאֶת־נִבְלָתָם תְּשַׁקֵּצוּ: 12כֹּל אֲשֶׁר אֵין־לֹו סְנַפִּיר וְקַשְׂקֶשֶׂת בַּמָּיִם שֶׁקֶץ הוּא לָכֶם: 13וְאֶת־אֵלֶּה תְּשַׁקְּצוּ מִן־הָעֹוף לֹא יֵאָכְלוּ שֶׁקֶץ הֵם אֶת־הַנֶּשֶׁר וְאֶת־הַפֶּרֶס וְאֵת הָעָזְנִיָּה: 14וְאֶת־הַדָּאָה וְאֶת־הָאַיָּה לְמִינָהּ: 15אֵת כָּל־עֹרֵב לְמִינֹו: 16וְאֵת בַּת הַיַּעֲנָה וְאֶת־הַתַּחְמָס וְאֶת־הַשָּׁחַף וְאֶת־הַנֵּץ לְמִינֵהוּ: 17וְאֶת־הַכֹּוס וְאֶת־הַשָּׁלָךְ וְאֶת־הַיַּנְשׁוּף: 18וְאֶת־הַתִּנְשֶׁמֶת וְאֶת־הַקָּאָת וְאֶת־הָרָחָם: 19וְאֵת הַחֲסִידָה הָאֲנָפָה לְמִינָהּ וְאֶת־הַדּוּכִיפַת וְאֶת־הָעֲטַלֵּף: 20כֹּל שֶׁרֶץ הָעֹוף הַהֹלֵךְ עַל־אַרְבַּע שֶׁקֶץ הוּא לָכֶם: ס 21אַךְ

11:9. **all that are in the water.** There is no differentiation of species of water creatures in the entire *Tanak*. All fish are simply called *dāg*. My colleague Jacob Milgrom has proposed that the reason for this is that ancient Israelites knew little of fish because the eastern Mediterranean was not suitable for fish until the opening of the Suez Canal in our era, which changed the ecology of that sea. But even if this were so—that there were no fish in the eastern Mediterranean—the Israelites still had the Red Sea, the Sea of Galilee, and the Jordan River. Surely those who lived near these bodies of water knew one fish from another. A more likely explanation is that the list of permitted and forbidden animals came from the Jerusalem priesthood, and before the invention of refrigeration it would have been extremely rare for anyone in Jerusalem to have an opportunity to eat fish.

11:16. **eagle owl.** Hebrew *bat hayya'ănāh.* It has usually been identified as an ostrich. Milgrom has thrown that identification into doubt. I agree. Moreover, ostriches are primarily plant-eating, like the permitted birds. Therefore: the ostrich is not necessarily forbidden for food.

thing to you. 21Except you shall eat this out of every swarming thing of flying creatures that goes on four: that which has jointed legs above its feet, to leap by them on the earth. 22You shall eat these out of them: the locust by its kind and the bald locust by its kind and the cricket by its kind and the grasshopper by its kind. 23And every swarming thing of flying creatures that has four legs—it is a detestable thing to you.

24"And you will become impure by these—everyone who touches their carcass will be impure until evening, 25and everyone who carries their carcass shall wash his clothes and be impure until evening— 26by every animal that has a hoof and does not have a split of hooves and does not regurgitate its cud. They are impure to you. Everyone who touches them will be impure. 27And every one that goes on its paws among all the animals that go on four, they are impure to you. Everyone who touches their carcass will be impure until evening, 28and one who carries their carcass shall wash his clothes and be impure until evening. They are impure to you.

29"And this is the impure to you among the things that swarm on the earth: the rat, the mouse, and the great lizard by its kind 30and the gecko and the spotted lizard and the lizard and the sand lizard and the chameleon. 31These are the impure to you among all the swarming things. Everyone who touches them when they are dead will be impure until evening. 32And everything on which one of them will fall when they are dead will be impure, out of every wooden item or clothing or leather or sack, every item with which work may be done shall be put in water and will be impure until evening and then will be pure. 33And every clay container into which any of them will fall: everything that is inside it will be impure, and you shall break it. 34Every food that may be eaten on which water will come will be impure, and every liquid that

אֶת־זֶה֙ תֹּאכְל֔וּ מִכֹּל֙ שֶׁ֣רֶץ הָע֔וֹף הַהֹלֵ֖ךְ עַל־אַרְבַּ֑ע אֲשֶׁר־ל֤וֹ כְרָעַ֨יִם֙ מִמַּ֣עַל לְרַגְלָ֔יו לְנַתֵּ֥ר בָּהֵ֖ן עַל־הָאָֽרֶץ׃ 22אֶת־אֵ֣לֶּה מֵהֶם֮ תֹּאכֵ֒לוּ֒ אֶת־הָֽאַרְבֶּ֣ה לְמִינ֔וֹ וְאֶת־הַסָּלְעָ֖ם לְמִינֵ֑הוּ וְאֶת־הַֽחַרְגֹּ֣ל לְמִינֵ֔הוּ וְאֶת־הֶחָגָ֖ב לְמִינֵֽהוּ׃ 23וְכֹל֙ שֶׁ֣רֶץ הָע֔וֹף אֲשֶׁר־ל֖וֹ אַרְבַּ֣ע רַגְלָ֑יִם שֶׁ֥קֶץ ה֖וּא לָכֶֽם׃ 24וּלְאֵ֖לֶּה תִּטַּמָּ֑אוּ כָּל־הַנֹּגֵ֥עַ בְּנִבְלָתָ֖ם יִטְמָ֥א עַד־הָעָֽרֶב׃ 25וְכָל־הַנֹּשֵׂ֖א מִנִּבְלָתָ֑ם יְכַבֵּ֥ס בְּגָדָ֖יו וְטָמֵ֥א עַד־הָעָֽרֶב׃ 26לְכָל־הַבְּהֵמָ֡ה אֲשֶׁ֣ר הִוא֩ מַפְרֶ֨סֶת פַּרְסָ֜ה וְשֶׁ֣סַע ׀ אֵינֶ֣נָּה שֹׁסַ֗עַת וְגֵרָה֙ אֵינֶ֣נָּה מַֽעֲלָ֔ה טְמֵאִ֥ים הֵ֖ם לָכֶ֑ם כָּל־הַנֹּגֵ֥עַ בָּהֶ֖ם יִטְמָֽא׃ 27וְכֹ֣ל ׀ הוֹלֵ֣ךְ עַל־כַּפָּ֗יו בְּכָל־הַֽחַיָּה֙ הַהֹלֶ֣כֶת עַל־אַרְבַּ֔ע טְמֵאִ֥ים הֵ֖ם לָכֶ֑ם כָּל־הַנֹּגֵ֥עַ בְּנִבְלָתָ֖ם יִטְמָ֥א עַד־הָעָֽרֶב׃ 28וְהַנֹּשֵׂא֙ אֶת־נִבְלָתָ֔ם יְכַבֵּ֥ס בְּגָדָ֖יו וְטָמֵ֣א עַד־הָעָ֑רֶב טְמֵאִ֥ים הֵ֖מָּה לָכֶֽם׃ ס 29וְזֶ֤ה לָכֶם֙ הַטָּמֵ֔א בַּשֶּׁ֖רֶץ הַשֹּׁרֵ֣ץ עַל־הָאָ֑רֶץ הַחֹ֥לֶד וְהָעַכְבָּ֖ר וְהַצָּ֥ב לְמִינֵֽהוּ׃ 30וְהָאֲנָקָ֥ה וְהַכֹּ֖חַ וְהַלְּטָאָ֑ה וְהַחֹ֖מֶט וְהַתִּנְשָֽׁמֶת׃ 31אֵ֛לֶּה הַטְּמֵאִ֥ים לָכֶ֖ם בְּכָל־הַשָּׁ֑רֶץ כָּל־הַנֹּגֵ֧עַ בָּהֶ֛ם בְּמֹתָ֖ם יִטְמָ֥א עַד־הָעָֽרֶב׃ 32וְכֹ֣ל אֲשֶׁר־יִפֹּל־עָלָיו֩ מֵהֶ֨ם ׀ בְּמֹתָ֜ם יִטְמָ֗א מִכָּל־כְּלִי־עֵץ֙ א֣וֹ בֶ֤גֶד אוֹ־ע֨וֹר א֣וֹ שָׂ֔ק כָּל־כְּלִ֕י אֲשֶׁר־יֵעָשֶׂ֥ה מְלָאכָ֖ה בָּהֶ֑ם בַּמַּ֧יִם יוּבָ֛א וְטָמֵ֥א עַד־הָעֶ֖רֶב וְטָהֵֽר׃ 33וְכָל־כְּלִי־חֶ֔רֶשׂ אֲשֶׁר־יִפֹּ֥ל מֵהֶ֖ם אֶל־תּוֹכ֑וֹ כֹּ֣ל אֲשֶׁ֧ר בְּתוֹכ֛וֹ יִטְמָ֖א וְאֹת֥וֹ תִשְׁבֹּֽרוּ׃ 34מִכָּל־הָאֹ֜כֶל אֲשֶׁ֣ר יֵֽאָכֵ֗ל אֲשֶׁ֨ר יָב֥וֹא עָלָ֛יו מַ֖יִם יִטְמָ֑א וְכָל־מַשְׁקֶה֙ אֲשֶׁ֣ר יִשָּׁתֶ֔ה

11:21 קְ לֹו

11:30. **spotted lizard**. The identification of several of the animals on this list is uncertain. Milgrom favors the spotted lizard for this one.

may be drunk in any container will be impure. ³⁵And everything on which some of their carcass will fall will be impure. An oven or stove shall be demolished. They are impure, and they *shall be* impure to you. ³⁶Except a spring or a cistern with a concentration of waters will be pure. And one who touches their carcass will be impure. ³⁷And if some of their carcass will fall on any sowing seed that will be sown, it is pure. ³⁸And if water will be put on a seed, and some of their carcass will fall on it, it is impure to you.

³⁹"And if any of the animals that are yours for food will die, the one who touches its carcass will be impure until evening, ⁴⁰and the one who eats some of its carcass shall wash his clothes and is impure until evening, and the one who carries its carcass shall wash his clothes and is impure until evening.

⁴¹"And every swarming creature that swarms on the earth, it is a detestable thing. It shall not be eaten. ⁴²Everything going on a belly and everything going on four as well as everything having a great number of legs of every swarming creature that swarms on the earth: you shall not eat them because they are a detestable thing. ⁴³Do not make yourselves detestable with any swarming creature that swarms, and you shall not become impure with them, so that you will be impure through them. ⁴⁴Because I am YHWH, your God, and you shall make yourselves holy, and you shall be holy because I am holy. And you shall not make yourselves impure with any swarming creature that creeps on the earth. ⁴⁵Because I am YHWH, who brought you up from the land of Egypt to be God to you, and you shall be holy because I am holy.

⁴⁶"This is the instruction for animal and bird and every living being that moves in the water and for every being that swarms on the earth, ⁴⁷to distinguish between the impure and the pure, and between the living thing that is eaten and the living thing that shall not be eaten."

בְּכָל־כְּלִי יִטְמָא: ³⁵וְכֹל אֲשֶׁר־יִפֹּל מִנִּבְלָתָם ׀ עָלָיו יִטְמָא תַּנּוּר וְכִירַיִם יֻתָּץ טְמֵאִים הֵם וּטְמֵאִים יִהְיוּ לָכֶם: ³⁶אַךְ מַעְיָן וּבוֹר מִקְוֵה־מַיִם יִהְיֶה טָהוֹר וְנֹגֵעַ בְּנִבְלָתָם יִטְמָא: ³⁷וְכִי יִפֹּל מִנִּבְלָתָם עַל־כָּל־זֶרַע זֵרוּעַ אֲשֶׁר יִזָּרֵעַ טָהוֹר הוּא: ³⁸וְכִי יֻתַּן־מַיִם עַל־זֶרַע וְנָפַל מִנִּבְלָתָם עָלָיו טָמֵא הוּא לָכֶם: ס ³⁹וְכִי יָמוּת מִן־הַבְּהֵמָה אֲשֶׁר־הִיא לָכֶם לְאָכְלָה הַנֹּגֵעַ בְּנִבְלָתָהּ יִטְמָא עַד־הָעָרֶב: ⁴⁰וְהָאֹכֵל מִנִּבְלָתָהּ יְכַבֵּס בְּגָדָיו וְטָמֵא עַד־הָעָרֶב וְהַנֹּשֵׂא אֶת־נִבְלָתָהּ יְכַבֵּס בְּגָדָיו וְטָמֵא עַד־הָעָרֶב: ⁴¹וְכָל־הַשֶּׁרֶץ הַשֹּׁרֵץ עַל־הָאָרֶץ שֶׁקֶץ הוּא לֹא יֵאָכֵל: ⁴²כֹּל הוֹלֵךְ עַל־גָּחוֹן וְכֹל ׀ הוֹלֵךְ עַל־אַרְבַּע עַד כָּל־מַרְבֵּה רַגְלַיִם לְכָל־הַשֶּׁרֶץ הַשֹּׁרֵץ עַל־הָאָרֶץ לֹא תֹאכְלוּם כִּי־שֶׁקֶץ הֵם: ⁴³אַל־תְּשַׁקְּצוּ אֶת־נַפְשֹׁתֵיכֶם בְּכָל־הַשֶּׁרֶץ הַשֹּׁרֵץ וְלֹא תִטַּמְּאוּ בָּהֶם וְנִטְמֵתֶם בָּם: ⁴⁴כִּי אֲנִי יְהוָה אֱלֹהֵיכֶם וְהִתְקַדִּשְׁתֶּם וִהְיִיתֶם קְדֹשִׁים כִּי קָדוֹשׁ אָנִי וְלֹא תְטַמְּאוּ אֶת־נַפְשֹׁתֵיכֶם בְּכָל־הַשֶּׁרֶץ הָרֹמֵשׂ עַל־הָאָרֶץ: ⁴⁵כִּי ׀ אֲנִי יְהוָה הַמַּעֲלֶה אֶתְכֶם מֵאֶרֶץ מִצְרַיִם לִהְיֹת לָכֶם לֵאלֹהִים וִהְיִיתֶם קְדֹשִׁים כִּי קָדוֹשׁ אָנִי: ⁴⁶זֹאת תּוֹרַת הַבְּהֵמָה וְהָעוֹף וְכֹל נֶפֶשׁ הַחַיָּה הָרֹמֶשֶׂת בַּמָּיִם וּלְכָל־נֶפֶשׁ הַשֹּׁרֶצֶת עַל־הָאָרֶץ: ⁴⁷לְהַבְדִּיל בֵּין הַטָּמֵא וּבֵין הַטָּהֹר וּבֵין הַחַיָּה הַנֶּאֱכֶלֶת וּבֵין הַחַיָּה אֲשֶׁר לֹא תֵאָכֵל: פ

11:42. **belly**. The third letter of this word in the Hebrew text is written extra large, thus: גחון—and it is the middle of the Torah in terms of letters.

SHE WILL BEAR SEED

תזריע

12 ¹And YHWH spoke to Moses, saying, ²"Speak to the children of Israel, saying: A woman, when she will bear seed and give birth to a male, will be impure seven days. She will be impure like the days of the impurity of her menstruation. ³And on the eighth day the flesh of his foreskin shall be circumcised. ⁴And thirty days and three days she shall remain in blood of purity. She shall not touch any holy thing, and she shall not come to the holy place until the completion of the days of her purification. ⁵And if she will give birth to a female, then she will be impure two weeks, like her impurity. And sixty days and six days she shall remain with blood of purity. ⁶And at the completion of the days of her purification, for a son or for a daughter, she shall bring a lamb in its first year for a burnt offering

12 ¹וַיְדַבֵּ֥ר יְהוָ֖ה אֶל־מֹשֶׁ֥ה לֵּאמֹֽר: ²דַּבֵּ֞ר אֶל־
בְּנֵ֤י יִשְׂרָאֵל֙ לֵאמֹ֔ר אִשָּׁה֙ כִּ֣י תַזְרִ֔יעַ וְיָלְדָ֖ה זָכָ֑ר
וְטָֽמְאָה֙ שִׁבְעַ֣ת יָמִ֔ים כִּימֵ֛י נִדַּ֥ת דְּוֹתָ֖הּ תִּטְמָֽא:
³וּבַיֹּ֖ום הַשְּׁמִינִ֑י יִמֹּ֖ול בְּשַׂ֥ר עָרְלָתֹֽו: ⁴וּשְׁלֹשִׁ֥ים יֹום֙
וּשְׁלֹ֣שֶׁת יָמִ֔ים תֵּשֵׁ֖ב בִּדְמֵ֣י טָהֳרָ֑ה בְּכָל־קֹ֣דֶשׁ לֹֽא־
תִגָּ֗ע וְאֶל־הַמִּקְדָּשׁ֙ לֹ֣א תָבֹ֔א עַד־מְלֹ֖את יְמֵ֥י
טָהֳרָֽהּ: ⁵וְאִם־נְקֵבָ֥ה תֵלֵ֖ד וְטָמְאָ֥ה שְׁבֻעַ֖יִם כְּנִדָּתָ֑הּ
וְשִׁשִּׁ֥ים יֹום֙ וְשֵׁ֣שֶׁת יָמִ֔ים תֵּשֵׁ֖ב עַל־דְּמֵ֥י טָהֳרָֽה:
⁶וּבִמְלֹ֣את ׀ יְמֵ֣י טָהֳרָ֗הּ לְבֵן֙ אֹ֣ו לְבַ֔ת תָּבִ֥יא כֶּ֖בֶשׂ

12:2. the impurity of her menstruation. This is the first occurrence of this matter in a portion dealing with law. Prior to this it has come up in the story of Rachel's hiding her father Laban's teraphim. There Rachel keeps Laban at a distance by telling him, "I have the way of women." What attitudes toward menstruation do the Torah's laws and stories reflect? The most neutral view is that menstruation was a specific condition with a particular legal status. But that is stretching in order to downplay the negative conception of menstruation that is contained here. Indeed, some people have regarded it as a kind of contamination, and some have even imagined some kind of invisible creatures on a person who is in this impure condition. Freud elucidated the psychological component in explaining why this subject is so mysterious and even intimidating to males. Or, even at a more conscious level, blood is intimidating to a large proportion of us, who look away when blood is drawn from ourselves or others, or who cannot bear to watch bloody scenes in drama, or who are distressed at the idea of contact with another person's blood, or who, like Lady Macbeth, associate blood with guilt. This list could easily be extended. The point is that blood is powerful: physically, symbolically, and emotionally. For a woman it is a natural part of her life from the time of puberty, visible each month. But for a man it is a sign that something is wrong, almost always associated with injury or illness. And so menstruation is a mysterious and intimidating subject even to a male who fully understands the biology of it. Laban wants his teraphim back, but not enough to approach his daughter when she has "the way of women."

12:5. two weeks. . . . And sixty days and six days. But it is one week plus thirty-three days for a male (12:2–4): a total of forty for a male but eighty for a female. No one knows the reason why it is double for a female.

352

and a pigeon or a turtledove for a sin offering to the entrance of the Tent of Meeting, to the priest. [7]And he shall bring it forward in front of YHWH and make atonement over her, and she will be purified from the source of her blood. This is the instruction for the one giving birth to a male or to a female. [8]And if her hand will not find enough for a sheep, then she shall take two turtledoves or two pigeons, one for a burnt offering and one for a sin offering, and the priest shall make atonement over her, and she will be purified."

13 [1]And YHWH spoke to Moses and to Aaron, saying, [2]"When a person will have a swelling or a rash or a bright spot in his flesh's skin, and it becomes an affliction of leprosy in his flesh's skin, and he will be brought to Aaron, the priest, or to one of his sons, the priests, [3]and

בֶּן־שְׁנָתוֹ לְעֹלָה וּבֶן־יוֹנָה אוֹ־תֹר לְחַטָּאת אֶל־פֶּתַח אֹהֶל־מוֹעֵד אֶל־הַכֹּהֵן: [7]וְהִקְרִיבוֹ לִפְנֵי יְהוָה וְכִפֶּר עָלֶיהָ וְטָהֲרָה מִמְּקֹר דָּמֶיהָ זֹאת תּוֹרַת הַיֹּלֶדֶת לַזָּכָר אוֹ לַנְּקֵבָה: [8]וְאִם־לֹא תִמְצָא יָדָהּ דֵּי שֶׂה וְלָקְחָה שְׁתֵּי־תֹרִים אוֹ שְׁנֵי בְּנֵי יוֹנָה אֶחָד לְעֹלָה וְאֶחָד לְחַטָּאת וְכִפֶּר עָלֶיהָ הַכֹּהֵן וְטָהֵרָה:

פ

13 [1]וַיְדַבֵּר יְהוָה אֶל־מֹשֶׁה וְאֶל־אַהֲרֹן לֵאמֹר: [2]אָדָם כִּי־יִהְיֶה בְעוֹר־בְּשָׂרוֹ שְׂאֵת אוֹ־סַפַּחַת אוֹ בַהֶרֶת וְהָיָה בְעוֹר־בְּשָׂרוֹ לְנֶגַע צָרָעַת וְהוּבָא אֶל־אַהֲרֹן הַכֹּהֵן אוֹ אֶל־אַחַד מִבָּנָיו הַכֹּהֲנִים: [3]וְרָאָה

12:8. **her hand will not find enough**. Meaning: if she will not be able to afford. (See comment on Lev 5:7,11.)

13:2. **a swelling or a rash or a bright spot**. All these terms for skin conditions are rare and their meanings uncertain.

13:2. **in his flesh's skin**. This phrase occurs five times in these first few verses. When one has a visible problem on his or her skin—sore, rash, discoloration, injury, scab, allergic reaction, loss of hair because of a medical treatment—it is a special distress: embarrassing, frightening. One feels ugly. One does not know how long it will last. One wonders if others are making fun or pitying or feeling disgusted. The laws in this section convey that it is not that the person has done something *wrong,* that it is not something *intrinsic* in the person's behavior. Being impure because of a skin condition does not mean that one has done something wrong any more than being impure because one happens to be menstruating means that one has done something wrong. The issue is that a qualified person (a priest) should identify the condition, steps should be taken to prevent it from spreading, and the afflicted person should become well and return to the community. We no longer treat these conditions through priests at the Temple, but we can still learn from this to be sensitive to the added distress, embarrassment, and vulnerability that are felt by those who suffer from illnesses that affect their appearance.

13:2. **it becomes an affliction of leprosy**. The one thing that does appear to be certain is that this term does not refer to the illness known as leprosy in postbiblical times (Hansen's disease, which showed up in the Near East much later and is thought to have been brought back from India by the troops of Alexander the Great). It refers to certain skin conditions whose nature varies. The main points we must note are:

the priest will see the affliction in the flesh's skin, and hair in the affliction will have turned white, and the affliction's appearance is deeper than his flesh's skin, it is an affliction of leprosy. And when the priest will see it he shall identify him as impure. ⁴And if it is a white bright spot in his flesh's skin, and its appearance is not deeper than the skin, and its hair has not turned white, then the priest shall shut in the one with the affliction seven days. ⁵And the priest shall see him on the seventh day; and, here, in his eyes the affliction will have stayed the same—the affliction has not spread in the skin—then the priest shall shut him in seven days a second time. ⁶And the priest shall see him on the seventh day a second time; and, here, the affliction has become dim, and the affliction has not spread in the skin, then the priest shall identify him as pure. It is a rash. And he shall wash his clothes and be pure. ⁷But

הַכֹּהֵן אֶת־הַנֶּגַע בְּעוֹר־הַבָּשָׂר וְשֵׂעָר בַּנֶּגַע הָפַךְ ׀ לָבָן וּמַרְאֵה הַנֶּגַע עָמֹק מֵעוֹר בְּשָׂרוֹ נֶגַע צָרַעַת הוּא וְרָאָהוּ הַכֹּהֵן וְטִמֵּא אֹתוֹ: ⁴וְאִם־בַּהֶרֶת לְבָנָה הִוא בְּעוֹר בְּשָׂרוֹ וְעָמֹק אֵין־מַרְאֶהָ מִן־הָעוֹר וּשְׂעָרָה לֹא־הָפַךְ לָבָן וְהִסְגִּיר הַכֹּהֵן אֶת־הַנֶּגַע שִׁבְעַת יָמִים: ⁵וְרָאָהוּ הַכֹּהֵן בַּיּוֹם הַשְּׁבִיעִי וְהִנֵּה הַנֶּגַע עָמַד בְּעֵינָיו לֹא־פָשָׂה הַנֶּגַע בָּעוֹר וְהִסְגִּירוֹ הַכֹּהֵן שִׁבְעַת יָמִים שֵׁנִית: ⁶וְרָאָה הַכֹּהֵן אֹתוֹ בַּיּוֹם הַשְּׁבִיעִי שֵׁנִית וְהִנֵּה כֵּהָה הַנֶּגַע וְלֹא־פָשָׂה הַנֶּגַע בָּעוֹר וְטִהֲרוֹ הַכֹּהֵן מִסְפַּחַת הִיא וְכִבֶּס בְּגָדָיו

---

1. This is not medicine. It is not about illness in the same sense as other illnesses. It is not about disease as a category, as a subject to be studied in medical school. It is about a specific group of skin diseases. They are dealt with by priests, not physicians. And the priests' task is to diagnose the condition, not to treat it. (There is very little about medicine in the *Tanak*.)

2. Leprosy is not a punishment from God. There are individual cases in which it is a direct punishment: Miriam's white-as-snow leprosy (Numbers 12) and King Uzziah's leprosy (2 Chr 26:16–21), but these are treated as extraordinary occurrences; they should not be used to prove anything about standard occurrences of skin afflictions. The reasons for such afflictions are not stated here in the laws of Leviticus.

3. This is not about morality. An affliction of this kind does not mean that the person has committed some ethical offense. There is a frequently quoted midrashic play on the word for leprosy: מצרע (*měṣōrāʾ*), that it is shorthand for מוציא שם רע (*môṣîʾ šēm raʿ*), meaning someone who brings out a bad name about someone else, that is, a slanderer. This has an intriguing reflex in the story of Miriam's leprosy (Numbers 12), because she is stricken with it in the wake of having criticized Moses. But the plain sense of the biblical laws of leprosy in general still does not point to any direct connection with morality.

4. It is not the leprosy that they are trying to prevent from spreading. It is the *impurity*. This matter thus remains part of the larger issue of categories—holy and secular, pure and impure—which is a recurring concern of Leviticus and of the comments on it here.

if the rash *has* spread in the skin after his being seen by the priest for pronouncing him pure, and he is seen a second time by the priest, [8]and the priest sees, and, here, the rash has spread in the skin, then the priest shall identify him as impure. It is leprosy.

[9]"When an affliction of leprosy will be in a human, and he will be brought to the priest, [10]and the priest will see; and, here, a white swelling will be in the skin, and it will have turned hair white, and some vital flesh will be in the swelling, [11]it is chronic leprosy in his flesh's skin, and the priest shall identify him as impure. He shall not shut him in, because he is impure. [12]And if the leprosy will *develop* in the skin, and the leprosy will cover all the skin of the one with the affliction from his head to his feet, to wherever it is within sight of the priest's eyes, [13]and the priest will see, and, here, the leprosy has covered all his flesh, then he shall identify the one with the affliction as pure. All of him has turned white. He is pure. [14]And on the day that vital flesh will appear in him he will be impure. [15]And the priest will see the vital flesh and shall identify him as impure. The vital flesh: it is impure. It is leprosy. [16]Or when the vital flesh will go back and turn to white, and he will come to the priest, [17]and the priest will see him, and, here, the affliction has turned to white, then the priest shall identify the affliction as pure. He is pure.

[18]"And when flesh will have a boil in it, in its skin, and will be healed, [19]and in place of the boil there will be a white swelling or a reddish white bright spot, and he will be seen by the priest, [20]and the priest will see, and, here, its appearance is lower than the skin, and its hair has turned white, then the priest shall identify him as impure. It is an affliction of leprosy. It has developed in the boil. [21]And if the priest will see it, and, here, there is not white hair in it, and it is not lower than the skin, and it has become dim, then the priest shall shut him in seven days. [22]And if it will *spread* in the skin, then the priest shall identify him as impure. It is an affliction.

וְטָהֵר: ⁷וְאִם־פָּשֹׂה תִפְשֶׂה הַמִּסְפַּחַת בָּעוֹר אַחֲרֵי הֵרָאֹתוֹ אֶל־הַכֹּהֵן לְטָהֳרָתוֹ וְנִרְאָה שֵׁנִית אֶל־הַכֹּהֵן: ⁸וְרָאָה הַכֹּהֵן וְהִנֵּה פָּשְׂתָה הַמִּסְפַּחַת בָּעוֹר וְטִמְּאוֹ הַכֹּהֵן צָרַעַת הִוא: פ ⁹נֶגַע צָרַעַת כִּי תִהְיֶה בְּאָדָם וְהוּבָא אֶל־הַכֹּהֵן: ¹⁰וְרָאָה הַכֹּהֵן וְהִנֵּה שְׂאֵת־לְבָנָה בָּעוֹר וְהִיא הָפְכָה שֵׂעָר לָבָן וּמִחְיַת בָּשָׂר חַי בַּשְׂאֵת: ¹¹צָרַעַת נוֹשֶׁנֶת הִוא בְּעוֹר בְּשָׂרוֹ וְטִמְּאוֹ הַכֹּהֵן לֹא יַסְגִּרֶנּוּ כִּי טָמֵא הוּא: ¹²וְאִם־פָּרוֹחַ תִּפְרַח הַצָּרַעַת בָּעוֹר וְכִסְּתָה הַצָּרַעַת אֵת כָּל־עוֹר הַנֶּגַע מֵרֹאשׁוֹ וְעַד־רַגְלָיו לְכָל־מַרְאֵה עֵינֵי הַכֹּהֵן: ¹³וְרָאָה הַכֹּהֵן וְהִנֵּה כִסְּתָה הַצָּרַעַת אֶת־כָּל־בְּשָׂרוֹ וְטִהַר אֶת־הַנָּגַע כֻּלּוֹ הָפַךְ לָבָן טָהוֹר הוּא: ¹⁴וּבְיוֹם הֵרָאוֹת בּוֹ בָּשָׂר חַי יִטְמָא: ¹⁵וְרָאָה הַכֹּהֵן אֶת־הַבָּשָׂר הַחַי וְטִמְּאוֹ הַבָּשָׂר הַחַי טָמֵא הוּא צָרַעַת הוּא: ¹⁶אוֹ כִי יָשׁוּב הַבָּשָׂר הַחַי וְנֶהְפַּךְ לְלָבָן וּבָא אֶל־הַכֹּהֵן: ¹⁷וְרָאָהוּ הַכֹּהֵן וְהִנֵּה נֶהְפַּךְ הַנֶּגַע לְלָבָן וְטִהַר הַכֹּהֵן אֶת־הַנֶּגַע טָהוֹר הוּא: פ ¹⁸וּבָשָׂר כִּי־יִהְיֶה בוֹ־בְעֹרוֹ שְׁחִין וְנִרְפָּא: ¹⁹וְהָיָה בִּמְקוֹם הַשְּׁחִין שְׂאֵת לְבָנָה אוֹ בַהֶרֶת לְבָנָה אֲדַמְדָּמֶת וְנִרְאָה אֶל־הַכֹּהֵן: ²⁰וְרָאָה הַכֹּהֵן וְהִנֵּה מַרְאֶהָ שָׁפָל מִן־הָעוֹר וּשְׂעָרָהּ הָפַךְ לָבָן וְטִמְּאוֹ הַכֹּהֵן נֶגַע־צָרַעַת הִוא בַּשְּׁחִין פָּרָחָה: ²¹וְאִם יִרְאֶנָּה הַכֹּהֵן וְהִנֵּה אֵין־בָּהּ שֵׂעָר לָבָן וּשְׁפָלָה אֵינֶנָּה מִן־הָעוֹר וְהִיא כֵהָה וְהִסְגִּירוֹ הַכֹּהֵן שִׁבְעַת יָמִים: ²²וְאִם־פָּשֹׂה תִפְשֶׂה בָּעוֹר וְטִמֵּא הַכֹּהֵן אֹתוֹ נֶגַע הוּא: ²³וְאִם־תַּחְתֶּיהָ תַעֲמֹד

23And if the bright spot will have stayed the same in its place—it has not spread—it is the scar of the boil, and the priest shall identify him as pure.

24"Or when flesh will have a burn from a fire in its skin, and the vital part of the burn is a bright spot of reddish white or white, 25and the priest will see it, and, here, hair has turned white in the bright spot, and its appearance is lower than the skin, it is leprosy. It has developed in the burn. And the priest shall identify him as impure. It is an affliction of leprosy. 26And if the priest will see it, and, here, there is not white hair in the bright spot, and it is not lower than the skin, and it has become dim, then the priest shall shut him in seven days. 27And the priest shall see him on the seventh day. If it will *spread* in the skin, then the priest shall identify him as impure. It is an affliction of leprosy. 28And if the bright spot will have stayed the same in its place—it has not spread in the skin—and it has become dim, it is the swelling of the burn, and the priest shall identify him as pure, because it is the scar of the burn.

29"And when a man or woman will have an affliction in the head or beard, 30and the priest will see the affliction, and, here, its appearance is deeper than the skin, and there is thin yellow hair in it, then the priest shall identify him as impure. It is a scab. It is leprosy of the head or the beard. 31And when the priest will see the affliction of the scab, and, here, its appearance is not deeper than the skin, and there is not black hair in it, then the priest shall shut in the affliction of the scab seven days. 32And the priest shall see the affliction on the seventh day. And, here, the scab has not spread, and there is not yellow hair in it, and the scab's appearance is not deeper than the skin. 33Then he shall shave himself, and he shall not shave the scab. And the priest shall shut in the one with the scab seven days a second time. 34And the priest shall see the scab on the seventh day. And, here, the scab has not spread in the skin, and its appearance is not deeper than the skin. Then the priest shall identify him as pure. And he shall wash his clothes, and he shall be

הַבַּהֶ֙רֶת֙ לֹ֣א פָשָׂ֔תָה צָרֶ֥בֶת הַשְּׁחִ֖ין הִ֑וא וְטִהֲר֖וֹ הַכֹּהֵֽן׃ ס 24אֽוֹ בָשָׂ֕ר כִּֽי־יִהְיֶ֥ה בְעֹר֖וֹ מִכְוַת־אֵ֑שׁ וְֽהָיְתָ֞ה מִֽחְיַ֣ת הַמִּכְוָ֗ה בַּהֶ֛רֶת לְבָנָ֥ה אֲדַמְדֶּ֖מֶת א֥וֹ לְבָנָֽה׃ 25וְרָאָ֣ה אֹתָ֣הּ הַכֹּהֵ֡ן וְהִנֵּ֣ה נֶהְפַּךְ֩ שֵׂעָ֨ר לָבָ֜ן בַּבַּהֶ֗רֶת וּמַרְאֶ֙הָ֙ עָמֹ֣ק מִן־הָע֔וֹר צָרַ֣עַת הִ֔וא בַּמִּכְוָ֖ה פָּרָ֑חָה וְטִמֵּ֙א אֹת֜וֹ הַכֹּהֵ֗ן נֶ֥גַע צָרַ֖עַת הִֽוא׃ 26וְאִ֣ם ׀ יִרְאֶ֣נָּה הַכֹּהֵ֗ן וְהִנֵּ֤ה אֵֽין־בַּבַּהֶ֙רֶת֙ שֵׂעָ֣ר לָבָ֔ן וּשְׁפָלָ֥ה אֵינֶ֛נָּה מִן־הָע֖וֹר וְהִ֣וא כֵהָ֑ה וְהִסְגִּיר֥וֹ הַכֹּהֵ֖ן שִׁבְעַ֥ת יָמִֽים׃ 27וְרָאָ֥הוּ הַכֹּהֵ֖ן בַּיּ֣וֹם הַשְּׁבִיעִ֑י אִם־פָּשֹׂ֤ה תִפְשֶׂה֙ בָּע֔וֹר וְטִמֵּ֤א הַכֹּהֵן֙ אֹת֔וֹ נֶ֥גַע צָרַ֖עַת הִֽוא׃ 28וְאִם־תַּחְתֶּ֩יהָ֩ תַעֲמֹ֨ד הַבַּהֶ֜רֶת לֹא־פָשְׂתָ֤ה בָעוֹר֙ וְהִ֣וא כֵהָ֔ה שְׂאֵ֥ת הַמִּכְוָ֖ה הִ֑וא וְטִֽהֲרוֹ֙ הַכֹּהֵ֔ן כִּֽי־צָרֶ֥בֶת הַמִּכְוָ֖ה הִֽוא׃ פ 29וְאִישׁ֙ א֣וֹ אִשָּׁ֔ה כִּֽי־יִהְיֶ֥ה ב֖וֹ נָ֑גַע בְּרֹ֖אשׁ א֥וֹ בְזָקָֽן׃ 30וְרָאָ֨ה הַכֹּהֵ֜ן אֶת־הַנֶּ֗גַע וְהִנֵּ֤ה מַרְאֵ֙הוּ֙ עָמֹ֣ק מִן־הָע֔וֹר וּב֛וֹ שֵׂעָ֥ר צָהֹ֖ב דָּ֑ק וְטִמֵּ֙א אֹת֤וֹ הַכֹּהֵן֙ נֶ֣תֶק ה֔וּא צָרַ֧עַת הָרֹ֛אשׁ א֥וֹ הַזָּקָ֖ן הֽוּא׃ 31וְכִֽי־יִרְאֶ֨ה הַכֹּהֵ֜ן אֶת־נֶ֣גַע הַנֶּ֗תֶק וְהִנֵּ֤ה אֵֽין־מַרְאֵ֙הוּ֙ עָמֹ֣ק מִן־הָע֔וֹר וְשֵׂעָ֥ר שָׁחֹ֖ר אֵ֣ין בּ֑וֹ וְהִסְגִּ֧יר הַכֹּהֵ֛ן אֶת־נֶ֥גַע הַנֶּ֖תֶק שִׁבְעַ֥ת יָמִֽים׃ 32וְרָאָ֨ה הַכֹּהֵ֣ן אֶת־הַנֶּגַע֮ בַּיּ֣וֹם הַשְּׁבִיעִי֒ וְהִנֵּה֙ לֹא־פָשָׂ֣ה הַנֶּ֔תֶק וְלֹא־הָ֥יָה ב֖וֹ שֵׂעָ֣ר צָהֹ֑ב וּמַרְאֵ֣ה הַנֶּ֔תֶק אֵ֥ין עָמֹ֖ק מִן־הָעֽוֹר׃ 33וְהִ֨תְגַּלָּ֔ח וְאֶת־הַנֶּ֖תֶק לֹ֣א יְגַלֵּ֑חַ וְהִסְגִּ֧יר הַכֹּהֵ֛ן אֶת־הַנֶּ֖תֶק שִׁבְעַ֥ת יָמִ֖ים שֵׁנִֽית׃ 34וְרָאָה֩ הַכֹּהֵ֨ן אֶת־הַנֶּ֜תֶק בַּיּ֣וֹם הַשְּׁבִיעִ֗י וְהִנֵּ֡ה לֹא־פָשָׂ֤ה הַנֶּ֙תֶק֙ בָּע֔וֹר וּמַרְאֵ֕הוּ אֵינֶ֥נּוּ עָמֹ֖ק מִן־הָע֑וֹר וְטִהַ֤ר אֹתוֹ֙ הַכֹּהֵ֔ן וְכִבֶּ֥ס בְּגָדָ֖יו וְטָהֵֽר׃ 35וְאִם־פָּשֹׂ֤ה

pure. 35But if the scab *has* spread in the skin, after his purification, 36and the priest will see him, and, here, the scab has spread in the skin, the priest shall not inspect for the yellow hair. He is impure. 37And if, in his eyes, the scab has stayed the same, and black hair has developed in it, the scab has been healed. He is pure. And the priest shall identify him as pure.

38"And when a man or woman will have bright spots in the skin of their flesh, white bright spots, 39and the priest will see, and, here, bright spots in the skin of their flesh are dim white, it is a tetter. It has developed in the skin. He is pure.

40"And when a man's head will become hairless, he is bald. He is pure. 41And if his head will become hairless from the corner of his face, he has a bald forehead. He is pure. 42And when there will be in the bald head or in the bald forehead a reddish white affliction, it is leprosy developing in his bald head or in his bald forehead. 43And the priest will see it, and, here, the affliction's swelling is reddish white in his bald head or in his bald forehead, like the appearance of leprosy of skin of flesh, 44he is a leprous man. He is impure. The priest shall *identify him as impure*. His affliction is in his head. 45And the leper in whom is the affliction: his clothes shall be torn, and the hair of his head shall be loosed, and he shall cover over his mustache. And he shall call, 'Impure! Impure!' 46All the days that the affliction is in him he will be impure. He is impure. He shall live separate. His home is outside of the camp.

47"And when clothing will have an affliction of leprosy in it—in clothing of wool or in clothing of linen, 48either in the warp or in the woof of the linen or of the wool, or in leather or in anything made of leather: 49if the affliction will be greenish or reddish in the clothing or in the

יִפְשֶׂה הַנֶּתֶק בָּעוֹר אַחֲרֵי טָהֳרָתוֹ: 36וְרָאָהוּ הַכֹּהֵן וְהִנֵּה פָּשָׂה הַנֶּתֶק בָּעוֹר לֹא־יְבַקֵּר הַכֹּהֵן לַשֵּׂעָר הַצָּהֹב טָמֵא הוּא: 37וְאִם־בְּעֵינָיו עָמַד הַנֶּתֶק וְשֵׂעָר שָׁחֹר צָמַח־בּוֹ נִרְפָּא הַנֶּתֶק טָהוֹר הוּא וְטִהֲרוֹ הַכֹּהֵן: ס 38וְאִישׁ אוֹ־אִשָּׁה כִּי־יִהְיֶה בְעוֹר־בְּשָׂרָם בֶּהָרֹת בֶּהָרֹת לְבָנֹת: 39וְרָאָה הַכֹּהֵן וְהִנֵּה בְעוֹר־בְּשָׂרָם בֶּהָרֹת כֵּהוֹת לְבָנֹת בֹּהַק הוּא פָּרַח בָּעוֹר טָהוֹר הוּא: ס 40וְאִישׁ כִּי יִמָּרֵט רֹאשׁוֹ קֵרֵחַ הוּא טָהוֹר הוּא: 41וְאִם מִפְּאַת פָּנָיו יִמָּרֵט רֹאשׁוֹ גִּבֵּחַ הוּא טָהוֹר הוּא: 42וְכִי־יִהְיֶה בַקָּרַחַת אוֹ בַגַּבַּחַת נֶגַע לָבָן אֲדַמְדָּם צָרַעַת פֹּרַחַת הִוא בְּקָרַחְתּוֹ אוֹ בְגַבַּחְתּוֹ: 43וְרָאָה אֹתוֹ הַכֹּהֵן וְהִנֵּה שְׂאֵת־הַנֶּגַע לְבָנָה אֲדַמְדֶּמֶת בְּקָרַחְתּוֹ אוֹ בְגַבַּחְתּוֹ כְּמַרְאֵה צָרַעַת עוֹר בָּשָׂר: 44אִישׁ־צָרוּעַ הוּא טָמֵא הוּא טַמֵּא יְטַמְּאֶנּוּ הַכֹּהֵן בְּרֹאשׁוֹ נִגְעוֹ: 45וְהַצָּרוּעַ אֲשֶׁר־בּוֹ הַנֶּגַע בְּגָדָיו יִהְיוּ פְרֻמִים וְרֹאשׁוֹ יִהְיֶה פָרוּעַ וְעַל־שָׂפָם יַעְטֶה וְטָמֵא ׀ טָמֵא יִקְרָא: 46כָּל־יְמֵי אֲשֶׁר הַנֶּגַע בּוֹ יִטְמָא טָמֵא הוּא בָּדָד יֵשֵׁב מִחוּץ לַמַּחֲנֶה מוֹשָׁבוֹ: ס 47וְהַבֶּגֶד כִּי־יִהְיֶה בוֹ נֶגַע צָרַעַת בְּבֶגֶד צֶמֶר אוֹ בְּבֶגֶד פִּשְׁתִּים: 48אוֹ בִשְׁתִי אוֹ בְעֵרֶב לַפִּשְׁתִּים וְלַצָּמֶר אוֹ בְעוֹר אוֹ בְּכָל־מְלֶאכֶת עוֹר: 49וְהָיָה הַנֶּגַע יְרַקְרַק ׀ אוֹ אֲדַמְדָּם

13:41. **the corner of his face.** The hair around the forehead.

13:45. **he shall call, 'Impure! Impure!'** It has been said that the reason for this is so that people will pray for the afflicted person. The apparent reason, however, is to warn people away, to avoid the spread of impurity.

leather or in the warp or in the woof or in any item of leather, it is an affliction of leprosy—and it will be shown to the priest, ⁵⁰and the priest will see the affliction, and he shall shut in the thing with the affliction seven days. ⁵¹And he shall see the affliction on the seventh day: if the affliction has spread in the clothing or in the warp or in the woof or in the leather, or any work into which the leather will be made, the affliction is malignant leprosy. It is impure. ⁵²And he shall burn the clothing or the warp or the woof in the wool or in the linen or any item of leather in which the affliction will be, because it is malignant leprosy. It shall be burned in fire. ⁵³And if the priest will look, and, here, the affliction has not spread in the clothing or in the warp or in the woof or any item of leather, ⁵⁴then the priest shall command, and they shall wash the thing in which the affliction is, and he shall shut it in seven days a second time. ⁵⁵And the priest shall see the affliction after it will be washed, and, here, the affliction has not changed its appearance, and the affliction will not have spread, it is impure. You shall burn it in fire. It is a deterioration, in its 'bald head' or in its 'forehead.' ⁵⁶If the priest will see, and, here, the affliction has become dim after it was washed, then he shall rip it from the clothing or from the leather or from the warp or from the woof. ⁵⁷And if it will appear again in the clothing or in the warp or in the woof or in any item of leather, it is developing. You shall burn it, the thing in which the affliction is, in fire. ⁵⁸And the clothing or the warp or the woof or any item of leather that you will wash: if the affliction will turn away from them, then it shall be washed a second time, and it will be pure.

⁵⁹"This is the instruction for the affliction of leprosy of clothing of wool or linen or warp or woof or any item of leather, to identify it as pure or to identify it as impure."

בַּבֶּ֙גֶד֙ א֣וֹ בָע֔וֹר אֽוֹ־בַשְּׁתִ֥י אֽוֹ־בָעֵ֖רֶב א֣וֹ בְכָל־כְּלִי־ע֑וֹר נֶ֤גַע צָרַ֙עַת֙ ה֔וּא וְהָרְאָ֖ה אֶת־הַכֹּהֵֽן: ⁵⁰וְרָאָ֣ה הַכֹּהֵ֖ן אֶת־הַנָּ֑גַע וְהִסְגִּ֥יר אֶת־הַנֶּ֖גַע שִׁבְעַ֥ת יָמִֽים: ⁵¹וְרָאָ֨ה אֶת־הַנֶּ֜גַע בַּיּ֣וֹם הַשְּׁבִיעִ֗י כִּֽי־פָשָׂ֤ה הַנֶּ֙גַע֙ בַּבֶּ֜גֶד אֽוֹ־בַשְּׁתִ֤י אֽוֹ־בָעֵ֙רֶב֙ א֣וֹ בָע֔וֹר לְכֹ֛ל אֲשֶׁר־יֵעָשֶׂ֥ה הָע֖וֹר לִמְלָאכָ֑ה צָרַ֧עַת מַמְאֶ֛רֶת הַנֶּ֖גַע טָמֵ֥א הֽוּא: ⁵²וְשָׂרַ֞ף אֶת־הַבֶּ֗גֶד א֤וֹ אֶֽת־הַשְּׁתִי֙ א֣וֹ אֶת־הָעֵ֜רֶב בַּצֶּ֤מֶר א֣וֹ בַפִּשְׁתִּ֗ים א֤וֹ אֶת־כָּל־כְּלִ֣י הָע֔וֹר אֲשֶׁר־יִהְיֶ֥ה ב֖וֹ הַנָּ֑גַע כִּֽי־צָרַ֤עַת מַמְאֶ֙רֶת֙ הִ֔וא בָּאֵ֖שׁ תִּשָּׂרֵֽף: ⁵³וְאִם֙ יִרְאֶ֣ה הַכֹּהֵ֔ן וְהִנֵּה֙ לֹֽא־פָשָׂ֣ה הַנֶּ֔גַע בַּבֶּ֖גֶד א֣וֹ בַשְּׁתִ֑י א֣וֹ בָעֵ֔רֶב א֖וֹ בְּכָל־כְּלִי־עֽוֹר: ⁵⁴וְצִוָּה֙ הַכֹּהֵ֔ן וְכִ֨בְּס֔וּ אֵ֛ת אֲשֶׁר־בּ֥וֹ הַנָּ֖גַע וְהִסְגִּיר֥וֹ שִׁבְעַת־יָמִ֖ים שֵׁנִֽית: ⁵⁵וְרָאָ֣ה הַכֹּהֵ֗ן אַחֲרֵ֣י ׀ הֻכַּבֵּ֣ס אֶת־הַנֶּ֗גַע וְ֠הִנֵּה לֹֽא־הָפַ֨ךְ הַנֶּ֤גַע אֶת־עֵינוֹ֙ וְהַנֶּ֣גַע לֹֽא־פָשָׂ֗ה טָמֵ֥א הוּא֙ בָּאֵ֣שׁ תִּשְׂרְפֶ֔נּוּ פְּחֶ֣תֶת הִ֔וא בְּקָרַחְתּ֖וֹ א֥וֹ בְגַבַּחְתּֽוֹ: ⁵⁶וְאִם֩ רָאָ֨ה הַכֹּהֵ֜ן וְהִנֵּה֙ כֵּהָ֣ה הַנֶּ֔גַע אַחֲרֵ֖י הֻכַּבֵּ֣ס אֹת֑וֹ וְקָרַ֣ע אֹת֗וֹ מִן־הַבֶּ֙גֶד֙ א֣וֹ מִן־הָע֔וֹר א֥וֹ מִן־הַשְּׁתִ֖י א֥וֹ מִן־הָעֵֽרֶב: ⁵⁷וְאִם־תֵּרָאֶ֨ה ע֜וֹד בַּבֶּ֤גֶד אֽוֹ־בַשְּׁתִי֙ אֽוֹ־בָעֵ֔רֶב א֖וֹ בְכָל־כְּלִי־עוֹר֙ פֹּרַ֣חַת הִ֔וא בָּאֵ֣שׁ תִּשְׂרְפֶ֔נּוּ אֵ֥ת אֲשֶׁר־בּ֖וֹ הַנָּֽגַע: ⁵⁸וְהַבֶּ֡גֶד אֽוֹ־הַשְּׁתִ֨י אֽוֹ־הָעֵ֜רֶב אֽוֹ־כָל־כְּלִ֣י הָע֗וֹר אֲשֶׁ֤ר תְּכַבֵּס֙ וְסָ֣ר מֵהֶ֣ם הַנָּ֔גַע וְכֻבַּ֥ס שֵׁנִ֖ית וְטָהֵֽר: ⁵⁹זֹ֠את תּוֹרַ֨ת נֶֽגַע־צָרַ֜עַת בֶּ֤גֶד הַצֶּ֙מֶר֙ א֣וֹ הַפִּשְׁתִּ֔ים א֥וֹ הַשְּׁתִ֖י א֣וֹ הָעֵ֑רֶב א֖וֹ כָּל־כְּלִי־ע֑וֹר לְטַהֲר֖וֹ א֥וֹ לְטַמְּאֽוֹ: פ

13:55. **in its "bald head" or in its "forehead."** Meaning: on the clothing's inside or its outside.

LEPER

מצורע

14 [1]And YHWH spoke to Moses, saying, [2]"This shall be the instruction for the leper in the day of his purification: And he shall be brought to the priest, [3]and the priest shall go outside the camp, and the priest shall see, and if, here, the affliction of leprosy has been healed from the leper, [4]then the priest shall command, and one shall take two live, pure birds and cedarwood and scarlet and hyssop for the one being purified. [5]And the priest shall command, and he shall slaughter one of the birds in a clay container over living water. [6]The live bird: he shall take it and the cedarwood and the scarlet and the hyssop, and he shall dip them and the live bird in the slaughtered bird's blood over the living water. [7]And he shall sprinkle it on the one being purified from the leprosy seven times. And he shall identify him as pure. And he shall let the live bird go at the open field. [8]And the one being purified shall wash his clothes and shave all his hair and wash in water, and he will be pure, and after that he shall come to the camp. And he shall live outside his tent seven days. [9]And it will be, on the seventh day: he shall shave all his hair—he shall shave his head and his beard and his eyebrows and all his hair—and he shall wash his clothes and wash his flesh in water, and he will be pure. [10]And on the eighth day he shall take two unblemished he-lambs and one unblemished ewe-lamb in its first year and three-

14 ‏1וַיְדַבֵּ֥ר יְהוָ֖ה אֶל־מֹשֶׁ֥ה לֵּאמֹֽר: ‏2זֹ֤את תִּֽהְיֶה֙ תּוֹרַ֣ת הַמְּצֹרָ֔ע בְּי֖וֹם טָהֳרָת֑וֹ וְהוּבָ֖א אֶל־הַכֹּהֵֽן: ‏3וְיָצָא֙ הַכֹּהֵ֔ן אֶל־מִח֖וּץ לַֽמַּחֲנֶ֑ה וְרָאָה֙ הַכֹּהֵ֔ן וְהִנֵּ֛ה נִרְפָּ֥א נֶֽגַע־הַצָּרַ֖עַת מִן־הַצָּרֽוּעַ: ‏4וְצִוָּה֙ הַכֹּהֵ֔ן וְלָקַ֧ח לַמִּטַּהֵ֛ר שְׁתֵּֽי־צִפֳּרִ֥ים חַיּ֖וֹת טְהֹר֑וֹת וְעֵ֣ץ אֶ֔רֶז וּשְׁנִ֥י תוֹלַ֖עַת וְאֵזֹֽב: ‏5וְצִוָּה֙ הַכֹּהֵ֔ן וְשָׁחַ֖ט אֶת־הַצִּפּ֣וֹר הָאֶחָ֑ת אֶל־כְּלִי־חֶ֖רֶשׂ עַל־מַ֥יִם חַיִּֽים: ‏6אֶת־הַצִּפֹּ֣ר הַֽחַיָּ֗ה יִקַּ֣ח אֹתָ֔הּ וְאֶת־עֵ֥ץ הָאֶ֛רֶז וְאֶת־שְׁנִ֥י הַתּוֹלַ֖עַת וְאֶת־הָאֵזֹ֑ב וְטָבַ֣ל אוֹתָ֗ם וְאֵ֣ת ׀ הַצִּפֹּ֣ר הַֽחַיָּ֔ה בְּדַם֙ הַצִּפֹּ֣ר הַשְּׁחֻטָ֔ה עַ֖ל הַמַּ֥יִם הַֽחַיִּֽים: ‏7וְהִזָּ֗ה עַ֧ל הַמִּטַּהֵ֛ר מִן־הַצָּרַ֖עַת שֶׁ֣בַע פְּעָמִ֑ים וְטִ֣הֲר֔וֹ וְשִׁלַּ֛ח אֶת־הַצִּפֹּ֥ר הַֽחַיָּ֖ה עַל־פְּנֵ֥י הַשָּׂדֶֽה: ‏8וְכִבֶּס֩ הַמִּטַּהֵ֨ר אֶת־בְּגָדָ֜יו וְגִלַּ֣ח אֶת־כָּל־שְׂעָר֗וֹ וְרָחַ֤ץ בַּמַּ֙יִם֙ וְטָהֵ֔ר וְאַחַ֖ר יָב֣וֹא אֶל־הַֽמַּחֲנֶ֑ה וְיָשַׁ֛ב מִח֥וּץ לְאָֽהֳל֖וֹ שִׁבְעַ֥ת יָמִֽים: ‏9וְהָיָה֩ בַיּ֨וֹם הַשְּׁבִיעִ֜י יְגַלַּ֣ח אֶת־כָּל־שְׂעָר֗וֹ אֶת־רֹאשׁ֤וֹ וְאֶת־זְקָנוֹ֙ וְאֵת֙ גַּבֹּ֣ת עֵינָ֔יו וְאֶת־כָּל־שְׂעָר֖וֹ יְגַלֵּ֑חַ וְכִבֶּ֣ס אֶת־בְּגָדָ֗יו וְרָחַ֧ץ אֶת־בְּשָׂר֛וֹ בַּמַּ֖יִם וְטָהֵֽר: ‏10וּבַיּ֣וֹם הַשְּׁמִינִ֗י יִקַּ֤ח שְׁנֵֽי־כְבָשִׂים֙ תְּמִימִ֔ם וְכַבְשָׂ֥ה אַחַ֛ת בַּת־שְׁנָתָ֖הּ תְּמִימָ֑ה וּשְׁלֹשָׁ֣ה

14:3. the priest shall see. Again, the priest is not a physician. The priest has identified the condition (in the preceding chapter) and now sees that the condition is healed. So what follows is not a ritual of healing. The person is already healed. It is a ritual of purification.

14:5. living water. On the meaning of מַיִם חַיִּים (*mayim ḥayyîm*): this seems to be indicated by Gen 26:19 and Song of Songs 4:15 to be freshwater flowing from a well or other natural source, as opposed to stagnant or stored water. I have heard it compared to a *mikveh* by Rabbi Martin Lawson. That is especially interesting in the light of Jer 17:13, where God is referred to first as "Israel's hope" (מִקְוֵה יִשְׂרָאֵל—*miqwēh yiśrā'ēl*) and then in the same verse as "source of living water" (מְקוֹר מַיִם חַיִּים—*mĕqôr mayim ḥayyîm*).

tenths of a measure of fine flour as a grain offering mixed with oil and one log of oil. 11And the priest who is purifying shall have the man being purified and them stand in front of YHWH at the entrance of the Tent of Meeting. 12And the priest shall take one of the lambs and bring it forward as a guilt offering and the log of oil, and he shall elevate them, an elevation offering in front of YHWH. 13And he shall slaughter the lamb in the place where he slaughters the sin offering and the burnt offering, in the place of the Holy, because, like the sin offering, the guilt offering is the priest's. It is the holy of holies. 14And the priest shall take some of the blood of the guilt offering, and the priest shall put it on the right earlobe of the one being purified and on the thumb of his right hand and on the big toe of his right foot. 15And the priest shall take some of the log of oil and pour it on the priest's left hand. 16And the priest shall dip his right finger in some of the oil that is on his left hand and sprinkle some of the oil with his finger seven times in front of YHWH. 17And the priest shall put some of the remaining oil that is on his hand on the right earlobe of the one being purified and on the thumb of his right hand and on the big toe of his right foot, over the blood of the guilt offering. 18And he shall put what is left of the oil that is on the priest's hand on the head of the one being purified. And the priest shall make atonement over him in front of YHWH. 19And the priest shall make the sin offering and make atonement over the one being purified from his impurity, and after that he shall slaughter the burnt offering. 20And the priest shall make the burnt offering and the grain offering at the altar.

עֶשְׂרֹנִים סֹלֶת מִנְחָה בְּלוּלָה בַשֶּׁמֶן וְלֹג אֶחָד שָׁמֶן: 11וְהֶעֱמִיד הַכֹּהֵן הַמְטַהֵר אֵת הָאִישׁ הַמִּטַּהֵר וְאֹתָם לִפְנֵי יְהוָה פֶּתַח אֹהֶל מוֹעֵד: 12וְלָקַח הַכֹּהֵן אֶת־הַכֶּבֶשׂ הָאֶחָד וְהִקְרִיב אֹתוֹ לְאָשָׁם וְאֶת־לֹג הַשָּׁמֶן וְהֵנִיף אֹתָם תְּנוּפָה לִפְנֵי יְהוָה: 13וְשָׁחַט אֶת־הַכֶּבֶשׂ בִּמְקוֹם אֲשֶׁר יִשְׁחַט אֶת־הַחַטָּאת וְאֶת־הָעֹלָה בִּמְקוֹם הַקֹּדֶשׁ כִּי כַּחַטָּאת הָאָשָׁם הוּא לַכֹּהֵן קֹדֶשׁ קָדָשִׁים הוּא: 14וְלָקַח הַכֹּהֵן מִדַּם הָאָשָׁם וְנָתַן הַכֹּהֵן עַל־תְּנוּךְ אֹזֶן הַמִּטַּהֵר הַיְמָנִית וְעַל־בֹּהֶן יָדוֹ הַיְמָנִית וְעַל־בֹּהֶן רַגְלוֹ הַיְמָנִית: 15וְלָקַח הַכֹּהֵן מִלֹּג הַשָּׁמֶן וְיָצַק עַל־כַּף הַכֹּהֵן הַשְּׂמָאלִית: 16וְטָבַל הַכֹּהֵן אֶת־אֶצְבָּעוֹ הַיְמָנִית מִן־הַשֶּׁמֶן אֲשֶׁר עַל־כַּפּוֹ הַשְּׂמָאלִית וְהִזָּה מִן־הַשֶּׁמֶן בְּאֶצְבָּעוֹ שֶׁבַע פְּעָמִים לִפְנֵי יְהוָה: 17וּמִיֶּתֶר הַשֶּׁמֶן אֲשֶׁר עַל־כַּפּוֹ יִתֵּן הַכֹּהֵן עַל־תְּנוּךְ אֹזֶן הַמִּטַּהֵר הַיְמָנִית וְעַל־בֹּהֶן יָדוֹ הַיְמָנִית וְעַל־בֹּהֶן רַגְלוֹ הַיְמָנִית עַל דַּם הָאָשָׁם: 18וְהַנּוֹתָר בַּשֶּׁמֶן אֲשֶׁר עַל־כַּף הַכֹּהֵן יִתֵּן עַל־רֹאשׁ הַמִּטַּהֵר וְכִפֶּר עָלָיו הַכֹּהֵן לִפְנֵי יְהוָה: 19וְעָשָׂה הַכֹּהֵן אֶת־הַחַטָּאת וְכִפֶּר עַל־הַמִּטַּהֵר מִטֻּמְאָתוֹ וְאַחַר יִשְׁחַט אֶת־הָעֹלָה: 20וְהֶעֱלָה הַכֹּהֵן אֶת־הָעֹלָה וְאֶת־הַמִּנְחָה הַמִּזְבֵּחָה וְכִפֶּר עָלָיו

14:10. **log.** A liquid measure (thought to be about one-half liter).

14:14. **blood on the right earlobe, thumb, and big toe.** This is the same as the ceremony for ordaining Aaron and his sons as priests (Lev 8:23–24). In both cases, there is a transition. Here it is from impure to pure. In the priestly case it is from secular to holy. Both apparently call for placing blood on the body's three extremities (ear, thumb, toe) to convey that the entire body is thus covered by this purification.

And the priest shall make atonement over him, and he will be pure.

21"And if he is poor, and his hand cannot attain enough, then he shall take one lamb, a guilt offering, for elevation, for making atonement over him, and one-tenth of a measure of fine flour mixed with oil for a grain offering and a log of oil 22and two turtledoves or two pigeons, whichever his hand can attain, and one shall be a sin offering and one a burnt offering. 23And he shall bring them on the eighth day of his purification to the priest, to the entrance of the Tent of Meeting, in front of YHWH. 24And the priest shall take the lamb of the guilt offering and the log of oil, and the priest shall elevate them, an elevation offering in front of YHWH. 25And he shall slaughter the lamb of the guilt offering, and the priest shall take some of the blood of the guilt offering and put it on the right earlobe of the one being purified and on the thumb of his right hand and on the big toe of his right foot. 26And the priest shall pour some of the oil on the priest's left hand, 27and the priest shall sprinkle some of the oil that is on his left hand with his right finger seven times in front of YHWH. 28And the priest shall put some of the oil that is on his hand on the right earlobe of the one being purified and on the thumb of his right hand and on the big toe of his right foot, over the place of the blood of the guilt offering. 29And what is left of the oil that is on the priest's hand he shall put on the head of the one being purified to make atonement over him in front of YHWH. 30And he shall make one of the turtledoves or the pi-

הַכֹּהֵן וְטָהֵר: ס 21וְאִם־דַּל הוּא וְאֵין יָדוֹ מַשֶּׂגֶת וְלָקַח כֶּבֶשׂ אֶחָד אָשָׁם לִתְנוּפָה לְכַפֵּר עָלָיו וְעִשָּׂרוֹן סֹלֶת אֶחָד בָּלוּל בַּשֶּׁמֶן לְמִנְחָה וְלֹג שָׁמֶן: 22וּשְׁתֵּי תֹרִים אוֹ שְׁנֵי בְּנֵי יוֹנָה אֲשֶׁר תַּשִּׂיג יָדוֹ וְהָיָה אֶחָד חַטָּאת וְהָאֶחָד עֹלָה: 23וְהֵבִיא אֹתָם בַּיּוֹם הַשְּׁמִינִי לְטָהֳרָתוֹ אֶל־הַכֹּהֵן אֶל־פֶּתַח אֹהֶל־מוֹעֵד לִפְנֵי יְהוָה: 24וְלָקַח הַכֹּהֵן אֶת־כֶּבֶשׂ הָאָשָׁם וְאֶת־לֹג הַשָּׁמֶן וְהֵנִיף אֹתָם הַכֹּהֵן תְּנוּפָה לִפְנֵי יְהוָה: 25וְשָׁחַט אֶת־כֶּבֶשׂ הָאָשָׁם וְלָקַח הַכֹּהֵן מִדַּם הָאָשָׁם וְנָתַן עַל־תְּנוּךְ אֹזֶן־הַמִּטַּהֵר הַיְמָנִית וְעַל־בֹּהֶן יָדוֹ הַיְמָנִית וְעַל־בֹּהֶן רַגְלוֹ הַיְמָנִית: 26וּמִן־הַשֶּׁמֶן יִצֹק הַכֹּהֵן עַל־כַּף הַכֹּהֵן הַשְּׂמָאלִית: 27וְהִזָּה הַכֹּהֵן בְּאֶצְבָּעוֹ הַיְמָנִית מִן־הַשֶּׁמֶן אֲשֶׁר עַל־כַּפּוֹ הַשְּׂמָאלִית שֶׁבַע פְּעָמִים לִפְנֵי יְהוָה: 28וְנָתַן הַכֹּהֵן מִן־הַשֶּׁמֶן אֲשֶׁר עַל־כַּפּוֹ עַל־תְּנוּךְ אֹזֶן הַמִּטַּהֵר הַיְמָנִית וְעַל־בֹּהֶן יָדוֹ הַיְמָנִית וְעַל־בֹּהֶן רַגְלוֹ הַיְמָנִית עַל־מְקוֹם דַּם הָאָשָׁם: 29וְהַנּוֹתָר מִן־הַשֶּׁמֶן אֲשֶׁר עַל־כַּף הַכֹּהֵן יִתֵּן עַל־רֹאשׁ הַמִּטַּהֵר לְכַפֵּר עָלָיו לִפְנֵי יְהוָה: 30וְעָשָׂה אֶת־הָאֶחָד מִן־הַתֹּרִים אוֹ מִן־בְּנֵי הַיּוֹנָה מֵאֲשֶׁר תַּשִּׂיג

14:20. **and he will be pure.** My old classmate Danny Siegel says concerning Parashat Meṣora that it is about bringing people who are infirm back into the community. As derivative practices in our own time he gives as examples: (1) synagogues that have installed ramps to the *bimah* for handicapped persons; and (2) balloons for the deaf so they can experience the vibrating sound of the shofar on Rosh Hashanah. As we were once responsible to return and include those who were impure to the congregation, so we may learn to include the handicapped as well. It is inspirational that we can derive this essential principle from a parashah in the Torah that seems so remote to readers in this age.

geons, from those which his hand can attain—
31whichever his hand will attain—one a sin offering and one a burnt offering, with the grain
offering, and the priest shall make atonement
over the one being purified in front of YHWH.

32"This is the instruction for one who has an
affliction of leprosy in him, whose hand cannot
attain enough for his purification."

33And YHWH spoke to Moses and to Aaron,
saying, 34"When you will come to the land of Canaan, which I am giving to you as a possession,
and I shall put an affliction of leprosy in a house
at the land of your possession, 35and the one
whose house it is will come and tell the priest,
saying, 'It appears like an affliction to me in the
house,' 36then the priest shall command, and
they shall clear the house before the priest will
come to see the affliction, so everything that is in
the house will not become impure. And, after
that, the priest shall come to see the house.
37And he shall see the affliction, and, here, the
affliction in the walls of the house is greenish or
reddish streaks, and their appearance is deeper
than the wall; 38then the priest shall come out
from the house, to the entrance of the house, and
he shall shut the house up seven days. 39And the
priest shall go back on the seventh day and see,
and, here, the affliction has spread in the walls of
the house; 40then the priest shall command, and
they shall extract the stones in which is the affliction, and they shall throw them outside the
city, to an impure place. 41And he shall have the
house scraped inside, all around, and they shall

יָדֽוֹ: 31אֵ֣ת אֲשֶׁר־תַּשִּׂ֣יג יָד֗וֹ אֶת־הָאֶחָ֤ד חַטָּאת֙ וְאֶת־
הָאֶחָ֣ד עֹלָ֔ה עַל־הַמִּנְחָ֑ה וְכִפֶּ֧ר הַכֹּהֵ֛ן עַ֥ל הַמִּטַּהֵ֖ר
לִפְנֵ֥י יְהוָֽה: 32זֹ֣את תּוֹרַ֔ת אֲשֶׁר־בּ֖וֹ נֶ֣גַע צָרָ֑עַת אֲשֶׁ֛ר
לֹֽא־תַשִּׂ֥יג יָד֖וֹ בְּטָהֳרָתֽוֹ: פ

33וַיְדַבֵּ֣ר יְהוָ֔ה אֶל־מֹשֶׁ֥ה וְאֶֽל־אַהֲרֹ֖ן לֵאמֹֽר:
34כִּ֤י תָבֹ֙אוּ֙ אֶל־אֶ֣רֶץ כְּנַ֔עַן אֲשֶׁ֥ר אֲנִ֛י נֹתֵ֥ן לָכֶ֖ם
לַאֲחֻזָּ֑ה וְנָתַתִּי֙ נֶ֣גַע צָרַ֔עַת בְּבֵ֖ית אֶ֥רֶץ אֲחֻזַּתְכֶֽם:
35וּבָ֙א אֲשֶׁר־ל֣וֹ הַבַּ֔יִת וְהִגִּ֥יד לַכֹּהֵ֖ן לֵאמֹ֑ר כְּנֶ֕גַע
נִרְאָ֥ה לִ֖י בַּבָּֽיִת: 36וְצִוָּ֣ה הַכֹּהֵ֗ן וּפִנּ֤וּ אֶת־הַבַּ֙יִת֙
בְּטֶ֨רֶם יָבֹ֤א הַכֹּהֵן֙ לִרְא֣וֹת אֶת־הַנֶּ֔גַע וְלֹ֥א יִטְמָ֖א
כָּל־אֲשֶׁ֣ר בַּבָּ֑יִת וְאַ֣חַר כֵּ֗ן יָבֹ֥א הַכֹּהֵ֖ן לִרְא֥וֹת אֶת־
הַבָּֽיִת: 37וְרָאָ֣ה אֶת־הַנֶּ֗גַע וְהִנֵּ֤ה הַנֶּ֙גַע֙ בְּקִירֹ֣ת הַבַּ֔יִת
שְׁקַֽעֲרוּרֹת֙ יְרַקְרַקֹּ֔ת א֖וֹ אֲדַמְדַּמֹּ֑ת וּמַרְאֵיהֶ֥ן שָׁפָ֖ל
מִן־הַקִּֽיר: 38וְיָצָ֧א הַכֹּהֵ֛ן מִן־הַבַּ֖יִת אֶל־פֶּ֣תַח הַבָּ֑יִת
וְהִסְגִּ֥יר אֶת־הַבַּ֖יִת שִׁבְעַ֥ת יָמִֽים: 39וְשָׁ֥ב הַכֹּהֵ֖ן בַּיּ֣וֹם
הַשְּׁבִיעִ֑י וְרָאָ֕ה וְהִנֵּ֛ה פָּשָׂ֥ה הַנֶּ֖גַע בְּקִירֹ֥ת הַבָּֽיִת:
40וְצִוָּה֙ הַכֹּהֵ֔ן וְחִלְּצוּ֙ אֶת־הָ֣אֲבָנִ֔ים אֲשֶׁ֥ר בָּהֵ֖ן הַנָּ֑גַע
וְהִשְׁלִ֤יכוּ אֶתְהֶן֙ אֶל־מִח֣וּץ לָעִ֔יר אֶל־מָק֖וֹם טָמֵֽא:
41וְאֶת־הַבַּ֛יִת יַקְצִ֥עַ מִבַּ֖יִת סָבִ֑יב וְשָׁפְכ֗וּ אֶת־הֶֽעָפָר֙

14:36. **they shall clear the house**. They clear the house before the priest comes to
examine the house "so everything that is in the house will not become impure." One
might ask why the house's contents are exempted from the examination? What if the
impurity has already spread? But when the priest comes to examine the house, if he
finds an affliction in the walls he has the house sealed for a week. It is when the house
is thus sealed that the affliction can spread. (Thus the people who have been in the
house prior to the sealing are not rendered impure, but anyone who enters the house
during the week that it is sealed *is* rendered impure; v. 46.) Therefore, they clear the
house before the priest's examination.

spill the dust that they have scraped outside the city, to an impure place. ⁴²And they shall take other stones and bring them in place of the stones, and he shall take other dust and coat the house. ⁴³And if the affliction will come back and develop in the house after he has extracted the stones and after scraping the house and after being coated, ⁴⁴then the priest shall come and see, and, here, the affliction has spread in the house, it is malignant leprosy in the house. It is impure. ⁴⁵And he shall demolish the house: its stones and its wood and all the dust of the house; and he shall take it outside the city, to an impure place. ⁴⁶And one who comes into the house all the days that it is shut up will be impure until evening, ⁴⁷and one who lies in the house shall wash his clothes, and one who eats in the house shall wash his clothes. ⁴⁸And if the priest will come and see, and, here, the affliction has not spread in the house after coating the house, then the priest shall identify the house as pure, because the affliction has been healed. ⁴⁹And, to decontaminate the house, he shall take two birds and cedarwood and scarlet and hyssop, ⁵⁰and he shall slaughter one of the birds in a clay container over living water. ⁵¹And he shall take the cedarwood and the hyssop and the scarlet and the live bird and dip them in the blood of the slaughtered bird and in the living water, and he shall sprinkle it at the house seven times. ⁵²And he shall decontaminate the house with the bird's blood and with the living water and with the live bird and with the cedarwood and with the hyssop and with the scarlet. ⁵³And he shall let the live bird go outside the city at the open field. And he shall make atonement over the house, and it will be pure.

⁵⁴"This is the instruction for every affliction of leprosy and for a scab ⁵⁵and for leprosy of clothing and for a house ⁵⁶and for a swelling and for a rash and for a bright spot, ⁵⁷to instruct on the day of the impure and on the day of the pure. This is the instruction for leprosy."

אֲשֶׁ֣ר הִקְצ֗וּ אֶל־מִח֛וּץ לָעִ֖יר אֶל־מָק֥וֹם טָמֵֽא׃
⁴²וְלָקְחוּ֙ אֲבָנִ֣ים אֲחֵר֔וֹת וְהֵבִ֖יאוּ אֶל־תַּ֣חַת הָאֲבָנִ֑ים וְעָפָ֥ר אַחֵ֛ר יִקַּ֖ח וְטָ֥ח אֶת־הַבָּֽיִת׃ ⁴³וְאִם־יָשׁ֤וּב הַנֶּ֨גַע֙ וּפָרַ֣ח בַּבַּ֔יִת אַחַ֖ר חִלֵּ֣ץ אֶת־הָאֲבָנִ֑ים וְאַחֲרֵ֛י הִקְצ֥וֹת אֶת־הַבַּ֖יִת וְאַחֲרֵ֥י הִטּֽוֹחַ׃ ⁴⁴וּבָא֙ הַכֹּהֵ֔ן וְרָאָ֕ה וְהִנֵּ֛ה פָּשָׂ֥ה הַנֶּ֖גַע בַּבָּ֑יִת צָרַ֨עַת מַמְאֶ֧רֶת הִ֛וא בַּבַּ֖יִת טָמֵ֥א הֽוּא׃ ⁴⁵וְנָתַ֣ץ אֶת־הַבַּ֗יִת אֶת־אֲבָנָיו֙ וְאֶת־עֵצָ֔יו וְאֵ֖ת כָּל־עֲפַ֣ר הַבָּ֑יִת וְהוֹצִיא֙ אֶל־מִח֣וּץ לָעִ֔יר אֶל־מָק֖וֹם טָמֵֽא׃ ⁴⁶וְהַבָּא֙ אֶל־הַבַּ֔יִת כָּל־יְמֵ֖י הִסְגִּ֣יר אֹת֑וֹ יִטְמָ֖א עַד־הָעָֽרֶב׃ ⁴⁷וְהַשֹּׁכֵ֣ב בַּבַּ֔יִת יְכַבֵּ֖ס אֶת־בְּגָדָ֑יו וְהָאֹכֵ֣ל בַּבַּ֔יִת יְכַבֵּ֖ס אֶת־בְּגָדָֽיו׃ ⁴⁸וְאִם־בֹּ֨א יָבֹ֜א הַכֹּהֵ֗ן וְרָאָה֙ וְ֠הִנֵּה לֹא־פָשָׂ֤ה הַנֶּ֨גַע֙ בַּבַּ֔יִת אַחֲרֵ֖י הִטֹּ֣חַ אֶת־הַבָּ֑יִת וְטִהַ֤ר הַכֹּהֵן֙ אֶת־הַבַּ֔יִת כִּ֥י נִרְפָּ֖א הַנָּֽגַע׃ ⁴⁹וְלָקַ֛ח לְחַטֵּ֥א אֶת־הַבַּ֖יִת שְׁתֵּ֣י צִפֳּרִ֑ים וְעֵ֣ץ אֶ֔רֶז וּשְׁנִ֥י תוֹלַ֖עַת וְאֵזֹֽב׃ ⁵⁰וְשָׁחַ֖ט אֶת־הַצִּפֹּ֣ר הָאֶחָ֑ת אֶל־כְּלִי־חֶ֖רֶשׂ עַל־מַ֥יִם חַיִּֽים׃ ⁵¹וְלָקַ֣ח אֶת־עֵץ־הָ֠אֶרֶז וְאֶת־הָ֨אֵזֹ֜ב וְאֵ֣ת ׀ שְׁנִ֣י הַתּוֹלַ֗עַת וְאֵת֮ הַצִּפֹּ֣ר הַֽחַיָּה֒ וְטָבַ֣ל אֹתָ֗ם בְּדַם֙ הַצִּפֹּ֣ר הַשְּׁחוּטָ֔ה וּבַמַּ֖יִם הַֽחַיִּ֑ים וְהִזָּ֥ה אֶל־הַבַּ֖יִת שֶׁ֥בַע פְּעָמִֽים׃ ⁵²וְחִטֵּ֣א אֶת־הַבַּ֗יִת בְּדַם֙ הַצִּפּ֔וֹר וּבַמַּ֖יִם הַֽחַיִּ֑ים וּבַצִּפֹּ֣ר הַחַיָּ֗ה וּבְעֵ֥ץ הָאֶ֛רֶז וּבָאֵזֹ֖ב וּבִשְׁנִ֥י הַתּוֹלָֽעַת׃ ⁵³וְשִׁלַּ֞ח אֶת־הַצִּפֹּ֧ר הַֽחַיָּ֛ה אֶל־מִח֥וּץ לָעִ֖יר אֶל־פְּנֵ֣י הַשָּׂדֶ֑ה וְכִפֶּ֥ר עַל־הַבַּ֖יִת וְטָהֵֽר׃ ⁵⁴זֹ֖את הַתּוֹרָ֑ה לְכָל־נֶ֥גַע הַצָּרַ֖עַת וְלַנָּֽתֶק׃ ⁵⁵וּלְצָרַ֥עַת הַבֶּ֖גֶד וְלַבָּֽיִת׃ ⁵⁶וְלַשְׂאֵ֥ת וְלַסַּפַּ֖חַת וְלַבֶּהָֽרֶת׃ ⁵⁷לְהוֹרֹ֕ת בְּי֥וֹם הַטָּמֵ֖א וּבְי֣וֹם הַטָּהֹ֑ר זֹ֥את תּוֹרַ֖ת הַצָּרָֽעַת׃ ס

15 ¹And YHWH spoke to Moses and to Aaron, saying, ²"Speak to the children of Israel, and you shall say to them: When any man will have an emission from his flesh, his emission: it is impure. ³And this shall be his impurity when he has an emission: his flesh leaks with his emission, or his flesh is obstructed from his emission. It is his impurity. ⁴Any bed on which the one with the emission will lie will be impure, and any item on which he will sit will be impure. ⁵And a man who will touch his bed shall wash his clothes and shall wash in water and will be impure until evening. ⁶And one who sits on an item on which the one with the emission has sat shall wash his clothes and shall wash in water and will be impure until evening. ⁷And one who touches the flesh of the one with the emission shall wash his clothes and shall wash in water and will be impure until evening. ⁸And if the one with the emission will spit on one who is pure, then he shall wash his clothes and shall wash in water and will be impure until evening. ⁹And any conveyance on which the one with the emission will ride will be impure. ¹⁰And anyone who touches anything that has been under him will be impure until evening. And one who carries them shall wash his clothes and shall wash in water and will be impure until evening. ¹¹And anyone whom the one with the emission will touch when he has not rinsed his hands in water shall wash his clothes and shall wash in water and will be impure until evening. ¹²And a clay container that the one with the emission will touch shall be broken, and any wood container shall be rinsed in water. ¹³And when the one with the emission will be purified from his emission, he shall count seven days for his purification and shall wash his clothes and shall wash his flesh in living water and will be pure. ¹⁴And on the eighth day he shall take two turtledoves or two pigeons and shall come in front of YHWH, to

15 ¹וַיְדַבֵּ֣ר יְהֹוָ֔ה אֶל־מֹשֶׁ֥ה וְאֶֽל־אַהֲרֹ֖ן לֵאמֹֽר׃ ²דַּבְּרוּ֙ אֶל־בְּנֵ֣י יִשְׂרָאֵ֔ל וַאֲמַרְתֶּ֖ם אֲלֵהֶ֑ם אִ֣ישׁ אִ֗ישׁ כִּ֤י יִהְיֶה֙ זָ֣ב מִבְּשָׂר֔וֹ זוֹב֖וֹ טָמֵ֥א הֽוּא׃ ³וְזֹ֛את תִּהְיֶ֥ה טֻמְאָת֖וֹ בְּזוֹב֑וֹ רָ֣ר בְּשָׂר֞וֹ אֶת־זוֹב֗וֹ אֽוֹ־הֶחְתִּ֤ים בְּשָׂרוֹ֙ מִזּוֹב֔וֹ טֻמְאָת֖וֹ הִֽוא׃ ⁴כׇּל־הַמִּשְׁכָּ֞ב אֲשֶׁ֨ר יִשְׁכַּ֥ב עָלָ֛יו הַזָּ֖ב יִטְמָ֑א וְכׇֽל־הַכְּלִ֛י אֲשֶׁר־יֵשֵׁ֥ב עָלָ֖יו יִטְמָֽא׃ ⁵וְאִ֕ישׁ אֲשֶׁ֥ר יִגַּ֖ע בְּמִשְׁכָּב֑וֹ יְכַבֵּ֧ס בְּגָדָ֛יו וְרָחַ֥ץ בַּמַּ֖יִם וְטָמֵ֥א עַד־הָעָֽרֶב׃ ⁶וְהַיֹּשֵׁב֙ עַֽל־הַכְּלִ֔י אֲשֶׁר־יֵשֵׁ֥ב עָלָ֖יו הַזָּ֑ב יְכַבֵּ֧ס בְּגָדָ֛יו וְרָחַ֥ץ בַּמַּ֖יִם וְטָמֵ֥א עַד־הָעָֽרֶב׃ ⁷וְהַנֹּגֵ֖עַ בִּבְשַׂ֣ר הַזָּ֑ב יְכַבֵּ֧ס בְּגָדָ֛יו וְרָחַ֥ץ בַּמַּ֖יִם וְטָמֵ֥א עַד־הָעָֽרֶב׃ ⁸וְכִֽי־יָרֹ֥ק הַזָּ֖ב בַּטָּה֑וֹר וְכִבֶּ֧ס בְּגָדָ֛יו וְרָחַ֥ץ בַּמַּ֖יִם וְטָמֵ֥א עַד־הָעָֽרֶב׃ ⁹וְכׇל־הַמֶּרְכָּ֗ב אֲשֶׁ֨ר יִרְכַּ֥ב עָלָ֛יו הַזָּ֖ב יִטְמָֽא׃ ¹⁰וְכׇל־הַנֹּגֵ֗עַ בְּכֹל֙ אֲשֶׁ֣ר יִהְיֶ֣ה תַחְתָּ֔יו יִטְמָ֖א עַד־הָעָ֑רֶב וְהַנּוֹשֵׂ֣א אוֹתָ֔ם יְכַבֵּ֧ס בְּגָדָ֛יו וְרָחַ֥ץ בַּמַּ֖יִם וְטָמֵ֥א עַד־הָעָֽרֶב׃ ¹¹וְכֹ֨ל אֲשֶׁ֤ר יִגַּע־בּוֹ֙ הַזָּ֔ב וְיָדָ֖יו לֹא־שָׁטַ֣ף בַּמָּ֑יִם וְכִבֶּ֧ס בְּגָדָ֛יו וְרָחַ֥ץ בַּמַּ֖יִם וְטָמֵ֥א עַד־הָעָֽרֶב׃ ¹²וּכְלִי־חֶ֛רֶשׂ אֲשֶׁר־יִגַּע־בּ֥וֹ הַזָּ֖ב יִשָּׁבֵ֑ר וְכׇ֨ל־כְּלִי־עֵ֔ץ יִשָּׁטֵ֖ף בַּמָּֽיִם׃ ¹³וְכִֽי־יִטְהַ֤ר הַזָּב֙ מִזּוֹב֔וֹ וְסָ֨פַר ל֜וֹ שִׁבְעַ֥ת יָמִ֛ים לְטׇהֳרָת֖וֹ וְכִבֶּ֣ס בְּגָדָ֑יו וְרָחַ֧ץ בְּשָׂר֛וֹ בְּמַ֥יִם חַיִּ֖ים וְטָהֵֽר׃ ¹⁴וּבַיּ֣וֹם הַשְּׁמִינִ֗י יִֽקַּֽח־לוֹ֙ שְׁתֵּ֣י תֹרִ֔ים א֥וֹ שְׁנֵ֖י בְּנֵ֣י יוֹנָ֑ה וּבָ֣א ׀ לִפְנֵ֣י יְהֹוָ֗ה אֶל־

15:2. **an emission from his flesh.** A spontaneous discharge from the penis.

15:3. **this shall be his impurity.** That is, the following shall be the nature of his impure condition.

the entrance of the Tent of Meeting, and shall give them to the priest. [15]And the priest shall do them: one a sin offering and one a burnt offering, and the priest shall make atonement over him in front of YHWH from his emission.

[16]"And when a man's intercourse seed will come out from him: he shall wash all his flesh in water and will be impure until evening. [17]And any clothing and any leather on which there will be intercourse seed: it shall be washed with water and will be impure until evening. [18]And a woman with whom a man will lie—an intercourse of seed—they shall wash with water and will be impure until evening.

[19]"And when a woman will have an emission—her emission will be blood in her flesh—she shall be in her impurity seven days. And anyone who touches her will be impure until evening. [20]And anything on which she will lie during her impurity will be impure, and anything on which she will sit will be impure. [21]And anyone who touches her bed shall wash his clothes and shall wash in water and will be impure until evening. [22]And anyone who touches any item on which she will sit shall wash his clothes and shall wash in water and will be impure until evening. [23]And if he is on the bed or on the item on which she sits while he is touching it, he will be impure until evening. [24]And if a

פֶּתַח אֹהֶל מוֹעֵד וּנְתָנָם אֶל־הַכֹּהֵן: [15]וְעָשָׂה אֹתָם הַכֹּהֵן אֶחָד חַטָּאת וְהָאֶחָד עֹלָה וְכִפֶּר עָלָיו הַכֹּהֵן לִפְנֵי יְהוָה מִזּוֹבוֹ: ס [16]וְאִישׁ כִּי־תֵצֵא מִמֶּנּוּ שִׁכְבַת־זָרַע וְרָחַץ בַּמַּיִם אֶת־כָּל־בְּשָׂרוֹ וְטָמֵא עַד־הָעָרֶב: [17]וְכָל־בֶּגֶד וְכָל־עוֹר אֲשֶׁר־יִהְיֶה עָלָיו שִׁכְבַת־זָרַע וְכֻבַּס בַּמַּיִם וְטָמֵא עַד־הָעָרֶב: פ [18]וְאִשָּׁה אֲשֶׁר יִשְׁכַּב אִישׁ אֹתָהּ שִׁכְבַת־זָרַע וְרָחֲצוּ בַמַּיִם וְטָמְאוּ עַד־הָעָרֶב: [19]וְאִשָּׁה כִּי־תִהְיֶה זָבָה דָּם יִהְיֶה זֹבָהּ בִּבְשָׂרָהּ שִׁבְעַת יָמִים תִּהְיֶה בְנִדָּתָהּ וְכָל־הַנֹּגֵעַ בָּהּ יִטְמָא עַד־הָעָרֶב: [20]וְכֹל אֲשֶׁר תִּשְׁכַּב עָלָיו בְּנִדָּתָהּ יִטְמָא וְכֹל אֲשֶׁר־תֵּשֵׁב עָלָיו יִטְמָא: [21]וְכָל־הַנֹּגֵעַ בְּמִשְׁכָּבָהּ יְכַבֵּס בְּגָדָיו וְרָחַץ בַּמַּיִם וְטָמֵא עַד־הָעָרֶב: [22]וְכָל־הַנֹּגֵעַ בְּכָל־כְּלִי אֲשֶׁר־תֵּשֵׁב עָלָיו יְכַבֵּס בְּגָדָיו וְרָחַץ בַּמַּיִם וְטָמֵא עַד־הָעָרֶב: [23]וְאִם עַל־הַמִּשְׁכָּב הוּא אוֹ עַל־הַכְּלִי אֲשֶׁר־הִוא יֹשֶׁבֶת־עָלָיו בְּנָגְעוֹ־בוֹ יִטְמָא עַד־הָעָרֶב:

15:16. **intercourse seed will come out from him.** This refers to a spontaneous flow of semen, as in a nocturnal emission.

15:23. **he is on the bed or on the item on which she sits while he is touching it.** Most other translators make it: "if he is on the bed or on the item on which she sits, when he touches it he is impure." That is, they make it that the impurity starts when he touches it. I think that the text is rather saying that even if he was on the bed first, and then she sat down on it, he is still rendered impure. (The Masoretic Text's placement of the *etnaḥ*, the symbol that marks the end of the phrase, agrees with my reading; that is, it comes after the words "he touches it.") Now, since he was there first, there is no question but that she has not had direct contact with him and that she has not touched the part of the bed on which he is sitting. But *still* he is impure—indicating that her contact with the bed or seat makes it impure (1) *entirely* and (2) *instantly*. This tells us something about the nature of impurity. It spreads throughout a person or object. And it is not any kind of creatures, like bacteria. It is a pervasive condition.

man will *lie* with her, and her impurity will be on him, then he will be impure seven days. And any bed on which he will lie will be impure.

25"And when a woman will have an emission of her blood many days when it is not the time of her impurity, or when she will have an emission beyond her impurity, for all the days of her impure emission she shall be like the days of her impurity. She is impure. 26Any bed on which she will lie all the days of her emission will be like a bed of her impurity for her, and any item on which she will sit will be impure like the impurity of her menstruation. 27And anyone who touches them will be impure. And he shall wash his clothes and shall wash with water and will be impure until evening.

28"And if she has become purified from her emission, then she shall count seven days, and after that she will be pure. 29And on the eighth day she shall take two turtledoves or two pigeons, and she shall bring them to the priest at the entrance of the Tent of Meeting. 30And the priest shall make one a sin offering and one a burnt offering, and the priest shall make atonement over her in front of YHWH from her impure emission.

31"And you shall alert the children of Israel regarding their impurity so they will not die through their impurity when they defile my Tabernacle that is among them. 32This is the instruction for one who has an emission and for one from whom seed of intercourse will come out, so as to become impure by it, 33and one who is in her menstrual impurity and one who

24וְאִם שָׁכֹב יִשְׁכַּב אִישׁ אֹתָהּ וּתְהִי נִדָּתָהּ עָלָיו
וְטָמֵא שִׁבְעַת יָמִים וְכָל־הַמִּשְׁכָּב אֲשֶׁר־יִשְׁכַּב עָלָיו
יִטְמָא: פ 25וְאִשָּׁה כִּי־יָזוּב זוֹב דָּמָהּ יָמִים רַבִּים
בְּלֹא עֶת־נִדָּתָהּ אוֹ כִי־תָזוּב עַל־נִדָּתָהּ כָּל־יְמֵי זוֹב
טֻמְאָתָהּ כִּימֵי נִדָּתָהּ תִּהְיֶה טְמֵאָה הִוא: 26כָּל־
הַמִּשְׁכָּב אֲשֶׁר־תִּשְׁכַּב עָלָיו כָּל־יְמֵי זוֹבָהּ כְּמִשְׁכַּב
נִדָּתָהּ יִהְיֶה־לָּהּ וְכָל־הַכְּלִי אֲשֶׁר תֵּשֵׁב עָלָיו טָמֵא
יִהְיֶה כְּטֻמְאַת נִדָּתָהּ: 27וְכָל־הַנּוֹגֵעַ בָּם יִטְמָא
וְכִבֶּס בְּגָדָיו וְרָחַץ בַּמַּיִם וְטָמֵא עַד־הָעָרֶב:
28וְאִם־טָהֲרָה מִזּוֹבָהּ וְסָפְרָה לָּהּ שִׁבְעַת יָמִים
וְאַחַר תִּטְהָר: 29וּבַיּוֹם הַשְּׁמִינִי תִּקַּח־לָהּ שְׁתֵּי
תֹרִים אוֹ שְׁנֵי בְּנֵי יוֹנָה וְהֵבִיאָה אוֹתָם אֶל־הַכֹּהֵן
אֶל־פֶּתַח אֹהֶל מוֹעֵד: 30וְעָשָׂה הַכֹּהֵן אֶת־הָאֶחָד
חַטָּאת וְאֶת־הָאֶחָד עֹלָה וְכִפֶּר עָלֶיהָ הַכֹּהֵן לִפְנֵי
יְהוָה מִזּוֹב טֻמְאָתָהּ: 31וְהִזַּרְתֶּם אֶת־בְּנֵי־יִשְׂרָאֵל
מִטֻּמְאָתָם וְלֹא יָמֻתוּ בְּטֻמְאָתָם בְּטַמְּאָם אֶת־מִשְׁכָּנִי
אֲשֶׁר בְּתוֹכָם: 32זֹאת תּוֹרַת הַזָּב וַאֲשֶׁר תֵּצֵא מִמֶּנּוּ
שִׁכְבַת־זֶרַע לְטָמְאָה־בָהּ: 33וְהַדָּוָה בְּנִדָּתָהּ וְהַזָּב

15:29. **at the entrance of the Tent of Meeting.** It has been noted that the instruction is the same for a man and for a woman except that a man is said to bring this offering "in front of YHWH," whereas these words do not occur here in the instruction about a woman. And it has been suggested that women's "cultic access" is thus not equal to men's. But the words "in front of YHWH" appear to apply regularly to the place at the entrance of the Tent. Both women and men have access to this place. The absence of the extra phrase here must therefore mean something else. (Or, since the phrase is not used in every reference to the entrance of the Tent, perhaps its absence here means nothing in particular.)

has an emission—for a male and for a female—and for a man who will lie with a woman who is impure."

אֶת־זוֹבוֹ לַזָּכָר וְלַנְּקֵבָה וּלְאִישׁ אֲשֶׁר יִשְׁכַּב עִם־טְמֵאָה: פ

AFTER THE DEATH

אַחֲרֵי מוֹת

16 ¹And YHWH spoke to Moses after the death of Aaron's two sons—when they came forward in front of YHWH and died. ²And YHWH said to Moses, "Speak to Aaron, your brother, and let him not come at all times to the Holy, inside the pavilion, in front of the atonement dais that is over the ark, so he will not die, because I shall appear in a cloud over the atonement dais. ³Aaron shall come to the Holy with this: with a bull of the cattle for a sin offering and a ram for a burnt offering. ⁴He shall wear a holy linen coat, and linen drawers shall be on his flesh, and he shall be belted with a linen sash, and he shall wear a linen headdress. They are holy clothes: and he shall wash his flesh with water and put them on. ⁵And he shall take from the congregation of the children of Israel two goats for a sin offering and one ram for a burnt offering. ⁶And Aaron shall bring forward the bull of the sin offering that is his and shall make atonement for himself and for his house. ⁷And

16 ¹וַיְדַבֵּר יְהוָה אֶל־מֹשֶׁה אַחֲרֵי מוֹת שְׁנֵי בְּנֵי אַהֲרֹן בְּקָרְבָתָם לִפְנֵי־יְהוָה וַיָּמֻתוּ: ²וַיֹּאמֶר יְהוָה אֶל־מֹשֶׁה דַּבֵּר אֶל־אַהֲרֹן אָחִיךָ וְאַל־יָבֹא בְכָל־עֵת אֶל־הַקֹּדֶשׁ מִבֵּית לַפָּרֹכֶת אֶל־פְּנֵי הַכַּפֹּרֶת אֲשֶׁר עַל־הָאָרֹן וְלֹא יָמוּת כִּי בֶּעָנָן אֵרָאֶה עַל־הַכַּפֹּרֶת: ³בְּזֹאת יָבֹא אַהֲרֹן אֶל־הַקֹּדֶשׁ בְּפַר בֶּן־בָּקָר לְחַטָּאת וְאַיִל לְעֹלָה: ⁴כְּתֹנֶת־בַּד קֹדֶשׁ יִלְבָּשׁ וּמִכְנְסֵי־בַד יִהְיוּ עַל־בְּשָׂרוֹ וּבְאַבְנֵט בַּד יַחְגֹּר וּבְמִצְנֶפֶת בַּד יִצְנֹף בִּגְדֵי־קֹדֶשׁ הֵם וְרָחַץ בַּמַּיִם אֶת־בְּשָׂרוֹ וּלְבֵשָׁם: ⁵וּמֵאֵת עֲדַת בְּנֵי יִשְׂרָאֵל יִקַּח שְׁנֵי־שְׂעִירֵי עִזִּים לְחַטָּאת וְאַיִל אֶחָד לְעֹלָה: ⁶וְהִקְרִיב אַהֲרֹן אֶת־פַּר הַחַטָּאת אֲשֶׁר־לוֹ וְכִפֶּר בַּעֲדוֹ וּבְעַד בֵּיתוֹ: ⁷וְלָקַח אֶת־שְׁנֵי הַשְּׂעִירִם

16:1. **after death**. The title of this parashah is *'aḥărê môt*, meaning "after death." The title of the following week's parashah is *qĕdōšîm*, meaning "holy" (19:2). In some years these two portions are read together, and so their titles merge as *'aḥărê môt qĕdōšîm*, meaning "after death: holy." My grandfather wrote a letter to my father when my father was about to be married, and he noted a traditional comment on this merger: that after people die we make them holy, speaking of them as if they were saints. "But," my grandfather told my father, "you have always shown me respect while I am still alive." And so one of the greatest lessons of these portions of the Torah is the result of a merger of titles that are three chapters apart and that were inserted centuries after the Torah was completed. Thus wisdom can emerge in a variety of ways if the reader is wise and sensitive.

16:2. **inside the pavilion**. The Hebrew is *mibbêt lappārōket*. The use of the term *bêt* (house, building) may be further evidence that the *pārōket* is a four-sided structure, not a curtain. See the comments on Tabernacle architecture at Exodus 26.

16:6. **his house**. Meaning: his family, his household.

he shall take the two goats and stand them in front of YHWH, at the entrance of the Tent of Meeting. ⁸And Aaron shall cast lots on the two goats, one lot for YHWH and one lot for Azazel. ⁹And Aaron shall bring forward the goat on which the lot for YHWH arose, and he shall make it a sin offering. ¹⁰And the goat on which the lot for Azazel arose shall be stood alive in front of YHWH to make atonement over it, to let it go to Azazel, into the wilderness. ¹¹And Aaron shall bring forward the bull of the sin offering that is his and shall make atonement for him and for his house, and he shall slaughter the bull

וְהֶעֱמִיד אֹתָם לִפְנֵי יְהוָה פֶּתַח אֹהֶל מוֹעֵד: ⁸וְנָתַן אַהֲרֹן עַל־שְׁנֵי הַשְּׂעִירִם גּוֹרָלוֹת גּוֹרָל אֶחָד לַיהוָה וְגוֹרָל אֶחָד לַעֲזָאזֵל: ⁹וְהִקְרִיב אַהֲרֹן אֶת־הַשָּׂעִיר אֲשֶׁר עָלָה עָלָיו הַגּוֹרָל לַיהוָה וְעָשָׂהוּ חַטָּאת: ¹⁰וְהַשָּׂעִיר אֲשֶׁר עָלָה עָלָיו הַגּוֹרָל לַעֲזָאזֵל יָעֳמַד־חַי לִפְנֵי יְהוָה לְכַפֵּר עָלָיו לְשַׁלַּח אֹתוֹ לַעֲזָאזֵל הַמִּדְבָּרָה: ¹¹וְהִקְרִיב אַהֲרֹן אֶת־פַּר הַחַטָּאת אֲשֶׁר־לוֹ וְכִפֶּר בַּעֲדוֹ וּבְעַד בֵּיתוֹ וְשָׁחַט אֶת־פַּר

16:8. **lots**. Why use lots? Lots are used frequently in the *Tanak*. In some cases they are understood to reflect divine determination, and in some they are not. They reflect the hand of God in the case of the lot that identifies Jonah to the sailors (1:7), the lot that identifies Achan as the Israelite who has violated the law of *herem* and taken spoils for himself at Jericho (Joshua 7), the lot that identifies Saul as the first king of Israel (1 Sam 10:17–21), and the lot that identifies Saul's son Jonathan as the one who has unwittingly violated an oath by his father (1 Sam 14:40–42). They appear to be a matter of chance rather than divine direction here in the case of the goats, in the case of the apportionment of the promised land to the Israelites (Num 26:52–56; Joshua 14–19; Judg 1:3), in assigning priests to their divisions (1 Chronicles 24), in drafting Israelites for a battle (Judg 20:9), in assigning population to Jerusalem (Nehemiah 11), and in sharing in spoils and captives (Joel 4:3; Obadiah 11; Nah 3:10; Ps 22:19). (The case of Haman's lots in Esther is anomalous and requires separate explanation.)

What is the distinction between these two groups of cases? It appears to be that all the cases that involve divine determination are about identifying a single individual in a specific situation. All the cases that do not imply divine determination are about assigning things that relate to groups or the community. The issue in the former cases is finding the right person. The issue in the latter cases is fairness—showing no favor in assignments. The goats are the first case of such assignment by lot in the *Tanak,* and they are the only case that is an annual event. All the others are onetime occurrences. The ritual of the goats thus sets the principle and the model for all subsequent cases involving lotteries for fairness in assignments.

It has been said that this is a denial of "Divine Providence." But this is an act by the *community,* seeking atonement for things that *they* have done. This is not a situation calling for "Divine Providence." On the contrary, the point here is precisely to convey the will of the community to express their atonement to God. The deity is the recipient, not the controller, of this message.

16:8. **Azazel**. This word occurs only in this chapter and nowhere else in the *Tanak*. There have been many attempts to explain it (the common view being that it refers to some sort of desert demon), but the simple fact is that we do not know who or what it is.

of the sin offering that he has. 12And he shall take a fire-holder-full of coals of fire from on the altar, from in front of YHWH, and handfuls of fine incense of fragrances, and he shall bring it inside the pavilion 13and put the incense on the fire in front of YHWH so that the cloud of the incense will cover the atonement dais that is over the Testimony, and he will not die. 14And he shall take some of the bull's blood and sprinkle with his finger on the front of the atonement dais eastward, and he shall sprinkle some of the blood with his finger in front of the atonement dais seven times. 15And he shall slaughter the goat of the sin offering that is the people's and shall bring its blood inside the pavilion and shall do its blood as he did to the bull's blood: and he shall sprinkle it on the atonement dais and in front of the atonement dais. 16And he shall make atonement over the Holy from the impurities of the children of Israel and from their offenses, for all their sins, and he shall do so for the Tent of Meeting that tents with them among their impurities. 17And no human shall be in the Tent of Meeting when he comes to make atonement in the Holy until he comes out. And he shall make atonement for him and for his house and for all the community of Israel.

18"And he shall go out to the altar that is in front of YHWH and make atonement over it, and he shall take some of the bull's blood and some of the goat's blood and put it on the altar's horns all around. 19And he shall sprinkle some of the blood on it with his finger seven times and purify it and make it holy from the impurities of the children of Israel.

20"And when he will finish making atonement for the Holy and the Tent of Meeting and the altar, then he shall bring forward the live goat. 21And Aaron shall lay his two hands on the live goat's head and confess over it all the crimes of the children of Israel and all their offenses, for all their sins, and he shall put them on the goat's head and let it go by the hand of an appointed man to the wilderness. 22And the goat will carry

הַחַטָּאת אֲשֶׁר־לֽוֹ: 12וְלָקַ֣ח מְלֹֽא־הַ֠מַּחְתָּה גַּֽחֲלֵי־אֵ֞שׁ מֵעַ֤ל הַמִּזְבֵּ֨חַ֙ מִלִּפְנֵ֣י יְהוָ֔ה וּמְלֹ֣א חָפְנָ֔יו קְטֹ֥רֶת סַמִּ֖ים דַּקָּ֑ה וְהֵבִ֖יא מִבֵּ֥ית לַפָּרֹֽכֶת: 13וְנָתַ֧ן אֶֽת־הַקְּטֹ֛רֶת עַל־הָאֵ֖שׁ לִפְנֵ֣י יְהוָ֑ה וְכִסָּ֣ה ׀ עֲנַ֣ן הַקְּטֹ֗רֶת אֶת־הַכַּפֹּ֛רֶת אֲשֶׁ֥ר עַל־הָֽעֵד֖וּת וְלֹ֥א יָמֽוּת: 14וְלָקַח֮ מִדַּ֣ם הַפָּר֒ וְהִזָּ֧ה בְאֶצְבָּע֛וֹ עַל־פְּנֵ֥י הַכַּפֹּ֖רֶת קֵ֑דְמָה וְלִפְנֵ֣י הַכַּפֹּ֗רֶת יַזֶּ֧ה שֶֽׁבַע־פְּעָמִ֛ים מִן־הַדָּ֖ם בְּאֶצְבָּעֽוֹ: 15וְשָׁחַ֞ט אֶת־שְׂעִ֤יר הַֽחַטָּאת֙ אֲשֶׁ֣ר לָעָ֔ם וְהֵבִיא֙ אֶת־דָּמ֔וֹ אֶל־מִבֵּ֖ית לַפָּרֹ֑כֶת וְעָשָׂ֣ה אֶת־דָּמ֗וֹ כַּֽאֲשֶׁ֤ר עָשָׂה֙ לְדַ֣ם הַפָּ֔ר וְהִזָּ֥ה אֹת֛וֹ עַל־הַכַּפֹּ֖רֶת וְלִפְנֵ֥י הַכַּפֹּֽרֶת: 16וְכִפֶּ֣ר עַל־הַקֹּ֗דֶשׁ מִטֻּמְאֹת֙ בְּנֵ֣י יִשְׂרָאֵ֔ל וּמִפִּשְׁעֵיהֶ֖ם לְכָל־חַטֹּאתָ֑ם וְכֵ֤ן יַֽעֲשֶׂה֙ לְאֹ֣הֶל מוֹעֵ֔ד הַשֹּׁכֵ֣ן אִתָּ֔ם בְּת֖וֹךְ טֻמְאֹתָֽם: 17וְכָל־אָדָ֞ם לֹֽא־יִֽהְיֶ֣ה ׀ בְּאֹ֣הֶל מוֹעֵ֗ד בְּבֹא֛וֹ לְכַפֵּ֥ר בַּקֹּ֖דֶשׁ עַד־צֵאת֑וֹ וְכִפֶּ֣ר בַּֽעֲד֗וֹ וּבְעַ֣ד בֵּית֔וֹ וּבְעַ֖ד כָּל־קְהַ֥ל יִשְׂרָאֵֽל: 18וְיָצָ֗א אֶל־הַמִּזְבֵּ֛חַ אֲשֶׁ֥ר לִפְנֵֽי־יְהוָ֖ה וְכִפֶּ֣ר עָלָ֑יו וְלָקַ֞ח מִדַּ֤ם הַפָּר֙ וּמִדַּ֣ם הַשָּׂעִ֔יר וְנָתַ֛ן עַל־קַרְנ֥וֹת הַמִּזְבֵּ֖חַ סָבִֽיב: 19וְהִזָּ֨ה עָלָ֧יו מִן־הַדָּ֛ם בְּאֶצְבָּע֖וֹ שֶׁ֣בַע פְּעָמִ֑ים וְטִֽהֲר֣וֹ וְקִדְּשׁ֔וֹ מִטֻּמְאֹ֖ת בְּנֵ֥י יִשְׂרָאֵֽל: 20וְכִלָּה֙ מִכַּפֵּ֣ר אֶת־הַקֹּ֔דֶשׁ וְאֶת־אֹ֥הֶל מוֹעֵ֖ד וְאֶת־הַמִּזְבֵּ֑חַ וְהִקְרִ֖יב אֶת־הַשָּׂעִ֥יר הֶחָֽי: 21וְסָמַ֨ךְ אַֽהֲרֹ֜ן אֶת־שְׁתֵּ֣י יָדָ֗ו עַ֣ל רֹ֣אשׁ הַשָּׂעִיר֮ הַחַי֒ וְהִתְוַדָּ֣ה עָלָ֗יו אֶת־כָּל־עֲוֺנֹת֙ בְּנֵ֣י יִשְׂרָאֵ֔ל וְאֶת־כָּל־פִּשְׁעֵיהֶ֖ם לְכָל־חַטֹּאתָ֑ם וְנָתַ֤ן אֹתָם֙ עַל־רֹ֣אשׁ הַשָּׂעִ֔יר וְשִׁלַּ֛ח בְּיַד־אִ֥ישׁ עִתִּ֖י הַמִּדְבָּֽרָה: 22וְנָשָׂ֨א

קְ יָדָ֖יו 16:21

all their crimes on it to an inaccessible land. And he shall let the goat go in the wilderness.

23"And Aaron shall come to the Tent of Meeting and take off the linen clothes that he wore when he came to the Holy, and he shall leave them there. 24And he shall wash his flesh with water in a holy place and put on his clothes, and he shall go out and make his burnt offering and the people's burnt offering and make atonement for him and for the people. 25And he shall burn the fat of the sin offering into smoke at the altar. 26And the one who let the goat go to Azazel shall wash his clothes and wash his flesh with water, and after that he shall come to the camp. 27And he shall take the bull of the sin offering and the goat of the sin offering, whose blood was brought to make atonement in the Holy, outside the camp; and they shall burn their skin and their meat and their dung in fire. 28And the one who burns them shall wash his clothes and wash his flesh with water, and after that he shall come to the camp.

29"And it shall be an eternal law for you: in the seventh month, on the tenth of the month, you shall degrade yourselves, and you shall not do any work: the citizen and the alien who resides among you. 30Because on this day he shall make atonement over you, to purify you. You will be pure from all your sins in front of YHWH. 31It is a Sabbath, a ceasing, to you. And you shall degrade yourselves—an eternal law. 32And the priest whom one will anoint and who will fill his hand to function as a priest in his father's place shall make atonement. And he shall wear the linen clothes, the holy clothes. 33And he shall make atonement for the holy place of the Holy, and he shall make atonement for the Tent of Meeting and for the altar, and he shall make

הַשָּׂעִיר עָלָיו אֶת־כָּל־עֲוֹנֹתָם אֶל־אֶרֶץ גְּזֵרָה וְשִׁלַּח אֶת־הַשָּׂעִיר בַּמִּדְבָּר: 23וּבָא אַהֲרֹן אֶל־אֹהֶל מוֹעֵד וּפָשַׁט אֶת־בִּגְדֵי הַבָּד אֲשֶׁר לָבַשׁ בְּבֹאוֹ אֶל־הַקֹּדֶשׁ וְהִנִּיחָם שָׁם: 24וְרָחַץ אֶת־בְּשָׂרוֹ בַמַּיִם בְּמָקוֹם קָדוֹשׁ וְלָבַשׁ אֶת־בְּגָדָיו וְיָצָא וְעָשָׂה אֶת־עֹלָתוֹ וְאֶת־עֹלַת הָעָם וְכִפֶּר בַּעֲדוֹ וּבְעַד הָעָם: 25וְאֵת חֵלֶב הַחַטָּאת יַקְטִיר הַמִּזְבֵּחָה: 26וְהַמְשַׁלֵּחַ אֶת־הַשָּׂעִיר לַעֲזָאזֵל יְכַבֵּס בְּגָדָיו וְרָחַץ אֶת־בְּשָׂרוֹ בַּמָּיִם וְאַחֲרֵי־כֵן יָבוֹא אֶל־הַמַּחֲנֶה: 27וְאֵת פַּר הַחַטָּאת וְאֵת ׀ שְׂעִיר הַחַטָּאת אֲשֶׁר הוּבָא אֶת־דָּמָם לְכַפֵּר בַּקֹּדֶשׁ יוֹצִיא אֶל־מִחוּץ לַמַּחֲנֶה וְשָׂרְפוּ בָאֵשׁ אֶת־עֹרֹתָם וְאֶת־בְּשָׂרָם וְאֶת־פִּרְשָׁם: 28וְהַשֹּׂרֵף אֹתָם יְכַבֵּס בְּגָדָיו וְרָחַץ אֶת־בְּשָׂרוֹ בַּמָּיִם וְאַחֲרֵי־כֵן יָבוֹא אֶל־הַמַּחֲנֶה: 29וְהָיְתָה לָכֶם לְחֻקַּת עוֹלָם בַּחֹדֶשׁ הַשְּׁבִיעִי בֶּעָשׂוֹר לַחֹדֶשׁ תְּעַנּוּ אֶת־נַפְשֹׁתֵיכֶם וְכָל־מְלָאכָה לֹא תַעֲשׂוּ הָאֶזְרָח וְהַגֵּר הַגָּר בְּתוֹכְכֶם: 30כִּי־בַיּוֹם הַזֶּה יְכַפֵּר עֲלֵיכֶם לְטַהֵר אֶתְכֶם מִכֹּל חַטֹּאתֵיכֶם לִפְנֵי יְהוָה תִּטְהָרוּ: 31שַׁבַּת שַׁבָּתוֹן הִיא לָכֶם וְעִנִּיתֶם אֶת־נַפְשֹׁתֵיכֶם חֻקַּת עוֹלָם: 32וְכִפֶּר הַכֹּהֵן אֲשֶׁר־יִמְשַׁח אֹתוֹ וַאֲשֶׁר יְמַלֵּא אֶת־יָדוֹ לְכַהֵן תַּחַת אָבִיו וְלָבַשׁ אֶת־בִּגְדֵי הַבָּד בִּגְדֵי הַקֹּדֶשׁ: 33וְכִפֶּר אֶת־מִקְדַּשׁ הַקֹּדֶשׁ וְאֶת־אֹהֶל מוֹעֵד וְאֶת־הַמִּזְבֵּחַ יְכַפֵּר וְעַל הַכֹּהֲנִים

16:29. **degrade yourselves**. The verb here is the same word that is used to describe what the Egyptians did to the Israelites (Exod 1:11–12): degradation, affliction. It has been understood to mean that one does not eat or drink or bathe or wear fine shoes on the Day of Atonement; rather, one humbles oneself.

16:32. **fill his hand to function as a priest**. See comment on Exod 29:29.

atonement over the priests and over all the people of the community. 34And this shall become an eternal law for you, to make atonement over the children of Israel from all their sins, once in the year."

And he did as YHWH had commanded Moses.

17 1And YHWH spoke to Moses, saying, 2"Speak to Aaron and to his sons and to all the children of Israel and say to them: This is the thing that YHWH has commanded, saying: 3Any man from the house of Israel who slaughters an ox or a sheep or a goat in the camp or who slaughters outside the camp 4and has not

וְעַל־כָּל־עַם הַקָּהָל יְכַפֵּר: 34וְהָיְתָה־זֹּאת לָכֶם לְחֻקַּת עוֹלָם לְכַפֵּר עַל־בְּנֵי יִשְׂרָאֵל מִכָּל־חַטֹּאתָם אַחַת בַּשָּׁנָה וַיַּעַשׂ כַּאֲשֶׁר צִוָּה יְהוָה אֶת־מֹשֶׁה: פ 17 1וַיְדַבֵּר יְהוָה אֶל־מֹשֶׁה לֵּאמֹר: 2דַּבֵּר אֶל־אַהֲרֹן וְאֶל־בָּנָיו וְאֶל כָּל־בְּנֵי יִשְׂרָאֵל וְאָמַרְתָּ אֲלֵיהֶם זֶה הַדָּבָר אֲשֶׁר־צִוָּה יְהוָה לֵאמֹר: 3אִישׁ אִישׁ מִבֵּית יִשְׂרָאֵל אֲשֶׁר יִשְׁחַט שׁוֹר אוֹ־כֶשֶׂב אוֹ־עֵז בַּמַּחֲנֶה אוֹ אֲשֶׁר יִשְׁחַט מִחוּץ לַמַּחֲנֶה: 4וְאֶל־

17:3. Any man . . . who slaughters. Most sacrifices involve the ritual slaughter of an animal that is to be used for food. In Leviticus, YHWH forbids the slaughter of animals outside of a formal ritual setting. For Leviticus there is no such occupation as butcher. If one wants to eat meat, one must bring the animal to the priest, who sacrifices it in the prescribed manner at the altar, retains a portion of it for the sustenance of the priesthood, and gives back the rest for consumption. The priests eat their portion according to prescription as well: specifically, priests eat meat with unleavened bread. As with the laws of Exodus, the reasons for requiring ritual slaughter are not stated explicitly, but there appears to be more at stake than the support of the priesthood. In the initial state of creation in Genesis, humans are vegetarian. Genesis depicts animals, but not plants, as sharing with humans the quality of being living beings (*nepeš ḥayyāh*, Gen 1:20,21,24,30; 2:7,19). Following the flood, animals are permitted as food. Now the sacrificial laws of Leviticus recognize that this involves the taking of life, and they decree that life cannot be taken as a secular act of slaughter. It must be done in a setting that reflects sensitivity to what is at stake. An indicator that this is the orientation of the Levitical law is that it permits one to hunt game animals such as deer, which one cannot easily lead to an altar, but then one must perform the act of pouring off the blood of the animal because, it says, "the flesh's life (*nepeš*) is in the blood" (17:11).

At several places in my comments on Leviticus, I have noted that we have lost the feeling of ritual as it was known in the biblical world. Here I would add that if we still had a greater feeling for ritual we would have more of a feeling for the life of an animal. For most humans in this age, we are farther removed from the life and death of the animals (and plants!) that we eat than in any previous generation. We buy meat in sealed packages, so that it no longer resembles the animal from which it came. We have lost the awareness of how this food came to be on our table. Part of life is the consumption of life-forms by other life-forms. But whether one is vegetarian or carnivorous, one will enrich one's life—and understand better one's place in the world— if one connects a ritual with that consumption. If it can no longer be sacrifice, then

brought it to the entrance of the Tent of Meeting to bring forward an offering to YHWH in front of YHWH's Tabernacle: blood will be counted to that man. He has spilled blood. And that man will be cut off from among his people. 5So that the children of Israel will bring their sacrifices—

פֶּ֣תַח אֹ֤הֶל מוֹעֵד֙ לֹ֣א הֱבִיא֔וֹ לְהַקְרִ֥יב קָרְבָּן֙ לַֽיהוָ֔ה לִפְנֵ֖י מִשְׁכַּ֣ן יְהוָ֑ה דָּ֣ם יֵחָשֵׁ֞ב לָאִ֤ישׁ הַהוּא֙ דָּ֣ם שָׁפָ֔ךְ וְנִכְרַ֛ת הָאִ֥ישׁ הַה֖וּא מִקֶּ֥רֶב עַמּֽוֹ׃ 5לְמַ֩עַן֩ אֲשֶׁ֨ר יָבִ֜יאוּ בְּנֵ֣י יִשְׂרָאֵ֗ל אֶת־זִבְחֵיהֶם֙ אֲשֶׁ֣ר הֵ֔ם

---

perhaps it can be saying grace, or a blessing, or occasionally visiting a farm or ranch and observing the animals and plants: watching, touching, listening to them.

17:4. **Tent of Meeting**. There is a long additional line here in the Septuagint, Qumran, and Samaritan texts, which has been lost in the Masoretic Text. The verse reads: "and has not brought it to the entrance of the Tent of Meeting *to make it a burnt offering or peace offering to YHWH to be acceptable for you as a pleasant smell, and he slaughters it outside and has not brought it to the entrance of the Tent of Meeting . . . "* The eye of the scribe writing the Masoretic Text apparently skipped the line because his eye jumped from one occurrence of the phrase "brought it to the entrance of the Tent of Meeting" to the next. This shows how much of a text can be changed by scribal error and is a warning to take account of all the available versions of the text. (It is also a reminder that systems of seeking patterns or codes by counting the text's letters are erroneous. See the comment on Exod 1:5.)

17:4. **blood will be counted to that man. He has spilled blood**. This person has slaughtered an animal, but the text speaks of it as an equivalent of murdering a human! Why does this act merit such extraordinary severity? Because it merges two of the most essential commandments of the Torah. First, it involves taking a life without respect for life's sanctity—as discussed in the comment on 17:3. And, second, it violates the law of centralization of worship, which is declared for the first time in this chapter. According to the law, one can sacrifice only at one place on earth: at the altar at the entrance of the Tent of Meeting. If one wants to eat lamb or beef, one must bring one's sheep or cow to that central altar. In the wilderness it is at the Tent. Later, in the land, it is at the Temple. (The Tent of Meeting is inside the Temple. See the comment on Exod 26:30.) But the all-important point is centralization of worship. As I commented earlier (Exod 26:6), centralization and monotheism go together: one God, one altar. Each town in Israel does not have its own altar or its own Tabernacle. This is explicitly forbidden here. In the books of Kings, it is the standard for judging *every* king of Israel and Judah: did he allow "high places" (Hebrew *bāmôt*) outside of the Jerusalem Temple or not? The only two kings to get nearly perfect ratings (Hezekiah and Josiah) are the two kings who most zealously enforce centralization. Today, one does not see a multiplicity of synagogues, churches, or mosques and assume that this means that a multiplicity of gods is being worshiped. But in the biblical world, when monotheism is a new idea, the principle of one God–one Temple–one altar is presented as supremely important.

17:4. **cut off from among his people**. This may mean to die without heirs or not to be buried in the ancestral tomb or not to join one's ancestors in an afterlife. See the comment on Exod 30:33.

which they are making at the open field—and will bring them to YHWH, to the entrance of the Tent of Meeting, to the priest, and make them sacrifices of peace offerings to YHWH. 6And the priest shall fling the blood on YHWH's altar at the entrance of the Tent of Meeting and burn the fat to smoke as a pleasant smell to YHWH. 7And they shall not make their sacrifices anymore to the satyrs, after whom they are whoring. This shall be an eternal law to them through their generations.

8"And you shall say to them: Any man from the house of Israel and from the aliens who will reside among them who will make a burnt offering or a sacrifice 9and will not bring it to the entrance of the Tent of Meeting to make it to YHWH: that man will be cut off from his people.

10"And any man from the house of Israel and from the aliens who will reside among them who will eat any blood: then I shall set my face against the person who eats the blood, and I shall cut him off from among his people. 11Because the *flesh's* life is in the blood, and *I* have given it to you on the altar to make atonement over *your* lives, because it is the blood that makes atonement for life. 12On account of this I have said to the children of Israel: every person among you shall not eat blood, and the alien who resides among you shall not eat blood.

13"And any man from the children of Israel and from the aliens who reside among them who will hunt game, animal or bird, that may be eaten: he shall spill out its blood and cover it with dust. 14Because all flesh's life: its blood is one with its life. So I say to the children of Israel: you shall not eat the blood of all flesh—because

זְבָחִים עַל־פְּנֵי הַשָּׂדֶה וֶהֱבִיאֻם לַיהוָה אֶל־פֶּתַח אֹהֶל מוֹעֵד אֶל־הַכֹּהֵן וְזָבְחוּ זִבְחֵי שְׁלָמִים לַיהוָה אוֹתָם: 6וְזָרַק הַכֹּהֵן אֶת־הַדָּם עַל־מִזְבַּח יְהוָה פֶּתַח אֹהֶל מוֹעֵד וְהִקְטִיר הַחֵלֶב לְרֵיחַ נִיחֹחַ לַיהוָה: 7וְלֹא־יִזְבְּחוּ עוֹד אֶת־זִבְחֵיהֶם לַשְּׂעִירִם אֲשֶׁר הֵם זֹנִים אַחֲרֵיהֶם חֻקַּת עוֹלָם תִּהְיֶה־זֹּאת לָהֶם לְדֹרֹתָם: 8וַאֲלֵהֶם תֹּאמַר אִישׁ אִישׁ מִבֵּית יִשְׂרָאֵל וּמִן־הַגֵּר אֲשֶׁר־יָגוּר בְּתוֹכָם אֲשֶׁר־יַעֲלֶה עֹלָה אוֹ־זָבַח: 9וְאֶל־פֶּתַח אֹהֶל מוֹעֵד לֹא יְבִיאֶנּוּ לַעֲשׂוֹת אֹתוֹ לַיהוָה וְנִכְרַת הָאִישׁ הַהוּא מֵעַמָּיו: 10וְאִישׁ אִישׁ מִבֵּית יִשְׂרָאֵל וּמִן־הַגֵּר הַגָּר בְּתוֹכָם אֲשֶׁר יֹאכַל כָּל־דָּם וְנָתַתִּי פָנַי בַּנֶּפֶשׁ הָאֹכֶלֶת אֶת־הַדָּם וְהִכְרַתִּי אֹתָהּ מִקֶּרֶב עַמָּהּ: 11כִּי נֶפֶשׁ הַבָּשָׂר בַּדָּם הִוא וַאֲנִי נְתַתִּיו לָכֶם עַל־הַמִּזְבֵּחַ לְכַפֵּר עַל־נַפְשֹׁתֵיכֶם כִּי־הַדָּם הוּא בַּנֶּפֶשׁ יְכַפֵּר: 12עַל־כֵּן אָמַרְתִּי לִבְנֵי יִשְׂרָאֵל כָּל־נֶפֶשׁ מִכֶּם לֹא־תֹאכַל דָּם וְהַגֵּר הַגָּר בְּתוֹכְכֶם לֹא־יֹאכַל דָּם: ס 13וְאִישׁ אִישׁ מִבְּנֵי יִשְׂרָאֵל וּמִן־הַגֵּר הַגָּר בְּתוֹכָם אֲשֶׁר יָצוּד צֵיד חַיָּה אוֹ־עוֹף אֲשֶׁר יֵאָכֵל וְשָׁפַךְ אֶת־דָּמוֹ וְכִסָּהוּ בֶּעָפָר: 14כִּי־נֶפֶשׁ כָּל־בָּשָׂר דָּמוֹ בְנַפְשׁוֹ הוּא וָאֹמַר לִבְנֵי יִשְׂרָאֵל דַּם כָּל־בָּשָׂר לֹא תֹאכֵלוּ

17:7. **satyrs**. It is not certain what these are. The term "satyrs" is used because the Hebrew term has to do with goats. They are mentioned in Isa 13:21; 34:14 and in 2 Chr 11:15.

17:10,12. **person**. This is very difficult to capture in translation. The word for "person," Hebrew *nepeš*, is the same word that means "life" three times in v. 11. In the Hebrew, therefore, it is more obvious that the issue is that a living creature is eating blood, which bears the life of another living creature.

all flesh's life: it is its blood. Everyone of those who eat it will be cut off. 15And any living being, whether a citizen or an alien, who will eat carcass or a torn animal shall wash his clothes and shall wash with water and will be impure until evening and then will be pure. 16And if he will not wash them and will not wash his flesh, then he shall bear his crime."

18 1And YHWH spoke to Moses, saying, 2"Speak to the children of Israel, and you shall say to them: I am YHWH, your God. 3You shall not do like what is done in the land of Egypt, in which you lived; and you shall not do like what is done in the land of Canaan, to which I'm bringing you; and you shall not go by their laws. 4You shall do *my* judgments, and you shall observe *my* laws, to go by them. I am YHWH, your God. 5And you shall observe my laws and

כִּי נֶפֶשׁ כָּל־בָּשָׂר דָּמוֹ הוּא כָּל־אֹכְלָיו יִכָּרֵת:

15וְכָל־נֶפֶשׁ אֲשֶׁר תֹּאכַל נְבֵלָה וּטְרֵפָה בָּאֶזְרָח וּבַגֵּר וְכִבֶּס בְּגָדָיו וְרָחַץ בַּמַּיִם וְטָמֵא עַד־הָעֶרֶב וְטָהֵר: 16וְאִם לֹא יְכַבֵּס וּבְשָׂרוֹ לֹא יִרְחָץ וְנָשָׂא עֲוֺנוֹ: פ

18 1וַיְדַבֵּר יְהוָה אֶל־מֹשֶׁה לֵּאמֹר: 2דַּבֵּר אֶל־בְּנֵי יִשְׂרָאֵל וְאָמַרְתָּ אֲלֵהֶם אֲנִי יְהוָה אֱלֹהֵיכֶם: 3כְּמַעֲשֵׂה אֶרֶץ־מִצְרַיִם אֲשֶׁר יְשַׁבְתֶּם־בָּהּ לֹא תַעֲשׂוּ וּכְמַעֲשֵׂה אֶרֶץ־כְּנַעַן אֲשֶׁר אֲנִי מֵבִיא אֶתְכֶם שָׁמָּה לֹא תַעֲשׂוּ וּבְחֻקֹּתֵיהֶם לֹא תֵלֵכוּ: 4אֶת־מִשְׁפָּטַי תַּעֲשׂוּ וְאֶת־חֻקֹּתַי תִּשְׁמְרוּ לָלֶכֶת בָּהֶם אֲנִי יְהוָה אֱלֹהֵיכֶם: 5וּשְׁמַרְתֶּם אֶת־חֻקֹּתַי וְאֶת־מִשְׁפָּטַי אֲשֶׁר

17:15. **carcass or a torn animal**. See the comments on Lev 7:24.

18:4. **You shall do *my* judgments, and you shall observe *my* laws.** Why is this said now, after we have already had seventeen chapters of laws in Leviticus? This juncture at the beginning of chapter 18 is a turning point: Until now the laws of Leviticus have had to do with *ritual*: sacrifices, permitted and forbidden food, leprosy. But the rest of Leviticus (especially chapter 19) will give *ethical* laws as well—not separately, but interspersed with ritual laws. Turning to the ethical laws, we find that, on one hand, they are easier to deal with than ritual laws, first, simply because they are fewer and, second, because the reasons behind ethical law tend to be more readily apparent than these of ritual. We are inclined to question why cows are permitted for food and pigs are not, but when we read a command that "You shall not steal, and you shall not lie, and you shall not act false" (19:11), we do not generally feel the need to ask, "Why not?" On the other hand, what is harder about dealing with ethical laws is that they are not as easily grouped by types, and they in fact usually do not occur in long sections of related laws as do the sacrificial, food, purity, or leprosy laws. The exceptions are the lists of forbidden sexual relations (18:6–30; 20:10–20) and a group of economic laws (Leviticus 25). The ethical laws include such diverse matters as leaving portions of harvests for the poor, judging cases without bias (toward the rich or toward the poor), honoring the aged, fearing one's parents, not injuring the blind or deaf, not gossiping, not making one's daughter a prostitute, and not committing adultery. If there is any common denominator to these diverse laws it is: feeling empathy with other human beings and attributing value to the lives of all of them.

374

my judgments, which, when a human will do them, he'll live through them! I am YHWH.

6 "Any man, to any close relative of his: you shall not come close to expose nudity. I am YHWH. 7You shall not expose your father's nudity and your mother's nudity. She is your mother. You shall not expose her nudity. 8You shall not expose your father's wife's nudity. It is your father's nudity. 9Your sister's nudity—your father's daughter or your mother's daughter, born home or born outside—you shall not expose their nudity. 10The nudity of your son's daughter or your daughter's daughter—you shall not expose their nudity, because they are *your* nudity. 11The nudity of your father's wife's daughter, born of your father: she is your sister; you shall not expose her nudity. 12You shall not expose your father's sister's nudity. She is your father's close relative. 13You shall not expose your mother's sister's nudity. She is your mother's close relative. 14You shall not expose your father's brother's nudity: you shall not come close to his wife. She is your aunt. 15You shall not expose your daughter-in-law's nudity. She is your son's wife. You shall not expose her nudity. 16You shall not expose your

6 ס אִישׁ֩ אִ֨ישׁ אֶל־כָּל־שְׁאֵ֤ר בְּשָׂרוֹ֙ לֹ֣א תִקְרְב֔וּ לְגַלּ֖וֹת עֶרְוָ֑ה אֲנִ֖י יְהוָֽה׃ ס 7 עֶרְוַ֨ת אָבִ֜יךָ וְעֶרְוַ֤ת אִמְּךָ֙ לֹ֣א תְגַלֵּ֔ה אִמְּךָ֣ הִ֔וא לֹ֥א תְגַלֶּ֖ה עֶרְוָתָֽהּ׃ ס 8 עֶרְוַ֥ת אֵֽשֶׁת־אָבִ֖יךָ לֹ֣א תְגַלֵּ֑ה עֶרְוַ֥ת אָבִ֖יךָ הִֽוא׃ ס 9 עֶרְוַ֨ת אֲחֽוֹתְךָ֤ בַת־אָבִ֙יךָ֙ א֣וֹ בַת־אִמֶּ֔ךָ מוֹלֶ֣דֶת בַּ֔יִת א֖וֹ מוֹלֶ֣דֶת ח֑וּץ לֹ֥א תְגַלֶּ֖ה עֶרְוָתָֽן׃ ס 10 עֶרְוַ֤ת בַּת־בִּנְךָ֙ א֣וֹ בַֽת־בִּתְּךָ֔ לֹ֥א תְגַלֶּ֖ה עֶרְוָתָ֑ן כִּ֥י עֶרְוָתְךָ֖ הֵֽנָּה׃ ס 11 עֶרְוַ֨ת בַּת־אֵ֤שֶׁת אָבִ֙יךָ֙ מוֹלֶ֣דֶת אָבִ֔יךָ אֲחוֹתְךָ֖ הִ֑וא לֹ֥א תְגַלֶּ֖ה עֶרְוָתָֽהּ׃ ס 12 עֶרְוַ֥ת אֲחוֹת־אָבִ֖יךָ לֹ֣א תְגַלֵּ֑ה שְׁאֵ֥ר אָבִ֖יךָ הִֽוא׃ ס 13 עֶרְוַ֥ת אֲחֽוֹת־אִמְּךָ֖ לֹ֣א תְגַלֵּ֑ה כִּֽי־שְׁאֵ֥ר אִמְּךָ֖ הִֽוא׃ ס 14 עֶרְוַ֥ת אֲחִֽי־אָבִ֖יךָ לֹ֣א תְגַלֵּ֑ה אֶל־אִשְׁתּוֹ֙ לֹ֣א תִקְרָ֔ב דֹּדָתְךָ֖ הִֽוא׃ ס 15 עֶרְוַ֥ת כַּלָּֽתְךָ֖ לֹ֣א תְגַלֵּ֑ה אֵ֤שֶׁת בִּנְךָ֙ הִ֔וא לֹ֥א תְגַלֶּ֖ה עֶרְוָתָֽהּ׃ ס 16 עֶרְוַ֨ת

18:5. **when a human will do them, he'll live through them!** This way of picturing the laws, as a path to *life,* begins here. It returns as the climax of the Torah in Deuteronomy. The path to the Tree of Life is blocked at the Torah's beginning, and the way to recover it is emphasized at the Torah's end. The laws are not presented as a burden but as a blessing. Those who have characterized the law as a weight that no human can possibly bear, as a curse from which one needs to be saved, may insufficiently appreciate the positive, fulfilling quality of the law as experienced by those who live it. It is presented here as something that humans *can* do. And those who add so much to the law that it does become a weight, forcing those who observe it into separation from fellow Jews and from the world, risk diminishing the positive force of the law and its value as being ultimately a source of blessing for all the families of the earth.

18:6. **expose nudity.** This means sexual intimacy. In 18:14 the text indicates that, if one has sexual relations with one's aunt, one exposes one's *uncle's* nudity. So to "expose nudity" must be understood broadly as meaning to enter the zone of another person's sexuality.

18:15. **You shall not expose her nudity.** The command occurs twice in the case of sex with one's daughter-in-law. It is a particularly emphatic order to one who may well be in a position of sufficient power in a family to commit this act. And it is a particu-

brother's wife's nudity. It is your brother's nudity. ¹⁷You shall not expose the nudity of a woman and her daughter. You shall not take her son's daughter or her daughter's daughter to expose her nudity. They are close relatives. It is perversion. ¹⁸And you shall not take a woman to her sister to rival, to expose her nudity along with her in her lifetime. ¹⁹And you shall not come close to a woman during her menstrual impurity to expose her nudity. ²⁰And you shall not give your intercourse of seed to your fellow's wife, to become impure by it. ²¹And you shall not give any of your seed for passing to the Molech, and

אֵשֶׁת־אָחִיךָ לֹא תְגַלֵּה עֶרְוַת אָחִיךָ הִוא: ס
¹⁷עֶרְוַת אִשָּׁה וּבִתָּהּ לֹא תְגַלֵּה אֶת־בַּת־בְּנָהּ וְאֶת־בַּת־בִּתָּהּ לֹא תִקַּח לְגַלּוֹת עֶרְוָתָהּ שַׁאֲרָה הֵנָּה זִמָּה הִוא: ¹⁸וְאִשָּׁה אֶל־אֲחֹתָהּ לֹא תִקָּח לִצְרֹר לְגַלּוֹת עֶרְוָתָהּ עָלֶיהָ בְּחַיֶּיהָ: ¹⁹וְאֶל־אִשָּׁה בְּנִדַּת טֻמְאָתָהּ לֹא תִקְרַב לְגַלּוֹת עֶרְוָתָהּ: ²⁰וְאֶל־אֵשֶׁת עֲמִיתְךָ לֹא־תִתֵּן שְׁכָבְתְּךָ לְזָרַע לְטָמְאָה־בָהּ: ²¹וּמִזַּרְעֲךָ לֹא־תִתֵּן לְהַעֲבִיר לַמֹּלֶךְ וְלֹא תְחַלֵּל

larly emphatic prohibition of an act that may be especially hurtful and psychologically damaging.

18:18. along with her. The Hebrew and this English translation both contain an ambiguity: does it mean to marry two sisters (as it is frequently understood), to have sexual relations (whether married or not) with two sisters, or to have sexual relations with two sisters at the same time (as Rashi understands it)? It says, "in her lifetime"— which sounds as though it means marriage.

18:20. give your intercourse of seed. Why is the wording different in this verse from those that precede it—i.e., "give your intercourse of seed" instead of "expose nudity"? Perhaps it is to connect to the next verse. See the next comment.

18:21. give any of your seed. It has been asked why this commandment is placed here, grouped with the commandments against particular sexual unions. It must be relevant that this commandment and the commandment against adultery that precedes it both use the expression "to give seed." Perhaps the command against adultery and the command against sacrificing one's children came to be connected precisely because of the parallel of the wording in which each had come to be known. Or perhaps it is the reverse: that the "seed" wording was used in the preceding verse precisely to make the transition to the "Molech" law. A third possibility is that the point is precisely the *seed*: that sexual intercourse with a married woman involves a potential abuse of children, and the fact that the law against child sacrifice is adjacent to this prohibition serves to emphasize this danger.

18:21. for passing to the Molech. This "passing" must be understood in the light of the earlier commandment that requires the sacrifice of every firstborn: "you will *pass* every first birth of a womb to YHWH" (Exod 13:12). There, the Israelite is told to explain to his children: "I am *sacrificing* to YHWH every first birth of a womb, and I shall redeem every firstborn of my sons" (13:15). We learn from this that the term "passing" in such contexts refers to sacrifice and that Israelites are not permitted to sacrifice their children, either to the God of Israel or to a foreign deity. This is supported by a reference in 2 Kings 23:10 to "a man's passing his son or his daughter *in fire* to the Molech."

you shall not desecrate your God's name. I am YHWH. 22And you shall not lie with a male like lying with a woman. It is an offensive thing. 23And you shall not give your intercourse with

אֶת־שֵׁם אֱלֹהֶיךָ אֲנִי יְהוָה: 22וְאֶת־זָכָר לֹא תִשְׁכַּב מִשְׁכְּבֵי אִשָּׁה תּוֹעֵבָה הִוא: 23וּבְכָל־בְּהֵמָה לֹא־

18:21. **Molech.** Some have taken this to be the name of a pagan god to whom human sacrifices were made. But there is little evidence of any human sacrifice in the ancient Near East, and no evidence of such sacrifice to a god named Molech (or any similar name). There is evidence of human sacrifice at the Phoenician colony at Carthage, but there it is to the god Baal-Hammon. There is evidence that the term Molech refers rather to the *institution*, the *practice* of human sacrifice. The law here would thus mean that one should not bring one's offspring for the practice of Molech. The reference in Lev 20:2 below may shed further light on this.

18:22. **you shall not lie with a male like lying with a woman.** Why is male homosexuality explicitly forbidden in the Torah but not female? Some would surmise that it is because women are controlled in a patriarchal Israelite society; and so a woman would simply have no choice but to marry a man. But this is not an adequate explanation, because there would still be opportunities for female homosexual liaisons. Some would say that the concern is the *seed*, which is understood to come from the male, and therefore is "wasted" in another male. But the text calls homosexuality "an offensive thing" (in older translations: "an abomination"), which certainly sounds like an abhorrence of the act, and not just a concern with the practical matter of reproduction. The reason may rather be because the Torah comes from a world in which there is polygamy. A man can have sex with his two wives simultaneously. That this is understood to be permissible is implied by the fact that the law in v. 18 above forbids it only with sisters (see the comment). Or, even if the above case means marriage and not simultaneous sex, then simultaneous sex still is not forbidden anywhere in the Torah. If simultaneous sex with one's two (or more) wives is practiced, it would be difficult to allow this while forbidding female homosexuality. (At minimum, it could require a number of laws specifying what sort of contact is permissible and under what circumstances.)

In the present state of knowledge concerning homosexuality, it is difficult to justify its prohibition in the Torah. All of the movements in Judaism (and other religions) are currently contending with this issue. Its resolution ultimately must lie in the law of Deuteronomy that states that, for difficult matters of the law, people must turn to the authorities of their age, to those who are competent to judge, and those judges must decide (Deut 17:8–9).

In my own view, the present understanding of the nature of homosexuality indicates that it is not an "offensive thing" (also translated "abomination") as described in this verse. The Hebrew term for "offensive thing" (*tôʿēbāh*) is understood to be a *relative* term, which varies according to human perceptions. For example, in Genesis, Joseph tells his brothers that "any shepherd is an offensive thing to Egypt" (46:34); but, obviously, it is not an offensive thing to the Israelites. In light of the evidence at present, homosexuality cannot be said to be unnatural, nor is it an illness. Its prohi-

any animal, to become impure by it. And a woman shall not stand in front of an animal to mate with it. It is an aberration.

24"You shall not become impure by all of these, because the nations that I am putting out from in front of you became impure by all of these, 25and the land became impure, and I reckoned its sin on it, and the land vomited out its residents. 26But you: you shall observe my laws and my judgments and not do any of all these offensive things, the citizen and the alien who resides among you— 27because the people of the land who were before you did all of these offensive things, and the land became impure— 28so the land will not vomit you out for your making it impure as it vomited out the nation that was before you. 29Because anyone who will do any of these offensive things: the persons who do will be cut off from among their people. 30And you shall keep my charge: not to do any of the abominable customs that were done before you; and you will not become impure by them. I am YHWH, your God."

HOLY

19 1And YHWH spoke to Moses, saying, 2"Speak to all the congregation of the children of Israel, and you shall say to them: You shall be holy, because *I, YHWH, your God,* am holy.

תִּתֵּן שְׁכָבְתְּךָ לְטָמְאָה־בָהּ וְאִשָּׁה לֹא־תַעֲמֹד לִפְנֵי בְהֵמָה לְרִבְעָהּ תֶּבֶל הוּא: 24אַל־תִּטַּמְּאוּ בְּכָל־אֵלֶּה כִּי בְכָל־אֵלֶּה נִטְמְאוּ הַגּוֹיִם אֲשֶׁר־אֲנִי מְשַׁלֵּחַ מִפְּנֵיכֶם: 25וַתִּטְמָא הָאָרֶץ וָאֶפְקֹד עֲוֺנָהּ עָלֶיהָ וַתָּקִא הָאָרֶץ אֶת־יֹשְׁבֶיהָ: 26וּשְׁמַרְתֶּם אַתֶּם אֶת־חֻקֹּתַי וְאֶת־מִשְׁפָּטַי וְלֹא תַעֲשׂוּ מִכֹּל הַתּוֹעֵבֹת הָאֵלֶּה הָאֶזְרָח וְהַגֵּר הַגָּר בְּתוֹכְכֶם: 27כִּי אֶת־כָּל־הַתּוֹעֵבֹת הָאֵל עָשׂוּ אַנְשֵׁי־הָאָרֶץ אֲשֶׁר לִפְנֵיכֶם וַתִּטְמָא הָאָרֶץ: 28וְלֹא־תָקִיא הָאָרֶץ אֶתְכֶם בְּטַמַּאֲכֶם אֹתָהּ כַּאֲשֶׁר קָאָה אֶת־הַגּוֹי אֲשֶׁר לִפְנֵיכֶם: 29כִּי כָּל־אֲשֶׁר יַעֲשֶׂה מִכֹּל הַתּוֹעֵבוֹת הָאֵלֶּה וְנִכְרְתוּ הַנְּפָשׁוֹת הָעֹשֹׂת מִקֶּרֶב עַמָּם: 30וּשְׁמַרְתֶּם אֶת־מִשְׁמַרְתִּי לְבִלְתִּי עֲשׂוֹת מֵחֻקּוֹת הַתּוֹעֵבֹת אֲשֶׁר נַעֲשׂוּ לִפְנֵיכֶם וְלֹא תִטַּמְּאוּ בָּהֶם אֲנִי יְהוָה אֱלֹהֵיכֶם: פ

קדשים

19 1וַיְדַבֵּר יְהוָה אֶל־מֹשֶׁה לֵּאמֹר: 2דַּבֵּר אֶל־כָּל־עֲדַת בְּנֵי־יִשְׂרָאֵל וְאָמַרְתָּ אֲלֵהֶם קְדֹשִׁים תִּהְיוּ כִּי קָדוֹשׁ אֲנִי יְהוָה אֱלֹהֵיכֶם: 3אִישׁ אִמּוֹ וְאָבִיו

---

bition in this verse explicitly applies only so long as it *is* properly perceived to be offensive, and therefore the current state of the evidence suggests that the period in which this commandment was binding has come to an end.

19:2. **be holy**. What is meant here by being holy? The chapter that begins with this statement stands out because, perhaps more than any other in the Torah, it merges major commandments of so many different sorts. It includes most of the Ten Commandments, sacrifices, justice, caring for the poor and the infirm, treatment of women, of the elderly, food, magic, loving one's neighbor as oneself, loving an alien as oneself. If one had to choose only one chapter out of the Torah to make known, it might well be this one.

The strange mixing of so many different kinds of commandments may convey that every commandment is important. Even if we are naturally inclined to regard some

3"You shall each fear his mother and his father, and you shall observe my Sabbaths. I am
YHWH, your God.

4"Do not turn to idols, and you shall not
make molten gods for yourselves. I am YHWH,
your God.

5"And when you will make a peace-offering

תִּירָאוּ וְאֶת־שַׁבְּתֹתַי תִּשְׁמֹרוּ אֲנִי יְהוָה אֱלֹהֵיכֶם:
4אַל־תִּפְנוּ אֶל־הָאֱלִילִים וֵאלֹהֵי מַסֵּכָה לֹא תַעֲשׂוּ
לָכֶם אֲנִי יְהוָה אֱלֹהֵיכֶם: 5וְכִי תִזְבְּחוּ זֶבַח שְׁלָמִים

---

commandments as more important than others, and some commandments as most
important of all, this tapestry presses us to see what is important and valuable in every
commandment, even commandments that one may question.

19:3. **You shall each fear his mother and his father**. Mother comes before father
(the reverse of the order in the Ten Commandments). Rashi says this is because one
naturally fears the father more than the mother, so the text needs to emphasize fearing the mother. And he says that the Fifth Commandment has the reverse because it
says to *honor* your father and your mother," and one naturally honors the mother
more than the father, so the text needs to emphasize honoring the father. But this is
not necessarily true. Whatever the reason for the word order here, though, at the very
least it shows that the text sometimes puts father first and sometimes mother. And the
fact that it says to *fear* them, rather than the Decalogue's command to *honor* them, is
yet another parallel between parents and God, whom the Israelites are told to fear as
well (Deut 8:6). This in turn reminds us that this linkage between parents and God is
established at the beginning of the Torah: God is said to create humans in the divine
image and likeness (Gen 1:26), and then the first human is said to produce a son in
his image and likeness (Gen 5:3). And it reminds us that the fifth commandment (to
honor parents) comes between the first four, which relate to God, and the latter five,
which relate to fellow humans. And, to this day, the most natural and common analogy that people use when talking about conceptions of God is: parents. Indeed, it is
hardly a psychological insight to recognize that most people's conceptions of a deity
derive precisely from their experience of their parents. Especially in infancy, one's parents *are* godlike in their power and their caring for their children. Thus in a variety of
ways parents are seen in this role in the Torah.

19:3. **You shall each fear his mother and his father, and you shall observe my
Sabbaths**. Why are parents and Sabbaths put together here? (They come next to each
other in the Ten Commandments as well, in reverse order.) It reminds us of the enormous power of the Sabbath to bind a family together. My first Jewish memory in my
life is the image of my mother lighting the Sabbath candles and giving my sister and
me a kiss. Then my father would say the kiddush over the wine and give us each a sip.
In many families the parents say a blessing over each child: "May you be like Sarah,
Rebekah, Leah, and Rachel"; "May you be like Ephraim and Manasseh." In many, the
husband recites "A Woman of Valor" from the book of Proverbs to his wife. The potential for making something beautiful that will last through a person's life is tremendous. Even more: when one grows up, recalls these things from childhood, and repeats them with one's own children, one encounters the extraordinary feeling of being
linked through generations: both generations past and those to come.

sacrifice to YHWH, you shall sacrifice it so that it will be accepted for you. 6It shall be eaten on the day of your sacrifice and on the next day; and what is left until the third day shall be burned in fire. 7And if it *will* be eaten on the third day it is a repugnant thing. It shall not be acceptable. 8And anyone who eats it shall bear his crime, because he desecrated YHWH's holy thing, and that person will be cut off from his people. 9And when you reap your land's harvest, you shall not finish harvesting your field's corner, and you shall not gather your harvest's gleaning. 10And you shall not strip your vineyard, and you shall not collect the vineyard's fallen fruit. You shall leave them for the poor and for the alien. I am YHWH, your God.

11"You shall not steal, and you shall not lie, and you shall not act false, each against his fellow. 12And you shall not swear by my name falsely, so that you would desecrate your God's name. I am YHWH.

13"You shall not exploit your neighbor, and you shall not rob. An employee's wages shall not stay through the night with you until morning. 14You shall not curse a deaf person, and you shall not place a stumbling block in front of a blind person. And you shall fear your God. I am YHWH.

15"You shall not do an injustice in judgment. You shall not be partial to a weak person, and you shall not favor a big person. You shall judge your fellow with justice. 16You shall not go with

לַיהוָה לִרְצֹנְכֶם תִּזְבָּחֻהוּ: 6בְּיוֹם זִבְחֲכֶם יֵאָכֵל וּמִמָּחֳרָת וְהַנּוֹתָר עַד־יוֹם הַשְּׁלִישִׁי בָּאֵשׁ יִשָּׂרֵף: 7וְאִם הֵאָכֹל יֵאָכֵל בַּיּוֹם הַשְּׁלִישִׁי פִּגּוּל הוּא לֹא יֵרָצֶה: 8וְאֹכְלָיו עֲוֹנוֹ יִשָּׂא כִּי־אֶת־קֹדֶשׁ יְהוָה חִלֵּל וְנִכְרְתָה הַנֶּפֶשׁ הַהִוא מֵעַמֶּיהָ: 9וּבְקֻצְרְכֶם אֶת־קְצִיר אַרְצְכֶם לֹא תְכַלֶּה פְּאַת שָׂדְךָ לִקְצֹר וְלֶקֶט קְצִירְךָ לֹא תְלַקֵּט: 10וְכַרְמְךָ לֹא תְעוֹלֵל וּפֶרֶט כַּרְמְךָ לֹא תְלַקֵּט לֶעָנִי וְלַגֵּר תַּעֲזֹב אֹתָם אֲנִי יְהוָה אֱלֹהֵיכֶם:

11לֹא תִּגְנֹבוּ וְלֹא־תְכַחֲשׁוּ וְלֹא־תְשַׁקְּרוּ אִישׁ בַּעֲמִיתוֹ: 12וְלֹא־תִשָּׁבְעוּ בִשְׁמִי לַשָּׁקֶר וְחִלַּלְתָּ אֶת־שֵׁם אֱלֹהֶיךָ אֲנִי יְהוָה: 13לֹא־תַעֲשֹׁק אֶת־רֵעֲךָ וְלֹא תִגְזֹל לֹא־תָלִין פְּעֻלַּת שָׂכִיר אִתְּךָ עַד־בֹּקֶר: 14לֹא־תְקַלֵּל חֵרֵשׁ וְלִפְנֵי עִוֵּר לֹא תִתֵּן מִכְשֹׁל וְיָרֵאתָ מֵּאֱלֹהֶיךָ אֲנִי יְהוָה: 15לֹא־תַעֲשׂוּ עָוֶל בַּמִּשְׁפָּט לֹא־תִשָּׂא פְנֵי־דָל וְלֹא תֶהְדַּר פְּנֵי גָדוֹל בְּצֶדֶק תִּשְׁפֹּט עֲמִיתֶךָ: 16לֹא־תֵלֵךְ רָכִיל בְּעַמֶּיךָ

19:13. **stay through the night**. The term commonly has this meaning of spending the night (Gen 24:54; 31:54; 32:14).

19:14. **you shall fear your God**. One might think that he or she has nothing to fear from the deaf or blind persons who cannot know who is wronging them, but one is warned that God knows and that one should be afraid of the consequences. In this matter of divine knowledge, one is reminded of the case of David's affair with Bathsheba and his elimination of her husband—which are then known, revealed, and paid back by God (2 Samuel 11–12); and one is reminded of Jacob's deception of his father, Isaac (who is blind!)—which is paid back in kind when Jacob is in turn deceived by his sons with the same items that he used to deceive *his* father: his brother's cloak and the parts of a goat (Gen 27:9–16; 37:31; see the comment on Gen 37:31).

slander among your people. You shall not stand by at your neighbor's blood. I am YHWH.

17"You shall not hate your brother in your heart. You shall *criticize* your fellow, so you shall not bear sin over him. 18You shall not take revenge, and you shall not keep on at the children

לֹא תַעֲמֹד עַל־דַּם רֵעֶךָ אֲנִי יְהוָה: 17לֹא־תִשְׂנָא אֶת־אָחִיךָ בִּלְבָבֶךָ הוֹכֵחַ תּוֹכִיחַ אֶת־עֲמִיתֶךָ וְלֹא־תִשָּׂא עָלָיו חֵטְא: 18לֹא־תִקֹּם וְלֹא־תִטֹּר אֶת־בְּנֵי

19:16. **stand by at your neighbor's blood.** The meaning of this wording is uncertain. It has usually been understood to mean: to stand by when someone's life is in danger and one could do something to save it (also: to fail to come forward as a witness when one has knowledge concerning a taking of life). This is the opposite of the principle in American law that one does not have an "affirmative duty to rescue." The biblical principle is that one has to help a fellow human being if one is able.

19:17. **so you shall not bear sin over him.** If one fails to tell a person that he is doing wrong, then one bears some responsibility for things that this person goes on to do that might have been prevented.

19:18. **You shall not take revenge.** This general principle does not apply to the legal case of the "avenger of blood," which is a different term in Hebrew (Num 35:12,19; Deut 19:6). That case involves the execution of someone who is found to be guilty of premeditated murder. Revenge is such a threatening matter that it is understood in the Torah to belong to God alone, not to humans. The essential statement of this is the famous "Vengeance and recompense are mine" (Deut 32:35). Only God takes revenge (Deut 32:41,43) or can command humans to take revenge (Num 31:2). The notable exception is the law "If a man will strike his slave or his maid with a rod, and he dies by his hand, he shall be *avenged*" (Exod 21:20). The special issue there apparently is that God takes an interest in the life of a slave. Since the Israelites themselves were slaves, and since God brought them out, it is a matter of divine interest that Israel never mistreat a slave.

This command comes in the chapter of the Torah that most conveys the idea of humans being like God (*imitatio Dei*). It begins: "Be holy because I am holy" (19:2). And so those beginning words should not be taken to mean imitation of God in just any way. The command is specifically to be *holy*, as God is—to live a life of holiness *as defined for a human being*, because God is holy.

19:18. **you shall not keep on.** Meaning: to maintain hostility over time. One must not go on feeling anger, resentment, or a grudge against someone. Note that these commands against taking revenge or persisting in hostile feelings do not address the question of whether the revenge or the keeping on is justified or not. The issue here is that one believes oneself to have been wronged, and the instruction is: don't get even, don't harbor the feeling forever. It is destructive to one's energy and one's spirit.

19:18. **the children of your people.** Fellow Israelites. This section refers to ways in which Israelites are commanded by law to behave toward one another. Next, the laws requiring equal treatment for aliens will expand this. And, ultimately, this behavior of a community's members toward one another is meant to be observed by others, who

of your people. And you shall love your neighbor as yourself. I am YHWH.

¹⁹"You shall observe my laws. Your animal: you shall not mate two kinds. Your field: you shall not seed two kinds. And a garment of two kinds, *sha'atnez:* it shall not go on you.

עַמֶּ֔ךָ וְאָהַבְתָּ֥ לְרֵעֲךָ֖ כָּמ֑וֹךָ אֲנִ֖י יְהוָֽה׃
¹⁹אֶֽת־חֻקֹּתַי֮ תִּשְׁמֹרוּ֒ בְּהֶמְתְּךָ֙ לֹא־תַרְבִּ֣יעַ כִּלְאַ֔יִם
שָֽׂדְךָ֖ לֹא־תִזְרַ֣ע כִּלְאָ֑יִם וּבֶ֤גֶד כִּלְאַ֨יִם֙ שַֽׁעַטְנֵ֔ז לֹ֖א

---

will choose to do likewise. And thus Abraham's descendants would behave in such a way as to be a source of blessing to all the families of the earth.

19:18. love your neighbor as yourself. Also translated as "companion" or "fellow," the word (Hebrew *rea'*) means a member of one's own group, a peer. In some contexts that will mean one's fellow human being. In others it will mean a friend or neighbor. (Thus, in Gen 38:12,20 it refers to Judah's "friend," who is an Adullamite.) In others it will mean a fellow member of a particular community. Some understand "Love your neighbor as yourself" as applying only to one's fellow Israelites. Even if one takes that view of this commandment, one must acknowledge that in this same chapter there is also the commandment to love the alien, the foreigner, as oneself as well (19:34). The people of Israel are thus commanded to love all human beings, not just their own people, no matter how one understands the term. And this is extraordinary.

The law of Leviticus is pervaded with the notion of distinction: between priest and layperson, between holy and secular, between pure and impure, between Israel and the other nations, between good and bad, and sometimes simply between permitted and forbidden with no reasons given. The book defines the priest's task (to *distinguish,* Lev 10:10) in terms that explicitly recall God's creation by distinction in Genesis 1. The law of the eternal light recalls God's first distinction in the creation (between light and darkness). Leviticus forbids one to merge that which has been distinguished in creation: to breed two species of animals together, to sow a field with mixed seed, or to wear clothing of mixed fabric, *ša'atnēz* (19:19). It establishes a specific location for sacrifice and excludes all others. Nadab and Abihu are killed for an act that exceeds their defined function. However, Leviticus does include one exception to this pervasive idea of differentiating, which, ironically, is perhaps the most famous line in the book, namely: "Love your neighbor as yourself!" Besides everything else that is impressive about this instruction, it stands out as anomalous in a book that so regularly makes distinctions. In relations with one's fellow human beings one is commanded instead to *equate* them—to oneself and, by necessary implication, to one another. The exception improves the rule. The distinctions in ritual and ethical matters serve various needs of the people and the will of their God, but underpinning the distinctions is a principle of equality of treatment for all.

Another point: Note the progression: Love yourself. Love your neighbor. Love the alien. Love God (coming later, in Deut 6:5).

19:19. you shall not mate two kinds. One is not permitted to mate one's animal with an animal of a different species.

19:19. you shall not seed two kinds. One is not permitted to mix seeds of different species of plants together.

20"And when a man will lie with a woman—an intercourse of seed—and she is a maid designated to a man, and she has not been *redeemed*, or freedom has not been given to her, there will be a reparation. They shall not be put to death, because she was not freed. 21And he shall bring his guilt offering to YHWH, to the entrance of the Tent of Meeting, a ram for a guilt offering. 22And the priest shall atone over him with the ram for the guilt offering in front of YHWH over his sin that he committed, and it will be forgiven for him from his sin that he committed.

23"And when you will come to the land, and you will plant any tree for eating, you shall leave its top with its fruit uncircumcised. It shall be uncircumcised for three years for you. It shall not be eaten. 24And in the fourth year all of its fruit shall be holy, tributes for YHWH. 25And in the fifth year you shall eat its fruit, to increase its produce for you. I am YHWH, your God.

26"You shall not eat with the blood. You shall not practice divination, and you shall not prac-

20וְאִ֗ישׁ כִּֽי־יִשְׁכַּ֤ב אֶת־אִשָּׁה֙ פ יַעֲלֶ֖ה עָלֶֽיךָ׃
שִׁכְבַת־זֶ֔רַע וְהִ֣וא שִׁפְחָ֗ה נֶחֱרֶ֙פֶת֙ לְאִ֔ישׁ וְהָפְדֵּה֙ לֹ֣א נִפְדָּ֔תָה א֖וֹ חֻפְשָׁ֣ה לֹ֣א נִתַּן־לָ֑הּ בִּקֹּ֧רֶת תִּהְיֶ֛ה לֹ֥א יוּמְת֖וּ כִּֽי־לֹ֥א חֻפָּֽשָׁה׃ 21וְהֵבִ֤יא אֶת־אֲשָׁמוֹ֙ לַֽיהוָ֔ה אֶל־פֶּ֖תַח אֹ֣הֶל מוֹעֵ֑ד אֵ֖יל אָשָֽׁם׃ 22וְכִפֶּר֩ עָלָ֨יו הַכֹּהֵ֜ן בְּאֵ֤יל הָֽאָשָׁם֙ לִפְנֵ֣י יְהוָ֔ה עַל־חַטָּאת֖וֹ אֲשֶׁ֣ר חָטָ֑א וְנִסְלַ֣ח ל֔וֹ מֵחַטָּאת֖וֹ אֲשֶׁ֥ר חָטָֽא׃ פ 23וְכִֽי־תָבֹ֣אוּ אֶל־הָאָ֗רֶץ וּנְטַעְתֶּם֙ כָּל־עֵ֣ץ מַאֲכָ֔ל וַעֲרַלְתֶּ֥ם עָרְלָת֖וֹ אֶת־פִּרְי֑וֹ שָׁלֹ֣שׁ שָׁנִ֗ים יִהְיֶ֥ה לָכֶ֛ם עֲרֵלִ֖ים לֹ֥א יֵאָכֵֽל׃ 24וּבַשָּׁנָה֙ הָרְבִיעִ֔ת יִהְיֶ֖ה כָּל־פִּרְי֑וֹ קֹ֥דֶשׁ הִלּוּלִ֖ים לַֽיהוָֽה׃ 25וּבַשָּׁנָ֣ה הַחֲמִישִׁ֗ת תֹּֽאכְלוּ֙ אֶת־פִּרְי֔וֹ לְהוֹסִ֥יף לָכֶ֖ם תְּבוּאָת֑וֹ אֲנִ֛י יְהוָ֖ה אֱלֹהֵיכֶֽם׃ 26לֹ֥א תֹאכְל֖וּ עַל־הַדָּ֑ם לֹ֥א תְנַחֲשׁ֖וּ וְלֹ֥א תְעוֹנֵֽנוּ׃

19:19. *sha'atnez*. One is not permitted to wear an item of clothing made of two different species of fabric. This is specified in Deuteronomy as wool and linen together. The former comes from an animal, a sheep; and the latter comes from a plant, flax. On these laws against mixtures, see the comments on Deut 22:9,11.

It is a curious juxtaposition: the commandment to love one's neighbor *as oneself* directly followed by three commandments to maintain *distinctions*. It seems to be saying: distinctions among animals, plants, and clothing are appropriate, but making distinctions in one's love of humankind is an offense.

19:20. a maid designated to a man. A female slave has been designated for marriage to a particular man (either her owner or another man), but the marriage has not yet taken place. If another man has sexual relations with her, it is not adultery since she is not yet married, and therefore there is no death penalty for either the man or the woman; but there is still a reparation to be paid to the owner for the infringement on his maid.

19:23. leave its top with its fruit uncircumcised. The Hebrew uses the same word that is used for an uncircumcised foreskin. The treetop, including its fruit, is not to be cut until it is three years old. Thus one may not eat a tree's fruit for the first three years, one takes it to the priests in the fourth year, and one may eat it in the fifth.

19:26. You shall not eat with the blood. One is not to eat meat with blood still in it.

19:26. divination. Discovering what is going on by means of magic.

tice soothsaying. ²⁷You shall not trim your head's edge, and you shall not destroy your beard's edge. ²⁸You shall not put a cut in your flesh for a person, and you shall not put an inscription of a tattoo in you. I am YHWH.

²⁹"Do not desecrate your daughter to make her a prostitute, so the land will not go to prostitution, and the land will fill with perversion. ³⁰You shall observe my Sabbaths and fear my holy place. I am YHWH.

³¹"Do not turn to ghosts, and do not seek spirits of acquaintances, to become impure by them. I am YHWH, your God.

²⁷לֹא תַקִּפוּ פְּאַת רֹאשְׁכֶם וְלֹא תַשְׁחִית אֵת פְּאַת זְקָנֶךָ: ²⁸וְשֶׂרֶט לָנֶפֶשׁ לֹא תִתְּנוּ בִּבְשַׂרְכֶם וּכְתֹבֶת קַעֲקַע לֹא תִתְּנוּ בָּכֶם אֲנִי יְהוָה: ²⁹אַל־תְּחַלֵּל אֶת־בִּתְּךָ לְהַזְנוֹתָהּ וְלֹא־תִזְנֶה הָאָרֶץ וּמָלְאָה הָאָרֶץ זִמָּה: ³⁰אֶת־שַׁבְּתֹתַי תִּשְׁמֹרוּ וּמִקְדָּשִׁי תִּירָאוּ אֲנִי יְהוָה: ³¹אַל־תִּפְנוּ אֶל־הָאֹבֹת וְאֶל־הַיִּדְּעֹנִים אַל־תְּבַקְשׁוּ לְטָמְאָה בָהֶם אֲנִי יְהוָה אֱלֹהֵיכֶם: ³²מִפְּנֵי שֵׂיבָה

19:26. **soothsaying**. Telling the future by means of magic.

19:27. **your head's edge**. Sideburns.

19:28. **for a person**. Meaning: for a *dead* person; as a sign of mourning for someone who has died. Hebrew *nepeš* can mean soul, person, or life, depending on its context. Its root meaning, like other Hebrew words relating to life, has to do with respiration.

19:28. **inscription of a tattoo**. Writing in the skin.

19:30. **fear my holy place**. Commentators and translators often soften the Hebrew word for "fear" here, taking it to mean "revere" or "hold in awe." But there is reason to believe that it really does mean "fear," because it refers to a sacred place, applying first to the Tabernacle and later to the Temple. Laypersons are not even permitted to enter this place. We are told four times: "An outsider who comes close shall be put to death" (Num 1:51; 3:10,38; 18:7).

19:31. **ghosts, spirits of acquaintances**. There is archaeological and textual evidence that ancient Israelites engaged in ancestor veneration, i.e., worship at the site of the tombs of known relations. The Israelite priests were opposed to this, and the biblical law codes forbid it. It appears to have come to an end during the reign of Hezekiah, king of Judah. My colleague Baruch Halpern has shown that it was an ironic consequence of the Assyrians' destruction of the Israelite countryside, which cut the people off from these traditional sites. My student Shawna Dolansky Overton and I have written about this matter: In several places in which wizards, sorcerers, and other practitioners of forbidden magic are mentioned, we also find this phrase, Hebrew *'ôb wĕyiddĕ'ōnî(m)* (Deut 18:11; 1 Samuel 28; 2 Kings 23:24; Isa 8:19). Although the precise meaning of each term is uncertain, the phrase is almost always understood as "necromancer" or "medium." The term *'ôb* is particularly ambiguous because it is found in a variety of contexts in which it can be understood as "spirit, ancestral spirit, the person controlled by a spirit, a bag of skin, the pit from which spirits are called up, a ghost, or a demon." It has also been suggested that its etymology should be sought in the Ugaritic phrase *il 'ib*, usually understood as cognate to Hebrew *'ĕlōhê*

³²"You shall get up in front of an aged person, and you shall show respect in front of an elderly person. And you shall fear your God. I am YHWH.

³³"And if an alien will reside with you in your land, you shall not persecute him. ³⁴The alien who resides with you shall be to you like a citizen of yours, and you shall love him as yourself, because you were aliens in the land of Egypt. I am YHWH, your God.

³⁵"You shall not do an injustice in judgment, in measurement, in weight, and in quantity. ³⁶You shall have just scales, just weights, a just ephah, and a just hin. I am YHWH, your God, who brought you out from the land of Egypt.

³⁷"And you shall observe all my laws and all my judgments and do them. I am YHWH."

20 ¹And YHWH spoke to Moses, saying, ²"And to the children of Israel you shall say: Any man from the children of Israel and from the alien who resides in Israel who will give any of his seed to the Molech shall be *put to*

תָּקוּם וְהָדַרְתָּ פְּנֵי זָקֵן וְיָרֵאתָ מֵּאֱלֹהֶיךָ אֲנִי יְהוָה:
ס ³³וְכִי־יָגוּר אִתְּךָ גֵּר בְּאַרְצְכֶם לֹא תוֹנוּ אֹתוֹ:
³⁴כְּאֶזְרָח מִכֶּם יִהְיֶה לָכֶם הַגֵּר ׀ הַגָּר אִתְּכֶם
וְאָהַבְתָּ לוֹ כָּמוֹךָ כִּי־גֵרִים הֱיִיתֶם בְּאֶרֶץ מִצְרָיִם
אֲנִי יְהוָה אֱלֹהֵיכֶם: ³⁵לֹא־תַעֲשׂוּ עָוֶל בַּמִּשְׁפָּט
בַּמִּדָּה בַּמִּשְׁקָל וּבַמְּשׂוּרָה: ³⁶מֹאזְנֵי צֶדֶק אַבְנֵי־
צֶדֶק אֵיפַת צֶדֶק וְהִין צֶדֶק יִהְיֶה לָכֶם אֲנִי יְהוָה
אֱלֹהֵיכֶם אֲשֶׁר־הוֹצֵאתִי אֶתְכֶם מֵאֶרֶץ מִצְרָיִם:
³⁷וּשְׁמַרְתֶּם אֶת־כָּל־חֻקֹּתַי וְאֶת־כָּל־מִשְׁפָּטַי
וַעֲשִׂיתֶם אֹתָם אֲנִי יְהוָה: פ

20 ¹וַיְדַבֵּר יְהוָה אֶל־מֹשֶׁה לֵּאמֹר: ²וְאֶל־בְּנֵי
יִשְׂרָאֵל תֹּאמַר אִישׁ אִישׁ מִבְּנֵי יִשְׂרָאֵל וּמִן־הַגֵּר ׀
הַגָּר בְּיִשְׂרָאֵל אֲשֶׁר יִתֵּן מִזַּרְעוֹ לַמֹּלֶךְ מוֹת יוּמָת

'ābîw but plausibly meaning "god of the pit" rather than "god of the father(s)" (William Propp). Although *'ôb* is often found on its own (usually when it means "pit" or "bag of skin"), the word *yiddě'ōnî(m)* occurs only in tandem with *'ôb*. Some scholars take the phrase as a hendiadys while others, along with most translations, see it as referring to separate persons (e.g., medium and wizard). The root seems to be *yd'*, but what remains unclear is whether the "one who knows" is the spirit being consulted or the necromancer who does the consulting. This phrase is also frequently translated as "one who has a familiar spirit." No matter how these words are translated, each translation conveys the basic idea of communication between the living and the dead. *Although the biblical references to life after death are often noted to be fewer than one would have expected, the fact remains: these references plus the archaeological evidence show that Israelites in biblical times believed in an afterlife.* (For more discussion of the belief in afterlife in biblical Israel, and for citations and references, see our article, "Death and Afterlife: The Biblical Silence," in *Judaism in Late Antiquity*, vol. 4: *Death, Afterlife, Resurrection, and the World to Come*, edited by Alan J. Avery-Peck and Jacob Neusner.)

19:35. You shall not do an injustice in judgment. These exact words are already said in 19:15. Why are they repeated here? Because the law here is adding weights and measures to the picture. This conveys that an abuse in doing business is in the same category as an abuse in court. The issues are equity, fairness, honesty.

20:2. Molech. See the comment on 18:21. The evidence appears to me to favor the

death. The people of the land shall batter him with stone. [3]And I shall set my face against that man, and I shall cut him off from among his people because he gave any of his seed for the Molech so as to make my holy place impure and to desecrate my holy name. [4]And if the people of the land will *hide* their eyes from that man when he gives any of his seed for the Molech, not to put him to death, [5]then I shall set my face at that man and at his family, and I shall cut off him and all who whore after him, to whore after the Molech, from among their people. [6]And the person who will turn to ghosts and to spirits of acquaintances to whore after them: I shall set my face against that person and cut him off from among his people.

[7]"And you shall make yourselves holy, and you shall *be* holy, because I am YHWH, your God. [8]And you shall observe my laws and do them. I am YHWH, who makes you holy.

[9]"Because any man who will curse his father and his mother shall be *put to death.* He has cursed his father and his mother: his blood is on him!

[10]"And a man who will commit adultery with a man's wife—who will commit adultery with his neighbor's wife!—shall be *put to death:* the adulterer and the adulteress. [11]And a man who will lie with his father's wife, he has exposed his father's nudity: the two of them shall be *put to death.* Their blood is on them. [12]And a man who will lie with his daughter-in-law: the two of them shall be *put to death.* They have done an aberra-

עַם הָאָרֶץ יִרְגְּמֻהוּ בָאָבֶן: [3]וַאֲנִי אֶתֵּן אֶת־פָּנַי בָּאִישׁ הַהוּא וְהִכְרַתִּי אֹתוֹ מִקֶּרֶב עַמּוֹ כִּי מִזַּרְעוֹ נָתַן לַמֹּלֶךְ לְמַעַן טַמֵּא אֶת־מִקְדָּשִׁי וּלְחַלֵּל אֶת־שֵׁם קָדְשִׁי: [4]וְאִם הַעְלֵם יַעְלִימוּ עַם הָאָרֶץ אֶת־עֵינֵיהֶם מִן־הָאִישׁ הַהוּא בְּתִתּוֹ מִזַּרְעוֹ לַמֹּלֶךְ לְבִלְתִּי הָמִית אֹתוֹ: [5]וְשַׂמְתִּי אֲנִי אֶת־פָּנַי בָּאִישׁ הַהוּא וּבְמִשְׁפַּחְתּוֹ וְהִכְרַתִּי אֹתוֹ וְאֵת ׀ כָּל־הַזֹּנִים אַחֲרָיו לִזְנוֹת אַחֲרֵי הַמֹּלֶךְ מִקֶּרֶב עַמָּם: [6]וְהַנֶּפֶשׁ אֲשֶׁר תִּפְנֶה אֶל־הָאֹבֹת וְאֶל־הַיִּדְּעֹנִים לִזְנֹת אַחֲרֵיהֶם וְנָתַתִּי אֶת־פָּנַי בַּנֶּפֶשׁ הַהִוא וְהִכְרַתִּי אֹתוֹ מִקֶּרֶב עַמּוֹ: [7]וְהִתְקַדִּשְׁתֶּם וִהְיִיתֶם קְדֹשִׁים כִּי אֲנִי יְהוָה אֱלֹהֵיכֶם: [8]וּשְׁמַרְתֶּם אֶת־חֻקֹּתַי וַעֲשִׂיתֶם אֹתָם אֲנִי יְהוָה מְקַדִּשְׁכֶם: [9]כִּי־אִישׁ אִישׁ אֲשֶׁר יְקַלֵּל אֶת־אָבִיו וְאֶת־אִמּוֹ מוֹת יוּמָת אָבִיו וְאִמּוֹ קִלֵּל דָּמָיו בּוֹ: [10]וְאִישׁ אֲשֶׁר יִנְאַף אֶת־אֵשֶׁת אִישׁ אֲשֶׁר יִנְאַף אֶת־אֵשֶׁת רֵעֵהוּ מוֹת־יוּמַת הַנֹּאֵף וְהַנֹּאָפֶת: [11]וְאִישׁ אֲשֶׁר יִשְׁכַּב אֶת־אֵשֶׁת אָבִיו עֶרְוַת אָבִיו גִּלָּה מוֹת־יוּמְתוּ שְׁנֵיהֶם דְּמֵיהֶם בָּם: [12]וְאִישׁ אֲשֶׁר יִשְׁכַּב אֶת־כַּלָּתוֹ מוֹת יוּמְתוּ שְׁנֵיהֶם תֶּבֶל עָשׂוּ

---

understanding of Molech as the term for the *practice* of human sacrifice, and not as the name of a god to whom such sacrifices were made. The reference in v. 3 here, "to make my holy place impure and to desecrate my holy name," sounds as if it is forbidding making human sacrifices at the *Temple,* to YHWH. This is further evidence that the mention of Molech here refers to the practice, not to a god.

20:2. batter him with stone. Stone him to death.

20:12. a man who will lie with his daughter-in-law. That is precisely what Judah (unknowingly) does with Tamar (knowingly) in Genesis 38. But she is not punished. On the contrary, Judah acknowledges that she is right; and their union maintains the family line, from which David and the royal family of Israel will be descended. What

tion. Their blood is on them. ¹³And a man who will lie with a male like lying with a woman: the two of them have done an offensive thing. They shall be *put to death*. Their blood is on them. ¹⁴And a man who will take a woman and her mother: it is a perversion. You shall burn him and them in fire, so there will not be perversion among you. ¹⁵And a man who will have his intercourse with an animal shall be *put to death*. And you shall kill the animal. ¹⁶And a woman who will go up to any animal to mate with it: you shall kill the woman and the animal. They shall be *put to death*. Their blood is on them. ¹⁷And a man who will take his sister, his father's daughter or his mother's daughter, and see her nudity, and she will see his nudity, it is shame; and they will be cut off in the eyes of the children of their people. He has exposed his sister's nudity. He shall bear his crime. ¹⁸And a man who will lie with a menstruating woman and will expose her nudity: he has uncovered her source, and she has exposed the source of her blood. And the two of them will be cut off from among their people. ¹⁹And you shall not expose the nudity of your mother's sister or your father's sister, because one has thus uncovered his close relative. They shall bear their crime. ²⁰And a man who will lie with his aunt: he has exposed his uncle's

דְּמֵיהֶם בָּם: ¹³וְאִישׁ אֲשֶׁר יִשְׁכַּב אֶת־זָכָר מִשְׁכְּבֵי אִשָּׁה תּוֹעֵבָה עָשׂוּ שְׁנֵיהֶם מוֹת יוּמָתוּ דְּמֵיהֶם בָּם: ¹⁴וְאִישׁ אֲשֶׁר יִקַּח אֶת־אִשָּׁה וְאֶת־אִמָּהּ זִמָּה הִוא בָּאֵשׁ יִשְׂרְפוּ אֹתוֹ וְאֶתְהֶן וְלֹא־תִהְיֶה זִמָּה בְּתוֹכְכֶם: ¹⁵וְאִישׁ אֲשֶׁר יִתֵּן שְׁכָבְתּוֹ בִּבְהֵמָה מוֹת יוּמָת וְאֶת־הַבְּהֵמָה תַּהֲרֹגוּ: ¹⁶וְאִשָּׁה אֲשֶׁר תִּקְרַב אֶל־כָּל־בְּהֵמָה לְרִבְעָה אֹתָהּ וְהָרַגְתָּ אֶת־הָאִשָּׁה וְאֶת־הַבְּהֵמָה מוֹת יוּמָתוּ דְּמֵיהֶם בָּם: ¹⁷וְאִישׁ אֲשֶׁר־יִקַּח אֶת־אֲחֹתוֹ בַּת־אָבִיו אוֹ בַת־אִמּוֹ וְרָאָה אֶת־עֶרְוָתָהּ וְהִיא־תִרְאֶה אֶת־עֶרְוָתוֹ חֶסֶד הוּא וְנִכְרְתוּ לְעֵינֵי בְּנֵי עַמָּם עֶרְוַת אֲחֹתוֹ גִּלָּה עֲוֹנוֹ יִשָּׂא: ¹⁸וְאִישׁ אֲשֶׁר־יִשְׁכַּב אֶת־אִשָּׁה דָּוָה וְגִלָּה אֶת־עֶרְוָתָהּ אֶת־מְקֹרָהּ הֶעֱרָה וְהִיא גִּלְּתָה אֶת־מְקוֹר דָּמֶיהָ וְנִכְרְתוּ שְׁנֵיהֶם מִקֶּרֶב עַמָּם: ¹⁹וְעֶרְוַת אֲחוֹת אִמְּךָ וַאֲחוֹת אָבִיךָ לֹא תְגַלֵּה כִּי אֶת־שְׁאֵרוֹ הֶעֱרָה עֲוֹנָם יִשָּׂאוּ: ²⁰וְאִישׁ אֲשֶׁר יִשְׁכַּב אֶת־דֹּדָתוֹ עֶרְוַת דֹּדוֹ גִּלָּה

---

this law in Moses' age establishes is that the Judah-and-Tamar event is no longer permissible, just as some other acts of the patriarchal days become forbidden in the laws given to Moses.

20:13. **an offensive thing**. See the comment on Lev 18:22.

20:16. **mate**. It is the same word that is used earlier (Lev 19:19) to describe mating animals of two different species.

20:17. **they will be cut off in the eyes of the children of their people. . . . He shall bear his crime**. Why are the brother and sister not killed as in the preceding cases? Perhaps the case of sex between a brother and sister is regarded as more specifically internal (same family, same generation) than any other. And perhaps an observed history of genetic weaknesses in the offspring of sibling unions led Israel to see this offense as carrying its own punishment. The words "He shall bear his crime" mean that the punishment is to come from God, as I discussed earlier, and this fits with the idea that this is outside the jurisdiction of human courts.

nudity. They shall bear their sin. They shall die childless. ²¹And a man who will take his brother's wife: it is an impurity. He has exposed his brother's nudity. They will be childless.

²²"And you shall observe all my laws and all my judgments and do them, and the land to which I am bringing you to live in it will not vomit you out. ²³And you shall not go by the laws of the nation that I am ejecting from in front of you, because they have done all of these, and I am disgusted with them. ²⁴And I have said to you: You shall possess their land, and I shall give it to you to possess it, a land flowing with milk and honey. I am YHWH, your God, who has distinguished you from the peoples, ²⁵and you shall distinguish between the pure animal and the impure, and between the impure bird and the pure, and you shall not make yourselves detestable by an animal or by a bird or by anything that creeps on the ground that I have distinguished as impure for you. ²⁶And you shall be holy to me because I, YHWH, am holy, and I have distinguished you from the peoples to be mine.

²⁷"And a man or woman: if there will be among them a ghost or a spirit of an acquaintance, they shall be *put to death*. They shall batter them with stone. Their blood is on them."

SAY

21 ¹And YHWH said to Moses, "Say to the priests, the sons of Aaron, and say to

כְּתָאָם יִשָּׂאוּ עֲרִירִים יָמֻתוּ: ²¹וְאִישׁ אֲשֶׁר יִקַּח אֶת־אֵשֶׁת אָחִיו נִדָּה הִוא עֶרְוַת אָחִיו גִּלָּה עֲרִירִים יִהְיוּ:

²²וּשְׁמַרְתֶּם אֶת־כָּל־חֻקֹּתַי וְאֶת־כָּל־מִשְׁפָּטַי וַעֲשִׂיתֶם אֹתָם וְלֹא־תָקִיא אֶתְכֶם הָאָרֶץ אֲשֶׁר אֲנִי מֵבִיא אֶתְכֶם שָׁמָּה לָשֶׁבֶת בָּהּ: ²³וְלֹא תֵלְכוּ בְּחֻקֹּת הַגּוֹי אֲשֶׁר־אֲנִי מְשַׁלֵּחַ מִפְּנֵיכֶם כִּי אֶת־כָּל־אֵלֶּה עָשׂוּ וָאָקֻץ בָּם: ²⁴וָאֹמַר לָכֶם אַתֶּם תִּירְשׁוּ אֶת־אַדְמָתָם וַאֲנִי אֶתְּנֶנָּה לָכֶם לָרֶשֶׁת אֹתָהּ אֶרֶץ זָבַת חָלָב וּדְבָשׁ אֲנִי יְהוָה אֱלֹהֵיכֶם אֲשֶׁר־הִבְדַּלְתִּי אֶתְכֶם מִן־הָעַמִּים: ²⁵וְהִבְדַּלְתֶּם בֵּין־הַבְּהֵמָה הַטְּהֹרָה לַטְּמֵאָה וּבֵין־הָעוֹף הַטָּמֵא לַטָּהֹר וְלֹא־תְשַׁקְּצוּ אֶת־נַפְשֹׁתֵיכֶם בַּבְּהֵמָה וּבָעוֹף וּבְכֹל אֲשֶׁר תִּרְמֹשׂ הָאֲדָמָה אֲשֶׁר־הִבְדַּלְתִּי לָכֶם לְטַמֵּא: ²⁶וִהְיִיתֶם לִי קְדֹשִׁים כִּי קָדוֹשׁ אֲנִי יְהוָה וָאַבְדִּל אֶתְכֶם מִן־הָעַמִּים לִהְיוֹת לִי: ²⁷וְאִישׁ אוֹ־אִשָּׁה כִּי־יִהְיֶה בָהֶם אוֹב אוֹ יִדְּעֹנִי מוֹת יוּמָתוּ בָּאֶבֶן יִרְגְּמוּ אֹתָם דְּמֵיהֶם בָּם: פ

אמור

21 ¹וַיֹּאמֶר יְהוָה אֶל־מֹשֶׁה אֱמֹר אֶל־הַכֹּהֲנִים

20:24. **distinguished**. The word "distinguished" in English may connote a sense of higher status over others, but that is not at all applicable here. God is distinguishing Israel from other nations just as God distinguishes light from darkness and distinguishes sea from dry land in Genesis 1. It is a matter of separating and making distinctions among things, not a matter of hierarchies.

20:26. **I have distinguished you from the peoples to be mine**. On the meaning of this for the people of Israel, see the preceding comment and the comments on Exod 19:5 and Deut 7:6.

them: One shall not become impure for a person among his people ²except for his relative who is close to him: for his mother and for his father and for his son and for his daughter and for his brother ³and for his virgin sister who is close to him, who has not been a husband's; he may become impure for her. ⁴He shall not become impure as a husband among his people, for him to be desecrated. ⁵They shall not make a bald place on their head and shall not shave the corner of their beard and not make a cut in their flesh. ⁶They shall be holy to their God and shall not desecrate their God's name, because they are bringing forward YHWH's offerings by fire, their God's bread, so they shall be a holy thing. ⁷They shall not take a woman who is a prostitute and desecrated, and they shall not take a woman who is divorced from her husband, because he is holy to his God. ⁸And you shall regard him as holy because he is bringing forward your God's bread. He shall be holy to you because I, YHWH, who makes you holy, am holy. ⁹And the daughter of a man who is a priest who will become desecrated, to whore: she is desecrating her father. She shall be burned in fire.

¹⁰"And the priest who is the most senior of his

בְּנֵי אַהֲרֹן וְאָמַרְתָּ אֲלֵהֶם לְנֶפֶשׁ לֹא־יִטַּמָּא בְּעַמָּיו: ²כִּי אִם־לִשְׁאֵרוֹ הַקָּרֹב אֵלָיו לְאִמּוֹ וּלְאָבִיו וְלִבְנוֹ וּלְבִתּוֹ וּלְאָחִיו: ³וְלַאֲחֹתוֹ הַבְּתוּלָה הַקְּרוֹבָה אֵלָיו אֲשֶׁר לֹא־הָיְתָה לְאִישׁ לָהּ יִטַּמָּא: ⁴לֹא יִטַּמָּא בַּעַל בְּעַמָּיו לְהֵחַלּוֹ: ⁵לֹא־יִקְרְחֻה קָרְחָה בְּרֹאשָׁם וּפְאַת זְקָנָם לֹא יְגַלֵּחוּ וּבִבְשָׂרָם לֹא יִשְׂרְטוּ שָׂרָטֶת: ⁶קְדֹשִׁים יִהְיוּ לֵאלֹהֵיהֶם וְלֹא יְחַלְּלוּ שֵׁם אֱלֹהֵיהֶם כִּי אֶת־אִשֵּׁי יְהוָה לֶחֶם אֱלֹהֵיהֶם הֵם מַקְרִיבִם וְהָיוּ קֹדֶשׁ: ⁷אִשָּׁה זֹנָה וַחֲלָלָה לֹא יִקָּחוּ וְאִשָּׁה גְּרוּשָׁה מֵאִישָׁהּ לֹא יִקָּחוּ כִּי־קָדֹשׁ הוּא לֵאלֹהָיו: ⁸וְקִדַּשְׁתּוֹ כִּי־אֶת־לֶחֶם אֱלֹהֶיךָ הוּא מַקְרִיב קָדֹשׁ יִהְיֶה־לָּךְ כִּי קָדוֹשׁ אֲנִי יְהוָה מְקַדִּשְׁכֶם: ⁹וּבַת אִישׁ כֹּהֵן כִּי תֵחֵל לִזְנוֹת אֶת־אָבִיהָ הִיא מְחַלֶּלֶת בָּאֵשׁ תִּשָּׂרֵף: ס ¹⁰וְהַכֹּהֵן הַגָּדוֹל מֵאֶחָיו אֲשֶׁר־

21:5 קֿ יְקָרְחוּ

21:1. **become impure for a person.** Meaning: to become impure by coming into contact with a *dead* person.

21:6. **bread.** Hebrew *leḥem* here refers broadly to the food of the sacrifices.

21:8. **holy . . . holy . . . holy.** The word occurs seven times in three verses, and four times just in this last verse. It is not redundant, but rather emphatic. This entire section of the Torah is concerned with holiness—it is referred to in biblical scholarship as the Holiness Code—and in these verses it is focused on the persons who are designated to ensure and carry out that holiness and to be holy themselves.

21:8. *He shall be holy . . . I make you holy.* Note that there are degrees of holiness. All the people are holy, but the priests still are holy in a singular way because of their role. This matter of degree between the people's holiness and the priests' holiness will become an issue in the matter of Korah's rebellion (Num 16:3–7).

21:10. **most senior.** Literally, "the biggest priest," Hebrew *hakkōhēn haggādôl*. It is the standard term for the high priest and could therefore also be translated "the high priest from among his brothers." Israel's first two high priests, Aaron and Eliezer, are

brothers, on whose head the anointing oil will be poured and who has filled his hand to wear the clothes, he shall not let loose the hair of his head and not tear his clothes 11and he shall not come to any dead persons; he shall not become impure for his father and for his mother. 12And he shall not go out from the holy place, so he will not desecrate his God's holy place, because the crown with his God's anointing oil is on him. I am YHWH.

13"And he shall take a woman in her virginity. 14A widow and a divorcée and a desecrated woman, a prostitute: he shall not take these; he shall take none except a virgin from his people. 15And he shall not desecrate his seed among his people, because I, YHWH, make him holy."

16And YHWH spoke to Moses, saying, 17"Speak to Aaron, saying: A man from your seed, through their generations, in whom will be an injury shall not come forward to bring forward his God's bread. 18Because any man in whom is an injury shall not come forward: a blind man or a cripple or mutilated or who has an elongated limb 19or a man who has a break of the leg or a break of the arm in him 20or a hunchback or a dwarf or who has a spotting in his eye or is scabbed or scurvied or has crushed

יוּצַק עַל־רֹאשׁוֹ ׀ שֶׁמֶן הַמִּשְׁחָה וּמִלֵּא אֶת־יָדוֹ לִלְבֹּשׁ אֶת־הַבְּגָדִים אֶת־רֹאשׁוֹ לֹא יִפְרָע וּבְגָדָיו לֹא יִפְרֹם: 11וְעַל כָּל־נַפְשֹׁת מֵת לֹא יָבֹא לְאָבִיו וּלְאִמּוֹ לֹא יִטַּמָּא: 12וּמִן־הַמִּקְדָּשׁ לֹא יֵצֵא וְלֹא יְחַלֵּל אֵת מִקְדַּשׁ אֱלֹהָיו כִּי נֵזֶר שֶׁמֶן מִשְׁחַת אֱלֹהָיו עָלָיו אֲנִי יְהֹוָה: 13וְהוּא אִשָּׁה בִבְתוּלֶיהָ יִקָּח: 14אַלְמָנָה וּגְרוּשָׁה וַחֲלָלָה זֹנָה אֶת־אֵלֶּה לֹא יִקָּח כִּי אִם־בְּתוּלָה מֵעַמָּיו יִקַּח אִשָּׁה: 15וְלֹא־יְחַלֵּל זַרְעוֹ בְּעַמָּיו כִּי אֲנִי יְהֹוָה מְקַדְּשׁוֹ: פ

16וַיְדַבֵּר יְהֹוָה אֶל־מֹשֶׁה לֵּאמֹר: 17דַּבֵּר אֶל־אַהֲרֹן לֵאמֹר אִישׁ מִזַּרְעֲךָ לְדֹרֹתָם אֲשֶׁר יִהְיֶה בוֹ מוּם לֹא יִקְרַב לְהַקְרִיב לֶחֶם אֱלֹהָיו: 18כִּי כָל־אִישׁ אֲשֶׁר־בּוֹ מוּם לֹא יִקְרָב אִישׁ עִוֵּר אוֹ פִסֵּחַ אוֹ חָרֻם אוֹ שָׂרוּעַ: 19אוֹ אִישׁ אֲשֶׁר־יִהְיֶה בוֹ שֶׁבֶר רָגֶל אוֹ שֶׁבֶר יָד: 20אוֹ־גִבֵּן אוֹ־דַק אוֹ תְּבַלֻּל בְּעֵינוֹ אוֹ גָרָב אוֹ יַלֶּפֶת אוֹ מְרוֹחַ אָשֶׁךְ: 21כָּל־

---

each the oldest living son; but the high priests in the following centuries may or may not be the eldest sons of the preceding high priests.

21:10. **filled his hand.** See comment on Exod 29:29.

21:12. **crown with anointing oil.** It is unclear whether this term (Hebrew *nēzer*) refers to the priest's crown or to his hair (the crown of his head). The high priest's crown is associated with the anointing in Exod 29:6–7; but elsewhere in Priestly law this term refers to consecrated hair (Num 6:19). Here it is consecrated by the anointing oil. There it is consecrated by a vow taken by a Nazirite.

21:17. **injury.** Meaning: a hurt or impairment to his body. This has commonly been understood as "blemish" or "defect," but those terms may connote something like a shortcoming in the person, denigrating the person as being marred or unworthy. But the actual list indicates that these are injuries or impairments that occurred either at birth or later in the person's life. They do not reflect on the character or quality of the person. But they do disqualify the person from offering sacrifices. For examples of what constitutes an injury, see 21:18–20 and 24:19–20.

testicles. 21Any man from the seed of Aaron the priest in whom is an injury shall not come near to bring forward YHWH's offerings by fire. He has an injury in him. He shall not come near to bring forward his God's bread. 22He shall eat his God's bread, from the holies of holies and from the holies. 23Just: he shall not come to the pavilion, and he shall not come near to the altar, because he has an injury in him. And he shall not desecrate my holy places, because I, YHWH, make them holy."

24So Moses spoke to Aaron and to his sons and to all the children of Israel.

22 1And YHWH spoke to Moses, saying, 2"Speak to Aaron and to his sons that they be alerted regarding the holy things of the children of Israel that they consecrate to me, so they will not desecrate my holy name. I am YHWH. 3Say to them: Through your generations, any man who will come close, from all of your seed, to the holy things that the children of Israel will consecrate to YHWH, while his impurity is on him: that person will be cut off from in front of me. I am YHWH.

4"Any man from Aaron's seed and who is a leper or has an emission shall not eat any of the holy things until he becomes pure. And one who touches anything that is impure by a person, or a

אִישׁ אֲשֶׁר־בּוֹ מוּם מִזֶּרַע אַהֲרֹן הַכֹּהֵן לֹא יִגַּשׁ לְהַקְרִיב אֶת־אִשֵּׁי יְהוָה מוּם בּוֹ אֵת לֶחֶם אֱלֹהָיו לֹא יִגַּשׁ לְהַקְרִיב: 22לֶחֶם אֱלֹהָיו מִקָּדְשֵׁי הַקֳּדָשִׁים וּמִן־הַקֳּדָשִׁים יֹאכֵל: 23אַךְ אֶל־הַפָּרֹכֶת לֹא יָבֹא וְאֶל־הַמִּזְבֵּחַ לֹא יִגַּשׁ כִּי־מוּם בּוֹ וְלֹא יְחַלֵּל אֶת־מִקְדָּשַׁי כִּי אֲנִי יְהוָה מְקַדְּשָׁם: 24וַיְדַבֵּר מֹשֶׁה אֶל־אַהֲרֹן וְאֶל־בָּנָיו וְאֶל־כָּל־בְּנֵי יִשְׂרָאֵל: פ

22 1וַיְדַבֵּר יְהוָה אֶל־מֹשֶׁה לֵּאמֹר: 2דַּבֵּר אֶל־אַהֲרֹן וְאֶל־בָּנָיו וְיִנָּזְרוּ מִקָּדְשֵׁי בְנֵי־יִשְׂרָאֵל וְלֹא יְחַלְּלוּ אֶת־שֵׁם קָדְשִׁי אֲשֶׁר הֵם מַקְדִּשִׁים לִי אֲנִי יְהוָה: 3אֱמֹר אֲלֵהֶם לְדֹרֹתֵיכֶם כָּל־אִישׁ ׀ אֲשֶׁר־יִקְרַב מִכָּל־זַרְעֲכֶם אֶל־הַקֳּדָשִׁים אֲשֶׁר יַקְדִּישׁוּ בְנֵי־יִשְׂרָאֵל לַיהוָה וְטֻמְאָתוֹ עָלָיו וְנִכְרְתָה הַנֶּפֶשׁ הַהִוא מִלְּפָנַי אֲנִי יְהוָה: 4אִישׁ אִישׁ מִזֶּרַע אַהֲרֹן וְהוּא צָרוּעַ אוֹ זָב בַּקֳּדָשִׁים לֹא יֹאכַל עַד אֲשֶׁר יִטְהָר וְהַנֹּגֵעַ בְּכָל־טְמֵא־נֶפֶשׁ אוֹ אִישׁ אֲשֶׁר־תֵּצֵא

21:23. he shall not come near to the altar, because he has an injury in him. And he shall not desecrate my holy places. What should we make of the fact that someone who is injured physically is disqualified from various priestly services? As I indicated in the preceding comment, it is not a denigration of the person's worth or of his ethical merit. It is rather another case that relates to the ritual versus the ethical realm. At the time that I am writing this, we have lost the sense of zones of holiness, impurity, and so on. The Torah contains the element of awe for the sacred, inspiring great care regarding who enters the zone, what fits the zone, and what the zone's boundaries are. By present standards, most would judge it to be unkind and hurtful to exclude an injured person from the priesthood. The same standard applies in the biblical world in *ethical* matters: one must be considerate of persons who are handicapped (Lev 19:14). But in the ritual matter of the priesthood, physical conditions supersede such considerations.

22:4. impure by a person. Meaning: something that has become impure because of contact with the dead body of a person.

man from whom intercourse seed will come out, ⁵or a man who will touch any swarming creature by which he will become impure or a human by whom he will become impure, whatever his impurity: ⁶a person who will touch him will be impure until evening; and he shall not eat from the holy things unless he has washed his flesh in water. ⁷And when the sun has set, he shall be pure, and after that he shall eat from the holy things, because it is his food. ⁸He shall not eat a carcass or a torn animal, to become impure by it. I am YHWH.

⁹"And they shall keep my charge so they will not bear sin over it and die through it when they desecrate it. I, YHWH, make them holy.

¹⁰"And any outsider shall not eat what is holy: a priest's visitor and an employee shall not eat what is holy. ¹¹But when a priest buys a person as a possession by his money, he may eat it; and one who is born in his household: they may eat his bread. ¹²And a priest's daughter who will become an outsider's: she shall not eat the donated holy things; ¹³but a priest's daughter who will be a widow or a divorcée and has no seed and returns to her father's house as in her youth, she may eat from her father's bread. But any outsider shall not eat it. ¹⁴And a man who eats what is holy by mistake shall add to it a fifth of it and shall give the holy thing to the priest. ¹⁵And they shall not desecrate the holy things of the children of Israel that they will donate to YHWH ¹⁶so that they would make them bear a crime requiring a guilt offering by their eating their holy things, because I, YHWH, make them holy."

¹⁷And YHWH spoke to Moses, saying, ¹⁸"Speak to Aaron and to his sons and to all the children of Israel, and you shall say to them: Any man from the house of Israel or from the aliens in Israel who will make his offering—for all their vows and all their contributions that they bring forward to YHWH as a burnt offering— ¹⁹for acceptance

מִמֶּ֖נּוּ שִׁכְבַת־זָ֑רַע: ⁵אֽוֹ־אִ֗ישׁ אֲשֶׁ֤ר יִגַּע֙ בְּכָל־שֶׁ֣רֶץ אֲשֶׁ֣ר יִטְמָא־ל֔וֹ א֤וֹ בְאָדָם֙ אֲשֶׁ֣ר יִטְמָא־ל֔וֹ לְכֹ֖ל טֻמְאָתֽוֹ: ⁶נֶ֚פֶשׁ אֲשֶׁ֣ר תִּגַּע־בּ֔וֹ וְטָמְאָ֖ה עַד־הָעָ֑רֶב וְלֹ֤א יֹאכַל֙ מִן־הַקֳּדָשִׁ֔ים כִּ֛י אִם־רָחַ֥ץ בְּשָׂר֖וֹ בַּמָּֽיִם: ⁷וּבָ֣א הַשֶּׁ֔מֶשׁ וְטָהֵ֑ר וְאַחַר֙ יֹאכַ֣ל מִן־הַקֳּדָשִׁ֔ים כִּ֥י לַחְמ֖וֹ הֽוּא: ⁸נְבֵלָ֤ה וּטְרֵפָה֙ לֹ֣א יֹאכַ֔ל לְטָמְאָה־בָ֑הּ אֲנִ֖י יְהוָֽה: ⁹וְשָׁמְר֣וּ אֶת־מִשְׁמַרְתִּ֗י וְלֹֽא־יִשְׂא֤וּ עָלָיו֙ חֵ֔טְא וּמֵ֥תוּ ב֖וֹ כִּ֣י יְחַלְּלֻ֑הוּ אֲנִ֥י יְהוָ֖ה מְקַדְּשָֽׁם: ¹⁰וְכָל־זָ֖ר לֹא־יֹ֣אכַל קֹ֑דֶשׁ תּוֹשַׁ֥ב כֹּהֵ֛ן וְשָׂכִ֖יר לֹא־יֹ֥אכַל קֹֽדֶשׁ: ¹¹וְכֹהֵ֗ן כִּֽי־יִקְנֶ֥ה נֶ֙פֶשׁ֙ קִנְיַ֣ן כַּסְפּ֔וֹ ה֖וּא יֹ֣אכַל בּ֑וֹ וִילִ֣יד בֵּית֔וֹ הֵ֖ם יֹאכְל֥וּ בְלַחְמֽוֹ: ¹²וּבַת־כֹּהֵ֔ן כִּ֥י תִהְיֶ֖ה לְאִ֣ישׁ זָ֑ר הִ֕וא בִּתְרוּמַ֥ת הַקֳּדָשִׁ֖ים לֹ֥א תֹאכֵֽל: ¹³וּבַת־כֹּהֵן֩ כִּ֨י תִהְיֶ֜ה אַלְמָנָ֣ה וּגְרוּשָׁ֗ה וְזֶ֘רַע֮ אֵ֣ין לָהּ֒ וְשָׁבָ֞ה אֶל־בֵּ֤ית אָבִ֙יהָ֙ כִּנְעוּרֶ֔יהָ מִלֶּ֥חֶם אָבִ֖יהָ תֹּאכֵ֑ל וְכָל־זָ֖ר לֹא־יֹ֥אכַל בּֽוֹ: ס ¹⁴וְאִ֕ישׁ כִּֽי־יֹאכַ֥ל קֹ֖דֶשׁ בִּשְׁגָגָ֑ה וְיָסַ֤ף חֲמִֽשִׁיתוֹ֙ עָלָ֔יו וְנָתַ֥ן לַכֹּהֵ֖ן אֶת־הַקֹּֽדֶשׁ: ¹⁵וְלֹ֣א יְחַלְּל֔וּ אֶת־קָדְשֵׁ֖י בְּנֵ֣י יִשְׂרָאֵ֑ל אֵ֥ת אֲשֶׁר־יָרִ֖ימוּ לַֽיהוָֽה: ¹⁶וְהִשִּׂ֤יאוּ אוֹתָם֙ עֲוֺ֣ן אַשְׁמָ֔ה בְּאָכְלָ֖ם אֶת־קָדְשֵׁיהֶ֑ם כִּ֛י אֲנִ֥י יְהוָ֖ה מְקַדְּשָֽׁם: פ

¹⁷וַיְדַבֵּ֥ר יְהוָ֖ה אֶל־מֹשֶׁ֥ה לֵּאמֹֽר: ¹⁸דַּבֵּ֨ר אֶֽל־אַהֲרֹ֜ן וְאֶל־בָּנָ֗יו וְאֶל֙ כָּל־בְּנֵ֣י יִשְׂרָאֵ֔ל וְאָמַרְתָּ֖ אֲלֵהֶ֑ם אִ֣ישׁ אִישׁ֩ מִבֵּ֨ית יִשְׂרָאֵ֜ל וּמִן־הַגֵּ֣ר בְּיִשְׂרָאֵ֗ל אֲשֶׁ֨ר יַקְרִ֤יב קָרְבָּנוֹ֙ לְכָל־נִדְרֵיהֶ֔ם וּלְכָל־נִדְבוֹתָ֔ם אֲשֶׁר־יַקְרִ֥יבוּ לַיהוָ֖ה לְעֹלָֽה: ¹⁹לִֽרְצֹנְכֶ֖ם תָּמִ֣ים

22:10. **outsider**. See comment on Exod 29:33.

for you it is to be unblemished, male of the cattle, of the sheep, or of the goats. ²⁰You shall not bring forward any that has an injury in it, because it will not be acceptable for you. ²¹And a man who will bring forward a peace-offering sacrifice to YHWH to express a vow or as a contribution of the cattle or of the flock: it shall be unblemished for acceptance; there shall not be any injury in it. ²²Blind or broken or slashed or sore or scabbed or scurvied: you shall not bring these forward to YHWH, and you shall not give an offering by fire of them on the altar to YHWH. ²³An ox or a sheep that has an elongated limb or a short limb: you may make it a contribution, but it shall not be accepted for a vow. ²⁴And you shall not bring forward to YHWH one that is bruised, crushed, torn, or cut. And you shall not do it in your land, ²⁵and you shall not bring forward your God's bread from any of these from a foreigner's hand, because their flaw is in them, an injury is in them; they shall not be accepted for you."

²⁶And YHWH spoke to Moses, saying, ²⁷"When an ox or a sheep or a goat will be born, it will be under its mother seven days, and from the eighth day on it will be accepted as an offering, an offering by fire to YHWH. ²⁸And an ox or a sheep: you shall not slaughter it and its child on one day. ²⁹And if you will make a sacrifice of thanks to YHWH, you shall sacrifice it so it will be acceptable for you. ³⁰It shall be eaten on that day. Do not leave any of it until morning. I am YHWH.

³¹"And you shall observe my commandments and do them. I am YHWH.

³²"And you shall not desecrate my holy name, so I shall be sanctified among the children of Israel. I am YHWH, who makes you holy, ³³who

זָכָר בַּבָּקָר בַּכְּשָׂבִים וּבָעִזִּים: ²⁰כָּל אֲשֶׁר־בּוֹ מוּם לֹא תַקְרִיבוּ כִּי־לֹא לְרָצוֹן יִהְיֶה לָכֶם: ²¹וְאִישׁ כִּי־יַקְרִיב זֶבַח־שְׁלָמִים לַיהוָה לְפַלֵּא־נֶדֶר אוֹ לִנְדָבָה בַּבָּקָר אוֹ בַצֹּאן תָּמִים יִהְיֶה לְרָצוֹן כָּל־מוּם לֹא יִהְיֶה־בּוֹ: ²²עַוֶּרֶת אוֹ שָׁבוּר אוֹ־חָרוּץ אוֹ־יַבֶּלֶת אוֹ גָרָב אוֹ יַלֶּפֶת לֹא־תַקְרִיבוּ אֵלֶּה לַיהוָה וְאִשֶּׁה לֹא־תִתְּנוּ מֵהֶם עַל־הַמִּזְבֵּחַ לַיהוָה: ²³וְשׁוֹר וָשֶׂה שָׂרוּעַ וְקָלוּט נְדָבָה תַּעֲשֶׂה אֹתוֹ וּלְנֵדֶר לֹא יֵרָצֶה: ²⁴וּמָעוּךְ וְכָתוּת וְנָתוּק וְכָרוּת לֹא תַקְרִיבוּ לַיהוָה וּבְאַרְצְכֶם לֹא תַעֲשׂוּ: ²⁵וּמִיַּד בֶּן־נֵכָר לֹא תַקְרִיבוּ אֶת־לֶחֶם אֱלֹהֵיכֶם מִכָּל־אֵלֶּה כִּי מָשְׁחָתָם בָּהֶם מוּם בָּם לֹא יֵרָצוּ לָכֶם: פ

²⁶וַיְדַבֵּר יְהוָה אֶל־מֹשֶׁה לֵּאמֹר: ²⁷שׁוֹר אוֹ־כֶשֶׂב אוֹ־עֵז כִּי יִוָּלֵד וְהָיָה שִׁבְעַת יָמִים תַּחַת אִמּוֹ וּמִיּוֹם הַשְּׁמִינִי וָהָלְאָה יֵרָצֶה לְקָרְבַּן אִשֶּׁה לַיהוָה: ²⁸וְשׁוֹר אוֹ־שֶׂה אֹתוֹ וְאֶת־בְּנוֹ לֹא תִשְׁחֲטוּ בְּיוֹם אֶחָד: ²⁹וְכִי־תִזְבְּחוּ זֶבַח־תּוֹדָה לַיהוָה לִרְצֹנְכֶם תִּזְבָּחוּ: ³⁰בַּיּוֹם הַהוּא יֵאָכֵל לֹא־תוֹתִירוּ מִמֶּנּוּ עַד־בֹּקֶר אֲנִי יְהוָה: ³¹וּשְׁמַרְתֶּם מִצְוֹתַי וַעֲשִׂיתֶם אֹתָם אֲנִי יְהוָה: ³²וְלֹא תְחַלְּלוּ אֶת־שֵׁם קָדְשִׁי וְנִקְדַּשְׁתִּי בְּתוֹךְ בְּנֵי יִשְׂרָאֵל אֲנִי יְהוָה מְקַדִּשְׁכֶם: ³³הַמּוֹצִיא

22:28. it and its child on one day. It is possible that this is a parallel to the commandment against cooking a kid in its mother's milk. This case is more commonly understood to be a moral matter—a respect for the animals, accepting that although we eat animals we must appreciate that they are living beings—whereas the case of the kid also has a ritual dimension, reflected in a Ugaritic text. See comment on Exod 23:19.

brought you out from the land of Egypt to be God to you. I am YHWH."

23 ¹And YHWH spoke to Moses, saying, ²"Speak to the children of Israel, and you shall say to them: YHWH's appointed times, which you shall call holy assemblies—these are my appointed times: ³Six days work shall be done, and in the seventh day is a Sabbath, a ceasing, a holy assembly. You shall not do any work. It is a Sabbath to YHWH in all your homes.

⁴"These are YHWH's appointed times, holy assemblies that you shall proclaim at their appointed time: ⁵In the first month, on the fourteenth of the month, 'between the two evenings,' is YHWH's Passover. ⁶And on the fifteenth day of this month is YHWH's Festival of Unleavened Bread. You shall eat unleavened bread seven days. ⁷On the first day you shall have a holy assembly. You shall not do any act of work. ⁸And you shall bring forward an offering by fire to YHWH for seven days. On the seventh day you shall have a holy assembly. You shall not do any act of work."

אֶתְכֶם֙ מֵאֶ֣רֶץ מִצְרַ֔יִם לִהְי֥וֹת לָכֶ֖ם לֵאלֹהִ֑ים אֲנִ֖י יְהוָֽה: פ

23 ¹וַיְדַבֵּ֥ר יְהוָ֖ה אֶל־מֹשֶׁ֥ה לֵּאמֹֽר: ²דַּבֵּ֞ר אֶל־בְּנֵ֤י יִשְׂרָאֵל֙ וְאָמַרְתָּ֣ אֲלֵהֶ֔ם מוֹעֲדֵ֣י יְהוָ֔ה אֲשֶׁר־תִּקְרְא֥וּ אֹתָ֖ם מִקְרָאֵ֣י קֹ֑דֶשׁ אֵ֥לֶּה הֵ֖ם מוֹעֲדָֽי: ³שֵׁ֣שֶׁת יָמִים֮ תֵּעָשֶׂ֣ה מְלָאכָה֒ וּבַיּ֣וֹם הַשְּׁבִיעִ֗י שַׁבַּ֤ת שַׁבָּתוֹן֙ מִקְרָא־קֹ֔דֶשׁ כָּל־מְלָאכָ֖ה לֹ֣א תַעֲשׂ֑וּ שַׁבָּ֥ת הִוא֙ לַֽיהוָ֔ה בְּכֹ֖ל מֽוֹשְׁבֹתֵיכֶֽם: פ

⁴אֵ֚לֶּה מוֹעֲדֵ֣י יְהוָ֔ה מִקְרָאֵ֖י קֹ֑דֶשׁ אֲשֶׁר־תִּקְרְא֥וּ אֹתָ֖ם בְּמוֹעֲדָֽם: ⁵בַּחֹ֣דֶשׁ הָרִאשׁ֗וֹן בְּאַרְבָּעָ֥ה עָשָׂ֛ר לַחֹ֖דֶשׁ בֵּ֣ין הָעַרְבָּ֑יִם פֶּ֖סַח לַיהוָֽה: ⁶וּבַחֲמִשָּׁ֨ה עָשָׂ֥ר יוֹם֙ לַחֹ֣דֶשׁ הַזֶּ֔ה חַ֥ג הַמַּצּ֖וֹת לַיהוָ֑ה שִׁבְעַ֥ת יָמִ֖ים מַצּ֥וֹת תֹּאכֵֽלוּ: ⁷בַּיּוֹם֙ הָרִאשׁ֔וֹן מִקְרָא־קֹ֖דֶשׁ יִהְיֶ֣ה לָכֶ֑ם כָּל־מְלֶ֥אכֶת עֲבֹדָ֖ה לֹ֥א תַעֲשֽׂוּ: ⁸וְהִקְרַבְתֶּ֥ם אִשֶּׁ֛ה לַיהוָ֖ה שִׁבְעַ֣ת יָמִ֑ים בַּיּ֤וֹם הַשְּׁבִיעִי֙ מִקְרָא־קֹ֔דֶשׁ כָּל־מְלֶ֥אכֶת עֲבֹדָ֖ה לֹ֥א תַעֲשֽׂוּ: פ ⁹וַיְדַבֵּ֥ר

23:2. these are my appointed times. The laws of the holidays as expressed in Leviticus reflect a concern with order and arrangement as well. YHWH tells Moses to tell the people what the nation's holidays are to be, specifically: the Sabbath, the holiday of unleavened bread (*maṣṣôt*), an unnamed holiday related to firstfruits, an unnamed holiday involving horn blowing (known subsequently in Judaism, but not biblically, as the New Year), the Day of Atonement, and the holiday of booths (*sukkôt*). In each case the text gives information on how to celebrate the holiday. In all but one case it gives the date on which the holiday is to be celebrated. Interestingly, it does not make historical associations for the holidays, not even connecting the feast of unleavened bread to the exodus from Egypt, or the Sabbath to God's rest at the end of the creation. (The single exception is an instruction in 23:39–43 that the Israelites should live in booths during the feast of *sukkôt* in order to remember that YHWH had Israel live in booths when He brought them out of Egypt.) It appears that the main concern, as with the food and purity laws, is not to explicate the background and purposes of the holidays—these things are a concern of Genesis, Exodus, Numbers, and Deuteronomy—but rather to instruct the people on how to observe them properly. In the case of the holidays, the concern of Leviticus with categorization and organization is applied to the temporal as well as the spatial, thus institutionalizing the sanctification of time more than in any text thus far. Organization through ritual is thus designed to pervade the people's life.

9And YHWH spoke to Moses, saying, 10"Speak to the children of Israel, and you shall say to them: When you will come to the land that I am giving to you and you reap its harvest, you shall bring the first sheaf of your harvest to the priest, 11and he shall elevate the sheaf in front of YHWH for acceptance for you. The priest shall elevate it on the day after the Sabbath. 12And on the day of your elevating the sheaf, you shall do an unblemished lamb in its first year as a burnt offering to YHWH, 13and its grain offering shall be two-tenths of a measure of fine flour mixed with oil, an offering by fire to YHWH, a pleasant smell, and its libation shall be wine, a fourth of a hin. 14And you shall not eat bread or parched or fresh grain until that very day, until you have brought your God's offering. It is an eternal law through your generations in all your homes. 15And you shall count from the day after the Sabbath, from the day of your bringing the sheaf for an elevation offering, seven Sabbaths. They shall be complete. 16You shall count until the day after the seventh Sabbath: fifty days. And you shall bring forward a new grain offering to YHWH. 17From your homes you shall bring bread for an elevation offering: two of them. They shall be two-tenths of a measure of fine flour, baked with leaven, firstfruits to YHWH. 18And you shall bring forward with the bread seven lambs, unblemished one-year-olds, and one bull of the cattle and two rams. They shall be a burnt offering to YHWH, with their grain offering and their libations, an offering by fire, a pleasant smell to YHWH. 19And you shall do one goat as a sin offering and two one-year-old lambs as a peace-offering sacrifice. 20And the priest shall elevate them with the bread of firstfruits, an elevation offering in front of YHWH with the two sheep. They shall be a holy thing to YHWH: for the priest. 21And you shall proclaim on that very day: you shall have a holy assembly. You shall not do any act of work: an eternal law in all your homes

יְהוָה אֶל־מֹשֶׁה לֵּאמֹר: 10דַּבֵּר אֶל־בְּנֵי יִשְׂרָאֵל וְאָמַרְתָּ אֲלֵהֶם כִּי־תָבֹאוּ אֶל־הָאָרֶץ אֲשֶׁר אֲנִי נֹתֵן לָכֶם וּקְצַרְתֶּם אֶת־קְצִירָהּ וַהֲבֵאתֶם אֶת־עֹמֶר רֵאשִׁית קְצִירְכֶם אֶל־הַכֹּהֵן: 11וְהֵנִיף אֶת־הָעֹמֶר לִפְנֵי יְהוָה לִרְצֹנְכֶם מִמָּחֳרַת הַשַּׁבָּת יְנִיפֶנּוּ הַכֹּהֵן: 12וַעֲשִׂיתֶם בְּיוֹם הֲנִיפְכֶם אֶת־הָעֹמֶר כֶּבֶשׂ תָּמִים בֶּן־שְׁנָתוֹ לְעֹלָה לַיהוָה: 13וּמִנְחָתוֹ שְׁנֵי עֶשְׂרֹנִים סֹלֶת בְּלוּלָה בַשֶּׁמֶן אִשֶּׁה לַיהוָה רֵיחַ נִיחֹחַ וְנִסְכֹּה יַיִן רְבִיעִת הַהִין: 14וְלֶחֶם וְקָלִי וְכַרְמֶל לֹא תֹאכְלוּ עַד־עֶצֶם הַיּוֹם הַזֶּה עַד הֲבִיאֲכֶם אֶת־קָרְבַּן אֱלֹהֵיכֶם חֻקַּת עוֹלָם לְדֹרֹתֵיכֶם בְּכֹל מֹשְׁבֹתֵיכֶם: ס 15וּסְפַרְתֶּם לָכֶם מִמָּחֳרַת הַשַּׁבָּת מִיּוֹם הֲבִיאֲכֶם אֶת־עֹמֶר הַתְּנוּפָה שֶׁבַע שַׁבָּתוֹת תְּמִימֹת תִּהְיֶינָה: 16עַד מִמָּחֳרַת הַשַּׁבָּת הַשְּׁבִיעִת תִּסְפְּרוּ חֲמִשִּׁים יוֹם וְהִקְרַבְתֶּם מִנְחָה חֲדָשָׁה לַיהוָה: 17מִמּוֹשְׁבֹתֵיכֶם תָּבִיאוּ לֶחֶם תְּנוּפָה שְׁתַּיִם שְׁנֵי עֶשְׂרֹנִים סֹלֶת תִּהְיֶינָה חָמֵץ תֵּאָפֶינָה בִּכּוּרִים לַיהוָה: 18וְהִקְרַבְתֶּם עַל־הַלֶּחֶם שִׁבְעַת כְּבָשִׂים תְּמִימִם בְּנֵי שָׁנָה וּפַר בֶּן־בָּקָר אֶחָד וְאֵילִם שְׁנָיִם יִהְיוּ עֹלָה לַיהוָה וּמִנְחָתָם וְנִסְכֵּיהֶם אִשֵּׁה רֵיחַ־נִיחֹחַ לַיהוָה: 19וַעֲשִׂיתֶם שְׂעִיר־עִזִּים אֶחָד לְחַטָּאת וּשְׁנֵי כְבָשִׂים בְּנֵי שָׁנָה לְזֶבַח שְׁלָמִים: 20וְהֵנִיף הַכֹּהֵן אֹתָם עַל לֶחֶם הַבִּכּוּרִים תְּנוּפָה לִפְנֵי יְהוָה עַל־שְׁנֵי כְּבָשִׂים קֹדֶשׁ יִהְיוּ לַיהוָה לַכֹּהֵן: 21וּקְרָאתֶם בְּעֶצֶם הַיּוֹם הַזֶּה מִקְרָא־קֹדֶשׁ יִהְיֶה לָכֶם כָּל־מְלֶאכֶת עֲבֹדָה לֹא תַעֲשׂוּ חֻקַּת עוֹלָם

23:15. **seven Sabbaths**. Meaning: seven full weeks.

through your generations. 22And when you reap your land's harvest, you shall not finish your field's corner when you harvest, and you shall not gather your harvest's gleaning. You shall leave them for the poor and for the alien. I am YHWH, your God."

23And YHWH spoke to Moses, saying, 24"Speak to the children of Israel, saying: In the seventh month, on the first of the month you shall have a ceasing, a commemoration with horn-blasting, a holy assembly. 25You shall not do any act of work. And you shall bring forward an offering by fire to YHWH."

26And YHWH spoke to Moses, saying, 27"Just: On the tenth of this seventh month, it is the Day of Atonement. You shall have a holy assembly, and you shall degrade yourselves. And you shall bring forward an offering by fire to YHWH. 28And you shall not do any work on this very day, because it is a day of atonement, to atone for you in front of YHWH, your God. 29Because any person who will not be degraded on this very day will be cut off from his people. 30And any person

22וּבְקֻצְרְכֶם אֶת־קְצִיר אַרְצְכֶם לֹא־תְכַלֶּה פְּאַת שָׂדְךָ בְּקֻצְרֶךָ וְלֶקֶט קְצִירְךָ לֹא תְלַקֵּט לֶעָנִי וְלַגֵּר תַּעֲזֹב אֹתָם אֲנִי יְהוָה אֱלֹהֵיכֶם: ס 23וַיְדַבֵּר יְהוָה אֶל־מֹשֶׁה לֵּאמֹר: 24דַּבֵּר אֶל־בְּנֵי יִשְׂרָאֵל לֵאמֹר בַּחֹדֶשׁ הַשְּׁבִיעִי בְּאֶחָד לַחֹדֶשׁ יִהְיֶה לָכֶם שַׁבָּתוֹן זִכְרוֹן תְּרוּעָה מִקְרָא־קֹדֶשׁ: 25כָּל־מְלֶאכֶת עֲבֹדָה לֹא תַעֲשׂוּ וְהִקְרַבְתֶּם אִשֶּׁה לַיהוָה: ס 26וַיְדַבֵּר יְהוָה אֶל־מֹשֶׁה לֵּאמֹר: 27אַךְ בֶּעָשׂוֹר לַחֹדֶשׁ הַשְּׁבִיעִי הַזֶּה יוֹם הַכִּפֻּרִים הוּא מִקְרָא־קֹדֶשׁ יִהְיֶה לָכֶם וְעִנִּיתֶם אֶת־נַפְשֹׁתֵיכֶם וְהִקְרַבְתֶּם אִשֶּׁה לַיהוָה: 28וְכָל־מְלָאכָה לֹא תַעֲשׂוּ בְּעֶצֶם הַיּוֹם הַזֶּה כִּי יוֹם כִּפֻּרִים הוּא לְכַפֵּר עֲלֵיכֶם לִפְנֵי יְהוָה אֱלֹהֵיכֶם: 29כִּי כָל־הַנֶּפֶשׁ אֲשֶׁר לֹא־תְעֻנֶּה בְּעֶצֶם הַיּוֹם הַזֶּה וְנִכְרְתָה מֵעַמֶּיהָ: 30וְכָל־הַנֶּפֶשׁ אֲשֶׁר תַּעֲשֶׂה כָל־

***

23:24. **In the seventh month, on the first of the month**. This holiday is not named; but, coming nine days before Yom Kippur and involving the blasting of a horn, it is clearly the holiday that is now known as the Jewish New Year, Rosh Hashanah. It is not known by this name in the Torah because, as this verse indicates, it came in the seventh month of the calendar. In the Torah's calendar, the first month comes in spring, and the first holiday is Passover (see Exod 12:2).

23:24. **blasting**. Sounding a shofar or trumpet.

23:27. **Just**. This term of special emphasis (Hebrew *'ak*) introduces commands concerning certain holidays: the Sabbath (Exod 31:13), Passover (12:16), the Day of Atonement (Lev 23:27), and Sukkot (23:39).

23:27. **degrade yourselves**. The word "degrade" is the same term that is used for what the Egyptians did to the Israelites (Exod 1:11–12). As a noun or adjective, the word means "poor." As a verb, it means "to abuse, afflict, oppress." It suggests that on the Day of Atonement one is to be hard on oneself and not to give care to making one-self look attractive or materially successful. It is understood to include fasting.

23:29,30. **his people**. The Hebrew word for "person" or "soul" (*nepeš*) is feminine, and so this is a case in which the feminine form stands for both men and women— contrary to the usual practice in Hebrew (and English). A more neutral English trans- lation could be "I shall destroy that soul from among its people." But the word "soul"

who will do any work in this very day: I shall destroy that person from among his people. 31You shall not do any work: an eternal law through your generations in all your homes. 32It is a Sabbath, a ceasing, for you, and you shall degrade yourselves: on the ninth of the month in the evening, from evening to evening, you shall keep your Sabbath."

33And YHWH spoke to Moses, saying, 34"Speak to the children of Israel, saying: On the fifteenth day of this seventh month is the Festival of Booths, seven days, for YHWH. 35On the first day is a holy assembly. You shall not do any act of work. 36For seven days you shall bring forward an offering by fire to YHWH. On the eighth day you shall have a holy assembly, and you shall bring forward an offering by fire to YHWH. It is a convocation. You shall not do any act of work.

37"These are YHWH's appointed times, which you shall call holy assemblies, to bring forward an offering by fire to YHWH: burnt offering and grain offering, sacrifice and libations, each day's thing on its day, 38aside from YHWH's Sabbaths and aside from your gifts and aside from all of your vows and aside from all of your contributions that you will give to YHWH.

39"Just: On the fifteenth day of the seventh month when you gather the land's produce, you shall celebrate YHWH's holiday seven days. On the first day is a ceasing, and on the eighth day is a ceasing. 40And on the first day you shall take

מְלָאכָה בְּעֶ֫צֶם הַיּ֣וֹם הַזֶּ֑ה וְהַאֲבַדְתִּ֛י אֶת־הַנֶּ֥פֶשׁ הַהִ֖וא מִקֶּ֥רֶב עַמָּֽהּ׃ 31כָּל־מְלָאכָ֖ה לֹ֣א תַעֲשׂ֑וּ חֻקַּ֤ת עוֹלָם֙ לְדֹרֹ֣תֵיכֶ֔ם בְּכֹ֖ל מֹשְׁבֹֽתֵיכֶֽם׃ 32שַׁבַּ֨ת שַׁבָּת֥וֹן הוּא֙ לָכֶ֔ם וְעִנִּיתֶ֖ם אֶת־נַפְשֹׁתֵיכֶ֑ם בְּתִשְׁעָ֤ה לַחֹ֨דֶשׁ֙ בָּעֶ֔רֶב מֵעֶ֣רֶב עַד־עֶ֔רֶב תִּשְׁבְּת֖וּ שַׁבַּתְּכֶֽם׃ פ

33וַיְדַבֵּ֥ר יְהוָ֖ה אֶל־מֹשֶׁ֥ה לֵּאמֹֽר׃ 34דַּבֵּ֞ר אֶל־בְּנֵ֤י יִשְׂרָאֵל֙ לֵאמֹ֔ר בַּחֲמִשָּׁ֨ה עָשָׂ֜ר י֗וֹם לַחֹ֤דֶשׁ הַשְּׁבִיעִי֙ הַזֶּ֔ה חַ֧ג הַסֻּכּ֛וֹת שִׁבְעַ֥ת יָמִ֖ים לַֽיהֹוָֽה׃ 35בַּיּ֥וֹם הָרִאשׁ֖וֹן מִקְרָא־קֹ֑דֶשׁ כָּל־מְלֶ֥אכֶת עֲבֹדָ֖ה לֹ֥א תַעֲשֽׂוּ׃ 36שִׁבְעַ֣ת יָמִ֔ים תַּקְרִ֥יבוּ אִשֶּׁ֖ה לַיהֹוָ֑ה בַּיּ֣וֹם הַשְּׁמִינִ֡י מִֽקְרָא־קֹ֩דֶשׁ֩ יִהְיֶ֨ה לָכֶ֜ם וְהִקְרַבְתֶּ֨ם אִשֶּׁ֤ה לַֽיהֹוָה֙ עֲצֶ֣רֶת הִ֔וא כָּל־מְלֶ֥אכֶת עֲבֹדָ֖ה לֹ֥א תַעֲשֽׂוּ׃ 37אֵ֚לֶּה מוֹעֲדֵ֣י יְהֹוָ֔ה אֲשֶׁר־תִּקְרְא֥וּ אֹתָ֖ם מִקְרָאֵ֣י קֹ֑דֶשׁ לְהַקְרִ֨יב אִשֶּׁ֤ה לַֽיהֹוָה֙ עֹלָ֣ה וּמִנְחָ֔ה זֶ֥בַח וּנְסָכִ֖ים דְּבַר־י֥וֹם בְּיוֹמֽוֹ׃ 38מִלְּבַ֖ד שַׁבְּתֹ֣ת יְהֹוָ֑ה וּמִלְּבַ֣ד מַתְּנֽוֹתֵיכֶ֗ם וּמִלְּבַד֙ כָּל־נִדְרֵיכֶ֔ם וּמִלְּבַד֙ כָּל־נִדְבֹֽתֵיכֶ֔ם אֲשֶׁ֥ר תִּתְּנ֖וּ לַֽיהֹוָֽה׃ 39אַ֡ךְ בַּחֲמִשָּׁה֩ עָשָׂ֨ר י֜וֹם לַחֹ֣דֶשׁ הַשְּׁבִיעִ֗י בְּאָסְפְּכֶם֙ אֶת־תְּבוּאַ֣ת הָאָ֔רֶץ תָּחֹ֥גּוּ אֶת־חַג־יְהֹוָ֖ה שִׁבְעַ֣ת יָמִ֑ים בַּיּ֤וֹם הָרִאשׁוֹן֙ שַׁבָּת֔וֹן וּבַיּ֥וֹם הַשְּׁמִינִ֖י שַׁבָּתֽוֹן׃ 40וּלְקַחְתֶּ֨ם לָכֶ֜ם בַּיּ֤וֹם הָרִאשׁוֹן֙ פְּרִ֨י עֵ֤ץ הָדָר֙

---

carries a wide range of meanings, which go beyond the point of this verse. And it is worth noting that there are occasions when the feminine as well as the masculine is used to stand for all humans.

23:34. **Booths**. Hebrew *sukkôt*. This term is used to describe the function of the *pārōket*, the pavilion that covers over the ark (Exod 40:3; Ps 27:5; Lam 2:6; see my comment on Exod 26:31). It thus reflects simultaneously both the simple, makeshift dwellings that house the Israelites in the wilderness period and the beautiful, most sacred structure that houses the ark.

23:36. **convocation**. The meaning of this term, Hebrew *'ăṣeret*, is uncertain. It occurs six times in the *Tanak*, and five of them refer specifically to this holiday, now known as Shemini Atzeret. The sixth (Jer 9:1) suggests that it means a gathering of people. It is thus understood to mean a special assembly.

fruit of appealing trees, branches of palms, boughs of thick trees, and willows of a wadi, and you shall be happy in front of YHWH, your God, seven days. 41And you shall celebrate it, a holiday to YHWH, seven days in the year, an eternal law through your generations; you shall celebrate it in the seventh month. 42You shall live in booths seven days. Every citizen in Israel shall live in booths, 43so your generations will know that I had the children of Israel live in booths when I brought them out from the land of Egypt. I am YHWH, your God."

44And Moses spoke YHWH's appointed times to the children of Israel.

24 1And YHWH spoke to Moses, saying, 2"Command the children of Israel that they shall take clear pressed olive oil to you for the light, to keep up a lamp always. 3Outside of the pavilion of the Testimony, in the Tent of Meeting, Aaron shall arrange it from evening until morning in front of YHWH always, an eternal law through your generations. 4He shall arrange the lamps on the pure menorah in front of YHWH always.

5"And you shall take fine flour and bake it into twelve loaves: each loaf shall be two-tenths of a measure. 6And you shall set them in two rows, six to a row, on the pure table in front of YHWH. 7And you shall put clear frankincense on each row, and it will be a representative portion for the bread, an offering by fire to YHWH. 8On the Sabbath day, on the Sabbath day, he shall arrange it in front of YHWH always from the children of Israel, an eternal covenant. 9And it shall be Aaron's and his sons', and they shall eat it in a holy place, because it is the holy of holies to him from YHWH's offerings by fire, an eternal law."

כַּפֹּת תְּמָרִים וַעֲנַף עֵץ־עָבֹת וְעַרְבֵי־נָחַל וּשְׂמַחְתֶּם לִפְנֵי יְהוָה אֱלֹהֵיכֶם שִׁבְעַת יָמִים: 41וְחַגֹּתֶם אֹתוֹ חַג לַיהוָה שִׁבְעַת יָמִים בַּשָּׁנָה חֻקַּת עוֹלָם לְדֹרֹתֵיכֶם בַּחֹדֶשׁ הַשְּׁבִיעִי תָּחֹגּוּ אֹתוֹ: 42בַּסֻּכֹּת תֵּשְׁבוּ שִׁבְעַת יָמִים כָּל־הָאֶזְרָח בְּיִשְׂרָאֵל יֵשְׁבוּ בַּסֻּכֹּת: 43לְמַעַן יֵדְעוּ דֹרֹתֵיכֶם כִּי בַסֻּכּוֹת הוֹשַׁבְתִּי אֶת־בְּנֵי יִשְׂרָאֵל בְּהוֹצִיאִי אוֹתָם מֵאֶרֶץ מִצְרַיִם אֲנִי יְהוָה אֱלֹהֵיכֶם: 44וַיְדַבֵּר מֹשֶׁה אֶת־מֹעֲדֵי יְהוָה אֶל־בְּנֵי יִשְׂרָאֵל: פ

24 1וַיְדַבֵּר יְהוָה אֶל־מֹשֶׁה לֵּאמֹר: 2צַו אֶת־בְּנֵי יִשְׂרָאֵל וְיִקְחוּ אֵלֶיךָ שֶׁמֶן זַיִת זָךְ כָּתִית לַמָּאוֹר לְהַעֲלֹת נֵר תָּמִיד: 3מִחוּץ לְפָרֹכֶת הָעֵדֻת בְּאֹהֶל מוֹעֵד יַעֲרֹךְ אֹתוֹ אַהֲרֹן מֵעֶרֶב עַד־בֹּקֶר לִפְנֵי יְהוָה תָּמִיד חֻקַּת עוֹלָם לְדֹרֹתֵיכֶם: 4עַל הַמְּנֹרָה הַטְּהֹרָה יַעֲרֹךְ אֶת־הַנֵּרוֹת לִפְנֵי יְהוָה תָּמִיד: פ 5וְלָקַחְתָּ סֹלֶת וְאָפִיתָ אֹתָהּ שְׁתֵּים עֶשְׂרֵה חַלּוֹת שְׁנֵי עֶשְׂרֹנִים יִהְיֶה הַחַלָּה הָאֶחָת: 6וְשַׂמְתָּ אוֹתָם שְׁתַּיִם מַעֲרָכוֹת שֵׁשׁ הַמַּעֲרָכֶת עַל הַשֻּׁלְחָן הַטָּהֹר לִפְנֵי יְהוָה: 7וְנָתַתָּ עַל־הַמַּעֲרֶכֶת לְבֹנָה זַכָּה וְהָיְתָה לַלֶּחֶם לְאַזְכָּרָה אִשֶּׁה לַיהוָה: 8בְּיוֹם הַשַּׁבָּת בְּיוֹם הַשַּׁבָּת יַעַרְכֶנּוּ לִפְנֵי יְהוָה תָּמִיד מֵאֵת בְּנֵי־יִשְׂרָאֵל בְּרִית עוֹלָם: 9וְהָיְתָה לְאַהֲרֹן וּלְבָנָיו וַאֲכָלֻהוּ בְּמָקוֹם קָדֹשׁ כִּי קֹדֶשׁ קָדָשִׁים הוּא לוֹ מֵאִשֵּׁי יְהוָה חָק־עוֹלָם: ס 10וַיֵּצֵא

23:42. **booths.** Hebrew *sukkôt.* See comment on 23:34.

24:8. **On the Sabbath day, on the Sabbath day.** Meaning: on every Sabbath.

10And a son of an Israelite woman—and he was a son of an Egyptian man—went out among the children of Israel, and the son of the Israelite woman fought with an Israelite man in the camp. 11And the son of the Israelite woman profaned the name and cursed. And they brought him to Moses. And his mother's name was Shelomith, daughter of Dibri, of the tribe of Dan. 12And they left him under watch, to determine it for them by YHWH's word.

13And YHWH spoke to Moses, saying, 14"Take out the one who cursed to the outside of the camp, and let all who heard lay their hands on his head, and all the congregation shall batter him.

בֶּן־אִשָּׁה יִשְׂרְאֵלִית וְהוּא בֶּן־אִישׁ מִצְרִי בְּתוֹךְ בְּנֵי יִשְׂרָאֵל וַיִּנָּצוּ בַּמַּחֲנֶה בֶּן הַיִּשְׂרְאֵלִית וְאִישׁ הַיִּשְׂרְאֵלִי: 11וַיִּקֹּב בֶּן־הָאִשָּׁה הַיִּשְׂרְאֵלִית אֶת־הַשֵּׁם וַיְקַלֵּל וַיָּבִיאוּ אֹתוֹ אֶל־מֹשֶׁה וְשֵׁם אִמּוֹ שְׁלֹמִית בַּת־דִּבְרִי לְמַטֵּה־דָן: 12וַיַּנִּיחֻהוּ בַּמִּשְׁמָר לִפְרֹשׁ לָהֶם עַל־פִּי יְהוָה: פ 13וַיְדַבֵּר יְהוָה אֶל־מֹשֶׁה לֵּאמֹר: 14הוֹצֵא אֶת־הַמְקַלֵּל אֶל־מִחוּץ לַמַּחֲנֶה וְסָמְכוּ כָל־הַשֹּׁמְעִים אֶת־יְדֵיהֶם עַל־רֹאשׁוֹ וְרָגְמוּ

24:10–23. a son of an Israelite woman. . . . they battered him with stone. It is curious that this single story occurs here in a section fifteen chapters long that otherwise simply states the law without any accompanying narratives. This story's significance may lie in the fact that it states that the man in question is the son of an Israelite woman and an Egyptian father, and the deity's decision includes the notation that the law applies equally to an alien and to a citizen. It therefore appears that the offender in this story is an alien (see the comment on Lev 24:16,22), and the account therefore has the value not only of dramatizing the law concerning blasphemy, but also of dramatizing the principle of equality before the law: "You shall have one judgment: it will be the same for the alien and the citizen" (24:22). Indeed, the group of laws that were described above as reflecting the notion of equivalence of justice ("eye for eye . . . ") is embedded in the middle of this very story. The story may appear here, therefore, because it illustrates several important laws and an extremely important legal principle.

The story is also interesting in parallel with the only other narrative in Leviticus, the story of the consecration of the priesthood. Like that other story, which culminates in the deaths of Aaron's sons, the account of the blasphemy expresses what is at stake in the people's young relationship with their God. Further, in the earlier account, it is God who deals with the offenders, Nadab and Abihu, directly; whereas in this account of the blasphemy, humans themselves must deal justice. The two stories thus convey together the idea that the law is both a divine and a human concern.

24:14. lay their hands on his head. The community's elders lay their hands on the head of a bull that is slaughtered as a sacrifice for a sin (4:15); and Aaron and his sons lay their hands on the head of the animal that is sacrificed as a sin offering (Lev 8:14). And so the mention of this ritual here brings up a frightful image of what is to come for the man who cursed, and it emphasizes the unusual solemnity of this execution for the crime of cursing God.

24:14. batter. Meaning: stone to death.

15"And you shall speak to the children of Israel, saying: Any man who curses his God: he shall bear his sin. 16And one who profanes YHWH's name shall be *put to death*. All the congregation shall *batter* him. The same for the alien and the citizen: when he profanes the name he shall be put to death.

17"And a man who will strike any human's life shall be *put to death*, 18and one who strikes an animal's life shall pay for it: a life for a life. 19And a man who will make an injury in his fellow: as he has done, so it shall be done to him. 20A break for a break, an eye for an eye, a tooth for a tooth: as he will make an injury in a human, so it shall

אֹתֽוֹ כָּל־הָעֵדָֽה: 15וְאֶל־בְּנֵ֣י יִשְׂרָאֵל֮ תְּדַבֵּ֣ר לֵאמֹר֒ אִ֥ישׁ אִ֖ישׁ כִּֽי־יְקַלֵּ֣ל אֱלֹהָ֑יו וְנָשָׂ֖א חֶטְאֽוֹ: 16וְנֹקֵ֤ב שֵׁם־יְהוָה֙ מ֣וֹת יוּמָ֔ת רָג֥וֹם יִרְגְּמוּ־ב֖וֹ כָּל־הָעֵדָ֑ה כַּגֵּר֙ כָּֽאֶזְרָ֔ח בְּנָקְבוֹ־שֵׁ֖ם יוּמָֽת: 17וְאִ֕ישׁ כִּ֥י יַכֶּ֖ה כָּל־נֶ֣פֶשׁ אָדָ֑ם מ֖וֹת יוּמָֽת: 18וּמַכֵּ֥ה נֶֽפֶשׁ־בְּהֵמָ֖ה יְשַׁלְּמֶ֑נָּה נֶ֖פֶשׁ תַּ֥חַת נָֽפֶשׁ: 19וְאִ֕ישׁ כִּֽי־יִתֵּ֥ן מ֖וּם בַּעֲמִית֑וֹ כַּאֲשֶׁ֣ר עָשָׂ֔ה כֵּ֖ן יֵעָ֥שֶׂה לּֽוֹ: 20שֶׁ֚בֶר תַּ֣חַת שֶׁ֔בֶר עַ֚יִן תַּ֣חַת עַ֔יִן שֵׁ֖ן תַּ֣חַת שֵׁ֑ן כַּאֲשֶׁ֨ר יִתֵּ֥ן מוּם֙

24:16,22. **the same for the alien and the citizen**. This phrase occurs at both the beginning and the end of this section on equivalence in justice. This principle of treating an alien like a citizen comes up often in the Torah, but its double emphasis here in the story of a man who has an Israelite mother and an Egyptian father is significant. It indicates that this man is an alien, because there would be no reason to make a special point of this principle if he were a citizen (that is, a native Israelite). It is further evidence that in biblical times a person's identification was based on the father (patrilineal descent). In every case we have encountered thus far, the woman and children take the ethnic and religious identity of the woman's husband—Sarah, Rebekah, Leah, Rachel, Zipporah, and their children. And all sons of Levite fathers are Levites, regardless of the tribal origins of their mothers. Likewise, all tribal identification is through the father (see the comment on Num 36:3). Identification in the Torah is patrilineal. This continues through the *Tanak* until the time of Ezra and Nehemiah. At that point it appears to change, because when Nehemiah opposes marriages of Jewish men to women from certain other groups, he instructs that their children be excluded (Nehemiah 13). And in postbiblical Judaism, identification came to be based on the mother (matrilineal descent). In the Torah, however, it follows the father in every case. Identification by patrilineal descent (in addition to matrilineal descent, not in place of it) is at present a matter of dispute among the movements in Judaism.

24:17. **strike any human's life**. Meaning: strike to death.

24:20. **an eye for an eye**. Perhaps the most perplexing of the ethical laws is the principle of justice expressed in the formulation "an eye for an eye." It has frequently been cited as evidence of the stern character of YHWH, but that is a misunderstanding. In its context in Leviticus it applies solely to human justice. YHWH Himself frequently follows a more relenting course than that, from the golden calf event to a series of reprieves for seemingly undeserving individuals and communities in subsequent books of the *Tanak*. As for the meaning of this formulation for human justice, we must read it in its context, where the basic principle appears to be that punishment should correspond to the crime and never exceed it:

be made in him. 21And one who strikes an animal shall pay for it, and one who strikes a human shall be put to death. 22You shall have one judgment: it will be the same for the alien and the citizen; because I am YHWH, your God."

23And Moses spoke to the children of Israel. And they brought out the one who cursed to the outside of the camp, and they battered him with stone.

And the children of Israel had done as YHWH commanded Moses.

בָּאָדָם כֵּן יִנָּתֶן בּוֹ: 21וּמַכֵּה בְהֵמָה יְשַׁלְּמֶנָּה וּמַכֵּה אָדָם יוּמָת: 22מִשְׁפַּט אֶחָד יִהְיֶה לָכֶם כַּגֵּר כָּאֶזְרָח יִהְיֶה כִּי אֲנִי יְהוָה אֱלֹהֵיכֶם: 23וַיְדַבֵּר מֹשֶׁה אֶל־בְּנֵי יִשְׂרָאֵל וַיּוֹצִיאוּ אֶת־הַמְקַלֵּל אֶל־מִחוּץ לַמַּחֲנֶה וַיִּרְגְּמוּ אֹתוֹ אָבֶן וּבְנֵי־יִשְׂרָאֵל עָשׂוּ כַּאֲשֶׁר צִוָּה יְהוָה אֶת־מֹשֶׁה: פ

A man who will make an injury in his fellow: as he has done, so it shall be done to him.

A break for a break, an eye for an eye, a tooth for a tooth: as he will make an injury in a human, so it shall be made in him.

And one who strikes [mortally] an animal shall pay for it, and one who strikes [mortally] a human shall be put to death.

You shall have one judgment: it will be the same for the alien and the citizen.

The common principle of all the instances in this group appears to be one of equivalence in justice. To that extent it is a prohibition against imposing punishments that do not suit the crime; e.g., execution as a punishment for killing an animal or for wounding a man; or more severe punishments for lower-class defendants or foreigners than for others. The question remains as to whether "a break for a break, an eye for an eye" was meant literally or if it likewise referred figuratively to equivalence of punishment: not requiring the court actually to gouge the eye of a man convicted of gouging, but only to exact an appropriate monetary compensation for the victim. The text certainly appears to be speaking quite literally. It is set in the middle of a story of an actual stoning, and the wording would not ordinarily be taken as figurative were it not for our surprise at the severity of it in comparison to our own current laws. Still, we must be cautious about our ability to judge the meaning of idiomatic expressions in the Hebrew of an ancient age, a Hebrew in which, for example, the expression "to know God face-to-face" explicitly did *not* mean actually to see the deity's face (Exod 33:11; cf. 33:20,23). Further, the earliest postbiblical Jewish sources already understood "an eye for an eye" to mean monetary, and not literal, compensation. In the present state of our knowledge, therefore, we may be limited to saying that this text either (1) meant equivalent monetary compensation, or else (2) initially meant literal physical punishment but was reinterpreted as monetary equivalence at a relatively early stage in legal history (in the early postbiblical period at the latest).

IN THE MOUNTAIN

בהר

25 ¹And YHWH spoke to Moses in Mount Sinai, saying, ²"Speak to the children of Israel. And you shall say to them: When you will come to the land that I am giving to you, then the land shall have a Sabbath for YHWH. ³Six years you shall seed your field, and six years you shall prune your vineyard, and you shall gather its produce. ⁴And in the seventh year the land shall have a Sabbath, a ceasing, a Sabbath for YHWH: you shall not seed your field, and you shall not prune your vineyard, ⁵you shall not reap your harvest's free growth, and you shall not cut off your untrimmed grapes. The land shall have a year of ceasing. ⁶And the land's Sabbath shall be yours for food: for you and for your servant and for your maid and for your employee and for your visitor who are residing with you ⁷and for your domestic animal and for the wild animal that are in your land shall be all of its produce to eat.

⁸"And you shall count seven Sabbaths of years: seven years, seven times. And the days of the seven Sabbaths of years shall be for you forty-nine years. ⁹And you shall pass a blasting horn in the seventh month on the tenth of the month: on the Day of Atonement you shall have the horn pass through all your land. ¹⁰And you shall consecrate the year that makes fifty years and proclaim liberty in the land, to all its inhabitants. It shall be a jubilee for you. And you shall go back, each to his possession; and you shall go back, each to his family. ¹¹It, the year that makes

25 ¹וַיְדַבֵּ֥ר יְהוָ֖ה אֶל־מֹשֶׁ֑ה בְּהַ֥ר סִינַ֖י לֵאמֹֽר׃
²דַּבֵּ֞ר אֶל־בְּנֵ֤י יִשְׂרָאֵל֙ וְאָמַרְתָּ֣ אֲלֵהֶ֔ם כִּ֤י תָבֹ֨אוּ֙ אֶל־הָאָ֔רֶץ אֲשֶׁ֥ר אֲנִ֖י נֹתֵ֣ן לָכֶ֑ם וְשָׁבְתָ֣ה הָאָ֔רֶץ שַׁבָּ֖ת לַיהוָֽה׃ ³שֵׁ֤שׁ שָׁנִים֙ תִּזְרַ֣ע שָׂדֶ֔ךָ וְשֵׁ֥שׁ שָׁנִ֖ים תִּזְמֹ֣ר כַּרְמֶ֑ךָ וְאָסַפְתָּ֖ אֶת־תְּבוּאָתָֽהּ׃ ⁴וּבַשָּׁנָ֣ה הַשְּׁבִיעִ֗ת שַׁבַּ֤ת שַׁבָּתוֹן֙ יִהְיֶ֣ה לָאָ֔רֶץ שַׁבָּ֖ת לַיהוָ֑ה שָׂדְךָ֙ לֹ֣א תִזְרָ֔ע וְכַרְמְךָ֖ לֹ֥א תִזְמֹֽר׃ ⁵אֵ֣ת סְפִ֤יחַ קְצִֽירְךָ֙ לֹ֣א תִקְצ֔וֹר וְאֶת־עִנְּבֵ֥י נְזִירֶ֖ךָ לֹ֣א תִבְצֹ֑ר שְׁנַ֥ת שַׁבָּת֖וֹן יִהְיֶ֥ה לָאָֽרֶץ׃ ⁶וְֽהָיְתָ֠ה שַׁבַּ֨ת הָאָ֤רֶץ לָכֶם֙ לְאָכְלָ֔ה לְךָ֖ וּלְעַבְדְּךָ֣ וְלַאֲמָתֶ֑ךָ וְלִשְׂכִֽירְךָ֙ וּלְתוֹשָׁ֣בְךָ֔ הַגָּרִ֖ים עִמָּֽךְ׃ ⁷וְלִ֨בְהֶמְתְּךָ֔ וְלַֽחַיָּ֖ה אֲשֶׁ֣ר בְּאַרְצֶ֑ךָ תִּהְיֶ֥ה כָל־תְּבוּאָתָ֖הּ לֶאֱכֹֽל׃ ס ⁸וְסָפַרְתָּ֣ לְךָ֗ שֶׁ֚בַע שַׁבְּתֹ֣ת שָׁנִ֔ים שֶׁ֥בַע שָׁנִ֖ים שֶׁ֣בַע פְּעָמִ֑ים וְהָי֣וּ לְךָ֗ יְמֵי֙ שֶׁ֣בַע שַׁבְּתֹ֣ת הַשָּׁנִ֔ים תֵּ֥שַׁע וְאַרְבָּעִ֖ים שָׁנָֽה׃ ⁹וְהַֽעֲבַרְתָּ֞ שׁוֹפַ֤ר תְּרוּעָה֙ בַּחֹ֣דֶשׁ הַשְּׁבִעִ֔י בֶּעָשׂ֖וֹר לַחֹ֑דֶשׁ בְּיוֹם֙ הַכִּפֻּרִ֔ים תַּעֲבִ֥ירוּ שׁוֹפָ֖ר בְּכָל־אַרְצְכֶֽם׃ ¹⁰וְקִדַּשְׁתֶּ֗ם אֵ֣ת שְׁנַ֤ת הַחֲמִשִּׁים֙ שָׁנָ֔ה וּקְרָאתֶ֥ם דְּר֛וֹר בָּאָ֖רֶץ לְכָל־יֹשְׁבֶ֑יהָ יוֹבֵ֥ל הִוא֙ תִּהְיֶ֣ה לָכֶ֔ם וְשַׁבְתֶּ֗ם אִ֚ישׁ אֶל־אֲחֻזָּת֔וֹ וְאִ֥ישׁ אֶל־מִשְׁפַּחְתּ֖וֹ תָּשֻֽׁבוּ׃ ¹¹יוֹבֵ֥ל הִוא֙

25:5,11. **free growth.** Plants that sprout on their own after a harvest rather than having been planted.

25:10. **possession.** Meaning: each person's ancestral property.

25:10,13. **a jubilee: you shall go back, each to his possession.** In the law of the jubilee, YHWH commands that every fifty years all property is to return to the original owners. This appears to be an economic program designed to prevent the feudal system, common in the rest of the ancient Near East, from developing in Israel. That is, it functions to prevent the establishment of a class of wealthy landowners at the top

fifty years, shall be a jubilee for you. You shall not seed, and you shall not harvest its free growths, and you shall not cut off its untrimmed fruits, [12]because it is a jubilee; it shall be a holy thing to you. You shall eat its produce from the field. [13]In this jubilee year you shall go back, each to his possession. [14]And when you will make a sale to your fellow or buy from your fellow's hand: each of you, do not persecute his brother. [15]You shall buy from your fellow by the number of years after the jubilee. He shall sell to you by the number of years of yields— [16]corresponding to a greater amount of the years, you shall make its price greater; and corresponding to a smaller amount of the years, you shall make its price smaller—because it is a number of yields that he is selling to you. [17]And you shall not persecute—each of you—his brother, but you shall fear your God, because I am YHWH, your God.

[18]"And you shall do my laws and observe my judgments and do them, so you will live on the land in security. [19]And the land will give its fruit, and you will eat to the full, and you will live in security on it. [20]And if you will say, 'What shall we eat in the seventh year? Here, we won't seed and won't gather our produce,' [21]I shall command my blessing for you in the sixth year, and it will make the produce for the three years. [22]And you will seed the eighth year and eat from the old produce until the ninth year; you will eat the old until its produce comes. [23]But the land shall not be sold permanently, because the land is *mine*, because you are aliens and visitors with me! [24]So in all the land in your possession you

שְׁנַת הַחֲמִשִּׁים שָׁנָה תִּהְיֶה לָכֶם לֹא תִזְרָעוּ וְלֹא תִקְצְרוּ אֶת־סְפִיחֶיהָ וְלֹא תִבְצְרוּ אֶת־נְזִרֶיהָ: [12]כִּי יוֹבֵל הִוא קֹדֶשׁ תִּהְיֶה לָכֶם מִן־הַשָּׂדֶה תֹּאכְלוּ אֶת־תְּבוּאָתָהּ:

[13]בִּשְׁנַת הַיּוֹבֵל הַזֹּאת תָּשֻׁבוּ אִישׁ אֶל־אֲחֻזָּתוֹ: [14]וְכִי־תִמְכְּרוּ מִמְכָּר לַעֲמִיתֶךָ אוֹ קָנֹה מִיַּד עֲמִיתֶךָ אַל־תּוֹנוּ אִישׁ אֶת־אָחִיו: [15]בְּמִסְפַּר שָׁנִים אַחַר הַיּוֹבֵל תִּקְנֶה מֵאֵת עֲמִיתֶךָ בְּמִסְפַּר שְׁנֵי־תְבוּאֹת יִמְכָּר־לָךְ: [16]לְפִי ׀ רֹב הַשָּׁנִים תַּרְבֶּה מִקְנָתוֹ וּלְפִי מְעֹט הַשָּׁנִים תַּמְעִיט מִקְנָתוֹ כִּי מִסְפַּר תְּבוּאֹת הוּא מֹכֵר לָךְ: [17]וְלֹא תוֹנוּ אִישׁ אֶת־עֲמִיתוֹ וְיָרֵאתָ מֵאֱלֹהֶיךָ כִּי אֲנִי יְהוָֹה אֱלֹהֵיכֶם: [18]וַעֲשִׂיתֶם אֶת־חֻקֹּתַי וְאֶת־מִשְׁפָּטַי תִּשְׁמְרוּ וַעֲשִׂיתֶם אֹתָם וִישַׁבְתֶּם עַל־הָאָרֶץ לָבֶטַח: [19]וְנָתְנָה הָאָרֶץ פִּרְיָהּ וַאֲכַלְתֶּם לָשֹׂבַע וִישַׁבְתֶּם לָבֶטַח עָלֶיהָ: [20]וְכִי תֹאמְרוּ מַה־נֹּאכַל בַּשָּׁנָה הַשְּׁבִיעִת הֵן לֹא נִזְרָע וְלֹא נֶאֱסֹף אֶת־תְּבוּאָתֵנוּ: [21]וְצִוִּיתִי אֶת־בִּרְכָתִי לָכֶם בַּשָּׁנָה הַשִּׁשִּׁית וְעָשָׂת אֶת־הַתְּבוּאָה לִשְׁלֹשׁ הַשָּׁנִים: [22]וּזְרַעְתֶּם אֵת הַשָּׁנָה הַשְּׁמִינִת וַאֲכַלְתֶּם מִן־הַתְּבוּאָה יָשָׁן עַד ׀ הַשָּׁנָה הַתְּשִׁיעִת עַד־בּוֹא תְּבוּאָתָהּ תֹּאכְלוּ יָשָׁן: [23]וְהָאָרֶץ לֹא תִמָּכֵר לִצְמִתֻת כִּי־לִי הָאָרֶץ כִּי־גֵרִים וְתוֹשָׁבִים אַתֶּם עִמָּדִי: [24]וּבְכֹל אֶרֶץ אֲחֻזַּתְכֶם גְּאֻלָּה תִּתְּנוּ

---

of the economic scale and a mass of landless peasants at the bottom. Every Israelite is to be apportioned some land (described in the books of Numbers and Joshua), and the deity commands that in every fiftieth year the system returns to where it started. If an Israelite has lost his ancestral land as a result of debt or calamity, he regains ownership of it in the jubilee year. *Land is unalienable.* Individuals can suffer difficult times, but there is a divinely decreed limit to their loss, and the nation as a whole can never degenerate into a two-tiered system of the very rich and the very poor.

25:21. **three years.** The sixth year, the seventh year, and the eighth year (the first year of the next seven-year cycle, until the first planting of that year produces a crop).

shall give a redemption for the land. 25When your brother will be low so that he will sell any of his possession, then his redeemer who is the closest relative to him shall come and redeem his brother's sale. 26And when a man will not have a redeemer, but his hand has come to attain it and he has found enough for his redemption, 27then he shall figure the years of his sale and pay back what is left over to the man to whom he sold it, and he shall go back to his possession. 28And if his hand has not found enough to pay it back to him, then his sale shall be in the hand of the one who bought it until the jubilee year, and it shall come out in the jubilee, and he shall go back to his possession.

29"And when a man will sell a home in a walled city, then its redemption shall be until the end of the year of its sale. Its redemption shall be for days. 30And if it will not be redeemed by the completion of a full year for it, then the house that is in a city that has a wall shall be estab-

25 כִּֽי־יָמ֣וּךְ אָחִ֔יךָ וּמָכַ֖ר מֵאֲחֻזָּת֑וֹ וּבָ֤א גֹֽאֲלוֹ֙ הַקָּרֹ֣ב אֵלָ֔יו וְגָאַ֕ל אֵ֖ת מִמְכַּ֥ר אָחִֽיו: 26 וְאִ֕ישׁ כִּ֛י לֹ֥א יִֽהְיֶה־לּ֖וֹ גֹּאֵ֑ל וְהִשִּׂ֣יגָה יָד֔וֹ וּמָצָ֖א כְּדֵ֥י גְאֻלָּתֽוֹ: 27 וְחִשַּׁב֙ אֶת־שְׁנֵ֣י מִמְכָּר֔וֹ וְהֵשִׁיב֙ אֶת־הָ֣עֹדֵ֔ף לָאִ֖ישׁ אֲשֶׁ֣ר מָֽכַר־ל֑וֹ וְשָׁ֖ב לַאֲחֻזָּתֽוֹ: 28 וְאִ֨ם לֹֽא־מָצְאָ֜ה יָד֗וֹ דֵּי֘ הָשִׁ֣יב לוֹ֒ וְהָיָ֣ה מִמְכָּר֗וֹ בְּיַד֙ הַקֹּנֶ֣ה אֹת֔וֹ עַ֖ד שְׁנַ֣ת הַיּוֹבֵ֑ל וְיָצָא֙ בַּיֹּבֵ֔ל וְשָׁ֖ב לַאֲחֻזָּתֽוֹ: 29 וְאִ֗ישׁ כִּֽי־יִמְכֹּ֤ר בֵּית־מוֹשַׁב֙ עִ֣יר חוֹמָ֔ה וְהָיְתָה֙ גְּאֻלָּת֔וֹ עַד־תֹּ֖ם שְׁנַ֣ת מִמְכָּר֑וֹ יָמִ֖ים תִּהְיֶ֥ה גְאֻלָּתֽוֹ: 30 וְאִ֣ם לֹֽא־יִגָּאֵ֗ל עַד־מְלֹ֣את לוֹ֘ שָׁנָ֣ה תְמִימָה֒ וְ֠קָם הַבַּ֨יִת אֲשֶׁר־בָּעִ֜יר אֲשֶׁר־ל֣וֹ חֹמָ֗ה לַצְּמִיתֻ֛ת לַקֹּנֶ֥ה

ק׳ לֽוֹ 25:30

25:25,35,39. **when your brother will be low**. Meaning: when your fellow Israelite will be so poor that he has difficulty holding on to his land. It has long been noted that the three times that this phrase occurs in this chapter reflect three stages of increasing hardship. In the first, the person has to sell his land. In the second, he has both lost his land and is without money. And in the third, he himself is sold (or sells himself) into servitude. And at each stage, the man's fellow Israelite is commanded to help him. If he has to sell his land, one must redeem it for him and then give it back to him in the jubilee year. If he is without money, one must lend him money without any charge or interest. And if he is sold, one must not treat him as a slave.

Here the units of law convey the specific requirements while the arrangement conveys the basic principle, namely, that as one's brother's need increases, so does one's responsibility to help him. Further, one must thus help one's fellow as a matter of law. The chapter never speaks of charity, nor does it appeal to one's feelings of compassion or generosity. An unfortunate Israelite need not feel degraded to be poor nor ashamed to be pitied. Economic suffering is rather treated as a reality of life, which one is required by law to remedy. The poor man thus can know that his brother is helping him because the system requires brothers to help one another and that, if the shoe were on the other foot, he would do the same for his brother. This is not to say that the text denies or discourages feelings of compassion, but only that the fulfillment of the law is not made dependent upon the presence or absence of such feelings.

25:29. **for days**. The word "days" is understood here to mean the rest of the days of the year—up to one full year. His redemption period can amount to days, not years.

lished permanently for the one who bought it, through his generations. It shall not come out in the jubilee.

31"As for houses of the villages that do not have a wall around them: it shall be figured along with the land's field. It shall have redemption, and it shall come out in the jubilee.

32"As for the Levites' cities, the houses in the cities of their possession: the Levites shall have eternal redemption. 33And that which one from the Levites will redeem: it shall come out, a sale of a house and of a city of his possession, in the jubilee, because that—the houses of the Levites' cities—is their possession among the children of Israel. 34But a field of their cities' surrounding land shall not be sold, because it is an eternal possession for them.

35"And when your brother will be low so that his hand is slipping with you, then you shall take hold of him—an alien and a visitor—and he shall live with you. 36Do not take interest or a charge from him; but you shall fear your God, and your brother will live with you. 37You shall not give him your money for interest, and you shall not give him your food for a charge. 38I am YHWH, your God, who brought you out from the land of Egypt to give you the land of Canaan, to be God to you.

39"And when your brother will be low with you so that he is sold to you, you shall not have him work a slave's work. 40He shall be like an employee, like a visitor, with you. He shall work with you until the jubilee year. 41And he shall go out from you, he and his children with him, and go back to his family, and he shall go back to his fathers' possession. 42Because they are *my* servants, whom I brought out from the land of Egypt; they shall not be sold like the sale of a slave. 43You

31וּבָתֵּי הַחֲצֵרִים אֲשֶׁר אֵין־לָהֶם חֹמָה סָבִיב עַל־שְׂדֵה הָאָרֶץ יֵחָשֵׁב גְּאֻלָּה תִּהְיֶה־לּוֹ וּבַיֹּבֵל יֵצֵא: 32וְעָרֵי הַלְוִיִּם בָּתֵּי עָרֵי אֲחֻזָּתָם גְּאֻלַּת עוֹלָם תִּהְיֶה לַלְוִיִּם: 33וַאֲשֶׁר יִגְאַל מִן־הַלְוִיִּם וְיָצָא מִמְכַּר־בַּיִת וְעִיר אֲחֻזָּתוֹ בַּיֹּבֵל כִּי בָתֵּי עָרֵי הַלְוִיִּם הִוא אֲחֻזָּתָם בְּתוֹךְ בְּנֵי יִשְׂרָאֵל: 34וּשְׂדֵה מִגְרַשׁ עָרֵיהֶם לֹא יִמָּכֵר כִּי־ אֲחֻזַּת עוֹלָם הוּא לָהֶם: ס 35וְכִי־יָמוּךְ אָחִיךָ וּמָטָה יָדוֹ עִמָּךְ וְהֶחֱזַקְתָּ בּוֹ גֵּר וְתוֹשָׁב וָחַי עִמָּךְ: 36אַל־תִּקַּח מֵאִתּוֹ נֶשֶׁךְ וְתַרְבִּית וְיָרֵאתָ מֵאֱלֹהֶיךָ וְחֵי אָחִיךָ עִמָּךְ: 37אֶת־כַּסְפְּךָ לֹא־תִתֵּן לוֹ בְּנֶשֶׁךְ וּבְמַרְבִּית לֹא־תִתֵּן אָכְלֶךָ: 38אֲנִי יְהוָה אֱלֹהֵיכֶם אֲשֶׁר־הוֹצֵאתִי אֶתְכֶם מֵאֶרֶץ מִצְרַיִם לָתֵת לָכֶם אֶת־אֶרֶץ כְּנַעַן לִהְיוֹת לָכֶם לֵאלֹהִים: ס 39וְכִי־ יָמוּךְ אָחִיךָ עִמָּךְ וְנִמְכַּר־לָךְ לֹא־תַעֲבֹד בּוֹ עֲבֹדַת עָבֶד: 40כְּשָׂכִיר כְּתוֹשָׁב יִהְיֶה עִמָּךְ עַד־שְׁנַת הַיֹּבֵל יַעֲבֹד עִמָּךְ: 41וְיָצָא מֵעִמָּךְ הוּא וּבָנָיו עִמּוֹ וְשָׁב אֶל־מִשְׁפַּחְתּוֹ וְאֶל־אֲחֻזַּת אֲבֹתָיו יָשׁוּב: 42כִּי־עֲבָדַי הֵם אֲשֶׁר־הוֹצֵאתִי אֹתָם מֵאֶרֶץ מִצְרָיִם לֹא יִמָּכְרוּ

25:35. **his hand is slipping**. Meaning: he does not have enough food and money to live.

25:35. **an alien and a visitor**. Being landless, he is now like an alien or a visitor.

25:42. **servant, slave**. The same Hebrew root (*ʻbd*) is used for "servant" and "slave."

shall not dominate him with harshness, but you shall fear your God.

⁴⁴"And your slave and your maid that you will have: from the nations that are around you, you shall buy a slave or a maid from them. ⁴⁵And also from the children of the visitors who reside with you—you shall buy from them and from their families that are with you—to whom they gave birth in your land. And they shall become a possession for you. ⁴⁶And you shall make them a legacy for your children after you to inherit as a possession. You may have them work forever, but as for your brothers, the children of Israel—a man toward his brother—you shall not dominate him with harshness.

⁴⁷"And if the hand of an alien and visitor with you will attain it, and your brother is low with him and is sold to the alien and visitor with you or to an offshoot of an alien's family, ⁴⁸after he is sold he shall have redemption. One of his brothers shall redeem him, ⁴⁹or his uncle or his uncle's son shall redeem him, or some close relative of his from his family shall redeem him; or if his hand can attain it then he can redeem himself. ⁵⁰And he shall figure with the one who buys

מִמְכֶּ֥רֶת עָֽבֶד׃ ⁴³לֹא־תִרְדֶּ֥ה ב֖וֹ בְּפָ֑רֶךְ וְיָרֵ֖אתָ מֵאֱלֹהֶֽיךָ׃ ⁴⁴וְעַבְדְּךָ֥ וַאֲמָֽתְךָ֖ אֲשֶׁ֣ר יִֽהְיוּ־לָ֑ךְ מֵאֵ֣ת הַגּוֹיִ֗ם אֲשֶׁר֙ סְבִיבֹ֣תֵיכֶ֔ם מֵהֶ֥ם תִּקְנ֖וּ עֶ֥בֶד וְאָמָֽה׃ ⁴⁵וְ֠גַם מִבְּנֵ֨י הַתּוֹשָׁבִ֜ים הַגָּרִ֤ים עִמָּכֶם֙ מֵהֶ֣ם תִּקְנ֔וּ וּמִמִּשְׁפַּחְתָּם֙ אֲשֶׁ֣ר עִמָּכֶ֔ם אֲשֶׁ֥ר הוֹלִ֖ידוּ בְּאַרְצְכֶ֑ם וְהָי֥וּ לָכֶ֖ם לַֽאֲחֻזָּֽה׃ ⁴⁶וְהִתְנַחַלְתֶּ֨ם אֹתָ֜ם לִבְנֵיכֶ֤ם אַֽחֲרֵיכֶם֙ לָרֶ֣שֶׁת אֲחֻזָּ֔ה לְעֹלָ֖ם בָּהֶ֣ם תַּעֲבֹ֑דוּ וּבְאַ֨חֵיכֶ֤ם בְּנֵֽי־יִשְׂרָאֵל֙ אִ֣ישׁ בְּאָחִ֔יו לֹא־תִרְדֶּ֥ה ב֖וֹ בְּפָֽרֶךְ׃ ⁴⁷וְכִ֣י תַשִּׂ֗יג יַ֣ד גֵּ֤ר וְתוֹשָׁב֙ עִמָּ֔ךְ וּמָ֥ךְ אָחִ֖יךָ עִמּ֑וֹ וְנִמְכַּ֗ר לְגֵ֤ר תּוֹשָׁב֙ עִמָּ֔ךְ א֛וֹ לְעֵ֖קֶר מִשְׁפַּ֥חַת גֵּֽר׃ ⁴⁸אַחֲרֵ֣י נִמְכַּ֔ר גְּאֻלָּ֖ה תִּהְיֶה־לּ֑וֹ אֶחָ֥ד מֵאֶחָ֖יו יִגְאָלֶֽנּוּ׃ ⁴⁹אֽוֹ־דֹד֞וֹ א֤וֹ בֶן־דֹּדוֹ֙ יִגְאָלֶ֔נּוּ אֽוֹ־מִשְּׁאֵ֧ר בְּשָׂר֛וֹ מִמִּשְׁפַּחְתּ֖וֹ יִגְאָלֶ֑נּוּ אֽוֹ־הִשִּׂ֥יגָה יָד֖וֹ וְנִגְאָֽל׃ ⁵⁰וְחִשַּׁב֙ עִם־קֹנֵ֔הוּ מִשְּׁנַת֙ הִמָּ֣כְרוֹ ל֔וֹ עַ֚ד

It has a wider range of meaning in Hebrew than either word has in English. Here it results in the use of its two different translations in the very same sentence, but this still conveys the Torah's meaning more correctly than leveling the nuances of the Hebrew into a single English word.

25:43. **dominate.** "You shall not *dominate* him." This is the term that is used for human dominion over animals in Genesis 1. Israelites are explicitly denied the kind of power over other human beings, even a slave, that they might exert over animals.

25:43. **with harshness.** This is the term that is used for the way the Egyptians made the Israelites work (Exod 1:14). Eliminating slavery on earth has been a gradual process rather than a revolution. The Israelites are permitted to have slaves themselves, but not in the manner of the Egyptians. They cannot overwork them. They cannot mistreat them (so an Israelite who knocks out his slave's tooth must set the slave free; Exod 21:2). The rules that are imposed on treatment of slaves in the Torah involve a recognition of a slave's *humanity* and *dignity*, and they establish that a slave has *rights*. This was a crucial first stage in the long process leading to opposition to slavery altogether.

25:47. **attain it.** That is, be able to provide the money to buy the poor Israelite.

him: from the year he was sold to him to the jubilee year; and the price of his sale shall be by the
number of years. It shall be with him like the
days of an employee: 51If there are still a great
number of years, he shall pay back his redemption according to them from his purchase price.
52And if a small amount of years remain until
the jubilee year, then he shall figure it for him.
He shall pay back his redemption according to
his years. 53He shall be with him like a year-by-
year employee. He shall not dominate him with
harshness before your eyes. 54And if he will not
be redeemed by these, then he shall go out in the
jubilee year, he and his children with him. 55Be-
cause the children of Israel are servants to *me*.
They are *my* servants, whom I brought out from
the land of Egypt. I am YHWH, your God.

26 1"You shall not make idols, and you
shall not set up an image or a pillar, and
you shall not put a carved stone in your land to
bow at it, because I am YHWH, your God.

2"You shall observe my Sabbaths and fear my
sanctuary. I am YHWH.

שְׁנַת הַיֹּבֵל וְהָיָה כֶּסֶף מִמְכָּרוֹ בְּמִסְפַּר שָׁנִים כִּימֵי
שָׂכִיר יִהְיֶה עִמּוֹ: 51אִם־עוֹד רַבּוֹת בַּשָּׁנִים לְפִיהֶן
יָשִׁיב גְּאֻלָּתוֹ מִכֶּסֶף מִקְנָתוֹ: 52וְאִם־מְעַט נִשְׁאַר
בַּשָּׁנִים עַד־שְׁנַת הַיֹּבֵל וְחִשַּׁב־לוֹ כְּפִי שָׁנָיו יָשִׁיב
אֶת־גְּאֻלָּתוֹ: 53כִּשְׂכִיר שָׁנָה בְּשָׁנָה יִהְיֶה עִמּוֹ לֹא־
יִרְדֶּנּוּ בְּפֶרֶךְ לְעֵינֶיךָ: 54וְאִם־לֹא יִגָּאֵל בְּאֵלֶּה
וְיָצָא בִּשְׁנַת הַיֹּבֵל הוּא וּבָנָיו עִמּוֹ:

55כִּי־לִי בְנֵי־יִשְׂרָאֵל עֲבָדִים עֲבָדַי הֵם אֲשֶׁר־
הוֹצֵאתִי אוֹתָם מֵאֶרֶץ מִצְרָיִם אֲנִי יְהוָה אֱלֹהֵיכֶם:
26 1לֹא־תַעֲשׂוּ לָכֶם אֱלִילִם וּפֶסֶל וּמַצֵּבָה לֹא־
תָקִימוּ לָכֶם וְאֶבֶן מַשְׂכִּית לֹא תִתְּנוּ בְּאַרְצְכֶם
לְהִשְׁתַּחֲוֹת עָלֶיהָ כִּי אֲנִי יְהוָה אֱלֹהֵיכֶם: 2אֶת־
שַׁבְּתֹתַי תִּשְׁמֹרוּ וּמִקְדָּשִׁי תִּירָאוּ אֲנִי יְהוָה: ס

BY MY LAWS

3"If you will go by my laws, and if you will observe my commandments, and you will do them:

בחקתי

3אִם־בְּחֻקֹּתַי תֵּלֵכוּ וְאֶת־מִצְוֹתַי תִּשְׁמְרוּ

26:2. **observe my Sabbaths and fear my sanctuary**. What is the reason for mentioning these two here together: Sabbaths and sanctuary? This pronouncement brings
together the sanctification of time and the sanctification of space. The Sabbath is the
most sacred time. The sanctuary (meaning first the Tabernacle and later the Temple)
is the most sacred space. This dual command thus embraces everything.

26:3. **If you will go by my laws**. The key to the relationship between Leviticus's laws
and the Bible's story is the list of blessings and curses here in Leviticus 26. The list
comes at the conclusion and is arguably the culmination of the book. It indicates that
all of this law has implications. Leviticus has definite connections to what has come
before it. The blessings-and-curses list is the connection to what will follow. It says,
plainly enough: the people's fate will depend on whether they follow these laws or
not. The blessings include rain, produce, satiety, security, peace, victory, population,
divine presence, and divine relationship. The curses include illness, defeat, wild ani-

4 then I shall give your rains in their time,
and the earth will give its crop,
and the tree of the field will give its fruit,

5 and threshing will extend to vintage for
you,
and vintage will extend to seeding,
and you will eat your bread to the full,
and you will live in security in your land,

6 and I shall give peace in the land,
and you will lie down with no one
making you afraid,
and I shall make wild animals cease from
the land,
and a sword will not pass through your
land,

7 and you will chase your enemies,
and they will fall in front of you by the
sword,

8 and five of you will chase a hundred,
and a hundred of you will chase ten
thousand,
and your enemies will fall in front of you
by the sword,

9 and I shall turn to you,
and I shall make you fruitful and make
you multiply,

וַעֲשִׂיתֶ֖ם אֹתָֽם: 4וְנָתַתִּ֥י גִשְׁמֵיכֶ֖ם בְּעִתָּ֑ם וְנָתְנָ֤ה
הָאָ֨רֶץ֙ יְבוּלָ֔הּ וְעֵ֥ץ הַשָּׂדֶ֖ה יִתֵּ֥ן פִּרְיֽוֹ: 5וְהִשִּׂ֨יג לָכֶ֥ם
דַּ֜יִשׁ אֶת־בָּצִ֗יר וּבָצִ֙יר֙ יַשִּׂ֣יג אֶת־זָ֔רַע וַאֲכַלְתֶּ֤ם
לַחְמְכֶם֙ לָשֹׂ֔בַע וִֽישַׁבְתֶּ֥ם לָבֶ֖טַח בְּאַרְצְכֶֽם: 6וְנָתַתִּ֤י
שָׁלוֹם֙ בָּאָ֔רֶץ וּשְׁכַבְתֶּ֖ם וְאֵ֣ין מַחֲרִ֑יד וְהִשְׁבַּתִּ֞י חַיָּ֤ה
רָעָה֙ מִן־הָאָ֔רֶץ וְחֶ֖רֶב לֹא־תַעֲבֹ֥ר בְּאַרְצְכֶֽם: 7וּרְדַפְתֶּ֖ם
אֶת־אֹיְבֵיכֶ֑ם וְנָפְל֥וּ לִפְנֵיכֶ֖ם לֶחָֽרֶב: 8וְרָדְפ֨וּ מִכֶּ֤ם
חֲמִשָּׁה֙ מֵאָ֔ה וּמֵאָ֥ה מִכֶּ֖ם רְבָבָ֣ה
יִרְדֹּ֑פוּ וְנָפְל֧וּ אֹיְבֵיכֶ֛ם לִפְנֵיכֶ֖ם לֶחָֽרֶב: 9וּפָנִ֣יתִי
אֲלֵיכֶ֗ם וְהִפְרֵיתִ֤י אֶתְכֶם֙ וְהִרְבֵּיתִ֣י אֶתְכֶ֔ם וַהֲקִימֹתִ֥י

---

mals, pestilence, famine, divine rejection, destruction, dispersion, and exile. The blessings and curses thus provide for the eventuality of a variety of essential matters in the
realms of nature, human relations (especially political relations), and divine-human
relationship. All future stories of the fortunes of the people of Israel in these realms
are to be understood, according to this text, as being the results of whether "you will
go by my laws, and if you will observe my commandments, and you will do them"
(26:3) or "if you will reject my laws, and if your souls will scorn my judgments so as
not to do all my commandments, so that you break my covenant" (26:15). Under-
scoring the literary force of these promises and threats is not only their placement at
the conclusion of the book but the fact that the list of curses is the most artfully written section in the book. I call it the most artfully written on the basis of its wording
as much as its content, including words of irony ("you will flee though no one is pursuing you," 26:17), words of horror ("you will eat your sons' flesh, and your daughters' flesh you will eat," 26:29), and words of pathos ("the sound of a driven leaf will
chase them," 26:36). The commandments thus are not presented as a loosely relevant
list. They are woven into the fabric of the narrative as essential to the life of the community.

and I shall establish my covenant with
   you,

10   and you will eat the oldest of the old,

and you will take out the old because of
   the new,

11   and I shall put my Tabernacle among
   you,

and my soul will not scorn you,

12   and I shall walk among you,

and I shall be God to you,

and you will be a people to me.

אֶת־בְּרִיתִי אִתְּכֶם: 10וַאֲכַלְתֶּם יָשָׁן נוֹשָׁן וְיָשָׁן מִפְּנֵי
חָדָשׁ תּוֹצִיאוּ: 11וְנָתַתִּי מִשְׁכָּנִי בְּתוֹכְכֶם וְלֹא־תִגְעַל
נַפְשִׁי אֶתְכֶם: 12וְהִתְהַלַּכְתִּי בְּתוֹכְכֶם וְהָיִיתִי לָכֶם
לֵאלֹהִים וְאַתֶּם תִּהְיוּ־לִי לְעָם: 13אֲנִי יְהוָה

26:10. the oldest of the old. Old, stored produce will still make good food.

26:10. take out the old because of the new. One will never run out of food. There will be good stored produce right up to the time that the new crops come in, and the old will have to be taken out in order to make room for the new.

26:11,30. my soul. Does God have a soul? This is the only place in the Torah that refers to the deity's *nepeš* (although a related verbal form, *wayyinnāpaš*, occurs in Exod 31:17). Elsewhere, the word refers to the living quality in humans and animals and is associated with breath. It is usually understood to mean soul, person, being, and life. It might possibly help us to understand what is meant by creation in the image of God, but that seems unlikely since animals are said to have a *nepeš* there as well, but they are not said to be in the divine image (Gen 1:24–27). We must be cautious in using the word's occurrences here to conclude anything about the Torah's conception of God, because both of these occurrences are in the phrase "my soul will scorn." This phrase may simply have been a known expression. It also occurs here with humans as the subject (26:15); and it occurs in Jeremiah as well (14:19). It may refer to the personal aspect of God, or it may rather refer to God in no specific way. Rashi (following Siphra) takes the phrase to refer to the departure of the divine presence (Shechinah). Here, too, we must be cautious, first, because that is also the understanding of other metaphorical phrases in the *Tanak*. Thus the Targum takes the phrase "God hides His face" to mean the departure of the Shechinah as well. And, second, the word *Shechinah* never occurs in the Torah or anywhere in the Hebrew Bible.

26:12. walk among you. This same term is used to describe God's walking among humans in the garden of Eden (the Hebrew root הלך in the *Hitpael*; Gen 3:8). This blessing thus hints at a return of the closeness to the divine presence that existed prior to the initial divine-human conflict in Eden.

26:12. I shall be God to you, and you will be a people to me. The last blessing of the list echoes what is thought to be the wording of the marriage ceremony in ancient Israel: "I shall be a husband to you, and you will be a wife to me"—as well as the adoption ceremony: "I shall be a parent to you, and you will be a son/daughter to me" (see, e.g., 2 Sam 7:14).

13I am YHWH, your God, who brought you out from the land of Egypt, from being slaves to them, and I broke the beams of your yoke and had you go standing tall.

14"But if you will not listen to me and not do all these commandments, 15and if you will reject my laws, and if your souls will scorn my judgments so as not to do all my commandments, so that you break my covenant, 16I, too, I shall do this to you:

> Then I shall appoint terror over you with consumption and with fever, exhausting eyes and grieving the soul,
>
> and you will sow your seed in vain, for your enemies will eat it,

17
> and I shall set my face against you,
> and you will be struck before your enemies,
>
> and ones who hate you will dominate you,
>
> and you will flee though no one is pursuing you.

18And if, even after these, you will not listen to me, then I shall add seven times more to discipline you for your sins:

19
> and I shall break your strong pride,
> and I shall make your skies like iron and your land like bronze,

20
> and your power will be used up in vain,
> and your land will not give its crop,
> and the tree of the land will not give its fruit.

21And if you will go on with me in defiance and will not be willing to listen to me, then I shall add seven times more striking on you, corresponding to your sins:

22
> and I shall let loose the wild animal among you,
> and it will bereave you,
> and it will cut off your cattle,
> and it will diminish you,
> and your roads will be desolated.

23And if you will not be disciplined for me by

אֱלֹהֵיכֶ֗ם אֲשֶׁ֨ר הוֹצֵ֤אתִי אֶתְכֶם֙ מֵאֶ֣רֶץ מִצְרַ֔יִם מִהְיֹ֥ת לָהֶ֖ם עֲבָדִ֑ים וָאֶשְׁבֹּר֙ מֹטֹ֣ת עֻלְּכֶ֔ם וָאוֹלֵ֥ךְ אֶתְכֶ֖ם קֽוֹמְמִיּֽוּת׃ פ 14וְאִם־לֹ֥א תִשְׁמְע֖וּ לִ֑י וְלֹ֣א תַעֲשׂ֔וּ אֵ֥ת כָּל־הַמִּצְוֹ֖ת הָאֵֽלֶּה׃ 15וְאִם־בְּחֻקֹּתַ֣י תִּמְאָ֔סוּ וְאִ֥ם אֶת־מִשְׁפָּטַ֖י תִּגְעַ֣ל נַפְשְׁכֶ֑ם לְבִלְתִּ֤י עֲשׂוֹת֙ אֶת־כָּל־מִצְוֹתַ֔י לְהַפְרְכֶ֖ם אֶת־בְּרִיתִֽי׃ 16אַף־ אֲנִ֞י אֶֽעֱשֶׂה־זֹּ֣את לָכֶ֗ם וְהִפְקַדְתִּ֨י עֲלֵיכֶ֤ם בֶּֽהָלָה֙ אֶת־הַשַּׁחֶ֣פֶת וְאֶת־הַקַּדַּ֔חַת מְכַלּ֥וֹת עֵינַ֖יִם וּמְדִיבֹ֣ת נָ֑פֶשׁ וּזְרַעְתֶּ֤ם לָרִיק֙ זַרְעֲכֶ֔ם וַאֲכָלֻ֖הוּ אֹיְבֵיכֶֽם׃ 17וְנָתַתִּ֤י פָנַי֙ בָּכֶ֔ם וְנִגַּפְתֶּ֖ם לִפְנֵ֣י אֹיְבֵיכֶ֑ם וְרָד֤וּ בָכֶם֙ שֹׂנְאֵיכֶ֔ם וְנַסְתֶּ֖ם וְאֵין־רֹדֵ֥ף אֶתְכֶֽם׃ ס 18וְאִ֨ם־ עַד־אֵ֔לֶּה לֹ֥א תִשְׁמְע֖וּ לִ֑י וְיָסַפְתִּי֙ לְיַסְּרָ֣ה אֶתְכֶ֔ם שֶׁ֖בַע עַל־חַטֹּאתֵיכֶֽם׃ 19וְשָׁבַרְתִּ֖י אֶת־גְּא֣וֹן עֻזְּכֶ֑ם וְנָתַתִּ֤י אֶת־שְׁמֵיכֶם֙ כַּבַּרְזֶ֔ל וְאֶת־אַרְצְכֶ֖ם כַּנְּחֻשָֽׁה׃ 20וְתַ֥ם לָרִ֖יק כֹּחֲכֶ֑ם וְלֹֽא־תִתֵּ֤ן אַרְצְכֶם֙ אֶת־יְבוּלָ֔הּ וְעֵ֣ץ הָאָ֔רֶץ לֹ֥א יִתֵּ֖ן פִּרְיֽוֹ׃ 21וְאִם־תֵּֽלְכ֤וּ עִמִּי֙ קֶ֔רִי וְלֹ֥א תֹאב֖וּ לִשְׁמֹ֣עַֽ לִ֑י וְיָסַפְתִּ֤י עֲלֵיכֶם֙ מַכָּ֔ה שֶׁ֖בַע כְּחַטֹּאתֵיכֶֽם׃ 22וְהִשְׁלַחְתִּ֨י בָכֶ֜ם אֶת־חַיַּ֣ת הַשָּׂדֶ֗ה וְשִׁכְּלָ֤ה אֶתְכֶם֙ וְהִכְרִ֙יתָה֙ אֶת־בְּהֶמְתְּכֶ֔ם וְהִמְעִ֖יטָה אֶתְכֶ֑ם וְנָשַׁ֖מּוּ דַּרְכֵיכֶֽם׃ 23וְאִ֨ם־בְּאֵ֔לֶּה לֹ֥א תִוָּסְר֖וּ

these, and you will go on with me in defiance, 24then I shall go on with you, I also, in defiance. And I shall strike you, I too, seven times more for your sins:

25 and I shall bring a sword over you,
    requiting covenant retribution,
  and you will be gathered to your cities,
  and I shall let an epidemic go among you,
  and you will be put in your enemy's
    hand.

26 When I break the staff of bread for you,
  then ten women will bake your bread in
    one oven,
  and they will give back your bread by
    weight,
  and you will eat and not be full.

27And if, through this, you will not listen to me, and you will go on with me in defiance, 28then I shall go on with you in a fury of defiance, and I shall discipline you, I also, seven times more for your sins:

29 and you will eat your sons' flesh,
  and your daughters' flesh you will eat,

30 and I shall destroy your high places,

לִי וַהֲלַכְתֶּם עִמִּי קֶרִי: 24וְהָלַכְתִּי אַף־אֲנִי עִמָּכֶם בְּקֶרִי וְהִכֵּיתִי אֶתְכֶם גַּם־אָנִי שֶׁבַע עַל־חַטֹּאתֵיכֶם: 25וְהֵבֵאתִי עֲלֵיכֶם חֶרֶב נֹקֶמֶת נְקַם־בְּרִית וְנֶאֱסַפְתֶּם אֶל־עָרֵיכֶם וְשִׁלַּחְתִּי דֶבֶר בְּתוֹכְכֶם וְנִתַּתֶּם בְּיַד־אוֹיֵב: 26בְּשִׁבְרִי לָכֶם מַטֵּה־לֶחֶם וְאָפוּ עֶשֶׂר נָשִׁים לַחְמְכֶם בְּתַנּוּר אֶחָד וְהֵשִׁיבוּ לַחְמְכֶם בַּמִּשְׁקָל וַאֲכַלְתֶּם וְלֹא תִשְׂבָּעוּ: ס 27וְאִם־בְּזֹאת לֹא תִשְׁמְעוּ לִי וַהֲלַכְתֶּם עִמִּי בְּקֶרִי: 28וְהָלַכְתִּי עִמָּכֶם בַּחֲמַת־קֶרִי וְיִסַּרְתִּי אֶתְכֶם אַף־אָנִי שֶׁבַע עַל־חַטֹּאתֵיכֶם: 29וַאֲכַלְתֶּם בְּשַׂר בְּנֵיכֶם וּבְשַׂר בְּנֹתֵיכֶם תֹּאכֵלוּ: 30וְהִשְׁמַדְתִּי אֶת־בָּמֹתֵיכֶם

26:29. **you will eat your sons' flesh and your daughters' flesh**. The blessings and curses are not rewards and punishments. They are a formal part of the biblical covenants (Leviticus 26; Deuteronomy 28)—with exact parallels in legal contracts of the ancient Near East. They express the *outcomes* of fulfillment or nonfulfillment of the covenant's terms. A people who is faithful to its God and keeps the Sabbath and honors its parents and does not steal will be prosperous and enduring in its land. A people who loses sight of its commitments and values will suffer. (It should not be hard to think of contemporary parallels.) The frightful curse of eating one's own children comes true centuries later in one of the most horrifying stories in the Bible (2 Kings 6:24–30). It is not presented there as a punishment. It rather conveys the terrible state of things in Israel in the wake of the heretical reigns of Kings Ahab and Jehoram. There is a big difference between a punishment and a curse, between a threat and a warning.

This explanation is still distressing, but it does not so easily picture the deity as malicious, as people have sometimes taken these curses to mean. The God of the Hebrew Bible is not the "Old Testament God of Wrath," but rather a deity who is torn between mercy and justice, between affection for humankind and regret over the continuous conflict with them. The curses are a sad outcome of a certain kind of human behavior. But, then, the blessings are the outcome of the other kind.

26:30. **high places**. These were large stone platforms where sacrifices were per-

and I shall cut off your incense altars,
and I shall put your carcasses on your
    idols' carcasses,
and my soul will scorn you,

31   and I shall make your cities a ruin,
and I shall devastate your holy places,
and I shall not smell your pleasant smell,

32   and I, *I*, shall devastate the land,
so your enemies who live in it will be
    astonished,

33   and you: I shall scatter among the
    nations,
and I shall unsheathe my sword after
    you,
and your land will be a devastation,
and your cities will be a ruin.

³⁴Then the land will accept its Sabbaths: all the days of devastation, while you are in your enemies' land. Then the land will cease and accept its Sabbaths. ³⁵All the days of the desolation it

וְהִכְרַתִּי אֶת־חַמָּנֵיכֶם וְנָתַתִּי אֶת־פִּגְרֵיכֶם עַל־פִּגְרֵי
גִּלּוּלֵיכֶם וְגָעֲלָה נַפְשִׁי אֶתְכֶם: 31וְנָתַתִּי אֶת־עָרֵיכֶם
חָרְבָּה וַהֲשִׁמּוֹתִי אֶת־מִקְדְּשֵׁיכֶם וְלֹא אָרִיחַ בְּרֵיחַ
נִיחֹחֲכֶם: 32וַהֲשִׁמֹּתִי אֲנִי אֶת־הָאָרֶץ וְשָׁמְמוּ עָלֶיהָ
אֹיְבֵיכֶם הַיֹּשְׁבִים בָּהּ: 33וְאֶתְכֶם אֱזָרֶה בַגּוֹיִם
וַהֲרִיקֹתִי אַחֲרֵיכֶם חָרֶב וְהָיְתָה אַרְצְכֶם שְׁמָמָה
וְעָרֵיכֶם יִהְיוּ חָרְבָּה: 34אָז תִּרְצֶה הָאָרֶץ אֶת־
שַׁבְּתֹתֶיהָ כֹּל יְמֵי הֳשַׁמָּה וְאַתֶּם בְּאֶרֶץ אֹיְבֵיכֶם אָז
תִּשְׁבַּת הָאָרֶץ וְהִרְצָת אֶת־שַׁבְּתֹתֶיהָ: 35כָּל־יְמֵי

---

formed. Some were used for worship of YHWH, and others were used for worship of pagan gods; but both kinds are regularly forbidden in the *Tanak*. High places to the God of Israel are regarded as violations of the laws of centralization of worship at a single site (see comments on Lev 1:3 and 17:4).

26:30. **incense altars**. These were stands, usually designed, on which incense was burned. Both high places and incense altars have been excavated in Israel.

26:31. **not smell your pleasant smell**. The "pleasant smell" has been referred to many times as the product of the burning incense that accompanies the sacrifices. Starting with Noah's sacrifice after the flood, the smell of sacrifices is meant to be attractive to the deity, but the curse here is that God will refuse to smell it.

26:33. **scatter among the nations**. Among the worst curses was the curse of exile: for a people to be driven off their land and scattered around the world. This possibility was a reality in the ancient Near East, where exile was a horrifying fate. This curse would come to pass for Israel later in the *Tanak*, when they would come to know exile at the hands of the Assyrians; and it would come to pass for Judah still later at the hands of the Babylonians. But they would also come to know the blessing of return.

26:33. **unsheathe my sword**. To appreciate the horror of the metaphor of God saying He will go after Israel unsheathing a sword, one should recall that this is exactly what the Egyptians say that they will do to Israel in the Song of the Sea (Exod 15:9). That is, God, who is Israel's protector, threatens a curse in which God would become like Israel's enemies. It is one's worst nightmare: that one's loving, protecting parents become a horrible threat.

will cease, the amount that it did not cease on your Sabbaths when you lived on it. 36And those of you who remain:

    I shall bring faintness in their hearts in their enemies' lands,

    and the sound of a driven leaf will chase them,

    and they will flee like the flight from a sword,

    and they will fall when there is no one pursuing,

37 and they will stumble, each over his brother, as in front of a sword,

    when there is no one pursuing,

    and you will not have a footing in front of your enemies,

38   and you will perish among the nations,

    and your enemies' land will eat you up,

39 and those of you who remain will rot for their crime in your enemies' lands,

    and also for their fathers' crimes with them they will rot.

40"When they will confess their crime and their fathers' crime for their breach that they made against me, and also that they went on with me in defiance, 41so I, I also, would go on with them in defiance, and I brought them into their enemies' land; or if then their uncircumcised heart will be humbled and then they will accept their crime, 42then I shall remember my covenant of Jacob, and I shall remember also my covenant of Isaac and also my covenant of Abra-

הַשַּׁמָּה תִּשְׁבֹּת אֵת אֲשֶׁר לֹא־שָׁבְתָה בְּשַׁבְּתֹתֵיכֶם בְּשִׁבְתְּכֶם עָלֶיהָ: 36וְהַנִּשְׁאָרִים בָּכֶם וְהֵבֵאתִי מֹרֶךְ בִּלְבָבָם בְּאַרְצֹת אֹיְבֵיהֶם וְרָדַף אֹתָם קוֹל עָלֶה נִדָּף וְנָסוּ מְנֻסַת־חֶרֶב וְנָפְלוּ וְאֵין רֹדֵף: 37וְכָשְׁלוּ אִישׁ־בְּאָחִיו כְּמִפְּנֵי־חֶרֶב וְרֹדֵף אָיִן וְלֹא־תִהְיֶה לָכֶם תְּקוּמָה לִפְנֵי אֹיְבֵיכֶם: 38וַאֲבַדְתֶּם בַּגּוֹיִם וְאָכְלָה אֶתְכֶם אֶרֶץ אֹיְבֵיכֶם: 39וְהַנִּשְׁאָרִים בָּכֶם יִמַּקּוּ בַּעֲוֺנָם בְּאַרְצֹת אֹיְבֵיכֶם וְאַף בַּעֲוֺנֹת אֲבֹתָם אִתָּם יִמָּקּוּ: 40וְהִתְוַדּוּ אֶת־עֲוֺנָם וְאֶת־עֲוֺן אֲבֹתָם בְּמַעֲלָם אֲשֶׁר מָעֲלוּ־בִי וְאַף אֲשֶׁר־הָלְכוּ עִמִּי בְּקֶרִי: 41אַף־אֲנִי אֵלֵךְ עִמָּם בְּקֶרִי וְהֵבֵאתִי אֹתָם בְּאֶרֶץ אֹיְבֵיהֶם אוֹ־אָז יִכָּנַע לְבָבָם הֶעָרֵל וְאָז יִרְצוּ אֶת־עֲוֺנָם: 42וְזָכַרְתִּי אֶת־בְּרִיתִי יַעֲקוֹב וְאַף אֶת־בְּרִיתִי יִצְחָק וְאַף אֶת־בְּרִיתִי אַבְרָהָם אֶזְכֹּר

26:40. **their crime and their fathers' crime.** On one hand, this is yet another reminder that it takes *generations* before the God of Israel will take such actions. On the other hand, it means that the Israelites must recognize that it is not only their own offenses that have led to these things. They must come to terms with their parents' offenses as well. The ultimate revelation of the divine at Sinai includes the fact that the deity "reckons fathers' crime on children and on children's children, on third generations and on fourth generations." Now the perspective is turned to those children, generations later; and we learn from the Torah, no less than from Freud, that humans must look back not only at the good that their parents and grandparents did but also at their errors and faults. It is an essential part of understanding how we came to be what we are.

ham, and I shall remember the land. 43And the land will be left from them, and it will accept its Sabbaths while it is devastated from them, and they will accept their crime, because and *only* because they rejected my judgments and their soul scorned my laws.

44"And even despite this, when they were in their enemies' land I did not reject them and did not scorn them, to finish them, to break my covenant with them, because I am YHWH, their God! 45So I shall remember for them the covenant of the first ones, whom I brought out from the land of Egypt before the eyes of the nations to be God to them. I am YHWH."

46These are the laws and the judgments and the instructions that YHWH gave between Him and the children of Israel in Mount Sinai by Moses' hand.

וְהָאָרֶץ אֶזְכֹּר: 43וְהָאָרֶץ תֵּעָזֵב מֵהֶם וְתִרֶץ אֶת־שַׁבְּתֹתֶיהָ בָּהְשַׁמָּה מֵהֶם וְהֵם יִרְצוּ אֶת־עֲוֹנָם יַעַן וּבְיַעַן בְּמִשְׁפָּטַי מָאָסוּ וְאֶת־חֻקֹּתַי גָּעֲלָה נַפְשָׁם: 44וְאַף־גַּם־זֹאת בִּהְיוֹתָם בְּאֶרֶץ אֹיְבֵיהֶם לֹא־מְאַסְתִּים וְלֹא־גְעַלְתִּים לְכַלֹּתָם לְהָפֵר בְּרִיתִי אִתָּם כִּי אֲנִי יְהוָה אֱלֹהֵיהֶם: 45וְזָכַרְתִּי לָהֶם בְּרִית רִאשֹׁנִים אֲשֶׁר הוֹצֵאתִי־אֹתָם מֵאֶרֶץ מִצְרַיִם לְעֵינֵי הַגּוֹיִם לִהְיֹת לָהֶם לֵאלֹהִים אֲנִי יְהוָה: 46אֵלֶּה הַחֻקִּים וְהַמִּשְׁפָּטִים וְהַתּוֹרֹת אֲשֶׁר נָתַן יְהוָה בֵּינוֹ וּבֵין בְּנֵי יִשְׂרָאֵל בְּהַר סִינַי בְּיַד־מֹשֶׁה: פ

26:46. **These are the laws and the judgments and the instructions.** The present age plainly appears to value the ethical more than the ritual in religion. Some even feel the need to justify ritual by attempting to connect each ritual act to some ethical value: "We keep kosher to remind us to care about animals; we wear fringes to remind us to be kind. . . ." This is misleading. Certainly ritual acts can have consequences in the ethical realm, but that is not their reason for being. If we are to understand Leviticus, we must have an appreciation of what ritual meant in its society intrinsically. Ritual can have aesthetic, psychological, and inspirational value. It has the potential of generating feelings of closeness to the sacred as well as feelings of identity, stability, and security. For some, it means, in a world of uncertainty, to be told what the "right" things are, what acts one can perform to feel that one is acting in accordance with nothing less than the will of the creator of the universe. In the matter of purity, for example, one can believe that, when one has had contact with any of a group of things that intimidate us but that are physiological facts of life (blood and other bodily fluids, bodily sores, death), one can do things that remove the condition that this contact has produced—and thus remove the fear. In the matter of sacrifice, as we have observed, the ritual has an impact on one's feeling of guilt. In the observance of the holidays, the ritual contributes to feelings of festivity and communal celebration—and the sanctification of time. And in the variety of elaborate ceremonies performed at the Tent of Meeting, officiated by the specially garbed priests, accompanied by the burning of incense, the ritual contributes an aesthetic component to religion as well. All of this is known—consciously or intuitively—to those who have found meaning and even enjoyment in the practice of the rituals of their own religion. The ritual and the ethical are two components of religion—and of Leviticus—that do not justify each other, but rather unite and produce mutual support. Indeed, it is instructive that

27 ¹And YHWH spoke to Moses, saying, ²"Speak to the children of Israel. And you shall say to them: When a man will express a vow by your appraisal of persons for YHWH, ³then your appraisal shall be:

"A male from twenty years old up to sixty years old: then your appraisal shall be fifty shekels of silver by the shekel of the Holy. ⁴And if it is a female, then your appraisal shall be thirty shekels. ⁵And if one is from five years old up to twenty years old, then your appraisal for a male shall be twenty shekels and for a female ten shekels. ⁶And if one is from a month old up to five years old, then your appraisal for a male shall be five shekels of silver and your appraisal for a female three shekels. ⁷And if one is from sixty years old and up, if a male then your appraisal shall be fifteen shekels, and for a female ten shekels. ⁸And if he is lower than your estimate, then one shall stand him in front of the priest, and the priest shall appraise him. The priest shall appraise him on the basis of what the hand of the one making the vow can attain.

⁹"And if it is an animal from which people would bring an offering to YHWH, everything that he will give of it to YHWH will be a holy thing. ¹⁰And he shall not exchange it and shall not trade it, good for bad or bad for good; and if he *does* trade an animal for an animal, then both it and the one traded for it shall be a holy thing.

27 ¹וַיְדַבֵּ֥ר יְהוָ֖ה אֶל־מֹשֶׁ֥ה לֵּאמֹֽר׃ ²דַּבֵּ֞ר אֶל־בְּנֵ֤י יִשְׂרָאֵל֙ וְאָמַרְתָּ֣ אֲלֵהֶ֔ם אִ֕ישׁ כִּ֥י יַפְלִ֖א נֶ֑דֶר בְּעֶרְכְּךָ֥ נְפָשֹׁ֖ת לַיהוָֽה׃ ³וְהָיָ֤ה עֶרְכְּךָ֙ הַזָּכָ֔ר מִבֶּן֙ עֶשְׂרִ֣ים שָׁנָ֔ה וְעַ֖ד בֶּן־שִׁשִּׁ֣ים שָׁנָ֑ה וְהָיָ֣ה עֶרְכְּךָ֗ חֲמִשִּׁ֛ים שֶׁ֥קֶל כֶּ֖סֶף בְּשֶׁ֥קֶל הַקֹּֽדֶשׁ׃ ⁴וְאִם־נְקֵבָ֖ה הִ֑וא וְהָיָ֥ה עֶרְכְּךָ֖ שְׁלֹשִׁ֥ים שָֽׁקֶל׃ ⁵וְאִ֨ם מִבֶּן־חָמֵ֜שׁ שָׁנִ֗ים וְעַד֙ בֶּן־עֶשְׂרִ֣ים שָׁנָ֔ה וְהָיָ֧ה עֶרְכְּךָ֛ הַזָּכָ֖ר עֶשְׂרִ֣ים שְׁקָלִ֑ים וְלַנְּקֵבָ֖ה עֲשֶׂ֥רֶת שְׁקָלִֽים׃ ⁶וְאִ֣ם מִבֶּן־חֹ֗דֶשׁ וְעַד֙ בֶּן־חָמֵ֣שׁ שָׁנִ֔ים וְהָיָ֤ה עֶרְכְּךָ֙ הַזָּכָ֔ר חֲמִשָּׁ֥ה שְׁקָלִ֖ים כָּ֑סֶף וְלַנְּקֵבָ֣ה עֶרְכְּךָ֔ שְׁלֹ֥שֶׁת שְׁקָלִ֖ים כָּֽסֶף׃ ⁷וְ֠אִם מִבֶּן־שִׁשִּׁ֨ים שָׁנָ֤ה וָמַ֨עְלָה֙ אִם־זָכָ֔ר וְהָיָ֣ה עֶרְכְּךָ֔ חֲמִשָּׁ֥ה עָשָׂ֖ר שָׁ֑קֶל וְלַנְּקֵבָ֖ה עֲשָׂרָ֥ה שְׁקָלִֽים׃ ⁸וְאִם־מָ֥ךְ הוּא֙ מֵֽעֶרְכֶּ֔ךָ וְהֶֽעֱמִידוֹ֙ לִפְנֵ֣י הַכֹּהֵ֔ן וְהֶעֱרִ֥יךְ אֹת֖וֹ הַכֹּהֵ֑ן עַל־פִּ֗י אֲשֶׁ֤ר תַּשִּׂיג֙ יַ֣ד הַנֹּדֵ֔ר יַעֲרִיכֶ֖נּוּ הַכֹּהֵֽן׃ ס ⁹וְאִם־בְּהֵמָ֔ה אֲשֶׁ֨ר יַקְרִ֧יבוּ מִמֶּ֛נָּה קָרְבָּ֖ן לַֽיהוָ֑ה כֹּל֩ אֲשֶׁ֨ר יִתֵּ֥ן מִמֶּ֛נּוּ לַיהוָ֖ה יִֽהְיֶה־קֹּֽדֶשׁ׃ ¹⁰לֹ֣א יַחֲלִיפֶ֗נּוּ וְלֹֽא־יָמִ֥יר אֹת֛וֹ ט֥וֹב בְּרָ֖ע אוֹ־רַ֣ע בְּט֑וֹב וְאִם־הָמֵ֨ר יָמִ֤יר בְּהֵמָה֙ בִּבְהֵמָ֔ה וְהָֽיָה־ה֥וּא וּתְמוּרָת֖וֹ יִֽהְיֶה־קֹּֽדֶשׁ׃ ¹¹וְאִם֙

Leviticus, a book that is so fundamentally concerned with distinction, does not make any explicit distinction between its ethical and its ritual laws. Sometimes they occur in separate units and sometimes they are mixed together, but they are never identified as two distinct categories of law.

We do a disservice when we interpret ritual matters in terms of ethical justifications. We move ourselves even farther from the appreciation of ritual and the awe before the holy. Similarly, when we say that the Hebrew word *qādōš* means a neutral kind of "separate" rather than meaning "holy, sacred," we further lose our feeling for holiness. And perhaps we err similarly when we say that Hebrew *ḥāṭā'* means "to miss the mark" rather than "to sin," to do something wrong that places us in a state that needs to be remedied through atonement and/or sacrifice and/or compensation.

27:9. an animal from which people would bring an offering. Meaning: an animal that is permissible for sacrifice, as opposed to an impure animal (see v. 11).

11And if it is any impure animal, from which people would not bring an offering to YHWH, then he shall stand the animal in front of the priest, 12and the priest shall appraise it. Whether good or bad: according to your appraisal by the priest, so it shall be. 13And if he will *redeem* it, then he shall add a fifth of it to your appraisal.

14"And when a man will consecrate his house to be a holy thing to YHWH, then the priest shall appraise it. Whether good or bad: as the priest will appraise it, so it shall stand. 15And if the one who consecrates it will redeem his house, then he shall add a fifth of the money of your appraisal to it, and it shall be his.

16"And if a man will consecrate any of a field of his possession to YHWH, then your appraisal shall be on the basis of its seed: the seed of a homer of barley at fifty shekels of silver. 17If he will consecrate his field from the jubilee year, it shall stand according to your appraisal; 18and if he will consecrate his field after the jubilee, then the priest shall figure the money for him on the basis of the years that are left until the jubilee year, and it shall be subtracted from your appraisal. 19And if the one who consecrates it will *redeem* the field, then he shall add a fifth of the money of your appraisal to it, and it will stand as his. 20And if he will not redeem the field, or if he has sold the field to another man, it shall not be redeemed anymore. 21And when it goes out in the jubilee, the field shall be a holy thing to YHWH, like a devoted field; his possession shall be the priest's.

22"And if he will consecrate any of a field that he has bought, that is not from a field of his possession, to YHWH, 23then the priest shall figure for him the count of your appraisal up to the jubilee year, and he shall give your appraisal on

כָּל־בְּהֵמָה טְמֵאָה אֲשֶׁר לֹא־יַקְרִיבוּ מִמֶּנָּה קָרְבָּן
לַיהוָה וְהֶעֱמִיד אֶת־הַבְּהֵמָה לִפְנֵי הַכֹּהֵן:
12וְהֶעֱרִיךְ הַכֹּהֵן אֹתָהּ בֵּין טוֹב וּבֵין רָע כְּעֶרְכְּךָ
הַכֹּהֵן כֵּן יִהְיֶה: 13וְאִם־גָּאֹל יִגְאָלֶנָּה וְיָסַף חֲמִישִׁתוֹ
עַל־עֶרְכֶּךָ: 14וְאִישׁ כִּי־יַקְדִּשׁ אֶת־בֵּיתוֹ קֹדֶשׁ
לַיהוָה וְהֶעֱרִיכוֹ הַכֹּהֵן בֵּין טוֹב וּבֵין רָע כַּאֲשֶׁר
יַעֲרִיךְ אֹתוֹ הַכֹּהֵן כֵּן יָקוּם: 15וְאִם־הַמַּקְדִּישׁ יִגְאַל
אֶת־בֵּיתוֹ וְיָסַף חֲמִישִׁית כֶּסֶף־עֶרְכְּךָ עָלָיו וְהָיָה
לוֹ: 16וְאִם । מִשְּׂדֵה אֲחֻזָּתוֹ יַקְדִּישׁ אִישׁ לַיהוָה
וְהָיָה עֶרְכְּךָ לְפִי זַרְעוֹ זֶרַע חֹמֶר שְׂעֹרִים בַּחֲמִשִּׁים
שֶׁקֶל כָּסֶף: 17אִם־מִשְּׁנַת הַיֹּבֵל יַקְדִּישׁ שָׂדֵהוּ
כְּעֶרְכְּךָ יָקוּם: 18וְאִם־אַחַר הַיֹּבֵל יַקְדִּישׁ שָׂדֵהוּ
וְחִשַּׁב־לוֹ הַכֹּהֵן אֶת־הַכֶּסֶף עַל־פִּי הַשָּׁנִים הַנּוֹתָרֹת
עַד שְׁנַת הַיֹּבֵל וְנִגְרַע מֵעֶרְכֶּךָ: 19וְאִם־גָּאֹל יִגְאַל
אֶת־הַשָּׂדֶה הַמַּקְדִּישׁ אֹתוֹ וְיָסַף חֲמִשִׁית כֶּסֶף־
עֶרְכְּךָ עָלָיו וְקָם לוֹ: 20וְאִם־לֹא יִגְאַל אֶת־הַשָּׂדֶה
וְאִם־מָכַר אֶת־הַשָּׂדֶה לְאִישׁ אַחֵר לֹא יִגָּאֵל עוֹד:
21וְהָיָה הַשָּׂדֶה בְּצֵאתוֹ בַיֹּבֵל קֹדֶשׁ לַיהוָה כִּשְׂדֵה
הַחֵרֶם לַכֹּהֵן תִּהְיֶה אֲחֻזָּתוֹ:

22וְאִם אֶת־שְׂדֵה מִקְנָתוֹ אֲשֶׁר לֹא מִשְּׂדֵה
אֲחֻזָּתוֹ יַקְדִּישׁ לַיהוָה: 23וְחִשַּׁב־לוֹ הַכֹּהֵן אֵת
מִכְסַת הָעֶרְכְּךָ עַד שְׁנַת הַיֹּבֵל וְנָתַן אֶת־הָעֶרְכְּךָ

27:16. **on the basis of its seed.** The value of the land is determined by how much seed one can plant in it.

27:21. **like a devoted field.** Anything that one formally devotes to God cannot ever be sold or redeemed, and it becomes the priests' property (Lev 27:28–29; Num 18:14).

that day, a holy thing to YHWH. 24In the jubilee year the field shall go back to the one from whom it was bought, to the one to whom the possession of the land belongs. 25And all of your appraisal shall be by the shekel of the Holy. (The shekel shall be twenty gerah.)

26"Except: a firstling of the animals—which as a firstling is committed to YHWH—no man shall consecrate it. Whether an ox or a sheep, it is YHWH's. 27And if it is of the impure animals, then he shall redeem it at your appraisal, and he shall add to it a fifth of it. And if it will not be redeemed then it shall be sold at your appraisal.

28"Except: any devoted thing that a man will devote to YHWH from anything that he has—from human or animal or from a field of his possession—shall not be sold and shall not be redeemed. Any devoted thing: it is a holy of holies to YHWH. 29Anyone who will be devoted from humans shall not be redeemed. He shall be put to *death*.

30"And all the tithe of the land, from the land's seed, from the tree's fruit: it is YHWH's, a holy thing to YHWH. 31And if a man will *redeem* some of his tithe, he shall add to it a fifth of it. 32And all the tithe of a herd or a flock, everything that passes under the rod: the tenth shall be a holy thing to YHWH. 33He shall not inspect it either for good or for bad. And he shall not trade it. And if he *will* trade it, then both it and the one traded for it shall be a holy thing. It shall not be redeemed."

34These are the commandments that YHWH commanded Moses for the children of Israel in Mount Sinai.

בַּיּוֹם הַהוּא קֹדֶשׁ לַיהוָה: 24בִּשְׁנַת הַיּוֹבֵל יָשׁוּב הַשָּׂדֶה לַאֲשֶׁר קָנָהוּ מֵאִתּוֹ לַאֲשֶׁר־לוֹ אֲחֻזַּת הָאָרֶץ: 25וְכָל־עֶרְכְּךָ יִהְיֶה בְּשֶׁקֶל הַקֹּדֶשׁ עֶשְׂרִים גֵּרָה יִהְיֶה הַשָּׁקֶל: ס 26אַךְ־בְּכוֹר אֲשֶׁר־יְבֻכַּר לַיהוָה בִּבְהֵמָה לֹא־יַקְדִּישׁ אִישׁ אֹתוֹ אִם־שׁוֹר אִם־שֶׂה לַיהוָה הוּא: 27וְאִם בַּבְּהֵמָה הַטְּמֵאָה וּפָדָה בְעֶרְכֶּךָ וְיָסַף חֲמִשִׁתוֹ עָלָיו וְאִם־לֹא יִגָּאֵל וְנִמְכַּר בְּעֶרְכֶּךָ: 28אַךְ־כָּל־חֵרֶם אֲשֶׁר יַחֲרִם אִישׁ לַיהוָה מִכָּל־אֲשֶׁר־לוֹ מֵאָדָם וּבְהֵמָה וּמִשְּׂדֵה אֲחֻזָּתוֹ לֹא יִמָּכֵר וְלֹא יִגָּאֵל כָּל־חֵרֶם קֹדֶשׁ־קָדָשִׁים הוּא לַיהוָה: 29כָּל־חֵרֶם אֲשֶׁר יָחֳרַם מִן־הָאָדָם לֹא יִפָּדֶה מוֹת יוּמָת: 30וְכָל־מַעְשַׂר הָאָרֶץ מִזֶּרַע הָאָרֶץ מִפְּרִי הָעֵץ לַיהוָה הוּא קֹדֶשׁ לַיהוָה: 31וְאִם־גָּאֹל יִגְאַל אִישׁ מִמַּעַשְׂרוֹ חֲמִשִׁיתוֹ יֹסֵף עָלָיו: 32וְכָל־מַעְשַׂר בָּקָר וָצֹאן כֹּל אֲשֶׁר־יַעֲבֹר תַּחַת הַשָּׁבֶט הָעֲשִׂירִי יִהְיֶה־קֹדֶשׁ לַיהוָה: 33לֹא יְבַקֵּר בֵּין־טוֹב לָרַע וְלֹא יְמִירֶנּוּ וְאִם־הָמֵר יְמִירֶנּוּ וְהָיָה־הוּא וּתְמוּרָתוֹ יִהְיֶה־קֹדֶשׁ לֹא יִגָּאֵל: 34אֵלֶּה הַמִּצְוֹת אֲשֶׁר צִוָּה יְהוָה אֶת־מֹשֶׁה אֶל־בְּנֵי יִשְׂרָאֵל בְּהַר סִינָי:

27:34. **These are the commandments that YHWH commanded Moses for the children of Israel in Mount Sinai.** Literary studies of Leviticus are likely to begin by raising the question of whether this book that contains so much law and so little narrative belongs in a literary study at all. But at bottom we do not have to argue that Leviticus is great literature in order to justify its inclusion in a literary analysis. It is not literature, not in the way in which almost anyone ever means that term. But the literary study of the Hebrew Bible has to come to terms with Leviticus, for it is embedded

in the biblical narrative. Indeed, the fact that no law code from ancient Israel survived independently, that law codes survived only in contexts of narrative, is notable in itself. Leviticus's laws are integral—and assumed thereafter. The book begins with the notation that YHWH speaks these things to Moses from the Tabernacle (1:1), and it ends here with the reminder that "These are the commandments that YHWH commanded Moses for the children of Israel at Mount Sinai." Some of the laws presume the preceding narrative, e.g., "You shall not do like what is done in the land of Egypt, in which you lived . . . " (18:3), which presumes the bondage in Egypt. Legal authority is vested in the priests (the power to teach and enforce, 10:10–11), which is an essential element in narratives in subsequent books. As new political figures, especially kings, will rise, the compatibility or conflict between them and the priests will be critical to the narrative, as it was critical in history.

Leviticus thus is a design for an organized society of people who help one another, who do not intentionally injure one another, who respect one another's property and relationships, who regularly assemble to celebrate together, who acknowledge their errors and atone for them, who regard life—in humans and in animals—as sacred, who pursue purity in various forms, who respect law, and who are utterly loyal to one God. It is against the background of this design that the book of Numbers must be understood.

418

NUMBERS

—◆—

במדבר

*T*he book of Numbers is the story of a journey. Against the backdrop of the book of Leviticus, with its absence of movement, Numbers is entirely about movement. The journey as a literary theme has been a recurring component of world literature from the epic of *Gilgamesh*, the oldest known book, and the *Odyssey* to *Alice's Adventures in Wonderland* and *The Wonderful Wizard of Oz*. It reflects real experience, it is a ready metaphor for human lives, and it is a connector between the world of literature and the world of dreams, in which experiences of journeys are common. The journey in literature can be the experience of an individual or a group. In the book of Numbers it is both. It is the people of Israel's journey from Sinai to the border of Canaan, from the site of the establishment of the covenant to the place where it is to be fulfilled. And it is Moses' journey from Mount Sinai to Mount Abarim, from the place where he has seen God to the place of his death.

One must read the story in Numbers with a sense of what is pictured: a great mass of people (603,550 adult males, plus the junior and elderly males and the females of all ages), an entire nation, in movement—with a visible miracle (the column of cloud and fire) and miraculous feeding (manna) happening in their presence at all times over a span of nearly forty years. It is the only age in the Bible in which miracle is a daily fact of life. There is an organization for travel, a hierarchy for community life (Moses, judges, priests), and formal rituals of time (Sabbath, holidays, and new moons) and of space (sacrifice, incense, vestments, the Tabernacle, fringes on clothing). There is a destination anticipated in a future in which some of them will participate and some will not. They are in an interim condition, conscious of the life in Egypt behind them and the promised life in front of them. Their mentality is a mentality of slaves. There are various groups and individuals among them with an interest in positions of leadership. On the evidence of the episodes of the story, they are to be pictured as deeply afraid.

Against this setting, the deity is pictured frequently as speaking and acting in response to human events rather than by divine initiative. Divine communications are fewer and briefer than in the preceding books. Leviticus is primarily concerned with God's giving the rules to the people. Now Numbers is concerned with their first experiences living under these rules and with God's responses to the courses of action they

take. Against the backdrop of the commandments of Leviticus, Numbers is the story of a people coming to terms with having a constitution of laws, and coming to terms with their relationship of holiness with the deity. And in the middle of this stands Moses. The story is about the people and God, but it is focused more than ever on Moses, his personality and especially his conflicts.

IN THE WILDERNESS

במדבר

1 ¹And YHWH spoke to Moses in the wilderness of Sinai in the Tent of Meeting on the first day of the second month in the second year of their exodus from the land of Egypt, saying, ²"Add up the heads of all of the congregation of Israel by their families, by their fathers' houses, with the number of names of every male by their heads. ³From twenty years old and up, everyone going out to the army in Israel: you shall count them by their army units, you and Aaron.

⁴"And a man for each tribe shall be with you; each is the head of his fathers' house. ⁵And these are the names of the men who will stand with you: For Reuben, Elizur son of Shedeur. ⁶For Simeon, Shelumiel son of Zurishadday. ⁷For Judah, Nahshon son of Amminadab. ⁸For Issachar, Nethanel son of Zuar. ⁹For Zebulun, Eliab son of Helon. ¹⁰For the children of Joseph: for Ephraim, Elishama son of Ammihud; for Manas-

1 ¹וַיְדַבֵּ֨ר יְהוָ֧ה אֶל־מֹשֶׁ֛ה בְּמִדְבַּ֥ר סִינַ֖י בְּאֹ֣הֶל
מוֹעֵ֑ד בְּאֶחָד֩ לַחֹ֨דֶשׁ הַשֵּׁנִ֜י בַּשָּׁנָ֣ה הַשֵּׁנִ֗ית לְצֵאתָ֛ם
מֵאֶ֥רֶץ מִצְרַ֖יִם לֵאמֹֽר: ²שְׂא֗וּ אֶת־רֹאשׁ֙ כָּל־עֲדַ֣ת
בְּנֵֽי־יִשְׂרָאֵ֔ל לְמִשְׁפְּחֹתָ֖ם לְבֵ֣ית אֲבֹתָ֑ם בְּמִסְפַּ֣ר
שֵׁמ֔וֹת כָּל־זָכָ֖ר לְגֻלְגְּלֹתָֽם: ³מִבֶּ֨ן עֶשְׂרִ֤ים שָׁנָה֙
וָמַ֔עְלָה כָּל־יֹצֵ֥א צָבָ֖א בְּיִשְׂרָאֵ֑ל תִּפְקְד֥וּ אֹתָ֛ם
לְצִבְאֹתָ֖ם אַתָּ֥ה וְאַהֲרֹֽן: ⁴וְאִתְּכֶ֣ם יִהְי֔וּ אִ֣ישׁ אִ֣ישׁ
לַמַּטֶּ֑ה אִ֛ישׁ רֹ֥אשׁ לְבֵית־אֲבֹתָ֖יו הֽוּא: ⁵וְאֵ֙לֶּה֙ שְׁמ֣וֹת
הָֽאֲנָשִׁ֔ים אֲשֶׁ֥ר יַֽעַמְד֖וּ אִתְּכֶ֑ם לִרְאוּבֵ֕ן אֱלִיצ֖וּר בֶּן־
שְׁדֵיאֽוּר: ⁶לְשִׁמְע֕וֹן שְׁלֻֽמִיאֵ֖ל בֶּן־צוּרִֽישַׁדָּֽי:
⁷לִֽיהוּדָ֕ה נַחְשׁ֖וֹן בֶּן־עַמִּֽינָדָֽב: ⁸לְיִ֨שָּׂשכָ֔ר נְתַנְאֵ֖ל בֶּן־
צוּעָֽר: ⁹לִזְבוּלֻ֕ן אֱלִיאָ֖ב בֶּן־חֵלֹֽן: ¹⁰לִבְנֵ֣י יוֹסֵ֔ף
לְאֶפְרַ֕יִם אֱלִֽישָׁמָ֖ע בֶּן־עַמִּיה֑וּד לִמְנַשֶּׁ֕ה גַּמְלִיאֵ֖ל
בֶּן־פְּדָהצֽוּר: ¹¹לְבִנְיָמִ֕ן אֲבִידָ֖ן בֶּן־גִּדְעֹנִֽי: ¹²לְדָ֕ן

1:1. **wilderness**. Wilderness emerges through the narrative not only as a setting but also as a theme of considerable significance. The Hebrew title of the book, *běmidbar*, "In the Wilderness," which derives from the opening verse ("And YHWH spoke to Moses in the wilderness of Sinai *[běmidbar sînay]* . . . "), is a better indicator of the book's contents than the Greek title, *arithmoi* (from which comes the English "Numbers"). It also better captures the pervasive feeling of the book. The wilderness depiction conveys two quite different qualities. On the one hand, the wilderness years constitute a kind of ideal. The people's life is orderly, protected, close to God. It is a period of incubation, of nurturing. All is provided: food, water, direction. The miraculous is the norm. At the same time, though, the wilderness is depicted as terrible. Conditions are bad. The environment is hostile. There is rebellion from within and fighting with peoples whom they encounter on the way. There are power struggles and fear. And this is pictured as having been almost entirely avoidable, a fate that has come upon the people for having rejected the opportunity to enter the land. Numbers thus expresses pervasively a notion that is only begun in Leviticus, namely that closeness to the divine is both glorious and dangerous. This dual picture of the ideal and the awesome sides of the wilderness years is perhaps the most striking and singular aspect of the book of Numbers. Numbers alone among the books of the Hebrew Bible recounts the story of a single generation of the nation, involving the entire nation, in a condition unlike that of any other time. In the earthly events and in the cosmic aspect of both continuous and situational miracles, the wilderness generation is like no other, and the book that tells its story is correspondingly unique.

seh, Gamaliel son of Pedahzur. 11For Benjamin, Abidan son of Gideoni. 12For Dan, Ahiezer son of Ammishadday. 13For Asher, Pagiel son of Ochran. 14For Gad, Eliasaph son of Deuel. 15For Naphtali, Ahira son of Enan." 16These were the prominent ones of the congregation, chieftains of their fathers' tribes. They were heads of Israel's thousands. 17And Moses and Aaron took these men who were designated by name, 18and they assembled all of the congregation on the first day of the second month, and they were recorded by their families, by their fathers' houses, with the number of names, from twenty years old and up, by their heads, 19as YHWH commanded Moses. And he counted them in the wilderness of Sinai.

20And the children of Reuben, Israel's first-born, were: by their records, by their families, by their fathers' house, with the number of names, by their heads, every male from twenty years old and up, everyone going out to the army, 21the tribe of Reuben's counts were forty-six thousand five hundred.

22For the children of Simeon: by their records, by their families, by their fathers' house, their counts with the number of names, by their heads, every male from twenty years old and up, everyone going out to the army, 23the tribe of Simeon's counts were fifty-nine thousand three hundred.

24For the children of Gad: by their records, by their families, by their fathers' house, with the number of names, from twenty years old and up, everyone going out to the army, 25the tribe of Gad's counts were forty-five thousand six hundred fifty.

26For the children of Judah: by their records, by their families, by their fathers' house, with the number of names, from twenty years old and up, everyone going out to the army, 27the tribe of Judah's counts were seventy-four thousand six hundred.

28For the children of Issachar: by their records, by their families, by their fathers' house, with the number of names, from twenty years old and up,

אֲחִיעֶ֕זֶר בֶּן־עַמִּֽישַׁדָּֽי: 13לְאָשֵׁ֕ר פַּגְעִיאֵ֖ל בֶּן־עָכְרָֽן: 14לְגָ֕ד אֶלְיָסָ֖ף בֶּן־דְּעוּאֵֽל: 15לְנַפְתָּלִ֕י אֲחִירַ֖ע בֶּן־עֵינָֽן: 16אֵ֚לֶּה קְרִיאֵ֣י הָֽעֵדָ֔ה נְשִׂיאֵ֖י מַטּ֣וֹת אֲבוֹתָ֑ם רָאשֵׁ֛י אַלְפֵ֥י יִשְׂרָאֵ֖ל הֵֽם: 17וַיִּקַּ֥ח מֹשֶׁ֖ה וְאַהֲרֹ֑ן אֵ֚ת הָאֲנָשִׁ֣ים הָאֵ֔לֶּה אֲשֶׁ֥ר נִקְּב֖וּ בְּשֵׁמֽוֹת: 18וְאֵ֨ת כָּל־הָעֵדָ֜ה הִקְהִ֗ילוּ בְּאֶחָד֙ לַחֹ֣דֶשׁ הַשֵּׁנִ֔י וַיִּתְיַלְד֥וּ עַל־מִשְׁפְּחֹתָ֖ם לְבֵ֣ית אֲבֹתָ֑ם בְּמִסְפַּ֣ר שֵׁמ֗וֹת מִבֶּ֨ן עֶשְׂרִ֥ים שָׁנָ֛ה וָמַ֖עְלָה לְגֻלְגְּלֹתָֽם: 19כַּאֲשֶׁ֛ר צִוָּ֥ה יְהוָ֖ה אֶת־מֹשֶׁ֑ה וַֽיִּפְקְדֵ֖ם בְּמִדְבַּ֥ר סִינָֽי: פ 20וַיִּהְי֤וּ בְנֵֽי־רְאוּבֵן֙ בְּכֹ֣ר יִשְׂרָאֵ֔ל תּוֹלְדֹתָ֥ם לְמִשְׁפְּחֹתָ֖ם לְבֵ֣ית אֲבֹתָ֑ם בְּמִסְפַּ֣ר שֵׁמֹ֗ות לְגֻלְגְּלֹתָם֙ כָּל־זָכָ֔ר מִבֶּ֨ן עֶשְׂרִ֥ים שָׁנָ֛ה וָמַ֖עְלָה כֹּ֥ל יֹצֵ֖א צָבָֽא: 21פְּקֻדֵיהֶ֖ם לְמַטֵּ֣ה רְאוּבֵ֑ן שִׁשָּׁ֧ה וְאַרְבָּעִ֛ים אֶ֖לֶף וַחֲמֵ֥שׁ מֵאֽוֹת: פ 22לִבְנֵ֣י שִׁמְע֔וֹן תּוֹלְדֹתָ֥ם לְמִשְׁפְּחֹתָ֖ם לְבֵ֣ית אֲבֹתָ֑ם פְּקֻדָ֗יו בְּמִסְפַּ֤ר שֵׁמוֹת֙ לְגֻלְגְּלֹתָ֔ם כָּל־זָכָ֗ר מִבֶּ֨ן עֶשְׂרִ֥ים שָׁנָ֛ה וָמַ֖עְלָה כֹּ֥ל יֹצֵ֖א צָבָֽא: 23פְּקֻדֵיהֶ֖ם לְמַטֵּ֣ה שִׁמְע֑וֹן תִּשְׁעָ֧ה וַחֲמִשִּׁ֛ים אֶ֖לֶף וּשְׁלֹ֥שׁ מֵאֽוֹת: פ 24לִבְנֵ֣י גָ֔ד תּוֹלְדֹתָ֥ם לְמִשְׁפְּחֹתָ֖ם לְבֵ֣ית אֲבֹתָ֑ם בְּמִסְפַּ֣ר שֵׁמ֗וֹת מִבֶּ֨ן עֶשְׂרִ֥ים שָׁנָ֛ה וָמַ֖עְלָה כֹּ֥ל יֹצֵ֖א צָבָֽא: 25פְּקֻדֵיהֶ֖ם לְמַטֵּ֣ה גָ֑ד חֲמִשָּׁ֧ה וְאַרְבָּעִים֙ אֶ֔לֶף וְשֵׁ֥שׁ מֵא֖וֹת וַחֲמִשִּֽׁים: פ 26לִבְנֵ֣י יְהוּדָ֔ה תּוֹלְדֹתָ֥ם לְמִשְׁפְּחֹתָ֖ם לְבֵ֣ית אֲבֹתָ֑ם בְּמִסְפַּ֣ר שֵׁמֹ֗ת מִבֶּ֨ן עֶשְׂרִ֥ים שָׁנָ֛ה וָמַ֖עְלָה כֹּ֥ל יֹצֵ֖א צָבָֽא: 27פְּקֻדֵיהֶ֖ם לְמַטֵּ֣ה יְהוּדָ֑ה אַרְבָּעָ֧ה וְשִׁבְעִ֛ים אֶ֖לֶף וְשֵׁ֥שׁ מֵאֽוֹת: פ 28לִבְנֵ֣י יִשָּׂשכָ֔ר תּוֹלְדֹתָ֥ם לְמִשְׁפְּחֹתָ֖ם לְבֵ֣ית אֲבֹתָ֑ם בְּמִסְפַּ֣ר שֵׁמֹ֗ת מִבֶּ֨ן עֶשְׂרִ֥ים שָׁנָ֛ה וָמַ֖עְלָה כֹּ֥ל

1:16 קְרוּאֵ֖י ק

everyone going out to the army, 29the tribe of Issachar's counts were fifty-four thousand four hundred.

30For the children of Zebulun: by their records, by their families, by their fathers' house, with the number of names, from twenty years old and up, everyone going out to the army, 31the tribe of Zebulun's counts were fifty-seven thousand four hundred.

32For the children of Joseph:

For the children of Ephraim: by their records, by their families, by their fathers' house, with the number of names, from twenty years old and up, everyone going out to the army, 33the tribe of Ephraim's counts were forty thousand five hundred.

34For the children of Manasseh: by their records, by their families, by their fathers' house, with the number of names, from twenty years old and up, everyone going out to the army, 35the tribe of Manasseh's counts were thirty-two thousand two hundred.

36For the children of Benjamin: by their records, by their families, by their fathers' house, with the number of names, from twenty years old and up, everyone going out to the army, 37the tribe of Benjamin's counts were thirty-five thousand four hundred.

38For the children of Dan: by their records, by their families, by their fathers' house, with the number of names, from twenty years old and up, everyone going out to the army, 39the tribe of Dan's counts were sixty-two thousand seven hundred.

40For the children of Asher: by their records, by their families, by their fathers' house, with the number of names, from twenty years old and up, everyone going out to the army, 41the tribe of Asher's counts were forty-one thousand five hundred.

42The children of Naphtali: by their records, by their families, by their fathers' house, with the number of names, from twenty years old and up, everyone going out to the army, 43the tribe of

יֹצֵא צָבָא: 29פְּקֻדֵיהֶם לְמַטֵּה יִשָּׂשכָר אַרְבָּעָה וַחֲמִשִּׁים אֶלֶף וְאַרְבַּע מֵאוֹת: פ 30לִבְנֵי זְבוּלֻן תּוֹלְדֹתָם לְמִשְׁפְּחֹתָם לְבֵית אֲבֹתָם בְּמִסְפַּר שֵׁמֹת מִבֶּן עֶשְׂרִים שָׁנָה וָמַעְלָה כֹּל יֹצֵא צָבָא: 31פְּקֻדֵיהֶם לְמַטֵּה זְבוּלֻן שִׁבְעָה וַחֲמִשִּׁים אֶלֶף וְאַרְבַּע מֵאוֹת: פ 32לִבְנֵי יוֹסֵף לִבְנֵי אֶפְרַיִם תּוֹלְדֹתָם לְמִשְׁפְּחֹתָם לְבֵית אֲבֹתָם בְּמִסְפַּר שֵׁמֹת מִבֶּן עֶשְׂרִים שָׁנָה וָמַעְלָה כֹּל יֹצֵא צָבָא: 33פְּקֻדֵיהֶם לְמַטֵּה אֶפְרָיִם אַרְבָּעִים אֶלֶף וַחֲמֵשׁ מֵאוֹת: פ 34לִבְנֵי מְנַשֶּׁה תּוֹלְדֹתָם לְמִשְׁפְּחֹתָם לְבֵית אֲבֹתָם בְּמִסְפַּר שֵׁמוֹת מִבֶּן עֶשְׂרִים שָׁנָה וָמַעְלָה כֹּל יֹצֵא צָבָא: 35פְּקֻדֵיהֶם לְמַטֵּה מְנַשֶּׁה שְׁנַיִם וּשְׁלֹשִׁים אֶלֶף וּמָאתָיִם: פ 36לִבְנֵי בִנְיָמִן תּוֹלְדֹתָם לְמִשְׁפְּחֹתָם לְבֵית אֲבֹתָם בְּמִסְפַּר שֵׁמֹת מִבֶּן עֶשְׂרִים שָׁנָה וָמַעְלָה כֹּל יֹצֵא צָבָא: 37פְּקֻדֵיהֶם לְמַטֵּה בִנְיָמִן חֲמִשָּׁה וּשְׁלֹשִׁים אֶלֶף וְאַרְבַּע מֵאוֹת: פ 38לִבְנֵי דָן תּוֹלְדֹתָם לְמִשְׁפְּחֹתָם לְבֵית אֲבֹתָם בְּמִסְפַּר שֵׁמֹת מִבֶּן עֶשְׂרִים שָׁנָה וָמַעְלָה כֹּל יֹצֵא צָבָא: 39פְּקֻדֵיהֶם לְמַטֵּה דָן שְׁנַיִם וְשִׁשִּׁים אֶלֶף וּשְׁבַע מֵאוֹת: פ 40לִבְנֵי אָשֵׁר תּוֹלְדֹתָם לְמִשְׁפְּחֹתָם לְבֵית אֲבֹתָם בְּמִסְפַּר שֵׁמֹת מִבֶּן עֶשְׂרִים שָׁנָה וָמַעְלָה כֹּל יֹצֵא צָבָא: 41פְּקֻדֵיהֶם לְמַטֵּה אָשֵׁר אֶחָד וְאַרְבָּעִים אֶלֶף וַחֲמֵשׁ מֵאוֹת: פ 42בְּנֵי נַפְתָּלִי תּוֹלְדֹתָם לְמִשְׁפְּחֹתָם לְבֵית אֲבֹתָם בְּמִסְפַּר שֵׁמֹת מִבֶּן עֶשְׂרִים שָׁנָה וָמַעְלָה כֹּל יֹצֵא צָבָא: 43פְּקֻדֵיהֶם

Naphtali's counts were fifty-three thousand four hundred.

⁴⁴These are the counts that Moses and Aaron and Israel's chieftains made. (They were twelve men, one each for his fathers' house.) ⁴⁵And they were all of the counts of the children of Israel, by their fathers' house, from twenty years old and up, everyone going out to the army in Israel. ⁴⁶And all of the counts were six hundred three thousand five hundred fifty.

⁴⁷And the Levites, by their fathers' tribe, were not counted among them, ⁴⁸for YHWH spoke to Moses, saying, ⁴⁹"Except: you shall not count the tribe of Levi, and you shall not add up their heads among the children of Israel. ⁵⁰And you: appoint the Levites over the Tabernacle of the Testimony and over all its equipment and over everything it has. They shall carry the Tabernacle and all its equipment, and they shall attend to it, and they shall camp around the Tabernacle. ⁵¹And when the Tabernacle travels, the Levites shall take it down; and when the Tabernacle camps, the Levites shall set it up. And an outsider who comes close shall be put to death. ⁵²And the children of Israel shall camp, each at his camp, each at his flag, by their army units, ⁵³and the Levites shall camp all around the Tabernacle of the Testimony, so there will not be a rage on the congregation of the children of Israel, and the Levites shall keep the charge of the Tabernacle of the Testimony."

⁵⁴And the children of Israel did according to everything that YHWH had commanded Moses. They did so.

לְמַטֵּה נַפְתָּלִי שְׁלֹשָׁה וַחֲמִשִּׁים אֶלֶף וְאַרְבַּע מֵאוֹת:
⁴⁴אֵלֶּה הַפְּקֻדִים אֲשֶׁר פָּקַד מֹשֶׁה וְאַהֲרֹן ס
וּנְשִׂיאֵי יִשְׂרָאֵל שְׁנֵים עָשָׂר אִישׁ אִישׁ־אֶחָד לְבֵית־
אֲבֹתָיו הָיוּ: ⁴⁵וַיִּהְיוּ כָּל־פְּקוּדֵי בְנֵי־יִשְׂרָאֵל לְבֵית
אֲבֹתָם מִבֶּן עֶשְׂרִים שָׁנָה וָמַעְלָה כָּל־יֹצֵא צָבָא
בְּיִשְׂרָאֵל: ⁴⁶וַיִּהְיוּ כָּל־הַפְּקֻדִים שֵׁשׁ־מֵאוֹת אֶלֶף
וּשְׁלֹשֶׁת אֲלָפִים וַחֲמֵשׁ מֵאוֹת וַחֲמִשִּׁים: ⁴⁷וְהַלְוִיִּם
לְמַטֵּה אֲבֹתָם לֹא הָתְפָּקְדוּ בְּתוֹכָם: פ ⁴⁸וַיְדַבֵּר
יְהוָה אֶל־מֹשֶׁה לֵּאמֹר: ⁴⁹אַךְ אֶת־מַטֵּה לֵוִי לֹא
תִפְקֹד וְאֶת־רֹאשָׁם לֹא תִשָּׂא בְּתוֹךְ בְּנֵי יִשְׂרָאֵל:
⁵⁰וְאַתָּה הַפְקֵד אֶת־הַלְוִיִּם עַל־מִשְׁכַּן הָעֵדֻת וְעַל
כָּל־כֵּלָיו וְעַל כָּל־אֲשֶׁר־לוֹ הֵמָּה יִשְׂאוּ אֶת־הַמִּשְׁכָּן
וְאֶת־כָּל־כֵּלָיו וְהֵם יְשָׁרְתֻהוּ וְסָבִיב לַמִּשְׁכָּן יַחֲנוּ:
⁵¹וּבִנְסֹעַ הַמִּשְׁכָּן יוֹרִידוּ אֹתוֹ הַלְוִיִּם וּבַחֲנֹת
הַמִּשְׁכָּן יָקִימוּ אֹתוֹ הַלְוִיִּם וְהַזָּר הַקָּרֵב יוּמָת:
⁵²וְחָנוּ בְּנֵי יִשְׂרָאֵל אִישׁ עַל־מַחֲנֵהוּ וְאִישׁ עַל־דִּגְלוֹ
לְצִבְאֹתָם: ⁵³וְהַלְוִיִּם יַחֲנוּ סָבִיב לְמִשְׁכַּן הָעֵדֻת
וְלֹא־יִהְיֶה קֶצֶף עַל־עֲדַת בְּנֵי יִשְׂרָאֵל וְשָׁמְרוּ
הַלְוִיִּם אֶת־מִשְׁמֶרֶת מִשְׁכַּן הָעֵדוּת: ⁵⁴וַיַּעֲשׂוּ בְּנֵי
יִשְׂרָאֵל כְּכֹל אֲשֶׁר צִוָּה יְהוָה אֶת־מֹשֶׁה כֵּן
עָשׂוּ: פ

1:52. **flag**. Hebrew *degel* refers to some visible sign of the group to which each Israelite belongs: a standard, banner, or flag of some sort.

1:53. **a rage**. The Levites are to form a protective barrier to prevent anyone from violating the Tabernacle, its equipment, and its functions. When such a violation occurs in the Korah rebellion and its aftermath, such a rage occurs, producing a plague that Aaron prevents from spreading (Num 17:11); and then the Levites are again commanded to perform this protective function (18:2–5).

2 ¹And YHWH spoke to Moses and to Aaron, saying, ²"The children of Israel shall camp, each by his flag with the signs of their fathers' house; they shall camp opposite, all around the Tent of Meeting. ³And the ones camping on the east: to the east is the flag of Judah's camp by their armies. And the chieftain of the children of Judah is Nahshon son of Amminadab, ⁴and his army and its counts are seventy-four thousand six hundred. ⁵And the ones camping next to it are: the tribe of Issachar. And the chieftain of the children of Issachar is Nethanel son of Zuar, ⁶and his army and its counts are fifty-four thousand four hundred. ⁷The tribe of Zebulun. And the chieftain of the children of Zebulun is Eliab son of Helon, ⁸and his army and its counts are fifty-seven thousand four hundred. ⁹All the counts of Judah's camp are one hundred eighty-six thousand four hundred by their army units. They shall travel first.

¹⁰"The flag of Reuben's camp on the south by their armies. And the chieftain of the children of Reuben is Elizur son of Shedeur, ¹¹and his army and its counts are forty-six thousand five hundred. ¹²And the ones camping next to it are: the tribe of Simeon. And the chieftain of the children of Simeon is Shelumiel son of Zurishadday, ¹³and his army and their counts are fifty-nine thousand three hundred. ¹⁴And the tribe of Gad. And the chieftain of the children of Gad is Eliasaph son of Reuel, ¹⁵and his army and their counts are forty-five thousand six hundred fifty. ¹⁶All the counts of Reuben's camp are one hundred fifty-one thousand four hundred fifty by their army units. And they shall travel second.

¹⁷"And the Tent of Meeting, the Levites' camp, shall travel inside the camps. As they camp, so they shall travel: each at his position by their flags.

¹⁸"The flag of Ephraim's camp by their armies on the west. And the chieftain of the children of Ephraim is Elishama son of Ammihud, ¹⁹and his army and their counts are forty thousand five hundred. ²⁰And next to it: the camp of Manas-

2 ¹וַיְדַבֵּ֣ר יְהוָ֔ה אֶל־מֹשֶׁ֥ה וְאֶֽל־אַהֲרֹ֖ן לֵאמֹֽר׃ ²אִ֣ישׁ עַל־דִּגְל֣וֹ בְאֹתֹ֗ת לְבֵ֤ית אֲבֹתָם֙ יַחֲנ֣וּ בְּנֵ֣י יִשְׂרָאֵ֑ל מִנֶּ֕גֶד סָבִ֥יב לְאֹֽהֶל־מוֹעֵ֖ד יַחֲנֽוּ׃ ³וְהַחֹנִים֙ קֵ֣דְמָה מִזְרָ֔חָה דֶּ֛גֶל מַחֲנֵ֥ה יְהוּדָ֖ה לְצִבְאֹתָ֑ם וְנָשִׂיא֙ לִבְנֵ֣י יְהוּדָ֔ה נַחְשׁ֖וֹן בֶּן־עַמִּינָדָֽב׃ ⁴וּצְבָא֖וֹ וּפְקֻדֵיהֶ֑ם אַרְבָּעָ֧ה וְשִׁבְעִ֛ים אֶ֖לֶף וְשֵׁ֥שׁ מֵאֽוֹת׃ ⁵וְהַחֹנִ֥ים עָלָ֖יו מַטֵּ֣ה יִשָּׂשכָ֑ר וְנָשִׂיא֙ לִבְנֵ֣י יִשָּׂשכָ֔ר נְתַנְאֵ֖ל בֶּן־צוּעָֽר׃ ⁶וּצְבָא֖וֹ וּפְקֻדָ֑יו אַרְבָּעָ֧ה וַחֲמִשִּׁ֛ים אֶ֖לֶף וְאַרְבַּ֥ע מֵאֽוֹת׃ ⁷מַטֵּ֖ה זְבוּלֻ֑ן וְנָשִׂיא֙ לִבְנֵ֣י זְבוּלֻ֔ן אֱלִיאָ֖ב בֶּן־חֵלֹֽן׃ ⁸וּצְבָא֖וֹ וּפְקֻדָ֑יו שִׁבְעָ֧ה וַחֲמִשִּׁ֛ים אֶ֖לֶף וְאַרְבַּ֥ע מֵאֽוֹת׃ ⁹כָּֽל־הַפְּקֻדִ֞ים לְמַחֲנֵ֣ה יְהוּדָ֗ה מְאַ֣ת אֶ֡לֶף וּשְׁמֹנִ֣ים אֶ֩לֶף֩ וְשֵֽׁשֶׁת־אֲלָפִ֨ים וְאַרְבַּע־מֵא֛וֹת לְצִבְאֹתָ֖ם רִאשֹׁנָ֥ה יִסָּֽעוּ׃ ¹⁰דֶּ֣גֶל מַחֲנֵ֧ה רְאוּבֵ֛ן תֵּימָ֖נָה לְצִבְאֹתָ֑ם וְנָשִׂיא֙ לִבְנֵ֣י רְאוּבֵ֔ן אֱלִיצ֖וּר בֶּן־שְׁדֵיאֽוּר׃ ¹¹וּצְבָא֖וֹ וּפְקֻדָ֑יו שִׁשָּׁ֧ה וְאַרְבָּעִ֛ים אֶ֖לֶף וַחֲמֵ֥שׁ מֵאֽוֹת׃ ¹²וְהַחוֹנִ֥ם עָלָ֖יו מַטֵּ֣ה שִׁמְע֑וֹן וְנָשִׂיא֙ לִבְנֵ֣י שִׁמְע֔וֹן שְׁלֻמִיאֵ֖ל בֶּן־צוּרִֽי־שַׁדָּֽי׃ ¹³וּצְבָא֖וֹ וּפְקֻדֵיהֶ֑ם תִּשְׁעָ֧ה וַחֲמִשִּׁ֛ים אֶ֖לֶף וּשְׁלֹ֥שׁ מֵאֽוֹת׃ ¹⁴וְמַטֵּ֖ה גָּ֑ד וְנָשִׂיא֙ לִבְנֵ֣י גָ֔ד אֶלְיָסָ֖ף בֶּן־רְעוּאֵֽל׃ ¹⁵וּצְבָא֖וֹ וּפְקֻדֵיהֶ֑ם חֲמִשָּׁ֧ה וְאַרְבָּעִ֛ים אֶ֖לֶף וְשֵׁ֥שׁ מֵא֖וֹת וַחֲמִשִּֽׁים׃ ¹⁶כָּֽל־הַפְּקֻדִ֞ים לְמַחֲנֵ֣ה רְאוּבֵ֗ן מְאַ֨ת אֶ֜לֶף וְאֶחָ֤ד וַחֲמִשִּׁים֙ אֶ֔לֶף וְאַרְבַּע־מֵא֖וֹת וַחֲמִשִּׁ֑ים לְצִבְאֹתָ֖ם וּשְׁנִיִּ֥ם יִסָּֽעוּ׃ ¹⁷וְנָסַ֧ע אֹֽהֶל־מוֹעֵ֛ד מַחֲנֵ֥ה הַלְוִיִּ֖ם בְּת֣וֹךְ הַֽמַּחֲנֹ֑ת כַּאֲשֶׁ֤ר יַחֲנוּ֙ כֵּ֣ן יִסָּ֔עוּ אִ֥ישׁ עַל־יָד֖וֹ לְדִגְלֵיהֶֽם׃ ¹⁸דֶּ֣גֶל מַחֲנֵ֥ה אֶפְרַ֛יִם לְצִבְאֹתָ֖ם יָ֑מָּה וְנָשִׂיא֙ לִבְנֵ֣י אֶפְרַ֔יִם אֱלִישָׁמָ֖ע בֶּן־עַמִּיהֽוּד׃ ¹⁹וּצְבָא֖וֹ וּפְקֻדֵיהֶ֑ם אַרְבָּעִ֥ים אֶ֖לֶף וַחֲמֵ֥שׁ מֵאֽוֹת׃ ²⁰וְעָלָ֖יו מַטֵּ֣ה מְנַשֶּׁ֑ה וְנָשִׂיא֙

seh. And the chieftain of the children of Manasseh is Gamaliel son of Pedahzur, 21and his army and their counts are thirty-two thousand two hundred. 22And the tribe of Benjamin. And the chieftain of the children of Benjamin is Abidan son of Gideoni, 23and his army and their counts are thirty-five thousand four hundred. 24All the counts of Ephraim's camp are one hundred eight thousand one hundred by their army units. And they shall travel third.

25"The flag of Dan's camp on the north by their armies. And the chieftain of the children of Dan is Ahiezer son of Ammishadday, 26and his army and their counts are sixty-two thousand seven hundred. 27And the ones camping next to it are: the tribe of Asher. And the chieftain of the children of Asher is Pagiel son of Ochran, 28and his army and their counts are forty-one thousand five hundred. 29And the tribe of Naphtali. And the chieftain of the children of Naphtali is Ahira son of Enan, 30and his army and their counts are fifty-three thousand four hundred. 31All the counts of Dan's camp are one hundred fifty-seven thousand six hundred. They shall travel last, by their flags."

32These are the counts of the children of Isra-

21וּצְבָא֑וֹ לִבְנֵ֣י מְנַשֶּׁ֔ה גַּמְלִיאֵ֖ל בֶּן־פְּדָהצֽוּר׃ 21וּפְקֻדֵיהֶ֕ם שְׁנַ֧יִם וּשְׁלֹשִׁ֛ים אֶ֖לֶף וּמָאתָֽיִם׃ 22וּמַטֵּ֖ה בִנְיָמִ֑ן וְנָשִׂיא֙ לִבְנֵ֣י בִנְיָמִ֔ן אֲבִידָ֖ן בֶּן־גִּדְעֹנִֽי׃ 23וּצְבָא֖וֹ וּפְקֻדֵיהֶ֑ם חֲמִשָּׁ֧ה וּשְׁלֹשִׁ֛ים אֶ֖לֶף וְאַרְבַּ֥ע מֵאֽוֹת׃ 24כׇּל־הַפְּקֻדִ֞ים לְמַחֲנֵ֣ה אֶפְרַ֗יִם מְאַ֥ת אֶ֛לֶף וּשְׁמֹנַֽת־אֲלָפִ֥ים וּמֵאָ֖ה לְצִבְאֹתָ֑ם וּשְׁלִשִׁ֖ים יִסָּֽעוּ׃ ס 25דֶּ֣גֶל מַחֲנֵ֥ה דָ֛ן צָפֹ֖נָה לְצִבְאֹתָ֑ם וְנָשִׂיא֙ לִבְנֵ֣י דָ֔ן אֲחִיעֶ֖זֶר בֶּן־עַמִּֽישַׁדָּֽי׃ 26וּצְבָא֖וֹ וּפְקֻדֵיהֶ֑ם שְׁנַ֧יִם וְשִׁשִּׁ֛ים אֶ֖לֶף וּשְׁבַ֥ע מֵאֽוֹת׃ 27וְהַחֹנִ֥ים עָלָ֖יו מַטֵּ֣ה אָשֵׁ֑ר וְנָשִׂיא֙ לִבְנֵ֣י אָשֵׁ֔ר פַּגְעִיאֵ֖ל בֶּן־עׇכְרָֽן׃ 28וּצְבָא֖וֹ וּפְקֻדֵיהֶ֑ם אֶחָ֧ד וְאַרְבָּעִ֛ים אֶ֖לֶף וַחֲמֵ֥שׁ מֵאֽוֹת׃ 29וּמַטֵּ֖ה נַפְתָּלִ֑י וְנָשִׂיא֙ לִבְנֵ֣י נַפְתָּלִ֔י אֲחִירַ֖ע בֶּן־עֵינָֽן׃ 30וּצְבָא֖וֹ וּפְקֻדֵיהֶ֑ם שְׁלֹשָׁ֧ה וַחֲמִשִּׁ֛ים אֶ֖לֶף וְאַרְבַּ֥ע מֵאֽוֹת׃ 31כׇּל־הַפְּקֻדִים֙ לְמַחֲנֵ֣ה דָ֔ן מְאַ֣ת אֶ֗לֶף וְשִׁבְעָ֧ה וַחֲמִשִּׁ֛ים אֶ֖לֶף וְשֵׁ֣שׁ מֵא֑וֹת לָאַחֲרֹנָ֥ה יִסְע֖וּ לְדִגְלֵיהֶֽם׃ פ 32אֵ֜לֶּה פְּקוּדֵ֥י בְנֵֽי־יִשְׂרָאֵ֖ל

2:32. six hundred three thousand five hundred fifty. Add to this the underage and elderly men, the women of all ages, and the Levites, and the total number of Israelites must approach two million. It has been calculated that by these numbers, marching eight across, when the first Israelites reach Mount Sinai, half of them would still be in Egypt! The extraordinary size of this population is a famous old problem in traditional and critical biblical scholarship. The numbers appear far too high; but they do not appear to be entirely invented either, because what would be the motive for contriving them in all of this tribe-by-tribe detail for the first four chapters of Numbers? Some suggest that the word for "thousand" here means rather a "clan," but that is not correct (see the comment on Num 3:43). One possibility is that these are the numbers from the census that is attributed to King David (2 Samuel 24; see the comment on Exod 30:12). (There are just three censuses in the *Tanak*, the two censuses of Moses and the census of David.) Coming centuries later, in a period in which Israel is settled in the land, the numbers are more understandable in the Davidic era (though they are questionably high even for that period). In this scenario, the records here would have come from old documents among the archives which would have come to be mixed in with documents that were used as sources for the Torah.

el by their fathers' house, all the counts of the camps by their armies: six hundred three thousand five hundred fifty. 33And the Levites were not counted among the children of Israel, as YHWH had commanded Moses. 34And the children of Israel did according to all that YHWH commanded Moses. So they camped by their flags, and so they traveled, each by his families, by his fathers' house.

3 1These are the records of Aaron and Moses in the day YHWH spoke to Moses in Mount Sinai. 2And these are the names of Aaron's sons: the firstborn Nadab, and Abihu and Eleazar and Ithamar. 3These are the names of Aaron's sons, the anointed priests, who filled their hand to function as priests. 4And Nadab and Abihu died in front of YHWH when they brought forward unfitting fire in front of YHWH in the wilderness of Sinai, and they had no sons; and Eleazar and Ithamar functioned as priests in front of Aaron, their father.

5And YHWH spoke to Moses, saying, 6"Bring forward the tribe of Levi and stand it in front of Aaron, the priest, so they will attend to him. 7And they shall keep his charge and the charge of all the congregation in front of the Tent of Meeting, to do the work of the Tabernacle. 8And they shall keep all the equipment of the Tent of Meeting and the charge of the children of Israel, to do the work of the Tabernacle. 9And you shall give the Levites to Aaron and to his sons. They are given—*given*—to him from the children of Israel. 10And you shall appoint Aaron and his sons, that they shall keep their priesthood, and an outsider who comes close shall be put to death."

11And YHWH spoke to Moses, saying, 12"And I, here, I have taken the Levites from among the children of Israel in place of every firstborn, the first birth of the womb, from the children of Israel. And the Levites shall be mine. 13Because every firstborn is mine. In the day that I struck

לְבֵית אֲבֹתָם כָּל־פְּקוּדֵי הַמַּחֲנֹת לְצִבְאֹתָם שֵׁשׁ־
מֵאוֹת אֶלֶף וּשְׁלֹשֶׁת אֲלָפִים וַחֲמֵשׁ מֵאוֹת וַחֲמִשִּׁים׃
33וְהַלְוִיִּם לֹא הָתְפָּקְדוּ בְּתוֹךְ בְּנֵי יִשְׂרָאֵל כַּאֲשֶׁר
צִוָּה יְהוָה אֶת־מֹשֶׁה׃ 34וַיַּעֲשׂוּ בְּנֵי יִשְׂרָאֵל כְּכֹל
אֲשֶׁר־צִוָּה יְהוָה אֶת־מֹשֶׁה כֵּן־חָנוּ לְדִגְלֵיהֶם וְכֵן
נָסָעוּ אִישׁ לְמִשְׁפְּחֹתָיו עַל־בֵּית אֲבֹתָיו׃

3 1וְאֵלֶּה תּוֹלְדֹת אַהֲרֹן וּמֹשֶׁה בְּיוֹם דִּבֶּר יְהוָה
אֶת־מֹשֶׁה בְּהַר סִינָי׃ 2וְאֵלֶּה שְׁמוֹת בְּנֵי־אַהֲרֹן
הַבְּכוֹר ׀ נָדָב וַאֲבִיהוּא אֶלְעָזָר וְאִיתָמָר׃ 3אֵלֶּה
שְׁמוֹת בְּנֵי אַהֲרֹן הַכֹּהֲנִים הַמְּשֻׁחִים אֲשֶׁר־מִלֵּא יָדָם
לְכַהֵן׃ 4וַיָּמָת נָדָב וַאֲבִיהוּא לִפְנֵי יְהוָה בְּהַקְרִבָם
אֵשׁ זָרָה לִפְנֵי יְהוָה בְּמִדְבַּר סִינַי וּבָנִים לֹא־הָיוּ
לָהֶם וַיְכַהֵן אֶלְעָזָר וְאִיתָמָר עַל־פְּנֵי אַהֲרֹן
אֲבִיהֶם׃ פ 5וַיְדַבֵּר יְהוָה אֶל־מֹשֶׁה לֵּאמֹר׃
6הַקְרֵב אֶת־מַטֵּה לֵוִי וְהַעֲמַדְתָּ אֹתוֹ לִפְנֵי אַהֲרֹן
הַכֹּהֵן וְשֵׁרְתוּ אֹתוֹ׃ 7וְשָׁמְרוּ אֶת־מִשְׁמַרְתּוֹ וְאֶת־
מִשְׁמֶרֶת כָּל־הָעֵדָה לִפְנֵי אֹהֶל מוֹעֵד לַעֲבֹד אֶת־
עֲבֹדַת הַמִּשְׁכָּן׃ 8וְשָׁמְרוּ אֶת־כָּל־כְּלֵי אֹהֶל מוֹעֵד
וְאֶת־מִשְׁמֶרֶת בְּנֵי יִשְׂרָאֵל לַעֲבֹד אֶת־עֲבֹדַת
הַמִּשְׁכָּן׃ 9וְנָתַתָּה אֶת־הַלְוִיִּם לְאַהֲרֹן וּלְבָנָיו נְתוּנִם
נְתוּנִם הֵמָּה לוֹ מֵאֵת בְּנֵי יִשְׂרָאֵל׃ 10וְאֶת־אַהֲרֹן
וְאֶת־בָּנָיו תִּפְקֹד וְשָׁמְרוּ אֶת־כְּהֻנָּתָם וְהַזָּר הַקָּרֵב
יוּמָת׃ פ 11וַיְדַבֵּר יְהוָה אֶל־מֹשֶׁה לֵּאמֹר׃ 12וַאֲנִי
הִנֵּה לָקַחְתִּי אֶת־הַלְוִיִּם מִתּוֹךְ בְּנֵי יִשְׂרָאֵל תַּחַת
כָּל־בְּכוֹר פֶּטֶר רֶחֶם מִבְּנֵי יִשְׂרָאֵל וְהָיוּ לִי
הַלְוִיִּם׃ 13כִּי לִי כָּל־בְּכוֹר בְּיוֹם הַכֹּתִי כָל־בְּכוֹר

3:3. **filled their hand to function as priests**. See comment on Exod 29:29.

every firstborn in the land of Egypt, I consecrated every firstborn in Israel to me, from human to animal. They shall be mine. I am YHWH."

14And YHWH spoke to Moses in the wilderness of Sinai, saying, 15"Count the children of Levi by their fathers' house, by their families. You shall count them: every male from a month old and up." 16And Moses counted them by YHWH's word as he was commanded. 17And these were Levi's sons by their names: Gershon and Kohath and Merari. 18And these are the names of Gershon's sons by their families: Libni and Shimei. 19And Kohath's sons by their families: Amram and Izhar, Hebron and Uzziel. 20And Merari's sons by their families: Mahli and Mushi. These are the Levite families by their fathers' house.

21Gershon had the Libnite family and the Shimeite family. These are the Gershonite families. 22Their counts by the number of every male from a month old and up: their counts were seven thousand five hundred. 23The Gershonite families were to camp behind the Tabernacle, to the west. 24And the chieftain of the Gershonite father's house was Eliasaph son of Lael. 25And the charge of the sons of Gershon in the Tent of Meeting was the Tabernacle and the tent, its covering and the cover of the entrance of the Tent of Meeting 26and the courtyard's hangings and the cover for the entrance of the courtyard that is all around the Tabernacle and the altar, and its cords, for all of its service.

27And Kohath had the Amramite family and the Izharite family and the Hebronite family and the Uzzielite family. These are the Kohathite families. 28By the number of every male from a month old and up: eight thousand six hundred keeping the charge of the Holy. 29The families of the children of Kohath were to camp to the south. 30And the chieftain of the father's house for the Kohathite families was Elizaphan son of Uzziel. 31And their charge was the ark and the

בְּאֶ֣רֶץ מִצְרַ֔יִם הִקְדַּ֣שְׁתִּי לִ֤י כָל־בְּכוֹר֙ בְּיִשְׂרָאֵ֔ל
מֵאָדָ֖ם עַד־בְּהֵמָ֑ה לִ֥י יִהְי֖וּ אֲנִ֥י יְהוָֽה׃ ס 14וַיְדַבֵּ֧ר
יְהוָ֛ה אֶל־מֹשֶׁ֖ה בְּמִדְבַּ֣ר סִינַ֣י לֵאמֹֽר׃ 15פְּקֹד֙ אֶת־
בְּנֵ֣י לֵוִ֗י לְבֵ֥ית אֲבֹתָ֖ם לְמִשְׁפְּחֹתָ֑ם כָּל־זָכָ֗ר מִבֶּן־
חֹ֛דֶשׁ וָמַ֖עְלָה תִּפְקְדֵֽם׃ 16וַיִּפְקֹ֨ד אֹתָ֤ם מֹשֶׁה֙ עַל־פִּ֣י
יְהוָ֔ה כַּאֲשֶׁ֖ר צֻוָּֽה׃ 17וַיִּֽהְיוּ־אֵ֥לֶּה בְנֵֽי־לֵוִ֖י בִּשְׁמֹתָ֑ם
גֵּרְשׁ֕וֹן וּקְהָ֖ת וּמְרָרִֽי׃ 18וְאֵ֛לֶּה שְׁמ֥וֹת בְּנֵֽי־גֵרְשׁ֖וֹן
לְמִשְׁפְּחֹתָ֑ם לִבְנִ֖י וְשִׁמְעִֽי׃ 19וּבְנֵ֥י קְהָ֖ת לְמִשְׁפְּחֹתָ֑ם
עַמְרָ֣ם וְיִצְהָ֔ר חֶבְר֖וֹן וְעֻזִּיאֵֽל׃ 20וּבְנֵ֧י מְרָרִ֛י
לְמִשְׁפְּחֹתָ֖ם מַחְלִ֣י וּמוּשִׁ֑י אֵ֣לֶּה הֵ֤ם מִשְׁפְּחֹ֣ת הַלֵּוִ֔י
לְבֵ֖ית אֲבֹתָֽם׃ 21לְגֵ֣רְשׁ֔וֹן מִשְׁפַּ֙חַת֙ הַלִּבְנִ֔י וּמִשְׁפַּ֖חַת
הַשִּׁמְעִ֑י אֵ֣לֶּה הֵ֔ם מִשְׁפְּחֹ֖ת הַגֵּרְשֻׁנִּֽי׃ 22פְּקֻדֵיהֶם֙
בְּמִסְפַּ֣ר כָּל־זָכָ֔ר מִבֶּן־חֹ֖דֶשׁ וָמָ֑עְלָה פְּקֻ֣דֵיהֶ֔ם
שִׁבְעַ֥ת אֲלָפִ֖ים וַחֲמֵ֥שׁ מֵאֽוֹת׃ 23מִשְׁפְּחֹ֖ת הַגֵּרְשֻׁנִּ֑י
אַחֲרֵ֧י הַמִּשְׁכָּ֛ן יַחֲנ֖וּ יָֽמָּה׃ 24וּנְשִׂ֥יא בֵֽית־אָ֖ב לַגֵּרְשֻׁנִּ֑י
אֶלְיָסָ֖ף בֶּן־לָאֵֽל׃ 25וּמִשְׁמֶ֤רֶת בְּנֵֽי־גֵרְשׁוֹן֙ בְּאֹ֣הֶל
מוֹעֵ֔ד הַמִּשְׁכָּ֖ן וְהָאֹ֑הֶל מִכְסֵ֕הוּ וּמָסַ֕ךְ פֶּ֖תַח אֹ֥הֶל
מוֹעֵֽד׃ 26וְקַלְעֵ֣י הֶֽחָצֵ֗ר וְאֶת־מָסַךְ֙ פֶּ֣תַח הֶֽחָצֵ֔ר
אֲשֶׁ֧ר עַל־הַמִּשְׁכָּ֛ן וְעַל־הַמִּזְבֵּ֖חַ סָבִ֑יב וְאֵת֙ מֵֽיתָרָ֔יו
לְכֹ֖ל עֲבֹדָתֽוֹ׃ 27וְלִקְהָ֗ת מִשְׁפַּ֤חַת הַֽעַמְרָמִי֙
וּמִשְׁפַּ֣חַת הַיִּצְהָרִ֔י וּמִשְׁפַּ֙חַת֙ הַֽחֶבְרֹנִ֔י וּמִשְׁפַּ֖חַת
הָֽעָזִּיאֵלִ֑י אֵ֣לֶּה הֵ֔ם מִשְׁפְּחֹ֖ת הַקְּהָתִֽי׃ 28בְּמִסְפַּר֙
כָּל־זָכָ֔ר מִבֶּן־חֹ֖דֶשׁ וָמָ֑עְלָה שְׁמֹנַ֤ת אֲלָפִים֙ וְשֵׁ֣שׁ
מֵא֔וֹת שֹׁמְרֵ֖י מִשְׁמֶ֥רֶת הַקֹּֽדֶשׁ׃ 29מִשְׁפְּחֹ֥ת בְּנֵֽי־קְהָ֖ת
יַחֲנ֑וּ עַ֛ל יֶ֥רֶךְ הַמִּשְׁכָּ֖ן תֵּימָֽנָה׃ 30וּנְשִׂ֥יא בֵֽית־אָ֖ב
לְמִשְׁפְּחֹ֣ת הַקְּהָתִ֑י אֱלִיצָפָ֖ן בֶּן־עֻזִּיאֵֽל׃ 31וּמִשְׁמַרְתָּ֞ם

3:31; 4:9. **menorah.** The lampstand has been compared in appearance—and as a symbol—to a tree, and especially to the tree of life. It is therefore notable that it is

table and the menorah and the altars and the equipment of the Holy with which they minister and the cover and all of its service.

³²And the chieftain of chieftains of the Levites was Eleazar son of Aaron, the priest, with responsibility for those who keep the charge of the Holy.

³³And Merari had the Mahlite family and the Mushite family. These are the Merarite families. ³⁴And their counts by the number of every male from a month old and up: six thousand two hundred. ³⁵And the chieftain of the father's house for the Merarite families was Zuriel son of Abihail. They were to camp on the side of the Tabernacle to the north. ³⁶And the responsibility of the charge of the children of Merari was the Tabernacle's frames and its bars and its columns and its bases and all of its equipment and all of its service ³⁷and the courtyard's columns all around and their bases and their pegs and their cords.

³⁸And those who camped in front of the Tabernacle, on the east, in front of the Tent of Meeting, to the east, were Moses and Aaron and his sons, keeping the charge of the holy place, for the charge of the children of Israel. And the outsider who will come close shall be put to death.

³⁹All the counts of the Levites that Moses and Aaron made by YHWH's word, by their families, every male from a month old and up were twenty-two thousand.

⁴⁰And YHWH said to Moses, "Count every male firstborn of the children of Israel from a month old and up, and add up the number of their names. ⁴¹And you shall take the Levites for me—I am YHWH—in place of every firstborn in the children of Israel, and the Levites' animals in place of every firstborn in the animals of the

הָאָרֹן וְהַשֻּׁלְחָן וְהַמְּנֹרָה וְהַמִּזְבְּחֹת וּכְלֵי הַקֹּדֶשׁ אֲשֶׁר יְשָׁרְתוּ בָּהֶם וְהַמָּסָךְ וְכֹל עֲבֹדָתוֹ: ³²וּנְשִׂיא נְשִׂיאֵי הַלֵּוִי אֶלְעָזָר בֶּן־אַהֲרֹן הַכֹּהֵן פְּקֻדַּת שֹׁמְרֵי מִשְׁמֶרֶת הַקֹּדֶשׁ: ³³לִמְרָרִי מִשְׁפַּחַת הַמַּחְלִי וּמִשְׁפַּחַת הַמּוּשִׁי אֵלֶּה הֵם מִשְׁפְּחֹת מְרָרִי: ³⁴וּפְקֻדֵיהֶם בְּמִסְפַּר כָּל־זָכָר מִבֶּן־חֹדֶשׁ וָמָעְלָה שֵׁשֶׁת אֲלָפִים וּמָאתָיִם: ³⁵וּנְשִׂיא בֵית־אָב לְמִשְׁפְּחֹת מְרָרִי צוּרִיאֵל בֶּן־אֲבִיחָיִל עַל יֶרֶךְ הַמִּשְׁכָּן יַחֲנוּ צָפֹנָה: ³⁶וּפְקֻדַּת מִשְׁמֶרֶת בְּנֵי מְרָרִי קַרְשֵׁי הַמִּשְׁכָּן וּבְרִיחָיו וְעַמֻּדָיו וַאֲדָנָיו וְכָל־כֵּלָיו וְכֹל עֲבֹדָתוֹ: ³⁷וְעַמֻּדֵי הֶחָצֵר סָבִיב וְאַדְנֵיהֶם וִיתֵדֹתָם וּמֵיתְרֵיהֶם: ³⁸וְהַחֹנִים לִפְנֵי הַמִּשְׁכָּן קֵדְמָה לִפְנֵי אֹהֶל־מוֹעֵד ׀ מִזְרָחָה מֹשֶׁה ׀ וְאַהֲרֹן וּבָנָיו שֹׁמְרִים מִשְׁמֶרֶת הַמִּקְדָּשׁ לְמִשְׁמֶרֶת בְּנֵי יִשְׂרָאֵל וְהַזָּר הַקָּרֵב יוּמָת: ³⁹כָּל־פְּקוּדֵי הַלְוִיִּם אֲשֶׁר פָּקַד מֹשֶׁה וְאַהֲרֹן עַל־פִּי יְהוָה לְמִשְׁפְּחֹתָם כָּל־זָכָר מִבֶּן־חֹדֶשׁ וָמָעְלָה שְׁנַיִם וְעֶשְׂרִים אָלֶף: ס ⁴⁰וַיֹּאמֶר יְהוָה אֶל־מֹשֶׁה פְּקֹד כָּל־בְּכֹר זָכָר לִבְנֵי יִשְׂרָאֵל מִבֶּן־חֹדֶשׁ וָמָעְלָה וְשָׂא אֵת מִסְפַּר שְׁמֹתָם: ⁴¹וְלָקַחְתָּ אֶת־הַלְוִיִּם לִי אֲנִי יְהוָה תַּחַת כָּל־בְּכֹר בִּבְנֵי יִשְׂרָאֵל וְאֵת בֶּהֱמַת הַלְוִיִּם תַּחַת כָּל־בְּכוֹר

---

mentioned here as being the responsibility of the Kohathites. And then just a few verses later the Kohathites are identified as the Levite group who must be careful that their closeness to the holy not cause them to die (see the comment on 4:15). The menorah, the sacred object, which became a symbol of Israel (more properly so than the six-pointed star that became a symbol some two thousand years after this text), is also a reminder of the essential human relationship to life and death that begins the Torah.

children of Israel." 42And Moses counted, as YHWH commanded him, every firstborn in the children of Israel. 43And every male firstborn, by the number of names, from a month old and up, by their counts were twenty-two thousand two hundred seventy-three. 44And YHWH spoke to Moses, saying, 45"Take the Levites in place of every firstborn in the children of Israel, and the Levites' animals in place of their animals, and the Levites shall be mine. I am YHWH. 46And for the redemption of the two hundred seventy-three who are left over above the Levites from the firstborn of the children of Israel, 47you shall take five shekels each per head; you shall take it by the shekel of the Holy. (The shekel is twenty gerah.) 48And you shall give the money to Aaron and to his sons for the redemption of those left over among them." 49And Moses took the money of the redemption from those left over above those who were redeemed by the Levites. 50He took the money from the firstborn of the children of Israel: one thousand three hundred sixty-five by the shekel of the Holy. 51And Moses gave the money for those who were redeemed to Aaron and to his sons by YHWH's word, as YHWH commanded Moses.

בְּבֶהֱמַת בְּנֵי יִשְׂרָאֵל: 42וַיִּפְקֹד מֹשֶׁה כַּאֲשֶׁר צִוָּה יְהוָה אֹתוֹ אֶת־כָּל־בְּכֹר בִּבְנֵי יִשְׂרָאֵל: 43וַיְהִי כָל־בְּכוֹר זָכָר בְּמִסְפַּר שֵׁמוֹת מִבֶּן־חֹדֶשׁ וָמַעְלָה לִפְקֻדֵיהֶם שְׁנַיִם וְעֶשְׂרִים אֶלֶף שְׁלֹשָׁה וְשִׁבְעִים וּמָאתָיִם: פ 44וַיְדַבֵּר יְהוָה אֶל־מֹשֶׁה לֵּאמֹר: 45קַח אֶת־הַלְוִיִּם תַּחַת כָּל־בְּכוֹר בִּבְנֵי יִשְׂרָאֵל וְאֶת־בֶּהֱמַת הַלְוִיִּם תַּחַת בְּהֶמְתָּם וְהָיוּ־לִי הַלְוִיִּם אֲנִי יְהוָה: 46וְאֵת פְּדוּיֵי הַשְּׁלֹשָׁה וְהַשִּׁבְעִים וְהַמָּאתָיִם הָעֹדְפִים עַל־הַלְוִיִּם מִבְּכוֹר בְּנֵי יִשְׂרָאֵל: 47וְלָקַחְתָּ חֲמֵשֶׁת חֲמֵשֶׁת שְׁקָלִים לַגֻּלְגֹּלֶת בְּשֶׁקֶל הַקֹּדֶשׁ תִּקָּח עֶשְׂרִים גֵּרָה הַשָּׁקֶל: 48וְנָתַתָּה הַכֶּסֶף לְאַהֲרֹן וּלְבָנָיו פְּדוּיֵי הָעֹדְפִים בָּהֶם: 49וַיִּקַּח מֹשֶׁה אֵת כֶּסֶף הַפִּדְיוֹם מֵאֵת הָעֹדְפִים עַל פְּדוּיֵי הַלְוִיִּם: 50מֵאֵת בְּכוֹר בְּנֵי יִשְׂרָאֵל לָקַח אֶת־הַכָּסֶף חֲמִשָּׁה וְשִׁשִּׁים וּשְׁלֹשׁ מֵאוֹת וָאֶלֶף בְּשֶׁקֶל הַקֹּדֶשׁ: 51וַיִּתֵּן מֹשֶׁה אֶת־כֶּסֶף הַפְּדֻיִם לְאַהֲרֹן וּלְבָנָיו עַל־פִּי יְהוָה כַּאֲשֶׁר צִוָּה יְהוָה אֶת־מֹשֶׁה: פ

3:43. **twenty-two thousand.** The number of firstborn Israelite males is given here as 22,273. This indicates that those who take the word for "thousand" (Hebrew *'elep*) to mean "clan" are mistaken, since firstborn sons as a group do not constitute clans. Those who try to understand this term as "clan" do this because they are troubled by the high numbers of Israelites in the census in Numbers. But we cannot escape the problem by redefining a term. Whatever we believe to have been the historical case, the fact is that the text depicts a vast population in the wilderness. And my concern is not to debate the numbers but rather to recognize the significance of the numbers to the Torah and to its story. Historically, only a portion of the Israelites may have had the experience of slavery in Egypt, but all of Israel came to see the experience as their own. For the Torah, it is important that the entire people of Israel be seen as present at Mount Sinai.

The complication of this number of 22,273 firstborn males of all ages is that it is utterly out of proportion to the number of over 600,000 adult males. I have seen no satisfactory solution to this problem.

4 ¹And YHWH spoke to Moses and to Aaron, saying, ²"Add up the heads of the children of Kohath from among the children of Levi by their families, by their fathers' house, ³from thirty years old and up to fifty years old, everyone who would come to the army to do work in the Tent of Meeting. ⁴This is the work of the sons of Kohath in the Tent of Meeting: the Holy of Holies.

⁵"And Aaron and his sons shall come when the camp is to travel, and they shall take down the covering pavilion and cover the ark of the testimony with it. ⁶And they shall put a cover of leather and shall spread a fabric all of blue above it and put in its poles. ⁷And on the table of show bread they shall spread a blue fabric, and they shall put on it the dishes and the pans and the bowls and the libation jars; and the continual bread shall be on it. ⁸And they shall spread a scarlet fabric over them and cover it with a leather covering and set its poles. ⁹And they shall take a blue fabric and cover the menorah for lighting and its lamps and its tongs and its fire-holders and all its equipment for oil with which they will minister for it. ¹⁰And they shall put it and all its equipment into a leather covering and put it on a beam. ¹¹And on the gold altar they shall spread a blue fabric, and they shall cover it with a leather covering and set its poles. ¹²And they shall take all the equipment for ministering with which they minister in the Holy and put them into a blue fabric and cover them with a leather covering and put them on a beam. ¹³And they shall clear the ashes from the altar and spread a purple fabric over it. ¹⁴And they shall put on it all its equipment with which they minister at it—the fire-holders, the forks and the shovels and the basins—all the altar's equipment, and they shall spread a leather covering on it and set its poles. ¹⁵And Aaron and his sons will finish covering the Holy and all the equipment of the Holy when the camp is to travel, and after that the children of Kohath shall come to carry,

4 ¹וַיְדַבֵּ֣ר יְהוָ֔ה אֶל־מֹשֶׁ֥ה וְאֶֽל־אַהֲרֹ֖ן לֵאמֹֽר׃ ²נָשֹׂ֗א אֶת־רֹאשׁ֙ בְּנֵ֣י קְהָ֔ת מִתּ֖וֹךְ בְּנֵ֣י לֵוִ֑י לְמִשְׁפְּחֹתָ֖ם לְבֵ֥ית אֲבֹתָֽם׃ ³מִבֶּ֨ן שְׁלֹשִׁ֤ים שָׁנָה֙ וָמַ֔עְלָה וְעַ֖ד בֶּן־חֲמִשִּׁ֣ים שָׁנָ֑ה כָּל־בָּא֙ לַצָּבָ֔א לַעֲשׂ֥וֹת מְלָאכָ֖ה בְּאֹ֥הֶל מוֹעֵֽד׃ ⁴זֹ֛את עֲבֹדַ֥ת בְּנֵֽי־קְהָ֖ת בְּאֹ֣הֶל מוֹעֵ֑ד קֹ֖דֶשׁ הַקֳּדָשִֽׁים׃ ⁵וּבָ֨א אַהֲרֹ֤ן וּבָנָיו֙ בִּנְסֹ֣עַ הַֽמַּחֲנֶ֔ה וְהוֹרִ֕דוּ אֵ֖ת פָּרֹ֣כֶת הַמָּסָ֑ךְ וְכִ֨סּוּ־בָ֔הּ אֵ֖ת אֲרֹ֥ן הָעֵדֻֽת׃ ⁶וְנָתְנ֣וּ עָלָ֗יו כְּסוּי֙ ע֣וֹר תַּ֔חַשׁ וּפָרְשׂ֧וּ בֶֽגֶד־כְּלִ֛יל תְּכֵ֖לֶת מִלְמָ֑עְלָה וְשָׂמ֖וּ בַּדָּֽיו׃ ⁷וְעַ֣ל ׀ שֻׁלְחַ֣ן הַפָּנִ֗ים יִפְרְשׂוּ֙ בֶּ֣גֶד תְּכֵ֔לֶת וְנָתְנ֣וּ עָ֠לָיו אֶת־הַקְּעָרֹ֤ת וְאֶת־הַכַּפֹּת֙ וְאֶת־הַמְּנַקִּיֹּ֔ת וְאֵ֖ת קְשׂ֣וֹת הַנָּ֑סֶךְ וְלֶ֥חֶם הַתָּמִ֖יד עָלָ֥יו יִהְיֶֽה׃ ⁸וּפָרְשׂ֣וּ עֲלֵיהֶ֗ם בֶּ֚גֶד תּוֹלַ֣עַת שָׁנִ֔י וְכִסּ֣וּ אֹת֔וֹ בְּמִכְסֵ֖ה ע֣וֹר תָּ֑חַשׁ וְשָׂמ֖וּ אֶת־בַּדָּֽיו׃ ⁹וְלָקְח֣וּ ׀ בֶּ֣גֶד תְּכֵ֗לֶת וְכִסּ֞וּ אֶת־מְנֹרַ֤ת הַמָּאוֹר֙ וְאֶת־נֵ֣רֹתֶ֔יהָ וְאֶת־מַלְקָחֶ֖יהָ וְאֶת־מַחְתֹּתֶ֑יהָ וְאֵת֙ כָּל־כְּלֵ֣י שַׁמְנָ֔הּ אֲשֶׁ֥ר יְשָׁרְתוּ־לָ֖הּ בָּהֶֽם׃ ¹⁰וְנָתְנ֣וּ אֹתָ֗הּ וְאֶת־כָּל־כֵּלֶ֙יהָ֙ אֶל־מִכְסֵ֖ה ע֣וֹר תָּ֑חַשׁ וְנָתְנ֖וּ עַל־הַמּֽוֹט׃ ¹¹וְעַ֣ל ׀ מִזְבַּ֣ח הַזָּהָ֗ב יִפְרְשׂוּ֙ בֶּ֣גֶד תְּכֵ֔לֶת וְכִסּ֣וּ אֹת֔וֹ בְּמִכְסֵ֖ה ע֣וֹר תָּ֑חַשׁ וְשָׂמ֖וּ אֶת־בַּדָּֽיו׃ ¹²וְלָקְחוּ֩ אֶת־כָּל־כְּלֵ֨י הַשָּׁרֵ֜ת אֲשֶׁ֧ר יְשָֽׁרְתוּ־בָ֣ם בַּקֹּ֗דֶשׁ וְנָֽתְנוּ֙ אֶל־בֶּ֣גֶד תְּכֵ֔לֶת וְכִסּ֣וּ אוֹתָ֔ם בְּמִכְסֵ֖ה ע֣וֹר תָּ֑חַשׁ וְנָתְנ֖וּ עַל־הַמּֽוֹט׃ ¹³וְדִשְּׁנ֖וּ אֶת־הַמִּזְבֵּ֑חַ וּפָרְשׂ֣וּ עָלָ֔יו בֶּ֖גֶד אַרְגָּמָֽן׃ ¹⁴וְנָתְנ֣וּ עָ֠לָיו אֶֽת־כָּל־כֵּלָ֞יו אֲשֶׁ֣ר יְֽשָׁרְת֧וּ עָלָ֣יו בָּהֶ֗ם אֶת־הַמַּחְתֹּ֤ת אֶת־הַמִּזְלָגֹת֙ וְאֶת־הַיָּעִ֣ים וְאֶת־הַמִּזְרָקֹ֔ת כֹּ֖ל כְּלֵ֣י הַמִּזְבֵּ֑חַ וּפָרְשׂ֣וּ עָלָ֗יו כְּס֛וּי ע֥וֹר תַּ֖חַשׁ וְשָׂמ֥וּ בַדָּֽיו׃ ¹⁵וְכִלָּ֣ה אַֽהֲרֹן־וּ֠בָנָיו לְכַסֹּ֨ת אֶת־הַקֹּ֜דֶשׁ וְאֶת־כָּל־כְּלֵ֣י הַקֹּדֶשׁ֮ בִּנְסֹ֣עַ הַֽמַּחֲנֶה֒ וְאַחֲרֵי־כֵ֗ן יָבֹ֤אוּ בְנֵי־קְהָת֙ לָשֵׂ֔את וְלֹֽא־יִגְּע֥וּ אֶל־הַקֹּ֖דֶשׁ

so they shall not touch the holy and die. These are what the children of Kohath are to carry in the Tent of Meeting.

16"And the responsibility of Eleazar son of Aaron, the priest, is the oil for lighting and the incense of fragrances and the continual grain offering and the anointing oil—the responsibility for all of the Tabernacle and everything that is in it, in the Holy and in its equipment."

17And YHWH spoke to Moses and to Aaron, saying, 18"You shall not cut off the tribe of the Kohathite families from among the Levites, 19but do this to them so they will live and not die when they come close to the Holy of Holies: Aaron and his sons shall come, and they shall set them each at his work and to what he is to carry, 20and they shall not come to see as the Holy is covered up and die."

וְמֵתוּ אֵלֶּה מַשָּׂא בְנֵי־קְהָת בְּאֹהֶל מוֹעֵד: 16וּפְקֻדַּת אֶלְעָזָר ׀ בֶּן־אַהֲרֹן הַכֹּהֵן שֶׁמֶן הַמָּאוֹר וּקְטֹרֶת הַסַּמִּים וּמִנְחַת הַתָּמִיד וְשֶׁמֶן הַמִּשְׁחָה פְּקֻדַּת כָּל־הַמִּשְׁכָּן וְכָל־אֲשֶׁר־בּוֹ בְּקֹדֶשׁ וּבְכֵלָיו: ס 17וַיְדַבֵּר יְהֹוָה אֶל־מֹשֶׁה וְאֶל־אַהֲרֹן לֵאמֹר: 18אַל־תַּכְרִיתוּ אֶת־שֵׁבֶט מִשְׁפְּחֹת הַקְּהָתִי מִתּוֹךְ הַלְוִיִּם: 19וְזֹאת ׀ עֲשׂוּ לָהֶם וְחָיוּ וְלֹא יָמֻתוּ בְּגִשְׁתָּם אֶת־קֹדֶשׁ הַקֳּדָשִׁים אַהֲרֹן וּבָנָיו יָבֹאוּ וְשָׂמוּ אוֹתָם אִישׁ אִישׁ עַל־עֲבֹדָתוֹ וְאֶל־מַשָּׂאוֹ: 20וְלֹא־יָבֹאוּ לִרְאוֹת כְּבַלַּע אֶת־הַקֹּדֶשׁ וָמֵתוּ: פ

ADD UP

21And YHWH spoke to Moses, saying, 22"Add up the heads of the children of Gershon, them as well, by their fathers' house, by their families. 23You shall count them from thirty years old and up to fifty years old, everyone who would come to do army service, to do work in the Tent of Meeting. 24This is the work of the Gershonite families, for work and for carrying: 25And they shall carry the curtains of the Tabernacle, and the Tent of Meeting, its covering, and the leather covering that is on it above, and the cover of the entrance of the Tent of Meeting 26and the courtyard's hangings and the cover for the entrance of the gate of the courtyard that is all around the

נשא

21וַיְדַבֵּר יְהֹוָה אֶל־מֹשֶׁה לֵּאמֹר: 22נָשֹׂא אֶת־רֹאשׁ בְּנֵי גֵרְשׁוֹן גַּם־הֵם לְבֵית אֲבֹתָם לְמִשְׁפְּחֹתָם: 23מִבֶּן שְׁלֹשִׁים שָׁנָה וָמַעְלָה עַד בֶּן־חֲמִשִּׁים שָׁנָה תִּפְקֹד אוֹתָם כָּל־הַבָּא לִצְבֹא צָבָא לַעֲבֹד עֲבֹדָה בְּאֹהֶל מוֹעֵד: 24זֹאת עֲבֹדַת מִשְׁפְּחֹת הַגֵּרְשֻׁנִּי לַעֲבֹד וּלְמַשָּׂא: 25וְנָשְׂאוּ אֶת־יְרִיעֹת הַמִּשְׁכָּן וְאֶת־אֹהֶל מוֹעֵד מִכְסֵהוּ וּמִכְסֵה הַתַּחַשׁ אֲשֶׁר־עָלָיו מִלְמָעְלָה וְאֶת־מָסַךְ פֶּתַח אֹהֶל מוֹעֵד: 26וְאֵת קַלְעֵי הֶחָצֵר וְאֶת־מָסַךְ ׀ פֶּתַח ׀ שַׁעַר הֶחָצֵר אֲשֶׁר עַל־הַמִּשְׁכָּן וְעַל־הַמִּזְבֵּחַ

4:15. **so they shall not touch the holy and die.** This is followed by: "they shall not come to see as the Holy is covered up and die" (4:20). Thus, twice more the text reminds us that closeness to the divine is dangerous. The death of Aaron's sons stands in the background of these warnings. (In fact, it is mentioned in the preceding chapter; 3:4.) And these warnings also remind us of the distinction between the ritual and moral realms. Whatever their intentions, whatever their moral condition, if these Kohathites touch what they are not supposed to touch or see what they are not supposed to see, they will die.

Tabernacle and the altar, and their cords and all the equipment for their service. And everything that will be done for them: they shall do the work. 27All the work of the children of the Gershonites shall be by the word of Aaron and his sons, for all their carrying and all their work. And you shall supervise them in the task: all their carrying. 28This is the work of the families of the children of the Gershonites in the Tent of Meeting. And their charge is in the hand of Ithamar son of Aaron, the priest.

29"The children of Merari by their families, by their fathers' house: you shall count them. 30You shall count them from thirty years old and up to fifty years old, everyone who would come to the army, to do the work of the Tent of Meeting. 31And this is their carrying task, for all their work in the Tent of Meeting: the Tabernacle's frames and its bars and its columns and its bases 32and the courtyard's columns all around and their bases and their pegs and their cords, for all their equipment and all their service. And you shall take account of the equipment for their carrying task by name. 33This is the work of the families of the children of Merari, for all their work in the Tent of Meeting in the hand of Ithamar son of Aaron, the priest."

34And Moses and Aaron and the congregation's chieftains counted the Kohathite children by their families and by their fathers' house 35from thirty years old and up to fifty years old, everyone who would come to the army for the work of the Tent of Meeting. 36And their counts by their families were two thousand seven hundred fifty. 37These are the counts of the Kohathite families, everyone who worked in the Tent of Meeting, whom Moses and Aaron counted by YHWH's word through Moses' hand.

38And the counts of the children of Gershon by their families and by their fathers' house 39from thirty years old and up to fifty years old, everyone who would come to the army for work in the Tent of Meeting: 40And their counts by their families, by their fathers' house, were two

סָבִ֗יב וְאֵ֤ת מֵֽיתְרֵיהֶם֙ וְאֶת־כָּל־כְּלֵ֣י עֲבֹֽדָתָ֔ם וְאֵ֨ת כָּל־אֲשֶׁ֧ר יֵעָשֶׂ֛ה לָהֶ֖ם וְעָבָֽדוּ׃ 27עַל־פִּ֩י אַהֲרֹ֨ן וּבָנָ֜יו תִּֽהְיֶ֗ה כָּל־עֲבֹדַת֙ בְּנֵ֣י הַגֵּֽרְשֻׁנִּ֔י לְכָל־מַשָּׂאָ֖ם וּלְכֹ֣ל עֲבֹֽדָתָ֑ם וּפְקַדְתֶּ֤ם עֲלֵהֶם֙ בְּמִשְׁמֶ֔רֶת אֵ֖ת כָּל־מַשָּׂאָֽם׃ 28זֹ֣את עֲבֹדַ֗ת מִשְׁפְּחֹת֙ בְּנֵ֣י הַגֵּֽרְשֻׁנִּ֔י בְּאֹ֖הֶל מוֹעֵ֑ד וּמִ֨שְׁמַרְתָּ֔ם בְּיַד֙ אִֽיתָמָ֔ר בֶּֽן־אַהֲרֹ֖ן הַכֹּהֵֽן׃ פ 29בְּנֵ֖י מְרָרִ֑י לְמִשְׁפְּחֹתָ֥ם לְבֵית־אֲבֹתָ֖ם תִּפְקֹ֥ד אֹתָֽם׃ 30מִבֶּן֩ שְׁלֹשִׁ֨ים שָׁנָ֜ה וָמַ֗עְלָה וְעַ֛ד בֶּן־חֲמִשִּׁ֥ים שָׁנָ֖ה תִּפְקְדֵ֑ם כָּל־הַבָּא֙ לַצָּבָ֔א לַעֲבֹ֕ד אֶת־עֲבֹדַ֖ת אֹ֥הֶל מוֹעֵֽד׃ 31וְזֹאת֙ מִשְׁמֶ֣רֶת מַשָּׂאָ֔ם לְכָל־עֲבֹדָתָ֖ם בְּאֹ֣הֶל מוֹעֵ֑ד קַרְשֵׁי֙ הַמִּשְׁכָּ֔ן וּבְרִיחָ֖יו וְעַמּוּדָ֥יו וַאֲדָנָֽיו׃ 32וְעַמּוּדֵי֩ הֶחָצֵ֨ר סָבִ֜יב וְאַדְנֵיהֶ֗ם וִיתֵֽדֹתָם֙ וּמֵ֣יתְרֵיהֶ֔ם לְכָל־כְּלֵיהֶ֖ם וּלְכֹ֣ל עֲבֹדָתָ֑ם וּבְשֵׁמֹ֣ת תִּפְקְד֔וּ אֶת־כְּלֵ֖י מִשְׁמֶ֥רֶת מַשָּׂאָֽם׃ 33זֹ֣את עֲבֹדַ֗ת מִשְׁפְּחֹת֙ בְּנֵ֣י מְרָרִ֔י לְכָל־עֲבֹֽדָתָ֖ם בְּאֹ֣הֶל מוֹעֵ֑ד בְּיַד֙ אִֽיתָמָ֔ר בֶּֽן־אַהֲרֹ֖ן הַכֹּהֵֽן׃ 34וַיִּפְקֹ֨ד מֹשֶׁ֧ה וְאַהֲרֹ֛ן וּנְשִׂיאֵ֥י הָעֵדָ֖ה אֶת־בְּנֵ֣י הַקְּהָתִ֑י לְמִשְׁפְּחֹתָ֖ם וּלְבֵ֥ית אֲבֹתָֽם׃ 35מִבֶּ֨ן שְׁלֹשִׁ֤ים שָׁנָה֙ וָמַ֔עְלָה וְעַ֖ד בֶּן־חֲמִשִּׁ֣ים שָׁנָ֑ה כָּל־הַבָּא֙ לַצָּבָ֔א לַעֲבֹדָ֖ה בְּאֹ֥הֶל מוֹעֵֽד׃ 36וַיִּהְי֥וּ פְקֻדֵיהֶ֖ם לְמִשְׁפְּחֹתָ֑ם אַלְפַּ֕יִם שְׁבַ֥ע מֵא֖וֹת וַחֲמִשִּֽׁים׃ 37אֵ֣לֶּה פְקוּדֵי֩ מִשְׁפְּחֹ֨ת הַקְּהָתִ֜י כָּל־הָעֹבֵ֖ד בְּאֹ֣הֶל מוֹעֵ֑ד אֲשֶׁ֨ר פָּקַ֤ד מֹשֶׁה֙ וְאַהֲרֹ֔ן עַל־פִּ֥י יְהוָ֖ה בְּיַד־מֹשֶֽׁה׃ ס 38וּפְקוּדֵ֖י בְּנֵ֣י גֵרְשׁ֑וֹן לְמִשְׁפְּחוֹתָ֖ם וּלְבֵ֥ית אֲבֹתָֽם׃ 39מִבֶּ֨ן שְׁלֹשִׁ֤ים שָׁנָה֙ וָמַ֔עְלָה וְעַ֖ד בֶּן־חֲמִשִּׁ֣ים שָׁנָ֑ה כָּל־הַבָּא֙ לַצָּבָ֔א לַעֲבֹדָ֖ה בְּאֹ֥הֶל מוֹעֵֽד׃ 40וַיִּֽהְיוּ֙ פְּקֻ֣דֵיהֶ֔ם לְמִשְׁפְּחֹתָ֖ם לְבֵ֣ית אֲבֹתָ֑ם אַלְפַּ֕יִם וְשֵׁ֖שׁ מֵא֖וֹת

thousand six hundred thirty. 41These are the counts of the families of the children of Gershon, everyone who worked in the Tent of Meeting, whom Moses and Aaron counted by YHWH's word.

42And the counts of the families of the children of Merari by their families, by their fathers' house 43from thirty years old and up to fifty years old, everyone who would come to the army for work in the Tent of Meeting: 44And their counts by their families were three thousand two hundred. 45These are the counts of the families of the children of Merari whom Moses and Aaron counted by YHWH's word through Moses' hand.

46All the counts that Moses and Aaron and Israel's chieftains made of the Levites by their families and by their fathers' house 47from thirty years old and up to fifty years old, everyone who was coming to do the service of work and the service of carrying in the Tent of Meeting: 48And their counts were eight thousand five hundred eighty. 49By YHWH's word he counted them by Moses' hand, each man by his work or by his carrying, and his counts were as YHWH commanded Moses.

5 1And YHWH spoke to Moses, saying, 2"Command the children of Israel that they shall have every leper and everyone who has an emission and everyone who is impure by a person go from the camp. 3Male or female, you shall have them go; you shall have them go outside the camp so they will not make their camps, among which I tent, impure." 4And the children of Israel did so, and they had them go outside the camp. As YHWH spoke to Moses, so the children of Israel did.

5And YHWH spoke to Moses, saying, 6"Speak to the children of Israel: A man or a woman—

וּשְׁלֹשִֽׁים: 41אֵ֣לֶּה פְקוּדֵ֔י מִשְׁפְּחֹת֙ בְּנֵ֣י גֵרְשׁ֔וֹן כָּל־הָעֹבֵ֖ד בְּאֹ֣הֶל מוֹעֵ֑ד אֲשֶׁ֨ר פָּקַ֥ד מֹשֶׁ֛ה וְאַהֲרֹ֖ן עַל־פִּ֥י יְהוָֽה: 42וּפְקוּדֵ֕י מִשְׁפְּחֹ֖ת בְּנֵ֣י מְרָרִ֑י לְמִשְׁפְּחֹתָ֖ם לְבֵ֥ית אֲבֹתָֽם: 43מִבֶּן֩ שְׁלֹשִׁ֨ים שָׁנָ֜ה וָמַ֗עְלָה וְעַ֛ד בֶּן־חֲמִשִּׁ֥ים שָׁנָ֖ה כָּל־הַבָּ֣א לַצָּבָ֑א לַעֲבֹדָ֖ה בְּאֹ֥הֶל מוֹעֵֽד: 44וַיִּהְי֣וּ פְקֻדֵיהֶ֔ם לְמִשְׁפְּחֹתָ֑ם שְׁלֹ֥שֶׁת אֲלָפִ֖ים וּמָאתָֽיִם: 45אֵ֣לֶּה פְקוּדֵ֔י מִשְׁפְּחֹ֖ת בְּנֵ֣י מְרָרִ֑י אֲשֶׁ֨ר פָּקַ֤ד מֹשֶׁה֙ וְאַהֲרֹ֔ן עַל־פִּ֥י יְהוָ֖ה בְּיַד־מֹשֶֽׁה: 46כָּל־הַפְּקֻדִ֡ים אֲשֶׁר֩ פָּקַ֨ד מֹשֶׁ֤ה וְאַהֲרֹן֙ וּנְשִׂיאֵ֣י יִשְׂרָאֵ֔ל אֶת־הַלְוִיִּ֑ם לְמִשְׁפְּחֹתָ֖ם וּלְבֵ֥ית אֲבֹתָֽם: 47מִבֶּ֨ן שְׁלֹשִׁ֤ים שָׁנָה֙ וָמַ֔עְלָה וְעַ֖ד בֶּן־חֲמִשִּׁ֣ים שָׁנָ֑ה כָּל־הַבָּ֗א לַעֲבֹ֨ד עֲבֹדַ֤ת עֲבֹדָה֙ וַעֲבֹדַ֣ת מַשָּׂ֔א בְּאֹ֖הֶל מוֹעֵֽד: 48וַיִּהְי֖וּ פְּקֻדֵיהֶ֑ם שְׁמֹנַ֣ת אֲלָפִ֔ים וַחֲמֵ֥שׁ מֵא֖וֹת וּשְׁמֹנִֽים: 49עַל־פִּ֤י יְהוָה֙ פָּקַ֣ד אוֹתָ֔ם בְּיַד־מֹשֶׁ֑ה אִ֥ישׁ אִ֛ישׁ עַל־עֲבֹדָת֖וֹ וְעַל־מַשָּׂא֑וֹ וּפְקֻדָ֕יו אֲשֶׁר־צִוָּ֥ה יְהוָ֖ה אֶת־מֹשֶֽׁה: פ

5 1וַיְדַבֵּ֥ר יְהוָ֖ה אֶל־מֹשֶׁ֥ה לֵּאמֹֽר: 2צַ֚ו אֶת־בְּנֵ֣י יִשְׂרָאֵ֔ל וִֽישַׁלְּחוּ֙ מִן־הַֽמַּחֲנֶ֔ה כָּל־צָר֖וּעַ וְכָל־זָ֑ב וְכֹ֖ל טָמֵ֥א לָנָֽפֶשׁ: 3מִזָּכָ֤ר עַד־נְקֵבָה֙ תְּשַׁלֵּ֔חוּ אֶל־מִח֥וּץ לַֽמַּחֲנֶ֖ה תְּשַׁלְּח֑וּם וְלֹ֤א יְטַמְּאוּ֙ אֶת־מַ֣חֲנֵיהֶ֔ם אֲשֶׁ֥ר אֲנִ֖י שֹׁכֵ֥ן בְּתוֹכָֽם: 4וַיַּֽעֲשׂוּ־כֵן֙ בְּנֵ֣י יִשְׂרָאֵ֔ל וַיְשַׁלְּח֣וּ אוֹתָ֔ם אֶל־מִח֖וּץ לַֽמַּחֲנֶ֑ה כַּאֲשֶׁ֨ר דִּבֶּ֤ר יְהוָה֙ אֶל־מֹשֶׁ֔ה כֵּ֥ן עָשׂ֖וּ בְּנֵ֥י יִשְׂרָאֵֽל: פ 5וַיְדַבֵּ֥ר יְהוָ֖ה אֶל־מֹשֶׁ֥ה לֵּאמֹֽר: 6דַּבֵּר֙ אֶל־בְּנֵ֣י יִשְׂרָאֵ֔ל אִ֥ישׁ אֽוֹ־אִשָּׁ֖ה

5:2. **impure by a person.** Meaning: something that has become impure because of contact with the dead body of a person.

when they will do any of the sins of humans, to make a breach against YHWH—so that person has guilt, [7]then they shall confess their sin that they have done. And he shall pay back for his guilt with its principal, and he shall add to it a fifth of it, and he shall give it to the one whom he wronged. [8]And if the man does not have a redeemer, to pay him back for the guilt, the guilt that is paid back is YHWH's, for the priest, apart from the ram of atonement by which he will make atonement for him. [9]And every donation of all the holy things of the children of Israel that they will bring forward to the priest shall be his. [10]And each man's holy things shall be his; what each man gives to the priest shall be his."

[11]And YHWH spoke to Moses, saying, [12]"Speak to the children of Israel, and you shall say to them: Any man whose wife will go astray and will make a breach of faith with him, [13]and a man has lain with her—an intercourse of

כִּי יַעֲשׂוּ מִכָּל־חַטֹּאת הָאָדָם לִמְעֹל מַעַל בַּיהוָה וְאָשְׁמָה הַנֶּפֶשׁ הַהִוא: [7]וְהִתְוַדּוּ אֶת־חַטָּאתָם אֲשֶׁר עָשׂוּ וְהֵשִׁיב אֶת־אֲשָׁמוֹ בְּרֹאשׁוֹ וַחֲמִישִׁתוֹ יֹסֵף עָלָיו וְנָתַן לַאֲשֶׁר אָשַׁם לוֹ: [8]וְאִם־אֵין לָאִישׁ גֹּאֵל לְהָשִׁיב הָאָשָׁם אֵלָיו הָאָשָׁם הַמּוּשָׁב לַיהוָה לַכֹּהֵן מִלְּבַד אֵיל הַכִּפֻּרִים אֲשֶׁר יְכַפֶּר־בּוֹ עָלָיו: [9]וְכָל־תְּרוּמָה לְכָל־קָדְשֵׁי בְנֵי־יִשְׂרָאֵל אֲשֶׁר־יַקְרִיבוּ לַכֹּהֵן לוֹ יִהְיֶה: [10]וְאִישׁ אֶת־קֳדָשָׁיו לוֹ יִהְיוּ אִישׁ אֲשֶׁר־יִתֵּן לַכֹּהֵן לוֹ יִהְיֶה: פ

[11]וַיְדַבֵּר יְהוָה אֶל־מֹשֶׁה לֵּאמֹר: [12]דַּבֵּר אֶל־בְּנֵי יִשְׂרָאֵל וְאָמַרְתָּ אֲלֵהֶם אִישׁ אִישׁ כִּי־תִשְׂטֶה אִשְׁתּוֹ וּמָעֲלָה בוֹ מָעַל: [13]וְשָׁכַב אִישׁ אֹתָהּ שִׁכְבַת־

5:10. **shall be his.** Meaning: shall be the priest's.

5:12. **go astray.** Hebrew root *śṭh.* This situation is known therefore as the case of the *śōṭāh.*

5:12. **go astray.** This section deals with the case of the suspected *śōṭāh:* a woman whose husband suspects her of adultery, but who has not been proved guilty by evidence or witnesses. It would not merit special notice as anything more than any other law, especially since it has not been practiced for at least two millennia (and, I would say, probably more than two-and-a-half millennia), but it has acquired special importance because, first, it is regarded as the only case of trial by ordeal in the Torah and, second, because questions about the legal status of women have risen to prominence in this generation.

The woman is made to drink a mixture of holy water, dust from the Tabernacle's floor, and ink from a document expressing a curse if she is guilty. Then, if "her womb swells and her thigh sags" she is understood to be guilty. There have been many attempts to understand what is going on in this strange case. The traditional Talmudic belief is that a miracle is expected to occur through this procedure. Another view is that the procedure is designed to scare guilty women into confessing rather than face the ceremony and the curse. Another is that, since drinking water with dust and ink does not produce these symptoms, this is a law that is designed to find all women not guilty—and thus protect suspected women from their husbands' or town's vengeance. Another view is that this procedure can result in the condition of a prolapsed uterus.

seed—and it has been hidden from her husband's eyes, and she has kept concealed, and she has been made impure, and there is no witness against her, and she has not been caught, [14]and

זֶרַע וְנֶעְלַם מֵעֵינֵי אִישָׁהּ וְנִסְתְּרָה וְהִיא נִטְמָאָה וְעֵד אֵין בָּהּ וְהִוא לֹא נִתְפָּשָׂה: 14וְעָבַר עָלָיו

All the views leave questions: Why not have some procedure like this for a *man* who is suspected of adultery? In fact, why not have a procedure like this for *any* other crime, by a man *or* a woman? Also, even if the woman is shown guilty, she is not executed, which elsewhere is the penalty for adultery (Lev 20:10; Deut 22:22). So, to begin with: this procedure must relate specifically to something (1) about women and not men, and (2) about sex and adultery. I believe that all of the past explanations are mistaken, and I offer the following explanation of this case:

If we were told that a woman's "womb is swelling and her thigh is sagging," nearly 100 percent of us would understand this to mean: she is pregnant. So, in this case, it is explicitly about a woman who has had sex with another man in place of her husband. That is, she has not slept with her husband recently, and that is why her pregnancy is proof of adultery. The purpose of drinking the mixture is not to prove her guilt but to bring about the *curse* through her pregnancy. (Thus it is called "the bitter cursing water"; and the priest says, "Let YHWH make you a curse and an oath among your people when YHWH sets your thigh sagging and your womb swelling.") This is why the law applies only to women and only to the matter of adultery: it is the only offense in the Torah in which guilt can be determined by this biological fact, even when there are no witnesses and no other evidence. And this is why the woman cannot be executed: She has not been proved guilty in front of judges in a court of law through witnesses. She has been shown to have done this in front of priests at the Tabernacle. Therefore, she "shall bear her crime" (see the comment on 5:31).

This has a more general implication as well. The reason that we have had such difficulty understanding this case for millennia is that *law is constructed on analogy:* we decide cases by precedents, by consistent principles that apply to cases in a variety of circumstances. But pregnancy is a condition that is without analogy in human experience. That is why this case reads like no other. And that is why there are agonizing, passionate debates in the present age over whether to save the mother or the baby in a medical crisis during labor, over rights to sperm and eggs that have been preserved, over surrogate mothers, and, above all, over abortion: with arguments about when the developing being inside the womb is a living human in its own right, and about the legal rights of the mother over her own body in balance with the legal protection of the fetus. There simply is no other experience in which two lives are so utterly interconnected.

Why are the rabbis of the Talmudic era so unclear about the actual procedure if it had been practiced in recent memory? Because, I think, it had *not* been practiced since the time of the *First* Temple in Jerusalem. It required dust from the Tabernacle floor, and the Tabernacle was only in the First Temple, not in the Second. (A report in the Mishnah that Rabbi Yohanan ben Zakkai abolished this procedure makes no sense historically. By the time of his authority, even the Second Temple was gone.) And so

a spirit of jealousy has come over him, and he is jealous about his wife, and she has been made impure, or a spirit of jealousy has come over him, and he is jealous about his wife, and she has not been made impure: 15then the man shall bring his wife to the priest and shall bring her offering along with her: a tenth of an ephah of barley flour. He shall not pour oil on it and shall not put frankincense on it, because it is an offering about jealousies, an offering of bringing to mind: causing a crime to be brought to mind.

16"And the priest shall bring her forward and stand her in front of YHWH. 17And the priest shall take holy water in a clay container, and the priest shall take some of the dust that will be on the Tabernacle's floor and put it into the water. 18And the priest shall stand the woman in front of YHWH and loosen the hair of the woman's head and put the offering of bringing to mind on her hands; it is an offering of jealousies. And in the priest's hand shall be the bitter cursing water. 19And the priest shall have her swear, and he shall say to the woman: 'If a man has not lain with you, and if you have not gone astray in im-

רוּחַ־קִנְאָה וְקִנֵּא אֶת־אִשְׁתּוֹ וְהִוא נִטְמָאָה אוֹ־עָבַר עָלָיו רוּחַ־קִנְאָה וְקִנֵּא אֶת־אִשְׁתּוֹ וְהִיא לֹא נִטְמָאָה: 15וְהֵבִיא הָאִישׁ אֶת־אִשְׁתּוֹ אֶל־הַכֹּהֵן וְהֵבִיא אֶת־קָרְבָּנָהּ עָלֶיהָ עֲשִׂירִת הָאֵיפָה קֶמַח שְׂעֹרִים לֹא־יִצֹק עָלָיו שֶׁמֶן וְלֹא־יִתֵּן עָלָיו לְבֹנָה כִּי־מִנְחַת קְנָאֹת הוּא מִנְחַת זִכָּרוֹן מַזְכֶּרֶת עָוֹן: 16וְהִקְרִיב אֹתָהּ הַכֹּהֵן וְהֶעֱמִדָהּ לִפְנֵי יְהוָה: 17וְלָקַח הַכֹּהֵן מַיִם קְדֹשִׁים בִּכְלִי־חָרֶשׂ וּמִן־הֶעָפָר אֲשֶׁר יִהְיֶה בְּקַרְקַע הַמִּשְׁכָּן יִקַּח הַכֹּהֵן וְנָתַן אֶל־הַמָּיִם: 18וְהֶעֱמִיד הַכֹּהֵן אֶת־הָאִשָּׁה לִפְנֵי יְהוָה וּפָרַע אֶת־רֹאשׁ הָאִשָּׁה וְנָתַן עַל־כַּפֶּיהָ אֵת מִנְחַת הַזִּכָּרוֹן מִנְחַת קְנָאֹת הִוא וּבְיַד הַכֹּהֵן יִהְיוּ מֵי הַמָּרִים הַמְאָרֲרִים: 19וְהִשְׁבִּיעַ אֹתָהּ הַכֹּהֵן וְאָמַר אֶל־הָאִשָּׁה אִם־לֹא שָׁכַב אִישׁ אֹתָךְ וְאִם־לֹא שָׂטִית

---

it came about that the actual meaning of this ceremony was forgotten after many centuries of not being practiced, and the result has been uncertainty and confusion about its meaning.

5:17. **holy water**. This is the only reference to holy water in the Torah. It may be the water from the basin that the priests use for washing (Exod 30:17–21); the basin is among the things that are identified as "holy of holies" (30:28–29).

5:17. **dust**. The woman must drink the water containing this dust (5:24). Some have claimed that there is a parallel between this case and the episode of the golden calf. Moses grinds the golden calf thin as dust (Exod 32:20; Deut 9:21), scatters it in water, and makes the people drink (Exodus 32). My reaction is that such a view is tenuous at best. The people in Exodus are guilty! The *sōṭāh* case is a process designed to *determine* guilt. And the dust from the Tabernacle is something positive, while the dust of the calf is the opposite. It is true that the people of Israel's turning to pagan gods is sometimes compared to adultery in the *Tanak*: Israel is described as a faithless wife. And the term that means "a breach of faith" (*ma'al*) with a husband here refers to breaches of faith with *God* in all its other occurrences in the Torah. But the cases of the *sōṭāh* and the golden calf have so many fundamental differences that drawing a connection between them may mislead more than shed light.

purity with someone in place of your husband, be cleared by this bitter cursing water. 20But you, if you have gone astray with someone in place of your husband and if you have been made impure, and if a man other than your husband has had his intercourse with you,' 21then the priest shall have the woman swear a curse oath, and the priest shall say to the woman, 'let YHWH make you a curse and an oath among your people when YHWH sets your thigh sagging and your womb swelling, 22and this cursing water will come in your insides, to swell the womb and make the thigh sag.'

"And the woman shall say, 'Amen, amen.'

23"And the priest shall write these curses in a scroll and rub them into the bitter water. 24And he shall have the woman drink the bitter cursing water, and the bitter cursing water will come into

טְמֵאָה תַּחַת אִישֵׁךְ הַנָּקִי מִמֵּי הַמָּרִים הַמְאָרֲרִים הָאֵלֶּה: 20וְאַתְּ כִּי שָׂטִית תַּחַת אִישֵׁךְ וְכִי נִטְמֵאת וַיִּתֵּן אִישׁ בָּךְ אֶת־שְׁכָבְתּוֹ מִבַּלְעֲדֵי אִישֵׁךְ: 21וְהִשְׁבִּיעַ הַכֹּהֵן אֶת־הָאִשָּׁה בִּשְׁבֻעַת הָאָלָה וְאָמַר הַכֹּהֵן לָאִשָּׁה יִתֵּן יְהוָה אוֹתָךְ לְאָלָה וְלִשְׁבֻעָה בְּתוֹךְ עַמֵּךְ בְּתֵת יְהוָה אֶת־יְרֵכֵךְ נֹפֶלֶת וְאֶת־בִּטְנֵךְ צָבָה: 22וּבָאוּ הַמַּיִם הַמְאָרֲרִים הָאֵלֶּה בְּמֵעַיִךְ לַצְבּוֹת בֶּטֶן וְלַנְפִּל יָרֵךְ וְאָמְרָה הָאִשָּׁה אָמֵן ׀ אָמֵן: 23וְכָתַב אֶת־הָאָלֹת הָאֵלֶּה הַכֹּהֵן בַּסֵּפֶר וּמָחָה אֶל־מֵי הַמָּרִים: 24וְהִשְׁקָה אֶת־הָאִשָּׁה אֶת־מֵי הַמָּרִים הַמְאָרֲרִים וּבָאוּ בָהּ הַמַּיִם הַמְאָרֲרִים

5:19. **in place of your husband**. Suggesting that if she is pregnant it must be by the other man, not the husband. Those who have other views of the *śōṭāh* procedure understand this phrase to mean "*under* your husband," and they interpret it as meaning "under his authority." But there is no reason why that had to be mentioned in the context of these instructions. Moreover, the term here, Hebrew *taḥat*, means "in place of" sixteen times in the Torah but never means "under someone's authority" (the term for that is "under the hand of," Hebrew *taḥat yad*; cf. Gen 41:35).

5:21. **womb**. Hebrew *beṭen*. This word is commonly understood to mean the woman's "belly," but in every one of its other ten occurrences in the Torah it means "womb" (see, e.g. Gen 25:23). This is further evidence that pregnancy is what this is all about.

5:22. **to swell the womb and make the thigh sag**. It is not clear whether this refers to God's making this happen (as is explicit in the preceding verse) or to the water's making it happen. It appears to me that God is understood here to bring about the pregnancy—in the sense that all pregnancies are understood to be enabled by God—and that the water brings about the curse: "the bitter cursing water."

5:24. **the bitter cursing water**. Hebrew *mê hammārîm hamme'ărěrîm*. The obvious alliteration is one of several cases of wordplay in this text: Hebrew נעלם (it has been hidden) reverses the root letters of מעל (breach). Hebrew עשׂירת (a tenth) reverses the root letters of שׂערים (barley). Hebrew פרע (loosen the hair) reverses עפר (dust). And Hebrew מאררים (cursing) has strong alliteration with מרים (bitter). This wordplay involves much more than artistry with language. Each of these puns is linked to an aspect of this ceremony that is unique in some way: This is the only case in which מעל (to make a breach) is used for an offense against a human rather than God (see the comment on Lev 5:15). It is the only time that שׂערים (barley flour) is used for a grain offering. It is the only use of the עפר (dust) from the Tabernacle. And this strange use

440

her. 25And the priest shall take the offering of jealousies from the woman's hand and elevate the offering in front of YHWH, and he shall bring her forward to the altar. 26And the priest shall take a fistful from the grain offering, a representative portion of it, and burn it to smoke at the altar, and after that he shall have the woman drink the water. 27When he has had her drink the water, then it will be, if she has been made impure and has made a breach of faith with her husband, when the bitter cursing water will come into her, and her womb will swell and her thigh will sag, then the woman will become a curse among her people. 28And if the woman has not been made impure, and she is pure, then she shall be cleared and shall conceive seed.

29"This is the instruction for jealousies, when a woman will go astray with someone in place of her husband and be made impure, 30or when a spirit of jealousy will come over a man and he will be jealous about his wife. And the priest shall stand the woman in front of YHWH and do all of this instruction to her. 31And the man shall be clear of a crime, and that woman shall bear her crime."

לְמֻרִֽים׃ 25וְלָקַ֨ח הַכֹּהֵ֜ן מִיַּ֣ד הָאִשָּׁ֗ה אֵ֚ת מִנְחַ֣ת הַקְּנָאֹ֔ת וְהֵנִ֥יף אֶת־הַמִּנְחָ֖ה לִפְנֵ֣י יְהוָ֑ה וְהִקְרִ֥יב אֹתָ֖הּ אֶל־הַמִּזְבֵּֽחַ׃ 26וְקָמַ֨ץ הַכֹּהֵ֤ן מִן־הַמִּנְחָה֙ אֶת־אַזְכָּ֣רָתָ֔הּ וְהִקְטִ֖יר הַמִּזְבֵּ֑חָה וְאַחַ֛ר יַשְׁקֶ֥ה אֶת־הָאִשָּׁ֖ה אֶת־הַמָּֽיִם׃ 27וְהִשְׁקָ֣הּ אֶת־הַמַּ֗יִם וְהָיְתָ֣ה אִֽם־נִטְמְאָה֮ וַתִּמְעֹ֣ל מַ֣עַל בְּאִישָׁהּ֒ וּבָ֨אוּ בָ֜הּ הַמַּ֤יִם הַמְאָֽרֲרִים֙ לְמָרִ֔ים וְצָבְתָ֣ה בִטְנָ֔הּ וְנָפְלָ֖ה יְרֵכָ֑הּ וְהָיְתָ֧ה הָאִשָּׁ֛ה לְאָלָ֖ה בְּקֶ֥רֶב עַמָּֽהּ׃ 28וְאִם־לֹ֤א נִטְמְאָה֙ הָֽאִשָּׁ֔ה וּטְהֹרָ֖ה הִ֑וא וְנִקְּתָ֖ה וְנִזְרְעָ֥ה זָֽרַע׃ 29זֹ֥את תּוֹרַ֖ת הַקְּנָאֹ֑ת אֲשֶׁ֨ר תִּשְׂטֶ֥ה אִשָּׁ֛ה תַּ֥חַת אִישָׁ֖הּ וְנִטְמָֽאָה׃ 30א֣וֹ אִ֗ישׁ אֲשֶׁ֨ר תַּעֲבֹ֤ר עָלָיו֙ ר֣וּחַ קִנְאָ֔ה וְקִנֵּ֖א אֶת־אִשְׁתּ֑וֹ וְהֶעֱמִ֤יד אֶת־הָֽאִשָּׁה֙ לִפְנֵ֣י יְהוָ֔ה וְעָ֤שָׂה לָהּ֙ הַכֹּהֵ֔ן אֵ֥ת כָּל־הַתּוֹרָ֖ה הַזֹּֽאת׃ 31וְנִקָּ֥ה הָאִ֖ישׁ מֵעָוֺ֑ן וְהָאִשָּׁ֣ה הַהִ֔וא תִּשָּׂ֖א אֶת־עֲוֺנָֽהּ׃ פ

of water (holy water, with a curse melted into it) is the most unusual of all. Puns are common in the Torah's *stories*, but their appearance in a *law* is extremely unusual and unexpected. They highlight the unusual aspect of this case, and they summon to mind associations with the realm of magic, in which the artistry of language and poetry figure in incantations and ceremonies. Likewise, the dissolving of the words of the curse into the water, the dust from the Tabernacle, the water from the priests' basin, the act of drinking a mixture that produces a curse: much of this has parallels in magic in other cultures, and all of this renders this ceremony mysterious. And it fits with the fact that the function of this procedure is not to establish legal guilt but rather to produce the curse.

5:31. **the man shall be clear of a crime.** This is usually understood to mean that the *husband* is innocent of the crime of making a false charge against his wife. But this is a questionable reading since the text does not say that he has made any charge against her; he has just brought her to the priest to make the determination of whether his jealousy is correct or not. This may rather refer to the *other* man, the one who had intercourse with the woman. The procedure proves only that the *woman* has had intercourse; it cannot prove who the man was. It is therefore not possible to convict the man by this procedure.

6 ¹And YHWH spoke to Moses, saying, ²"Speak to the children of Israel, and you shall say to them: When a man or a woman will expressly make a Nazirite vow to make a separation for YHWH, ³he shall separate from wine

6 ¹וַיְדַבֵּר יְהוָה אֶל־מֹשֶׁה לֵּאמֹר: ²דַּבֵּר אֶל־בְּנֵי יִשְׂרָאֵל וְאָמַרְתָּ אֲלֵהֶם אִישׁ אוֹ־אִשָּׁה כִּי יַפְלִא לִנְדֹּר נֶדֶר נָזִיר לְהַזִּיר לַיהוָה: ³מִיַּיִן וְשֵׁכָר יַזִּיר

This also answers the question of why this procedure applies only to women. A man accused of adultery does not go through this. Because only women can become pregnant, it is only women who can be proved to have committed adultery in the absence of witnesses or any other evidence. (This brings to mind the case of Bathsheba, who becomes pregnant through adultery with David. Her pregnancy while her husband has been away at war is what would make her adultery known; 2 Samuel 11.)

5:31. **that woman shall bear her crime**. Even though the procedure has indicated her guilt, she still has not been convicted in the manner of any other case. There have been no witnesses. It is explicitly a hidden matter. It is therefore not in human hands to do anything to her. (On the requirement of two or more witnesses in order to execute, see Deut 17:6.) Even though adultery is a capital crime in the Torah, she cannot be executed. (Another possible reason: in many cultures it is not permissible to execute a pregnant woman in any case.) The words "she shall bear her crime" mean that it is a matter between her and God.

6:2. **a man or a woman**. Although the rest of the law is stated in the masculine, the entire matter of choosing to be a Nazirite applies to both men and women.

6:2. **make a separation for YHWH**. A Nazirite vows to give up certain things and live in a state of holiness. There is the general idea in the Torah that all the people are holy (Lev 19:1), but the Nazirite vow refers to a singular state that exceeds that. The Nazirite gives up three things: consuming alcohol, coming near to dead persons, and cutting his or her hair. Why these three things? These three things are related to priesthood—and particularly to the high priest. Israel's priests are forbidden to consume alcohol at the Tent of Meeting, and this is the first command in the Torah that God gives directly to Aaron, the high priest, not to Moses (Lev 10:9). Priests are forbidden to come to dead persons except their closest relatives (Lev 21:1–3), and the high priest is commanded that "he shall not come to *any* dead persons; he shall not become impure for his father and for his mother" (21:11)—which is the wording here for the Nazirite as well: "he shall not come to a dead person. For his father and for his mother, for his brother and for his sister: he shall not become impure for them" (Num 6:6–7). But in the matter of the hair, the high priest is commanded to do the opposite of the Nazirite: The Nazirite shall "grow the hair of his head loose" (Num 6:5), but the high priest "shall not let loose the hair of his head" (Lev 21:10). What does it mean that a Nazirite is someone who chooses to live in certain respects like a high priest but that a high priest is commanded not to have the most obvious characteristic of the Nazirite?

The issue appears to me to relate to the fact that the clergy in Israel is not open to most Israelites to choose, but only to members of the tribe of Levi by heredity, and then only to males; and the priesthood comes to be limited only to a certain family within Levi, the family of Aaron; and the high priesthood is limited to a son of the

442

and beer; he shall not drink any vinegar of wine or vinegar of beer, and he shall not drink any juice of grapes, and he shall not eat fresh or dried grapes. 4All the days of his being a Nazirite, he shall not eat anything that is made from the grapevine, from seeds to skin. 5All the days of his Nazirite vow, a razor shall not pass on his head; until the fulfillment of the days that he will make a separation for YHWH, he shall be holy, growing the hair of his head loose. 6All the days of his making a separation for YHWH he shall not come to a dead person. 7For his father and for his mother, for his brother and for his sister: he shall not become impure for them when they die, because the crown of his God is on his head. 8All the days of his being a Nazirite he is holy to

חֹמֶץ יַיִן וְחֹמֶץ שֵׁכָר לֹא יִשְׁתֶּה וְכָל־מִשְׁרַת עֲנָבִים לֹא יִשְׁתֶּה וַעֲנָבִים לַחִים וִיבֵשִׁים לֹא יֹאכֵל: 4כֹּל יְמֵי נִזְרוֹ מִכֹּל אֲשֶׁר יֵעָשֶׂה מִגֶּפֶן הַיַּיִן מֵחַרְצַנִּים וְעַד־זָג לֹא יֹאכֵל: 5כָּל־יְמֵי נֶדֶר נִזְרוֹ תַּעַר לֹא־יַעֲבֹר עַל־רֹאשׁוֹ עַד־מְלֹאת הַיָּמִם אֲשֶׁר־יַזִּיר לַיהוָה קָדֹשׁ יִהְיֶה גַּדֵּל פֶּרַע שְׂעַר רֹאשׁוֹ: 6כָּל־יְמֵי הַזִּירוֹ לַיהוָה עַל־נֶפֶשׁ מֵת לֹא יָבֹא: 7לְאָבִיו וּלְאִמּוֹ לְאָחִיו וּלְאַחֹתוֹ לֹא־יִטַּמָּא לָהֶם בְּמֹתָם כִּי נֵזֶר אֱלֹהָיו עַל־רֹאשׁוֹ: 8כֹּל יְמֵי נִזְרוֹ קָדֹשׁ הוּא

---

preceding high priest. Prophets can be from any tribe and can be male or female; one becomes a prophet by being called by God. Postbiblically, rabbis replace priests as the primary clergy of the Jews, and membership in the rabbinate is open to anyone who chooses it and proves capable of qualifying and carrying it out. Originally it was limited to males, but in the present generation the Reform, Conservative, and Reconstructionist movements have included both females and males. So what option does a person in the biblical world have who is drawn to the holy life of a priest but who is not a male Levite from the family of Aaron? Such a person can choose to be a Nazirite. And note the case of Samuel: he becomes a priest, seemingly the high priest, even though he is not a Levite—and Samuel is a Nazirite! He replaces the Levite high priest Eli at the Tabernacle at Shiloh, and he performs sacrifices, which no nonpriest, even the king, may do (1 Samuel 1–13). Historically, the law forbidding the high priest to let his hair grow loose may have been composed precisely to establish that this could never happen again. No one outside the Aaronid Levite clan could just choose to enter the clergy and rise in the priesthood. As the law stands in the Torah now, preceding the story of Samuel, it means that the case of Samuel must be regarded as unique, with Samuel's rise in the priesthood being the result of a special selection by God.

6:5. **he shall be holy**. This, too, is like priests ("They shall be holy to their God," Lev 21:6). And since it especially mentions the name of God ("a separation for YHWH"), it is especially like the high priest ("I, YHWH, make him holy," Lev 21:15).

6:6. **come to a dead person**. Meaning: touch a dead body. Interestingly, the case of Samson is different. Like Samuel, he is a Nazirite from birth, and he is forbidden to cut his hair—which becomes the key to his story. But he is not forbidden to have contact with dead bodies—which is also essential to the story, because he becomes a warrior and personally makes thousands of dead bodies!

6:7. **the crown of his God is on his head**. As I noted in the case of the high priest, the Hebrew term *nēzer* has the same range as the English word *crown*, denoting either

YHWH. 9And if someone will die by chance suddenly by him and will make his head's crown impure, then he shall shave his head on the day of his purification: he shall shave it on the seventh day. 10And on the eighth day he shall bring two turtledoves or two pigeons to the priest, to the entrance of the Tent of Meeting. 11And the priest shall do one as a sin offering and one as a burnt offering and shall make atonement over him in that he has sinned over a person. And he shall make his head holy on that day. 12And he shall make a separation for YHWH for the days of his being a Nazirite, and he shall bring a lamb in its first year for a guilt offering, and the first days shall fall because his Nazirite state became impure.

13"And this is the instruction for the Nazirite: On the day of the fulfillment of the days of his being a Nazirite one shall bring him to the entrance of the Tent of Meeting. 14And he shall make his offering to YHWH: one unblemished lamb in its first year for a burnt offering and one unblemished ewe-lamb in its first year for a sin offering and one unblemished ram for a peace offering 15and a basket of unleavened bread of fine flour, cakes mixed with oil and unleavened wafers with oil poured on them with their grain offering and their libations. 16And the priest shall bring it forward in front of YHWH and shall do his sin offering and his burnt offering. 17And he shall make the ram a peace-offering sacrifice to YHWH with the basket of unleavened bread, and the priest shall do his grain offering and his libation. 18And the Nazirite shall shave

לַיהוָה: 9וְכִי־יָמוּת מֵת עָלָיו בְּפֶתַע פִּתְאֹם וְטִמֵּא רֹאשׁ נִזְרוֹ וְגִלַּח רֹאשׁוֹ בְּיוֹם טָהֳרָתוֹ בַּיּוֹם הַשְּׁבִיעִי יְגַלְּחֶנּוּ: 10וּבַיּוֹם הַשְּׁמִינִי יָבֹא שְׁתֵּי תֹרִים אוֹ שְׁנֵי בְּנֵי יוֹנָה אֶל־הַכֹּהֵן אֶל־פֶּתַח אֹהֶל מוֹעֵד: 11וְעָשָׂה הַכֹּהֵן אֶחָד לְחַטָּאת וְאֶחָד לְעֹלָה וְכִפֶּר עָלָיו מֵאֲשֶׁר חָטָא עַל־הַנָּפֶשׁ וְקִדַּשׁ אֶת־רֹאשׁוֹ בַּיּוֹם הַהוּא: 12וְהִזִּיר לַיהוָה אֶת־יְמֵי נִזְרוֹ וְהֵבִיא כֶּבֶשׂ בֶּן־שְׁנָתוֹ לְאָשָׁם וְהַיָּמִים הָרִאשֹׁנִים יִפְּלוּ כִּי טָמֵא נִזְרוֹ: 13וְזֹאת תּוֹרַת הַנָּזִיר בְּיוֹם מְלֹאת יְמֵי נִזְרוֹ יָבִיא אֹתוֹ אֶל־פֶּתַח אֹהֶל מוֹעֵד: 14וְהִקְרִיב אֶת־קָרְבָּנוֹ לַיהוָה כֶּבֶשׂ בֶּן־שְׁנָתוֹ תָמִים אֶחָד לְעֹלָה וְכַבְשָׂה אַחַת בַּת־שְׁנָתָהּ תְּמִימָה לְחַטָּאת וְאַיִל־אֶחָד תָּמִים לִשְׁלָמִים: 15וְסַל מַצּוֹת סֹלֶת חַלֹּת בְּלוּלֹת בַּשֶּׁמֶן וּרְקִיקֵי מַצּוֹת מְשֻׁחִים בַּשָּׁמֶן וּמִנְחָתָם וְנִסְכֵּיהֶם: 16וְהִקְרִיב הַכֹּהֵן לִפְנֵי יְהוָה וְעָשָׂה אֶת־חַטָּאתוֹ וְאֶת־עֹלָתוֹ: 17וְאֶת־הָאַיִל יַעֲשֶׂה זֶבַח שְׁלָמִים לַיהוָה עַל סַל הַמַּצּוֹת וְעָשָׂה הַכֹּהֵן אֶת־מִנְחָתוֹ וְאֶת־נִסְכּוֹ: 18וְגִלַּח הַנָּזִיר פֶּתַח אֹהֶל

---

the top of the head or the headdress worn by a king or priest (see my comment on Lev 21:12). Here it refers to the hair on the Nazirite's head, which may not be cut. As long as the man or woman wears the uncut Nazirite hair, he or she also follows the high priest's practice of not touching a corpse.

6:11. **a person**. Meaning: a dead person.

6:12. **the first days shall fall**. The time that he spent as a Nazirite before becoming impure by contact with a corpse does not count toward the time that he vowed to spend as a Nazirite. It is nullified by the contact.

his head's crown at the entrance of the Tent of Meeting and shall take the hair of his head's crown and put it on the fire that is under the peace-offering sacrifice. ¹⁹And the priest shall take the cooked shoulder from the ram and one unleavened cake from the basket and one unleavened wafer and put them on the Nazirite's hands after his crown is shaved. ²⁰And the priest shall elevate them, an elevation offering in front of YHWH. It is holy for the priest along with the breast of the elevation offering and the thigh of the donation. And after that the Nazirite may drink wine. ²¹This is the instruction for the Nazirite who will vow his offering to YHWH for his being a Nazirite outside of what his hand may attain. According to his vow that he will make, so he shall do along with the instruction of his being a Nazirite."

²²And YHWH spoke to Moses, saying, ²³"Speak to Aaron and to his sons, saying, This is how you shall bless the children of Israel; say to them:

24   May YHWH bless you and watch over
      you.

מוֹעֵ֑ד אֶת־רֹ֣אשׁ נִזְר֔וֹ וְלָקַ֗ח אֶת־שְׂעַר֙ רֹ֣אשׁ נִזְר֔וֹ
וְנָתַן֙ עַל־הָאֵ֔שׁ אֲשֶׁר־תַּ֖חַת זֶ֣בַח הַשְּׁלָמִֽים׃ ¹⁹וְלָקַ֨ח
הַכֹּהֵ֜ן אֶת־הַזְּרֹ֣עַ בְּשֵׁלָה֮ מִן־הָאַיִל֒ וְֽחַלַּ֥ת מַצָּ֛ה אַחַ֖ת
מִן־הַסַּ֗ל וּרְקִ֥יק מַצָּ֖ה אֶחָ֑ד וְנָתַן֙ עַל־כַּפֵּ֣י הַנָּזִ֔יר
אַחַ֖ר הִֽתְגַּלְּח֥וֹ אֶת־נִזְרֽוֹ׃ ²⁰וְהֵנִ֨יף אוֹתָ֥ם הַכֹּהֵ֣ן ׀
תְּנוּפָה֮ לִפְנֵ֣י יְהוָה֒ קֹ֤דֶשׁ הוּא֙ לַכֹּהֵ֔ן עַ֚ל חֲזֵ֣ה
הַתְּנוּפָ֔ה וְעַ֖ל שׁ֣וֹק הַתְּרוּמָ֑ה וְאַחַ֛ר יִשְׁתֶּ֥ה הַנָּזִ֖יר
יָֽיִן׃ ²¹זֹ֣את תּוֹרַ֣ת הַנָּזִיר֮ אֲשֶׁ֣ר יִדֹּר֒ קׇרְבָּנ֤וֹ לַֽיהוָה֙
עַל־נִזְר֔וֹ מִלְּבַ֖ד אֲשֶׁר־תַּשִּׂ֣יג יָד֑וֹ כְּפִ֤י נִדְרוֹ֙ אֲשֶׁ֣ר
יִדֹּ֔ר כֵּ֣ן יַעֲשֶׂ֔ה עַ֖ל תּוֹרַ֥ת נִזְרֽוֹ׃ פ ²²וַיְדַבֵּ֥ר יְהוָ֖ה
אֶל־מֹשֶׁ֥ה לֵּאמֹֽר׃ ²³דַּבֵּ֤ר אֶֽל־אַהֲרֹן֙ וְאֶל־בָּנָ֣יו
לֵאמֹ֔ר כֹּ֥ה תְבָרְכ֖וּ אֶת־בְּנֵ֣י יִשְׂרָאֵ֑ל אָמ֖וֹר לָהֶֽם׃ ס
²⁴יְבָרֶכְךָ֥ יְהוָ֖ה וְיִשְׁמְרֶֽךָ׃ ס

6:21. **outside of what his hand may attain.** Meaning: this is what the Nazirite is required to do, outside of whatever else he or she can afford to do by choice.

6:23. **This is how you shall bless.** A new form of expression that enters biblical narrative in the book of Numbers is prayer. In earlier books there have been depictions of individuals in prayer, but Numbers includes a formal prayer, commanded to be said verbatim by the priests, known as the priestly benediction (6:22–27). This blessing has been pronounced upon the congregation by those of priestly descent presumably from the biblical period until the present day (in some synagogues). It has come to be of special interest recently. While staying in Jerusalem in the summer of 1978, I looked out my window and watched a team of archaeologists working below. They had uncovered Jewish tombs of the Iron Age. I (and they) did not know it then, but inscriptions in thin silver foil that they discovered were later painstakingly unrolled and found to bear the words of the priestly benediction. The silver foil inscriptions are the oldest known texts of a passage from the Bible. (Their wording differs slightly from the biblical text and from each other.)

6:24. **you.** The language of the priestly benediction, like the Decalogue, is formulated in the second-person singular. Although the priests are instructed to bless the

25 May YHWH make His face shine to you
and be gracious to you.

26 May YHWH raise His face to you and
give you peace.

27And they shall set my name on the children of
Israel, and I shall bless them."

7 1And it was on the day that Moses finished
setting up the Tabernacle, and he anointed it
and made it and all its equipment and the altar
and all its equipment holy. He anointed them
and made them holy. 2And Israel's chieftains, the
heads of their fathers' house brought forward—
they were the tribes' chieftains; they were the ones
standing over those who were counted— 3and

25יָאֵ֨ר יְהוָ֧ה ׀ פָּנָ֛יו אֵלֶ֖יךָ וִֽיחֻנֶּֽךָּ׃ ס
26יִשָּׂ֨א יְהוָ֤ה ׀ פָּנָיו֙ אֵלֶ֔יךָ וְיָשֵׂ֥ם לְךָ֖ שָׁלֽוֹם׃ ס
27וְשָׂמ֥וּ אֶת־שְׁמִ֖י עַל־בְּנֵ֣י יִשְׂרָאֵ֑ל וַאֲנִ֖י אֲבָרֲכֵֽם׃ פ
7 1וַיְהִ֡י בְּיוֹם֩ כַּלּ֨וֹת מֹשֶׁ֜ה לְהָקִ֣ים אֶת־הַמִּשְׁכָּ֗ן
וַיִּמְשַׁ֨ח אֹת֜וֹ וַיְקַדֵּ֤שׁ אֹתוֹ֙ וְאֶת־כָּל־כֵּלָ֔יו וְאֶת־
הַמִּזְבֵּ֖חַ וְאֶת־כָּל־כֵּלָ֑יו וַיִּמְשָׁחֵ֖ם וַיְקַדֵּ֥שׁ אֹתָֽם׃
2וַיַּקְרִ֙יבוּ֙ נְשִׂיאֵ֣י יִשְׂרָאֵ֔ל רָאשֵׁ֖י בֵּ֣ית אֲבֹתָ֑ם הֵ֚ם
נְשִׂיאֵ֣י הַמַּטֹּ֔ת הֵ֥ם הָעֹמְדִ֖ים עַל־הַפְּקֻדִֽים׃ 3וַיָּבִ֣יאוּ

---

entire people with it, and although it historically has been pronounced as a congregational blessing, it is both a personal and a communal wish. In three brief lines the priests wish each individual Israelite divine blessing, protection, favor, grace, attention, and peace.

6:26. **and give you peace**. The culminating wish of peace in the priestly benediction is particularly poignant because Numbers is the first book of the Bible so far to concentrate on war. Certainly peace can mean a secure condition for an individual generally rather than being limited to meaning an absence of war, but the issue of war is so much a part of Numbers that the reference to peace in this significant position is nonetheless quite striking. It appears in the beginning section of the book as part of the preparation at Mount Sinai for the journey to come. The people's journey then comes to include substantial doses of reality in the form of confrontations with hostile groups. Israel's only experience of war before this is in the brief account of an attack by the Amalekites shortly after the exodus as the people first approach Horeb (Exod 17:8–16). Indeed, the book of Exodus reports that the reason the Israelites go to the Red Sea on the way out of Egypt instead of taking the more obvious route, overland through Philistine territory, is that YHWH is concerned that they are not yet ready to face war (13:17). When the Egyptian army pursues them, Moses instructs them, "YHWH will fight for you, and you'll keep quiet!" (14:14); and again in the Song of the Sea, it is the deity who is described as a warrior (15:3). Genesis recounts only one battle, in which Abraham becomes involved because of the capture of his nephew Lot (Genesis 14). Leviticus includes no battles, and the word "war" does not occur in it. Deuteronomy, as I shall discuss, treats the subject of war through remarkable legislation but not through narrative other than to refer to the war episodes of Numbers. It is Numbers alone among the Five Books of Moses that especially develops this worst of human conditions through narrative of specific military encounters. And it is Numbers that says, "May YHWH give you peace"!

they brought their offering in front of YHWH: six covered wagons and twelve oxen, a wagon for two chieftains and an ox for each one. And they brought them in front of the Tabernacle.

4And YHWH said to Moses, saying, 5"Take them from them, and they will be for doing the work of the Tent of Meeting. And you shall give them to the Levites, to each man according to his work."

6And Moses took the wagons and the oxen and gave them to the Levites. 7He gave two wagons and four oxen to the sons of Gershon according to their work. 8And he gave four wagons and eight oxen to the sons of Merari according to their work in the hand of Ithamar son of Aaron, the priest. 9And he did not give to the sons of Kohath, because the service of the Holy is their responsibility. They would carry on the shoulder. 10And the chieftains brought forward the altar's dedication offering on the day it was anointed, and the chieftains made their offering in front of the altar.

11And YHWH said to Moses, "One chieftain on a day, one chieftain on the next day, they shall make their offering for the altar's dedication offering."

12And the one who made his offering on the

אֶת־קׇרְבָּנָם לִפְנֵי יְהֹוָה שֵׁשׁ־עֶגְלֹת צָב וּשְׁנֵי עָשָׂר בָּקָר עֲגָלָה עַל־שְׁנֵי הַנְּשִׂאִים וְשׁוֹר לְאֶחָד וַיַּקְרִיבוּ אוֹתָם לִפְנֵי הַמִּשְׁכָּן: 4וַיֹּאמֶר יְהֹוָה אֶל־מֹשֶׁה לֵּאמֹר: 5קַח מֵאִתָּם וְהָיוּ לַעֲבֹד אֶת־עֲבֹדַת אֹהֶל מוֹעֵד וְנָתַתָּה אוֹתָם אֶל־הַלְוִיִּם אִישׁ כְּפִי עֲבֹדָתוֹ: 6וַיִּקַּח מֹשֶׁה אֶת־הָעֲגָלֹת וְאֶת־הַבָּקָר וַיִּתֵּן אוֹתָם אֶל־הַלְוִיִּם: 7אֵת ׀ שְׁתֵּי הָעֲגָלֹת וְאֵת אַרְבַּעַת הַבָּקָר נָתַן לִבְנֵי גֵרְשׁוֹן כְּפִי עֲבֹדָתָם: 8וְאֵת ׀ אַרְבַּע הָעֲגָלֹת וְאֵת שְׁמֹנַת הַבָּקָר נָתַן לִבְנֵי מְרָרִי כְּפִי עֲבֹדָתָם בְּיַד אִיתָמָר בֶּן־אַהֲרֹן הַכֹּהֵן: 9וְלִבְנֵי קְהָת לֹא נָתָן כִּי־עֲבֹדַת הַקֹּדֶשׁ עֲלֵהֶם בַּכָּתֵף יִשָּׂאוּ: 10וַיַּקְרִיבוּ הַנְּשִׂאִים אֵת חֲנֻכַּת הַמִּזְבֵּחַ בְּיוֹם הִמָּשַׁח אֹתוֹ וַיַּקְרִיבוּ הַנְּשִׂיאִם אֶת־קׇרְבָּנָם לִפְנֵי הַמִּזְבֵּחַ: 11וַיֹּאמֶר יְהֹוָה אֶל־מֹשֶׁה נָשִׂיא אֶחָד לַיּוֹם נָשִׂיא אֶחָד לַיּוֹם יַקְרִיבוּ אֶת־קׇרְבָּנָם לַחֲנֻכַּת הַמִּזְבֵּחַ: ס 12וַיְהִי הַמַּקְרִיב בַּיּוֹם הָרִאשׁוֹן אֶת־

7:10. **the altar's dedication offering**. What is the function of this lengthy, repetitive list of the donations that each tribe brings for the dedication? First, it establishes the importance of donations for maintaining the religious establishment. People tend to be cynical about the financial aspect of religious institutions, sometimes with good reason, sometimes mistakenly, and sometimes as a rationalization for declining to contribute. But the services that the institution provides require support from those in the community who can give it. The issue is not the need for donations, but that this need should not be abused. Second, this list conveys that all the people have a share in what goes on at the altar. No tribe is favored. No tribe gets special treatment for giving more than others. And no tribe fails to contribute. Support must come from every part of the community. If there are twelve tribes, then twelve need to contribute. (See the comment on 7:84.) Third, note that the tribe of Levi, which takes charge of the donations, does not itself make a donation. That may seem obvious, but it conveys that the donation of religious leaders is their lifework, and that monetary donations should not be expected of them. They may make such contributions if they choose, but that is an act of generosity beyond what is required.

first day was Nahshon son of Amminadab for the tribe of Judah. 13And his offering was one silver dish, its weight in shekels a hundred thirty; one silver basin, seventy shekels by the shekel of the Holy; both of them were full of fine flour mixed with oil for a grain offering; 14one gold pan, ten shekels, full of incense; 15one bull of the cattle, one ram, one lamb in its first year for a burnt offering; 16one goat for a sin offering; 17and for a peace-offering sacrifice two oxen, five rams, five he-goats, five lambs a year old. This was the offering of Nahshon son of Amminadab.

18On the second day, Nethanel son of Zuar, chieftain of Issachar, brought forward. 19He made his offering: one silver dish, its weight in shekels a hundred thirty; one silver basin, seventy shekels by the shekel of the Holy; both of them were full of fine flour mixed with oil for a grain offering; 20one gold pan, ten shekels, full of incense; 21one bull of the cattle, one ram, one lamb in its first year for a burnt offering; 22one goat for a sin offering; 23and for a peace-offering sacrifice two oxen, five rams, five he-goats, five lambs a year old. This was the offering of Nethanel son of Zuar.

24On the third day, the chieftain of the children of Zebulun, Eliab son of Helon. 25His offering was one silver dish, its weight in shekels a hundred thirty; one silver basin, seventy shekels by the shekel of the Holy; both of them were full of fine flour mixed with oil for a grain offering; 26one gold pan, ten shekels, full of incense; 27one bull of the cattle, one ram, one lamb in its first year for a burnt offering; 28one goat for a sin offering; 29and for a peace-offering sacrifice two oxen, five rams, five he-goats, five lambs a year old. This was the offering of Eliab son of Helon.

30On the fourth day, the chieftain of the children of Reuben, Elizur son of Shedeur. 31His offering was one silver dish, its weight in shekels a hundred thirty; one silver basin, seventy shekels by the shekel of the Holy; both of them were full of fine flour mixed with oil for a grain offering; 32one gold pan, ten shekels, full of incense;

13 וְקָרְבָּנֹו נַחְשֹׁון בֶּן־עַמִּינָדָב לְמַטֵּה יְהוּדָה: וְקָרְבָּנֹו קַעֲרַת־כֶּסֶף אַחַת שְׁלֹשִׁים וּמֵאָה מִשְׁקָלָהּ מִזְרָק אֶחָד כֶּסֶף שִׁבְעִים שֶׁקֶל בְּשֶׁקֶל הַקֹּדֶשׁ שְׁנֵיהֶם ׀ מְלֵאִים סֹלֶת בְּלוּלָה בַשֶּׁמֶן לְמִנְחָה: 14כַּף אַחַת עֲשָׂרָה זָהָב מְלֵאָה קְטֹרֶת: 15פַּר אֶחָד בֶּן־בָּקָר אַיִל אֶחָד כֶּבֶשׂ־אֶחָד בֶּן־שְׁנָתֹו לְעֹלָה: 16שְׂעִיר־עִזִּים אֶחָד לְחַטָּאת: 17וּלְזֶבַח הַשְּׁלָמִים בָּקָר שְׁנַיִם אֵילִם חֲמִשָּׁה עַתּוּדִים חֲמִשָּׁה כְּבָשִׂים בְּנֵי־שָׁנָה חֲמִשָּׁה זֶה קָרְבַּן נַחְשֹׁון בֶּן־עַמִּינָדָב: פ 18בַּיֹּום הַשֵּׁנִי הִקְרִיב נְתַנְאֵל בֶּן־צוּעָר נְשִׂיא יִשָּׂשכָר: 19הִקְרִב אֶת־קָרְבָּנֹו קַעֲרַת־כֶּסֶף אַחַת שְׁלֹשִׁים וּמֵאָה מִשְׁקָלָהּ מִזְרָק אֶחָד כֶּסֶף שִׁבְעִים שֶׁקֶל בְּשֶׁקֶל הַקֹּדֶשׁ שְׁנֵיהֶם ׀ מְלֵאִים סֹלֶת בְּלוּלָה בַשֶּׁמֶן לְמִנְחָה: 20כַּף אַחַת עֲשָׂרָה זָהָב מְלֵאָה קְטֹרֶת: 21פַּר אֶחָד בֶּן־בָּקָר אַיִל אֶחָד כֶּבֶשׂ־אֶחָד בֶּן־שְׁנָתֹו לְעֹלָה: 22שְׂעִיר־עִזִּים אֶחָד לְחַטָּאת: 23וּלְזֶבַח הַשְּׁלָמִים בָּקָר שְׁנַיִם אֵילִם חֲמִשָּׁה עַתּוּדִים חֲמִשָּׁה כְּבָשִׂים בְּנֵי־שָׁנָה חֲמִשָּׁה זֶה קָרְבַּן נְתַנְאֵל בֶּן־צוּעָר: פ 24בַּיֹּום הַשְּׁלִישִׁי נָשִׂיא לִבְנֵי זְבוּלֻן אֱלִיאָב בֶּן־חֵלֹן: 25קָרְבָּנֹו קַעֲרַת־כֶּסֶף אַחַת שְׁלֹשִׁים וּמֵאָה מִשְׁקָלָהּ מִזְרָק אֶחָד כֶּסֶף שִׁבְעִים שֶׁקֶל בְּשֶׁקֶל הַקֹּדֶשׁ שְׁנֵיהֶם ׀ מְלֵאִים סֹלֶת בְּלוּלָה בַשֶּׁמֶן לְמִנְחָה: 26כַּף אַחַת עֲשָׂרָה זָהָב מְלֵאָה קְטֹרֶת: 27פַּר אֶחָד בֶּן־בָּקָר אַיִל אֶחָד כֶּבֶשׂ־אֶחָד בֶּן־שְׁנָתֹו לְעֹלָה: 28שְׂעִיר־עִזִּים אֶחָד לְחַטָּאת: 29וּלְזֶבַח הַשְּׁלָמִים בָּקָר שְׁנַיִם אֵילִם חֲמִשָּׁה עַתֻּדִים חֲמִשָּׁה כְּבָשִׂים בְּנֵי־שָׁנָה חֲמִשָּׁה זֶה קָרְבַּן אֱלִיאָב בֶּן־חֵלֹן: פ 30בַּיֹּום הָרְבִיעִי נָשִׂיא לִבְנֵי רְאוּבֵן אֱלִיצוּר בֶּן־שְׁדֵיאוּר: 31קָרְבָּנֹו קַעֲרַת־כֶּסֶף אַחַת שְׁלֹשִׁים וּמֵאָה מִשְׁקָלָהּ מִזְרָק אֶחָד כֶּסֶף שִׁבְעִים שֶׁקֶל בְּשֶׁקֶל הַקֹּדֶשׁ שְׁנֵיהֶם ׀ מְלֵאִים סֹלֶת בְּלוּלָה בַשֶּׁמֶן לְמִנְחָה: 32כַּף אַחַת עֲשָׂרָה זָהָב מְלֵאָה

33one bull of the cattle, one ram, one lamb in its first year for a burnt offering; 34one goat for a sin offering; 35and for a peace-offering sacrifice two oxen, five rams, five he-goats, five lambs a year old. This was the offering of Elizur son of Shedeur.

36On the fifth day, the chieftain of the children of Simeon, Shelumiel son of Zurishadday. 37His offering was one silver dish, its weight in shekels a hundred thirty; one silver basin, seventy shekels by the shekel of the Holy; both of them were full of fine flour mixed with oil for a grain offering; 38one gold pan, ten shekels, full of incense; 39one bull of the cattle, one ram, one lamb in its first year for a burnt offering; 40one goat for a sin offering; 41and for a peace-offering sacrifice two oxen, five rams, five he-goats, five lambs a year old. This was the offering of Shelumiel son of Zurishadday.

42On the sixth day, the chieftain of the children of Gad, Eliasaph son of Deuel. 43His offering was one silver dish, its weight in shekels a hundred thirty; one silver basin, seventy shekels by the shekel of the Holy; both of them were full of fine flour mixed with oil for a grain offering; 44one gold pan, ten shekels, full of incense; 45one bull of the cattle, one ram, one lamb in its first year for a burnt offering; 46one goat for a sin offering; 47and for a peace-offering sacrifice two oxen, five rams, five he-goats, five lambs a year old. This was the offering of Eliasaph son of Deuel.

48On the seventh day, the chieftain of the children of Ephraim, Elishama son of Ammihud. 49His offering was one silver dish, its weight in shekels a hundred thirty; one silver basin, seventy shekels by the shekel of the Holy; both of them were full of fine flour mixed with oil for a grain offering; 50one gold pan, ten shekels, full of incense; 51one bull of the cattle, one ram, one

33 פַּ֨ר אֶחָ֜ד בֶּן־בָּקָ֗ר אַ֤יִל אֶחָד֙ כֶּ֣בֶשׂ־אֶחָ֔ד בֶּן־שְׁנָת֖וֹ לְעֹלָֽה: 34שְׂעִיר־עִזִּ֥ים אֶחָ֖ד לְחַטָּֽאת: 35וּלְזֶ֣בַח הַשְּׁלָמִים֮ בָּקָ֣ר שְׁנַיִם֒ אֵילִ֤ם חֲמִשָּׁה֙ עַתֻּדִ֣ים חֲמִשָּׁ֔ה כְּבָשִׂ֥ים בְּנֵֽי־שָׁנָ֖ה חֲמִשָּׁ֑ה זֶ֛ה קָרְבַּ֥ן אֱלִיצ֖וּר בֶּן־שְׁדֵיאֽוּר: פ 36בַּיּוֹם֙ הַחֲמִישִׁ֔י נָשִׂ֖יא לִבְנֵ֣י שִׁמְע֑וֹן שְׁלֻֽמִיאֵ֖ל בֶּן־צוּרִֽישַׁדָּֽי: 37קָרְבָּנ֞וֹ קַֽעֲרַת־כֶּ֣סֶף אַחַ֗ת שְׁלֹשִׁ֣ים וּמֵאָה֮ מִשְׁקָלָהּ֒ מִזְרָ֤ק אֶחָד֙ כֶּ֔סֶף שִׁבְעִ֥ים שֶׁ֖קֶל בְּשֶׁ֣קֶל הַקֹּ֑דֶשׁ שְׁנֵיהֶ֣ם ׀ מְלֵאִ֗ים סֹ֛לֶת בְּלוּלָ֥ה בַשֶּׁ֖מֶן לְמִנְחָֽה: 38כַּ֥ף אַחַ֛ת עֲשָׂרָ֥ה זָהָ֖ב מְלֵאָ֥ה קְטֹֽרֶת: 39פַּ֣ר אֶחָ֞ד בֶּן־בָּקָ֗ר אַ֤יִל אֶחָד֙ כֶּֽבֶשׂ־אֶחָ֣ד בֶּן־שְׁנָת֖וֹ לְעֹלָֽה: 40שְׂעִיר־עִזִּ֥ים אֶחָ֖ד לְחַטָּֽאת: 41וּלְזֶ֣בַח הַשְּׁלָמִים֮ בָּקָ֣ר שְׁנַיִם֒ אֵילִ֤ם חֲמִשָּׁה֙ עַתֻּדִ֣ים חֲמִשָּׁ֔ה כְּבָשִׂ֥ים בְּנֵֽי־שָׁנָ֖ה חֲמִשָּׁ֑ה זֶ֛ה קָרְבַּ֥ן שְׁלֻמִיאֵ֖ל בֶּן־צוּרִֽישַׁדָּֽי: פ 42בַּיּוֹם֙ הַשִּׁשִּׁ֔י נָשִׂ֖יא לִבְנֵ֣י גָ֑ד אֶלְיָסָ֖ף בֶּן־דְּעוּאֵֽל: 43קָרְבָּנ֞וֹ קַֽעֲרַת־כֶּ֣סֶף אַחַ֗ת שְׁלֹשִׁ֣ים וּמֵאָה֮ מִשְׁקָלָהּ֒ מִזְרָ֤ק אֶחָד֙ כֶּ֔סֶף שִׁבְעִ֥ים שֶׁ֖קֶל בְּשֶׁ֣קֶל הַקֹּ֑דֶשׁ שְׁנֵיהֶ֣ם ׀ מְלֵאִ֗ים סֹ֛לֶת בְּלוּלָ֥ה בַשֶּׁ֖מֶן לְמִנְחָֽה: 44כַּ֚ף אַחַ֣ת עֲשָׂרָ֣ה זָהָ֔ב מְלֵאָ֖ה קְטֹֽרֶת: 45פַּ֣ר אֶחָ֞ד בֶּן־בָּקָ֗ר אַ֤יִל אֶחָד֙ כֶּֽבֶשׂ־אֶחָ֛ד בֶּן־שְׁנָת֖וֹ לְעֹלָֽה: 46שְׂעִיר־עִזִּ֥ים אֶחָ֖ד לְחַטָּֽאת: 47וּלְזֶ֣בַח הַשְּׁלָמִים֮ בָּקָ֣ר שְׁנַיִם֒ אֵילִ֤ם חֲמִשָּׁה֙ עַתֻּדִ֣ים חֲמִשָּׁ֔ה כְּבָשִׂ֥ים בְּנֵֽי־שָׁנָ֖ה חֲמִשָּׁ֑ה זֶ֛ה קָרְבַּ֥ן אֶלְיָסָ֖ף בֶּן־דְּעוּאֵֽל: פ 48בַּיּוֹם֙ הַשְּׁבִיעִ֔י נָשִׂ֖יא לִבְנֵ֣י אֶפְרָ֑יִם אֱלִֽישָׁמָ֖ע בֶּן־עַמִּיהֽוּד: 49קָרְבָּנ֞וֹ קַֽעֲרַת־כֶּ֣סֶף אַחַ֗ת שְׁלֹשִׁ֣ים וּמֵאָה֮ מִשְׁקָלָהּ֒ מִזְרָ֤ק אֶחָד֙ כֶּ֔סֶף שִׁבְעִ֥ים שֶׁ֖קֶל בְּשֶׁ֣קֶל הַקֹּ֑דֶשׁ שְׁנֵיהֶ֣ם ׀ מְלֵאִ֗ים סֹ֛לֶת בְּלוּלָ֥ה בַשֶּׁ֖מֶן לְמִנְחָֽה: 50כַּ֚ף אַחַ֣ת עֲשָׂרָ֣ה זָהָ֔ב מְלֵאָ֖ה קְטֹֽרֶת: 51פַּ֣ר אֶחָ֞ד בֶּן־

7:42. **Deuel**. The Greek (Septuagint) reads Reuel, as does the Hebrew (Masoretic Text) above (Num 2:14). The letters *r* (*resh*) and *d* (*dalet*) looked similar in ancient Hebrew script (and in the script down to our own times), and scribes occasionally confused them.

lamb in its first year for a burnt offering; 52one goat for a sin offering; 53and for a peace-offering sacrifice two oxen, five rams, five he-goats, five lambs a year old. This was the offering of Elishama son of Ammihud.

54On the eighth day, the chieftain of the children of Manasseh, Gamaliel son of Pedahzur. 55His offering was one silver dish, its weight in shekels a hundred thirty; one silver basin, seventy shekels by the shekel of the Holy; both of them were full of fine flour mixed with oil for a grain offering; 56one gold pan, ten shekels, full of incense; 57one bull of the cattle, one ram, one lamb in its first year for a burnt offering; 58one goat for a sin offering; 59and for a peace-offering sacrifice two oxen, five rams, five he-goats, five lambs a year old. This was the offering of Gamaliel son of Pedahzur.

60On the ninth day, the chieftain of the children of Benjamin, Abidan son of Gideoni. 61His offering was one silver dish, its weight in shekels a hundred thirty; one silver basin, seventy shekels by the shekel of the Holy; both of them were full of fine flour mixed with oil for a grain offering; 62one gold pan, ten shekels, full of incense; 63one bull of the cattle, one ram, one lamb in its first year for a burnt offering; 64one goat for a sin offering; 65and for a peace-offering sacrifice two oxen, five rams, five he-goats, five lambs a year old. This was the offering of Abidan son of Gideoni.

66On the tenth day, the chieftain of the children of Dan, Ahiezer son of Ammishadday. 67His offering was one silver dish, its weight in shekels a hundred thirty; one silver basin, seventy shekels by the shekel of the Holy; both of them were full of fine flour mixed with oil for a grain offering; 68one gold pan, ten shekels, full of incense; 69one bull of the cattle, one ram, one lamb in its first year for a burnt offering; 70one goat for a sin offering; 71and for a peace-offering sacrifice two oxen, five rams, five he-goats, five lambs a year old. This was the offering of Ahiezer son of Ammishadday.

בָּקָר אַיִל אֶחָד כֶּבֶשׂ־אֶחָד בֶּן־שְׁנָתוֹ לְעֹלָה: 52שְׂעִיר־עִזִּים אֶחָד לְחַטָּאת: 53וּלְזֶבַח הַשְּׁלָמִים בָּקָר שְׁנַיִם אֵילִם חֲמִשָּׁה עַתֻּדִים חֲמִשָּׁה כְּבָשִׂים בְּנֵי־שָׁנָה חֲמִשָּׁה זֶה קָרְבַּן אֱלִישָׁמָע בֶּן־עַמִּיהוּד: פ 54בַּיּוֹם הַשְּׁמִינִי נָשִׂיא לִבְנֵי מְנַשֶּׁה גַּמְלִיאֵל בֶּן־פְּדָהצוּר: 55קָרְבָּנוֹ קַעֲרַת־כֶּסֶף אַחַת שְׁלֹשִׁים וּמֵאָה מִשְׁקָלָהּ מִזְרָק אֶחָד כֶּסֶף שִׁבְעִים שֶׁקֶל בְּשֶׁקֶל הַקֹּדֶשׁ שְׁנֵיהֶם ׀ מְלֵאִים סֹלֶת בְּלוּלָה בַשֶּׁמֶן לְמִנְחָה: 56כַּף אַחַת עֲשָׂרָה זָהָב מְלֵאָה קְטֹרֶת: 57פַּר אֶחָד בֶּן־בָּקָר אַיִל אֶחָד כֶּבֶשׂ־אֶחָד בֶּן־שְׁנָתוֹ לְעֹלָה: 58שְׂעִיר־עִזִּים אֶחָד לְחַטָּאת: 59וּלְזֶבַח הַשְּׁלָמִים בָּקָר שְׁנַיִם אֵילִם חֲמִשָּׁה עַתֻּדִים חֲמִשָּׁה כְּבָשִׂים בְּנֵי־שָׁנָה חֲמִשָּׁה זֶה קָרְבַּן גַּמְלִיאֵל בֶּן־פְּדָהצוּר: פ 60בַּיּוֹם הַתְּשִׁיעִי נָשִׂיא לִבְנֵי בִנְיָמִן אֲבִידָן בֶּן־גִּדְעֹנִי: 61קָרְבָּנוֹ קַעֲרַת־כֶּסֶף אַחַת שְׁלֹשִׁים וּמֵאָה מִשְׁקָלָהּ מִזְרָק אֶחָד כֶּסֶף שִׁבְעִים שֶׁקֶל בְּשֶׁקֶל הַקֹּדֶשׁ שְׁנֵיהֶם ׀ מְלֵאִים סֹלֶת בְּלוּלָה בַשֶּׁמֶן לְמִנְחָה: 62כַּף אַחַת עֲשָׂרָה זָהָב מְלֵאָה קְטֹרֶת: 63פַּר אֶחָד בֶּן־בָּקָר אַיִל אֶחָד כֶּבֶשׂ־אֶחָד בֶּן־שְׁנָתוֹ לְעֹלָה: 64שְׂעִיר־עִזִּים אֶחָד לְחַטָּאת: 65וּלְזֶבַח הַשְּׁלָמִים בָּקָר שְׁנַיִם אֵילִם חֲמִשָּׁה עַתֻּדִים חֲמִשָּׁה כְּבָשִׂים בְּנֵי־שָׁנָה חֲמִשָּׁה זֶה קָרְבַּן אֲבִידָן בֶּן־גִּדְעֹנִי: פ 66בַּיּוֹם הָעֲשִׂירִי נָשִׂיא לִבְנֵי דָן אֲחִיעֶזֶר בֶּן־עַמִּישַׁדָּי: 67קָרְבָּנוֹ קַעֲרַת־כֶּסֶף אַחַת שְׁלֹשִׁים וּמֵאָה מִשְׁקָלָהּ מִזְרָק אֶחָד כֶּסֶף שִׁבְעִים שֶׁקֶל בְּשֶׁקֶל הַקֹּדֶשׁ שְׁנֵיהֶם ׀ מְלֵאִים סֹלֶת בְּלוּלָה בַשֶּׁמֶן לְמִנְחָה: 68כַּף אַחַת עֲשָׂרָה זָהָב מְלֵאָה קְטֹרֶת: 69פַּר אֶחָד בֶּן־בָּקָר אַיִל אֶחָד כֶּבֶשׂ־אֶחָד בֶּן־שְׁנָתוֹ לְעֹלָה: 70שְׂעִיר־עִזִּים אֶחָד לְחַטָּאת: 71וּלְזֶבַח הַשְּׁלָמִים בָּקָר שְׁנַיִם אֵילִם חֲמִשָּׁה עַתֻּדִים חֲמִשָּׁה כְּבָשִׂים בְּנֵי־שָׁנָה חֲמִשָּׁה זֶה קָרְבַּן אֲחִיעֶזֶר

72On the eleventh day, the chieftain of the children of Asher, Pagiel son of Ochran. 73His offering was one silver dish, its weight in shekels a hundred thirty; one silver basin, seventy shekels by the shekel of the Holy; both of them were full of fine flour mixed with oil for a grain offering; 74one gold pan, ten shekels, full of incense; 75one bull of the cattle, one ram, one lamb in its first year for a burnt offering; 76one goat for a sin offering; 77and for a peace-offering sacrifice two oxen, five rams, five he-goats, five lambs a year old. This was the offering of Pagiel son of Ochran.

78On the twelfth day, the chieftain of the children of Naphtali, Ahira son of Enan. 79His offering was one silver dish, its weight in shekels a hundred thirty; one silver basin, seventy shekels by the shekel of the Holy; both of them were full of fine flour mixed with oil for a grain offering; 80one gold pan, ten shekels, full of incense; 81one bull of the cattle, one ram, one lamb in its first year for a burnt offering; 82one goat for a sin offering; 83and for a peace-offering sacrifice two oxen, five rams, five he-goats, five lambs a year old. This was the offering of Ahira son of Enan.

84This was the dedication offering of the altar from Israel's chieftains on the day of its being anointed: Twelve silver dishes, twelve silver basins, twelve gold pans, 85each dish being a hundred thirty of silver, and each basin seventy; all the silver of the items was two thousand four hundred by the shekel of the Holy. 86Twelve gold pans full of incense, the pans being ten each by the shekel of the Holy; all the gold of the pans was a hundred twenty. 87All the oxen for the burnt offering were twelve bulls, twelve rams, twelve lambs a year old and their grain offering and twelve goats for a sin offering. 88And all the

בֶּן־עַמִּישַׁדָּֽי: פ 72בְּיוֹם֙ עַשְׁתֵּ֣י עָשָׂ֣ר י֔וֹם נָשִׂ֖יא לִבְנֵ֣י אָשֵׁ֑ר פַּגְעִיאֵ֖ל בֶּן־עָכְרָֽן: 73קָרְבָּנ֞וֹ קַֽעֲרַת־כֶּ֣סֶף אַחַ֗ת שְׁלֹשִׁ֣ים וּמֵאָה֮ מִשְׁקָלָהּ֒ מִזְרָ֤ק אֶחָד֙ כֶּ֔סֶף שִׁבְעִ֥ים שֶׁ֖קֶל בְּשֶׁ֣קֶל הַקֹּ֑דֶשׁ שְׁנֵיהֶ֣ם ׀ מְלֵאִ֗ים סֹ֛לֶת בְּלוּלָ֥ה בַשֶּׁ֖מֶן לְמִנְחָֽה: 74כַּ֥ף אַחַ֛ת עֲשָׂרָ֥ה זָהָ֖ב מְלֵאָ֥ה קְטֹֽרֶת: 75פַּ֣ר אֶחָ֞ד בֶּן־בָּקָ֗ר אַ֧יִל אֶחָ֛ד כֶּֽבֶשׂ־אֶחָ֥ד בֶּן־שְׁנָת֖וֹ לְעֹלָֽה: 76שְׂעִיר־עִזִּ֥ים אֶחָ֖ד לְחַטָּֽאת: 77וּלְזֶ֣בַח הַשְּׁלָמִים֮ בָּקָ֣ר שְׁנַ֒יִם֒ אֵילִ֤ם חֲמִשָּׁה֙ עַתֻּדִ֣ים חֲמִשָּׁ֔ה כְּבָשִׂ֥ים בְּנֵֽי־שָׁנָ֖ה חֲמִשָּׁ֑ה זֶ֛ה קָרְבַּ֥ן פַּגְעִיאֵ֖ל בֶּן־עָכְרָֽן: פ 78בְּיוֹם֙ שְׁנֵ֣ים עָשָׂ֣ר י֔וֹם נָשִׂ֖יא לִבְנֵ֣י נַפְתָּלִ֑י אֲחִירַ֖ע בֶּן־עֵינָֽן: 79קָרְבָּנ֞וֹ קַֽעֲרַת־כֶּ֣סֶף אַחַ֗ת שְׁלֹשִׁ֣ים וּמֵאָה֮ מִשְׁקָלָהּ֒ מִזְרָ֤ק אֶחָד֙ כֶּ֔סֶף שִׁבְעִ֥ים שֶׁ֖קֶל בְּשֶׁ֣קֶל הַקֹּ֑דֶשׁ שְׁנֵיהֶ֣ם ׀ מְלֵאִ֗ים סֹ֛לֶת בְּלוּלָ֥ה בַשֶּׁ֖מֶן לְמִנְחָֽה: 80כַּ֥ף אַחַ֛ת עֲשָׂרָ֥ה זָהָ֖ב מְלֵאָ֥ה קְטֹֽרֶת: 81פַּ֣ר אֶחָ֞ד בֶּן־בָּקָ֗ר אַ֧יִל אֶחָ֛ד כֶּֽבֶשׂ־אֶחָ֥ד בֶּן־שְׁנָת֖וֹ לְעֹלָֽה: 82שְׂעִיר־עִזִּ֥ים אֶחָ֖ד לְחַטָּֽאת: 83וּלְזֶ֣בַח הַשְּׁלָמִים֮ בָּקָ֣ר שְׁנַ֒יִם֒ אֵילִ֤ם חֲמִשָּׁה֙ עַתֻּדִ֣ים חֲמִשָּׁ֔ה כְּבָשִׂ֥ים בְּנֵֽי־שָׁנָ֖ה חֲמִשָּׁ֑ה זֶ֛ה קָרְבַּ֥ן אֲחִירַ֖ע בֶּן־עֵינָֽן: פ 84זֹ֣את ׀ חֲנֻכַּ֣ת הַמִּזְבֵּ֗חַ בְּיוֹם֙ הִמָּשַׁ֣ח אֹת֔וֹ מֵאֵ֖ת נְשִׂיאֵ֣י יִשְׂרָאֵ֑ל קַֽעֲרֹ֨ת כֶּ֜סֶף שְׁתֵּ֣ים עֶשְׂרֵ֗ה מִֽזְרְקֵי־כֶ֙סֶף֙ שְׁנֵ֣ים עָשָׂ֔ר כַּפּ֥וֹת זָהָ֖ב שְׁתֵּ֥ים עֶשְׂרֵֽה: 85שְׁלֹשִׁ֣ים וּמֵאָ֗ה הַקְּעָרָ֤ה הָֽאַחַת֙ כֶּ֔סֶף וְשִׁבְעִ֖ים הַמִּזְרָ֣ק הָֽאֶחָ֑ד כֹּ֚ל כֶּ֣סֶף הַכֵּלִ֔ים אַלְפַּ֥יִם וְאַרְבַּע־מֵא֖וֹת בְּשֶׁ֥קֶל הַקֹּֽדֶשׁ: 86כַּפּ֨וֹת זָהָ֤ב שְׁתֵּים־עֶשְׂרֵה֙ מְלֵאֹ֣ת קְטֹ֔רֶת עֲשָׂרָ֧ה עֲשָׂרָ֛ה הַכַּ֖ף בְּשֶׁ֣קֶל הַקֹּ֑דֶשׁ כָּל־זְהַ֥ב הַכַּפּ֖וֹת עֶשְׂרִ֥ים וּמֵאָֽה: 87כָּל־הַבָּקָ֨ר לָעֹלָ֜ה שְׁנֵ֧ים עָשָׂ֣ר פָּרִ֗ים אֵילִ֤ם שְׁנֵים־עָשָׂר֙ כְּבָשִׂ֧ים בְּנֵֽי־שָׁנָ֛ה שְׁנֵ֥ים עָשָׂ֖ר וּמִנְחָתָ֑ם וּשְׂעִירֵ֥י עִזִּ֛ים שְׁנֵ֥ים עָשָׂ֖ר

7:84. **from Israel's chieftains**. Why does the text have to repeat the detailed list of offerings from each of the twelve chieftains, when all their offerings are exactly, word for word, the same? It is notable that earlier the text gave detailed records of the number of persons in each tribe. Now we learn that, even though the tribes are all different sizes, their chieftains all bring the same offering. It would appear to establish that all the tribes, whether large or small in population, are equal.

oxen of the peace-offering sacrifice were twenty-four bulls, sixty rams, sixty he-goats, sixty lambs a year old. This was the dedication offering of the altar after its being anointed.

89And when Moses came into the Tent of Meeting to speak with Him, then he heard the voice speaking to him from above the atonement dais that was on the Ark of the Testimony, from between the two cherubs, and He spoke to him.

WHEN YOU PUT UP

8 1And YHWH spoke to Moses, saying, 2"Speak to Aaron, and you shall say to him: 'When you put up the lamps, the seven lamps shall shed light opposite the front of the menorah.'" 3And Aaron did so. He put up its lamps opposite the front of the menorah as YHWH had commanded Moses. 4And this was the menorah's construction: hammered work of gold; including its shaft, including its flower, it was hammered work. According to the appearance that YHWH had shown Moses, so he made the menorah.

5And YHWH spoke to Moses, saying, 6"Take the Levites from among the children of Israel, and make them pure. 7And this is what you shall do to them to make them pure: you shall sprinkle water of sin expiation on them, and they shall pass a razor over all of their flesh, and they shall wash their clothes, and so they will be made pure. 8And they shall take a bull of the cattle and its grain offering, fine flour mixed with oil; and you shall take a second bull of the cattle for a sin offering. 9And you shall bring the Levites forward in front of the Tent of Meeting, and you shall assemble all of the congregation of the children of Israel. 10And you shall bring the Levites forward in front of YHWH, and the children of Israel shall lay their hands on the Levites.

לְחַטָּאת: 88וְכֹל בְּקַר ׀ זֶבַח הַשְּׁלָמִים עֶשְׂרִים וְאַרְבָּעָה פָּרִים אֵילִם שִׁשִּׁים עַתֻּדִים שִׁשִּׁים כְּבָשִׂים בְּנֵי־שָׁנָה שִׁשִּׁים זֹאת חֲנֻכַּת הַמִּזְבֵּחַ אַחֲרֵי הִמָּשַׁח אֹתוֹ: 89וּבְבֹא מֹשֶׁה אֶל־אֹהֶל מוֹעֵד לְדַבֵּר אִתּוֹ וַיִּשְׁמַע אֶת־הַקּוֹל מִדַּבֵּר אֵלָיו מֵעַל הַכַּפֹּרֶת אֲשֶׁר עַל־אֲרֹן הָעֵדֻת מִבֵּין שְׁנֵי הַכְּרֻבִים וַיְדַבֵּר אֵלָיו: פ

בהעלתך

8 1וַיְדַבֵּר יְהוָה אֶל־מֹשֶׁה לֵּאמֹר: 2דַּבֵּר אֶל־אַהֲרֹן וְאָמַרְתָּ אֵלָיו בְּהַעֲלֹתְךָ אֶת־הַנֵּרֹת אֶל־מוּל פְּנֵי הַמְּנוֹרָה יָאִירוּ שִׁבְעַת הַנֵּרוֹת: 3וַיַּעַשׂ כֵּן אַהֲרֹן אֶל־מוּל פְּנֵי הַמְּנוֹרָה הֶעֱלָה נֵרֹתֶיהָ כַּאֲשֶׁר צִוָּה יְהוָה אֶת־מֹשֶׁה: 4וְזֶה מַעֲשֵׂה הַמְּנֹרָה מִקְשָׁה זָהָב עַד־יְרֵכָהּ עַד־פִּרְחָהּ מִקְשָׁה הִוא כַּמַּרְאֶה אֲשֶׁר הֶרְאָה יְהוָה אֶת־מֹשֶׁה כֵּן עָשָׂה אֶת־הַמְּנֹרָה: פ

5וַיְדַבֵּר יְהוָה אֶל־מֹשֶׁה לֵּאמֹר: 6קַח אֶת־הַלְוִיִּם מִתּוֹךְ בְּנֵי יִשְׂרָאֵל וְטִהַרְתָּ אֹתָם: 7וְכֹה־תַעֲשֶׂה לָהֶם לְטַהֲרָם הַזֵּה עֲלֵיהֶם מֵי חַטָּאת וְהֶעֱבִירוּ תַעַר עַל־כָּל־בְּשָׂרָם וְכִבְּסוּ בִגְדֵיהֶם וְהִטֶּהָרוּ: 8וְלָקְחוּ פַּר בֶּן־בָּקָר וּמִנְחָתוֹ סֹלֶת בְּלוּלָה בַשָּׁמֶן וּפַר־שֵׁנִי בֶן־בָּקָר תִּקַּח לְחַטָּאת: 9וְהִקְרַבְתָּ אֶת־הַלְוִיִּם לִפְנֵי אֹהֶל מוֹעֵד וְהִקְהַלְתָּ אֶת־כָּל־עֲדַת בְּנֵי יִשְׂרָאֵל: 10וְהִקְרַבְתָּ אֶת־הַלְוִיִּם לִפְנֵי יְהוָה וְסָמְכוּ בְנֵי־יִשְׂרָאֵל אֶת־יְדֵיהֶם עַל־

8:7. water of sin expiation. The nature and preparation of water of sin expiation are described in Num 19:1–9.

11And Aaron shall make the Levites an elevation offering in front of YHWH from the children of Israel, and they shall be to do YHWH's service. 12And the Levites shall lay their hands on the bulls' heads. And make one a sin offering and one a burnt offering for YHWH to make atonement for the Levites. 13And you shall stand the Levites in front of Aaron and in front of his sons and make them an elevation offering for YHWH. 14And you shall distinguish the Levites from among the children of Israel, and the Levites shall be mine. 15And after that the Levites shall come to work at the Tent of Meeting, when you have made them pure and made them an elevation offering. 16Because they are given, *given*, to me from among the children of Israel. I have taken them to me in place of the first birth of every womb, the firstborn of everyone from the children of Israel. 17Because every firstborn of the children Israel is mine, of human and of animal; on the day that I struck every firstborn in the land of Egypt I consecrated them to me. 18And I took the Levites in place of every firstborn of the children of Israel 19and gave the Levites—they are given—to Aaron and to his sons from among the children of Israel to do the work of the children of Israel in the Tent of Meeting and to make atonement for the children of Israel, so there will not be a plague in the children of Israel when the children of Israel would come near to the Holy."

20And Moses and Aaron and all the congregation of the children of Israel did to the Levites according to all that YHWH commanded Moses about the Levites; the children of Israel did so to them. 21And the Levites did sin expiation and

הַלְוִיִּם: 11וְהֵנִיף֩ אַהֲרֹ֨ן אֶת־הַלְוִיִּ֤ם תְּנוּפָה֙ לִפְנֵ֣י יְהֹוָ֔ה מֵאֵ֖ת בְּנֵ֣י יִשְׂרָאֵ֑ל וְהָי֕וּ לַעֲבֹ֖ד אֶת־עֲבֹדַ֥ת יְהֹוָֽה: 12וְהַלְוִיִּם֙ יִסְמְכ֣וּ אֶת־יְדֵיהֶ֔ם עַ֖ל רֹ֣אשׁ הַפָּרִ֑ים וַ֠עֲשֵׂה אֶת־הָאֶחָ֨ד חַטָּ֜את וְאֶת־הָאֶחָ֤ד עֹלָה֙ לַֽיהֹוָ֔ה לְכַפֵּ֖ר עַל־הַלְוִיִּֽם: 13וְהַעֲמַדְתָּ֙ אֶת־הַלְוִיִּ֔ם לִפְנֵ֥י אַהֲרֹ֖ן וְלִפְנֵ֣י בָנָ֑יו וְהֵנַפְתָּ֥ אֹתָ֛ם תְּנוּפָ֖ה לַֽיהֹוָֽה: 14וְהִבְדַּלְתָּ֙ אֶת־הַלְוִיִּ֔ם מִתּ֖וֹךְ בְּנֵ֣י יִשְׂרָאֵ֑ל וְהָ֥יוּ לִ֖י הַלְוִיִּֽם: 15וְאַֽחֲרֵי־כֵ֗ן יָבֹ֙אוּ֙ הַלְוִיִּ֔ם לַעֲבֹ֖ד אֶת־אֹ֣הֶל מוֹעֵ֑ד וְטִֽהַרְתָּ֣ אֹתָ֔ם וְהֵנַפְתָּ֥ אֹתָ֖ם תְּנוּפָֽה: 16כִּי֩ נְתֻנִ֨ים נְתֻנִ֥ים הֵ֙מָּה֙ לִ֔י מִתּ֖וֹךְ בְּנֵ֣י יִשְׂרָאֵ֑ל תַּ֣חַת פִּטְרַ֣ת כָּל־רֶ֗חֶם בְּכ֨וֹר כֹּ֜ל מִבְּנֵ֤י יִשְׂרָאֵל֙ לָקַ֥חְתִּי אֹתָ֖ם לִֽי: 17כִּ֣י לִ֤י כָל־בְּכוֹר֙ בִּבְנֵ֣י יִשְׂרָאֵ֔ל בָּאָדָ֖ם וּבַבְּהֵמָ֑ה בְּי֗וֹם הַכֹּתִ֤י כָל־בְּכוֹר֙ בְּאֶ֣רֶץ מִצְרַ֔יִם הִקְדַּ֥שְׁתִּי אֹתָ֖ם לִֽי: 18וָאֶקַּ֖ח אֶת־הַלְוִיִּ֑ם תַּ֥חַת כָּל־בְּכ֖וֹר בִּבְנֵ֥י יִשְׂרָאֵֽל: 19וָאֶתְּנָ֨ה אֶת־הַלְוִיִּ֜ם נְתֻנִ֣ים ׀ לְאַהֲרֹ֣ן וּלְבָנָ֗יו מִתּוֹךְ֮ בְּנֵ֣י יִשְׂרָאֵל֒ לַעֲבֹ֞ד אֶת־עֲבֹדַ֤ת בְּנֵֽי־יִשְׂרָאֵל֙ בְּאֹ֣הֶל מוֹעֵ֔ד וּלְכַפֵּ֖ר עַל־בְּנֵ֣י יִשְׂרָאֵ֑ל וְלֹ֨א יִהְיֶ֜ה בִּבְנֵ֤י יִשְׂרָאֵל֙ נֶ֔גֶף בְּגֶ֥שֶׁת בְּנֵֽי־יִשְׂרָאֵ֖ל אֶל־הַקֹּֽדֶשׁ: 20וַיַּ֣עַשׂ מֹשֶׁ֣ה וְאַהֲרֹ֣ן וְכָל־עֲדַ֣ת בְּנֵֽי־יִשְׂרָאֵל֩ לַלְוִיִּ֨ם כְּ֠כֹל אֲשֶׁר־צִוָּ֨ה יְהֹוָ֤ה אֶת־מֹשֶׁה֙ לַלְוִיִּ֔ם כֵּן־עָשׂ֥וּ לָהֶ֖ם בְּנֵ֥י יִשְׂרָאֵֽל: 21וַיִּֽתְחַטְּא֣וּ

8:19. **plague.** Only Levites come near to the holy zone at the Tabernacle. This notice that a plague would occur if the children of Israel would come near to the Holy proves to be disastrously true later in the account of Phinehas, in which an encroachment on the *qubbāh*, the inside of the Tabernacle, is associated with a plague that kills thousands (Num 25:8–9).

8:21. **the Levites did sin expiation.** Meaning: they used the water of sin expiation. See the comment on 8:7.

washed their clothes, and Aaron made them an elevation offering in front of YHWH, and Aaron made atonement for them to make them pure. ²²And after that the Levites came to do their work in the Tent of Meeting in front of Aaron and in front of his sons. As YHWH commanded Moses about the Levites, so they did to them.

²³And YHWH spoke to Moses, saying, ²⁴"This is what the Levites have: from twenty-five years old and up each shall come to do army service by the work of the Tent of Meeting; ²⁵and from fifty years old he shall go back from the army service and shall not work anymore; ²⁶and he shall minister with his brothers in the Tent of Meeting to keep the charge, but he shall not do work. You shall do thus to the Levites regarding their charge."

9 ¹And YHWH had spoken to Moses in the wilderness of Sinai in the second year of their exodus from the land of Egypt, in the first month, saying, ²"And the children of Israel shall do the Passover at its appointed time. ³On the fourteenth day in this month 'between the two evenings' you shall do it at its appointed time. You shall do it according to all of its law and according to all of its judgments."

⁴And Moses had spoken to the children of Israel to do the Passover, ⁵and they had done the Passover in the first month on the fourteenth day

הַלְוִיִּם וַיְכַבְּסוּ בִּגְדֵיהֶם וַיָּנֶף אַהֲרֹן אֹתָם תְּנוּפָה לִפְנֵי יְהוָה וַיְכַפֵּר עֲלֵיהֶם אַהֲרֹן לְטַהֲרָם: ²²וְאַחֲרֵי־כֵן בָּאוּ הַלְוִיִּם לַעֲבֹד אֶת־עֲבֹדָתָם בְּאֹהֶל מוֹעֵד לִפְנֵי אַהֲרֹן וְלִפְנֵי בָנָיו כַּאֲשֶׁר צִוָּה יְהוָה אֶת־מֹשֶׁה עַל־הַלְוִיִּם כֵּן עָשׂוּ לָהֶם: ס ²³וַיְדַבֵּר יְהוָה אֶל־מֹשֶׁה לֵּאמֹר: ²⁴זֹאת אֲשֶׁר לַלְוִיִּם מִבֶּן חָמֵשׁ וְעֶשְׂרִים שָׁנָה וָמַעְלָה יָבוֹא לִצְבֹא צָבָא בַּעֲבֹדַת אֹהֶל מוֹעֵד: ²⁵וּמִבֶּן חֲמִשִּׁים שָׁנָה יָשׁוּב מִצְּבָא הָעֲבֹדָה וְלֹא יַעֲבֹד עוֹד: ²⁶וְשֵׁרֵת אֶת־אֶחָיו בְּאֹהֶל מוֹעֵד לִשְׁמֹר מִשְׁמֶרֶת וַעֲבֹדָה לֹא יַעֲבֹד כָּכָה תַּעֲשֶׂה לַלְוִיִּם בְּמִשְׁמְרֹתָם: פ

9 ¹וַיְדַבֵּר יְהוָה אֶל־מֹשֶׁה בְמִדְבַּר־סִינַי בַּשָּׁנָה הַשֵּׁנִית לְצֵאתָם מֵאֶרֶץ מִצְרַיִם בַּחֹדֶשׁ הָרִאשׁוֹן לֵאמֹר: ²וְיַעֲשׂוּ בְנֵי־יִשְׂרָאֵל אֶת־הַפָּסַח בְּמוֹעֲדוֹ: ³בְּאַרְבָּעָה עָשָׂר־יוֹם בַּחֹדֶשׁ הַזֶּה בֵּין הָעַרְבַּיִם תַּעֲשׂוּ אֹתוֹ בְּמוֹעֲדוֹ כְּכָל־חֻקֹּתָיו וּכְכָל־מִשְׁפָּטָיו תַּעֲשׂוּ אֹתוֹ: ⁴וַיְדַבֵּר מֹשֶׁה אֶל־בְּנֵי יִשְׂרָאֵל לַעֲשֹׂת הַפָּסַח: ⁵וַיַּעֲשׂוּ אֶת־הַפֶּסַח בָּרִאשׁוֹן בְּאַרְבָּעָה עָשָׂר

9:1. **had spoken**. This is a rare occurrence in the Torah: telling an event out of order. The book of Numbers begins with God speaking to Moses in the second month of the year. Now it tells of God speaking to Moses back in the first month of the year. Why? Because it tells of a case in which some people had been unable to observe Passover, which falls in the first month, and so God tells Moses in this flashback that the law in that situation is that they should observe Passover one month later, on the evening of the fourteenth day of the second month. Their observance on that date thus belongs here in the sequence of the narrative. The flashback is placed here to explain it. The point is that the Torah adheres to chronological order in its story, and exceptional breaks in that pattern such as this one occur very rarely and for specific narrative purposes.

9:3. **between the two evenings**. Understood to mean the early evening hours: "dusk" or "twilight." (The Hebrew has the dual ending, which produces the meaning of being between two evenings.)

454

of the month "between the two evenings" in the wilderness of Sinai. According to all that YHWH had commanded Moses, so the children of Israel had done.

6And there had been people who were impure by a human being and so had not been able to do the Passover on that day, and they had come forward in front of Moses and in front of Aaron on that day, 7and those people had said to him, "We're impure by a human being. Why should we be excluded so as not to make YHWH's offering at its appointed time among the children of Israel?"

8And Moses had said, "Stay, and let me hear what YHWH will command about you."

9And YHWH had spoken to Moses, saying, 10"Speak to the children of Israel, saying: Any man who will be impure by a person or on a far-away journey—among you or through your generations—and will do the Passover for YHWH, 11they shall do it in the second month on the fourteenth day 'between the two evenings.' They shall eat it with unleavened bread and bitter herbs. 12They shall not leave any of it until morning, and they shall not break a bone of it. They shall do it according to all of the law of the Passover. 13But a man who is pure and has not been on a journey and has failed to do the Passover: that person will be cut off from his people, because he did not make YHWH's offering at its appointed time. That man shall bear his sin. 14And if an alien will reside with you and will do the Passover for YHWH: according to the law of the Passover and according to its required manner, so he shall do it. You shall have one law, for the alien and for the citizen of the land."

15And on the day that the Tabernacle was set

יֹ֣ום לַחֹ֗דֶשׁ בֵּ֣ין הָעַרְבַּ֛יִם בְּמִדְבַּ֥ר סִינָ֖י כְּכֹ֥ל אֲשֶׁ֨ר צִוָּ֤ה יְהוָה֙ אֶת־מֹשֶׁ֔ה כֵּ֥ן עָשׂ֖וּ בְּנֵ֥י יִשְׂרָאֵֽל׃ 6וַיְהִ֣י אֲנָשִׁ֗ים אֲשֶׁ֨ר הָי֤וּ טְמֵאִים֙ לְנֶ֣פֶשׁ אָדָ֔ם וְלֹא־יָכְל֥וּ לַעֲשֹׂת־הַפֶּ֖סַח בַּיֹּ֣ום הַה֑וּא וַֽיִּקְרְב֞וּ לִפְנֵ֥י מֹשֶׁ֛ה וְלִפְנֵ֥י אַהֲרֹ֖ן בַּיֹּ֥ום הַהֽוּא׃ 7וַ֠יֹּאמְרוּ הָאֲנָשִׁ֤ים הָהֵ֨מָּה֙ אֵלָ֔יו אֲנַ֥חְנוּ טְמֵאִ֖ים לְנֶ֣פֶשׁ אָדָ֑ם לָ֣מָּה נִגָּרַ֗ע לְבִלְתִּ֡י הַקְרִ֣ב אֶת־קָרְבַּן֩ יְהוָ֨ה בְּמֹעֲדֹ֜ו בְּתֹ֖וךְ בְּנֵ֥י יִשְׂרָאֵֽל׃ 8וַיֹּ֥אמֶר אֲלֵהֶ֖ם מֹשֶׁ֑ה עִמְד֣וּ וְאֶשְׁמְעָ֔ה מַה־יְצַוֶּ֥ה יְהוָ֖ה לָכֶֽם׃ פ 9וַיְדַבֵּ֥ר יְהוָ֖ה אֶל־מֹשֶׁ֥ה לֵּאמֹֽר׃ 10דַּבֵּ֞ר אֶל־בְּנֵ֤י יִשְׂרָאֵל֙ לֵאמֹ֔ר אִ֣ישׁ אִ֣ישׁ כִּי־יִהְיֶֽה־טָמֵ֣א ׀ לָנֶ֡פֶשׁ אֹו֩ בְדֶ֨רֶךְ רְחֹקָ֜ה לָכֶ֗ם אֹ֚ו לְדֹרֹ֣תֵיכֶ֔ם וְעָ֥שָׂה פֶ֖סַח לַיהוָֽה׃ 11בַּחֹ֨דֶשׁ הַשֵּׁנִ֜י בְּאַרְבָּעָ֨ה עָשָׂ֥ר יֹ֛ום בֵּ֥ין הָעַרְבַּ֖יִם יַעֲשׂ֣וּ אֹתֹ֑ו עַל־מַצֹּ֥ות וּמְרֹרִ֖ים יֹאכְלֻֽהוּ׃ 12לֹֽא־יַשְׁאִ֤ירוּ מִמֶּ֨נּוּ֙ עַד־בֹּ֔קֶר וְעֶ֖צֶם לֹ֣א יִשְׁבְּרוּ־בֹ֑ו כְּכָל־חֻקַּ֥ת הַפֶּ֖סַח יַעֲשׂ֥וּ אֹתֹֽו׃ 13וְהָאִישׁ֩ אֲשֶׁר־ה֨וּא טָהֹ֜ור וּבְדֶ֣רֶךְ לֹא־הָיָ֗ה וְחָדַל֙ לַעֲשֹׂ֣ות הַפֶּ֔סַח וְנִכְרְתָ֛ה הַנֶּ֥פֶשׁ הַהִ֖וא מֵֽעַמֶּ֑יהָ כִּ֣י ׀ קָרְבַּ֣ן יְהוָ֗ה לֹ֤א הִקְרִיב֙ בְּמֹ֣עֲדֹ֔ו חֶטְאֹ֥ו יִשָּׂ֖א הָאִ֥ישׁ הַהֽוּא׃ 14וְכִֽי־יָגוּר֩ אִתְּכֶ֨ם גֵּ֜ר וְעָ֤שָׂה פֶ֨סַח֙ לַֽיהוָ֔ה כְּחֻקַּ֥ת הַפֶּ֛סַח וּכְמִשְׁפָּטֹ֖ו כֵּ֣ן יַעֲשֶׂ֑ה חֻקָּ֤ה אַחַת֙ יִהְיֶ֣ה לָכֶ֔ם וְלַגֵּ֖ר וּלְאֶזְרַ֥ח הָאָֽרֶץ׃ פ 15וּבְיֹום֙ הָקִ֣ים אֶת־

9:6. **impure by a human being.** See comment on Num 5:2.

9:13. **cut off from his people.** On the meaning of this phrase, see the comment on Gen 17:14.

up, the cloud covered the Tabernacle of the tent of the Testimony, and in the evening it would be over the Tabernacle like the appearance of fire until morning. ¹⁶So it would be always: the cloud would cover it and the appearance of fire at night. ¹⁷And according to when the cloud was lifted from over the tent, after that the children of Israel would travel. And in a place where the cloud would tent, the children of Israel would camp there. ¹⁸By YHWH's word the children of Israel would travel, and by YHWH's word they would camp. All the days that the cloud would tent over the Tabernacle they would camp. ¹⁹And when the cloud would extend many days over the Tabernacle, then the children of Israel kept YHWH's charge and would not travel. ²⁰And there were times that the cloud would be over the Tabernacle for a number of days: by YHWH's word they would camp, and by YHWH's word they would travel. ²¹And there were times that the cloud would be there from evening until morning, and the cloud was lifted in the morning, and then they would travel; or for a day and a night, and the cloud was lifted, and then they traveled. ²²Whether two days or a month or a year, when the cloud would extend long over the Tabernacle, to tent over it, the children of Israel would camp and would not travel, and when it was lifted they would travel. ²³By YHWH's word they would camp, and by YHWH's word they would travel. They kept YHWH's charge, by YHWH's word through Moses' hand.

הַמִּשְׁכָּן כִּסָּה הֶעָנָן אֶת־הַמִּשְׁכָּן לְאֹהֶל הָעֵדֻת וּבָעֶרֶב יִהְיֶה עַל־הַמִּשְׁכָּן כְּמַרְאֵה־אֵשׁ עַד־בֹּקֶר: ¹⁶כֵּן יִהְיֶה תָמִיד הֶעָנָן יְכַסֶּנּוּ וּמַרְאֵה־אֵשׁ לָיְלָה: ¹⁷וּלְפִי הֵעָלֹת הֶעָנָן מֵעַל הָאֹהֶל וְאַחֲרֵי־כֵן יִסְעוּ בְּנֵי יִשְׂרָאֵל וּבִמְקוֹם אֲשֶׁר יִשְׁכָּן־שָׁם הֶעָנָן שָׁם יַחֲנוּ בְּנֵי יִשְׂרָאֵל: ¹⁸עַל־פִּי יְהוָה יִסְעוּ בְּנֵי יִשְׂרָאֵל וְעַל־פִּי יְהוָה יַחֲנוּ כָּל־יְמֵי אֲשֶׁר יִשְׁכֹּן הֶעָנָן עַל־הַמִּשְׁכָּן יַחֲנוּ: ¹⁹וּבְהַאֲרִיךְ הֶעָנָן עַל־הַמִּשְׁכָּן יָמִים רַבִּים וְשָׁמְרוּ בְנֵי־יִשְׂרָאֵל אֶת־מִשְׁמֶרֶת יְהוָה וְלֹא יִסָּעוּ: ²⁰וְיֵשׁ אֲשֶׁר יִהְיֶה הֶעָנָן יָמִים מִסְפָּר עַל־הַמִּשְׁכָּן עַל־פִּי יְהוָה יַחֲנוּ וְעַל־פִּי יְהוָה יִסָּעוּ: ²¹וְיֵשׁ אֲשֶׁר־יִהְיֶה הֶעָנָן מֵעֶרֶב עַד־בֹּקֶר וְנַעֲלָה הֶעָנָן בַּבֹּקֶר וְנָסָעוּ אוֹ יוֹמָם וָלַיְלָה וְנַעֲלָה הֶעָנָן וְנָסָעוּ: ²²אוֹ־יֹמַיִם אוֹ־חֹדֶשׁ אוֹ־יָמִים בְּהַאֲרִיךְ הֶעָנָן עַל־הַמִּשְׁכָּן לִשְׁכֹּן עָלָיו יַחֲנוּ בְנֵי־יִשְׂרָאֵל וְלֹא יִסָּעוּ וּבְהֵעָלֹתוֹ יִסָּעוּ: ²³עַל־פִּי יְהוָה יַחֲנוּ וְעַל־פִּי יְהוָה יִסָּעוּ אֶת־מִשְׁמֶרֶת יְהוָה שָׁמָרוּ עַל־פִּי יְהוָה בְּיַד־מֹשֶׁה: פ

9:15. the tent of the Testimony. This is the first occurrence of this phrase. The usual phrase until now has been "Tent of Meeting." The phrase here may not refer to the entire Tent of Meeting, but rather to the inner pavilion, the *pārōket*, which is associated with the Testimony (the tablets of the Ten Commandments) four times (Exod 27:21; 30:6; Lev 24:3; Num 4:5) and is called explicitly "the pavilion of the Testimony" (Lev 24:3).

9:17. the cloud would tent. Forms of this Hebrew verb (*yiškān*) are frequently taken to mean "to dwell"; but, when it refers to God or to the cloud, this verb is a denominative from the noun *miškān*: Tabernacle. The deity cannot be pictured as *residing* on the earth, but God rather is understood to *tent* among humans, that is, to be present in association with an impermanent, movable structure. For references, see the comment on Exod 25:8.

10 ¹And YHWH spoke to Moses, saying, ²"Make two trumpets of silver. You shall make them hammered work. And you shall have them for calling the congregation and for having the camps travel. ³And when they will blow them, then all the congregation shall be gathered to you, to the entrance of the Tent of Meeting. ⁴And if they will blow with one, then the chieftains, the heads of thousands of Israel shall be gathered to you. ⁵And when you will blow a blasting sound, then the camps that are camping on the east shall travel. ⁶And when you will blow a second blasting sound, then the camps that are camping on the west shall travel. They shall blow a blasting sound for their travels. ⁷And for assembling the community you shall blow, but you shall not make a blast. ⁸And the sons of Aaron, the priests, shall blow the trumpets; and they shall be an eternal law for you through your generations. ⁹And when you will go to war in your land against a foe who afflicts you, then you shall blast the trumpets, and you will be brought to mind in front of YHWH, your God, and you will be saved from your enemies. ¹⁰And on your happy occasion and at your appointed times and on your new moons, you shall blow the trumpets over your burnt offerings and over your peace-offering sacrifices, and they shall be for a commemoration for you in front of your God. I am YHWH, your God."

¹¹And it was in the second year, in the second month, on the twentieth of the month that the cloud was lifted from over the Tabernacle of the Testimony. ¹²And the children of Israel set out on their travels from the wilderness of Sinai. And the cloud tented in the wilderness of Paran. ¹³And they traveled from the first by YHWH's word through Moses' hand.

¹⁴And the flag of the camp of the children of Judah traveled first by their armies, and over its

10 ¹וַיְדַבֵּ֥ר יְהוָ֖ה אֶל־מֹשֶׁ֥ה לֵּאמֹֽר׃ ²עֲשֵׂ֣ה לְךָ֗ שְׁתֵּי֙ חֲצֽוֹצְרֹ֣ת כֶּ֔סֶף מִקְשָׁ֖ה תַּעֲשֶׂ֣ה אֹתָ֑ם וְהָי֤וּ לְךָ֙ לְמִקְרָ֣א הָֽעֵדָ֔ה וּלְמַסַּ֖ע אֶת־הַֽמַּחֲנֽוֹת׃ ³וְתָקְע֖וּ בָּהֵ֑ן וְנֽוֹעֲד֤וּ אֵלֶ֙יךָ֙ כָּל־הָ֣עֵדָ֔ה אֶל־פֶּ֖תַח אֹ֥הֶל מוֹעֵֽד׃ ⁴וְאִם־בְּאַחַ֖ת יִתְקָ֑עוּ וְנֽוֹעֲד֤וּ אֵלֶ֙יךָ֙ הַנְּשִׂיאִ֔ים רָאשֵׁ֖י אַלְפֵ֥י יִשְׂרָאֵֽל׃ ⁵וּתְקַעְתֶּ֖ם תְּרוּעָ֑ה וְנָֽסְעוּ֙ הַֽמַּחֲנ֔וֹת הַֽחֹנִ֖ים קֵֽדְמָה׃ ⁶וּתְקַעְתֶּ֤ם תְּרוּעָה֙ שֵׁנִ֔ית וְנָֽסְעוּ֙ הַֽמַּחֲנ֔וֹת הַֽחֹנִ֖ים תֵּימָ֑נָה תְּרוּעָ֥ה יִתְקְע֖וּ לְמַסְעֵיהֶֽם׃ ⁷וּבְהַקְהִ֥יל אֶת־הַקָּהָ֖ל תִּתְקְע֑וּ וְלֹ֖א תָרִֽיעוּ׃ ⁸וּבְנֵ֤י אַהֲרֹן֙ הַכֹּ֣הֲנִ֔ים יִתְקְע֖וּ בַּחֲצֹֽצְר֑וֹת וְהָי֥וּ לָכֶ֛ם לְחֻקַּ֥ת עוֹלָ֖ם לְדֹרֹֽתֵיכֶֽם׃ ⁹וְכִֽי־תָבֹ֨אוּ מִלְחָמָ֜ה בְּאַרְצְכֶ֗ם עַל־הַצַּר֙ הַצֹּרֵ֣ר אֶתְכֶ֔ם וַהֲרֵֽעֹתֶ֖ם בַּחֲצֹֽצְר֑וֹת וְנִזְכַּרְתֶּ֗ם לִפְנֵי֙ יְהוָ֣ה אֱלֹֽהֵיכֶ֔ם וְנֽוֹשַׁעְתֶּ֖ם מֵאֹֽיְבֵיכֶֽם׃ ¹⁰וּבְי֨וֹם שִׂמְחַתְכֶ֥ם וּֽבְמוֹעֲדֵיכֶם֮ וּבְרָאשֵׁ֣י חָדְשֵׁיכֶם֒ וּתְקַעְתֶּ֣ם בַּחֲצֹֽצְרֹ֗ת עַ֚ל עֹלֹ֣תֵיכֶ֔ם וְעַ֖ל זִבְחֵ֣י שַׁלְמֵיכֶ֑ם וְהָי֨וּ לָכֶ֤ם לְזִכָּרוֹן֙ לִפְנֵ֣י אֱלֹֽהֵיכֶ֔ם אֲנִ֖י יְהוָ֥ה אֱלֹֽהֵיכֶֽם׃ פ ¹¹וַיְהִ֞י בַּשָּׁנָ֧ה הַשֵּׁנִ֛ית בַּחֹ֥דֶשׁ הַשֵּׁנִ֖י בְּעֶשְׂרִ֣ים בַּחֹ֑דֶשׁ נַעֲלָה֙ הֶֽעָנָ֔ן מֵעַ֖ל מִשְׁכַּ֥ן הָעֵדֻֽת׃ ¹²וַיִּסְע֧וּ בְנֵֽי־יִשְׂרָאֵ֛ל לְמַסְעֵיהֶ֖ם מִמִּדְבַּ֣ר סִינָ֑י וַיִּשְׁכֹּ֥ן הֶעָנָ֖ן בְּמִדְבַּ֥ר פָּארָֽן׃ ¹³וַיִּסְע֖וּ בָּרִֽאשֹׁנָ֑ה עַל־פִּ֥י יְהוָ֖ה בְּיַד־מֹשֶֽׁה׃ ¹⁴וַיִּסַּ֞ע דֶּ֣גֶל מַחֲנֵ֥ה בְנֵֽי־

10:5. **blasting.** We do not know what sort of trumpet sound this was.

10:12. **the cloud tented.** See the comment on 9:17.

army was Nahshon son of Amminadab. 15And over the army of the tribe of the children of Issachar was Nethanel son of Zuar. 16And over the army of the tribe of the children of Zebulun was Eliab son of Helon. 17And the Tabernacle was taken down; and the children of Gershon and the children of Merari, who carried the Tabernacle, traveled. 18And the flag of Reuben's camp by their armies traveled, and over its army was Elizur son of Shedeur. 19And over the army of the tribe of the children of Simeon was Shelumiel son of Zurishadday. 20And over the army of the tribe of the children of Gad was Eliasaph son of Deuel. 21And the Kohathites, who carried the holy place, traveled; and they set up the Tabernacle by the time they came. 22And the flag of the camp of the children of Ephraim by their armies traveled, and over its army was Elishama son of Ammihud. 23And over the army of the tribe of the children of Manasseh was Gamaliel son of Pedahzur. 24And over the army of the tribe of the children of Benjamin was Abidan son of Gideoni. 25And the flag of the camp of the children of Dan, the final one of all the camps, by their armies, traveled, and over its army was Ahiezer son of Ammishadday. 26And over the army of the tribe of the children of Asher was Pagiel son of Ochran. 27And over the army of the tribe of the children of Naphtali was Ahira son of Enan.

28These were the orders of travel of the children of Israel by their armies when they traveled.

29And Moses said to Hobab, the son of Reuel the Midianite, Moses' father-in-law, "We're traveling to the place that YHWH said, 'I'll give it to you.' Come with us, and we'll be good to you,

יְהוּדָה בָּרִאשֹׁנָה לְצִבְאֹתָם וְעַל־צְבָאוֹ נַחְשׁוֹן בֶּן־
עַמִּינָדָב: 15וְעַל־צְבָא מַטֵּה בְּנֵי יִשָּׂשכָר נְתַנְאֵל בֶּן־
צוּעָר: 16וְעַל־צְבָא מַטֵּה בְּנֵי זְבוּלֻן אֱלִיאָב בֶּן־
חֵלוֹן: 17וְהוּרַד הַמִּשְׁכָּן וְנָסְעוּ בְנֵי־גֵרְשׁוֹן וּבְנֵי
מְרָרִי נֹשְׂאֵי הַמִּשְׁכָּן: ס 18וְנָסַע דֶּגֶל מַחֲנֵה רְאוּבֵן
לְצִבְאֹתָם וְעַל־צְבָאוֹ אֱלִיצוּר בֶּן־שְׁדֵיאוּר: 19וְעַל־
צְבָא מַטֵּה בְּנֵי שִׁמְעוֹן שְׁלֻמִיאֵל בֶּן־צוּרִישַׁדָּי:
20וְעַל־צְבָא מַטֵּה בְּנֵי־גָד אֶלְיָסָף בֶּן־דְּעוּאֵל:
21וְנָסְעוּ הַקְּהָתִים נֹשְׂאֵי הַמִּקְדָּשׁ וְהֵקִימוּ אֶת־
הַמִּשְׁכָּן עַד־בֹּאָם: ס 22וְנָסַע דֶּגֶל מַחֲנֵה בְנֵי־
אֶפְרַיִם לְצִבְאֹתָם וְעַל־צְבָאוֹ אֱלִישָׁמָע בֶּן־
עַמִּיהוּד: 23וְעַל־צְבָא מַטֵּה בְּנֵי מְנַשֶּׁה גַּמְלִיאֵל בֶּן־
פְּדָהצוּר: 24וְעַל־צְבָא מַטֵּה בְּנֵי בִנְיָמִן אֲבִידָן בֶּן־
גִּדְעֹנִי: ס 25וְנָסַע דֶּגֶל מַחֲנֵה בְנֵי־דָן מְאַסֵּף
לְכָל־הַמַּחֲנֹת לְצִבְאֹתָם וְעַל־צְבָאוֹ אֲחִיעֶזֶר בֶּן־
עַמִּישַׁדָּי: 26וְעַל־צְבָא מַטֵּה בְּנֵי אָשֵׁר פַּגְעִיאֵל בֶּן־
עָכְרָן: 27וְעַל־צְבָא מַטֵּה בְּנֵי נַפְתָּלִי אֲחִירַע בֶּן־
עֵינָן: 28אֵלֶּה מַסְעֵי בְנֵי־יִשְׂרָאֵל לְצִבְאֹתָם וַיִּסָּעוּ: ס
29וַיֹּאמֶר מֹשֶׁה לְחֹבָב בֶּן־רְעוּאֵל הַמִּדְיָנִי חֹתֵן
מֹשֶׁה נֹסְעִים ׀ אֲנַחְנוּ אֶל־הַמָּקוֹם אֲשֶׁר אָמַר יְהוָה
אֹתוֹ אֶתֵּן לָכֶם לְכָה אִתָּנוּ וְהֵטַבְנוּ לָךְ כִּי־יְהוָה

10:21. **holy place.** The Kohathites' charge was the sacred objects that went inside the holy place (the interior of the Tabernacle), namely: the ark, the table, the menorah, and the altars and the equipment of the Holy (Num 3:31).

10:21. **they set up the Tabernacle by the time they came.** The Gershonite and Merarite priests traveled first and set up the Tabernacle so that it was ready when the Kohathite priests arrived with the ark, table, menorah, altars, and equipment.

because YHWH has spoken of good regarding Israel."

30And he said to him, "I won't go, but rather I'll go to my land and to my birthplace."

31And he said, "Don't leave us, because you know the way we should camp in the wilderness, and you'll be eyes for us. 32And it will be, when you go with us, that we'll do good for you in proportion to the good that YHWH will do for us."

33And they traveled from the mountain of YHWH three days' journey. And the ark of the covenant of YHWH traveled in front of them three days' journey to scout a resting place for them. 34And YHWH's cloud was over them by day as they traveled from the camp. 35And it was, when the ark traveled, that Moses said, "Arise, YHWH, and let your enemies be scattered, and let those who hate you flee from your presence," 36and when it rested, he said, "Come back, YHWH, the ten thousands of thousands of Israel."

דִּבֶּר־טֹוב עַל־יִשְׂרָאֵל: 30וַיֹּאמֶר אֵלָיו לֹא אֵלֵךְ כִּי
אִם־אֶל־אַרְצִי וְאֶל־מֹולַדְתִּי אֵלֵךְ: 31וַיֹּאמֶר אַל־נָא
תַּעֲזֹב אֹתָנוּ כִּי ׀ עַל־כֵּן יָדַעְתָּ חֲנֹתֵנוּ בַּמִּדְבָּר ׀
וְהָיִיתָ לָּנוּ לְעֵינָיִם: 32וְהָיָה כִּי־תֵלֵךְ עִמָּנוּ וְהָיָה ׀
הַטֹּוב הַהוּא אֲשֶׁר יֵיטִיב יְהוָה עִמָּנוּ וְהֵטַבְנוּ לָךְ:
33וַיִּסְעוּ מֵהַר יְהוָה דֶּרֶךְ שְׁלֹשֶׁת יָמִים וַאֲרֹון
בְּרִית־יְהוָה נֹסֵעַ לִפְנֵיהֶם דֶּרֶךְ שְׁלֹשֶׁת יָמִים לָתוּר
לָהֶם מְנוּחָה: 34וַעֲנַן יְהוָה עֲלֵיהֶם יֹומָם בְּנָסְעָם
מִן־הַמַּחֲנֶה: נ ס 35וַיְהִי בִּנְסֹעַ הָאָרֹן וַיֹּאמֶר מֹשֶׁה
קוּמָה ׀ יְהוָה וְיָפֻצוּ אֹיְבֶיךָ
וְיָנֻסוּ מְשַׂנְאֶיךָ מִפָּנֶיךָ:
36וּבְנֻחֹה יֹאמַר
שׁוּבָה יְהוָה רִבְבֹות אַלְפֵי יִשְׂרָאֵל:] פ

10:35. **let your enemies be scattered**. Moses' ceremonial words that are associated with the respective lifting and resting of the ark have been taken as poetry in several scholarly treatments of Numbers:

> And it was, when the ark traveled, that Moses said, "Arise, YHWH, and let your enemies be scattered, and let those who hate you flee from your presence," 36and when it rested, he said, "Come back, YHWH, the ten thousands of thousands of Israel."

Many identify this as poetry without any explanation. One elaborates that it is "4:4 meter." Given the complexities of speaking of meter in biblical Hebrew poetry, and given that the lines in question here do not add up to 4:4 by any metrical reckoning in any case, we are better advised to be cautious of calling these lines poetry. Presumably the element that has led some to assume that this is poetry is the parallel of scattered enemies and fleeing adversaries, but simple parallels within a single verse such as this may be found in both prose and poetry in the Hebrew Bible. Some scholars have more circumspectly spoken of these lines simply as "sayings."

The significance of this point is that it directs us to recognize the effect of the late introduction of short poems further on in the book (in Numbers 21–24). More broadly, it should serve as a methodological caution in our identification of verses as poetry in the Hebrew Bible. As a matter of method, it is precarious to call a single verse in a prose context poetry. Biblical poetry rarely rhymes and has no obvious meter. Its best-known feature is the use of parallels ("Hear YHWH's word, rulers of Sodom. / Listen to our God's teaching, people of Gomorrah," Isa 1:10), and it is also frequently

11 ¹And the people were like grumblers, bad in YHWH's ears, and YHWH heard, and His anger flared, and a fire of YHWH burned among them and consumed at the edge of the camp. ²And the people cried out to Moses, and Moses prayed to YHWH, and the fire subsided. ³And he called that place's name Taberah because a fire of YHWH burned among them.

⁴And the gathered mass who were among them had a longing, and the children of Israel, as well, went back and cried, and they said, "Who will feed us meat? ⁵We remember the fish that we would eat in Egypt for free: the cucumbers and the melons and the leek and the onions and the garlics. ⁶And now, our soul is dried up. There isn't anything—except the manna before our eyes."

⁷And the manna: it was like a seed of coriander, and its appearance was like the appearance of bdellium. ⁸The people went around and col-

וַיְהִ֤י הָעָם֙ כְּמִתְאֹ֣נְנִ֔ים רַ֖ע בְּאָזְנֵ֣י יְהֹוָ֑ה 11 ¹
וַיִּשְׁמַ֤ע יְהֹוָה֙ וַיִּ֣חַר אַפּ֔וֹ וַתִּבְעַר־בָּם֙ אֵ֣שׁ יְהֹוָ֔ה
וַתֹּ֖אכַל בִּקְצֵ֥ה הַֽמַּחֲנֶֽה: ²וַיִּצְעַ֥ק הָעָ֖ם אֶל־מֹשֶׁ֑ה
וַיִּתְפַּלֵּ֤ל מֹשֶׁה֙ אֶל־יְהֹוָ֔ה וַתִּשְׁקַ֖ע הָאֵֽשׁ: ³וַיִּקְרָ֛א
שֵֽׁם־הַמָּק֥וֹם הַה֖וּא תַּבְעֵרָ֑ה כִּֽי־בָעֲרָ֥ה בָ֖ם אֵ֥שׁ
יְהֹוָֽה: ⁴וְהָֽאסַפְסֻף֙ אֲשֶׁ֣ר בְּקִרְבּ֔וֹ הִתְאַוּ֖וּ תַּאֲוָ֑ה
וַיָּשֻׁ֣בוּ וַיִּבְכּ֗וּ גַּ֚ם בְּנֵ֣י יִשְׂרָאֵ֔ל וַיֹּ֣אמְר֔וּ מִ֥י יַאֲכִלֵ֖נוּ
בָּשָֽׂר: ⁵זָכַ֙רְנוּ֙ אֶת־הַדָּגָ֔ה אֲשֶׁר־נֹאכַ֥ל בְּמִצְרַ֖יִם חִנָּ֑ם
אֵ֣ת הַקִּשֻּׁאִ֗ים וְאֵת֙ הָֽאֲבַטִּחִ֔ים וְאֶת־הֶחָצִ֥יר וְאֶת־
הַבְּצָלִ֖ים וְאֶת־הַשּׁוּמִֽים: ⁶וְעַתָּ֛ה נַפְשֵׁ֥נוּ יְבֵשָׁ֖ה אֵ֣ין
כֹּ֑ל בִּלְתִּ֖י אֶל־הַמָּ֥ן עֵינֵֽינוּ: ⁷וְהַמָּ֕ן כִּזְרַע־גַּ֖ד ה֑וּא
וְעֵינ֖וֹ כְּעֵ֥ין הַבְּדֹֽלַח: ⁸שָׁ֣טוּ הָעָם֩ וְלָֽקְט֨וּ וְטָֽחֲנ֜וּ

---

characterized by puns and alliteration. But parallels, puns, and alliteration are all to be found in biblical prose as well. Without entering into a tedious discussion of the respective definitions of prose and poetry in the Bible, we can say at this point that in almost any passage that is more than a few verses long there will be little scholarly disagreement over the simple identification of the passage as prose or poetry. But making a judgment of a single verse in the middle of a narrative and calling it poetry—and sometimes even proceeding thereafter to analyze the author's use of these poetic lines in prose contexts as an artistic device—is a delicate and subjective practice. This is not to say that there are no cases of single lines of poetry embedded in biblical prose. It is rather a call for recognition, as a matter of method, that whenever one identifies a verse as poetry one must feel obliged to support that claim with analysis and evidence. In the case of this passage, if I were to make such a case, it would be based on the absence of prose particles (the definite article, the direct object marker *'et*, the relative pronoun *'ašer*). But my point is not to enter into this technical matter here, but rather to make the larger point about poetry in the Torah in general.

11:1. **the people were like grumblers**. This is just the first of many accounts of their complaining in Numbers, and, interestingly, it is the only one in which the reason for their dissatisfaction is not told. The story's function, therefore, is not to point to any of the obstacles in the wilderness but rather to indicate the people's state of mind: negative, volatile, unconfident.

11:2. **the people cried out to Moses**. The people appeal to Moses rather than to God, and Moses acts as intercessor. They still turn to the human leader rather than directly to the mysterious, invisible divine source.

11:4. **the gathered mass**. See the comment on Num 12:2.

lected and ground it in mills or pounded it in a mortar and cooked it in a pot and made it into cakes. And its taste was like the taste of something creamy made with oil. 9And when the dew descended on the camp at night, the manna would descend on it.

10And Moses heard the people crying by their families, each at his tent entrance, and YHWH's anger flared very much, and it was bad in Moses' eyes. 11And Moses said to YHWH, "Why have you done bad to your servant, and why have I not found favor in your eyes, to set the burden of this entire people on me? 12Did *I* conceive this entire people? Did *I* give birth to it, that you

בְּרֵחַיִם אוֹ דָכוּ בַּמְּדֹכָה וּבִשְּׁלוּ בַּפָּרוּר וְעָשׂוּ אֹתוֹ עֻגוֹת וְהָיָה טַעְמוֹ כְּטַעַם לְשַׁד הַשָּׁמֶן: 9וּבְרֶדֶת הַטַּל עַל־הַמַּחֲנֶה לָיְלָה יֵרֵד הַמָּן עָלָיו: 10וַיִּשְׁמַע מֹשֶׁה אֶת־הָעָם בֹּכֶה לְמִשְׁפְּחֹתָיו אִישׁ לְפֶתַח אָהֳלוֹ וַיִּחַר־אַף יְהוָה מְאֹד וּבְעֵינֵי מֹשֶׁה רָע: 11וַיֹּאמֶר מֹשֶׁה אֶל־יְהוָה לָמָה הֲרֵעֹתָ לְעַבְדֶּךָ וְלָמָּה לֹא־מָצָתִי חֵן בְּעֵינֶיךָ לָשׂוּם אֶת־מַשָּׂא כָּל־הָעָם הַזֶּה עָלָי: 12הֶאָנֹכִי הָרִיתִי אֵת כָּל־הָעָם הַזֶּה אִם־אָנֹכִי

11:11. Why have you done bad to your servant. Is this a way to talk to God?! In what is the most extraordinary speech spoken by a human to God in the Torah, Moses begins with these words and ends with: "And if this is how you treat me, *kill me!*" We have seen a dramatic change in the way humans speak to God: Adam and Cain speak like children caught in a naughty act. Abraham dares to question a divine decision (the destruction of Sodom) and says, "Far be it from you to do a thing like this. . . . Will the judge of all the earth not do justice?" (Gen 18:25). Moses pleads for the people after the golden calf event and says that if God will not forgive them, then "wipe me out from your scroll that you've written" (Exod 32:32). And now Moses, pleading for himself, speaks to the creator in a way that we would never imagine Adam or Abraham or Jacob or even Moses himself speaking until now. It can only be understood in the light of everything that has happened up to this moment: God's speaking to Moses in a personal way from the beginning ("I'm your father's God"), Moses' spending long hours in conversation with God, Moses' performance of the miracles. The same Moses whose first reaction to the deity was to "hide his face, because he was afraid of looking at God" (Exod 3:6) now dares to speak forcefully. It is the opposite of when an atheist uses some audacious or outrageous language about gods. Moses is pictured as the human who has come the closest to God, the one person who has seen God, and it is precisely Moses who speaks the most audaciously of all. And Moses in turn thus epitomizes humankind: it is precisely the wilderness generation, the generation that is closest to God, who hear God's voice and see miracles daily, who are the most rebellious generation in the Bible. This in turn may remind us of the Bible's first story: when humans live in the garden where God walks, they make the initial act of rebellion. An ongoing point of the Torah is thus that humans and their creator have an underlying basis of conflict, something in the very nature of the divine-human condition. And the relations between God and Abraham's descendants are aimed at eventually resolving this. Thus Moses is not seen as bad for speaking this way to God, and he is not punished. It is rather part of his close relationship with God, and part of the Torah's central story.

should say to me, 'Carry it in your bosom,' the way a nurse carries a suckling, to the land that you swore to its fathers? 13From where do I have meat to give to this entire people, that they cry at me, saying, 'Give us meat, and let's eat'? 14I'm not able, I, by myself, to carry this entire people, because it's too heavy for me. 15And if this is how you treat me, *kill me*, if I've found favor in your eyes, and let me not see my suffering."

16And YHWH said to Moses, "Gather to me seventy men from Israel's elders whom you've known because they're the people's elders and its officers, and you'll take them to the Tent of Meeting, and they'll stand up there with you. 17And I'll come down and speak with you there, and I'll take some of the spirit that is on you, and I'll set it on them, and they'll carry the burden of the people with you, and you won't bear it, you, by yourself. 18And you shall say to the people, 'Consecrate yourselves for tomorrow, and you'll eat meat, because you cried in YHWH's ears saying: Who will feed us meat, because we had it good in Egypt. And YHWH will give you meat, and you'll eat. 19You'll eat not for one day and not two days and not five days and not ten days and not twenty days. 20Until a month of days! Until it will come out of your nose, and it will be a revulsion to you! Because you rejected YHWH, who was

יְלַדְתִּ֔יהוּ כִּי־תֹאמַ֨ר אֵלַ֜י שָׂאֵ֣הוּ בְחֵיקֶ֗ךָ כַּאֲשֶׁ֨ר יִשָּׂ֤א הָאֹמֵן֙ אֶת־הַיֹּנֵ֔ק עַ֚ל הָֽאֲדָמָ֔ה אֲשֶׁ֥ר נִשְׁבַּ֖עְתָּ לַאֲבֹתָֽיו׃ 13מֵאַ֤יִן לִי֙ בָּשָׂ֔ר לָתֵ֖ת לְכָל־הָעָ֣ם הַזֶּ֑ה כִּֽי־יִבְכּ֤וּ עָלַי֙ לֵאמֹ֔ר תְּנָה־לָּ֥נוּ בָשָׂ֖ר וְנֹאכֵֽלָה׃ 14לֹֽא־אוּכַ֤ל אָֽנֹכִי֙ לְבַדִּ֔י לָשֵׂ֖את אֶת־כָּל־הָעָ֣ם הַזֶּ֑ה כִּ֥י כָבֵ֖ד מִמֶּֽנִּי׃ 15וְאִם־כָּ֣כָה ׀ אַתְּ־עֹ֣שֶׂה לִּ֗י הָרְגֵ֤נִי נָא֙ הָרֹ֔ג אִם־מָצָ֥אתִי חֵ֖ן בְּעֵינֶ֑יךָ וְאַל־אֶרְאֶ֖ה בְּרָעָתִֽי׃ פ 16וַיֹּ֨אמֶר יְהוָ֜ה אֶל־מֹשֶׁ֗ה אֶסְפָה־לִּ֞י שִׁבְעִ֣ים אִישׁ֮ מִזִּקְנֵ֣י יִשְׂרָאֵל֒ אֲשֶׁ֣ר יָדַ֔עְתָּ כִּי־הֵ֛ם זִקְנֵ֥י הָעָ֖ם וְשֹׁטְרָ֑יו וְלָקַחְתָּ֤ אֹתָם֙ אֶל־אֹ֣הֶל מוֹעֵ֔ד וְהִֽתְיַצְּב֥וּ שָׁ֖ם עִמָּֽךְ׃ 17וְיָרַדְתִּ֗י וְדִבַּרְתִּ֣י עִמְּךָ֮ שָׁם֒ וְאָצַלְתִּ֗י מִן־הָר֛וּחַ אֲשֶׁ֥ר עָלֶ֖יךָ וְשַׂמְתִּ֣י עֲלֵיהֶ֑ם וְנָשְׂא֤וּ אִתְּךָ֙ בְּמַשָּׂ֣א הָעָ֔ם וְלֹא־תִשָּׂ֥א אַתָּ֖ה לְבַדֶּֽךָ׃ 18וְאֶל־הָעָ֨ם תֹּאמַ֜ר הִתְקַדְּשׁ֣וּ לְמָחָר֮ וַאֲכַלְתֶּ֣ם בָּשָׂר֒ כִּ֤י בְּכִיתֶם֙ בְּאָזְנֵ֣י יְהוָ֔ה לֵאמֹ֗ר מִ֤י יַאֲכִלֵ֙נוּ֙ בָּשָׂ֔ר כִּי־ט֥וֹב לָ֖נוּ בְּמִצְרָ֑יִם וְנָתַ֨ן יְהוָ֥ה לָכֶ֛ם בָּשָׂ֖ר וַאֲכַלְתֶּֽם׃ 19לֹ֣א י֥וֹם אֶחָ֛ד תֹּאכְל֖וּן וְלֹ֣א יוֹמָ֑יִם וְלֹ֣א ׀ חֲמִשָּׁ֣ה יָמִ֗ים וְלֹא֙ עֲשָׂרָ֣ה יָמִ֔ים וְלֹ֖א עֶשְׂרִ֥ים יֽוֹם׃ 20עַ֣ד ׀ חֹ֣דֶשׁ יָמִ֗ים עַ֤ד אֲשֶׁר־יֵצֵא֙ מֵֽאַפְּכֶ֔ם וְהָיָ֥ה לָכֶ֖ם לְזָרָ֑א יַ֗עַן כִּֽי־מְאַסְתֶּ֤ם אֶת־יְהוָה֙ אֲשֶׁ֣ר

11:12,14. **by myself, to carry.** Moses complains that he has to bear the burden of the people alone. This is in explicit contrast to the report about Jethro's advice to Moses in Exod 18:22, in which Jethro tells him to pick judges to help him with the weight of his task, "and they'll bear it with you." Moses takes Jethro's advice there and appoints judges to help him, so why does he say now that he is carrying the burden alone? Notably, that earlier matter did not come from God, and the text never says that God sanctioned it. It was specifically Moses' own arrangement, on the advice of his father-in-law. He still complains now to God that God has left so much to him.

11:14. **too heavy for me.** The recurring adjective "heavy," which persisted through the exodus account and culminated with the heavy cloud and the divine glory (*kābôd*), now returns, with Moses using it to describe the impossible burden on him, just as Jethro had told Moses earlier (Exod 18:18). Note the parallels in Jethro's words there and Moses' words here, which indicate that Moses' father-in-law indeed had much influence on him. Moses' use of the term "heavy" now recalls the exodus, arguably to remind God of Moses' past service.

among you, and you cried in front of him, saying: Why is this that we went out from Egypt?'"

21And Moses said, "The people among whom I am are six hundred thousand on foot, and you've said, 'I'll give them meat, and they'll eat for a month of days!' 22Will flock and herd be slaughtered for them, and would it provide for them? Or will all the sea's fish be gathered for them, and would it provide for them?"

23And YHWH said to Moses, "Is YHWH's hand getting short?! Now you'll see if my word happens to you or not."

24And Moses went out and spoke YHWH's words to the people. And he gathered seventy men from the people's elders, and he stood them around the tent. 25And YHWH came down in a cloud and spoke to him and took some of the spirit that was on him and put it on the seventy men of the elders. And it was when the spirit rested on them: and they prophesied. Then they did not do it anymore.

בְּקִרְבְּכֶ֔ם וַתִּבְכּ֤וּ לְפָנָיו֙ לֵאמֹ֔ר לָ֥מָּה זֶּ֖ה יָצָ֥אנוּ
מִמִּצְרָֽיִם׃ 21וַיֹּ֗אמֶר מֹשֶׁ֔ה שֵׁשׁ־מֵא֥וֹת אֶ֙לֶף֙ רַגְלִ֔י
הָעָ֕ם אֲשֶׁ֥ר אָנֹכִ֖י בְּקִרְבּ֑וֹ וְאַתָּ֣ה אָמַ֗רְתָּ בָּשָׂר֙ אֶתֵּ֣ן
לָהֶ֔ם וְאָכְל֖וּ חֹ֥דֶשׁ יָמִֽים׃ 22הֲצֹ֧אן וּבָקָ֛ר יִשָּׁחֵ֥ט
לָהֶ֖ם וּמָצָ֣א לָהֶ֑ם אִ֣ם אֶֽת־כָּל־דְּגֵ֥י הַיָּ֛ם יֵאָסֵ֥ף לָהֶ֖ם
וּמָצָ֥א לָהֶֽם׃ פ 23וַיֹּ֤אמֶר יְהוָה֙ אֶל־מֹשֶׁ֔ה הֲיַ֥ד יְהוָ֖ה
תִּקְצָ֑ר עַתָּ֥ה תִרְאֶ֛ה הֲיִקְרְךָ֥ דְבָרִ֖י אִם־לֹֽא׃ 24וַיֵּצֵ֣א
מֹשֶׁ֔ה וַיְדַבֵּ֤ר אֶל־הָעָם֙ אֵ֖ת דִּבְרֵ֣י יְהוָ֑ה וַיֶּאֱסֹ֞ף
שִׁבְעִ֥ים אִישׁ֙ מִזִּקְנֵ֣י הָעָ֔ם וַֽיַּעֲמֵ֥ד אֹתָ֖ם סְבִיבֹ֥ת
הָאֹֽהֶל׃ 25וַיֵּ֨רֶד יְהוָ֣ה ׀ בֶּעָנָן֮ וַיְדַבֵּ֣ר אֵלָיו֒ וַיָּ֗אצֶל
מִן־הָר֙וּחַ֙ אֲשֶׁ֣ר עָלָ֔יו וַיִּתֵּ֕ן עַל־שִׁבְעִ֥ים אִ֖ישׁ הַזְּקֵנִ֑ים
וַיְהִ֗י כְּנ֤וֹחַ עֲלֵיהֶם֙ הָר֔וּחַ וַיִּֽתְנַבְּא֖וּ וְלֹ֥א יָסָֽפוּ׃

11:25. **they prophesied**. What exactly do they do? Prophecy in the Bible does not primarily involve prediction. It is not that they are going about telling the future. What is happening that makes it obvious to Moses, Joshua, and apparently everyone that they are doing something that is associated with prophets? Some suggest that they are in some sort of trance, but trance behavior is not generally part of what is pictured in the fifteen books of the prophets in the *Tanak* or in the cases of prophecy in the *Tanak*'s narrative books. What is typical of prophecy, as opposed to historical narrative, in the Bible is that *prophecy is in poetry* (or in combinations of poetry and prose). Biblical prophecy has the characteristics of oral formulaic poetry. That is, the prophet composes it on the spot, using lines that he or she has already composed and memorized, and mixing these "formulas" with new lines that occur to him or her spontaneously. When such poems occurred to the ancient poets, the poets must have truly felt inspired. And the people who watched and listened to them must have perceived them to be inspired as well. When a man *spontaneously* says:

> They'll beat their swords into plowshares
> and their spears into pruning hooks.
> A nation won't lift a sword against a nation,
> and they won't learn war anymore.

we can easily imagine him and his audience feeling that it is God moving through him. Further evidence that they are doing something musical or poetic comes from the other most famous biblical instance of such group prophecy: King Saul joins in a group of prophets, and he prophesies with them, which astounds everyone. And in

26And two men had been left in the camp. One's name was Eldad, and the second's name was Medad. And the spirit rested on them. And they were among the ones who were written, but they did not go out to the tent, and they prophesied in the camp. 27And a boy ran and told Moses, and he said, "Eldad and Medad are prophesying in the camp!"

28And Joshua, son of Nun, Moses' attendant from his chosen ones, answered, and he said, "My lord Moses, restrain them!"

29And Moses said to him, "Are you jealous for me? And who would make it so that *all* of YHWH's people were prophets, that YHWH would put His spirit on them!" 30And Moses was gathered back to the camp, he and Israel's elders.

26וַיִּשָּׁאֲרוּ שְׁנֵי־אֲנָשִׁים ׀ בַּמַּחֲנֶה שֵׁם הָאֶחָד ׀ אֶלְדָּד וְשֵׁם הַשֵּׁנִי מֵידָד וַתָּנַח עֲלֵיהֶם הָרוּחַ וְהֵמָּה בַּכְּתֻבִים וְלֹא יָצְאוּ הָאֹהֱלָה וַיִּתְנַבְּאוּ בַּמַּחֲנֶה: 27וַיָּרָץ הַנַּעַר וַיַּגֵּד לְמֹשֶׁה וַיֹּאמַר אֶלְדָּד וּמֵידָד מִתְנַבְּאִים בַּמַּחֲנֶה: 28וַיַּעַן יְהוֹשֻׁעַ בִּן־נוּן מְשָׁרֵת מֹשֶׁה מִבְּחֻרָיו וַיֹּאמַר אֲדֹנִי מֹשֶׁה כְּלָאֵם: 29וַיֹּאמֶר לוֹ מֹשֶׁה הַמְקַנֵּא אַתָּה לִי וּמִי יִתֵּן כָּל־עַם יְהוָה נְבִיאִים כִּי־יִתֵּן יְהוָה אֶת־רוּחוֹ עֲלֵיהֶם: 30וַיֵּאָסֵף מֹשֶׁה אֶל־הַמַּחֲנֶה הוּא וְזִקְנֵי יִשְׂרָאֵל: 31וְרוּחַ נָסַע ׀

that case the text notes that these prophets are accompanied by musical instruments (1 Sam 10:5).

See also the story of Aaron's and Miriam's challenge to Moses in the coming chapter. They have experienced prophecy, and they say, "Has YHWH only just spoken through Moses? Hasn't He also spoken through us?" God responds with a declaration about the nature of prophecy, saying that Moses' experience is different from all others, and the important thing to note here is that the words of God are in poetry (see Num 12:6–8).

Some think that biblical prophecy involved some sort of ecstatic state. That is possible, but it may be more of an *inspired* state, both in an Isaiah and in a case like Saul's or the seventy elders here, in which one who does not normally speak in poetry is now moved and enabled to do so.

11:26. they were among the ones who were written. Meaning: they were among the seventy who were written about in the preceding verse.

11:28. his chosen ones. The seventy whom Moses had chosen earlier on Jethro's advice (Exod 18:25). The Aramaic translation (Targum Onkelos) and others read different vowels here and understand this to say: "from his youth." The Greek (Septuagint) takes it as "chosen," as does Ibn Ezra. The explicit reference to Moses' "choosing" a group of seventy in the Jethro episode seems to me to make this the more probable reading here. It also makes Joshua's concern now more intriguing, as he questions the behavior of members of the second group of seventy. They go beyond what the seventy whom Moses himself had chosen had done, and he wants them to stop. But Moses says, Don't be jealous for me.

11:29. who would make it so. Literally, "who would give" or "who would put it." Meaning: "if only it were so" or "I wish it were so." This is the only time that Moses uses this expression. The people use it once (Exod 16:3); it occurs once as part of a

464

31And a wind traveled from YHWH and transported quails from the sea and left them on the camp, about a day's journey in one direction and about a day's journey in the other around the camp, and about two cubits on the face of the earth. 32And the people got up all that day and all night and all the next day and gathered the quail. The one who had the least gathered ten homers. And they spread them out, spreading around the camp. 33And the meat was still between their teeth, not yet chewed, and YHWH's anger flared at the people, and YHWH struck at the people, a very great strike. 34And he called that place's name Kibroth Hattaavah, because they buried the people who were longing there. 35From Kibroth Hattaavah the people traveled to Hazeroth, and they were in Hazeroth.

12 1And Miriam and Aaron spoke against Moses about the Cushite wife whom he had taken—because he had taken a Cushite wife.

מֵאֵת יְהוָה וַיָּגָז שַׂלְוִים מִן־הַיָּם וַיִּטֹּשׁ עַל־הַמַּחֲנֶה כְּדֶרֶךְ יוֹם כֹּה וּכְדֶרֶךְ יוֹם כֹּה סְבִיבוֹת הַמַּחֲנֶה וּכְאַמָּתַיִם עַל־פְּנֵי הָאָרֶץ: 32וַיָּקָם הָעָם כָּל־הַיּוֹם הַהוּא וְכָל־הַלַּיְלָה וְכֹל ׀ יוֹם הַמָּחֳרָת וַיַּאַסְפוּ אֶת־הַשְּׂלָו הַמַּמְעִיט אָסַף עֲשָׂרָה חֳמָרִים וַיִּשְׁטְחוּ לָהֶם שָׁטוֹחַ סְבִיבוֹת הַמַּחֲנֶה: 33הַבָּשָׂר עוֹדֶנּוּ בֵּין שִׁנֵּיהֶם טֶרֶם יִכָּרֵת וְאַף יְהוָה חָרָה בָעָם וַיַּךְ יְהוָה בָּעָם מַכָּה רַבָּה מְאֹד: 34וַיִּקְרָא אֶת־שֵׁם־הַמָּקוֹם הַהוּא קִבְרוֹת הַתַּאֲוָה כִּי־שָׁם קָבְרוּ אֶת־הָעָם הַמִּתְאַוִּים: 35מִקִּבְרוֹת הַתַּאֲוָה נָסְעוּ הָעָם חֲצֵרוֹת וַיִּהְיוּ בַּחֲצֵרוֹת: פ

12 1וַתְּדַבֵּר מִרְיָם וְאַהֲרֹן בְּמֹשֶׁה עַל־אֹדוֹת הָאִשָּׁה הַכֻּשִׁית אֲשֶׁר לָקָח כִּי־אִשָּׁה כֻשִׁית לָקָח:

---

curse (Deut 28:67); and, most extraordinarily, Moses reports that God used it after the revelation at Sinai (Deut 5:29).

11:31. a wind from YHWH. The wording plays exquisitely on the double meaning of the Hebrew word *rûaḥ*, which means both spirit and wind. (See the comment on Gen 1:2.) Moses has just said, "If only YHWH would put His *spirit*" on all the people; and now YHWH brings His *wind*, carrying food for the people. It appears that, in the divine wisdom, the provision of sustenance is of more immediate importance than the bestowing of the spirit. It reminds one of the later rabbinic expression אֵין קֶמַח אֵין תּוֹרָה (*'ên qemaḥ 'ên tôrāh*; No flour, no Torah!).

11:31. two cubits on the face of the earth. Piled three feet high.

11:34. Kibroth Hattaavah. Meaning "Graves of Longing."

12:1. the Cushite wife. Cush is usually understood to be Ethiopia. Its people are identified as descendants of Noah's son Ham (Gen 10:6–7). On this understanding, Moses has taken an Ethiopian wife in addition to his first, Midianite wife, Zipporah. This has been confused somewhat by the fact that the prophet Habakkuk refers to a place called Cushan in parallel with Midian (Hab 3:7). Some scholars, therefore, have concluded that the Cushite wife is Zipporah herself (so Ibn Ezra). But this latter view does not explain why the text should suddenly refer to her here as a Cushite. Also, the words "because he had taken a Cushite wife" certainly appear to be here in the verse in order to inform us of an essential *new* fact, but we already knew that he was married to Zipporah (so Rashbam). This story, therefore, is about a second, probably Ethiopian wife.

²And they said, "Has YHWH only just spoken through Moses? Hasn't He also spoken through us?"

²וַיֹּאמְרוּ הֲרַק אַךְ־בְּמֹשֶׁה֙ דִּבֶּר יְהוָה הֲלֹא גַּם־בָּ֫נוּ

12:2. only just spoken. Aaron and Miriam say, "Has YHWH only just spoken through Moses?" "Only just" sounds redundant. The redundant word "only," though, is Hebrew *raq*, and the story concludes with YHWH demanding a measure of punishment of Miriam comparable to the shame she would have experienced if her father "had *spit* in her face," which is Hebrew *yārōq yāraq* (12:14), an intensive form that doubles the verb—and doubly emphasizes the pun. And the pun confirms that Miriam's punishment is meant to fit the crime: see the comment on v. 10.

One might regard this last pun as a relatively minor item of wordplay, but it is in fact part of an elaborate chain of puns that are stitched through this section of Numbers. The chain encompasses this story and the one that precedes it, the story of Moses' anguished complaint and the appointment of the seventy elders to share his load. The first word of that story is the extremely unusual and uncertain term *'sapsup* (spelled with an unvocalized *aleph* at the beginning because it is preceded by the definite article), meaning a "gathered mass" (classically translated as a "mixed multitude") among the Israelites. The root letters of this strange word (*'SP*) then resurface in a showcase of forms through this story and the next one:

11:4	gathered mass	*ha'SaPSuP*
11:16	Gather to me	*'ĕSĕPâ lî*
11:20	out of your nose . . .	*mē'aPPĕkem . . .*
	because you rejected	*kî mĕ'aStem*
11:22	will be gathered	*yē'āSēP*
11:24	and he gathered	*wayye'ĕSōP*
11:25	they did not do it anymore	*lō' yāSāPû*
11:30	and he was gathered back	*wayyē'āSēP*
11:32	and they gathered	*wayya'aSĕPû*
11:32	[he] gathered	*'āSaP*
11:33	anger	*'aP*
12:9	anger	*'aP*
12:14	let her be gathered back	*tē'āSēP*
12:15	Miriam was gathered back	*hē'āSēP miryām*

Through fourteen variations on the root letters, we are brought from the crisis that is generated by the "gathered mass" to resolution when Miriam is "gathered back" (*hē'āsēp*). Moreover, this chain of paronomasia may serve to stitch these two stories more tightly together and thus suggest a relationship between the seventy elders'

And YHWH heard.

³And the man Moses was very humble, more than every human who was on the face of the earth.

⁴And YHWH said suddenly to Moses and to Aaron and to Miriam, "Go out, the three of you, to the Tent of Meeting." And the three of them went out. ⁵And YHWH came down in a column of cloud and stood at the entrance of the tent. And He called, "Aaron and Miriam." And the two of them went out. ⁶And He said, "Hear my words:

If there will be a prophet among you,
I, YHWH, shall be known to him in a
    vision;
in a dream I shall speak through him.

דָּבֶר וַיִּשְׁמַע יְהוָה: ³וְהָאִישׁ מֹשֶׁה עָנָו מְאֹד מִכֹּל
הָאָדָם אֲשֶׁר עַל־פְּנֵי הָאֲדָמָה: ס ⁴וַיֹּאמֶר יְהוָה
פִּתְאֹם אֶל־מֹשֶׁה וְאֶל־אַהֲרֹן וְאֶל־מִרְיָם צְאוּ
שְׁלָשְׁתְּכֶם אֶל־אֹהֶל מוֹעֵד וַיֵּצְאוּ שְׁלָשְׁתָּם: ⁵וַיֵּרֶד
יְהוָה בְּעַמּוּד עָנָן וַיַּעֲמֹד פֶּתַח הָאֹהֶל וַיִּקְרָא אַהֲרֹן
וּמִרְיָם וַיֵּצְאוּ שְׁנֵיהֶם: ⁶וַיֹּאמֶר
שִׁמְעוּ־נָא דְבָרָי אִם־יִהְיֶה נְבִיאֲכֶם יְהוָה
בַּמַּרְאָה אֵלָיו אֶתְוַדָּע בַּחֲלוֹם אֲדַבֶּר־בּוֹ:
⁷לֹא־כֵן עַבְדִּי מֹשֶׁה בְּכָל־בֵּיתִי נֶאֱמָן הוּא:

12:3 קְ עָנָיו

---

prophesying in Numbers 11 and Aaron's and Miriam's complaint in Numbers 12 ("Has YHWH only just spoken through Moses?").

12:2. **they said, "Has YHWH only just spoken through Moses?"** What does this complaint have to do with Moses' wife?! Answer: nothing. Like someone who has had a bad day and comes home and complains about dinner, Aaron and Miriam do not voice what is really bothering them. They redirect their annoyance at Moses himself. Aaron and Miriam have been identified as prophets (Exod 7:1; 15:20). God has spoken to Aaron, and Aaron was part of the group that had a vision of God on Sinai (Exodus 24). And so they question Moses' position: is he the only one close to God? It is common for people to redirect anger, but it has risks in every case, especially when it occurs within a family. This episode dramatizes that danger: Miriam and Aaron bring God into what was a family dispute. This is a mistake! God appears, and they suffer.

12:3. **humble, more than every human who was on the face of the earth.** Is this the humblest man on earth? But he is the man who has just said things to *God* like "Why have you done bad to your servant?" and "If this is how you treat me, *kill me!*" We might say that his closeness to God enables him to speak this way to the deity while still being humble when dealing with other human beings. But then how are we to account for the way he spoke to the Pharaoh before the last plague in Egypt: "All these servants of yours will come down to *me*, and they'll bow to *me*" (Exod 11:8)? Perhaps it is precisely his experiences in Egypt and at Sinai that have made him *now* the humblest of humans. Having seen the extent of God's power, he feels humble. Having seen his inability to handle the people and their complaints on his own, he feels humbler still. Thus, even when he speaks to God with his audacious closeness, he says, "I'm not able, I, by myself, to carry this entire people, because it's too heavy for me" (11:14).

12:6. **in a vision; in a dream.** All prophetic experience in the *Tanak* is understood to be through visions and dreams—except Moses'. The fifteen books of the Hebrew Bible that are named for prophets either identify the prophets' experiences as visions

7   Not so is my servant Moses;
     in all my house he is faithful.
8   Mouth to mouth I shall speak through
       him
     and vision and not in enigmas,
     and he will see the form of YHWH.
     And why did you not fear to speak
       against my servant,
     against Moses?"

8פֶּה אֶל־פֶּה אֲדַבֶּר־בּוֹ וּמַרְאֶה וְלֹא בְחִידֹת
וּתְמֻנַת יְהוָה יַבִּיט
וּמַדּוּעַ לֹא יְרֵאתֶם לְדַבֵּר בְּעַבְדִּי בְמֹשֶׁה:
9וַיִּחַר אַף יְהוָה בָּם וַיֵּלַךְ: 10וְהֶעָנָן סָר מֵעַל
הָאֹהֶל וְהִנֵּה מִרְיָם מְצֹרַעַת כַּשָּׁלֶג וַיִּפֶן אַהֲרֹן אֶל־
מִרְיָם וְהִנֵּה מְצֹרָעַת: 11וַיֹּאמֶר אַהֲרֹן אֶל־מֹשֶׁה בִּי
אֲדֹנִי אַל־נָא תָשֵׁת עָלֵינוּ חַטָּאת אֲשֶׁר נוֹאַלְנוּ

9And YHWH's anger flared against them, and He went. 10And the cloud turned from over the tent; and, here, Miriam was leprous, like snow. And Aaron turned to Miriam, and, here, she was leprous. 11And Aaron said to Moses, "In me, my lord. Don't set a sin on us, which we did foolish-

---

or else leave the form of the experiences undescribed (Ezek 12:27; 40:2; Hos 12:11; Hab 2:2; Mic 3:6). Many begin by identifying the book's contents as the prophet's vision: "The vision of Isaiah" (Isa 1:1; cf. 2 Chr 32:32); "The vision of Obadiah" (Oba 1); "The book of the vision of Nahum" (Nah 1:1); "The words of Amos . . . which he envisioned" (Amos 1:1); "The word of YHWH that came to Micah . . . which he envisioned" (Mic 1:1); "The oracle that Habakkuk the prophet envisioned" (Hab 1:1).

12:7. **Not so is my servant Moses.** Some experiences are impressive or inspiring or powerful in themselves; and some experiences change a person's life ever after. The moment at which Moses sees the form of God from the back on Sinai separates him from all other prophets (Exod 33:21–23). It is understood that no other prophet has a standing that is equal to that of Moses.

12:10. **leprous, like snow.** Miriam is left with a kind of leprosy in which her flesh is devoid of pigment. If we understand correctly that the Cushite wife is Ethiopian, then this is a provocative case of punishment to suit the crime and a powerful biblical statement regarding racism. It is as if God says to Miriam: "You don't like a woman with dark pigmentation? Then you don't have to have *any* pigmentation!" Or: "You don't like a woman who is black? Try being completely white!"

12:11. **my lord.** Aaron addressed Moses as "my lord" one other time: in the golden calf episode. On each of the two occasions on which he has acted inappropriately toward Moses, he has ended up having to acknowledge Moses' status humbly and politely.

12:11. **Don't set a sin on us.** Aaron acknowledges that both he and Miriam are guilty. He says, "Don't set a sin on *us,* which *we* did foolishly and which *we* sinned." Why is there no consequence here for Aaron? Why does Miriam suffer while Aaron does not? As I commented in the case of Aaron's making the golden calf, the answer may be that Aaron is the high priest. In that position he cannot suffer any direct pun-

ly and which we sinned. 12Let her not be like the dead who, when he comes out of his mother's womb, half of his flesh is eaten up!"

13And Moses cried out to YHWH, saying, "Oh, God, heal her!"

14And YHWH said to Moses, "And if her father had *spit* in her face, wouldn't she be humiliated seven days? Let her be closed up seven days outside the camp, and after that let her be gathered back." 15And Miriam was closed up outside the camp seven days. And the people did not travel until Miriam was gathered back, and after that the people traveled from Hazeroth. And they camped in the Paran wilderness.

SEND

13 1And YHWH spoke to Moses, saying, 2"Send men and let them scout the land of Canaan that I'm giving to the children of Israel. You shall send one man for each tribe of his fathers, every one of them a chieftain."

וַאֲשֶׁר חָטָאנוּ: 12אַל־נָא תְהִי כַּמֵּת אֲשֶׁר בְּצֵאתוֹ מֵרֶחֶם אִמּוֹ וַיֵּאָכֵל חֲצִי בְשָׂרוֹ: 13וַיִּצְעַק מֹשֶׁה אֶל־יְהוָה לֵאמֹר אֵל נָא רְפָא נָא לָהּ: פ 14וַיֹּאמֶר יְהוָה אֶל־מֹשֶׁה וְאָבִיהָ יָרֹק יָרַק בְּפָנֶיהָ הֲלֹא תִכָּלֵם שִׁבְעַת יָמִים תִּסָּגֵר שִׁבְעַת יָמִים מִחוּץ לַמַּחֲנֶה וְאַחַר תֵּאָסֵף: 15וַתִּסָּגֵר מִרְיָם מִחוּץ לַמַּחֲנֶה שִׁבְעַת יָמִים וְהָעָם לֹא נָסַע עַד־הֵאָסֵף מִרְיָם: 16וְאַחַר נָסְעוּ הָעָם מֵחֲצֵרוֹת וַיַּחֲנוּ בְּמִדְבַּר פָּארָן: פ

שְׁלַח לְךָ

13 1וַיְדַבֵּר יְהוָה אֶל־מֹשֶׁה לֵּאמֹר: 2שְׁלַח־לְךָ אֲנָשִׁים וְיָתֻרוּ אֶת־אֶרֶץ כְּנַעַן אֲשֶׁר־אֲנִי נֹתֵן לִבְנֵי יִשְׂרָאֵל אִישׁ אֶחָד אִישׁ אֶחָד לְמַטֵּה אֲבֹתָיו תִּשְׁלָחוּ

ishment from God, which would both disqualify him and demean the office of high priest. And so what is left is for Aaron to make amends through personal atonement. What is impressive here is that he frames his atonement entirely in terms of Miriam. He acknowledges his own equal culpability, and he pleads with Moses to intercede for his sister.

12:13. **Oh, God, heal her!** The untranslatable Hebrew *nā'* particle occurs twice in Moses' words, conveying that this is a fervent plea, something like: "God, please, heal her, please!"

13:2. **send one man for each tribe**. One scout is named for each tribe *except Levi*. Why is the priestly tribe not represented? Perhaps no one from Levi is sent to scout the territory because Levi is the one tribe that will not be assigned any territory in the land. They derive their support from the sacrifices, tithes, and donations of the other tribes.

13:2. **every one of them a chieftain**. This story is commonly referred to as the episode of the *spies*, but the men whom Moses sends are tribal leaders, not ordinary scouts. The function of their mission is not espionage but observation, to bring back a description of the land to their people. They are leaders. That is why their negativity when they return is so devastating. It is not just a disappointing bit of intelligence. It is a failure to lead and encourage.

3And Moses sent them from the wilderness of Paran by YHWH's word. They were all men who were heads of the children of Israel. 4And these are their names: For the tribe of Reuben, Shammua son of Zaccur. 5For the tribe of Simeon, Shaphat son of Hori. 6For the tribe of Judah, Caleb son of Jephunneh. 7For the tribe of Issachar, Igal son of Joseph. 8For the tribe of Ephraim, Hoshea son of Nun. 9For the tribe of Benjamin, Palti son of Raphu. 10For the tribe of Zebulun, Gaddiel son of Sodi. 11For the tribe of Joseph: of the tribe of Manasseh, Gaddi son of Susi. 12For the tribe of Dan, Ammiel son of Gemalli. 13For the tribe of Asher, Sethur son of Michael. 14For the tribe of Naphtali, Nahbi son of Vophsi. 15For the tribe of Gad, Geuel son of Machi.

16These are the names of the men whom Moses sent to scout the land. And Moses called Hoshea son of Nun Joshua. 17And Moses sent them to scout the land of Canaan. And he said to them, "Go up there in the Negeb, and you shall go up the mountain 18and see the land, how it is; and the people who live on it, are they strong or weak, are they few or many; 19and how is the land in which they live, is it good or bad; and how are the cities in which they live, are they in camps or in fortified places; 20and how is the land, is it fat or meager; does it have trees or not; and exert strength and take some fruit of the land."

And it was the days of the first grapes. 21And they went up and scouted the land from the wilderness of Zin to Rehob at the entrance of Hamath. 22And they went up in the Negeb and came to Hebron. And Ahiman, Sheshai, and Talmai, the offspring of the giants, were there. (And Hebron was built seven years before Zoan of Egypt.) 23And they came to the Wadi Eshcol, and

כָּל נָשִׂיא בָהֶם: 3וַיִּשְׁלַח אֹתָם מֹשֶׁה מִמִּדְבַּר פָּארָן עַל־פִּי יְהוָה כֻּלָּם אֲנָשִׁים רָאשֵׁי בְנֵי־יִשְׂרָאֵל הֵמָּה: 4וְאֵלֶּה שְׁמוֹתָם לְמַטֵּה רְאוּבֵן שַׁמּוּעַ בֶּן־זַכּוּר: 5לְמַטֵּה שִׁמְעוֹן שָׁפָט בֶּן־חוֹרִי: 6לְמַטֵּה יְהוּדָה כָּלֵב בֶּן־יְפֻנֶּה: 7לְמַטֵּה יִשָּׂשכָר יִגְאָל בֶּן־יוֹסֵף: 8לְמַטֵּה אֶפְרָיִם הוֹשֵׁעַ בִּן־נוּן: 9לְמַטֵּה בִנְיָמִן פַּלְטִי בֶּן־רָפוּא: 10לְמַטֵּה זְבוּלֻן גַּדִּיאֵל בֶּן־סוֹדִי: 11לְמַטֵּה יוֹסֵף לְמַטֵּה מְנַשֶּׁה גַּדִּי בֶּן־סוּסִי: 12לְמַטֵּה דָן עַמִּיאֵל בֶּן־גְּמַלִּי: 13לְמַטֵּה אָשֵׁר סְתוּר בֶּן־מִיכָאֵל: 14לְמַטֵּה נַפְתָּלִי נַחְבִּי בֶּן־וָפְסִי: 15לְמַטֵּה גָד גְּאוּאֵל בֶּן־מָכִי: 16אֵלֶּה שְׁמוֹת הָאֲנָשִׁים אֲשֶׁר־שָׁלַח מֹשֶׁה לָתוּר אֶת־הָאָרֶץ וַיִּקְרָא מֹשֶׁה לְהוֹשֵׁעַ בִּן־נוּן יְהוֹשֻׁעַ: 17וַיִּשְׁלַח אֹתָם מֹשֶׁה לָתוּר אֶת־אֶרֶץ כְּנָעַן וַיֹּאמֶר אֲלֵהֶם עֲלוּ זֶה בַּנֶּגֶב וַעֲלִיתֶם אֶת־הָהָר: 18וּרְאִיתֶם אֶת־הָאָרֶץ מַה־הִוא וְאֶת־הָעָם הַיֹּשֵׁב עָלֶיהָ הֶחָזָק הוּא הֲרָפֶה הַמְעַט הוּא אִם־רָב: 19וּמָה הָאָרֶץ אֲשֶׁר־הוּא יֹשֵׁב בָּהּ הֲטוֹבָה הִוא אִם־רָעָה וּמָה הֶעָרִים אֲשֶׁר־הוּא יוֹשֵׁב בָּהֵנָּה הַבְּמַחֲנִים אִם בְּמִבְצָרִים: 20וּמָה הָאָרֶץ הַשְּׁמֵנָה הִוא אִם־רָזָה הֲיֵשׁ־בָּהּ עֵץ אִם־אַיִן וְהִתְחַזַּקְתֶּם וּלְקַחְתֶּם מִפְּרִי הָאָרֶץ וְהַיָּמִים יְמֵי בִּכּוּרֵי עֲנָבִים: 21וַיַּעֲלוּ וַיָּתֻרוּ אֶת־הָאָרֶץ מִמִּדְבַּר־צִן עַד־רְחֹב לְבֹא חֲמָת: 22וַיַּעֲלוּ בַנֶּגֶב וַיָּבֹא עַד־חֶבְרוֹן וְשָׁם אֲחִימַן שֵׁשַׁי וְתַלְמַי יְלִידֵי הָעֲנָק וְחֶבְרוֹן שֶׁבַע שָׁנִים נִבְנְתָה לִפְנֵי צֹעַן מִצְרָיִם: 23וַיָּבֹאוּ עַד־נַחַל

13:22. **came to Hebron.** They return to a place where Abraham lived (Gen 13:18), where he met the three visitors and first questioned God (Genesis 18; Mamre is at Hebron), and where the patriarchs and matriarchs are buried (Gen 23:19). It is also the place from which Jacob sent Joseph to find his brothers, which, in a sense, initiated the sequence of events that led to Israel's being in Egypt. It is therefore, meaningful in

they cut a branch and one cluster of grapes from there—and carried it on a pole by two people—and some pomegranates and some figs. 24That place was called Wadi Eshcol on account of the cluster that the children of Israel cut from there. 25And they came back from scouting the land at the end of forty days. 26And they went and came to Moses and to Aaron and to all the congregation of the children of Israel, to the wilderness of Paran, at Kadesh; and they brought back word to them and all the congregation and showed them the land's fruit.

27And they told him and said, "We came to the land where you sent us, and also it's flowing with milk and honey, and this is its fruit. 28Nonetheless: the people who live in the land are strong. And the cities are fortified, very big. And also we saw the offspring of the giants there. 29Amalek lives in the land of the Negeb, and the Hittite and the Jebusite and the Amorite live in the mountains, and the Canaanite lives by the sea and along the Jordan."

30And Caleb quieted the people toward Moses and said, "*Let's go up,* and we'll take possession of it, because *we'll be able* to handle it."

31And the men who went up with him said, "We won't be able to go up against the people, because they're stronger than we are." 32And they brought out a report of the land that they had scouted to the children of Israel, saying, "The land through which we passed to scout it: it's a land that eats those who live in it, and all the people whom we saw in it were people of *size!* 33And we saw the Nephilim there, sons of giants from the Nephilim, and we were like grasshoppers in our eyes, and so were we in *their* eyes."

אֶשְׁכֹּל וַיִּכְרְתוּ מִשָּׁם זְמוֹרָה וְאֶשְׁכּוֹל עֲנָבִים אֶחָד וַיִּשָּׂאֻהוּ בַמּוֹט בִּשְׁנָיִם וּמִן־הָרִמֹּנִים וּמִן־הַתְּאֵנִים: 24לַמָּקוֹם הַהוּא קָרָא נַחַל אֶשְׁכּוֹל עַל אֹדוֹת הָאֶשְׁכּוֹל אֲשֶׁר־כָּרְתוּ מִשָּׁם בְּנֵי יִשְׂרָאֵל: 25וַיָּשֻׁבוּ מִתּוּר הָאָרֶץ מִקֵּץ אַרְבָּעִים יוֹם: 26וַיֵּלְכוּ וַיָּבֹאוּ אֶל־מֹשֶׁה וְאֶל־אַהֲרֹן וְאֶל־כָּל־עֲדַת בְּנֵי־יִשְׂרָאֵל אֶל־מִדְבַּר פָּארָן קָדֵשָׁה וַיָּשִׁיבוּ אוֹתָם דָּבָר וְאֶת־כָּל־הָעֵדָה וַיַּרְאוּם אֶת־פְּרִי הָאָרֶץ: 27וַיְסַפְּרוּ־לוֹ וַיֹּאמְרוּ בָּאנוּ אֶל־הָאָרֶץ אֲשֶׁר שְׁלַחְתָּנוּ וְגַם זָבַת חָלָב וּדְבַשׁ הִוא וְזֶה־פִּרְיָהּ: 28אֶפֶס כִּי־עַז הָעָם הַיֹּשֵׁב בָּאָרֶץ וְהֶעָרִים בְּצֻרוֹת גְּדֹלֹת מְאֹד וְגַם־יְלִדֵי הָעֲנָק רָאִינוּ שָׁם: 29עֲמָלֵק יוֹשֵׁב בְּאֶרֶץ הַנֶּגֶב וְהַחִתִּי וְהַיְבוּסִי וְהָאֱמֹרִי יוֹשֵׁב בָּהָר וְהַכְּנַעֲנִי יֹשֵׁב עַל־הַיָּם וְעַל יַד הַיַּרְדֵּן: 30וַיַּהַס כָּלֵב אֶת־הָעָם אֶל־מֹשֶׁה וַיֹּאמֶר עָלֹה נַעֲלֶה וְיָרַשְׁנוּ אֹתָהּ כִּי־יָכוֹל נוּכַל לָהּ: 31וְהָאֲנָשִׁים אֲשֶׁר־עָלוּ עִמּוֹ אָמְרוּ לֹא נוּכַל לַעֲלוֹת אֶל־הָעָם כִּי־חָזָק הוּא מִמֶּנּוּ: 32וַיֹּצִיאוּ דִּבַּת הָאָרֶץ אֲשֶׁר תָּרוּ אֹתָהּ אֶל־בְּנֵי יִשְׂרָאֵל לֵאמֹר הָאָרֶץ אֲשֶׁר עָבַרְנוּ בָהּ לָתוּר אֹתָהּ אֶרֶץ אֹכֶלֶת יוֹשְׁבֶיהָ הִוא וְכָל־הָעָם אֲשֶׁר־רָאִינוּ בְתוֹכָהּ אַנְשֵׁי מִדּוֹת: 33וְשָׁם רָאִינוּ אֶת־הַנְּפִילִים בְּנֵי עֲנָק מִן־הַנְּפִלִים וַנְּהִי בְעֵינֵינוּ כַּחֲגָבִים וְכֵן

a variety of ways that the scouts are especially noted to come to Hebron. It particularly symbolizes that this is a return home. It might have been the perfect place to begin Israel's return to the land, but the people's resistance will change all that.

13:33. sons of giants from the Nephilim. The huge creatures known as the Nephilim come up in a chain of references that are spread far apart through several books of the *Tanak.* Their origin is explained near the beginning of the Torah, in the story of the "sons of God" who have relations with human women who then give birth to

14

¹And all the congregation raised and let out their voices! And the people wept that night. ²And all the children of Israel complained at Moses and at Aaron, and all the congregation said to them, "If only we had died in the land of Egypt! Or in this wilderness, if only we had died! ³And why is YHWH bringing us to this land to fall by the sword? Our wives and our infants will become a spoil! Isn't it better for us to go back to Egypt?" ⁴And they said, each man to his brother, "Let's appoint a chief and go back to Egypt."

⁵And Moses and Aaron fell on their faces in front of all the community of the congregation of the children of Israel.

⁶And Joshua son of Nun and Caleb son of Jephunneh, from those who had scouted the land, had torn their clothes. ⁷And they said to all the congregation of the children of Israel, saying, "The land through which we passed to scout it: the land is very, very good! ⁸If YHWH desires us, then He'll bring us to this land and give it to us, a land that flows with milk and honey! ⁹Just don't revolt against YHWH. And you, don't fear the people of the land, because they're our bread! Their protection has turned from them, while YHWH is with us. Don't fear them."

¹⁰And all the congregation said to batter them with stones.

And YHWH's glory appeared at the Tent of Meeting to all the children of Israel!

¹¹And YHWH said to Moses, "How long will this people reject me, and how long will they not trust in me, with all the signs that I've done

הָיִינוּ בְּעֵינֵיהֶם: 14 ¹וַתִּשָּׂא כָּל־הָעֵדָה וַיִּתְּנוּ אֶת־
קוֹלָם וַיִּבְכּוּ הָעָם בַּלַּיְלָה הַהוּא: ²וַיִּלֹּנוּ עַל־מֹשֶׁה
וְעַל־אַהֲרֹן כֹּל בְּנֵי יִשְׂרָאֵל וַיֹּאמְרוּ אֲלֵהֶם כָּל־
הָעֵדָה לוּ־מַתְנוּ בְּאֶרֶץ מִצְרַיִם אוֹ בַּמִּדְבָּר הַזֶּה
לוּ־מָתְנוּ: ³וְלָמָה יְהֹוָה מֵבִיא אֹתָנוּ אֶל־הָאָרֶץ
הַזֹּאת לִנְפֹּל בַּחֶרֶב נָשֵׁינוּ וְטַפֵּנוּ יִהְיוּ לָבַז הֲלוֹא
טוֹב לָנוּ שׁוּב מִצְרָיְמָה: ⁴וַיֹּאמְרוּ אִישׁ אֶל־אָחִיו
נִתְּנָה רֹאשׁ וְנָשׁוּבָה מִצְרָיְמָה: ⁵וַיִּפֹּל מֹשֶׁה וְאַהֲרֹן
עַל־פְּנֵיהֶם לִפְנֵי כָּל־קְהַל עֲדַת בְּנֵי יִשְׂרָאֵל:
⁶וִיהוֹשֻׁעַ בִּן־נוּן וְכָלֵב בֶּן־יְפֻנֶּה מִן־הַתָּרִים אֶת־
הָאָרֶץ קָרְעוּ בִּגְדֵיהֶם: ⁷וַיֹּאמְרוּ אֶל־כָּל־עֲדַת בְּנֵי־
יִשְׂרָאֵל לֵאמֹר הָאָרֶץ אֲשֶׁר עָבַרְנוּ בָהּ לָתוּר אֹתָהּ
טוֹבָה הָאָרֶץ מְאֹד מְאֹד: ⁸אִם־חָפֵץ בָּנוּ יְהֹוָה
וְהֵבִיא אֹתָנוּ אֶל־הָאָרֶץ הַזֹּאת וּנְתָנָהּ לָנוּ אֶרֶץ
אֲשֶׁר־הִוא זָבַת חָלָב וּדְבָשׁ: ⁹אַךְ בַּיהֹוָה אַל־
תִּמְרֹדוּ וְאַתֶּם אַל־תִּירְאוּ אֶת־עַם הָאָרֶץ כִּי לַחְמֵנוּ
הֵם סָר צִלָּם מֵעֲלֵיהֶם וַיהֹוָה אִתָּנוּ אַל־תִּירָאֻם:
¹⁰וַיֹּאמְרוּ כָּל־הָעֵדָה לִרְגּוֹם אֹתָם בָּאֲבָנִים וּכְבוֹד
יְהֹוָה נִרְאָה בְּאֹהֶל מוֹעֵד אֶל־כָּל־בְּנֵי יִשְׂרָאֵל: פ
¹¹וַיֹּאמֶר יְהֹוָה אֶל־מֹשֶׁה עַד־אָנָה יְנַאֲצֻנִי הָעָם הַזֶּה
וְעַד־אָנָה לֹא־יַאֲמִינוּ בִי בְּכֹל הָאֹתוֹת אֲשֶׁר עָשִׂיתִי

---

giants (Gen 6:1–4). Now in the spies episode, the Israelite spies see the descendants of these giants (Numbers 13). Later, Joshua eliminates the giants from all of the land except from the Philistine cities, including Gath (Josh 11:21–22). And later still, the Philistine giant Goliath comes from *Gath* (1 Sam 17:4). These widespread references are among the many stitches that bind the *Tanak* together as a continuing story. Those who see the Bible as a loose collection of stories fail to take proper account of the substantial number of such widely distributed binding elements.

14:11. **how long will they not trust in me, with all the signs that I've done among them?** Why in fact do the people not trust? Why are they still afraid and doubtful?

among them? 12I'll strike them with an epidemic and dispossess them, and I'll make you into a
bigger and more powerful nation than they are."

13And Moses said to YHWH, "And Egypt will
hear it, for you brought this people up from
among them with your power, 14and they'll say it
to those who live in this land. They've heard that
you, YHWH, are among this people; that you,
YHWH, have appeared eye-to-eye; and your cloud
stands over them; and you go in front of them in
a column of cloud by day and in a column of fire

בְּקִרְבּוֹ: 12אַכֶּנּוּ בַדֶּבֶר וְאוֹרִשֶׁנּוּ וְאֶעֱשֶׂה אֹתְךָ
לְגוֹי־גָּדוֹל וְעָצוּם מִמֶּנּוּ: 13וַיֹּאמֶר מֹשֶׁה אֶל־יְהוָה
וְשָׁמְעוּ מִצְרַיִם כִּי־הֶעֱלִיתָ בְכֹחֲךָ אֶת־הָעָם הַזֶּה
מִקִּרְבּוֹ: 14וְאָמְרוּ אֶל־יוֹשֵׁב הָאָרֶץ הַזֹּאת שָׁמְעוּ
כִּי־אַתָּה יְהוָה בְּקֶרֶב הָעָם הַזֶּה אֲשֶׁר־עַיִן בְּעַיִן
נִרְאָה ׀ אַתָּה יְהוָה וַעֲנָנְךָ עֹמֵד עֲלֵהֶם וּבְעַמֻּד עָנָן
אַתָּה הֹלֵךְ לִפְנֵיהֶם יוֹמָם וּבְעַמּוּד אֵשׁ לָיְלָה:

They have seen their God handle *Egypt,* the major power of the world. Why would they
doubt that He can handle the Canaanites? They have seen Him manipulate the whole
of nature with the ten plagues and the splitting of the sea. They have seen water come
from a mountain crag. They have heard God's voice from the sky at Sinai. They are eating miraculous manna every day. They have just miraculously been provided with
quail to eat. Even as they complain in this moment, there is a miraculous column of
cloud and fire right in front of them. Why are they afraid? Recall that the reason they
are directed to the Red Sea when they leave Egypt, rather than through Philistine territory, is that YHWH is concerned that they will be afraid of facing war with the Philistines. As I commented there (Exod 13:18), the Red Sea required no decisions or action on their part, but facing the Philistines would have required them to take up
arms. Likewise, in every case so far, from the plagues to the quail, God and Moses have
acted for them, and they have had to do very little. Even in the battle against the
Amalekites, it was the Amalekites who attacked them, and then Joshua chose a select
group to fight on their behalf (Exod 17:8–13). But now, for the first time, the people
perceive that *they* will have to act. The scouts speak in terms of the people of Israel
themselves having to fight: "*We* won't be able to go up against the people, because
they're stronger than *we* are" (13:31). The scouts do not even mention God. What was
true when they left Egypt is still true: They are still slaves in their hearts. They are not
yet capable of independence, responsibility, or action. And so God's decision is precisely to leave the entry into the land for their children. See the comment on Num
14:29.

14:12. **I'll make you.** The Septuagint and Samaritan texts have "I'll make you *and
your father's house.*" The extra words appear to have been lost by haplography. (That
is, in the Hebrew, the word for "make you" and the phrase for "your father's house"
both end in the same letter, *kaf,* so a scribe's eye skipped from one *kap* to the next and
left out the words in between.) The addition of the reference to Moses' father's house
may suggest that Aaron's family is to be spared as well, or it may mean more broadly
that the Levites as a whole are to survive. Alternatively, it may still mean that only
Moses is to survive to start over a new people, but it is still described as the survival of
his father's house because God's relationship with Moses has focused on that link
from the beginning—God's self-introduction to Moses at the bush is: "I am your father's God" (Exod 3:6).

by night. 15And if you kill this people as one man, then the nations that have heard about you will say it, saying, 16'Because YHWH wasn't able to bring this people to the land that He swore to them, He slaughtered them in the wilderness.' 17And now, let my Lord's power be big, as you spoke, saying, 18'YHWH is slow to anger and abounding in kindness, bearing crime and offense; though not making one *innocent*: reckoning fathers' crime on children, on third generations and on fourth generations.' 19Forgive this people's crime in proportion to the magnitude of your kindness and as you've borne this people from Egypt to here."

20And YHWH said, "I've forgiven according to your word. 21But indeed, as I live, and as

וְהֵמַתָּה אֶת־הָעָם הַזֶּה כְּאִישׁ אֶחָד וְאָמְרוּ הַגּוֹיִם 15 אֲשֶׁר־שָׁמְעוּ אֶת־שִׁמְעֲךָ לֵאמֹר: 16מִבִּלְתִּי יְכֹלֶת יְהוָה לְהָבִיא אֶת־הָעָם הַזֶּה אֶל־הָאָרֶץ אֲשֶׁר־נִשְׁבַּע לָהֶם וַיִּשְׁחָטֵם בַּמִּדְבָּר: 17וְעַתָּה יִגְדַּל־נָא כֹּחַ אֲדֹנָי כַּאֲשֶׁר דִּבַּרְתָּ לֵאמֹר: 18יְהוָה אֶרֶךְ אַפַּיִם וְרַב־ חֶסֶד נֹשֵׂא עָוֹן וָפָשַׁע וְנַקֵּה לֹא יְנַקֶּה פֹּקֵד עֲוֹן אָבוֹת עַל־בָּנִים עַל־שִׁלֵּשִׁים וְעַל־רִבֵּעִים: 19סְלַח־ נָא לַעֲוֹן הָעָם הַזֶּה כְּגֹדֶל חַסְדֶּךָ וְכַאֲשֶׁר נָשָׂאתָה לָעָם הַזֶּה מִמִּצְרַיִם וְעַד־הֵנָּה: 20וַיֹּאמֶר יְהוָה סָלַחְתִּי כִּדְבָרֶךָ: 21וְאוּלָם חַי־אָנִי וְיִמָּלֵא כְבוֹד־

14:17. **let my Lord's power be big**. Moses suggests that it is more powerful to be merciful than to punish. In some circumstances, compassion is weakness. In others, it requires enormous strength.

14:18. **slow to anger** . . . Moses quotes God's own words from the moment of the great revelation, when Moses saw God at Sinai (Exod 34:6–7). So he is not only appealing to God's mercy; he is citing God's own description of Himself as if to say that God must be true to Himself.

14:18. **on children, on third generations and on fourth generations**. The passage that Moses is quoting says: "on children and on children's children, on third generations and on fourth generations" (Exod 34:7). It looks like "and on children's children" has been lost, presumably by another haplography: a scribe's eye skipped from one occurrence of the word "children" to the next. It is the easiest kind of scribal error to make, and in fact this same omission occurs in the Ten Commandments (Exod 20:5 and Deut 5:9). As a less banal and more homiletical explanation of this case, we might suggest that the text pictures Moses as shortening the long formula so as to keep focused on the larger point. Or perhaps, by leaving it out, he subtly presses God to make the correction and thus to be reminded of the extent of His compassion according to His own words. Deliberately misquoting someone may actually be an effective tool of persuasion.

14:19. **Forgive this people's crime**. Moses' fourfold defense of the people is brilliantly merged: What will the Egyptians say! What will the nations say! You swore the land to them (namely, in the covenant)! You are merciful.

14:20. **I've forgiven according to your word**. Abraham questioned God regarding Sodom and Gomorrah, but his conversation did not change anything. Ten virtuous persons were not found, and the cities were destroyed. But Moses is pictured as actually making a difference in a divine decision and in the fate of the people. This is another case in which there is growth in the human stance relative to God.

474

YHWH's glory has filled all the earth, 22I swear that all of these people, who have seen my glory and my signs that I did in Egypt and in the wilderness and who have tested me ten times now and haven't listened to my voice, 23won't see the land that I swore to their fathers, and all those who rejected me won't see it. 24And my servant Caleb, because a different spirit was with him, and he went after me completely, I'll bring him to the land where he went, and his seed will possess it. 25And the Amalekite and the Canaanite live in the valley. Turn and travel tomorrow to the wilderness by the way of the Red Sea."

26And YHWH spoke to Moses and to Aaron, saying, 27"How much further for this bad congregation, that they're complaining against me? I've heard the complaints of the children of Israel that they're making against me. 28Say to them: As I live—word of YHWH—what you have spoken in my ears, that is what I'll do to you! 29In this wilderness your carcasses will fall; and all of you who were counted, for all your number, from twenty years old and up, who complained against me, 30I swear that you won't come to the land that I raised my hand to have you reside there—except Caleb son of Jephunneh and Joshua son of Nun. 31And your infants, whom you said would become a spoil: I'll bring *them*, and

יְהוָה אֶת־כָּל־הָאָרֶץ: 22כִּי כָל־הָאֲנָשִׁים הָרֹאִים אֶת־כְּבֹדִי וְאֶת־אֹתֹתַי אֲשֶׁר־עָשִׂיתִי בְמִצְרַיִם וּבַמִּדְבָּר וַיְנַסּוּ אֹתִי זֶה עֶשֶׂר פְּעָמִים וְלֹא שָׁמְעוּ בְּקוֹלִי: 23אִם־יִרְאוּ אֶת־הָאָרֶץ אֲשֶׁר נִשְׁבַּעְתִּי לַאֲבֹתָם וְכָל־מְנַאֲצַי לֹא יִרְאוּהָ: 24וְעַבְדִּי כָלֵב עֵקֶב הָיְתָה רוּחַ אַחֶרֶת עִמּוֹ וַיְמַלֵּא אַחֲרָי וַהֲבִיאֹתִיו אֶל־הָאָרֶץ אֲשֶׁר־בָּא שָׁמָּה וְזַרְעוֹ יוֹרִשֶׁנָּה: 25וְהָעֲמָלֵקִי וְהַכְּנַעֲנִי יוֹשֵׁב בָּעֵמֶק מָחָר פְּנוּ וּסְעוּ לָכֶם הַמִּדְבָּר דֶּרֶךְ יַם־סוּף: פ 26וַיְדַבֵּר יְהוָה אֶל־מֹשֶׁה וְאֶל־אַהֲרֹן לֵאמֹר: 27עַד־מָתַי לָעֵדָה הָרָעָה הַזֹּאת אֲשֶׁר הֵמָּה מַלִּינִים עָלַי אֶת־תְּלֻנּוֹת בְּנֵי יִשְׂרָאֵל אֲשֶׁר הֵמָּה מַלִּינִים עָלַי שָׁמָעְתִּי: 28אֱמֹר אֲלֵהֶם חַי־אָנִי נְאֻם־יְהוָה אִם־לֹא כַּאֲשֶׁר דִּבַּרְתֶּם בְּאָזְנָי כֵּן אֶעֱשֶׂה לָכֶם: 29בַּמִּדְבָּר הַזֶּה יִפְּלוּ פִגְרֵיכֶם וְכָל־פְּקֻדֵיכֶם לְכָל־מִסְפַּרְכֶם מִבֶּן עֶשְׂרִים שָׁנָה וָמָעְלָה אֲשֶׁר הֲלִינֹתֶם עָלָי: 30אִם־אַתֶּם תָּבֹאוּ אֶל־הָאָרֶץ אֲשֶׁר נָשָׂאתִי אֶת־יָדִי לְשַׁכֵּן אֶתְכֶם בָּהּ כִּי אִם־כָּלֵב בֶּן־יְפֻנֶּה וִיהוֹשֻׁעַ בִּן־נוּן: 31וְטַפְּכֶם אֲשֶׁר אֲמַרְתֶּם לָבַז יִהְיֶה

14:28. **what you have spoken in my ears, that is what I'll do to you!** Another case of ironic divine punishment to suit the crime: They could have had the land and lived, but they were afraid and said that they would die and their children would be made captives. So now they will in fact die, but their children will live and one day be free in the land. This is the most dramatic demonstration yet of the people's persistent slave mentality. God says that He has forgiven them, and they are not stricken with an epidemic as God had originally said; but they are also not ready for the life of free people in a land of their own. And so this is left for their children, who grow up not knowing the experience of having been slaves. An entire generation's experience is not easily reversed. In our own age we see the impact on the lives of survivors of the holocaust. Some become more religious, some reject religion. Some cannot speak of it, and some speak of it constantly. Some return to the sites where they suffered, and some will never go back. It affects their medical decisions, their ways of raising their children, their trust of other human beings, their work, their thoughts, their opinions, and their memories. Their children carry tremendous loads of guilt and obligation, but they have a chance of knowing a kind of freedom that their parents cannot know.

they will know the land that you rejected! 32And *you:* your carcasses will fall in this wilderness. 33And your children will be roving in the wilderness forty years, and they'll bear your whoring until the end of your carcasses in the wilderness. 34For the number of days that you scouted the land, forty days, you shall bear your crimes a day for each year, forty years, and you shall know my frustration! 35I, YHWH, have spoken: If I shall not do this to all this bad congregation who are gathered against me: in this wilderness they shall end, and they shall die there!"

36And the men whom Moses sent to scout the land and came back and caused all the congregation to complain against him, bringing out a report about the land: 37the men who brought out the bad report of the land died in a plague in front of YHWH. 38But, out of those men who went to scout the land, Joshua son of Nun and Caleb son of Jephunneh lived.

39And Moses spoke these things to all the children of Israel, and the people mourned very much. 40And they got up in the morning and went up to the top of the mountain, saying, "Here we are, and we'll go up to the place that YHWH said, because we've sinned."

41And Moses said, "Why are you violating YHWH's word? And it won't succeed. 42Don't go up, so you won't be stricken in front of your enemies, because YHWH isn't among you. 43Because the Amalekite and the Canaanite are there in front of you, and you'll fall by the sword because of the fact that you've gone back from following YHWH, and YHWH won't be with you."

44And they acted heedlessly, going up to the top of the mountain. And the ark of the covenant of YHWH and Moses did not draw away from the camp. 45And the Amalekite and the Canaanite who lived in that mountain came down, and they struck them and crushed them as far as Hormah.

וְהֵבֵאתִי אֹתָם וְיָדְעוּ אֶת־הָאָרֶץ אֲשֶׁר מְאַסְתֶּם
בָּהּ: 32וּפִגְרֵיכֶם אַתֶּם יִפְּלוּ בַּמִּדְבָּר הַזֶּה:
33וּבְנֵיכֶם יִהְיוּ רֹעִים בַּמִּדְבָּר אַרְבָּעִים שָׁנָה וְנָשְׂאוּ
אֶת־זְנוּתֵיכֶם עַד־תֹּם פִּגְרֵיכֶם בַּמִּדְבָּר: 34בְּמִסְפַּר
הַיָּמִים אֲשֶׁר־תַּרְתֶּם אֶת־הָאָרֶץ אַרְבָּעִים יוֹם יוֹם
לַשָּׁנָה יוֹם לַשָּׁנָה תִּשְׂאוּ אֶת־עֲוֹנֹתֵיכֶם אַרְבָּעִים
שָׁנָה וִידַעְתֶּם אֶת־תְּנוּאָתִי: 35אֲנִי יְהוָה דִּבַּרְתִּי אִם־
לֹא ׀ זֹאת אֶעֱשֶׂה לְכָל־הָעֵדָה הָרָעָה הַזֹּאת
הַנּוֹעָדִים עָלָי בַּמִּדְבָּר הַזֶּה יִתַּמּוּ וְשָׁם יָמֻתוּ:
36וְהָאֲנָשִׁים אֲשֶׁר־שָׁלַח מֹשֶׁה לָתוּר אֶת־הָאָרֶץ
וַיָּשֻׁבוּ וַיַּלִּינוּ עָלָיו אֶת־כָּל־הָעֵדָה לְהוֹצִיא דִבָּה
עַל־הָאָרֶץ: 37וַיָּמֻתוּ הָאֲנָשִׁים מוֹצִאֵי דִבַּת־הָאָרֶץ
רָעָה בַּמַּגֵּפָה לִפְנֵי יְהוָה: 38וִיהוֹשֻׁעַ בִּן־נוּן וְכָלֵב
בֶּן־יְפֻנֶּה חָיוּ מִן־הָאֲנָשִׁים הָהֵם הַהֹלְכִים לָתוּר
אֶת־הָאָרֶץ: 39וַיְדַבֵּר מֹשֶׁה אֶת־הַדְּבָרִים הָאֵלֶּה
אֶל־כָּל־בְּנֵי יִשְׂרָאֵל וַיִּתְאַבְּלוּ הָעָם מְאֹד:
40וַיַּשְׁכִּמוּ בַבֹּקֶר וַיַּעֲלוּ אֶל־רֹאשׁ־הָהָר לֵאמֹר הִנֶּנּוּ
וְעָלִינוּ אֶל־הַמָּקוֹם אֲשֶׁר־אָמַר יְהוָה כִּי חָטָאנוּ:
41וַיֹּאמֶר מֹשֶׁה לָמָּה זֶּה אַתֶּם עֹבְרִים אֶת־פִּי יְהוָה
וְהִוא לֹא תִצְלָח: 42אַל־תַּעֲלוּ כִּי אֵין יְהוָה
בְּקִרְבְּכֶם וְלֹא תִּנָּגְפוּ לִפְנֵי אֹיְבֵיכֶם: 43כִּי
הָעֲמָלֵקִי וְהַכְּנַעֲנִי שָׁם לִפְנֵיכֶם וּנְפַלְתֶּם בֶּחָרֶב כִּי־
עַל־כֵּן שַׁבְתֶּם מֵאַחֲרֵי יְהוָה וְלֹא־יִהְיֶה יְהוָה
עִמָּכֶם: 44וַיַּעְפִּלוּ לַעֲלוֹת אֶל־רֹאשׁ הָהָר וַאֲרוֹן
בְּרִית־יְהוָה וּמֹשֶׁה לֹא־מָשׁוּ מִקֶּרֶב הַמַּחֲנֶה: 45וַיֵּרֶד
הָעֲמָלֵקִי וְהַכְּנַעֲנִי הַיֹּשֵׁב בָּהָר הַהוּא וַיַּכּוּם וַיַּכְּתוּם
עַד־הַחָרְמָה: פ

קֹ וַיַּלִּינוּ 14:36

14:35. **If I shall not do this.** This wording is an oath formulation. It means, "I shall surely do this."

15 ¹And YHWH spoke to Moses, saying, ²"Speak to the children of Israel, and you shall say to them: When you will come to the land of your homes that I am giving to you, ³and you will make a fire offering to YHWH, a burnt offering or a sacrifice, to express a vow or as a contribution or at your appointed times, to make a pleasant smell to YHWH from the cattle or from the flock, ⁴then the one bringing his offering to YHWH shall bring forward a grain offering, fine flour, one-tenth of a measure, mixed with a fourth of a hin of oil. ⁵And you shall make wine for a libation with the burnt offering or the sacrifice, a fourth of a hin for one lamb. ⁶Or for a ram, you shall make a grain offering, fine flour, two tenths, mixed with oil, a third of a hin, ⁷and you shall bring forward wine for a libation, a third of a hin, a pleasant smell to YHWH. ⁸And if you will make a bull a burnt offering or a sacrifice, to express a vow, or a peace offering to YHWH, ⁹then he shall bring forward with the bull a grain offering, fine flour, three tenths, mixed with oil, half of a hin, ¹⁰and you shall bring forward wine for a libation, half of a hin, an offering by fire of a pleasant smell to YHWH. ¹¹It shall be done this way for one ox or for one ram or for a lamb of the sheep or of the goats. ¹²By the number that you will do, you shall do each one of their number this way. ¹³Every citizen shall do these this way when bringing forward an offering by fire of a pleasant smell to YHWH. ¹⁴And when an alien will reside with you—or someone who is among you—through your generations and will make an offering by fire of a pleasant smell to YHWH, as you will do so he shall do. ¹⁵You, congregation, and the resident alien have one law, an eternal law through your generations: it will be the same for you and for the alien in front of YHWH. ¹⁶You and the alien who resides with you shall have one instruction and one judgment."

15 ²דַּבֵּ֣ר אֶל־ ¹וַיְדַבֵּ֥ר יְהֹוָ֖ה אֶל־מֹשֶׁ֥ה לֵּאמֹֽר׃
בְּנֵ֣י יִשְׂרָאֵל֮ וְאָמַרְתָּ֣ אֲלֵהֶם֒ כִּ֣י תָבֹ֗אוּ אֶל־אֶ֨רֶץ֙
מוֹשְׁבֹ֣תֵיכֶ֔ם אֲשֶׁ֥ר אֲנִ֖י נֹתֵ֥ן לָכֶֽם׃ ³וַעֲשִׂיתֶ֨ם אִשֶּׁ֤ה
לַֽיהֹוָה֙ עֹלָ֣ה אוֹ־זֶ֔בַח לְפַלֵּא־נֶ֨דֶר֙ א֣וֹ בִנְדָבָ֔ה א֖וֹ
בְּמֹעֲדֵיכֶ֑ם לַעֲשׂ֞וֹת רֵ֤יחַ נִיחֹ֨חַ֙ לַֽיהֹוָ֔ה מִן־הַבָּקָ֖ר א֥וֹ
מִן־הַצֹּֽאן׃ ⁴וְהִקְרִ֛יב הַמַּקְרִ֥יב קׇרְבָּנ֖וֹ לַֽיהֹוָ֑ה מִנְחָה֙
סֹ֣לֶת עִשָּׂר֔וֹן בָּל֕וּל בִּרְבִעִ֥ית הַהִ֖ין שָֽׁמֶן׃ ⁵וְיַ֤יִן
לַנֶּ֨סֶךְ֙ רְבִיעִ֣ית הַהִ֔ין תַּעֲשֶׂ֥ה עַל־הָעֹלָ֖ה א֣וֹ לַזָּ֑בַח
לַכֶּ֖בֶשׂ הָאֶחָֽד׃ ⁶א֤וֹ לָאַ֨יִל֙ תַּעֲשֶׂ֣ה מִנְחָ֔ה סֹ֖לֶת שְׁנֵ֣י
עֶשְׂרֹנִ֑ים בְּלוּלָ֥ה בַשֶּׁ֖מֶן שְׁלִשִׁ֥ית הַהִֽין׃ ⁷וְיַ֥יִן לַנֶּ֖סֶךְ
שְׁלִשִׁ֣ית הַהִ֑ין תַּקְרִ֥יב רֵֽיחַ־נִיחֹ֖חַ לַֽיהֹוָֽה׃ ⁸וְכִֽי־
תַעֲשֶׂ֥ה בֶן־בָּקָ֖ר עֹלָ֣ה אוֹ־זָ֑בַח לְפַלֵּא־נֶ֨דֶר֙ אֽוֹ־
שְׁלָמִ֖ים לַֽיהֹוָֽה׃ ⁹וְהִקְרִ֥יב עַל־בֶּן־הַבָּקָ֖ר מִנְחָ֑ה
סֹ֣לֶת שְׁלֹשָׁ֣ה עֶשְׂרֹנִ֔ים בָּל֥וּל בַּשֶּׁ֖מֶן חֲצִ֥י הַהִֽין׃
¹⁰וְיַ֛יִן תַּקְרִ֥יב לַנֶּ֖סֶךְ חֲצִ֣י הַהִ֑ין אִשֵּׁ֥ה רֵֽיחַ־נִיחֹ֖חַ
לַֽיהֹוָֽה׃ ¹¹כָּ֣כָה יֵעָשֶׂ֗ה לַשּׁוֹר֙ הָֽאֶחָ֔ד א֖וֹ לָאַ֣יִל
הָאֶחָ֑ד אֽוֹ־לַשֶּׂ֥ה בַכְּבָשִׂ֖ים א֥וֹ בָעִזִּֽים׃ ¹²כַּמִּסְפָּ֖ר
אֲשֶׁ֣ר תַּעֲשׂ֑וּ כָּ֚כָה תַּעֲשׂ֣וּ לָֽאֶחָ֔ד כְּמִסְפָּרָֽם׃ ¹³כׇּל־
הָאֶזְרָ֛ח יַעֲשֶׂה־כָּ֖כָה אֶת־אֵ֑לֶּה לְהַקְרִ֛יב אִשֵּׁ֥ה רֵֽיחַ־
נִיחֹ֖חַ לַֽיהֹוָֽה׃ ¹⁴וְכִֽי־יָגוּר֩ אִתְּכֶ֨ם גֵּ֜ר א֤וֹ אֲשֶֽׁר־
בְּתֽוֹכְכֶם֙ לְדֹרֹ֣תֵיכֶ֔ם וְעָשָׂ֛ה אִשֵּׁ֥ה רֵֽיחַ־נִיחֹ֖חַ לַֽיהֹוָ֑ה
כַּאֲשֶׁ֥ר תַּעֲשׂ֖וּ כֵּ֥ן יַעֲשֶֽׂה׃ ¹⁵הַקָּהָ֕ל חֻקָּ֥ה אַחַ֛ת לָכֶ֖ם
וְלַגֵּ֣ר הַגָּ֑ר חֻקַּ֤ת עוֹלָם֙ לְדֹרֹ֣תֵיכֶ֔ם כָּכֶ֛ם כַּגֵּ֥ר יִהְיֶ֖ה
לִפְנֵ֥י יְהֹוָֽה׃ ¹⁶תּוֹרָ֥ה אַחַ֛ת וּמִשְׁפָּ֥ט אֶחָ֖ד יִהְיֶ֣ה לָכֶ֑ם
וְלַגֵּ֖ר הַגָּ֥ר אִתְּכֶֽם׃ פ ¹⁷וַיְדַבֵּ֥ר יְהֹוָ֖ה אֶל־מֹשֶׁ֥ה

15:16. You and the alien. In these verses (14–16) the text says in four different ways that the law is the same for a citizen and a resident alien. Thus it again emphasizes that this is an essential principle of the Torah: Israelites are not privileged over anyone else. A country must treat everyone who lives in it fairly, with equality under the law.

17And YHWH spoke to Moses, saying, 18"Speak to the children of Israel, and you shall say to them: When you come to the land where I'm bringing you, 19then it will be that when you eat some of the land's bread you shall make a donation to YHWH. 20The first of your dough: you shall make a loaf as a donation. Like a donation from the threshing floor, so you shall donate it. 21From the first of your dough you shall give a donation to YHWH through your generations.

22"And when you will make a mistake and not do all of these commandments that YHWH has spoken to Moses, 23everything that YHWH has commanded you by Moses' hand, from the day that YHWH commanded and on through your generations, 24then it will be that, if it was done by mistake, out of the congregation's sight, then all the congregation shall do one bull of the cattle as a burnt offering for a pleasant smell to YHWH and its grain offering and its libation according to the required manner and one goat for a sin offering. 25And the priest shall make atonement for all the congregation of the children of Israel, and it will be forgiven for them, because it was a mistake, and they brought their offering, an offering by fire to YHWH, and their sin offering in front of YHWH for their mistake. 26And it will be forgiven for all the congregation of the children of Israel and the alien who resides among them, because it was by mistake for all the people.

27"And if one person will sin by mistake, then he shall bring a she-goat in its first year for a sin offering. 28And the priest shall make atonement for the person who made the mistake, sinning by mistake, in front of YHWH to make atonement for him, and it will be forgiven for him. 29The citizen among the children of Israel and for the alien who resides among them: you shall have one instruction for one who acts by mistake.

30"But the person who will act with a high hand, a citizen or an alien, he is blaspheming YHWH, and that person will be cut off from

לֵאמֹר: 18דַּבֵּר אֶל־בְּנֵי יִשְׂרָאֵל וְאָמַרְתָּ אֲלֵהֶם בְּבֹאֲכֶם אֶל־הָאָרֶץ אֲשֶׁר אֲנִי מֵבִיא אֶתְכֶם שָׁמָּה: 19וְהָיָה בַּאֲכָלְכֶם מִלֶּחֶם הָאָרֶץ תָּרִימוּ תְרוּמָה לַיהוָה: 20רֵאשִׁית עֲרִסֹתֵכֶם חַלָּה תָּרִימוּ תְרוּמָה כִּתְרוּמַת גֹּרֶן כֵּן תָּרִימוּ אֹתָהּ: 21מֵרֵאשִׁית עֲרִסֹתֵיכֶם תִּתְּנוּ לַיהוָה תְּרוּמָה לְדֹרֹתֵיכֶם: ס

22וְכִי תִשְׁגּוּ וְלֹא תַעֲשׂוּ אֵת כָּל־הַמִּצְוֹת הָאֵלֶּה אֲשֶׁר־דִּבֶּר יְהוָה אֶל־מֹשֶׁה: 23אֵת כָּל־אֲשֶׁר צִוָּה יְהוָה אֲלֵיכֶם בְּיַד־מֹשֶׁה מִן־הַיּוֹם אֲשֶׁר צִוָּה יְהוָה וָהָלְאָה לְדֹרֹתֵיכֶם: 24וְהָיָה אִם מֵעֵינֵי הָעֵדָה נֶעֶשְׂתָה לִשְׁגָגָה וְעָשׂוּ כָל־הָעֵדָה פַּר בֶּן־בָּקָר אֶחָד לְעֹלָה לְרֵיחַ נִיחֹחַ לַיהוָה וּמִנְחָתוֹ וְנִסְכּוֹ כַּמִּשְׁפָּט וּשְׂעִיר־עִזִּים אֶחָד לְחַטָּת: 25וְכִפֶּר הַכֹּהֵן עַל־כָּל־עֲדַת בְּנֵי יִשְׂרָאֵל וְנִסְלַח לָהֶם כִּי־שְׁגָגָה הִוא וְהֵם הֵבִיאוּ אֶת־קָרְבָּנָם אִשֶּׁה לַיהוָה וְחַטָּאתָם לִפְנֵי יְהוָה עַל־שִׁגְגָתָם: 26וְנִסְלַח לְכָל־עֲדַת בְּנֵי יִשְׂרָאֵל וְלַגֵּר הַגָּר בְּתוֹכָם כִּי לְכָל־הָעָם בִּשְׁגָגָה: ס

27וְאִם־נֶפֶשׁ אַחַת תֶּחֱטָא בִשְׁגָגָה וְהִקְרִיבָה עֵז בַּת־שְׁנָתָהּ לְחַטָּאת: 28וְכִפֶּר הַכֹּהֵן עַל־הַנֶּפֶשׁ הַשֹּׁגֶגֶת בְּחֶטְאָה בִשְׁגָגָה לִפְנֵי יְהוָה לְכַפֵּר עָלָיו וְנִסְלַח לוֹ: 29הָאֶזְרָח בִּבְנֵי יִשְׂרָאֵל וְלַגֵּר הַגָּר בְּתוֹכָם תּוֹרָה אַחַת יִהְיֶה לָכֶם לָעֹשֶׂה בִּשְׁגָגָה: 30וְהַנֶּפֶשׁ אֲשֶׁר־תַּעֲשֶׂה בְּיָד רָמָה מִן־הָאֶזְרָח וּמִן־הַגֵּר אֶת־יְהוָה הוּא מְגַדֵּף וְנִכְרְתָה הַנֶּפֶשׁ הַהִוא מִקֶּרֶב

among his people, 31because he disdained YHWH's word and broke His commandment. That person will be *cut off*. His crime is in him."

32And the children of Israel were in the wilderness, and they found a man collecting wood on the Sabbath day. 33And those who found him collecting wood brought him forward to Moses and to Aaron and to all the congregation. 34And they left him under watch because it had not been determined what should be done to him.

35And YHWH said to Moses, "The man shall be *put to death*! All the congregation is to batter him with stones outside the camp."

36And all the congregation brought him outside the camp and battered him with stones, and he died, as YHWH commanded Moses.

37And YHWH said to Moses, saying, 38"Speak to the children of Israel, and you shall say to them that they shall make fringe on the corners of their clothes through their generations. And they shall put a blue string on the fringe of the corner. 39And you shall have the fringe so you will see it and bring to mind all of YHWH's commandments and will do them, and you will not

עַמָּה: 31כִּי דְבַר־יְהוָה בָּזָה וְאֶת־מִצְוָתוֹ הֵפַר הִכָּרֵת | תִּכָּרֵת הַנֶּפֶשׁ הַהִוא עֲוֺנָה בָהּ: פ 32וַיִּהְיוּ בְנֵי־יִשְׂרָאֵל בַּמִּדְבָּר וַיִּמְצְאוּ אִישׁ מְקֹשֵׁשׁ עֵצִים בְּיוֹם הַשַּׁבָּת: 33וַיַּקְרִיבוּ אֹתוֹ הַמֹּצְאִים אֹתוֹ מְקֹשֵׁשׁ עֵצִים אֶל־מֹשֶׁה וְאֶל־אַהֲרֹן וְאֶל כָּל־הָעֵדָה: 34וַיַּנִּיחוּ אֹתוֹ בַּמִּשְׁמָר כִּי לֹא פֹרַשׁ מַה־יֵּעָשֶׂה לוֹ: ס 35וַיֹּאמֶר יְהוָה אֶל־מֹשֶׁה מוֹת יוּמַת הָאִישׁ רָגוֹם אֹתוֹ בָאֲבָנִים כָּל־הָעֵדָה מִחוּץ לַמַּחֲנֶה: 36וַיֹּצִיאוּ אֹתוֹ כָּל־הָעֵדָה אֶל־מִחוּץ לַמַּחֲנֶה וַיִּרְגְּמוּ אֹתוֹ בָּאֲבָנִים וַיָּמֹת כַּאֲשֶׁר צִוָּה יְהוָה אֶת־מֹשֶׁה: פ 37וַיֹּאמֶר יְהוָה אֶל־מֹשֶׁה לֵּאמֹר: 38דַּבֵּר אֶל־בְּנֵי יִשְׂרָאֵל וְאָמַרְתָּ אֲלֵהֶם וְעָשׂוּ לָהֶם צִיצִת עַל־כַּנְפֵי בִגְדֵיהֶם לְדֹרֹתָם וְנָתְנוּ עַל־צִיצִת הַכָּנָף פְּתִיל תְּכֵלֶת: 39וְהָיָה לָכֶם לְצִיצִת וּרְאִיתֶם אֹתוֹ וּזְכַרְתֶּם אֶת־כָּל־מִצְוֺת יְהוָה וַעֲשִׂיתֶם אֹתָם וְלֹא־תָתֻרוּ

15:34. it had not been determined. There had already been commandments to observe the Sabbath, not to work on that day, and not to make a fire on that day; and it had already been stated that one who violates the Sabbath is to be executed and cut off. But it was yet to be determined whether this particular case of collecting wood constituted work or whether (if the collection of wood was for building a fire) the collection itself constituted a violation. This account thus not only teaches a law about the Sabbath but also demonstrates the relationship between a legal *principle* and the application of that principle to each individual *case*. No case is to be prejudged. Every case deserves an inquiry and a decision.

15:38. blue string. Blue string is used in the garments of the high priest (Exod 28:28,37). The blue string in the fringe of every Israelite's clothing is an element of the holy in everyone's daily life. The fringe in general is a reminder to keep all the commandments; the blue string is a reminder of holiness. (See the next comment.)

15:39. see it and bring to mind. Most of the commandments in the Torah are given without any reason being stated. We are not told why we are not allowed to eat a pig or to steal, or why the Tabernacle must have twenty frames on each side. If we want to know the reasons, we have to ponder and try to determine them ourselves. For some commandments the reason is obvious, and for some it is extremely difficult to know. The commandment to wear fringes stands out, therefore, as being one for which the

go around after your heart and after your eyes, because you whore after them. 40So you will bring to mind and do all my commandments, and you will be holy to your God. 41I am YHWH, your God, who brought you out from the land of Egypt to be God to you. I am YHWH, your God."

אַחֲרֵי לְבַבְכֶם וְאַחֲרֵי עֵינֵיכֶם אֲשֶׁר־אַתֶּם זֹנִים אַחֲרֵיהֶם: 40לְמַעַן תִּזְכְּרוּ וַעֲשִׂיתֶם אֶת־כָּל־מִצְוֺתָי וִהְיִיתֶם קְדֹשִׁים לֵאלֹהֵיכֶם: 41אֲנִי יְהוָה אֱלֹהֵיכֶם אֲשֶׁר הוֹצֵאתִי אֶתְכֶם מֵאֶרֶץ מִצְרַיִם לִהְיוֹת לָכֶם לֵאלֹהִים אֲנִי יְהוָה אֱלֹהֵיכֶם: פ

KORAH

קרח

16 ¹And Korah son of Izhar son of Kohath son of Levi, and Dathan and Abiram, sons of Eliab, and On, son of Peleth, sons of Reuben, took ²and got up in front of Moses—and two hundred fifty people from the children of Israel, chieftains of the congregation, prominent ones of the assembly, people of repute. ³And they assembled against Moses and against Aaron and said to them, "You have much! Because all of the congregation, all of them, are holy, and YHWH is among them. And why do you raise yourselves up over YHWH's community?"

16 ¹וַיִּקַּח קֹרַח בֶּן־יִצְהָר בֶּן־קְהָת בֶּן־לֵוִי וְדָתָן וַאֲבִירָם בְּנֵי אֱלִיאָב וְאוֹן בֶּן־פֶּלֶת בְּנֵי רְאוּבֵן: ²וַיָּקֻמוּ לִפְנֵי מֹשֶׁה וַאֲנָשִׁים מִבְּנֵי־יִשְׂרָאֵל חֲמִשִּׁים וּמָאתָיִם נְשִׂיאֵי עֵדָה קְרִאֵי מוֹעֵד אַנְשֵׁי־ שֵׁם: ³וַיִּקָּהֲלוּ עַל־מֹשֶׁה וְעַל־אַהֲרֹן וַיֹּאמְרוּ אֲלֵהֶם רַב־לָכֶם כִּי כָל־הָעֵדָה כֻּלָּם קְדֹשִׁים וּבְתוֹכָם יְהוָה וּמַדּוּעַ תִּתְנַשְּׂאוּ עַל־קְהַל יְהוָה: ⁴וַיִּשְׁמַע

---

reason is stated explicitly: the fringe is a reminder; it is always present on one's clothing so that one will see it and be reminded of the existence of all the commandments, so one will do them, and so the people will be holy.

15:39. go around. Hebrew *tûr*. This is the same word that is used for the scouting of the land by the spies in the preceding chapters. This both helps us understand the word—meaning to go looking all over, here with the sense of looking for trouble— and helps to connect the laws of this chapter with the story of the spies that just precedes it. This chapter of law is often seen as intrusive between a series of stories, but the language used in the laws bring the stories to mind, and vice versa.

16:1. Korah. He is a first cousin of Moses and Aaron (Exod 6:18–21).

16:1. Korah . . . took. He assembles a group with him, and he frames his argument in terms of the people ("all of them are holy"). He is the prototype of some politicians, religious leaders, and others, who act as though they represent a group and are working for the people—when their motives are suspect.

16:3. all of the congregation, all of them, are holy. It is true that all the people have been described as a holy nation. Korah uses this now to enhance his claim that he has as much right to the priesthood as Aaron. But it is a deception, mixing two different meanings and degrees of holiness. It is like telling a child that he or she is now "big" or "grown up"—and then the child demands all the rights and privileges of grownups.

4And Moses listened, and he fell on his face. 5And he spoke to Korah and to all of his congregation, saying, "In the morning YHWH will make known who is His and who is holy, and He will bring him close to Him. And He will bring the one He chooses close to Him. 6Do this: Take incense burners, Korah and all his congregation, 7and put fire in them and set incense on them in front of YHWH tomorrow. And it will be that the man whom YHWH will choose, he will be the holy one. *You* have much, sons of Levi!" 8And Moses said to Korah, "Listen, sons of Levi, 9is it too small a thing for you that Israel's God has distinguished you from the congregation of Israel to bring you close to him, to do the work of YHWH's Tabernacle and to stand in front of the congregation to minister for them, 10and that He has brought you and all your brothers, the sons of Levi, with you close to Him? And you seek priesthood as well?! 11Therefore you and all your congregation who are gathering are against YHWH! And Aaron, what is he that you complain against him?"

12And Moses sent to call Dathan and Abiram, sons of Eliab, and they said, "We won't come up.

מֹשֶׁה וַיִּפֹּל עַל־פָּנָיו: 5וַיְדַבֵּר אֶל־קֹרַח וְאֶל־כָּל־עֲדָתוֹ לֵאמֹר בֹּקֶר וְיֹדַע יְהוָה אֶת־אֲשֶׁר־לוֹ וְאֶת־הַקָּדוֹשׁ וְהִקְרִיב אֵלָיו וְאֵת אֲשֶׁר יִבְחַר־בּוֹ יַקְרִיב אֵלָיו: 6זֹאת עֲשׂוּ קְחוּ־לָכֶם מַחְתּוֹת קֹרַח וְכָל־עֲדָתוֹ: 7וּתְנוּ בָהֵן ׀ אֵשׁ וְשִׂימוּ עֲלֵיהֶן קְטֹרֶת לִפְנֵי יְהוָה מָחָר וְהָיָה הָאִישׁ אֲשֶׁר־יִבְחַר יְהוָה הוּא הַקָּדוֹשׁ רַב־לָכֶם בְּנֵי לֵוִי: 8וַיֹּאמֶר מֹשֶׁה אֶל־קֹרַח שִׁמְעוּ־נָא בְּנֵי לֵוִי: 9הַמְעַט מִכֶּם כִּי־הִבְדִּיל אֱלֹהֵי יִשְׂרָאֵל אֶתְכֶם מֵעֲדַת יִשְׂרָאֵל לְהַקְרִיב אֶתְכֶם אֵלָיו לַעֲבֹד אֶת־עֲבֹדַת מִשְׁכַּן יְהוָה וְלַעֲמֹד לִפְנֵי הָעֵדָה לְשָׁרְתָם: 10וַיַּקְרֵב אֹתְךָ וְאֶת־כָּל־אַחֶיךָ בְנֵי־לֵוִי אִתָּךְ וּבִקַּשְׁתֶּם גַּם־כְּהֻנָּה: 11לָכֵן אַתָּה וְכָל־עֲדָתְךָ הַנֹּעָדִים עַל־יְהוָה וְאַהֲרֹן מַה־הוּא כִּי תַלִּינוּ עָלָיו: 12וַיִּשְׁלַח מֹשֶׁה לִקְרֹא לְדָתָן וְלַאֲבִירָם בְּנֵי אֱלִיאָב וַיֹּאמְרוּ לֹא נַעֲלֶה: 13הַמְעַט

16:11 קְ תַלִּינוּ

16:5. **who is holy.** Moses sets up a test of who is holy, to establish what it means to be holy in the priestly sense, as opposed to the general concept that the people should strive to be holy. The test will be the use of incense, because only the holy—namely, priests—are permitted to burn incense. The test will establish this, and it will be declared formally following this episode (Num 17:5). And Korah and his company cannot be unaware of the significance of the correct burning of incense, because it was precisely a misuse of incense that led to the death of Aaron's sons, Nadab and Abihu (Lev 10:1-2).

16:6. **Do this.** Why does Korah go along with the test? Do he and his followers really believe that God would support them? Answer: they have no choice. Moses does not *propose* a test. He *commands* Korah and his group. His verbs are four imperatives in a row: do, take, put, set! And Korah cannot refuse. The whole point, after all, is that Korah is seeking priesthood (Num 16:10). What Moses challenges him to do is to perform one of the acts that he would commonly have to do if he were to become a priest: burn incense. Korah's claim on the priesthood would evaporate if he were to decline the opportunity he has been offered to do a priestly task.

16:12. **Moses sent to call Dathan and Abiram.** Two groups with two different complaints have joined together to challenge Moses. Korah's company challenge Aaron's

13Is it a small thing that you brought us up from a land flowing with milk and honey to kill us in the wilderness, that you lord it over us as well? 14Besides, you haven't brought us to a land flowing with milk and honey or given us possession of field or vineyard. Will you put out those people's eyes? We won't come up."

15And Moses was very angry, and he said to YHWH, "Don't turn to their offering. Not one ass of theirs have I taken away, and I haven't wronged one of them."

16And Moses said to Korah, "You and all your congregation, be in front of YHWH—you and they and Aaron—tomorrow. 17And each man take his fire-holder, and put incense on them, and each man bring his fire-holder forward in front of YHWH, two hundred fifty fire-holders, and you and Aaron, each man his fire-holder."

18And each man took his fire-holder, and they put fire on them and set incense on them, and they stood at the entrance of the Tent of Meeting,

כִּי הֶעֱלִיתָ֫נוּ מֵאֶ֫רֶץ זָבַת חָלָב֙ וּדְבַשׁ֙ לַהֲמִיתֵ֫נוּ בַּמִּדְבָּ֑ר כִּי־תִשְׂתָּרֵ֥ר עָלֵ֖ינוּ גַּם־הִשְׂתָּרֵֽר: 14אַ֡ף לֹ֣א אֶל־אֶ֩רֶץ֩ זָבַ֨ת חָלָ֤ב וּדְבַשׁ֙ הֲבִ֣יאֹתָ֔נוּ וַתִּֽתֶּן־לָ֔נוּ נַחֲלַ֖ת שָׂדֶ֣ה וָכָ֑רֶם הַעֵינֵ֞י הָאֲנָשִׁ֤ים הָהֵם֙ תְּנַקֵּ֔ר לֹ֥א נַעֲלֶֽה: 15וַיִּ֤חַר לְמֹשֶׁה֙ מְאֹ֔ד וַיֹּ֨אמֶר֙ אֶל־יְהוָ֔ה אַל־תֵּ֖פֶן אֶל־מִנְחָתָ֑ם לֹ֠א חֲמ֨וֹר אֶחָ֤ד מֵהֶם֙ נָשָׂ֔אתִי וְלֹ֥א הֲרֵעֹ֖תִי אֶת־אַחַ֥ד מֵהֶֽם: 16וַיֹּ֤אמֶר מֹשֶׁה֙ אֶל־קֹ֔רַח אַתָּה֙ וְכָל־עֲדָ֣תְךָ֔ הֱי֖וּ לִפְנֵ֣י יְהוָ֑ה אַתָּ֥ה וָהֵ֛ם וְאַהֲרֹ֖ן מָחָֽר: 17וּקְח֣וּ ׀ אִ֣ישׁ מַחְתָּת֗וֹ וּנְתַתֶּ֤ם עֲלֵיהֶם֙ קְטֹ֔רֶת וְהִקְרַבְתֶּ֞ם לִפְנֵ֤י יְהוָה֙ אִ֣ישׁ מַחְתָּת֔וֹ חֲמִשִּׁ֥ים וּמָאתַ֖יִם מַחְתֹּ֑ת וְאַתָּ֥ה וְאַהֲרֹ֖ן אִ֥ישׁ מַחְתָּתֽוֹ: 18וַיִּקְח֞וּ אִ֣ישׁ מַחְתָּת֗וֹ וַיִּתְּנ֤וּ עֲלֵיהֶם֙ אֵ֔שׁ וַיָּשִׂ֥ימוּ עֲלֵיהֶ֖ם קְטֹ֑רֶת וַיַּֽעַמְד֗וּ פֶּ֛תַח אֹ֥הֶל מוֹעֵ֖ד וּמֹשֶׁ֥ה

---

hold on the priesthood; Dathan and Abiram challenge Moses' hold on the leadership of Israel. This political union of two agendas is presumably arranged to strengthen the positions of both. Moses, however, keeps them separate. He has responded first to Korah and his company who are challenging the priestly prerogatives of Moses and Aaron. Now he turns to Dathan and Abiram and summons them. By separating them, he weakens their position.

16:13. you brought us up from a land flowing with milk and honey. They are referring to Egypt! They use the rhetorical device of reversing their opponent's position: they say that Moses has taken them *out* of a land flowing with milk and honey. It is a clever device (common in political debate). And it is outrageous: accusing the liberator of being the source of their problems, picturing the land of slavery as the land of milk and honey, and, as usual, focusing on Moses rather than on God. And then they say, "Will you put out those people's eyes?"—accusing Moses of being the one who is deceiving the people, when it is they who are the deceivers. This is a battle for leadership, which is to say it is a political battle, which is to say it is a battle for power; and it dramatizes the danger of the power-seeking politician who is a skillful speaker. Moses defeats his opponents because God intervenes with a miracle. We who cannot count on earthquakes to identify the corrupt ones among us must be thoughtful, sensitive, and diligent when we listen to political argument.

16:14. you haven't brought us to a land flowing with milk and honey or given us possession of field or vineyard. This is true. Part of a persuasive lie is to mix in something that is true.

482

and Moses and Aaron. ¹⁹And Korah assembled all the congregation against them, to the entrance of the Tent of Meeting. And YHWH's glory appeared to all the congregation.

²⁰And YHWH spoke to Moses and to Aaron, saying, ²¹"Separate from among this congregation, and I'll finish them in an instant!"

²²And they fell on their faces and said, "God, the God of the spirits of all flesh, will one man sin and you be angry at all the congregation?"

²³And YHWH spoke to Moses, saying, ²⁴"Speak to the congregation, saying, 'Get up from around the tabernacle of Korah, Dathan and Abiram.'"

²⁵And Moses got up and went to Dathan and Abiram, and Israel's elders went after him. ²⁶And he spoke to the congregation, saying, "Turn away from the tents of these wicked men and don't touch anything that is theirs, or else you'll be annihilated through all their sins."

²⁷And they got up from around the tabernacle of Korah, Dathan and Abiram. And Dathan and Abiram came out, standing at the entrance of their tents, and their wives and their children and their infants. ²⁸And Moses said, "By this you'll know that YHWH sent me to do all these things, because it's not from my own heart. ²⁹If these die like the death of every human, and the event of every human happens to them, then YHWH hasn't sent me. ³⁰But if YHWH will create something, and the ground will open its mouth and swallow them and all that they have, and

וְאַהֲרֹן: ¹⁹וַיַּקְהֵל עֲלֵיהֶם קֹרַח אֶת־כָּל־הָעֵדָה אֶל־פֶּתַח אֹהֶל מוֹעֵד וַיֵּרָא כְבוֹד־יְהוָה אֶל־כָּל־הָעֵדָה: פ ²⁰וַיְדַבֵּר יְהוָה אֶל־מֹשֶׁה וְאֶל־אַהֲרֹן לֵאמֹר: ²¹הִבָּדְלוּ מִתּוֹךְ הָעֵדָה הַזֹּאת וַאֲכַלֶּה אֹתָם כְּרָגַע: ²²וַיִּפְּלוּ עַל־פְּנֵיהֶם וַיֹּאמְרוּ אֵל אֱלֹהֵי הָרוּחֹת לְכָל־בָּשָׂר הָאִישׁ אֶחָד יֶחֱטָא וְעַל כָּל־הָעֵדָה תִּקְצֹף: פ ²³וַיְדַבֵּר יְהוָה אֶל־מֹשֶׁה לֵּאמֹר: ²⁴דַּבֵּר אֶל־הָעֵדָה לֵאמֹר הֵעָלוּ מִסָּבִיב לְמִשְׁכַּן־קֹרַח דָּתָן וַאֲבִירָם: ²⁵וַיָּקָם מֹשֶׁה וַיֵּלֶךְ אֶל־דָּתָן וַאֲבִירָם וַיֵּלְכוּ אַחֲרָיו זִקְנֵי יִשְׂרָאֵל: ²⁶וַיְדַבֵּר אֶל־הָעֵדָה לֵאמֹר סוּרוּ נָא מֵעַל אָהֳלֵי הָאֲנָשִׁים הָרְשָׁעִים הָאֵלֶּה וְאַל־תִּגְּעוּ בְּכָל־אֲשֶׁר לָהֶם פֶּן־תִּסָּפוּ בְּכָל־חַטֹּאתָם: ²⁷וַיֵּעָלוּ מֵעַל מִשְׁכַּן־קֹרַח דָּתָן וַאֲבִירָם מִסָּבִיב וְדָתָן וַאֲבִירָם יָצְאוּ נִצָּבִים פֶּתַח אָהֳלֵיהֶם וּנְשֵׁיהֶם וּבְנֵיהֶם וְטַפָּם: ²⁸וַיֹּאמֶר מֹשֶׁה בְּזֹאת תֵּדְעוּן כִּי־יְהוָה שְׁלָחַנִי לַעֲשׂוֹת אֵת כָּל־הַמַּעֲשִׂים הָאֵלֶּה כִּי־לֹא מִלִּבִּי: ²⁹אִם־כְּמוֹת כָּל־הָאָדָם יְמֻתוּן אֵלֶּה וּפְקֻדַּת כָּל־הָאָדָם יִפָּקֵד עֲלֵיהֶם לֹא יְהוָה שְׁלָחָנִי: ³⁰וְאִם־בְּרִיאָה יִבְרָא יְהוָה וּפָצְתָה הָאֲדָמָה אֶת־פִּיהָ וּבָלְעָה אֹתָם וְאֶת־

16:22. will one man sin and you be angry at all the congregation. Korah has brought the whole congregation of Israel along (16:19), and God has threatened to destroy all of them (16:21), and so Moses and Aaron plead that only those who have done something wrong should suffer. "One man" here cannot mean literally only a single person; it must refer to every individual in Korah's congregation, as opposed to the entire congregation of Israel. It is reminiscent of Abraham's plea in the case of Sodom and Gomorrah ("Will you also annihilate the virtuous with the wicked?" Gen 18:23). The connection to the case of Sodom is highlighted by the fact that Moses then tells the people to get away "or else you'll be annihilated," which are the words that the angels say at Sodom—and these words occur nowhere else in the Torah (see Gen 18:23,24; 19:15,17).

they'll go down alive to Sheol, then you'll know that these people have rejected YHWH."

31And it was as he was finishing speaking all these things, and the ground that was under them was broken up, 32and the earth opened its mouth and swallowed them and their households and all the people who were with Korah and all the property, 33and they went down, they and all that they had, alive to Sheol. And the earth covered them over, and they perished from among the community. 34And all Israel that was around them fled at the sound of them, for they said, "Or else the earth will swallow us."

35And fire had gone out from YHWH and consumed the two hundred fifty people offering the incense.

כָּל־אֲשֶׁר לָהֶם וְיָרְדוּ חַיִּים שְׁאֹלָה וִידַעְתֶּם כִּי נִאֲצוּ הָאֲנָשִׁים הָאֵלֶּה אֶת־יְהוָה: 31וַיְהִי כְּכַלֹּתוֹ לְדַבֵּר אֵת כָּל־הַדְּבָרִים הָאֵלֶּה וַתִּבָּקַע הָאֲדָמָה אֲשֶׁר תַּחְתֵּיהֶם: 32וַתִּפְתַּח הָאָרֶץ אֶת־פִּיהָ וַתִּבְלַע אֹתָם וְאֶת־בָּתֵּיהֶם וְאֵת כָּל־הָאָדָם אֲשֶׁר לְקֹרַח וְאֵת כָּל־הָרְכוּשׁ: 33וַיֵּרְדוּ הֵם וְכָל־אֲשֶׁר לָהֶם חַיִּים שְׁאֹלָה וַתְּכַס עֲלֵיהֶם הָאָרֶץ וַיֹּאבְדוּ מִתּוֹךְ הַקָּהָל: 34וְכָל־יִשְׂרָאֵל אֲשֶׁר סְבִיבֹתֵיהֶם נָסוּ לְקֹלָם כִּי אָמְרוּ פֶּן־תִּבְלָעֵנוּ הָאָרֶץ: 35וְאֵשׁ יָצְאָה מֵאֵת יְהוָה וַתֹּאכַל אֵת הַחֲמִשִּׁים וּמָאתַיִם אִישׁ מַקְרִיבֵי הַקְּטֹרֶת: פ

16:32. them and their households. Meaning: their entire families die with them. Why does the entire household suffer? Elsewhere in the law we are told that each person is responsible for his or her own crimes. Children are not to suffer for their parents' acts (Deut 24:16). But that principle applies only to ethical law: crimes between one human and another. In ritual law—violations against God, such as blasphemy or, in this case, openly opposing an instruction from God ("these people have rejected YHWH")—anyone who comes in contact with the source of the offense is tainted by it, regardless of that person's own intent. Thus, for example, in the book of Joshua, Achan keeps some of the forbidden spoils of Jericho, which are designated for complete destruction (*ḥerem*). He conceals them in his tent. When his offense is revealed he and the spoils "and his sons and his daughters and his ox and his ass and his flock and his tent and everything he had" are stoned and burned (Josh 7:24). It is difficult to understand in the postbiblical age, but the concepts of ritual, sacred realms, purity and impurity, and violation of sacred zones are fundamental to Israel's life as pictured in the Bible's early books. It may be that the advance in psychology and especially of psychoanalysis in this century can help us to appreciate the mind-set of those who conceived of this notion of guilt by contact. We can recognize that people feel guilt even about things that are not their fault morally. Victims of childhood incest frequently feel guilt through their adult lives. As a closer example: as a child I observed another boy tear a Torah scroll, and I recall how upsetting this was to him and others even though he did not necessarily do it out of lack of care. I also recall, from my student days, knocking a pious rabbi's black hat from a hook onto the floor and feeling terrible even though it was an accident. (He was wise; he just said lightly, "Praise God that my head wasn't in it at the time.") The point is that we do have feelings of guilt in connection with things that we hold in awe. And this is multiplied a thousandfold in the narrative of the age of the Torah: when the divine is believed to be close at hand.

16:35. fire had gone out. This is worded in the past perfect. (The noun precedes the verb in the Hebrew.) That is, this must be understood to have happened to Korah's

17 ¹And YHWH spoke to Moses, saying, ²"Say to Eleazar son of Aaron, the priest, that he should pick up the fire-holders from the burning and disperse the fire, because they have become holy. ³And the fire-holders of these who sinned at the cost of their lives: let them make them into hammered plates as plating for the altar, because they brought them forward in front of YHWH, and they became holy, and let them become a sign to the children of Israel."

⁴And Eleazar, the priest, took the fire-holders of bronze that those who were burned had brought forward, and they hammered them into a plating for the altar, ⁵a commemoration for the children of Israel so that no outsider, one who is not from Aaron's seed, will come forward to burn incense in front of YHWH, so he will not be like Korah and like his congregation, as YHWH spoke to him by Moses' hand.

⁶And all the congregation of the children of Israel complained the next day against Moses and against Aaron, saying, "*You* killed YHWH's people!"

17 ¹וַיְדַבֵּ֥ר יְהוָ֖ה אֶל־מֹשֶׁ֥ה לֵּאמֹֽר: ²אֱמֹ֨ר אֶל־אֶלְעָזָ֜ר בֶּן־אַהֲרֹ֣ן הַכֹּהֵ֗ן וְיָרֵ֤ם אֶת־הַמַּחְתֹּת֙ מִבֵּ֣ין הַשְּׂרֵפָ֔ה וְאֶת־הָאֵ֖שׁ זְרֵה־הָ֑לְאָה כִּ֖י קָדֵֽשׁוּ: ³אֵ֡ת מַחְתּוֹת֩ הַֽחַטָּאִ֨ים הָאֵ֜לֶּה בְּנַפְשֹׁתָ֗ם וְעָשׂ֨וּ אֹתָ֜ם רִקֻּעֵ֤י פַחִים֙ צִפּ֣וּי לַמִּזְבֵּ֔חַ כִּֽי־הִקְרִיבֻ֥ם לִפְנֵֽי־יְהוָ֖ה וַיִּקְדָּ֑שׁוּ וְיִֽהְי֥וּ לְא֖וֹת לִבְנֵ֥י יִשְׂרָאֵֽל: ⁴וַיִּקַּ֞ח אֶלְעָזָ֣ר הַכֹּהֵ֗ן אֵ֚ת מַחְתּ֣וֹת הַנְּחֹ֔שֶׁת אֲשֶׁ֥ר הִקְרִ֖יבוּ הַשְּׂרֻפִ֑ים וַֽיְרַקְּע֖וּם צִפּ֥וּי לַמִּזְבֵּֽחַ: ⁵זִכָּר֞וֹן לִבְנֵ֣י יִשְׂרָאֵ֗ל לְ֠מַעַן אֲשֶׁ֨ר לֹֽא־יִקְרַ֜ב אִ֣ישׁ זָ֗ר אֲ֠שֶׁר לֹ֣א מִזֶּ֤רַע אַהֲרֹן֙ ה֔וּא לְהַקְטִ֥יר קְטֹ֖רֶת לִפְנֵ֣י יְהוָ֑ה וְלֹֽא־יִהְיֶ֤ה כְקֹ֙רַח֙ וְכַ֣עֲדָת֔וֹ כַּאֲשֶׁ֨ר דִּבֶּ֧ר יְהוָ֛ה בְּיַד־מֹשֶׁ֖ה לֽוֹ: ⁶וַיִּלֹּ֜נוּ כָּל־עֲדַ֤ת בְּנֵֽי־יִשְׂרָאֵל֙ מִֽמָּחֳרָ֔ת עַל־מֹשֶׁ֥ה וְעַֽל־אַהֲרֹ֖ן לֵאמֹ֑ר אַתֶּ֥ם הֲמִתֶּ֖ם אֶת־עַ֥ם יְהוָֽה:

---

incense-burning group before the earthquake swallowed them along with Dathan's and Abiram's households.

17:6. all the congregation of the children of Israel complained the next day. Sometimes a solution may give rise to worse conditions than the original problem. Korah, Dathan, and Abiram had 250 persons in their congregation challenging Moses and Aaron. They are all killed, but now the *entire* congregation of Israel challenges them.

17:6. *You* killed YHWH's people! Not only do they focus, once again, on Moses and Aaron instead of on their God, they say that Moses and Aaron caused the deaths of Korah and his group. And they turn the truth around even further by saying, "*You* killed YHWH's people!"—seemingly placing Moses and Aaron on the *opposite* side from God. Their attack turns the truth on its head, and so God's response is ironic: they have said that Moses and Aaron have killed God's people, so God now threatens to kill His people Himself for their attack on Moses and Aaron! And the irony is extended because Moses and Aaron are the ones who *save* the people from the rage and plague that come.

One might look at a summary of these episodes of challenges to Moses and be inclined to think that the book of Numbers ultimately has only one story to tell and simply keeps repeating it with slight changes of detail. However, that is not likely to be the sense one gets while reading through the stories themselves. The stories act

7And it was when the congregation was assembled against Moses and against Aaron, and they turned to the Tent of Meeting; and, here, the cloud had covered it, and YHWH's glory appeared. 8And Moses and Aaron came to the front of the Tent of Meeting.

9And YHWH spoke to Moses, saying, 10"Move away from among this congregation, and I'll finish them in an instant!" And they fell on their faces.

11And Moses said to Aaron, "Take a fire-holder and put fire from the altar on it and set incense and carry it quickly to the congregation and make atonement for them, because a rage has come out from in front of YHWH! The plague has begun!"

12And Aaron took it as Moses had spoken, and he ran among the community. And, here, the plague had begun among the people. And he put in incense and made atonement for the people. 13And he stood between the dead and the living. And the plague was halted. 14And the dead in the plague were fourteen thousand seven hundred, apart from the dead over the matter of Korah. 15And Aaron went back to Moses, to the entrance of the Tent of Meeting, when the plague had been halted.

16And YHWH spoke to Moses, saying,

7וַיְהִ֗י בְּהִקָּהֵ֤ל הָֽעֵדָה֙ עַל־מֹשֶׁ֣ה וְעַֽל־אַהֲרֹ֔ן וַיִּפְנוּ֙ אֶל־אֹ֣הֶל מוֹעֵ֔ד וְהִנֵּ֥ה כִסָּ֖הוּ הֶעָנָ֑ן וַיֵּרָ֖א כְּב֥וֹד יְהוָֽה׃ 8וַיָּבֹ֤א מֹשֶׁה֙ וְאַהֲרֹ֔ן אֶל־פְּנֵ֖י אֹ֥הֶל מוֹעֵֽד׃ פ 9וַיְדַבֵּ֥ר יְהוָ֖ה אֶל־מֹשֶׁ֥ה לֵּאמֹֽר׃ 10הֵרֹ֗מּוּ מִתּוֹךְ֙ הָעֵדָ֣ה הַזֹּ֔את וַאֲכַלֶּ֥ה אֹתָ֖ם כְּרָ֑גַע וַֽיִּפְּל֖וּ עַל־פְּנֵיהֶֽם׃ 11וַיֹּ֨אמֶר מֹשֶׁ֜ה אֶֽל־אַהֲרֹ֗ן קַ֣ח אֶת־הַ֠מַּחְתָּ֠ה וְתֶן־עָלֶ֨יהָ אֵ֜שׁ מֵעַ֤ל הַמִּזְבֵּ֙חַ֙ וְשִׂ֣ים קְטֹ֔רֶת וְהוֹלֵ֧ךְ מְהֵרָ֛ה אֶל־הָעֵדָ֖ה וְכַפֵּ֣ר עֲלֵיהֶ֑ם כִּֽי־יָצָ֥א הַקֶּ֛צֶף מִלִּפְנֵ֥י יְהוָ֖ה הֵחֵ֥ל הַנָּֽגֶף׃ 12וַיִּקַּ֨ח אַהֲרֹ֜ן כַּֽאֲשֶׁ֣ר ׀ דִּבֶּ֣ר מֹשֶׁ֗ה וַיָּ֙רָץ֙ אֶל־תּ֣וֹךְ הַקָּהָ֔ל וְהִנֵּ֛ה הֵחֵ֥ל הַנֶּ֖גֶף בָּעָ֑ם וַיִּתֵּן֙ אֶֽת־הַקְּטֹ֔רֶת וַיְכַפֵּ֖ר עַל־הָעָֽם׃ 13וַיַּֽעֲמֹ֥ד בֵּֽין־הַמֵּתִ֖ים וּבֵ֣ין הַֽחַיִּ֑ים וַתֵּֽעָצַ֖ר הַמַּגֵּפָֽה׃ 14וַיִּֽהְי֗וּ הַמֵּתִים֙ בַּמַּגֵּפָ֔ה אַרְבָּעָ֥ה עָשָׂ֛ר אֶ֖לֶף וּשְׁבַ֣ע מֵא֑וֹת מִלְּבַ֥ד הַמֵּתִ֖ים עַל־דְּבַר־קֹֽרַח׃ 15וַיָּ֤שָׁב אַהֲרֹן֙ אֶל־מֹשֶׁ֔ה אֶל־פֶּ֖תַח אֹ֣הֶל מוֹעֵ֑ד וְהַמַּגֵּפָ֖ה נֶעֱצָֽרָה׃ פ 16וַיְדַבֵּ֥ר יְהוָ֖ה אֶל־מֹשֶׁ֥ה לֵּאמֹֽר׃ 17דַּבֵּ֣ר ׀ אֶל־בְּנֵ֣י

---

more like variations on a theme. They are each attractive and instructive in themselves, while the recurring elements of theme and language provide sufficient commonality to relate them sensibly to one another and thus give shape to Numbers as a book. When one reads that the people make the same error again and again, directing their complaints toward their human leaders rather than toward the deity who is in fact responsible for their fortunes, one errs to see in this mere repetition. More fruitful would be a consideration of what is to be learned from this picture of a human community who will not learn from experience on this point—or who apparently refuse to accept the reality of it. As in Exodus, closeness to the divine, witnessing the intervention of the cosmic into the mundane, is pictured more as frightening than as uplifting. Despite all that they have seen, they resist coming to terms with the invisible God who has gotten them their freedom and made a covenant with them. And so each new episode of conflict and divine response does not resolve the problem but only leads to another stage of it. But they will finally begin to recognize that their conflicts are also with their God in one of their last rebellions (see Num 21:4–9 and the comments on 21:5).

486

17"Speak to the children of Israel and take from them a staff for each father's house, from all their chieftains by their fathers' house, twelve staffs. You shall write each man's name on his staff, 18and you shall write Aaron's name on the staff of Levi, because there shall be one staff for the head of their fathers' house. 19And you shall leave them in the Tent of Meeting in front of the Testimony where I shall meet with you. 20And it will be that the man I shall choose: his staff will bloom. And I'll decrease from me the complaints of the children of Israel that they're making against you."

21And Moses spoke to the children of Israel, and all their chieftains gave him a staff for each chieftain by their fathers' house, twelve staffs, and Aaron's staff was among their staffs. 22And Moses left the staffs in front of YHWH in the Tent of the Testimony. 23And it was the next day, and Moses came to the Tent of the Testimony; and, here, Aaron's staff, of the house of Levi, had bloomed; and it brought out a bloom, and it made a blossom, and it produced almonds! 24And Moses brought out all the staffs from in front of YHWH to the children of Israel. And they saw, and each took his staff.

25And YHWH said to Moses, "Put back Aaron's staff in front of the Testimony for watching over, for a sign to rebels, and you'll end their complaints against me so they won't die!" 26And Moses did it. As YHWH had commanded him, he did so.

27And the children of Israel said to Moses, saying, "Here, we're expiring, we're perishing, we're all perishing! 28Everyone who comes close— who comes close to YHWH's Tabernacle—will die. Have we come to the end of expiring?!"

יִשְׂרָאֵל֒ וְקַ֣ח מֵֽאִתָּ֡ם מַטֶּ֣ה מַטֶּה֩ לְבֵ֨ית אָ֜ב מֵאֵ֣ת
כָּל־נְשִׂיאֵהֶ֗ם לְבֵ֤ית אֲבֹתָם֙ שְׁנֵ֣ים עָשָׂ֣ר מַטּ֔וֹת אִ֕ישׁ
אֶת־שְׁמ֖וֹ תִּכְתֹּ֥ב עַל־מַטֵּֽהוּ: 18וְאֵת֙ שֵׁ֣ם אַהֲרֹ֔ן
תִּכְתֹּ֖ב עַל־מַטֵּ֣ה לֵוִ֑י כִּ֚י מַטֶּ֣ה אֶחָ֔ד לְרֹ֖אשׁ בֵּ֥ית
אֲבוֹתָֽם: 19וְהִנַּחְתָּ֖ם בְּאֹ֣הֶל מוֹעֵ֑ד לִפְנֵי֙ הָֽעֵד֔וּת
אֲשֶׁ֛ר אִוָּעֵ֥ד לָכֶ֖ם שָֽׁמָּה: 20וְהָיָ֗ה הָאִ֛ישׁ אֲשֶׁ֥ר
אֶבְחַר־בּ֖וֹ מַטֵּ֣הוּ יִפְרָ֑ח וַהֲשִׁכֹּתִ֣י מֵֽעָלַ֗י אֶת־תְּלֻנּוֹת֙
בְּנֵ֣י יִשְׂרָאֵ֔ל אֲשֶׁ֛ר הֵ֥ם מַלִּינִ֖ם עֲלֵיכֶֽם: 21וַיְדַבֵּ֨ר
מֹשֶׁ֜ה אֶל־בְּנֵ֣י יִשְׂרָאֵ֗ל וַיִּתְּנ֣וּ אֵלָ֣יו ׀ כָּֽל־נְשִׂיאֵיהֶ֡ם
מַטֶּה֩ לְנָשִׂ֨יא אֶחָ֜ד מַטֶּ֣ה לְנָשִׂ֣יא אֶחָ֗ד לְבֵ֤ית אֲבֹתָם֙
שְׁנֵ֣ים עָשָׂ֣ר מַטּ֑וֹת וּמַטֵּ֥ה אַהֲרֹ֖ן בְּת֥וֹךְ מַטּוֹתָֽם:
22וַיַּנַּ֥ח מֹשֶׁ֛ה אֶת־הַמַּטֹּ֖ת לִפְנֵ֣י יְהוָ֑ה בְּאֹ֖הֶל הָעֵדֻֽת:
23וַיְהִ֣י מִֽמָּחֳרָ֗ת וַיָּבֹ֤א מֹשֶׁה֙ אֶל־אֹ֣הֶל הָעֵד֔וּת וְהִנֵּ֛ה
פָּרַ֥ח מַטֵּֽה־אַהֲרֹ֖ן לְבֵ֣ית לֵוִ֑י וַיֹּ֤צֵֽא פֶ֨רַח֙ וַיָּ֣צֵֽץ צִ֔יץ
וַיִּגְמֹ֖ל שְׁקֵדִֽים: 24וַיֹּצֵ֨א מֹשֶׁ֤ה אֶת־כָּל־הַמַּטֹּת֙ מִלִּפְנֵ֣י
יְהוָ֔ה אֶֽל־כָּל־בְּנֵ֖י יִשְׂרָאֵ֑ל וַיִּרְא֥וּ וַיִּקְח֖וּ אִ֥ישׁ מַטֵּֽהוּ: ס
25וַיֹּ֨אמֶר יְהוָ֜ה אֶל־מֹשֶׁ֗ה הָשֵׁ֞ב אֶת־מַטֵּ֤ה אַהֲרֹן֙
לִפְנֵ֣י הָעֵד֔וּת לְמִשְׁמֶ֥רֶת לְא֖וֹת לִבְנֵי־מֶ֑רִי וּתְכַ֧ל
תְּלוּנֹּתָ֛ם מֵעָלַ֖י וְלֹ֥א יָמֻֽתוּ: 26וַיַּ֖עַשׂ מֹשֶׁ֑ה כַּאֲשֶׁ֨ר
צִוָּ֧ה יְהוָ֛ה אֹת֖וֹ כֵּ֥ן עָשָֽׂה: ס 27וַיֹּֽאמְרוּ֙ בְּנֵ֣י יִשְׂרָאֵ֔ל
אֶל־מֹשֶׁ֖ה לֵאמֹ֑ר הֵ֥ן גָּוַ֛עְנוּ אָבַ֖דְנוּ כֻּלָּ֥נוּ אָבָֽדְנוּ:
28כֹּ֞ל הַקָּרֵ֧ב ׀ הַקָּרֵ֛ב אֶל־מִשְׁכַּ֥ן יְהוָ֖ה יָמ֑וּת הַאִ֥ם
תַּמְנוּ לִגְוֹֽעַ: ס

17:25. Put back Aaron's staff in front of the Testimony for watching over, for a sign to rebels. Aaron's staff that miraculously blossomed is now saved by the ark as a reminder when people will rebel in the future. This will be crucial to the event that will determine Aaron's fate later, when the people will rebel at Meribah. See the comment on Num 20:8.

18

¹And YHWH said to Aaron, "You and your sons and your father's house with you shall bear any crime of the holy place, and you and your sons with you shall bear any crime of your priesthood. ²And bring forward your brothers, the tribe of Levi, your father's tribe, with you as well, and they shall be connected to you and shall minister to you, and you and your sons with you shall be in front of the Tent of the Testimony. ³And they shall keep your charge, the charge of all of the tent, but they shall not come close to the equipment of the holy and to the altar, so they will not die, both they and you. ⁴And they shall be connected to you and shall keep the charge of the Tent of Meeting, for all the work of the tent, but an outsider shall not come close to you. ⁵And you shall keep the charge of the holy and the charge of the altar, so there will not be any more rage at the children of Israel. ⁶And I, here, I have taken your brothers, the Levites from among the children of Israel as a gift to you, given for YHWH, to do the work of the Tent of Meeting. ⁷And you and your sons with you shall watch over your priesthood for everything of the altar's and for inside the pavilion, and you shall serve. I give your priesthood as a gift of service. And the outsider who comes close shall be put to death."

⁸And YHWH said to Aaron, "And I, here, I have given charge of my donations to you for all the holy things of the children of Israel. I have given them to you as an anointing and to your sons as an eternal law. ⁹This shall be yours from the holy of holies, from the fire: every offering of theirs, every grain offering of theirs and every sin

18 ¹וַיֹּאמֶר יְהוָה אֶל־אַהֲרֹן אַתָּה וּבָנֶיךָ וּבֵית־אָבִיךָ אִתָּךְ תִּשְׂאוּ אֶת־עֲוֹן הַמִּקְדָּשׁ וְאַתָּה וּבָנֶיךָ אִתָּךְ תִּשְׂאוּ אֶת־עֲוֹן כְּהֻנַּתְכֶם: ²וְגַם אֶת־אַחֶיךָ מַטֵּה לֵוִי שֵׁבֶט אָבִיךָ הַקְרֵב אִתָּךְ וְיִלָּווּ עָלֶיךָ וִישָׁרְתוּךָ וְאַתָּה וּבָנֶיךָ אִתָּךְ לִפְנֵי אֹהֶל הָעֵדֻת: ³וְשָׁמְרוּ מִשְׁמַרְתְּךָ וּמִשְׁמֶרֶת כָּל־הָאֹהֶל אַךְ אֶל־כְּלֵי הַקֹּדֶשׁ וְאֶל־הַמִּזְבֵּחַ לֹא יִקְרָבוּ וְלֹא־יָמֻתוּ גַם־הֵם גַם־אַתֶּם: ⁴וְנִלְווּ עָלֶיךָ וְשָׁמְרוּ אֶת־מִשְׁמֶרֶת אֹהֶל מוֹעֵד לְכֹל עֲבֹדַת הָאֹהֶל וְזָר לֹא־יִקְרַב אֲלֵיכֶם: ⁵וּשְׁמַרְתֶּם אֵת מִשְׁמֶרֶת הַקֹּדֶשׁ וְאֵת מִשְׁמֶרֶת הַמִּזְבֵּחַ וְלֹא־יִהְיֶה עוֹד קֶצֶף עַל־בְּנֵי יִשְׂרָאֵל: ⁶וַאֲנִי הִנֵּה לָקַחְתִּי אֶת־אֲחֵיכֶם הַלְוִיִּם מִתּוֹךְ בְּנֵי יִשְׂרָאֵל לָכֶם מַתָּנָה נְתֻנִים לַיהוָה לַעֲבֹד אֶת־עֲבֹדַת אֹהֶל מוֹעֵד: ⁷וְאַתָּה וּבָנֶיךָ אִתְּךָ תִּשְׁמְרוּ אֶת־כְּהֻנַּתְכֶם לְכָל־דְּבַר הַמִּזְבֵּחַ וּלְמִבֵּית לַפָּרֹכֶת וַעֲבַדְתֶּם עֲבֹדַת מַתָּנָה אֶתֵּן אֶת־כְּהֻנַּתְכֶם וְהַזָּר הַקָּרֵב יוּמָת: ס ⁸וַיְדַבֵּר יְהוָה אֶל־אַהֲרֹן וַאֲנִי הִנֵּה נָתַתִּי לְךָ אֶת־מִשְׁמֶרֶת תְּרוּמֹתָי לְכָל־קָדְשֵׁי בְנֵי־יִשְׂרָאֵל לְךָ נְתַתִּים לְמָשְׁחָה וּלְבָנֶיךָ לְחָק־עוֹלָם: ⁹זֶה־יִהְיֶה לְךָ מִקֹּדֶשׁ הַקֳּדָשִׁים מִן־הָאֵשׁ כָּל־קָרְבָּנָם לְכָל־מִנְחָתָם וּלְכָל־חַטָּאתָם וּלְכָל־

18:2. **connected**. The word is the verbal form of the word "Levite." Some would say that it might shed light on the original meaning of the term Levite as being someone who is joined or attached to the sacred in order to perform service; in other words, a priest. In this verse, it is used to mean that these persons are rather attached to the priests, in order to perform service to the priests; in other words, Levites are designated as secondary clergy, whose task is to assist the priests.

18:8. **anointing**. Meaning the donations that they acquire by virtue of being anointed as Israel's priests (see Exod 29:27–28; Lev 7:35–36).

offering of theirs and every guilt offering of theirs that they will pay back to me. It is holy of holies for you and for your sons. ¹⁰You shall eat it in the holy of holies. Every male shall eat it. It shall be holy to you.

¹¹"And this is yours: their gift donation, all the elevation offerings of the children of Israel. I have given them to you and to your sons and to your daughters with you as an eternal law. Everyone who is pure in your house shall eat it.

¹²"All the best of the oil and all the best of the wine and grain, the first of them that they will give to YHWH: I have given them to you. ¹³The firstfruits of everything that is in their land that they will bring to YHWH shall be yours. Everyone who is pure in your house shall eat it. ¹⁴Every devoted thing in Israel shall be yours. ¹⁵Every first birth of a womb of all flesh that they will bring forward to YHWH, human and animal, shall be yours. Just: you shall *redeem* the human firstborn, and you shall redeem the firstborn of an impure animal. ¹⁶And their redemption price: from one month old you shall redeem it at your appraisal, five shekels of silver by the shekel of the Holy. It is twenty gerah. ¹⁷Just: you shall not redeem a firstborn of an ox or firstborn of a sheep or firstborn of a goat. They are holy. You shall fling their blood on the altar and burn their fat to smoke, a fire offering for a pleasant smell to YHWH. ¹⁸And their meat shall be yours; like the breast of the elevation offering and the right thigh it shall be yours. ¹⁹All the donations of the holy things that the children of Israel will donate to YHWH I have given to you and to your sons and to your daughters with you as an eternal law. It is an eternal covenant of salt in front of YHWH for you and for your seed with you."

אַשְׁמָם אֲשֶׁר יָשִׁיבוּ לִי קֹדֶשׁ קָדָשִׁים לְךָ הוּא וּלְבָנֶיךָ: ¹⁰בְּקֹדֶשׁ הַקֳּדָשִׁים תֹּאכֲלֶנּוּ כָּל־זָכָר יֹאכַל אֹתוֹ קֹדֶשׁ יִהְיֶה־לָּךְ: ¹¹וְזֶה־לְּךָ תְּרוּמַת מַתָּנָם לְכָל־תְּנוּפֹת בְּנֵי יִשְׂרָאֵל לְךָ נְתַתִּים וּלְבָנֶיךָ וְלִבְנֹתֶיךָ אִתְּךָ לְחָק־עוֹלָם כָּל־טָהוֹר בְּבֵיתְךָ יֹאכַל אֹתוֹ: ¹²כֹּל חֵלֶב יִצְהָר וְכָל־חֵלֶב תִּירוֹשׁ וְדָגָן רֵאשִׁיתָם אֲשֶׁר־יִתְּנוּ לַיהוָה לְךָ נְתַתִּים: ¹³בִּכּוּרֵי כָּל־אֲשֶׁר בְּאַרְצָם אֲשֶׁר־יָבִיאוּ לַיהוָה לְךָ יִהְיֶה כָּל־טָהוֹר בְּבֵיתְךָ יֹאכֲלֶנּוּ: ¹⁴כָּל־חֵרֶם בְּיִשְׂרָאֵל לְךָ יִהְיֶה: ¹⁵כָּל־פֶּטֶר רֶחֶם לְכָל־בָּשָׂר אֲשֶׁר־יַקְרִיבוּ לַיהוָה בָּאָדָם וּבַבְּהֵמָה יִהְיֶה־לָּךְ אַךְ פָּדֹה תִפְדֶּה אֵת בְּכוֹר הָאָדָם וְאֵת בְּכוֹר־הַבְּהֵמָה הַטְּמֵאָה תִּפְדֶּה: ¹⁶וּפְדוּיָו מִבֶּן־חֹדֶשׁ תִּפְדֶּה בְּעֶרְכְּךָ כֶּסֶף חֲמֵשֶׁת שְׁקָלִים בְּשֶׁקֶל הַקֹּדֶשׁ עֶשְׂרִים גֵּרָה הוּא: ¹⁷אַךְ בְּכוֹר־שׁוֹר אוֹ־בְכוֹר כֶּשֶׂב אוֹ־בְכוֹר עֵז לֹא תִפְדֶּה קֹדֶשׁ הֵם אֶת־דָּמָם תִּזְרֹק עַל־הַמִּזְבֵּחַ וְאֶת־חֶלְבָּם תַּקְטִיר אִשֶּׁה לְרֵיחַ נִיחֹחַ לַיהוָה: ¹⁸וּבְשָׂרָם יִהְיֶה־לָּךְ כַּחֲזֵה הַתְּנוּפָה וּכְשׁוֹק הַיָּמִין לְךָ יִהְיֶה: ¹⁹כֹּל תְּרוּמֹת הַקֳּדָשִׁים אֲשֶׁר יָרִימוּ בְנֵי־יִשְׂרָאֵל לַיהוָה נָתַתִּי לְךָ וּלְבָנֶיךָ וְלִבְנֹתֶיךָ אִתְּךָ לְחָק־עוֹלָם בְּרִית מֶלַח עוֹלָם הִוא לִפְנֵי יְהוָה לְךָ וּלְזַרְעֲךָ אִתָּךְ: ²⁰וַיֹּאמֶר יְהוָה אֶל־

18:9. **guilt offering that they will pay back**. See the case in Num 5:7-8.

18:10. **in the holy of holies**. Meaning in the holiest of holy conditions.

18:14. **devoted thing**. Anything that one formally devotes to God cannot ever be sold or redeemed, and it becomes the priests' property.

18:19. **covenant of salt**. Salt is associated with the offerings that are given to the

20And YHWH said to Aaron, "You shall not have a legacy in their land, and you shall not have a portion among them. I am your portion and your legacy among the children of Israel. 21And to the children of Levi, here, I've given every tithe in Israel as a legacy in exchange for their work that they're doing, the service of the Tent of Meeting. 22And the children of Israel shall not come near to the Tent of Meeting anymore so as to bear sin and die. 23But he, the Levite, shall do the service of the Tent of Meeting, and they shall bear their crime. It is an eternal law through your generations. And they shall not have a legacy among the children of Israel, 24because I've given to the Levites as a legacy the tithe of the children of Israel that they will give to YHWH as a donation. On account of this I've said to them: they shall not have a legacy among the children of Israel."

25And YHWH spoke to Moses, saying, 26"And you shall speak to the Levites and say to them: 'When you will take the tithe from the children of Israel that I have given you from them as your legacy, then you shall make a donation for YHWH from it, a tithe of the tithe. 27And it will be counted for you as your donation, like grain from the threshing floor and like the fill of the winepress. 28So you shall donate, you too, a donation for YHWH from all your tithes that you will take from the children of Israel, and you shall give a donation for YHWH to Aaron, the priest, from them. 29From all your gifts you shall make every donation for YHWH, from all the best of it, its holy part from it.' 30And you shall say to them: 'When you donate the best of it from it, then it shall be counted to the Levites like the produce of the threshing floor and like

אַהֲרֹן בְּאַרְצָם לֹא תִנְחָל וְחֵלֶק לֹא־יִהְיֶה לְךָ
בְּתוֹכָם אֲנִי חֶלְקְךָ וְנַחֲלָתְךָ בְּתוֹךְ בְּנֵי יִשְׂרָאֵל: ס
21וְלִבְנֵי לֵוִי הִנֵּה נָתַתִּי כָּל־מַעֲשֵׂר בְּיִשְׂרָאֵל
לְנַחֲלָה חֵלֶף עֲבֹדָתָם אֲשֶׁר־הֵם עֹבְדִים אֶת־עֲבֹדַת
אֹהֶל מוֹעֵד: 22וְלֹא־יִקְרְבוּ עוֹד בְּנֵי יִשְׂרָאֵל אֶל־
אֹהֶל מוֹעֵד לָשֵׂאת חֵטְא לָמוּת: 23וְעָבַד הַלֵּוִי הוּא
אֶת־עֲבֹדַת אֹהֶל מוֹעֵד וְהֵם יִשְׂאוּ עֲוֹנָם חֻקַּת עוֹלָם
לְדֹרֹתֵיכֶם וּבְתוֹךְ בְּנֵי יִשְׂרָאֵל לֹא יִנְחֲלוּ נַחֲלָה:
24כִּי אֶת־מַעְשַׂר בְּנֵי־יִשְׂרָאֵל אֲשֶׁר יָרִימוּ לַיהוָה
תְּרוּמָה נָתַתִּי לַלְוִיִּם לְנַחֲלָה עַל־כֵּן אָמַרְתִּי לָהֶם
בְּתוֹךְ בְּנֵי יִשְׂרָאֵל לֹא יִנְחֲלוּ נַחֲלָה: פ 25וַיְדַבֵּר
יְהוָה אֶל־מֹשֶׁה לֵּאמֹר: 26וְאֶל־הַלְוִיִּם תְּדַבֵּר
וְאָמַרְתָּ אֲלֵהֶם כִּי־תִקְחוּ מֵאֵת בְּנֵי־יִשְׂרָאֵל אֶת־
הַמַּעֲשֵׂר אֲשֶׁר נָתַתִּי לָכֶם מֵאִתָּם בְּנַחֲלַתְכֶם
וַהֲרֵמֹתֶם מִמֶּנּוּ תְּרוּמַת יְהוָה מַעֲשֵׂר מִן־הַמַּעֲשֵׂר:
27וְנֶחְשַׁב לָכֶם תְּרוּמַתְכֶם כַּדָּגָן מִן־הַגֹּרֶן וְכַמְלֵאָה
מִן־הַיָּקֶב: 28כֵּן תָּרִימוּ גַם־אַתֶּם תְּרוּמַת יְהוָה מִכֹּל
מַעְשְׂרֹתֵיכֶם אֲשֶׁר תִּקְחוּ מֵאֵת בְּנֵי יִשְׂרָאֵל וּנְתַתֶּם
מִמֶּנּוּ אֶת־תְּרוּמַת יְהוָה לְאַהֲרֹן הַכֹּהֵן: 29מִכֹּל
מַתְּנֹתֵיכֶם תָּרִימוּ אֵת כָּל־תְּרוּמַת יְהוָה מִכָּל־חֶלְבּוֹ
אֶת־מִקְדְּשׁוֹ מִמֶּנּוּ: 30וְאָמַרְתָּ אֲלֵהֶם בַּהֲרִימְכֶם
אֶת־חֶלְבּוֹ מִמֶּנּוּ וְנֶחְשַׁב לַלְוִיִּם כִּתְבוּאַת גֹּרֶן

---

priests. Lev 2:13 emphasizes, "You shall sprinkle every offering of a grain offering with salt. And you shall not let the salt of your God's covenant cease from on your grain offering; you shall bring salt on all your offerings." (Some take the fact that salt is a preservative to imply that "covenant of salt" means a long-lasting covenant.) It is a custom to this day to sprinkle some salt on the bread at the Sabbath meal as a memorial of this practice.

the produce of the winepress. ³¹And you shall eat it in every place, you and your house, because it is compensation for you in exchange for your work in the Tent of Meeting. ³²And you will not bear sin over it, when you have donated its best from it, so you will not desecrate the holy things of the children of Israel, and you will not die.'"

LAW

19 ¹And YHWH spoke to Moses and to Aaron, saying, ²"This is the law of the instruction that YHWH commanded, saying: Speak to the children of Israel that they should take to you an unblemished red cow that has no injury, on which a yoke has not gone. ³And you shall give it to Eleazar, the priest, and one shall bring it outside the camp and slaughter it in front of him. ⁴And Eleazar, the priest, shall take some of its blood with his finger and sprinkle some of its blood toward the front of the Tent of Meeting seven times. ⁵And one shall burn the cow before his eyes. He shall burn its skin and its meat and its blood and its dung. ⁶And the priest shall take cedarwood and hyssop and scarlet and throw them into the fire of the cow. ⁷And the priest shall wash his clothes and wash his flesh with water, and after that he shall come to the camp,

חקת

וּכְתְבוּאַ֖ת יָֽקֶב׃ ³¹וַאֲכַלְתֶּ֤ם אֹתוֹ֙ בְּכָל־מָק֔וֹם אַתֶּ֖ם וּבֵיתְכֶ֑ם כִּֽי־שָׂכָ֥ר הוּא֙ לָכֶ֔ם חֵ֥לֶף עֲבֹֽדַתְכֶ֖ם בְּאֹ֥הֶל מוֹעֵֽד׃ ³²וְלֹֽא־תִשְׂא֤וּ עָלָיו֙ חֵ֔טְא בַּהֲרִֽימְכֶ֥ם אֶת־חֶלְבּ֖וֹ מִמֶּ֑נּוּ וְאֶת־קָדְשֵׁ֧י בְנֵֽי־יִשְׂרָאֵ֛ל לֹ֥א תְחַלְּל֖וּ וְלֹ֥א תָמֽוּתוּ׃ פ

19 ¹וַיְדַבֵּ֣ר יְהוָ֔ה אֶל־מֹשֶׁ֥ה וְאֶֽל־אַהֲרֹ֖ן לֵאמֹֽר׃ ²זֹ֚את חֻקַּ֣ת הַתּוֹרָ֔ה אֲשֶׁר־צִוָּ֥ה יְהוָ֖ה לֵאמֹ֑ר דַּבֵּ֣ר ׀ אֶל־בְּנֵ֣י יִשְׂרָאֵ֗ל וְיִקְח֣וּ אֵלֶיךָ֩ פָרָ֨ה אֲדֻמָּ֜ה תְּמִימָ֗ה אֲשֶׁ֤ר אֵֽין־בָּהּ֙ מ֔וּם אֲשֶׁ֛ר לֹא־עָלָ֥ה עָלֶ֖יהָ עֹֽל׃ ³וּנְתַתֶּ֣ם אֹתָ֔הּ אֶל־אֶלְעָזָ֖ר הַכֹּהֵ֑ן וְהוֹצִ֤יא אֹתָהּ֙ אֶל־מִחוּץ֙ לַֽמַּחֲנֶ֔ה וְשָׁחַ֥ט אֹתָ֖הּ לְפָנָֽיו׃ ⁴וְלָקַ֞ח אֶלְעָזָ֧ר הַכֹּהֵ֛ן מִדָּמָ֖הּ בְּאֶצְבָּע֑וֹ וְהִזָּ֞ה אֶל־נֹ֨כַח פְּנֵ֧י אֹֽהֶל־מוֹעֵ֛ד מִדָּמָ֖הּ שֶׁ֥בַע פְּעָמִֽים׃ ⁵וְשָׂרַ֥ף אֶת־הַפָּרָ֖ה לְעֵינָ֑יו אֶת־עֹרָ֤הּ וְאֶת־בְּשָׂרָהּ֙ וְאֶת־דָּמָ֔הּ עַל־פִּרְשָׁ֖הּ יִשְׂרֹֽף׃ ⁶וְלָקַ֣ח הַכֹּהֵ֗ן עֵ֥ץ אֶ֛רֶז וְאֵז֖וֹב וּשְׁנִ֣י תוֹלָ֑עַת וְהִשְׁלִ֕יךְ אֶל־תּ֖וֹךְ שְׂרֵפַ֥ת הַפָּרָֽה׃ ⁷וְכִבֶּ֨ס בְּגָדָ֜יו הַכֹּהֵ֗ן וְרָחַ֤ץ בְּשָׂרוֹ֙ בַּמַּ֔יִם וְאַחַ֖ר יָבֹ֣א אֶל־הַֽמַּחֲנֶ֑ה

19:2. **law.** Legal texts are worked in at various points of the wilderness narrative, thus conveying that not all of the law has been revealed at Sinai, but that the law rather continues to be elaborated upon and added to as the people move closer to the land. Also through this construction the revelation of the law comes to be pictured as an ongoing part of the people's life, and it is understood to be part of the new, post–exodus generation's experience—and thus the possession of the people who will carry it into the promised land.

19:3. **Eleazar.** Here and in the matter of the fire-holders after the Korah rebellion (17:2), Eleazar, Aaron's oldest surviving son, is directly commanded for the first time. It is as if the text is anticipating the events of the next chapter (20), in which Aaron will suffer the same fate as Moses: to die before reaching the promised land. The conclusion of that story recounts the succession of Eleazar to Aaron's place as high priest (20:23–28). These first commands to Eleazar thus appear to be a preparation for the moment of succession. Part of the task of a wise leader is to prepare a successor.

and the priest shall be impure until evening. 8And the one who burns it shall wash his clothes with water and wash his flesh with water and be impure until evening. 9And a man who is pure shall gather the cow's ashes and leave them outside the camp in a pure place, and it shall be for the congregation of the children of Israel to be kept for water of impurity, for sin expiation. 10And the one who gathers the cow's ashes shall wash his clothes and be impure until evening. And it will be for the children of Israel and for the alien who resides among them as an eternal law.

11"One who touches a dead body of any human being will be impure seven days. 12He shall do sin expiation with it on the third day, and on the seventh day he will be pure. And if he will not do sin expiation on the third day, then on the seventh day he will not be pure. 13Anyone who touches a dead body of a human being who has died and does not do sin expiation has made YHWH's Tabernacle impure, and that person will be cut off from Israel. Because the water of impurity was not flung on him, he shall be impure. His impurity is still in him.

14"This is the instruction: When a human will die in a tent, anyone who comes into the tent and everything that is in the tent will be impure seven days. 15And any open container, on which there is not a fastened cover: it is impure. 16And anyone who, at an open field, will touch a corpse slain by the sword or a dead body or a human bone or a grave will be impure seven days. 17And they shall take for the one who is impure some of the ashes of the fire of sin expiation, and one shall put living water on it in a container. 18And a man who is pure shall take hyssop and dip it in the water and sprinkle it on the tent and on all the items and on the persons who were there and on the one who touched the bone or the slain corpse or

וְטָמֵא הַכֹּהֵן עַד־הָעָרֶב: 8וְהַשֹּׂרֵף אֹתָהּ יְכַבֵּס בְּגָדָיו בַּמַּיִם וְרָחַץ בְּשָׂרוֹ בַּמָּיִם וְטָמֵא עַד־הָעָרֶב: 9וְאָסַף ׀ אִישׁ טָהוֹר אֵת אֵפֶר הַפָּרָה וְהִנִּיחַ מִחוּץ לַמַּחֲנֶה בְּמָקוֹם טָהוֹר וְהָיְתָה לַעֲדַת בְּנֵי־יִשְׂרָאֵל לְמִשְׁמֶרֶת לְמֵי נִדָּה חַטָּאת הִוא: 10וְכִבֶּס הָאֹסֵף אֶת־אֵפֶר הַפָּרָה אֶת־בְּגָדָיו וְטָמֵא עַד־הָעָרֶב וְהָיְתָה לִבְנֵי יִשְׂרָאֵל וְלַגֵּר הַגָּר בְּתוֹכָם לְחֻקַּת עוֹלָם: 11הַנֹּגֵעַ בְּמֵת לְכָל־נֶפֶשׁ אָדָם וְטָמֵא שִׁבְעַת יָמִים: 12הוּא יִתְחַטָּא־בוֹ בַּיּוֹם הַשְּׁלִישִׁי וּבַיּוֹם הַשְּׁבִיעִי יִטְהָר וְאִם־לֹא יִתְחַטָּא בַּיּוֹם הַשְּׁלִישִׁי וּבַיּוֹם הַשְּׁבִיעִי לֹא יִטְהָר: 13כָּל־הַנֹּגֵעַ בְּמֵת בְּנֶפֶשׁ הָאָדָם אֲשֶׁר־יָמוּת וְלֹא יִתְחַטָּא אֶת־מִשְׁכַּן יְהוָה טִמֵּא וְנִכְרְתָה הַנֶּפֶשׁ הַהִוא מִיִּשְׂרָאֵל כִּי מֵי נִדָּה לֹא־זֹרַק עָלָיו טָמֵא יִהְיֶה עוֹד טֻמְאָתוֹ בוֹ: 14זֹאת הַתּוֹרָה אָדָם כִּי־יָמוּת בְּאֹהֶל כָּל־הַבָּא אֶל־הָאֹהֶל וְכָל־אֲשֶׁר בָּאֹהֶל יִטְמָא שִׁבְעַת יָמִים: 15וְכֹל כְּלִי פָתוּחַ אֲשֶׁר אֵין־צָמִיד פָּתִיל עָלָיו טָמֵא הוּא: 16וְכֹל אֲשֶׁר־יִגַּע עַל־פְּנֵי הַשָּׂדֶה בַּחֲלַל־חֶרֶב אוֹ בְמֵת אוֹ־בְעֶצֶם אָדָם אוֹ בְקָבֶר יִטְמָא שִׁבְעַת יָמִים: 17וְלָקְחוּ לַטָּמֵא מֵעֲפַר שְׂרֵפַת הַחַטָּאת וְנָתַן עָלָיו מַיִם חַיִּים אֶל־כֶּלִי: 18וְלָקַח אֵזוֹב וְטָבַל בַּמַּיִם אִישׁ טָהוֹר וְהִזָּה עַל־הָאֹהֶל וְעַל־כָּל־הַכֵּלִים וְעַל־הַנְּפָשׁוֹת אֲשֶׁר הָיוּ־שָׁם וְעַל־הַנֹּגֵעַ בַּעֶצֶם אוֹ

19:12. **with it**. With the ashes of the red cow.

19:17. **living water**. Freshwater flowing from a well or other natural source. See the comment on Lev 14:5.

the dead body or the grave. ¹⁹And the one who is pure shall sprinkle it on the impure on the third day and on the seventh day, so he shall expiate sin from him on the seventh day, and he shall wash his clothes and wash in water and be pure in the evening. ²⁰And if a man will be impure and will not do sin expiation, then that person will be cut off from among the community, because he has made YHWH's holy place impure. The water of impurity has not been flung on him: he is impure. ²¹And it will become an eternal law for them. And one who sprinkles the water of impurity shall wash his clothes, and one who touches the water of impurity will be impure until evening. ²²And whatever the impure one will touch will be impure, and the person who touches it will be impure until evening."

20 ¹And the children of Israel, all the congregation, came to the wilderness of Zin in the first month, and the people stayed in Kadesh. And Miriam died there and was buried there. ²And there was no water for the congregation, and they assembled against Moses and against Aaron. ³And the people quarreled with Moses, and they said, saying, "If only we had expired when our brothers expired in front of YHWH! ⁴And why have you brought YHWH's community to this wilderness to die there, we and our cattle? ⁵And why did you bring us up from Egypt to bring us to this bad place? It's not a place of seed and fig and vine and pomegranate, and there's no water to drink!"

⁶And Moses and Aaron came from in front of the community to the entrance of the Tent of Meeting, and they fell on their faces. And YHWH's glory appeared to them. ⁷And YHWH spoke to Moses, saying, ⁸"Take the staff and assemble the congregation, you and Aaron, your brother. And you shall speak to the rock before

בֶּחָלָ֛ל א֥וֹ בְמֵ֖ת א֣וֹ בְקָ֑בֶר: ¹⁹וְהִזָּ֨ה הַטָּהֹר֙ עַל־הַטָּמֵ֔א בַּיּ֥וֹם הַשְּׁלִישִׁ֖י וּבַיּ֣וֹם הַשְּׁבִיעִ֑י וְחִטְּאוֹ֙ בַּיּ֣וֹם הַשְּׁבִיעִ֔י וְכִבֶּ֧ס בְּגָדָ֛יו וְרָחַ֥ץ בַּמַּ֖יִם וְטָהֵ֥ר בָּעָֽרֶב: ²⁰וְאִ֤ישׁ אֲשֶׁר־יִטְמָא֙ וְלֹ֣א יִתְחַטָּ֔א וְנִכְרְתָ֛ה הַנֶּ֥פֶשׁ הַהִ֖וא מִתּ֣וֹךְ הַקָּהָ֑ל כִּ֤י אֶת־מִקְדַּ֤שׁ יְהוָה֙ טִמֵּ֔א מֵ֥י נִדָּ֛ה לֹא־זֹרַ֥ק עָלָ֖יו טָמֵ֥א הֽוּא: ²¹וְהָיְתָ֥ה לָהֶ֖ם לְחֻקַּ֣ת עוֹלָ֑ם וּמַזֵּ֤ה מֵֽי־הַנִּדָּה֙ יְכַבֵּ֣ס בְּגָדָ֔יו וְהַנֹּגֵ֙עַ֙ בְּמֵ֣י הַנִּדָּ֔ה יִטְמָ֖א עַד־הָעָֽרֶב: ²²וְכֹ֛ל אֲשֶׁר־יִגַּע־בּ֥וֹ הַטָּמֵ֖א יִטְמָ֑א וְהַנֶּ֥פֶשׁ הַנֹּגַ֖עַת תִּטְמָ֥א עַד־הָעָֽרֶב: פ

20 ¹וַיָּבֹ֣אוּ בְנֵֽי־יִ֠שְׂרָאֵל כָּל־הָ֨עֵדָ֤ה מִדְבַּר־צִן֙ בַּחֹ֣דֶשׁ הָֽרִאשׁ֔וֹן וַיֵּ֥שֶׁב הָעָ֖ם בְּקָדֵ֑שׁ וַתָּ֤מָת שָׁם֙ מִרְיָ֔ם וַתִּקָּבֵ֖ר שָֽׁם: ²וְלֹא־הָ֥יָה מַ֖יִם לָעֵדָ֑ה וַיִּקָּ֣הֲל֔וּ עַל־מֹשֶׁ֖ה וְעַֽל־אַהֲרֹֽן: ³וַיָּ֥רֶב הָעָ֖ם עִם־מֹשֶׁ֑ה וַיֹּאמְר֣וּ לֵאמֹ֔ר וְל֥וּ גָוַ֛עְנוּ בִּגְוַ֥ע אַחֵ֖ינוּ לִפְנֵ֥י יְהוָֽה: ⁴וְלָמָ֤ה הֲבֵאתֶם֙ אֶת־קְהַ֣ל יְהוָ֔ה אֶל־הַמִּדְבָּ֖ר הַזֶּ֑ה לָמ֣וּת שָׁ֔ם אֲנַ֖חְנוּ וּבְעִירֵֽנוּ: ⁵וְלָמָ֤ה הֶֽעֱלִיתֻ֨נוּ֙ מִמִּצְרַ֔יִם לְהָבִ֣יא אֹתָ֔נוּ אֶל־הַמָּק֥וֹם הָרָ֖ע הַזֶּ֑ה לֹ֣א ׀ מְק֣וֹם זֶ֗רַע וּתְאֵנָ֤ה וְגֶ֨פֶן֙ וְרִמּ֔וֹן וּמַ֥יִם אַ֖יִן לִשְׁתּֽוֹת: ⁶וַיָּבֹא֩ מֹשֶׁ֨ה וְאַהֲרֹ֜ן מִפְּנֵ֣י הַקָּהָ֗ל אֶל־פֶּ֨תַח֙ אֹ֣הֶל מוֹעֵ֔ד וַֽיִּפְּל֖וּ עַל־פְּנֵיהֶ֑ם וַיֵּרָ֥א כְבוֹד־יְהוָ֖ה אֲלֵיהֶֽם: פ ⁷וַיְדַבֵּ֥ר יְהוָ֖ה אֶל־מֹשֶׁ֥ה לֵּאמֹֽר: ⁸קַ֣ח אֶת־הַמַּטֶּ֗ה וְהַקְהֵ֤ל אֶת־הָעֵדָה֙ אַתָּה֙ וְאַהֲרֹ֣ן אָחִ֔יךָ וְדִבַּרְתֶּ֧ם

20:8. Take the staff and . . . speak to the rock. Why does he need the staff if he is only supposed to speak to the rock?! Some might say that God is testing Moses. But the reason for taking the staff is already given in the story of Aaron's blossoming staff.

their eyes, and it will give its water. So you shall bring water out of the rock for them and give a drink to the congregation and their cattle."

9And Moses took the staff from in front of YHWH as He commanded him. 10And Moses and Aaron assembled the community opposite the rock. And he said to them, "Listen, rebels, shall we bring water out of this rock for you?" 11And Moses lifted his hand and struck the rock with his staff twice. And much water came out! And the congregation and their cattle drank.

אֶל־הַסֶּלַע לְעֵינֵיהֶם וְנָתַן מֵימָיו וְהוֹצֵאתָ לָהֶם מַיִם מִן־הַסֶּלַע וְהִשְׁקִיתָ אֶת־הָעֵדָה וְאֶת־בְּעִירָם: 9וַיִּקַּח מֹשֶׁה אֶת־הַמַּטֶּה מִלִּפְנֵי יְהוָה כַּאֲשֶׁר צִוָּהוּ: 10וַיַּקְהִלוּ מֹשֶׁה וְאַהֲרֹן אֶת־הַקָּהָל אֶל־פְּנֵי הַסֶּלַע וַיֹּאמֶר לָהֶם שִׁמְעוּ־נָא הַמֹּרִים הֲמִן־הַסֶּלַע הַזֶּה נוֹצִיא לָכֶם מָיִם: 11וַיָּרֶם מֹשֶׁה אֶת־יָדוֹ וַיַּךְ אֶת־הַסֶּלַע בְּמַטֵּהוּ פַּעֲמָיִם וַיֵּצְאוּ מַיִם רַבִּים וַתֵּשְׁתְּ

Moses is told there to "put back Aaron's staff in front of the Testimony . . . *for a sign to rebels*" (Num 17:25). The text now says that Moses "took the staff from in front of YHWH" (20:9). This expression would normally be expected to mean that he took a staff that was located at the ark in the Tent of Meeting, "in front of YHWH." William Propp has pointed out that this connects back to the staff of Aaron that miraculously blossomed and was placed before the ark in the preceding episode. As quoted above, its purpose, explicitly, was to be "a sign to rebels." That is why Moses is supposed to carry it in his hand in the people's sight while dealing with their rebellion. As he holds it, his first words to the people are in fact "Listen, rebels" (19:10). And that is why Aaron is implicated by its misuse even though Aaron does not say or do anything at the rock. It is his staff, with his name on it, to be kept in a holy place and used in specific circumstances. As we have seen in Leviticus, intent is not the issue in the realm of ritual. Rather, actions relating to sacred objects and boundaries bring necessary consequences of themselves. Whether or not Aaron has thought or done anything improper, he is tied to what has happened.

20:8. **you shall speak**. It is a plural: both Moses and Aaron are supposed to speak to the rock.

20:8. **rock**. This is a different word from the one in the other story of Moses striking a rock to get water (Exod 17:1–7). There it is a crag (*ṣûr*) of Mount Horeb (Sinai). Here it is a rock (*selaʿ*) in the wilderness. In Moses' last blessings to the people before he dies, he will speak of God as Israel's *ṣûr* (Deut 32:4,15,18,30,31,37); i.e., he uses the word that recalls the water-from-the-rock episode that came out well, not the present episode, which comes out disastrously for himself and Aaron.

20:11. **water came out!** Moses is supposed to speak to the rock, but he hits it. So why does the miracle still work?! We might surmise that it means that God makes it happen so as not to humiliate Moses. Or the explanation may be that the miraculous power is in the staff, which is the one that miraculously blossomed. Whatever the reason, though, the fact remains: for the first time in the Bible, a human has changed a miracle. This is an all-important step in a gradual shift in the balance of control of miraculous phenomena in the *Tanak*. Adam, Noah, Abraham, and Isaac perform no miracles. But Jacob manipulates the coloring of Laban's flock. Then Joseph interprets dreams. Then Moses and Aaron perform God's miracles. And now Moses changes a

12And YHWH said to Moses and to Aaron, "Because you did not trust in me, to make me holy before the eyes of the children of Israel, therefore you shall not bring this community to the land that I have given them!"

וַיֹּ֣אמֶר יְהוָה֮ אֶל־מֹשֶׁה֮ וְאֶֽל־12 ס :הָעֵדָ֖ה וּבְעִירָֽם אַהֲרֹן֒ יַ֚עַן לֹא־הֶאֱמַנְתֶּ֣ם בִּ֔י לְהַ֨קְדִּישֵׁ֔נִי לְעֵינֵ֖י בְּנֵ֣י יִשְׂרָאֵ֑ל לָכֵ֗ן לֹ֤א תָבִ֙יאוּ֙ אֶת־הַקָּהָ֣ל הַזֶּ֔ה אֶל־הָאָ֖רֶץ

miracle. This shift will continue in the biblical books that follow the Torah, and it is one of the central developments of the Bible: Joshua will call for the sun to stand still in the skies. By calling for a miracle on his own, without direction from God, he goes even further than Moses. Later, Samson has powers implanted in him at birth, so that he is free to use them as he wishes all his life. Later still, Elijah and Elisha use miracles for a variety of personal purposes. It appears that, starting with Moses, God is entrusting humans with ever more responsibility and control of their destiny. By the end of the *Tanak*, miracles cease. There are no visible miracles in the late books of Ezra, Nehemiah, and Esther. Humans rather must direct their destiny with their own natural human powers, not with endowments of miraculous powers from God. Through the course of the *Tanak*, humans are forced to grow up and become more self-reliant.

20:12. **you did not trust in me, to make me holy**. What is Moses' offense? What has he done that is so horrible as to deserve what is probably the worst possible thing that could have been done to him: that he will not live to enter the land? Many answers have been proposed to the question of what the sin of Moses is. He calls the people rebels. He says, "Shall *we* bring water out of this rock" instead of "Shall *God* . . . " He strikes the rock instead of speaking to it. The answer may lie in the wording of YHWH's reprimand: "You did not trust in me, to make me holy." By hitting the rock Moses makes it appear more as if it is his own agency that is producing the water than if he had just spoken to the rock and watched the water flow out. His saying "we" has the same effect verbally that his physical action has visually. True, YHWH had said to him in his instructions, "So *you* shall bring water out," but Moses' saying it to the people before hitting the rock still makes those words appear to mean something quite different from their meaning in the original instructions. By word and act Moses is thus appropriating to himself an act of God. In doing this he is undoing the message that God and Moses himself have been conveying to the people up to this point. The people have continuously directed their attention to Moses instead of to God. In this story, as in the others so far, they say to Moses and Aaron, "Why have *you* brought YHWH's community to this wilderness . . . ? Why did *you* bring us up from Egypt?" Until this episode Moses has repeatedly told the people, "It is not from my own heart" and "You are congregating against YHWH," but now his words and actions confirm the people's own perception. He has come a considerable way from his timid attempts to avoid the assignment at the burning bush. At Meribah Moses oversteps a divine limit, and he pays a maximal price. The severity of the punishment demonstrates the seriousness of the offense.

20:12. **you shall not bring this community to the land**. In a way, the sin of Moses is like the sin of Adam and Eve: stepping over the line, taking a power from the divine realm. His punishment is not death. He lives to be 120 years old, the maximum (as decreed in Gen 6:3); his punishment is exile—he is not permitted to enter the land—

13They are the waters of Meribah, over which the children of Israel quarreled with YHWH, and He was made holy among them.

14And Moses sent messengers from Kadesh to the king of Edom. "Your brother, Israel, says this: You know all the hardship that has found us: 15And our fathers went down to Egypt, and we lived in Egypt many days. And Egypt was bad to us and to our fathers, 16and we cried to YHWH, and He heard our voice and sent an angel and brought us from Egypt. And here we are in Kadesh, a city at the edge of your border. 17Let us pass through your land. We won't pass through a field or through a vineyard, and we won't drink the water of a well. We'll go by the king's road, we won't turn right or left, until we pass your border."

18And Edom said to him, "You won't pass through me, or else I'll go out to you with the sword."

אֲשֶׁר־נָתַ֖תִּי לָהֶ֑ם: 13הֵ֚מָּה מֵ֣י מְרִיבָ֔ה אֲשֶׁר־רָב֧וּ בְנֵֽי־יִשְׂרָאֵ֛ל אֶת־יְהוָ֖ה וַיִּקָּדֵ֥שׁ בָּֽם: ס 14וַיִּשְׁלַ֨ח מֹשֶׁ֧ה מַלְאָכִ֛ים מִקָּדֵ֖שׁ אֶל־מֶ֣לֶךְ אֱד֑וֹם כֹּ֤ה אָמַר֙ אָחִ֣יךָ יִשְׂרָאֵ֔ל אַתָּ֣ה יָדַ֔עְתָּ אֵ֥ת כָּל־הַתְּלָאָ֖ה אֲשֶׁ֥ר מְצָאָֽתְנוּ: 15וַיֵּרְד֤וּ אֲבֹתֵ֙ינוּ֙ מִצְרַ֔יְמָה וַנֵּ֥שֶׁב בְּמִצְרַ֖יִם יָמִ֣ים רַבִּ֑ים וַיָּרֵ֥עוּ לָ֛נוּ מִצְרַ֖יִם וְלַאֲבֹתֵֽינוּ: 16וַנִּצְעַ֤ק אֶל־יְהוָה֙ וַיִּשְׁמַ֣ע קֹלֵ֔נוּ וַיִּשְׁלַ֣ח מַלְאָ֔ךְ וַיֹּצִאֵ֖נוּ מִמִּצְרָ֑יִם וְהִנֵּה֙ אֲנַ֣חְנוּ בְקָדֵ֔שׁ עִ֖יר קְצֵ֥ה גְבוּלֶֽךָ: 17נַעְבְּרָה־נָּ֣א בְאַרְצֶ֗ךָ לֹ֤א נַעֲבֹר֙ בְּשָׂדֶ֣ה וּבְכֶ֔רֶם וְלֹ֥א נִשְׁתֶּ֖ה מֵ֣י בְאֵ֑ר דֶּ֧רֶךְ הַמֶּ֣לֶךְ נֵלֵ֗ךְ לֹ֤א נִטֶּה֙ יָמִ֣ין וּשְׂמֹ֔אול עַ֥ד אֲשֶֽׁר־נַעֲבֹ֖ר גְּבוּלֶֽךָ: 18וַיֹּ֤אמֶר אֵלָיו֙ אֱד֔וֹם לֹ֥א תַעֲבֹ֖ר בִּ֑י פֶּן־בַּחֶ֖רֶב אֵצֵ֥א לִקְרָאתֶֽךָ: 19וַיֹּאמְר֨וּ אֵלָ֤יו בְּנֵֽי־

---

which is also like the punishment of Adam and Eve, who are prevented from reentering Eden.

20:14. **sent messengers**. There are implicit reflections of the acts of the ancestors in the accounts of the descendants. The account of Israel's passing by the territory of the Edomites, who are the descendants of Esau, on their return to their patriarchal homeland begins here with the words "And Moses sent messengers (*wayyišlaḥ mal'ākîm*) to the king of Edom." This recalls the story of Jacob's first meeting with their ancestor Esau on his return to his homeland in Genesis, which begins with the words "And Jacob sent messengers (*wayyišlaḥ mal'ākîm*) before him to Esau" (Gen 32:4). The text in Genesis refers to the twin seemingly redundantly as "Esau his brother," but this underscores that the relationship is not merely figurative when Moses now protests it to the Edomites, beginning his plea for passage with the words "Your brother, Israel, says this." (The text omits the word "brother" in Moses' similar message to the Amorite king Sihon.) The wording thus (1) develops the patriarchal background of the story in Numbers; (2) includes an element of recapitulation (or reflection) of the ancestors' acts by their descendants; and (3) invites comparison and interpretation. In the Genesis story, Esau approaches Jacob with an armed force and seemingly has in his power the brother who took his blessing, but Esau is forgiving and shows fraternal affection in a remarkably touching scene: "And Esau ran to him and embraced him and fell on his neck and kissed him. And they wept" (Gen 33:4). In the story of their descendants, however, the roles are reversed. Israel makes overtures of peace to Edom, but the Edomites approach with an armed force and no fraternal affection. That is, in these biblical terms, qualities of character are not hereditary. Edom may not be as brotherly as Esau, and Israel may not be as obedient as Abraham or as deceptive as Jacob.

19And the children of Israel said to him, "We'll go up by the highway, and if we drink your water, I and my cattle, then I'll pay its price. Only, it's nothing: let me pass through by foot."

20And he said, "You won't pass." And Edom went out to him with a heavy mass of people and a strong hand, 21and Edom refused to allow Israel to pass through his border. And Israel turned away from him.

22And they traveled from Kadesh, and the children of Israel, all the congregation, came to Mount Hor.

23And YHWH said to Moses and to Aaron at Mount Hor, on the border of the land of Edom, saying, 24"Let Aaron be gathered to his people, because he shall not come to the land that I have given to the children of Israel, because you rebelled against my word at the waters of Meribah. 25Take Aaron and Eleazar, his son, and take them up Mount Hor, 26and take off Aaron's clothes, and you shall put them on Eleazar, his son. And Aaron will be gathered and die there."

27And Moses did as YHWH commanded him. And they went up to Mount Hor before the eyes of all the congregation. 28And Moses took off Aaron's clothes and put them on Eleazar, his son. And Aaron died there on the top of the mountain. And Moses and Eleazar came down from the mountain. 29And all the congregation saw that Aaron had expired, and all the house of Israel mourned Aaron thirty days.

21 1And the Canaanite, the king of Arad, who lived in the Negeb, heard that Israel was coming by the way of Atharim, and he fought against Israel and took some of them prisoners. 2And Israel made a vow to YHWH and said, "If you will *deliver* this people into my hand, then I shall completely destroy their

יִשְׂרָאֵל בַּֽמְסִלָּה נַעֲלֶה וְאִם־מֵימֶיךָ נִשְׁתֶּה אֲנִי וּמִקְנַי וְנָתַתִּי מִכְרָם רַק אֵין־דָּבָר בְּרַגְלַי אֶעֱבֹֽרָה: 20וַיֹּאמֶר לֹא תַעֲבֹר וַיֵּצֵא אֱדוֹם לִקְרָאתוֹ בְּעַם כָּבֵד וּבְיָד חֲזָקָֽה: 21וַיְמָאֵן ׀ אֱדוֹם נְתֹן אֶת־יִשְׂרָאֵל עֲבֹר בִּגְבֻלוֹ וַיֵּט יִשְׂרָאֵל מֵעָלָֽיו: פ 22וַיִּסְעוּ מִקָּדֵשׁ וַיָּבֹאוּ בְנֵֽי־יִשְׂרָאֵל כָּל־הָעֵדָה הֹר הָהָֽר: 23וַיֹּאמֶר יְהוָה אֶל־מֹשֶׁה וְאֶֽל־אַהֲרֹן בְּהֹר הָהָר עַל־גְּבוּל אֶֽרֶץ־אֱדוֹם לֵאמֹֽר: 24יֵאָסֵף אַהֲרֹן אֶל־עַמָּיו כִּי לֹא יָבֹא אֶל־הָאָרֶץ אֲשֶׁר נָתַתִּי לִבְנֵי יִשְׂרָאֵל עַל אֲשֶׁר־מְרִיתֶם אֶת־פִּי לְמֵי מְרִיבָֽה: 25קַח אֶֽת־אַהֲרֹן וְאֶת־אֶלְעָזָר בְּנוֹ וְהַעַל אֹתָם הֹר הָהָֽר: 26וְהַפְשֵׁט אֶֽת־אַהֲרֹן אֶת־בְּגָדָיו וְהִלְבַּשְׁתָּם אֶת־אֶלְעָזָר בְּנוֹ וְאַהֲרֹן יֵאָסֵף וּמֵת שָֽׁם: 27וַיַּעַשׂ מֹשֶׁה כַּאֲשֶׁר צִוָּה יְהוָה וַיַּעֲלוּ אֶל־הֹר הָהָר לְעֵינֵי כָּל־הָעֵדָֽה: 28וַיַּפְשֵׁט מֹשֶׁה אֶֽת־אַהֲרֹן אֶת־בְּגָדָיו וַיַּלְבֵּשׁ אֹתָם אֶת־אֶלְעָזָר בְּנוֹ וַיָּמָת אַהֲרֹן שָׁם בְּרֹאשׁ הָהָר וַיֵּרֶד מֹשֶׁה וְאֶלְעָזָר מִן־הָהָֽר: 29וַיִּרְאוּ כָּל־הָעֵדָה כִּי גָוַע אַהֲרֹן וַיִּבְכּוּ אֶֽת־אַהֲרֹן שְׁלֹשִׁים יוֹם כֹּל בֵּית יִשְׂרָאֵֽל: ס

21 1וַיִּשְׁמַע הַכְּנַעֲנִי מֶֽלֶךְ־עֲרָד יֹשֵׁב הַנֶּגֶב כִּי בָּא יִשְׂרָאֵל דֶּרֶךְ הָאֲתָרִים וַיִּלָּחֶם בְּיִשְׂרָאֵל וַיִּשְׁבְּ ׀ מִמֶּנּוּ שֶֽׁבִי: 2וַיִּדַּר יִשְׂרָאֵל נֶדֶר לַֽיהוָה וַיֹּאמַר אִם־נָתֹן תִּתֵּן אֶת־הָעָם הַזֶּה בְּיָדִי וְהַחֲרַמְתִּי אֶת־

20:24. **you rebelled.** *You* rebelled—meaning Moses and Aaron! God tells them that they themselves did exactly what they were supposed to stop the people from doing. It is especially painful for Moses, who said "Listen, rebels," to hear his God apply that word now to him. Leaders of a congregation cannot violate the very instruction that they uphold and teach to others.

cities." ³And YHWH listened to Israel's voice and delivered the Canaanite, and they completely destroyed them and their cities. And the name of the place was called Hormah.

⁴And they traveled from Mount Hor by way of the Red Sea road to go around the land of Edom. And the people's soul was getting short on the way. ⁵And the people spoke against God and against Moses: "Why did you bring us up from Egypt to die in the wilderness? Because there's no bread, and there's no water, and our soul is disgusted with the cursed bread."

עֲרֵיהֶֽם: ³וַיִּשְׁמַ֨ע יְהוָ֜ה בְּק֣וֹל יִשְׂרָאֵל֮ וַיִּתֵּ֣ן אֶת־הַֽכְּנַעֲנִי֒ וַיַּחֲרֵ֥ם אֶתְהֶ֖ם וְאֶת־עָרֵיהֶ֑ם וַיִּקְרָ֥א שֵׁם־הַמָּק֖וֹם חָרְמָֽה: פ ⁴וַיִּסְע֞וּ מֵהֹ֤ר הָהָר֙ דֶּ֣רֶךְ יַם־ס֔וּף לִסְבֹ֖ב אֶת־אֶ֣רֶץ אֱד֑וֹם וַתִּקְצַ֥ר נֶֽפֶשׁ־הָעָ֖ם בַּדָּֽרֶךְ: ⁵וַיְדַבֵּ֣ר הָעָ֗ם בֵּֽאלֹהִים֮ וּבְמֹשֶׁה֒ לָמָ֤ה הֶֽעֱלִיתֻ֨נוּ֙ מִמִּצְרַ֔יִם לָמ֖וּת בַּמִּדְבָּ֑ר כִּ֣י אֵ֥ין לֶ֨חֶם֙ וְאֵ֣ין מַ֔יִם וְנַפְשֵׁ֣נוּ קָ֔צָה בַּלֶּ֖חֶם הַקְּלֹקֵֽל: ⁶וַיְשַׁלַּ֨ח

21:4. **the Red Sea**. Hebrew *yam sûp*. People argue that the sea that splits in Exodus 14 is not the Red Sea but rather the "Reed Sea," an otherwise unknown body of water. But the reference to the *yam sûp* here, when the Israelites are no longer anywhere near Egypt, must refer to the eastern arm of the Red Sea, which is the only body of water that extends both up into Egypt and to a location far away in the Sinai. See my comment on Exod 13:8.

21:4. **the people's soul was getting short**. The image is of getting short of breath or short of temper. The word here stands in contrast to its last occurrence in the Torah: when the people cried for meat, and Moses doubted whether so much meat could be provided, God said, "Is YHWH's hand getting short?!" (Num 11:23). Now they are crying for food again, and it is the people's soul or breath that is "getting short." And all of this is doubly ironic because back in Egypt the people were unable to respond to Moses' announcement of their coming freedom owing to "shortage of spirit" (קֹצֶר רוּחַ—Exod 6:9). Freedom has not produced a speedy transformation of their nature. When faced with stress they think of returning to Egypt, which now looks attractive even though their condition there was described with the same term.

21:5. **the people spoke against God and against Moses**. The notable new element in their complaint this time is that they finally seem to have assimilated the fact that it is not merely Moses but God who is directing them. What made them finally see this? It certainly appears to be the aftermath of the events at Meribah. When Moses stopped saying "It's God, not I," and just one time said instead "Shall *we* bring water out," he paid such a terrible price that the people have now seen the proof that it is God, and not just Moses, who controls their fortunes.

21:5. **Why did you bring us up**. The word "you" here is plural, further reflecting that the people are, for once, not directing their entire complaint against Moses. They are at least beginning to acknowledge the divine power in what happened in Egypt. Even though it comes in the context of a complaint, this is still a step for the people, who have, all along, been unable to accept the terrifying wonder of the closeness of divinity.

6And YHWH let fiery snakes go among the people, and they bit the people, and a great many people from Israel died. 7And the people came to Moses, and they said, "We've sinned, because we spoke against YHWH and against you. Pray to YHWH, that He will turn the snake away from us." And Moses prayed on behalf of the people.

8And YHWH said to Moses, "Make a fiery one and set it on a pole, and it will be that everyone who is bitten and sees it will live." 9And Moses made a bronze snake and set it on a pole, and it was, if a snake bit a man, then he would look at the bronze snake and live.

10And the children of Israel traveled, and they camped in Oboth. 11And they traveled from Oboth, and they camped in Iye-abarim, in the wilderness that is toward Moab, toward the sun's rising. 12From there they traveled, and they camped in the Wadi Zered. 13From there they traveled, and they camped across the Arnon, which is in the wilderness that extends from the

יְהוָֹה בָּעָם אֵת הַנְּחָשִׁים הַשְּׂרָפִים וַיְנַשְּׁכוּ אֶת־הָעָם
וַיָּמָת עַם־רָב מִיִּשְׂרָאֵל: 7וַיָּבֹא הָעָם אֶל־מֹשֶׁה
וַיֹּאמְרוּ חָטָאנוּ כִּי־דִבַּרְנוּ בַיהוָה וָבָךְ הִתְפַּלֵּל
אֶל־יְהוָה וְיָסֵר מֵעָלֵינוּ אֶת־הַנָּחָשׁ וַיִּתְפַּלֵּל מֹשֶׁה
בְּעַד הָעָם: 8וַיֹּאמֶר יְהוָה אֶל־מֹשֶׁה עֲשֵׂה לְךָ שָׂרָף
וְשִׂים אֹתוֹ עַל־נֵס וְהָיָה כָּל־הַנָּשׁוּךְ וְרָאָה אֹתוֹ וָחָי:
9וַיַּעַשׂ מֹשֶׁה נְחַשׁ נְחֹשֶׁת וַיְשִׂמֵהוּ עַל־הַנֵּס וְהָיָה
אִם־נָשַׁךְ הַנָּחָשׁ אֶת־אִישׁ וְהִבִּיט אֶל־נְחַשׁ הַנְּחֹשֶׁת
וָחָי: 10וַיִּסְעוּ בְּנֵי יִשְׂרָאֵל וַיַּחֲנוּ בְּאֹבֹת: 11וַיִּסְעוּ
מֵאֹבֹת וַיַּחֲנוּ בְּעִיֵּי הָעֲבָרִים בַּמִּדְבָּר אֲשֶׁר עַל־פְּנֵי
מוֹאָב מִמִּזְרַח הַשָּׁמֶשׁ: 12מִשָּׁם נָסָעוּ וַיַּחֲנוּ בְּנַחַל
זָרֶד: 13מִשָּׁם נָסָעוּ וַיַּחֲנוּ מֵעֵבֶר אַרְנוֹן אֲשֶׁר

21:9. **a bronze snake.** When someone is bitten by a snake, the victim can look at the bronze snake of Moses and be healed. This story is the only case of what appears to be sympathetic magic in these books. It is also the only depiction of a sacred object that is not associated with the Tent of Meeting and its contents. Related to this fact, and perhaps more significant, it is the only sacred object that is not connected in any way with Aaron and the priests of his family. Rather, it is personally made and mounted by Moses himself. This fits with the fact that it was *Moses'* staff that miraculously became a snake at the burning bush and in Egypt (Exod 4:2–3); Aaron's staff became a different kind of serpent (Exod 7:8–10; see the comment on 7:9). The text is unclear as to whether the snake is used only on the occasion of this crisis or if it continues to be mounted in some visible location. On the evidence of an event reported in the book of 2 Kings (18:4), it seems likely that we should understand it as continuing to be in public view even after the crisis is past. In that account, we are told that Moses' snake was called Nehushtan and that King Hezekiah destroyed it because the Israelites had been burning incense to it. (Concerning the reason why a Judean king would have dared to destroy something that was believed to have been made by Moses himself, see my *Who Wrote the Bible?* pp. 126, 210–211.)

Another point: The two signs that God gives Moses at the burning bush are that his staff becomes a snake and his hand becomes leprous like snow (Exod 4:1–8). These now are seen to foreshadow events in Numbers: the snake on a pole (Num 21:5–9) and Miriam's becoming leprous like snow (Numbers 12).

border of the Amorite, because Arnon is Moab's border, between Moab and the Amorite. 14On account of this it is said in the Scroll of the Wars of YHWH:

> Waheb in Suphah and the wadis of Arnon,
> 15and the slope of the wadis that reached to the settlement of Ar, and pressed to Moab's border.

16And from there to Beer: that is the well of which YHWH said to Moses, "Gather the people, so I may give them water." 17Then Israel sang this song:

> Spring up, well. Sing to it.
> 18 The commanders hewed the well, the
>   people's nobles dug it,
>   with a scepter, with their staffs.

And from the wilderness to Mattanah, 19and from Mattanah to Nahaliel, and from Nahaliel to Bamoth, 20and from Bamoth in the valley, that is in the field of Moab, to the top of Pisgah, which looks toward Jeshimon.

21And Israel sent messengers to Sihon, king of the Amorites, saying, 22"Let me pass through your land. We won't turn in at a field and at a vineyard and won't drink well waters. We'll go by the king's road until we pass your border." 23And Sihon did not allow Israel to pass within his border. And Sihon gathered all his people and went out to Israel at the wilderness and came to Jahaz and fought against Israel. 24And Israel struck him by the sword and took possession of his land from Arnon to Jabbok, to the children of Ammon, because the border of the children of

בַּמִּדְבָּר הַיֹּצֵא מִגְּבֻל הָאֱמֹרִי כִּי אַרְנוֹן גְּבוּל
מוֹאָב בֵּין מוֹאָב וּבֵין הָאֱמֹרִי: 14עַל־כֵּן יֵאָמַר
בְּסֵפֶר מִלְחֲמֹת יְהוָה

אֶת־וָהֵב בְּסוּפָה וְאֶת־הַנְּחָלִים אַרְנוֹן:

15וְאֶשֶׁד הַנְּחָלִים

אֲשֶׁר נָטָה לְשֶׁבֶת עָר וְנִשְׁעַן לִגְבוּל מוֹאָב:

16וּמִשָּׁם בְּאֵרָה הִוא הַבְּאֵר אֲשֶׁר אָמַר יְהוָה
לְמֹשֶׁה אֱסֹף אֶת־הָעָם וְאֶתְּנָה לָהֶם מָיִם: ס 17אָז
יָשִׁיר יִשְׂרָאֵל אֶת־הַשִּׁירָה הַזֹּאת

עֲלִי בְאֵר עֱנוּ־לָהּ:

18בְּאֵר חֲפָרוּהָ שָׂרִים כָּרוּהָ נְדִיבֵי הָעָם
בִּמְחֹקֵק בְּמִשְׁעֲנֹתָם וּמִמִּדְבָּר מַתָּנָה:

19וּמִמַּתָּנָה נַחֲלִיאֵל וּמִנַּחֲלִיאֵל בָּמוֹת: 20וּמִבָּמוֹת
הַגַּיְא אֲשֶׁר בִּשְׂדֵה מוֹאָב רֹאשׁ הַפִּסְגָּה וְנִשְׁקָפָה
עַל־פְּנֵי הַיְשִׁימֹן: פ 21וַיִּשְׁלַח יִשְׂרָאֵל מַלְאָכִים
אֶל־סִיחֹן מֶלֶךְ־הָאֱמֹרִי לֵאמֹר: 22אֶעְבְּרָה בְאַרְצֶךָ
לֹא נִטֶּה בְּשָׂדֶה וּבְכֶרֶם לֹא נִשְׁתֶּה מֵי בְאֵר בְּדֶרֶךְ
הַמֶּלֶךְ נֵלֵךְ עַד אֲשֶׁר־נַעֲבֹר גְּבֻלֶךָ: 23וְלֹא־נָתַן
סִיחֹן אֶת־יִשְׂרָאֵל עֲבֹר בִּגְבֻלוֹ וַיֶּאֱסֹף סִיחֹן אֶת־
כָּל־עַמּוֹ וַיֵּצֵא לִקְרַאת יִשְׂרָאֵל הַמִּדְבָּרָה וַיָּבֹא
יָהְצָה וַיִּלָּחֶם בְּיִשְׂרָאֵל: 24וַיַּכֵּהוּ יִשְׂרָאֵל לְפִי־חָרֶב
וַיִּירַשׁ אֶת־אַרְצוֹ מֵאַרְנֹן עַד־יַבֹּק עַד־בְּנֵי עַמּוֹן כִּי

21:14. **the Scroll of the Wars of YHWH.** The Torah here indicates that there are known older, written sources, which it may sometimes use or cite.

21:17. **Then Israel sang.** The poems come relatively late in the book (with the possible exception of Num 12:6–8), and their effect is likely to be heightened for many readers on account of this. After twenty-and-a-half chapters of rebellion episodes, lists, and laws, we read that "Then Israel sang" (21:17). It is the first report of song since the account of the crossing of the Red Sea, which culminated with the Song of the Sea (introduced with comparable words: "Then Moses and the children of Israel sang," Exod 15:1).

Ammon was strong. 25And Israel took all of these cities, and Israel lived in all the Amorite cities in Heshbon and all of its environs, 26because Heshbon was the city of Sihon, the king of the Amorite, and he fought against the former king of Moab and took all of his land from his hand as far as Arnon. 27On account of this they say proverbially:

> Come to Heshbon.
> Built and founded is Sihon's city.

28　For fire went out of Heshbon,
　　flame from Sihon's town;
　　it consumed Ar of Moab,
　　the lords of the high places of Arnon.

29　Woe unto you, Moab:
　　you've perished, Chemosh's people.
　　He's made his sons refugees
　　and his daughters captive
　　to the king of the Amorite, Sihon.

30　And their fiefdom perished,
　　Heshbon to Dibon,
　　and we devastated up to Nophah
　　which reaches to Medeba.

31And Israel lived in the Amorite's land. 32And Moses sent to spy on Jazer, and they captured its environs and dispossessed the Amorite who was there. 33And they turned and went up the road of Bashan, and Og, the king of Bashan, went out to them, he and all his people, to war at Edrei. 34And YHWH said to Moses, "Don't fear him, because I've delivered him and all his people and his land into your hand, and you'll do to him as you did to Sihon, king of the Amorite, who lived in Heshbon." 35And they struck him and his sons and all his people until he did not have a remnant left, and they took possession of his land.

עֹז גְּב֖וּל בְּנֵ֣י עַמּֽוֹן׃ 25וַיִּקַּח֙ יִשְׂרָאֵ֔ל אֵ֥ת כָּל־הֶעָרִ֖ים הָאֵ֑לֶּה וַיֵּ֨שֶׁב יִשְׂרָאֵל֙ בְּכָל־עָרֵ֣י הָֽאֱמֹרִ֔י בְּחֶשְׁבּ֖וֹן וּבְכָל־בְּנֹתֶֽיהָ׃ 26כִּ֣י חֶשְׁבּ֔וֹן עִ֗יר סִיחֹ֛ן מֶ֥לֶךְ הָאֱמֹרִ֖י הִ֑וא וְה֣וּא נִלְחַ֗ם בְּמֶ֤לֶךְ מוֹאָב֙ הָ֣רִאשׁ֔וֹן וַיִּקַּ֧ח אֶת־כָּל־אַרְצ֛וֹ מִיָּד֖וֹ עַד־אַרְנֹֽן׃ 27עַל־כֵּ֛ן יֹאמְר֥וּ הַמֹּשְׁלִ֖ים

בֹּ֣אוּ חֶשְׁבּ֑וֹן תִּבָּנֶ֥ה וְתִכּוֹנֵ֖ן עִ֥יר סִיחֽוֹן׃

28כִּי־אֵשׁ֙ יָֽצְאָ֣ה מֵֽחֶשְׁבּ֔וֹן לֶהָבָ֖ה מִקִּרְיַ֣ת סִיחֹ֑ן אָֽכְלָה֙ עָ֣ר מוֹאָ֔ב בַּעֲלֵ֖י בָּמ֥וֹת אַרְנֹֽן׃

29אוֹי־לְךָ֣ מוֹאָ֗ב אָבַ֖דְתָּ עַם־כְּמ֑וֹשׁ נָתַ֨ן בָּנָ֤יו פְּלֵיטִם֙ וּבְנֹתָ֣יו בַּשְּׁבִ֔ית לְמֶ֥לֶךְ אֱמֹרִ֖י סִיחֽוֹן׃

30וַנִּירָ֛ם אָבַ֥ד חֶשְׁבּ֖וֹן עַד־דִּיבֹ֑ן וַנַּשִּׁ֣ים עַד־נֹ֔פַח אֲשֶׁ֖ר עַד־מֵֽידְבָֽא׃

31וַיֵּ֨שֶׁב֙ יִשְׂרָאֵ֔ל בְּאֶ֖רֶץ הָאֱמֹרִֽי׃ 32וַיִּשְׁלַ֤ח מֹשֶׁה֙ לְרַגֵּ֣ל אֶת־יַעְזֵ֔ר וַֽיִּלְכְּד֖וּ בְּנֹתֶ֑יהָ וַיּ֖וֹרֶשׁ אֶת־הָאֱמֹרִ֥י אֲשֶׁר־שָֽׁם׃ 33וַיִּפְנוּ֙ וַֽיַּעֲל֔וּ דֶּ֖רֶךְ הַבָּשָׁ֑ן וַיֵּצֵ֣א עוֹג֩ מֶֽלֶךְ־הַבָּשָׁ֨ן לִקְרָאתָ֜ם ה֧וּא וְכָל־עַמּ֛וֹ לַמִּלְחָמָ֖ה אֶדְרֶֽעִי׃ 34וַיֹּ֨אמֶר יְהוָ֤ה אֶל־מֹשֶׁה֙ אַל־תִּירָ֣א אֹת֔וֹ כִּ֣י בְיָדְךָ֞ נָתַ֧תִּי אֹת֛וֹ וְאֶת־כָּל־עַמּ֖וֹ וְאֶת־אַרְצ֑וֹ וְעָשִׂ֣יתָ לּ֔וֹ כַּאֲשֶׁ֣ר עָשִׂ֗יתָ לְסִיחֹן֙ מֶ֣לֶךְ הָֽאֱמֹרִ֔י אֲשֶׁ֥ר יוֹשֵׁ֖ב בְּחֶשְׁבּֽוֹן׃ 35וַיַּכּ֨וּ אֹת֤וֹ וְאֶת־בָּנָיו֙ וְאֶת־כָּל־עַמּ֔וֹ עַד־בִּלְתִּ֥י הִשְׁאִֽיר־ל֖וֹ שָׂרִ֑יד וַיִּֽירְשׁ֖וּ אֶת־אַרְצֽוֹ׃

21:32　וַיּוֹרֶשׁ ק

21:28. high places. High places are large flat platforms where sacrificial worship takes place. They are used among the Canaanites; and later the Israelites use them, sometimes for worship of YHWH and sometimes for worship of pagan gods. High places are forbidden to Israelites, whether for YHWH or for pagan gods. Israelites are allowed to sacrifice in only one place: at the Tent of Meeting, "the place where YHWH tents His name" (Lev 17:5; Deut 12:5–6).

　21:35. they took possession of his land. The Israelites' eastern route next takes

22

¹And the children of Israel traveled, and they camped in the plains of Moab, across the Jordan from Jericho.

בלק 22 ¹וַיִּסְעוּ בְּנֵי יִשְׂרָאֵל וַיַּחֲנוּ בְּעַרְבוֹת מוֹאָב מֵעֵבֶר לְיַרְדֵּן יְרֵחוֹ: ס

BALAK

בלק

²And Balak, son of Zippor, saw everything that Israel had done to the Amorite. ³And Moab was very fearful because of the people because it was numerous, and Moab felt a disgust at the children of Israel. ⁴And Moab said to the elders of Midian, "Now the community will lick up all of our surroundings the way an ox licks up the plants of a field!"

And Balak, son of Zippor, was king of Moab at that time. ⁵And he sent messengers to Balaam, son of Beor, at Pethor, which is on the river—the

²וַיַּרְא בָּלָק בֶּן־צִפּוֹר אֵת כָּל־אֲשֶׁר־עָשָׂה יִשְׂרָאֵל לָאֱמֹרִי: ³וַיָּגָר מוֹאָב מִפְּנֵי הָעָם מְאֹד כִּי רַב־הוּא וַיָּקָץ מוֹאָב מִפְּנֵי בְּנֵי יִשְׂרָאֵל: ⁴וַיֹּאמֶר מוֹאָב אֶל־זִקְנֵי מִדְיָן עַתָּה יְלַחֲכוּ הַקָּהָל אֶת־כָּל־סְבִיבֹתֵינוּ כִּלְחֹךְ הַשּׁוֹר אֵת יֶרֶק הַשָּׂדֶה וּבָלָק בֶּן־צִפּוֹר מֶלֶךְ לְמוֹאָב בָּעֵת הַהִוא: ⁵וַיִּשְׁלַח מַלְאָכִים אֶל־בִּלְעָם בֶּן־בְּעוֹר פְּתוֹרָה אֲשֶׁר עַל־הַנָּהָר אֶרֶץ

---

them to the territory of the Amorite kings Sihon and Og, and Israel makes the same request for peaceful passage that it has made to Edom. Both Sihon and Og attack Israel militarily, and both are utterly defeated. Thus Israel comes to acquire territory on the eastern side of the Jordan River, outside the borders of the promised land (Num 21:21–35).

22:3. Moab. The descendants of Lot and his daughter (Gen 19:36–37).

22:3. it was numerous, and Moab felt a disgust. History repeats itself. Moab's fears are expressly like those of Egypt at the time of the oppression of the Israelites. A cluster of parallel wordings conveys this: Israel was "numerous" (cf. Exod 1:9). Moab "felt a disgust at the children of Israel"; these exact words are used with regard to the Egyptians (Exod 1:12). Israel is "more powerful than I" (Num 22:6; cf. Exod 1:9). Israel "has covered the eye of the land"; these words are used to describe the locust plague (Exod 10:5,15). Egypt set out to control the too-numerous Israelites; Moab sets out to drive them away. But the irony in both cases is that they *perceive* Israel to be a threat because it is so big, but Israel is in fact no threat at all. Israel is not said to have any hostile intentions at all. It is the actions that Egypt and Moab take on the basis of their mistaken perceptions that bring catastrophes on them. It is a strange human characteristic, taking the very existence of someone who is different and strong to be a threat.

22:4. Moab . . . Midian. The Moabites, who are descendants of Lot, ally with the Midianites, who are direct descendants of Abraham himself (Gen 25:2). The forces that caused the ancestors to separate from one another now escalate into hostility among the descendants. And the kindness and family fidelity that Abraham showed when he rescued Lot (Genesis 14) are no longer factors in the minds of Lot's descendants.

22:5. Balaam, son of Beor. Balaam, son of Beor, is described in a plaster inscrip-

land of the children of his people—to call him, saying, "Here, a people has come out from Egypt. Here, it has covered the eye of the land. And it's sitting across from me! 6And now, go, curse this people for me, because it's more powerful than I—maybe I'll be able: we'll strike it, and I'll drive it out from the land—because I know that whoever you'll bless will be blessed, and whoever you'll curse will be cursed."

7And Moab's elders and Midian's elders went, and divination implements were in their hand, and they came to Balaam and spoke Balak's words to him. 8And he said to them, "Spend the night here tonight, and I'll bring back word to you as YHWH will speak to me." And the chiefs of Moab stayed with Balaam.

9And God came to Balaam and said, "Who are these people with you?"

10And Balaam said to God, "Balak, son of Zippor, king of Moab, sent to me: 11'Here is a people who came out from Egypt and has covered the eye of the land. Now go, execrate it for me. Maybe I'll be able to fight against it, and I'll drive it out.'"

12And God said to Balaam, "You shall not go with them. You shall not curse the people, because it is blessed."

בְּנֵי־עַמּוֹ לִקְרֹא־לוֹ לֵאמֹר הִנֵּה עַם יָצָא מִמִּצְרַיִם הִנֵּה כִסָּה אֶת־עֵין הָאָרֶץ וְהוּא יֹשֵׁב מִמֻּלִי: 6וְעַתָּה לְכָה־נָּא אָרָה־לִּי אֶת־הָעָם הַזֶּה כִּי־עָצוּם הוּא מִמֶּנִּי אוּלַי אוּכַל נַכֶּה־בּוֹ וַאֲגָרְשֶׁנּוּ מִן־הָאָרֶץ כִּי יָדַעְתִּי אֵת אֲשֶׁר־תְּבָרֵךְ מְבֹרָךְ וַאֲשֶׁר תָּאֹר יוּאָר: 7וַיֵּלְכוּ זִקְנֵי מוֹאָב וְזִקְנֵי מִדְיָן וּקְסָמִים בְּיָדָם וַיָּבֹאוּ אֶל־בִּלְעָם וַיְדַבְּרוּ אֵלָיו דִּבְרֵי בָלָק: 8וַיֹּאמֶר אֲלֵיהֶם לִינוּ פֹה הַלַּיְלָה וַהֲשִׁבֹתִי אֶתְכֶם דָּבָר כַּאֲשֶׁר יְדַבֵּר יְהֹוָה אֵלָי וַיֵּשְׁבוּ שָׂרֵי־מוֹאָב עִם־בִּלְעָם: 9וַיָּבֹא אֱלֹהִים אֶל־בִּלְעָם וַיֹּאמֶר מִי הָאֲנָשִׁים הָאֵלֶּה עִמָּךְ: 10וַיֹּאמֶר בִּלְעָם אֶל־הָאֱלֹהִים בָּלָק בֶּן־צִפֹּר מֶלֶךְ מוֹאָב שָׁלַח אֵלָי: 11הִנֵּה הָעָם הַיֹּצֵא מִמִּצְרַיִם וַיְכַס אֶת־עֵין הָאָרֶץ עַתָּה לְכָה קָבָה־לִּי אֹתוֹ אוּלַי אוּכַל לְהִלָּחֶם בּוֹ וְגֵרַשְׁתִּיו: 12וַיֹּאמֶר אֱלֹהִים אֶל־בִּלְעָם לֹא תֵלֵךְ עִמָּהֶם לֹא תָאֹר אֶת־הָעָם כִּי בָרוּךְ הוּא: 13וַיָּקָם

---

tion from Deir 'Alla that was discovered in 1967. He is the earliest person mentioned in the Bible who is also mentioned in an archaeological source.

22:5,11. covered the eye of the land. Meaning: the Israelites are so many that they make the ground invisible. This is the same expression that is used to describe the plague of the locust swarm in Egypt.

22:9. God came to Balaam. It is surely significant that the Torah, a work that comes from Israel, pictures the creator as communicating with a non-Israelite prophet as well. It is a reminder that the Torah begins with the story of the connection between God and all of the earth. The narrowing of focus to Abraham and to his descendants is said to be so that they will be a blessing to all the families of the earth. Indeed the connection between Balaam and that promise given in God's first words to Abraham is explicit. The full wording to Abraham is: "And I'll bless those who bless you, and those who affront you I'll curse. And all the families of the earth will be blessed through you" (Gen 12:3). And soon Balaam will bless Israel with the parallel words: "Those who bless you: he's blessed. And those who curse you: he's cursed" (Num 24:9).

13And Balaam got up in the morning and said to Balak's chiefs, "Go to your land, because YHWH refused to allow me to go with you."

14And the chiefs of Moab got up and came to Balak and said, "Balaam refused to go with us."

15And Balak went on again to send more numerous and prestigious chiefs than these. 16And they came to Balaam and said to him, "Balak, son of Zippor, said this: 'Don't be held back from coming to me, 17because I'll *honor* you very much, and I'll do everything that you'll say to me. And go, *execrate* this people for me.'"

18And Balaam answered, and he said to Balak's servants, "If Balak would give me a houseful of silver and gold of his I wouldn't be able to go against the mouth of YHWH, my God, to do something small or big. 19And now, stay here, you as well, tonight, so I may know what YHWH will add to speak with me."

20And God came to Balaam at night and said to him, "If these people have come to call you, get up, go with them. And just the thing that I shall speak to you—you shall do *that.*"

21And Balaam got up in the morning and harnessed his ass and went with the chiefs of Moab. 22And God's anger flared because he was going. And an angel of YHWH stood up in the road as an adversary to him. And he was riding on his ass, and his two boys were with him. 23And the

בִּלְעָם בַּבֹּקֶר וַיֹּאמֶר אֶל־שָׂרֵי בָלָק לְכוּ אֶל־אַרְצְכֶם כִּי מֵאֵן יְהוָה לְתִתִּי לַהֲלֹךְ עִמָּכֶם: 14וַיָּקוּמוּ שָׂרֵי מוֹאָב וַיָּבֹאוּ אֶל־בָּלָק וַיֹּאמְרוּ מֵאֵן בִּלְעָם הֲלֹךְ עִמָּנוּ: 15וַיֹּסֶף עוֹד בָּלָק שְׁלֹחַ שָׂרִים רַבִּים וְנִכְבָּדִים מֵאֵלֶּה: 16וַיָּבֹאוּ אֶל־בִּלְעָם וַיֹּאמְרוּ לוֹ כֹּה אָמַר בָּלָק בֶּן־צִפּוֹר אַל־נָא תִמָּנַע מֵהֲלֹךְ אֵלָי: 17כִּי־כַבֵּד אֲכַבֶּדְךָ מְאֹד וְכֹל אֲשֶׁר־תֹּאמַר אֵלַי אֶעֱשֶׂה וּלְכָה־נָּא קָבָה־לִּי אֵת הָעָם הַזֶּה: 18וַיַּעַן בִּלְעָם וַיֹּאמֶר אֶל־עַבְדֵי בָלָק אִם־יִתֶּן־לִי בָלָק מְלֹא בֵיתוֹ כֶּסֶף וְזָהָב לֹא אוּכַל לַעֲבֹר אֶת־פִּי יְהוָה אֱלֹהָי לַעֲשׂוֹת קְטַנָּה אוֹ גְדוֹלָה: 19וְעַתָּה שְׁבוּ נָא בָזֶה גַּם־אַתֶּם הַלָּיְלָה וְאֵדְעָה מַה־יֹּסֵף יְהוָה דַּבֵּר עִמִּי: 20וַיָּבֹא אֱלֹהִים ׀ אֶל־בִּלְעָם לַיְלָה וַיֹּאמֶר לוֹ אִם־לִקְרֹא לְךָ בָּאוּ הָאֲנָשִׁים קוּם לֵךְ אִתָּם וְאַךְ אֶת־הַדָּבָר אֲשֶׁר־אֲדַבֵּר אֵלֶיךָ אֹתוֹ תַעֲשֶׂה: 21וַיָּקָם בִּלְעָם בַּבֹּקֶר וַיַּחֲבֹשׁ אֶת־אֲתֹנוֹ וַיֵּלֶךְ עִם־שָׂרֵי מוֹאָב: 22וַיִּחַר־אַף אֱלֹהִים כִּי־הוֹלֵךְ הוּא וַיִּתְיַצֵּב מַלְאַךְ יְהוָה בַּדֶּרֶךְ לְשָׂטָן לוֹ וְהוּא רֹכֵב עַל־אֲתֹנוֹ וּשְׁנֵי נְעָרָיו עִמּוֹ: 23וַתֵּרֶא הָאָתוֹן

22:14. **Balaam refused.** Like the Egyptians toward Joseph, and like the Israelites toward Moses, the Moabites focus on the human rather than on God. What Balaam said was, "YHWH refused to allow me to go with you." But the Moabite emissaries report, "*Balaam* refused to go with us." Relating to the prophet rather than to the God who communicates through the prophet is presented as a fundamental human characteristic.

22:22. **God's anger flared because he was going.** But did God not just tell him to go (v. 20)?! The answer may lie in v. 32; see below.

22:22. **an angel . . . his ass . . . his two boys.** Note the parallels to the story of the binding of Isaac: he takes an ass and two servant boys, and he encounters an angel. And a life is spared. And altars are built. And a ram is sacrificed as a burnt offering. And both stories involve the doubled, emphatic form of the verb "to bless" (Gen 22:17; Num 24:10). And both involve the number three. And both end with the same three verbs: got up, went, returned. This may thus be another signal that the merit of

504

ass saw the angel of YHWH standing up in the road and his sword drawn in his hand, and the ass turned from the road and went into the field. And Balaam hit the ass to turn her back to the road.

24And the angel of YHWH stood in the pathway of the vineyards, a fence on this side and a fence on that side. 25And the ass saw the angel of YHWH, and she was pressed against the wall, and she pressed Balaam's foot against the wall, and he continued hitting her.

26And the angel continued passing on and stood in a narrow place where there was no way to turn right or left. 27And the ass saw the angel of YHWH, and she lay down under Balaam. And Balaam's anger flared, and he struck the ass with a stick. 28And YHWH opened the ass's mouth, and she said to Balaam, "What have I done to you that you've struck me these three times?!"

29And Balaam said to the ass, "Because you abused me! If there had been a sword in my hand I would have killed you by now!"

30And the ass said to Balaam, "Aren't I your ass, on whom you've ridden? From your start until this day, have I *been accustomed* to do like this to you?"

And he said, "No."

31And YHWH uncovered Balaam's eyes, and he saw the angel of YHWH standing up in the road, and his sword drawn in his hand. And he knelt and bowed to his nose. 32And the angel of

אֶת־מַלְאַ֣ךְ יְהוָ֗ה נִצָּ֤ב בַּדֶּ֙רֶךְ֙ וְחַרְבּ֣וֹ שְׁלוּפָ֣ה בְּיָד֔וֹ וַתֵּ֤ט הָֽאָתוֹן֙ מִן־הַדֶּ֔רֶךְ וַתֵּ֖לֶךְ בַּשָּׂדֶ֑ה וַיַּ֤ךְ בִּלְעָם֙ אֶת־הָ֣אָת֔וֹן לְהַטֹּתָ֖הּ הַדָּֽרֶךְ׃ 24וַֽיַּעֲמֹד֙ מַלְאַ֣ךְ יְהוָ֔ה בְּמִשְׁע֖וֹל הַכְּרָמִ֑ים גָּדֵ֥ר מִזֶּ֖ה וְגָדֵ֥ר מִזֶּֽה׃ 25וַתֵּ֨רֶא הָאָת֜וֹן אֶת־מַלְאַ֣ךְ יְהוָ֗ה וַתִּלָּחֵץ֙ אֶל־הַקִּ֔יר וַתִּלְחַ֛ץ אֶת־רֶ֥גֶל בִּלְעָ֖ם אֶל־הַקִּ֑יר וַיֹּ֖סֶף לְהַכֹּתָֽהּ׃ 26וַיּ֥וֹסֶף מַלְאַךְ־יְהוָ֖ה עֲב֑וֹר וַֽיַּעֲמֹד֙ בְּמָק֣וֹם צָ֔ר אֲשֶׁ֛ר אֵֽין־דֶּ֥רֶךְ לִנְט֖וֹת יָמִ֥ין וּשְׂמֹֽאול׃ 27וַתֵּ֤רֶא הָֽאָתוֹן֙ אֶת־מַלְאַ֣ךְ יְהוָ֔ה וַתִּרְבַּ֖ץ תַּ֣חַת בִּלְעָ֑ם וַיִּֽחַר־אַ֣ף בִּלְעָ֔ם וַיַּ֥ךְ אֶת־הָאָת֖וֹן בַּמַּקֵּֽל׃ 28וַיִּפְתַּ֥ח יְהוָ֖ה אֶת־פִּ֣י הָאָת֑וֹן וַתֹּ֤אמֶר לְבִלְעָם֙ מֶה־עָשִׂ֣יתִי לְךָ֔ כִּ֣י הִכִּיתַ֔נִי זֶ֖ה שָׁלֹ֥שׁ רְגָלִֽים׃ 29וַיֹּ֤אמֶר בִּלְעָם֙ לָֽאָת֔וֹן כִּ֖י הִתְעַלַּ֣לְתְּ בִּ֑י ל֤וּ יֶשׁ־חֶ֙רֶב֙ בְּיָדִ֔י כִּ֥י עַתָּ֖ה הֲרַגְתִּֽיךְ׃ 30וַתֹּ֨אמֶר הָאָת֜וֹן אֶל־בִּלְעָ֗ם הֲלוֹא֩ אָנֹכִ֨י אֲתֹֽנְךָ֜ אֲשֶׁר־רָכַ֣בְתָּ עָלַ֗י מֵעֽוֹדְךָ֙ עַד־הַיּ֣וֹם הַזֶּ֔ה הַֽהַסְכֵּ֣ן הִסְכַּ֔נְתִּי לַעֲשׂ֥וֹת לְךָ֖ כֹּ֑ה וַיֹּ֖אמֶר לֹֽא׃ 31וַיְגַ֣ל יְהוָה֮ אֶת־עֵינֵ֣י בִלְעָם֒ וַיַּ֞רְא אֶת־מַלְאַ֤ךְ יְהוָה֙ נִצָּ֣ב בַּדֶּ֔רֶךְ וְחַרְבּ֥וֹ שְׁלֻפָ֖ה בְּיָד֑וֹ וַיִּקֹּ֥ד וַיִּשְׁתַּ֖חוּ לְאַפָּֽיו׃ 32וַיֹּ֣אמֶר

---

the patriarchs protects their descendants, the children of Israel. On the basis of Abraham's obedience at Moriah, God promises (Gen 22:17) to make his descendants *numerous*, which is the thing that now distresses Balak (22:3); and God promises to *bless* his descendants, which He now does through Balaam (24:10).

22:29. Balaam said to the ass. As usual, the text does not provide details about emotions, and so we do not know if Balaam's answer is expressed with amazement at hearing his ass talk or if he is to be pictured as just answering matter-of-factly without yet realizing that something extraordinary is happening. This heightens the comic effect. Some people resist seeing humor in the Bible, as if being funny is contrary to the book's dignity. Their error is not that they value the Bible too much but rather that they value humor too little. Humor is such an essential part of human life that the Bible would be strange and incomplete without it.

YHWH said to him, "For what have you struck your ass these three times? Here, I came out as an adversary because the way was precipitous with regard to me. ³³And the ass saw me and turned in front of me these three times. If she hadn't turned from in front of me, I would have killed you, too, by now and kept her alive!"

³⁴And Balaam said to the angel of YHWH, "I've sinned, because I didn't know that you were standing up toward me in the road. And now, if it's bad in your eyes, let me go back."

³⁵And the angel of YHWH said to Balaam, "Go with the people. And nothing but the thing that I shall speak to you: that is what you shall speak." And Balaam went with Balak's chiefs.

³⁶And Balak heard that Balaam was coming, and he went out to him, to a city of Moab that was on the Arnon border, that was at the edge of the border. ³⁷And Balak said to Balaam, "Didn't I *send* to you, to call you? Why didn't you come to me? Am I indeed not able to honor you?!"

³⁸And Balaam said to Balak, "Here, I've come to you. Now: will I be *able* to speak anything? The thing that God will set in my mouth: that is what I'll speak." ³⁹And Balaam went with Balak, and they came to Kiriath Huzoth. ⁴⁰And Balak sacrificed oxen and sheep, and he let them go to Balaam and to the chiefs who were with them. ⁴¹And it was in the morning, and Balak took Balaam and brought him up to the High Places of Baal, and he saw the outer edge of the people from there.

אֵלָיו מַלְאַךְ יְהוָה עַל־מָה הִכִּיתָ אֶת־אֲתֹנְךָ זֶה שָׁלוֹשׁ רְגָלִים הִנֵּה אָנֹכִי יָצָאתִי לְשָׂטָן כִּי־יָרַט הַדֶּרֶךְ לְנֶגְדִּי: ³³וַתִּרְאַנִי הָאָתוֹן וַתֵּט לְפָנַי זֶה שָׁלֹשׁ רְגָלִים אוּלַי נָטְתָה מִפָּנַי כִּי עַתָּה גַּם־אֹתְכָה הָרַגְתִּי וְאוֹתָהּ הֶחֱיֵיתִי: ³⁴וַיֹּאמֶר בִּלְעָם אֶל־מַלְאַךְ יְהוָה חָטָאתִי כִּי לֹא יָדַעְתִּי כִּי אַתָּה נִצָּב לִקְרָאתִי בַּדָּרֶךְ וְעַתָּה אִם־רַע בְּעֵינֶיךָ אָשׁוּבָה לִּי: ³⁵וַיֹּאמֶר מַלְאַךְ יְהוָה אֶל־בִּלְעָם לֵךְ עִם־הָאֲנָשִׁים וְאֶפֶס אֶת־הַדָּבָר אֲשֶׁר־אֲדַבֵּר אֵלֶיךָ אֹתוֹ תְדַבֵּר וַיֵּלֶךְ בִּלְעָם עִם־שָׂרֵי בָלָק: ³⁶וַיִּשְׁמַע בָּלָק כִּי בָא בִלְעָם וַיֵּצֵא לִקְרָאתוֹ אֶל־עִיר מוֹאָב אֲשֶׁר עַל־גְּבוּל אַרְנֹן אֲשֶׁר בִּקְצֵה הַגְּבוּל: ³⁷וַיֹּאמֶר בָּלָק אֶל־בִּלְעָם הֲלֹא שָׁלֹחַ שָׁלַחְתִּי אֵלֶיךָ לִקְרֹא־לָךְ לָמָּה לֹא־הָלַכְתָּ אֵלָי הַאֻמְנָם לֹא אוּכַל כַּבְּדֶךָ: ³⁸וַיֹּאמֶר בִּלְעָם אֶל־בָּלָק הִנֵּה־בָאתִי אֵלֶיךָ עַתָּה הֲיָכוֹל אוּכַל דַּבֵּר מְאוּמָה הַדָּבָר אֲשֶׁר יָשִׂים אֱלֹהִים בְּפִי אֹתוֹ אֲדַבֵּר: ³⁹וַיֵּלֶךְ בִּלְעָם עִם־בָּלָק וַיָּבֹאוּ קִרְיַת חֻצוֹת: ⁴⁰וַיִּזְבַּח בָּלָק בָּקָר וָצֹאן וַיְשַׁלַּח לְבִלְעָם וְלַשָּׂרִים אֲשֶׁר אִתּוֹ: ⁴¹וַיְהִי בַבֹּקֶר וַיִּקַּח בָּלָק אֶת־בִּלְעָם וַיַּעֲלֵהוּ בָּמוֹת בַּעַל וַיַּרְא

22:32. **the way was precipitous with regard to me**. This verse may provide the answer to the question of why God was angry at Balaam for going. The problem is that the meaning of the key word here (Hebrew *yāraṭ*) is uncertain. This is its only occurrence in the Torah. (Its only other occurrence in the *Tanak* is in Job 16:11.) It may mean that Balaam was too quick to go with the Moabite chiefs. Still, this remains one of the classic unsolved enigmas of the Torah. Balaam appears to be doing just what he was told by God to do, yet God is angry.

22:40. **he let them go**. He gave the sacrificed animals to Balaam and the chiefs as a great meal prior to the intended cursing of Israel.

22:41. **High Places**. See the comment on Num 21:28.

23

¹And Balaam said to Balak, "Build seven altars for me here, and prepare seven bulls and seven rams for me here." ²And Balak did as Balaam spoke, and Balak and Balaam offered a bull and a ram on each altar. ³And Balaam said to Balak, "Stand up by your burnt offering, and let me go. Maybe YHWH will communicate to me. And whatever He'll show me, I'll tell you." And he went to a viewpoint. ⁴And God communicated to Balaam. And he said to Him, "I've arranged the seven altars and offered a bull and a ram on each altar."

⁵And YHWH put a word in Balaam's mouth, and He said, "Go back to Balak, and speak like this."

⁶And he went back to him, and here he was, standing up by his burnt offering, he and all the chiefs of Moab. ⁷And he took up his pronouncement, and he said:

Balak led me from Aram,
Moab's king from mountains of the East.
"Come, curse Jacob for me!
Come, denounce Israel!"

8 How shall I execrate whom God hasn't
    execrated?
And how shall I denounce whom YHWH
    hasn't denounced?

9 For from the top of rocks I see it,

מִשָּׁם קְצֵה הָעָם: 23 ¹וַיֹּאמֶר בִּלְעָם אֶל־בָּלָק בְּנֵה־לִי בָזֶה שִׁבְעָה מִזְבְּחֹת וְהָכֵן לִי בָּזֶה שִׁבְעָה פָרִים וְשִׁבְעָה אֵילִים: ²וַיַּעַשׂ בָּלָק כַּאֲשֶׁר דִּבֶּר בִּלְעָם וַיַּעַל בָּלָק וּבִלְעָם פָּר וָאַיִל בַּמִּזְבֵּחַ: ³וַיֹּאמֶר בִּלְעָם לְבָלָק הִתְיַצֵּב עַל־עֹלָתֶךָ וְאֵלְכָה אוּלַי יִקָּרֵה יְהוָה לִקְרָאתִי וּדְבַר מַה־יַּרְאֵנִי וְהִגַּדְתִּי לָךְ וַיֵּלֶךְ שֶׁפִי: ⁴וַיִּקָּר אֱלֹהִים אֶל־בִּלְעָם וַיֹּאמֶר אֵלָיו אֶת־שִׁבְעַת הַמִּזְבְּחֹת עָרַכְתִּי וָאַעַל פָּר וָאַיִל בַּמִּזְבֵּחַ: ⁵וַיָּשֶׂם יְהוָה דָּבָר בְּפִי בִלְעָם וַיֹּאמֶר שׁוּב אֶל־בָּלָק וְכֹה תְדַבֵּר: ⁶וַיָּשָׁב אֵלָיו וְהִנֵּה נִצָּב עַל־עֹלָתוֹ הוּא וְכָל־שָׂרֵי מוֹאָב: ⁷וַיִּשָּׂא מְשָׁלוֹ וַיֹּאמַר

מִן־אֲרָם יַנְחֵנִי בָלָק מֶלֶךְ־מוֹאָב מֵהַרְרֵי־קֶדֶם
לְכָה אָרָה־לִּי יַעֲקֹב וּלְכָה זֹעֲמָה יִשְׂרָאֵל:
⁸מָה אֶקֹּב לֹא קַבֹּה אֵל
וּמָה אֶזְעֹם לֹא זָעַם יְהוָה:
⁹כִּי־מֵרֹאשׁ צֻרִים אֶרְאֶנּוּ וּמִגְּבָעוֹת אֲשׁוּרֶנּוּ

23:7. **pronouncement**. There is no adequate way of conveying the sense of Hebrew *māšāl*, a pronouncement reflecting wisdom, inspiration, and, in some instances, revelation, usually in poetry. It can refer to a proverb or parable, but that does not fit here.

23:7. **Balak led me from Aram, Moab's king from mountains of the East**. We should particularly note the beauty of the poems of the Balaam episode. The poetry is embroidered more intimately in its prose context than most biblical poetry that is housed in the narrative books. Neither the narrative nor the poetry is complete without the other. The narrative context sets the scene and creates the ironic character of the poetry: the Moabite king has hired Balaam to curse Israel, but Balaam blesses them instead. The poems themselves refer back to the narrative context and are referred to in turn in the course of the narrative: Balak hears the poems and complains about them. The Balaam episode is a splendid example of the merging of poetry and prose in the Hebrew Bible.

23:9. **rocks**. The word "rock" refers not to a small stone but to a crag of the mountain. See Exodus 17 text and comments.

and from hills I view it.
Here: a people dwelling separate
and not reckoned among the nations.

10 Who has counted the dust of Jacob
and the number of a fourth of Israel?
May my soul die the death of the
righteous,
and may my future be like his!

11And Balak said to Balaam, "What have you done to me?! I took you to execrate my enemies. And, here, you've *blessed* them!"

12And he answered and said, "Isn't it that whatever YHWH sets in my mouth, *that* is what I'll watch out to say?!"

13And Balak said to him, "Come on with me to another place from which you'll see it. You'll see nothing but its edge, and you won't see all of it. And execrate it for me from there." 14And he took him to the field of Zophim, to the top of Pisgah, and he built seven altars and offered a bull and a ram on each altar.

15And he said to Balak, "Stand up here by your burnt offering, and I'll be communicated with here." 16And YHWH was communicated to Balaam, and He set a word in his mouth and said, "Go back to Balak, and you shall speak this."

17And he came to him, and here he was, standing up by his burnt offering, and the chiefs of Moab were with him. And Balak said to him, "What did YHWH speak?"

18And he took up his pronouncement, and he said:

Get up, Balak, and listen.
Hear me, son of Zippor.

19 God is not a man, that He would lie,
or a human being, that He would regret.
Has He said and will not do
or spoken and will not bring it about?

20 Here, I was taken to bless,
and He blessed, and I won't take it back.

21 He didn't find harm in Jacob,
and He didn't see trouble in Israel.

הֶן־עָם֙ לְבָדָ֣ד יִשְׁכֹּ֔ן וּבַגּוֹיִ֖ם לֹ֥א יִתְחַשָּֽׁב׃
10 מִ֤י מָנָה֙ עֲפַ֣ר יַעֲקֹ֔ב
וּמִסְפָּ֖ר אֶת־רֹ֣בַע יִשְׂרָאֵ֑ל
תָּמֹ֤ת נַפְשִׁי֙ מ֣וֹת יְשָׁרִ֔ים וּתְהִ֥י אַחֲרִיתִ֖י כָּמֹֽהוּ׃
11 וַיֹּ֤אמֶר בָּלָק֙ אֶל־בִּלְעָ֔ם מֶ֥ה עָשִׂ֖יתָ לִ֑י לָקֹ֤ב אֹיְבַי֙ לְקַחְתִּ֔יךָ וְהִנֵּ֖ה בֵּרַ֥כְתָּ בָרֵֽךְ׃ 12 וַיַּ֖עַן וַיֹּאמַ֑ר הֲלֹ֗א אֵת֩ אֲשֶׁ֨ר יָשִׂ֤ים יְהוָה֙ בְּפִ֔י אֹת֥וֹ אֶשְׁמֹ֖ר לְדַבֵּֽר׃ 13 וַיֹּ֨אמֶר אֵלָ֜יו בָּלָ֗ק לְךָ־נָּ֨א אִתִּ֜י אֶל־מָק֤וֹם אַחֵר֙ אֲשֶׁ֣ר תִּרְאֶ֣נּוּ מִשָּׁ֔ם אֶ֚פֶס קָצֵ֣הוּ תִרְאֶ֔ה וְכֻלּ֖וֹ לֹ֣א תִרְאֶ֑ה וְקָבְנוֹ־לִ֖י מִשָּֽׁם׃ 14 וַיִּקָּחֵ֙הוּ֙ שְׂדֵ֣ה צֹפִ֔ים אֶל־רֹ֖אשׁ הַפִּסְגָּ֑ה וַיִּ֙בֶן֙ שִׁבְעָ֣ה מִזְבְּחֹ֔ת וַיַּ֛עַל פָּ֥ר וָאַ֖יִל בַּמִּזְבֵּֽחַ׃ 15 וַיֹּ֙אמֶר֙ אֶל־בָּלָ֔ק הִתְיַצֵּ֥ב כֹּ֖ה עַל־עֹלָתֶ֑ךָ וְאָנֹכִ֖י אִקָּ֥רֶה כֹּֽה׃ 16 וַיִּקָּ֤ר יְהוָה֙ אֶל־בִּלְעָ֔ם וַיָּ֥שֶׂם דָּבָ֖ר בְּפִ֑יו וַיֹּ֛אמֶר שׁ֥וּב אֶל־בָּלָ֖ק וְכֹ֥ה תְדַבֵּֽר׃ 17 וַיָּבֹ֣א אֵלָ֗יו וְהִנּ֤וֹ נִצָּב֙ עַל־עֹ֣לָת֔וֹ וְשָׂרֵ֥י מוֹאָ֖ב אִתּ֑וֹ וַיֹּ֤אמֶר לוֹ֙ בָּלָ֔ק מַה־דִּבֶּ֖ר יְהוָֽה׃ 18 וַיִּשָּׂ֥א מְשָׁל֖וֹ וַיֹּאמַֽר׃

ק֤וּם בָּלָק֙ וּֽשֲׁמָ֔ע הַאֲזִ֥ינָה עָדַ֖י בְּנ֥וֹ צִפֹּֽר׃
19 לֹ֣א אִ֥ישׁ אֵל֙ וִֽיכַזֵּ֔ב וּבֶן־אָדָ֖ם וְיִתְנֶחָ֑ם
הַה֥וּא אָמַ֛ר וְלֹ֥א יַעֲשֶׂ֖ה וְדִבֶּ֥ר וְלֹ֥א יְקִימֶֽנָּה׃
20 הִנֵּ֥ה בָרֵ֖ךְ לָקָ֑חְתִּי וּבֵרֵ֖ךְ וְלֹ֥א אֲשִׁיבֶֽנָּה׃
21 לֹֽא־הִבִּ֥יט אָ֙וֶן֙ בְּיַעֲקֹ֔ב
וְלֹא־רָאָ֥ה עָמָ֖ל בְּיִשְׂרָאֵ֑ל

23:13 ק֤ לְכָ֣ה

23:14. **Zophim.** Meaning "lookouts"—a place with a view.

YHWH, its God, is with it,
and a shout for a king is in it.

22 God who brought them out from Egypt
is like a wild ox's horns for it.

23 For there's no divination against Jacob
and no enchantment against Israel.
At this time it will be said to Jacob
and to Israel: "What has God done?"

24 Here, a people will get up like a feline
and like a lion will raise itself.
It won't lie down until it has eaten prey
and until it has drunk blood of carcasses.

25And Balak said to Balaam, "Don't do either: *execrate* them or *bless* them!"

26And Balaam answered, and he said to Balak, "Didn't I speak to you, saying, 'Everything that YHWH will speak, that is what I'll do'?"

27And Balak said to Balaam, "Come on. I'll take you to another place. Maybe it will be right in God's eyes, and you'll execrate it for me from there." 28And Balak took Balaam to the top of Peor, which looks out over Jeshimon.

29And Balaam said to Balak, "Build seven altars for me here and prepare seven bulls and seven rams for me here." 30And Balak did as Balaam had said, and he offered a bull and a ram on each altar.

24 1And Balaam saw that it was good in YHWH's eyes to bless Israel, and he did not go as in previous times to divinations. And he turned his face to the wilderness, 2and Balaam raised his eyes and saw Israel, tenting according to its tribes, and God's spirit came on him. 3And he took up his pronouncement, and he said:

Word of Balaam, son of Beor,
and word of the man, opened of eye;

4 word of the one who hears God's sayings,
who sees Shadday's vision,
falling, but with eyes uncovered.

5 How good your tents are, Jacob,
your tabernacles, Israel.

6 They spread like palms,
like gardens by a river,

יְהוָה אֱלֹהָיו עִמּוֹ וּתְרוּעַת מֶלֶךְ בּוֹ:
22 אֵל מוֹצִיאָם מִמִּצְרָיִם כְּתוֹעֲפֹת רְאֵם לוֹ:
23 כִּי לֹא־נַחַשׁ בְּיַעֲקֹב וְלֹא־קֶסֶם בְּיִשְׂרָאֵל
כָּעֵת יֵאָמֵר לְיַעֲקֹב וּלְיִשְׂרָאֵל מַה־פָּעַל אֵל:
24 הֶן־עָם כְּלָבִיא יָקוּם וְכַאֲרִי יִתְנַשָּׂא
לֹא יִשְׁכַּב עַד־יֹאכַל טֶרֶף וְדַם־חֲלָלִים יִשְׁתֶּה:
25 וַיֹּאמֶר בָּלָק אֶל־בִּלְעָם גַּם־קֹב לֹא תִקֳּבֶנּוּ גַּם־
בָּרֵךְ לֹא תְבָרֲכֶנּוּ: 26 וַיַּעַן בִּלְעָם וַיֹּאמֶר אֶל־בָּלָק
הֲלֹא דִּבַּרְתִּי אֵלֶיךָ לֵאמֹר כֹּל אֲשֶׁר־יְדַבֵּר יְהוָה
אֹתוֹ אֶעֱשֶׂה:
27 וַיֹּאמֶר בָּלָק אֶל־בִּלְעָם לְכָה־נָּא אֶקָּחֲךָ אֶל־
מָקוֹם אַחֵר אוּלַי יִישַׁר בְּעֵינֵי הָאֱלֹהִים וְקַבֹּתוֹ לִי
מִשָּׁם: 28 וַיִּקַּח בָּלָק אֶת־בִּלְעָם רֹאשׁ הַפְּעוֹר
הַנִּשְׁקָף עַל־פְּנֵי הַיְשִׁימֹן: 29 וַיֹּאמֶר בִּלְעָם אֶל־בָּלָק
בְּנֵה־לִי בָזֶה שִׁבְעָה מִזְבְּחֹת וְהָכֵן לִי בָּזֶה שִׁבְעָה
פָרִים וְשִׁבְעָה אֵילִים: 30 וַיַּעַשׂ בָּלָק כַּאֲשֶׁר אָמַר
בִּלְעָם וַיַּעַל פָּר וָאַיִל בַּמִּזְבֵּחַ: 24 1 וַיַּרְא בִּלְעָם
כִּי טוֹב בְּעֵינֵי יְהוָה לְבָרֵךְ אֶת־יִשְׂרָאֵל וְלֹא־הָלַךְ
כְּפַעַם־בְּפַעַם לִקְרַאת נְחָשִׁים וַיָּשֶׁת אֶל־הַמִּדְבָּר
פָּנָיו: 2 וַיִּשָּׂא בִלְעָם אֶת־עֵינָיו וַיַּרְא אֶת־יִשְׂרָאֵל
שֹׁכֵן לִשְׁבָטָיו וַתְּהִי עָלָיו רוּחַ אֱלֹהִים: 3 וַיִּשָּׂא
מְשָׁלוֹ וַיֹּאמַר
נְאֻם בִּלְעָם בְּנוֹ בְעֹר וּנְאֻם הַגֶּבֶר שְׁתֻם הָעָיִן:
4 נְאֻם שֹׁמֵעַ אִמְרֵי־אֵל
אֲשֶׁר מַחֲזֵה שַׁדַּי יֶחֱזֶה נֹפֵל וּגְלוּי עֵינָיִם:
5 מַה־טֹּבוּ אֹהָלֶיךָ יַעֲקֹב מִשְׁכְּנֹתֶיךָ יִשְׂרָאֵל:
6 כִּנְחָלִים נִטָּיוּ כְּגַנֹּת עֲלֵי נָהָר

509

like aloes YHWH planted,
like cedars by water.

7 It drips water from its branches
and its seed in plentiful water.
And its king will be higher than Agag,
and its kingdom will be elevated.

8 God who brought it out from Egypt
is like a wild ox's horns for it.
He shall eat up nations, its foes,
and break their bones
and pierce with His arrows.

9 It bent, lay down, like a lion;
and, like a feline, who will rouse it?
Those who bless you: he's blessed.
And those who curse you: he's cursed.

כַּאֲהָלִים֙ נָטַ֣ע יְהֹוָ֔ה כַּאֲרָזִ֖ים עֲלֵי־מָֽיִם׃
7 יִֽזַּל־מַ֙יִם֙ מִדָּ֣לְיָ֔ו וְזַרְע֖וֹ בְּמַ֣יִם רַבִּ֑ים
וְיָרֹ֤ם מֵֽאֲגַג֙ מַלְכּ֔וֹ וְתִנַּשֵּׂ֖א מַלְכֻתֽוֹ׃
8 אֵ֚ל מוֹצִיא֣וֹ מִמִּצְרַ֔יִם כְּתוֹעֲפֹ֥ת רְאֵ֖ם ל֑וֹ
יֹאכַ֞ל גּוֹיִ֣ם צָרָ֗יו וְעַצְמֹתֵיהֶ֛ם יְגָרֵ֖ם
וְחִצָּ֥יו יִמְחָֽץ׃
9 כָּרַ֨ע שָׁכַ֧ב כַּאֲרִ֛י וּכְלָבִ֖יא מִ֣י יְקִימֶ֑נּוּ
מְבָרְכֶ֣יךָ בָר֔וּךְ וְאֹרְרֶ֖יךָ אָרֽוּר׃

24:8. pierce with His arrows. This is a pun, *ḥṣyw mḥṣ*, which culminates a chain of puns on the letters of the word "Egypt," Hebrew *miṣrayim*, in this verse:

מוציאו ממצרים . . . צריו עצמת . . . חציו ימחץ

The chain of alliteration may be wordplay for its own sake, or it may be an intentional linkage between Egypt and the words for "foes" and breaking "bones" and "piercing with arrows"—thus conveying through puns the defeat of Egypt.

24:9. It bent . . . who will rouse it. This line of Balaam's blessing is almost identical to a line of Jacob's deathbed blessing of his son Judah (Gen 49:9). We may say that, as a matter of poetic technique, this was a poetic formula that happened to be used in two different biblical poems. This occurs elsewhere in the *Tanak* as well, as in the case of the famous words "They shall beat their swords into plowshares and their spears into pruning hooks," which are said by both Isaiah and Micah (Isa 2:4; Mic 4:3). But we may also ask what it means that both Jacob and Balaam use these same words in prophecies. It may be understood to convey the authenticity of Balaam's prophetic experience from the God of Israel. Israel presumably becomes aware of these prophecies and blessings that Balaam has pronounced, because they come to be contained in the Torah. And so this informs Israel that, even though they are spoken by a foreigner, they are from Israel's God.

24:9. Those who bless you: he's blessed. And those who curse you: he's cursed. God had already promised Abraham generations earlier that those who bless his descendants would be blessed and that those who curse them would be cursed. But Balaam's pronouncement now adds a new dimension. The text here refers to those who bless Israel in the plural. But when it then says that they themselves will be blessed, it is in the singular. It uses the same plural-to-singular pattern for those who curse Israel. This pattern conveys the implication that people frequently follow a group in their attitudes—positive or negative—toward others. But they should be aware that the consequences of their attitudes fall on each and every one of them as individuals. If one becomes anti-Jew or anti-Arab or anti-anyone because one is part of a group or cul-

510

10And Balak's anger flared at Balaam, and he wrung his hands, and Balak said to Balaam, "I called you to execrate my enemies; and, here, you've *blessed* these three times! 11And now, flee to your place! I said I would *honor* you; and, here, YHWH has held you back from honor!"

12And Balaam said to Balak, "Didn't I speak to your messengers whom you sent to me as well, saying, 13'If Balak would give me a houseful of silver and gold of his I wouldn't be able to go against the mouth of YHWH, to do good or bad from my own heart. Whatever YHWH speaks, that is what I'll speak.' 14And now, here, I'm going to my people. Come. I'll advise you of what this people will do to your people in the future days." 15And he took up his pronouncement, and he said:

Word of Balaam, son of Beor,
and word of the man whose eye is whole;
16   word of the one who hears God's sayings
and who knows the Highest's knowledge,
who sees Shadday's vision,
falling, but with eyes uncovered.
17   I see it—and not now;
I view it—and not close:
a star has stepped from Jacob,
and a scepter has come up from Israel
and pierced the temples of Moab
and the crown of all the children of Seth.
18   And Edom was a possession,
and Seir was a possession of its enemies,
and Israel was making triumph.
19   And one from Jacob dominated
and destroyed a remnant from a city.

10וַיִּחַר־אַף בָּלָק אֶל־בִּלְעָם וַיִּסְפֹּק אֶת־כַּפָּיו וַיֹּאמֶר בָּלָק אֶל־בִּלְעָם לָקֹב אֹיְבַי קְרָאתִיךָ וְהִנֵּה בֵּרַכְתָּ בָרֵךְ זֶה שָׁלֹשׁ פְּעָמִים: 11וְעַתָּה בְּרַח־לְךָ אֶל־מְקוֹמֶךָ אָמַרְתִּי כַּבֵּד אֲכַבֶּדְךָ וְהִנֵּה מְנָעֲךָ יְהוָה מִכָּבוֹד: 12וַיֹּאמֶר בִּלְעָם אֶל־בָּלָק הֲלֹא גַם אֶל־מַלְאָכֶיךָ אֲשֶׁר־שָׁלַחְתָּ אֵלַי דִּבַּרְתִּי לֵאמֹר: 13אִם־יִתֶּן־לִי בָלָק מְלֹא בֵיתוֹ כֶּסֶף וְזָהָב לֹא אוּכַל לַעֲבֹר אֶת־פִּי יְהוָה לַעֲשׂוֹת טוֹבָה אוֹ רָעָה מִלִּבִּי אֲשֶׁר־יְדַבֵּר יְהוָה אֹתוֹ אֲדַבֵּר: 14וְעַתָּה הִנְנִי הוֹלֵךְ לְעַמִּי לְכָה אִיעָצְךָ אֲשֶׁר יַעֲשֶׂה הָעָם הַזֶּה לְעַמְּךָ בְּאַחֲרִית הַיָּמִים: 15וַיִּשָּׂא מְשָׁלוֹ וַיֹּאמַר נְאֻם בִּלְעָם בְּנוֹ בְעֹר וּנְאֻם הַגֶּבֶר שְׁתֻם הָעָיִן: 16נְאֻם שֹׁמֵעַ אִמְרֵי־אֵל וְיֹדֵעַ דַּעַת עֶלְיוֹן מַחֲזֵה שַׁדַּי יֶחֱזֶה נֹפֵל וּגְלוּי עֵינָיִם: 17אֶרְאֶנּוּ וְלֹא עַתָּה אֲשׁוּרֶנּוּ וְלֹא קָרוֹב דָּרַךְ כּוֹכָב מִיַּעֲקֹב וְקָם שֵׁבֶט מִיִּשְׂרָאֵל וּמָחַץ פַּאֲתֵי מוֹאָב וְקַרְקַר כָּל־בְּנֵי־שֵׁת: 18וְהָיָה אֱדוֹם יְרֵשָׁה וְהָיָה יְרֵשָׁה שֵׂעִיר אֹיְבָיו וְיִשְׂרָאֵל עֹשֶׂה חָיִל: 19וְיֵרְדְּ מִיַּעֲקֹב וְהֶאֱבִיד שָׂרִיד מֵעִיר:

---

ture that bears such a prejudice, one is still individually culpable for his or her bias—and one must bear the consequences as an individual as well.

24:17. **pierced the temples of Moab.** Moab is pictured metaphorically as a man, who is struck at the temples, i.e., the corners of his head.

24:17. **and the crown of all the children of Seth.** In parallel with the temples of the head comes the crown, i.e., the top of his head. Like others, I read "crown," translating Hebrew קָדְקֹד instead of קַרְקַר in the text. The Hebrew letters *resh* and *dalet* are frequently mistaken for each other in the old Hebrew script, and there is also support for this reading in Jer 48:45, which pairs Moab's temple with קָדְקֹד.

20And he saw Amalek, and he took up his pronouncement, and he said:

> Amalek was foremost of nations,
> and its future arrives at destruction.

21And he saw the Kenites, and he took up his pronouncement and said:

> Your residence is strong,
> and set your nest in a cliff.

22 But Cain will be for burning
> How long will Asshur hold you prisoner?

23And he took up his pronouncement, and he said:

> Woe. Who will live more than what God set him?

24 And ships from the hand of Kittim:
> And they degraded Asshur, and they degraded Eber.
> And it, too, arrives at destruction.

25And Balaam got up and went, and he went back to his place. And Balak, too, went his way.

25 1And Israel lived in Shittim, and the people began to prostitute themselves to the daughters of Moab: 2And they attracted the people to the sacrifices of their gods, and the people ate and bowed to their gods, 3and Israel was associated with Baal Peor. And YHWH's anger flared at Israel. 4And YHWH said to Moses, "Take all of the leaders of the people and hang them in front of the sun, and YHWH's flaring anger will go back from Israel."

20וַיַּרְא אֶת־עֲמָלֵק וַיִּשָּׂא מְשָׁלוֹ וַיֹּאמַר
רֵאשִׁית גּוֹיִם עֲמָלֵק וְאַחֲרִיתוֹ עֲדֵי אֹבֵד:
21וַיַּרְא אֶת־הַקֵּינִי וַיִּשָּׂא מְשָׁלוֹ וַיֹּאמַר
אֵיתָן מוֹשָׁבֶךָ וְשִׂים בַּסֶּלַע קִנֶּךָ:
22כִּי אִם־יִהְיֶה לְבָעֵר קָיִן
עַד־מָה אַשּׁוּר תִּשְׁבֶּךָּ:
23וַיִּשָּׂא מְשָׁלוֹ וַיֹּאמַר
אוֹי מִי יִחְיֶה מִשֻּׂמוֹ אֵל: 24וְצִים מִיַּד כִּתִּים
וְעִנּוּ אַשּׁוּר וְעִנּוּ־עֵבֶר וְגַם־הוּא עֲדֵי אֹבֵד:
25וַיָּקָם בִּלְעָם וַיֵּלֶךְ וַיָּשָׁב לִמְקֹמוֹ וְגַם־בָּלָק הָלַךְ
לְדַרְכּוֹ: פ

25 1וַיֵּשֶׁב יִשְׂרָאֵל בַּשִּׁטִּים וַיָּחֶל הָעָם לִזְנוֹת
אֶל־בְּנוֹת מוֹאָב: 2וַתִּקְרֶאןָ לָעָם לְזִבְחֵי אֱלֹהֵיהֶן
וַיֹּאכַל הָעָם וַיִּשְׁתַּחֲווּ לֵאלֹהֵיהֶן: 3וַיִּצָּמֶד יִשְׂרָאֵל
לְבַעַל פְּעוֹר וַיִּחַר־אַף יְהוָה בְּיִשְׂרָאֵל: 4וַיֹּאמֶר
יְהוָה אֶל־מֹשֶׁה קַח אֶת־כָּל־רָאשֵׁי הָעָם וְהוֹקַע
אוֹתָם לַיהוָה נֶגֶד הַשָּׁמֶשׁ וְיָשֹׁב חֲרוֹן אַף־יְהוָה

25:2. sacrifices of their gods. Hebrew זבחי אלהיהן. Ps 106:28 refers to these sacrifices at Baal Peor as זבחי מתים, meaning "sacrifices of the dead" instead of "sacrifices of their gods." This episode may therefore refer to ancestor veneration: offering sacrifices to the spirits of the dead. Forms of ancestor veneration are known in ancient Israel, involving the provision of food and fluid for ancestors' tombs. It reflected belief in an afterlife. It was practiced until the time of King Hezekiah, at which time the devastation of the countryside by the Assyrian emperor Sennacherib cut the people off from the family burial sites, and the centralization of religion at the Temple prohibited sacrifices anywhere but at the Temple. (See the comment on Lev 19:31.)

25:4. in front of the sun. This expression apparently means "publicly" (and possibly with a negative connotation). It occurs in one other place in the *Tanak* (2 Sam

5And Moses said to Israel's judges, "Each of you, kill those of his people who are associated with Baal Peor."

6And, here, a man from the children of Israel came and brought forward a Midianite woman to his brothers before the eyes of Moses and before the eyes of all the congregation of the children of Israel while they were mourning at the entrance of the Tent of Meeting. 7And Phinehas son of Eleazar son of Aaron, the priest, saw, and he got up from among the congregation and took a spear in his hand. 8And he came after the Israelite man to the enclosure and ran the two of them through, the Israelite man and the woman,

מִישְׂרָאֵל: 5וַיֹּאמֶר מֹשֶׁה אֶל־שֹׁפְטֵי יִשְׂרָאֵל הִרְגוּ
אִישׁ אֲנָשָׁיו הַנִּצְמָדִים לְבַעַל פְּעוֹר: 6וְהִנֵּה אִישׁ
מִבְּנֵי יִשְׂרָאֵל בָּא וַיַּקְרֵב אֶל־אֶחָיו אֶת־הַמִּדְיָנִית
לְעֵינֵי מֹשֶׁה וּלְעֵינֵי כָּל־עֲדַת בְּנֵי־יִשְׂרָאֵל וְהֵמָּה
בֹכִים פֶּתַח אֹהֶל מוֹעֵד: 7וַיַּרְא פִּינְחָס בֶּן־אֶלְעָזָר
בֶּן־אַהֲרֹן הַכֹּהֵן וַיָּקָם מִתּוֹךְ הָעֵדָה וַיִּקַּח רֹמַח
בְּיָדוֹ: 8וַיָּבֹא אַחַר אִישׁ־יִשְׂרָאֵל אֶל־הַקֻּבָּה וַיִּדְקֹר
אֶת־שְׁנֵיהֶם אֵת אִישׁ יִשְׂרָאֵל וְאֶת־הָאִשָּׁה אֶל־

12:12), in the curse on David's house over his adultery with Bathsheba: he took another man's wife in secret, but a man will take *David's* wives "in front of the sun."

25:6. **they were mourning**. The last reference to mourning was that "all the house of Israel mourned Aaron thirty days" (20:29). Thus this episode occurs during the thirty days that they were mourning Aaron.

25:8. **enclosure**. Hebrew *qubbāh*. The *qubbāh* is a tent, as Rashi understood. Moreover, as my teacher Frank Cross discussed, the *qubbāh* is known in the pre-Islamic Near East. It was a tent used to house sacred objects, and, like the biblical Tabernacle, it was made of red leather. Since this episode begins precisely at the entrance to the Tabernacle (the Tent of Meeting; v. 6), it certainly appears that the *qubbāh* here refers to the inside of the Tabernacle. This is confirmed by what happens next. See the next comment.

25:8. **he ran them through**. Commentators have been troubled by Phinehas's zeal in killing these two people. But the point is that it is a *ritual* crime. The crime is not that an Israelite and a Midianite have sexual relations. It is that they have violated the Tabernacle. As non-Levites, they are not even permitted to enter it, let alone to have sexual relations—whether it is for procreation, pleasure, or a fertility rite. Note that there is no trial. If it were solely an ethical offense, there would be a trial and an inquiry into their motives. But, for a ritual violation of the holy place, there is no trial because there is no possible defense, no satisfactory motive or explanation. Phinehas, as a priest, can enter, and he executes them—as the law requires (Num 1:51; 3:10,38; 18:4,7). Thus the Torah goes on to tell us that (1) this stops a plague and (2) God is pleased with what Phinehas has done and gives him a reward for it: a covenant of eternal priesthood. These harsh consequences for ritual offenses—here and in the case of Nadab and Abihu and elsewhere—are extremely difficult to comprehend in the present age, in which most people (I think), including me, respond with shock to their severity.

to her stomach, and the plague was halted from the children of Israel. 9And the dead in the plague were twenty-four thousand.

קְבָתָהּ וַתֵּעָצַר הַמַּגֵּפָה מֵעַל בְּנֵי יִשְׂרָאֵל: 9וַיִּהְיוּ הַמֵּתִים בַּמַּגֵּפָה אַרְבָּעָה וְעֶשְׂרִים אָלֶף: פ

PHINEHAS

פינחס

10And YHWH spoke to Moses, saying, 11"Phinehas son of Eleazar son of Aaron, the priest, has turned back my fury from the children of Israel by his carrying out my jealousy among them, so I didn't finish the children of Israel in my jealousy. 12Therefore, say: Here, I'm giving him my covenant of peace, 13and it shall be his, and his seed's after him, a covenant of eternal priesthood, because he was jealous for his God, and he made atonement for the children of Israel."

14And the name of the stricken Israelite man, who was struck with the Midianite woman, was Zimri son of Salu, chieftain of a father's house of the Simeonites. 15And the name of the stricken Midianite woman was Cozbi daughter of Zur. He was head of the people of a father's house in Midian.

16And YHWH spoke to Moses, saying, 17"Afflict the Midianites—and you shall strike them— 18because they have been afflicting you with their conspiracies that they made against you over the matter of Peor and over the matter of

10וַיְדַבֵּר יְהוָה אֶל־מֹשֶׁה לֵּאמֹר: 11פִּינְחָס בֶּן־ אֶלְעָזָר בֶּן־אַהֲרֹן הַכֹּהֵן הֵשִׁיב אֶת־חֲמָתִי מֵעַל בְּנֵי־יִשְׂרָאֵל בְּקַנְאוֹ אֶת־קִנְאָתִי בְּתוֹכָם וְלֹא־כִלִּיתִי אֶת־בְּנֵי־יִשְׂרָאֵל בְּקִנְאָתִי: 12לָכֵן אֱמֹר הִנְנִי נֹתֵן לוֹ אֶת־בְּרִיתִי שָׁלוֹם: 13וְהָיְתָה לּוֹ וּלְזַרְעוֹ אַחֲרָיו בְּרִית כְּהֻנַּת עוֹלָם תַּחַת אֲשֶׁר קִנֵּא לֵאלֹהָיו וַיְכַפֵּר עַל־בְּנֵי יִשְׂרָאֵל: 14וְשֵׁם אִישׁ יִשְׂרָאֵל הַמֻּכֶּה אֲשֶׁר הֻכָּה אֶת־הַמִּדְיָנִית זִמְרִי בֶּן־סָלוּא נְשִׂיא בֵית־אָב לַשִּׁמְעֹנִי: 15וְשֵׁם הָאִשָּׁה הַמֻּכָּה הַמִּדְיָנִית כָּזְבִּי בַת־ צוּר רֹאשׁ אֻמּוֹת בֵּית־אָב בְּמִדְיָן הוּא: פ 16וַיְדַבֵּר יְהוָה אֶל־מֹשֶׁה לֵּאמֹר: 17צָרוֹר אֶת־הַמִּדְיָנִים וְהִכִּיתֶם אוֹתָם: 18כִּי צֹרְרִים הֵם לָכֶם בְּנִכְלֵיהֶם אֲשֶׁר־נִכְּלוּ לָכֶם עַל־דְּבַר־פְּעוֹר וְעַל־דְּבַר כָּזְבִּי

25:8. **her stomach.** Hebrew קבתה (*qābātāh*), a pun on the word for the enclosure, Hebrew קבה (*qubbāh*). The pun hints that it is an ironic punishment to suit the crime. The word may mean her genital area rather than her stomach. Either way, though, it is a most extraordinary sexual image, as the spear strikes the man and then protrudes from him into her belly or genital area, bizarrely paralleling their sexual intercourse.

25:8. **the plague.** What plague?! No plague has been mentioned until now. Some would say that this sudden mention of a plague is the result of the combining of two originally separate sources to make this chapter, but I do not think that this point is a source issue. The plague is a direct, unannounced consequence of the violation of the holy place, just as it was in the aftermath of the Korah rebellion (Num 17:11–14). This is precisely what is warned in Num 8:19, "so there will not be a plague . . . when the children of Israel would come near to the Holy." This further confirms that the crime here is the ritual offense of entering the Holy.

Cozbi, the daughter of a chieftain of Midian, their sister who was struck on the day of the plague over the matter of Peor."

¹⁹And it was after the plague.

26 ¹And YHWH said to Moses and to Eleazar son of Aaron, the priest, saying, ²"Add up the heads of all of the congregation of Israel from twenty years old and up, by their fathers' house, everyone going out to Israel's army."

³And Moses and Eleazar, the priest, spoke with them in the plains of Moab by the Jordan toward Jericho, saying, ⁴"From twenty years old and up," as YHWH commanded Moses and the children of Israel who had gone out from the land of Egypt.

⁵Reuben, Israel's firstborn; the children of Reuben:

Hanoch: the family of the Hanochites. Of Pallu: the family of the Palluites. ⁶Of Hezron: the family of the Hezronites. Of Carmi: the family of the Carmites. ⁷These are the families of the Reubenites, and their counts were forty-three thousand seven hundred thirty. ⁸And Pallu's sons: Eliab. ⁹And Eliab's sons: Nemuel and Dathan and Abiram. That is the Dathan and Abiram, prominent ones of the congregation, who fought against Moses and against Aaron in Korah's congregation when they fought against YHWH, ¹⁰and the earth opened its mouth and swallowed them and Korah when the congregation died, when the fire consumed the two hundred fifty men, and they became a sign. ¹¹But Korah's sons did not die.

בַת־נְשִׂיא מִדְיָן אֲחֹתָם הַמֻּכָּה בְיוֹם־הַמַּגֵּפָה עַל־דְּבַר־פְּעוֹר:

פ 26 ‏¹⁹וַיְהִי אַחֲרֵי הַמַּגֵּפָה: ‏¹וַיֹּאמֶר יְהוָה אֶל־מֹשֶׁה וְאֶל אֶלְעָזָר בֶּן־אַהֲרֹן הַכֹּהֵן לֵאמֹר: ‏²שְׂאוּ אֶת־רֹאשׁ ׀ כָּל־עֲדַת בְּנֵי־יִשְׂרָאֵל מִבֶּן עֶשְׂרִים שָׁנָה וָמַעְלָה לְבֵית אֲבֹתָם כָּל־יֹצֵא צָבָא בְּיִשְׂרָאֵל: ‏³וַיְדַבֵּר מֹשֶׁה וְאֶלְעָזָר הַכֹּהֵן אֹתָם בְּעַרְבֹת מוֹאָב עַל־יַרְדֵּן יְרֵחוֹ לֵאמֹר: ‏⁴מִבֶּן עֶשְׂרִים שָׁנָה וָמָעְלָה כַּאֲשֶׁר צִוָּה יְהוָה אֶת־מֹשֶׁה וּבְנֵי יִשְׂרָאֵל הַיֹּצְאִים מֵאֶרֶץ מִצְרָיִם: ‏⁵רְאוּבֵן בְּכוֹר יִשְׂרָאֵל בְּנֵי רְאוּבֵן חֲנוֹךְ מִשְׁפַּחַת הַחֲנֹכִי לְפַלּוּא מִשְׁפַּחַת הַפַּלֻּאִי: ‏⁶לְחֶצְרֹן מִשְׁפַּחַת הַחֶצְרוֹנִי לְכַרְמִי מִשְׁפַּחַת הַכַּרְמִי: ‏⁷אֵלֶּה מִשְׁפְּחֹת הָראוּבֵנִי וַיִּהְיוּ פְקֻדֵיהֶם שְׁלֹשָׁה וְאַרְבָּעִים אֶלֶף וּשְׁבַע מֵאוֹת וּשְׁלֹשִׁים: ‏⁸וּבְנֵי פַלּוּא אֱלִיאָב: ‏⁹וּבְנֵי אֱלִיאָב נְמוּאֵל וְדָתָן וַאֲבִירָם הוּא־דָתָן וַאֲבִירָם קריאי הָעֵדָה אֲשֶׁר הִצּוּ עַל־מֹשֶׁה וְעַל־אַהֲרֹן בַּעֲדַת־קֹרַח בְּהַצֹּתָם עַל־יְהוָה: ‏¹⁰וַתִּפְתַּח הָאָרֶץ אֶת־פִּיהָ וַתִּבְלַע אֹתָם וְאֶת־קֹרַח בְּמוֹת הָעֵדָה בַּאֲכֹל הָאֵשׁ אֵת חֲמִשִּׁים וּמָאתַיִם אִישׁ וַיִּהְיוּ לְנֵס: ‏¹¹וּבְנֵי־קֹרַח לֹא־מֵתוּ: ס ‏¹²בְּנֵי שִׁמְעוֹן לְמִשְׁפְּחֹתָם

קְרִיאֵי ק 26:9

26:11. **Korah's sons did not die.** Indeed, their descendants later become the composers or singers of psalms in the Temple (see Pss 42; 44; 45; 46; 47; 48; 49; 84; 85; 87; 88), and they are mentioned in an inscription on a bowl from a temple excavated at Arad that functioned during the preexilic biblical period. So, if they were known in Israel, why was it necessary to mention the obvious fact that they did not die? It may be to distinguish them from the children of Dathan and Abiram. The wives and children of Dathan and Abiram die with them (Num 16:27,32). Why do Korah's children not die with Korah? Korah's ritual offense is the improper burning of incense. His 250 followers commit this offense as well. And so all those who have had contact with the forbidden incense are killed. There is no suggestion that their sons play any part or

12The children of Simeon by their families:

Of Nemuel: the family of the Nemuelites. Of Jamin: the family of the Jaminites. Of Jachin: the family of the Jachinites. 13Of Zerah: the family of the Zerahites. Of Saul: the family of the Saulites. 14These are the families of the Simeonites: twenty-two thousand two hundred.

15The children of Gad by their families:

Of Zephon: the family of the Zephonites. Of Haggi: the family of the Haggites. Of Shuni: the family of the Shunites. 16Of Ozni: the family of the Oznites. Of Eri: the family of the Erites. 17Of Arod: the family of the Arodites. Of Areli: the family of the Arelites. 18These are the families of the children of Gad by their counts: forty thousand five hundred.

19Judah's sons were Er and Onan, but Er and Onan died in the land of Canaan. 20Then the children of Judah by their families were:

Of Shelah: the family of the Shelanites. Of Perez: the family of the Perezites. Of Zerah: the family of the Zerahites. 21And the children of Perez were: Of Hezron: the family of the Hezronites. Of Hamul: the family of the Hamulites. 22These are the families of Judah by their counts: seventy-six thousand five hundred.

23The children of Issachar by their families:

Tola: the family of the Tolaites. Of Puwah, the family of the Punites. 24Of Jashub: the family of the Jashubites. Of Shimron: the family of the Shimronites. 25These are the families of Issachar by their counts: sixty-four thousand three hundred.

26The children of Zebulun by their families:

Of Sered: the family of the Seredites. Of Elon: the family of the Elonites. Of Jahleel: the family of the Jahleelites. 27These are the families of the Zebulunites by their counts: sixty thousand five hundred.

לִנְמוּאֵל מִשְׁפַּחַת הַנְּמוּאֵלִי לְיָמִין מִשְׁפַּחַת הַיָּמִינִי לְיָכִין מִשְׁפַּחַת הַיָּכִינִי: 13לְזֶרַח מִשְׁפַּחַת הַזַּרְחִי לְשָׁאוּל מִשְׁפַּחַת הַשָּׁאוּלִי: 14אֵלֶּה מִשְׁפְּחֹת הַשִּׁמְעֹנִי שְׁנַיִם וְעֶשְׂרִים אֶלֶף וּמָאתָיִם: ס 15בְּנֵי גָד לְמִשְׁפְּחֹתָם לִצְפוֹן מִשְׁפַּחַת הַצְּפוֹנִי לְחַגִּי מִשְׁפַּחַת הַחַגִּי לְשׁוּנִי מִשְׁפַּחַת הַשּׁוּנִי: 16לְאָזְנִי מִשְׁפַּחַת הָאָזְנִי לְעֵרִי מִשְׁפַּחַת הָעֵרִי: 17לַאֲרוֹד מִשְׁפַּחַת הָאֲרוֹדִי לְאַרְאֵלִי מִשְׁפַּחַת הָאַרְאֵלִי: 18אֵלֶּה מִשְׁפְּחֹת בְּנֵי־גָד לִפְקֻדֵיהֶם אַרְבָּעִים אֶלֶף וַחֲמֵשׁ מֵאוֹת: ס 19בְּנֵי יְהוּדָה עֵר וְאוֹנָן וַיָּמָת עֵר וְאוֹנָן בְּאֶרֶץ כְּנָעַן: 20וַיִּהְיוּ בְנֵי־יְהוּדָה לְמִשְׁפְּחֹתָם לְשֵׁלָה מִשְׁפַּחַת הַשֵּׁלָנִי לְפֶרֶץ מִשְׁפַּחַת הַפַּרְצִי לְזֶרַח מִשְׁפַּחַת הַזַּרְחִי: 21וַיִּהְיוּ בְנֵי־פֶרֶץ לְחֶצְרֹן מִשְׁפַּחַת הַחֶצְרֹנִי לְחָמוּל מִשְׁפַּחַת הֶחָמוּלִי: 22אֵלֶּה מִשְׁפְּחֹת יְהוּדָה לִפְקֻדֵיהֶם שִׁשָּׁה וְשִׁבְעִים אֶלֶף וַחֲמֵשׁ מֵאוֹת: ס 23בְּנֵי יִשָּׂשכָר לְמִשְׁפְּחֹתָם תּוֹלָע מִשְׁפַּחַת הַתּוֹלָעִי לְפֻוָה מִשְׁפַּחַת הַפּוּנִי: 24לְיָשׁוּב מִשְׁפַּחַת הַיָּשׁוּבִי לְשִׁמְרֹן מִשְׁפַּחַת הַשִּׁמְרֹנִי: 25אֵלֶּה מִשְׁפְּחֹת יִשָּׂשכָר לִפְקֻדֵיהֶם אַרְבָּעָה וְשִׁשִּׁים אֶלֶף וּשְׁלֹשׁ מֵאוֹת: ס 26בְּנֵי זְבוּלֻן לְמִשְׁפְּחֹתָם לְסֶרֶד מִשְׁפַּחַת הַסַּרְדִּי לְאֵלוֹן מִשְׁפַּחַת הָאֵלֹנִי לְיַחְלְאֵל מִשְׁפַּחַת הַיַּחְלְאֵלִי: 27אֵלֶּה מִשְׁפְּחֹת הַזְּבוּלֹנִי לִפְקֻדֵיהֶם שִׁשִּׁים אֶלֶף וַחֲמֵשׁ מֵאוֹת: ס 28בְּנֵי

---

come into contact with the incense. But Dathan and Abiram's ritual offense is different. It is the direct rejection of Moses' and God's authority: "These people have rejected YHWH" (Num 16:30). All those who stand with them in their refusal to respond to Moses (Num 16:27b) participate in the sin and suffer the consequence.

28The children of Joseph by their families were Manasseh and Ephraim.

29Of the children of Manasseh: Of Machir: the family of the Machirites. And Machir fathered Gilead. Of Gilead: the family of the Gileadites. 30These are the children of Gilead: Of Iezer: the family of the Iezerites. Of Helek: the family of the Helekites. 31And Asriel: the family of the Asrielites. And Shechem: the family of the Shechemites. 32And Shemida: the family of the Shemidaites. And Hepher: the family of the Hepherites. 33And Zelophehad son of Hepher had no sons, just daughters, and the names of Zelophehad's daughters were Mahlah and Noah, Hoglah, Milcah, and Tirzah. 34These are the families of Manasseh; and their counts: fifty-two thousand seven hundred.

35These are the children of Ephraim by their families:

Of Shuthelah: the family of the Shuthelahites. Of Becher: the family of the Becherites. Of Tahan: the family of the Tahanites. 36And these are the children of Shuthelah: Of Eran: the family of the Eranites. 37These are the families of the children of Ephraim by their counts: thirty-two thousand five hundred. These are the sons of Joseph after their families.

38The children of Benjamin by their families:

Of Bela: the family of the Belaites. Of Ashbel: the family of the Ashbelites. Of Ahiram: the family of the Ahiramites. 39Of Shephupham: the family of the Shuphamites. Of Hupham: the family of the Huphamites. 40And the children of Bela were Ard and Naaman: the family of the Ardites. Of Naaman: the family of the Naamites. 41These are the children of Benjamin by their families; and their counts: forty-five thousand six hundred.

42These are the children of Dan by their families:

Of Shuham: the family of the Shuhamites. These are the families of Dan after their families. 43All the families of the Shuhamites by their counts: sixty-four thousand four hundred.

יוֹסֵף לְמִשְׁפְּחֹתָם מְנַשֶּׁה וְאֶפְרָיִם: 29בְּנֵי מְנַשֶּׁה לְמָכִיר מִשְׁפַּחַת הַמָּכִירִי וּמָכִיר הוֹלִיד אֶת־גִּלְעָד לְגִלְעָד מִשְׁפַּחַת הַגִּלְעָדִי: 30אֵלֶּה בְּנֵי גִלְעָד אִיעֶזֶר מִשְׁפַּחַת הָאִיעֶזְרִי לְחֵלֶק מִשְׁפַּחַת הַחֶלְקִי: 31וְאַשְׂרִיאֵל מִשְׁפַּחַת הָאַשְׂרִאֵלִי וְשֶׁכֶם מִשְׁפַּחַת הַשִּׁכְמִי: 32וּשְׁמִידָע מִשְׁפַּחַת הַשְּׁמִידָעִי וְחֵפֶר מִשְׁפַּחַת הַחֶפְרִי: 33וּצְלָפְחָד בֶּן־חֵפֶר לֹא־הָיוּ לוֹ בָּנִים כִּי אִם־בָּנוֹת וְשֵׁם בְּנוֹת צְלָפְחָד מַחְלָה וְנֹעָה חָגְלָה מִלְכָּה וְתִרְצָה: 34אֵלֶּה מִשְׁפְּחֹת מְנַשֶּׁה וּפְקֻדֵיהֶם שְׁנַיִם וַחֲמִשִּׁים אֶלֶף וּשְׁבַע מֵאוֹת: ס

35אֵלֶּה בְנֵי־אֶפְרַיִם לְמִשְׁפְּחֹתָם לְשׁוּתֶלַח מִשְׁפַּחַת הַשֻּׁתַלְחִי לְבֶכֶר מִשְׁפַּחַת הַבַּכְרִי לְתַחַן מִשְׁפַּחַת הַתַּחֲנִי: 36וְאֵלֶּה בְּנֵי שׁוּתָלַח לְעֵרָן מִשְׁפַּחַת הָעֵרָנִי: 37אֵלֶּה מִשְׁפְּחֹת בְּנֵי־אֶפְרַיִם לִפְקֻדֵיהֶם שְׁנַיִם וּשְׁלֹשִׁים אֶלֶף וַחֲמֵשׁ מֵאוֹת אֵלֶּה בְנֵי־יוֹסֵף לְמִשְׁפְּחֹתָם: ס 38בְּנֵי בִנְיָמִן לְמִשְׁפְּחֹתָם לְבֶלַע מִשְׁפַּחַת הַבַּלְעִי לְאַשְׁבֵּל מִשְׁפַּחַת הָאַשְׁבֵּלִי לַאֲחִירָם מִשְׁפַּחַת הָאֲחִירָמִי: 39לִשְׁפוּפָם מִשְׁפַּחַת הַשּׁוּפָמִי לְחוּפָם מִשְׁפַּחַת הַחוּפָמִי: 40וַיִּהְיוּ בְנֵי־בֶלַע אַרְדְּ וְנַעֲמָן מִשְׁפַּחַת הָאַרְדִּי לְנַעֲמָן מִשְׁפַּחַת הַנַּעֲמִי: 41אֵלֶּה בְנֵי־בִנְיָמִן לְמִשְׁפְּחֹתָם וּפְקֻדֵיהֶם חֲמִשָּׁה וְאַרְבָּעִים אֶלֶף וְשֵׁשׁ מֵאוֹת: ס 42אֵלֶּה בְנֵי־דָן לְמִשְׁפְּחֹתָם לְשׁוּחָם מִשְׁפַּחַת הַשּׁוּחָמִי אֵלֶּה מִשְׁפְּחֹת דָּן לְמִשְׁפְּחֹתָם: 43כָּל־מִשְׁפְּחֹת הַשּׁוּחָמִי לִפְקֻדֵיהֶם אַרְבָּעָה וְשִׁשִּׁים אֶלֶף וְאַרְבַּע מֵאוֹת: ס

44The children of Asher by their families:

Of Imnah: the family of Imnah. Of Ishvi: the family of the Ishvites. Of Beriah: the family of the Beriites. 45Of the children of Beriah: Of Heber: the family of the Heberites. Of Malchiel: the family of the Malchielites. 46And Asher's daughter's name was Serah. 47These are the families of the children of Asher by their counts: fifty-three thousand four hundred.

48The children of Naphtali by their families:

Of Jahzeel: the family of the Jahzeelites. Of Guni: the family of the Gunites. 49Of Jezer: the family of the Jezerites. Of Shillem: the family of the Shillemites. 50These are the families of Naphtali by their families, and their counts: forty-five thousand four hundred.

51These are the counts of the children of Israel: six hundred one thousand seven hundred thirty.

52And YHWH spoke to Moses, saying, 53"The land shall be distributed to these as a legacy with the number of names. 54For the large you shall make its legacy larger, and for the small you shall make its legacy smaller. Each man will be given his legacy according to his counts. 55Just: the land shall be distributed by lot. They shall have a legacy by the names of their fathers' tribes. 56Its legacy shall be distributed according to the lot, whether large or small."

57And these are the counts of the Levites by their families:

Of Gershon: the family of the Gershonites. Of Kohath: the family of the Kohathites. Of Merari: the family of the Merarites. 58These are the families of the Levites: the family of the Libnites, the family of the Hebronites, the family of the Mahlites, the family of the Mushites, the family of the Korahites.

And Kohath fathered Amram. 59And the name of Amram's wife was Jochebed, a daughter of Levi, who was born to Levi in Egypt. And she gave birth for Amram to Aaron and Moses and Miriam, their sister. 60And Nadab and Abihu, El-

בְּנֵי אָשֵׁר לְמִשְׁפְּחֹתָם לְיִמְנָה מִשְׁפַּחַת הַיִּמְנָה 44 לְיִשְׁוִי מִשְׁפַּחַת הַיִּשְׁוִי לִבְרִיעָה מִשְׁפַּחַת הַבְּרִיעִי: 45 לִבְנֵי בְרִיעָה לְחֶבֶר מִשְׁפַּחַת הַחֶבְרִי לְמַלְכִּיאֵל מִשְׁפַּחַת הַמַּלְכִּיאֵלִי: 46 וְשֵׁם בַּת־אָשֵׁר שָׂרַח: 47 אֵלֶּה מִשְׁפְּחֹת בְּנֵי־אָשֵׁר לִפְקֻדֵיהֶם שְׁלֹשָׁה וַחֲמִשִּׁים אֶלֶף וְאַרְבַּע מֵאוֹת: ס 48 בְּנֵי נַפְתָּלִי לְמִשְׁפְּחֹתָם לְיַחְצְאֵל מִשְׁפַּחַת הַיַּחְצְאֵלִי לְגוּנִי מִשְׁפַּחַת הַגּוּנִי: 49 לְיֵצֶר מִשְׁפַּחַת הַיִּצְרִי לְשִׁלֵּם מִשְׁפַּחַת הַשִּׁלֵּמִי: 50 אֵלֶּה מִשְׁפְּחֹת נַפְתָּלִי לְמִשְׁפְּחֹתָם וּפְקֻדֵיהֶם חֲמִשָּׁה וְאַרְבָּעִים אֶלֶף וְאַרְבַּע מֵאוֹת: 51 אֵלֶּה פְּקוּדֵי בְּנֵי יִשְׂרָאֵל שֵׁשׁ־מֵאוֹת אֶלֶף וָאָלֶף שְׁבַע מֵאוֹת וּשְׁלֹשִׁים: פ 52 וַיְדַבֵּר יְהוָה אֶל־מֹשֶׁה לֵּאמֹר: 53 לָאֵלֶּה תֵּחָלֵק הָאָרֶץ בְּנַחֲלָה בְּמִסְפַּר שֵׁמוֹת: 54 לָרַב תַּרְבֶּה נַחֲלָתוֹ וְלַמְעַט תַּמְעִיט נַחֲלָתוֹ אִישׁ לְפִי פְקֻדָיו יֻתַּן נַחֲלָתוֹ: 55 אַךְ־בְּגוֹרָל יֵחָלֵק אֶת־הָאָרֶץ לִשְׁמוֹת מַטּוֹת־אֲבֹתָם יִנְחָלוּ: 56 עַל־פִּי הַגּוֹרָל תֵּחָלֵק נַחֲלָתוֹ בֵּין רַב לִמְעָט: ס 57 וְאֵלֶּה פְקוּדֵי הַלֵּוִי לְמִשְׁפְּחֹתָם לְגֵרְשׁוֹן מִשְׁפַּחַת הַגֵּרְשֻׁנִּי לִקְהָת מִשְׁפַּחַת הַקְּהָתִי לִמְרָרִי מִשְׁפַּחַת הַמְּרָרִי: 58 אֵלֶּה מִשְׁפְּחֹת לֵוִי מִשְׁפַּחַת הַלִּבְנִי מִשְׁפַּחַת הַחֶבְרֹנִי מִשְׁפַּחַת הַמַּחְלִי מִשְׁפַּחַת הַמּוּשִׁי מִשְׁפַּחַת הַקָּרְחִי וּקְהָת הוֹלִד אֶת־עַמְרָם: 59 וְשֵׁם אֵשֶׁת עַמְרָם יוֹכֶבֶד בַּת־לֵוִי אֲשֶׁר יָלְדָה אֹתָהּ לְלֵוִי בְּמִצְרָיִם וַתֵּלֶד לְעַמְרָם אֶת־אַהֲרֹן וְאֶת־מֹשֶׁה וְאֵת מִרְיָם אֲחֹתָם: 60 וַיִּוָּלֵד לְאַהֲרֹן אֶת־נָדָב וְאֶת־אֲבִיהוּא

eazar and Ithamar were born to Aaron. 61And Nadab and Abihu died when they brought forward unfitting fire in front of YHWH.

62And their counts were twenty-three thousand, every male from a month old and up, because they were not counted among the children of Israel because a legacy was not given to them among the children of Israel.

63These are the counts of Moses and Eleazar, the priest, who counted the children of Israel in the plains of Moab by the Jordan toward Jericho; 64and there was not a man among these from the counts of Moses and Aaron, the priest, who counted the children of Israel in the wilderness of Sinai, 65because YHWH said of them, "They shall *die* in the wilderness," and not a man was left of them except Caleb son of Jephunneh and Joshua son of Nun.

27 1And the daughters of Zelophehad son of Hepher son of Gilead son of Machir son of Manasseh, of the families of Manasseh son of Joseph, came forward. And these are his daughters' names: Mahlah, Noah, and Hoglah and Milcah and Tirzah. 2And they stood in front of Moses and in front of Eleazar, the priest, and in front of the chieftains and all the congregation at the entrance of the Tent of Meeting, saying, 3"Our father died in the wilderness. And he wasn't among the congregation who were gathered against YHWH: in Korah's congregation. Rather, he died through his own sin. And he had no sons. 4Why should our father's name be subtracted from among his family because he didn't

אֶת־אֶלְעָזָר וְאֶת־אִיתָמָר: 61וַיָּמָת נָדָב וַאֲבִיהוּא בְּהַקְרִיבָם אֵשׁ־זָרָה לִפְנֵי יְהוָה: 62וַיִּהְיוּ פְקֻדֵיהֶם שְׁלֹשָׁה וְעֶשְׂרִים אֶלֶף כָּל־זָכָר מִבֶּן־חֹדֶשׁ וָמָעְלָה כִּי ׀ לֹא הָתְפָּקְדוּ בְּתוֹךְ בְּנֵי יִשְׂרָאֵל כִּי לֹא־נִתַּן לָהֶם נַחֲלָה בְּתוֹךְ בְּנֵי יִשְׂרָאֵל: 63אֵלֶּה פְּקוּדֵי מֹשֶׁה וְאֶלְעָזָר הַכֹּהֵן אֲשֶׁר פָּקְדוּ אֶת־בְּנֵי יִשְׂרָאֵל בְּעַרְבֹת מוֹאָב עַל יַרְדֵּן יְרֵחוֹ: 64וּבְאֵלֶּה לֹא־הָיָה אִישׁ מִפְּקוּדֵי מֹשֶׁה וְאַהֲרֹן הַכֹּהֵן אֲשֶׁר פָּקְדוּ אֶת־בְּנֵי יִשְׂרָאֵל בְּמִדְבַּר סִינָי: 65כִּי־אָמַר יְהוָה לָהֶם מוֹת יָמֻתוּ בַּמִּדְבָּר וְלֹא־נוֹתַר מֵהֶם אִישׁ כִּי אִם־כָּלֵב בֶּן־יְפֻנֶּה וִיהוֹשֻׁעַ בִּן־נוּן: ס

27 1וַתִּקְרַבְנָה בְּנוֹת צְלָפְחָד בֶּן־חֵפֶר בֶּן־גִּלְעָד בֶּן־מָכִיר בֶּן־מְנַשֶּׁה לְמִשְׁפְּחֹת מְנַשֶּׁה בֶן־יוֹסֵף וְאֵלֶּה שְׁמוֹת בְּנֹתָיו מַחְלָה נֹעָה וְחָגְלָה וּמִלְכָּה וְתִרְצָה: 2וַתַּעֲמֹדְנָה לִפְנֵי מֹשֶׁה וְלִפְנֵי אֶלְעָזָר הַכֹּהֵן וְלִפְנֵי הַנְּשִׂיאִם וְכָל־הָעֵדָה פֶּתַח אֹהֶל־מוֹעֵד לֵאמֹר: 3אָבִינוּ מֵת בַּמִּדְבָּר וְהוּא לֹא־הָיָה בְּתוֹךְ הָעֵדָה הַנּוֹעָדִים עַל־יְהוָה בַּעֲדַת־קֹרַח כִּי־בְחֶטְאוֹ מֵת וּבָנִים לֹא־הָיוּ לוֹ: 4לָמָּה יִגָּרַע שֵׁם־אָבִינוּ מִתּוֹךְ מִשְׁפַּחְתּוֹ כִּי אֵין לוֹ בֵּן תְּנָה־לָּנוּ

26:64. **there was not a man among these from the counts of Moses and Aaron.** The main result of this second census is the confirmation that YHWH's condemnation of the exodus generation has come true. Because of their rejection of the promised land in the spies episode, all the adults of that generation have died. The exceptions are Joshua and Caleb, the two scouts who remained faithful, and Moses. Moses' death will be told at the end of the Torah, and only Caleb and Joshua will live to lead the new generation into the promised land.

27:4. **Why should our father's name be subtracted**. They do not make their case in terms of their own rights or of women's rights in general. They put it in terms of

have a son? Give us a possession among our father's brothers."

⁵And Moses brought their case forward in front of YHWH.

⁶And YHWH said to Moses, saying, ⁷"Zelophehad's daughters speak right. You *shall* give them a possession for a legacy among their father's brothers, and you shall pass their father's legacy to them. ⁸And you shall speak to the children of Israel, saying, 'A man who will die and not have a son: you shall pass his legacy to his daughter. ⁹And if he does not have a daughter, then you shall give his legacy to his brothers.

אֲחֻזָּה בְּתוֹךְ אֲחֵי אָבִינוּ: ⁵וַיַּקְרֵב מֹשֶׁה אֶת־מִשְׁפָּטָן לִפְנֵי יְהוָה: ס ⁶וַיֹּאמֶר יְהוָה אֶל־מֹשֶׁה לֵּאמֹר: ⁷כֵּן בְּנוֹת צְלָפְחָד דֹּבְרֹת נָתֹן תִּתֵּן לָהֶם אֲחֻזַּת נַחֲלָה בְּתוֹךְ אֲחֵי אֲבִיהֶם וְהַעֲבַרְתָּ אֶת־נַחֲלַת אֲבִיהֶן לָהֶן: ⁸וְאֶל־בְּנֵי יִשְׂרָאֵל תְּדַבֵּר לֵאמֹר אִישׁ כִּי־יָמוּת וּבֵן אֵין לוֹ וְהַעֲבַרְתֶּם אֶת־נַחֲלָתוֹ לְבִתּוֹ: ⁹וְאִם־אֵין לוֹ בַּת וּנְתַתֶּם אֶת־נַחֲלָתוֹ לְאֶחָיו:

their father, that his name would be eliminated from the territorial holdings of Israel. The issue is the one that arises in the law of the jubilee. Land is unalienable. It is to be distributed among the Israelites when they arrive in the land. If a man ever loses his land, it is returned to him in the jubilee year. If he has died by then, it is returned to his sons. But the property in his name stays in the family forever. Zelophehad's daughters now protest that the property that would have gone to their father will go to his brothers instead, and the family holding in his name will be lost.

27:7. Zelophehad's daughters speak right. See the comment on Num 36:5.

27:8. A man who will die and not have a son: you shall pass his legacy to his daughter. This judgment is an important step in the development of women's rights, but its message is mixed. On one hand, it says that women can inherit property, and their right of inheritance precedes the rights of their father's male siblings or any other male relatives who are more distantly related to their father than the women themselves. On the other hand, this applies only if their father had no sons. If a father has even one son and ten daughters, the son inherits the family land. The daughters are dependent on that brother or on their husbands for property. (This matter of women's inheritance will become even more complex in the last chapter of Numbers; see the comments on Num 36:3; 36:5; and 36:6.) There is little point in debating whether this step means that the Torah is supportive of women, on the grounds that it provides for them to inherit, or whether it means that the Torah is unfair to women, on the grounds that sons still precede daughters. The fact is that social transformations take time: generations, centuries, even millennia. The Torah does not command a revolution in the status of women. It provides for steps such as this one, which in the short run established that women do have rights, and which ultimately participated in the development of women's rights more generally. We can praise the Bible for how far it went, or we can be critical that it did not go farther. But we would do better to examine how far it went in its age, and how much this contributed to the transformation in the balance between men and women in the millennia that followed. The larger point is the same that I made with regard to slavery: The Torah does not forbid it and attempt to bring it to an end overnight. It rather gives laws of treatment of slaves—which involved granting respect, rights, and compassion for slaves. And this eventual-

10And if he does not have brothers, then you shall give his legacy to his father's brothers. 11And if there are no brothers of his father, then you shall give his legacy to his relative who is closest to him of his family, and he shall possess it.' And it shall become a law of judgment for the children of Israel, as YHWH commanded Moses."

12And YHWH said to Moses, "Go up to this mountain of Abarim and see the land that I've given to the children of Israel. 13And you'll see it, and then you'll be gathered to your people, you as well, as Aaron, your brother, was gathered, 14because you rebelled against my word in the wilderness of Zin in the congregation's quarrel to make me holy with water before their eyes. That is the water of Meribah of Kadesh at the wilderness of Zin."

15And Moses spoke to YHWH, saying, 16"Let YHWH, God of the spirits of all flesh, appoint a man over the congregation 17who will go out in front of them and who will come in in front of

10וְאִם־אֵין לוֹ אַחִים וּנְתַתֶּם אֶת־נַחֲלָתוֹ לַאֲחֵי אָבִיו: 11וְאִם־אֵין אַחִים לְאָבִיו וּנְתַתֶּם אֶת־נַחֲלָתוֹ לִשְׁאֵרוֹ הַקָּרֹב אֵלָיו מִמִּשְׁפַּחְתּוֹ וְיָרַשׁ אֹתָהּ וְהָיְתָה לִבְנֵי יִשְׂרָאֵל לְחֻקַּת מִשְׁפָּט כַּאֲשֶׁר צִוָּה יְהוָה אֶת־מֹשֶׁה: ס

12וַיֹּאמֶר יְהוָה אֶל־מֹשֶׁה עֲלֵה אֶל־הַר הָעֲבָרִים הַזֶּה וּרְאֵה אֶת־הָאָרֶץ אֲשֶׁר נָתַתִּי לִבְנֵי יִשְׂרָאֵל: 13וְרָאִיתָה אֹתָהּ וְנֶאֱסַפְתָּ אֶל־עַמֶּיךָ גַּם־אָתָּה כַּאֲשֶׁר נֶאֱסַף אַהֲרֹן אָחִיךָ: 14כַּאֲשֶׁר מְרִיתֶם פִּי בְּמִדְבַּר־צִן בִּמְרִיבַת הָעֵדָה לְהַקְדִּישֵׁנִי בַמַּיִם לְעֵינֵיהֶם הֵם מֵי־מְרִיבַת קָדֵשׁ מִדְבַּר־צִן: פ

15וַיְדַבֵּר מֹשֶׁה אֶל־יְהוָה לֵאמֹר: 16יִפְקֹד יְהוָה אֱלֹהֵי הָרוּחֹת לְכָל־בָּשָׂר אִישׁ עַל־הָעֵדָה: 17אֲשֶׁר־יֵצֵא לִפְנֵיהֶם וַאֲשֶׁר יָבֹא לִפְנֵיהֶם וַאֲשֶׁר יוֹצִיאֵם

---

ly undermined slavery as an institution. The diminution of slavery and the increase of women's rights are two of the major developments of the past century. The Torah's laws played an early and determinative part in birthing and nurturing both of these revolutions.

27:11. **law of judgment**. This term is used twice in the Torah: here for cases of inheritance, and later for cases involving cities of refuge (Num 35:29). In both occurrences it involves the stating of a legal procedure for deciding cases—civil procedure in this instance, and criminal procedure in the later instance—which judges will then apply to the particular cases before them.

27:15. **Moses spoke to YHWH**. This is the last time that Moses is quoted as saying anything to God. In Deuteronomy Moses will report to the people his *past* conversations with God, but *these are the last words of Moses to God in the Torah*. And his last concern is: the *people*—that they should have a leader. And note that all of this draws us back to Moses' first meeting with God, at the burning bush. God begins the charge to Moses there by expressing concern for the people: "I've *seen* the degradation of my people" (Exod 3:7). So God's first charge to Moses and Moses' last request of God are both about the good of the people. And the connection to Moses' origins is underscored by Moses' choice of metaphor here. The episode at the bush begins: "Moses had been shepherding the flock" (Exod 3:1); and now Moses asks for a leader so the people won't be "like sheep that don't have a shepherd" (Num 27:17).

them and who will bring them out and who will bring them in, so YHWH's congregation won't be like sheep that don't have a shepherd." ¹⁸And YHWH said to Moses, "Take Joshua son of Nun, a man with spirit in him, and lay your hand on him. ¹⁹And you shall stand him in front of Eleazar, the priest, and in front of all the congregation, and you shall command him before their eyes. ²⁰And you shall put some of your eminence on him so that all the congregation of the children of Israel will hear. ²¹And he shall stand in front of Eleazar, the priest; and he shall ask him in judgment of the Urim in front of YHWH. By his word they shall go out, and by his word they shall come in, he and all the children of Israel with him and all the congregation."

²²And Moses did as YHWH commanded him, and he took Joshua and stood him in front of Eleazar, the priest, and in front of all the congregation. ²³And he laid his hands on him and commanded him, as YHWH had spoken by Moses' hand.

28 ¹And YHWH spoke to Moses, saying, ²"Command the children of Israel, and you shall say to them: You shall observe to bring forward my sacrifice to me, my bread, for my offering by fire, my pleasant smell, at its appointed time.

וַאֲשֶׁ֤ר יְבִיאֵם֙ וְלֹ֣א תִהְיֶ֔ה עֲדַ֣ת יְהוָ֔ה כַּצֹּ֕אן אֲשֶׁ֥ר אֵין־לָהֶ֖ם רֹעֶֽה׃ ¹⁸וַיֹּ֨אמֶר יְהוָ֜ה אֶל־מֹשֶׁ֗ה קַח־לְךָ֙ אֶת־יְהוֹשֻׁ֣עַ בִּן־נ֔וּן אִ֖ישׁ אֲשֶׁר־ר֣וּחַ בּ֑וֹ וְסָמַכְתָּ֥ אֶת־יָדְךָ֖ עָלָֽיו׃ ¹⁹וְהַעֲמַדְתָּ֣ אֹת֗וֹ לִפְנֵי֙ אֶלְעָזָ֣ר הַכֹּהֵ֔ן וְלִפְנֵ֖י כָּל־הָעֵדָ֑ה וְצִוִּיתָ֥ה אֹת֖וֹ לְעֵינֵיהֶֽם׃ ²⁰וְנָתַתָּ֥ה מֵהוֹדְךָ֖ עָלָ֑יו לְמַ֣עַן יִשְׁמְע֔וּ כָּל־עֲדַ֖ת בְּנֵ֥י יִשְׂרָאֵֽל׃ ²¹וְלִפְנֵ֨י אֶלְעָזָ֤ר הַכֹּהֵן֙ יַעֲמֹ֔ד וְשָׁ֥אַל ל֛וֹ בְּמִשְׁפַּ֥ט הָאוּרִ֖ים לִפְנֵ֣י יְהוָ֑ה עַל־פִּ֨יו יֵצְא֜וּ וְעַל־פִּ֣יו יָבֹ֗אוּ ה֛וּא וְכָל־בְּנֵי־יִשְׂרָאֵ֥ל אִתּ֖וֹ וְכָל־הָעֵדָֽה׃ ²²וַיַּ֣עַשׂ מֹשֶׁ֔ה כַּאֲשֶׁ֛ר צִוָּ֥ה יְהוָ֖ה אֹת֑וֹ וַיִּקַּ֣ח אֶת־יְהוֹשֻׁ֗עַ וַיַּֽעֲמִדֵ֙הוּ֙ לִפְנֵי֙ אֶלְעָזָ֣ר הַכֹּהֵ֔ן וְלִפְנֵ֖י כָּל־הָעֵדָֽה׃ ²³וַיִּסְמֹ֧ךְ אֶת־יָדָ֛יו עָלָ֖יו וַיְצַוֵּ֑הוּ כַּאֲשֶׁ֛ר דִּבֶּ֥ר יְהוָ֖ה בְּיַד־מֹשֶֽׁה׃ פ

28 ¹וַיְדַבֵּ֥ר יְהוָ֖ה אֶל־מֹשֶׁ֥ה לֵּאמֹֽר׃ ²צַ֚ו אֶת־בְּנֵ֣י יִשְׂרָאֵ֔ל וְאָמַרְתָּ֖ אֲלֵהֶ֑ם אֶת־קָרְבָּנִ֨י לַחְמִ֜י לְאִשַּׁ֗י רֵ֚יחַ נִֽיחֹחִ֔י תִּשְׁמְר֕וּ לְהַקְרִ֥יב לִ֖י בְּמוֹעֲדֽוֹ׃ ³וְאָמַרְתָּ֣ לָהֶ֗ם זֶ֤ה הָֽאִשֶּׁה֙ אֲשֶׁ֣ר תַּקְרִ֣יבוּ לַֽיהוָ֔ה כְּבָשִׂ֧ים בְּנֵֽי־שָׁנָ֛ה תְמִימִ֥ם שְׁנַ֖יִם לַיּ֑וֹם עֹלָ֥ה תָמִֽיד׃ ⁴אֶת־הַכֶּ֣בֶשׂ

27:23. **he laid his hands**. God used the singular: "Lay your *hand*." But Moses lays both hands on Joshua. It is as if he wants to make the appointment of his successor as visible and unmistakable as possible. And he indicates in this way that this appointment is his own choice as well. He fulfills the divine command with one hand. The second hand is his own affirmation of Joshua, which bolsters Joshua's appointment and preempts anyone from criticizing Joshua later as not having been Moses' choice. The successor to a great leader is always in a vulnerable position, and it is a gracious act by the great leader to support that successor.

28:2. **Command the children of Israel**. Numbers 28 and 29 contain commands concerning sacrifices and holidays. Much of this has been treated already. There is a notable difference here, though: nowhere in these two chapters is there a mention of the Tabernacle (or Tent of Meeting). Other laws clearly indicate that sacrifice can be performed only at the entrance of the Tabernacle. If I was correct in my commentary on the Tabernacle (Exodus 26)—that the Tabernacle was actually located in the First

³"And you shall say to them: This is the offering by fire that you shall bring forward to YHWH: two unblemished one-year-old lambs per day as a continual burnt offering. ⁴You shall do one lamb in the morning, and you shall do the second lamb 'between the two evenings.' ⁵And a tenth of an ephah of fine flour for a grain offering, mixed with a fourth of a hin of pressed oil, ⁶the continual burnt offering that was done at Mount Sinai for a pleasant smell, an offering by fire to YHWH. ⁷And its libation shall be a fourth of a hin for one lamb. Pour a libation of beer in the holy place for YHWH. ⁸And you shall do the second lamb 'between the two evenings,' and you shall do it like the morning grain offering and like its libation, an offering by fire of a pleasant smell to YHWH.

⁹"And on the Sabbath day two unblemished one-year-old lambs and two tenths of fine flour, a grain offering, mixed with oil, and its libation: ¹⁰the burnt offering of each Sabbath in its week, beside the continual burnt offering and its libation.

¹¹"And at the beginning of your months you shall bring forward a burnt offering to YHWH: two bulls of the cattle and one ram, seven unblemished one-year-old lambs, ¹²with three tenths of fine flour, a grain offering, mixed with oil for one bull and two tenths of fine flour mixed with oil for the one ram, ¹³and one tenth

אֶחָ֖ד תַּעֲשֶׂ֣ה בַבֹּ֑קֶר וְאֵת֙ הַכֶּ֣בֶשׂ הַשֵּׁנִ֔י תַּעֲשֶׂ֖ה בֵּ֥ין הָעַרְבָּֽיִם: ⁵וַעֲשִׂירִ֧ית הָאֵיפָ֛ה סֹ֖לֶת לְמִנְחָ֑ה בְּלוּלָ֣ה בְּשֶׁ֔מֶן רְבִיעִ֖ת הַהִֽין: ⁶עֹלַ֖ת תָּמִ֑יד הָעֲשֻׂיָה֙ בְּהַ֣ר סִינַ֔י לְרֵ֣יחַ נִיחֹ֔חַ אִשֶּׁ֖ה לַֽיהוָֽה: ⁷וְנִסְכּוֹ֙ רְבִיעִ֣ת הַהִ֔ין לַכֶּ֖בֶשׂ הָאֶחָ֑ד בַּקֹּ֗דֶשׁ הַסֵּ֛ךְ נֶ֥סֶךְ שֵׁכָ֖ר לַֽיהוָֽה: ⁸וְאֵת֙ הַכֶּ֣בֶשׂ הַשֵּׁנִ֔י תַּעֲשֶׂ֖ה בֵּ֣ין הָעַרְבָּ֑יִם כְּמִנְחַ֨ת הַבֹּ֤קֶר וּכְנִסְכּוֹ֙ תַּעֲשֶׂ֔ה אִשֵּׁ֛ה רֵ֥יחַ נִיחֹ֖חַ לַֽיהוָֽה: פ ⁹וּבְיוֹם֙ הַשַּׁבָּ֔ת שְׁנֵֽי־כְבָשִׂ֥ים בְּנֵֽי־שָׁנָ֖ה תְּמִימִ֑ם וּשְׁנֵ֣י עֶשְׂרֹנִ֗ים סֹ֧לֶת מִנְחָ֛ה בְּלוּלָ֥ה בַשֶּׁ֖מֶן וְנִסְכּֽוֹ: ¹⁰עֹלַ֥ת שַׁבַּ֖ת בְּשַׁבַּתּ֑וֹ עַל־עֹלַ֥ת הַתָּמִ֖יד וְנִסְכָּֽהּ: ס ¹¹וּבְרָאשֵׁי֙ חָדְשֵׁיכֶ֔ם תַּקְרִ֥יבוּ עֹלָ֖ה לַֽיהוָ֑ה פָּרִ֨ים בְּנֵֽי־בָקָ֤ר שְׁנַ֙יִם֙ וְאַ֣יִל אֶחָ֔ד כְּבָשִׂ֧ים בְּנֵֽי־שָׁנָ֛ה שִׁבְעָ֖ה תְּמִימִֽם: ¹²וּשְׁלֹשָׁ֣ה עֶשְׂרֹנִ֗ים סֹ֤לֶת מִנְחָה֙ בְּלוּלָ֣ה בַשֶּׁ֔מֶן לַפָּ֖ר הָֽאֶחָ֑ד וּשְׁנֵ֣י עֶשְׂרֹנִ֗ים סֹ֤לֶת מִנְחָה֙ בְּלוּלָ֣ה בַשֶּׁ֔מֶן לָאַ֖יִל הָֽאֶחָֽד: ¹³וְעִשָּׂרֹ֣ן

Temple—then it is critically important that these laws come now picturing sacrifice even without reference to the Tabernacle. By no reckoning was the Tabernacle in the Second Temple. (Nor were the ark, the tablets, the cherubs, or the Urim and Tummim.) It is these two chapters (and Num 15:1–31, which likewise does not mention the Tabernacle) that make it possible for there to be sacrificial worship at the Second Temple.

28:7. **beer**. I have consistently translated Hebrew *yayin* and *šĕkār* as "wine" and "beer," respectively, because wine and beer are the alcoholic beverages of the ancient Near East. Still, I admit that a libation of beer here presents a difficulty because beer involves fermentation, and normally fermented substances are not used in the holy place. Thus the priests eat the meat of their sacrifices on unleavened bread. The translation "beer" is therefore uncertain in this passage (and possibly in other occurrences as well).

of fine flour, a grain offering, mixed with oil for each lamb, a burnt offering as a pleasant smell, an offering by fire to YHWH. 14And their libations: half a hin will be for a bull and a third of a hin for a ram and a fourth of a hin for a lamb—wine. This is the burnt offering of each new month in its month for the months of the year. 15And one goat for a sin offering to YHWH shall be done, beside the continual burnt offering and its libation.

16"And in the first month on the fourteenth day of the month is a Passover to YHWH. 17And on the fifteenth day of this month is a holiday. For seven days unleavened bread shall be eaten. 18On the first day is a holy assembly. You shall not do any act of work. 19And you shall bring forward an offering by fire, a burnt offering to YHWH. You shall have two bulls of the cattle and one ram and seven unblemished one-year-old lambs. 20And their grain offering shall be fine flour mixed with oil. You shall do three tenths for a bull and two tenths for a ram. 21And you shall do one tenth for each lamb, for the seven lambs. 22And one goat for a sin offering to make atonement over you. 23You shall do these aside from the morning burnt offering that is for the continual burnt offering. 24You shall do food as a fire offering, a pleasant smell to YHWH, like these daily for seven days. It shall be done beside the continual burnt offering and its libation. 25And on the seventh day you shall have a holy assembly. You shall not do any act of work.

26"And on the Day of Firstfruits, when you bring a new grain offering to YHWH on your Feast of Weeks, you shall have a holy assembly. You shall not do any act of work. 27And you shall bring forward a burnt offering for a pleasant smell to YHWH: two bulls of the cattle, one ram, seven one-year-old lambs 28and their grain offering, fine flour mixed with oil, three tenths for one bull, two tenths for one ram, 29one tenth for each lamb, for the seven lambs, 30one goat to make atonement over you. 31You shall do it aside from the continual burnt offering and its grain

עִשָּׂרוֹן סֹלֶת מִנְחָה בְּלוּלָה בַשֶּׁמֶן לַכֶּבֶשׂ הָאֶחָד
עֹלָה רֵיחַ נִיחֹחַ אִשֶּׁה לַיהוָה: 14וְנִסְכֵּיהֶם חֲצִי
הַהִין יִהְיֶה לַפָּר וּשְׁלִישִׁת הַהִין לָאַיִל וּרְבִיעִת
הַהִין לַכֶּבֶשׂ יָיִן זֹאת עֹלַת חֹדֶשׁ בְּחָדְשׁוֹ לְחָדְשֵׁי
הַשָּׁנָה: 15וּשְׂעִיר עִזִּים אֶחָד לְחַטָּאת לַיהוָה עַל־
עֹלַת הַתָּמִיד יֵעָשֶׂה וְנִסְכּוֹ: ס 16וּבַחֹדֶשׁ הָרִאשׁוֹן
בְּאַרְבָּעָה עָשָׂר יוֹם לַחֹדֶשׁ פֶּסַח לַיהוָה:
17וּבַחֲמִשָּׁה עָשָׂר יוֹם לַחֹדֶשׁ הַזֶּה חָג שִׁבְעַת יָמִים
מַצּוֹת יֵאָכֵל: 18בַּיּוֹם הָרִאשׁוֹן מִקְרָא־קֹדֶשׁ כָּל־
מְלֶאכֶת עֲבֹדָה לֹא תַעֲשׂוּ: 19וְהִקְרַבְתֶּם אִשֶּׁה עֹלָה
לַיהוָה פָּרִים בְּנֵי־בָקָר שְׁנַיִם וְאַיִל אֶחָד וְשִׁבְעָה
כְבָשִׂים בְּנֵי שָׁנָה תְּמִימִם יִהְיוּ לָכֶם: 20וּמִנְחָתָם
סֹלֶת בְּלוּלָה בַשֶּׁמֶן שְׁלֹשָׁה עֶשְׂרֹנִים לַפָּר וּשְׁנֵי
עֶשְׂרֹנִים לָאַיִל תַּעֲשׂוּ: 21עִשָּׂרוֹן עִשָּׂרוֹן תַּעֲשֶׂה
לַכֶּבֶשׂ הָאֶחָד לְשִׁבְעַת הַכְּבָשִׂים: 22וּשְׂעִיר חַטָּאת
אֶחָד לְכַפֵּר עֲלֵיכֶם: 23מִלְּבַד עֹלַת הַבֹּקֶר אֲשֶׁר
לְעֹלַת הַתָּמִיד תַּעֲשׂוּ אֶת־אֵלֶּה: 24כָּאֵלֶּה תַּעֲשׂוּ
לַיּוֹם שִׁבְעַת יָמִים לֶחֶם אִשֵּׁה רֵיחַ־נִיחֹחַ לַיהוָה
עַל־עוֹלַת הַתָּמִיד יֵעָשֶׂה וְנִסְכּוֹ: 25וּבַיּוֹם הַשְּׁבִיעִי
מִקְרָא־קֹדֶשׁ יִהְיֶה לָכֶם כָּל־מְלֶאכֶת עֲבֹדָה לֹא
תַעֲשׂוּ: ס 26וּבְיוֹם הַבִּכּוּרִים בְּהַקְרִיבְכֶם מִנְחָה
חֲדָשָׁה לַיהוָה בְּשָׁבֻעֹתֵיכֶם מִקְרָא־קֹדֶשׁ יִהְיֶה לָכֶם
כָּל־מְלֶאכֶת עֲבֹדָה לֹא תַעֲשׂוּ: 27וְהִקְרַבְתֶּם עוֹלָה
לְרֵיחַ נִיחֹחַ לַיהוָה פָּרִים בְּנֵי־בָקָר שְׁנַיִם אַיִל
אֶחָד שִׁבְעָה כְבָשִׂים בְּנֵי שָׁנָה: 28וּמִנְחָתָם סֹלֶת
בְּלוּלָה בַשֶּׁמֶן שְׁלֹשָׁה עֶשְׂרֹנִים לַפָּר הָאֶחָד שְׁנֵי
עֶשְׂרֹנִים לָאַיִל הָאֶחָד: 29עִשָּׂרוֹן עִשָּׂרוֹן לַכֶּבֶשׂ
הָאֶחָד לְשִׁבְעַת הַכְּבָשִׂים: 30שְׂעִיר עִזִּים אֶחָד
לְכַפֵּר עֲלֵיכֶם: 31מִלְּבַד עֹלַת הַתָּמִיד וּמִנְחָתוֹ

offering—they shall be unblemished for you—and their libations.

29 [1]"And in the seventh month on the first of the month you shall have a holy assembly. You shall not do any act of work. You shall have a day of horn-blasting. [2]And you shall do a burnt offering for a pleasant smell for YHWH: one bull of the cattle, one ram, seven unblemished one-year-old lambs, [3]and their grain offering, fine flour mixed with oil, three tenths for a bull, two tenths for a ram, [4]and one tenth for each lamb, for the seven lambs, [5]and one goat for a sin offering to make atonement over you, [6]aside from the burnt offering of the new month and its grain offering and the continual burnt offering and its grain offering and their libations as required, for a pleasant smell, an offering by fire to YHWH.

[7]"And on the tenth of this seventh month you shall have a holy assembly. And you shall degrade yourselves. You shall not do any act of work. [8]And you shall bring forward a burnt offering to YHWH for a pleasant smell: you shall have one bull of the cattle, one ram, seven unblemished one-year-old lambs, [9]and their grain offering, fine flour mixed with oil, three tenths for a bull, two tenths for one ram, [10]one tenth for each lamb, for the seven lambs, [11]one goat for a sin offering, aside from the sin offering of atonement and the continual burnt offering and its grain offering and their libations.

[12]"And on the fifteenth day of the seventh month you shall have a holy assembly. You shall not do any act of work. And you shall celebrate a holiday for YHWH for seven days. [13]And you shall bring forward a burnt offering, an offering by fire for a pleasant smell to YHWH: thirteen bulls of the cattle, two rams, fourteen one-year-

תַּעֲשׂוּ תְּמִימִ֥ם יִֽהְיוּ־לָכֶ֖ם וְנִסְכֵּיהֶֽם: פ
29 ¹וּבַחֹ֨דֶשׁ הַשְּׁבִיעִ֜י בְּאֶחָ֣ד לַחֹ֗דֶשׁ מִֽקְרָא־קֹ֙דֶשׁ֙ יִהְיֶ֣ה לָכֶ֔ם כָּל־מְלֶ֥אכֶת עֲבֹדָ֖ה לֹ֣א תַעֲשׂ֑וּ י֥וֹם תְּרוּעָ֖ה יִהְיֶ֥ה לָכֶֽם: ²וַעֲשִׂיתֶ֨ם עֹלָ֜ה לְרֵ֤יחַ נִיחֹ֙חַ֙ לַֽיהֹוָ֔ה פַּ֧ר בֶּן־בָּקָ֛ר אֶחָ֖ד אַ֣יִל אֶחָ֑ד כְּבָשִׂ֧ים בְּנֵֽי־שָׁנָ֛ה שִׁבְעָ֖ה תְּמִימִֽם: ³וּמִנְחָתָ֗ם סֹ֤לֶת בְּלוּלָ֣ה בַשֶּׁ֔מֶן שְׁלֹשָׁ֣ה עֶשְׂרֹנִ֗ים לַפָּ֛ר שְׁנֵ֥י עֶשְׂרֹנִ֖ים לָאָֽיִל: ⁴וְעִשָּׂר֣וֹן אֶחָ֔ד לַכֶּ֖בֶשׂ הָאֶחָ֑ד לְשִׁבְעַ֖ת הַכְּבָשִֽׂים: ⁵וּשְׂעִיר־עִזִּ֥ים אֶחָ֖ד חַטָּ֑את לְכַפֵּ֖ר עֲלֵיכֶֽם: ⁶מִלְּבַד֩ עֹלַ֨ת הַחֹ֜דֶשׁ וּמִנְחָתָ֗הּ וְעֹלַ֤ת הַתָּמִיד֙ וּמִנְחָתָ֔הּ וְנִסְכֵּיהֶ֖ם כְּמִשְׁפָּטָ֑ם לְרֵ֣יחַ נִיחֹ֔חַ אִשֶּׁ֖ה לַֽיהֹוָֽה: ס ⁷וּבֶעָשׂ֜וֹר לַחֹ֣דֶשׁ הַשְּׁבִיעִ֣י הַזֶּ֗ה מִֽקְרָא־קֹ֙דֶשׁ֙ יִהְיֶ֣ה לָכֶ֔ם וְעִנִּיתֶ֖ם אֶת־נַפְשֹֽׁתֵיכֶ֑ם כָּל־מְלָאכָ֖ה לֹ֥א תַעֲשֽׂוּ: ⁸וְהִקְרַבְתֶּ֨ם עֹלָ֤ה לַֽיהֹוָה֙ רֵ֣יחַ נִיחֹ֔חַ פַּ֧ר בֶּן־בָּקָ֛ר אֶחָ֖ד אַ֣יִל אֶחָ֑ד כְּבָשִׂ֤ים בְּנֵֽי־שָׁנָה֙ שִׁבְעָ֔ה תְּמִימִ֖ם יִהְי֥וּ לָכֶֽם: ⁹וּמִנְחָתָ֗ם סֹ֤לֶת בְּלוּלָ֣ה בַשֶּׁ֔מֶן שְׁלֹשָׁ֣ה עֶשְׂרֹנִים֙ לַפָּ֔ר שְׁנֵי֙ עֶשְׂרֹנִ֔ים לָאַ֖יִל הָאֶחָֽד: ¹⁰עִשָּׂרוֹן֙ עִשָּׂר֔וֹן לַכֶּ֖בֶשׂ הָאֶחָ֑ד לְשִׁבְעַ֖ת הַכְּבָשִֽׂים: ¹¹שְׂעִיר־עִזִּ֥ים אֶחָ֖ד חַטָּ֑את מִלְּבַ֞ד חַטַּ֤את הַכִּפֻּרִים֙ וְעֹלַ֣ת הַתָּמִ֔יד וּמִנְחָתָ֖הּ וְנִסְכֵּיהֶֽם: פ ¹²וּבַחֲמִשָּׁה֩ עָשָׂ֨ר י֜וֹם לַחֹ֣דֶשׁ הַשְּׁבִיעִ֗י מִֽקְרָא־קֹ֙דֶשׁ֙ יִהְיֶ֣ה לָכֶ֔ם כָּל־מְלֶ֥אכֶת עֲבֹדָ֖ה לֹ֣א תַעֲשׂ֑וּ וְחַגֹּתֶ֥ם חַ֛ג לַֽיהֹוָ֖ה שִׁבְעַ֥ת יָמִֽים: ¹³וְהִקְרַבְתֶּ֨ם עֹלָ֜ה אִשֵּׁ֨ה רֵ֤יחַ נִיחֹ֙חַ֙ לַֽיהֹוָ֔ה פָּרִ֧ים בְּנֵֽי־בָקָ֛ר שְׁלֹשָׁ֥ה עָשָׂ֖ר אֵילִ֣ם שְׁנָ֑יִם כְּבָשִׂ֧ים

29:1. **seventh month on the first of the month**. This is the holiday that later came to be known as Rosh Hashanah, the New Year. It is never called by that name in the Torah, where it is rather counted as the seventh month.

29:7. **on the tenth of this seventh month**. This is the Day of Atonement, Yom Kippur.

old lambs. They shall be unblemished. 14And their grain offering shall be fine flour mixed with oil, three tenths for each bull, for thirteen bulls, two tenths for each ram, for two rams, 15and one tenth for each lamb, for fourteen lambs, 16and one goat for a sin offering, aside from the continual burnt offering, its grain offering, and its libation.

17"And on the second day: twelve bulls of the cattle, two rams, fourteen unblemished one-year-old lambs 18and their grain offering and their libations for the bulls, for the rams, and for the lambs by their number as required, 19and one goat for a sin offering, aside from the continual burnt offering and its grain offering and their libations.

20"And on the third day: eleven bulls, two rams, fourteen unblemished one-year-old lambs 21and their grain offering and their libations for the bulls, for the rams, and for the lambs by their number as required, 22and one goat for a sin offering, aside from the continual burnt offering and its grain offering and its libation.

23"And on the fourth day: ten bulls, two rams, fourteen unblemished one-year-old lambs, 24their grain offering and their libations for the bulls, for the rams, and for the lambs by their number as required, 25and one goat for a sin offering, aside from the continual burnt offering, its grain offering, and its libation.

26"And on the fifth day: nine bulls, two rams, fourteen unblemished one-year-old lambs 27and their grain offering and their libations for the bulls, for the rams, and for the lambs by their number as required, 28and one goat for a sin offering, aside from the continual burnt offering and its grain offering and its libation.

29"And on the sixth day: eight bulls, two rams, fourteen unblemished one-year-old lambs 30and their grain offering and their libations for the bulls, for the rams, and for the lambs by their number as required, 31and one goat for a sin offering, aside from the continual burnt offering, its grain offering, and its libations.

14וּמִנְחָתָם בְּנֵי־שָׁנָה אַרְבָּעָה עָשָׂר תְּמִימִם יִהְיוּ: סֹלֶת בְּלוּלָה בַשֶּׁמֶן שְׁלֹשָׁה עֶשְׂרֹנִים לַפָּר הָאֶחָד לִשְׁלֹשָׁה עָשָׂר פָּרִים שְׁנֵי עֶשְׂרֹנִים לָאַיִל הָאֶחָד לִשְׁנֵי הָאֵילִם: 15וְעִשָּׂרוֹן עִשָּׂרוֹן לַכֶּבֶשׂ הָאֶחָד לְאַרְבָּעָה עָשָׂר כְּבָשִׂים: 16וּשְׂעִיר־עִזִּים אֶחָד חַטָּאת מִלְּבַד עֹלַת הַתָּמִיד מִנְחָתָהּ וְנִסְכָּהּ: ס

17וּבַיּוֹם הַשֵּׁנִי פָּרִים בְּנֵי־בָקָר שְׁנֵים עָשָׂר אֵילִם שְׁנָיִם כְּבָשִׂים בְּנֵי־שָׁנָה אַרְבָּעָה עָשָׂר תְּמִימִם: 18וּמִנְחָתָם וְנִסְכֵּיהֶם לַפָּרִים לָאֵילִם וְלַכְּבָשִׂים בְּמִסְפָּרָם כַּמִּשְׁפָּט: 19וּשְׂעִיר־עִזִּים אֶחָד חַטָּאת מִלְּבַד עֹלַת הַתָּמִיד וּמִנְחָתָהּ וְנִסְכֵּיהֶם: ס

20וּבַיּוֹם הַשְּׁלִישִׁי פָּרִים עַשְׁתֵּי־עָשָׂר אֵילִם שְׁנָיִם כְּבָשִׂים בְּנֵי־שָׁנָה אַרְבָּעָה עָשָׂר תְּמִימִם: 21וּמִנְחָתָם וְנִסְכֵּיהֶם לַפָּרִים לָאֵילִם וְלַכְּבָשִׂים בְּמִסְפָּרָם כַּמִּשְׁפָּט: 22וּשְׂעִיר חַטָּאת אֶחָד מִלְּבַד עֹלַת הַתָּמִיד וּמִנְחָתָהּ וְנִסְכָּהּ: ס 23וּבַיּוֹם הָרְבִיעִי פָּרִים עֲשָׂרָה אֵילִם שְׁנָיִם כְּבָשִׂים בְּנֵי־שָׁנָה אַרְבָּעָה עָשָׂר תְּמִימִם: 24מִנְחָתָם וְנִסְכֵּיהֶם לַפָּרִים לָאֵילִם וְלַכְּבָשִׂים בְּמִסְפָּרָם כַּמִּשְׁפָּט: 25וּשְׂעִיר־עִזִּים אֶחָד חַטָּאת מִלְּבַד עֹלַת הַתָּמִיד מִנְחָתָהּ וְנִסְכָּהּ: ס 26וּבַיּוֹם הַחֲמִישִׁי פָּרִים תִּשְׁעָה אֵילִם שְׁנָיִם כְּבָשִׂים בְּנֵי־שָׁנָה אַרְבָּעָה עָשָׂר תְּמִימִם: 27וּמִנְחָתָם וְנִסְכֵּיהֶם לַפָּרִים לָאֵילִם וְלַכְּבָשִׂים בְּמִסְפָּרָם כַּמִּשְׁפָּט: 28וּשְׂעִיר חַטָּאת אֶחָד מִלְּבַד עֹלַת הַתָּמִיד וּמִנְחָתָהּ וְנִסְכָּהּ: ס 29וּבַיּוֹם הַשִּׁשִּׁי פָּרִים שְׁמֹנָה אֵילִם שְׁנָיִם כְּבָשִׂים בְּנֵי־שָׁנָה אַרְבָּעָה עָשָׂר תְּמִימִם: 30וּמִנְחָתָם וְנִסְכֵּיהֶם לַפָּרִים לָאֵילִם וְלַכְּבָשִׂים בְּמִסְפָּרָם כַּמִּשְׁפָּט: 31וּשְׂעִיר חַטָּאת אֶחָד מִלְּבַד עֹלַת הַתָּמִיד מִנְחָתָהּ וּנְסָכֶיהָ: פ

32"And on the seventh day: seven bulls, two rams, fourteen unblemished one-year-old lambs 33and their grain offering and their libations for the bulls, for the rams, and for the lambs by their number according to their requirement, 34and one goat for a sin offering, aside from the continual burnt offering, its grain offering, and its libation.

35"On the eighth day you shall have a convocation. You shall not do any act of work. 36And you shall bring forward a burnt offering, an offering by fire, a pleasant smell to YHWH: one bull, one ram, seven unblemished one-year-old lambs, 37their grain offering and their libations for the bull, for the ram, and for the lambs by their number as required, 38and one goat for a sin offering, aside from the continual burnt offering and its grain offering and its libation.

39"You shall do these for YHWH at your appointed times, aside from your vows and your contributions for your burnt offerings and for your grain offerings and for your libations and for your peace offerings."

30 ¹And Moses said it to the children of Israel, according to everything that YHWH commanded Moses.

TRIBES

²And Moses spoke to the heads of the tribes of the children of Israel, saying, "This is the thing that YHWH commanded: ³A man who will make a vow to YHWH or has sworn an oath to make a restriction on himself shall not desecrate his word. He shall do it according to everything that comes out of his mouth.

⁴"And a woman who will make a vow to YHWH and made a restriction in her father's house in her youth, ⁵and her father hears her vow and her restriction that she made on herself, and her father keeps quiet to her, then all her vows shall stand, and every restriction that she

32וּבַיּוֹם הַשְּׁבִיעִי פָּרִים שִׁבְעָה אֵילִם שְׁנָיִם כְּבָשִׂים בְּנֵי־שָׁנָה אַרְבָּעָה עָשָׂר תְּמִימִם: 33וּמִנְחָתָם וְנִסְכֵּהֶם לַפָּרִים לָאֵילִם וְלַכְּבָשִׂים בְּמִסְפָּרָם כַּמִּשְׁפָּט: 34וּשְׂעִיר חַטָּאת אֶחָד מִלְּבַד עֹלַת הַתָּמִיד מִנְחָתָהּ וְנִסְכָּהּ: פ 35בַּיּוֹם הַשְּׁמִינִי עֲצֶרֶת תִּהְיֶה לָכֶם כָּל־מְלֶאכֶת עֲבֹדָה לֹא תַעֲשׂוּ: 36וְהִקְרַבְתֶּם עֹלָה אִשֵּׁה רֵיחַ נִיחֹחַ לַיהוָה פַּר אֶחָד אַיִל אֶחָד כְּבָשִׂים בְּנֵי־שָׁנָה שִׁבְעָה תְּמִימִם: 37מִנְחָתָם וְנִסְכֵּיהֶם לַפָּר לָאַיִל וְלַכְּבָשִׂים בְּמִסְפָּרָם כַּמִּשְׁפָּט: 38וּשְׂעִיר חַטָּאת אֶחָד מִלְּבַד עֹלַת הַתָּמִיד וּמִנְחָתָהּ וְנִסְכָּהּ: 39אֵלֶּה תַּעֲשׂוּ לַיהוָה בְּמוֹעֲדֵיכֶם לְבַד מִנִּדְרֵיכֶם וְנִדְבֹתֵיכֶם לְעֹלֹתֵיכֶם וּלְמִנְחֹתֵיכֶם וּלְנִסְכֵּיכֶם וּלְשַׁלְמֵיכֶם: 30 ¹וַיֹּאמֶר מֹשֶׁה אֶל־בְּנֵי יִשְׂרָאֵל כְּכֹל אֲשֶׁר־צִוָּה יְהוָה אֶת־מֹשֶׁה: פ

מטות

²וַיְדַבֵּר מֹשֶׁה אֶל־רָאשֵׁי הַמַּטּוֹת לִבְנֵי יִשְׂרָאֵל לֵאמֹר זֶה הַדָּבָר אֲשֶׁר צִוָּה יְהוָה: ³אִישׁ כִּי־יִדֹּר נֶדֶר לַיהוָה אוֹ־הִשָּׁבַע שְׁבֻעָה לֶאְסֹר אִסָּר עַל־נַפְשׁוֹ לֹא יַחֵל דְּבָרוֹ כְּכָל־הַיֹּצֵא מִפִּיו יַעֲשֶׂה: ⁴וְאִשָּׁה כִּי־תִדֹּר נֶדֶר לַיהוָה וְאָסְרָה אִסָּר בְּבֵית אָבִיהָ בִּנְעֻרֶיהָ: ⁵וְשָׁמַע אָבִיהָ אֶת־נִדְרָהּ וֶאֱסָרָהּ אֲשֶׁר אָסְרָה עַל־נַפְשָׁהּ וְהֶחֱרִישׁ לָהּ אָבִיהָ וְקָמוּ כָּל־נְדָרֶיהָ וְכָל־אִסָּר אֲשֶׁר־אָסְרָה עַל־נַפְשָׁהּ

made on herself shall stand. ⁶But if her father held her back on the day he heard all her vows and her restrictions that she made on herself, it will not stand. And YHWH will forgive her because her father held her back.

⁷"And if she will have a husband while her vows or the thing she let out of her lips with which she restricted herself are on her, ⁸and her husband hears and keeps quiet on the day he heard it, then her vows will stand, and her restrictions that she made on herself will stand. ⁹But if, on the day her husband hears it, he will hold her back and will break her vow that is on her and what was let out of her lips by which she restricted herself, then YHWH will forgive her.

¹⁰"And a widow's or divorced woman's vow, everything by which she has restricted herself, shall stand regarding her.

¹¹"And if she vowed or made a restriction on herself by an oath at her husband's house, ¹²and her husband heard it and kept quiet to her—he did not hold her back—then all her vows shall stand, and every restriction that she made on herself shall stand. ¹³But if her husband broke them on the day he heard all that came out of her lips for her vows and for restricting herself, it shall not stand. Her husband had broken them, and YHWH will forgive her. ¹⁴Every vow and every oath of restriction to degrade oneself: her husband shall make it stand, and her husband shall break it. ¹⁵And if her husband will keep *quiet* in regard to her from that day to the next, then he has made all her vows and all her restrictions that are on her stand. He has made them stand because he kept quiet to her on the day he heard it. ¹⁶And if he will *break* them after he has heard them, then he shall bear her crime."

¹⁷These are the laws that YHWH commanded Moses between a man and his wife, between a

יָקֽוּם׃ ⁶וְאִם־הֵנִ֨יא אָבִ֣יהָ אֹתָהּ֮ בְּי֣וֹם שָׁמְעוֹ֒ כָּל־
נְדָרֶ֗יהָ וֶֽאֱסָרֶ֛יהָ אֲשֶׁר־אָסְרָ֥ה עַל־נַפְשָׁ֖הּ לֹ֣א יָק֑וּם
וַֽיהוָה֙ יִֽסְלַח־לָ֔הּ כִּֽי־הֵנִ֥יא אָבִ֖יהָ אֹתָֽהּ׃ ⁷וְאִם־הָי֤וֹ
תִֽהְיֶה֙ לְאִ֔ישׁ וּנְדָרֶ֖יהָ עָלֶ֑יהָ א֚וֹ מִבְטָ֣א שְׂפָתֶ֔יהָ אֲשֶׁ֥ר
אָסְרָ֖ה עַל־נַפְשָֽׁהּ׃ ⁸וְשָׁמַ֤ע אִישָׁהּ֙ בְּי֣וֹם שָׁמְע֔וֹ
וְהֶחֱרִ֖ישׁ לָ֑הּ וְקָ֣מוּ נְדָרֶ֗יהָ וֶֽאֱסָרֶ֛הָ אֲשֶׁר־אָסְרָ֥ה
עַל־נַפְשָׁ֖הּ יָקֻֽמוּ׃ ⁹וְ֠אִם בְּי֨וֹם שְׁמֹ֣עַ אִישָׁהּ֮ יָנִ֣יא
אוֹתָהּ֒ וְהֵפֵ֗ר אֶת־נִדְרָהּ֙ אֲשֶׁ֣ר עָלֶ֔יהָ וְאֵת֙ מִבְטָ֣א
שְׂפָתֶ֔יהָ אֲשֶׁ֥ר אָסְרָ֖ה עַל־נַפְשָׁ֑הּ וַֽיהוָ֖ה יִֽסְלַֽח־לָֽהּ׃
¹⁰וְנֵ֥דֶר אַלְמָנָ֖ה וּגְרוּשָׁ֑ה כֹּ֛ל אֲשֶׁר־אָסְרָ֥ה עַל־נַפְשָׁ֖הּ
יָק֥וּם עָלֶֽיהָ׃ ¹¹וְאִם־בֵּ֥ית אִישָׁ֖הּ נָדָ֑רָה אֽוֹ־אָסְרָ֥ה
אִסָּ֛ר עַל־נַפְשָׁ֖הּ בִּשְׁבֻעָֽה׃ ¹²וְשָׁמַ֤ע אִישָׁהּ֙ וְהֶחֱרִ֣שׁ
לָ֔הּ לֹ֥א הֵנִ֖יא אֹתָ֑הּ וְקָ֙מוּ֙ כָּל־נְדָרֶ֔יהָ וְכָל־אִסָּ֛ר
אֲשֶׁר־אָסְרָ֥ה עַל־נַפְשָׁ֖הּ יָקֽוּם׃ ¹³וְאִם־הָפֵר֩ יָפֵ֨ר
אֹתָ֥ם ׀ אִישָׁהּ֮ בְּי֣וֹם שָׁמְעוֹ֒ כָּל־מוֹצָ֥א שְׂפָתֶ֛יהָ
לִנְדָרֶ֥יהָ וּלְאִסַּ֥ר נַפְשָׁ֖הּ לֹ֣א יָק֑וּם אִישָׁ֣הּ הֲפֵרָ֗ם
וַֽיהוָ֖ה יִֽסְלַֽח־לָֽהּ׃ ¹⁴כָּל־נֵ֥דֶר וְכָל־שְׁבֻעַ֖ת אִסָּ֑ר
לְעַנֹּ֣ת נָ֑פֶשׁ אִישָׁ֥הּ יְקִימֶ֖נּוּ וְאִישָׁ֥הּ יְפֵרֶֽנּוּ׃ ¹⁵וְאִם־
הַחֲרֵשׁ֩ יַחֲרִ֨ישׁ לָ֥הּ אִישָׁהּ֮ מִיּ֣וֹם אֶל־יוֹם֒ וְהֵקִים֙ אֶת־
כָּל־נְדָרֶ֔יהָ א֥וֹ אֶת־כָּל־אֱסָרֶ֖יהָ אֲשֶׁ֣ר עָלֶ֑יהָ הֵקִ֣ים
אֹתָ֔ם כִּֽי־הֶחֱרִ֥שׁ לָ֖הּ בְּי֥וֹם שָׁמְעֽוֹ׃ ¹⁶וְאִם־הָפֵ֥ר יָפֵ֛ר
אֹתָ֖ם אַחֲרֵ֣י שָׁמְע֑וֹ וְנָשָׂ֖א אֶת־עֲוֺנָֽהּ׃ ¹⁷אֵ֣לֶּה הַֽחֻקִּ֗ים
אֲשֶׁ֨ר צִוָּ֤ה יְהוָה֙ אֶת־מֹשֶׁ֔ה בֵּ֥ין אִ֖ישׁ לְאִשְׁתּ֑וֹ בֵּֽין־אָ֕ב

30:16. he shall bear her crime. Having power over another person also means taking responsibility for that person's actions. If a man causes his wife to violate a vow she made, then it is he who must live with the consequences.

30:17. between a man and his wife, between a father and his daughter. This law,

father and his daughter in her youth at her father's house.

31 ¹And YHWH spoke to Moses, saying, ²"Get revenge for the children of Israel from the Midianites. After that you'll be gathered to your people."

³And Moses spoke to the people, saying, "Let people from you be equipped for the army, so they'll be against Midian to put YHWH's revenge in Midian. ⁴You shall send a thousand per tribe, a thousand per tribe, for all Israel's tribes, to the army."

⁵And, from Israel's thousands, a thousand per tribe were delivered, twelve thousand equipped for the army. ⁶And Moses sent them, a thousand per tribe, to the army; them and Phinehas son of Eleazar, the priest, to the army, with the equipment of the Holy and the trumpets for blasting in his hand. ⁷And they made war on Midian as YHWH had commanded Moses. And they killed every male. ⁸And they killed the kings of Midian—Evi and Rekem and Zur and Hur and Reba, the five kings of Midian—over their corpses. And they killed Balaam son of Beor by the sword.

לְבִתּוֹ בִּנְעֻרֶיהָ בֵּית אָבִיהָ: פ

31 ¹וַיְדַבֵּר יְהוָה אֶל־מֹשֶׁה לֵּאמֹר: ²נְקֹם נִקְמַת בְּנֵי יִשְׂרָאֵל מֵאֵת הַמִּדְיָנִים אַחַר תֵּאָסֵף אֶל־עַמֶּיךָ: ³וַיְדַבֵּר מֹשֶׁה אֶל־הָעָם לֵאמֹר הֵחָלְצוּ מֵאִתְּכֶם אֲנָשִׁים לַצָּבָא וְיִהְיוּ עַל־מִדְיָן לָתֵת נִקְמַת־יְהוָה בְּמִדְיָן: ⁴אֶלֶף לַמַּטֶּה אֶלֶף לַמַּטֶּה לְכֹל מַטּוֹת יִשְׂרָאֵל תִּשְׁלְחוּ לַצָּבָא: ⁵וַיִּמָּסְרוּ מֵאַלְפֵי יִשְׂרָאֵל אֶלֶף לַמַּטֶּה שְׁנֵים־עָשָׂר אֶלֶף חֲלוּצֵי צָבָא: ⁶וַיִּשְׁלַח אֹתָם מֹשֶׁה אֶלֶף לַמַּטֶּה לַצָּבָא אֹתָם וְאֶת־פִּינְחָס בֶּן־אֶלְעָזָר הַכֹּהֵן לַצָּבָא וּכְלֵי הַקֹּדֶשׁ וַחֲצֹצְרוֹת הַתְּרוּעָה בְּיָדוֹ: ⁷וַיִּצְבְּאוּ עַל־מִדְיָן כַּאֲשֶׁר צִוָּה יְהוָה אֶת־מֹשֶׁה וַיַּהַרְגוּ כָּל־זָכָר: ⁸וְאֶת־מַלְכֵי מִדְיָן הָרְגוּ עַל־חַלְלֵיהֶם אֶת־אֱוִי וְאֶת־רֶקֶם וְאֶת־צוּר וְאֶת־חוּר וְאֶת־רֶבַע חֲמֵשֶׁת מַלְכֵי מִדְיָן וְאֵת בִּלְעָם בֶּן־בְּעוֹר הָרְגוּ בֶּחָרֶב:

---

like several others in the Torah, stands at a juncture in the development of the balance between women and men. On one hand, it accepts the fact that men are in a position of such power over women that they can prevent their daughters and wives from keeping vows that they have made to their God—and it gives this power the force of law. But, on the other hand, it places a tremendous burden of responsibility on the men. If they dare to prevent their daughters and wives from keeping these vows, they bear the guilt themselves for whatever comes of it.

31:3. **YHWH's revenge**. God had said "*Israel's* revenge [revenge for the children of Israel]" (31:2), but Moses tells the people to get *YHWH's* revenge. Perhaps this is because the Israelites willingly participated in the matter of Baal Peor, and so in their minds there is no reason for revenge; therefore Moses tells them that it is for God. But the deity sees the event at Baal Peor as an injury to the people, not to God.

31:8. **they killed Balaam**. This is a shock. Balaam has been pictured as a prophet who faithfully pronounces YHWH's words, who blesses Israel and thus offends the Moabite king who hires him. Why is he killed? Moses relates a few verses later that the Midianite women who seduced the Israelites at Baal Peor did so at Balaam's direction: "Here, they came to bring about a breach against YHWH by the children of Israel, at Balaam's word, over the matter of Peor" (31:16). But there is no indication of why

9And the children of Israel took the women of Midian and their infants prisoner, and they despoiled all their animals and all their livestock and all their wealth. 10And they burned all their cities with their homes and all their encampments in fire. 11And they took all the spoil and all the prey, human and animal. 12And they brought the prisoners and the prey and the spoil to Moses and to Eleazar, the priest, and to the congregation of the children of Israel, to the camp, to the plains of Moab, which is by the Jordan toward Jericho.

13And Moses and Eleazar, the priest, and all the congregation's chieftains went out to them, outside the camp. 14And Moses was angry at the officers of the army, the chiefs of thousands and the chiefs of hundreds who were coming from the army of the war. 15And Moses said to them, "Did you keep every female alive?! 16Here, they came to bring about a breach against YHWH by the children of Israel, at Balaam's word, over the matter of Peor, so there was the plague in

9וַיִּשְׁבּוּ בְנֵי־יִשְׂרָאֵל אֶת־נְשֵׁי מִדְיָן וְאֶת־טַפָּם וְאֵת כָּל־בְּהֶמְתָּם וְאֶת־כָּל־מִקְנֵהֶם וְאֶת־כָּל־חֵילָם בָּזָזוּ: 10וְאֵת כָּל־עָרֵיהֶם בְּמוֹשְׁבֹתָם וְאֵת כָּל־טִירֹתָם שָׂרְפוּ בָּאֵשׁ: 11וַיִּקְחוּ אֶת־כָּל־הַשָּׁלָל וְאֵת כָּל־הַמַּלְקוֹחַ בָּאָדָם וּבַבְּהֵמָה: 12וַיָּבִאוּ אֶל־מֹשֶׁה וְאֶל־אֶלְעָזָר הַכֹּהֵן וְאֶל־עֲדַת בְּנֵי־יִשְׂרָאֵל אֶת־הַשְּׁבִי וְאֶת־הַמַּלְקוֹחַ וְאֶת־הַשָּׁלָל אֶל־הַמַּחֲנֶה אֶל־עַרְבֹת מוֹאָב אֲשֶׁר עַל־יַרְדֵּן יְרֵחוֹ: ס 13וַיֵּצְאוּ מֹשֶׁה וְאֶלְעָזָר הַכֹּהֵן וְכָל־נְשִׂיאֵי הָעֵדָה לִקְרָאתָם אֶל־מִחוּץ לַמַּחֲנֶה: 14וַיִּקְצֹף מֹשֶׁה עַל פְּקוּדֵי הֶחָיִל שָׂרֵי הָאֲלָפִים וְשָׂרֵי הַמֵּאוֹת הַבָּאִים מִצְּבָא הַמִּלְחָמָה: 15וַיֹּאמֶר אֲלֵיהֶם מֹשֶׁה הַחִיִּיתֶם כָּל־נְקֵבָה: 16הֵן הֵנָּה הָיוּ לִבְנֵי יִשְׂרָאֵל בִּדְבַר בִּלְעָם לִמְסָר־מַעַל בַּיהוָה עַל־דְּבַר־פְּעוֹר וַתְּהִי הַמַּגֵּפָה

Balaam would have done that. The ambiguity prods us to imagine possibilities and conceive connections. One possibility is that he gives the advice to the Moabites and Midianites, thinking that it will do them no good, since he himself has prophesied God's words promising a bright future for Israel. Another is that he himself has no affection for Israel; he pronounces blessings for them because he is a true prophet and faithfully says what he is told, but he still acts on his own to injure them. These are mere speculations. The text only lets us know that human motives are complex. And so we should be circumspect in judging and admiring persons whom we think, by their words, to be great benefactors of humankind.

31:16. **plague.** The extraordinary severity of the command—to kill all males, even infants, and all females who have had sexual relations with men is due to the fact that this is about a *ritual* crime. The plague is the indication of this. Plague is a divine response to ritual crimes, such as trespass on the Holy (Num 8:19) and the events of the Korah rebellion and its aftermath (Num 17:11–12). The harshness of treatment for ritual crimes, including the execution of persons who had no evil intent (including babies in this case), has been one of the hardest elements of the Torah for people to comprehend in the past two millennia. Since the destruction of the last Temple, we have lost the feeling for holy zones and sacred boundaries. Whether we are better off or worse, the fact remains that we are mystified and horrified by the seeming barbarism of a massacre of women and children that Moses commands here. On the crucial distinction between treatment of ritual and ethical offenses, see the comments on Num 4:15; 16:32; 25:8.

YHWH's congregation! 17So now, kill every male among the infants, and kill every woman who has known a man for male intercourse. 18But all infants among the women who have not known a male's intercourse: keep alive. 19And you, camp outside the camp for seven days: everyone who killed a life and everyone who touched a corpse, do sin expiation on the third day and on the seventh day, you and your prisoners. 20And for every piece of clothing and every leather item and

בַּעֲדַת יְהֹוָה: 17וְעַתָּה הִרְגוּ כָל־זָכָר בַּטָּף וְכָל־
אִשָּׁה יֹדַעַת אִישׁ לְמִשְׁכַּב זָכָר הֲרֹגוּ: 18וְכֹל הַטַּף
בַּנָּשִׁים אֲשֶׁר לֹא־יָדְעוּ מִשְׁכַּב זָכָר הַחֲיוּ לָכֶם:
19וְאַתֶּם חֲנוּ מִחוּץ לַמַּחֲנֶה שִׁבְעַת יָמִים כֹּל הֹרֵג
נֶפֶשׁ וְכֹל ׀ נֹגֵעַ בֶּחָלָל תִּתְחַטְּאוּ בַּיּוֹם הַשְּׁלִישִׁי
וּבַיּוֹם הַשְּׁבִיעִי אַתֶּם וּשְׁבִיכֶם: 20וְכָל־בֶּגֶד וְכָל־

31:17. **kill every woman** . . . If Moses' anger over the fact that they have not killed the women and children is difficult to accept, how much more amazing is the fact that the women in question are Midianite—like Moses' wife! The command to attack the Midianites comes from God, and the text does not state what Moses' personal reaction is. He must order a war against his wife's people, with whom he once lived, whose priest was his father-in-law and adviser. He married a Midianite woman, but now he has all the other married Midianite women killed. The lack of any comment about Moses' thoughts and feelings here is the most powerful silence since the story of the near-sacrifice of Isaac, in which we were told nothing of Abraham's heart. The Torah's way is to leave these things unspoken, and thus to leave us to ponder them.

Remarkably, the fearful order to kill the women and children comes from Moses himself. The text does not say whether it originates from God. To conceive of Moses' thoughts, perhaps we must go back to the point of the Midianite seductions at Baal Peor and start with the question of what Moses might feel when he learns that women of his wife's people are seducing the Israelites into heresy: shock, embarrassment, betrayal, fury. What conversation can we imagine between Moses and Zipporah? What humiliation might Zipporah suffer from the Israelites in the aftermath of Baal Peor? How much are both Moses and Zipporah undermined? Moses' command to eliminate the Midianite women can be conceived of as coming from the depth of his outrage and pain.

Another point: The text never reports that Moses' order was carried out! There is a mention of retaining the virgin women as captives (31:35) but no mention of the execution of the women who have known men or of the male infants. It is possible to imagine that they are released or allowed to escape—and that Moses acquiesces in this. Alternatively, perhaps it is not reported simply because it is so horrible to describe.

31:19. **do sin expiation**. Moses is directing them to follow the procedure for persons who have had contact with the dead, which God had instructed him earlier (Num 19:11–13).

31:19. **on the third day and on the seventh day**. Based on the law in Num 19:12, the text here should say: "Do sin expiation on the third day, and on the seventh day be pure." The term for "be pure" may have been lost here by a scribe.

everything made from goats and every wood item you shall do expiation."

21And Eleazar, the priest, said to the men of the army who had come to the war, "This is the law of the instruction that YHWH commanded Moses: 22Just the gold and the silver, the bronze, the iron, the tin, and the lead, 23every thing that will go in fire, you shall pass through fire and purify. It shall be expiated from sin just in water of impurity. And everything that will not go in fire, you shall pass through water. 24And you shall wash your clothes on the seventh day, and you will be pure, and after that you shall come to the camp."

25And YHWH said to Moses, saying, 26"Add up the heads of the prey, the prisoners, human and animal, you and Eleazar, the priest, and the heads of the fathers of the congregation. 27And you shall split the prey between the warriors who went out to the army and all the congregation. 28And you shall levy a tax for YHWH from the men of war who went out to the army, one individual out of five hundred, from humans and from cattle and from asses and from sheep. 29You shall take from their half and you shall give to Eleazar, the priest, YHWH's donation. 30From the half of the children of Israel you shall take one share out of fifty, from humans, from cattle, from asses, and from sheep, from all the animals, and you shall give them to the Levites, who keep the watch of YHWH's Tabernacle."

31And Moses and Eleazar, the priest, did as YHWH commanded Moses. 32And the prey, over and above the spoil that the people of the army had taken, was: six hundred seventy-five thousand sheep 33and seventy-two thousand cattle 34and sixty-one thousand asses 35and human beings—from the women who had not known male intercourse—all the persons were thirty-two thousand. 36So the half, the portion of those who went out in the army was: the number of sheep was three hundred thirty-seven thousand

כְּלִי־עוֹר וְכָל־מַעֲשֵׂה עִזִּים וְכָל־כְּלִי־עֵץ תִּתְחַטָּאוּ:
21 ס וַיֹּאמֶר אֶלְעָזָר הַכֹּהֵן אֶל־אַנְשֵׁי הַצָּבָא הַבָּאִים לַמִּלְחָמָה זֹאת חֻקַּת הַתּוֹרָה אֲשֶׁר־צִוָּה יְהוָה אֶת־מֹשֶׁה: 22 אַךְ אֶת־הַזָּהָב וְאֶת־הַכָּסֶף אֶת־הַנְּחֹשֶׁת אֶת־הַבַּרְזֶל אֶת־הַבְּדִיל וְאֶת־הָעֹפָרֶת: 23 כָּל־דָּבָר אֲשֶׁר־יָבֹא בָאֵשׁ תַּעֲבִירוּ בָאֵשׁ וְטָהֵר אַךְ בְּמֵי נִדָּה יִתְחַטָּא וְכֹל אֲשֶׁר לֹא־יָבֹא בָּאֵשׁ תַּעֲבִירוּ בַמָּיִם: 24 וְכִבַּסְתֶּם בִּגְדֵיכֶם בַּיּוֹם הַשְּׁבִיעִי וּטְהַרְתֶּם וְאַחַר תָּבֹאוּ אֶל־הַמַּחֲנֶה: פ 25 וַיֹּאמֶר יְהוָה אֶל־מֹשֶׁה לֵּאמֹר: 26 שָׂא אֵת רֹאשׁ מַלְקוֹחַ הַשְּׁבִי בָּאָדָם וּבַבְּהֵמָה אַתָּה וְאֶלְעָזָר הַכֹּהֵן וְרָאשֵׁי אֲבוֹת הָעֵדָה: 27 וְחָצִיתָ אֶת־הַמַּלְקוֹחַ בֵּין תֹּפְשֵׂי הַמִּלְחָמָה הַיֹּצְאִים לַצָּבָא וּבֵין כָּל־הָעֵדָה: 28 וַהֲרֵמֹתָ מֶכֶס לַיהוָה מֵאֵת אַנְשֵׁי הַמִּלְחָמָה הַיֹּצְאִים לַצָּבָא אֶחָד נֶפֶשׁ מֵחֲמֵשׁ הַמֵּאוֹת מִן־הָאָדָם וּמִן־הַבָּקָר וּמִן־הַחֲמֹרִים וּמִן־הַצֹּאן: 29 מִמַּחֲצִיתָם תִּקָּחוּ וְנָתַתָּה לְאֶלְעָזָר הַכֹּהֵן תְּרוּמַת יְהוָה: 30 וּמִמַּחֲצִת בְּנֵי־יִשְׂרָאֵל תִּקַּח אֶחָד אָחֻז מִן־הַחֲמִשִּׁים מִן־הָאָדָם מִן־הַבָּקָר מִן־הַחֲמֹרִים וּמִן־הַצֹּאן מִכָּל־הַבְּהֵמָה וְנָתַתָּה אֹתָם לַלְוִיִּם שֹׁמְרֵי מִשְׁמֶרֶת מִשְׁכַּן יְהוָה: 31 וַיַּעַשׂ מֹשֶׁה וְאֶלְעָזָר הַכֹּהֵן כַּאֲשֶׁר צִוָּה יְהוָה אֶת־מֹשֶׁה: 32 וַיְהִי הַמַּלְקוֹחַ יֶתֶר הַבָּז אֲשֶׁר בָּזְזוּ עַם הַצָּבָא צֹאן שֵׁשׁ־מֵאוֹת אֶלֶף וְשִׁבְעִים אֶלֶף וַחֲמֵשֶׁת־אֲלָפִים: 33 וּבָקָר שְׁנַיִם וְשִׁבְעִים אָלֶף: 34 וַחֲמֹרִים אֶחָד וְשִׁשִּׁים אָלֶף: 35 וְנֶפֶשׁ אָדָם מִן־הַנָּשִׁים אֲשֶׁר לֹא־יָדְעוּ מִשְׁכַּב זָכָר כָּל־נֶפֶשׁ שְׁנַיִם וּשְׁלֹשִׁים אָלֶף: 36 וַתְּהִי הַמֶּחֱצָה חֵלֶק הַיֹּצְאִים בַּצָּבָא מִסְפַּר הַצֹּאן שְׁלֹשׁ־מֵאוֹת אֶלֶף וּשְׁלֹשִׁים אֶלֶף וְשִׁבְעַת אֲלָפִים וַחֲמֵשׁ מֵאוֹת:

31:23. **water of impurity.** See Num 19:9.

five hundred. ³⁷And the tax for YHWH from the sheep was six hundred seventy-five. ³⁸And the cattle were thirty-six thousand, and their tax for YHWH was seventy-two. ³⁹And asses were thirty thousand five hundred, and their tax for YHWH was sixty-one. ⁴⁰And human beings were sixteen thousand, and their tax for YHWH was thirty-two persons. ⁴¹And Moses gave the tax, a donation for YHWH, to Eleazar, the priest, as YHWH commanded Moses. ⁴²And of the half for the children of Israel, which Moses had split from the people who were serving in the army: ⁴³and the congregation's half of the sheep was three hundred thirty-seven thousand five hundred. ⁴⁴And the cattle were thirty-six thousand. ⁴⁵And asses were thirty thousand five hundred. ⁴⁶And human beings were sixteen thousand. ⁴⁷And Moses took from the half of the children of Israel one share out of fifty, from humans and from animals, and gave them to the Levites, who kept the watch of YHWH's Tabernacle, as YHWH commanded Moses.

⁴⁸And the officers who were over the thousands of the army came forward to Moses, the chiefs of the thousands and the chiefs of the hundreds. ⁴⁹And they said to Moses, "Your servants have added up the heads of the men of war who are in our hands, and not a man of them is lacking. ⁵⁰And we have made an offering for YHWH—whatever each man found: an item of gold, an armlet or bracelet, a ring, an earring, or an ornament—to make atonement for ourselves in front of YHWH." ⁵¹And Moses and Eleazar, the priest, took the gold from them, every item of handiwork. ⁵²And all the gold of the donation that they donated to YHWH was sixteen thousand seven hundred fifty shekels, from the chiefs of the thousands and from the chiefs of the hundreds. ⁵³The men of the army each had kept as spoil what was his. ⁵⁴And Moses and Eleazar, the priest, took the gold from the chiefs of the thousands and the hundreds and brought it to the Tent of Meeting, a commemoration for the children of Israel in front of YHWH.

³⁷וַיְהִ֣י הַמֶּ֗כֶס לַֽיהוָה֙ מִן־הַצֹּ֔אן שֵׁ֥שׁ מֵא֖וֹת חָמֵ֥שׁ וְשִׁבְעִֽים: ³⁸וְהַ֨בָּקָ֔ר שִׁשָּׁ֥ה וּשְׁלֹשִׁ֖ים אָ֑לֶף וּמִכְסָ֥ם לַֽיהוָ֖ה שְׁנַ֥יִם וְשִׁבְעִֽים: ³⁹וַחֲמֹרִ֕ים שְׁלֹשִׁ֥ים אֶ֖לֶף וַחֲמֵ֣שׁ מֵא֑וֹת וּמִכְסָ֥ם לַֽיהוָ֖ה אֶחָ֥ד וְשִׁשִּֽׁים: ⁴⁰וְנֶ֣פֶשׁ אָדָ֔ם שִׁשָּׁ֥ה עָשָׂ֖ר אָ֑לֶף וּמִכְסָם֙ לַֽיהוָ֔ה שְׁנַ֥יִם וּשְׁלֹשִׁ֖ים נָֽפֶשׁ: ⁴¹וַיִּתֵּ֣ן מֹשֶׁ֗ה אֶת־מֶ֙כֶס֙ תְּרוּמַ֣ת יְהוָ֔ה לְאֶלְעָזָ֖ר הַכֹּהֵ֑ן כַּאֲשֶׁ֛ר צִוָּ֥ה יְהוָ֖ה אֶת־מֹשֶֽׁה: ⁴²וּמִֽמַּחֲצִ֖ית בְּנֵ֣י יִשְׂרָאֵ֑ל אֲשֶׁר֙ חָצָ֣ה מֹשֶׁ֔ה מִן־הָאֲנָשִׁ֖ים הַצֹּבְאִֽים: ⁴³וַתְּהִ֛י מֶחֱצַ֥ת הָעֵדָ֖ה מִן־הַצֹּ֑אן שְׁלֹשׁ־מֵא֥וֹת אֶ֛לֶף וּשְׁלֹשִׁ֥ים אֶ֖לֶף שִׁבְעַ֣ת אֲלָפִ֑ים וַחֲמֵ֖שׁ מֵאֽוֹת: ⁴⁴וּבָקָ֕ר שִׁשָּׁ֥ה וּשְׁלֹשִׁ֖ים אָֽלֶף: ⁴⁵וַחֲמֹרִ֕ים שְׁלֹשִׁ֥ים אֶ֖לֶף וַחֲמֵ֥שׁ מֵאֽוֹת: ⁴⁶וְנֶ֣פֶשׁ אָדָ֔ם שִׁשָּׁ֥ה עָשָׂ֖ר אָֽלֶף: ⁴⁷וַיִּקַּ֨ח מֹשֶׁ֜ה מִמַּחֲצִ֣ת בְּנֵֽי־יִשְׂרָאֵ֗ל אֶת־הָֽאָחֻז֙ אֶחָ֣ד מִן־הַחֲמִשִּׁ֔ים מִן־הָאָדָ֖ם וּמִן־הַבְּהֵמָ֑ה וַיִּתֵּ֨ן אֹתָ֜ם לַלְוִיִּ֗ם שֹֽׁמְרֵי֙ מִשְׁמֶ֙רֶת֙ מִשְׁכַּ֣ן יְהוָ֔ה כַּאֲשֶׁ֛ר צִוָּ֥ה יְהוָ֖ה אֶת־מֹשֶֽׁה: ⁴⁸וַֽיִּקְרְבוּ֙ אֶל־מֹשֶׁ֔ה הַפְּקֻדִ֕ים אֲשֶׁ֖ר לְאַלְפֵ֣י הַצָּבָ֑א שָׂרֵ֥י הָאֲלָפִ֖ים וְשָׂרֵ֥י הַמֵּאֽוֹת: ⁴⁹וַיֹּֽאמְרוּ֙ אֶל־מֹשֶׁ֔ה עֲבָדֶ֣יךָ נָֽשְׂא֗וּ אֶת־רֹ֛אשׁ אַנְשֵׁ֥י הַמִּלְחָמָ֖ה אֲשֶׁ֣ר בְּיָדֵ֑נוּ וְלֹא־נִפְקַ֥ד מִמֶּ֖נּוּ אִֽישׁ: ⁵⁰וַנַּקְרֵ֞ב אֶת־קָרְבַּ֣ן יְהוָ֗ה אִישׁ֩ אֲשֶׁ֨ר מָצָ֤א כְלִֽי־זָהָב֙ אֶצְעָדָ֣ה וְצָמִ֔יד טַבַּ֖עַת עָגִ֣יל וְכוּמָ֑ז לְכַפֵּ֥ר עַל־נַפְשֹׁתֵ֖ינוּ לִפְנֵ֥י יְהוָֽה: ⁵¹וַיִּקַּ֨ח מֹשֶׁ֜ה וְאֶלְעָזָ֧ר הַכֹּהֵ֛ן אֶת־הַזָּהָ֖ב מֵֽאִתָּ֑ם כֹּ֖ל כְּלִ֥י מַעֲשֶֽׂה: ⁵²וַיְהִ֣י ׀ כָּל־זְהַ֣ב הַתְּרוּמָ֗ה אֲשֶׁ֤ר הֵרִ֙ימוּ֙ לַֽיהוָ֔ה שִׁשָּׁ֨ה עָשָׂ֥ר אֶ֛לֶף שְׁבַע־מֵא֥וֹת וַחֲמִשִּׁ֖ים שָׁ֑קֶל מֵאֵת֙ שָׂרֵ֣י הָאֲלָפִ֔ים וּמֵאֵ֖ת שָׂרֵ֥י הַמֵּאֽוֹת: ⁵³אַנְשֵׁי֙ הַצָּבָ֔א בָּזְז֖וּ אִ֥ישׁ לֽוֹ: ⁵⁴וַיִּקַּ֨ח מֹשֶׁ֜ה וְאֶלְעָזָ֣ר הַכֹּהֵ֗ן אֶת־הַזָּהָב֙ מֵאֵת֙ שָׂרֵ֣י הָֽאֲלָפִ֔ים וְהַמֵּא֑וֹת וַיָּבִ֤אוּ אֹתוֹ֙ אֶל־אֹ֣הֶל מוֹעֵ֔ד זִכָּר֥וֹן לִבְנֵֽי־יִשְׂרָאֵ֖ל לִפְנֵ֥י יְהוָֽה: פ

32

¹And the children of Reuben and the children of Gad had a great amount of livestock, very substantial. And they saw the land of Jazer and the land of Gilead, and here: the place was a place for livestock. ²And the children of Gad and the children of Reuben came and said to Moses and to Eleazar, the priest, and to the chieftains of the congregation, saying, ³"Ataroth and Dibon and Jazer and Nimrah and Heshbon and Elealeh and Sebam and Nebo and Beon, ⁴the land that YHWH struck in front of the congregation of Israel: it's livestock land, and your servants have livestock." ⁵And they said, "If we've found favor in your eyes, let this land be given to your servants for a possession. Don't have us cross the Jordan."

⁶And Moses said to the children of Gad and to the children of Reuben, "Will your brothers go to war while you sit here?! ⁷And why do you hold back the heart of the children of Israel from crossing to the land that YHWH has given them? ⁸That's what your fathers did when I sent them from Kadesh-barnea to see the land. ⁹And they went up to the Wadi Eshcol and saw the land, but they held back the heart of the children of Israel so as not to go to the land that YHWH had given them. ¹⁰And YHWH's anger flared on that day, and he swore saying, ¹¹'The people who came up from Egypt, from twenty years old and up, won't see the land that I swore to Abraham, to Isaac, and to Jacob, because they didn't go after me completely, ¹²except Caleb son of Jephunneh, the Kenizzite, and Joshua son of Nun because they went after YHWH completely.' ¹³And YHWH's anger flared at Israel, and he made them roam in the wilderness forty years, until the end of all the generation who were doing bad in YHWH's eyes. ¹⁴And, here, you've gotten up in your fathers' place, a group of sinning people, to add more onto YHWH's flaring anger at Israel. ¹⁵If you go back from behind Him, then He'll add more to leave them in the wilderness, and you'll have destroyed all of this people!"

32 ¹וּמִקְנֶ֣ה ׀ רַ֗ב הָיָ֞ה לִבְנֵ֧י רְאוּבֵ֛ן וְלִבְנֵי־גָ֖ד עָצ֣וּם מְאֹ֑ד וַיִּרְא֞וּ אֶת־אֶ֤רֶץ יַעְזֵר֙ וְאֶת־אֶ֣רֶץ גִּלְעָ֔ד וְהִנֵּ֥ה הַמָּק֖וֹם מְק֥וֹם מִקְנֶֽה׃ ²וַיָּבֹ֥אוּ בְנֵי־גָ֖ד וּבְנֵ֣י רְאוּבֵ֑ן וַיֹּאמְר֤וּ אֶל־מֹשֶׁה֙ וְאֶל־אֶלְעָזָ֣ר הַכֹּהֵ֔ן וְאֶל־נְשִׂיאֵ֥י הָעֵדָ֖ה לֵאמֹֽר׃ ³עֲטָר֤וֹת וְדִיבֹן֙ וְיַעְזֵ֣ר וְנִמְרָ֔ה וְחֶשְׁבּ֖וֹן וְאֶלְעָלֵ֑ה וּשְׂבָ֥ם וּנְב֖וֹ וּבְעֹֽן׃ ⁴הָאָ֗רֶץ אֲשֶׁ֨ר הִכָּ֤ה יְהוָה֙ לִפְנֵי֙ עֲדַ֣ת יִשְׂרָאֵ֔ל אֶ֥רֶץ מִקְנֶ֖ה הִ֑וא וְלַעֲבָדֶ֖יךָ מִקְנֶֽה׃ ס ⁵וַיֹּאמְר֗וּ אִם־מָצָ֤אנוּ חֵן֙ בְּעֵינֶ֔יךָ יֻתַּ֞ן אֶת־הָאָ֧רֶץ הַזֹּ֛את לַעֲבָדֶ֖יךָ לַאֲחֻזָּ֑ה אַל־תַּעֲבִרֵ֖נוּ אֶת־הַיַּרְדֵּֽן׃ ⁶וַיֹּ֣אמֶר מֹשֶׁ֔ה לִבְנֵי־גָ֖ד וְלִבְנֵ֣י רְאוּבֵ֑ן הַאַֽחֵיכֶ֗ם יָבֹ֨אוּ֙ לַמִּלְחָמָ֔ה וְאַתֶּ֖ם תֵּ֥שְׁבוּ פֹֽה׃ ⁷וְלָ֣מָּה תְנִיא֔וּן אֶת־לֵ֖ב בְּנֵ֣י יִשְׂרָאֵ֑ל מֵֽעֲבֹר֙ אֶל־הָאָ֔רֶץ אֲשֶׁר־נָתַ֥ן לָהֶ֖ם יְהוָֽה׃ ⁸כֹּ֤ה עָשׂוּ֙ אֲבֹ֣תֵיכֶ֔ם בְּשָׁלְחִ֥י אֹתָ֛ם מִקָּדֵ֥שׁ בַּרְנֵ֖עַ לִרְא֥וֹת אֶת־הָאָֽרֶץ׃ ⁹וַֽיַּעֲל֞וּ עַד־נַ֣חַל אֶשְׁכּ֗וֹל וַיִּרְאוּ֙ אֶת־הָאָ֔רֶץ וַיָּנִ֕יאוּ אֶת־לֵ֖ב בְּנֵ֣י יִשְׂרָאֵ֑ל לְבִלְתִּי־בֹא֙ אֶל־הָאָ֔רֶץ אֲשֶׁר־נָתַ֥ן לָהֶ֖ם יְהוָֽה׃ ¹⁰וַיִּֽחַר־אַ֥ף יְהוָ֖ה בַּיּ֣וֹם הַה֑וּא וַיִּשָּׁבַ֖ע לֵאמֹֽר׃ ¹¹אִם־יִרְא֨וּ הָאֲנָשִׁ֜ים הָעֹלִ֣ים מִמִּצְרַ֗יִם מִבֶּ֨ן עֶשְׂרִ֤ים שָׁנָה֙ וָמַ֔עְלָה אֵ֚ת הָאֲדָמָ֔ה אֲשֶׁ֥ר נִשְׁבַּ֛עְתִּי לְאַבְרָהָ֥ם לְיִצְחָ֖ק וּֽלְיַעֲקֹ֑ב כִּ֥י לֹא־מִלְא֖וּ אַחֲרָֽי׃ ¹²בִּלְתִּ֞י כָּלֵ֤ב בֶּן־יְפֻנֶּה֙ הַקְּנִזִּ֔י וִיהוֹשֻׁ֖עַ בִּן־נ֑וּן כִּ֥י מִלְא֖וּ אַחֲרֵ֥י יְהוָֽה׃ ¹³וַיִּֽחַר־אַ֤ף יְהוָה֙ בְּיִשְׂרָאֵ֔ל וַיְנִעֵם֙ בַּמִּדְבָּ֔ר אַרְבָּעִ֖ים שָׁנָ֑ה עַד־תֹּם֙ כָּל־הַדּ֔וֹר הָעֹשֶׂ֥ה הָרַ֖ע בְּעֵינֵ֥י יְהוָֽה׃ ¹⁴וְהִנֵּ֣ה קַמְתֶּ֗ם תַּ֚חַת אֲבֹ֣תֵיכֶ֔ם תַּרְבּ֖וּת אֲנָשִׁ֣ים חַטָּאִ֑ים לִסְפּ֣וֹת ע֗וֹד עַ֛ל חֲר֥וֹן אַף־יְהוָ֖ה אֶל־יִשְׂרָאֵֽל׃ ¹⁵כִּ֤י תְשׁוּבֻן֙ מֵאַ֣חֲרָ֔יו וְיָסַ֣ף ע֔וֹד לְהַנִּיח֖וֹ בַּמִּדְבָּ֑ר וְשִׁחַתֶּ֖ם לְכָל־

32:7 ק תְּנִיא֔וּן

16And they came over to him and said, "We'll build walls for our livestock here, and cities for our infants. 17And *we* shall be equipped, ready in front of the children of Israel until we've brought them to their place, and our infants will live in fortified cities because of the residents of the land. 18We won't go back to our houses until the children of Israel take possession, each of his legacy. 19Because we won't have a possession with them from the farther side of the Jordan, because our possession has come to us from the eastward side of the Jordan."

20And Moses said to them, "If you'll do this thing: if you'll get equipped for war in front of YHWH, 21and every one of you will cross the Jordan equipped in front of YHWH until He dispossesses his enemies in front of him, 22and the land will be subdued in front of YHWH, then, after that, you'll go back, and, from YHWH and from Israel, you'll be free, and this land will become yours for a possession in front of YHWH. 23But if you won't do this, here, you've sinned to YHWH, and know that your sin will find you. 24Build cities for your infants and fences for your flocks, and do what has come out of your mouths."

25And the children of Gad and the children of Reuben said to Moses, saying, "Your servants will do as my lord commands. 26Our infants, our women, our livestock, and all our animals will be there in the cities of Gilead. 27And your servants will cross, everyone equipped for the army, in front of YHWH for war as my lord speaks."

28And Moses commanded Eleazar, the priest, and Joshua son of Nun and the heads of the fathers of the tribes of the children of Israel for them. 29And Moses said to them, "If the children

הָעָם הַזֶּה: ס 16וַיִּגְּשׁוּ אֵלָיו וַיֹּאמְרוּ גִּדְרֹת צֹאן
נִבְנֶה לְמִקְנֵנוּ פֹּה וְעָרִים לְטַפֵּנוּ: 17וַאֲנַחְנוּ נֵחָלֵץ
חֻשִׁים לִפְנֵי בְּנֵי יִשְׂרָאֵל עַד אֲשֶׁר אִם־הֲבִיאֹנֻם
אֶל־מְקוֹמָם וְיָשַׁב טַפֵּנוּ בְּעָרֵי הַמִּבְצָר מִפְּנֵי יֹשְׁבֵי
הָאָרֶץ: 18לֹא נָשׁוּב אֶל־בָּתֵּינוּ עַד הִתְנַחֵל בְּנֵי
יִשְׂרָאֵל אִישׁ נַחֲלָתוֹ: 19כִּי לֹא נִנְחַל אִתָּם מֵעֵבֶר
לַיַּרְדֵּן וָהָלְאָה כִּי בָאָה נַחֲלָתֵנוּ אֵלֵינוּ מֵעֵבֶר
הַיַּרְדֵּן מִזְרָחָה: פ 20וַיֹּאמֶר אֲלֵיהֶם מֹשֶׁה אִם־
תַּעֲשׂוּן אֶת־הַדָּבָר הַזֶּה אִם־תֵּחָלְצוּ לִפְנֵי יְהוָה
לַמִּלְחָמָה: 21וְעָבַר לָכֶם כָּל־חָלוּץ אֶת־הַיַּרְדֵּן
לִפְנֵי יְהוָה עַד הוֹרִישׁוֹ אֶת־אֹיְבָיו מִפָּנָיו:
22וְנִכְבְּשָׁה הָאָרֶץ לִפְנֵי יְהוָה וְאַחַר תָּשֻׁבוּ וִהְיִיתֶם
נְקִיִּים מֵיהוָה וּמִיִּשְׂרָאֵל וְהָיְתָה הָאָרֶץ הַזֹּאת לָכֶם
לַאֲחֻזָּה לִפְנֵי יְהוָה: 23וְאִם־לֹא תַעֲשׂוּן כֵּן הִנֵּה
חֲטָאתֶם לַיהוָה וּדְעוּ חַטַּאתְכֶם אֲשֶׁר תִּמְצָא
אֶתְכֶם: 24בְּנוּ־לָכֶם עָרִים לְטַפְּכֶם וּגְדֵרֹת לְצֹנַאֲכֶם
וְהַיֹּצֵא מִפִּיכֶם תַּעֲשׂוּ: 25וַיֹּאמֶר בְּנֵי־גָד וּבְנֵי רְאוּבֵן
אֶל־מֹשֶׁה לֵאמֹר עֲבָדֶיךָ יַעֲשׂוּ כַּאֲשֶׁר אֲדֹנִי מְצַוֶּה:
26טַפֵּנוּ נָשֵׁינוּ מִקְנֵנוּ וְכָל־בְּהֶמְתֵּנוּ יִהְיוּ־שָׁם בְּעָרֵי
הַגִּלְעָד: 27וַעֲבָדֶיךָ יַעַבְרוּ כָּל־חֲלוּץ צָבָא לִפְנֵי
יְהוָה לַמִּלְחָמָה כַּאֲשֶׁר אֲדֹנִי דֹּבֵר: 28וַיְצַו לָהֶם
מֹשֶׁה אֵת אֶלְעָזָר הַכֹּהֵן וְאֵת יְהוֹשֻׁעַ בִּן־נוּן וְאֶת־
רָאשֵׁי אֲבוֹת הַמַּטּוֹת לִבְנֵי יִשְׂרָאֵל: 29וַיֹּאמֶר מֹשֶׁה

32:28. **Moses commanded Eleazar and Joshua** . . . Moses is now directing his successors to handle a matter that will not arise until after Moses himself is dead. This is the first indication that Moses has accepted the reality of his condemnation to die and never set foot in the promised land. So, even though this fact is never mentioned explicitly in this episode, it stands as a powerful background to what is going on in the foreground. And, at the same time, it is a lesson about the preparation of a successor—and the humble acceptance that one's own time of leadership must end and that

of Gad and the children of Reuben will cross the Jordan with you, everyone equipped for war, in front of YHWH, and the land will be subdued in front of you, then you shall give them the land of Gilead for a possession. ³⁰But if they will not cross equipped with you, then they will have possessions among you in the land of Canaan."

³¹And the children of Gad and the children of Reuben answered, saying, "What YHWH has spoken to your servants: we shall do so. ³²We'll cross equipped in front of YHWH to the land of Canaan while we'll have our legacy possession across the Jordan."

³³And Moses gave them, the children of Gad and the children of Reuben and half of the tribe of Manasseh son of Joseph, the kingdom of Sihon, king of the Amorites, and the kingdom of Og, king of Bashan, the land with its cities, with the borders of the land's cities all around. ³⁴And the children of Gad built Dibon and Ataroth and Aroer ³⁵and Atroth-shophan and Jazer and Jogbehah ³⁶and Beth-Nimrah and Beth-Haran, fortified cities and fences for flocks. ³⁷And the children of Reuben built Heshbon and Elealeh and Kiriathaim ³⁸and Nebo and Baal-meon—with changes of name—and Sibmah, and they called the names of the cities that they built by new names. ³⁹And the children of Machir son of Manasseh went to Gilead and captured it and dispossessed the Amorite who was in it. ⁴⁰And Moses gave Gilead to Machir son of Manasseh, and they lived in it. ⁴¹And Jair son of Manasseh went and captured their villages, and he called

אֲלֵהֶם אִם־יַעַבְרוּ בְנֵי־גָד וּבְנֵי־רְאוּבֵן ׀ אִתְּכֶם אֶת־הַיַּרְדֵּן כָּל־חָלוּץ לַמִּלְחָמָה לִפְנֵי יְהוָה וְנִכְבְּשָׁה הָאָרֶץ לִפְנֵיכֶם וּנְתַתֶּם לָהֶם אֶת־אֶרֶץ הַגִּלְעָד לַאֲחֻזָּה: ³⁰וְאִם־לֹא יַעַבְרוּ חֲלוּצִים אִתְּכֶם וְנֹאחֲזוּ בְתֹכְכֶם בְּאֶרֶץ כְּנָעַן: ³¹וַיַּעֲנוּ בְנֵי־גָד וּבְנֵי רְאוּבֵן לֵאמֹר אֵת אֲשֶׁר דִּבֶּר יְהוָה אֶל־עֲבָדֶיךָ כֵּן נַעֲשֶׂה: ³²נַחְנוּ נַעֲבֹר חֲלוּצִים לִפְנֵי יְהוָה אֶרֶץ כְּנָעַן וְאִתָּנוּ אֲחֻזַּת נַחֲלָתֵנוּ מֵעֵבֶר לַיַּרְדֵּן: ³³וַיִּתֵּן לָהֶם ׀ מֹשֶׁה לִבְנֵי־גָד וְלִבְנֵי רְאוּבֵן וְלַחֲצִי ׀ שֵׁבֶט ׀ מְנַשֶּׁה בֶן־יוֹסֵף אֶת־מַמְלֶכֶת סִיחֹן מֶלֶךְ הָאֱמֹרִי וְאֶת־מַמְלֶכֶת עוֹג מֶלֶךְ הַבָּשָׁן הָאָרֶץ לְעָרֶיהָ בִּגְבֻלֹת עָרֵי הָאָרֶץ סָבִיב: ³⁴וַיִּבְנוּ בְנֵי־גָד אֶת־דִּיבֹן וְאֶת־עֲטָרֹת וְאֵת עֲרֹעֵר: ³⁵וְאֶת־עַטְרֹת שׁוֹפָן וְאֶת־יַעְזֵר וְיָגְבֳּהָה: ³⁶וְאֶת־בֵּית נִמְרָה וְאֶת־בֵּית הָרָן עָרֵי מִבְצָר וְגִדְרֹת צֹאן: ³⁷וּבְנֵי רְאוּבֵן בָּנוּ אֶת־חֶשְׁבּוֹן וְאֶת־אֶלְעָלֵא וְאֵת קִרְיָתָיִם: ³⁸וְאֶת־נְבוֹ וְאֶת־בַּעַל מְעוֹן מוּסַבֹּת שֵׁם וְאֶת־שִׂבְמָה וַיִּקְרְאוּ בְשֵׁמֹת אֶת־שְׁמוֹת הֶעָרִים אֲשֶׁר בָּנוּ: ³⁹וַיֵּלְכוּ בְּנֵי מָכִיר בֶּן־מְנַשֶּׁה גִּלְעָדָה וַיִּלְכְּדֻהָ וַיּוֹרֶשׁ אֶת־הָאֱמֹרִי אֲשֶׁר־בָּהּ: ⁴⁰וַיִּתֵּן מֹשֶׁה אֶת־הַגִּלְעָד לְמָכִיר בֶּן־מְנַשֶּׁה וַיֵּשֶׁב בָּהּ: ⁴¹וְיָאִיר בֶּן־מְנַשֶּׁה הָלַךְ וַיִּלְכֹּד

---

someone else will take one's place. It is a natural inclination to hope that one's successor will not be as good as oneself. But a wise leader understands that it is in his or her own interest to have a good successor. Thus one's accomplishments live on and grow.

32:33. half of the tribe of Manasseh. Some understand and translate this as "the half-tribe of Manasseh," apparently thinking that Manasseh and Ephraim are merely half-tribes because they are both traced to one ancestor, Joseph. But that is wrong, because there is later a reference to the nine and a half tribes on the west side of the Jordan (Num 34:13). Thus, as is commonly pictured on maps, Manasseh was split, half on each side of the Jordan.

them Havvoth-Jair. 42And Nobah went and captured Kenath and its towns, and he called it Nobah after his own name.

אֶת־חַוֺּתֵיהֶם וַיִּקְרָא אֶתְהֶן חַוֺּת יָאִיר: 42וְנֹבַח הָלַךְ וַיִּלְכֹּד אֶת־קְנָת וְאֶת־בְּנֹתֶיהָ וַיִּקְרָא לָהּ נֹבַח בִּשְׁמוֹ: פ

TRAVELS

מסעי

33 1These are the travels of the children of Israel who went out from the land of Egypt by their armies by the hand of Moses and Aaron. 2And Moses wrote their stops for their travels by YHWH's word, and these are their travels and their stops.

3And they traveled from Rameses in the first month on the fifteenth day of the first month. On the day after the Passover, the children of Israel went out with a high hand before the eyes of all Egypt. 4And the Egyptians were burying those whom YHWH had struck among them: every firstborn. And YHWH had made judgments on their gods.

5And the children of Israel traveled from Rameses and camped in Succoth. 6And they traveled from Succoth and camped in Etham, which is at the edge of the wilderness. 7And they traveled from Etham and turned back toward Pi-hahiroth, which is in front of Baal-Zephon: and they camped in front of Migdol. 8And they traveled from before Pi-hahiroth and passed through the sea to the wilderness. And they went three days' journey in the wilderness of Etham and camped in Marah. 9And they traveled from Marah and came to Elim. And in Elim were twelve springs of water and seventy palm trees. And they camped there. 10And they traveled from Elim and camped by the Red Sea. 11And they traveled from the Red

33 1אֵלֶּה מַסְעֵי בְנֵי־יִשְׂרָאֵל אֲשֶׁר יָצְאוּ מֵאֶרֶץ מִצְרַיִם לְצִבְאֹתָם בְּיַד־מֹשֶׁה וְאַהֲרֹן: 2וַיִּכְתֹּב מֹשֶׁה אֶת־מוֹצָאֵיהֶם לְמַסְעֵיהֶם עַל־פִּי יְהוָה וְאֵלֶּה מַסְעֵיהֶם לְמוֹצָאֵיהֶם: 3וַיִּסְעוּ מֵרַעְמְסֵס בַּחֹדֶשׁ הָרִאשׁוֹן בַּחֲמִשָּׁה עָשָׂר יוֹם לַחֹדֶשׁ הָרִאשׁוֹן מִמָּחֳרַת הַפֶּסַח יָצְאוּ בְנֵי־יִשְׂרָאֵל בְּיָד רָמָה לְעֵינֵי כָּל־מִצְרָיִם: 4וּמִצְרַיִם מְקַבְּרִים אֵת אֲשֶׁר הִכָּה יְהוָה בָּהֶם כָּל־בְּכוֹר וּבֵאלֹהֵיהֶם עָשָׂה יְהוָה שְׁפָטִים: 5וַיִּסְעוּ בְנֵי־יִשְׂרָאֵל מֵרַעְמְסֵס וַיַּחֲנוּ בְּסֻכֹּת: 6וַיִּסְעוּ מִסֻּכֹּת וַיַּחֲנוּ בְאֵתָם אֲשֶׁר בִּקְצֵה הַמִּדְבָּר: 7וַיִּסְעוּ מֵאֵתָם וַיָּשָׁב עַל־פִּי הַחִירֹת אֲשֶׁר עַל־פְּנֵי בַּעַל צְפוֹן וַיַּחֲנוּ לִפְנֵי מִגְדֹּל: 8וַיִּסְעוּ מִפְּנֵי הַחִירֹת וַיַּעַבְרוּ בְתוֹךְ־הַיָּם הַמִּדְבָּרָה וַיֵּלְכוּ דֶּרֶךְ שְׁלֹשֶׁת יָמִים בְּמִדְבַּר אֵתָם וַיַּחֲנוּ בְּמָרָה: 9וַיִּסְעוּ מִמָּרָה וַיָּבֹאוּ אֵילִמָה וּבְאֵילִם שְׁתֵּים עֶשְׂרֵה עֵינֹת מַיִם וְשִׁבְעִים תְּמָרִים וַיַּחֲנוּ־שָׁם: 10וַיִּסְעוּ מֵאֵילִם וַיַּחֲנוּ עַל־יַם־סוּף: 11וַיִּסְעוּ מִיַּם־סוּף וַיַּחֲנוּ

33:1. **These are the travels.** This chapter gives a summary of Israel's travels through the wilderness. Many readers may find it uninteresting or unnecessary, but it is important. A connecting line of cause and effect runs through the stories in the book of Numbers so that, like the Jacob cycle of stories in Genesis, they can be read both as individual stories and as a meaningful chain of events. This list of the Israelites' itinerary formally shows the sequence of the journey to be the theme and unifying line of the book. See the closing comment at the end of Numbers (page 548).

Sea and camped in the wilderness of Sin. ¹²And they traveled from the wilderness of Sin and camped in Dophkah. ¹³And they traveled from Dophkah and camped in Alush. ¹⁴And they traveled from Alush and camped at Rephidim. And there was no water there for the people to drink. ¹⁵And they traveled from Rephidim and camped in the wilderness of Sinai. ¹⁶And they traveled from the wilderness of Sinai and camped at Kibroth Hattaavah. ¹⁷And they traveled from Kibroth Hattaavah and camped at Hazeroth. ¹⁸And they traveled from Hazeroth and camped in Rithmah. ¹⁹And they traveled from Rithmah and camped at Rimmon-parez. ²⁰And they traveled from Rimmon-parez and camped in Libnah. ²¹And they traveled from Libnah and camped at Rissah. ²²And they traveled from Rissah and camped in Kehelathah. ²³And they traveled from Kehelathah and camped at Mount Shapher. ²⁴And they traveled from Mount Shapher and camped in Haradah. ²⁵And they traveled from Haradah and camped in Makheloth. ²⁶And they traveled from Makheloth and camped at Tahath. ²⁷And they traveled from Tahath and camped at Tarah. ²⁸And they traveled from Tarah and camped in Mithkah. ²⁹And they went from Mithkah and camped in Hashmonah. ³⁰And they traveled from Hashmonah and camped at Moseroth. ³¹And they traveled from Moseroth and camped in Bene-jaakan. ³²And they traveled from Bene-jaakan and camped at Hor-haggidgad. ³³And they went from Hor-haggidgad and camped in Jotbathah. ³⁴And they traveled from Jotbathah and camped at Ebronah. ³⁵And they traveled from Ebronah and camped at Eziongeber. ³⁶And they traveled from Ezion-geber and camped in the wilderness of Zin. That is Kadesh. ³⁷And they traveled from Kadesh and camped in Mount Hor, at the edge of the land of Edom.

³⁸And Aaron, the priest, went up into Mount Hor at the word of YHWH and died there in the fortieth year after the children of Israel came out of the land of Egypt, in the fifth month, on the first day of the month. ³⁹And Aaron was a hun-

בְּמִדְבַּר־סִין: ¹²וַיִּסְעוּ מִמִּדְבַּר־סִין וַיַּחֲנוּ בְּדָפְקָה: ¹³וַיִּסְעוּ מִדָּפְקָה וַיַּחֲנוּ בְּאָלוּשׁ: ¹⁴וַיִּסְעוּ מֵאָלוּשׁ וַיַּחֲנוּ בִּרְפִידִם וְלֹא־הָיָה שָׁם מַיִם לָעָם לִשְׁתּוֹת: ¹⁵וַיִּסְעוּ מֵרְפִידִם וַיַּחֲנוּ בְּמִדְבַּר סִינָי: ¹⁶וַיִּסְעוּ מִמִּדְבַּר סִינָי וַיַּחֲנוּ בְּקִבְרֹת הַתַּאֲוָה: ¹⁷וַיִּסְעוּ מִקִּבְרֹת הַתַּאֲוָה וַיַּחֲנוּ בַּחֲצֵרֹת: ¹⁸וַיִּסְעוּ מֵחֲצֵרֹת וַיַּחֲנוּ בְּרִתְמָה: ¹⁹וַיִּסְעוּ מֵרִתְמָה וַיַּחֲנוּ בְּרִמֹּן פָּרֶץ: ²⁰וַיִּסְעוּ מֵרִמֹּן פָּרֶץ וַיַּחֲנוּ בְּלִבְנָה: ²¹וַיִּסְעוּ מִלִּבְנָה וַיַּחֲנוּ בְּרִסָּה: ²²וַיִּסְעוּ מֵרִסָּה וַיַּחֲנוּ בִּקְהֵלָתָה: ²³וַיִּסְעוּ מִקְּהֵלָתָה וַיַּחֲנוּ בְּהַר־שָׁפֶר: ²⁴וַיִּסְעוּ מֵהַר־שָׁפֶר וַיַּחֲנוּ בַּחֲרָדָה: ²⁵וַיִּסְעוּ מֵחֲרָדָה וַיַּחֲנוּ בְּמַקְהֵלֹת: ²⁶וַיִּסְעוּ מִמַּקְהֵלֹת וַיַּחֲנוּ בְּתָחַת: ²⁷וַיִּסְעוּ מִתָּחַת וַיַּחֲנוּ בְּתָרַח: ²⁸וַיִּסְעוּ מִתָּרַח וַיַּחֲנוּ בְּמִתְקָה: ²⁹וַיִּסְעוּ מִמִּתְקָה וַיַּחֲנוּ בְּחַשְׁמֹנָה: ³⁰וַיִּסְעוּ מֵחַשְׁמֹנָה וַיַּחֲנוּ בְּמֹסֵרוֹת: ³¹וַיִּסְעוּ מִמֹּסֵרוֹת וַיַּחֲנוּ בִּבְנֵי יַעֲקָן: ³²וַיִּסְעוּ מִבְּנֵי יַעֲקָן וַיַּחֲנוּ בְּחֹר הַגִּדְגָּד: ³³וַיִּסְעוּ מֵחֹר הַגִּדְגָּד וַיַּחֲנוּ בְּיָטְבָתָה: ³⁴וַיִּסְעוּ מִיָּטְבָתָה וַיַּחֲנוּ בְּעַבְרֹנָה: ³⁵וַיִּסְעוּ מֵעַבְרֹנָה וַיַּחֲנוּ בְּעֶצְיוֹן גָּבֶר: ³⁶וַיִּסְעוּ מֵעֶצְיוֹן גָּבֶר וַיַּחֲנוּ בְמִדְבַּר־צִן הִוא קָדֵשׁ: ³⁷וַיִּסְעוּ מִקָּדֵשׁ וַיַּחֲנוּ בְּהֹר הָהָר בִּקְצֵה אֶרֶץ אֱדוֹם: ³⁸וַיַּעַל אַהֲרֹן הַכֹּהֵן אֶל־הֹר הָהָר עַל־פִּי יְהוָה וַיָּמָת שָׁם בִּשְׁנַת הָאַרְבָּעִים לְצֵאת בְּנֵי־יִשְׂרָאֵל מֵאֶרֶץ מִצְרַיִם בַּחֹדֶשׁ הַחֲמִישִׁי בְּאֶחָד לַחֹדֶשׁ: ³⁹וְאַהֲרֹן בֶּן־שָׁלֹשׁ

dred twenty-three years old when he died in Mount Hor.

⁴⁰And the Canaanite, the king of Arad, who lived in the Negeb in the land of Canaan, heard of the coming of the children of Israel. ⁴¹And they traveled from Mount Hor and camped in Zalmonah. ⁴²And they traveled from Zalmonah and camped in Punon. ⁴³And they traveled from Punon and camped in Oboth. ⁴⁴And they traveled from Oboth and camped in Iyye-abarim, in the border of Moab. ⁴⁵And they traveled from Iyyim and camped in Dibon-gad. ⁴⁶And they traveled from Dibon-gad and camped in Almon-diblathaim. ⁴⁷And they traveled from Almon-diblathaim and camped in the mountains of Abarim in front of Nebo. ⁴⁸And they traveled from the mountains of Abarim and camped in the plains of Moab by the Jordan toward Jericho. ⁴⁹And they camped by the Jordan from Beth-jeshimoth to Abel-shittim in the plains of Moab.

⁵⁰And YHWH spoke to Moses in the plains of Moab by the Jordan toward Jericho, saying, ⁵¹"Speak to the children of Israel, and you shall say to them: When you cross the Jordan to the land of Canaan, ⁵²you shall dispossess all the residents of the land in front of you, and destroy all their carved figures, and you shall destroy all their molten images and demolish all their high places. ⁵³And you shall take possession of the land and live in it, because I've given the land to you to possess it. ⁵⁴And you shall give legacies of the land by lot, by your families: for the large you shall make its legacy larger, and for the small you shall make its legacy smaller. Wherever the lot indicates for it shall belong to it. You shall give legacies to the tribes of your fathers. ⁵⁵And if you don't dispossess the residents of the land in front of you, then those whom you leave of them will become sticks in your eyes and thorns in your sides, and they'll afflict you on the land in which you're living. ⁵⁶And it will be that, as I meant to do to them, I'll do to you!"

וְעֶשְׂרִים וּמְאַת שָׁנָה בְּמֹתוֹ בְּהֹר הָהָר: ס ⁴⁰וַיִּשְׁמַע הַכְּנַעֲנִי מֶלֶךְ עֲרָד וְהוּא־יֹשֵׁב בַּנֶּגֶב בְּאֶרֶץ כְּנַעַן בְּבֹא בְּנֵי יִשְׂרָאֵל: ⁴¹וַיִּסְעוּ מֵהֹר הָהָר וַיַּחֲנוּ בְּצַלְמֹנָה: ⁴²וַיִּסְעוּ מִצַּלְמֹנָה וַיַּחֲנוּ בְּפוּנֹן: ⁴³וַיִּסְעוּ מִפּוּנֹן וַיַּחֲנוּ בְּאֹבֹת: ⁴⁴וַיִּסְעוּ מֵאֹבֹת וַיַּחֲנוּ בְּעִיֵּי הָעֲבָרִים בִּגְבוּל מוֹאָב: ⁴⁵וַיִּסְעוּ מֵעִיִּים וַיַּחֲנוּ בְּדִיבֹן גָּד: ⁴⁶וַיִּסְעוּ מִדִּיבֹן גָּד וַיַּחֲנוּ בְּעַלְמֹן דִּבְלָתָיְמָה: ⁴⁷וַיִּסְעוּ מֵעַלְמֹן דִּבְלָתָיְמָה וַיַּחֲנוּ בְּהָרֵי הָעֲבָרִים לִפְנֵי נְבוֹ: ⁴⁸וַיִּסְעוּ מֵהָרֵי הָעֲבָרִים וַיַּחֲנוּ בְּעַרְבֹת מוֹאָב עַל יַרְדֵּן יְרֵחוֹ: ⁴⁹וַיַּחֲנוּ עַל־הַיַּרְדֵּן מִבֵּית הַיְשִׁמֹת עַד אָבֵל הַשִּׁטִּים בְּעַרְבֹת מוֹאָב: ס

⁵⁰וַיְדַבֵּר יְהוָה אֶל־מֹשֶׁה בְּעַרְבֹת מוֹאָב עַל־יַרְדֵּן יְרֵחוֹ לֵאמֹר: ⁵¹דַּבֵּר אֶל־בְּנֵי יִשְׂרָאֵל וְאָמַרְתָּ אֲלֵהֶם כִּי אַתֶּם עֹבְרִים אֶת־הַיַּרְדֵּן אֶל־אֶרֶץ כְּנָעַן: ⁵²וְהוֹרַשְׁתֶּם אֶת־כָּל־יֹשְׁבֵי הָאָרֶץ מִפְּנֵיכֶם וְאִבַּדְתֶּם אֵת כָּל־מַשְׂכִּיֹּתָם וְאֵת כָּל־צַלְמֵי מַסֵּכֹתָם תְּאַבֵּדוּ וְאֵת כָּל־בָּמֹתָם תַּשְׁמִידוּ: ⁵³וְהוֹרַשְׁתֶּם אֶת־הָאָרֶץ וִישַׁבְתֶּם־בָּהּ כִּי לָכֶם נָתַתִּי אֶת־הָאָרֶץ לָרֶשֶׁת אֹתָהּ: ⁵⁴וְהִתְנַחַלְתֶּם אֶת־הָאָרֶץ בְּגוֹרָל לְמִשְׁפְּחֹתֵיכֶם לָרַב תַּרְבּוּ אֶת־נַחֲלָתוֹ וְלַמְעַט תַּמְעִיט אֶת־נַחֲלָתוֹ אֶל אֲשֶׁר־יֵצֵא לוֹ שָׁמָּה הַגּוֹרָל לוֹ יִהְיֶה לְמַטּוֹת אֲבֹתֵיכֶם תִּתְנֶחָלוּ: ⁵⁵וְאִם־לֹא תוֹרִישׁוּ אֶת־יֹשְׁבֵי הָאָרֶץ מִפְּנֵיכֶם וְהָיָה אֲשֶׁר תּוֹתִירוּ מֵהֶם לְשִׂכִּים בְּעֵינֵיכֶם וְלִצְנִינִם בְּצִדֵּיכֶם וְצָרֲרוּ אֶתְכֶם עַל־הָאָרֶץ אֲשֶׁר אַתֶּם יֹשְׁבִים בָּהּ: ⁵⁶וְהָיָה כַּאֲשֶׁר דִּמִּיתִי לַעֲשׂוֹת לָהֶם אֶעֱשֶׂה לָכֶם:

33:52. **high places.** See the comment on Num 21:28.

34

1And YHWH spoke to Moses, saying, 2"Command the children of Israel, and you shall say to them: When you come to the land of Canaan, this is the land that will fall to you as a legacy, the land of Canaan by its borders: 3And the southern side for you shall be from the wilderness of Zin next to Edom, and the southern border for you shall be from the edge of the Dead Sea to the east. 4And the border for you shall turn from the south to the ascent of Akrabim and will pass to Zin, and its extent shall be from the south to Kadesh-barnea, and it shall go out to Hazar-addar and pass to Azmon. 5And the border shall turn from Azmon to the Wadi of Egypt, and its extent shall be to the sea. 6And the western border: and the big sea shall be a border for you. This shall be the western border for you. 7And this shall be the northern border for you: you shall mark from the big sea to Mount Hor, 8from Mount Hor you shall mark to the entrance of Hamath, and the border's extent shall be to Zedad, 9and the border shall go out to Ziphron, and its extent shall be to Hazar-enan. This shall be the northern border for you. 10And you shall mark for the border to the east from Hazar-enan to Shepham, 11and the border shall go down from Shepham to Riblah at the east of Ain, and the border shall go down and rub on the shoulder of the Sea of Kinneret on the east, 12and the border shall go down to the Jordan, and its extent will be to the Dead Sea. This shall be the land for you by its borders all around."

13And Moses commanded the children of Israel, saying, "This is the land that you shall give as legacies by lot, which YHWH commanded to

פ 34 ‏1וַיְדַבֵּ֥ר יְהוָ֖ה אֶל־מֹשֶׁ֥ה לֵּאמֹֽר׃ 2צַ֞ו אֶת־בְּנֵ֤י יִשְׂרָאֵל֙ וְאָמַרְתָּ֣ אֲלֵהֶ֔ם כִּֽי־אַתֶּ֥ם בָּאִ֖ים אֶל־הָאָ֣רֶץ כְּנָ֑עַן זֹ֣את הָאָ֗רֶץ אֲשֶׁ֨ר תִּפֹּ֤ל לָכֶם֙ בְּנַחֲלָ֔ה אֶ֥רֶץ כְּנַ֖עַן לִגְבֻלֹתֶֽיהָ׃ 3וְהָיָ֥ה לָכֶ֛ם פְּאַת־נֶ֖גֶב מִמִּדְבַּר־צִ֣ן עַל־יְדֵ֣י אֱד֑וֹם וְהָיָ֤ה לָכֶם֙ גְּב֣וּל נֶ֔גֶב מִקְצֵ֥ה יָם־הַמֶּ֖לַח קֵֽדְמָה׃ 4וְנָסַ֣ב לָכֶם֩ הַגְּב֨וּל מִנֶּ֜גֶב לְמַעֲלֵ֣ה עַקְרַבִּ֗ים וְעָ֤בַר צִ֨נָה֙ וְהָיָה֙ תּוֹצְאֹתָ֔יו מִנֶּ֖גֶב לְקָדֵ֣שׁ בַּרְנֵ֑עַ וְיָצָ֥א חֲצַר־אַדָּ֖ר וְעָבַ֥ר עַצְמֹֽנָה׃ 5וְנָסַ֧ב הַגְּב֛וּל מֵעַצְמ֖וֹן נַ֣חְלָה מִצְרָ֑יִם וְהָי֥וּ תוֹצְאֹתָ֖יו הַיָּֽמָּה׃ 6וּגְב֣וּל יָ֔ם וְהָ֥יָה לָכֶ֛ם הַיָּ֥ם הַגָּד֖וֹל וּגְב֑וּל זֶֽה־יִּהְיֶ֥ה לָכֶ֖ם גְּב֥וּל יָֽם׃ 7וְזֶֽה־יִהְיֶ֥ה לָכֶ֖ם גְּב֣וּל צָפ֑וֹן מִן־הַיָּם֙ הַגָּדֹ֔ל תְּתָא֥וּ לָכֶ֖ם הֹ֥ר הָהָֽר׃ 8מֵהֹ֣ר הָהָ֔ר תְּתָא֖וּ לְבֹ֣א חֲמָ֑ת וְהָי֛וּ תּוֹצְאֹ֥ת הַגְּבֻ֖ל צְדָֽדָה׃ 9וְיָצָ֤א הַגְּבֻל֙ זִפְרֹ֔נָה וְהָי֥וּ תוֹצְאֹתָ֖יו חֲצַ֣ר עֵינָ֑ן זֶה־יִהְיֶ֥ה לָכֶ֖ם גְּב֥וּל צָפֽוֹן׃ 10וְהִתְאַוִּיתֶ֥ם לָכֶ֖ם לִגְב֣וּל קֵ֑דְמָה מֵחֲצַ֥ר עֵינָ֖ן שְׁפָֽמָה׃ 11וְיָרַ֨ד הַגְּבֻ֜ל מִשְּׁפָ֣ם הָרִבְלָ֗ה מִקֶּ֛דֶם לָעָ֑יִן וְיָרַ֣ד הַגְּב֔וּל וּמָחָ֛ה עַל־כֶּ֥תֶף יָם־כִּנֶּ֖רֶת קֵֽדְמָה׃ 12וְיָרַ֤ד הַגְּבוּל֙ הַיַּרְדֵּ֔נָה וְהָי֥וּ תוֹצְאֹתָ֖יו יָ֣ם הַמֶּ֑לַח זֹאת֩ תִּהְיֶ֨ה לָכֶ֥ם הָאָ֛רֶץ לִגְבֻלֹתֶ֖יהָ סָבִֽיב׃ 13וַיְצַ֣ו מֹשֶׁ֗ה אֶת־בְּנֵ֤י יִשְׂרָאֵל֙ לֵאמֹ֔ר זֹ֣את הָאָ֗רֶץ אֲשֶׁ֨ר תִּתְנַחֲל֤וּ אֹתָהּ֙ בְּגוֹרָ֔ל

‏34:4 ק וְהָיֽוּ

34:5. **the wadi of Egypt**. This refers to the Wadi el-'Arîsh.

34:6. **the big sea**. The Mediterranean Sea.

34:11. **Sea of Kinneret**. The Sea of Galilee.

34:11. **shoulder . . . on the east**. On the east side of the Sea of Galilee is a mountain wall, a "shoulder," known as the Golan Heights.

34:12. **the Dead Sea**. In Hebrew it is called "the Salt Sea."

give to the nine tribes and the half of a tribe." ¹⁴Because the tribe of the children of the Reubenites by their fathers' house and the tribe of the children of the Gadites by their fathers' house had taken and half of the tribe of Manasseh had taken their legacy. ¹⁵The two tribes and the half of a tribe had taken their legacy from across the Jordan toward Jericho on the east side—to the east.

¹⁶And YHWH spoke to Moses, saying, ¹⁷"These are the names of the people who will give the land as legacies to you: Eleazar, the priest, and Joshua son of Nun; ¹⁸and you shall take one chieftain for each tribe to give the land as legacies. ¹⁹And these are the people's names: For the tribe of Judah, Caleb son of Jephunneh. ²⁰And for the tribe of the children of Simeon, Samuel son of Ammihud. ²¹For the tribe of Benjamin, Elidad son of Chislon. ²²And for the tribe of the children of Dan, a chieftain, Bukki son of Jogli. ²³For the children of Joseph: for the tribe of the children of Manasseh, a chieftain, Hanniel son of Ephod; ²⁴and for the tribe of the children of Ephraim, a chieftain, Kemuel son of Shiphtan. ²⁵And for the tribe of the children of Zebulun, a chieftain, Elizaphan son of Parnach. ²⁶And for the tribe of the children of Issachar, a chieftain, Paltiel son of Azzan. ²⁷And for the tribe of the children of Asher, a chieftain, Ahihud son of Shelomi. ²⁸And for the tribe of the children of Naphtali, a chieftain, Pedahel son of Ammihud."

²⁹These are the ones whom YHWH commanded to give the children of Israel legacies in the land of Canaan.

אֲשֶׁר צִוָּה יְהוָה לָתֵת לְתִשְׁעַת הַמַּטּוֹת וַחֲצִי הַמַּטֶּה: ¹⁴כִּי לָקְחוּ מַטֵּה בְנֵי הָראוּבֵנִי לְבֵית אֲבֹתָם וּמַטֵּה בְנֵי־הַגָּדִי לְבֵית אֲבֹתָם וַחֲצִי מַטֵּה מְנַשֶּׁה לָקְחוּ נַחֲלָתָם: ¹⁵שְׁנֵי הַמַּטּוֹת וַחֲצִי הַמַּטֶּה לָקְחוּ נַחֲלָתָם מֵעֵבֶר לְיַרְדֵּן יְרֵחוֹ קֵדְמָה מִזְרָחָה: פ ¹⁶וַיְדַבֵּר יְהוָה אֶל־מֹשֶׁה לֵּאמֹר: ¹⁷אֵלֶּה שְׁמוֹת הָאֲנָשִׁים אֲשֶׁר־יִנְחֲלוּ לָכֶם אֶת־הָאָרֶץ אֶלְעָזָר הַכֹּהֵן וִיהוֹשֻׁעַ בִּן־נוּן: ¹⁸וְנָשִׂיא אֶחָד נָשִׂיא אֶחָד מִמַּטֶּה תִּקְחוּ לִנְחֹל אֶת־הָאָרֶץ: ¹⁹וְאֵלֶּה שְׁמוֹת הָאֲנָשִׁים לְמַטֵּה יְהוּדָה כָּלֵב בֶּן־יְפֻנֶּה: ²⁰וּלְמַטֵּה בְּנֵי שִׁמְעוֹן שְׁמוּאֵל בֶּן־עַמִּיהוּד: ²¹לְמַטֵּה בִנְיָמִן אֱלִידָד בֶּן־כִּסְלוֹן: ²²וּלְמַטֵּה בְנֵי־דָן נָשִׂיא בֻּקִּי בֶּן־יָגְלִי: ²³לִבְנֵי יוֹסֵף לְמַטֵּה בְנֵי־מְנַשֶּׁה נָשִׂיא חַנִּיאֵל בֶּן־אֵפֹד: ²⁴וּלְמַטֵּה בְנֵי־אֶפְרַיִם נָשִׂיא קְמוּאֵל בֶּן־שִׁפְטָן: ²⁵וּלְמַטֵּה בְנֵי־זְבוּלֻן נָשִׂיא אֱלִיצָפָן בֶּן־פַּרְנָךְ: ²⁶וּלְמַטֵּה בְנֵי־יִשָּׂשכָר נָשִׂיא פַּלְטִיאֵל בֶּן־עַזָּן: ²⁷וּלְמַטֵּה בְנֵי־אָשֵׁר נָשִׂיא אֲחִיהוּד בֶּן־שְׁלֹמִי: ²⁸וּלְמַטֵּה בְנֵי־נַפְתָּלִי נָשִׂיא פְּדַהְאֵל בֶּן־עַמִּיהוּד: ²⁹אֵלֶּה אֲשֶׁר צִוָּה יְהוָה לְנַחֵל אֶת־בְּנֵי־יִשְׂרָאֵל בְּאֶרֶץ כְּנָעַן: פ

34:13. nine tribes and the half of a tribe. The half of a tribe is half of the tribe of Manasseh. The other half of Manasseh took land on the east side of the Jordan along with the tribes of Reuben and Gad.

34:17. the names of the people. Over and over, the tribes and their leaders are named in the book of Numbers. From the wilderness period to the time of the judges to the time of the monarchy, Israel is never ruled by an individual political authority. There are always tribal chiefs, councils of leaders, priests, judges, and military officers. An individual human's rule is never absolute—not even for Moses, not even for David.

35 ¹And YHWH spoke to Moses in the plains of Moab by the Jordan toward Jericho, saying, ²"Command the children of Israel that, from the legacy of their possession, they shall give the Levites cities in which to live, and you shall give the Levites surrounding land for the cities all around them. ³And the cities shall be theirs to live in, and their surrounding lands shall be for their cattle and for their property and for their animals. ⁴And the surrounding lands of the cities that you shall give to the Levites: from the city wall outward, a thousand cubits all around. ⁵And you shall measure outside the city: on the eastern side two thousand in cubits, and on the southern side two thousand in cubits, and on the western side two thousand in cubits, and on the northern side two thousand in cubits, and the city in the middle. This shall be the surrounding lands of the cities for them. ⁶And the cities that you shall give to the Levites: six cities of refuge that you shall give for the manslayer to flee there, and you shall give in addition to them forty-two cities. ⁷All the cities that you shall give to the Levites: forty-eight cities, them and their surrounding lands. ⁸And the cities that you shall give from the possession of the children of Israel: from the larger you shall give more, and from the smaller you shall give fewer. Each shall give some of his cities to the Levites according to his legacy that they will give."

⁹And YHWH spoke to Moses, saying, ¹⁰"Speak to the children of Israel, and you shall say to them: When you cross the Jordan to the land of Canaan, ¹¹you shall establish cities; they shall be cities of refuge for you, and a manslayer who strikes a life by mistake shall flee there. ¹²And you shall have the cities for refuge from an avenger so the manslayer will not die until he

‫35 ¹וַיְדַבֵּר יְהוָה אֶל־מֹשֶׁה בְּעַרְבֹת מוֹאָב עַל־‬
‫יַרְדֵּן יְרֵחוֹ לֵאמֹר: ²צַו אֶת־בְּנֵי יִשְׂרָאֵל וְנָתְנוּ‬
‫לַלְוִיִּם מִנַּחֲלַת אֲחֻזָּתָם עָרִים לָשָׁבֶת וּמִגְרָשׁ‬
‫לֶעָרִים סְבִיבֹתֵיהֶם תִּתְּנוּ לַלְוִיִּם: ³וְהָיוּ הֶעָרִים‬
‫לָהֶם לָשָׁבֶת וּמִגְרְשֵׁיהֶם יִהְיוּ לִבְהֶמְתָּם וְלִרְכֻשָׁם‬
‫וּלְכֹל חַיָּתָם: ⁴וּמִגְרְשֵׁי הֶעָרִים אֲשֶׁר תִּתְּנוּ לַלְוִיִּם‬
‫מִקִּיר הָעִיר וָחוּצָה אֶלֶף אַמָּה סָבִיב: ⁵וּמַדֹּתֶם‬
‫מִחוּץ לָעִיר אֶת־פְּאַת־קֵדְמָה אַלְפַּיִם בָּאַמָּה וְאֶת־‬
‫פְּאַת־נֶגֶב אַלְפַּיִם בָּאַמָּה וְאֶת־פְּאַת־יָם | אַלְפַּיִם‬
‫בָּאַמָּה וְאֵת פְּאַת צָפוֹן אַלְפַּיִם בָּאַמָּה וְהָעִיר‬
‫בַּתָּוֶךְ זֶה יִהְיֶה לָהֶם מִגְרְשֵׁי הֶעָרִים: ⁶וְאֵת הֶעָרִים‬
‫אֲשֶׁר תִּתְּנוּ לַלְוִיִּם אֵת שֵׁשׁ־עָרֵי הַמִּקְלָט אֲשֶׁר‬
‫תִּתְּנוּ לָנֻס שָׁמָּה הָרֹצֵחַ וַעֲלֵיהֶם תִּתְּנוּ אַרְבָּעִים‬
‫וּשְׁתַּיִם עִיר: ⁷כָּל־הֶעָרִים אֲשֶׁר תִּתְּנוּ לַלְוִיִּם‬
‫אַרְבָּעִים וּשְׁמֹנֶה עִיר אֶתְהֶן וְאֶת־מִגְרְשֵׁיהֶן:‬
‫⁸וְהֶעָרִים אֲשֶׁר תִּתְּנוּ מֵאֲחֻזַּת בְּנֵי־יִשְׂרָאֵל מֵאֵת‬
‫הָרַב תַּרְבּוּ וּמֵאֵת הַמְעַט תַּמְעִיטוּ אִישׁ כְּפִי נַחֲלָתוֹ‬
‫אֲשֶׁר יִנְחָלוּ יִתֵּן מֵעָרָיו לַלְוִיִּם: פ‬

‫⁹וַיְדַבֵּר יְהוָה אֶל־מֹשֶׁה לֵּאמֹר: ¹⁰דַּבֵּר אֶל־בְּנֵי‬
‫יִשְׂרָאֵל וְאָמַרְתָּ אֲלֵהֶם כִּי אַתֶּם עֹבְרִים אֶת־הַיַּרְדֵּן‬
‫אַרְצָה כְּנָעַן: ¹¹וְהִקְרִיתֶם לָכֶם עָרִים עָרֵי מִקְלָט‬
‫תִּהְיֶינָה לָכֶם וְנָס שָׁמָּה רֹצֵחַ מַכֵּה־נֶפֶשׁ בִּשְׁגָגָה:‬
‫¹²וְהָיוּ לָכֶם הֶעָרִים לְמִקְלָט מִגֹּאֵל וְלֹא יָמוּת‬

35:6,16. **manslayer . . . murderer.** These two words are both used to translate the same Hebrew word throughout this chapter. In Hebrew the word is the same for an unintentional manslayer and for a murderer. We determine which is meant in each sentence by the context. In English we have two words available, and so the appropriate word is used for each case.

stands in front of the congregation for judgment. 13And the cities that you shall give: You shall have six cities of refuge. 14You shall put three of the cities across the Jordan, and you shall put three of the cities in the land of Canaan. They shall be cities of refuge.

15"These six cities shall be for refuge for the children of Israel and for the alien and for the visitor among them, for anyone who strikes a life by mistake to flee there. 16But if he struck him with an iron item so that he died, he is a murderer. The murderer shall be put to *death*. 17And if he struck him with a stone in the hand by which one could die, so that he died, he is a murderer. The murderer shall be put to *death*. 18Or if he struck him with a wooden object in the hand by which one could die, so that he died, he is a murderer. The murderer shall be put to *death*. 19The blood avenger, he shall kill the murderer. When he comes upon him, *he* shall kill him. 20And if he pushed him in hatred or threw something on him through scheming so that he died, 21or if he struck him with his hand in enmity so that he died, the one who struck shall be put to *death*. He is a murderer. The blood avenger shall kill the murderer when he comes upon him. 22But if by chance, not in enmity, he pushed him or threw any object on him not through scheming, 23or with any stone by which one could die, without seeing, so that he dropped it on him so that he died, and he was not an enemy to him and was not seeking to harm him, 24then the congregation shall judge between the one who struck and the blood avenger on the basis of these judgments. 25And the congregation shall rescue the manslayer from the blood avenger's hand, and the congregation shall bring him back to his city of refuge to which he fled, and he shall live in it until the death of the high priest whom one anointed with the holy oil. 26But if the

הָרֹצֵחַ עַד־עָמְדֹו לִפְנֵי הָעֵדָה לַמִּשְׁפָּט: 13וְהֶעָרִים אֲשֶׁר תִּתֵּנוּ שֵׁשׁ־עָרֵי מִקְלָט תִּהְיֶינָה לָכֶם: 14אֵת ׀ שְׁלֹשׁ הֶעָרִים תִּתְּנוּ מֵעֵבֶר לַיַּרְדֵּן וְאֵת שְׁלֹשׁ הֶעָרִים תִּתְּנוּ בְּאֶרֶץ כְּנָעַן עָרֵי מִקְלָט תִּהְיֶינָה: 15לִבְנֵי יִשְׂרָאֵל וְלַגֵּר וְלַתֹּושָׁב בְּתֹוכָם תִּהְיֶינָה שֵׁשׁ־הֶעָרִים הָאֵלֶּה לְמִקְלָט לָנוּס שָׁמָּה כָּל־מַכֵּה־נֶפֶשׁ בִּשְׁגָגָה: 16וְאִם־בִּכְלִי בַרְזֶל ׀ הִכָּהוּ וַיָּמֹת רֹצֵחַ הוּא מֹות יוּמַת הָרֹצֵחַ: 17וְאִם בְּאֶבֶן יָד אֲשֶׁר־יָמוּת בָּהּ הִכָּהוּ וַיָּמֹת רֹצֵחַ הוּא מֹות יוּמַת הָרֹצֵחַ: 18אֹו בִּכְלִי עֵץ־יָד אֲשֶׁר־יָמוּת בֹּו הִכָּהוּ וַיָּמֹת רֹצֵחַ הוּא מֹות יוּמַת הָרֹצֵחַ: 19גֹּאֵל הַדָּם הוּא יָמִית אֶת־הָרֹצֵחַ בְּפִגְעֹו־בֹו הוּא יְמִיתֶנּוּ: 20וְאִם־בְּשִׂנְאָה יֶהְדָּפֶנּוּ אֹו־הִשְׁלִיךְ עָלָיו בִּצְדִיָּה וַיָּמֹת: 21אֹו בְאֵיבָה הִכָּהוּ בְיָדֹו וַיָּמֹת מֹות־יוּמַת הַמַּכֶּה רֹצֵחַ הוּא גֹּאֵל הַדָּם יָמִית אֶת־הָרֹצֵחַ בְּפִגְעֹו־בֹו: 22וְאִם־בְּפֶתַע בְּלֹא־אֵיבָה הֲדָפֹו אֹו־הִשְׁלִיךְ עָלָיו כָּל־כְּלִי בְּלֹא צְדִיָּה: 23אֹו בְכָל־אֶבֶן אֲשֶׁר־יָמוּת בָּהּ בְּלֹא רְאֹות וַיַּפֵּל עָלָיו וַיָּמֹת וְהוּא לֹא־אֹויֵב לֹו וְלֹא מְבַקֵּשׁ רָעָתֹו: 24וְשָׁפְטוּ הָעֵדָה בֵּין הַמַּכֶּה וּבֵין גֹּאֵל הַדָּם עַל הַמִּשְׁפָּטִים הָאֵלֶּה: 25וְהִצִּילוּ הָעֵדָה אֶת־הָרֹצֵחַ מִיַּד גֹּאֵל הַדָּם וְהֵשִׁיבוּ אֹתֹו הָעֵדָה אֶל־עִיר מִקְלָטֹו אֲשֶׁר־נָס שָׁמָּה וְיָשַׁב בָּהּ עַד־מֹות הַכֹּהֵן הַגָּדֹל אֲשֶׁר־מָשַׁח אֹתֹו בְּשֶׁמֶן הַקֹּדֶשׁ:

35:25. **the death of the high priest**. Why does the high priest's death release him? It makes atonement for the crime. After that, the person who killed by accident is innocent, and if a blood avenger would kill him it would be murder.

murderer will go *out* of the border of his city of refuge to which he will flee, 27and the blood avenger will find him outside of the border of his city of refuge, and the blood avenger will murder the murderer, he does not have blood, 28because he shall live in his city of refuge until the high priest's death, and after the high priest's death the murderer shall go back to the land of his possession.

29"And these shall become a law of judgment for you through your generations in all your homes. 30Anyone who strikes a life, the murderer shall be murdered by the mouth of witnesses. And one witness shall not testify against a person so as to die. 31And you shall not take a ransom for a murderer's life, because he did wrong so as to die, but he shall be put to *death*. 32And you shall not take a ransom to flee to his city of refuge, to go back to live in the land until the priest's death. 33So you shall not pollute the land in which you are. Because blood: it will pollute the land, and the land will not have expiation for blood that is spilled in it except by the blood of the one who spilled it! 34And you shall not make the land impure in which you are living, in

26וְאִם־יָצֹא יֵצֵא הָרֹצֵחַ אֶת־גְּבוּל' עִיר מִקְלָטֹו אֲשֶׁר יָנוּס שָׁמָּה: 27וּמָצָא אֹתֹו גֹּאֵל הַדָּם מִחוּץ לִגְבוּל' עִיר מִקְלָטֹו וְרָצַח גֹּאֵל הַדָּם אֶת־הָרֹצֵחַ אֵין לֹו דָּם: 28כִּי בְעִיר מִקְלָטֹו יֵשֵׁב עַד־מֹות הַכֹּהֵן הַגָּדֹל וְאַחֲרֵי מֹות הַכֹּהֵן הַגָּדֹל יָשׁוּב הָרֹצֵחַ אֶל־אֶרֶץ אֲחֻזָּתֹו: 29וְהָיוּ אֵלֶּה לָכֶם לְחֻקַּת מִשְׁפָּט לְדֹרֹתֵיכֶם בְּכֹל מֹושְׁבֹתֵיכֶם: 30כָּל־מַכֵּה־נֶפֶשׁ לְפִי עֵדִים יִרְצַח אֶת־הָרֹצֵחַ וְעֵד אֶחָד לֹא־יַעֲנֶה בְנֶפֶשׁ לָמֽוּת: 31וְלֹא־תִקְחוּ כֹפֶר' לְנֶפֶשׁ רֹצֵחַ אֲשֶׁר־הוּא רָשָׁע לָמֽוּת כִּי־מֹות יוּמָת: 32וְלֹא־תִקְחוּ כֹפֶר לָנוּס אֶל־עִיר מִקְלָטֹו לָשׁוּב' לָשֶׁבֶת בָּאָרֶץ עַד־מֹות הַכֹּהֵן: 33וְלֹא־תַחֲנִיפוּ אֶת־הָאָרֶץ אֲשֶׁר אַתֶּם בָּהּ כִּי הַדָּם הוּא יַחֲנִיף אֶת־הָאָרֶץ וְלָאָרֶץ לֹא־יְכֻפַּר לַדָּם' אֲשֶׁר שֻׁפַּךְ־בָּהּ כִּי־אִם בְּדַם שֹׁפְכֹו: 34וְלֹא תְטַמֵּא אֶת־הָאָרֶץ אֲשֶׁר אַתֶּם יֹשְׁבִים בָּהּ אֲשֶׁר אֲנִי

35:27. he does not have blood. Meaning: he does not have guilt for shedding the blood of the person who killed someone by accident.

35:29. law of judgment. See the comment on Num 27:11.

35:30. one witness. A person cannot be executed on the testimony of only one witness. There must be two or more.

35:33. blood will pollute the land. As conveyed at the beginning of the Torah from the stories of Eden, Cain and Abel, and the flood, the earth's environment suffers from human wrongdoing: "The ground is cursed on your account." "You're cursed from the ground that opened its mouth to take your brother's blood." "The earth was corrupted, because all flesh had corrupted its way on the earth." Human violence and corruption have consequences not only for the immediate victims, and not even only for other humans, but for the condition of the earth and nature. Murder is not only a sin against the victim. It is a sin against the earth.

35:34. you shall not make the land impure. As we have seen in other instances, blood can make impure (for example, Lev 15:33), and it can expiate impurity (for example, Lev 14:49–53). It can be contaminating, and it can be protective. As blood can make a person impure, so blood(shed) can render the *land* impure.

which I tent, because I, YHWH, tent among the children of Israel."

36

¹And the heads of the fathers of the family of the children of Gilead son of Machir son of Manasseh, from the families of the children of Joseph, came forward and spoke in front of Moses and in front of the chieftains, heads of fathers of the children of Israel. ²And they said, "YHWH commanded my lord to give the land as legacy by lot to the children of Israel, and my lord was commanded by YHWH to give the legacy of Zelophehad, our brother, to his daughters. ³If they will become wives to one of the sons of the tribes of the children of Israel, then their legacy will be subtracted from our fathers' legacy and added onto the legacy of the tribe to whom they will belong, and it will be subtracted from our legacy by the lot. ⁴And if the children of Israel will have the jubilee, then their legacy will be added onto the legacy of the tribe to whom they will belong, and their legacy will be subtracted from the legacy of our fathers' tribe."

⁵And Moses commanded the children of Israel

שֹׁכֵן בְּתוֹכָה כִּי אֲנִי יְהוָה שֹׁכֵן בְּתוֹךְ בְּנֵי יִשְׂרָאֵל: פ

36 ¹וַיִּקְרְבוּ רָאשֵׁי הָאָבוֹת לְמִשְׁפַּחַת בְּנֵי־גִלְעָד בֶּן־מָכִיר בֶּן־מְנַשֶּׁה מִמִּשְׁפְּחֹת בְּנֵי יוֹסֵף וַיְדַבְּרוּ לִפְנֵי מֹשֶׁה וְלִפְנֵי הַנְּשִׂאִים רָאשֵׁי אָבוֹת לִבְנֵי יִשְׂרָאֵל: ²וַיֹּאמְרוּ אֶת־אֲדֹנִי צִוָּה יְהוָה לָתֵת אֶת־הָאָרֶץ בְּנַחֲלָה בְּגוֹרָל לִבְנֵי יִשְׂרָאֵל וַאדֹנִי צֻוָּה בַיהוָה לָתֵת אֶת־נַחֲלַת צְלָפְחָד אָחִינוּ לִבְנֹתָיו: ³וְהָיוּ לְאֶחָד מִבְּנֵי שִׁבְטֵי בְנֵי־יִשְׂרָאֵל לְנָשִׁים וְנִגְרְעָה נַחֲלָתָן מִנַּחֲלַת אֲבֹתֵינוּ וְנוֹסַף עַל נַחֲלַת הַמַּטֶּה אֲשֶׁר תִּהְיֶינָה לָהֶם וּמִגֹּרַל נַחֲלָתֵנוּ יִגָּרֵעַ: ⁴וְאִם־יִהְיֶה הַיֹּבֵל לִבְנֵי יִשְׂרָאֵל וְנוֹסְפָה נַחֲלָתָן עַל נַחֲלַת הַמַּטֶּה אֲשֶׁר תִּהְיֶינָה לָהֶם וּמִנַּחֲלַת מַטֵּה אֲבֹתֵינוּ יִגָּרַע נַחֲלָתָן: ⁵וַיְצַו מֹשֶׁה אֶת־בְּנֵי יִשְׂרָאֵל

35:34. I tent. On God's tenting presence among humans, see the comments on Exod 25:8 and Num 9:17.

36:3. their legacy will be subtracted. Whenever a new law arises that makes a social change, there will be consequences that will make the matter complex. Earlier (27:4), Zelophehad's daughters protested that since their father had no sons, his land would not be passed on. And so, they said, "Why should our father's name be subtracted?" It was therefore determined that, in such a situation, women can inherit their father's land. But now their tribe (Manasseh) realizes that this leads to a new problem. If these women marry men from other tribes, then their land will pass by inheritance to the sons whom they will have. But tribal identification goes by the father, not the mother. (Identification in the Torah is always patrilineal; see the comment on Lev 24:16,22.) And so their sons will be members of their fathers' tribes, not members of Manasseh. And so some of the territory of Manasseh would be subtracted from Manasseh and passed to another tribe. (A contemporary analogy would be if parts of a state or country could be transferred away to another state or country without the former having any say in the matter.)

by YHWH's word, saying, "The children of Joseph speak right. ⁶This is the thing that YHWH has commanded Zelophehad's daughters, saying: They shall become wives for any in whose eyes it is good, except: they shall become wives to the family of their father's tribe. ⁷So a legacy of the children of Israel will not turn from tribe to tribe, but the children of Israel shall each cling to the legacy of his fathers' tribe. ⁸And any daughter who inherits a legacy from the tribes of the children of Israel shall become a wife to someone from a family of her father's tribe, so that the children of Israel will each inherit his fathers' legacy, ⁹and a legacy will not turn from a tribe to another tribe, but the tribes of the children of Israel shall each cling to its legacy."

¹⁰As YHWH commanded Moses, so Zelophehad's daughters did. ¹¹And Mahlah, Tirzah, and Hoglah and Milcah and Noah, Zelophehad's

עַל־פִּי יְהוָה לֵאמֹר כֵּן מַטֵּה בְנֵי־יוֹסֵף דֹּבְרִים:
⁶זֶה הַדָּבָר אֲשֶׁר־צִוָּה יְהוָה לִבְנוֹת צְלָפְחָד לֵאמֹר לַטּוֹב בְּעֵינֵיהֶם תִּהְיֶינָה לְנָשִׁים אַךְ לְמִשְׁפַּחַת מַטֵּה אֲבִיהֶם תִּהְיֶינָה לְנָשִׁים: ⁷וְלֹא־תִסֹּב נַחֲלָה לִבְנֵי יִשְׂרָאֵל מִמַּטֶּה אֶל־מַטֶּה כִּי אִישׁ בְּנַחֲלַת מַטֵּה אֲבֹתָיו יִדְבְּקוּ בְּנֵי יִשְׂרָאֵל: ⁸וְכָל־בַּת יֹרֶשֶׁת נַחֲלָה מִמַּטּוֹת בְּנֵי יִשְׂרָאֵל לְאֶחָד מִמִּשְׁפַּחַת מַטֵּה אָבִיהָ תִּהְיֶה לְאִשָּׁה לְמַעַן יִירְשׁוּ בְּנֵי יִשְׂרָאֵל אִישׁ נַחֲלַת אֲבֹתָיו: ⁹וְלֹא־תִסֹּב נַחֲלָה מִמַּטֶּה לְמַטֶּה אַחֵר כִּי־אִישׁ בְּנַחֲלָתוֹ יִדְבְּקוּ מַטּוֹת בְּנֵי יִשְׂרָאֵל: ¹⁰כַּאֲשֶׁר צִוָּה יְהוָה אֶת־מֹשֶׁה כֵּן עָשׂוּ בְּנוֹת צְלָפְחָד: ¹¹וַתִּהְיֶינָה מַחְלָה תִרְצָה וְחָגְלָה וּמִלְכָּה וְנֹעָה בְּנוֹת

36:5. The tribe of the children of Joseph speak right. These are the exact words that Moses had said about the case that Zelophehad's daughters made: "Zelophehad's daughters speak right" (Num 27:7). This case thus involves a conflict between two legitimate positions.

36:6. they shall become wives to the family of their father's tribe. The decision on the conflicting claims of Zelophehad's daughters and the leaders of their tribe (Manasseh) results in a limitation on the rights of women that were established in the original case. If there are no sons, daughters may still inherit their father's property, but they must then marry only men from their own tribe. If they choose to marry outside their tribe, they lose their legacy, and it passes to their father's brothers instead.

Beside the immediate issues of this case, it teaches a broader principle of law as well. When any law is instituted, there may be situations and consequences later that require a modification of the law. There must be a mechanism for dealing with such situations. In the wilderness Moses can turn directly to God for an answer. But later that is no longer possible. And so we must rely on human judgment on questions of new consequences of laws. This requires turning to those who have both learning and wisdom.

36:10. Zelophehad's daughters. Numbers concludes with this account of a ruling on a point of law that has arisen out of an earlier ruling on women's property rights in the case of the daughters of Zelophehad. It is a strange ending, not only because it is anticlimactic but because it is not remotely a denouement to all that has been narrated so far in the book. The slave mentality of the people, their rebellions, their rejection of the land, the development of Moses' character and of his relationship with

daughters, became wives to their uncles' sons. [12]They became wives within the families of the children of Manasseh son of Joseph, and their legacy was on the tribe of their father's family.

[13]These are the commandments and the judgments that YHWH commanded by Moses' hand to the children of Israel in the plains of Moab by the Jordan toward Jericho.

מִמִּשְׁפְּחֹת בְּנֵי־ ‏[12] צְלָפְחָד לִבְנֵי דֹדֵיהֶן לְנָשִׁים:
מְנַשֶּׁה בֶן־יוֹסֵף הָיוּ לְנָשִׁים וַתְּהִי נַחֲלָתָן עַל־מַטֵּה
מִשְׁפַּחַת אֲבִיהֶן: ‏[13] אֵלֶּה הַמִּצְוֹת וְהַמִּשְׁפָּטִים אֲשֶׁר
צִוָּה יְהוָה בְּיַד־מֹשֶׁה אֶל־בְּנֵי יִשְׂרָאֵל בְּעַרְבֹת
מוֹאָב עַל יַרְדֵּן יְרֵחוֹ:

God, the challenges to his authority, the great miraculous events and the continuous divine nurturing, the entire theme of the journey from Sinai to the promised land itself—all of these things seem to be left without a finish at the end of Numbers. This, however, is consistent with what we have already observed: that Numbers is less self-contained than the other books of the Five Books of Moses. The natural culmination and conclusion to all these things is the death of Moses, which is pictured as resulting from the spiral of all these elements. But Moses' death is to be preceded by an exceptionally long address by the prophet, which would have been too long to include in Numbers. It would have doubled the length of the book. And so the division of the originally continuous biblical text into five books has left Numbers with a finish that is unsatisfactory in itself but that serves to point us to a coming climax and resolution in the book of Deuteronomy.

36:13. by Moses' hand. Numbers develops what was begun in Exodus in the matter of the man Moses himself. Exodus began to present the complex and conflicting sides of his personality. Now in Numbers we see these elements of Moses' character operating and metamorphosing through a variety of circumstances. There are fewer glimpses of him alone in conversation with God and more portrayals of his deepening connection with the people to whom he has been bound not by choice but by divine decision. Through the course of Numbers he emerges as the most textured personality in the Hebrew Bible, the closest to God and yet perhaps the most empathetically human. His humility is depicted in conflict with his anger; his love of his fellow humans is set in tension with his repeated disappointments over their rebelliousness and lack of wisdom. Precisely in his closeness to God he speaks to the deity in language that appears audacious by usual human conceptions of reverence before the divine, even more audacious than his own words at Sinai in Exodus (32:32; 33:12–16). And, despite his protests to the people that it is not against him but God that they are complaining, after years of closeness to the divine-human boundary of authority he comes to infringe on that boundary and thus brings upon himself the condemnation of death. Whether or not one regards this depiction as tragic in the Greek sense, one must appreciate its power and its irony. One can also appreciate that it exemplifies the issue of the danger of coming close to the divine, which is present through the course of the book of Numbers. The cosmic and the historical are bound in a particularly pervasive way in Numbers: in the record of the people, who witness and are sustained by constant miracles and whose closeness to the cosmic occasionally brings them into contact with fearful phenomena; in the life of the priesthood,

where closeness to the cosmic realm is an ongoing and threatening concern; and in the life of Moses himself, where his extraordinary position on that boundary is at the heart of the episodes about him in this book.

A closing comment on the book of Numbers

Scholars have often described the book of Numbers as a hodgepodge of relatively unconnected narratives, laws, and poems. They say it is heterogeneous and the least unified composition in the Torah. But, on the contrary, the book is coherent and tightly woven. The *journey* is the unifying element. It functions both through time (by its chronology of events) and space (by the geographical placement of the events along the route of travel) to organize the episodes into a related story. Elements of language and recurring themes contribute to this unity. Most of all, though, the events of the journey themselves bind the story, for they are not a collection of unrelated episodes. A connecting line of cause and effect runs through them so that they can be read both as individual stories and as a meaningful chain of events. Indeed, the episodes of the journey described in the book of Numbers are much more clearly related to one another than those of the epic of *Gilgamesh* or *The Odyssey*.

Here is a review of the book with attention to the narrative's progression:

The story of the journey begins with an account of preparations for the departure. There is a census, the Levites are numbered and assigned to care for the Tabernacle, YHWH gives a group of laws relating to maintaining purity in the camp, a number of ritual matters are described (the priestly blessing, the menorah, the Passover sacrifice), the tribal offerings for the Tabernacle are enumerated, and instructions for travel are given: travel is to follow the movements of the cloud and fire over the Tabernacle and is to be signaled by blasts on two silver trumpets.

This takes up the great majority of the first ten chapters of the book. Then the moment of departure arrives. The journey begins with the people complaining (11:1–3). The reason for their grumbling is not told. The story's function, therefore, is rather to establish the people's state of mind as they set out. With the usual biblical economy of wording, the text, which is only three verses long, conveys the dynamic of the triangle of God, the people, and Moses. The people anger YHWH, He plagues them (in this case with fire), they cry to Moses, Moses pleads on their behalf, and the plague stops. Most notably about this dynamic: the people still address Moses rather than God. They still focus on the human leader.

This role for Moses has direct implications for the episode that immediately follows (11:4–34). The people's complaint in this case is over food. They find the manna that they have been eating to be unsatisfactory compared to the food that they received—"free"!—in Egypt (11:5). They cry for meat. Moses, apparently unable to bear the burden of being the sole leader any longer, pours out his heart to YHWH in one of the most remarkable speeches in the Scriptures. Having come closer to God than any other human being has, Moses speaks to God as no other human being in the Hebrew Bible does: "Why have you done bad to your servant . . . if this is how you treat me, kill me" (11:11–15).

God's response to this anguished yet audacious speech is seemingly to ignore its emotional content and to go directly to the solution of the problem. This mode of divine response is akin to earlier accounts we have observed, in which the deity addresses what is in the person's heart rather than what the person says. YHWH instructs Moses to gather seventy of the elders of Israel and to inform the people that they will receive meat the next day. The meat comes in the form of birds that a divine wind carries to the camp. The assistance to Moses comes as God takes some of the spirit that is on Moses and sets it on the seventy elders, who then prophesy. Despite the uncertainty about the terms, it is understood that Moses' special role as the people's prophet is now shared in some way with others.

This in turn sets the stage for the episode that follows, the story of "snow-white" Miriam in Numbers 12. Miriam and Aaron speak against Moses. On the heels of the story of the sharing of Moses' prophetic status, they ask, "Has YHWH only just spoken through Moses? Hasn't He also spoken through us?" Their concern is a personal matter, but they involve God. This error of judgment draws God personally into the matter and proves costly. Moses does not defend himself, but YHWH defends him to Aaron and Miriam, declaring that Moses' experience of the divine is indeed qualitatively different from the prophetic experience of others—Moses has actually seen God—and the deity concludes with the ominous words, "And why did you not fear to speak against my servant, against Moses?" (12:8). Miriam is left with the leprosy. Aaron, like the people in the first episode, appeals to Moses, whose superiority he now appears to acknowledge by addressing him as "my lord." Moses in turn intercedes with God, and Miriam is healed after a week passes. The story thus establishes by word and action that Moses' singular experience of God at Sinai has left him with a singular relationship with God.

This unique status of Moses out of all the people of Israel then plays a part at a crucial moment in the destiny of the people, depicted in the next episode of the journey, the episode of the scouts (Numbers 13–14). Once again the people complain against Moses (and Aaron) and speak of appointing new leaders and returning to Egypt. On the verge of their arrival and of the fulfillment of the promise to be free people in their own land, they want to turn back to Egypt. YHWH's response is the same as in the matter of the golden calf. He tells Moses that he plans to destroy the nation and start over with Moses' descendants. In the wake of the preceding episodes, which establish Moses' exceptional status and closeness to God, this divine plan—making Moses a sort of new Abraham—is even more understandable, and therefore more frightening, than in the golden calf episode; and Moses' appeal to the deity to relent is about 50 percent longer. Again Moses raises the point of "what will the Egyptians say?" but this time he adds references to what the inhabitants of the land, and the other nations as well, will say, namely, "Because YHWH wasn't able to bring this people to the land that He swore to them, He slaughtered them in the wilderness" (14:16). Moses' second ground for appeal this time is to quote YHWH's own words back to Him, the words of the divine formula that YHWH had said to Moses in the moment that Moses had actually seen God: "as you spoke, saying, 'YHWH is slow to anger and abounding in kindness, bearing crime and offense. . . .'" Once again Moses' appeal is successful, but it is important to see that in this instance the decree and the appeal have a greater depth in the narrative than in the golden calf account. In particular, the Miriam

episode, which immediately precedes this, has underscored the uniqueness of Moses' relationship with God, and in identifying this relationship it has referred to the very moment that now figures crucially in Moses' appeal to save the people—the moment in which Moses saw God and was told the qualities of the divine personality. The episodes of the journey in Numbers are thus linked together both in a general thematic way and in specific connecting elements.

Although Moses is successful in his appeal that the people not be wiped out, the divine reprieve is only a partial one. The fact remains that their slave mentality has surfaced again, and they have shown themselves to be not only fearful and ungrateful but unprepared for the responsibilities that go with being a free people in their own land. YHWH decrees that none of these people of the generation who have seen His power since they were in Egypt will live to arrive in the promised land. They are condemned to extend their journey in the wilderness to forty years, during which time everyone from the age of twenty and older will die, with the exception of the two dissenting scouts Caleb and Joshua. (We can deduce from subsequent events that Moses and Aaron, too, do not fall under this decree.) The journey is thus transformed horribly for the exodus generation from a short trip to a promised land into a lengthy movement with no end until death. They are undeserving of bondage and unequipped for freedom, but these are the two known conditions of residence in a land in their world, and this dilemma leaves them in an interim state on a journey without a destination.

In the following chapter, YHWH gives Moses a series of commands concerning the nation's sacrifices when they arrive in the land (15:2), which seems like a confirmation that God does intend to bring the younger generation there ultimately, and it is a painful indication to the older generation of what they have lost. He also instructs the people to wear fringes on their clothing forever, and, in a rare explanation for a law, tells them that the purpose of the fringe is to serve as a visible reminder to keep all the other commandments and thus be holy to their God (15:39–40). The decree that the exodus generation will not be brought to the land and this reminder that they are to be a holy people are then entwined together to figure centrally in the next episode of the journey, the story of the rebellion of Korah, Dathan, and Abiram. The rebellion story combines the two issues. Dathan and Abiram protest that Moses has not brought them to the land flowing with milk and honey that they were promised (16:14); and Korah and his group accuse Moses and Aaron of putting themselves above the people when "all of the congregation, all of them, are holy" (16:3). The unity in the chain of episodes in the journey is particularly visible here, in the substance of the narrative and in its specific language.

The unity is also thematic. Leadership and the prerogatives thereof are again the issue. Dathan and Abiram direct their challenge, like earlier challenges, to Moses personally, rather than to the deity, as being the one who has brought them out of Egypt—which they outrageously describe as "a land flowing with milk and honey" (16:13)—but who has not brought them to the promised land. Moses promises proof "that YHWH sent me to do all these things, because it's not from my own heart" (16:28). And the continuing issue of leadership of the priesthood is combined with this general issue of leadership, for Korah is a Levite, Moses' and Aaron's first cousin (Exod 6:18–21), and Moses takes Korah's group's complaint as a claim on the priesthood (Num 16:10). Their challenge, too, takes the form of a personal attack on Moses

and Aaron, and Moses refocuses this attack as well, informing the challengers that they are "gathering against *YHWH*," and he adds, "And Aaron, what is he that you complain against him?" (16:11). The full story therefore appears to recount an alliance among several dissident groups who, despite their having witnessed considerable miraculous evidence that Moses' (and Aaron's) authority is divinely supported, choose nonetheless to raise challenges to their status. As in the preceding episodes, the attack on Moses is handled by God, and an earthquake and miraculous fire consume the rebels.

The next episode is built explicitly on this. The people now complain to Moses and Aaron that "*You* killed YHWH's people!" (17:6). Apparently slow learners, they once again direct their complaints, about an act that was manifestly the deity's, at Moses and Aaron personally. Again the attack is handled by God, this time by a plague. Again it is the interceding actions of Moses and especially Aaron that save the nation from further destruction. At divine command, Moses places the staffs that represent each of the tribes inside the Tent of Meeting. On the next day the staff of the tribe of Levi, with Aaron's name inscribed on it, has blossomed and grown almonds, clearly confirming once and for all YHWH's selection of Aaron for the priesthood. YHWH orders Moses to place Aaron's staff in front of the ark "for a sign to rebels" (17:25). We learn the consequence of this in the subsequent episode: Meribah. There Moses refers to the people as rebels, strikes the rock with this miraculous staff of Aaron's, and so Aaron shares Moses' fate: they both are to die without reaching the promised land.

As a consequence of being condemned to forty years in the wilderness in the episode of the scouts, Israel abandons its direct route of entry into the land from the south. After spending time moving about in the Sinai, the people take a longer route that will lead them through the territory to the east of the land and eventually to an entry from the east. This brings them into contact with the peoples of this area, who are already familiar from the book of Genesis: Edomites, Amorites, Moabites, and Midianites. The next several episodes relate Israel's encounters with these groups. They come first to the territory of Edom, the land of Esau's descendants, and the Israelites appeal with due diplomacy to their "brothers" to allow them to pass through their territory. The Edomites refuse and threaten an armed response (20:14–21). Israel therefore avoids Edom, which means a circuitous route and lost access to food and water. It comes as no surprise, then, when the people rebel again in the next chapter over the lack of food and water. The notable new element in their complaint this time is that they finally seem to have assimilated the fact that it is not merely Moses but God who is directing them. Therefore: "the people spoke against God—and against Moses" (21:5). This time YHWH plagues them with deadly snakes. Again they appeal to Moses ("We've sinned, because we spoke against YHWH and against you"), again Moses intercedes, and God provides a remedy: the bronze snake on a pole.

The Israelites' eastern route next takes them to the territory of the Amorite kings Sihon and Og, and Israel makes the same request for peaceful passage that they have made to Edom. Both Sihon and Og attack Israel militarily, and both are utterly defeated. Thus Israel comes to acquire territory on the eastern side of the Jordan River, outside the borders of the promised land (Num 21:21–35).

Israel's conquest of the Amorite territories in turn leads to conflict with the Moab-

ites, who are the descendants of Abraham's nephew Lot (Gen 19:36–37), and the Midianites, who are descendants of Abraham himself (Gen 25:2). Explicitly as a consequence of Israel's conquests of the Amorites, the Moabite king Balak acts preemptively against Israel (22:2–3). Military might has not been successful against Israel, and so Balak, allied with Midian, turns to more transcendent means, hiring the seer Balaam to put a curse on Israel. But instead of cursing Israel, Balaam blesses them, and Balak's plan is frustrated. Moab and Midian then try another nonmilitary, albeit more earthy, approach to the Israelites. Moabite and Midianite women seduce the Israelites, first sexually and then to their religious worship at Baal Peor. Moses orders the execution of those who were associated with Baal Peor, but the culminating event of the Baal Peor apostasy is not Moses' action but rather that of Phinehas, Aaron's grandson. When an Israelite man and a Midianite woman openly pass before Moses and the people at the Tent of Meeting to enter the tent's inner sanctum, it is Phinehas who goes after them and impales them both on his spear while they are in the sexual act on the floor (25:8). The Israelites subsequently take revenge on the Midianites, involving the slaughter of the males and adult females (the severity of the recompense being apparently the consequence of the severity of the offense in the ritual realm) and the execution of Balaam, who, we learn, had devised the Baal Peor scheme (31:8,16).

When Phinehas plunges his spear through the couple in the Tent, he halts a plague that had stricken the people (25:8–9,18–19). The account of the revenge on the Midianites also refers to this plague (31:16). Earlier we noted an account of a plague in the aftermath of the Korah episode. The matter of plagues in cases of ritual offense is another cohesive element uniting the chain of events in Numbers. The first section of the book, covering the preparations for the journey, includes the establishment of the Levites as the Israelite group that is to perform the religious services at the Tent of Meeting. YHWH commands the Levites to serve at the Tabernacle and "make atonement" for the people so that "there will not be a *plague* in the children of Israel when the children of Israel would *come near to the Holy*" (8:19). Both the Korah and the Phinehas episodes are then about persons who step beyond the formal limits of the holy. Korah and his people, declaring that "all the people are holy," dare to burn incense; and the Israelite man and Midianite woman dare to enter the interior of the Tabernacle, an area known precisely as "the Holy" (Exod 26:33). Both actions result in plagues, the two plagues are halted by the intervention of Aaron and Phinehas respectively, and thus the divisions and status of the Levites and the Aaronid priests are established. YHWH awards Phinehas a covenant of eternal priesthood in Israel for having "made atonement" for the people (Num 25:11–13).

Following the plague, YHWH orders a second census, which likewise recalls the preparatory actions of the first section of Numbers, in which the first census was taken. It is now confirmed that no one who was counted in the census at the beginning of the book has survived except Caleb and Joshua, as decreed in the episode of the scouts (26:63–65). God designates Joshua as Moses' successor as leader of the nation, preparing for the fulfillment of the decree of Moses' death in the Meribah episode (27:15–23). In sum, various lines of action and law run as threads that bind the episodes together and now converge in the concluding chapters of the book. Everything follows naturally. The new census is naturally followed by matters of the

distribution of the land and laws of inheritance of property, including inheritance by women and Levites. There is also a section on the calendar that is to be followed in the land, including the proper observance of the Sabbath, new moons, and holidays (28; 29). The book thus concludes by picturing the people at the end of the journey, ready to arrive in the land, with a leader, a priestly establishment, a constitution of laws, and a system to distribute the land. To bring it together, the list of Israel's itinerary in Numbers 33 formally shows the sequence of the journey to be the unifying line of the book.

Like the Jacob cycle of stories in Genesis, the book of Numbers is a collection of stories that appear superficially to be loosely connected but that are in fact bound by chronological and geographical flow, by continuous themes, and by a causal sequence in the progression of the story. This prepares us for Moses' great speech in Deuteronomy.

DEUTERONOMY

*T*he book of Deuteronomy pictures the last events of Israel's forty years in the wilderness and the last events of Moses' life. It ends with Moses' death, which is the climax and culmination that the book of Numbers lacked. The scene: The people are at the end of a journey. They are located east of the Jordan River, at the border of their promised land, in the plains of Moab. They are about to enter a new land and a settled life. And their leader is about to die. It is no surprise that Moses tells them not to be afraid. There is every reason for them to be in need of such reassurance. As for Moses, he knows he is about to die, and he is not accepting it with wise acquiescence. He pleads with YHWH to let him live to cross over into the land; but YHWH tells him, "Don't go on speaking to me anymore of this thing." And Moses gives a glorious farewell speech. It starts off unattractively to the audience, a review of history, mostly unpleasant, a criticism of the people's unworthiness; then a lengthy list of laws, reviewing some old ones and adding many new ones; then a list of blessings and horrible curses; then a beautiful conclusion: encouraging, inspiring. And then he ends with songs.

The narrative has come a long distance from the cosmic Genesis 1. Now, for the whole of the last book of the Five Books of Moses, it is a picture of a group of people listening to the speech of a man. No seas split; no angels appear; there are in fact no miracles at all in Deuteronomy. There is rather the retelling of the miracles. The acts of God, of Moses, and of the people now themselves become part of the background, and the foreground belongs to Moses' words.

WORDS

דברים

1 ¹These are the words that Moses spoke to all of Israel across the Jordan in the wilderness, in the plain opposite Suph between Paran and

1 ¹אֵ֣לֶּה הַדְּבָרִ֗ים אֲשֶׁ֨ר דִּבֶּ֤ר מֹשֶׁה֙ אֶל־כָּל־
יִשְׂרָאֵ֔ל בְּעֵ֖בֶר הַיַּרְדֵּ֑ן בַּמִּדְבָּ֡ר בָּֽעֲרָבָה֩ מ֨וֹל ס֜וּף

1:1. **words.** The last verse in Numbers is, "These are the commandments and the judgments that YHWH commanded by Moses' hand to the children of Israel." The first verse in Deuteronomy is, "These are the words that Moses spoke to all of Israel." The difference between *commandments and judgments* in Numbers and *words* in Deuteronomy marks an essential change. Commandments and judgments are laws. Now, in the last book of the Torah, Moses does more than give law. Deuteronomy is a book of Words. That is its name in Hebrew: *děbārîm*, and that is what it is about. Its first thirty chapters are Moses' farewell address to his people before his death. It would have taken close to three hours to say it all to them. It contains history, law, and great wisdom. In places, especially near its end, it is beautiful—inspired and inspirational. Moses is eloquent. And that is ironic and instructive when we turn back to Moses' first meeting with God, at the burning bush. There he tries to escape from the assignment to go speak to the Pharaoh by saying, "I'm not a man of words" (Exod 4:10)! Now he has become a man of words. It is interesting, remarkable, ironic, and inspiring to see Moses' development through all that has happened in forty years into a man of words. More than any other human in the Bible, Moses grows and changes in the course of his life. One can change: change professions, change values, change lifestyle, change character. One can grow and become stronger and better.

This is also a change in the presentation of law in the Torah. Most of the commandments in the Torah have been given without reasons or explanations. From the law of the "red cow" (Numbers 19) to the Ten Commandments, one is not told *why* one must perform them, but only that God commands it (with a few notable exceptions). But the law code of Deuteronomy (12–28) is preceded by eleven chapters of history, explanation, and inspiration, and it is followed by two chapters of exquisite revelation of the relevance and value of the commandments. The Torah thus concludes with the message that the law is meant to be relevant, comprehensible, and meaningful in the people's lives. It is appropriate to seek out the meanings of the laws and, when interpreting the law, to understand that it is explicitly meant to enhance lives. One must not apply it in a way that causes injury or undermines its positive function in life.

1:1. **Moses.** In the Hebrew Bible's picture of human history, Moses is the first great man—and the first great leader. In Deuteronomy, our acquaintance with Moses reaches a summit. Deuteronomy is the book that is about Moses more than any other in the Torah. All are called "the Five Books of Moses," but Deuteronomy is the most focused on Moses himself: a speech by him, expressions of his own views, descriptions of his last acts. By virtue of the book's being a speech, Moses now speaks for himself, as it were, rather than the narrator's speaking for and about him. Moses has moved from "heavy mouth" to eloquence.

Tophel and Laban and Hazeroth and Di-zahab, ²eleven days from Horeb by way of Mount Seir up to Kadesh-barnea. ³And it was in the fortieth year, in the eleventh month, on the first of the

בֵּין־פָּארָן וּבֵין־תֹּפֶל וְלָבָן וַחֲצֵרֹת וְדִי זָהָב: ²אַחַד עָשָׂר יוֹם מֵחֹרֵב דֶּרֶךְ הַר־שֵׂעִיר עַד קָדֵשׁ בַּרְנֵעַ: ³וַיְהִי בְּאַרְבָּעִים שָׁנָה בְּעַשְׁתֵּי־עָשָׂר חֹדֶשׁ בְּאֶחָד

Essentially an unknown quantity at the burning bush, he has become probably the most known person in the Bible. So known and still so enigmatic: the man who wears a veil; who feared to take the assignment to go to Egypt but whose temper flared at the king of Egypt; who ran from a staff that turned to a snake at the burning bush but who disobediently struck a rock with a staff at Meribah; who pleaded with God not to be angry with the people over their golden calf but who smashed the tablets when he saw the calf himself; the humblest man on earth who spoke to the deity more audaciously than any other human.

In analyzing and interpreting Moses, one is more likely to reveal things about oneself than about Moses. Moses is so much a Rorschach test because he is so much a regular human being, with weaknesses, a temper, fears, and flaws—with key pieces unrevealed—who comes to be the leader of a nation, a spokesman for God, and the founder of a faith that plays a role in the destiny of humankind. That is Moses as portrayed in the text. The reader's knowledge, moreover, that Moses is to some degree—to whatever degree—historical behind this portrayal fuels this phenomenon. This real, regular, unique, meek, powerful, audacious figure cries out for understanding and interpretation.

1:1. **the words that Moses spoke**. In developing from a man of actions to a man of words, Moses imitates God. The *Tanak* depicts God as becoming more and more hidden over the course of history. In the first books of the Bible God appears to humans, is seen and heard at Sinai, makes His presence known through miracles, angels, and the column of cloud and fire. But these visible signs of divine action in history disappear from the story one by one. And by the last books of the *Tanak*, there are no angels or miracles. The words "YHWH appeared to" and "YHWH spoke to" do not occur to anyone. Instead, the priest Ezra reads the Torah aloud to the people. In the place of the acts of God there is the *word* of God. When the Torah pictures Moses ending his life in words, he imitates and prefigures the transformation of the human experience of God that will occur in the Bible.

1:2. **eleven days from Horeb**. The journey from Horeb (the other name for Mount Sinai) to the promised land only needed to take eleven days! Now, as the people stand at the entrance to the land after forty years, after everyone with adult memories of slavery has died, the meaning of the loss of forty years can be deeply felt, appreciated, and regretted. The new generation can think: "If only my mother and father had lived to see this." So they quintessentially reflect the human experience of wishing, when we experience some joy after our parents or grandparents have died, that they had lived to see it.

1:3. **in the fortieth year**. The juxtaposition of this notice (that it was in the fortieth year) to the preceding verse (that it was only eleven days' journey) underscores the point that I made in my preceding comment. These two verses should always be read

month, Moses spoke to the children of Israel of everything that YHWH commanded him to them. [4]After he struck Sihon, king of the Amorites, who lived in Heshbon, and Og, king of Bashan, who lived in Ashtaroth at Edrei, [5]across the Jordan in the land of Moab, Moses undertook to make this instruction clear, saying, [6]"YHWH our God spoke to us in Horeb, saying, 'You've had enough of staying at this mountain. [7]Turn and travel and come to the Amorite hill country and to all its neighboring places, in the plain, in the hill country, and in the lowland and in the Negeb and by the seashore, the land of the Canaanite and Lebanon as far as the big river, the Euphrates River. [8]See: I've put the land in front of you. Come and possess the land that YHWH swore to your fathers, to Abraham, to Isaac, and to Jacob, to give to them and to their seed after them.'

לַחֹדֶשׁ דִּבֶּר מֹשֶׁה אֶל־בְּנֵי יִשְׂרָאֵל כְּכֹל אֲשֶׁר צִוָּה יְהוָה אֹתוֹ אֲלֵהֶם: ⁴אַחֲרֵי הַכֹּתוֹ אֵת סִיחֹן מֶלֶךְ הָאֱמֹרִי אֲשֶׁר יוֹשֵׁב בְּחֶשְׁבּוֹן וְאֵת עוֹג מֶלֶךְ הַבָּשָׁן אֲשֶׁר־יוֹשֵׁב בְּעַשְׁתָּרֹת בְּאֶדְרֶעִי: ⁵בְּעֵבֶר הַיַּרְדֵּן בְּאֶרֶץ מוֹאָב הוֹאִיל מֹשֶׁה בֵּאֵר אֶת־הַתּוֹרָה הַזֹּאת לֵאמֹר: ⁶יְהוָה אֱלֹהֵינוּ דִּבֶּר אֵלֵינוּ בְּחֹרֵב לֵאמֹר רַב־לָכֶם שֶׁבֶת בָּהָר הַזֶּה: ⁷פְּנוּ | וּסְעוּ לָכֶם וּבֹאוּ הַר הָאֱמֹרִי וְאֶל־כָּל־שְׁכֵנָיו בָּעֲרָבָה בָהָר וּבַשְּׁפֵלָה וּבַנֶּגֶב וּבְחוֹף הַיָּם אֶרֶץ הַכְּנַעֲנִי וְהַלְּבָנוֹן עַד־הַנָּהָר הַגָּדֹל נְהַר־פְּרָת: ⁸רְאֵה נָתַתִּי לִפְנֵיכֶם אֶת־הָאָרֶץ בֹּאוּ וּרְשׁוּ אֶת־הָאָרֶץ אֲשֶׁר נִשְׁבַּע יְהוָה לַאֲבֹתֵיכֶם לְאַבְרָהָם לְיִצְחָק וּלְיַעֲקֹב לָתֵת לָהֶם וּלְזַרְעָם

together as a unit: "It is eleven days from Horeb . . . but it was in the fortieth year . . ." And this juxtaposition cries out for us to consider all the ways of interpreting this fact: the irony, the waste, the necessity, the experience, the growth, the suffering, the need for a new generation who had not known slavery, the inability of humans to outgrow a trauma of mammoth proportions to an entire nation (I write this in the generation after the holocaust, in which the psychological effects of what happened still afflict us).

1:5. **undertook.** This is the word that Abraham uses twice in his attempt to affect God's decision about the fate of Sodom. He says: "Here I've undertaken to speak to my Lord, and I'm dust and ashes" (Gen 18:27,31). That is the first time in the *Tanak* that a human argues with God. Now the same term is used for Moses' setting out to convey a message from God to the people. Again it is a reminder of how far humans have come, and it may even hint that such growth was necessary: humans had to rise to that level, at which one (Abraham) could question God, before they could move to the level of receiving the commandments. Humans have to be able to question commandments—even divine commandments, *especially* divine commandments—in order for there to be any merit in performing them.

1:5. **make clear.** Hebrew *bē'ēr*. This term occurs just twice in the Torah: here at the beginning of Moses' speech and, later, near the end of the speech (Deut 27:8). There it refers to the way in which this instruction is to be written on stones: very clearly. Here Moses seeks to accomplish in words what is accomplished there in writing, to make the instructions clear. Among his final words he will tell the people that this is not a hidden or distant thing. It is close and is meant to be practiced (29:28; 30:11–14).

⁹"And I said to you at that time, saying, 'I'm not able to carry you by myself. ¹⁰YHWH, your God, has made you multiply, and here today you're like the stars of the skies for multitude. ¹¹(May YHWH, your fathers' God, add on to you a thousand times more like you! And may He bless you as He spoke to you.) ¹²How shall I carry your stress and your burden and your quarrels by myself? ¹³Get wise and understanding and knowledgeable people for your tribes, and I'll set them among your heads.'

¹⁴"And you answered me, and you said, 'The thing that you've spoken is good to do.'

¹⁵"And I took heads of your tribes, wise and knowledgeable people, and I set them as heads over you, chiefs of thousands and chiefs of hundreds and chiefs of fifties and chiefs of tens and officers for your tribes. ¹⁶And I commanded your judges at that time, saying, 'Hear between your brothers, and you shall judge with justice between a man and his brother or between him and his alien. ¹⁷You shall not recognize a face in judgment: you shall hear the same for small and for big. Don't be fearful in front of a man—because justice is *God's*. And a matter that will be too hard for you, you shall bring forward to me, and I'll hear it.' ¹⁸And I commanded you at that time all the things that you should do.

אַחֲרֵיהֶֽם: ⁹וָאֹמַ֣ר אֲלֵכֶ֔ם בָּעֵ֥ת הַהִ֖וא לֵאמֹ֑ר לֹא־ אוּכַ֥ל לְבַדִּ֖י שְׂאֵ֥ת אֶתְכֶֽם: ¹⁰יְהוָ֥ה אֱלֹהֵיכֶ֖ם הִרְבָּ֣ה אֶתְכֶ֑ם וְהִנְּכֶ֣ם הַיּ֔וֹם כְּכוֹכְבֵ֥י הַשָּׁמַ֖יִם לָרֹֽב: ¹¹יְהוָ֞ה אֱלֹהֵ֣י אֲבֽוֹתֵכֶ֗ם יֹסֵ֧ף עֲלֵיכֶ֛ם כָּכֶ֖ם אֶ֣לֶף פְּעָמִ֑ים וִיבָרֵ֣ךְ אֶתְכֶ֔ם כַּאֲשֶׁ֖ר דִּבֶּ֥ר לָכֶֽם: ¹²אֵיכָ֥ה אֶשָּׂ֖א לְבַדִּ֑י טָרְחֲכֶ֥ם וּמַשַּׂאֲכֶ֖ם וְרִֽיבְכֶֽם: ¹³הָב֣וּ לָכֶ֡ם אֲנָשִׁים֩ חֲכָמִ֨ים וּנְבֹנִ֜ים וִידֻעִ֣ים לְשִׁבְטֵיכֶ֗ם וַאֲשִׂימֵ֖ם בְּרָאשֵׁיכֶֽם: ¹⁴וַֽתַּעֲנ֖וּ אֹתִ֑י וַתֹּ֣אמְר֔וּ טֽוֹב־הַדָּבָ֥ר אֲשֶׁר־דִּבַּ֖רְתָּ לַעֲשֽׂוֹת: ¹⁵וָאֶקַּ֞ח אֶת־רָאשֵׁ֣י שִׁבְטֵיכֶ֗ם אֲנָשִׁ֤ים חֲכָמִים֙ וִֽידֻעִ֔ים וָאֶתֵּ֥ן אֹתָ֛ם רָאשִׁ֖ים עֲלֵיכֶ֑ם שָׂרֵ֨י אֲלָפִ֜ים וְשָׂרֵ֣י מֵא֗וֹת וְשָׂרֵ֤י חֲמִשִּׁים֙ וְשָׂרֵ֣י עֲשָׂרֹ֔ת וְשֹׁטְרִ֖ים לְשִׁבְטֵיכֶֽם: ¹⁶וָאֲצַוֶּה֙ אֶת־שֹׁפְטֵיכֶ֔ם בָּעֵ֥ת הַהִ֖וא לֵאמֹ֑ר שָׁמֹ֤עַ בֵּין־אֲחֵיכֶם֙ וּשְׁפַטְתֶּ֣ם צֶ֔דֶק בֵּֽין־אִ֥ישׁ וּבֵין־אָחִ֖יו וּבֵ֥ין גֵּרֽוֹ: ¹⁷לֹֽא־תַכִּ֨ירוּ פָנִ֜ים בַּמִּשְׁפָּ֗ט כַּקָּטֹ֤ן כַּגָּדֹל֙ תִּשְׁמָע֔וּן לֹ֤א תָג֙וּרוּ֙ מִפְּנֵי־אִ֔ישׁ כִּ֥י הַמִּשְׁפָּ֖ט לֵאלֹהִ֣ים ה֑וּא וְהַדָּבָר֙ אֲשֶׁ֣ר יִקְשֶׁ֣ה מִכֶּ֔ם תַּקְרִב֥וּן אֵלַ֖י וּשְׁמַעְתִּֽיו: ¹⁸וָאֲצַוֶּ֥ה אֶתְכֶ֖ם בָּעֵ֣ת הַהִ֑וא אֵ֥ת כָּל־הַדְּבָרִ֖ים אֲשֶׁ֥ר תַּעֲשֽׂוּן:

1:9. **I said to you at that time**. Moses says, "I said to *you* at that time," even though most of the people he is addressing now were not even born yet at the time he is discussing. And Moses will continue to speak this way in this address. He conveys to the people that they are part of history, that they receive the burden and the legacy of their parents and ancestors. And in the course of his speech he will extend this beyond his immediate audience as well. He mixes past, present, and future generations. So in the end it becomes the message for each generation who reads this text.

1:16. **Hear between your brothers**. "Hear" is meant in the same sense as the phrase in English: judges "hear a case."

1:16. **his alien**. The possessive (*his* alien) is used here and in the Ten Commandments (*your* alien; Exod 20:10; Deut 5:14), conveying how one must feel about—and treat—a non-Israelite living among the people of Israel.

1:17. **recognize a face in judgment**. Meaning: you shall not show favoritism to anyone in a legal proceeding.

19"And we traveled from Horeb and went through all that big and fearful wilderness that you've seen by way of the Amorite hill country as YHWH, our God, commanded us, and we came to Kadesh-barnea. 20And I said to you, 'You've come to the Amorite hill country that YHWH, our God, is giving us. 21See: YHWH, our God, has put the land in front of you. Go up, possess it as YHWH, your fathers' God, spoke to you. Don't be afraid and don't be dismayed.'

22"And you came forward to me, all of you, and said, 'Let's send men ahead of us, and let them explore the land for us and bring us back word of the way by which we'll go up and of the cities to which we'll come.' 23And the thing was good in my eyes, and I took twelve men from you, one man per tribe. 24And they turned and went up to the hill country and came to the Wadi Eshcol and spied it out. 25And they took some of the land's fruit in their hand and brought it down to us, and they brought us back word and said, the land that YHWH, our God, is giving us is good. 26But you weren't willing to go up, and you rebelled against the word of YHWH, your God, 27and you grumbled in your tents and said, 'Because of YHWH's *hatred* for us He brought us out from the land of Egypt, to put us in the Amorite's hand to destroy us! 28To *where* are we going up? Our brothers have melted our heart, saying, "We saw a bigger and taller people than we are, big cities and fortified to the skies, and also giants!"'

29"And I said to you, 'Don't be scared and don't be afraid of them. 30YHWH, your God,

וַנִּסַּע מֵחֹרֵב וַנֵּלֶךְ אֵת כָּל־הַמִּדְבָּר הַגָּדוֹל 19
וְהַנּוֹרָא הַהוּא אֲשֶׁר רְאִיתֶם דֶּרֶךְ הַר הָאֱמֹרִי
כַּאֲשֶׁר צִוָּה יְהוָה אֱלֹהֵינוּ אֹתָנוּ וַנָּבֹא עַד קָדֵשׁ
בַּרְנֵעַ: 20 וָאֹמַר אֲלֵכֶם בָּאתֶם עַד־הַר הָאֱמֹרִי
אֲשֶׁר־יְהוָה אֱלֹהֵינוּ נֹתֵן לָנוּ: 21 רְאֵה נָתַן יְהוָה
אֱלֹהֶיךָ לְפָנֶיךָ אֶת־הָאָרֶץ עֲלֵה רֵשׁ כַּאֲשֶׁר דִּבֶּר
יְהוָה אֱלֹהֵי אֲבֹתֶיךָ לָךְ אַל־תִּירָא וְאַל־תֵּחָת:
22 וַתִּקְרְבוּן אֵלַי כֻּלְּכֶם וַתֹּאמְרוּ נִשְׁלְחָה אֲנָשִׁים
לְפָנֵינוּ וְיַחְפְּרוּ־לָנוּ אֶת־הָאָרֶץ וְיָשִׁבוּ אֹתָנוּ דָּבָר
אֶת־הַדֶּרֶךְ אֲשֶׁר נַעֲלֶה־בָּהּ וְאֵת הֶעָרִים אֲשֶׁר נָבֹא
אֲלֵיהֶן: 23 וַיִּיטַב בְּעֵינַי הַדָּבָר וָאֶקַּח מִכֶּם שְׁנֵים
עָשָׂר אֲנָשִׁים אִישׁ אֶחָד לַשָּׁבֶט: 24 וַיִּפְנוּ וַיַּעֲלוּ
הָהָרָה וַיָּבֹאוּ עַד־נַחַל אֶשְׁכֹּל וַיְרַגְּלוּ אֹתָהּ:
25 וַיִּקְחוּ בְיָדָם מִפְּרִי הָאָרֶץ וַיּוֹרִדוּ אֵלֵינוּ וַיָּשִׁבוּ
אֹתָנוּ דָבָר וַיֹּאמְרוּ טוֹבָה הָאָרֶץ אֲשֶׁר־יְהוָה
אֱלֹהֵינוּ נֹתֵן לָנוּ: 26 וְלֹא אֲבִיתֶם לַעֲלֹת וַתַּמְרוּ אֶת־
פִּי יְהוָה אֱלֹהֵיכֶם: 27 וַתֵּרָגְנוּ בְאָהֳלֵיכֶם וַתֹּאמְרוּ
בְּשִׂנְאַת יְהוָה אֹתָנוּ הוֹצִיאָנוּ מֵאֶרֶץ מִצְרָיִם לָתֵת
אֹתָנוּ בְּיַד הָאֱמֹרִי לְהַשְׁמִידֵנוּ: 28 אָנָה ׀ אֲנַחְנוּ עֹלִים
אַחֵינוּ הֵמַסּוּ אֶת־לְבָבֵנוּ לֵאמֹר עַם גָּדוֹל וָרָם
מִמֶּנּוּ עָרִים גְּדֹלֹת וּבְצוּרֹת בַּשָּׁמָיִם וְגַם־בְּנֵי עֲנָקִים
רָאִינוּ שָׁם: 29 וָאֹמַר אֲלֵכֶם לֹא־תַעַרְצוּן וְלֹא־
תִירְאוּן מֵהֶם: 30 יְהוָה אֱלֹהֵיכֶם הַהֹלֵךְ לִפְנֵיכֶם

1:19. **from Horeb . . . to Kadesh-barnea.** Moses covers the trip from Horeb to the area near the promised land in a single sentence. Thus the text again conveys that the journey could have been a simple thing—eleven days, as in v. 2—but the people's condition turned it into forty years.

1:21. **See. . . . Go up, possess.** Not only does Moses mix past, present, and future generations in his wording. Now he mixes the whole community and each individual. Until now he has spoken in the plural, to all of Israel in front of him. But now he changes to the singular, telling each person, young and old, male and female: YHWH has put this land in front of *you*.

who is going in front of you, *He* will fight for you—like everything that He did with you in Egypt before your eyes ³¹and in the wilderness, as you've seen that YHWH, your God, carried you the way a man would carry his child through all the way that you've gone until you came to this place. ³²And in this thing, don't you trust in YHWH, your God, ³³who was going in front of you on the way to scout a camping place for you, in fire at night to let you see the way in which you would go, and in a cloud by day?!'

³⁴"And YHWH heard the sound of your words and was angry and swore, saying, ³⁵'Not a man of these people, this bad generation, will see the good land that I swore to give to your fathers; ³⁶just Caleb son of Jephunneh: *he* will see it, and I shall give the land on which he went to him and to his children because he went after YHWH fully.' ³⁷(YHWH was incensed at me, too, because of you, saying, 'You, too, shall not come there. ³⁸Joshua son of Nun, who is standing in front of you: *he* shall come there. Strengthen him, because *he* shall get Israel its legacy.') ³⁹'And your infants

הוּא יִלָּחֵם לָכֶם כְּכֹל אֲשֶׁר עָשָׂה אִתְּכֶם בְּמִצְרַיִם לְעֵינֵיכֶם: ³¹וּבַמִּדְבָּר אֲשֶׁר רָאִיתָ אֲשֶׁר נְשָׂאֲךָ יְהוָה אֱלֹהֶיךָ כַּאֲשֶׁר יִשָּׂא־אִישׁ אֶת־בְּנוֹ בְּכָל־הַדֶּרֶךְ אֲשֶׁר הֲלַכְתֶּם עַד־בֹּאֲכֶם עַד־הַמָּקוֹם הַזֶּה: ³²וּבַדָּבָר הַזֶּה אֵינְכֶם מַאֲמִינִם בַּיהוָה אֱלֹהֵיכֶם: ³³הַהֹלֵךְ לִפְנֵיכֶם בַּדֶּרֶךְ לָתוּר לָכֶם מָקוֹם לַחֲנֹתְכֶם בָּאֵשׁ ׀ לַיְלָה לַרְאֹתְכֶם בַּדֶּרֶךְ אֲשֶׁר תֵּלְכוּ־בָהּ וּבֶעָנָן יוֹמָם: ³⁴וַיִּשְׁמַע יְהוָה אֶת־קוֹל דִּבְרֵיכֶם וַיִּקְצֹף וַיִּשָּׁבַע לֵאמֹר: ³⁵אִם־יִרְאֶה אִישׁ בָּאֲנָשִׁים הָאֵלֶּה הַדּוֹר הָרָע הַזֶּה אֵת הָאָרֶץ הַטּוֹבָה אֲשֶׁר נִשְׁבַּעְתִּי לָתֵת לַאֲבֹתֵיכֶם: ³⁶זוּלָתִי כָּלֵב בֶּן־יְפֻנֶּה הוּא יִרְאֶנָּה וְלוֹ־אֶתֵּן אֶת־הָאָרֶץ אֲשֶׁר דָּרַךְ־בָּהּ וּלְבָנָיו יַעַן אֲשֶׁר מִלֵּא אַחֲרֵי יְהוָה: ³⁷גַּם־בִּי הִתְאַנַּף יְהוָה בִּגְלַלְכֶם לֵאמֹר גַּם־אַתָּה לֹא־תָבֹא שָׁם: ³⁸יְהוֹשֻׁעַ בִּן־נוּן הָעֹמֵד לְפָנֶיךָ הוּא יָבֹא שָׁמָּה אֹתוֹ חַזֵּק כִּי־הוּא יַנְחִלֶנָּה אֶת־יִשְׂרָאֵל: ³⁹וְטַפְּכֶם אֲשֶׁר אֲמַרְתֶּם

1:37. **me, too.** This is the first of many times that Moses will mention the fact that he, too, will not live to see the land. Here he connects it with the people's actions, even though the reason that he cannot enter the land is because of his sin at the rock in Meribah (Numbers 20). Even though his comment comes in the context of the spies episode, he may still be understood to be referring to the Meribah episode in this comment. His point is to let the Israelites know that he shares their fate. Like everyone else of his generation, he will not live to set foot in the promised land.

1:37. **because of you.** If he is referring to the Meribah episode, then he is blaming his actions there on the people, whose rebellion moved him to act as he did. Alternatively, if he is referring to the spies episode, then it is particularly striking that Moses says "because of *you*," since none of the people standing in front of him was culpable for that sin. They were all the "infants" at the time (v. 39), who are now adults; and they are to inherit the land precisely because they were *not* part of the generation that rejected the land in the spies episode. The point may be that Moses is especially emphasizing the message that they are still a part of the history that preceded them. Or this may convey that the concept of a "nation" or "people" is a fluid one, crossing lines of generations. Like a river, which is constantly being made up of new molecules of water yet is always the same river ("You cannot step into the same river twice"), so a people retains its identity even though its individual members are constantly changing over time.

whom you said would become a spoil, and your children today who haven't known good and bad, *they* will come there, and I'll give it to them, and *they* will possess it. 40But *you:* turn and travel to the wilderness by way of the Red Sea.'

41"And you answered and said to me, 'We've sinned against YHWH. *We'll* go up! And we'll fight, according to everything that YHWH, our God, commanded us.' And you each put on his weapons of war, and you were willing to go up to the hill country.

42"And YHWH said to me, 'Say to them: You shall not go up, and you shall not fight, because I am not among you, so you won't be stricken before your enemies.' 43And I spoke to you, but you didn't listen, and you rebelled against YHWH's word and acted presumptuously and went up to the hill country. 44And the Amorite who lives in

לְבַז יִהְיֶה וּבְנֵיכֶם אֲשֶׁר לֹא־יָדְעוּ הַיּוֹם טוֹב וָרָע הֵמָּה יָבֹאוּ שָׁמָּה וְלָהֶם אֶתְּנֶנָּה וְהֵם יִירָשׁוּהָ: 40וְאַתֶּם פְּנוּ לָכֶם וּסְעוּ הַמִּדְבָּרָה דֶּרֶךְ יַם־סוּף: 41וַתַּעֲנוּ ׀ וַתֹּאמְרוּ אֵלַי חָטָאנוּ לַיהוָה אֲנַחְנוּ נַעֲלֶה וְנִלְחַמְנוּ כְּכֹל אֲשֶׁר־צִוָּנוּ יְהוָה אֱלֹהֵינוּ וַתַּחְגְּרוּ אִישׁ אֶת־כְּלֵי מִלְחַמְתּוֹ וַתָּהִינוּ לַעֲלֹת הָהָרָה: 42וַיֹּאמֶר יְהוָה אֵלַי אֱמֹר לָהֶם לֹא תַעֲלוּ וְלֹא־תִלָּחֲמוּ כִּי אֵינֶנִּי בְּקִרְבְּכֶם וְלֹא תִּנָּגְפוּ לִפְנֵי אֹיְבֵיכֶם: 43וָאֲדַבֵּר אֲלֵיכֶם וְלֹא שְׁמַעְתֶּם וַתַּמְרוּ אֶת־פִּי יְהוָה וַתָּזִדוּ וַתַּעֲלוּ הָהָרָה: 44וַיֵּצֵא הָאֱמֹרִי

1:39. **haven't known good and bad**. Elsewhere in the *Tanak* this expression refers to a small child who is not yet old enough to know the difference between good and bad (Isa 7:14–16). The reference to the knowledge of good and bad is also one of many reminiscences here in the Torah's last book of things that occur at the beginning of the Torah's first book. In Genesis humans acquire knowledge of good and bad. Now Moses quotes God from the spies episode, giving a clearer explanation of why only the youngsters will live to enter the promised land: because they have not yet "known good and bad." Again knowledge of good and bad is tied up with life and death.

1:40; 2:1. **by way of the Red Sea**. The Israelites never go back near any place that could be the site of the splitting of the sea. This reference therefore must be to the *eastern* arm of the Red Sea. It is further confirmation that the name of that entire body of water, Hebrew *yam sûp*, in the Torah refers to what is known today as the Red Sea, and not to any imagined "Reed Sea." See the comments on Exod 13:8 and Num 21:4.

1:41. **you were willing**. This verb (Hebrew *tāhînû*) occurs only here. No one is sure what it means. Rashi connects it with the text of the spies episode, in which the people say, "Here we are (Hebrew *hinnennû*), and we'll go up" (Num 14:40), which appears to be what Moses alludes to here: "you were willing to go up." That seems most probable to me, in which case the text here makes a verb out of the word *hinnennû* (here we are), conveying one's willingness to do something.

1:43,45. **didn't listen**. Moses reminds the people that "*You* didn't listen," and so later "*YHWH* didn't listen." This foreshadows developments coming in the *Tanak* in which God will be described as hiding His face, not seeing, and not listening—always in response to the people's not listening to God. It will be stated explicitly among God's last words to Moses at the end of the Torah (Deut 31:16–18).

that hill country came out at you and pursued you the way bees do, and they crushed you in Seir as far as Hormah. ⁴⁵And you came back and wept in front of YHWH, but *YHWH* didn't listen to your voices and didn't hear you!

⁴⁶"So you lived in Kadesh many days—as many days as you lived there— 2 ¹and we turned and traveled to the wilderness by way of the Red Sea as YHWH spoke to me, and we stayed around Mount Seir many days.

²"And YHWH said to me, saying, ³'You've had enough of staying around this mountain. Turn north. ⁴And command the people, saying: You're crossing the border of your brothers, the children of Esau, who live in Seir. And they'll be afraid of you, so be very watchful. ⁵Don't get agitated at them, because I won't give you any of their land, even as much as a footstep, because I've given Mount Seir to Esau as a possession. ⁶Food: you shall buy from them with money, and then you'll eat. And water, too: you shall purchase from them with money, and then you'll drink. ⁷Because YHWH, your God, has blessed you in all your hand's work. He has known your walking in this big wilderness. These forty years, YHWH, your God, has been with you. You haven't lacked

הַיֵּ֤שֶׁב בָּהָר֙ הַה֔וּא לִקְרַאתְכֶ֖ם וַיִּרְדְּפ֣וּ אֶתְכֶ֗ם כַּאֲשֶׁ֤ר תַּעֲשֶׂ֙ינָה֙ הַדְּבֹרִ֔ים וַיַּכְּת֥וּ אֶתְכֶ֖ם בְּשֵׂעִ֥יר עַד־חָרְמָֽה: ⁴⁵וַתָּשֻׁ֣בוּ וַתִּבְכּ֣וּ לִפְנֵ֣י יְהוָ֑ה וְלֹא־שָׁמַ֤ע יְהוָה֙ בְּקֹ֣לְכֶ֔ם וְלֹ֥א הֶאֱזִ֖ין אֲלֵיכֶֽם: ⁴⁶וַתֵּשְׁב֥וּ בְקָדֵ֖שׁ יָמִ֣ים רַבִּ֑ים כַּיָּמִ֖ים אֲשֶׁ֥ר יְשַׁבְתֶּֽם:

2 ¹וַנֵּ֜פֶן וַנִּסַּ֤ע הַמִּדְבָּ֙רָה֙ דֶּ֣רֶךְ יַם־ס֔וּף כַּאֲשֶׁ֛ר דִּבֶּ֥ר יְהוָ֖ה אֵלָ֑י וַנָּ֥סָב אֶת־הַר־שֵׂעִ֖יר יָמִ֥ים רַבִּֽים: ס ²וַיֹּ֥אמֶר יְהוָ֖ה אֵלַ֥י לֵאמֹֽר: ³רַב־לָכֶ֕ם סֹ֖ב אֶת־הָהָ֣ר הַזֶּ֑ה פְּנ֥וּ לָכֶ֖ם צָפֹֽנָה: ⁴וְאֶת־הָעָם֮ צַ֣ו לֵאמֹר֒ אַתֶּ֣ם עֹֽבְרִ֗ים בִּגְבוּל֙ אֲחֵיכֶ֣ם בְּנֵי־עֵשָׂ֔ו הַיֹּשְׁבִ֖ים בְּשֵׂעִ֑יר וְיִֽירְא֣וּ מִכֶּ֔ם וְנִשְׁמַרְתֶּ֖ם מְאֹֽד: ⁵אַל־תִּתְגָּר֣וּ בָ֔ם כִּ֠י לֹֽא־אֶתֵּ֤ן לָכֶם֙ מֵֽאַרְצָ֔ם עַ֖ד מִדְרַ֣ךְ כַּף־רָ֑גֶל כִּֽי־יְרֻשָּׁ֣ה לְעֵשָׂ֔ו נָתַ֖תִּי אֶת־הַ֥ר שֵׂעִֽיר: ⁶אֹ֣כֶל תִּשְׁבְּר֧וּ מֵֽאִתָּ֛ם בַּכֶּ֖סֶף וַאֲכַלְתֶּ֑ם וְגַם־מַ֜יִם תִּכְר֧וּ מֵֽאִתָּ֛ם בַּכֶּ֖סֶף וּשְׁתִיתֶֽם: ⁷כִּי֩ יְהוָ֨ה אֱלֹהֶ֜יךָ בֵּֽרַכְךָ֗ בְּכֹל֙ מַעֲשֵׂ֣ה יָדֶ֔ךָ יָדַ֣ע לֶכְתְּךָ֔ אֶת־הַמִּדְבָּ֥ר הַגָּדֹ֖ל הַזֶּ֑ה זֶ֣ה ׀ אַרְבָּעִ֣ים שָׁנָ֗ה יְהוָ֤ה אֱלֹהֶ֙יךָ֙ עִמָּ֔ךְ לֹ֥א

2:4. **they'll be afraid of you**. The shoe is on the other foot. When Jacob approached his brother Esau at Seir, "Jacob was very afraid" (Gen 32:8,12). Now Jacob's children are close to Seir, and Esau's children will be afraid. But YHWH tells Israel to leave them alone. The stated reason is that God gave this land to Esau (Num 2:5). Another reason may be that Esau did not harm Jacob and his children, and so, on the merit of Esau's act of forgiveness, Jacob's children should now not harm Esau's children. In any case, we should take note of the benign attitude that the Torah takes toward Edom, who are identified as the descendants of Esau. This changes radically later on. First Edom is conquered by David and then held in subjugation by Judah for many years during the monarchy. The bad relations with Edom culminate following the destruction of Jerusalem, with bitter denunciations of Edom (in Psalm 137, the book of Lamentations, and the book of Obadiah).

2:7. **These forty years**. He has known his people for forty years, and the text conveys a depth of acquaintance with them that is not apparent in the preceding books. Never hesitant to criticize the people of Israel, he nonetheless speaks to them now with affection. He begins and ends his speech with blessings on the people. In his opening he says to them (1:11):

a thing.' ⁸So we passed by our brothers, the children of Esau, who live in Seir, from the way of the plain, from Eilat, and from Ezion-geber, and we turned and passed by way of the wilderness of Moab.

⁹"And YHWH said to me, 'Don't oppose Moab and don't agitate them with war, because I won't give you a possession from its land, because I've given Ar as a possession to the children of Lot. ¹⁰The Emim had lived there before, a people that was big and numerous and tall as giants. ¹¹They were also thought to be Rephaim, like the giants, but the Moabites call them Emim. ¹²And the Horites lived in Seir before, but the children of Esau dispossessed them and destroyed them in front of them and lived in their place, as Israel

חָסַ֖רְתָּ דָּבָֽר: ⁸וַֽנַּעֲבֹ֞ר מֵאֵ֧ת אַחֵ֣ינוּ בְנֵי־עֵשָׂ֗ו הַיֹּֽשְׁבִים֙ בְּשֵׂעִ֔יר מִדֶּ֙רֶךְ֙ הָֽעֲרָבָ֔ה מֵֽאֵילַ֖ת וּמֵעֶצְיֹ֣ן גָּ֑בֶר ס וַנֵּ֙פֶן֙ וַֽנַּעֲבֹ֔ר דֶּ֖רֶךְ מִדְבַּ֥ר מוֹאָֽב: ⁹וַיֹּ֨אמֶר יְהֹוָ֜ה אֵלַ֗י אַל־תָּ֙צַר֙ אֶת־מוֹאָ֔ב וְאַל־תִּתְגָּ֥ר בָּ֖ם מִלְחָמָ֑ה כִּ֠י לֹֽא־אֶתֵּ֨ן לְךָ֤ מֵֽאַרְצוֹ֙ יְרֻשָּׁ֔ה כִּ֣י לִבְנֵי־ל֔וֹט נָתַ֥תִּי אֶת־עָ֖ר יְרֻשָּֽׁה: ¹⁰הָאֵמִ֥ים לְפָנִ֖ים יָ֣שְׁבוּ בָ֑הּ עַ֣ם גָּד֥וֹל וְרַ֛ב וָרָ֖ם כָּֽעֲנָקִֽים: ¹¹רְפָאִ֞ים יֵחָֽשְׁב֤וּ אַף־הֵם֙ כָּֽעֲנָקִ֔ים וְהַמֹּ֣אָבִ֔ים יִקְרְא֥וּ לָהֶ֖ם אֵמִֽים: ¹²וּבְשֵׂעִ֞יר יָֽשְׁב֤וּ הַחֹרִים֙ לְפָנִ֔ים וּבְנֵ֤י עֵשָׂו֙ יִֽירָשׁ֔וּם וַיַּשְׁמִידוּם֙ מִפְּנֵיהֶ֔ם וַיֵּֽשְׁב֖וּ תַּחְתָּ֑ם כַּֽאֲשֶׁ֣ר עָשָׂ֣ה

May YHWH, your fathers' God, add on to you a thousand times more like you! And may He bless you as He spoke to you.

And in his very last words, he sings to them (33:29):

Happy are you, Israel!
Who is like you,
a people saved by YHWH.

He has also known his God for forty years, but their singular acquaintance—unique among all divine-human encounters in the Hebrew Bible—is now among the most thunderous of the Bible's loud silences. God speaks very little to Moses in Deuteronomy, and Moses never says a word to God, even in the chapters following his speech. (He only quotes *previous* conversations he has had with God.)

2:9. **Ar.** A Moabite city mentioned in Num 21:15.

2:11. **Rephaim.** In some places we have references to the Rephaim (and the Emim, who are connected with the Rephaim here) among the indigenous peoples of Canaan (Gen 14:5; Deut 2:20), but in other places the Rephaim are the dead, continuing some sort of existence in an underworld (Isa 14:9; 26:14; Ps 88:11; see also Prov 2:18; 9:18; 21:16; Job 26:5). Fifth-century Phoenician inscriptions identify the Rephaim as those whom the living join in dying (KAI 13:7–8, 14:8). The term is also found in Ugaritic (*rapi'uma*, KTU 1.61), referring to a line of dead kings and heroes (cf. Isa 14:9). The deceased are invoked to assist in bestowing blessings upon the reigning king. Alan Cooper has traced the etymology of Rephaim to Ugaritic *Rp'u*, a chthonic deity and patron god of the king of Ugarit, associated with healing, in the sense of granting health, strength, fertility, and fecundity; hence the Hebrew *rāpā'*, to heal. These associations are important in discussing ancestor veneration in the ancient Near East, since the purposes for revering one's dead ancestors were often requests for health, strength, and progeny.

did to the land of its possession that YHWH gave them. ¹³Now get up and cross the Wadi Zered.' And we crossed the Wadi Zered. ¹⁴And the days that we went from Kadesh-barnea until we crossed the Wadi Zered were thirty-eight years, until the end of all the generation, the men of war, from among the camp, as YHWH swore to them. ¹⁵And YHWH's hand was against them, to eliminate them from among the camp until their end.

¹⁶"And it was when all the men of war had ended, dying from among the people, ¹⁷and YHWH spoke to me, saying, ¹⁸'You're crossing the border of Moab, Ar, today. ¹⁹And when you come close opposite the children of Ammon, don't oppose them and don't get agitated at them, because I won't give you a possession from the land of the children of Ammon, because I've given it as a possession to the children of Lot.' ²⁰(It, too, was thought to be a land of Rephaim: Rephaim had lived there before, and the Ammonites call them Zamzummim, ²¹a people that was big and numerous and tall as giants, but YHWH destroyed them in front of them, and they dispossessed them and lived in their place, ²²as He did for the children of Esau, who live in Seir, in that He destroyed the Horite in front of them, and they dispossessed them and have lived in their place to this day. ²³So the Avvim, who lived in villages as far as Gaza: the Caphtorites who left Caphtor destroyed them, and they dwelled in their place.) ²⁴'Get up, travel, and cross the Wadi Arnon. See: I've put Sihon,

יִשְׂרָאֵל֙ לְאֶ֣רֶץ יְרֻשָּׁת֔וֹ אֲשֶׁר־נָתַ֥ן יְהוָ֖ה לָהֶֽם: ¹³עַתָּ֗ה קֻ֚מוּ וְעִבְר֣וּ לָכֶ֔ם אֶת־נַ֖חַל זָ֑רֶד וַֽנַּעֲבֹ֖ר אֶת־נַ֥חַל זָֽרֶד: ¹⁴וְהַיָּמִ֞ים אֲשֶׁר־הָלַ֣כְנוּ ׀ מִקָּדֵ֣שׁ בַּרְנֵ֗עַ עַ֤ד אֲשֶׁר־עָבַ֙רְנוּ֙ אֶת־נַ֣חַל זֶ֔רֶד שְׁלֹשִׁ֥ים וּשְׁמֹנֶ֖ה שָׁנָ֑ה עַד־תֹּ֨ם כָּל־הַדּ֜וֹר אַנְשֵׁ֤י הַמִּלְחָמָה֙ מִקֶּ֣רֶב הַֽמַּחֲנֶ֔ה כַּאֲשֶׁ֛ר נִשְׁבַּ֥ע יְהוָ֖ה לָהֶֽם: ¹⁵וְגַ֤ם יַד־יְהוָה֙ הָ֣יְתָה בָּ֔ם לְהֻמָּ֛ם מִקֶּ֥רֶב הַֽמַּחֲנֶ֖ה עַ֥ד תֻּמָּֽם: ¹⁶וַיְהִ֨י כַאֲשֶׁר־תַּ֜מּוּ כָּל־אַנְשֵׁ֧י הַמִּלְחָמָ֛ה לָמ֖וּת מִקֶּ֥רֶב הָעָֽם: ס ¹⁷וַיְדַבֵּ֥ר יְהוָ֖ה אֵלַ֥י לֵאמֹֽר: ¹⁸אַתָּ֨ה עֹבֵ֥ר הַיּ֛וֹם אֶת־גְּב֥וּל מוֹאָ֖ב אֶת־עָֽר: ¹⁹וְקָרַבְתָּ֗ מ֚וּל בְּנֵ֣י עַמּ֔וֹן אַל־תְּצֻרֵ֖ם וְאַל־תִּתְגָּ֣ר בָּ֑ם כִּ֣י לֹֽא־אֶ֠תֵּן מֵאֶ֨רֶץ בְּנֵי־עַמּ֤וֹן לְךָ֙ יְרֻשָּׁ֔ה כִּ֥י לִבְנֵי־ל֖וֹט נְתַתִּ֥יהָ יְרֻשָּֽׁה: ²⁰אֶֽרֶץ־רְפָאִ֥ים תֵּחָשֵׁ֖ב אַף־הִ֑וא רְפָאִ֤ים יָֽשְׁבוּ־בָהּ֙ לְפָנִ֔ים וְהָֽעַמֹּנִ֔ים יִקְרְא֥וּ לָהֶ֖ם זַמְזֻמִּֽים: ²¹עַ֣ם גָּד֥וֹל וְרַ֖ב וָרָ֣ם כָּעֲנָקִ֑ים וַיַּשְׁמִידֵ֤ם יְהוָה֙ מִפְּנֵיהֶ֔ם וַיִּירָשֻׁ֖ם וַיֵּשְׁב֥וּ תַחְתָּֽם: ²²כַּאֲשֶׁ֤ר עָשָׂה֙ לִבְנֵ֣י עֵשָׂ֔ו הַיֹּשְׁבִ֖ים בְּשֵׂעִ֑יר אֲשֶׁ֨ר הִשְׁמִ֤יד אֶת־הַֽחֹרִי֙ מִפְּנֵיהֶ֔ם וַיִּֽירָשֻׁם֙ וַיֵּשְׁב֣וּ תַחְתָּ֔ם עַ֖ד הַיּ֥וֹם הַזֶּֽה: ²³וְהָֽעַוִּ֛ים הַיֹּשְׁבִ֥ים בַּחֲצֵרִ֖ים עַד־עַזָּ֑ה כַּפְתֹּרִים֙ הַיֹּצְאִ֣ים מִכַּפְתּ֔וֹר הִשְׁמִידֻ֖ם וַיֵּשְׁב֥וּ תַחְתָּֽם: ²⁴ק֣וּמוּ סְּע֗וּ וְעִבְרוּ֮ אֶת־נַ֣חַל אַרְנֹן֒ רְאֵ֣ה נָתַ֣תִּי בְ֠יָדְךָ אֶת־סִיחֹ֨ן מֶֽלֶךְ־חֶשְׁבּ֤וֹן

2:19. the children of Lot. The stories in Genesis now return to mind with yet another layer of significance. Israel is not to be hostile to Edom (because they are Esau's children) or Moab and Ammon (because they are Lot's children). So the stories of individuals and families in Genesis now become the stories of nations in Deuteronomy. Ancient Israel understood its neighboring peoples to be *relatives*. Israel was expected to act out of kinship to them. And hostility from any of them was regarded as betrayal by a family member. This attitude continues past the Torah into the narrative of Israel's history in its land.

2:23. Caphtor. Crete or another of the Greek islands. It is associated with the Philistines (Gen 10:14; Amos 9:7; Jer 47:4; 1 Chr 1:12).

king of Heshbon, the Amorite, and his land in your hand. Begin. Dispossess! And you shall agitate him with war. 25This day I'll begin to put an awe of you and a fear of you on the faces of the peoples under all the skies so that when they'll hear the news of you they'll tremble and writhe in front of you.'

26"And I sent messengers from the wilderness of Kedemoth to Sihon, king of Heshbon, words of peace, saying, 27'Let me pass through your land. I'll go on the road, *on the road!* I won't turn right or left. 28Food: you'll sell me for money, and I'll eat. And water: you'll give me for money, and I'll drink. Only let me pass on my feet 29as the children of Esau, who live in Seir, and the Moabites who live in Ar did for me, until I'll cross the Jordan to the land that YHWH, our God, is giving us.' 30But Sihon, king of Heshbon, was not willing to let us pass through it, because YHWH, your God, had hardened his spirit and made his heart bold in order to put him in your hand—as it is this day.

31"And YHWH said to me, 'See: I've begun to put Sihon and his land before you. Begin. Dispossess, so as to possess his land.'

32"And Sihon came out at us, he and all his people, for war at Jahaz. 33And YHWH, our God, put him before us, and we struck him and his sons and all his people. 34And we captured all his cities at that time, and we put every city to complete destruction: men and women and infants. We didn't leave a remnant. 35Only the animals we despoiled for ourselves, and the spoil of the cities that we captured. 36From Aroer, which is on the edge of the Wadi Arnon and the city that is in the wadi, to Gilead, there wasn't a town that was too high for us. YHWH, our God, put it all before us. 37Only to the land of the children of Ammon did you not come close, all along the

הָאֱמֹרִי וְאֶת־אַרְצוֹ הָחֵל רָשׁ וְהִתְגָּר בּוֹ מִלְחָמָה: 25הַיּוֹם הַזֶּה אָחֵל תֵּת פַּחְדְּךָ וְיִרְאָתְךָ עַל־פְּנֵי הָעַמִּים תַּחַת כָּל־הַשָּׁמָיִם אֲשֶׁר יִשְׁמְעוּן שִׁמְעֲךָ וְרָגְזוּ וְחָלוּ מִפָּנֶיךָ: 26וָאֶשְׁלַח מַלְאָכִים מִמִּדְבַּר קְדֵמוֹת אֶל־סִיחוֹן מֶלֶךְ חֶשְׁבּוֹן דִּבְרֵי שָׁלוֹם לֵאמֹר: 27אֶעְבְּרָה בְאַרְצֶךָ בַּדֶּרֶךְ בַּדֶּרֶךְ אֵלֵךְ לֹא אָסוּר יָמִין וּשְׂמֹאול: 28אֹכֶל בַּכֶּסֶף תַּשְׁבִּרֵנִי וְאָכַלְתִּי וּמַיִם בַּכֶּסֶף תִּתֶּן־לִי וְשָׁתִיתִי רַק אֶעְבְּרָה בְרַגְלָי: 29כַּאֲשֶׁר עָשׂוּ־לִי בְּנֵי עֵשָׂו הַיֹּשְׁבִים בְּשֵׂעִיר וְהַמּוֹאָבִים הַיֹּשְׁבִים בְּעָר עַד אֲשֶׁר־אֶעֱבֹר אֶת־הַיַּרְדֵּן אֶל־הָאָרֶץ אֲשֶׁר־יְהוָה אֱלֹהֵינוּ נֹתֵן לָנוּ: 30וְלֹא אָבָה סִיחֹן מֶלֶךְ חֶשְׁבּוֹן הַעֲבִרֵנוּ בּוֹ כִּי־הִקְשָׁה יְהוָה אֱלֹהֶיךָ אֶת־רוּחוֹ וְאִמֵּץ אֶת־לְבָבוֹ לְמַעַן תִּתּוֹ בְיָדְךָ כַּיּוֹם הַזֶּה: ס 31וַיֹּאמֶר יְהוָה אֵלַי רְאֵה הַחִלֹּתִי תֵּת לְפָנֶיךָ אֶת־סִיחֹן וְאֶת־אַרְצוֹ הָחֵל רָשׁ לָרֶשֶׁת אֶת־אַרְצוֹ: 32וַיֵּצֵא סִיחֹן לִקְרָאתֵנוּ הוּא וְכָל־עַמּוֹ לַמִּלְחָמָה יָהְצָה: 33וַיִּתְּנֵהוּ יְהוָה אֱלֹהֵינוּ לְפָנֵינוּ וַנַּךְ אֹתוֹ וְאֶת־בָּנָו וְאֶת־כָּל־עַמּוֹ: 34וַנִּלְכֹּד אֶת־כָּל־עָרָיו בָּעֵת הַהִוא וַנַּחֲרֵם אֶת־כָּל־עִיר מְתִם וְהַנָּשִׁים וְהַטָּף לֹא הִשְׁאַרְנוּ שָׂרִיד: 35רַק הַבְּהֵמָה בָּזַזְנוּ לָנוּ וּשְׁלַל הֶעָרִים אֲשֶׁר לָכָדְנוּ: 36מֵעֲרֹעֵר אֲשֶׁר עַל־שְׂפַת־נַחַל אַרְנֹן וְהָעִיר אֲשֶׁר בַּנַּחַל וְעַד־הַגִּלְעָד לֹא הָיְתָה קִרְיָה אֲשֶׁר שָׂגְבָה מִמֶּנּוּ אֶת־הַכֹּל נָתַן יְהוָה אֱלֹהֵינוּ לְפָנֵינוּ: 37רַק אֶל־אֶרֶץ בְּנֵי־עַמּוֹן לֹא קָרָבְתָּ כָּל־

2:33 קְ בָּנָיו

2:34. **complete destruction.** In contexts that do not have to do with war, the Hebrew word *ḥerem* refers to something that is devoted to God (Lev 27:21,28–29; Num 18:14). In contexts of war, as in this verse, *ḥerem* refers to the rule, in divinely commanded wars only, against taking spoils or slaves, but rather destroying all of these and thus dedicating them to the deity. The point: the war is not for profit.

Wadi Jabbok, and the cities of the hill country, and whatever YHWH, our God, commanded.

3 1"And we turned and went up the way to Bashan. And Og, king of Bashan, came out at us, he and all his people, for war at Edrei. 2And YHWH said to me, 'Don't be afraid of him, because I've put him and all his people and his land in your hand, and you shall do to him as you did to Sihon, king of the Amorites, who lived in Heshbon.' 3And YHWH, our God, put Og, king of Bashan, and all his people in our hand as well, and we struck him until he did not have a remnant left. 4And we captured all his cities at that time. There wasn't a town that we didn't take from them: sixty cities—all the region of Argob, Og's kingdom in Bashan. 5All of these were fortified cities—a high wall, double gates, and a bar—aside from a great many unwalled cities. 6And we completely destroyed them as we did to Sihon, king of Heshbon, completely destroying every city: men, women, and infants. 7And we despoiled all the animals and the spoil of the cities for ourselves. 8And at that time we took the land from the hand of the two kings of the Amorites that was across the Jordan, from the

יַד נַחַל יַבֹּק וְעָרֵי הָהָר וְכֹל אֲשֶׁר־צִוָּה יְהוָה
אֱלֹהֵינוּ:

3 1וַנֵּפֶן וַנַּעַל דֶּרֶךְ הַבָּשָׁן וַיֵּצֵא עוֹג מֶלֶךְ־
הַבָּשָׁן לִקְרָאתֵנוּ הוּא וְכָל־עַמּוֹ לַמִּלְחָמָה אֶדְרֶעִי:
2וַיֹּאמֶר יְהוָה אֵלַי אַל־תִּירָא אֹתוֹ כִּי בְיָדְךָ נָתַתִּי
אֹתוֹ וְאֶת־כָּל־עַמּוֹ וְאֶת־אַרְצוֹ וְעָשִׂיתָ לּוֹ כַּאֲשֶׁר
עָשִׂיתָ לְסִיחֹן מֶלֶךְ הָאֱמֹרִי אֲשֶׁר יוֹשֵׁב בְּחֶשְׁבּוֹן:
3וַיִּתֵּן יְהוָה אֱלֹהֵינוּ בְּיָדֵנוּ גַּם אֶת־עוֹג מֶלֶךְ־הַבָּשָׁן
וְאֶת־כָּל־עַמּוֹ וַנַּכֵּהוּ עַד־בִּלְתִּי הִשְׁאִיר־לוֹ שָׂרִיד:
4וַנִּלְכֹּד אֶת־כָּל־עָרָיו בָּעֵת הַהִוא לֹא הָיְתָה קִרְיָה
אֲשֶׁר לֹא־לָקַחְנוּ מֵאִתָּם שִׁשִּׁים עִיר כָּל־חֶבֶל
אַרְגֹּב מַמְלֶכֶת עוֹג בַּבָּשָׁן: 5כָּל־אֵלֶּה עָרִים
בְּצֻרוֹת חוֹמָה גְבֹהָה דְּלָתַיִם וּבְרִיחַ לְבַד מֵעָרֵי
הַפְּרָזִי הַרְבֵּה מְאֹד: 6וַנַּחֲרֵם אוֹתָם כַּאֲשֶׁר עָשִׂינוּ
לְסִיחֹן מֶלֶךְ חֶשְׁבּוֹן הַחֲרֵם כָּל־עִיר מְתִם הַנָּשִׁים
וְהַטָּף: 7וְכָל־הַבְּהֵמָה וּשְׁלַל הֶעָרִים בַּזּוֹנוּ לָנוּ:
8וַנִּקַּח בָּעֵת הַהִוא אֶת־הָאָרֶץ מִיַּד שְׁנֵי מַלְכֵי
הָאֱמֹרִי אֲשֶׁר בְּעֵבֶר הַיַּרְדֵּן מִנַּחַל אַרְנֹן עַד־הַר

3:6. **completely destroyed**. See the comment on Deut 2:34.

3:8. **across the Jordan**. This phrase occurs several times in Moses' speech in Deuteronomy. Ibn Ezra hinted at a secret implied by this and several other matters in the Torah, and he added, "One who understands should keep silent." But scholars of later centuries no longer kept silent. The issue, presumably, was that the land in question is *across* the Jordan only from the point of view of someone writing in Israel. Moses, who never set foot in Israel, would not be expected to refer to the place where he was standing as *across* the Jordan. Of course we might say that Moses says this phrase with a future audience in mind, a people settled in Israel. But Ibn Ezra's comments are important as being among the first hints that some of the traditional rabbinic commentators questioned whether Moses wrote the Torah. That question—how the Torah came to exist—has become a central concern of biblical scholarship in the last two centuries. I have written about it elsewhere, but it is not the subject of this commentary. Those who want to pursue it can look at my *Who Wrote the Bible?* and *The Hidden Book in the Bible*. Those books look at the persons and events that gave birth to the Torah. This commentary is focused on the Torah itself, the work that those persons and events produced.

Wadi Arnon to Mount Hermon 9(Sidonians call Hermon Sirion, and the Amorites call it Senir), 10all the cities of the plain and all of Gilead and all of Bashan as far as Salcah and Edrei, cities of Og's kingdom in Bashan. 11Because only Og, king of Bashan, was left from the rest of the Rephaim. Here, his bedstead was a bedstead of iron. Isn't it in Rabbah of the children of Ammon? Its length is nine cubits and its width is four cubits by a man's cubit. 12And we took possession of this land at that time. I gave the Reubenites and the Gadites from Aroer, which is on the Wadi Arnon, and half of the hill country of Gilead and its cities. 13And I gave the rest of Gilead and all of Bashan, Og's kingdom, to half of the tribe of Manasseh. All the region of Argob: all of that Bashan is called 'the land of the Rephaim.' 14Jair son of Manasseh had taken all the region of Argob as far as the border of the Geshurites and the Maachathites, and he called them, the Bashan, by his name, Havvoth-Jair, to this day. 15And I gave Gilead to Machir. 16And I gave the Reubenites and the Gadites from Gilead to the Wadi Arnon, the middle of the wadi being the border, and to the Wadi Jabbok, the border of the children of Ammon, 17and the plain, with the Jordan being the border, from the Kinneret to the sea of the plain, the Dead Sea, below the slopes of Pisgah eastward.

18"And I commanded you at that time, saying, 'YHWH, your God, has given you this land to

חֶרְמֽוֹן: 9צִידֹנִים יִקְרְאוּ לְחֶרְמוֹן שְׂרִיֹן וְהָאֱמֹרִי יִקְרְאוּ־לוֹ שְׂנִיר: 10כֹּל | עָרֵי הַמִּישֹׁר וְכָל־הַגִּלְעָד וְכָל־הַבָּשָׁן עַד־סַלְכָה וְאֶדְרֶעִי עָרֵי מַמְלֶכֶת עֽוֹג בַּבָּשָֽׁן: 11כִּי רַק־עוֹג מֶלֶךְ הַבָּשָׁן נִשְׁאַר מִיֶּתֶר הָרְפָאִים הִנֵּה עַרְשׂוֹ עֶרֶשׂ בַּרְזֶל הֲלֹה הִוא בְּרַבַּת בְּנֵי עַמּוֹן תֵּשַׁע אַמּוֹת אָרְכָּהּ וְאַרְבַּע אַמּוֹת רָחְבָּהּ בְּאַמַּת־אִֽישׁ: 12וְאֶת־הָאָרֶץ הַזֹּאת יָרַשְׁנוּ בָּעֵת הַהִוא מֵעֲרֹעֵר אֲשֶׁר־עַל־נַחַל אַרְנֹן וַחֲצִי הַר־ הַגִּלְעָד וְעָרָיו נָתַתִּי לָרֻאוּבֵנִי וְלַגָּדִֽי: 13וְיֶתֶר הַגִּלְעָד וְכָל־הַבָּשָׁן מַמְלֶכֶת עוֹג נָתַתִּי לַחֲצִי שֵׁבֶט הַמְנַשֶּׁה כֹּל חֶבֶל הָאַרְגֹּב לְכָל־הַבָּשָׁן הַהוּא יִקָּרֵא אֶרֶץ רְפָאִֽים: 14יָאִיר בֶּן־מְנַשֶּׁה לָקַח אֶת־כָּל־חֶבֶל אַרְגֹּב עַד־גְּבוּל הַגְּשׁוּרִי וְהַמַּעֲכָתִי וַיִּקְרָא אֹתָם עַל־שְׁמוֹ אֶת־הַבָּשָׁן חַוֹּת יָאִיר עַד הַיּוֹם הַזֶּֽה: 15וּלְמָכִיר נָתַתִּי אֶת־הַגִּלְעָֽד: 16וְלָרֻאוּבֵנִי וְלַגָּדִי נָתַתִּי מִן־הַגִּלְעָד וְעַד־נַחַל אַרְנֹן תּוֹךְ הַנַּחַל וּגְבֻל וְעַד יַבֹּק הַנַּחַל גְּבוּל בְּנֵי עַמּֽוֹן: 17וְהָעֲרָבָה וְהַיַּרְדֵּן וּגְבֻל מִכִּנֶּרֶת וְעַד יָם הָעֲרָבָה יָם הַמֶּלַח תַּחַת אַשְׁדֹּת הַפִּסְגָּה מִזְרָֽחָה: 18וָאֲצַו אֶתְכֶם בָּעֵת הַהִוא לֵאמֹר יְהוָה אֱלֹהֵיכֶם נָתַן לָכֶם אֶת־הָאָרֶץ

3:11. **his bedstead was a bedstead of iron**. Og is pictured as a giant, requiring a tremendous bed that had to made of iron in order to bear his weight. This may also relate to his being the last of the Rephaim, being connected with beings who are now associated with the world of the dead. (See the comment on 2:11.)

3:11. **by a man's cubit**. A cubit is measured from a man's elbow to his hand's second knuckle: eighteen inches.

3:14. **Geshurites**. Later in the *Tanak*, Geshur becomes extremely important, a Canaanite people who reside close to the Israelites. King David marries Maacah, a Geshurite princess, and they have a son, Absalom. Absalom kills his elder half-brother, Amnon (for raping Absalom's full sister, Tamar), who would have been first in line to succeed their father, David. And later Absalom leads a rebellion to usurp his father's throne (2 Sam 3:3; 13:1–19:1).

take possession of it. You shall pass equipped, all the warriors, in front of your brothers, the children of Israel. 19Only your wives and your infants and your livestock (I knew that you have a great amount of livestock) shall stay in your cities that I've given you 20until YHWH will give your brothers rest like you, and they, too, will get possession of the land that YHWH, your God, is giving them across the Jordan. Then you shall go back, each to his possession that I've given you.' 21And I commanded Joshua at that time, saying, 'Your eyes, that have seen everything that YHWH, your God, has done to these two kings: so may YHWH do to all the kingdoms to which you're crossing. 22You shall not fear them, because YHWH, your God: He is the one fighting for you.'

הַזֹּאת֙ לְרִשְׁתָּ֔הּ חֲלוּצִ֣ים תַּֽעַבְר֗וּ לִפְנֵ֛י אֲחֵיכֶ֖ם בְּנֵֽי־
יִשְׂרָאֵ֑ל כָּל־בְּנֵי־חָֽיִל׃ 19רַ֤ק נְשֵׁיכֶם֙ וְטַפְּכֶ֔ם
וּמִקְנֵכֶ֕ם יָדַ֕עְתִּי כִּֽי־מִקְנֶ֥ה רַ֖ב לָכֶ֑ם יֵשְׁבוּ֙ בְּעָ֣רֵיכֶ֔ם
אֲשֶׁ֥ר נָתַ֖תִּי לָכֶֽם׃ 20עַ֠ד אֲשֶׁר־יָנִ֨יחַ יְהוָ֥ה ׀ לַֽאֲחֵיכֶם֮
כָּכֶם֒ וְיָרְשׁ֣וּ גַם־הֵ֔ם אֶת־הָאָ֕רֶץ אֲשֶׁ֨ר יְהוָ֧ה
אֱלֹֽהֵיכֶ֛ם נֹתֵ֥ן לָהֶ֖ם בְּעֵ֣בֶר הַיַּרְדֵּ֑ן וְשַׁבְתֶּ֗ם אִ֚ישׁ
לִֽירֻשָּׁת֔וֹ אֲשֶׁ֥ר נָתַ֖תִּי לָכֶֽם׃ 21וְאֶת־יְהוֹשׁ֣וּעַ צִוֵּ֔יתִי
בָּעֵ֥ת הַהִ֖וא לֵאמֹ֑ר עֵינֶ֣יךָ הָרֹאֹ֗ת אֵת֩ כָּל־אֲשֶׁ֨ר
עָשָׂ֜ה יְהוָ֤ה אֱלֹֽהֵיכֶם֙ לִשְׁנֵי֙ הַמְּלָכִ֣ים הָאֵ֔לֶּה כֵּֽן־
יַעֲשֶׂ֤ה יְהוָה֙ לְכָל־הַמַּמְלָכ֔וֹת אֲשֶׁ֥ר אַתָּ֖ה עֹבֵ֥ר
שָֽׁמָּה׃ 22לֹ֖א תִּֽירָא֑וּם כִּ֚י יְהוָ֣ה אֱלֹֽהֵיכֶ֔ם ה֖וּא
הַנִּלְחָ֥ם לָכֶֽם׃ ס

AND I IMPLORED

23"And I implored YHWH at that time, saying, 24'My Lord, YHWH, you've begun to show your servant your greatness and your strong hand, for

וָאֶתְחַנַּן

23וָאֶתְחַנַּ֖ן אֶל־יְהוָ֑ה בָּעֵ֥ת הַהִ֖וא לֵאמֹֽר׃ 24אֲדֹנָ֣י
יְהוִ֗ה אַתָּ֤ה הַֽחִלּ֙וֹתָ֙ לְהַרְא֣וֹת אֶֽת־עַבְדְּךָ֔ אֶ֨ת־גָּדְלְךָ֔

3:23. **I implored**. Moses' report of his anguished plea to God, begging to be allowed to go to the promised land, is an exquisite reminder of another report of anguish and begging: when Joseph's brothers are accused of spying in Egypt, they recall with shame and guilt that Joseph *implored* them and they would not *listen* (Gen 42:21). Now Moses says that he *implored* God, using the same word that Joseph's brothers used—and these are the only two occurrences of this word in the Torah—and that God would not *listen*. And to cement the connection: Moses says that God told him not to add anything more ("to go on speaking") about this matter, which in Hebrew is: Don't *tôsep*—the root of the name Joseph! What is the point of the parallel? When Joseph's brothers do not listen to his plea, he is the innocent one, and they are guilty. (They explicitly admit: "But we're guilty over our brother"—42:21.) But when Moses pleads, he is not innocent. His fate has been sealed as a matter of justice. This is extraordinary because when Moses pleads for the people in the matter of the golden calf and the spies episode, he is successful: God forgives them. There he is an innocent man pleading for mercy on behalf of the guilty people. But now, as he pleads on his own behalf, he stands guilty, and justice outweighs mercy.

Another view: God is hardest on those who are closest, like parents who may be tougher on their own children than on the children of their friends. God shows no favoritism for Moses. And the message is also that Moses' serious public sin cannot go unpunished. As God says in the matter of the death of Aaron's sons: "I shall be made holy through those who are close to me, and I shall be honored in front of all

who is a god in the skies and in the earth who can do anything like your acts and like your victories?! 25Let me cross and see the good land that's across the Jordan, this good hill country and the Lebanon.'

26"But YHWH was cross at me for your sakes, and He would not listen to me. And YHWH said to me, 'You have much. Don't go on speaking to me anymore of this thing. 27Go up to the top of Pisgah and raise your eyes west and north and south and east and see it with your eyes, because you won't cross this Jordan. 28And command Joshua and strengthen him and make him bold,

וְאֶת־יָדְךָ הַחֲזָקָה אֲשֶׁר מִי־אֵל בַּשָּׁמַיִם וּבָאָרֶץ אֲשֶׁר־יַעֲשֶׂה כְמַעֲשֶׂיךָ וְכִגְבוּרֹתֶךָ: 25אֶעְבְּרָה־נָּא וְאֶרְאֶה אֶת־הָאָרֶץ הַטּוֹבָה אֲשֶׁר בְּעֵבֶר הַיַּרְדֵּן הָהָר הַטּוֹב הַזֶּה וְהַלְּבָנֹון: 26וַיִּתְעַבֵּר יְהוָה בִּי לְמַעַנְכֶם וְלֹא שָׁמַע אֵלָי וַיֹּאמֶר יְהוָה אֵלַי רַב־לָךְ אַל־תֹּוסֶף דַּבֵּר אֵלַי עֹוד בַּדָּבָר הַזֶּה: 27עֲלֵה ׀ רֹאשׁ הַפִּסְגָּה וְשָׂא עֵינֶיךָ יָמָּה וְצָפֹנָה וְתֵימָנָה וּמִזְרָחָה וּרְאֵה בְעֵינֶיךָ כִּי־לֹא תַעֲבֹר אֶת־הַיַּרְדֵּן הַזֶּה: 28וְצַו אֶת־יְהֹושֻׁעַ וְחַזְּקֵהוּ וְאַמְּצֵהוּ כִּי־הוּא

---

the people" (Lev 10:3). Moses tells this to Aaron on that occasion, and "Aaron was silent." Now that message comes back hauntingly to Moses, and God tells Moses that it is he who must be silent.

Thus it is here in Deuteronomy, the last book of the Torah, that we see the Torah's extraordinary embroidery. Words and themes wind, in this case, from Genesis through Leviticus and Numbers into Deuteronomy, like threads through a fabric.

3:25. **Let me cross and see the good land that's across the Jordan.** Moses' life ends, as it began, at a river. On the continuing role that water plays in his life, from the Nile to the Jordan, see the comment on Exod 17:6. Recall also that the creation account in Genesis 1 begins with water, and the account in Genesis 2 begins with rivers flowing out of Eden. Moses' life is thus a reflection in an individual human of the nature of the world.

3:26. **cross at me.** This is not the usual word for anger. It occurs only here in the Torah. It puns on the preceding verse: Moses says, "Let me cross (Hebrew אעברה)" to the land that is "across (בעבר) the Jordan." And then God is cross (ויתעבר) and says "you shall not cross (לא תעבר)." The pun (in English and in Hebrew) conveys irony as well as the idea that divine punishment in the Bible is often made to fit the crime.

3:26. **for your sakes.** This has been taken to mean that Moses is blaming the people for his fate. Alternatively, it can mean that God is thinking of the people and is angry because Moses failed to sanctify God in *their* eyes (Num 20:12). See also the comment on Deut 1:37.

3:26. **You have much.** These are the same words that Korah says to Moses and Aaron. There is a great difference when the same words are spoken by different persons—and with different motives. Korah uses them perhaps out of envy, perhaps as a device to make his claim on priesthood sound more justified. When God now uses them, it is more a reminder that Moses has lived 120 years and has done great things. Even in being denied his dream of coming to the land, he has much, perhaps more than any other human who has ever lived.

3:28. **command Joshua.** The story of the brothers' sale of Joseph into slavery again

because he will cross in front of this people, and he will get them the land that you'll see as a legacy.'

29"And we stayed in the valley opposite Beth-peor.

4 1"And now, Israel, listen to the laws and to the judgments that I'm teaching you to do, so that you'll live, and you'll come and take possession of the land that YHWH, your fathers' God, is giving you. 2You shall not add onto the thing that I command you, and you shall not subtract from it: observing the commandments of YHWH, your God, that I command you. 3It's

יַעֲבֹר לִפְנֵי הָעָם הַזֶּה וְהוּא יַנְחִיל אוֹתָם אֶת־
הָאָרֶץ אֲשֶׁר תִּרְאֶה: 29וַנֵּשֶׁב בַּגַּיְא מוּל בֵּית
פְּעוֹר: פ

4 1וְעַתָּה יִשְׂרָאֵל שְׁמַע אֶל־הַחֻקִּים וְאֶל־
הַמִּשְׁפָּטִים אֲשֶׁר אָנֹכִי מְלַמֵּד אֶתְכֶם לַעֲשׂוֹת לְמַעַן
תִּחְיוּ וּבָאתֶם וִירִשְׁתֶּם אֶת־הָאָרֶץ אֲשֶׁר יְהוָה אֱלֹהֵי
אֲבֹתֵיכֶם נֹתֵן לָכֶם: 2לֹא תֹסִפוּ עַל־הַדָּבָר אֲשֶׁר
אָנֹכִי מְצַוֶּה אֶתְכֶם וְלֹא תִגְרְעוּ מִמֶּנּוּ לִשְׁמֹר אֶת־
מִצְוֺת יְהוָה אֱלֹהֵיכֶם אֲשֶׁר אָנֹכִי מְצַוֶּה אֶתְכֶם:

---

comes to mind, because that was the beginning of the process that led the Israelites from their homeland to Egypt. And now, God's response to Moses ends with the charge to prepare Joshua to lead them, at last, back into their homeland. And note that Joshua is from the tribe of Ephraim; he is a descendant of Joseph! (And, like Joseph, he lives 110 years; Gen 50:26; Josh 24:29.)

4:1. **so that you'll live**. This theme of choosing life begins here and will recur several times in the course of Moses' speech, and culminate in his last sentences (Deut 30:19). See the comment there.

4:2. **You shall not add . . . and you shall not subtract**. This is an essential command: it governs the way Israel is to observe all the other commandments. The second part—not to subtract from the law—is more obvious than the first, but that makes the recognition of the first part all the more important. One may think that, by doing *more* than the law requires, one is doing better, being more religious, more observant, when one is in fact thus *violating* the law. And when one imposes such additions to the law on others, one puts them at risk of violation as well.

This is stated here in the last book of the Torah as a command, but it was already conveyed through a story at the beginning of the Torah, when the woman says to the snake that God commanded that they not eat from the tree *or touch it*, though God had said nothing about touching it (see the comment on Gen 3:3). Adding to a command is as dangerous as taking away from it. Indeed, as Rashi noted in his comment on that verse in Genesis, adding to it may *lead* to taking away from it. One must, therefore, use extreme caution in interpreting and expanding the laws in the Torah. This is sometimes a delicate task because in postbiblical Judaism a principle developed of "building a fence around the Torah." One starts to observe the Sabbath early, before sunset, so as not to risk violating the Sabbath by mistakenly starting late. But there is a difference between sincere care for the law, which is done out of reverence for it, and extreme expansion of the law, which is done for other motives: fear, power over others. The law is presented in the Torah as divine, but it requires human strength and wisdom to carry it out.

your eyes that saw what YHWH did at Baal Peor, that every man who went after Baal Peor: YHWH, your God, destroyed him from among you. [4]But you who were clinging to YHWH, your God: you're all alive today! [5]See: I've taught you laws and judgments as YHWH, my God, commanded me, to do so within the land to which you're coming to take possession of it. [6]And you shall observe and do them because it's your wisdom and your understanding before the eyes of the peoples, in that they will hear all these laws and will say, 'Only a wise and understanding people is this great nation.' [7]Because who is a great nation that has gods close to it like YHWH, our God, in all our calling to him? [8]And who is a great nation that has just laws and judgments like all this instruction that I'm putting in front of you today?

[9]"Only be watchful, and watch yourself very much, in case you'll forget the things that your eyes have seen and in case they'll turn away from your heart, all the days of your life. But you shall make them known to your children and to your children's children: [10]the day that you stood in front of YHWH, your God, at Horeb, when YHWH said to me, 'Assemble the people to me, and I'll make them hear my words so that they'll learn to fear me all the days that they're living on the land, and they'll teach their children.' [11]And you came forward and stood below the mountain, and the mountain was burning in fire to the heart of the skies: darkness, cloud, and nimbus.

³עֵינֵיכֶם֙ הָרֹאֹ֔ת אֵ֛ת אֲשֶׁר־עָשָׂ֥ה יְהוָ֖ה בְּבַ֣עַל פְּעֹ֑ור כִּ֣י כָל־הָאִ֗ישׁ אֲשֶׁ֤ר הָלַךְ֙ אַחֲרֵ֣י בַֽעַל־פְּעֹ֔ור הִשְׁמִידֹ֛ו יְהוָ֥ה אֱלֹהֶ֖יךָ מִקִּרְבֶּֽךָ׃ ⁴וְאַתֶּם֙ הַדְּבֵקִ֔ים בַּיהוָ֖ה אֱלֹהֵיכֶ֑ם חַיִּ֥ים כֻּלְּכֶ֖ם הַיֹּֽום׃ ⁵רְאֵ֣ה ׀ לִמַּ֣דְתִּי אֶתְכֶ֗ם חֻקִּים֙ וּמִשְׁפָּטִ֔ים כַּאֲשֶׁ֥ר צִוַּ֖נִי יְהוָ֣ה אֱלֹהָ֑י לַעֲשֹׂ֣ות כֵּ֔ן בְּקֶ֣רֶב הָאָ֔רֶץ אֲשֶׁ֥ר אַתֶּ֛ם בָּאִ֥ים שָׁ֖מָּה לְרִשְׁתָּֽהּ׃ ⁶וּשְׁמַרְתֶּם֮ וַעֲשִׂיתֶם֒ כִּ֣י הִ֤וא חָכְמַתְכֶם֙ וּבִ֣ינַתְכֶ֔ם לְעֵינֵ֖י הָעַמִּ֑ים אֲשֶׁ֣ר יִשְׁמְע֗וּן אֵ֚ת כָּל־הַחֻקִּ֣ים הָאֵ֔לֶּה וְאָמְר֗וּ רַ֚ק עַם־חָכָ֣ם וְנָבֹ֔ון הַגֹּ֥וי הַגָּדֹ֖ול הַזֶּֽה׃ ⁷כִּ֚י מִי־גֹ֣וי גָּדֹ֔ול אֲשֶׁר־לֹ֥ו אֱלֹהִ֖ים קְרֹבִ֣ים אֵלָ֑יו כַּיהוָ֣ה אֱלֹהֵ֔ינוּ בְּכָל־קָרְאֵ֖נוּ אֵלָֽיו׃ ⁸וּמִי֙ גֹּ֣וי גָּדֹ֔ול אֲשֶׁר־לֹ֛ו חֻקִּ֥ים וּמִשְׁפָּטִ֖ים צַדִּיקִ֑ם כְּכֹל֙ הַתֹּורָ֣ה הַזֹּ֔את אֲשֶׁ֧ר אָנֹכִ֛י נֹתֵ֥ן לִפְנֵיכֶ֖ם הַיֹּֽום׃ ⁹רַ֡ק הִשָּׁ֣מֶר לְךָ֩ וּשְׁמֹ֨ר נַפְשְׁךָ֜ מְאֹ֗ד פֶּן־תִּשְׁכַּ֣ח אֶת־הַדְּבָרִ֗ים אֲשֶׁר־רָא֣וּ עֵינֶ�a֮יךָ וּפֶ֣ן־יָס֮וּרוּ֮ מִלְּבָבְךָ֒ כֹּ֖ל יְמֵ֣י חַיֶּ֑יךָ וְהֹודַעְתָּ֥ם לְבָנֶ֖יךָ וְלִבְנֵ֣י בָנֶֽיךָ׃ ¹⁰יֹ֗ום אֲשֶׁ֨ר עָמַ֜דְתָּ לִפְנֵ֨י יְהוָ֣ה אֱלֹהֶיךָ֮ בְּחֹרֵב֒ בֶּאֱמֹ֨ר יְהוָ֜ה אֵלַ֗י הַקְהֶל־לִי֙ אֶת־הָעָ֔ם וְאַשְׁמִעֵ֖ם אֶת־דְּבָרָ֑י אֲשֶׁ֨ר יִלְמְד֜וּן לְיִרְאָ֣ה אֹתִ֗י כָּל־הַיָּמִים֙ אֲשֶׁ֨ר הֵ֤ם חַיִּים֙ עַל־הָ֣אֲדָמָ֔ה וְאֶת־בְּנֵיהֶ֖ם יְלַמֵּדֽוּן׃ ¹¹וַתִּקְרְב֣וּן וַתַּֽעַמְד֗וּן תַּ֣חַת הָהָ֑ר וְהָהָ֞ר בֹּעֵ֤ר בָּאֵשׁ֙ עַד־לֵ֣ב הַשָּׁמַ֔יִם חֹ֖שֶׁךְ עָנָ֥ן וַעֲרָפֶֽל׃

4:11. **the mountain was burning.** The text in Exodus does not in fact use this word for burning. It says that "Mount Sinai was all smoke because YHWH came down on it in fire" (Exod 19:18). This word was rather the term for the burning bush. And so we learn only now that the burning bush that Moses experienced was already a sign of what was to come. And this in turn may answer the old question of what is meant when God says to Moses at the bush, "This is the sign for you that I have sent you. When you bring out the people from Egypt you shall serve God on this mountain" (Exod 3:12). What is the sign? The miraculous burning bush itself. And it prefigures what will happen when the people come back to that mountain. This point is supported later in this chapter (4:36) when Moses reminds the people that at Sinai "you heard His voice from inside the fire"—which recalls how Moses himself heard God call "from inside the bush" that was on fire (Exod 3:4).

12And YHWH spoke to you from inside the fire. You were hearing the sound of words, but you weren't seeing a form, just sound. 13And He told you His covenant that He commanded you to do, the Ten Commandments, and He wrote them on two tablets of stones. 14And YHWH commanded me at that time to teach you laws and judgments, for you to do them in the land to which you're crossing to take possession of it. 15And you shall be very watchful of yourselves—because you didn't see any form in the day that YHWH spoke to you at Horeb from inside the fire— 16in case you'll be corrupted, and you'll make a statue, a form of any figure, a design of a male or a female, 17a design of any animal that's in the earth, a design of any winged bird that flies in the skies, 18a design of anything that creeps on the ground, a design of any fish that's in the water under the earth, 19and in case you'll raise your eyes to the skies, and you'll see the sun and the moon and the stars, all the array of the skies, and you'll be moved so that you'll bow to them and serve them, when YHWH, your God, has allocated them to all the peoples under all the skies. 20But YHWH has taken you, and He has brought you out from the iron furnace, from

וַיְדַבֵּ֨ר יְהוָ֤ה אֲלֵיכֶם֙ מִתּ֣וֹךְ הָאֵ֔שׁ ק֥וֹל דְּבָרִ֖ים 12
אַתֶּ֣ם שֹׁמְעִ֔ים וּתְמוּנָ֖ה אֵינְכֶ֣ם רֹאִ֑ים זוּלָתִ֖י קֽוֹל׃
וַיַּגֵּ֣ד לָכֶ֣ם אֶת־בְּרִית֗וֹ אֲשֶׁ֨ר צִוָּ֤ה אֶתְכֶם֙ לַעֲשׂ֔וֹת 13
עֲשֶׂ֖רֶת הַדְּבָרִ֑ים וַיִּכְתְּבֵ֔ם עַל־שְׁנֵ֖י לֻח֥וֹת אֲבָנִֽים׃
וְאֹתִ֞י צִוָּ֤ה יְהוָה֙ בָּעֵ֣ת הַהִ֔וא לְלַמֵּ֣ד אֶתְכֶ֔ם חֻקִּ֖ים 14
וּמִשְׁפָּטִ֑ים לַעֲשֹׂתְכֶ֣ם אֹתָ֔ם בָּאָ֕רֶץ אֲשֶׁ֥ר אַתֶּ֛ם
עֹבְרִ֥ים שָׁ֖מָּה לְרִשְׁתָּֽהּ׃ וְנִשְׁמַרְתֶּ֥ם מְאֹ֖ד 15
לְנַפְשֹׁתֵיכֶ֑ם כִּ֣י לֹ֤א רְאִיתֶם֙ כָּל־תְּמוּנָ֔ה בְּי֗וֹם דִּבֶּ֨ר
יְהוָ֧ה אֲלֵיכֶ֛ם בְּחֹרֵ֖ב מִתּ֥וֹךְ הָאֵֽשׁ׃ פֶּ֨ן־תַּשְׁחִת֔וּן 16
וַעֲשִׂיתֶ֥ם לָכֶ֛ם פֶּ֖סֶל תְּמוּנַ֣ת כָּל־סָ֑מֶל תַּבְנִ֥ית זָכָ֖ר
א֣וֹ נְקֵבָֽה׃ תַּבְנִ֕ית כָּל־בְּהֵמָ֖ה אֲשֶׁ֣ר בָּאָ֑רֶץ תַּבְנִית֙ 17
כָּל־צִפּ֣וֹר כָּנָ֔ף אֲשֶׁ֥ר תָּע֖וּף בַּשָּׁמָֽיִם׃ תַּבְנִ֕ית כָּל־ 18
רֹמֵ֖שׂ בָּאֲדָמָ֑ה תַּבְנִ֛ית כָּל־דָּגָ֥ה אֲשֶׁר־בַּמַּ֖יִם מִתַּ֥חַת
לָאָֽרֶץ׃ וּפֶן־תִּשָּׂ֨א עֵינֶ֜יךָ הַשָּׁמַ֗יְמָה וְֽ֠רָאִיתָ אֶת־ 19
הַשֶּׁ֣מֶשׁ וְאֶת־הַיָּרֵ֣חַ וְאֶת־הַכּֽוֹכָבִ֗ים כֹּ֚ל צְבָ֣א הַשָּׁמַ֔יִם
וְנִדַּחְתָּ֗ וְהִֽשְׁתַּחֲוִ֤יתָ לָהֶם֙ וַעֲבַדְתָּ֔ם אֲשֶׁ֣ר חָלַ֗ק יְהוָ֤ה
אֱלֹהֶ֨יךָ֙ אֹתָ֔ם לְכֹל֙ הָֽעַמִּ֔ים תַּ֖חַת כָּל־הַשָּׁמָֽיִם׃
וְאֶתְכֶם֙ לָקַ֣ח יְהוָ֔ה וַיּוֹצִ֥א אֶתְכֶ֖ם מִכּ֣וּר הַבַּרְזֶ֑ל 20

4:13. **His covenant . . . the Ten Commandments.** The Ten Commandments *are* the covenant. All the other commandments are important, and there are rewards for keeping them and consequences for breaking them. But the Ten Commandments on the tablets are different. Violation of them by the community (for example, widespread pagan worship or injustice) risks the breaking of the covenant. They are the essence of the covenant itself.

4:19. **the array of the skies.** Again the last book of the Torah recalls the beginning of the Torah. The term "array" has not been used to refer to the heavenly bodies since the creation story (Gen 2:1). There it was used in the account of God's creation of the cosmos. Now Moses warns that one might be inspired by their awesome quality to worship them.

4:19. **allocated them to all the peoples.** This is doubly extraordinary: (1) God is understood to have provided the pagan deities that the other nations worship. (2) There is no criticism here of the other nations for worshiping them. There is nothing wrong with other people's following their own faiths. They are only criticized elsewhere in the Torah for specific practices in their religions that are abhorrent to Israelites, such as human sacrifice.

Egypt, to become a legacy people for him, as it is this day.

21"And YHWH had been incensed at me over your matters, and He swore that I would not cross the Jordan and not come to the good land that YHWH, your God, is giving you as a legacy. 22So I am dying in this land. I'm not crossing the Jordan. But *you* are crossing, and you shall possess this good land. 23Watch yourselves, in case you'll forget the covenant of YHWH, your God, that He made with you, and you'll make a statue of any form about which YHWH, your God, has commanded you, 24because YHWH, your God: He is a consuming fire, a jealous God.

25"When you'll produce children and grandchildren and will have been in the land long, and you'll be corrupt and make a statue of any form and do what is bad in the eyes of YHWH, your God, to provoke Him, 26I call the skies and the earth to witness regarding you today that you'll *perish* quickly from the land to which you're crossing the Jordan to take possession of it. You won't extend days on it, but you'll be *destroyed!* 27And YHWH will scatter you among the peoples, and you'll be left few in number among the

מִמִּצְרָיִם לִהְיֹות לֹו לְעַם נַחֲלָה כַּיֹּום הַזֶּה: 21וַיהוָה הִתְאַנַּף־בִּי עַל־דִּבְרֵיכֶם וַיִּשָּׁבַע לְבִלְתִּי עָבְרִי אֶת־הַיַּרְדֵּן וּלְבִלְתִּי־בֹא אֶל־הָאָרֶץ הַטֹּובָה אֲשֶׁר יְהוָה אֱלֹהֶיךָ נֹתֵן לְךָ נַחֲלָה: 22כִּי אָנֹכִי מֵת בָּאָרֶץ הַזֹּאת אֵינֶנִּי עֹבֵר אֶת־הַיַּרְדֵּן וְאַתֶּם עֹבְרִים וִירִשְׁתֶּם אֶת־הָאָרֶץ הַטֹּובָה הַזֹּאת: 23הִשָּׁמְרוּ לָכֶם פֶּן־תִּשְׁכְּחוּ אֶת־בְּרִית יְהוָה אֱלֹהֵיכֶם אֲשֶׁר כָּרַת עִמָּכֶם וַעֲשִׂיתֶם לָכֶם פֶּסֶל תְּמוּנַת כֹּל אֲשֶׁר צִוְּךָ יְהוָה אֱלֹהֶיךָ: 24כִּי יְהוָה אֱלֹהֶיךָ אֵשׁ אֹכְלָה הוּא אֵל קַנָּא: פ

25כִּי־תֹולִיד בָּנִים וּבְנֵי בָנִים וְנֹושַׁנְתֶּם בָּאָרֶץ וְהִשְׁחַתֶּם וַעֲשִׂיתֶם פֶּסֶל תְּמוּנַת כֹּל וַעֲשִׂיתֶם הָרַע בְּעֵינֵי יְהוָה־אֱלֹהֶיךָ לְהַכְעִיסֹו: 26הַעִידֹתִי בָכֶם הַיֹּום אֶת־הַשָּׁמַיִם וְאֶת־הָאָרֶץ כִּי־אָבֹד תֹּאבֵדוּן מַהֵר מֵעַל הָאָרֶץ אֲשֶׁר אַתֶּם עֹבְרִים אֶת־הַיַּרְדֵּן שָׁמָּה לְרִשְׁתָּהּ לֹא־תַאֲרִיכֻן יָמִים עָלֶיהָ כִּי הִשָּׁמֵד תִּשָּׁמֵדוּן: 27וְהֵפִיץ יְהוָה אֶתְכֶם בָּעַמִּים וְנִשְׁאַרְתֶּם

4:22. **good**. The word "good" recurs nine times in the first chapters of Deuteronomy. It culminates when Moses ends this section of his speech with the instruction to keep all the commandments "so it will be *good* for you" (4:40). It is reminiscent of Genesis 1. There God declares each stage of the creation to be "good." That is, the world starts off in a state that is positive, but it soon goes into a variety of troubles relating to human behavior ("The ground is cursed on your account," Gen 3:17). And now Moses tells the people over and over that the land they are entering is "good." It too starts off in a positive state, and they have the opportunity to keep it good or to ruin it.

4:24. **a consuming fire, a jealous God**. Here Moses emphasizes the harsh, frightening side of God. But he immediately softens it in his next few sentences. See the comments on vv. 29 and 31 below. (On the term "jealous," see the comment on Exod 20:5.)

4:27. **scatter**. The threat of scattering a people is frightening itself, and, again, it harks back to the early part of Genesis, where YHWH scatters the people of the world in the matter of the tower of Babylon (Gen 11:9).

4:27. **few in number**. The other occurrence of this expression in the Torah is where Jacob reprimands his sons Simeon and Levi for massacring the city of Shechem; he

nations where YHWH will drive you. 28And you'll serve gods, the work of human hands, wood and stone, there, that don't see and don't hear and don't eat and don't smell.

29"But if you'll seek YHWH, your God, from there, then you'll find Him, when you'll inquire of Him with all your heart and all your soul. 30When you have trouble, and all these things have found you, in the future days, if you'll go back to YHWH, your God, and listen to His voice, 31He won't let you down, and he won't destroy you, *because YHWH, your God, is a merciful God,* and He won't forget your fathers' covenant that He swore to them. 32Because ask of the earliest days that were before you, from the day that God created a human on the earth, and from one end of the skies to the other end of the skies: has there been anything like this great thing? or has anything like it been heard of? 33Has a people heard God's voice speaking from inside a fire the

מְתֵי מִסְפָּר בַּגּוֹיִם אֲשֶׁר יְנַהֵג יְהוָה אֶתְכֶם שָׁמָּה: 28וַעֲבַדְתֶּם־שָׁם אֱלֹהִים מַעֲשֵׂה יְדֵי אָדָם עֵץ וָאֶבֶן אֲשֶׁר לֹא־יִרְאוּן וְלֹא יִשְׁמְעוּן וְלֹא יֹאכְלוּן וְלֹא יְרִיחֻן: 29וּבִקַּשְׁתֶּם מִשָּׁם אֶת־יְהוָה אֱלֹהֶיךָ וּמָצָאתָ כִּי תִדְרְשֶׁנּוּ בְּכָל־לְבָבְךָ וּבְכָל־נַפְשֶׁךָ: 30בַּצַּר לְךָ וּמְצָאוּךָ כֹּל הַדְּבָרִים הָאֵלֶּה בְּאַחֲרִית הַיָּמִים וְשַׁבְתָּ עַד־יְהוָה אֱלֹהֶיךָ וְשָׁמַעְתָּ בְּקֹלוֹ: 31כִּי אֵל רַחוּם יְהוָה אֱלֹהֶיךָ לֹא יַרְפְּךָ וְלֹא יַשְׁחִיתֶךָ וְלֹא יִשְׁכַּח אֶת־בְּרִית אֲבֹתֶיךָ אֲשֶׁר נִשְׁבַּע לָהֶם: 32כִּי שְׁאַל־נָא לְיָמִים רִאשֹׁנִים אֲשֶׁר־הָיוּ לְפָנֶיךָ לְמִן־הַיּוֹם אֲשֶׁר בָּרָא אֱלֹהִים אָדָם עַל־הָאָרֶץ וּלְמִקְצֵה הַשָּׁמַיִם וְעַד־קְצֵה הַשָּׁמָיִם הֲנִהְיָה כַּדָּבָר הַגָּדוֹל הַזֶּה אוֹ הֲנִשְׁמַע כָּמֹהוּ: 33הֲשָׁמַע עָם קוֹל אֱלֹהִים מְדַבֵּר מִתּוֹךְ־הָאֵשׁ כַּאֲשֶׁר־שָׁמַעְתָּ אַתָּה

---

says that he is vulnerable now because he is *few in number* (Gen 34:30). And the denouement of this matter comes when, on his deathbed, Jacob condemns Simeon and Levi to be *scattered* (Gen 49:7), using the same word that is used for scattering in the first half of this verse. The double parallel makes a notable reminiscence of Genesis here.

4:28. **work of human hands**. This verse is a brief expression of what is said in Ps 115:4–8.

4:29. **But if you'll seek . . . then you'll find**. Even though Moses has just told the people that God will destroy and scatter them, he still returns to the idea that they can repent and that God will forgive them. The conception of God is always based in compassion. No matter what the people's offense, God is forgiving and merciful, and there can be a new reconciliation.

4:31. *a merciful God*. This is the first time that Moses mentions to the people a portion of the divine formula that God revealed to him at Sinai in the moment of Moses' greatest revelation, when he saw God (Exod 34:6). Until this point, Moses had only spoken of it to God Himself (when Moses pleaded with God not to destroy the people in the spies episode; Num 14:18). Later these come to be the most quoted words of God in the *Tanak:* in the prophets (Joel 2:13; Jon 4:2; Nah 1:3), Psalms (86:15; 103:8; 111:4; 112:4; 145:8), and later history (2 Chr 30:9; Neh 9:17,31). During their travels the people have seen much of God's just, punishing side. But now, as they are about to begin their life in the promised land, Moses informs them that God is, in the first place, not a wrathful God, but a *merciful* God.

way *you* heard—and lived? 34Or has God put it to the test, to come to take for Himself a people from among another people with tests, with signs, and with wonders and with war and with a strong hand and with an outstretched arm and with great fears like everything that YHWH, your God, has done for you in Egypt before your eyes? 35You have been shown in order to know that YHWH: *He* is God. There is no other outside of Him. 36From the skies He had you hear His voice in order to discipline you, and on the earth He showed you His great fire, and you heard His words from inside the fire. 37And because He loved your fathers He chose their seed after them, so He brought you out in front of Him from Egypt by His great power, 38to dispossess bigger and more powerful nations than you in front of you, to bring you, to give you their land as a legacy as it is today. 39And you shall know today and store it in your heart that YHWH: *He* is God in the skies above and on the earth below. There isn't another. 40And you shall observe His laws and His commandments that I command you today so it will be *good* for you and for your

וַיְחִי: 34אוֹ ׀ הֲנִסָּה אֱלֹהִים לָבוֹא לָקַחַת לוֹ גוֹי מִקֶּרֶב גּוֹי בְּמַסֹּת בְּאֹתֹת וּבְמוֹפְתִים וּבְמִלְחָמָה וּבְיָד חֲזָקָה וּבִזְרוֹעַ נְטוּיָה וּבְמוֹרָאִים גְּדֹלִים כְּכֹל אֲשֶׁר־עָשָׂה לָכֶם יְהוָה אֱלֹהֵיכֶם בְּמִצְרַיִם לְעֵינֶיךָ: 35אַתָּה הָרְאֵתָ לָדַעַת כִּי יְהוָה הוּא הָאֱלֹהִים אֵין עוֹד מִלְבַדּוֹ: 36מִן־הַשָּׁמַיִם הִשְׁמִיעֲךָ אֶת־קֹלוֹ לְיַסְּרֶךָּ וְעַל־הָאָרֶץ הֶרְאֲךָ אֶת־אִשּׁוֹ הַגְּדוֹלָה וּדְבָרָיו שָׁמַעְתָּ מִתּוֹךְ הָאֵשׁ: 37וְתַחַת כִּי אָהַב אֶת־אֲבֹתֶיךָ וַיִּבְחַר בְּזַרְעוֹ אַחֲרָיו וַיּוֹצִאֲךָ בְּפָנָיו בְּכֹחוֹ הַגָּדֹל מִמִּצְרָיִם: 38לְהוֹרִישׁ גּוֹיִם גְּדֹלִים וַעֲצֻמִים מִמְּךָ מִפָּנֶיךָ לַהֲבִיאֲךָ לָתֶת־לְךָ אֶת־אַרְצָם נַחֲלָה כַּיּוֹם הַזֶּה: 39וְיָדַעְתָּ הַיּוֹם וַהֲשֵׁבֹתָ אֶל־לְבָבֶךָ כִּי יְהוָה הוּא הָאֱלֹהִים בַּשָּׁמַיִם מִמַּעַל וְעַל־הָאָרֶץ מִתָּחַת אֵין עוֹד: 40וְשָׁמַרְתָּ אֶת־חֻקָּיו וְאֶת־מִצְוֹתָיו אֲשֶׁר אָנֹכִי מְצַוְּךָ הַיּוֹם אֲשֶׁר יִיטַב לְךָ וּלְבָנֶיךָ

4:34. a strong hand and an outstretched arm. More correctly, the first noun (*yād*) means "forearm" and the second (*zĕrō'a*) means "arm." In Hebrew, *kāp* is the hand, up to the wrist; *yād* is the forearm, from the fingers up to the elbow; and *zĕrō'a* is the entire arm, from the fingers up to the shoulder (see Gen 49:24). I have retained the traditional translation, "a strong hand and an outstretched arm," because it is a famous biblical phrase. And I frequently translate *yād* as hand because the word sometimes can mean just the hand and because of factors of English usage. (See also the comment on Deut 11:24.)

4:35,39. *He* is God. The Hebrew is written with the definite article (literally, "He is *the* God," not just "He is God" or "He is a God"). Grammatically, it excludes the possibility of saying the same thing about any other god as well. That is, it is a purely monotheistic statement. The sentence that follows it in v. 35 confirms this: "There is no other outside of Him." The sentence that follows it in v. 39 does likewise: "There isn't another." And these sentences were written by the seventh century B.C.E. at the very latest. They weigh against the claim of some scholars that monotheism was a late concept in biblical Israel (later than the Babylonian exile in 587 B.C.E.).

4:37. their seed after them. Grammatically, the text reads "his seed after him"—using the singular even though the antecedent is the plural "your fathers." I do not know if there is some special meaning to this.

children after you, and so that you'll extend days on the land that YHWH, your God, is giving you forever."

⁴¹Then Moses distinguished three cities across the Jordan toward the sun's rising, ⁴²for the manslayer who would slay his neighbor without knowing—and he had not hated him from the day before yesterday—to flee there, so he would flee to one of these cities and would live: ⁴³Bezer in the wilderness of the plain for the Reubenites, and Ramoth in Gilead for the Gadites, and Golan in Bashan for the Manassites.

⁴⁴And this is the instruction that Moses set before the children of Israel. ⁴⁵These are the testimonies and the laws and the judgments that Moses spoke to the children of Israel when they went out from Egypt, ⁴⁶across the Jordan in the valley opposite Beth Peor, in the land of Sihon, king of the Amorites, who lived in Heshbon, whom Moses and the children of Israel struck when they came out from the land of Egypt. ⁴⁷And they took possession of his land, and of the land of Og, king of Bashan, the two kings of the Amorites who were across the Jordan at the sun's rising, ⁴⁸from Aroer, which is on the edge of the Wadi Arnon, to Mount Sion—that is Hermon— ⁴⁹and all the plain across the Jordan eastward to the sea of the plain below the slopes of Pisgah.

אַחֲרֶ֔יךָ וּלְמַ֨עַן֙ תַּאֲרִ֣יךְ יָמִ֔ים עַל־הָ֣אֲדָמָ֔ה אֲשֶׁ֨ר יהוה אֱלֹהֶ֜יךָ נֹתֵ֥ן לְךָ֖ כָּל־הַיָּמִֽים׃ פ

⁴¹אָ֣ז יַבְדִּ֤יל מֹשֶׁה֙ שָׁלֹ֣שׁ עָרִ֔ים בְּעֵ֖בֶר הַיַּרְדֵּ֑ן מִזְרְחָ֖ה שָֽׁמֶשׁ׃ ⁴²לָנֻ֨ס שָׁ֜מָּה רוֹצֵ֗חַ אֲשֶׁ֨ר יִרְצַ֤ח אֶת־רֵעֵ֙הוּ֙ בִּבְלִי־דַ֔עַת וְה֛וּא לֹא־שֹׂנֵ֥א ל֖וֹ מִתְּמֹ֣ל שִׁלְשֹׁ֑ם וְנָ֗ס אֶל־אַחַ֛ת מִן־הֶעָרִ֥ים הָאֵ֖ל וָחָֽי׃ ⁴³אֶת־בֶּ֧צֶר בַּמִּדְבָּ֛ר בְּאֶ֥רֶץ הַמִּישֹׁ֖ר לָרֻֽאוּבֵנִ֑י וְאֶת־רָאמֹ֤ת בַּגִּלְעָד֙ לַגָּדִ֔י וְאֶת־גּוֹלָ֥ן בַּבָּשָׁ֖ן לַֽמְנַשִּֽׁי׃

⁴⁴וְזֹ֖את הַתּוֹרָ֑ה אֲשֶׁר־שָׂ֣ם מֹשֶׁ֔ה לִפְנֵ֖י בְּנֵ֥י יִשְׂרָאֵֽל׃ ⁴⁵אֵ֚לֶּה הָֽעֵדֹ֔ת וְהַֽחֻקִּ֖ים וְהַמִּשְׁפָּטִ֑ים אֲשֶׁ֨ר דִּבֶּ֤ר מֹשֶׁה֙ אֶל־בְּנֵ֣י יִשְׂרָאֵ֔ל בְּצֵאתָ֖ם מִמִּצְרָֽיִם׃ ⁴⁶בְּעֵ֨בֶר הַיַּרְדֵּ֜ן בַּגַּ֗יְא מ֚וּל בֵּ֣ית פְּע֔וֹר בְּאֶ֗רֶץ סִיחֹן֙ מֶ֣לֶךְ הָֽאֱמֹרִ֔י אֲשֶׁ֥ר יוֹשֵׁ֖ב בְּחֶשְׁבּ֑וֹן אֲשֶׁ֨ר הִכָּ֤ה מֹשֶׁה֙ וּבְנֵ֣י יִשְׂרָאֵ֔ל בְּצֵאתָ֖ם מִמִּצְרָֽיִם׃ ⁴⁷וַיִּֽירְשׁ֨וּ אֶת־אַרְצ֜וֹ וְאֶת־אֶ֣רֶץ ׀ ע֣וֹג מֶֽלֶךְ־הַבָּשָׁ֗ן שְׁנֵי֙ מַלְכֵ֣י הָֽאֱמֹרִ֔י אֲשֶׁ֖ר בְּעֵ֣בֶר הַיַּרְדֵּ֑ן מִזְרַ֖ח שָֽׁמֶשׁ׃ ⁴⁸מֵעֲרֹעֵ֞ר אֲשֶׁ֨ר עַל־שְׂפַת־נַ֧חַל אַרְנֹ֛ן וְעַד־הַ֥ר שִׂיאֹ֖ן ה֥וּא חֶרְמֽוֹן׃ ⁴⁹וְכָל־הָ֨עֲרָבָ֜ה עֵ֤בֶר הַיַּרְדֵּן֙ מִזְרָ֔חָה וְעַ֖ד יָ֣ם הָֽעֲרָבָ֑ה תַּ֖חַת אַשְׁדֹּ֥ת הַפִּסְגָּֽה׃ פ

4:42. **from the day before yesterday**. Meaning: he had no prior hatred of the person he killed. The killing was accidental and without malice.

4:44. **this is the instruction**. In the original context here in Deuteronomy, the word "Torah/instruction" refers only to the things that Moses says to the people across the Jordan from Canaan in his last speech (4:44–46). Jews now sing this verse when the Torah is held up for all to see after it is read each week. These words, "this is the Torah that Moses set . . . ," have therefore come to be understood in that context to refer to the entire five books on the Torah scroll.

4:45. **testimonies**. Meaning: things that have been witnessed. Moses has called the skies and the earth to witness what he has instructed the people (4:26). He will do so again at the end of Deuteronomy (31:28; 32:1).

5 ¹And Moses called all of Israel and said to them, "Listen, Israel, to the laws and the judgments that I'm speaking in your ears today. And you shall learn them and be watchful to do them. ²YHWH, our God, had made a covenant with us at Horeb. ³YHWH did not make this covenant with our fathers, but with us! We! These! Here! Today! All of us! Living! ⁴Face-to-face, YHWH spoke with you at the mountain from inside the fire ⁵(I was standing between YHWH and you at that time to tell you YHWH's word because you were afraid on account of the fire, and you didn't go up in the mountain), saying:

⁶I am YHWH, your God, who brought you out from the land of Egypt, from a house of slaves.

5 ¹וַיִּקְרָ֣א מֹשֶׁה֮ אֶל־כָּל־יִשְׂרָאֵל֒ וַיֹּ֣אמֶר אֲלֵהֶ֔ם שְׁמַ֣ע יִשְׂרָאֵ֗ל אֶת־הַחֻקִּים֙ וְאֶת־הַמִּשְׁפָּטִ֔ים אֲשֶׁ֧ר אָנֹכִ֛י דֹּבֵ֥ר בְּאָזְנֵיכֶ֖ם הַיּ֑וֹם וּלְמַדְתֶּ֣ם אֹתָ֔ם וּשְׁמַרְתֶּ֖ם לַעֲשֹׂתָֽם: ²יְהוָ֣ה אֱלֹהֵ֗ינוּ כָּרַ֥ת עִמָּ֛נוּ בְּרִ֖ית בְּחֹרֵֽב: ³לֹ֣א אֶת־אֲבֹתֵ֔ינוּ כָּרַ֥ת יְהוָ֖ה אֶת־הַבְּרִ֣ית הַזֹּ֑את כִּ֣י אִתָּ֗נוּ אֲנַ֜חְנוּ אֵ֣לֶּה פֹ֥ה הַיּ֛וֹם כֻּלָּ֖נוּ חַיִּֽים: ⁴פָּנִ֣ים ׀ בְּפָנִ֗ים דִּבֶּ֨ר יְהוָ֧ה עִמָּכֶ֛ם בָּהָ֖ר מִתּ֥וֹךְ הָאֵֽשׁ: ⁵אָֽנֹכִ֞י עֹמֵ֨ד בֵּין־יְהוָ֤ה וּבֵֽינֵיכֶם֙ בָּעֵ֣ת הַהִ֔וא לְהַגִּ֥יד לָכֶ֖ם אֶת־דְּבַ֣ר יְהוָ֑ה כִּ֤י יְרֵאתֶם֙ מִפְּנֵ֣י הָאֵ֔שׁ וְלֹֽא־עֲלִיתֶ֥ם בָּהָ֖ר לֵאמֹֽר: ס

⁶אָֽנֹכִי֙ יְהוָ֣ה אֱלֹהֶ֔יךָ אֲשֶׁ֧ר הוֹצֵאתִ֛יךָ מֵאֶ֥רֶץ

5:1. **watchful.** This is the fifth time that Moses uses this word in his speech. Its concentration here calls to mind another element of the beginning of the Torah, where forms of this word are played upon: Humans are placed in the garden of Eden "to watch over it" (Gen 2:15); but when they eat from the forbidden tree they are removed from the garden, and cherubs are placed "to watch over the way to the tree of life" (3:24)—that is, to keep humans away; and in the next episode Cain lies about his brother Abel's whereabouts by saying "Am I my brother's watchman?" (4:9). The point of this: The word "watch" marks a gradual descent by humans away from their initial condition of closeness to God. But then the word is used in a new way when God says that the merit of Abraham is that he "kept my watch" (26:5). (This phrase is generally translated "keep my charge" in this work, but I used the word "watch" in Gen 26:5 in order to make known this development in Genesis.) The word thus comes to point the way to a return to harmony with the creator, and thus it resurfaces meaningfully here in the Torah's final book.

5:3. **us! We! These! Here! Today! All of us! Living!** As I commented above (1:9), Moses mixes past, present, and future. He speaks to the people in front of him as if they had all been at Sinai forty years earlier. Now he says it explicitly, powerfully, unmistakably, with seven different words: Each generation must see themselves as personally standing at Sinai, not just as inheriting their parents' covenant, but as making the covenant themselves. It is a present, living commitment.

5:4. **Face-to-face.** Just a short time earlier Moses had said, "You didn't see any form in the day that YHWH spoke to you at Horeb from inside the fire." But now he says, "Face-to-face, YHWH spoke with you at the mountain from inside the fire." This is further confirmation that "face-to-face" is not a literal expression. Like many Hebrew expressions involving the word "face," it is an idiom. It is used metaphorically to mean direct, personal communication, not mediated by any third party.

7You shall not have other gods before my face.

8You shall not make a statue, any form that is in the skies above or that is in the earth below or that is in the water below the earth. 9You shall not bow to them, and you shall not serve them. Because I, YHWH, your God, am a jealous God, counting parents' crime on children and on the third generation and on the fourth generation of those who hate me, 10but practicing kindness to thousands for those who love me and for those who observe my commandments.

11You shall not bring up the name of YHWH, your God, for a falsehood, because YHWH will not make one innocent who will bring up His name for a falsehood.

12Observe the Sabbath day, to make it holy, as YHWH, your God, commanded you. 13Six days you shall labor and do all your work, 14and the seventh day is a Sabbath to YHWH, your God. You shall not do

מִצְרַיִם מִבֵּית עֲבָדִים׃ 7לֹא יִהְיֶה־לְךָ אֱלֹהִים
אֲחֵרִים עַל־פָּנָי׃ 8לֹא־תַעֲשֶׂה־לְךָ פֶסֶל ׀ כָּל־תְּמוּנָה
אֲשֶׁר בַּשָּׁמַיִם ׀ מִמַּעַל וַאֲשֶׁר בָּאָרֶץ מִתָּחַת וַאֲשֶׁר
בַּמַּיִם ׀ מִתַּחַת לָאָרֶץ׃ 9לֹא־תִשְׁתַּחֲוֶה לָהֶם וְלֹא
תָעָבְדֵם כִּי אָנֹכִי יְהוָה אֱלֹהֶיךָ אֵל קַנָּא פֹּקֵד עֲוֺן
אָבוֹת עַל־בָּנִים וְעַל־שִׁלֵּשִׁים וְעַל־רִבֵּעִים לְשֹׂנְאָי׃
10וְעֹשֶׂה חֶסֶד לַאֲלָפִים לְאֹהֲבַי וּלְשֹׁמְרֵי מִצְוֺתָו ס
11לֹא תִשָּׂא אֶת־שֵׁם־יְהוָה אֱלֹהֶיךָ לַשָּׁוְא כִּי לֹא
יְנַקֶּה יְהוָה אֵת אֲשֶׁר־יִשָּׂא אֶת־שְׁמוֹ לַשָּׁוְא׃ ס
12שָׁמוֹר אֶת־יוֹם הַשַּׁבָּת לְקַדְּשׁוֹ כַּאֲשֶׁר צִוְּךָ ׀ יְהוָה
אֱלֹהֶיךָ׃ 13שֵׁשֶׁת יָמִים תַּעֲבֹד וְעָשִׂיתָ כָּל־
מְלַאכְתֶּךָ׃ 14וְיוֹם הַשְּׁבִיעִי שַׁבָּת ׀ לַיהוָה אֱלֹהֶיךָ

5:10 ק מִצְוֺתָי׃

5:7. **not have other gods**. This is a monotheistic command. It has been mistakenly taken to mean that other gods do exist but that Israelites are not to worship them. But that is a linguistic misunderstanding. See the comment on Exod 20:3.

5:12. **Observe**. Probably the most famous difference between the wording of the Ten Commandments at Sinai and the way that Moses quotes them here is this first word of the Sabbath commandment. At Sinai God says "Remember the Sabbath" (Exod 20:8), but Moses now says "Observe the Sabbath." Many have commented on the two words. The most basic explanation may be that the two are both necessary and are complementary: In the mind, one must remember it. In actions, one must observe it.

Another explanation: The most striking difference between the Decalogue at Sinai and Moses' quotation of it here is the *reason* for the Sabbath command. At Sinai it is

> Because for six days YHWH made the skies and the earth, the sea, and everything that is in them, and He rested on the seventh day. On account of this, YHWH blessed the Sabbath day and made it holy. (Exod 20:11)

But here it is so

> you shall remember that you were a slave in the land of Egypt and YHWH, your God, brought you out from there with a strong hand and an outstretched arm. On account of this, YHWH, your God, has commanded you to do the Sabbath day. (Deut 5:15)

any work: you and your son and your daughter and your servant and your maid and your ox and your ass or any animal and your alien who is in your gates—in order that your servant and your maid will rest like you, 15and you shall remember that you were a slave in the land of Egypt and YHWH, your God, brought you out from there with a strong hand and an outstretched arm. On account of this, YHWH, your God, has commanded you to do the Sabbath day.

16Honor your father and your mother, as YHWH, your God, commanded you, so

לֹא תַעֲשֶׂה כָל־מְלָאכָה אַתָּה וּבִנְךָ־וּבִתֶּךָ וְעַבְדְּךָ
וַאֲמָתֶךָ וְשׁוֹרְךָ וַחֲמֹרְךָ וְכָל־בְּהֶמְתֶּךָ וְגֵרְךָ אֲשֶׁר
בִּשְׁעָרֶיךָ לְמַעַן יָנוּחַ עַבְדְּךָ וַאֲמָתְךָ כָּמוֹךָ׃
15וְזָכַרְתָּ כִּי־עֶבֶד הָיִיתָ ׀ בְּאֶרֶץ מִצְרַיִם וַיֹּצִאֲךָ
יְהוָה אֱלֹהֶיךָ מִשָּׁם בְּיָד חֲזָקָה וּבִזְרֹעַ נְטוּיָה עַל־
כֵּן צִוְּךָ יְהוָה אֱלֹהֶיךָ לַעֲשׂוֹת אֶת־יוֹם הַשַּׁבָּת׃ ס
16כַּבֵּד אֶת־אָבִיךָ וְאֶת־אִמֶּךָ כַּאֲשֶׁר צִוְּךָ יְהוָה

What do we learn from this: When *God* states the commandment, God identifies the Sabbath with the creation of the universe and the sanctification of time (see the comments on Gen 2:2 and 2:3). But when a human, Moses, states the commandment, he identifies the Sabbath rather with history, with a divine action in human affairs. The Sabbath thus comes to have both dimensions: cosmic and historical. (A Dead Sea scroll text of Deuteronomy combines these and gives *both* reasons for the Sabbath.) This in turn may explain why the text here begins this command with the words "Observe the Sabbath" instead of "Remember the Sabbath"—namely, since it now adds the words "and you shall *remember* that you were a slave . . ." at the end of the commandment, it uses a different word at the beginning.

5:14. **you and your son and your daughter**. The text does not mention "your wife." One might take this to be male-chauvinist, but I think that, in this case, it is the opposite. The text mentions daughters as well as sons, and it mentions female as well as male servants here (and elsewhere: Deut 12:12,18). Therefore the words "you and your son and your daughter" must be understood to be directed to both men and women, husbands and wives, in the first place. Indeed, all of the Ten Commandments are directed to each individual Israelite, male and female, with the exception of the first part of the last commandment—"You shall not covet your neighbor's wife"—which is explicitly directed only to men and reflects a marital structure that men control.

5:16. **Honor your father and your mother**. Children ask, "What if your parents tell you to break one of the other commandments?" The question reveals an essential fact: all of the Ten Commandments are given to two people. The commandment to the child to honor one's parents is also a commandment to the parent to be worthy of honor. The parent cannot be utterly dishonorable, and cannot put the child in a position in which the child cannot possibly honor the parent. Similarly, the command not to steal is also a command not to deny food to the poor so that he or she might be obliged to steal.

that your days will be extended and so that it will be good for you on the land that YHWH, your God, is giving you.

17You shall not murder.

And you shall not commit adultery.

And you shall not steal.

And you shall not testify against your neighbor as a false witness.

18And you shall not covet your neighbor's wife, and you shall not long for your neighbor's house, his field, or his servant or his maid, his ox or his ass or anything that your neighbor has.

19"YHWH spoke these words to your entire community at the mountain from inside the fire, the cloud, and the nimbus, a powerful voice. And He did not add. And He wrote them on two tablets of stones and gave them to me.

20"And it was when you heard the voice from inside the darkness, as the mountain was burning in fire, that you came forward to me, all the heads of your tribes and your elders, 21and you said, 'Here, YHWH, our God, has shown us His glory and His greatness, and we've heard His voice from inside the fire. This day we've seen that God may speak to a human and he lives. 22So now why should we die? Because this big fire will consume us. If we go on hearing the voice of YHWH, our God, anymore, then we'll

אֱלֹהֶ֔יךָ לְמַ֤עַן ׀ יַאֲרִיכֻ֣ן יָמֶ֔יךָ וּלְמַ֙עַן֙ יִ֣יטַב לָ֔ךְ עַ֚ל הָ֣אֲדָמָ֔ה אֲשֶׁר־יְהוָ֥ה אֱלֹהֶ֖יךָ נֹתֵ֥ן לָֽךְ׃ ס 17לֹ֥א תִּרְצָֽח׃ ס 18וְלֹ֖א תִּנְאָֽף׃ ס 19וְלֹ֖א תִּגְנֹֽב׃ ס 20וְלֹֽא־תַעֲנֶ֥ה בְרֵעֲךָ֖ עֵ֣ד שָֽׁוְא׃ ס 21וְלֹ֥א תַחְמֹ֖ד אֵ֣שֶׁת רֵעֶ֑ךָ ס וְלֹ֨א תִתְאַוֶּ֜ה בֵּ֣ית רֵעֶ֗ךָ שָׂדֵ֜הוּ וְעַבְדּ֤וֹ וַאֲמָתוֹ֙ שׁוֹר֣וֹ וַחֲמֹר֔וֹ וְכֹ֖ל אֲשֶׁ֥ר לְרֵעֶֽךָ׃ ס 22אֶֽת־הַדְּבָרִ֣ים הָאֵ֡לֶּה דִּבֶּר֩ יְהוָ֨ה אֶל־כָּל־קְהַלְכֶ֜ם בָּהָ֗ר מִתּ֤וֹךְ הָאֵשׁ֙ הֶֽעָנָ֣ן וְהָֽעֲרָפֶ֔ל ק֥וֹל גָּד֖וֹל וְלֹ֣א יָסָ֑ף וַֽיִּכְתְּבֵ֗ם עַל־שְׁנֵי֙ לֻחֹ֣ת אֲבָנִ֔ים וַֽיִּתְּנֵ֖ם אֵלָֽי׃ 23וַיְהִ֗י כְּשָׁמְעֲכֶ֤ם אֶת־הַקּוֹל֙ מִתּ֣וֹךְ הַחֹ֔שֶׁךְ וְהָהָ֖ר בֹּעֵ֣ר בָּאֵ֑שׁ וַתִּקְרְב֣וּן אֵלַ֗י כָּל־רָאשֵׁ֥י שִׁבְטֵיכֶ֖ם וְזִקְנֵיכֶֽם׃ 24וַתֹּאמְר֗וּ הֵ֣ן הֶרְאָ֜נוּ יְהוָ֤ה אֱלֹהֵ֙ינוּ֙ אֶת־כְּבֹד֣וֹ וְאֶת־גָּדְל֔וֹ וְאֶת־קֹל֥וֹ שָׁמַ֖עְנוּ מִתּ֣וֹךְ הָאֵ֑שׁ הַיּ֤וֹם הַזֶּה֙ רָאִ֔ינוּ כִּֽי־יְדַבֵּ֧ר אֱלֹהִ֛ים אֶת־הָֽאָדָ֖ם וָחָֽי׃ 25וְעַתָּה֙ לָ֣מָּה נָמ֔וּת כִּ֣י תֹֽאכְלֵ֔נוּ הָאֵ֥שׁ הַגְּדֹלָ֖ה הַזֹּ֑את אִם־יֹסְפִ֣ים ׀ אֲנַ֗חְנוּ לִשְׁמֹ֛עַ אֶת־ק֥וֹל יְהוָ֛ה

Note: BHS numbers ET 17 as 17–19; thus there is a 3-verse discrepancy from ET 19–30 = BHS 22–33.

5:16. **and so that it will be good for you.** These words do not appear in the Decalogue at Sinai. Moses adds them here. See the comment on Deut 4:22. Again Moses conveys the idea that the commandments are a path back to the *good*, the condition that prevailed at the time of creation, prior to the event in Eden.

5:17. **adultery.** This is perhaps the most readily broken of the commandments (except for coveting?). It is the commandment that *good* people break. The temptation is extraordinary. The potential for hurt is substantial. The potential for leading to other behavior, especially lying, is tremendous as well.

5:19. **He did not add.** Again Moses reminds the people that the commandments as stated are not to be added to (see the comment on Deut 4:2). For two millennia Jews have struggled with the matter of additions to the law. Rabbinites and Karaites, Orthodox and Reform and Conservative Jews, have differed over the limits of the law and over where Jews have gone too far in adding to it.

584

die. 23Because who, of all flesh, is there who has heard the voice of the living God speaking from inside fire as we have and lived? 24*You* go forward and listen to everything that YHWH, our God, will say, and *you'll* speak to us everything that YHWH, our God, will speak to you, and we'll listen, and we'll do it.'

25"And YHWH listened to your words' voice when you were speaking to me, and YHWH said to me, 'I've listened to the voice of this people's words that they spoke to you. They've been good in everything that they've spoken. 26Who would make it so, that they would have such a heart, to fear me and observe all my commandments every day, so it would be good for them and for their children forever! 27Go say to them, "Go back to your tents." 28And you, stand here with me so I may speak to you all the commandment and the laws and the judgments that you shall teach them so they'll do them in the land that I'm giving them to take possession of it. 29And you shall be watchful to do as YHWH, your God, has commanded you. You shall not turn right or left. 30You shall go in all the way that YHWH, your God, has commanded you, so that you'll live, and it will be good for you, and you'll extend days in the land that you'll possess.'

אֱלֹהֵינוּ עוֹד וָמָתְנוּ: 26כִּי מִי כָל־בָּשָׂר אֲשֶׁר שָׁמַע קוֹל אֱלֹהִים חַיִּים מְדַבֵּר מִתּוֹךְ־הָאֵשׁ כָּמֹנוּ וַיֶּחִי: 27קְרַב אַתָּה וּשֲׁמָע אֵת כָּל־אֲשֶׁר יֹאמַר יְהוָה אֱלֹהֵינוּ וְאַתְּ ׀ תְּדַבֵּר אֵלֵינוּ אֵת כָּל־אֲשֶׁר יְדַבֵּר יְהוָה אֱלֹהֵינוּ אֵלֶיךָ וְשָׁמַעְנוּ וְעָשִׂינוּ: 28וַיִּשְׁמַע יְהוָה אֶת־קוֹל דִּבְרֵיכֶם בְּדַבֶּרְכֶם אֵלָי וַיֹּאמֶר יְהוָה אֵלַי שָׁמַעְתִּי אֶת־קוֹל דִּבְרֵי הָעָם הַזֶּה אֲשֶׁר דִּבְּרוּ אֵלֶיךָ הֵיטִיבוּ כָּל־אֲשֶׁר דִּבֵּרוּ: 29מִי־יִתֵּן וְהָיָה לְבָבָם זֶה לָהֶם לְיִרְאָה אֹתִי וְלִשְׁמֹר אֶת־כָּל־מִצְוֹתַי כָּל־הַיָּמִים לְמַעַן יִיטַב לָהֶם וְלִבְנֵיהֶם לְעֹלָם: 30לֵךְ אֱמֹר לָהֶם שׁוּבוּ לָכֶם לְאָהֳלֵיכֶם: 31וְאַתָּה פֹּה עֲמֹד עִמָּדִי וַאֲדַבְּרָה אֵלֶיךָ אֵת כָּל־הַמִּצְוָה וְהַחֻקִּים וְהַמִּשְׁפָּטִים אֲשֶׁר תְּלַמְּדֵם וְעָשׂוּ בָאָרֶץ אֲשֶׁר אָנֹכִי נֹתֵן לָהֶם לְרִשְׁתָּהּ: 32וּשְׁמַרְתֶּם לַעֲשׂוֹת כַּאֲשֶׁר צִוָּה יְהוָה אֱלֹהֵיכֶם אֶתְכֶם לֹא תָסֻרוּ יָמִין וּשְׂמֹאל: 33בְּכָל־הַדֶּרֶךְ אֲשֶׁר צִוָּה יְהוָה אֱלֹהֵיכֶם אֶתְכֶם תֵּלֵכוּ לְמַעַן תִּחְיוּן וְטוֹב לָכֶם וְהַאֲרַכְתֶּם יָמִים בָּאָרֶץ אֲשֶׁר תִּירָשׁוּן:

Note: BHS numbers ET 17 as 17–19; thus there is a 3-verse discrepancy from ET 19–30 = BHS 22–33.

5:26. **Who would make it so.** I asked in *The Hidden Face of God*: should *God* have to ask *who* when the answer seems so manifestly to be that God Himself could make it so? Even if "Who would make it so" was a known expression, it still seems inapplicable for God. All the classic English translations reword this verse, eliminating the phrase "who would make it so," presumably because it seems so incongruous. But we cannot translate the concept away. It suggests that, in the Torah's conception, even though God makes humans as God sees fit, humans are free thereafter to follow their hearts. God splits seas, makes animals talk, and makes water come from rocks, but God does not change the human heart. This in turn sheds light in retrospect on what God does to Pharaoh's heart during the plagues. English translators have often made it "God *hardened* Pharaoh's heart," but the Hebrew rather means "God *strengthened* Pharaoh's heart." God does not *change* the king's heart, but only gives the Pharaoh strength to follow his own resolve.

5:29. **not turn right or left.** This expression complements the command not to add to or subtract from the commandments (4:2; 5:19). The emphasis is on focusing on the law as given. Later, King Josiah will be singled out from all the kings of Israel and Judah because "he did not turn right or left" (2 Kings 22:2).

6 ¹"And this is the commandment, the laws, and the judgments that YHWH, your God, commanded to teach you to do in the land to which you're crossing to take possession of it, ²so that you'll fear YHWH, your God, to observe all His laws and His commandments that I'm commanding you: you and your child and your child's child, all the days of your life, and so that your days will be extended. ³And you shall listen, Israel, and be watchful to do it, that it will be good for you and that you'll multiply very much, as YHWH, your fathers' God, spoke to you: a land flowing with milk and honey.

⁴"Listen, Israel: YHWH is our God. YHWH is one. ⁵And you shall love YHWH, your God, with all your heart and with all your soul and with all your might. ⁶And these words that I command you today shall be on your heart. ⁷And you shall impart them to your children, and you shall speak about them when you sit in your house and when you go in the road and when you lie

1 וְזֹאת הַמִּצְוָה הַחֻקִּים וְהַמִּשְׁפָּטִים אֲשֶׁר צִוָּה 6
יְהוָה אֱלֹהֵיכֶם לְלַמֵּד אֶתְכֶם לַעֲשׂוֹת בָּאָרֶץ אֲשֶׁר
אַתֶּם עֹבְרִים שָׁמָּה לְרִשְׁתָּהּ: 2לְמַעַן תִּירָא אֶת־
יְהוָה אֱלֹהֶיךָ לִשְׁמֹר אֶת־כָּל־חֻקֹּתָיו וּמִצְוֹתָיו אֲשֶׁר
אָנֹכִי מְצַוֶּךָ אַתָּה וּבִנְךָ וּבֶן־בִּנְךָ כֹּל יְמֵי חַיֶּיךָ
וּלְמַעַן יַאֲרִכֻן יָמֶיךָ: 3וְשָׁמַעְתָּ יִשְׂרָאֵל וְשָׁמַרְתָּ
לַעֲשׂוֹת אֲשֶׁר יִיטַב לְךָ וַאֲשֶׁר תִּרְבּוּן מְאֹד כַּאֲשֶׁר
דִּבֶּר יְהוָה אֱלֹהֵי אֲבֹתֶיךָ לָךְ אֶרֶץ זָבַת חָלָב
וּדְבָשׁ: פ
4שְׁמַע יִשְׂרָאֵל יְהוָה אֱלֹהֵינוּ יְהוָה ׀ אֶחָד:
5וְאָהַבְתָּ אֵת יְהוָה אֱלֹהֶיךָ בְּכָל־לְבָבְךָ וּבְכָל־
נַפְשְׁךָ וּבְכָל־מְאֹדֶךָ: 6וְהָיוּ הַדְּבָרִים הָאֵלֶּה אֲשֶׁר
אָנֹכִי מְצַוְּךָ הַיּוֹם עַל־לְבָבֶךָ: 7וְשִׁנַּנְתָּם לְבָנֶיךָ
וְדִבַּרְתָּ בָּם בְּשִׁבְתְּךָ בְּבֵיתֶךָ וּבְלֶכְתְּךָ בַדֶּרֶךְ

6:4. **Listen**. Forms of this word (Hebrew *šĕmaʿ*) occur about eighty times in Deuteronomy. This emphasis on listening goes together with the title and theme of the book: words, Moses' speech. The great events of creation, patriarchs, exodus, Sinai, and the wilderness are at an end. What remains now is the words: the story of what happened, and the commandments to be fulfilled. Israel's task now—and in its future generations—is to *listen*, to learn the story and to do the commandments. And so this passage, probably the most commonly known and frequently repeated words in the Bible by Jews, begins with the commandment that necessarily precedes all others: Listen.

6:4. **YHWH is one**. This is a supremely monotheistic statement, especially when taken together with the preceding statements: "He is God" and "There is no other outside of Him" and "There isn't another." More evidence that monotheism is essential in Deuteronomy, in its early (preexilic) layers, will follow. Monotheism was an early concept in biblical Israel.

Some take these words to mean, "YHWH is our God, YHWH *alone*." But "alone" is an extremely uncommon meaning for the Hebrew word here: *ʾeḥād*.

6:4. **YHWH is one**. In comparing Israel's monotheism to pagan religion, we must appreciate that the difference between one and many is not the same sort of thing as the difference between two and three or between six and twenty. It is not numerical. It is a different concept of what a god is. A God who is outside of nature, known through acts in history, a creator, unseeable, without a mate, who makes legal covenants with humans, who is one, is a revolution in religious conception.

down and when you get up. 8And you shall bind them for a sign on your hand, and they shall become bands between your eyes. 9And you shall write them on the doorposts of your house and in your gates.

10"And it will be when YHWH, your God, will bring you to the land that He swore to your fathers, to Abraham, to Isaac, and to Jacob, to give you big and good cities that you didn't build, 11and houses filled with everything good that you didn't fill, and cisterns hewed that you didn't hew, vineyards and olives that you didn't plant, and you'll eat and be satisfied, 12watch yourself in case you'll forget YHWH, who brought you out from the land of Egypt, from a house of slaves. 13It's YHWH, your God, whom you'll fear, and it's He whom you'll serve, and it's in His name that you'll swear. 14You shall not go after other gods, from the gods of the peoples who are around you, 15because YHWH, your God, is a jealous God among you, in case the anger of YHWH, your God, will flare at you, and He'll destroy you from the face of the earth. 16You shall not test YHWH, your God, as you tested at Massah. 17You *shall* observe the commandments of YHWH, your God, and His testimonies and His laws that He commanded you. 18And you shall do what is right and good in YHWH's eyes so it will be good for you, and you'll come and take possession of the good land that YHWH swore to your fathers, 19to push all your enemies from in front of you, as YHWH has spoken.

20"When your child will ask you tomorrow, saying, 'What are the testimonies and the laws

וּבְשָׁכְבְּךָ֖ וּבְקוּמֶֽךָ׃ 8וּקְשַׁרְתָּ֥ם לְא֖וֹת עַל־יָדֶ֑ךָ וְהָי֥וּ לְטֹטָפֹ֖ת בֵּ֥ין עֵינֶֽיךָ׃ 9וּכְתַבְתָּ֛ם עַל־מְזוּזֹ֥ת בֵּיתֶ֖ךָ וּבִשְׁעָרֶֽיךָ׃ ס 10וְהָיָ֞ה כִּ֥י יְבִֽיאֲךָ֣ ׀ יְהוָ֣ה אֱלֹהֶ֗יךָ אֶל־הָאָ֜רֶץ אֲשֶׁ֨ר נִשְׁבַּ֧ע לַאֲבֹתֶ֛יךָ לְאַבְרָהָ֥ם לְיִצְחָ֖ק וּֽלְיַעֲקֹ֑ב לָ֤תֶת לָךְ֙ עָרִ֤ים גְּדֹלֹת֙ וְטֹבֹ֔ת אֲשֶׁ֥ר לֹא־בָנִֽיתָ׃ 11וּבָ֨תִּ֜ים מְלֵאִ֣ים כָּל־טוּב֮ אֲשֶׁ֣ר לֹא־מִלֵּ֒אתָ֒ וּבֹרֹ֤ת חֲצוּבִים֙ אֲשֶׁ֣ר לֹא־חָצַ֔בְתָּ כְּרָמִ֥ים וְזֵיתִ֖ים אֲשֶׁ֣ר לֹא־נָטָ֑עְתָּ וְאָכַלְתָּ֖ וְשָׂבָֽעְתָּ׃ 12הִשָּׁ֣מֶר לְךָ֔ פֶּן־תִּשְׁכַּ֖ח אֶת־יְהוָ֑ה אֲשֶׁ֧ר הוֹצִֽיאֲךָ֛ מֵאֶ֥רֶץ מִצְרַ֖יִם מִבֵּ֥ית עֲבָדִֽים׃ 13אֶת־יְהוָ֧ה אֱלֹהֶ֛יךָ תִּירָ֖א וְאֹת֣וֹ תַעֲבֹ֑ד וּבִשְׁמ֖וֹ תִּשָּׁבֵֽעַ׃ 14לֹ֣א תֵֽלְכ֔וּן אַחֲרֵ֖י אֱלֹהִ֣ים אֲחֵרִ֑ים מֵֽאֱלֹהֵי֙ הָֽעַמִּ֔ים אֲשֶׁ֖ר סְבִיבֽוֹתֵיכֶֽם׃ 15כִּ֣י אֵ֥ל קַנָּ֛א יְהוָ֥ה אֱלֹהֶ֖יךָ בְּקִרְבֶּ֑ךָ פֶּן־יֶ֠חֱרֶה אַף־יְהוָ֤ה אֱלֹהֶ֙יךָ֙ בָּ֔ךְ וְהִשְׁמִ֣ידְךָ֔ מֵעַ֖ל פְּנֵ֥י הָאֲדָמָֽה׃ ס 16לֹ֣א תְנַסּ֔וּ אֶת־יְהוָ֖ה אֱלֹהֵיכֶ֑ם כַּאֲשֶׁ֥ר נִסִּיתֶ֖ם בַּמַּסָּֽה׃ 17שָׁמ֣וֹר תִּשְׁמְר֔וּן אֶת־מִצְוֹ֖ת יְהוָ֣ה אֱלֹהֵיכֶ֑ם וְעֵדֹתָ֖יו וְחֻקָּ֖יו אֲשֶׁ֥ר צִוָּֽךְ׃ 18וְעָשִׂ֛יתָ הַיָּשָׁ֥ר וְהַטּ֖וֹב בְּעֵינֵ֣י יְהוָ֑ה לְמַ֙עַן֙ יִ֣יטַב לָ֔ךְ וּבָ֗אתָ וְיָֽרַשְׁתָּ֙ אֶת־הָאָ֣רֶץ הַטֹּבָ֔ה אֲשֶׁר־נִשְׁבַּ֥ע יְהוָ֖ה לַאֲבֹתֶֽיךָ׃ 19לַהֲדֹ֥ף אֶת־כָּל־אֹיְבֶ֖יךָ מִפָּנֶ֑יךָ כַּאֲשֶׁ֖ר דִּבֶּ֥ר יְהוָֽה׃ ס 20כִּֽי־יִשְׁאָלְךָ֥ בִנְךָ֛ מָחָ֖ר לֵאמֹ֑ר מָ֣ה הָעֵדֹ֗ת וְהַֽחֻקִּים֙

6:8. **bind them on your hand**. This came to be taken literally, requiring one to wear boxes (*tephillin*) on one's arm and head containing passages from the Torah. In the *Tanak*, however, this expression is meant figuratively, meaning to keep these teachings at hand. Thus, elsewhere it refers to binding religious teachings to one's neck (Prov 3:3), one's heart (6:21), and one's fingers (7:3).

6:8. **bands between your eyes**. This, too, is meant figuratively, meaning to keep these teachings right before one's eyes. Elsewhere it is used to refer to the law of redemption of the firstborn (Exod 13:16), where there is no connection to *tephillin*.

and the judgments that YHWH, our God, commanded you?' 21then you shall say to your child, 'We were slaves to Pharaoh in Egypt, and YHWH brought us out from Egypt with a strong hand. 22And YHWH put great and harsh signs and wonders in Egypt at Pharaoh and at all of his household before our eyes. 23And He brought us out from there in order to bring us to give us the land that He swore to our fathers. 24And YHWH commanded us to do all these laws, to fear YHWH, our God, for our good every day, to keep us alive as we are this day. 25And we'll have virtue when we are watchful to do all of this commandment in front of YHWH, our God, as He commanded us.'

7 1"When YHWH, your God, will bring you to the land to which you're coming to take possession of it and will eject numerous nations from in front of you—the Hittite and the Girgashite and the Amorite and the Canaanite and the Perizzite and the Hivite and the Jebusite—seven nations more numerous and powerful than you, 2and YHWH, your God, will put them in front of you, and you'll strike them: you shall completely destroy them! You shall not make a covenant with them, and you shall not show

וְהַמִּשְׁפָּטִים אֲשֶׁר צִוָּה יְהוָה אֱלֹהֵינוּ אֶתְכֶם: 21וְאָמַרְתָּ לְבִנְךָ עֲבָדִים הָיִינוּ לְפַרְעֹה בְּמִצְרָיִם וַיּוֹצִיאֵנוּ יְהוָה מִמִּצְרַיִם בְּיָד חֲזָקָה: 22וַיִּתֵּן יְהוָה אוֹתֹת וּמֹפְתִים גְּדֹלִים וְרָעִים ׀ בְּמִצְרַיִם בְּפַרְעֹה וּבְכָל־בֵּיתוֹ לְעֵינֵינוּ: 23וְאוֹתָנוּ הוֹצִיא מִשָּׁם לְמַעַן הָבִיא אֹתָנוּ לָתֶת לָנוּ אֶת־הָאָרֶץ אֲשֶׁר נִשְׁבַּע לַאֲבֹתֵינוּ: 24וַיְצַוֵּנוּ יְהוָה לַעֲשׂוֹת אֶת־כָּל־הַחֻקִּים הָאֵלֶּה לְיִרְאָה אֶת־יְהוָה אֱלֹהֵינוּ לְטוֹב לָנוּ כָּל־הַיָּמִים לְחַיֹּתֵנוּ כְּהַיּוֹם הַזֶּה: 25וּצְדָקָה תִּהְיֶה־לָּנוּ כִּי־נִשְׁמֹר לַעֲשׂוֹת אֶת־כָּל־הַמִּצְוָה הַזֹּאת לִפְנֵי יְהוָה אֱלֹהֵינוּ כַּאֲשֶׁר צִוָּנוּ: ס 7 1כִּי יְבִיאֲךָ יְהוָה אֱלֹהֶיךָ אֶל־הָאָרֶץ אֲשֶׁר־אַתָּה בָא־שָׁמָּה לְרִשְׁתָּהּ וְנָשַׁל גּוֹיִם־רַבִּים ׀ מִפָּנֶיךָ הַחִתִּי וְהַגִּרְגָּשִׁי וְהָאֱמֹרִי וְהַכְּנַעֲנִי וְהַפְּרִזִּי וְהַחִוִּי וְהַיְבוּסִי שִׁבְעָה גוֹיִם רַבִּים וַעֲצוּמִים מִמֶּךָּ: 2וּנְתָנָם יְהוָה אֱלֹהֶיךָ לְפָנֶיךָ וְהִכִּיתָם הַחֲרֵם תַּחֲרִים אֹתָם לֹא־תִכְרֹת לָהֶם

6:25. **we'll have virtue**. Again an issue from Genesis returns in Moses' farewell in Deuteronomy. The initial covenant with Abraham is made on the premise of Abraham's virtue (*ṣĕdāqāh*, Gen 15:6), and God later says of Abraham that "I've known him for the purpose that he'll command his children and his house after him, and they'll observe YHWH's way, to do *virtue* . . . " (18:19). His grandson Jacob later says that "my *virtue* will answer for me" (30:33). And then the word does not occur again in the Torah until this speech in Deuteronomy, where Moses repeatedly tells the people how they can come to have virtue.

7:1. **more numerous and powerful than you**. Ironically, these are the words that the Pharaoh who enslaved Israel used to describe the Israelites: "Here, the people of the children of Israel is more numerous and powerful than we" (Exod 1:9). But the situation is reversed. The Pharaoh tells his people that they should fear Israel on account of its great size. But God now tells the Israelites *not* to fear the Canaanite peoples on account of their size.

7:2. **completely destroy**. See the comment on Deut 2:34. Many people have been troubled by the idea of commanding the annihilation of the Canaanite residents of

grace to them. 3And you shall not marry with them. You shall not give your daughter to his son, and you shall not take his daughter for your son, 4because he'll turn your son from after me, and they'll serve other gods, and YHWH's anger will flare at you, and He'll destroy you quickly. 5But this is what you shall do to them: you shall demolish their altars and shatter their pillars and cut down their Asherahs and burn their statues in fire. 6Because you are a holy people to YHWH, your God. YHWH, your God, chose you to become a treasured people to Him out of all the peoples who are on the face of the earth. 7It

בְּרִית וְלֹא תְחָנֵּם: ³וְלֹא תִתְחַתֵּן בָּם בִּתְּךָ לֹא־תִתֵּן לִבְנוֹ וּבִתּוֹ לֹא־תִקַּח לִבְנֶךָ: ⁴כִּי־יָסִיר אֶת־בִּנְךָ מֵאַחֲרַי וְעָבְדוּ אֱלֹהִים אֲחֵרִים וְחָרָה אַף־יְהוָה בָּכֶם וְהִשְׁמִידְךָ מַהֵר: ⁵כִּי־אִם־כֹּה תַעֲשׂוּ לָהֶם מִזְבְּחֹתֵיהֶם תִּתֹּצוּ וּמַצֵּבֹתָם תְּשַׁבֵּרוּ וַאֲשֵׁירֵהֶם תְּגַדֵּעוּן וּפְסִילֵיהֶם תִּשְׂרְפוּן בָּאֵשׁ: ⁶כִּי עַם קָדוֹשׁ אַתָּה לַיהוָה אֱלֹהֶיךָ בְּךָ בָּחַר ׀ יְהוָה אֱלֹהֶיךָ לִהְיוֹת לוֹ לְעַם סְגֻלָּה מִכֹּל הָעַמִּים אֲשֶׁר עַל־פְּנֵי

---

the land. The archaeological evidence is that such a destruction never took place. This passage in the Torah was written long after the period of the Israelites' settlement in the land, and so it is ironic that the author of this text conceived of a degree of violence that appears never in fact to have happened, and then people are troubled by this degree of violence in Israel's history.

7:3. **you shall not marry with them**. Moses tells the Israelites that they are no longer free to marry persons from the seven peoples of Canaan. Their ancestors, like Judah (Gen 38:2), could marry Canaanite women because, biblically, a woman takes her husband's religion. Thus Abraham, Isaac, Jacob, Joseph, Moses, and Samson all marry women who come from other communities but who are understood to take on their husbands' religion. But Canaanite women are no longer included.

There is certainly the possibility that wives will not completely turn to their husbands' religion. This is what happens in the case of Solomon (1 Kings 11) and in the case of Ahab and Jezebel (1 Kings 16:30–33). And this possibility is given as the reason for the ban on marriage to Canaanites, as stated in the next verse (Deut 7:4).

This command is curious because in the preceding verse Moses has already said that the Canaanites are to be completely destroyed. The ban on marrying them appears to come from the recognition that the Israelites may fail to eliminate the Canaanites from the land or that it may be a very long process—which is in fact what happens (see Judg 2:1–3).

7:5. **Asherahs**. See the comment on Deut 16:21.

7:6. **chose you to become a treasured people**. As we see in an earlier occurrence of the term "treasured" for Israel, it applies only if they listen and fulfill their covenant (see the comment on Exod 19:5). The same applies to the term "chosen." It does not refer to any superiority of Israel. The reference to being chosen here is immediately followed by the statement that it is not because of size. And a little farther on, Moses will declare in vivid terms that it is not because of any special merit of Israel's (Deuteronomy 9). It is because of (*a*) YHWH's affection for Israel and (*b*) YHWH's oath to the patriarchs. Its practical consequence is that YHWH and Israel have a cov-

wasn't because of your being more numerous than all the peoples that YHWH was attracted to you so that He chose you, because you're the smallest of all the peoples. 8But because of YHWH's loving you and because of His keeping the oath that He swore to your fathers, YHWH brought you out with a strong hand and redeemed you from a house of slaves, from the hand of Pharaoh, king of Egypt. 9Therefore you shall know that YHWH, your God, *He* is God, the faithful God, keeping the covenant and kindness for those who love Him and who observe His commandments to the thousandth generation 10and paying back to those who hate Him to their faces to destroy them. He won't delay toward one who hates Him. He'll pay him back to his face. 11So you shall observe the commandment and the laws and the judgments that I command you today, to do them.

הָאֲדָמָה: ס ⁷לֹא מֵרֻבְּכֶם מִכָּל־הָעַמִּים חָשַׁק יְהוָה בָּכֶם וַיִּבְחַר בָּכֶם כִּי־אַתֶּם הַמְעַט מִכָּל־הָעַמִּים: ⁸כִּי מֵאַהֲבַת יְהוָה אֶתְכֶם וּמִשָּׁמְרוֹ אֶת־הַשְּׁבֻעָה אֲשֶׁר נִשְׁבַּע לַאֲבֹתֵיכֶם הוֹצִיא יְהוָה אֶתְכֶם בְּיָד חֲזָקָה וַיִּפְדְּךָ מִבֵּית עֲבָדִים מִיַּד פַּרְעֹה מֶלֶךְ־מִצְרָיִם: ⁹וְיָדַעְתָּ כִּי־יְהוָה אֱלֹהֶיךָ הוּא הָאֱלֹהִים הָאֵל הַנֶּאֱמָן שֹׁמֵר הַבְּרִית וְהַחֶסֶד לְאֹהֲבָיו וּלְשֹׁמְרֵי מִצְוֺתָו לְאֶלֶף דּוֹר: ¹⁰וּמְשַׁלֵּם לְשֹׂנְאָיו אֶל־פָּנָיו לְהַאֲבִידוֹ לֹא יְאַחֵר לְשֹׂנְאוֹ אֶל־פָּנָיו יְשַׁלֶּם־לוֹ: ¹¹וְשָׁמַרְתָּ אֶת־הַמִּצְוָה וְאֶת־הַחֻקִּים וְאֶת־הַמִּשְׁפָּטִים אֲשֶׁר אָנֹכִי מְצַוְּךָ הַיּוֹם לַעֲשׂוֹתָם: פ

BECAUSE

12"And it will be because you'll listen to these judgments and observe and do them that YHWH, your God, will keep the covenant and kindness for you that he swore to your fathers. 13And He'll love you and bless you and multiply you and bless the fruit of your womb and the fruit of your land: your grain and your wine and your oil, your cattle's offspring and your flock's young, on the

עקב

¹²וְהָיָה | עֵקֶב תִּשְׁמְעוּן אֵת הַמִּשְׁפָּטִים הָאֵלֶּה וּשְׁמַרְתֶּם וַעֲשִׂיתֶם אֹתָם וְשָׁמַר יְהוָה אֱלֹהֶיךָ לְךָ אֶת־הַבְּרִית וְאֶת־הַחֶסֶד אֲשֶׁר נִשְׁבַּע לַאֲבֹתֶיךָ: ¹³וַאֲהֵבְךָ וּבֵרַכְךָ וְהִרְבֶּךָ וּבֵרַךְ פְּרִי־בִטְנְךָ וּפְרִי־אַדְמָתֶךָ דְּגָנְךָ וְתִירֹשְׁךָ וְיִצְהָרֶךָ שְׁגַר־אֲלָפֶיךָ

7:9 ק מִצְוֺתָיו

enant. That is, being chosen has many sides: it is inspiring, uplifting, a burden, a challenge, a threat, an opportunity.

7:7. **attracted**. This is the same word that is used to describe Shechem's longing for Dinah (Gen 34:8) and a soldier's attraction to a female captive (Deut 21:11). It conveys a feeling of attachment that one soul has to another.

7:13. **your womb**. The word "your" in this phrase is masculine, and so some have interpreted it as meaning that the woman's womb was thought to belong to her husband. But that is questionable because the entire list of blessings in these verses (13–24) is formulated in the masculine singular, so the reference to the womb was just understood as taking a masculine possessive pronoun like the rest of the list. No conclusions should be drawn from this technical point of grammar regarding ancient Israelite conceptions of male-female ownership of the womb.

land that He swore to your fathers to give to you. ¹⁴You'll be more blessed than all the peoples. There won't be an infertile male or female among you or among your animals. ¹⁵And YHWH will turn away from you every illness. And all the bad diseases of Egypt that you knew: He won't set them among you but will put them among all who hate you. ¹⁶And you shall eat up all the peoples that YHWH, your God, is giving you. Your eye shall not pity them. And you shall not serve their gods, because that's a trap for you.

¹⁷"If you say in your heart, 'These nations are more numerous than I; how shall I be able to dispossess them?' ¹⁸you shall not fear them. You shall *remember* what YHWH, your God, did to Pharaoh and to all Egypt: ¹⁹the big tests that your eyes saw and the signs and the wonders and the strong hand and the outstretched arm by which YHWH, your God, brought you out. So YHWH, your God, will do to the peoples before whom you fear! ²⁰And YHWH, your God, will send the hornet against them as well until those who remain and those who are hidden perish from in front of you. ²¹Don't be scared in front of them, because YHWH, your God, is among you, a great and fearful God. ²²And YHWH, your God, will eject these nations from in front of you little by little. You won't be able to finish them quickly, or else the animal of the field will become many at you. ²³And YHWH, your God, will put them in front of you and put them into a big tumult until they're destroyed. ²⁴And He'll put their kings in your hand, and you'll destroy their name from under the skies. Not a man will stand in front of

וְעַשְׁתְּרֹת צֹאנֶךָ עַל הָאֲדָמָה אֲשֶׁר־נִשְׁבַּע לַאֲבֹתֶיךָ לָתֶת לָךְ: ¹⁴בָּרוּךְ תִּהְיֶה מִכָּל־הָעַמִּים לֹא־יִהְיֶה בְךָ עָקָר וַעֲקָרָה וּבִבְהֶמְתֶּךָ: ¹⁵וְהֵסִיר יְהוָה מִמְּךָ כָּל־חֹלִי וְכָל־מַדְוֵי מִצְרַיִם הָרָעִים אֲשֶׁר יָדַעְתָּ לֹא יְשִׂימָם בָּךְ וּנְתָנָם בְּכָל־שֹׂנְאֶיךָ: ¹⁶וְאָכַלְתָּ אֶת־כָּל־הָעַמִּים אֲשֶׁר יְהוָה אֱלֹהֶיךָ נֹתֵן לָךְ לֹא־תָחֹס עֵינְךָ עֲלֵיהֶם וְלֹא תַעֲבֹד אֶת־אֱלֹהֵיהֶם כִּי־מוֹקֵשׁ הוּא לָךְ: ס ¹⁷כִּי תֹאמַר בִּלְבָבְךָ רַבִּים הַגּוֹיִם הָאֵלֶּה מִמֶּנִּי אֵיכָה אוּכַל לְהוֹרִישָׁם: ¹⁸לֹא תִירָא מֵהֶם זָכֹר תִּזְכֹּר אֵת אֲשֶׁר־עָשָׂה יְהוָה אֱלֹהֶיךָ לְפַרְעֹה וּלְכָל־מִצְרָיִם: ¹⁹הַמַּסֹּת הַגְּדֹלֹת אֲשֶׁר־רָאוּ עֵינֶיךָ וְהָאֹתֹת וְהַמֹּפְתִים וְהַיָּד הַחֲזָקָה וְהַזְּרֹעַ הַנְּטוּיָה אֲשֶׁר הוֹצִאֲךָ יְהוָה אֱלֹהֶיךָ כֵּן־יַעֲשֶׂה יְהוָה אֱלֹהֶיךָ לְכָל־הָעַמִּים אֲשֶׁר־אַתָּה יָרֵא מִפְּנֵיהֶם: ²⁰וְגַם אֶת־הַצִּרְעָה יְשַׁלַּח יְהוָה אֱלֹהֶיךָ בָּם עַד־אֲבֹד הַנִּשְׁאָרִים וְהַנִּסְתָּרִים מִפָּנֶיךָ: ²¹לֹא תַעֲרֹץ מִפְּנֵיהֶם כִּי־יְהוָה אֱלֹהֶיךָ בְּקִרְבֶּךָ אֵל גָּדוֹל וְנוֹרָא: ²²וְנָשַׁל יְהוָה אֱלֹהֶיךָ אֶת־הַגּוֹיִם הָאֵל מִפָּנֶיךָ מְעַט מְעָט לֹא תוּכַל כַּלֹּתָם מַהֵר פֶּן־תִּרְבֶּה עָלֶיךָ חַיַּת הַשָּׂדֶה: ²³וּנְתָנָם יְהוָה אֱלֹהֶיךָ לְפָנֶיךָ וְהָמָם מְהוּמָה גְדֹלָה עַד הִשָּׁמְדָם: ²⁴וְנָתַן מַלְכֵיהֶם בְּיָדֶךָ וְהַאֲבַדְתָּ אֶת־שְׁמָם מִתַּחַת הַשָּׁמָיִם לֹא־יִתְיַצֵּב אִישׁ

7:14. blessed. This word in the Torah generally refers to being well off. Here it is explicitly connected with fertility and good health. So when it says that Israel will be more blessed than other peoples if they keep their covenant, it does not mean that Israel will have some special status, but rather it means that God will bless them with well-being.

7:23. a big tumult. This is the term for what God does to the Egyptians at the Red Sea. A few verses earlier Moses says that God will do to the Canaanites what was done to the Egyptians, and so he now describes what will happen to the Canaanites in the language of the defeat of the Egyptian army.

you, until you've destroyed them. 25You shall burn the statues of their gods in fire. You shall not covet the silver and gold on them and take them for yourself, in case you'll be trapped through it, because that is an offensive thing to YHWH, your God, 26and you shall not bring an offensive thing to your house, so that you'll be a thing to be completely destroyed like it. You shall *detest* it and find it *abhorrent*, because it is a thing to be completely destroyed.

8 1"All of the commandment that I command you today you shall be watchful to do, so that you'll live, and you'll multiply, and you'll come and take possession of the land that YHWH swore to your fathers. 2And you shall remember all the way that YHWH, your God, had you go these forty years in the wilderness in order to degrade you, to test you, to know what was in your heart: would you observe His commandments or not. 3So He degraded you and made you hunger and then fed you the manna, which you had not known and your fathers had not known, to let you know that a human doesn't live by bread alone, but a human lives by every product of YHWH's mouth. 4Your garment didn't wear out on you, and your foot didn't swell these forty years. 5So you shall know in your heart that, the way a man disciplines his child, so YHWH, your

בְּפָנֶיךָ עַד הִשָּׁמְדָךְ אֹתָם: 25פְּסִילֵי אֱלֹהֵיהֶם תִּשְׂרְפוּן בָּאֵשׁ לֹא־תַחְמֹד כֶּסֶף וְזָהָב עֲלֵיהֶם וְלָקַחְתָּ לָךְ פֶּן תִּוָּקֵשׁ בּוֹ כִּי תוֹעֲבַת יְהוָה אֱלֹהֶיךָ הוּא: 26וְלֹא־תָבִיא תוֹעֵבָה אֶל־בֵּיתֶךָ וְהָיִיתָ חֵרֶם כָּמֹהוּ שַׁקֵּץ ׀ תְּשַׁקְּצֶנּוּ וְתַעֵב ׀ תְּתַעֲבֶנּוּ כִּי־חֵרֶם הוּא: פ

8 1כָּל־הַמִּצְוָה אֲשֶׁר אָנֹכִי מְצַוְּךָ הַיּוֹם תִּשְׁמְרוּן לַעֲשׂוֹת לְמַעַן תִּחְיוּן וּרְבִיתֶם וּבָאתֶם וִירִשְׁתֶּם אֶת־הָאָרֶץ אֲשֶׁר־נִשְׁבַּע יְהוָה לַאֲבֹתֵיכֶם: 2וְזָכַרְתָּ אֶת־כָּל־הַדֶּרֶךְ אֲשֶׁר הֹלִיכֲךָ יְהוָה אֱלֹהֶיךָ זֶה אַרְבָּעִים שָׁנָה בַּמִּדְבָּר לְמַעַן עַנֹּתְךָ לְנַסֹּתְךָ לָדַעַת אֶת־אֲשֶׁר בִּלְבָבְךָ הֲתִשְׁמֹר מִצְוֹתָו אִם־לֹא: 3וַיְעַנְּךָ וַיַּרְעִבֶךָ וַיַּאֲכִלְךָ אֶת־הַמָּן אֲשֶׁר לֹא־יָדַעְתָּ וְלֹא יָדְעוּן אֲבֹתֶיךָ לְמַעַן הוֹדִיעֲךָ כִּי לֹא עַל־הַלֶּחֶם לְבַדּוֹ יִחְיֶה הָאָדָם כִּי עַל־כָּל־מוֹצָא פִי־יְהוָה יִחְיֶה הָאָדָם: 4שִׂמְלָתְךָ לֹא בָלְתָה מֵעָלֶיךָ וְרַגְלְךָ לֹא בָצֵקָה זֶה אַרְבָּעִים שָׁנָה: 5וְיָדַעְתָּ עִם־לְבָבֶךָ כִּי כַּאֲשֶׁר יְיַסֵּר אִישׁ אֶת־בְּנוֹ יְהוָה אֱלֹהֶיךָ

8:2 קֿ מִצְוֹתָיו

8:2. **to degrade you, to test you, to know.** This sequence of verbs is powerful because of the ways that they are used before this. The word "degrade" is used to describe what the Egyptians did to the Israelites as slaves (Exod 1:11). (It is also used for what Shechem did to Dinah, and for what the people of Israel are supposed to do to themselves on Yom Kippur.) It means to bring down, to humble, to lower someone. The difference is that the Egyptians do it to weaken the Israelites, whereas God does it to test their strength. The second word here, "test," is the word for what God does in commanding Abraham to sacrifice Isaac (Gen 22:1). The result of that test is that God says, "Now I *know* that you fear God" (22:12). And so the third word here, likewise, is "know," conveying that the purpose of a divine test is still to establish what is in a human's heart. Moses thus now tells the people that the reason for many of the tribulations that they experienced for forty years was to test them. We, the readers, were informed of this at the beginning of the account of the years in the wilderness, where testing is mentioned twice (Exod 15:25; 16:4), but this is the first time that Moses reveals it to the people.

God, disciplines you. 6And you shall observe the commandments of YHWH, your God, to go in His ways and to fear Him. 7Because YHWH, your God, is bringing you to a good land, a land of wadis of water, springs, and deeps coming out in valleys and in hills, 8a land of wheat and barley and vine and fig and pomegranate, a land of olive, oil, and honey, 9a land in which you won't eat bread in scarcity, in which you won't lack anything, a land whose stones are iron and from whose hills you'll hew bronze. 10And you'll eat and be full and bless YHWH, your God, for the good land that He has given you.

11"Watch yourself in case you'll forget YHWH, your God, so as not to observe His commandments and His judgments and His laws that I command you today, 12in case you'll eat, and you'll be full, and you'll build good houses, and you'll live there, 13and your oxen and your flock will multiply, and silver and gold will multiply for you, and everything that you'll have will multiply, 14and your heart will be lifted, and you'll forget YHWH, your God, who brought you out from the land of Egypt, from a house of slaves, 15who led you in the big and fearful wilderness of fiery snake and scorpion and thirst, where there isn't water, who brought out water for you from the flint rock, 16who fed you manna in the wilderness, which your fathers had not known, in order to degrade you and in order to test you to be good to you in your future; 17and you'll say in your heart: '*My* power and *my* hand's strength

מִיַסְּרֶֽךָ׃ 6וְשָׁמַרְתָּ֙ אֶת־מִצְוֺ֣ת יְהוָ֣ה אֱלֹהֶ֔יךָ לָלֶ֥כֶת בִּדְרָכָ֖יו וּלְיִרְאָ֥ה אֹתֽוֹ׃ 7כִּ֚י יְהוָ֣ה אֱלֹהֶ֔יךָ מְבִֽיאֲךָ֖ אֶל־אֶ֣רֶץ טוֹבָ֑ה אֶ֚רֶץ נַ֣חֲלֵי מָ֔יִם עֲיָנֹת֙ וּתְהֹמֹ֔ת יֹצְאִ֥ים בַּבִּקְעָ֖ה וּבָהָֽר׃ 8אֶ֤רֶץ חִטָּה֙ וּשְׂעֹרָ֔ה וְגֶ֥פֶן וּתְאֵנָ֖ה וְרִמּ֑וֹן אֶֽרֶץ־זֵ֥ית שֶׁ֖מֶן וּדְבָֽשׁ׃ 9אֶ֗רֶץ אֲשֶׁ֨ר לֹ֤א בְמִסְכֵּנֻת֙ תֹּֽאכַל־בָּ֣הּ לֶ֔חֶם לֹֽא־תֶחְסַ֥ר כֹּ֖ל בָּ֑הּ אֶ֚רֶץ אֲשֶׁ֣ר אֲבָנֶ֣יהָ בַרְזֶ֔ל וּמֵהֲרָרֶ֖יהָ תַּחְצֹ֥ב נְחֹֽשֶׁת׃ 10וְאָכַלְתָּ֖ וְשָׂבָ֑עְתָּ וּבֵֽרַכְתָּ֙ אֶת־יְהוָ֣ה אֱלֹהֶ֔יךָ עַל־הָאָ֥רֶץ הַטֹּבָ֖ה אֲשֶׁ֥ר נָֽתַן־לָֽךְ׃ 11הִשָּׁ֣מֶר לְךָ֔ פֶּן־תִּשְׁכַּ֖ח אֶת־יְהוָ֣ה אֱלֹהֶ֑יךָ לְבִלְתִּ֨י שְׁמֹ֤ר מִצְוֺתָיו֙ וּמִשְׁפָּטָ֣יו וְחֻקֹּתָ֔יו אֲשֶׁ֛ר אָנֹכִ֥י מְצַוְּךָ֖ הַיּֽוֹם׃ 12פֶּן־תֹּאכַ֖ל וְשָׂבָ֑עְתָּ וּבָתִּ֥ים טוֹבִ֛ים תִּבְנֶ֖ה וְיָשָֽׁבְתָּ׃ 13וּבְקָֽרְךָ֤ וְצֹֽאנְךָ֙ יִרְבְּיֻ֔ן וְכֶ֥סֶף וְזָהָ֖ב יִרְבֶּה־לָּ֑ךְ וְכֹ֥ל אֲשֶׁר־לְךָ֖ יִרְבֶּֽה׃ 14וְרָ֖ם לְבָבֶ֑ךָ וְשָֽׁכַחְתָּ֙ אֶת־יְהוָ֣ה אֱלֹהֶ֔יךָ הַמּוֹצִֽיאֲךָ֛ מֵאֶ֥רֶץ מִצְרַ֖יִם מִבֵּ֥ית עֲבָדִֽים׃ 15הַמּוֹלִֽיכֲךָ֗ בַּמִּדְבָּ֣ר ׀ הַגָּדֹ֣ל וְהַנּוֹרָ֡א נָחָ֣שׁ ׀ שָׂרָ֠ף וְעַקְרָ֤ב וְצִמָּאוֹן֙ אֲשֶׁ֣ר אֵֽין־מָ֔יִם הַמּוֹצִ֥יא לְךָ֙ מַ֔יִם מִצּ֖וּר הַֽחַלָּמִֽישׁ׃ 16הַמַּֽאֲכִֽלְךָ֨ מָ֜ן בַּמִּדְבָּ֗ר אֲשֶׁ֤ר לֹא־יָֽדְעוּן֙ אֲבֹתֶ֔יךָ לְמַ֣עַן עַנֹּֽתְךָ֔ וּלְמַ֖עַן נַסֹּתֶ֑ךָ לְהֵיטִֽבְךָ֖ בְּאַֽחֲרִיתֶֽךָ׃ 17וְאָֽמַרְתָּ֖ בִּלְבָבֶ֑ךָ כֹּחִי֙ וְעֹ֣צֶם

8:6. **fear.** Some may find the idea of being afraid of God to be strange or unattractive. But the fact remains that to experience the power of the creator of the universe is fearful. Thus Moses hides his face at the burning bush because he is afraid to look at God. Thus the people are terrified when they hear the divine voice at Sinai. Thus Nadab and Abihu die because of a misstep in closeness to the holy. When one appreciates what is at stake, one can understand why the idea of *fear* of God—literally, profoundly—is so significant here.

8:9. **you'll hew bronze.** Copper and tin.

8:10. **eat and be full and bless.** The Jewish practice of saying grace after meals, *birkāt hammāzōn*, is associated with this verse.

8:17. *My* **power.** The entire passage from v. 11 to v. 17 is one sentence. Moses uses

made this wealth for me.' 18Then you shall remember YHWH, your God, because *He* is the one who gave you power to make wealth so as to uphold His covenant that He swore to your fathers—as it is this day.

19"And it will be, if you'll *forget* YHWH, your God, and you'll go after other gods and serve them and bow to them, I call witness regarding you today that you'll *perish!* 20Like the nations that YHWH is making to perish in front of you, so will you perish, because you wouldn't listen to the voice of YHWH, your God.

9 1"Listen, Israel: you're crossing the Jordan today to come to dispossess nations bigger and stronger than you, big cities and fortified to the skies, 2a people big and tall, giants, of whom you have known, and of whom you have heard it said: 'Who can stand in front of the giants?!' 3So you shall know today that YHWH, your God: *He* is the one who is crossing in front of you, a consuming fire. *He* will destroy them, and *He* will subdue them in front of you, so you'll dispossess them and destroy them quickly as YHWH has spoken to you.

4"Don't say in your heart when YHWH pushes them from in front of you, saying, 'Because of my virtue YHWH has brought me to take possession of this land,' when it is because of these nations' wickedness that YHWH dispossesses them from before you. 5It's not because of your virtue and

וְיָדִי עֲשָׂה לִי אֶת־הַחַיִל הַזֶּה: 18וְזָכַרְתָּ אֶת־יְהוָה אֱלֹהֶיךָ כִּי הוּא הַנֹּתֵן לְךָ כֹּחַ לַעֲשׂוֹת חָיִל לְמַעַן הָקִים אֶת־בְּרִיתוֹ אֲשֶׁר־נִשְׁבַּע לַאֲבֹתֶיךָ כַּיּוֹם הַזֶּה: פ 19וְהָיָה אִם־שָׁכֹחַ תִּשְׁכַּח אֶת־יְהוָה אֱלֹהֶיךָ וְהָלַכְתָּ אַחֲרֵי אֱלֹהִים אֲחֵרִים וַעֲבַדְתָּם וְהִשְׁתַּחֲוִיתָ לָהֶם הַעִדֹתִי בָכֶם הַיּוֹם כִּי אָבֹד תֹּאבֵדוּן: 20כַּגּוֹיִם אֲשֶׁר יְהוָה מַאֲבִיד מִפְּנֵיכֶם כֵּן תֹּאבֵדוּן עֵקֶב לֹא תִשְׁמְעוּן בְּקוֹל יְהוָה אֱלֹהֵיכֶם: פ 9 1שְׁמַע יִשְׂרָאֵל אַתָּה עֹבֵר הַיּוֹם אֶת־הַיַּרְדֵּן לָבֹא לָרֶשֶׁת גּוֹיִם גְּדֹלִים וַעֲצֻמִים מִמֶּךָּ עָרִים גְּדֹלֹת וּבְצֻרֹת בַּשָּׁמָיִם: 2עַם־גָּדוֹל וָרָם בְּנֵי עֲנָקִים אֲשֶׁר אַתָּה יָדַעְתָּ וְאַתָּה שָׁמַעְתָּ מִי יִתְיַצֵּב לִפְנֵי בְּנֵי עֲנָק: 3וְיָדַעְתָּ הַיּוֹם כִּי יְהוָה אֱלֹהֶיךָ הוּא־הָעֹבֵר לְפָנֶיךָ אֵשׁ אֹכְלָה הוּא יַשְׁמִידֵם וְהוּא יַכְנִיעֵם לְפָנֶיךָ וְהוֹרַשְׁתָּם וְהַאֲבַדְתָּם מַהֵר כַּאֲשֶׁר דִּבֶּר יְהוָה לָךְ: 4אַל־תֹּאמַר בִּלְבָבְךָ בַּהֲדֹף יְהוָה אֱלֹהֶיךָ אֹתָם מִלְּפָנֶיךָ לֵאמֹר בְּצִדְקָתִי הֱבִיאַנִי יְהוָה לָרֶשֶׁת אֶת־הָאָרֶץ הַזֹּאת וּבְרִשְׁעַת הַגּוֹיִם הָאֵלֶּה יְהוָה מוֹרִישָׁם מִפָּנֶיךָ: 5לֹא בְצִדְקָתְךָ

---

this extraordinarily long sentence to convey the weight of the situation against which he is warning. So much will go well that the people can be drawn to forget the God who has done so much for them, so they think that they have achieved it all on their own. And then Moses answers in a simple sentence of ordinary length: You shall remember that *He* is the one who gives . . .

9:5. **not because of your virtue.** The point is made three times, in three verses in a row (9:4–6): it is not because of your virtue but rather because of these nations' wickedness. Some think that the repetition is just a scribe's error, repeating a line by mistake. (Such errors are known as dittography.) That is possible, but the repetition itself is not sufficient reason to make that conclusion. On the contrary, the text seems to me precisely to be making the point as emphatically as possible. Moses notes the people's own lack of virtue even more strongly in the next verse (7) and he begins with the words "Remember—don't forget!" which is redundant as well but is certainly

your heart's integrity that you're coming to take possession of their land, but it is because of these nations' wickedness that YHWH, your God, dispossesses them from before you, and in order to uphold the thing that YHWH swore to your fathers, to Abraham, to Isaac, and to Jacob. ⁶So you shall know that it is not because of your virtue that YHWH, your God, gives you this good land to take possession of it, because you're a hard-necked people. ⁷Remember—don't forget!—that you made YHWH, your God, angry in the wilderness. From the day that you went out from the land of Egypt until you came to this place, you've been rebellious toward YHWH. ⁸And you made YHWH angry at Horeb, and YHWH was so incensed at you as to destroy you. ⁹When I went up to the mountain to get the tablets of stones, the tablets of the covenant that YHWH made with you, and I stayed in the mountain forty days and forty nights, I didn't eat bread and didn't drink

וּבִישֶׁר֙ לְבָ֣בְךָ֔ אַתָּ֥ה בָ֖א לָרֶ֣שֶׁת אֶת־אַרְצָ֑ם כִּ֤י בְּרִשְׁעַת֙ הַגּוֹיִ֣ם הָאֵ֔לֶּה יְהוָ֥ה אֱלֹהֶ֖יךָ מוֹרִישָׁ֣ם מִפָּנֶ֔יךָ וּלְמַ֜עַן הָקִ֣ים אֶת־הַדָּבָ֗ר אֲשֶׁ֨ר נִשְׁבַּ֤ע יְהוָה֙ לַאֲבֹתֶ֔יךָ לְאַבְרָהָ֥ם לְיִצְחָ֖ק וּֽלְיַעֲקֹֽב: ⁶וְיָ֣דַעְתָּ֔ כִּ֠י לֹ֤א בְצִדְקָֽתְךָ֙ יְהוָ֣ה אֱלֹהֶ֗יךָ נֹתֵ֨ן לְךָ֜ אֶת־הָאָ֧רֶץ הַטּוֹבָ֛ה הַזֹּ֖את לְרִשְׁתָּ֑הּ כִּ֥י עַם־קְשֵׁה־עֹ֖רֶף אָֽתָּה: ⁷זְכֹר֙ אַל־תִּשְׁכַּ֔ח אֵ֧ת אֲשֶׁר־הִקְצַ֛פְתָּ אֶת־יְהוָ֥ה אֱלֹהֶ֖יךָ בַּמִּדְבָּ֑ר לְמִן־הַיּ֞וֹם אֲשֶׁר־יָצָ֣אתָ ׀ מֵאֶ֣רֶץ מִצְרַ֗יִם עַד־בֹּֽאֲכֶם֙ עַד־הַמָּק֣וֹם הַזֶּ֔ה מַמְרִ֥ים הֱיִיתֶ֖ם עִם־יְהוָֽה: ⁸וּבְחֹרֵ֥ב הִקְצַפְתֶּ֖ם אֶת־יְהוָ֑ה וַיִּתְאַנַּ֧ף יְהוָ֛ה בָּכֶ֖ם לְהַשְׁמִ֥יד אֶתְכֶֽם: ⁹בַּעֲלֹתִ֣י הָהָ֗רָה לָקַ֜חַת לוּחֹ֤ת הָאֲבָנִים֙ לוּחֹ֣ת הַבְּרִ֔ית אֲשֶׁר־כָּרַ֥ת יְהוָ֖ה עִמָּכֶ֑ם וָאֵשֵׁ֣ב בָּהָ֗ר אַרְבָּעִ֥ים יוֹם֙ וְאַרְבָּעִ֣ים לַ֔יְלָה לֶ֚חֶם לֹ֣א אָכַ֔לְתִּי וּמַ֖יִם לֹ֥א שָׁתִֽיתִי: ¹⁰וַיִּתֵּ֨ן

---

done on purpose for emphasis. And he then goes on for the rest of the chapter listing the people's record of rebellions. Moses thus gives a powerful warning against chauvinism and self-congratulation. And this also provides a profound balance to the declaration that Israel was chosen to become a treasured people, which came just two chapters earlier (7:6). Possession of the land is the result of a promise to Israel's ancestors. Status as a treasured people depends on actions: faithfulness to the covenant. Israel is not intrinsically better than anyone. What is special about Israel is rather that it has been given a singular opportunity to follow a path that will ultimately bring blessing to all the families of the earth.

9:4,5,6. **take possession.** Forms of this term occur more than sixty times in Deuteronomy. Here it is linked specifically to the promise to the patriarchs. This brings back to mind Abraham's exchange with YHWH just before their covenant, where this word occurs three times. Abraham says that he is childless, so someone else will "take possession" of what is his, but God assures him that his own offspring will "take possession" from him (Gen 15:3–4). The numerous repetitions of the term convey the central importance of the link and continuity between the episodes of the patriarchs' lives and the fate of their descendants.

9:9. **didn't eat bread and didn't drink water.** This is the first mention of this miracle that Moses personally experiences at Horeb. It is not reported in Exodus. Moses tells the people about it now, in his list of their rebellions, seemingly to convey to them that they rebelled in the golden calf episode precisely while something awesome was going on. While they were saying, "This man Moses, we don't know what's become of him," Moses was in fact experiencing a kind of physical transformation.

water. 10And YHWH gave me the two tablets of stones, written with God's finger, and on them were all the words that YHWH had spoken with you at the mountain from inside the fire in the day of the assembly. 11And it was: at the end of forty days and forty nights YHWH gave me the two tablets of stones, the tablets of the covenant.

12"And YHWH said to me, 'Get up. Go down quickly from here, because your people whom you brought out from Egypt has become corrupt. They've turned quickly from the way that I commanded them. They've made themselves a molten thing.' 13And YHWH said to me, saying, 'I've seen this people; and, here, it's a hard-necked people. 14Hold back from me, and I'll destroy them and wipe out their name from under the skies, and I'll make you into a more powerful and numerous people than they.'

15"And I turned and went down from the mountain—and the mountain was burning in fire—and the two tablets of the covenant were on my two hands. 16And I saw! And, here, you'd sinned against YHWH, your God. You'd made yourselves a molten calf. You'd turned quickly from the way that YHWH had commanded you. 17And I grasped the two tablets and threw them from on my two hands and shattered them before your eyes.

18"And I prostrated myself in front of YHWH like the first time, forty days and forty nights—I didn't eat bread and didn't drink water—over all your sin that you did, to do what was bad in YHWH's eyes, to provoke Him, 19because I was dreading on account of the anger and the fury, that YHWH was so angry at you as to destroy you. But YHWH listened to me that time as well.

יְהֹוָה אֵלַי אֶת־שְׁנֵי לוּחֹת הָאֲבָנִים כְּתֻבִים בְּאֶצְבַּע אֱלֹהִים וַעֲלֵיהֶם כְּכָל־הַדְּבָרִים אֲשֶׁר דִּבֶּר יְהֹוָה עִמָּכֶם בָּהָר מִתּוֹךְ הָאֵשׁ בְּיוֹם הַקָּהָל: 11וַיְהִי מִקֵּץ אַרְבָּעִים יוֹם וְאַרְבָּעִים לַיְלָה נָתַן יְהֹוָה אֵלַי אֶת־שְׁנֵי לֻחֹת הָאֲבָנִים לֻחֹת הַבְּרִית: 12וַיֹּאמֶר יְהֹוָה אֵלַי קוּם רֵד מַהֵר מִזֶּה כִּי שִׁחֵת עַמְּךָ אֲשֶׁר הוֹצֵאתָ מִמִּצְרָיִם סָרוּ מַהֵר מִן־הַדֶּרֶךְ אֲשֶׁר צִוִּיתִם עָשׂוּ לָהֶם מַסֵּכָה: 13וַיֹּאמֶר יְהֹוָה אֵלַי לֵאמֹר רָאִיתִי אֶת־הָעָם הַזֶּה וְהִנֵּה עַם־קְשֵׁה־עֹרֶף הוּא: 14הֶרֶף מִמֶּנִּי וְאַשְׁמִידֵם וְאֶמְחֶה אֶת־שְׁמָם מִתַּחַת הַשָּׁמָיִם וְאֶעֱשֶׂה אוֹתְךָ לְגוֹי־עָצוּם וָרָב מִמֶּנּוּ: 15וָאֵפֶן וָאֵרֵד מִן־הָהָר וְהָהָר בֹּעֵר בָּאֵשׁ וּשְׁנֵי לֻחֹת הַבְּרִית עַל שְׁתֵּי יָדָי: 16וָאֵרֶא וְהִנֵּה חֲטָאתֶם לַיהֹוָה אֱלֹהֵיכֶם עֲשִׂיתֶם לָכֶם עֵגֶל מַסֵּכָה סַרְתֶּם מַהֵר מִן־הַדֶּרֶךְ אֲשֶׁר־צִוָּה יְהֹוָה אֶתְכֶם: 17וָאֶתְפֹּשׂ בִּשְׁנֵי הַלֻּחֹת וָאַשְׁלִכֵם מֵעַל שְׁתֵּי יָדָי וָאֲשַׁבְּרֵם לְעֵינֵיכֶם: 18וָאֶתְנַפַּל לִפְנֵי יְהֹוָה כָּרִאשֹׁנָה אַרְבָּעִים יוֹם וְאַרְבָּעִים לַיְלָה לֶחֶם לֹא אָכַלְתִּי וּמַיִם לֹא שָׁתִיתִי עַל כָּל־חַטַּאתְכֶם אֲשֶׁר חֲטָאתֶם לַעֲשׂוֹת הָרַע בְּעֵינֵי יְהֹוָה לְהַכְעִיסוֹ: 19כִּי יָגֹרְתִּי מִפְּנֵי הָאַף וְהַחֵמָה אֲשֶׁר קָצַף יְהֹוָה עֲלֵיכֶם לְהַשְׁמִיד אֶתְכֶם וַיִּשְׁמַע יְהֹוָה אֵלַי גַּם בַּפַּעַם הַהִוא:

Another explanation: The people's rebellions up to that point (and frequently thereafter) were about food and water: the bitter water at Marah (Exod 22–26), the manna (16:2–36), and the water from the rock (17:1–7). And so Moses conveys to them that their worries and complaints were utterly unnecessary: in God's hands a man could even live without food or water for forty days. Indeed, this follows Moses' admonition in the preceding chapter that "a human doesn't live by bread alone" (Deut 8:3).

20And YHWH was very incensed at Aaron so as to destroy him, and I prayed for Aaron at that time as well. 21And your sin that you made, the calf: I took it and burned it in fire and crushed it, grinding it well until it was thin as dust, and I threw its dust into the wadi that comes down from the mountain.

22"And at Taberah and at Massah and at Kibroth Hattaavah you were making YHWH angry. 23And when YHWH sent you from Kadesh-barnea, saying, 'Go up and take possession of the land that I've given you,' then you rebelled at the word of YHWH, your God, and you didn't trust Him and didn't listen to His voice. 24You've been rebelling toward YHWH from the day I knew you.

25"So I prostrated myself in front of YHWH for the forty days and forty nights that I had

20וּבְאַהֲרֹן הִתְאַנַּף יְהוָה מְאֹד לְהַשְׁמִידוֹ וָאֶתְפַּלֵּל גַּם־בְּעַד אַהֲרֹן בָּעֵת הַהִוא: 21וְאֶת־חַטַּאתְכֶם אֲשֶׁר־עֲשִׂיתֶם אֶת־הָעֵגֶל לָקַחְתִּי וָאֶשְׂרֹף אֹתוֹ ׀ בָּאֵשׁ וָאֶכֹּת אֹתוֹ טָחוֹן הֵיטֵב עַד אֲשֶׁר־דַּק לְעָפָר וָאַשְׁלִךְ אֶת־עֲפָרוֹ אֶל־הַנַּחַל הַיֹּרֵד מִן־הָהָר: 22וּבְתַבְעֵרָה וּבְמַסָּה וּבְקִבְרֹת הַתַּאֲוָה מַקְצִפִים הֱיִיתֶם אֶת־יְהוָה: 23וּבִשְׁלֹחַ יְהוָה אֶתְכֶם מִקָּדֵשׁ בַּרְנֵעַ לֵאמֹר עֲלוּ וּרְשׁוּ אֶת־הָאָרֶץ אֲשֶׁר נָתַתִּי לָכֶם וַתַּמְרוּ אֶת־פִּי יְהוָה אֱלֹהֵיכֶם וְלֹא הֶאֱמַנְתֶּם לוֹ וְלֹא שְׁמַעְתֶּם בְּקֹלוֹ: 24מַמְרִים הֱיִיתֶם עִם־יְהוָה מִיּוֹם דַּעְתִּי אֶתְכֶם: 25וָאֶתְנַפַּל לִפְנֵי יְהוָה אֵת אַרְבָּעִים הַיּוֹם וְאֶת־אַרְבָּעִים הַלַּיְלָה אֲשֶׁר

9:20. **incensed at Aaron**. The text of the golden calf event (Exodus 32) never says that God was specifically angry at Aaron. We might understand the fact that Moses only makes it known now for the first time as indicating that he would not mention it until after Aaron's death. Thus he spares Aaron the humiliation. And he has thus deferred any doubts that this might have raised about the status of the high priest until now, when they can be considered in the light of the man's entire life and career as high priest.

9:21. **burned it . . . thin as dust**. The parallels between Aaron's golden calf and those of Jeroboam I, king of Israel, are unmistakable. Jeroboam erects golden calves at Dan and Beth-El (1 Kings 12:26–30). On that occasion he says, "Here are your gods, Israel, which brought you out from the land of Egypt"—which are the same words that the people say at the golden calf in Exodus. Jeroboam's sons are Nadab and Abiyah; Aaron's sons are Nadab and Abihu. And King Josiah destroys the high place where Jeroboam's golden calf stood at Beth-El, and, like Moses, "he burned it thin as dust" (2 Kings 23:15). Also like Moses, Josiah casts the dust of pagan altars into a wadi (23:6,12). A literary-historical analysis of this parallel appears in my *Who Wrote the Bible?* (pp. 111–116). In the terms of the full *Tanak* as it now stands, the parallel would suggest that history repeats itself. This is also one of many parallels between Josiah and Moses that serve to single out Josiah as the best of the kings of Israel, the one who comes closest to the standards that Moses taught by commandment and example. Thus the Torah says at the end of Moses' life: "And a prophet did not rise again in Israel like Moses" (Deut 34:10); and the *Tanak* says at the end of Josiah's life: "And after him one did not rise like him" (2 Kings 23:25)—and these are the only two occurrences of the expression "did not rise like him" in the Bible. Again the embroidery of connections through the *Tanak* is apparent.

fallen down because YHWH had said He would destroy you, 26and I prayed to YHWH and said, 'My Lord YHWH, don't destroy your people and your legacy whom you redeemed by your greatness, whom you brought out from Egypt with a strong hand. 27Remember your servants Abraham, Isaac, and Jacob. Don't look to this people's hardness and to its wickedness and to its sin, 28or else the land from which you brought us out will say: Because YHWH wasn't *able* to bring them to the land of which He spoke to them, and because He *hated* them, He brought them out to kill them in the wilderness! 29And they're your people and your legacy, whom you brought out by your great power and by your outstretched arm.'

10 1"At that time YHWH said to me, 'Carve two tablets of stones like the first ones, and come up to me at the mountain. And you shall make an ark of wood. 2And I'll write on the

הִתְנַפַּלְתִּי כִּי־אָמַר יְהוָה לְהַשְׁמִיד אֶתְכֶם: 26וָאֶתְפַּלֵּל אֶל־יְהוָה וָאֹמַר אֲדֹנָי יְהוִה אַל־תַּשְׁחֵת עַמְּךָ וְנַחֲלָתְךָ אֲשֶׁר פָּדִיתָ בְּגָדְלֶךָ אֲשֶׁר־הוֹצֵאתָ מִמִּצְרַיִם בְּיָד חֲזָקָה: 27זְכֹר לַעֲבָדֶיךָ לְאַבְרָהָם לְיִצְחָק וּלְיַעֲקֹב אַל־תֵּפֶן אֶל־קְשִׁי הָעָם הַזֶּה וְאֶל־רִשְׁעוֹ וְאֶל־חַטָּאתוֹ: 28פֶּן־יֹאמְרוּ הָאָרֶץ אֲשֶׁר הוֹצֵאתָנוּ מִשָּׁם מִבְּלִי יְכֹלֶת יְהוָה לַהֲבִיאָם אֶל־הָאָרֶץ אֲשֶׁר־דִּבֶּר לָהֶם וּמִשִּׂנְאָתוֹ אוֹתָם הוֹצִיאָם לַהֲמִתָם בַּמִּדְבָּר: 29וְהֵם עַמְּךָ וְנַחֲלָתֶךָ אֲשֶׁר הוֹצֵאתָ בְּכֹחֲךָ הַגָּדֹל וּבִזְרֹעֲךָ הַנְּטוּיָה: פ

10 1בָּעֵת הַהִוא אָמַר יְהוָה אֵלַי פְּסָל־לְךָ שְׁנֵי־לוּחֹת אֲבָנִים כָּרִאשֹׁנִים וַעֲלֵה אֵלַי הָהָרָה וְעָשִׂיתָ לְךָ אֲרוֹן עֵץ: 2וְאֶכְתֹּב עַל־הַלֻּחֹת אֶת־

9:26. destroy. The word in Hebrew, *tašḥēt*, has the same root meaning as the word for what the people have done: become corrupt, *hišḥît* (9:12). The same play on this root is used in the flood story (Gen 6:12–13). There and here it is not just wordplay for its own sake. It conveys the principle that punishment is meant to be in proportion to the crime. The repetition of the pun here in Deuteronomy conveys that what was true for all humankind in the early generations of creation is still true in relations between God and humans in the Torah's final book.

10:1. you shall make an ark of wood. It says "*you* shall make," but in Exodus it was Bezalel, not Moses, who made the ark. Rashi and Ramban and others therefore say that there must have been two arks. In current critical scholarship, the apparent contradiction would generally be taken to be a result of the fact that this text in Deuteronomy and the text in Exodus were written by two different authors. But, even without raising such solutions that are arrived at through critical approaches, we can understand Moses' words in Deuteronomy to be a brief account of what happened at Sinai, and so he speaks of himself as making the ark when he means that he directed Bezalel to do it. Likewise, he speaks of the ark as if it were finished and ready when he came down from the mountain when he knows that actually some time passed before the ark was made. J. H. Hertz proposed such an understanding as an alternative to Rashi's and Ramban's view even though Hertz harshly rejected literary-critical scholarship. This is important because an almost fundamentalist view of Rashi is growing at present in some communities, wherein it is practically heresy to question Rashi. This gives Rashi a status that I do not think he would have wanted for himself. And certainly the commentators of the generations that followed him, including his own grandson

598

tablets the words that were on the first tablets, which you shattered, and you shall set them in the ark.'

3"And I made an ark of acacia wood, and I carved two tablets of stones like the first ones, and I went up the mountain with the two tablets in my hands. 4And He wrote on the tablets like the first writing: the Ten Commandments that YHWH spoke to you at the mountain from inside the fire in the day of the assembly, and YHWH gave them to me. 5And I turned and went down from the mountain, and I set the tablets in the ark that I had made, and they have been there, as YHWH commanded me.

6"And the children of Israel had traveled from Beeroth-bene-Jaakan to Moserah. There Aaron died, and he was buried there; and Eleazar, his son, functioned as priest in his place. 7From there they traveled to Gudgod, and from Gudgod to Jotbah, a land of wadis of water. 8At that time YHWH distinguished the tribe of Levi to carry the ark of YHWH's covenant, to stand in front of YHWH to serve Him, and to bless in His name to this day. 9Therefore Levi has not had a portion and a legacy with its brothers. YHWH: *He* is its legacy, as YHWH, your God, spoke to it.

10"And I: I stood in the mountain as in the first days: forty days and forty nights. And YHWH listened to me that time as well. YHWH was not willing to destroy you. 11And YHWH said to me, 'Get up. Set out on the journey in front of the people, and they'll come and take possession of

הַדְּבָרִים אֲשֶׁר הָיוּ עַל־הַלֻּחֹת הָרִאשֹׁנִים אֲשֶׁר
שִׁבַּרְתָּ וְשַׂמְתָּם בָּאָרוֹן: ³וָאַעַשׂ אֲרוֹן עֲצֵי שִׁטִּים
וָאֶפְסֹל שְׁנֵי־לֻחֹת אֲבָנִים כָּרִאשֹׁנִים וָאַעַל הָהָרָה
וּשְׁנֵי הַלֻּחֹת בְּיָדִי: ⁴וַיִּכְתֹּב עַל־הַלֻּחֹת כַּמִּכְתָּב
הָרִאשׁוֹן אֵת עֲשֶׂרֶת הַדְּבָרִים אֲשֶׁר דִּבֶּר יְהוָה
אֲלֵיכֶם בָּהָר מִתּוֹךְ הָאֵשׁ בְּיוֹם הַקָּהָל וַיִּתְּנֵם יְהוָה
אֵלָי: ⁵וָאֵפֶן וָאֵרֵד מִן־הָהָר וָאָשִׂם אֶת־הַלֻּחֹת
בָּאָרוֹן אֲשֶׁר עָשִׂיתִי וַיִּהְיוּ שָׁם כַּאֲשֶׁר צִוַּנִי יְהוָה:
⁶וּבְנֵי יִשְׂרָאֵל נָסְעוּ מִבְּאֵרֹת בְּנֵי־יַעֲקָן מוֹסֵרָה שָׁם
מֵת אַהֲרֹן וַיִּקָּבֵר שָׁם וַיְכַהֵן אֶלְעָזָר בְּנוֹ תַּחְתָּיו:
⁷מִשָּׁם נָסְעוּ הַגֻּדְגֹּדָה וּמִן־הַגֻּדְגֹּדָה יָטְבָתָה אֶרֶץ
נַחֲלֵי מָיִם: ⁸בָּעֵת הַהִוא הִבְדִּיל יְהוָה אֶת־שֵׁבֶט
הַלֵּוִי לָשֵׂאת אֶת־אֲרוֹן בְּרִית־יְהוָה לַעֲמֹד לִפְנֵי
יְהוָה לְשָׁרְתוֹ וּלְבָרֵךְ בִּשְׁמוֹ עַד הַיּוֹם הַזֶּה: ⁹עַל־
כֵּן לֹא־הָיָה לְלֵוִי חֵלֶק וְנַחֲלָה עִם־אֶחָיו יְהוָה הוּא
נַחֲלָתוֹ כַּאֲשֶׁר דִּבֶּר יְהוָה אֱלֹהֶיךָ לוֹ: ¹⁰וְאָנֹכִי
עָמַדְתִּי בָהָר כַּיָּמִים הָרִאשֹׁנִים אַרְבָּעִים יוֹם
וְאַרְבָּעִים לָיְלָה וַיִּשְׁמַע יְהוָה אֵלַי גַּם בַּפַּעַם הַהִוא
לֹא־אָבָה יְהוָה הַשְׁחִיתֶךָ: ¹¹וַיֹּאמֶר יְהוָה אֵלַי קוּם
לֵךְ לְמַסַּע לִפְנֵי הָעָם וְיָבֹאוּ וְיִרְשׁוּ אֶת־הָאָרֶץ

Rashbam, were prepared to question his comments. We respect and admire the great commentators of past generations, but we should never forget to distinguish between Torah and commentary. The goal of refining our knowledge of the Torah and shedding new light from it in each new age is never-ending; and our commentaries—including my own—are always subject to criticism and improvement.

10:4. **the Ten Commandments**. Hebrew *'ăśeret haddĕbārîm*, literally, the ten things. This is what the Ten Commandments are called in Hebrew.

10:10. **And I**. Moses now resumes his account of his second forty days on Horeb, which had left off at 9:29. He had interrupted his story with mention of the ark and other matters.

the land that I swore to their fathers to give to them.'

12"And now, Israel, what is YHWH, your God, asking from you except to fear YHWH, your God, to go in all His ways, and to love Him and to serve YHWH, your God, with all your heart and all your soul, 13to observe YHWH's commandments and His laws that I command you today to be good for you. 14Here, YHWH, your God, has the skies—and the skies of the skies!—the earth and everything that's in it. 15Only, YHWH was attracted to your fathers, to love them, and He chose their seed after them: you, out of all the peoples, as it is this day. 16So you shall circumcise the foreskin of your *heart*, and you shall not harden your necks anymore. 17Because YHWH, your God: He is the God of gods and the Lord of

אֲשֶׁר־נִשְׁבַּ֥עְתִּי לַאֲבֹתָ֖ם לָתֵ֥ת לָהֶֽם: פ
12וְעַתָּה֙ יִשְׂרָאֵ֔ל מָ֚ה יְהֹוָ֣ה אֱלֹהֶ֔יךָ שֹׁאֵ֖ל מֵעִמָּ֑ךְ
כִּ֣י אִם־לְ֠יִרְאָה אֶת־יְהֹוָ֨ה אֱלֹהֶ֜יךָ לָלֶ֣כֶת בְּכָל־
דְּרָכָיו֙ וּלְאַהֲבָ֣ה אֹת֔וֹ וְלַֽעֲבֹד֙ אֶת־יְהֹוָ֣ה אֱלֹהֶ֔יךָ
בְּכָל־לְבָבְךָ֖ וּבְכָל־נַפְשֶֽׁךָ: 13לִשְׁמֹ֞ר אֶת־מִצְוֺ֣ת
יְהֹוָה֙ וְאֶת־חֻקֹּתָ֔יו אֲשֶׁ֧ר אָנֹכִ֛י מְצַוְּךָ֖ הַיּ֑וֹם לְט֖וֹב
לָֽךְ: 14הֵ֚ן לַֽיהֹוָ֣ה אֱלֹהֶ֔יךָ הַשָּׁמַ֖יִם וּשְׁמֵ֣י הַשָּׁמָ֑יִם
הָאָ֖רֶץ וְכָל־אֲשֶׁר־בָּֽהּ: 15רַ֧ק בַּאֲבֹתֶ֛יךָ חָשַׁ֥ק יְהֹוָ֖ה
לְאַהֲבָ֣ה אוֹתָ֑ם וַיִּבְחַ֞ר בְּזַרְעָ֤ם אַחֲרֵיהֶם֙ בָּכֶ֔ם
מִכָּל־הָֽעַמִּ֖ים כַּיּ֥וֹם הַזֶּֽה: 16וּמַלְתֶּ֕ם אֵ֖ת עָרְלַ֣ת
לְבַבְכֶ֑ם וְעָ֨רְפְּכֶ֔ם לֹ֥א תַקְשׁ֖וּ עֽוֹד: 17כִּ֚י יְהֹוָ֣ה
אֱלֹֽהֵיכֶ֔ם ה֚וּא אֱלֹהֵ֣י הָֽאֱלֹהִ֔ים וַאֲדֹנֵ֖י הָאֲדֹנִ֑ים הָאֵ֨ל

10:12. **what is God asking from you**. All the things that follow in this verse have been mentioned already in Moses' speech. They come now, therefore, as a summary, a statement of the basic things that underlie everything else: fear, love, deeds, service, complete commitment.

10:14. **the skies of the skies**. Meaning, presumably, that if one were in the sky and looked up, one would see a farther portion of the sky. So the phrase means the farthest reaches of the sky.

10:16. **the foreskin of your *heart***. This concept occurs in two books of the Torah (Deut 10:16; 30:6; Lev 26:41) and in two of the prophets (Jer 4:4; Ezek 44:7,9). The sign of the Abrahamic covenant, and probably the most commonly observed of the commandments by Jewish families for centuries, is circumcision. But the Torah *commands* the circumcision of one's heart as well. It establishes that outward fulfillment of practices without also feeling it in one's heart is insufficient. The concept of circumcising one's heart, moreover, unlike physical circumcision, applies to both women and men.

10:17. **the God of gods and the Lord of lords**. Admittedly, this sounds unmonotheistic, seemingly acknowledging the existence of other gods. But, earlier, Moses has said, "YHWH: *He* is God. There is no other outside of Him" (4:35) and "YHWH is one" (6:4). And, later, YHWH says, "There is no god with me" (32:39). How are we to reconcile the many monotheistic passages in Deuteronomy with "God of gods and Lord of lords"? As in the case of not having "other gods before my face," this is a linguistic matter. "God of gods" is an expression for conveying that YHWH is something that all other gods in whom people believe are not. It need not presume that such other gods exist.

lords, the great, the mighty, and the awesome God, who won't be partial and won't take a bribe, [18]doing judgment for an orphan and a widow and loving an alien, to give him bread and a garment. [19]So you shall love the alien, because you were aliens in the land of Egypt. [20]You shall fear YHWH, your God, you shall serve Him, and you shall cling to Him, and you shall swear by His name. [21]He is your splendor, and He is your God, who did these great and awesome things for you that your eyes have seen. Your fathers went down to Egypt with seventy persons, and now YHWH, your God, has made you like the stars of the skies for multitude.

11 [1]"And you shall love YHWH, your God, and keep His charge and His laws and His judgments and His commandments every day. [2]And you shall know today that it's not with your children, who didn't know and who didn't see the discipline of YHWH, your God, His greatness and His strong hand and His outstretched arm [3]and His signs and His deeds that He did in Egypt to Pharaoh, king of Egypt, and to all his land, [4]and what He did to Egypt's army and to his horses and his chariots, that He flowed the waters of the Red Sea over their faces when they pursued you so YHWH destroyed them to this day, [5]and what He did for you in the wilderness until you came to this place, [6]and what He did to Dathan and to Abiram, sons of Eliab son of Reuben, that the earth opened its mouth and swallowed them and their households and their tents and all the substance that was at their feet among the children of Israel— [7]but it's your eyes, that saw every great deed of YHWH's that He did. [8]And you shall observe all of the commandment that I command you today so that you'll be strong and you'll come and take possession of the land that you're crossing there to take pos-

הַגָּדֹל הַגִּבֹּר וְהַנּוֹרָא אֲשֶׁר לֹא־יִשָּׂא פָנִים וְלֹא יִקַּח שֹׁחַד: [18]עֹשֶׂה מִשְׁפַּט יָתוֹם וְאַלְמָנָה וְאֹהֵב גֵּר לָתֶת לוֹ לֶחֶם וְשִׂמְלָה: [19]וַאֲהַבְתֶּם אֶת־הַגֵּר כִּי־גֵרִים הֱיִיתֶם בְּאֶרֶץ מִצְרָיִם: [20]אֶת־יְהוָה אֱלֹהֶיךָ תִּירָא אֹתוֹ תַעֲבֹד וּבוֹ תִדְבָּק וּבִשְׁמוֹ תִּשָּׁבֵעַ: [21]הוּא תְהִלָּתְךָ וְהוּא אֱלֹהֶיךָ אֲשֶׁר־עָשָׂה אִתְּךָ אֶת־הַגְּדֹלֹת וְאֶת־הַנּוֹרָאֹת הָאֵלֶּה אֲשֶׁר רָאוּ עֵינֶיךָ: [22]בְּשִׁבְעִים נֶפֶשׁ יָרְדוּ אֲבֹתֶיךָ מִצְרָיְמָה וְעַתָּה שָׂמְךָ יְהוָה אֱלֹהֶיךָ כְּכוֹכְבֵי הַשָּׁמַיִם לָרֹב: 11 [1]וְאָהַבְתָּ אֵת יְהוָה אֱלֹהֶיךָ וְשָׁמַרְתָּ מִשְׁמַרְתּוֹ וְחֻקֹּתָיו וּמִשְׁפָּטָיו וּמִצְוֹתָיו כָּל־הַיָּמִים: [2]וִידַעְתֶּם הַיּוֹם כִּי ׀ לֹא אֶת־בְּנֵיכֶם אֲשֶׁר לֹא־יָדְעוּ וַאֲשֶׁר לֹא־רָאוּ אֶת־מוּסַר יְהוָה אֱלֹהֵיכֶם אֶת־גָּדְלוֹ אֶת־יָדוֹ הַחֲזָקָה וּזְרֹעוֹ הַנְּטוּיָה: [3]וְאֶת־אֹתֹתָיו וְאֶת־מַעֲשָׂיו אֲשֶׁר עָשָׂה בְּתוֹךְ מִצְרָיִם לְפַרְעֹה מֶלֶךְ־מִצְרַיִם וּלְכָל־אַרְצוֹ: [4]וַאֲשֶׁר עָשָׂה לְחֵיל מִצְרַיִם לְסוּסָיו וּלְרִכְבּוֹ אֲשֶׁר הֵצִיף אֶת־מֵי יַם־סוּף עַל־פְּנֵיהֶם בְּרָדְפָם אַחֲרֵיכֶם וַיְאַבְּדֵם יְהוָה עַד הַיּוֹם הַזֶּה: [5]וַאֲשֶׁר עָשָׂה לָכֶם בַּמִּדְבָּר עַד־בֹּאֲכֶם עַד־הַמָּקוֹם הַזֶּה: [6]וַאֲשֶׁר עָשָׂה לְדָתָן וְלַאֲבִירָם בְּנֵי אֱלִיאָב בֶּן־רְאוּבֵן אֲשֶׁר פָּצְתָה הָאָרֶץ אֶת־פִּיהָ וַתִּבְלָעֵם וְאֶת־בָּתֵּיהֶם וְאֶת־אָהֳלֵיהֶם וְאֵת כָּל־הַיְקוּם אֲשֶׁר בְּרַגְלֵיהֶם בְּקֶרֶב כָּל־יִשְׂרָאֵל: [7]כִּי עֵינֵיכֶם הָרֹאֹת אֶת־כָּל־מַעֲשֵׂה יְהוָה הַגָּדֹל אֲשֶׁר עָשָׂה: [8]וּשְׁמַרְתֶּם אֶת־כָּל־הַמִּצְוָה אֲשֶׁר אָנֹכִי מְצַוְּךָ הַיּוֹם לְמַעַן תֶּחֶזְקוּ וּבָאתֶם וִירִשְׁתֶּם אֶת־הָאָרֶץ אֲשֶׁר אַתֶּם עֹבְרִים שָׁמָּה

10:17. **won't take a bribe.** What could it mean to bribe God?! A sacrifice, a donation, a kindness, charity, prayer: one might do any of these to win the deity's favor, rather than doing them as fulfillment of the commandments or as free acts. Moses informs the people that this will not work.

session of it, 9and so that you'll extend days on the land that YHWH swore to your fathers to give to them and to their seed, a land flowing with milk and honey.

10"Because the land to which you're coming to take possession of it: it's not like the land of Egypt from which you've come out, where you plant your seed and water it at your feet like a garden of plants. 11But the land to which you're crossing to take possession of it is a land of hills and valleys. It drinks water by the skies' showers. 12A land that YHWH, your God, cares about; YHWH's eyes are always on it, from the year's beginning to year's end. 13So it will be, if you'll *listen* to my commandments that I command you today, to love YHWH, your God, and to serve Him with all your heart and with all your soul, 14then I'll give your land's showers at their time, early rain and late rain, and you'll gather your grain and your wine and your oil. 15And I'll give vegetation in your field for your animals, and you'll eat and be full.

16"Watch yourselves in case your heart will be deceived so you'll turn and serve other gods and bow to them, 17and YHWH's anger will flare at you, and He'll hold back the skies, and there won't be showers, and the earth won't give its crop, and you'll perish quickly from the good land that YHWH is giving you. 18So you shall set these words of mine on your heart and on your soul, and you shall bind them for a sign on your

לְרִשְׁתָּהּ: 9וּלְמַ֫עַן תַּאֲרִ֫יכוּ יָמִים֮ עַל־הָ֣אֲדָמָ֒ה אֲשֶׁר נִשְׁבַּ֫ע יְהֹוָ֛ה לַאֲבֹתֵיכֶ֖ם לָתֵ֣ת לָהֶ֑ם וּלְזַרְעָ֖ם אֶ֤רֶץ זָבַ֥ת חָלָ֖ב וּדְבָֽשׁ: ס 10כִּ֣י הָאָ֗רֶץ אֲשֶׁ֨ר אַתָּ֜ה בָא־ שָׁ֙מָּה֙ לְרִשְׁתָּ֔הּ לֹ֣א כְאֶ֤רֶץ מִצְרַ֙יִם֙ הִ֔וא אֲשֶׁ֤ר יְצָאתֶ֣ם מִשָּׁ֔ם אֲשֶׁ֤ר תִּזְרַע֙ אֶֽת־זַרְעֲךָ֔ וְהִשְׁקִ֥יתָ בְרַגְלְךָ֖ כְּגַ֥ן הַיָּרָֽק: 11וְהָאָ֗רֶץ אֲשֶׁ֤ר אַתֶּם֙ עֹבְרִ֤ים שָׁ֙מָּה֙ לְרִשְׁתָּ֔הּ אֶ֥רֶץ הָרִ֖ים וּבְקָעֹ֑ת לִמְטַ֥ר הַשָּׁמַ֖יִם תִּשְׁתֶּה־מָּֽיִם: 12אֶ֕רֶץ אֲשֶׁר־יְהֹוָ֥ה אֱלֹהֶ֖יךָ דֹּרֵ֣שׁ אֹתָ֑הּ תָּמִ֗יד עֵינֵ֨י יְהֹוָ֤ה אֱלֹהֶ֙יךָ֙ בָּ֔הּ מֵֽרֵשִׁית֙ הַשָּׁנָ֔ה וְעַ֖ד אַחֲרִ֥ית שָׁנָֽה: ס 13וְהָיָ֗ה אִם־שָׁמֹ֤עַ תִּשְׁמְעוּ֙ אֶל־ מִצְוֺתַ֔י אֲשֶׁ֧ר אָנֹכִ֛י מְצַוֶּ֥ה אֶתְכֶ֖ם הַיּ֑וֹם לְאַהֲבָ֞ה אֶת־ יְהֹוָ֤ה אֱלֹֽהֵיכֶם֙ וּלְעׇבְד֔וֹ בְּכׇל־לְבַבְכֶ֖ם וּבְכׇל־ נַפְשְׁכֶֽם: 14וְנָתַתִּ֧י מְטַֽר־אַרְצְכֶ֛ם בְּעִתּ֖וֹ יוֹרֶ֣ה וּמַלְק֑וֹשׁ וְאָסַפְתָּ֣ דְגָנֶ֔ךָ וְתִירֹֽשְׁךָ֖ וְיִצְהָרֶֽךָ: 15וְנָתַתִּ֛י עֵ֥שֶׂב בְּשָׂדְךָ֖ לִבְהֶמְתֶּ֑ךָ וְאָכַלְתָּ֖ וְשָׂבָֽעְתָּ: 16הִשָּׁמְר֣וּ לָכֶ֔ם פֶּ֫ן יִפְתֶּ֣ה לְבַבְכֶ֑ם וְסַרְתֶּ֗ם וַעֲבַדְתֶּם֙ אֱלֹהִ֣ים אֲחֵרִ֔ים וְהִשְׁתַּחֲוִיתֶ֖ם לָהֶֽם: 17וְחָרָ֨ה אַף־יְהֹוָ֜ה בָּכֶ֗ם וְעָצַ֤ר אֶת־הַשָּׁמַ֙יִם֙ וְלֹֽא־יִהְיֶ֣ה מָטָ֔ר וְהָ֣אֲדָמָ֔ה לֹ֥א תִתֵּ֖ן אֶת־יְבוּלָ֑הּ וַאֲבַדְתֶּ֣ם מְהֵרָ֗ה מֵעַל֙ הָאָ֣רֶץ הַטֹּבָ֔ה אֲשֶׁ֥ר יְהֹוָ֖ה נֹתֵ֥ן לָכֶֽם: 18וְשַׂמְתֶּם֙ אֶת־דְּבָרַ֣י אֵ֔לֶּה עַל־לְבַבְכֶ֖ם וְעַל־נַפְשְׁכֶ֑ם וּקְשַׁרְתֶּ֨ם אֹתָ֜ם

11:10. **water it at your feet like a garden.** Because the Nile's water is commonly present, the human's role is simply to get it to the plants, by conveying or irrigation. But in Israel much of the land is dependent on rain as its source of water; it "drinks water by the skies' showers" (11:11). And so one feels more dependent on God. But, Moses assures the people, God "cares about" the land, and God's "eyes are always on it" (11:12).

11:14,15. **I'll give.** The subject of "I'll give" must be God, and so Moses has apparently shifted in the middle of his discussion and is now quoting God when until now he has been speaking in his own name and referring to God in third person. It may convey a kind of intimacy in which Moses is now so close to the deity and so used to speaking in God's name and declaring the commandments that he moves into the divine first-person mode with ease.

hand, and they shall become bands between your eyes, 19and you shall teach them to your children, to speak about them when you sit in your house and when you go in the road and when you lie down and when you get up, 20and you shall write them on the doorposts of your house and in your gates, 21so that your days and your children's days will be many on the land that YHWH swore to your fathers to give them, like the days of the skies over the earth. 22Because, if you *will* observe all of this commandment that I command you, to do it, to love YHWH, your God, to go in all His ways and to cling to Him, 23then YHWH will dispossess all these nations in front of you, and you'll dispossess bigger and more powerful nations than you. 24Every place in which your foot will step shall be yours, from the wilderness and Lebanon, from the river, the Euphrates River, to the far sea shall be your border. 25Not a man will stand up in front of you. YHWH, your God, will put awe of you and fear of you on the face of all the land on which you'll step, as He spoke to you.

SEE

26"See: I'm putting in front of you today a blessing and a curse: 27the blessing when you'll listen to the commandments of YHWH, your

לְאוֹת֙ עַל־יֶדְכֶ֔ם וְהָי֥וּ לְטוֹטָפֹ֖ת בֵּ֥ין עֵינֵיכֶֽם: 19וְלִמַּדְתֶּ֥ם אֹתָ֛ם אֶת־בְּנֵיכֶ֖ם לְדַבֵּ֣ר בָּ֑ם בְּשִׁבְתְּךָ֤ בְּבֵיתֶ֙ךָ֙ וּבְלֶכְתְּךָ֣ בַדֶּ֔רֶךְ וּֽבְשָׁכְבְּךָ֖ וּבְקוּמֶֽךָ: 20וּכְתַבְתָּ֛ם עַל־מְזוּז֥וֹת בֵּיתֶ֖ךָ וּבִשְׁעָרֶֽיךָ: 21לְמַ֗עַן יִרְבּ֤וּ יְמֵיכֶם֙ וִימֵ֣י בְנֵיכֶ֔ם עַ֚ל הָֽאֲדָמָ֔ה אֲשֶׁ֨ר נִשְׁבַּ֧ע יְהֹוָ֛ה לַאֲבֹתֵיכֶ֖ם לָתֵ֣ת לָהֶ֑ם כִּימֵ֥י הַשָּׁמַ֖יִם עַל־הָאָֽרֶץ: ס 22כִּי֩ אִם־שָׁמֹ֨ר תִּשְׁמְר֜וּן אֶת־כׇּל־הַמִּצְוָ֣ה הַזֹּ֗את אֲשֶׁ֧ר אָנֹכִ֛י מְצַוֶּ֥ה אֶתְכֶ֖ם לַעֲשֹׂתָ֑הּ לְאַהֲבָ֞ה אֶת־יְהֹוָ֤ה אֱלֹֽהֵיכֶם֙ לָלֶ֣כֶת בְּכׇל־דְּרָכָ֔יו וּלְדׇבְקָה־בֽוֹ: 23וְהוֹרִ֧ישׁ יְהֹוָ֛ה אֶת־כׇּל־הַגּוֹיִ֥ם הָאֵ֖לֶּה מִלִּפְנֵיכֶ֑ם וִֽירִשְׁתֶּ֣ם גּוֹיִ֔ם גְּדֹלִ֥ים וַעֲצֻמִ֖ים מִכֶּֽם: 24כׇּל־הַמָּק֗וֹם אֲשֶׁ֨ר תִּדְרֹ֧ךְ כַּֽף־רַגְלְכֶ֛ם בּ֖וֹ לָכֶ֣ם יִהְיֶ֑ה מִן־הַמִּדְבָּ֨ר וְהַלְּבָנ֜וֹן מִן־הַנָּהָ֣ר נְהַר־פְּרָ֗ת וְעַד֙ הַיָּ֣ם הָאַֽחֲר֔וֹן יִהְיֶ֖ה גְּבֻלְכֶֽם: 25לֹא־יִתְיַצֵּ֥ב אִ֖ישׁ בִּפְנֵיכֶ֑ם פַּחְדְּכֶ֤ם וּמֽוֹרַאֲכֶם֙ יִתֵּ֣ן ׀ יְהֹוָ֣ה אֱלֹֽהֵיכֶ֔ם עַל־פְּנֵ֤י כׇל־הָאָ֙רֶץ֙ אֲשֶׁ֣ר תִּדְרְכוּ־בָ֔הּ כַּאֲשֶׁ֖ר דִּבֶּ֥ר לָכֶֽם: ס

ראה

26רְאֵ֗ה אָנֹכִ֛י נֹתֵ֥ן לִפְנֵיכֶ֖ם הַיּ֑וֹם בְּרָכָ֖ה וּקְלָלָֽה: 27אֶת־הַבְּרָכָ֑ה אֲשֶׁ֣ר תִּשְׁמְע֔וּ אֶל־מִצְוֺת֙

11:24. **foot.** Hebrew *kap regel* is often taken to mean "the sole of the foot," but that is not correct. *regel* refers to the leg in Hebrew (although we often translate it as "foot" in English because of the conventions of usage of the two words "leg" and "foot" in English), and *kap regel* refers to the portion of the leg from the ankle down, i.e., the foot. See Ezek 1:7, which says: "Their *kap regel* was like the *kap regel* of a calf"—which must mean the appearance of a foot and not of the sole of a foot.

The same goes for *kap yād*, which is often taken to mean "the palm of the hand," but which means the portion of the *yād* ("forearm," although, again, we often translate it as "hand" because of English usage) from the wrist down, i.e., the hand. See 2 Kings 9:35, where dogs have eaten Jezebel's body, and nothing can be found but her skull, legs, and *kappôt hayyādāyîm*—which must mean "hands" and not "palms." (See also the comment on Deut 4:34.)

603   11:24. **the far sea.** The Mediterranean Sea.

God, that I command you today, 28and the curse if you won't listen to the commandments of YHWH, your God, and you'll turn from the way that I command you today, to go after other gods, whom you haven't known. 29And it shall be, when YHWH, your God, will bring you to the land to which you're coming to take possession of it, that you shall put the blessing on Mount Gerizim and the curse on Mount Ebal. 30Aren't they across the Jordan, beyond the way of the sun's setting, in the land of the Canaanite who lives in the plain, opposite Gilgal, near the oaks of Moreh? 31Because you're crossing the Jordan to come to take possession of the land that YHWH, your God, is giving you; and you shall take possession of it and live in it 32and be watchful to do all the laws and the judgments that I'm putting in front of you today.

12 1"These are the laws and the judgments that you shall be watchful to do in the land that YHWH, your fathers' God, has given you to take possession of it, every day that you're living on the land:

2"You shall *destroy* all the places where the nations that you're dispossessing worshiped their gods there: on the high mountains and on the hills and under every lush tree. 3And you shall demolish their altars and shatter their pillars and burn their Asherahs in fire and cut down the statues of their gods in fire and destroy their name from that place.

יְהוָה אֱלֹהֵיכֶם אֲשֶׁר אָנֹכִי מְצַוֶּה אֶתְכֶם הַיּוֹם:
28וְהַקְּלָלָה אִם־לֹא תִשְׁמְעוּ אֶל־מִצְוֹת יְהוָה אֱלֹהֵיכֶם וְסַרְתֶּם מִן־הַדֶּרֶךְ אֲשֶׁר אָנֹכִי מְצַוֶּה אֶתְכֶם הַיּוֹם לָלֶכֶת אַחֲרֵי אֱלֹהִים אֲחֵרִים אֲשֶׁר לֹא־יְדַעְתֶּם: ס 29וְהָיָה כִּי יְבִיאֲךָ יְהוָה אֱלֹהֶיךָ אֶל־הָאָרֶץ אֲשֶׁר־אַתָּה בָא־שָׁמָּה לְרִשְׁתָּהּ וְנָתַתָּה אֶת־הַבְּרָכָה עַל־הַר גְּרִזִים וְאֶת־הַקְּלָלָה עַל־הַר עֵיבָל: 30הֲלֹא־הֵמָּה בְּעֵבֶר הַיַּרְדֵּן אַחֲרֵי דֶּרֶךְ מְבוֹא הַשֶּׁמֶשׁ בְּאֶרֶץ הַכְּנַעֲנִי הַיֹּשֵׁב בָּעֲרָבָה מוּל הַגִּלְגָּל אֵצֶל אֵלוֹנֵי מֹרֶה: 31כִּי אַתֶּם עֹבְרִים אֶת־הַיַּרְדֵּן לָבֹא לָרֶשֶׁת אֶת־הָאָרֶץ אֲשֶׁר־יְהוָה אֱלֹהֵיכֶם נֹתֵן לָכֶם וִירִשְׁתֶּם אֹתָהּ וִישַׁבְתֶּם־בָּהּ: 32וּשְׁמַרְתֶּם לַעֲשׂוֹת אֵת כָּל־הַחֻקִּים וְאֶת־הַמִּשְׁפָּטִים אֲשֶׁר אָנֹכִי נֹתֵן לִפְנֵיכֶם הַיּוֹם:

12 1אֵלֶּה הַחֻקִּים וְהַמִּשְׁפָּטִים אֲשֶׁר תִּשְׁמְרוּן לַעֲשׂוֹת בָּאָרֶץ אֲשֶׁר נָתַן יְהוָה אֱלֹהֵי אֲבֹתֶיךָ לְךָ לְרִשְׁתָּהּ כָּל־הַיָּמִים אֲשֶׁר־אַתֶּם חַיִּים עַל־הָאֲדָמָה: 2אַבֵּד תְּאַבְּדוּן אֶת־כָּל־הַמְּקֹמוֹת אֲשֶׁר עָבְדוּ־שָׁם הַגּוֹיִם אֲשֶׁר אַתֶּם יֹרְשִׁים אֹתָם אֶת־אֱלֹהֵיהֶם עַל־הֶהָרִים הָרָמִים וְעַל־הַגְּבָעוֹת וְתַחַת כָּל־עֵץ רַעֲנָן: 3וְנִתַּצְתֶּם אֶת־מִזְבְּחֹתָם וְשִׁבַּרְתֶּם אֶת־מַצֵּבֹתָם וַאֲשֵׁרֵיהֶם תִּשְׂרְפוּן בָּאֵשׁ וּפְסִילֵי אֱלֹהֵיהֶם תְּגַדֵּעוּן וְאִבַּדְתֶּם אֶת־שְׁמָם מִן־הַמָּקוֹם הַהוּא: 4לֹא־תַעֲשׂוּן

11:30. **oaks of Moreh**. The first place to which Abraham comes when he moves to Canaan is the oak of Moreh (Gen 12:6). There YHWH is said to appear to him for the first time (which is also the first time that God is said to have appeared to *anyone* in the Bible). There YHWH says for the first time that He will give the land to Abraham's descendants. And there Abraham builds the first altar to YHWH in Canaan. Now the oaks (or oak; the Septuagint has the singular) of Moreh are mentioned just before a statement that those descendants are now about "to come to take possession of the land." It is thus another signal that the merit of the ancestors is a source of protection and well-being for Israel many generations later. In this case, because Abraham listened to God's first command and left his home for a new land, his descendants now come to the land.

⁴"You shall not do that for YHWH, your God. ⁵But, rather, you shall inquire at the place that YHWH, your God, will choose from all your tribes to set His name there, to tent it. And you shall come there, ⁶and bring there your burnt offerings and your sacrifices and your tithes and your hand's donation and your vows and your contributions and the firstborn of your herd and your flock. ⁷And you shall eat there in front of

כֵּן לַיהוָה אֱלֹהֵיכֶם: ⁵כִּי אִם־אֶל־הַמָּקוֹם אֲשֶׁר־
יִבְחַר יְהוָה אֱלֹהֵיכֶם מִכָּל־שִׁבְטֵיכֶם לָשׂוּם אֶת־
שְׁמוֹ שָׁם לְשִׁכְנוֹ תִדְרְשׁוּ וּבָאתָ שָּׁמָּה: ⁶וַהֲבֵאתֶם
שָׁמָּה עֹלֹתֵיכֶם וְזִבְחֵיכֶם וְאֵת מַעְשְׂרֹתֵיכֶם וְאֵת
תְּרוּמַת יֶדְכֶם וְנִדְרֵיכֶם וְנִדְבֹתֵיכֶם וּבְכֹרֹת בְּקַרְכֶם
וְצֹאנְכֶם: ⁷וַאֲכַלְתֶּם־שָׁם לִפְנֵי יְהוָה אֱלֹהֵיכֶם

12:4. You shall not do that. Meaning: you shall not worship your God *in many places*. Moses has just told the people that the nations worshiped their gods all over the land—on hills, in valleys, and under every tree—and that the Israelites are to destroy "all the places." In the next verse Moses will tell them that they are to worship their God in *only one place*.

12:5. the place that YHWH, your God, will choose. This is the central point: There are not to be Temples of YHWH all over the world, or even all over Israel. There is to be only one place. I understand this to be a physical, visible expression of the principle of monotheism: one God, one place of worship. (This does not preclude the post-biblical Jewish practice of having synagogues, nor the Christian practice of having churches, as places of prayer, study, and gathering. It just means that worship involving *sacrifices* can be done only in the one sanctioned place.)

12:5. to set His name there. This is known as the Deuteronomistic Name Theology. The concept is that God cannot be contained in all of the universe, so how can a structure built on earth by humans possibly house God? Answer: God causes His name to be contained in the structure. The divine name becomes almost a tangible entity, and it is connected to the structure; that is, to the Tent of Meeting. The visible symbol of the presence of the divine name is the ark. And so every occurrence of this expression in Deuteronomy refers to the place where the ark is. Later the ark and the Tent of Meeting will be moved to the Temple that Solomon builds in Jerusalem (1 Kings 8:4), and on that occasion Solomon will use some of these same terms to convey that the Name is now housed in the Temple (8:12–30). For prayer and sacrifice, Israelites are to focus their attention in the direction of the place where the name of YHWH is housed.

12:5. to tent it. I follow Frank Moore Cross in the understanding of this word (Hebrew root *škn*) as denominative from the word *miškān*, a tent or tabernacle, so that it means that YHWH tents His name there. That is, the Tent of Meeting houses the ark and the divine name.

One can *pray* anywhere, but a great many of the commandments can be fulfilled only at that one place. Most notably, all sacrifices must be made there, and nowhere else on earth.

12:7. you shall eat there in front of YHWH. A sacrifice is a sacred meal eaten in the presence of God. The commandments of Leviticus 17 are conveyed again here. The

YHWH, your God. And you shall rejoice about everything your hand has taken on, you and your households, in that YHWH, your God, has blessed you. 8You shall not do it like everything that we're doing here today, each one, everything that's right in his own eyes, 9because up to now you haven't come to the resting place and to the legacy that YHWH, your God, is giving you. 10But when you'll cross the Jordan and live in the land that YHWH, your God, is giving you as a legacy, and He'll give you rest from all your enemies all around, and you'll live securely, 11then it shall be, the place that YHWH, your God, will choose to tent His name there: there you shall bring everything that I command you, your burnt offerings and your sacrifices, your tithes and your hand's donation and every choice one of your vows that you'll make to YHWH. 12And you shall rejoice in front of YHWH, your God: you and your sons and your daughters and your servants and your maids and the Levite who is in your gates because he doesn't have a portion or a legacy with you.

13"Watch yourself in case you would make your burnt offerings in any place that you'll see. 14But, rather, in the place that YHWH will choose in one of your tribes: there you shall make your burnt offerings, and there you shall do everything that I command you. 15Only, as much as your soul desires you may slaughter and may eat meat according to the blessing of YHWH, your God, that He has given you in all your gates. The impure and the pure may eat it: like a gazelle, like a deer. 16Only, you shall not

וּשְׂמַחְתֶּ֞ם בְּכֹ֣ל מִשְׁלַ֣ח יֶדְכֶ֗ם אַתֶּם֙ וּבָ֣תֵּיכֶ֔ם אֲשֶׁ֥ר בֵּרַכְךָ֖ יְהֹוָ֥ה אֱלֹהֶֽיךָ׃ 8לֹ֣א תַעֲשׂ֔וּן כְּ֠כֹל אֲשֶׁ֨ר אֲנַ֧חְנוּ עֹשִׂ֛ים פֹּ֖ה הַיּ֑וֹם אִ֖ישׁ כׇּל־הַיָּשָׁ֥ר בְּעֵינָֽיו׃ 9כִּ֥י לֹא־בָּאתֶ֖ם עַד־עָ֑תָּה אֶל־הַמְּנוּחָה֙ וְאֶל־הַֽנַּחֲלָ֔ה אֲשֶׁר־יְהֹוָ֥ה אֱלֹהֶ֖יךָ נֹתֵ֥ן לָֽךְ׃ 10וַעֲבַרְתֶּם֮ אֶת־הַיַּרְדֵּן֒ וִֽישַׁבְתֶּ֣ם בָּאָ֔רֶץ אֲשֶׁר־יְהֹוָ֥ה אֱלֹהֵיכֶ֖ם מַנְחִ֣יל אֶתְכֶ֑ם וְהֵנִ֨יחַ לָכֶ֧ם מִכׇּל־אֹיְבֵיכֶ֛ם מִסָּבִ֖יב וִֽישַׁבְתֶּם־בֶּֽטַח׃ 11וְהָיָ֣ה הַמָּק֗וֹם אֲשֶׁר־יִבְחַר֩ יְהֹוָ֨ה אֱלֹהֵיכֶ֥ם בּוֹ֙ לְשַׁכֵּ֤ן שְׁמוֹ֙ שָׁ֔ם שָׁ֣מָּה תָבִ֔יאוּ אֵ֛ת כׇּל־אֲשֶׁ֥ר אָנֹכִ֖י מְצַוֶּ֣ה אֶתְכֶ֑ם עוֹלֹתֵיכֶ֣ם וְזִבְחֵיכֶ֗ם מַעְשְׂרֹֽתֵיכֶם֙ וּתְרֻמַ֣ת יֶדְכֶ֔ם וְכֹל֙ מִבְחַ֣ר נִדְרֵיכֶ֔ם אֲשֶׁ֥ר תִּדְּר֖וּ לַֽיהֹוָֽה׃ 12וּשְׂמַחְתֶּ֗ם לִפְנֵי֮ יְהֹוָ֣ה אֱלֹהֵיכֶם֒ אַתֶּ֗ם וּבְנֵיכֶם֙ וּבְנֹ֣תֵיכֶ֔ם וְעַבְדֵיכֶ֖ם וְאַמְהֹתֵיכֶ֑ם וְהַלֵּוִי֙ אֲשֶׁ֣ר בְּשַֽׁעֲרֵיכֶ֔ם כִּ֣י אֵ֥ין ל֛וֹ חֵ֥לֶק וְנַחֲלָ֖ה אִתְּכֶֽם׃ 13הִשָּׁ֣מֶר לְךָ֔ פֶּֽן־תַּעֲלֶ֖ה עֹלֹתֶ֑יךָ בְּכׇל־מָק֖וֹם אֲשֶׁ֥ר תִּרְאֶֽה׃ 14כִּ֣י אִם־בַּמָּק֗וֹם אֲשֶׁר־יִבְחַ֤ר יְהֹוָה֙ בְּאַחַ֣ד שְׁבָטֶ֔יךָ שָׁ֖ם תַּעֲלֶ֣ה עֹלֹתֶ֑יךָ וְשָׁ֣ם תַּעֲשֶׂ֔ה כֹּ֥ל אֲשֶׁ֖ר אָנֹכִ֥י מְצַוֶּֽךָּ׃ 15רַק֩ בְּכׇל־אַוַּ֨ת נַפְשְׁךָ֜ תִּזְבַּ֣ח ׀ וְאָכַלְתָּ֣ בָשָׂ֗ר כְּבִרְכַּ֨ת יְהֹוָ֧ה אֱלֹהֶ֛יךָ אֲשֶׁ֥ר נָֽתַן־לְךָ֖ בְּכׇל־שְׁעָרֶ֑יךָ הַטָּמֵ֤א וְהַטָּהוֹר֙ יֹאכְלֶ֔נּוּ כַּצְּבִ֖י

---

language is different, but the principle is the same: Animals' lives cannot be taken in a thoughtless way. If one wishes to eat meat, the animal must be killed at the one central place of worship, called the Tabernacle in Leviticus and "the place where YHWH sets His name" in Deuteronomy. Then, instead of slaughter, one participates in holiness when one eats the meal. The meal then includes a component of reverence for the animal's life and affirms a belief in the unity of God.

12:15. **like a gazelle, like a deer.** Israelites may kill an animal as a *sacrifice* only at the one place that will be chosen (which will ultimately be the Temple). But they may slaughter an animal in a nonsacrificial way (that is, secular rather than ritual slaugh-

eat the blood. You shall spill it like water on the earth. 17You may not eat within your gates the tithe of your grain or your wine or your oil or the firstborn of your herd or your flock or all your vows that you'll make or your contributions or your hand's donation. 18But, rather, you shall eat them in front of YHWH, your God, in the place that YHWH, your God, will choose: you and your son and your daughter and your servant and your maid and the Levite who is in your gates. And you shall rejoice in front of YHWH, your God, about everything your hand has taken on. 19Watch yourself in case you would leave the Levite, all your days in your land.

20"When YHWH, your God, will widen your border as He spoke to you, and you'll say, 'Let me eat meat,' because your soul will desire to eat meat, you may eat meat as much as your soul desires. 21When the place that YHWH, your God, will choose to put His name there will be far from you, then you shall slaughter from your herd and from your flock that YHWH has given you as I've commanded you, and you may eat within your gates as much as your soul desires. 22Just: as a gazelle and a deer are eaten, so you shall eat it. The impure and the pure may eat it together. 23Only, be strong not to eat the blood, because the blood: it's the life; and you shall not eat the life with the meat. 24You shall not eat it. You shall spill it like water on the earth. 25You shall not eat it, so it will be good for you and for your children after you when you do what is right in YHWH's eyes.

26"Only, you shall carry your holy things that you'll have and your vows and shall come to the place that YHWH will choose. 27And you shall do your burnt offerings, the meat and the blood, on the altar of YHWH, your God. And the blood

וְכָאֱיָֽל: 16רַק הַדָּם לֹא תֹאכֵלוּ עַל־הָאָרֶץ תִּשְׁפְּכֶנּוּ כַּמָּיִם: 17לֹא־תוּכַל לֶאֱכֹל בִּשְׁעָרֶיךָ מַעְשַׂר דְּגָנְךָ וְתִירֹשְׁךָ וְיִצְהָרֶךָ וּבְכֹרֹת בְּקָרְךָ וְצֹאנֶךָ וְכָל־נְדָרֶיךָ אֲשֶׁר תִּדֹּר וְנִדְבֹתֶיךָ וּתְרוּמַת יָדֶךָ: 18כִּי אִם־לִפְנֵי יְהוָה אֱלֹהֶיךָ תֹּאכְלֶנּוּ בַּמָּקוֹם אֲשֶׁר יִבְחַר יְהוָה אֱלֹהֶיךָ בּוֹ אַתָּה וּבִנְךָ וּבִתֶּךָ וְעַבְדְּךָ וַאֲמָתֶךָ וְהַלֵּוִי אֲשֶׁר בִּשְׁעָרֶיךָ וְשָׂמַחְתָּ לִפְנֵי יְהוָה אֱלֹהֶיךָ בְּכֹל מִשְׁלַח יָדֶךָ: 19הִשָּׁמֶר לְךָ פֶּן־תַּעֲזֹב אֶת־הַלֵּוִי כָּל־יָמֶיךָ עַל־אַדְמָתֶךָ: ס 20כִּי־יַרְחִיב יְהוָה אֱלֹהֶיךָ אֶת־גְּבוּלְךָ כַּאֲשֶׁר דִּבֶּר־לָךְ וְאָמַרְתָּ אֹכְלָה בָשָׂר כִּי־תְאַוֶּה נַפְשְׁךָ לֶאֱכֹל בָּשָׂר בְּכָל־אַוַּת נַפְשְׁךָ תֹּאכַל בָּשָׂר: 21כִּי־יִרְחַק מִמְּךָ הַמָּקוֹם אֲשֶׁר יִבְחַר יְהוָה אֱלֹהֶיךָ לָשׂוּם שְׁמוֹ שָׁם וְזָבַחְתָּ מִבְּקָרְךָ וּמִצֹּאנְךָ אֲשֶׁר נָתַן יְהוָה לְךָ כַּאֲשֶׁר צִוִּיתִךָ וְאָכַלְתָּ בִּשְׁעָרֶיךָ בְּכֹל אַוַּת נַפְשֶׁךָ: 22אַךְ כַּאֲשֶׁר יֵאָכֵל אֶת־הַצְּבִי וְאֶת־הָאַיָּל כֵּן תֹּאכְלֶנּוּ הַטָּמֵא וְהַטָּהוֹר יַחְדָּו יֹאכְלֶנּוּ: 23רַק חֲזַק לְבִלְתִּי אֲכֹל הַדָּם כִּי הַדָּם הוּא הַנָּפֶשׁ וְלֹא־תֹאכַל הַנֶּפֶשׁ עִם־הַבָּשָׂר: 24לֹא תֹּאכְלֶנּוּ עַל־הָאָרֶץ תִּשְׁפְּכֶנּוּ כַּמָּיִם: 25לֹא תֹּאכְלֶנּוּ לְמַעַן יִיטַב לְךָ וּלְבָנֶיךָ אַחֲרֶיךָ כִּי־תַעֲשֶׂה הַיָּשָׁר בְּעֵינֵי יְהוָה: 26רַק קָדָשֶׁיךָ אֲשֶׁר־יִהְיוּ לְךָ וּנְדָרֶיךָ תִּשָּׂא וּבָאתָ אֶל־הַמָּקוֹם אֲשֶׁר־יִבְחַר יְהוָה: 27וְעָשִׂיתָ עֹלֹתֶיךָ הַבָּשָׂר וְהַדָּם עַל־מִזְבַּח יְהוָה אֱלֹהֶיךָ וְדַם־זְבָחֶיךָ

ter) at any other place. Then the same laws apply to this slaughter as would apply to animals that are killed by hunting, such as gazelles and deer: (1) the blood must be spilled off and not eaten; (2) only people who are in a condition of ritual purity may eat sacrificed meat, but this secularly slaughtered meat may be eaten by anyone, pure or impure.

of your sacrifices shall be spilled on the altar of YHWH, your God, and you shall eat the meat. 28Be watchful that you listen to all these things that I command you so that it will be good for you and for your children after you forever when you'll do what is good and right in the eyes of YHWH, your God.

29"When YHWH, your God, will cut off the nations that you're coming there to dispossess from in front of you, and you'll dispossess them and live in their land, 30watch yourself in case you'll be trapped after them, after their destruction from in front of you, and in case you'll inquire about their gods, saying, 'How did these nations serve their gods? And I'll do that—I, too.' 31You shall *not* do this for YHWH, your God, because they did every offensive thing of YHWH that He hates for their gods, because they would also burn their sons and their daughters in fire to their gods!

13 1"Everything that I command you: you shall be watchful to do it. You shall not add onto it, and you shall not subtract from it.

2"When a prophet or one who has a dream will get up among you and will give you a sign or a wonder, 3and the sign or the wonder of which he spoke to you—saying, 'Let's go after other gods,' whom you haven't known, 'and let's serve them'—will come to pass, 4you shall not listen to that prophet's words or to that one who has the dream, because YHWH, your God, is testing you, to know whether you are loving YHWH, your God, with all your heart and with all your soul. 5You shall go after YHWH, your God, and you shall fear *Him*, and you shall observe *His*

יִשָּׁפֵךְ֙ עַל־מִזְבַּח֙ יְהוָ֣ה אֱלֹהֶ֔יךָ וְהַבָּשָׂ֖ר תֹּאכֵֽל׃ 28שְׁמֹ֣ר וְשָׁמַעְתָּ֗ אֵ֣ת כָּל־הַדְּבָרִ֣ים הָאֵ֔לֶּה אֲשֶׁ֥ר אָנֹכִ֖י מְצַוֶּ֑ךָּ לְמַ֩עַן֩ יִיטַ֨ב לְךָ֜ וּלְבָנֶ֤יךָ אַחֲרֶ֙יךָ֙ עַד־ עוֹלָ֔ם כִּ֤י תַעֲשֶׂה֙ הַטּ֣וֹב וְהַיָּשָׁ֔ר בְּעֵינֵ֖י יְהוָ֥ה אֱלֹהֶֽיךָ׃ ס 29כִּֽי־יַכְרִית֩ יְהוָ֨ה אֱלֹהֶ֤יךָ אֶת־הַגּוֹיִם֙ אֲשֶׁ֨ר אַתָּ֥ה בָא־שָׁ֛מָּה לָרֶ֥שֶׁת אוֹתָ֖ם מִפָּנֶ֑יךָ וְיָרַשְׁתָּ֣ אֹתָ֔ם וְיָשַׁבְתָּ֖ בְּאַרְצָֽם׃ 30הִשָּׁ֣מֶר לְךָ֗ פֶּן־תִּנָּקֵשׁ֙ אַחֲרֵיהֶ֔ם אַחֲרֵ֖י הִשָּׁמְדָ֣ם מִפָּנֶ֑יךָ וּפֶן־תִּדְרֹ֨שׁ לֵאלֹֽהֵיהֶ֜ם לֵאמֹ֗ר אֵיכָ֨ה יַעַבְד֜וּ הַגּוֹיִ֤ם הָאֵ֙לֶּה֙ אֶת־ אֱלֹ֣הֵיהֶ֔ם וְאֶעֱשֶׂה־כֵּ֖ן גַּם־אָֽנִי׃ 31לֹא־תַעֲשֶׂ֣ה כֵ֔ן לַיהוָ֖ה אֱלֹהֶ֑יךָ כִּי֩ כָל־תּוֹעֲבַ֨ת יְהוָ֜ה אֲשֶׁ֣ר שָׂנֵ֗א עָשׂוּ֙ לֵאלֹ֣הֵיהֶ֔ם כִּ֣י גַ֤ם אֶת־בְּנֵיהֶם֙ וְאֶת־בְּנֹ֣תֵיהֶ֔ם יִשְׂרְפ֥וּ בָאֵ֖שׁ לֵאלֹהֵיהֶֽם׃

13 1אֵ֣ת כָּל־הַדָּבָ֗ר אֲשֶׁ֤ר אָנֹכִי֙ מְצַוֶּ֣ה אֶתְכֶ֔ם אֹת֥וֹ תִשְׁמְר֖וּ לַעֲשׂ֑וֹת לֹא־תֹסֵ֣ף עָלָ֔יו וְלֹ֥א תִגְרַ֖ע מִמֶּֽנּוּ׃ פ

2כִּֽי־יָק֤וּם בְּקִרְבְּךָ֙ נָבִ֔יא א֖וֹ חֹלֵ֣ם חֲל֑וֹם וְנָתַ֥ן אֵלֶ֛יךָ א֖וֹת א֥וֹ מוֹפֵֽת׃ 3וּבָ֤א הָאוֹת֙ וְהַמּוֹפֵ֔ת אֲשֶׁר־ דִּבֶּ֥ר אֵלֶ֖יךָ לֵאמֹ֑ר נֵֽלְכָ֞ה אַחֲרֵ֨י אֱלֹהִ֧ים אֲחֵרִ֛ים אֲשֶׁ֥ר לֹֽא־יְדַעְתָּ֖ם וְנָעָבְדֵֽם׃ 4לֹ֣א תִשְׁמַ֗ע אֶל־דִּבְרֵי֙ הַנָּבִ֣יא הַה֔וּא א֛וֹ אֶל־חוֹלֵ֥ם הַחֲל֖וֹם הַה֑וּא כִּ֣י מְנַסֶּ֞ה יְהוָ֤ה אֱלֹֽהֵיכֶם֙ אֶתְכֶ֔ם לָדַ֗עַת הֲיִשְׁכֶ֤ם אֹֽהֲבִים֙ אֶת־ יְהוָ֣ה אֱלֹֽהֵיכֶ֔ם בְּכָל־לְבַבְכֶ֖ם וּבְכָל־נַפְשְׁכֶֽם׃ 5אַחֲרֵ֨י יְהוָ֧ה אֱלֹהֵיכֶ֛ם תֵּלֵ֖כוּ וְאֹת֣וֹ תִירָ֑אוּ וְאֶת־

12:27. **sacrifices**. This refers to sacrifices that are for food (as opposed to burnt offerings, which the donor does not eat). The blood is to be poured off at the altar, and then one may eat the meat of the sacrifice.

13:1. **You shall not add onto it, and you shall not subtract from it**. Moses repeats the principle of not adding to or taking away from the law. This repetition emphasizes its extreme importance. It is a command that affects all other commandments. See the comment on Deut 4:2.

commandments and listen to *His* voice and serve *Him* and cling to *Him.* 6And that prophet or that one who has the dream shall be put to death, because he spoke a misrepresentation about YHWH, your God, who brought you out from the land of Egypt and who redeemed you from a house of slaves, to drive you from the way in which YHWH, your God, commanded you to go. So you shall burn away what is bad from among you.

7"When your brother, your mother's son or your father's son, or the wife of your bosom, or your friend who is as your own self will entice you in secret, saying, 'Let's go and serve other gods,' whom you haven't known, you and your fathers, 8from the gods of the peoples who are all around you, those close to you or those far from you, from one end of the earth to the other end of the earth, 9you shall not consent to him, and you shall not listen to him, and your eye shall not pity him, and you shall not have compassion and shall not cover it up for him. 10But you shall *kill* him. Your hand shall be on him first to put him to death, and all the people's hand thereafter. 11And you shall stone him with stones so he dies because he sought to drive you away from YHWH, your God, who brought you out from the land of Egypt, from a house of slaves. 12And all Israel will hear and fear and won't continue to do a bad thing like this among you.

13"When you'll hear in one of your cities that YHWH, your God, is giving you to live there, say-

מִצְוֺתָיו תִּשְׁמֹרוּ וּבְקֹלוֹ תִשְׁמָעוּ וְאֹתוֹ תַעֲבֹדוּ וּבוֹ תִדְבָּקוּן: 6וְהַנָּבִיא הַהוּא אוֹ חֹלֵם הַחֲלוֹם הַהוּא יוּמָת כִּי דִבֶּר־סָרָה עַל־יְהֹוָה אֱלֹהֵיכֶם הַמּוֹצִיא אֶתְכֶם ׀ מֵאֶרֶץ מִצְרַיִם וְהַפֹּדְךָ מִבֵּית עֲבָדִים לְהַדִּיחֲךָ מִן־הַדֶּרֶךְ אֲשֶׁר צִוְּךָ יְהֹוָה אֱלֹהֶיךָ לָלֶכֶת בָּהּ וּבִעַרְתָּ הָרָע מִקִּרְבֶּךָ: 7כִּי יְסִיתְךָ אָחִיךָ בֶן־אִמֶּךָ אוֹ־בִנְךָ אוֹ־בִתְּךָ אוֹ ׀ אֵשֶׁת חֵיקֶךָ אוֹ רֵעֲךָ אֲשֶׁר כְּנַפְשְׁךָ בַּסֵּתֶר לֵאמֹר נֵלְכָה וְנַעַבְדָה אֱלֹהִים אֲחֵרִים אֲשֶׁר לֹא יָדַעְתָּ אַתָּה וַאֲבֹתֶיךָ: 8מֵאֱלֹהֵי הָעַמִּים אֲשֶׁר סְבִיבֹתֵיכֶם הַקְּרֹבִים אֵלֶיךָ אוֹ הָרְחֹקִים מִמֶּךָּ מִקְצֵה הָאָרֶץ וְעַד־קְצֵה הָאָרֶץ: 9לֹא־תֹאבֶה לוֹ וְלֹא תִשְׁמַע אֵלָיו וְלֹא־תָחוֹס עֵינְךָ עָלָיו וְלֹא־תַחְמֹל וְלֹא־תְכַסֶּה עָלָיו: 10כִּי הָרֹג תַּהַרְגֶנּוּ יָדְךָ תִּהְיֶה־בּוֹ בָרִאשׁוֹנָה לַהֲמִיתוֹ וְיַד כָּל־הָעָם בָּאַחֲרֹנָה: 11וּסְקַלְתּוֹ בָאֲבָנִים וָמֵת כִּי בִקֵּשׁ לְהַדִּיחֲךָ מֵעַל יְהֹוָה אֱלֹהֶיךָ הַמּוֹצִיאֲךָ מֵאֶרֶץ מִצְרַיִם מִבֵּית עֲבָדִים: 12וְכָל־יִשְׂרָאֵל יִשְׁמְעוּ וְיִרָאוּן וְלֹא־יוֹסִפוּ לַעֲשׂוֹת כַּדָּבָר הָרָע הַזֶּה בְּקִרְבֶּךָ: ס 13כִּי־תִשְׁמַע בְּאַחַת עָרֶיךָ אֲשֶׁר יְהֹוָה אֱלֹהֶיךָ נֹתֵן לְךָ לָשֶׁבֶת שָׁם לֵאמֹר: 14יָצְאוּ אֲנָשִׁים

13:6. burn away what is bad. This is the first of nine occurrences of this expression in Deuteronomy. Until now Moses has used the word literally to describe the burning fire on Mount Sinai (see the comment on 4:11). Now he turns it from describing what God has done to conveying figuratively what the people of Israel must do themselves. This device of using a word in two ways so as to compare what God does and what humans do occurs elsewhere in Deuteronomy as well. Notably, in this very verse, the false prophet or dreamer is described as "driving" Israel from their God. Later God will be described as "driving" Israel from its land because of their apostasy (see the comment on Deut 30:1). In this way, Deuteronomy is an exquisitely woven tapestry of language, pointing to connections and to causes and effects in human behavior.

ing, 14'Good-for-nothing people have gone out from among you and driven away their city's residents, saying: "Let's go and serve other gods," whom you haven't known,' 15and you'll inquire and investigate and ask well, and, here, the thing is true—this offensive thing was done among you— 16you shall strike that city's residents by the sword, completely destroying it and everything in it and its animals with the sword. 17And you shall gather all its spoil into the middle of its square, and you shall burn the city and all its spoil in fire entirely to YHWH, your God, and it shall be a tell eternally. It shall not be rebuilt

בְּנֵי־בְלִיַּעַל מִקִּרְבֶּךָ וַיַּדִּיחוּ אֶת־יֹשְׁבֵי עִירָם לֵאמֹר נֵלְכָה וְנַעַבְדָה אֱלֹהִים אֲחֵרִים אֲשֶׁר לֹא־יְדַעְתֶּם: 15וְדָרַשְׁתָּ וְחָקַרְתָּ וְשָׁאַלְתָּ הֵיטֵב וְהִנֵּה אֱמֶת נָכוֹן הַדָּבָר נֶעֶשְׂתָה הַתּוֹעֵבָה הַזֹּאת בְּקִרְבֶּךָ: 16הַכֵּה תַכֶּה אֶת־יֹשְׁבֵי הָעִיר הַהִוא לְפִי־חָרֶב הַחֲרֵם אֹתָהּ וְאֶת־כָּל־אֲשֶׁר־בָּהּ וְאֶת־בְּהֶמְתָּהּ לְפִי־חָרֶב: 17וְאֶת־כָּל־שְׁלָלָהּ תִּקְבֹּץ אֶל־תּוֹךְ רְחֹבָהּ וְשָׂרַפְתָּ בָאֵשׁ אֶת־הָעִיר וְאֶת־כָּל־שְׁלָלָהּ כָּלִיל לַיהוָה אֱלֹהֶיךָ וְהָיְתָה תֵּל עוֹלָם לֹא תִבָּנֶה עוֹד: 18וְלֹא־יִדְבַּק

ק הַהִיא 13:16

13:14. **Good-for-nothing**. The Hebrew *bĕlîya'al* appears to be a compound of two words meaning "without value" or "without benefit." This corresponds to the English expression "good-for-nothing," which fits with every occurrence of the expression in the *Tanak*'s narrative books.

13:16. **completely destroying it and everything in it**. On the extreme violence that is commanded in destroying those (Israelites) who would lead one to worship other gods, or in destroying an entire Israelite town that worships other gods (including any righteous; cf. Sodom): again the Torah distinguishes between ethical sins and ritual sins. Ethical sins (those that occur between a human and one's fellow humans; theft, for example) are judged in terms of each individual person's actions, and the person's intent is taken into account. Ritual sins (those that are between a human and God; blasphemy, for example) are judged in terms of *groups* and *zones*, and intent is not an issue. Thus, when Achan violates the law of *ḥerem* in Joshua 7, the text says that "*the children of Israel*" violated the *ḥerem* (7:1)—and all of Israel suffers a defeat. Achan takes items that were forbidden to the Israelites, and he hides them in his tent; and the result is that not only is Achan stoned and burned, but his family, his animals, everything that was in the tent, and also the tent itself are stoned and burned.

Questions about the harsh response to Israelites who turn to (or seduce others to) pagan worship must be addressed in this light. Worship of other gods is the ultimate ritual sin in Deuteronomy. As with all ritual infringements, the perpetrators must be utterly eliminated from Israel. If it is an entire city, then that city must be eliminated from Israel—including any righteous members of the community and even the animals.

All of this may seem foreign and barbaric in our time. That is because (1) Israel has not been a religious state for 2000 years; and (2) after the destruction of the Second Temple, ritual became less central in Judaism, and emphasis on ethics rose. Also, (3) monotheism has defeated pagan religion in Western civilization, so we no longer feel the degree of threat that authors of the Bible felt toward it.

13:17. **a tell**. A tell is a hill that came to exist as a result of successive layers of cities being built on top of one another. Because a tell is composed of sand and rock and

again. ¹⁸And let nothing from the complete destruction cling in your hand, so that YHWH will turn back from His flaring anger and will give you mercy. And He'll be merciful to you and multiply you as He swore to your fathers ¹⁹when you'll listen to the voice of YHWH, your God, to observe all His commandments that I command you today, to do what is right in the eyes of YHWH, your God.

14 ¹"You are children of YHWH, your God. You shall not cut yourselves and shall not make a bald place between your eyes for the dead. ²Because you are a holy people to YHWH, your God, and YHWH has chosen you to become a treasured people to Him out of all the peoples who are on the face of the earth.

³"You shall not eat any offensive thing. ⁴This is the animal that you shall eat: ox, lamb of sheep, and lamb of goats, ⁵deer and gazelle and roebuck and wild goat and bison and antelope and mountain sheep ⁶and every animal that has a hoof and that has a split of hooves in two, that regurgitates cud, among animals, you shall eat it. ⁷Except you shall not eat this out of those that regurgitate the cud and out of those that have a hoof: the camel and the rock-badger and the hare, because they regurgitate cud and do not have a hoof; they are impure to you. ⁸And the

בְּיָדְךָ מְאוּמָה מִן־הַחֵרֶם לְמַעַן יָשׁוּב יְהוָה מֵחֲרוֹן אַפּוֹ וְנָתַן־לְךָ רַחֲמִים וְרִחַמְךָ וְהִרְבֶּךָ כַּאֲשֶׁר נִשְׁבַּע לַאֲבֹתֶיךָ: ¹⁹כִּי תִשְׁמַע בְּקוֹל יְהוָה אֱלֹהֶיךָ לִשְׁמֹר אֶת־כָּל־מִצְוֹתָיו אֲשֶׁר אָנֹכִי מְצַוְּךָ הַיּוֹם לַעֲשׂוֹת הַיָּשָׁר בְּעֵינֵי יְהוָה אֱלֹהֶיךָ: ס 14 ¹בָּנִים אַתֶּם לַיהוָה אֱלֹהֵיכֶם לֹא תִתְגֹּדְדוּ וְלֹא־תָשִׂימוּ קָרְחָה בֵּין עֵינֵיכֶם לָמֵת: ²כִּי עַם קָדוֹשׁ אַתָּה לַיהוָה אֱלֹהֶיךָ וּבְךָ בָּחַר יְהוָה לִהְיוֹת לוֹ לְעַם סְגֻלָּה מִכֹּל הָעַמִּים אֲשֶׁר עַל־פְּנֵי הָאֲדָמָה: ס ³לֹא תֹאכַל כָּל־תּוֹעֵבָה: ⁴זֹאת הַבְּהֵמָה אֲשֶׁר תֹּאכֵלוּ שׁוֹר שֵׂה כְשָׂבִים וְשֵׂה עִזִּים: ⁵אַיָּל וּצְבִי וְיַחְמוּר וְאַקּוֹ וְדִישֹׁן וּתְאוֹ וָזָמֶר: ⁶וְכָל־בְּהֵמָה מַפְרֶסֶת פַּרְסָה וְשֹׁסַעַת שֶׁסַע שְׁתֵּי פְרָסוֹת מַעֲלַת גֵּרָה בַּבְּהֵמָה אֹתָהּ תֹּאכֵלוּ: ⁷אַךְ אֶת־זֶה לֹא תֹאכְלוּ מִמַּעֲלֵי הַגֵּרָה וּמִמַּפְרִיסֵי הַפַּרְסָה הַשְּׁסוּעָה אֶת־הַגָּמָל וְאֶת־הָאַרְנֶבֶת וְאֶת־הַשָּׁפָן כִּי־מַעֲלֵה גֵרָה הֵמָּה וּפַרְסָה לֹא הִפְרִיסוּ טְמֵאִים הֵם לָכֶם: ⁸וְאֶת־

---

debris rather than soil, very little grass or vegetation grows on it. Such a mound is a treasure to an archaeologist, but it is a curse here in the text: not only is an apostate city to be destroyed, but it is to become a tell permanently, never to be rebuilt.

14:1. **cut yourselves.** This commandment is already given, in different language, in Lev 19:28. Now the commandment not to "make a bald place" is added to it. In Leviticus this latter commandment refers only to priests (21:5). In some matters, such as entry into the Tabernacle, priests are different from the rest of the people. But in certain other matters, all Israelites are to behave like priests, reflecting the idea that "you are a holy people to YHWH," which is stated in the next verse (Deut 14:2). These cases of imitation of the priests act as a sign and a reminder of what Israel was told at the beginning of the covenant at Sinai: if they will listen and observe the covenant, they will be a "kingdom of priests" (Exod 19:6).

14:4. **This is the animal that you shall eat.** On the dietary laws, cf. the comments on Leviticus 11.

pig, because it has a hoof but no cud; it is impure to you. You shall not eat from their meat, and you shall not touch their carcass.

9"You shall eat this out of all that are in the water: you shall eat every one that has fins and scales. 10And you shall not eat any one that does not have fins and scales; it is impure to you.

11"And you shall eat any pure bird. 12And this is what you shall not eat from them: the eagle and the vulture and the black vulture 13and the kite and the falcon by its kind 14and every raven by its kind 15and the eagle owl and the night-hawk and the seagull and the hawk by its kind, 16the little owl and the great owl and the white owl 17and the pelican and the fish hawk and the cormorant 18and the stork and the heron by its kind and the hoopoe and the bat.

19"And every swarming thing of flying creatures; it is impure to you. It shall not be eaten. 20You shall eat every pure bird.

21"You shall not eat any carcass. You shall give it to the alien who is in your gates, and he will eat it, or sell to a foreigner. Because you are a holy people to YHWH, your God.

"You shall not cook a kid in its mother's milk.

22"You shall *tithe* all of your seed's produce that comes out of the field year by year. 23And you shall eat the tithe of your grain, your wine, and your oil and the firstborn of your herd and your flock in front of YHWH, your God, in the place that He will choose to tent His name there, so that you'll learn to fear YHWH, your God, all

הַחֲזִיר כִּי־מַפְרִיס פַּרְסָה הוּא וְלֹא גֵרָה טָמֵא הוּא לָכֶם מִבְּשָׂרָם לֹא תֹאכֵלוּ וּבְנִבְלָתָם לֹא תִגָּעוּ: ס

9אֶת־זֶה תֹּאכְלוּ מִכֹּל אֲשֶׁר בַּמָּיִם כֹּל אֲשֶׁר־לוֹ סְנַפִּיר וְקַשְׂקֶשֶׂת תֹּאכֵלוּ: 10וְכֹל אֲשֶׁר אֵין־לוֹ סְנַפִּיר וְקַשְׂקֶשֶׂת לֹא תֹאכֵלוּ טָמֵא הוּא לָכֶם: ס

11כָּל־צִפּוֹר טְהֹרָה תֹּאכֵלוּ: 12וְזֶה אֲשֶׁר לֹא־תֹאכְלוּ מֵהֶם הַנֶּשֶׁר וְהַפֶּרֶס וְהָעָזְנִיָּה: 13וְהָרָאָה וְאֶת־הָאַיָּה וְהַדַּיָּה לְמִינָהּ: 14וְאֵת כָּל־עֹרֵב לְמִינוֹ: 15וְאֵת בַּת הַיַּעֲנָה וְאֶת־הַתַּחְמָס וְאֶת־הַשָּׁחַף וְאֶת־הַנֵּץ לְמִינֵהוּ: 16אֶת־הַכּוֹס וְאֶת־הַיַּנְשׁוּף וְהַתִּנְשָׁמֶת: 17וְהַקָּאָת וְאֶת־הָרָחָמָה וְאֶת־הַשָּׁלָךְ: 18וְהַחֲסִידָה וְהָאֲנָפָה לְמִינָהּ וְהַדּוּכִיפַת וְהָעֲטַלֵּף: 19וְכֹל שֶׁרֶץ הָעוֹף טָמֵא הוּא לָכֶם לֹא יֵאָכֵלוּ: 20כָּל־עוֹף טָהוֹר תֹּאכֵלוּ: 21לֹא תֹאכְלוּ כָל־נְבֵלָה לַגֵּר אֲשֶׁר־בִּשְׁעָרֶיךָ תִּתְּנֶנָּה וַאֲכָלָהּ אוֹ מָכֹר לְנָכְרִי כִּי עַם קָדוֹשׁ אַתָּה לַיהוָה אֱלֹהֶיךָ לֹא־תְבַשֵּׁל גְּדִי בַּחֲלֵב אִמּוֹ: פ

22עַשֵּׂר תְּעַשֵּׂר אֵת כָּל־תְּבוּאַת זַרְעֶךָ הַיֹּצֵא הַשָּׂדֶה שָׁנָה שָׁנָה: 23וְאָכַלְתָּ לִפְנֵי | יְהוָה אֱלֹהֶיךָ בַּמָּקוֹם אֲשֶׁר־יִבְחַר לְשַׁכֵּן שְׁמוֹ שָׁם מַעְשַׂר דְּגָנְךָ תִּירֹשְׁךָ וְיִצְהָרֶךָ וּבְכֹרֹת בְּקָרְךָ וְצֹאנֶךָ לְמַעַן תִּלְמַד לְיִרְאָה אֶת־יְהוָה אֱלֹהֶיךָ כָּל־הַיָּמִים:

14:13. **kite and the falcon.** There are problems, apparently scribal, in this verse. The first word, *rā'āh*, is an apparent *resh/dalet* scribal error for *dā'āh*, as it appears in Lev 11:14. The third word, *dayyāh*, may be a further confusion of *dā'āh*. It does not appear in the Septuagint.

14:21. **a kid in its mother's milk.** This is the third occurrence of this command (Exod 23:19; 34:26), and it is the first time that it is grouped with the laws of forbidden animals. It does not appear in the corresponding list in Leviticus 11. Its origin and purpose are thus different from the other dietary laws. Its original meaning may have been ritual or moral (see the comment on Exod 23:19), but it belongs to a different category of law from the prohibitions of eating pigs and other animals.

the days. 24And if the way will be too long for you because you won't be able to carry it because the place that YHWH, your God, will choose to set His name there will be far from you, because YHWH, your God, will bless you, 25then you shall give it by money. And you shall enclose the money in your hand and go to the place that YHWH, your God, will choose. 26And you shall spend the money for anything that your soul will desire: for herd and for flock and for wine and for beer and for anything that your soul will ask of you. And you shall eat there in front of YHWH, your God, and you shall rejoice, you and your household. 27And the Levite who is in your gates: you shall not leave him, because he doesn't have a portion and legacy with you.

28"At the end of three years you shall bring out all the tithe of your produce in that year and leave it within your gates, 29and the Levite will come, because he doesn't have a portion and legacy with you, and the alien and the orphan and the widow who are in your gates, and they shall eat and be full, so that YHWH, your God, will bless you in all your hand's work that you'll do.

15 1"At the end of seven years you shall make a remission. 2And this is the matter of the remission: every holder of a loan is to remit what he has lent his neighbor. He shall not demand it of his neighbor and his brother, because a remission for YHWH has been called. 3You may demand it of a foreigner, but your hand shall remit whatever of yours is with your brother. 4Nonetheless, there won't be an indigent one among you, because YHWH will *bless* you in the land that YHWH, your God, is giving you as a legacy, to take possession of it— 5only if you'll *listen* to the voice of YHWH, your God, to be watchful to do all of this commandment that

24וְכִי־יִרְבֶּה מִמְּךָ הַדֶּרֶךְ כִּי לֹא תוּכַל שְׂאֵתוֹ כִּי־יִרְחַק מִמְּךָ הַמָּקוֹם אֲשֶׁר יִבְחַר יְהוָה אֱלֹהֶיךָ לָשׂוּם שְׁמוֹ שָׁם כִּי יְבָרֶכְךָ יְהוָה אֱלֹהֶיךָ: 25וְנָתַתָּה בַּכָּסֶף וְצַרְתָּ הַכֶּסֶף בְּיָדְךָ וְהָלַכְתָּ אֶל־הַמָּקוֹם אֲשֶׁר יִבְחַר יְהוָה אֱלֹהֶיךָ בּוֹ: 26וְנָתַתָּה הַכֶּסֶף בְּכֹל אֲשֶׁר־תְּאַוֶּה נַפְשְׁךָ בַּבָּקָר וּבַצֹּאן וּבַיַּיִן וּבַשֵּׁכָר וּבְכֹל אֲשֶׁר תִּשְׁאָלְךָ נַפְשֶׁךָ וְאָכַלְתָּ שָּׁם לִפְנֵי יְהוָה אֱלֹהֶיךָ וְשָׂמַחְתָּ אַתָּה וּבֵיתֶךָ: 27וְהַלֵּוִי אֲשֶׁר־בִּשְׁעָרֶיךָ לֹא תַעַזְבֶנּוּ כִּי אֵין לוֹ חֵלֶק וְנַחֲלָה עִמָּךְ: ס 28מִקְצֵה ׀ שָׁלֹשׁ שָׁנִים תּוֹצִיא אֶת־כָּל־מַעְשַׂר תְּבוּאָתְךָ בַּשָּׁנָה הַהִוא וְהִנַּחְתָּ בִּשְׁעָרֶיךָ: 29וּבָא הַלֵּוִי כִּי אֵין־לוֹ חֵלֶק וְנַחֲלָה עִמָּךְ וְהַגֵּר וְהַיָּתוֹם וְהָאַלְמָנָה אֲשֶׁר בִּשְׁעָרֶיךָ וְאָכְלוּ וְשָׂבֵעוּ לְמַעַן יְבָרֶכְךָ יְהוָה אֱלֹהֶיךָ בְּכָל־מַעֲשֵׂה יָדְךָ אֲשֶׁר תַּעֲשֶׂה: ס 15 1מִקֵּץ שֶׁבַע־שָׁנִים תַּעֲשֶׂה שְׁמִטָּה: 2וְזֶה דְּבַר הַשְּׁמִטָּה שָׁמוֹט כָּל־בַּעַל מַשֵּׁה יָדוֹ אֲשֶׁר יַשֶּׁה בְּרֵעֵהוּ לֹא־יִגֹּשׂ אֶת־רֵעֵהוּ וְאֶת־אָחִיו כִּי־קָרָא שְׁמִטָּה לַיהוָה: 3אֶת־הַנָּכְרִי תִּגֹּשׂ וַאֲשֶׁר יִהְיֶה לְךָ אֶת־אָחִיךָ תַּשְׁמֵט יָדֶךָ: 4אֶפֶס כִּי לֹא יִהְיֶה־בְּךָ אֶבְיוֹן כִּי־בָרֵךְ יְבָרֶכְךָ יְהוָה בָּאָרֶץ אֲשֶׁר יְהוָה אֱלֹהֶיךָ נֹתֵן לְךָ נַחֲלָה לְרִשְׁתָּהּ: 5רַק אִם־שָׁמוֹעַ תִּשְׁמַע בְּקוֹל יְהוָה אֱלֹהֶיךָ לִשְׁמֹר לַעֲשׂוֹת אֶת־כָּל־הַמִּצְוָה הַזֹּאת אֲשֶׁר אָנֹכִי מְצַוְּךָ הַיּוֹם: 6כִּי־

15:2. **demand**. This is the same root that is understood in its noun form to mean taskmasters in the story of the enslavement in Egypt (Exod 3:7; 5:10). As a verb it means to require, demand, or exact something from someone.

I command you today. 6When YHWH, your God, will have blessed you as He spoke to you, then you'll lend to many nations, but you won't borrow; and you'll dominate many nations, but they won't dominate you.

7"When there will be an indigent one among you from one of your brothers within one of your gates in your land that YHWH, your God, is giving you, you shall not fortify your heart and shall not shut your hand from your brother who is indigent. 8But you shall *open* your hand to him and shall *lend* to him, enough for his shortage that he has. 9Watch yourself in case there will be something good-for-nothing in your heart, saying, 'The seventh year, the remission year, is getting close,' and your eye will be bad toward your brother who is indigent, and you won't give to him; and he'll call to YHWH about you, and it will be a sin in you. 10You *shall* give to him, and your heart shall not be bad when you're giving to him, because on account of this thing YHWH, your God, will bless you in everything you do and in everything your hand has taken on. 11Because there won't stop being an indigent in the land. On account of this I command you, saying: you shall *open* your hand to your brother, to your poor, and to your indigent in your land.

12"When your Hebrew brother or sister will be

יְהֹוָה אֱלֹהֶיךָ בֵּרַכְךָ כַּאֲשֶׁר דִּבֶּר־לָךְ וְהַעֲבַטְתָּ גוֹיִם רַבִּים וְאַתָּה לֹא תַעֲבֹט וּמָשַׁלְתָּ בְּגוֹיִם רַבִּים וּבְךָ לֹא יִמְשֹׁלוּ: ס 7כִּי־יִהְיֶה בְךָ אֶבְיוֹן מֵאַחַד אַחֶיךָ בְּאַחַד שְׁעָרֶיךָ בְּאַרְצְךָ אֲשֶׁר־יְהֹוָה אֱלֹהֶיךָ נֹתֵן לָךְ לֹא תְאַמֵּץ אֶת־לְבָבְךָ וְלֹא תִקְפֹּץ אֶת־יָדְךָ מֵאָחִיךָ הָאֶבְיוֹן: 8כִּי־פָתֹחַ תִּפְתַּח אֶת־יָדְךָ לוֹ וְהַעֲבֵט תַּעֲבִיטֶנּוּ דֵּי מַחְסֹרוֹ אֲשֶׁר יֶחְסַר לוֹ: 9הִשָּׁמֶר לְךָ פֶּן־יִהְיֶה דָבָר עִם־לְבָבְךָ בְלִיַּעַל לֵאמֹר קָרְבָה שְׁנַת־הַשֶּׁבַע שְׁנַת הַשְּׁמִטָּה וְרָעָה עֵינְךָ בְּאָחִיךָ הָאֶבְיוֹן וְלֹא תִתֵּן לוֹ וְקָרָא עָלֶיךָ אֶל־יְהֹוָה וְהָיָה בְךָ חֵטְא: 10נָתוֹן תִּתֵּן לוֹ וְלֹא־יֵרַע לְבָבְךָ בְּתִתְּךָ לוֹ כִּי בִּגְלַל ׀ הַדָּבָר הַזֶּה יְבָרֶכְךָ יְהֹוָה אֱלֹהֶיךָ בְּכָל־מַעֲשֶׂךָ וּבְכֹל מִשְׁלַח יָדֶךָ: 11כִּי לֹא־יֶחְדַּל אֶבְיוֹן מִקֶּרֶב הָאָרֶץ עַל־כֵּן אָנֹכִי מְצַוְּךָ לֵאמֹר פָּתֹחַ תִּפְתַּח אֶת־יָדְךָ לְאָחִיךָ לַעֲנִיֶּךָ וּלְאֶבְיֹנְךָ בְּאַרְצֶךָ: ס 12כִּי־יִמָּכֵר לְךָ אָחִיךָ

15:11. **there won't stop being an indigent in the land**. This is generally understood to mean that there will never cease to be poor people. And the problem is that just a few verses earlier the text says the opposite: "there won't be an indigent one among you" (15:4). Ibn Ezra and others have explained this apparent contradiction by noting that the statement that "there won't be an indigent one among you" goes on to say "only if you'll *listen*.. . . ." Since Israel will not, in fact, listen in the future, therefore "there won't stop being an indigent in the land." Ramban criticizes this view, saying that it is unimaginable that the Torah would say that the Jewish people will never come to listen to the Torah's commandments. It seems to me that the problem arises because everyone takes this verse to mean that there will *never* stop being indigent people. But it simply says "there won't stop." I take that to mean that poverty will not just come to a stop on its own one day—without any action by humans. That is one of the ways in which this word is used elsewhere in the Torah. Sarah's menopause is described as "Sarah had *stopped* having the way of women" (Gen 18:11). The end of the plague of hail in Egypt is described as "the shower and the hail *stopped*" (Exod 9:34). So here, too, the full verse says that poverty will not simply stop—the poor will not just disappear—

sold to you, then he shall work for you six years, and in the seventh year you shall let him go liberated from you. [13]And when you let him go liberated from you, you shall not let him go empty-handed. [14]You shall *provide* him from your flock and from your threshing floor and from your winepress; as YHWH, your God, has blessed you, you shall give to him. [15]And you shall remember that you were a slave in the land of Egypt, and YHWH, your God, redeemed you. On account of this, I command you this thing today.

[16]"And it will be, if he'll say to you, 'I won't go out from you' because he loves you and your house, because it is good for him with you, [17]then you shall take an awl and put it in his ear and in the door, and he shall be a slave forever to you. And you shall also do this to your maid. [18]It shall not be hard in your eyes when you let him go liberated from you, because he served you six years at twice the value of an employee, and YHWH, your God, will bless you in everything that you'll do.

[19]"Every male firstborn that will be born in your herd and in your flock you shall consecrate to YHWH, your God. You shall not work with your ox's firstborn, and you shall not shear your sheep's firstborn. [20]You shall eat it in front of YHWH, your God, year by year in the place that YHWH will choose—you and your household. [21]And if there will be an injury in it—crippled or blind, any bad injury—you shall not sacrifice it to YHWH, your God. [22]You shall eat it within your gates—the impure and the pure together, like a gazelle and like a deer. [23]Only: you shall not eat its blood. You shall spill it like water on the ground.

הָעִבְרִ֗י א֚וֹ הָעִבְרִיָּ֔ה וַעֲבָֽדְךָ֖ שֵׁ֣שׁ שָׁנִ֑ים וּבַשָּׁנָה֙ הַשְּׁבִיעִ֔ת תְּשַׁלְּחֶ֥נּוּ חָפְשִׁ֖י מֵעִמָּֽךְ׃ [13]וְכִֽי־תְשַׁלְּחֶ֥נּוּ חָפְשִׁ֖י מֵֽעִמָּ֑ךְ לֹ֥א תְשַׁלְּחֶ֖נּוּ רֵיקָֽם׃ [14]הַעֲנֵ֤יק תַּעֲנִיק֙ ל֔וֹ מִצֹּֽאנְךָ֙ וּמִֽגָּרְנְךָ֔ וּמִיִּקְבֶ֑ךָ אֲשֶׁ֧ר בֵּרַכְךָ֛ יְהוָ֥ה אֱלֹהֶ֖יךָ תִּתֶּן־לֽוֹ׃ [15]וְזָכַרְתָּ֗ כִּ֣י עֶ֤בֶד הָיִ֙יתָ֙ בְּאֶ֣רֶץ מִצְרַ֔יִם וַֽיִּפְדְּךָ֖ יְהוָ֣ה אֱלֹהֶ֑יךָ עַל־כֵּ֞ן אָנֹכִ֧י מְצַוְּךָ֛ אֶת־הַדָּבָ֥ר הַזֶּ֖ה הַיּֽוֹם׃ [16]וְהָיָה֙ כִּֽי־יֹאמַ֣ר אֵלֶ֔יךָ לֹ֥א אֵצֵ֖א מֵעִמָּ֑ךְ כִּ֤י אֲהֵֽבְךָ֙ וְאֶת־בֵּיתֶ֔ךָ כִּי־ט֥וֹב ל֖וֹ עִמָּֽךְ׃ [17]וְלָקַחְתָּ֣ אֶת־הַמַּרְצֵ֗עַ וְנָתַתָּ֤ה בְאָזְנוֹ֙ וּבַדֶּ֔לֶת וְהָיָ֥ה לְךָ֖ עֶ֣בֶד עוֹלָ֑ם וְאַ֥ף לַאֲמָתְךָ֖ תַּעֲשֶׂה־כֵּֽן׃ [18]לֹא־יִקְשֶׁ֣ה בְעֵינֶ֗ךָ בְּשַׁלֵּֽחֲךָ֙ אֹת֤וֹ חָפְשִׁי֙ מֵֽעִמָּ֔ךְ כִּ֗י מִשְׁנֶה֙ שְׂכַ֣ר שָׂכִ֔יר עֲבָֽדְךָ֖ שֵׁ֣שׁ שָׁנִ֑ים וּבֵֽרַכְךָ֙ יְהוָ֣ה אֱלֹהֶ֔יךָ בְּכֹ֖ל אֲשֶׁ֥ר תַּעֲשֶֽׂה׃ פ [19]כָּֽל־הַבְּכ֡וֹר אֲשֶׁר֩ יִוָּלֵ֨ד בִּבְקָרְךָ֤ וּבְצֹֽאנְךָ֙ הַזָּכָ֔ר תַּקְדִּ֖ישׁ לַיהוָ֣ה אֱלֹהֶ֑יךָ לֹ֤א תַעֲבֹד֙ בִּבְכֹ֣ר שׁוֹרֶ֔ךָ וְלֹ֥א תָגֹ֖ז בְּכ֥וֹר צֹאנֶֽךָ׃ [20]לִפְנֵי֩ יְהוָ֨ה אֱלֹהֶ֤יךָ תֹֽאכְלֶ֙נּוּ֙ שָׁנָ֣ה בְשָׁנָ֔ה בַּמָּק֖וֹם אֲשֶׁר־יִבְחַ֣ר יְהוָ֑ה אַתָּ֖ה וּבֵיתֶֽךָ׃ [21]וְכִֽי־יִהְיֶ֨ה ב֜וֹ מ֗וּם פִּסֵּ֙חַ֙ א֣וֹ עִוֵּ֔ר כֹּ֖ל מ֣וּם רָ֑ע לֹ֣א תִזְבָּחֶ֔נּוּ לַיהוָ֖ה אֱלֹהֶֽיךָ׃ [22]בִּשְׁעָרֶ֖יךָ תֹּאכְלֶ֑נּוּ הַטָּמֵ֤א וְהַטָּהוֹר֙ יַחְדָּ֔ו כַּצְּבִ֖י וְכָאַיָּֽל׃ [23]רַ֥ק אֶת־דָּמ֖וֹ לֹ֣א תֹאכֵ֑ל עַל־הָאָ֥רֶץ תִּשְׁפְּכֶ֖נּוּ כַּמָּֽיִם׃ פ

and "*On account of this* I command you, saying: you shall open your hand to your brother, to your poor, and to your indigent in your land." The statements here and in v. 4 are consistent: there will be no poverty only if people act to end it.

15:12. **let him go**. This is the same term that was used for Pharaoh's release of the Israelite slaves: "Let my people go." The Israelite should do no less than Pharaoh! The Israelite should let his slave go, without the coercion that Pharaoh needed, and after no more than six years.

16 [1]"Observe the month of Abib, and you shall make Passover for YHWH, your God, because in the month of Abib YHWH, your God, brought you out from Egypt at night. [2]And you shall make a Passover sacrifice to YHWH, your God, of the flock and herd, in the place that YHWH will choose to tent His name there. [3]You shall not eat leavened bread with it. Seven days you shall eat unleavened bread, the bread of degradation, with it, because you went out from the land of Egypt in haste—so that you will remember the day you went out from the land of Egypt all the days of your life. [4]And you shall not have leaven appear within all your borders for seven days, and none of the meat that you will sacrifice in the evening on the first day shall remain until the morning. [5]You may not make the Passover sacrifice within one of your gates that YHWH, your God, is giving you. [6]But, rather, to the place that YHWH, your God, will choose to tent His name: there you shall make the Passover sacrifice in the evening at sunset, the time when you went out from Egypt. [7]And you shall cook and eat it in the place that YHWH, your God, will choose; and you shall turn in the morning and go to your tents. [8]Six days you shall eat unleavened bread, and on the seventh day shall be a convocation to YHWH, your God. You shall not do work.

[9]"You shall count seven weeks. From when the sickle begins to be in the standing grain you shall begin to count seven weeks. [10]And you shall make a Festival of Weeks for YHWH, your God, the full amount of your hand's contribution that you can give insofar as YHWH, your God, will bless you. [11]And you shall rejoice in front of YHWH, your God—you and your son and your daughter and your servant and your maid and the Levite who is within your gates and the alien and the orphan and the widow who are among you—in the place that YHWH,

16 [1]שָׁמוֹר֙ אֶת־חֹ֣דֶשׁ הָֽאָבִ֔יב וְעָשִׂ֣יתָ פֶּ֔סַח לַיהוָ֖ה אֱלֹהֶ֑יךָ כִּ֞י בְּחֹ֣דֶשׁ הָֽאָבִ֗יב הוֹצִ֨יאֲךָ֜ יְהוָ֧ה אֱלֹהֶ֛יךָ מִמִּצְרַ֖יִם לָֽיְלָה׃ [2]וְזָבַ֥חְתָּ פֶּ֛סַח לַיהוָ֥ה אֱלֹהֶ֖יךָ צֹ֣אן וּבָקָ֑ר בַּמָּקוֹם֙ אֲשֶׁר־יִבְחַ֣ר יְהוָ֔ה לְשַׁכֵּ֥ן שְׁמ֖וֹ שָֽׁם׃ [3]לֹא־תֹאכַ֤ל עָלָיו֙ חָמֵ֔ץ שִׁבְעַ֥ת יָמִ֛ים תֹּֽאכַל־עָלָ֥יו מַצּ֖וֹת לֶ֣חֶם עֹ֑נִי כִּ֣י בְחִפָּז֗וֹן יָצָ֨אתָ֙ מֵאֶ֣רֶץ מִצְרַ֔יִם לְמַ֣עַן תִּזְכֹּר֙ אֶת־י֤וֹם צֵֽאתְךָ֙ מֵאֶ֣רֶץ מִצְרַ֔יִם כֹּ֖ל יְמֵ֥י חַיֶּֽיךָ׃ [4]וְלֹֽא־יֵרָאֶ֨ה לְךָ֥ שְׂאֹ֛ר בְּכָל־גְּבֻלְךָ֖ שִׁבְעַ֣ת יָמִ֑ים וְלֹא־יָלִ֣ין מִן־הַבָּשָׂ֗ר אֲשֶׁ֨ר תִּזְבַּ֥ח בָּעֶ֛רֶב בַּיּ֥וֹם הָרִאשׁ֖וֹן לַבֹּֽקֶר׃ [5]לֹ֥א תוּכַ֖ל לִזְבֹּ֣חַ אֶת־הַפָּ֑סַח בְּאַחַ֣ד שְׁעָרֶ֔יךָ אֲשֶׁר־יְהוָ֥ה אֱלֹהֶ֖יךָ נֹתֵ֥ן לָֽךְ׃ [6]כִּ֠י אִֽם־אֶל־הַמָּק֞וֹם אֲשֶׁר־יִבְחַ֨ר יְהוָ֤ה אֱלֹהֶ֙יךָ֙ לְשַׁכֵּ֣ן שְׁמ֔וֹ שָׁ֛ם תִּזְבַּ֥ח אֶת־הַפֶּ֖סַח בָּעָ֑רֶב כְּב֣וֹא הַשֶּׁ֔מֶשׁ מוֹעֵ֖ד צֵֽאתְךָ֥ מִמִּצְרָֽיִם׃ [7]וּבִשַּׁלְתָּ֙ וְאָ֣כַלְתָּ֔ בַּמָּק֕וֹם אֲשֶׁ֥ר יִבְחַ֖ר יְהוָ֣ה אֱלֹהֶ֣יךָ בּ֑וֹ וּפָנִ֣יתָ בַבֹּ֔קֶר וְהָלַכְתָּ֖ לְאֹהָלֶֽיךָ׃ [8]שֵׁ֥שֶׁת יָמִ֖ים תֹּאכַ֣ל מַצּ֑וֹת וּבַיּ֣וֹם הַשְּׁבִיעִ֗י עֲצֶ֙רֶת֙ לַיהוָ֣ה אֱלֹהֶ֔יךָ לֹ֥א תַעֲשֶׂ֖ה מְלָאכָֽה׃ ס [9]שִׁבְעָ֥ה שָׁבֻעֹ֖ת תִּסְפָּר־לָ֑ךְ מֵהָחֵ֤ל חֶרְמֵשׁ֙ בַּקָּמָ֔ה תָּחֵ֣ל לִסְפֹּ֔ר שִׁבְעָ֖ה שָׁבֻעֽוֹת׃ [10]וְעָשִׂ֜יתָ חַ֣ג שָׁבֻע֗וֹת לַיהוָ֤ה אֱלֹהֶ֙יךָ֙ מִסַּ֛ת נִדְבַ֥ת יָדְךָ֖ אֲשֶׁ֣ר תִּתֵּ֑ן כַּאֲשֶׁ֥ר יְבָרֶכְךָ֖ יְהוָ֥ה אֱלֹהֶֽיךָ׃ [11]וְשָׂמַחְתָּ֞ לִפְנֵ֣י ׀ יְהוָ֣ה אֱלֹהֶ֗יךָ אַתָּ֨ה וּבִנְךָ֣ וּבִתֶּךָ֮ וְעַבְדְּךָ֣ וַאֲמָתֶךָ֒ וְהַלֵּוִ֜י אֲשֶׁ֣ר בִּשְׁעָרֶ֗יךָ וְהַגֵּ֤ר וְהַיָּתוֹם֙ וְהָ֣אַלְמָנָ֔ה אֲשֶׁ֖ר בְּקִרְבֶּ֑ךָ בַּמָּק֗וֹם אֲשֶׁ֤ר יִבְחַר֙ יְהוָ֣ה

16:1. **the month of Abib**. See the comment on Exod 13:4.

your God, will choose to tent His name there. [12]And you shall remember that you were a slave in Egypt, and you shall be watchful and do these laws.

[13]"You shall make a Festival of Booths seven days, when you gather from your threshing floor and from your winepress. [14]And you shall rejoice on your festival—you and your son and your daughter and your servant and your maid and the Levite and the alien and the orphan and the widow who are within your gates. [15]Seven days you shall celebrate for YHWH, your God, in the place that YHWH will choose, because YHWH, your God, will bless you in all your produce and all your hands' work, and you shall just be happy.

[16]"Three times in the year every male of yours shall appear in front of YHWH, your God, in the place that He will choose: on the Festival of Unleavened Bread and on the Festival of Weeks and on the Festival of Booths. And he shall not appear in front of YHWH empty-handed: [17]each according to what his hand can give, according to the blessing of YHWH, your God, that He has given you.

JUDGES

[18]"You shall put judges and officers in all your gates that YHWH, your God, is giving you, for your tribes, and they shall judge the people: judgment with justice. [19]You shall not bend judgment, you shall not recognize a face, and you shall not take a bribe, because bribery will blind the eyes of the wise and undermine the

אֱלֹהֶ֔יךָ לְשַׁכֵּ֥ן שְׁמ֖וֹ שָֽׁם׃ ¹²וְזָ֣כַרְתָּ֔ כִּי־עֶ֥בֶד הָיִ֖יתָ בְּמִצְרָ֑יִם וְשָׁמַרְתָּ֣ וְעָשִׂ֔יתָ אֶת־הַֽחֻקִּ֖ים הָאֵֽלֶּה׃ פ

¹³חַ֧ג הַסֻּכֹּ֛ת תַּעֲשֶׂ֥ה לְךָ֖ שִׁבְעַ֣ת יָמִ֑ים בְּאָסְפְּךָ֔ מִֽגָּרְנְךָ֖ וּמִיִּקְבֶֽךָ׃ ¹⁴וְשָׂמַחְתָּ֖ בְּחַגֶּ֑ךָ אַתָּ֨ה וּבִנְךָ֤ וּבִתֶּ֙ךָ֙ וְעַבְדְּךָ֣ וַאֲמָתֶ֔ךָ וְהַלֵּוִ֗י וְהַגֵּ֛ר וְהַיָּת֥וֹם וְהָֽאַלְמָנָ֖ה אֲשֶׁ֥ר בִּשְׁעָרֶֽיךָ׃ ¹⁵שִׁבְעַ֣ת יָמִ֗ים תָּחֹג֙ לַיהֹוָ֣ה אֱלֹהֶ֔יךָ בַּמָּק֖וֹם אֲשֶׁר־יִבְחַ֣ר יְהֹוָ֑ה כִּ֣י יְבָרֶכְךָ֞ יְהֹוָ֣ה אֱלֹהֶ֗יךָ בְּכֹ֤ל תְּבוּאָֽתְךָ֙ וּבְכֹל֙ מַעֲשֵׂ֣ה יָדֶ֔יךָ וְהָיִ֖יתָ אַ֥ךְ שָׂמֵֽחַ׃

¹⁶שָׁל֣וֹשׁ פְּעָמִ֣ים ׀ בַּשָּׁנָ֡ה יֵרָאֶ֨ה כָל־זְכוּרְךָ֜ אֶת־פְּנֵ֣י ׀ יְהֹוָ֣ה אֱלֹהֶ֗יךָ בַּמָּקוֹם֙ אֲשֶׁ֣ר יִבְחָ֔ר בְּחַ֧ג הַמַּצּ֛וֹת וּבְחַ֥ג הַשָּׁבֻע֖וֹת וּבְחַ֣ג הַסֻּכּ֑וֹת וְלֹ֧א יֵרָאֶ֛ה אֶת־פְּנֵ֥י יְהֹוָ֖ה רֵיקָֽם׃ ¹⁷אִ֖ישׁ כְּמַתְּנַ֣ת יָד֑וֹ כְּבִרְכַּ֛ת יְהֹוָ֥ה אֱלֹהֶ֖יךָ אֲשֶׁ֥ר נָֽתַן־לָֽךְ׃ ס

שֹׁפְטִים

¹⁸שֹׁפְטִ֣ים וְשֹֽׁטְרִ֗ים תִּֽתֶּן־לְךָ֙ בְּכָל־שְׁעָרֶ֔יךָ אֲשֶׁ֨ר יְהֹוָ֧ה אֱלֹהֶ֛יךָ נֹתֵ֥ן לְךָ֖ לִשְׁבָטֶ֑יךָ וְשָׁפְט֥וּ אֶת־הָעָ֖ם מִשְׁפַּט־צֶֽדֶק׃ ¹⁹לֹא־תַטֶּ֣ה מִשְׁפָּ֗ט לֹ֤א תַכִּיר֙ פָּנִ֔ים וְלֹא־תִקַּ֖ח שֹׁ֑חַד כִּ֣י הַשֹּׁ֗חַד יְעַוֵּר֙ עֵינֵ֣י חֲכָמִ֔ים

16:18. **judgment with justice.** It should be obvious, but, regrettably, it needs to be said: judgment and justice are not the same thing. Judges and lawyers can be part of one of the noblest endeavors of humankind: the law. When they fail to pursue justice in their performance of judgment, they pervert and degrade the law, and thus they demean humankind—nothing less. The same goes for clerks, bailiffs, law enforcement officers, and everyone else involved in the execution of justice. They elevate or lower themselves—and all of us—by the degree of their commitment to justice.

words of the virtuous. 20Justice, justice you shall pursue, so that you'll *live*, and you'll take possession of the land that YHWH, your God, is giving you.

21"You shall not plant an Asherah of any wood near the altar of YHWH, your God, that you will make. 22And you shall not set up a pillar, which YHWH, your God, hates.

17 1"You shall not sacrifice to YHWH, your God, a bull or a sheep in which will be any injury, any bad thing, because that is an offensive thing of YHWH, your God.

וִיסַלֵּף דִּבְרֵי צַדִּיקִם: 20צֶדֶק צֶדֶק תִּרְדֹּף לְמַעַן תִּחְיֶה וְיָרַשְׁתָּ אֶת־הָאָרֶץ אֲשֶׁר־יְהֹוָה אֱלֹהֶיךָ נֹתֵן לָךְ: ס 21לֹא־תִטַּע לְךָ אֲשֵׁרָה כָּל־עֵץ אֵצֶל מִזְבַּח יְהֹוָה אֱלֹהֶיךָ אֲשֶׁר תַּעֲשֶׂה־לָּךְ: ס 22וְלֹא־תָקִים לְךָ מַצֵּבָה אֲשֶׁר שָׂנֵא יְהֹוָה אֱלֹהֶיךָ: ס 17 1לֹא־תִזְבַּח לַיהֹוָה אֱלֹהֶיךָ שׁוֹר וָשֶׂה אֲשֶׁר יִהְיֶה בוֹ מוּם כֹּל דָּבָר רָע כִּי תוֹעֲבַת יְהֹוָה אֱלֹהֶיךָ הוּא: ס

16:20. **Justice, justice.** Many interpretations have been given for the repetition of the word *justice* in this famous verse, from taking it to mean that one should go to a good court (Siphre; Rashi) to midrashic and Kabbalistic meanings (Ramban), as well as the most basic explanation: that it is repeated for emphasis. It has also been taken to mean "justice alone" (Jeffrey Tigay). And it is often said to mean that one must pursue justice in a just way: one cannot use improper means to achieve it. For example, police and prosecutors must not bend the law in order to get a conviction. The repetition might also be taken to mean that one must pursue justice for both sides: both the plaintiff and the defense in a civil matter, and both the defendant and the prosecution ("the people") in a criminal matter. Most probably, though, we should understand it with those who take it to be a matter of emphasis. Lacking italics or exclamation points, Biblical Hebrew has few ways other than repetition to express emphasis. That is the function of placing an infinitive before a cognate verb (see Notes on the Translation, paragraph 9, page xv), and here it is achieved by repeating the noun.

16:21. **Asherah.** The word is used for the goddess of that name or for a tree or wooden pole that was associated with the worship of Asherah (or possibly other deities as well).

16:22. **you shall not set up a pillar.** Moses set up pillars himself (Exod 24:4). So did Jacob (Gen 28:18; 32:45; 35:14,20). So why does Moses forbid it now? Rashi and some modern commentators have thought that pillars were originally acceptable but came to be associated with pagan worship and so were abandoned. That may or may not be the actual historical development behind these changes, but that does not seem to be what is presented here in the text, because Moses moves from making them to saying that God hates them, all within the forty years in the wilderness. Perhaps we should understand it to mean that Moses is prohibiting the people from making pillars after the formal altar and Temple are built in the land, because then an altar might be taken as an alternative locus of God. Here in Deuteronomy Moses repeatedly emphasizes that there can be only one place of worship, one structure in which God's name is housed. Thus, even Joshua sets up a large stone, which seems like a pillar (although the word is not used there; Josh 24:26), but this may be before the establishment of an official central place of worship.

2"If there will be found among you, in one of your gates that YHWH, your God, is giving you, a man or woman who will do what is bad in the eyes of YHWH, your God, to violate His covenant, 3and will go and serve other gods and bow to them and to the sun or to the moon or to any of the array of the skies, which I did not command, 4and it will be told to you and you will hear it, and you will inquire well, and, here, it is true, the thing is right, this offensive thing has been done in Israel, 5then you shall bring that man or that woman who did this bad thing out to your gates, the man or the woman, and you shall stone them with stones so they die.

6"On the word of two witnesses or three witnesses shall the one who is to die be put to death. One shall not be put to death on the word of one witness. 7The witnesses' hand shall be on him first to put him to death, and all the people's hand after that. So you shall burn away what is bad from among you.

8"If a matter for judgment will be too daunting

כִּי־יִמָּצֵא בְקִרְבְּךָ בְּאַחַד שְׁעָרֶיךָ אֲשֶׁר־יְהוָה אֱלֹהֶיךָ נֹתֵן לָךְ אִישׁ אוֹ־אִשָּׁה אֲשֶׁר יַעֲשֶׂה אֶת־הָרַע בְּעֵינֵי יְהוָה־אֱלֹהֶיךָ לַעֲבֹר בְּרִיתוֹ: 3וַיֵּלֶךְ וַיַּעֲבֹד אֱלֹהִים אֲחֵרִים וַיִּשְׁתַּחוּ לָהֶם וְלַשֶּׁמֶשׁ אוֹ לַיָּרֵחַ אוֹ לְכָל־צְבָא הַשָּׁמַיִם אֲשֶׁר לֹא־צִוִּיתִי: 4וְהֻגַּד־לְךָ וְשָׁמָעְתָּ וְדָרַשְׁתָּ הֵיטֵב וְהִנֵּה אֱמֶת נָכוֹן הַדָּבָר נֶעֶשְׂתָה הַתּוֹעֵבָה הַזֹּאת בְּיִשְׂרָאֵל: 5וְהוֹצֵאתָ אֶת־הָאִישׁ הַהוּא אוֹ אֶת־הָאִשָּׁה הַהִוא אֲשֶׁר עָשׂוּ אֶת־הַדָּבָר הָרַע הַזֶּה אֶל־שְׁעָרֶיךָ אֶת־הָאִישׁ אוֹ אֶת־הָאִשָּׁה וּסְקַלְתָּם בָּאֲבָנִים וָמֵתוּ: 6עַל־פִּי שְׁנַיִם עֵדִים אוֹ שְׁלֹשָׁה עֵדִים יוּמַת הַמֵּת לֹא יוּמַת עַל־פִּי עֵד אֶחָד: 7יַד הָעֵדִים תִּהְיֶה־בּוֹ בָרִאשֹׁנָה לַהֲמִיתוֹ וְיַד כָּל־הָעָם בָּאַחֲרֹנָה וּבִעַרְתָּ הָרָע מִקִּרְבֶּךָ: פ 8כִּי יִפָּלֵא מִמְּךָ דָבָר לַמִּשְׁפָּט בֵּין־

17:7. **witnesses first . . . all the people after**. Numerous commentators discuss the first half of this verse but not the second. It is of course significant that witnesses must know that, if they testify against someone in a capital case, they will have to strike the first blows against the defendant themselves. That conveys vividly how serious their testimony is. But it is at least as significant that *all the people* participate in the execution as well. Capital punishment is the act of a community—in ancient Israel and even more so in democracies. In biblical law, the community must know that if they are going to have capital punishment they must understand that this means that the community as a whole is taking lives. So that there can be no mistaking this point, the entire community must participate in the execution. In postbiblical societies where the entire people does not participate personally, this point may easily be forgotten, but it is true all the same: a community that has capital punishment is responsible *as a community* for the lives it takes. It is not just the executioner or just the witnesses or just the courts.

Perhaps this fact—that in ancient Israel all the people had to carry out the execution—was one of the forces that led Israel to make capital punishment almost impossible in rabbinic law.

17:8. **If a matter for judgment will be too daunting for you**. In every law code there must be a mechanism for change and for application to new and difficult situations. Even if the law is divine law, there must be such a mechanism, and *the Torah recognizes this* and *provides for it*. It directs that in such difficult questions, the authorities

for you, between blood and blood, between law and law, and between injury and injury, matters of disputes in your gates, then you shall get up and go up to the place that YHWH, your God, will choose. 9And you shall come to the Levite priests and to the judge who will be in those days, and you shall inquire, and they will tell you the matter of judgment. 10And you shall do according to the word on the matter that they will tell you from that place that YHWH will choose, and you shall be watchful to do according to everything that they will instruct you. 11You shall do it according to the word of the instruction that they will give you and according to the judgment that they will say to you. You shall not turn from the thing that they will tell you, right or left. 12And the man who will act presumptuously, not listening to the priest who is standing to serve YHWH,

דָּם ׀ לְדָם בֵּין־דִּין לְדִין וּבֵין נֶגַע לָנֶגַע דִּבְרֵי רִיבֹת בִּשְׁעָרֶיךָ וְקַמְתָּ וְעָלִיתָ אֶל־הַמָּקוֹם אֲשֶׁר יִבְחַר יְהוָה אֱלֹהֶיךָ בּוֹ: 9וּבָאתָ אֶל־הַכֹּהֲנִים הַלְוִיִּם וְאֶל־הַשֹּׁפֵט אֲשֶׁר יִהְיֶה בַּיָּמִים הָהֵם וְדָרַשְׁתָּ וְהִגִּידוּ לְךָ אֵת דְּבַר הַמִּשְׁפָּט: 10וְעָשִׂיתָ עַל־פִּי הַדָּבָר אֲשֶׁר יַגִּידוּ לְךָ מִן־הַמָּקוֹם הַהוּא אֲשֶׁר יִבְחַר יְהוָה וְשָׁמַרְתָּ לַעֲשׂוֹת כְּכֹל אֲשֶׁר יוֹרוּךָ: 11עַל־פִּי הַתּוֹרָה אֲשֶׁר יוֹרוּךָ וְעַל־הַמִּשְׁפָּט אֲשֶׁר־יֹאמְרוּ לְךָ תַּעֲשֶׂה לֹא תָסוּר מִן־הַדָּבָר אֲשֶׁר־יַגִּידוּ לְךָ יָמִין וּשְׂמֹאל: 12וְהָאִישׁ אֲשֶׁר־יַעֲשֶׂה בְזָדוֹן לְבִלְתִּי שְׁמֹעַ אֶל־הַכֹּהֵן הָעֹמֵד לְשָׁרֶת שָׁם אֶת־

(judges and priests; i.e., authorities in law and religion) in each age shall determine what to do. This has always been done in Judaism. The most obvious distinction among the movements in Judaism has been their different views of how the law changes. The primary consideration when authorities, including scholars and rabbis, determine that a law is changed is that they do so with wisdom and reverence, and not with arrogance.

17:8. **blood and blood.** Cases involving the taking of life.

17:8. **between law and law.** Cases that are complex because more than one law applies.

17:8. **between injury and injury.** Cases involving physical hurt.

17:8. **disputes.** The term (Hebrew *rîb*) meant a quarrel, as in the quarreling at the rock that leads to the name Meribah (Exodus 17; Numbers 20), and it came to refer to a lawsuit, a legal dispute. Israel's prophets use it to describe God's judgment of Israel in legal terms (Hos 12:3; Mic 6:2). This is known in biblical scholarship as a "covenant lawsuit." The covenant between God and Israel is a legal relationship, formulated in the legal terminology of the ancient Near East (see the comment on Exod 20:1). In a *rîb* oracle, the prophet describes God as bringing a case against His people for violating the covenant, which can end in judgment and punishment.

17:9. **the Levite priests.** Historically, originally all Levites were priests. Later the Levite group that identified itself as descendants of Aaron took exclusive hold of the priesthood and limited all the other Levites to a secondary role. Thereafter a distinction was made between priests and Levites. Deuteronomy reflects the original status of all Levites and does not make this distinction between priests and Levites. (I have discussed this history of priesthood in *Who Wrote the Bible?*)

620

your God, there, or to the judge: that man shall die. So you shall burn away what is bad from Israel. 13And all the people will listen and fear and won't act presumptuously anymore.

14"When you'll come to the land that YHWH, your God, is giving you, and you'll take possession of it and live in it, and you'll say, 'Let me set a king over me like all the nations that are around me,' 15you *shall* set a king over you whom YHWH, your God, will choose! You shall set a king from among your brothers over you. You may not put a foreign man, who is not your brother, over you. 16Only, he shall not get himself many horses, and he shall not bring the people back to Egypt in order to get many horses, when YHWH has said to you, 'You shall not go back this way ever again.'

יְהוָה אֱלֹהֶיךָ אוֹ אֶל־הַשֹּׁפֵט וּמֵת הָאִישׁ הַהוּא
וּבִעַרְתָּ הָרָע מִיִּשְׂרָאֵל: 13וְכָל־הָעָם יִשְׁמְעוּ וְיִרָאוּ
וְלֹא יְזִידוּן עוֹד: ס

14כִּי־תָבֹא אֶל־הָאָרֶץ אֲשֶׁר יְהוָה אֱלֹהֶיךָ נֹתֵן
לָךְ וִירִשְׁתָּהּ וְיָשַׁבְתָּה בָּהּ וְאָמַרְתָּ אָשִׂימָה עָלַי
מֶלֶךְ כְּכָל־הַגּוֹיִם אֲשֶׁר סְבִיבֹתָי: 15שׂוֹם תָּשִׂים
עָלֶיךָ מֶלֶךְ אֲשֶׁר יִבְחַר יְהוָה אֱלֹהֶיךָ בּוֹ מִקֶּרֶב
אַחֶיךָ תָּשִׂים עָלֶיךָ מֶלֶךְ לֹא תוּכַל לָתֵת עָלֶיךָ
אִישׁ נָכְרִי אֲשֶׁר לֹא־אָחִיךָ הוּא: 16רַק לֹא־יַרְבֶּה־
לּוֹ סוּסִים וְלֹא־יָשִׁיב אֶת־הָעָם מִצְרַיְמָה לְמַעַן
הַרְבּוֹת סוּס וַיהוָה אָמַר לָכֶם לֹא תֹסִפוּן לָשׁוּב

17:15. **you *shall* set a king over you**. The Torah permits Israel to have a king if they wish. It is placed in their hands to decide if they want one: "When . . . you'll say, 'Let me set a king over me . . . ,' you *shall* set a king over you." But the king must be chosen by God (see the next comment). Later, Gideon and Samuel will question whether it is right for Israel to have a king, saying that God should be Israel's king (Judg 8:23; 1 Sam 8:6). But they do not base their opposition to monarchy on the Torah. Both Gideon and Samuel are judges and also priests (Judg 8:24–27), and they naturally think of God's will as being properly expressed through priests, and so they see kings as a threat to the order that they know. But the Torah permits the people to have kings if they wish. And so God tells Samuel to give the people a king, even though their wish for a king, in that particular case, involves a rejection of God (1 Sam 8:7,22).

17:15. **whom God will choose**. This means that a prophet must designate the king as chosen by God. Thus Samuel designates Saul and David, Nathan designates Solomon, and Ahijah designates Jeroboam. The stories of the kings of Israel and Judah in the books of Samuel, Kings, and Chronicles convey that kings are acceptable if the people want them, but their power is limited and balanced by the power of prophets. And kings who do not listen to prophets, or who imprison or execute them, do so at their peril.

17:16. **not get himself many horses**. Maintaining forces with a great many horses means the development of a small upper class plus a large class of serfs or servants to support and serve them. This is one of several laws in the Torah that work to counter the development of such a two-tiered feudal system. And so, when King David defeats Hadadezer and captures 1,700 chariots and horsemen, he hamstrings all but a small number of the horses (2 Sam 8:4). Why would he deliberately give up a prize of such tremendous value? Because he is obeying this Law of the King.

17:16. **YHWH has said to you, 'You shall not go back.'** No such words from God are reported prior to this. This may appear to be a problem, but it may simply be that this *is* Moses' report of God's words on this matter.

17And he shall not get himself many wives, so his heart will not turn away. And he shall not get himself very much silver and gold. 18And it will be, when he sits on his kingdom's throne, that he shall write himself a copy of this instruction on a scroll from in front of the Levite priests. 19And it shall be with him, and he shall read it all the days of his life, so that he will learn to fear YHWH, his God, to observe all the words of this instruction and these laws, to do them, 20so his heart will not be elevated above his brothers, and so he will not turn from the commandment, right or left, and so he will extend days over his kingdom, he and his sons, within Israel.

18 1"The Levite priests, all the tribe of Levi, shall not have a portion and legacy with Israel. They shall eat YHWH's offerings by fire and *His* legacy. 2But he shall not have a legacy among his brothers. YHWH: *He* is his legacy, as He spoke to him. 3And this shall be the rule for the priests from the people, from those who make a sacrifice, whether an ox or a sheep: he shall give the shoulder, the cheeks, and the stomach. 4You shall give him the first of your grain, your wine, and your oil, and the first shearing of your sheep. 5Because YHWH, your God, has chosen him from all your tribes to stand to serve in YHWH's name, he and his sons, for all time.

6"And when a Levite will come from one of your gates, from all of Israel, where he lives, then he shall come as much as his soul desires to the

בַּדֶּרֶךְ הַזֶּה עוֹד: 17וְלֹא יַרְבֶּה־לּוֹ נָשִׁים וְלֹא יָסוּר לְבָבוֹ וְכֶסֶף וְזָהָב לֹא יַרְבֶּה־לּוֹ מְאֹד: 18וְהָיָה כְשִׁבְתּוֹ עַל כִּסֵּא מַמְלַכְתּוֹ וְכָתַב לוֹ אֶת־מִשְׁנֵה הַתּוֹרָה הַזֹּאת עַל־סֵפֶר מִלִּפְנֵי הַכֹּהֲנִים הַלְוִיִּם: 19וְהָיְתָה עִמּוֹ וְקָרָא בוֹ כָּל־יְמֵי חַיָּיו לְמַעַן יִלְמַד לְיִרְאָה אֶת־יְהוָה אֱלֹהָיו לִשְׁמֹר אֶת־כָּל־דִּבְרֵי הַתּוֹרָה הַזֹּאת וְאֶת־הַחֻקִּים הָאֵלֶּה לַעֲשֹׂתָם: 20לְבִלְתִּי רוּם־לְבָבוֹ מֵאֶחָיו וּלְבִלְתִּי סוּר מִן הַמִּצְוָה יָמִין וּשְׂמֹאול לְמַעַן יַאֲרִיךְ יָמִים עַל־מַמְלַכְתּוֹ הוּא וּבָנָיו בְּקֶרֶב יִשְׂרָאֵל: ס

18 1לֹא־יִהְיֶה לַכֹּהֲנִים הַלְוִיִּם כָּל־שֵׁבֶט לֵוִי חֵלֶק וְנַחֲלָה עִם־יִשְׂרָאֵל אִשֵּׁי יְהוָה וְנַחֲלָתוֹ יֹאכֵלוּן: 2וְנַחֲלָה לֹא־יִהְיֶה־לּוֹ בְּקֶרֶב אֶחָיו יְהוָה הוּא נַחֲלָתוֹ כַּאֲשֶׁר דִּבֶּר־לוֹ: ס 3וְזֶה יִהְיֶה מִשְׁפַּט הַכֹּהֲנִים מֵאֵת הָעָם מֵאֵת זֹבְחֵי הַזֶּבַח אִם־שׁוֹר אִם־שֶׂה וְנָתַן לַכֹּהֵן הַזְּרֹעַ וְהַלְּחָיַיִם וְהַקֵּבָה: 4רֵאשִׁית דְּגָנְךָ תִּירֹשְׁךָ וְיִצְהָרֶךָ וְרֵאשִׁית גֵּז צֹאנְךָ תִּתֶּן־לּוֹ: 5כִּי בוֹ בָּחַר יְהוָה אֱלֹהֶיךָ מִכָּל־שְׁבָטֶיךָ לַעֲמֹד לְשָׁרֵת בְּשֵׁם־יְהוָה הוּא וּבָנָיו כָּל־הַיָּמִים: ס 6וְכִי־יָבֹא הַלֵּוִי מֵאַחַד שְׁעָרֶיךָ מִכָּל־יִשְׂרָאֵל אֲשֶׁר־הוּא גָּר שָׁם וּבָא בְּכָל־אַוַּת נַפְשׁוֹ אֶל־הַמָּקוֹם

17:18. a copy of this instruction. It is unclear whether this means a copy of this Law of the King or a copy of the full law code of Deuteronomy in which it is now contained. In either case, this means that Israel has a constitutional monarchy. Baruch Halpern has shown substantial evidence that Israel's kings were bound by this Law of the King from the time of the first king, Saul (Halpern, *The Constitution of the Monarchy in Israel*). That means that Israel was historically a constitutional monarchy, with a written constitution, more than a thousand years B.C.E.

17:18. a copy . . . from in front of the Levite priests. That is, the Levites have the text of the law, and the king makes himself a copy from the text that they have before them.

place that YHWH will choose 7and serve in the name of YHWH, his God, like all of his Levite brothers who are standing there in front of YHWH. 8They shall eat, portion for portion, aside from his sales of patrimony.

9"When you come to the land that YHWH, your God, is giving you, you shall not learn to do like the offensive things of those nations. 10There shall not be found among you someone who passes his son or his daughter through fire, one who practices enchantment, a soothsayer or a diviner or a sorcerer 11or one who casts spells or who asks of a ghost or of a spirit of an acquaintance or inquires of the dead, 12because everyone who does these is an offensive thing of YHWH, and because of these offensive things YHWH, your God, is dispossessing them from in front of you. 13You shall be unblemished with YHWH, your God, 14because these nations whom you are dispossessing listen to soothsayers and enchanters, but you: YHWH, your God, has not permitted such for you. 15YHWH, your God, will raise up for you a prophet from among you, from your brothers, like me. You shall listen to him—16in accordance with everything that you asked

אֲשֶׁר־יִבְחַר יְהוָה: 7וְשֵׁרֵת בְּשֵׁם יְהוָה אֱלֹהָיו כְּכָל־ אֶחָיו הַלְוִיִּם הָעֹמְדִים שָׁם לִפְנֵי יְהוָה: 8חֵלֶק כְּחֵלֶק יֹאכֵלוּ לְבַד מִמְכָּרָיו עַל־הָאָבוֹת: ס

9כִּי אַתָּה בָּא אֶל־הָאָרֶץ אֲשֶׁר־יְהוָה אֱלֹהֶיךָ נֹתֵן לָךְ לֹא־תִלְמַד לַעֲשׂוֹת כְּתוֹעֲבֹת הַגּוֹיִם הָהֵם: 10לֹא־יִמָּצֵא בְךָ מַעֲבִיר בְּנוֹ־וּבִתּוֹ בָּאֵשׁ קֹסֵם קְסָמִים מְעוֹנֵן וּמְנַחֵשׁ וּמְכַשֵּׁף: 11וְחֹבֵר חָבֶר וְשֹׁאֵל אוֹב וְיִדְּעֹנִי וְדֹרֵשׁ אֶל־הַמֵּתִים: 12כִּי־תוֹעֲבַת יְהוָה כָּל־עֹשֵׂה אֵלֶּה וּבִגְלַל הַתּוֹעֵבֹת הָאֵלֶּה יְהוָה אֱלֹהֶיךָ מוֹרִישׁ אוֹתָם מִפָּנֶיךָ: 13תָּמִים תִּהְיֶה עִם יְהוָה אֱלֹהֶיךָ: ס 14כִּי הַגּוֹיִם הָאֵלֶּה אֲשֶׁר אַתָּה יוֹרֵשׁ אוֹתָם אֶל־מְעֹנְנִים וְאֶל־קֹסְמִים יִשְׁמָעוּ וְאַתָּה לֹא כֵן נָתַן לְךָ יְהוָה אֱלֹהֶיךָ: 15נָבִיא מִקִּרְבְּךָ מֵאַחֶיךָ כָּמֹנִי יָקִים לְךָ יְהוָה אֱלֹהֶיךָ אֵלָיו תִּשְׁמָעוּן: 16כְּכֹל אֲשֶׁר־שָׁאַלְתָּ מֵעִם יְהוָה אֱלֹהֶיךָ

18:8. **portion for portion.** Any Levite who comes to serve at the central place of worship is supposed to receive the same share of the priestly food as every other Levite. And this share is not affected by whether he has any other income from family property, i.e., "from his sales of patrimony."

18:13. **unblemished.** This word is the mark of the recipients of the first two covenants with God. It is the word that is used to describe the merit of Noah; and God tells Abraham to be unblemished as well in the opening words of the covenant (Gen 6:9; 17:1). (The only other person in the *Tanak* to be described by these words is Job.) Now *all* the people of Israel are recipients of the third covenant, and so all of them are instructed to be like Noah and Abraham. They may receive the covenant initially on the merit of Abraham, but they must maintain it on their own integrity.

18:15,18. **God will raise up a prophet like me.** But the end of the Torah says: "A prophet did *not* rise again in Israel like Moses" (Deut 34:10)! Still, this need not be a contradiction. The context of the passage here in Deuteronomy 18 is that Israel should not listen to soothsayers and enchanters, but only to a prophet from God, a "prophet like me." Moses reminds the people that this is what they asked for at Sinai: that they not hear God's voice directly anymore, but that they hear from God only through prophets. The passage at the end of the Torah visibly means that no other prophet was

from YHWH, your God, at Horeb in the day of the assembly, saying, 'Let me not continue to hear the voice of YHWH, my God, and let me not see this big fire anymore, so I won't die!'

¹⁷"And YHWH said to me, 'They've been good in what they've spoken. ¹⁸I'll raise up a prophet for them from among their brothers, like you, and I'll put my words in his mouth, and he'll speak to them everything that I'll command him. ¹⁹And it will be: the man who won't listen to my words that he'll speak in my name, *I* shall require it from him! ²⁰Just: the prophet who will presume to speak a thing in my name that I didn't command him to speak, and who will speak in the name of other gods—that prophet shall die.'

²¹"And if you'll say in your heart, 'How shall we know the thing, that YHWH didn't speak it?!'— ²²when the prophet will speak in YHWH's name, and the thing won't be and won't come to pass: that is the thing that YHWH did *not* say. The prophet spoke it presumptuously. You shall not be fearful of him.

19 ¹"When YHWH, your God, will cut off the nations whose land YHWH, your God, is giving you, and you'll dispossess them and live in their cities and in their houses, ²you shall distinguish three cities within your land that YHWH, your God, is giving you to take pos-

בְּחֹרֵב בְּיוֹם הַקָּהָל לֵאמֹר לֹא אֹסֵף לִשְׁמֹעַ אֶת־קוֹל יְהוָה אֱלֹהָי וְאֶת־הָאֵשׁ הַגְּדֹלָה הַזֹּאת לֹא־אֶרְאֶה עוֹד וְלֹא אָמוּת: ¹⁷וַיֹּאמֶר יְהוָה אֵלָי הֵיטִיבוּ אֲשֶׁר דִּבֵּרוּ: ¹⁸נָבִיא אָקִים לָהֶם מִקֶּרֶב אֲחֵיהֶם כָּמוֹךָ וְנָתַתִּי דְבָרַי בְּפִיו וְדִבֶּר אֲלֵיהֶם אֵת כָּל־אֲשֶׁר אֲצַוֶּנּוּ: ¹⁹וְהָיָה הָאִישׁ אֲשֶׁר לֹא־יִשְׁמַע אֶל־דְּבָרַי אֲשֶׁר יְדַבֵּר בִּשְׁמִי אָנֹכִי אֶדְרֹשׁ מֵעִמּוֹ: ²⁰אַךְ הַנָּבִיא אֲשֶׁר יָזִיד לְדַבֵּר דָּבָר בִּשְׁמִי אֵת אֲשֶׁר לֹא־צִוִּיתִיו לְדַבֵּר וַאֲשֶׁר יְדַבֵּר בְּשֵׁם אֱלֹהִים אֲחֵרִים וּמֵת הַנָּבִיא הַהוּא: ²¹וְכִי תֹאמַר בִּלְבָבֶךָ אֵיכָה נֵדַע אֶת־הַדָּבָר אֲשֶׁר לֹא־דִבְּרוֹ יְהוָה: ²²אֲשֶׁר יְדַבֵּר הַנָּבִיא בְּשֵׁם יְהוָה וְלֹא־יִהְיֶה הַדָּבָר וְלֹא יָבוֹא הוּא הַדָּבָר אֲשֶׁר לֹא־דִבְּרוֹ יְהוָה בְּזָדוֹן דִּבְּרוֹ הַנָּבִיא לֹא תָגוּר מִמֶּנּוּ: ס

19 ¹כִּי־יַכְרִית יְהוָה אֱלֹהֶיךָ אֶת־הַגּוֹיִם אֲשֶׁר יְהוָה אֱלֹהֶיךָ נֹתֵן לְךָ אֶת־אַרְצָם וִירִשְׁתָּם וְיָשַׁבְתָּ בְעָרֵיהֶם וּבְבָתֵּיהֶם: ²שָׁלוֹשׁ עָרִים תַּבְדִּיל לָךְ בְּתוֹךְ אַרְצֶךָ אֲשֶׁר יְהוָה אֱלֹהֶיךָ נֹתֵן לְךָ לְרִשְׁתָּהּ:

as great as Moses. It is simply a linguistic matter: the range of the expression "to be like someone" is wide enough to have these two meanings (and several more).

18:21. **How shall we know.** It is one of the Bible's central and most difficult questions: How does one tell a true prophet from a false one? Moses tells the people that the way to tell a false prophet is by seeing whether his prophecy comes true or not. But that is a little late, is it not? The question was how to know *at the time of the prophecy* whether it is from God. Moses' instruction appears to mean that one should go by the prophet's past record. Even then, people's inclination seems to be to disbelieve the true prophets. Even after Jeremiah's prophecies of Jerusalem's fall come to pass (and the prophecies of those who oppose him fail), as soon as he gives a prophecy that the people do not like they say, "You're speaking a lie. YHWH hasn't sent you" (Jer 43:2)! So Moses' criterion for identifying false prophets may seem simple and obvious, but the psychological point is that people miss the obvious and turn instead to the comfortable.

session of it. ³You shall prepare the way and divide the border of your land that YHWH, your God, will give you as a legacy into three sections, and it will be for any murderer to flee there. ⁴And this is the case of the manslayer who will flee there and live: one who will strike his neighbor without knowing, when he did not hate him from the day before yesterday; ⁵and one who will come with his neighbor into the forest to cut down trees, and his hand will be moved with the axe to cut down the tree, and the axe head will come off the wood and find his neighbor, and he dies. He shall flee to one of these cities and live. ⁶In case an avenger of blood will pursue the manslayer when his heart will be hot and will catch up to him because the way will be long, and he'll strike him mortally though he does not have a sentence of death, because he did not hate him from the day before yesterday, ⁷on account of this I command you, saying, 'You shall distinguish three cities.' ⁸And if YHWH, your God, will widen your border as He swore to your fathers and will give you all the land that He spoke to give to your fathers, ⁹when you'll observe all of this commandment to do it, that which I command you today, to love YHWH, your God, and to go in His ways every day, then you shall add three more cities to these three. ¹⁰So innocent blood will not be spilled within your land that YHWH, your God, is giving you as a legacy, and blood would be on you.

¹¹"But if there will be a man who hates his neighbor and will lie in wait for him and get up against him and strike him mortally, and he dies, and he will flee to one of these cities, ¹²then his city's elders shall send and take him from there and put him in the hand of the avenger of blood, so he will die. ¹³Your eye shall not pity him. And you shall burn away the innocent blood from Israel, and it will be well with you.

³תָּכִין לְךָ֨ הַדֶּ֗רֶךְ וְשִׁלַּשְׁתָּ֙ אֶת־גְּב֣וּל אַרְצְךָ֔ אֲשֶׁ֥ר יַנְחִֽילְךָ֖ יְהֹוָ֣ה אֱלֹהֶ֑יךָ וְהָיָ֕ה לָנ֥וּס שָׁ֖מָּה כָּל־רֹצֵֽחַ: ⁴וְזֶה֙ דְּבַ֣ר הָרֹצֵ֔חַ אֲשֶׁר־יָנ֥וּס שָׁ֖מָּה וָחָ֑י אֲשֶׁ֨ר יַכֶּ֤ה אֶת־רֵעֵ֙הוּ֙ בִּבְלִי־דַ֔עַת וְה֛וּא לֹא־שֹׂנֵ֥א ל֖וֹ מִתְּמֹ֥ל שִׁלְשֹֽׁם: ⁵וַאֲשֶׁר֩ יָבֹ֨א אֶת־רֵעֵ֥הוּ בַיַּעַר֮ לַחְטֹ֣ב עֵצִים֒ וְנִדְּחָ֨ה יָד֤וֹ בַגַּרְזֶן֙ לִכְרֹ֣ת הָעֵ֔ץ וְנָשַׁ֤ל הַבַּרְזֶל֙ מִן־הָעֵ֔ץ וּמָצָ֥א אֶת־רֵעֵ֖הוּ וָמֵ֑ת ה֗וּא יָנ֛וּס אֶל־אַחַ֥ת הֶעָרִים־הָאֵ֖לֶּה וָחָֽי: ⁶פֶּן־יִרְדֹּף֩ גֹּאֵ֨ל הַדָּ֜ם אַחֲרֵ֣י הָרֹצֵ֗חַ כִּֽי־יֵחַם֮ לְבָבוֹ֒ וְהִשִּׂיג֛וֹ כִּֽי־יִרְבֶּ֥ה הַדֶּ֖רֶךְ וְהִכָּ֣הוּ נָ֑פֶשׁ וְלוֹ֙ אֵ֣ין מִשְׁפַּט־מָ֔וֶת כִּ֠י לֹ֣א שֹׂנֵ֥א ה֛וּא ל֖וֹ מִתְּמ֥וֹל שִׁלְשֽׁוֹם: ⁷עַל־כֵּ֛ן אָנֹכִ֥י מְצַוְּךָ֖ לֵאמֹ֑ר שָׁלֹ֥שׁ עָרִ֖ים תַּבְדִּ֥יל לָֽךְ: ס ⁸וְאִם־יַרְחִ֞יב יְהֹוָ֤ה אֱלֹהֶ֙יךָ֙ אֶת־גְּבֻ֣לְךָ֔ כַּאֲשֶׁ֥ר נִשְׁבַּ֖ע לַאֲבֹתֶ֑יךָ וְנָ֤תַן לְךָ֙ אֶת־כָּל־הָאָ֔רֶץ אֲשֶׁ֥ר דִּבֶּ֖ר לָתֵ֥ת לַאֲבֹתֶֽיךָ: ⁹כִּֽי־תִשְׁמֹר֩ אֶת־כָּל־הַמִּצְוָ֨ה הַזֹּ֜את לַעֲשֹׂתָ֗הּ אֲשֶׁ֨ר אָנֹכִ֣י מְצַוְּךָ֮ הַיּוֹם֒ לְאַהֲבָ֞ה אֶת־יְהֹוָ֧ה אֱלֹהֶ֛יךָ וְלָלֶ֥כֶת בִּדְרָכָ֖יו כָּל־הַיָּמִ֑ים וְיָסַפְתָּ֨ לְךָ֥ עוֹד֙ שָׁלֹ֣שׁ עָרִ֔ים עַ֖ל הַשָּׁלֹ֥שׁ הָאֵֽלֶּה: ¹⁰וְלֹ֤א יִשָּׁפֵךְ֙ דָּ֣ם נָקִ֔י בְּקֶ֣רֶב אַרְצְךָ֔ אֲשֶׁר֙ יְהֹוָ֣ה אֱלֹהֶ֔יךָ נֹתֵ֥ן לְךָ֖ נַחֲלָ֑ה וְהָיָ֥ה עָלֶ֖יךָ דָּמִֽים: ס ¹¹וְכִֽי־יִהְיֶ֥ה אִישׁ֙ שֹׂנֵ֣א לְרֵעֵ֔הוּ וְאָ֤רַב לוֹ֙ וְקָ֣ם עָלָ֔יו וְהִכָּ֥הוּ נֶ֖פֶשׁ וָמֵ֑ת וְנָ֕ס אֶל־אַחַ֖ת הֶעָרִ֥ים הָאֵֽל: ¹²וְשָֽׁלְחוּ֙ זִקְנֵ֣י עִיר֔וֹ וְלָקְח֥וּ אֹת֖וֹ מִשָּׁ֑ם וְנָתְנ֣וּ אֹת֔וֹ בְּיַ֛ד גֹּאֵ֥ל הַדָּ֖ם וָמֵֽת: ¹³לֹא־תָח֥וֹס עֵֽינְךָ֖ עָלָ֑יו וּבִֽעַרְתָּ֧ דַֽם־הַנָּקִ֛י מִיִּשְׂרָאֵ֖ל וְט֥וֹב לָֽךְ: ס

19:4. from the day before yesterday. Meaning: he had no prior malice toward the person whom he killed.

19:10. blood would be on you. Meaning: you would incur guilt for spilled blood.

14"You shall not move your neighbor's landmark that the first ones set, in your legacy that you will have in the land that YHWH, your God, is giving you to take possession of it.

15"One witness shall not get up against a man for any crime or for any sin, in any sin that one will commit. On the word of two witnesses or on the word of three witnesses a case shall stand up. 16If a malicious witness will get up against a man to testify a misrepresentation against him, 17and the two people who have the dispute shall stand in front of YHWH, in front of the priests and the judges who will be in those days, 18and the judges will inquire well, and, here, the witness is a lying witness, he testified a lie against his brother, 19then you shall do to him as he schemed to do to his brother. So you shall burn away what is bad from among you. 20And those who remain will listen and fear and won't continue to do anything like this bad thing anymore among you. 21And your eye shall not pity: life for life, eye for eye, tooth for tooth, hand for hand, foot for foot.

14לֹ֤א תַסִּיג֙ גְּב֣וּל רֵֽעֲךָ֔ אֲשֶׁ֥ר גָּבְל֖וּ רִאשֹׁנִ֑ים בְּנַחֲלָֽתְךָ֙ אֲשֶׁ֣ר תִּנְחַ֔ל בָּאָ֕רֶץ אֲשֶׁר֙ יְהוָ֣ה אֱלֹהֶ֔יךָ נֹתֵ֥ן לְךָ֖ לְרִשְׁתָּֽהּ׃ ס 15לֹא־יָק֩וּם עֵ֨ד אֶחָ֜ד בְּאִ֗ישׁ לְכָל־עָוֹן֙ וּלְכָל־חַטָּ֔את בְּכָל־חֵ֖טְא אֲשֶׁ֣ר יֶֽחֱטָ֑א עַל־פִּ֣י ׀ שְׁנֵ֣י עֵדִ֗ים א֛וֹ עַל־פִּ֥י שְׁלֹשָֽׁה־עֵדִ֖ים יָק֥וּם דָּבָֽר׃ 16כִּֽי־יָק֥וּם עֵד־חָמָ֖ס בְּאִ֑ישׁ לַעֲנ֥וֹת בּ֖וֹ סָרָֽה׃ 17וְעָמְד֧וּ שְׁנֵֽי־הָאֲנָשִׁ֛ים אֲשֶׁר־לָהֶ֥ם הָרִ֖יב לִפְנֵ֣י יְהוָ֑ה לִפְנֵ֤י הַכֹּֽהֲנִים֙ וְהַשֹּׁ֣פְטִ֔ים אֲשֶׁ֥ר יִהְי֖וּ בַּיָּמִ֥ים הָהֵֽם׃ 18וְדָרְשׁ֥וּ הַשֹּׁפְטִ֖ים הֵיטֵ֑ב וְהִנֵּ֤ה עֵֽד־שֶׁ֨קֶר֙ הָעֵ֔ד שֶׁ֖קֶר עָנָ֥ה בְאָחִֽיו׃ 19וַעֲשִׂ֣יתֶם ל֔וֹ כַּאֲשֶׁ֥ר זָמַ֖ם לַעֲשׂ֣וֹת לְאָחִ֑יו וּבִֽעַרְתָּ֥ הָרָ֖ע מִקִּרְבֶּֽךָ׃ 20וְהַנִּשְׁאָרִ֖ים יִשְׁמְע֣וּ וְיִרָ֑אוּ וְלֹֽא־יֹסִ֨פוּ לַעֲשׂ֜וֹת ע֗וֹד כַּדָּבָ֥ר הָרָ֛ע הַזֶּ֖ה בְּקִרְבֶּֽךָ׃ 21וְלֹ֥א תָח֖וֹס עֵינֶ֑ךָ נֶ֣פֶשׁ בְּנֶ֗פֶשׁ עַ֤יִן בְּעַ֨יִן֙ שֵׁ֣ן בְּשֵׁ֔ן יָ֣ד בְּיָ֔ד רֶ֖גֶל בְּרָֽגֶל׃ ס

19:14. **your legacy that you will have in the land**. This chapter gives laws protecting lives and property, which will apply once the people arrive in the land. Most of the Torah thus looks toward the well-being of the land from outside it. Only about 29 of the Torah's 187 chapters take place in the promised land. Moses never sets foot in the land. And the phrase "Land of Israel" never occurs in the Torah. (The land acquires this name only after the people of Israel have settled there. It first occurs in 1 Sam 13:19.) Yet the Torah's story is focused on and directed toward Israel constantly. It is the promise of the covenant with Abraham. The promise is renewed to Isaac and Jacob. Jacob's body is returned from Egypt to be buried there. Joseph asks to be taken back for burial there someday as well. And almost the entire content of Exodus through Numbers is the story of the people's liberation and journey home. The Torah thus already relates to the experience of the Jewish people in the postbiblical world: For the last two millennia most of the Jews have lived outside the promised land. They have lived all over the world and have been good citizens of the countries where they settled while having affection for the land of Israel, a consciousness of their origin there, and a desire to contribute to it, travel there, and seek its well-being.

19:21. **life for life, eye for eye, tooth for tooth**. See the comments on Exod 21:23 and Lev 24:20.

20 ¹"When you'll go out to war against your enemies, and you'll see horses and chariots, a people more numerous than you, you shall not fear them, because YHWH, your God, is with you, who brought you up from the land of Egypt. ²And it will be, when you approach the war, that the priest shall go over and speak to the people. ³And he shall say to them, 'Listen, Israel, you're approaching war against your enemies today. Let your heart not be weak. Don't be afraid and don't panic and don't be scared in front of them, ⁴because YHWH, your God, is the one going with you to fight for you with your enemies, to save you.'

⁵"And the officers shall speak to the people, saying, 'Who is a man who has built a new house and has not dedicated it? Let him go, and let him go back to his house, in case he would die in the war and another man would dedicate it. ⁶And who is a man who has planted a vineyard and has not desanctified it? Let him go, and let him go back to his house, in case he would die in the war and another man would desanctify it. ⁷And who is a man who has betrothed a woman and has not taken her? Let him go, and let him go back to his house, in case he would die in the war and another man would take her.' ⁸And the officers shall continue to speak to the people and shall say, 'Who is a man who is afraid and weakhearted? Let him go, and go back to his house, so he won't melt his brothers' heart like his heart.' ⁹And it will be, when the officers finish speaking to the people, that they shall appoint officers of the armies at the head of the people.

¹⁰"When you'll approach a city to fight against it, then you shall call to it for peace. ¹¹And it will be, if it will answer you with peace and open up to you, then it will be that all the people who are

כִּי־תֵצֵא לַמִּלְחָמָה עַל־אֹיְבֶ֗ךָ וְרָאִ֜יתָ ס֣וּס 20 ¹ וָרֶ֗כֶב עַ֚ם רַ֣ב מִמְּךָ֔ לֹ֥א תִירָ֖א מֵהֶ֑ם כִּֽי־יְהוָ֣ה אֱלֹהֶ֔יךָ עִמָּ֔ךְ הַמַּעַלְךָ֖ מֵאֶ֥רֶץ מִצְרָֽיִם: ²וְהָיָ֕ה כְּקָרָבְכֶ֖ם אֶל־הַמִּלְחָמָ֑ה וְנִגַּ֥שׁ הַכֹּהֵ֖ן וְדִבֶּ֥ר אֶל־ הָעָֽם: ³וְאָמַ֣ר אֲלֵהֶ֗ם שְׁמַ֣ע יִשְׂרָאֵ֔ל אַתֶּ֨ם קְרֵבִ֥ים הַיּ֛וֹם לַמִּלְחָמָ֖ה עַל־אֹיְבֵיכֶ֑ם אַל־יֵרַ֣ךְ לְבַבְכֶ֔ם אַל־ תִּֽירְא֧וּ וְאַֽל־תַּחְפְּז֛וּ וְאַֽל־תַּֽעַרְצ֖וּ מִפְּנֵיהֶֽם: ⁴כִּ֚י יְהוָ֣ה אֱלֹֽהֵיכֶ֔ם הַהֹלֵ֖ךְ עִמָּכֶ֑ם לְהִלָּחֵ֥ם לָכֶ֛ם עִם־ אֹיְבֵיכֶ֖ם לְהוֹשִׁ֥יעַ אֶתְכֶֽם: ⁵וְדִבְּר֣וּ הַשֹּֽׁטְרִים֮ אֶל־ הָעָ֣ם לֵאמֹר֒ מִֽי־הָאִ֞ישׁ אֲשֶׁ֨ר בָּנָ֤ה בַֽיִת־חָדָשׁ֙ וְלֹ֣א חֲנָכ֔וֹ יֵלֵ֖ךְ וְיָשֹׁ֣ב לְבֵית֑וֹ פֶּן־יָמוּת֙ בַּמִּלְחָמָ֔ה וְאִ֥ישׁ אַחֵ֖ר יַחְנְכֶֽנּוּ: ⁶וּמִֽי־הָאִ֞ישׁ אֲשֶׁ֨ר נָטַ֥ע כֶּ֙רֶם֙ וְלֹ֣א חִלְּל֔וֹ יֵלֵ֖ךְ וְיָשֹׁ֣ב לְבֵית֑וֹ פֶּן־יָמוּת֙ בַּמִּלְחָמָ֔ה וְאִ֥ישׁ אַחֵ֖ר יְחַלְּלֶֽנּוּ: ⁷וּמִֽי־הָאִ֞ישׁ אֲשֶׁר־אֵרַ֤שׂ אִשָּׁה֙ וְלֹ֣א לְקָחָ֔הּ יֵלֵ֖ךְ וְיָשֹׁ֣ב לְבֵית֑וֹ פֶּן־יָמוּת֙ בַּמִּלְחָמָ֔ה וְאִ֥ישׁ אַחֵ֖ר יִקָּחֶֽנָּה: ⁸וְיָסְפ֣וּ הַשֹּֽׁטְרִים֮ לְדַבֵּ֣ר אֶל־הָעָם֒ וְאָמְר֗וּ מִֽי־הָאִ֤ישׁ הַיָּרֵא֙ וְרַ֣ךְ הַלֵּבָ֔ב יֵלֵ֖ךְ וְיָשֹׁ֣ב לְבֵית֑וֹ וְלֹ֥א יִמַּ֛ס אֶת־לְבַ֥ב אֶחָ֖יו כִּלְבָבֽוֹ: ⁹וְהָיָ֛ה כְּכַלֹּ֥ת הַשֹּֽׁטְרִ֖ים לְדַבֵּ֣ר אֶל־הָעָ֑ם וּפָֽקְד֛וּ שָׂרֵ֥י צְבָא֖וֹת בְּרֹ֥אשׁ הָעָֽם: ס ¹⁰כִּֽי־תִקְרַ֣ב אֶל־עִ֔יר לְהִלָּחֵ֖ם עָלֶ֑יהָ וְקָרָ֥אתָ אֵלֶ֖יהָ לְשָׁלֽוֹם: ¹¹וְהָיָה֙ אִם־ שָׁל֣וֹם תַּֽעַנְ֔ךָ וּפָֽתְחָ֖ה לָ֑ךְ וְהָיָ֗ה כָּל־הָעָ֤ם הַנִּמְצָא

20:6. **desanctified.** This may relate to a law such as that in Lev 19:23–25, whereby a newly planted tree goes through a period during which its fruit may not be eaten, followed by a period of being holy ("all of its fruit shall be holy"), and then a third period in which its period of sanctification ends and one may eat it. In the present context, then, it would refer to a man who has planted a vineyard but has not yet eaten any of its fruit.

found in it shall become yours for a work-company and shall serve you. 12And if it will not make peace with you, but it will make war with you, then you shall besiege it. 13And YHWH, your God, will put it in your hand, and you shall strike all its males by the sword. 14Only, you shall take as spoil the women and the infants and the animals and everything that will be in the city, all its spoil, and you shall eat your enemies' spoil that YHWH, your God, has given you. 15That is what you shall do to all the cities that are very distant from you, those that are not from these nations' cities. 16Only from these peoples' cities that YHWH, your God, is giving you as a legacy shall you not let any soul live. 17But you shall *completely* destroy them—the Hittite and the Amorite, the Canaanite and the Perizzite, the Hivite and the Jebusite—as YHWH, your God, has commanded you, 18so they won't teach you to do things like all their offensive things that they did for their gods, and you'll sin to YHWH, your God.

19"When you'll besiege a city many days, fighting against it to capture it, you shall not destroy a tree of it, moving an axe at it, because you'll eat from it, so you shall not cut it down; because is a tree of the field a human, to go from in front of you in a siege?! 20Only a tree that you'll know that it isn't a tree for eating: that one you may destroy and cut down so you may build a siegework against the city that is making war with you until its fall.

21 1"If a corpse will be found in the land that YHWH, your God, is giving you to take possession of it, fallen in the field, unknown who struck him, 2then your elders and your judges shall go out and measure to the cities that are around the corpse. 3And it will be, the closest city to the corpse: that city's elders shall take a heifer that has not been worked with, that has not pulled in a yoke. 4And that city's elders shall take the heifer down to a strongly flowing wadi that would not be worked with and would not be seeded, and they shall break the heifer's neck

בָּהּ יִהְיוּ לְךָ לָמַס וַעֲבָדוּךָ: 12וְאִם־לֹא תַשְׁלִים עִמָּךְ וְעָשְׂתָה עִמְּךָ מִלְחָמָה וְצַרְתָּ עָלֶיהָ: 13וּנְתָנָהּ יְהוָה אֱלֹהֶיךָ בְּיָדֶךָ וְהִכִּיתָ אֶת־כָּל־זְכוּרָהּ לְפִי־חָרֶב: 14רַק הַנָּשִׁים וְהַטַּף וְהַבְּהֵמָה וְכֹל אֲשֶׁר יִהְיֶה בָעִיר כָּל־שְׁלָלָהּ תָּבֹז לָךְ וְאָכַלְתָּ אֶת־שְׁלַל אֹיְבֶיךָ אֲשֶׁר נָתַן יְהוָה אֱלֹהֶיךָ לָךְ: 15כֵּן תַּעֲשֶׂה לְכָל־הֶעָרִים הָרְחֹקֹת מִמְּךָ מְאֹד אֲשֶׁר לֹא־מֵעָרֵי הַגּוֹיִם־הָאֵלֶּה הֵנָּה: 16רַק מֵעָרֵי הָעַמִּים הָאֵלֶּה אֲשֶׁר יְהוָה אֱלֹהֶיךָ נֹתֵן לְךָ נַחֲלָה לֹא תְחַיֶּה כָּל־נְשָׁמָה: 17כִּי־הַחֲרֵם תַּחֲרִימֵם הַחִתִּי וְהָאֱמֹרִי הַכְּנַעֲנִי וְהַפְּרִזִּי הַחִוִּי וְהַיְבוּסִי כַּאֲשֶׁר צִוְּךָ יְהוָה אֱלֹהֶיךָ: 18לְמַעַן אֲשֶׁר לֹא־יְלַמְּדוּ אֶתְכֶם לַעֲשׂוֹת כְּכֹל תּוֹעֲבֹתָם אֲשֶׁר עָשׂוּ לֵאלֹהֵיהֶם וַחֲטָאתֶם לַיהוָה אֱלֹהֵיכֶם: ס 19כִּי־תָצוּר אֶל־עִיר יָמִים רַבִּים לְהִלָּחֵם עָלֶיהָ לְתָפְשָׂהּ לֹא־תַשְׁחִית אֶת־עֵצָהּ לִנְדֹּחַ עָלָיו גַּרְזֶן כִּי מִמֶּנּוּ תֹאכֵל וְאֹתוֹ לֹא תִכְרֹת כִּי הָאָדָם עֵץ הַשָּׂדֶה לָבֹא מִפָּנֶיךָ בַּמָּצוֹר: 20רַק עֵץ אֲשֶׁר־תֵּדַע כִּי־לֹא־עֵץ מַאֲכָל הוּא אֹתוֹ תַשְׁחִית וְכָרָתָּ וּבָנִיתָ מָצוֹר עַל־הָעִיר אֲשֶׁר־הִוא עֹשָׂה עִמְּךָ מִלְחָמָה עַד רִדְתָּהּ: פ

21 1כִּי־יִמָּצֵא חָלָל בָּאֲדָמָה אֲשֶׁר יְהוָה אֱלֹהֶיךָ נֹתֵן לְךָ לְרִשְׁתָּהּ נֹפֵל בַּשָּׂדֶה לֹא נוֹדַע מִי הִכָּהוּ: 2וְיָצְאוּ זְקֵנֶיךָ וְשֹׁפְטֶיךָ וּמָדְדוּ אֶל־הֶעָרִים אֲשֶׁר סְבִיבֹת הֶחָלָל: 3וְהָיָה הָעִיר הַקְּרֹבָה אֶל־הֶחָלָל וְלָקְחוּ זִקְנֵי הָעִיר הַהִוא עֶגְלַת בָּקָר אֲשֶׁר לֹא־עֻבַּד בָּהּ אֲשֶׁר לֹא־מָשְׁכָה בְּעֹל: 4וְהוֹרִדוּ זִקְנֵי הָעִיר הַהִוא אֶת־הָעֶגְלָה אֶל־נַחַל אֵיתָן אֲשֶׁר לֹא־יֵעָבֵד בּוֹ וְלֹא יִזָּרֵעַ וְעָרְפוּ־שָׁם אֶת־הָעֶגְלָה בַּנָּחַל:

there in the wadi. 5And the priests, sons of Levi, shall go over, because YHWH, your God, chose them to serve Him and to bless in YHWH's name, and every dispute and every injury shall be by their word. 6And all of that city's elders, who are close to the corpse, shall wash their hands over the heifer whose neck was broken in the wadi. 7And they shall testify, and they shall say, 'Our hands did not spill this blood, and our eyes did not see it. 8Grant atonement for your people Israel, whom you redeemed, YHWH, and don't impute innocent blood among your people Israel.' And for them the blood will be atoned for. 9So you shall burn away the innocent blood from among you when you will do what is right in YHWH's eyes.

WHEN YOU'LL GO OUT

כי תצא

10"When you'll go out to war against your enemies, and YHWH, your God, will put him in your hand, and you'll take prisoners from him, 11and you'll see among the prisoners a woman with a beautiful figure, and you'll be attracted to her and take her for yourself as a wife, 12then you shall bring her into your house, and she shall shave her head and do her nails 13and take away her prisoner's garment from on her. And she

5וְנִגְּשׁוּ הַכֹּהֲנִים בְּנֵי לֵוִי כִּי בָּם בָּחַר יְהוָה אֱלֹהֶיךָ לְשָׁרְתוֹ וּלְבָרֵךְ בְּשֵׁם יְהוָה וְעַל־פִּיהֶם יִהְיֶה כָּל־רִיב וְכָל־נָגַע: 6וְכֹל זִקְנֵי הָעִיר הַהִוא הַקְּרֹבִים אֶל־הֶחָלָל יִרְחֲצוּ אֶת־יְדֵיהֶם עַל־הָעֶגְלָה הָעֲרוּפָה בַנָּחַל: 7וְעָנוּ וְאָמְרוּ יָדֵינוּ לֹא שָׁפְכָה אֶת־הַדָּם הַזֶּה וְעֵינֵינוּ לֹא רָאוּ: 8כַּפֵּר לְעַמְּךָ יִשְׂרָאֵל אֲשֶׁר־פָּדִיתָ יְהוָה וְאַל־תִּתֵּן דָּם נָקִי בְּקֶרֶב עַמְּךָ יִשְׂרָאֵל וְנִכַּפֵּר לָהֶם הַדָּם: 9וְאַתָּה תְּבַעֵר הַדָּם הַנָּקִי מִקִּרְבֶּךָ כִּי־תַעֲשֶׂה הַיָּשָׁר בְּעֵינֵי יְהוָה: ס

10כִּי־תֵצֵא לַמִּלְחָמָה עַל־אֹיְבֶיךָ וּנְתָנוֹ יְהוָה אֱלֹהֶיךָ בְּיָדֶךָ וְשָׁבִיתָ שִׁבְיוֹ: 11וְרָאִיתָ בַּשִּׁבְיָה אֵשֶׁת יְפַת־תֹּאַר וְחָשַׁקְתָּ בָהּ וְלָקַחְתָּ לְךָ לְאִשָּׁה: 12וַהֲבֵאתָהּ אֶל־תּוֹךְ בֵּיתֶךָ וְגִלְּחָה אֶת־רֹאשָׁהּ וְעָשְׂתָה אֶת־צִפָּרְנֶיהָ: 13וְהֵסִירָה אֶת־שִׂמְלַת שִׁבְיָהּ מֵעָלֶיהָ

21:7 ק שָׁפְכוּ

21:11. **a woman among the prisoners.** A number of this law's details have never been explained definitively. Some would say she cuts her hair and nails so as to be less attractive, so that the man who is attracted to her will become less infatuated. Some would say it is part of her mourning. But what pervades the elements of the law is an extraordinary sensitivity to the humanity of a captured woman. Contrary to one of the most common practices of war, the Israelite soldier is not permitted to rape her. He may take her as a wife. But even then he must give her time to mourn the loss of her family. And if he takes her as a wife but then rejects her, he must let her go completely free. The text uses the same verb as in the law of divorce (Deut 24:1). And the text recognizes that he has degraded her, and so he cannot treat her like a slave to be sold; he cannot receive money for her from anyone else. Notably, the words for degrading her and for letting her go are the same words that are used to describe the Egyptians' degrading of Israel and then letting Israel go (Exod 1:11–12; 5:1). Again Israel learns from its experience of enslavement. Israel not only celebrates its own release, but it learns to have compassion for others as well.

shall live in your house and shall mourn her father and her mother a month of days. And after that you may come to her and marry her, and she shall become your wife. 14And it will be, if you don't desire her then you shall let her go on her own, and you shall not *sell* her for money. You shall not get profit through her, because you degraded her.

15"When a man will have two wives, one loved and one hated, and they'll give birth to children for him, the loved and the hated, and the hated will have the firstborn son, 16then it will be, on the day that he gives what he has as a legacy to his children, he shall not be able to give a son of the loved one the birthright before the firstborn son of the hated one. 17But he shall recognize the firstborn son of the hated one, to give him a double portion of all that he has, because he is the beginning of his might. The legal due of the firstborn is his.

18"When a man will have a stubborn and rebellious son, not listening to his father's voice and his mother's voice, and they will discipline him, but he will not listen to them, 19then his father and his mother shall take hold of him and bring him out to his city's elders and to the gate of his place. 20And they shall say to his city's elders, 'This son of ours is stubborn and rebellious, he doesn't listen to our voice, a glutton, and a drunk.' 21And all his city's people shall batter him with stones so he dies. So you shall burn away what is bad from among you. And all Israel will listen and fear.

וְיָשְׁבָה בְּבֵיתֶךָ וּבָכְתָה אֶת־אָבִיהָ וְאֶת־אִמָּהּ יֶרַח יָמִים וְאַחַר כֵּן תָּבוֹא אֵלֶיהָ וּבְעַלְתָּהּ וְהָיְתָה לְךָ לְאִשָּׁה: 14וְהָיָה אִם־לֹא חָפַצְתָּ בָּהּ וְשִׁלַּחְתָּהּ לְנַפְשָׁהּ וּמָכֹר לֹא־תִמְכְּרֶנָּה בַּכָּסֶף לֹא־תִתְעַמֵּר בָּהּ תַּחַת אֲשֶׁר עִנִּיתָהּ: ס 15כִּי־תִהְיֶיןָ לְאִישׁ שְׁתֵּי נָשִׁים הָאַחַת אֲהוּבָה וְהָאַחַת שְׂנוּאָה וְיָלְדוּ־לוֹ בָנִים הָאֲהוּבָה וְהַשְּׂנוּאָה וְהָיָה הַבֵּן הַבְּכוֹר לַשְּׂנִיאָה: 16וְהָיָה בְּיוֹם הַנְחִילוֹ אֶת־בָּנָיו אֵת אֲשֶׁר־יִהְיֶה לוֹ לֹא יוּכַל לְבַכֵּר אֶת־בֶּן־הָאֲהוּבָה עַל־פְּנֵי בֶן־הַשְּׂנוּאָה הַבְּכֹר: 17כִּי אֶת־הַבְּכֹר בֶּן־הַשְּׂנוּאָה יַכִּיר לָתֶת לוֹ פִּי שְׁנַיִם בְּכֹל אֲשֶׁר־יִמָּצֵא לוֹ כִּי־הוּא רֵאשִׁית אֹנוֹ לוֹ מִשְׁפַּט הַבְּכֹרָה: ס 18כִּי־יִהְיֶה לְאִישׁ בֵּן סוֹרֵר וּמוֹרֶה אֵינֶנּוּ שֹׁמֵעַ בְּקוֹל אָבִיו וּבְקוֹל אִמּוֹ וְיִסְּרוּ אֹתוֹ וְלֹא יִשְׁמַע אֲלֵיהֶם: 19וְתָפְשׂוּ בוֹ אָבִיו וְאִמּוֹ וְהוֹצִיאוּ אֹתוֹ אֶל־זִקְנֵי עִירוֹ וְאֶל־שַׁעַר מְקֹמוֹ: 20וְאָמְרוּ אֶל־זִקְנֵי עִירוֹ בְּנֵנוּ זֶה סוֹרֵר וּמֹרֶה אֵינֶנּוּ שֹׁמֵעַ בְּקֹלֵנוּ זוֹלֵל וְסֹבֵא: 21וּרְגָמֻהוּ כָּל־אַנְשֵׁי עִירוֹ בָאֲבָנִים וָמֵת וּבִעַרְתָּ הָרָע מִקִּרְבֶּךָ וְכָל־יִשְׂרָאֵל יִשְׁמְעוּ וְיִרָאוּ:

21:17. **beginning of his might.** Moses uses the same phrase that Jacob uses to describe Reuben, his firstborn, when he speaks of his sons' legacies (Gen 49:3). Perhaps this was a known expression for firstborn sons, or perhaps we should picture Moses as deliberately bringing Jacob's words to mind. It is ironic because Jacob does in fact take away the double portion from Reuben, who is the son of the less-loved wife, Leah; and he gives it to Joseph, who is the son of the more-loved wife, Rachel (Gen 29:30). It may be that Moses is teaching that the Israelites may not do what Jacob did. Or it may be that Jacob's case demonstrates the point of the law that Moses is giving, since Jacob does not take the birthright away from Reuben because of Reuben's mother, Leah, being less loved. He takes it away because Reuben himself committed an offense, sleeping with his father's concubine (Gen 35:22; 49:4).

22"And if there will be a sin bringing a sentence of death on a man, and he will be put to death, and you will hang him on a tree, 23you shall not leave his corpse on the tree, but you shall *bury* him on that day, because a hanged person is an offense to God, and you shall not make impure your land that YHWH, your God, is giving you as a legacy.

22 1"You shall not see your brother's ox or his sheep driven off, and you hide yourself from them. You shall *bring them back* to your brother. 2And if your brother is not close to you, and you don't know him, then you shall gather it into your house, and it shall be with you until your brother inquires about it, and you shall give it back to him. 3And you shall do that with his ass, and you shall do that with his garment, and you shall do that with any lost thing of your brother's that will be lost by him and you find it. You may not hide yourself. 4You shall not see your brother's ass or his ox falling in the road, and you hide yourself from them. You shall *lift it up* with him.

5"There shall not be a man's item on a woman, and a man shall not wear a woman's garment, because everyone who does these is an offensive thing of YHWH, your God.

6"When a bird's nest will happen to be in front of you on the road in any tree or on the ground—chicks or eggs—and the mother is sitting over the chicks or over the eggs, you shall not take the mother along with the children. 7You shall *let the mother go*, and you may take the children for you, so that it will be good for you, and you will extend days.

ס 22 וְכִי־יִהְיֶה בְאִישׁ חֵטְא מִשְׁפַּט־מָוֶת וְהוּמָת וְתָלִיתָ אֹתוֹ עַל־עֵץ: 23 לֹא־תָלִין נִבְלָתוֹ עַל־הָעֵץ כִּי־קָבוֹר תִּקְבְּרֶנּוּ בַּיּוֹם הַהוּא כִּי־קִלְלַת אֱלֹהִים תָּלוּי וְלֹא תְטַמֵּא אֶת־אַדְמָתְךָ אֲשֶׁר יְהוָה אֱלֹהֶיךָ נֹתֵן לְךָ נַחֲלָה: ס

22 1 לֹא־תִרְאֶה אֶת־שׁוֹר אָחִיךָ אוֹ אֶת־שֵׂיוֹ נִדָּחִים וְהִתְעַלַּמְתָּ מֵהֶם הָשֵׁב תְּשִׁיבֵם לְאָחִיךָ: 2 וְאִם־לֹא קָרוֹב אָחִיךָ אֵלֶיךָ וְלֹא יְדַעְתּוֹ וַאֲסַפְתּוֹ אֶל־תּוֹךְ בֵּיתֶךָ וְהָיָה עִמְּךָ עַד דְּרֹשׁ אָחִיךָ אֹתוֹ וַהֲשֵׁבֹתוֹ לוֹ: 3 וְכֵן תַּעֲשֶׂה לַחֲמֹרוֹ וְכֵן תַּעֲשֶׂה לְשִׂמְלָתוֹ וְכֵן תַּעֲשֶׂה לְכָל־אֲבֵדַת אָחִיךָ אֲשֶׁר־תֹּאבַד מִמֶּנּוּ וּמְצָאתָהּ לֹא תוּכַל לְהִתְעַלֵּם: ס 4 לֹא־תִרְאֶה אֶת־חֲמוֹר אָחִיךָ אוֹ שׁוֹרוֹ נֹפְלִים בַּדֶּרֶךְ וְהִתְעַלַּמְתָּ מֵהֶם הָקֵם תָּקִים עִמּוֹ: ס 5 לֹא־יִהְיֶה כְלִי־גֶבֶר עַל־אִשָּׁה וְלֹא־יִלְבַּשׁ גֶּבֶר שִׂמְלַת אִשָּׁה כִּי תוֹעֲבַת יְהוָה אֱלֹהֶיךָ כָּל־עֹשֵׂה אֵלֶּה: פ 6 כִּי יִקָּרֵא קַן־צִפּוֹר לְפָנֶיךָ בַּדֶּרֶךְ בְּכָל־עֵץ אוֹ עַל־הָאָרֶץ אֶפְרֹחִים אוֹ בֵיצִים וְהָאֵם רֹבֶצֶת עַל־הָאֶפְרֹחִים אוֹ עַל־הַבֵּיצִים לֹא־תִקַּח הָאֵם עַל־הַבָּנִים: 7 שַׁלֵּחַ תְּשַׁלַּח אֶת־הָאֵם וְאֶת־הַבָּנִים תִּקַּח־לָךְ לְמַעַן יִיטַב לָךְ וְהַאֲרַכְתָּ יָמִים: ס 8 כִּי

22:6. the mother along with the children. The purpose of this law, like the law against cooking a kid in its mother's milk, is uncertain. Both laws may have to do with caring about animals, prohibiting unfeeling treatment of them. But both may also have purposes of a different sort. Both cases may have been regarded as unnatural combinations, offensive in themselves. In the case of the mother bird along with the eggs or chicks, that would explain why this law is grouped here with laws against forbidden mixtures of seeds, fabrics, and work animals, as well as the law against males wearing female clothing and females wearing male items. (For another explanation of the kid cooked in milk, see the comment on 22:9 below.)

8"When you'll build a new house, you shall make a railing for your roof, so you won't set blood in your house when someone will fall from it.

9"You shall not seed your vineyard with two kinds, or else the whole of the seed that you'll sow and the vineyard's produce will become holy. 10You shall not plow with an ox and an ass together. 11You shall not wear *sha'atnez:* wool and linen together.

12"You shall make braided threads on the four

תִּבְנֶה֙ בַּ֣יִת חָדָ֔שׁ וְעָשִׂ֥יתָ מַעֲקֶ֖ה לְגַגֶּ֑ךָ וְלֹֽא־תָשִׂ֤ים דָּמִים֙ בְּבֵיתֶ֔ךָ כִּֽי־יִפֹּ֥ל הַנֹּפֵ֖ל מִמֶּֽנּוּ: ס 9לֹא־תִזְרַ֤ע כַּרְמְךָ֙ כִּלְאָ֑יִם פֶּן־תִּקְדַּ֗שׁ הַֽמְלֵאָ֤ה הַזֶּ֨רַע֙ אֲשֶׁ֣ר תִּזְרָ֔ע וּתְבוּאַ֖ת הַכָּֽרֶם: ס 10לֹֽא־תַחֲרֹ֥שׁ בְּשֽׁוֹר־ וּבַחֲמֹ֖ר יַחְדָּֽו: ס 11לֹ֤א תִלְבַּשׁ֙ שַֽׁעַטְנֵ֔ז צֶ֥מֶר וּפִשְׁתִּ֖ים יַחְדָּֽו: ס 12גְּדִלִ֖ים תַּעֲשֶׂה־לָּ֑ךְ עַל־אַרְבַּ֛ע

22:8. **a railing for your roof.** This law seems to be out of place, in the middle of laws concerning mixtures. But there is apparently more than one principle of organization operating here. The first laws of this chapter concern caring about one's neighbor, but specifically expressed in terms of the neighbor's animals. Then it adds the neighbor's garment. These laws are followed by the law prohibiting men and women to mix each other's garments, followed by a return to laws regarding animals, followed by another law of caring about one's neighbor: this law of putting a railing on one's roof. This is followed by more laws of prohibited mixtures, including mixing certain animals. The full group is a complex mixture of moral and ritual laws, but as a group it also shows how the Torah's different kinds of laws are interconnected.

22:8. **set blood in your house.** Meaning: you won't bring the responsibility on your home for a loss of life.

22:9. **will become holy.** Why does mixing different seeds in a vineyard make the resulting crop holy? Several of the laws regarding mixtures have possible explanations having to do with the realm of the holy. The law against cooking a kid in its mother's milk may be because that was regarded as a food for a deity, since a Ugaritic text pictures the chief god, El, having kid cooked in milk (see the comment on Exod 23:19). The law against wearing wool and linen together may be because they were both used in the Tabernacle (see the comment on Deut 22:11 below). (Even the law against men wearing clothes of the opposite sex may have to do with pagan myths in which the gods and goddesses do that.) And so it may be in the case of mixed seeds, as well: the prohibition of mixing them may not be because the mixing is bad in some way but rather because some mixtures are regarded as divine. This is only a speculation, since the meaning of this law (and of the other laws concerning mixtures) has stymied scholars for centuries. But this speculation at least has the advantage of coming to terms with the word "holy" in this law. Other commentaries and translations have commonly ascribed some other meaning to the word because of the difficulty of making sense of it in this context.

22:11. **sha'atnez: wool and linen together.** The former comes from an animal, a sheep; and the latter comes from a plant, flax. Some think that such fabric is prohibited because it was thought to be an unnatural mixture. Others think that it is because the priests have both linen and wool in their clothing, and that therefore laypersons

corners of your apparel with which you cover yourself.

13"When a man will take a wife and come to her and then hate her, 14and he'll assert words of abuse toward her and bring out a bad name on her and say, 'I took this woman, and I came close to her, and I didn't find signs of virginity for her,' 15then the young woman's father and her mother shall take and bring out the signs of the young woman's virginity to the city's elders at the gate.

16"And the young woman's father shall say to the elders, 'I gave my daughter to this man for a wife, and he hated her. 17And, here, he has asserted words of abuse, saying: "I didn't find signs of virginity for your daughter." But these are the signs of my daughter's virginity!' And they shall spread out the garment in front of the city's elders.

18"And that city's elders shall take the man and discipline him. 19And they shall fine him a hundred weights of silver and give it to the young woman's father because he brought out a bad name on a virgin of Israel. And she shall be

13כִּי־יִקַּח ס כַּנְפוֹת כְּסוּתְךָ אֲשֶׁר תְּכַסֶּה־בָּהּ:
אִישׁ אִשָּׁה וּבָא אֵלֶיהָ וּשְׂנֵאָהּ: 14וְשָׂם לָהּ עֲלִילֹת
דְּבָרִים וְהוֹצִיא עָלֶיהָ שֵׁם רָע וְאָמַר אֶת־הָאִשָּׁה
הַזֹּאת לָקַחְתִּי וָאֶקְרַב אֵלֶיהָ וְלֹא־מָצָאתִי לָהּ
בְּתוּלִים: 15וְלָקַח אֲבִי הַנַּעֲרָ וְאִמָּהּ וְהוֹצִיאוּ אֶת־
בְּתוּלֵי הַנַּעֲרָ אֶל־זִקְנֵי הָעִיר הַשָּׁעְרָה: 16וְאָמַר
אֲבִי הַנַּעֲרָ אֶל־הַזְּקֵנִים אֶת־בִּתִּי נָתַתִּי לָאִישׁ הַזֶּה
לְאִשָּׁה וַיִּשְׂנָאֶהָ: 17וְהִנֵּה־הוּא שָׂם עֲלִילֹת דְּבָרִים
לֵאמֹר לֹא־מָצָאתִי לְבִתְּךָ בְּתוּלִים וְאֵלֶּה בְּתוּלֵי
בִתִּי וּפָרְשׂוּ הַשִּׂמְלָה לִפְנֵי זִקְנֵי הָעִיר: 18וְלָקְחוּ
זִקְנֵי הָעִיר־הַהִוא אֶת־הָאִישׁ וְיִסְּרוּ אֹתוֹ: 19וְעָנְשׁוּ
אֹתוֹ מֵאָה כֶסֶף וְנָתְנוּ לַאֲבִי הַנַּעֲרָה כִּי הוֹצִיא שֵׁם
רָע עַל בְּתוּלַת יִשְׂרָאֵל וְלוֹ־תִהְיֶה לְאִשָּׁה לֹא־

22:15 קְ הַנַּעֲרָה . קְ הַנַּעֲרָה
22:16 קְ הַנַּעֲרָה

---

must not wear what belongs to the realm of the sacred. The problem with the latter view is that the only description of priestly garments in the Torah mentions linen but does not mention wool explicitly. Still, it is likely that the priests have wool and linen, because some of their clothing is said to be dyed (Exod 28:4–6), and it is extremely difficult to dye linen (I learned this from Avigail Sheffer, a specialist in ancient textiles). Fabric excavated at Kuntillat 'Ajrud, which may have been a cultic site, contained linen and wool.

Alternatively, the Tabernacle is made of an inside layer of linen fabric and a second layer of wool (goats' hair) fabric over it. The *sha'atnez* prohibition may therefore relate to the sacred state of the Tabernacle rather than of the priesthood.

22:17. **garment.** It is either the clothing she wore on the wedding night or the cloth or sheet beneath the couple that night, on which a bloodstain would be evidence of her virginity.

22:18. **discipline him.** It is unclear if this means a verbal criticism, a flogging, or some other form of chastisement.

22:19. **a bad name on a virgin of Israel.** Premarital sex is not forbidden elsewhere in the Torah, and men marry women who are not virgins. Only the high priest is absolutely required to marry a virgin (Lev 21:13–14). The issue in this case must therefore be that the woman was *represented* to be a virgin at the time she was married, and now her husband claims that she was not.

his for a wife: he shall not be able to let her go, all his days.

20"But if this thing was true—signs of virginity for the young woman were not found— 21then they shall take the young woman out to the entrance of her father's house, and the people of her city shall stone her with stones so she dies, because she did a foolhardy thing in Israel, to whore at her father's house. So you shall burn away what is bad from among you.

22"If a man will be found lying with a woman who is a husband's wife, then the two of them shall die: the man who lay with the woman, and the woman. So you shall burn away what is bad from Israel.

23"If it will be that a virgin young woman will be betrothed to a man, and a man will find her in the city and lie with her, 24then you shall take the two of them to that city's gate and stone them with stones so they die: the young woman on account of the fact that she did not cry out in the city, and the man on account of the fact that he degraded his neighbor's wife. So you shall burn away what is bad from among you. 25But if the man will find the betrothed young woman in the field, and the man will take hold of her and lie with her, then only the man who lay with her shall die, 26but you shall not do a thing to the young woman. The young woman does not have a sin deserving death, because, just as a man would get up against his neighbor and murder him: this case is like that; 27because he found her in the field, the betrothed young woman cried out, and there was no one to save her.

28"If a man will find a virgin young woman who is not betrothed, and he'll grasp her and lie with her, and they'll be found, 29then the man who lay with her shall give the young woman's father fifty weights of silver, and she shall be his

יוּכַ֥ל לְשַׁלְּחָ֖הּ כָּל־יָמָֽיו׃ ס 20וְאִם־אֱמֶ֥ת הָיָ֖ה הַדָּבָ֣ר הַזֶּ֑ה לֹא־נִמְצְא֥וּ בְתוּלִ֖ים לַֽנַּעֲרָֽ׃ 21וְהוֹצִ֜יאוּ אֶת־הַֽנַּעֲרָ֗ אֶל־פֶּ֨תַח בֵּית־אָבִ֜יהָ וּסְקָל֩וּהָ אַנְשֵׁ֨י עִירָ֤הּ בָּֽאֲבָנִים֙ וָמֵ֔תָה כִּֽי־עָשְׂתָ֤ה נְבָלָה֙ בְּיִשְׂרָאֵ֔ל לִזְנ֖וֹת בֵּ֣ית אָבִ֑יהָ וּבִֽעַרְתָּ֥ הָרָ֖ע מִקִּרְבֶּֽךָ׃ ס 22כִּֽי־ יִמָּצֵ֨א אִ֜ישׁ שֹׁכֵ֣ב ׀ עִם־אִשָּׁ֣ה בְעֻֽלַת־בַּ֗עַל וּמֵ֨תוּ֙ גַּם־ שְׁנֵיהֶ֔ם הָאִ֛ישׁ הַשֹּׁכֵ֥ב עִם־הָאִשָּׁ֖ה וְהָאִשָּׁ֑ה וּבִֽעַרְתָּ֥ הָרָ֖ע מִיִּשְׂרָאֵֽל׃ ס 23כִּ֤י יִֽהְיֶה֙ נַעֲרָ֣ בְתוּלָ֔ה מְאֹרָשָׂ֖ה לְאִ֑ישׁ וּמְצָאָ֥הּ אִ֛ישׁ בָּעִ֖יר וְשָׁכַ֥ב עִמָּֽהּ׃ 24וְהֽוֹצֵאתֶ֨ם אֶת־שְׁנֵיהֶ֜ם אֶל־שַׁ֣עַר ׀ הָעִ֣יר הַהִ֗וא וּסְקַלְתֶּ֨ם אֹתָ֥ם בָּֽאֲבָנִים֮ וָמֵ֒תוּ֒ אֶֽת־הַֽנַּעֲרָ֗ עַל־דְּבַ֤ר אֲשֶׁ֣ר לֹא־צָֽעֲקָ֣ה בָעִ֔יר וְאֶ֨ת־הָאִ֔ישׁ עַל־דְּבַ֥ר אֲשֶׁר־ עִנָּ֖ה אֶת־אֵ֣שֶׁת רֵעֵ֑הוּ וּבִֽעַרְתָּ֥ הָרָ֖ע מִקִּרְבֶּֽךָ׃ ס 25וְֽאִם־בַּשָּׂדֶ֞ה יִמְצָ֣א הָאִ֗ישׁ אֶת־הַֽנַּעֲרָ֣ הַֽמְאֹרָשָׂ֔ה וְהֶחֱזִֽיק־בָּ֥הּ הָאִ֖ישׁ וְשָׁכַ֣ב עִמָּ֑הּ וּמֵ֗ת הָאִ֛ישׁ אֲשֶׁר־ שָׁכַ֥ב עִמָּ֖הּ לְבַדּֽוֹ׃ 26וְלַֽנַּעֲרָ֙ לֹא־תַעֲשֶׂ֣ה דָבָ֔ר אֵ֥ין לַֽנַּעֲרָ֖ חֵ֣טְא מָ֑וֶת כִּ֡י כַּֽאֲשֶׁר֩ יָק֨וּם אִ֤ישׁ עַל־רֵעֵ֙הוּ֙ וּרְצָח֣וֹ נֶ֔פֶשׁ כֵּ֖ן הַדָּבָ֥ר הַזֶּֽה׃ 27כִּ֥י בַשָּׂדֶ֖ה מְצָאָ֑הּ צָֽעֲקָ֗ה הַֽנַּעֲרָ֙ הַֽמְאֹ֣רָשָׂ֔ה וְאֵ֥ין מוֹשִׁ֖יעַ לָֽהּ׃ ס 28כִּֽי־ יִמְצָ֣א אִ֗ישׁ נַעֲרָ֤ בְתוּלָה֙ אֲשֶׁ֣ר לֹא־אֹרָ֔שָׂה וּתְפָשָׂ֖הּ וְשָׁכַ֣ב עִמָּ֑הּ וְנִמְצָֽאוּ׃ 29וְנָתַ֠ן הָאִ֨ישׁ הַשֹּׁכֵ֥ב עִמָּ֛הּ לַֽאֲבִ֥י הַֽנַּעֲרָ֖ חֲמִשִּׁ֣ים כָּ֑סֶף וְלֽוֹ־תִהְיֶ֣ה לְאִשָּׁ֗ה תַּ֚חַת

22:20 קֹ לַֽנַּעֲרָה · 22:23 קֹ הַֽנַּעֲרָ · 22:23 קֹ נַעֲרָה
22:24 קֹ הַֽנַּעֲרָ · 22:25 קֹ הַֽנַּעֲרָ
22:26 קֹ וְלַֽנַּעֲרָ · 22:26 קֹ לַֽנַּעֲרָה
22:27 קֹ הַֽנַּעֲרָ · 22:28 קֹ נַעֲרָה
22:29 קֹ הַֽנַּעֲרָ

22:19. **to let her go.** Meaning: to divorce her.

22:19,29. **the young woman's father.** Both the woman herself and her father receive some form of compensation. The woman can never be divorced. The father receives monetary compensation.

for a wife. Because he degraded her, he shall not be able to let her go, all his days.

23 ¹"A man shall not take his father's wife, so he will not expose his father's hem. ²One who is wounded by crushing or whose organ is cut off shall not come into YHWH's community. ³A bastard shall not come into YHWH's community; even in the tenth generation one shall not come into YHWH's community. ⁴An Ammonite and a Moabite shall not come into YHWH's community; even in the tenth gen-

אֲשֶׁר עִנָּהּ לֹא־יוּכַל שַׁלְּחָהּ כָּל־יָמָיו: ס
23 ¹לֹא־יִקַּח אִישׁ אֶת־אֵשֶׁת אָבִיו וְלֹא יְגַלֶּה כְּנַף אָבִיו: ס ²לֹא־יָבֹא פְצוּעַ־דַּכָּא וּכְרוּת שָׁפְכָה בִּקְהַל יְהוָה: ס ³לֹא־יָבֹא מַמְזֵר בִּקְהַל יְהוָה גַּם דּוֹר עֲשִׂירִי לֹא־יָבֹא לוֹ בִּקְהַל יְהוָה: ס ⁴לֹא־יָבֹא עַמּוֹנִי וּמוֹאָבִי בִּקְהַל יְהוָה גַּם דּוֹר עֲשִׂירִי

22:29. she shall be his for a wife. Married to the man who raped her?! Presumably, hopefully, this means that the choice was hers as well as her father's.

23:1. take his father's wife. Before or after his father's death. This law appears as part of the list of prohibited sexual mates in Leviticus (18:8; 20:11), but here it stands alone. Its apparent special significance is that this issue comes up several times in Israel's royal family. When David becomes king he takes Saul's wives, but Saul was not his father. But David is succeeded by his own sons, so the matter is relevant. When his son Absalom rebels, he takes ten of David's concubines (2 Sam 16:22). After David's death, his son Adonijah asks for David's concubine Abishag, a request that David's successor Solomon regards as a claim on the throne (1 Kings 2:22–25). This law also recalls Reuben's taking of his father Jacob's concubine Bilhah (Gen 35:22). Jacob takes away the birthright from Reuben because of this (Gen 49:3–4). The law against taking one's father's wife thus guards against dangerous situations (that a man would marry his half-brother's mother, or that a son might kill his father to get his wife) and especially guards the security of the royal succession.

23:1. expose his father's hem. Meaning: the son would have contact with the woman to whom the father has been exposed. "Exposing nudity" is the euphemism for prohibited sexual unions (see Leviticus 18).

23:2. wounded by crushing. The testicles.

23:2. whose organ is cut off. The penis.

23:2. come into YHWH's community. Meaning: may not marry an Israelite woman. It is also possible that there was some sort of conversion by which a non-Israelite might become an Israelite and that this was denied to those persons mentioned here in vv. 2–9. But this is uncertain because conversion is never mentioned in the Torah.

23:3. bastard. This has not been understood to mean someone born out of wedlock, but rather someone born from one of the forbidden sexual relationships.

23:4. a Moabite. Yet Ruth, a Moabite woman, marries an Israelite, and their descendant is King David—and all the royal line of Judah! Elsewhere, however, we have seen that biblically a woman automatically takes on her husband's religion. Therefore,

eration they shall not come into YHWH's community, forever, ⁵on account of the fact that they did not meet you with bread and with water on the way when you came out from Egypt, and the fact that it hired Balaam son of Beor from Pethor of Aram Naharaim against you to curse you. ⁶But YHWH, your God, was not willing to listen to Balaam, and YHWH, your God, turned the curse into a blessing for you because YHWH, your God, loved you. ⁷You shall not seek their well-being or their good, all your days, forever.

⁸"You shall not abhor an Edomite, because he is your brother. You shall not abhor an Egyptian, because you were an alien in his land. ⁹Third-generation children who will be born to them may come into YHWH's community.

¹⁰"When you'll go out encamped against your enemies, you shall be watchful against any bad thing. ¹¹If there will be among you a man who will not be pure by a night occurrence, then he shall go outside the camp. He shall not come inside the camp. ¹²And it shall be: toward evening he shall wash in water, and when the sun sets he shall come inside the camp. ¹³And you shall

לֹא־יָבֹא לָהֶם בִּקְהַל יְהוָה עַד־עוֹלָם: ⁵עַל־דְּבַ֗ר אֲשֶׁ֨ר לֹא־קִדְּמ֤וּ אֶתְכֶם֙ בַּלֶּ֣חֶם וּבַמַּ֔יִם בַּדֶּ֖רֶךְ בְּצֵאתְכֶ֣ם מִמִּצְרָ֑יִם וַאֲשֶׁר֩ שָׂכַ֨ר עָלֶ֜יךָ אֶת־בִּלְעָ֣ם בֶּן־בְּע֗וֹר מִפְּת֛וֹר אֲרַ֥ם נַהֲרַ֖יִם לְקַֽלְלֶֽךָ: ⁶וְלֹא־אָבָ֞ה יְהוָ֤ה אֱלֹהֶ֙יךָ֙ לִשְׁמֹ֣עַ אֶל־בִּלְעָ֔ם וַיַּהֲפֹךְ֩ יְהוָ֨ה אֱלֹהֶ֤יךָ לְּךָ֙ אֶת־הַקְּלָלָ֣ה לִבְרָכָ֔ה כִּ֥י אֲהֵֽבְךָ֖ יְהוָ֥ה אֱלֹהֶֽיךָ: ⁷לֹא־תִדְרֹ֥שׁ שְׁלֹמָ֖ם וְטֹבָתָ֑ם כָּל־יָמֶ֖יךָ לְעוֹלָֽם: ס ⁸לֹֽא־תְתַעֵ֣ב אֲדֹמִ֔י כִּ֥י אָחִ֖יךָ ה֑וּא ס לֹא־תְתַעֵ֣ב מִצְרִ֔י כִּי־גֵ֖ר הָיִ֥יתָ בְאַרְצֽוֹ: ⁹בָּנִ֛ים אֲשֶׁר־יִוָּלְד֥וּ לָהֶ֖ם דּ֣וֹר שְׁלִישִׁ֑י יָבֹ֥א לָהֶ֖ם בִּקְהַ֥ל יְהוָֽה: ס ¹⁰כִּֽי־תֵצֵ֥א מַחֲנֶ֖ה עַל־אֹיְבֶ֑יךָ וְנִ֨שְׁמַרְתָּ֔ מִכֹּ֖ל דָּבָ֥ר רָֽע: ¹¹כִּֽי־יִהְיֶ֤ה בְךָ֙ אִ֔ישׁ אֲשֶׁ֛ר לֹא־יִהְיֶ֥ה טָה֖וֹר מִקְּרֵה־לָ֑יְלָה וְיָצָא֙ אֶל־מִח֣וּץ לַֽמַּחֲנֶ֔ה לֹ֥א יָבֹ֖א אֶל־תּ֥וֹךְ הַֽמַּחֲנֶֽה: ¹²וְהָיָ֥ה לִפְנֽוֹת־עֶ֖רֶב יִרְחַ֣ץ בַּמָּ֑יִם וּכְבֹ֣א הַשֶּׁ֔מֶשׁ יָבֹ֖א אֶל־תּ֥וֹךְ הַֽמַּחֲנֶֽה: ¹³וְיָ֛ד

---

it is only a Moabite or Ammonite man who is prohibited from marrying an Israelite woman. A Moabite or Ammonite woman may marry an Israelite man. (This is also the rabbinic understanding of this law.)

23:8. an Edomite . . . he is your brother. Edomites are the descendants of Esau. As in Genesis, Esau is not regarded as an enemy. As earlier in Deuteronomy, Israelites are not to enter into conflict with Edom (2:4–8). Later in the biblical era and in postbiblical times, Israel and Edom became bitterly hostile (see, for example, Ps 137:7). But the benevolence toward Esau and Edom in the Torah is clear and a marked contrast to the later feelings and midrashim concerning Esau.

23:8. not abhor an Egyptian. Even more remarkable is this command not to disdain an Egyptian—despite everything that happened in Egypt. We have seen repeated laws requiring Israelites to give aliens the same protections as citizens. And apparently this is the ultimate expression of that principle (and possibly the reason for it): Israelites themselves were aliens in Egypt, and they were abhorred (Gen 46:34; the word translated "offensive thing" there is cognate to the word "abhor" here) and mistreated, and so they must now never abhor an Egyptian or mistreat any alien. It is the prime demonstration of the principle in Judaism: "What is hateful to you, don't do to your neighbor."

23:11. night occurrence. As in Lev 15:16—"when a man's intercourse seed will come out from him"—this refers to a flow of semen.

have a location outside the camp, and you shall go out there, outside; [14]and you shall have a spade among your equipment, and it shall be, when you sit outside, that you shall dig with it, and you shall go back and cover what comes out of you. [15]Because YHWH, your God, is going within your camp, to rescue you and to put your enemies in front of you, so your camp shall be holy, so He won't see an exposure of something in you and turn back from you.

[16]"You shall not turn over to his master a slave who will seek deliverance with you from his master. [17]He shall live with you, among you, in the place that he will choose in one of your gates, where it is good for him. You shall not persecute him.

[18]"There shall not be a sacred prostitute from the daughters of Israel, and there shall not be a sacred prostitute from the sons of Israel. [19]You

תִּהְיֶה לְךָ מִחוּץ לַמַּחֲנֶה וְיָצֵאתָ שָּׁמָּה חוּץ: [14]וְיָתֵד תִּהְיֶה לְךָ עַל־אֲזֵנֶךָ וְהָיָה בְּשִׁבְתְּךָ חוּץ וְחָפַרְתָּה בָהּ וְשַׁבְתָּ וְכִסִּיתָ אֶת־צֵאָתֶךָ: [15]כִּי יְהוָה אֱלֹהֶיךָ מִתְהַלֵּךְ ׀ בְּקֶרֶב מַחֲנֶךָ לְהַצִּילְךָ וְלָתֵת אֹיְבֶיךָ לְפָנֶיךָ וְהָיָה מַחֲנֶיךָ קָדוֹשׁ וְלֹא־יִרְאֶה בְךָ עֶרְוַת דָּבָר וְשָׁב מֵאַחֲרֶיךָ: ס [16]לֹא־תַסְגִּיר עֶבֶד אֶל־אֲדֹנָיו אֲשֶׁר־יִנָּצֵל אֵלֶיךָ מֵעִם אֲדֹנָיו: [17]עִמְּךָ יֵשֵׁב בְּקִרְבְּךָ בַּמָּקוֹם אֲשֶׁר־יִבְחַר בְּאַחַד שְׁעָרֶיךָ בַּטּוֹב לוֹ לֹא תּוֹנֶנּוּ: ס [18]לֹא־תִהְיֶה קְדֵשָׁה מִבְּנוֹת יִשְׂרָאֵל וְלֹא־יִהְיֶה קָדֵשׁ מִבְּנֵי יִשְׂרָאֵל: [19]לֹא־תָבִיא

23:15. an exposure of something. Meaning: something improper. The term for "exposure" (Hebrew *'erwāh*) elsewhere relates to nudity. It frequently involves sexual matters. Here it involves human excretion. The phrase here thus refers to something from the sexual or excremental realms that offends.

23:18. sacred prostitute. I realize that there is little evidence that there was such a thing as cultic prostitution in the ancient Near East, and I know that we should not derive the meaning of words solely from their roots (the etymological fallacy), so we cannot assume that this word (Hebrew *qĕdēšāh*) means "sacred" prostitute just because it has the same root as *qādōš*, meaning "holy." Still, I think that "sacred prostitute" is probably correct here because: (1) The female and male prostitutes in this verse are in parallel with bringing the price of female and male prostitutes to the Temple in the next verse, so the common issue seems to be the association of prostitution with the realm of the holy. (2) The story of Tamar (Genesis 38) plays upon the distinction between Hebrew *zōnāh*, meaning "prostitute," and Hebrew *qĕdēšāh*, meaning something higher than a regular prostitute. Judah is described as thinking that Tamar is a *zōnāh* (38:15), but Judah's friend uses the word *qĕdēšāh* when he discreetly inquires about her later (38:21). It is possible that the distinction there is between levels of prostitutes or between more and less pejorative terms (comparable to English "whore" versus "prostitute"). But, since this is uncertain, the combination of this point with the etymological factor and the parallel verse still weighs in favor of the meaning of "sacred prostitute." Regular prostitution is not necessarily prohibited by law in the *Tanak*, but it is disdained. The symbolism of the prophet Hosea's marriage to a prostitute indicates this (Hosea 1–3).

shall not bring the price of a prostitute or the cost of a dog to the house of YHWH, your God, for any vow, because the two of them are both an offensive thing of YHWH.

20"You shall not require interest for your brother: interest of money, interest of food, interest of anything that one might charge. 21For a foreigner you may require it, but for your brother you shall not require it, so that YHWH, your God, will bless you in everything your hand has taken on, on the land to which you're coming to take possession of it.

22"When you'll make a vow to YHWH, your God, you shall not delay to fulfill it, because YHWH, your God, will *require* it from you, and it will be a sin in you. 23But if you desist from vowing, that will not be a sin in you. 24You shall watch what comes out of your lips and do as you vowed to YHWH, your God, the contribution that you spoke with your mouth.

25"When you'll come into your neighbor's vineyard, then you may eat grapes as you wish, your fill; but you shall not put any into your container. 26When you'll come into your neighbor's standing grain, then you may pluck ears with your hand; but you shall not lift a sickle at your neighbor's grain.

אֶתְנַן זוֹנָה וּמְחִיר כֶּלֶב בֵּית יְהוָה אֱלֹהֶיךָ לְכָל־נֶדֶר כִּי תוֹעֲבַת יְהוָה אֱלֹהֶיךָ גַּם־שְׁנֵיהֶם: 20לֹא־תַשִּׁיךְ לְאָחִיךָ נֶשֶׁךְ כֶּסֶף נֶשֶׁךְ אֹכֶל נֶשֶׁךְ כָּל־דָּבָר אֲשֶׁר יִשָּׁךְ: 21לַנָּכְרִי תַשִּׁיךְ וּלְאָחִיךָ לֹא תַשִּׁיךְ לְמַעַן יְבָרֶכְךָ יְהוָה אֱלֹהֶיךָ בְּכֹל מִשְׁלַח יָדֶךָ עַל־הָאָרֶץ אֲשֶׁר־אַתָּה בָא־שָׁמָּה לְרִשְׁתָּהּ: ס 22כִּי־תִדֹּר נֶדֶר לַיהוָה אֱלֹהֶיךָ לֹא תְאַחֵר לְשַׁלְּמוֹ כִּי־דָּרֹשׁ יִדְרְשֶׁנּוּ יְהוָה אֱלֹהֶיךָ מֵעִמָּךְ וְהָיָה בְךָ חֵטְא: 23וְכִי תֶחְדַּל לִנְדֹּר לֹא־יִהְיֶה בְךָ חֵטְא: 24מוֹצָא שְׂפָתֶיךָ תִּשְׁמֹר וְעָשִׂיתָ כַּאֲשֶׁר נָדַרְתָּ לַיהוָה אֱלֹהֶיךָ נְדָבָה אֲשֶׁר דִּבַּרְתָּ בְּפִיךָ: ס 25כִּי תָבֹא בְּכֶרֶם רֵעֶךָ וְאָכַלְתָּ עֲנָבִים כְּנַפְשְׁךָ שָׂבְעֶךָ וְאֶל־כֶּלְיְךָ לֹא תִתֵּן: ס 26כִּי תָבֹא בְּקָמַת רֵעֶךָ וְקָטַפְתָּ מְלִילֹת בְּיָדֶךָ וְחֶרְמֵשׁ לֹא תָנִיף עַל קָמַת רֵעֶךָ: ס

23:19. **the price of a prostitute**. It is offensive to vow an amount for the Temple that is known to be the going rate for a prostitute.

23:19. **the cost of a dog**. "Dog" is widely understood to refer pejoratively to a male prostitute. There is little evidence for or against this understanding. It is based on the context, which is concerned with prostitutes.

23:20. **require interest**. This law is consistent with other laws that contribute to preventing the development of a small, wealthy upper class and a large poor class. Like the jubilee law and the law prohibiting the king from having many horses and the law against keeping an Israelite slave more than six years, this law aims to protect an Israelite in financial straits from entering a cycle that will keep him or her from ever recovering, and thus permanently locked into a dependent position. This is part of an economic system for the country, and so it applies only to "your brother," i.e., a fellow Israelite. Israelites may still require interest on loans to foreign borrowers.

24

1"When a man will take a woman and marry her, and it will be that, if she does not find favor in his eyes because he has found an exposure of something in her, and he will write a document of cutting-off for her and put it in her hand and let her go from his house, 2and she will go out from his house and go and become another man's, 3and the latter man will hate her and write a document of cutting-off for her and put it in her hand and let her go from his house, or if the latter man who took her to him for a wife will die: 4her first husband who let her go shall not be able to come back to take her to be his for a wife since she has been made impure, because that is an offensive thing in front of

כד 1 כִּי־יִקַּח אִישׁ אִשָּׁה וּבְעָלָהּ וְהָיָה אִם־לֹא תִמְצָא־חֵן בְּעֵינָיו כִּי־מָצָא בָהּ עֶרְוַת דָּבָר וְכָתַב לָהּ סֵפֶר כְּרִיתֻת וְנָתַן בְּיָדָהּ וְשִׁלְּחָהּ מִבֵּיתוֹ: 2 וְיָצְאָה מִבֵּיתוֹ וְהָלְכָה וְהָיְתָה לְאִישׁ־אַחֵר: 3 וּשְׂנֵאָהּ הָאִישׁ הָאַחֲרוֹן וְכָתַב לָהּ סֵפֶר כְּרִיתֻת וְנָתַן בְּיָדָהּ וְשִׁלְּחָהּ מִבֵּיתוֹ אוֹ כִי יָמוּת הָאִישׁ הָאַחֲרוֹן אֲשֶׁר־לְקָחָהּ לוֹ לְאִשָּׁה: 4 לֹא־יוּכַל בַּעְלָהּ הָרִאשׁוֹן אֲשֶׁר־שִׁלְּחָהּ לָשׁוּב לְקַחְתָּהּ לִהְיוֹת לוֹ לְאִשָּׁה אַחֲרֵי אֲשֶׁר הֻטַּמָּאָה כִּי־תוֹעֵבָה הִוא לִפְנֵי

24:1. **When a man will take a woman.** This law (vv. 1–4) has been taken as the biblical law of divorce, but it is not. It is the law governing a specific instance in which a couple might want to return to each other after they were divorced and she was remarried and then was divorced again or widowed. Divorce law in general has been derived in part from this case because of the curious fact that there is no law in the Torah telling how to get married and no law telling how to get divorced. Here, the divorce procedure appears to be *assumed,* as a known practice.

The absence of marriage and divorce procedures has been used as a proof of the existence of oral law that was given along with the law that is written in the Torah. But the case may be rather that these ceremonies were not regarded as having been given in detail by God—as few ceremonies outside of the sacrifices at the Tabernacle are so given. The divine interest is in the marriage *relationship* rather than in the ceremony: the husband's treatment of the wife, the prohibition of adultery, their relationship with their children, inheritance, making one's spouse happy (see 24:5). The same goes for funerals and bar mitzvah. Even such well-known Jewish practices as saying kaddish and sitting shivah are not mentioned in the Torah. And bar and bat mitzvah are not treated (or even mentioned): the concern is with *doing* the commandments. The details of the ceremony of arriving at the age of doing them are left for humans to choose. All of these ceremonies were detailed in rabbinic law and practice later. Ceremonial procedures are given in the Torah for less common cases, such as the slave who declines to leave a master (Deut 15:16–17), or the brother-in-law who declines to perform levirate marriage (25:7–10), or the present case of return marriage.

24:1. **an exposure of something.** See the comment on 23:15 above.

24:1. **a document of cutting-off.** A divorce.

24:4. **her first husband shall not be able to come back.** Jeremiah transforms this into a metaphor in which God has cut off Israel the way the husband in this law cuts off his wife (Jer 3:1), yet God would still take Israel back, seemingly against God's own law concerning human marriages (3:12,14,22)!

YHWH, and you shall not bring sin on the land that YHWH, your God, is giving you as a legacy.

5"When a man will take a new wife, he shall not go out in the army and not go along with it for any matter. He shall be free at his house for one year and shall make his wife whom he has taken happy. 6One shall not take a mill or an upper millstone as security, because he is taking one's *life* as security.

7"When a man will be found stealing a person from among his brothers, from the children of Israel, so he will get profit through him and sell him, then that thief shall die. So you shall burn away what is bad from among you.

8"Be watchful with the plague of leprosy, to be very watchful and to do according to everything that the Levite priests will instruct you. You shall be watchful to do according to what I commanded them. 9Remember what YHWH, your God, did to Miriam on the way when you were coming out from Egypt.

10"When you'll make a loan of anything to your neighbor, you shall not come into his house to get his pledge. 11You shall stand outside, and the man to whom you're lending shall bring the pledge outside to you. 12And if he is a poor man, you shall not lie down with his pledge. 13You shall give *back* the pledge to him as the sun sets, and he'll lie down with his clothing, and he'll bless you, and you'll have virtue in front of YHWH, your God.

יְהוָה וְלֹא תַחֲטִיא אֶת־הָאָרֶץ אֲשֶׁר יְהוָה אֱלֹהֶיךָ
נֹתֵן לְךָ נַחֲלָה: ס 5כִּי־יִקַּח אִישׁ אִשָּׁה חֲדָשָׁה לֹא
יֵצֵא בַּצָּבָא וְלֹא־יַעֲבֹר עָלָיו לְכָל־דָּבָר נָקִי יִהְיֶה
לְבֵיתוֹ שָׁנָה אֶחָת וְשִׂמַּח אֶת־אִשְׁתּוֹ אֲשֶׁר־לָקָח: ס
6לֹא־יַחֲבֹל רֵחַיִם וָרָכֶב כִּי־נֶפֶשׁ הוּא חֹבֵל: ס
7כִּי־יִמָּצֵא אִישׁ גֹּנֵב נֶפֶשׁ מֵאֶחָיו מִבְּנֵי יִשְׂרָאֵל
וְהִתְעַמֶּר־בּוֹ וּמְכָרוֹ וּמֵת הַגַּנָּב הַהוּא וּבִעַרְתָּ הָרָע
מִקִּרְבֶּךָ: 8הִשָּׁמֶר בְּנֶגַע־הַצָּרַעַת לִשְׁמֹר מְאֹד
וְלַעֲשׂוֹת כְּכֹל אֲשֶׁר־יוֹרוּ אֶתְכֶם הַכֹּהֲנִים הַלְוִיִּם
כַּאֲשֶׁר צִוִּיתִם תִּשְׁמְרוּ לַעֲשׂוֹת: ס 9זָכוֹר אֵת
אֲשֶׁר־עָשָׂה יְהוָה אֱלֹהֶיךָ לְמִרְיָם בַּדֶּרֶךְ בְּצֵאתְכֶם
מִמִּצְרָיִם: ס 10כִּי־תַשֶּׁה בְרֵעֲךָ מַשַּׁאת מְאוּמָה
לֹא־תָבֹא אֶל־בֵּיתוֹ לַעֲבֹט עֲבֹטוֹ: 11בַּחוּץ תַּעֲמֹד
וְהָאִישׁ אֲשֶׁר אַתָּה נֹשֶׁה בוֹ יוֹצִיא אֵלֶיךָ אֶת־
הַעֲבוֹט הַחוּצָה: 12וְאִם־אִישׁ עָנִי הוּא לֹא תִשְׁכַּב
בַּעֲבֹטוֹ: 13הָשֵׁב תָּשִׁיב לוֹ אֶת־הַעֲבוֹט כְּבֹא הַשֶּׁמֶשׁ
וְשָׁכַב בְּשַׂלְמָתוֹ וּבֵרֲכֶךָּ וּלְךָ תִּהְיֶה צְדָקָה לִפְנֵי

24:9. **Remember what God did to Miriam**. Why is this brought up here in the context of a general law about leprosy? Because the law here is not concerned only with the correct treatment for leprosy after one has contracted it (which is the concern of Leviticus 13–14). It also warns to be watchful (the term occurs three times) against behavior that would bring about leprosy as a consequence (see 24:8). Miriam does something that causes her to be stricken with leprosy. Rashi understands her offense to be slanderous gossip (*lāšôn hārā'*), but leprosy is more likely to be tied to a ritual offense. Miriam's words are not gossip; she is stricken with leprosy for having challenged Moses' status as a prophet compared with her own (Num 12:9–15; see the comment on 12:2). And later, King Uzziah is stricken with it for burning incense in the Temple, which only priests can do (2 Chr 26:16–21).

24:13. **you'll have virtue**. See the comment on Deut 6:25.

14"You shall not exploit a poor or an indigent employee, from your brothers or from your aliens who are in your land, in your gates. 15You shall give his pay in his day, and the sun shall not set on it—because he is poor, and he maintains his life by it—so he won't call against you to YHWH, and it will be a sin in you.

16"Fathers shall not be put to death for sons, and sons shall not be put to death for fathers. They shall each be put to death through his own sin.

17"You shall not bend judgment of an alien or an orphan, and you shall not take a widow's clothing as security. 18And you shall remember that you were a slave in Egypt, and YHWH, your God, redeemed you from there. On account of this I command you to do this thing. 19When you'll reap your harvest in your field, and you'll forget a sheaf in the field, you shall not go back to take it. It shall be the alien's and the orphan's and the widow's, so that YHWH, your God, will bless you in all your hands' work. 20When you'll beat your olive trees, you shall not do a bough afterward. It shall be the alien's and the orphan's and the widow's. 21When you'll cut off grapes of your vineyard, you shall not glean afterward. It shall be the alien's and the orphan's and the widow's. 22And you shall remember that you were a slave in the land of Egypt. On account of this I command you to do this thing.

25 1"When there will be a dispute between people, and they will go over to judgment, and they will judge them, then they shall find in favor of the one who is in the right and find against the one who is in the wrong. 2And it will be, if the one who is in the wrong is to be struck, that the judge shall have him laid down and have him struck in front of him, according

יְהוָה אֱלֹהֶיךָ: ס 14לֹא־תַעֲשֹׁק שָׂכִיר עָנִי וְאֶבְיוֹן מֵאַחֶיךָ אוֹ מִגֵּרְךָ אֲשֶׁר בְּאַרְצְךָ בִּשְׁעָרֶיךָ: 15בְּיוֹמוֹ תִתֵּן שְׂכָרוֹ וְלֹא־תָבוֹא עָלָיו הַשֶּׁמֶשׁ כִּי עָנִי הוּא וְאֵלָיו הוּא נֹשֵׂא אֶת־נַפְשׁוֹ וְלֹא־יִקְרָא עָלֶיךָ אֶל־יְהוָה וְהָיָה בְךָ חֵטְא: ס 16לֹא־יוּמְתוּ אָבוֹת עַל־בָּנִים וּבָנִים לֹא־יוּמְתוּ עַל־אָבוֹת אִישׁ בְּחֶטְאוֹ יוּמָתוּ: ס 17לֹא תַטֶּה מִשְׁפַּט גֵּר יָתוֹם וְלֹא תַחֲבֹל בֶּגֶד אַלְמָנָה: 18וְזָכַרְתָּ כִּי עֶבֶד הָיִיתָ בְּמִצְרַיִם וַיִּפְדְּךָ יְהוָה אֱלֹהֶיךָ מִשָּׁם עַל־כֵּן אָנֹכִי מְצַוְּךָ לַעֲשׂוֹת אֶת־הַדָּבָר הַזֶּה: ס 19כִּי תִקְצֹר קְצִירְךָ בְשָׂדֶךָ וְשָׁכַחְתָּ עֹמֶר בַּשָּׂדֶה לֹא תָשׁוּב לְקַחְתּוֹ לַגֵּר לַיָּתוֹם וְלָאַלְמָנָה יִהְיֶה לְמַעַן יְבָרֶכְךָ יְהוָה אֱלֹהֶיךָ בְּכֹל מַעֲשֵׂה יָדֶיךָ: 20כִּי תַחְבֹּט זֵיתְךָ לֹא תְפַאֵר אַחֲרֶיךָ לַגֵּר לַיָּתוֹם וְלָאַלְמָנָה יִהְיֶה: ס 21כִּי תִבְצֹר כַּרְמְךָ לֹא תְעוֹלֵל אַחֲרֶיךָ לַגֵּר לַיָּתוֹם וְלָאַלְמָנָה יִהְיֶה: 22וְזָכַרְתָּ כִּי־עֶבֶד הָיִיתָ בְּאֶרֶץ מִצְרָיִם עַל־כֵּן אָנֹכִי מְצַוְּךָ לַעֲשׂוֹת אֶת־הַדָּבָר הַזֶּה: ס 25 1כִּי־יִהְיֶה רִיב בֵּין אֲנָשִׁים וְנִגְּשׁוּ אֶל־הַמִּשְׁפָּט וּשְׁפָטוּם וְהִצְדִּיקוּ אֶת־הַצַּדִּיק וְהִרְשִׁיעוּ אֶת־הָרָשָׁע: 2וְהָיָה אִם־בִּן הַכּוֹת הָרָשָׁע וְהִפִּילוֹ הַשֹּׁפֵט וְהִכָּהוּ לְפָנָיו כְּדֵי רִשְׁעָתוֹ בְּמִסְפָּר:

24:16. **each through his own sin.** This does not contradict the statement that God "reckons fathers' crime on children and on children's children, on third generations and on fourth generations" (Exod 34:7). That applies to divine justice and may refer to the way in which behavior recurs through generations in a family. This applies to human justice and refers to the point of law that Israelite courts cannot execute people for their relatives' offenses.

to his wrongdoing in number. ³They shall strike him forty times. He shall not add, in case he would add onto these to strike him a great amount, and your brother would be treated as inconsequential before your eyes.

⁴"You shall not muzzle an ox when it is threshing.

⁵"When brothers will live together, and one of them will die, and he had no son, the dead man's wife shall not be an unrelated man's, outside. Her brother-in-law shall come to her and take her to him for a wife and shall do the brother-in-law's duty for her. ⁶And the firstborn to whom she will give birth shall be signified by the name of his brother who died, so his name will not be wiped out from Israel. ⁷And if the man won't desire to take his sister-in-law, then his sister-in-law shall go up at the gate to the elders and say, 'My brother-in-law refuses to preserve a name for his brother in Israel. He was not willing to do the brother-in-law's duty for me.' ⁸And his city's elders shall call him and speak to him, and if he'll stand and say, 'I don't desire to take her,' ⁹then his sister-in-law shall go over to him before the elders' eyes and take off his shoe from his foot and spit in front of him. And she shall answer and say, 'Thus shall be done to the man who will not build up his brother's house.' ¹⁰And his name shall be called in Israel 'the house of the one whose shoe was taken off.'

¹¹"If people will fight together, a man and his brother, and the wife of one will come close to rescue her husband from the hand of the one

³אַרְבָּעִ֥ים יַכֶּ֖נּוּ לֹ֣א יֹסִ֑יף פֶּן־יֹסִ֨יף לְהַכֹּת֤וֹ עַל־אֵ֨לֶּה֙ מַכָּ֣ה רַבָּ֔ה וְנִקְלָ֥ה אָחִ֖יךָ לְעֵינֶֽיךָ: ס ⁴לֹא־תַחְסֹ֥ם שׁ֖וֹר בְּדִישֽׁוֹ: ס ⁵כִּֽי־יֵשְׁב֨וּ אַחִ֜ים יַחְדָּ֗ו וּמֵ֨ת אַחַ֤ד מֵהֶם֙ וּבֵ֣ן אֵֽין־ל֔וֹ לֹא־תִֽהְיֶ֧ה אֵֽשֶׁת־הַמֵּ֛ת הַח֖וּצָה לְאִ֣ישׁ זָ֑ר יְבָמָהּ֙ יָבֹ֣א עָלֶ֔יהָ וּלְקָחָ֥הּ ל֛וֹ לְאִשָּׁ֖ה וְיִבְּמָֽהּ: ⁶וְהָיָ֗ה הַבְּכוֹר֙ אֲשֶׁ֣ר תֵּלֵ֔ד יָק֕וּם עַל־שֵׁ֥ם אָחִ֖יו הַמֵּ֑ת וְלֹֽא־יִמָּחֶ֥ה שְׁמ֖וֹ מִיִּשְׂרָאֵֽל: ⁷וְאִם־לֹ֤א יַחְפֹּץ֙ הָאִ֔ישׁ לָקַ֖חַת אֶת־יְבִמְתּ֑וֹ וְעָלְתָה֩ יְבִמְתּ֨וֹ הַשַּׁ֜עְרָה אֶל־הַזְּקֵנִ֗ים וְאָֽמְרָה֙ מֵאֵ֨ין יְבָמִ֜י לְהָקִ֥ים לְאָחִ֛יו שֵׁ֖ם בְּיִשְׂרָאֵ֑ל לֹ֥א אָבָ֖ה יַבְּמִֽי: ⁸וְקָֽרְאוּ־ל֥וֹ זִקְנֵֽי־עִיר֖וֹ וְדִבְּר֣וּ אֵלָ֑יו וְעָמַ֣ד וְאָמַ֔ר לֹ֥א חָפַ֖צְתִּי לְקַחְתָּֽהּ: ⁹וְנִגְּשָׁ֨ה יְבִמְתּ֣וֹ אֵלָיו֮ לְעֵינֵ֣י הַזְּקֵנִים֒ וְחָֽלְצָ֤ה נַֽעֲלוֹ֙ מֵעַ֣ל רַגְל֔וֹ וְיָֽרְקָ֖ה בְּפָנָ֑יו וְעָֽנְתָה֙ וְאָ֣מְרָ֔ה כָּ֚כָה יֵֽעָשֶׂ֣ה לָאִ֔ישׁ אֲשֶׁ֥ר לֹֽא־יִבְנֶ֖ה אֶת־בֵּ֥ית אָחִֽיו: ¹⁰וְנִקְרָ֥א שְׁמ֖וֹ בְּיִשְׂרָאֵ֑ל בֵּ֖ית חֲל֥וּץ הַנָּֽעַל: ס ¹¹כִּֽי־יִנָּצ֨וּ אֲנָשִׁ֤ים יַחְדָּו֙ אִ֣ישׁ וְאָחִ֔יו וְקָֽרְבָה֙ אֵ֣שֶׁת הָֽאֶחָ֔ד לְהַצִּ֥יל אֶת־אִישָׁ֖הּ מִיַּ֣ד מַכֵּ֑הוּ

25:5. **brother-in-law.** This is known as the law of levirate marriage, from the Latin *levir*, meaning brother-in-law.

25:6. **by the name of his brother who died.** The child is not called "son of" followed by the name of his biological father, but rather "son of" followed by the name of the deceased brother of his biological father. In this way the deceased brother's name is preserved after his death.

25:9. **spit in front of him.** This is commonly understood and translated as "spit in his face." But the only other occurrence of this term (בפניו) in the Torah clearly means "in front of him" (Deut 4:37), and there are no linguistic or contextual grounds for taking it to mean something more specific (and repugnant) than that here.

striking him, and she'll put out her hand and take hold of his private parts, 12then you shall cut off her hand. Your eye shall not pity.

13"You shall not have in your bag multiple stones, a big and a small. 14You shall not have in your house multiple ephah measures, a big and a small. 15You shall have a whole and honest stone; you shall have a whole and honest ephah measure, so your days will be extended on the land that YHWH, your God, is giving you. 16Because everyone who does these is an offensive thing of YHWH, everyone who does injustice.

17"Remember what Amalek did to you on the way when you came out from Egypt, 18how he fell upon you on the way and cut off all the weak ones at your rear, when you were exhausted and tired, and he didn't fear God. 19So it shall be, when YHWH, your God, will give you rest from all your enemies all around in the land that YHWH, your God, is giving you as a legacy to take possession of it, you shall wipe out the memory of Amalek from under the skies. You shall not forget.

WHEN YOU'LL COME

26 1"And it shall be, when you'll come to the land that YHWH, your God, is giving you as a legacy, and you'll take possession of it and live in it, 2that you shall take from the first of all the land's fruit that you'll bring in from your land that YHWH, your God, is giving you, and set it in a basket and go to the place that YHWH, your God, will choose to tent His name there. 3And you shall come to the priest who will be in those days and say to him:

I declare today to YHWH, your God, that I've come to the land that YHWH swore to our fathers to give to us.

וְשָׁלְחָה יָדָהּ וְהֶחֱזִיקָה בִּמְבֻשָׁיו: 12וְקַצֹּתָה אֶת־כַּפָּהּ לֹא תָחוֹס עֵינֶךָ: ס 13לֹא־יִהְיֶה לְךָ בְּכִיסְךָ אֶבֶן וָאָבֶן גְּדוֹלָה וּקְטַנָּה: ס 14לֹא־יִהְיֶה לְךָ בְּבֵיתְךָ אֵיפָה וְאֵיפָה גְּדוֹלָה וּקְטַנָּה: 15אֶבֶן שְׁלֵמָה וָצֶדֶק יִהְיֶה־לָּךְ אֵיפָה שְׁלֵמָה וָצֶדֶק יִהְיֶה־לָּךְ לְמַעַן יַאֲרִיכוּ יָמֶיךָ עַל הָאֲדָמָה אֲשֶׁר־יְהוָה אֱלֹהֶיךָ נֹתֵן לָךְ: 16כִּי תוֹעֲבַת יְהוָה אֱלֹהֶיךָ כָּל־עֹשֵׂה אֵלֶּה כֹּל עֹשֵׂה עָוֶל: פ 17זָכוֹר אֵת אֲשֶׁר־עָשָׂה לְךָ עֲמָלֵק בַּדֶּרֶךְ בְּצֵאתְכֶם מִמִּצְרָיִם: 18אֲשֶׁר קָרְךָ בַּדֶּרֶךְ וַיְזַנֵּב בְּךָ כָּל־הַנֶּחֱשָׁלִים אַחֲרֶיךָ וְאַתָּה עָיֵף וְיָגֵעַ וְלֹא יָרֵא אֱלֹהִים: 19וְהָיָה בְּהָנִיחַ יְהוָה אֱלֹהֶיךָ ׀ לְךָ מִכָּל־אֹיְבֶיךָ מִסָּבִיב בָּאָרֶץ אֲשֶׁר יְהוָה־אֱלֹהֶיךָ נֹתֵן לְךָ נַחֲלָה לְרִשְׁתָּהּ תִּמְחֶה אֶת־זֵכֶר עֲמָלֵק מִתַּחַת הַשָּׁמָיִם לֹא תִּשְׁכָּח: פ

כִּי תָבוֹא

26 1וְהָיָה כִּי־תָבוֹא אֶל־הָאָרֶץ אֲשֶׁר יְהוָה אֱלֹהֶיךָ נֹתֵן לְךָ נַחֲלָה וִירִשְׁתָּהּ וְיָשַׁבְתָּ בָּהּ: 2וְלָקַחְתָּ מֵרֵאשִׁית ׀ כָּל־פְּרִי הָאֲדָמָה אֲשֶׁר תָּבִיא מֵאַרְצְךָ אֲשֶׁר יְהוָה אֱלֹהֶיךָ נֹתֵן לָךְ וְשַׂמְתָּ בַטֶּנֶא וְהָלַכְתָּ אֶל־הַמָּקוֹם אֲשֶׁר יִבְחַר יְהוָה אֱלֹהֶיךָ לְשַׁכֵּן שְׁמוֹ שָׁם: 3וּבָאתָ אֶל־הַכֹּהֵן אֲשֶׁר יִהְיֶה בַּיָּמִים הָהֵם וְאָמַרְתָּ אֵלָיו הִגַּדְתִּי הַיּוֹם לַיהוָה אֱלֹהֶיךָ כִּי־בָאתִי אֶל־הָאָרֶץ אֲשֶׁר נִשְׁבַּע יְהוָה

25:13. multiple stones, a big and a small. Meaning: one should not have larger and smaller weights so as to weigh things dishonestly.

⁴And the priest shall take the basket from your hand and set it down in front of the altar of YHWH, your God. ⁵And you shall answer and say in front of YHWH, your God:

My father was a perishing Aramean, so he went down to Egypt and resided there with few persons and became a big, powerful, and numerous nation there. ⁶And the Egyptians were bad to us and degraded us and imposed hard work on us. ⁷And we cried out to YHWH, our fathers' God, and YHWH listened to our voice and saw our degradation and our trouble and our oppression. ⁸And YHWH brought us out from Egypt with a strong hand and an outstretched arm and with great fear and with signs and with wonders. ⁹And He brought us to this place and gave us this land, a land flowing with milk and honey. ¹⁰And now, here, I've brought the first of the fruit of the land that you've given me, YHWH.

And you shall set it down in front of YHWH, your God, and bow in front of YHWH, your God. ¹¹And you shall rejoice in all the good that YHWH, your God, has given to you and to your house, you and the Levite and the alien who is among you.

¹²"When you'll finish doing all the tithe of your produce in the third year, the year of the tithe, and you'll give it to the Levite, to the alien, to the orphan, and to the widow, and they'll eat in your gates and be full, ¹³then you shall say in front of YHWH, your God:

I have taken away what was holy from the house, and I have also given it to the Levite and to the alien, to the orphan, and to the widow according to all your commandment that you've commanded me. I have not violated and have not forgotten any of your commandments. ¹⁴I have not eaten any of it while I was mourning, and I have

לַאֲבֹתֵ֖ינוּ לָ֥תֶת לָֽנוּ׃ ⁴וְלָקַ֧ח הַכֹּהֵ֛ן הַטֶּ֖נֶא מִיָּדֶ֑ךָ וְהִ֨נִּיח֔וֹ לִפְנֵ֕י מִזְבַּ֖ח יְהוָ֥ה אֱלֹהֶֽיךָ׃ ⁵וְעָנִ֨יתָ וְאָמַרְתָּ֜ לִפְנֵ֣י ׀ יְהוָ֣ה אֱלֹהֶ֗יךָ אֲרַמִּי֙ אֹבֵ֣ד אָבִ֔י וַיֵּ֣רֶד מִצְרַ֔יְמָה וַיָּ֥גָר שָׁ֖ם בִּמְתֵ֣י מְעָ֑ט וַֽיְהִי־שָׁ֕ם לְג֥וֹי גָּד֖וֹל עָצ֥וּם וָרָֽב׃ ⁶וַיָּרֵ֧עוּ אֹתָ֛נוּ הַמִּצְרִ֖ים וַיְעַנּ֑וּנוּ וַיִּתְּנ֥וּ עָלֵ֖ינוּ עֲבֹדָ֥ה קָשָֽׁה׃ ⁷וַנִּצְעַ֕ק אֶל־יְהוָ֖ה אֱלֹהֵ֣י אֲבֹתֵ֑ינוּ וַיִּשְׁמַ֤ע יְהוָה֙ אֶת־קֹלֵ֔נוּ וַיַּ֧רְא אֶת־עָנְיֵ֛נוּ וְאֶת־עֲמָלֵ֖נוּ וְאֶת־לַחֲצֵֽנוּ׃ ⁸וַיּוֹצִאֵ֤נוּ יְהוָה֙ מִמִּצְרַ֔יִם בְּיָ֤ד חֲזָקָה֙ וּבִזְרֹ֣עַ נְטוּיָ֔ה וּבְמֹרָ֖א גָּדֹ֑ל וּבְאֹת֖וֹת וּבְמֹפְתִֽים׃ ⁹וַיְבִאֵ֖נוּ אֶל־הַמָּק֣וֹם הַזֶּ֑ה וַיִּתֶּן־לָ֨נוּ֙ אֶת־הָאָ֣רֶץ הַזֹּ֔את אֶ֛רֶץ זָבַ֥ת חָלָ֖ב וּדְבָֽשׁ׃ ¹⁰וְעַתָּ֗ה הִנֵּ֤ה הֵבֵ֙אתִי֙ אֶת־רֵאשִׁית֙ פְּרִ֣י הָאֲדָמָ֔ה אֲשֶׁר־נָתַ֥תָּה לִּ֖י יְהוָ֑ה וְהִנַּחְתּ֗וֹ לִפְנֵי֙ יְהוָ֣ה אֱלֹהֶ֔יךָ וְהִֽשְׁתַּחֲוִ֔יתָ לִפְנֵ֖י יְהוָ֥ה אֱלֹהֶֽיךָ׃ ¹¹וְשָׂמַחְתָּ֣ בְכָל־הַטּ֗וֹב אֲשֶׁ֧ר נָֽתַן־לְךָ֛ יְהוָ֥ה אֱלֹהֶ֖יךָ וּלְבֵיתֶ֑ךָ אַתָּה֙ וְהַלֵּוִ֔י וְהַגֵּ֖ר אֲשֶׁ֥ר בְּקִרְבֶּֽךָ׃ ס

¹²כִּ֣י תְכַלֶּ֞ה לַ֠עְשֵׂר אֶת־כָּל־מַעְשַׂ֧ר תְּבוּאָתְךָ֛ בַּשָּׁנָ֥ה הַשְּׁלִישִׁ֖ת שְׁנַ֣ת הַֽמַּעֲשֵׂ֑ר וְנָתַתָּ֣ה לַלֵּוִ֗י לַגֵּר֙ לַיָּת֣וֹם וְלָֽאַלְמָנָ֔ה וְאָכְל֥וּ בִשְׁעָרֶ֖יךָ וְשָׂבֵֽעוּ׃ ¹³וְאָמַרְתָּ֡ לִפְנֵי֩ יְהוָ֨ה אֱלֹהֶ֜יךָ בִּעַ֧רְתִּי הַקֹּ֣דֶשׁ מִן־הַבַּ֗יִת וְגַ֨ם נְתַתִּ֤יו לַלֵּוִי֙ וְלַגֵּר֙ לַיָּת֣וֹם וְלָֽאַלְמָנָ֔ה כְּכָל־מִצְוָתְךָ֖ אֲשֶׁ֣ר צִוִּיתָ֑נִי לֹֽא־עָבַ֥רְתִּי מִמִּצְוֹתֶ֖יךָ וְלֹ֥א שָׁכָֽחְתִּי׃ ¹⁴לֹא־אָכַ֨לְתִּי בְאֹנִי֙ מִמֶּ֔נּוּ וְלֹא־

not taken any of it away while impure, and I have not given any of it to the dead. I have listened to the voice of YHWH, my God. I have done according to everything that you commanded me. [15]Gaze from your holy abode, from the skies, and bless your people, Israel, and the land that you've given us as you swore to our fathers, a land flowing with milk and honey.

[16]"This day YHWH, your God, commands you to do these laws and judgments. And you shall be watchful and do them with all your heart and all your soul. [17]You have proclaimed YHWH today to be God to you, and to go in His ways and to observe His laws and His commandments and His judgments and to listen to His voice. [18]And YHWH proclaimed you today to be a treasured people to Him as He spoke to you—and to observe all His commandments— [19]and to set you high above all the nations that He has made in praise and name and beauty, and for you to be a holy people to YHWH, your God, as He spoke."

בִּעַרְתִּי מִמֶּנּוּ בְּטָמֵא וְלֹא־נָתַתִּי מִמֶּנּוּ לְמֵת שָׁמַעְתִּי בְּקוֹל יְהוָה אֱלֹהָי עָשִׂיתִי כְּכֹל אֲשֶׁר צִוִּיתָנִי: [15]הַשְׁקִיפָה מִמְּעוֹן קָדְשְׁךָ מִן־הַשָּׁמַיִם וּבָרֵךְ אֶת־עַמְּךָ אֶת־יִשְׂרָאֵל וְאֵת הָאֲדָמָה אֲשֶׁר נָתַתָּה לָנוּ כַּאֲשֶׁר נִשְׁבַּעְתָּ לַאֲבֹתֵינוּ אֶרֶץ זָבַת חָלָב וּדְבָשׁ: ס [16]הַיּוֹם הַזֶּה יְהוָה אֱלֹהֶיךָ מְצַוְּךָ לַעֲשׂוֹת אֶת־הַחֻקִּים הָאֵלֶּה וְאֶת־הַמִּשְׁפָּטִים וְשָׁמַרְתָּ וְעָשִׂיתָ אוֹתָם בְּכָל־לְבָבְךָ וּבְכָל־נַפְשֶׁךָ: [17]אֶת־יְהוָה הֶאֱמַרְתָּ הַיּוֹם לִהְיוֹת לְךָ לֵאלֹהִים וְלָלֶכֶת בִּדְרָכָיו וְלִשְׁמֹר חֻקָּיו וּמִצְוֹתָיו וּמִשְׁפָּטָיו וְלִשְׁמֹעַ בְּקֹלוֹ: [18]וַיהוָה הֶאֱמִירְךָ הַיּוֹם לִהְיוֹת לוֹ לְעַם סְגֻלָּה כַּאֲשֶׁר דִּבֶּר־לָךְ וְלִשְׁמֹר כָּל־מִצְוֹתָיו: [19]וּלְתִתְּךָ עֶלְיוֹן עַל כָּל־הַגּוֹיִם אֲשֶׁר עָשָׂה לִתְהִלָּה וּלְשֵׁם וּלְתִפְאָרֶת וְלִהְיֹתְךָ עַם־קָדֹשׁ לַיהוָה אֱלֹהֶיךָ כַּאֲשֶׁר דִּבֵּר: ס

26:14. **not given any of it to the dead**. The person declares that he has not misused his tithed produce in any way that associates it with death or impurity. This disallows offering the dead *tithed* food; but, as many scholars have observed, this prohibition is not against making *other* offerings of food to the dead. Giving food (and drink) for dead ancestors was practiced in Israel and Judah at least until the reign of King Hezekiah (c. 700 B.C.E.). Tombs have been excavated (at Megiddo, Hazor, Gezer, Beth-Shemesh, Dothan) that had apertures cut into their ceilings through which it would be possible to give offerings to the dead, or that had storage jars placed directly over the heads of the corpses. Beginning in the tenth century B.C.E., open ceramic bowls and flasks and jars for liquids, store-jars with dipper juglets, plates, cooking pots, and wine decanters were placed in tombs in Judah. The destruction of much of the countryside by the Assyrians, followed by the centralization of worship under Hezekiah, dramatically cut back on this practice.

26:16. **This day**. This passage, vv. 16–19, concludes Moses' speech that began at the start of chapter 5. In it, Moses formally pronounces that the people and God have each made a commitment. The people have declared that YHWH is to be their God and that they will keep His laws and listen to Him. YHWH has declared that Israel is to be His treasured people and that, if they will keep His laws, He will make them a renowned, holy people. The performance of the lengthy corpus of law that Moses has just taught (chapters 12–26, as well as the Decalogue in chapter 5) is thus said to be mutually confirmed by God and the people.

27 ¹And Moses and Israel's elders commanded the people, saying, "Observe all
the commandment that I command you today.
²And it shall be, in the day that you'll cross the
Jordan to the land that YHWH, your God, is giving you, that you shall set up big stones and
cover them with plaster. ³And you shall write on
them all the words of this instruction when you
cross so that you'll come to the land that YHWH,
your God, is giving you, a land flowing with milk
and honey, as YHWH, your fathers' God, spoke
to you. ⁴And it shall be, when you cross the Jordan, that you shall set up these stones that I command you today in Mount Ebal and cover them
with plaster. ⁵And you shall build an altar to
YHWH, your God, there, an altar of stones. You
shall not lift iron over them. ⁶You shall build the
altar of YHWH, your God, of whole stones, and
you shall offer burnt offerings on it to YHWH,
your God. ⁷And you shall sacrifice peace offerings and eat there and rejoice in front of YHWH,
your God. ⁸And you shall write on the stones all
the words of this instruction very clearly."

⁹And Moses and the Levite priests spoke to all
Israel, saying, "Be silent, and listen, Israel: this
day you have become a people to YHWH, your
God. ¹⁰And you shall listen to the voice of
YHWH, your God, and do His commandments
and His laws that I command you today."

¹¹And Moses commanded the people on that
day, saying, ¹²"These shall stand to bless the people on Mount Gerizim when you cross the Jordan: Simeon and Levi and Judah and Issachar
and Joseph and Benjamin. ¹³And these shall
stand for the curse on Mount Ebal: Reuben, Gad,
and Asher and Zebulun, Dan, and Naphtali.
¹⁴And the Levites shall answer, and they shall say
in a loud voice to every man of Israel:

¹⁵'Cursed be the man who will make a
statue or molten thing, an offensive thing
of YHWH, a stone engraver's work, and set
it up in secret.'

27:6. whole stones. Unhewn stones, not cut or shaped with tools.

And all the people shall answer, and they shall say: 'Amen.'

16'Cursed be one who disrespects one's father and his mother.'

And all the people shall say: 'Amen.'

17'Cursed be one who moves his neighbor's landmark.'

And all the people shall say: 'Amen.'

18'Cursed be one who misleads a blind person on the way.'

And all the people shall say: 'Amen.'

19'Cursed be one who bends the judgment of an alien, an orphan, or a widow.'

And all the people shall say: 'Amen.'

20'Cursed be one who lies with his father's wife, because he has exposed his father's hem.'

And all the people shall say: 'Amen.'

21'Cursed be one who lies with any animal.'

And all the people shall say: 'Amen.'

22'Cursed be one who lies with his sister —his father's daughter or his mother's daughter.'

And all the people shall say: 'Amen.'

23'Cursed be one who lies with his mother-in-law.'

And all the people shall say: 'Amen.'

24'Cursed be one who strikes his neighbor in secret.'

And all the people shall say: 'Amen.'

25'Cursed be one who takes a bribe to strike a person—innocent blood.'

And all the people shall say: 'Amen.'

26'Cursed be one who will not uphold the words of this instruction, to do them.'

And all the people shall say: 'Amen.'

אָמֵן: ס ¹⁶אָר֯וּר מַקְלֶה אָבִיו וְאִמּ֑וֹ וְאָמַר כָּל־
הָעָם אָמֵן: ס ¹⁷אָר֯וּר מַסִּיג גְּבוּל רֵעֵ֑הוּ וְאָמַר
כָּל־הָעָם אָמֵן: ס ¹⁸אָר֯וּר מַשְׁגֶּה עִוֵּר בַּדָּ֑רֶךְ
וְאָמַר כָּל־הָעָם אָמֵן: ס ¹⁹אָר֯וּר מַטֶּה מִשְׁפַּט גֵּר־
יָתוֹם וְאַלְמָנָ֑ה וְאָמַר כָּל־הָעָם אָמֵן: ס ²⁰אָר֯וּר
שֹׁכֵב֙ עִם־אֵשֶׁת אָבִיו כִּי גִלָּה כְּנַף אָבִ֑יו וְאָמַר
כָּל־הָעָם אָמֵן: ס ²¹אָר֯וּר שֹׁכֵב עִם־כָּל־בְּהֵמָ֑ה
וְאָמַר כָּל־הָעָם אָמֵן: ס ²²אָר֯וּר שֹׁכֵב֙ עִם־אֲחֹתוֹ
בַּת־אָבִיו א֖וֹ בַת־אִמּ֑וֹ וְאָמַר כָּל־הָעָם אָמֵן: ס
²³אָר֯וּר שֹׁכֵב עִם־חֹתַנְתּ֑וֹ וְאָמַר כָּל־הָעָם אָמֵן: ס
²⁴אָר֯וּר מַכֵּה רֵעֵ֖הוּ בַּסָּ֑תֶר וְאָמַר כָּל־הָעָם אָמֵן:
ס ²⁵אָרוּר֙ לֹקֵחַ שֹׁ֔חַד לְהַכּוֹת נֶפֶשׁ דָּם נָקִ֑י וְאָמַר
כָּל־הָעָם אָמֵן: ס ²⁶אָר֯וּר אֲשֶׁר לֹא־יָקִים אֶת־
דִּבְרֵי הַתּוֹרָה־הַזֹּאת לַעֲשׂוֹת אוֹתָ֑ם וְאָמַר כָּל־הָעָם
אָמֵן: פ

27:26. who will not uphold the words of this instruction. The curses seem like a list of sundry examples of the laws that Moses has given until now. Most of the things that are forbidden are uncommon and easy to avoid doing. So the people as a whole will readily say the "Amen" to them. But then the final curse is on anyone who will not support and perform "the words of this Torah"—in other words: the Torah as a whole. The people are led to a point at which they must say "Amen" to the full Torah.

28 [1]"And it will be, if you'll *listen* to the voice of YHWH, your God, to be watchful to do all His commandments that I command you today, that YHWH, your God, will set you high above all the nations of the earth. [2]And all these blessings will come on you and catch up with you when you'll listen to the voice of YHWH, your God: [3]You'll be blessed in the city, and you'll be blessed in the field. [4]The fruit of your womb and the fruit of your land and the fruit of your animals, your cattle's offspring and your flock's young, will be blessed. [5]Your basket and your bowl will be blessed. [6]You'll be blessed when you come in, and you'll be blessed when you go out. [7]YHWH will make your enemies who come up against you stricken in front of you. By one road they'll come out at you, and by seven roads they'll flee in front of you. [8]YHWH will command the blessing for you in your storehouses and in everything your hand takes on and will bless you in the land that YHWH, your God, is giving you. [9]YHWH will establish you for him as a holy people as He swore to you if you'll keep the commandments of YHWH, your God, and go in His ways. [10]And all the peoples of the earth will see that YHWH's name is called on you, and they'll be afraid of you. [11]And YHWH will give you a surplus of good in the fruit of your womb and in the fruit of your animals and in the fruit of your land, on the land that YHWH swore to your fathers to give you. [12]YHWH will open His good treasure, the skies, to you, to give your

וְהָיָ֗ה אִם־שָׁמֹ֤עַ תִּשְׁמַע֙ בְּקֹול֙ יְהוָ֣ה [1] 28
אֱלֹהֶ֔יךָ לִשְׁמֹ֤ר לַעֲשֹׂות֙ אֶת־כָּל־מִצְוֺתָ֔יו אֲשֶׁ֛ר אָנֹכִ֥י
מְצַוְּךָ֖ הַיֹּ֑ום וּנְתָֽנְךָ֞ יְהוָ֤ה אֱלֹהֶ֙יךָ֙ עֶלְיֹ֔ון עַ֖ל כָּל־גֹּויֵ֥י
הָאָֽרֶץ׃ [2] וּבָ֧אוּ עָלֶ֛יךָ כָּל־הַבְּרָכֹ֥ות הָאֵ֖לֶּה וְהִשִּׂיגֻ֑ךָ
כִּ֣י תִשְׁמַ֔ע בְּקֹ֖ול יְהוָ֥ה אֱלֹהֶֽיךָ׃ [3] בָּר֥וּךְ אַתָּ֖ה בָּעִ֑יר
וּבָר֥וּךְ אַתָּ֖ה בַּשָּׂדֶֽה׃ [4] בָּר֧וּךְ פְּרִֽי־בִטְנְךָ֛ וּפְרִ֥י
אַדְמָתְךָ֖ וּפְרִ֣י בְהֶמְתֶּ֑ךָ שְׁגַ֥ר אֲלָפֶ֖יךָ וְעַשְׁתְּרֹ֥ות
צֹאנֶֽךָ׃ [5] בָּר֥וּךְ טַנְאֲךָ֖ וּמִשְׁאַרְתֶּֽךָ׃ [6] בָּר֥וּךְ אַתָּ֖ה
בְּבֹאֶ֑ךָ וּבָר֥וּךְ אַתָּ֖ה בְּצֵאתֶֽךָ׃ [7] יִתֵּ֨ן יְהוָ֜ה אֶת־אֹיְבֶ֗יךָ
הַקָּמִ֤ים עָלֶ֙יךָ֙ נִגָּפִ֣ים לְפָנֶ֔יךָ בְּדֶ֥רֶךְ אֶחָ֖ד יֵצְא֣וּ
אֵלֶ֑יךָ וּבְשִׁבְעָ֥ה דְרָכִ֖ים יָנ֥וּסוּ לְפָנֶֽיךָ׃ [8] יְצַ֤ו יְהוָה֙
אִתְּךָ֙ אֶת־הַבְּרָכָ֔ה בַּאֲסָמֶ֕יךָ וּבְכֹ֖ל מִשְׁלַ֣ח יָדֶ֑ךָ
וּבֵ֣רַכְךָ֔ בָּאָ֕רֶץ אֲשֶׁר־יְהוָ֥ה אֱלֹהֶ֖יךָ נֹתֵ֥ן לָֽךְ׃
[9] יְקִֽימְךָ֨ יְהוָ֥ה לֹו֙ לְעַ֣ם קָדֹ֔ושׁ כַּאֲשֶׁ֖ר נִֽשְׁבַּֽע־לָ֑ךְ כִּ֣י
תִשְׁמֹ֗ר אֶת־מִצְוֺת֙ יְהוָ֣ה אֱלֹהֶ֔יךָ וְהָלַכְתָּ֖ בִּדְרָכָֽיו׃
[10] וְרָאוּ֙ כָּל־עַמֵּ֣י הָאָ֔רֶץ כִּ֛י שֵׁ֥ם יְהוָ֖ה נִקְרָ֣א עָלֶ֑יךָ
וְיָרְא֖וּ מִמֶּֽךָּ׃ [11] וְהֹותִֽרְךָ֤ יְהוָה֙ לְטֹובָ֔ה בִּפְרִ֧י בִטְנְךָ֛
וּבִפְרִ֥י בְהַמְתְּךָ֖ וּבִפְרִ֣י אַדְמָתֶ֑ךָ עַ֚ל הָֽאֲדָמָ֔ה אֲשֶׁ֨ר
נִשְׁבַּ֧ע יְהוָ֛ה לַאֲבֹתֶ֖יךָ לָ֥תֶת לָֽךְ׃ [12] יִפְתַּ֣ח יְהוָ֣ה ׀
לְךָ֡ אֶת־אֹוצָרֹ֣ו הַטֹּוב֩ אֶת־הַשָּׁמַ֜יִם לָתֵ֤ת מְטַֽר־

28:2,15. **blessings . . . curses.** The curses are four times the length of the blessings. Like the blessings and curses list in Leviticus 26 (where the curses are three times longer than the blessings), this list may convey that threats of punishment were thought to be more effective than promises of reward. Or it may convey the opposite: that threats are *less* effective, and therefore more are required. The remarkable thing is that, following all these blessings and curses, Moses speaks beautifully for two chapters about why the people should keep the covenant for *itself*. The blessings and curses are there out of a realistic recognition of human psychology: rewards and punishments are effective tools of instruction from childhood and up. But the aim is higher: that humans should come to see that what is being put in their hands is "life" and "good" and "love" (Deut 30:15–16).

lands showers at their time and to bless all your hand's work. And you'll lend to many nations, and you won't borrow; 13and YHWH will put you at the head and not at the tail; and you'll only be above, and you won't be below—if you'll listen to the commandments of YHWH, your God, that I command you today, to observe and to do, 14and you won't turn from all the things that I command you today, right or left, to go after other gods, to serve them.

15"And it will be, if you won't listen to the voice of YHWH, your God, to be watchful to do all His commandments and His laws that I command you today, that all these curses will come on you and catch up with you: 16You'll be cursed in the city, and you'll be cursed in the field. 17Your basket and your bowl will be cursed. 18The fruit of your womb and the fruit of your land, your cattle's offspring and your flock's young, will be cursed. 19You'll be cursed when you come in, and you'll be cursed when you go out. 20YHWH will send curse and tumult and annoyance at you in everything your hand takes on that you'll do, until you're destroyed and until you perish quickly because of your bad practices, in that you left me. 21YHWH will make an epidemic cling to you until He finishes you from the land to which you're coming to take possession of it. 22YHWH will strike you with consumption and with fever and with inflammation and with burning and with the sword and with blight and with mildew. And they'll pursue you until you perish. 23And your skies that are over your head will be bronze, and the land that is under you iron. 24YHWH will make your land's showers powder and dust; it will fall on you from the skies until you're destroyed. 25YHWH will make you stricken in front of your enemies. By one road you'll go out at him, and by seven roads you'll flee in front of him. And you'll be a horrifying thing to all the earth's kingdoms. 26And your carcass will become food for every bird of the skies and for the animals of the earth, with no one making them afraid. 27YHWH will strike

אַרְצְךָ֙ בְּעִתּ֔וֹ וּלְבָרֵ֕ךְ אֵ֖ת כָּל־מַעֲשֵׂ֣ה יָדֶ֑ךָ וְהִלְוִ֙יתָ֙ גּוֹיִ֣ם רַבִּ֔ים וְאַתָּ֖ה לֹ֥א תִלְוֶֽה: 13וּנְתָֽנְךָ֙ יְהוָ֤ה לְרֹאשׁ֙ וְלֹ֣א לְזָנָ֔ב וְהָיִ֙יתָ֙ רַ֣ק לְמַ֔עְלָה וְלֹ֥א תִהְיֶ֖ה לְמָ֑טָּה כִּֽי־תִשְׁמַ֞ע אֶל־מִצְוֺ֣ת ׀ יְהוָ֣ה אֱלֹהֶ֗יךָ אֲשֶׁ֧ר אָנֹכִ֛י מְצַוְּךָ֥ הַיּ֖וֹם לִשְׁמֹ֥ר וְלַעֲשֽׂוֹת: 14וְלֹ֣א תָס֗וּר מִכָּל־הַדְּבָרִים֙ אֲשֶׁ֨ר אָנֹכִ֜י מְצַוֶּ֥ה אֶתְכֶ֛ם הַיּ֖וֹם יָמִ֣ין וּשְׂמֹ֑אול לָלֶ֗כֶת אַחֲרֵ֛י אֱלֹהִ֥ים אֲחֵרִ֖ים לְעָבְדָֽם: ס

15וְהָיָ֗ה אִם־לֹ֤א תִשְׁמַע֙ בְּקוֹל֙ יְהוָ֣ה אֱלֹהֶ֔יךָ לִשְׁמֹ֤ר לַעֲשׂוֹת֙ אֶת־כָּל־מִצְוֺתָ֣יו וְחֻקֹּתָ֔יו אֲשֶׁ֛ר אָנֹכִ֥י מְצַוְּךָ֖ הַיּ֑וֹם וּבָ֧אוּ עָלֶ֛יךָ כָּל־הַקְּלָל֥וֹת הָאֵ֖לֶּה וְהִשִּׂיגֽוּךָ: 16אָר֥וּר אַתָּ֖ה בָּעִ֑יר וְאָר֥וּר אַתָּ֖ה בַּשָּׂדֶֽה: 17אָר֥וּר טַנְאֲךָ֖ וּמִשְׁאַרְתֶּֽךָ: 18אָר֥וּר פְּרִֽי־בִטְנְךָ֖ וּפְרִ֣י אַדְמָתֶ֑ךָ שְׁגַ֥ר אֲלָפֶ֖יךָ וְעַשְׁתְּר֥וֹת צֹאנֶֽךָ: 19אָר֥וּר אַתָּ֖ה בְּבֹאֶ֑ךָ וְאָר֥וּר אַתָּ֖ה בְּצֵאתֶֽךָ: 20יְשַׁלַּ֣ח יְהוָ֣ה ׀ בְּךָ֗ אֶת־הַמְּאֵרָ֤ה אֶת־הַמְּהוּמָה֙ וְאֶת־הַמִּגְעֶ֔רֶת בְּכָל־מִשְׁלַ֥ח יָדְךָ֖ אֲשֶׁ֣ר תַּעֲשֶׂ֑ה עַ֣ד הִשָּֽׁמֶדְךָ֤ וְעַד־אֲבָדְךָ֙ מַהֵ֔ר מִפְּנֵ֛י רֹ֥עַ מַֽעֲלָלֶ֖יךָ אֲשֶׁ֥ר עֲזַבְתָּֽנִי: 21יַדְבֵּ֧ק יְהוָ֛ה בְּךָ֖ אֶת־הַדָּ֑בֶר עַ֚ד כַּלֹּת֣וֹ אֹֽתְךָ֔ מֵעַל֙ הָֽאֲדָמָ֔ה אֲשֶׁר־אַתָּ֥ה בָא־שָׁ֖מָּה לְרִשְׁתָּֽהּ: 22יַכְּכָ֣ה יְ֠הוָה בַּשַּׁחֶ֨פֶת וּבַקַּדַּ֜חַת וּבַדַּלֶּ֗קֶת וּבַֽחַרְחֻר֙ וּבַחֶ֔רֶב וּבַשִּׁדָּפ֖וֹן וּבַיֵּרָק֑וֹן וּרְדָפ֖וּךָ עַ֥ד אָבְדֶֽךָ: 23וְהָי֥וּ שָׁמֶ֛יךָ אֲשֶׁ֥ר עַל־רֹאשְׁךָ֖ נְחֹ֑שֶׁת וְהָאָ֥רֶץ אֲשֶׁר־תַּחְתֶּ֖יךָ בַּרְזֶֽל: 24יִתֵּ֧ן יְהוָ֛ה אֶת־מְטַ֥ר אַרְצְךָ֖ אָבָ֣ק וְעָפָ֑ר מִן־הַשָּׁמַ֙יִם֙ יֵרֵ֣ד עָלֶ֔יךָ עַ֖ד הִשָּֽׁמְדָֽךְ: 25יִתֶּנְךָ֨ יְהוָ֥ה ׀ נִגָּף֮ לִפְנֵ֣י אֹיְבֶיךָ֒ בְּדֶ֤רֶךְ אֶחָד֙ תֵּצֵ֣א אֵלָ֔יו וּבְשִׁבְעָ֥ה דְרָכִ֖ים תָּנ֣וּס לְפָנָ֑יו וְהָיִ֣יתָ לְזַעֲוָ֔ה לְכֹ֖ל מַמְלְכ֥וֹת הָאָֽרֶץ: 26וְהָיְתָ֤ה נִבְלָֽתְךָ֙ לְמַאֲכָ֔ל לְכָל־ע֥וֹף הַשָּׁמַ֖יִם וּלְבֶהֱמַ֣ת הָאָ֑רֶץ וְאֵ֖ין מַחֲרִֽיד: 27יַכְּכָ֙ה

you with the boils of Egypt and with hemor-rhoids and with scabs and with itches, from which you won't be able to be healed. 28YHWH will strike you with madness and with blindness and with amazement of heart. 29And you'll be feeling around at noon the way the blind would feel around, in the dark. And you won't make your ways successful, but you'll just be exploited and robbed every day, and there will be no one to save you. 30You'll betroth a woman, and an-other man will ravish her. You'll build a house, and you won't live in it. You'll plant a vineyard, and you won't desanctify it. 31Your ox slaugh-tered before your eyes—and you won't eat any of it. Your ass stolen from in front of you—and it won't come back to you. Your sheep given to your enemies—and you'll have no one to save you. 32Your sons and your daughters given to an-other people—while your eyes are looking for them all day and giving out, and there's no God at your hand. 33A people whom you haven't known will eat your land's fruit and all the prod-

יְהֹוָה בִּשְׁחִין מִצְרַיִם֙ וּבַעְפֹלִ֔ים וּבַגָּרָ֖ב וּבֶחָ֑רֶס אֲשֶׁ֥ר לֹא־תוּכַ֖ל לְהֵרָפֵֽא׃ 28יַכְּכָ֣ה יְהֹוָ֔ה בְּשִׁגָּע֖וֹן וּבְעִוָּר֑וֹן וּבְתִמְה֖וֹן לֵבָֽב׃ 29וְהָיִ֜יתָ מְמַשֵּׁ֣שׁ בַּֽצׇּהֳרַ֗יִם כַּאֲשֶׁ֨ר יְמַשֵּׁ֤שׁ הָעִוֵּר֙ בָּאֲפֵלָ֔ה וְלֹ֥א תַצְלִ֖יחַ אֶת־דְּרָכֶ֑יךָ וְהָיִ֜יתָ אַ֣ךְ עָשׁ֧וּק וְגָז֛וּל כׇּל־הַיָּמִ֖ים וְאֵ֥ין מוֹשִֽׁיעַ׃ 30אִשָּׁ֣ה תְאָרֵ֗שׂ וְאִ֤ישׁ אַחֵר֙ יִשְׁגָּלֶ֔נָּה בַּ֥יִת תִּבְנֶ֖ה וְלֹא־תֵשֵׁ֣ב בּ֑וֹ כֶּ֥רֶם תִּטַּ֖ע וְלֹ֥א תְחַלְּלֶֽנּוּ׃ 31שֽׁוֹרְךָ֞ טָב֣וּחַ לְעֵינֶ֗יךָ וְלֹ֣א תֹאכַל֮ מִמֶּ֒נּוּ֒ חֲמֹֽרְךָ֙ גָּז֣וּל מִלְּפָנֶ֔יךָ וְלֹ֥א יָשׁ֖וּב לָ֑ךְ צֹֽאנְךָ֙ נְתֻנ֣וֹת לְאֹ֣יְבֶ֔יךָ וְאֵ֥ין לְךָ֖ מוֹשִֽׁיעַ׃ 32בָּנֶ֤יךָ וּבְנֹתֶ֙יךָ֙ נְתֻנִ֣ים לְעַ֣ם אַחֵ֔ר וְעֵינֶ֣יךָ רֹא֗וֹת וְכָל֧וֹת אֲלֵיהֶ֛ם כׇּל־הַיּ֖וֹם וְאֵ֥ין לְאֵ֥ל יָדֶֽךָ׃ 33פְּרִ֤י אַדְמָֽתְךָ֙ וְכָל־יְגִ֣יעֲךָ֔ יֹאכַ֥ל עַ֖ם אֲשֶׁ֣ר

קֿ וּבַטְּחֹרִ֖ים 28:27
קֿ יִשְׁכָּבֶֽנָּה 28:30

28:27. **the boils of Egypt.** The horror of the curses is multiplied by the fact that this and other curses are among the ten plagues that were imposed on Egypt. The thought that God would impose on Israel the very plagues that were used on Egypt to make YHWH known and set Israel free is terrifying. The reminder of Egypt will culminate in the last curse (v. 68 below).

28:29. **feeling around at noon the way the blind would feel around, in the dark.** This curse, too, reflects the plagues on Egypt. In Exod 10:22, the darkness is described with this same term, Hebrew *'ăpēlāh*, which occurs only in these two places in the Torah. Also, the related verb for "feeling" or "groping" is used there (10:21).

28:30. **ravish her.** The written text of the Torah (the *ketib*) uses this strong term. When it is read (the *qere'*), a milder term, "lie with her" (*yiškabenāh*), is substituted.

28:30. **desanctify.** See the comment on Deut 20:6.

28:32. **no God at your hand.** Laban uses this expression to convey to Jacob that he has power ("The god at my hand has the means to do bad to you," Gen 31:29). Here in the curse list of Deuteronomy it is formulated in the negative, conveying that the people will be powerless. Similarly, the curse in v. 29 uses the expression "you won't make your ways successful," which is a negative formulation of the words that are used to describe Abraham's servant's internal question ("to know if YHWH had made his trip successful or not," Gen 24:21). Thus there are reminiscences of the first book of the Torah that are reversed here in the curse list in the last book of the Torah—which doubles the force of these horrible threats.

650

uct of your exhaustion, and you'll only be exploited and crushed every day. 34And you'll be driven mad from the sight before your eyes that you'll see. 35YHWH will strike you with bad boils on the knees and on the thighs from which you won't be able to be healed, from your foot to the top of your head. 36YHWH will drive you and your king whom you'll set up over you to a nation whom you haven't known, you and your fathers, and you'll serve other gods, wood and stone, there. 37And you'll become an astonishment, a proverb, and an expression among all the peoples to which YHWH will drive you. 38You'll take out much seed to the field, but you'll gather little, because locusts will finish it off. 39You'll plant vineyards and work them, but you won't drink wine or gather grapes, because worms will eat it. 40You'll have olives within all your border, but you won't anoint with oil, because your olive will drop off. 41You'll give birth to sons and daughters, but you won't have them, because they'll go into captivity. 42Crickets will take possession of all your trees and your land's fruit. 43The alien who is among you will go up above you higher and higher, and *you* will go down lower and lower. 44*He* will lend to you, but *you* won't lend to him. *He* will become a head, and *you* will become a tail.

45"And all these curses will come over you and pursue you and catch up with you until you're destroyed because you didn't listen to the voice of YHWH, your God, to observe His commandments and His laws that He commanded you. 46And they'll be a sign and a wonder in you and in your seed forever. 47Because you didn't serve YHWH, your God, with joy and with good feeling from the abundance of everything, 48so you'll serve your enemies whom YHWH will send at you in hunger and in thirst and in nakedness and in lack of everything. And He'll put an iron yoke on your neck until He has destroyed you. 49YHWH will fetch a nation from far, from the end of the earth, over you the way an eagle soars, a nation whose language you won't understand,

לֹא־יָדַעְתָּ וְהָיִיתָ רַק עָשׁוּק וְרָצוּץ כָּל־הַיָּמִים: 34וְהָיִיתָ מְשֻׁגָּע מִמַּרְאֵה עֵינֶיךָ אֲשֶׁר תִּרְאֶה: 35יַכְּכָה יְהוָה בִּשְׁחִין רָע עַל־הַבִּרְכַּיִם וְעַל־הַשֹּׁקַיִם אֲשֶׁר לֹא־תוּכַל לְהֵרָפֵא מִכַּף רַגְלְךָ וְעַד קָדְקֳדֶךָ: 36יוֹלֵךְ יְהוָה אֹתְךָ וְאֶת־מַלְכְּךָ אֲשֶׁר תָּקִים עָלֶיךָ אֶל־גּוֹי אֲשֶׁר לֹא־יָדַעְתָּ אַתָּה וַאֲבֹתֶיךָ וְעָבַדְתָּ שָּׁם אֱלֹהִים אֲחֵרִים עֵץ וָאָבֶן: 37וְהָיִיתָ לְשַׁמָּה לְמָשָׁל וְלִשְׁנִינָה בְּכֹל הָעַמִּים אֲשֶׁר־יְנַהֶגְךָ יְהוָה שָׁמָּה: 38זֶרַע רַב תּוֹצִיא הַשָּׂדֶה וּמְעַט תֶּאֱסֹף כִּי יַחְסְלֶנּוּ הָאַרְבֶּה: 39כְּרָמִים תִּטַּע וְעָבָדְתָּ וְיַיִן לֹא־תִשְׁתֶּה וְלֹא תֶאֱגֹר כִּי תֹאכְלֶנּוּ הַתֹּלָעַת: 40זֵיתִים יִהְיוּ לְךָ בְּכָל־גְּבוּלֶךָ וְשֶׁמֶן לֹא תָסוּךְ כִּי יִשַּׁל זֵיתֶךָ: 41בָּנִים וּבָנוֹת תּוֹלִיד וְלֹא־יִהְיוּ לָךְ כִּי יֵלְכוּ בַּשֶּׁבִי: 42כָּל־עֵצְךָ וּפְרִי אַדְמָתֶךָ יְיָרֵשׁ הַצְּלָצַל: 43הַגֵּר אֲשֶׁר בְּקִרְבְּךָ יַעֲלֶה עָלֶיךָ מַעְלָה מָּעְלָה וְאַתָּה תֵרֵד מַטָּה מָּטָּה: 44הוּא יַלְוְךָ וְאַתָּה לֹא תַלְוֶנּוּ הוּא יִהְיֶה לְרֹאשׁ וְאַתָּה תִּהְיֶה לְזָנָב: 45וּבָאוּ עָלֶיךָ כָּל־הַקְּלָלוֹת הָאֵלֶּה וּרְדָפוּךָ וְהִשִּׂיגוּךָ עַד הִשָּׁמְדָךְ כִּי־לֹא שָׁמַעְתָּ בְּקוֹל יְהוָה אֱלֹהֶיךָ לִשְׁמֹר מִצְוֹתָיו וְחֻקֹּתָיו אֲשֶׁר צִוָּךְ: 46וְהָיוּ בְךָ לְאוֹת וּלְמוֹפֵת וּבְזַרְעֲךָ עַד־עוֹלָם: 47תַּחַת אֲשֶׁר לֹא־עָבַדְתָּ אֶת־יְהוָה אֱלֹהֶיךָ בְּשִׂמְחָה וּבְטוּב לֵבָב מֵרֹב כֹּל: 48וְעָבַדְתָּ אֶת־אֹיְבֶיךָ אֲשֶׁר יְשַׁלְּחֶנּוּ יְהוָה בָּךְ בְּרָעָב וּבְצָמָא וּבְעֵירֹם וּבְחֹסֶר כֹּל וְנָתַן עֹל בַּרְזֶל עַל־צַוָּארֶךָ עַד הִשְׁמִידוֹ אֹתָךְ: 49יִשָּׂא יְהוָה עָלֶיךָ גּוֹי מֵרָחוֹק מִקְצֵה הָאָרֶץ כַּאֲשֶׁר יִדְאֶה הַנָּשֶׁר גּוֹי אֲשֶׁר לֹא־תִשְׁמַע לְשֹׁנוֹ: 50גּוֹי עַז

50a fierce-faced nation who won't be partial to the old and won't show grace to the young— 51and it will eat the fruit of your animals and the fruit of your land until you are destroyed—who won't leave you grain, wine, and oil, your cattle's off-spring and your flock's young until it has made you perish. 52And it will close you in, in all your gates, until your high and fortified walls in which you trust come down in all your land; and it will close you in, in all your gates, in all your land that YHWH, your God, has given you. 53And you'll eat the fruit of your womb, the flesh of your sons and your daughters whom YHWH, your God, has given you, in the siege and in the constraint that your enemy will put on you. 54The tenderest man among you and the very delicate: his eye will look with evil intent at his brother and the wife of his bosom and the rest of his children that he'll have left 55from giving to one of them any of the flesh of his children that he'll eat, because nothing will be left to him in the siege and in the constraint that your enemy will put on you in all your gates. 56The tenderest and the most delicate woman among you, who wouldn't risk setting her foot on the ground out of delicacy and tenderness: her eye will look with evil intent at the man of her bosom and her son and her daughter 57and her afterbirth that comes out from between her legs and her children to whom she'll give birth, be-cause she'll eat them in secret due to the lack of everything in the siege and in the constraint that your enemy will put on you in your gates. 58If you won't be watchful to do the words of this instruc-tion that are written in this scroll, to fear this hon-ored and awesome name: YHWH, your God, 59then YHWH will make your plagues and your seed's plagues astonishing, great and enduring plagues, and great and enduring illnesses. 60And He'll bring back among you every disease of Egypt, which you were dreading, and they'll cling to you. 61YHWH will bring over you every illness

פָּנִ֔ים אֲשֶׁ֨ר לֹא־יִשָּׂ֤א פָנִים֙ לְזָקֵ֔ן וְנַ֖עַר לֹ֥א יָחֹֽן׃
‏51וְ֠אָכַל פְּרִ֨י בְהֶמְתְּךָ֥ וּפְרִֽי־אַדְמָתְךָ֮ עַ֣ד הִשָּֽׁמְדָךְ֒ אֲשֶׁ֨ר לֹֽא־יַשְׁאִ֜יר לְךָ֗ דָּגָ֤ן תִּירוֹשׁ֙ וְיִצְהָ֔ר שְׁגַ֥ר אֲלָפֶ֖יךָ וְעַשְׁתְּרֹ֣ת צֹאנֶ֑ךָ עַ֥ד הַאֲבִיד֖וֹ אֹתָֽךְ׃ ‏52וְהֵצַ֨ר לְךָ֜ בְּכָל־שְׁעָרֶ֗יךָ עַ֣ד רֶ֤דֶת חֹמֹתֶ֙יךָ֙ הַגְּבֹהֹ֣ת וְהַבְּצֻר֔וֹת אֲשֶׁ֥ר אַתָּ֛ה בֹּטֵ֥חַ בָּהֵ֖ן בְּכָל־אַרְצֶ֑ךָ וְהֵצַ֤ר לְךָ֙ בְּכָל־שְׁעָרֶ֔יךָ בְּכָל־אַרְצְךָ֔ אֲשֶׁ֥ר נָתַ֛ן יְהוָ֥ה אֱלֹהֶ֖יךָ לָֽךְ׃ ‏53וְאָכַלְתָּ֣ פְרִֽי־בִטְנְךָ֗ בְּשַׂ֤ר בָּנֶ֙יךָ֙ וּבְנֹתֶ֔יךָ אֲשֶׁ֥ר נָֽתַן־לְךָ֖ יְהוָ֣ה אֱלֹהֶ֑יךָ בְּמָצוֹר֙ וּבְמָצ֔וֹק אֲשֶׁר־יָצִ֥יק לְךָ֖ אֹיְבֶֽךָ׃ ‏54הָאִישׁ֙ הָרַ֣ךְ בְּךָ֔ וְהֶעָנֹ֖ג מְאֹ֑ד תֵּרַ֨ע עֵינ֤וֹ בְאָחִיו֙ וּבְאֵ֣שֶׁת חֵיק֔וֹ וּבְיֶ֥תֶר בָּנָ֖יו אֲשֶׁ֥ר יוֹתִֽיר׃ ‏55מִתֵּ֣ת ׀ לְאַחַ֣ד מֵהֶ֗ם מִבְּשַׂ֤ר בָּנָיו֙ אֲשֶׁ֣ר יֹאכֵ֔ל מִבְּלִ֥י הִשְׁאִֽיר־ל֖וֹ כֹּ֑ל בְּמָצוֹר֙ וּבְמָצ֔וֹק אֲשֶׁ֨ר יָצִ֥יק לְךָ֛ אֹיִבְךָ֖ בְּכָל־שְׁעָרֶֽיךָ׃ ‏56הָרַכָּ֨ה בְךָ֜ וְהָעֲנֻגָּ֗ה אֲשֶׁ֨ר לֹא־נִסְּתָ֤ה כַף־רַגְלָהּ֙ הַצֵּ֣ג עַל־הָאָ֔רֶץ מֵהִתְעַנֵּ֖ג וּמֵרֹ֑ךְ תֵּרַ֤ע עֵינָהּ֙ בְּאִ֣ישׁ חֵיקָ֔הּ וּבִבְנָ֖הּ וּבְבִתָּֽהּ׃ ‏57וּֽבְשִׁלְיָתָ֞הּ הַיּוֹצֵ֣ת ׀ מִבֵּ֣ין רַגְלֶ֗יהָ וּבְבָנֶ֙יהָ֙ אֲשֶׁ֣ר תֵּלֵ֔ד כִּֽי־תֹאכְלֵ֥ם בְּחֹֽסֶר־כֹּ֖ל בַּסָּ֑תֶר בְּמָצוֹר֙ וּבְמָצ֔וֹק אֲשֶׁ֨ר יָצִ֥יק לְךָ֛ אֹיִבְךָ֖ בִּשְׁעָרֶֽיךָ׃ ‏58אִם־לֹ֨א תִשְׁמֹ֜ר לַעֲשׂ֗וֹת אֶת־כָּל־דִּבְרֵי֙ הַתּוֹרָ֣ה הַזֹּ֔את הַכְּתוּבִ֖ים בַּסֵּ֣פֶר הַזֶּ֑ה לְ֠יִרְאָה אֶת־הַשֵּׁ֞ם הַנִּכְבָּ֤ד וְהַנּוֹרָא֙ הַזֶּ֔ה אֵ֖ת יְהוָ֥ה אֱלֹהֶֽיךָ׃ ‏59וְהִפְלָ֤א יְהוָה֙ אֶת־מַכֹּ֣תְךָ֔ וְאֵ֖ת מַכּ֣וֹת זַרְעֶ֑ךָ מַכּ֤וֹת גְּדֹלֹת֙ וְנֶ֣אֱמָנ֔וֹת וָחֳלָיִ֥ם רָעִ֖ים וְנֶאֱמָנִֽים׃ ‏60וְהֵשִׁ֣יב בְּךָ֗ אֵ֚ת כָּל־מַדְוֵ֣ה מִצְרַ֔יִם אֲשֶׁ֥ר יָגֹ֖רְתָּ מִפְּנֵיהֶ֑ם וְדָבְק֖וּ בָּֽךְ׃ ‏61גַּ֤ם כָּל־חֳלִי֙ וְכָל־מַכָּ֔ה אֲשֶׁר֙ לֹ֤א

28:53. you'll eat . . . the flesh of your sons. This horrid curse comes true four cen-turies later during the Aramean siege of Samaria (2 Kings 6:25–29).

and every plague that is not written in this scroll of instruction, as well, until you are destroyed. 62And you'll be left with few persons when you had been like the stars of the skies for multitude, because you didn't listen to the voice of YHWH, your God. 63And it will be: as YHWH had satisfaction over you to do good to you and to multiply you, so YHWH will have satisfaction over you to make you perish and to destroy you, and you'll be torn away from the land to which you're coming to take possession of it. 64And YHWH will scatter you among all the peoples from one end of the earth to the other end of the earth. And you'll serve other gods, whom you haven't known, you and your fathers, there, wood and stone. 65And among those nations you won't have a respite, and there won't be a resting place for your foot, and YHWH will give you there a trembling heart and a failing of eyes and a fainting of soul. 66And your life will be hanging opposite you, and you'll fear night and day, and you won't trust in your life. 67In the morning you'll say, 'Who would make it evening,' and in the evening you'll say, 'Who would make it morning,' because of your heart's fear that you'll have and because of the sight before your eyes that you'll see. 68And YHWH will bring you back to Egypt in

כָּתוּב בְּסֵפֶר הַתּוֹרָה הַזֹּאת יַעְלֵם יְהוָה עָלֶיךָ עַד הִשָּׁמְדָךְ: 62וְנִשְׁאַרְתֶּם בִּמְתֵי מְעָט תַּחַת אֲשֶׁר הֱיִיתֶם כְּכוֹכְבֵי הַשָּׁמַיִם לָרֹב כִּי־לֹא שָׁמַעְתָּ בְּקוֹל יְהוָה אֱלֹהֶיךָ: 63וְהָיָה כַּאֲשֶׁר־שָׂשׂ יְהוָה עֲלֵיכֶם לְהֵיטִיב אֶתְכֶם וּלְהַרְבּוֹת אֶתְכֶם כֵּן יָשִׂישׂ יְהוָה עֲלֵיכֶם לְהַאֲבִיד אֶתְכֶם וּלְהַשְׁמִיד אֶתְכֶם וְנִסַּחְתֶּם מֵעַל הָאֲדָמָה אֲשֶׁר־אַתָּה בָא־שָׁמָּה לְרִשְׁתָּהּ: 64וֶהֱפִיצְךָ יְהוָה בְּכָל־הָעַמִּים מִקְצֵה הָאָרֶץ וְעַד־קְצֵה הָאָרֶץ וְעָבַדְתָּ שָּׁם אֱלֹהִים אֲחֵרִים אֲשֶׁר לֹא־יָדַעְתָּ אַתָּה וַאֲבֹתֶיךָ עֵץ וָאָבֶן: 65וּבַגּוֹיִם הָהֵם לֹא תַרְגִּיעַ וְלֹא־יִהְיֶה מָנוֹחַ לְכַף־רַגְלֶךָ וְנָתַן יְהוָה לְךָ שָׁם לֵב רַגָּז וְכִלְיוֹן עֵינַיִם וְדַאֲבוֹן נָפֶשׁ: 66וְהָיוּ חַיֶּיךָ תְּלֻאִים לְךָ מִנֶּגֶד וּפָחַדְתָּ לַיְלָה וְיוֹמָם וְלֹא תַאֲמִין בְּחַיֶּיךָ: 67בַּבֹּקֶר תֹּאמַר מִי־יִתֵּן עֶרֶב וּבָעֶרֶב תֹּאמַר מִי־יִתֵּן בֹּקֶר מִפַּחַד לְבָבְךָ אֲשֶׁר תִּפְחָד וּמִמַּרְאֵה עֵינֶיךָ אֲשֶׁר תִּרְאֶה: 68וֶהֱשִׁיבְךָ

28:65. **a resting place for your foot.** Again an expression from the early part of Genesis reappears at the end of the Torah. The dove that Noah lets go "did not find a resting place for its foot" (Gen 8:9). The helplessness of the dove, with no place on earth to go, now turns out to have been a metaphoric image of the condition of the people of Israel if they do not keep their covenant.

28:68. **back to Egypt.** For the last curse of this list of horrors, what would be the worst threat specifically for the people of Israel: back to Egypt! This nightmare comes true seven hundred years later, after the Babylonian destruction of Jerusalem, described at the end of the book of Kings: "All the people, from the smallest to the biggest . . . got up and came to Egypt" (2 Kings 25:26; Jer 43:5–7). The last curse is that they will go back to Egypt, and the last page of the book of Kings reports that the entire people go back to Egypt. Yet, incredibly, this fact is almost never mentioned in commentaries on Deuteronomy or Kings or in biblical scholarship in general. The focus has been on the small portion of the nation who go into exile in Babylon, not on the mass of the people, who go as refugees to Egypt. It is time that we recognized, first, the full horror of the final curse of the covenant. Second, we must be sensitive to what it means to *Moses* to pronounce this curse: the heartbreak of what it would mean

boats, by the way that I said to you: 'You won't go on to see it anymore.' And you'll sell yourselves there to your enemies as slaves and as maids, and none will buy!"

69These are the words of the covenant that YHWH commanded Moses to make with the children of Israel in the land of Moab, aside from the covenant that He made with them at Horeb.

29 1And Moses called all of Israel and said to them, "You've seen everything that YHWH did before your eyes in the land of Egypt to Pharaoh and to all his servants and to all his land, 2the great tests that your eyes saw, those great signs and wonders. 3But YHWH did not give you a heart to know and eyes to see and ears to hear until this day. 4As I led you forty years in the wilderness, your clothing did not become worn on you, and your shoe did not become worn on your foot, 5you didn't eat bread, and you didn't drink wine and beer, so you would know that 'I am YHWH your God.' 6And you came to this place. (And Sihon, king of Heshbon,

יְהוָ֗ה ׀ מִצְרַ֙יִם֙ בָּֽאֳנִיּ֔וֹת בַּדֶּ֙רֶךְ֙ אֲשֶׁ֣ר אָמַ֣רְתִּי לְךָ֔
לֹא־תֹסִ֥יף ע֖וֹד לִרְאֹתָ֑הּ וְהִתְמַכַּרְתֶּ֙ם שָׁ֜ם לְאֹיְבֶ֛יךָ
לַעֲבָדִ֥ים וְלִשְׁפָח֖וֹת וְאֵ֥ין קֹנֶֽה׃ ס 69אֵ֣לֶּה דִבְרֵ֣י
הַבְּרִ֗ית אֲשֶׁר־צִוָּ֤ה יְהוָה֙ אֶת־מֹשֶׁ֔ה לִכְרֹ֥ת אֶת־בְּנֵ֖י
יִשְׂרָאֵ֑ל בְּאֶ֖רֶץ מוֹאָ֑ב מִלְּבַ֣ד הַבְּרִ֔ית אֲשֶׁר־כָּרַ֥ת
אִתָּ֖ם בְּחֹרֵֽב׃ פ

29 1וַיִּקְרָ֥א מֹשֶׁ֖ה אֶל־כָּל־יִשְׂרָאֵ֑ל וַיֹּ֣אמֶר
אֲלֵהֶ֗ם אַתֶּ֤ם רְאִיתֶם֙ אֵ֣ת כָּל־אֲשֶׁר֩ עָשָׂ֨ה יְהוָ֤ה
לְעֵֽינֵיכֶם֙ בְּאֶ֣רֶץ מִצְרַ֔יִם לְפַרְעֹ֥ה וּלְכָל־עֲבָדָ֖יו
וּלְכָל־אַרְצֽוֹ׃ 2הַמַּסּוֹת֙ הַגְּדֹלֹ֔ת אֲשֶׁ֥ר רָא֖וּ עֵינֶ֑יךָ
הָאֹתֹ֧ת וְהַמֹּפְתִ֛ים הַגְּדֹלִ֖ים הָהֵֽם׃ 3וְלֹא־נָתַן֩ יְהוָ֨ה
לָכֶ֥ם לֵב֙ לָדַ֔עַת וְעֵינַ֥יִם לִרְא֖וֹת וְאָזְנַ֣יִם לִשְׁמֹ֑עַ עַ֖ד
הַיּ֥וֹם הַזֶּֽה׃ 4וָאוֹלֵ֧ךְ אֶתְכֶ֛ם אַרְבָּעִ֥ים שָׁנָ֖ה בַּמִּדְבָּ֑ר
לֹֽא־בָל֤וּ שַׂלְמֹֽתֵיכֶם֙ מֵעֲלֵיכֶ֔ם וְנַֽעַלְךָ֥ לֹֽא־בָלְתָ֖ה
מֵעַ֥ל רַגְלֶֽךָ׃ 5לֶ֚חֶם לֹ֣א אֲכַלְתֶּ֔ם וְיַ֥יִן וְשֵׁכָ֖ר לֹ֣א
שְׁתִיתֶ֑ם לְמַ֙עַן֙ תֵּֽדְע֔וּ כִּ֛י אֲנִ֥י יְהוָ֖ה אֱלֹֽהֵיכֶֽם׃
6וַתָּבֹ֖אוּ אֶל־הַמָּק֣וֹם הַזֶּ֑ה וַיֵּצֵ֣א סִיחֹ֣ן מֶֽלֶךְ־חֶשְׁבּ֗וֹן

---

for his people to be back in Egypt, even worse off than before, the failure, the humiliation. Third, we must give due attention to the fate of the Jews who ended up back in Egypt. And, fourth, we should appreciate the significance of the fact that it was the small portion of the community who were taken to Babylon who produced the kernel who returned to Israel a generation later and rebuilt the Temple, Jerusalem, and the country—a second life for Israel in its land that lasted six hundred years.

28:68. in boats. The reference to boats has never been understood. It may be an *alef/ayin* scribal error for *'nywt* (afflictions) or a plural of *'ăniyyāh* (mourning; Isa 29:2; Lam 2:5), although these forms of the words are unattested in the *Tanak;* or it may refer to an historical event that is no longer known.

29:3. did not give you . . . until this day. This is an old enigma: have they not been able to understand the meaning of all the great wonders they have witnessed until now? I understand this to mean just that. Moses has just finished the long speech that takes up nearly all of Deuteronomy. Now he is beginning a much shorter speech, and he is telling them that he is about to reveal to them, in his last message to them, the key to understanding what their experience means. What follows is a speech like no other he has ever made in the Torah. Until now he has focused on facts: points of history, specific laws. But, starting in a few verses, he will turn philosophical, moral, and spiritual—and his message is formulated in some of the most beautiful words in the Torah.

654

and Og, king of Bashan, came out at us for war, and we struck them. ⁷And we took their land and gave it as a legacy to the Reubenite and to the Gadite and to half of the Manassite tribe.) ⁸And you shall observe the words of this covenant and do them so that you'll *understand* all that you'll do.

STANDING

⁹"You're standing today, all of you, in front of YHWH, your God—your heads, your tribes, your elders, and your officers, every man of Israel, ¹⁰your infants, your women, and your alien who is in your camps, from one who cuts your wood to one who draws your water— ¹¹for you to enter into the covenant of YHWH, your God, and into His oath, which YHWH, your God, is making with you today, ¹²in order to establish you today for Him as a people, and *He* will be a God to you, as He spoke to you and as He swore to your fathers: to Abraham, to Isaac, and to Jacob. ¹³And I am not making this covenant and this oath with you alone, ¹⁴but with the one who is here standing with us today in front of YHWH, our God, and with the one who isn't here with us today. ¹⁵Because *you* know that we lived in the land of Egypt and that we passed among the nations that you passed. ¹⁶And you've seen their disgraces and their idols, wood and stone, silver and gold, that were with them. ¹⁷In case there

נצבים

וְעוֹג מֶלֶךְ־הַבָּשָׁן לִקְרָאתֵנוּ לַמִּלְחָמָה וַנַּכֵּם: ⁷וַנִּקַּח אֶת־אַרְצָם וַנִּתְּנָהּ לְנַחֲלָה לָרֻאוּבֵנִי וְלַגָּדִי וְלַחֲצִי שֵׁבֶט הַמְנַשִּׁי: ⁸וּשְׁמַרְתֶּם אֶת־דִּבְרֵי הַבְּרִית הַזֹּאת וַעֲשִׂיתֶם אֹתָם לְמַעַן תַּשְׂכִּילוּ אֵת כָּל־אֲשֶׁר תַּעֲשׂוּן:

פ ⁹אַתֶּם נִצָּבִים הַיּוֹם כֻּלְּכֶם לִפְנֵי יְהוָה אֱלֹהֵיכֶם רָאשֵׁיכֶם שִׁבְטֵיכֶם זִקְנֵיכֶם וְשֹׁטְרֵיכֶם כֹּל אִישׁ יִשְׂרָאֵל: ¹⁰טַפְּכֶם נְשֵׁיכֶם וְגֵרְךָ אֲשֶׁר בְּקֶרֶב מַחֲנֶיךָ מֵחֹטֵב עֵצֶיךָ עַד שֹׁאֵב מֵימֶיךָ: ¹¹לְעָבְרְךָ בִּבְרִית יְהוָה אֱלֹהֶיךָ וּבְאָלָתוֹ אֲשֶׁר יְהוָה אֱלֹהֶיךָ כֹּרֵת עִמְּךָ הַיּוֹם: ¹²לְמַעַן הָקִים־אֹתְךָ הַיּוֹם ׀ לוֹ לְעָם וְהוּא יִהְיֶה־לְּךָ לֵאלֹהִים כַּאֲשֶׁר דִּבֶּר־לָךְ וְכַאֲשֶׁר נִשְׁבַּע לַאֲבֹתֶיךָ לְאַבְרָהָם לְיִצְחָק וּלְיַעֲקֹב: ¹³וְלֹא אִתְּכֶם לְבַדְּכֶם אָנֹכִי כֹּרֵת אֶת־הַבְּרִית הַזֹּאת וְאֶת־הָאָלָה הַזֹּאת: ¹⁴כִּי אֶת־אֲשֶׁר יֶשְׁנוֹ פֹּה עִמָּנוּ עֹמֵד הַיּוֹם לִפְנֵי יְהוָה אֱלֹהֵינוּ וְאֵת אֲשֶׁר אֵינֶנּוּ פֹּה עִמָּנוּ הַיּוֹם: ¹⁵כִּי־אַתֶּם יְדַעְתֶּם אֵת אֲשֶׁר־יָשַׁבְנוּ בְּאֶרֶץ מִצְרָיִם וְאֵת אֲשֶׁר־עָבַרְנוּ בְּקֶרֶב הַגּוֹיִם אֲשֶׁר עֲבַרְתֶּם: ¹⁶וַתִּרְאוּ אֶת־שִׁקּוּצֵיהֶם וְאֵת גִּלֻּלֵיהֶם עֵץ וָאֶבֶן כֶּסֶף וְזָהָב אֲשֶׁר

29:8. **understand**. Yet again the words of the beginning of the Torah return in the Torah's closing portions. In the garden of Eden, the woman is attracted to the fruit of the tree of knowledge of good and bad because it will "bring about understanding" (Hebrew *haśkîl*; 3:6). Humans acquire that ability—understanding—when they eat the forbidden fruit. The word then does not occur again in the Torah until here. Now Moses tells them that they can use the divine power of understanding for a purpose: comprehending the meaning of what they have experienced and of what they will do. The past and the future, the miracles and the performance of the covenant's commandments, are all within humans' power to grasp. What began as something taken in violation of a divine command now becomes something positive. Humans are not limited to following the commandments without comprehension. They can use what they took from the divine realm for their own good and for their relationship with their God.

will be among you a man or woman or family or tribe whose heart is turning today from YHWH, our God, to go to serve those nations' gods; in case there is among you a root bearing poison and wormwood, 18and it will be when he hears the words of this oath that he'll feel himself blessed in his heart, saying, 'I'll have peace, though I'll go on in my heart's obstinacy,' so as to annihilate the wet with the dry: 19YHWH will not be willing to forgive him, because YHWH's anger and His jealousy will then smoke against that man, and every curse that is written in this scroll will weigh on him, and YHWH will wipe out his name from under the skies. 20And YHWH will separate him from all of Israel's tribes for bad, according to all the curses of the covenant that is written in this scroll of instruction.

21"And a later generation will say—your children who will come up after you, and the foreigner who will come from a far land, when they'll see that land's plagues and its illnesses that YHWH put in it, 22brimstone and salt, all the land a burning, it won't be seeded and won't grow, and not any vegetation will come up in it, like the overturning of Sodom and Gomorrah, Admah and Zeboiim, which YHWH overturned in His anger and His fury— 23and all the nations

עִמָּהֶם: 17פֶּן־יֵשׁ בָּכֶם אִישׁ אוֹ־אִשָּׁה אוֹ מִשְׁפָּחָה אוֹ־שֵׁבֶט אֲשֶׁר לְבָבוֹ פֹנֶה הַיּוֹם מֵעִם יְהֹוָה אֱלֹהֵינוּ לָלֶכֶת לַעֲבֹד אֶת־אֱלֹהֵי הַגּוֹיִם הָהֵם פֶּן־יֵשׁ בָּכֶם שֹׁרֶשׁ פֹּרֶה רֹאשׁ וְלַעֲנָה: 18וְהָיָה בְּשָׁמְעוֹ אֶת־דִּבְרֵי הָאָלָה הַזֹּאת וְהִתְבָּרֵךְ בִּלְבָבוֹ לֵאמֹר שָׁלוֹם יִהְיֶה־לִּי כִּי בִּשְׁרִרוּת לִבִּי אֵלֵךְ לְמַעַן סְפוֹת הָרָוָה אֶת־הַצְּמֵאָה: 19לֹא־יֹאבֶה יְהֹוָה סְלֹחַ לוֹ כִּי אָז יֶעְשַׁן אַף־יְהֹוָה וְקִנְאָתוֹ בָּאִישׁ הַהוּא וְרָבְצָה בּוֹ כָּל־הָאָלָה הַכְּתוּבָה בַּסֵּפֶר הַזֶּה וּמָחָה יְהֹוָה אֶת־שְׁמוֹ מִתַּחַת הַשָּׁמָיִם: 20וְהִבְדִּילוֹ יְהֹוָה לְרָעָה מִכֹּל שִׁבְטֵי יִשְׂרָאֵל כְּכֹל אָלוֹת הַבְּרִית הַכְּתוּבָה בְּסֵפֶר הַתּוֹרָה הַזֶּה: 21וְאָמַר הַדּוֹר הָאַחֲרוֹן בְּנֵיכֶם אֲשֶׁר יָקוּמוּ מֵאַחֲרֵיכֶם וְהַנָּכְרִי אֲשֶׁר יָבֹא מֵאֶרֶץ רְחוֹקָה וְרָאוּ אֶת־מַכּוֹת הָאָרֶץ הַהִוא וְאֶת־תַּחֲלֻאֶיהָ אֲשֶׁר־חִלָּה יְהֹוָה בָּהּ: 22גָּפְרִית וָמֶלַח שְׂרֵפָה כָל־אַרְצָהּ לֹא תִזָּרַע וְלֹא תַצְמִחַ וְלֹא־יַעֲלֶה בָהּ כָּל־עֵשֶׂב כְּמַהְפֵּכַת סְדֹם וַעֲמֹרָה אַדְמָה וצְבֹיִים אֲשֶׁר הָפַךְ יְהֹוָה בְּאַפּוֹ וּבַחֲמָתוֹ: 23וְאָמְרוּ כָּל־הַגּוֹיִם עַל־מֶה

ק וּצְבוֹיִם 29:22

29:18. **oath**. The word can mean either "oath" or "curse." Here it can refer to the covenant oath mentioned in v. 11 or to the covenant curses; or it can mean the two together, since the covenant oath implicitly invokes the curses on the one who takes it.

29:18. **annihilate the wet with the dry**. Commentators and translators struggle with this phrase, which may have been an idiomatic expression whose context is no longer known. The answer may lie in the phenomenon that we have seen a number of times whereby expressions from Genesis recur here in Deuteronomy. The verb here ("annihilate" or "sweep away") occurs four times in the matter of Sodom and Gomorrah (Gen 18:23,24; 19:15,17) and in one other place in the Torah, the destruction of Korah and his group (Num 16:26). In all five occurrences there is an issue of whether good people will be annihilated along with the bad. And they all involve fire coming from God and destroying the offenders. The meaning of this expression here, therefore, may be that as a strong fire burns up what is dry and evaporates what is wet (or as a forest fire destroys both the dry and fresh trees), so the obstinate person, or group in this case, may bring down the community with them. This understanding is reinforced by the fact that Sodom and Gomorrah are referred to just four verses later (29:22).

656

will say, 'For *what* did YHWH do something like this to this land? What is this big flaring of anger?'

²⁴"And they'll say, 'For the fact that they left the covenant of YHWH, their fathers' God, which He made with them when He brought them out from the land of Egypt. ²⁵And they went and served other gods and bowed to them, gods whom they hadn't known and He hadn't allocated to them. ²⁶And YHWH's anger flared at that land, to bring over it every curse that was written in this scroll. ²⁷And YHWH plucked them from their land in anger and in fury and in great rage, and He threw them into another land, as it is this day.'

²⁸"The hidden things belong to YHWH, our God, and the revealed things belong to us and to our children forever, to do all the words of this instruction. **30** ¹And it will be, when all these things, the blessing and the curse that I've put in front of you, will come upon you, and you'll store it in your heart among the nations to which YHWH, your God, has driven you, ²and you'll come back to YHWH, your God, and listen to His voice, according to everything that I command you today, you and your children, with all your heart and with all your soul, ³that YHWH, your God, will bring back your captivity and be merciful to you. And He'll come back and gather

עָשָׂ֤ה יְהוָה֙ כָּ֔כָה לָאָ֖רֶץ הַזֹּ֑את מֶ֥ה חֳרִ֛י הָאַ֖ף הַגָּד֥וֹל הַזֶּֽה׃ ²⁴וְאָ֣מְר֔וּ עַ֚ל אֲשֶׁ֣ר עָֽזְב֔וּ אֶת־בְּרִ֗ית יְהוָ֖ה אֱלֹהֵ֣י אֲבֹתָ֑ם אֲשֶׁר֙ כָּרַ֣ת עִמָּ֔ם בְּהוֹצִיא֥וֹ אֹתָ֖ם מֵאֶ֥רֶץ מִצְרָֽיִם׃ ²⁵וַיֵּלְכ֗וּ וַיַּֽעַבְדוּ֙ אֱלֹהִ֣ים אֲחֵרִ֔ים וַיִּֽשְׁתַּחֲו֖וּ לָהֶ֑ם אֱלֹהִים֙ אֲשֶׁ֣ר לֹֽא־יְדָע֔וּם וְלֹ֥א חָלַ֖ק לָהֶֽם׃ ²⁶וַיִּֽחַר־אַ֥ף יְהוָ֖ה בָּאָ֣רֶץ הַהִ֑וא לְהָבִ֤יא עָלֶ֙יהָ֙ אֶת־כָּל־הַקְּלָלָ֔ה הַכְּתוּבָ֖ה בַּסֵּ֥פֶר הַזֶּֽה׃ ²⁷וַיִּתְּשֵׁ֤ם יְהוָה֙ מֵעַ֣ל אַדְמָתָ֔ם בְּאַ֥ף וּבְחֵמָ֖ה וּבְקֶ֣צֶף גָּד֑וֹל וַיַּשְׁלִכֵ֛ם אֶל־אֶ֥רֶץ אַחֶ֖רֶת כַּיּ֥וֹם הַזֶּֽה׃ ²⁸הַ֨נִּסְתָּרֹ֔ת לַיהוָ֖ה אֱלֹהֵ֑ינוּ וְהַנִּגְלֹ֞ת לָ֤ׄנׄוּׄ וּׄלְׄבָׄנֵׄ֙יׄנׄוּ֙ עַד־עוֹלָ֔ם לַעֲשׂ֕וֹת אֶת־כָּל־דִּבְרֵ֖י הַתּוֹרָ֥ה הַזֹּֽאת׃ ס ³⁰ ¹וְהָיָה֩ כִֽי־יָבֹ֨אוּ עָלֶ֜יךָ כָּל־הַדְּבָרִ֣ים הָאֵ֗לֶּה הַבְּרָכָה֙ וְהַקְּלָלָ֔ה אֲשֶׁ֥ר נָתַ֖תִּי לְפָנֶ֑יךָ וַהֲשֵׁבֹתָ֣ אֶל־לְבָבֶ֔ךָ בְּכָל־הַגּוֹיִ֔ם אֲשֶׁ֧ר הִדִּיחֲךָ֛ יְהוָ֥ה אֱלֹהֶ֖יךָ שָֽׁמָּה׃ ²וְשַׁבְתָּ֞ עַד־יְהוָ֤ה אֱלֹהֶ֙יךָ֙ וְשָׁמַעְתָּ֣ בְקֹל֔וֹ כְּכֹ֛ל אֲשֶׁר־אָנֹכִ֥י מְצַוְּךָ֖ הַיּ֑וֹם אַתָּ֣ה וּבָנֶ֔יךָ בְּכָל־לְבָבְךָ֖ וּבְכָל־נַפְשֶֽׁךָ׃ ³וְשָׁ֨ב יְהוָ֧ה אֱלֹהֶ֛יךָ אֶת־

29:28. The hidden things belong to YHWH. Moses tells the people that there are things that are solely in the divine realm, hidden from humans. Humans' task is here in this world: to live a certain kind of life. He breaks off from this matter and turns to a discussion of future exile and return to God (30:1–10). Then he returns to this picture of what humans must do, and how it is not something enigmatic, in v. 11.

30:1. your God has driven you. The word "driven" is ironic here. It has been used three times until now, always referring to persons who would drive Israelites away from their God (Deut 13:6,11,14). But now it describes how YHWH drives Israel away to other lands because of Israel's apostasy. The term is thus another allusion to the fact of divine punishment to fit the crime, which is to say: there is justice.

30:3. bring back your captivity. This expression occurs about twenty-five times in the *Tanak*. It is grammatically unclear. The verb (*šāb*) would normally be in the *Hiphil*, but here (and usually) it is in the intransitive *Qal*. The noun may reflect the root *šwb*, "bring back" (making it a cognate accusative with the verb), or it may reflect the root *šbh*, "captive." On the former root, the phrase would mean "to produce a coming

you from all the peoples to which YHWH, your God, has scattered you. 4If you'll be driven to the end of the skies, YHWH, your God, will gather you from there, and He'll take you from there. 5And YHWH, your God, will bring you to the land that your fathers possessed, and you'll take possession of it, and He'll be good to you and multiply you more than your fathers. 6And YHWH, your God, will circumcise your heart and your seed's heart so as to love YHWH, your God, with all your heart and with all your soul so that you'll live. 7And YHWH, your God, will put all these curses on your enemies and on those who hate you who have pursued you. 8And you'll come back and listen to YHWH's voice and do all His commandments that I command you today. 9And YHWH, your God, will give you extra of all your hand's work, of the fruit of your womb and of the fruit of your animals and the fruit of your land for good. Because YHWH will come back to have satisfaction over you for good as He had satisfaction over your fathers, 10when you'll listen to the voice of YHWH, your God, to observe His commandments and His laws, written in this scroll of instruction, when you'll come back to

שְׁבוּתְךָ וְרִחֲמֶךָ וְשָׁב וְקִבֶּצְךָ מִכָּל־הָעַמִּים אֲשֶׁר הֱפִיצְךָ יְהוָה אֱלֹהֶיךָ שָׁמָּה: 4אִם־יִהְיֶה נִדַּחֲךָ בִּקְצֵה הַשָּׁמָיִם מִשָּׁם יְקַבֶּצְךָ יְהוָה אֱלֹהֶיךָ וּמִשָּׁם יִקָּחֶךָ: 5וֶהֱבִיאֲךָ יְהוָה אֱלֹהֶיךָ אֶל־הָאָרֶץ אֲשֶׁר־יָרְשׁוּ אֲבֹתֶיךָ וִירִשְׁתָּהּ וְהֵיטִבְךָ וְהִרְבְּךָ מֵאֲבֹתֶיךָ: 6וּמָל יְהוָה אֱלֹהֶיךָ אֶת־לְבָבְךָ וְאֶת־לְבַב זַרְעֶךָ לְאַהֲבָה אֶת־יְהוָה אֱלֹהֶיךָ בְּכָל־לְבָבְךָ וּבְכָל־נַפְשְׁךָ לְמַעַן חַיֶּיךָ: 7וְנָתַן יְהוָה אֱלֹהֶיךָ אֵת כָּל־הָאָלוֹת הָאֵלֶּה עַל־אֹיְבֶיךָ וְעַל־שֹׂנְאֶיךָ אֲשֶׁר רְדָפוּךָ: 8וְאַתָּה תָשׁוּב וְשָׁמַעְתָּ בְּקוֹל יְהוָה וְעָשִׂיתָ אֶת־כָּל־מִצְוֹתָיו אֲשֶׁר אָנֹכִי מְצַוְּךָ הַיּוֹם: 9וְהוֹתִירְךָ יְהוָה אֱלֹהֶיךָ בְּכֹל ׀ מַעֲשֵׂה יָדֶךָ בִּפְרִי בִטְנְךָ וּבִפְרִי בְהֶמְתְּךָ וּבִפְרִי אַדְמָתְךָ לְטוֹבָה כִּי ׀ יָשׁוּב יְהוָה לָשׂוּשׂ עָלֶיךָ לְטוֹב כַּאֲשֶׁר־שָׂשׂ עַל־אֲבֹתֶיךָ: 10כִּי תִשְׁמַע בְּקוֹל יְהוָה אֱלֹהֶיךָ לִשְׁמֹר מִצְוֹתָיו וְחֻקֹּתָיו הַכְּתוּבָה בְּסֵפֶר הַתּוֹרָה הַזֶּה כִּי תָשׁוּב

---

back." On the latter root, it would mean "to bring back a captivity." These two meanings are very close to each other in any case. Those who take this phrase to mean figuratively "to restore your fortunes" have a good parallel in Job 42:10; but all the occurrences in Jeremiah, which is linked closely with Deuteronomy, fit the meaning of "coming back" or "captivity" far better. Note especially Jer 30:16–23 and 48:46–47, in which this expression occurs in proximity to the related word for captivity: *šebî*.

30:6. **God will circumcise your heart**. Earlier, Moses directs the people to circumcise their hearts themselves (see Deut 10:16 and the comment there), but now he speaks of God circumcising their hearts for them. The difference is that now he is speaking of a future condition: the people will have violated the covenant, suffered the curses, and turned back to their God; and God, in response, will bring them back and then will circumcise their hearts. This in turn will enable them to love the deity with all their hearts and souls—which Moses had commanded them to do earlier as well. The divine-human relationship is pictured as mutual. Humans require the experience of being away from their God, on their own. And then, more experienced, more understanding, having suffered and grown, humans look to God anew. And then the new encounter with the divine transforms them.

30:6. **your seed's heart**. Meaning: the hearts of your progeny.

YHWH, your God, with all your heart and with all your soul.

11"Because this commandment that I command you today: it's not too wondrous for you, and it's not too far. 12It's not in the skies, that one would say, 'Who will go up for us to the skies and get it for us and enable us to hear it so we'll do it?' 13And it's not across the sea, that one would say, 'Who will cross for us, across the sea, and get it for us and enable us to hear it so we'll do it?' 14But the thing is very close to you, in your mouth, and in your heart, to do it.

15"See: I've put in front of you today life and good, and death and bad, 16in that I command you today to love YHWH, your God, to go in His ways and to observe His commandments and His laws and His judgments so you'll live and multiply and bless YHWH, your God, in the land to which you're coming to take possession of it. 17But if your heart will turn away, and you won't listen, and you'll be driven so that you'll bow to other gods and serve them, 18I've told you today that you'll *perish*. You won't extend days on the land to which you're crossing the Jordan to come to take possession of it. 19I call the skies and the earth to witness regarding you today: I've put life and death in front of you, blessing and curse.

אֶל־יְהוָה אֱלֹהֶיךָ בְּכָל־לְבָבְךָ וּבְכָל־נַפְשֶׁךָ: פ
11 כִּי הַמִּצְוָה הַזֹּאת אֲשֶׁר אָנֹכִי מְצַוְּךָ הַיּוֹם לֹא־נִפְלֵאת הִוא מִמְּךָ וְלֹא רְחֹקָה הִוא: 12 לֹא בַשָּׁמַיִם הִוא לֵאמֹר מִי יַעֲלֶה־לָּנוּ הַשָּׁמַיְמָה וְיִקָּחֶהָ לָּנוּ וְיַשְׁמִעֵנוּ אֹתָהּ וְנַעֲשֶׂנָּה: 13 וְלֹא־מֵעֵבֶר לַיָּם הִוא לֵאמֹר מִי יַעֲבָר־לָנוּ אֶל־עֵבֶר הַיָּם וְיִקָּחֶהָ לָּנוּ וְיַשְׁמִעֵנוּ אֹתָהּ וְנַעֲשֶׂנָּה: 14 כִּי־קָרוֹב אֵלֶיךָ הַדָּבָר מְאֹד בְּפִיךָ וּבִלְבָבְךָ לַעֲשֹׂתוֹ: ס 15 רְאֵה נָתַתִּי לְפָנֶיךָ הַיּוֹם אֶת־הַחַיִּים וְאֶת־הַטּוֹב וְאֶת־הַמָּוֶת וְאֶת־הָרָע: 16 אֲשֶׁר אָנֹכִי מְצַוְּךָ הַיּוֹם לְאַהֲבָה אֶת־יְהוָה אֱלֹהֶיךָ לָלֶכֶת בִּדְרָכָיו וְלִשְׁמֹר מִצְוֹתָיו וְחֻקֹּתָיו וּמִשְׁפָּטָיו וְחָיִיתָ וְרָבִיתָ וּבֵרַכְךָ יְהוָה אֱלֹהֶיךָ בָּאָרֶץ אֲשֶׁר־אַתָּה בָא־שָׁמָּה לְרִשְׁתָּהּ: 17 וְאִם־יִפְנֶה לְבָבְךָ וְלֹא תִשְׁמָע וְנִדַּחְתָּ וְהִשְׁתַּחֲוִיתָ לֵאלֹהִים אֲחֵרִים וַעֲבַדְתָּם: 18 הִגַּדְתִּי לָכֶם הַיּוֹם כִּי אָבֹד תֹּאבֵדוּן לֹא־תַאֲרִיכֻן יָמִים עַל־הָאֲדָמָה אֲשֶׁר אַתָּה עֹבֵר אֶת־הַיַּרְדֵּן לָבֹא שָׁמָּה לְרִשְׁתָּהּ: 19 הַעִידֹתִי בָכֶם הַיּוֹם אֶת־הַשָּׁמַיִם וְאֶת־הָאָרֶץ הַחַיִּים וְהַמָּוֶת נָתַתִּי לְפָנֶיךָ הַבְּרָכָה וְהַקְּלָלָה

30:11. it's not too wondrous for you. Now Moses finishes what he started to say ten verses earlier about the hidden things belonging to God and the revealed things belonging to humans (29:28). In one of the most beautiful passages in the Torah (vv. 11–14), he explains what this meant: The commandments are not enigmatic, they do not reside in a distant realm, and they do not require an intermediary. They are already made known. And they are within a human's ability to do.

30:16. so you'll live and multiply. This is a change of wording from the beginning of the Torah, where the command is to "be fruitful and multiply" (Gen 1:28). The command to grow in numbers is for the purpose of *life*. As the human population grows to the point that its number is a threat to life, humankind and its leaders need enormous wisdom to determine what to do. The wording there in Genesis is: "And God *blessed* them, and God said to them, 'Be fruitful and multiply . . .'" (Gen 1:28). That first commandment of the Torah is thus presented not as a strict order, but as a blessing. And here at the end of the Torah as well, the text is: "so you'll live and multiply and *bless* YHWH." In the Torah, the creator blesses humans with the opportunity to grow, and humans will bless their creator for it once it is fulfilled. The Bible's first commandment is now becoming humankind's greatest challenge.

And you shall choose life, so you'll live, you and your seed, ²⁰to love YHWH, your God, to listen to His voice and to cling to Him, because He is your life and the extension of your days to reside on the land that YHWH swore to your fathers, to Abraham, to Isaac, and to Jacob, to give to them."

וּבָחַרְתָּ בַּחַיִּים לְמַעַן תִּחְיֶה אַתָּה וְזַרְעֶךָ: ²⁰לְאַהֲבָה אֶת־יְהוָה אֱלֹהֶיךָ לִשְׁמֹעַ בְּקֹלוֹ וּלְדָבְקָה־בוֹ כִּי הוּא חַיֶּיךָ וְאֹרֶךְ יָמֶיךָ לָשֶׁבֶת עַל־הָאֲדָמָה אֲשֶׁר נִשְׁבַּע יְהוָה לַאֲבֹתֶיךָ לְאַבְרָהָם לְיִצְחָק וּלְיַעֲקֹב לָתֵת לָהֶם: פ

AND HE WENT

ויקרא

31 ¹And Moses went and spoke these things to all Israel. ²And he said to them, "I'm a hundred twenty years old today. I'm not able to

31 ¹וַיֵּלֶךְ מֹשֶׁה וַיְדַבֵּר אֶת־הַדְּבָרִים הָאֵלֶּה אֶל־כָּל־יִשְׂרָאֵל: ²וַיֹּאמֶר אֲלֵהֶם בֶּן־מֵאָה וְעֶשְׂרִים

30:19. **choose life.** The theme of the path to life began early in Moses' speech (Deut 4:1) and culminates here in the last words of the speech. This focus at the conclusion of the Torah returns us to the Torah's opening: the loss of the tree of life. Humans lose access to the tree of life as the price of having gained access to the tree of knowledge of *good* and *bad*. Now the people are told, "I've put in front of you life and good, blessing and curse." Using the knowledge of good and bad, and choosing to do good, is the path back to life—not necessarily eternal life (though who knows?), but *meaningful* life, *fulfilling* life. As the book of Proverbs says about knowledge and wisdom: "It is a tree of life." And Jews sing this verse from Proverbs each Sabbath after reading the Torah and returning it to the ark.

30:20. **to cling to Him.** "Cling" is the same term that is used for man's attachment to woman at the beginning of the Torah (Gen 2:24). This is part of a string of terms in this passage (vv. 15–20) that call to mind the opening chapters of the Torah: life, death, good and bad, the skies and earth, the ground, the day (cf. "in the day" and "in the day you eat from it," Gen 2:4,17), "your seed," be fruitful, to give, to tell, to command (cf. Gen 3:11), to watch (or observe, Hebrew *šmr*), and to listen to the voice (of God; cf. "You listened to your woman's voice," Gen 3:17). And these are preceded by references to fruit (Deut 30:9), and to the skies and the sea (30:12–13). This cluster of language here in the last sentences of Moses' address forms a great connection back to the start of Genesis and a reminder of the unity of the Torah.

30:20. **He is your life.** This can also be understood to mean *"It is your life."* Translators are split on this. The former means that Moses is saying that *God* is the people's life and the source of their being in their land a long time. The latter means that the people's choice to love, listen, and cling to God is their life and the source of lengthy time in the land. That is, the question is whether it is God or it is people's feeling about God that brings this about. I do not know which is correct.

31:1. **And Moses went.** Went where? The Septuagint and Qumran texts have "And Moses finished speaking all these things"—reading Hebrew ויכל (finished) rather than וילך (went), reversing the last two letters. This makes better sense. It also adds a

660

go out and come in anymore. And YHWH said to me, 'You shall not cross this Jordan.' ³YHWH, your God: *He* is crossing in front of you. He'll destroy these nations in front of you, and you'll dispossess them. Joshua: *he* is crossing in front of you, as YHWH has spoken. ⁴And YHWH will do to them as He did to Sihon and to Og, the kings of the Amorites, and to their land, that He destroyed them. ⁵And YHWH will put them in front of you, and you shall do to them according to all of the commandment that I've commanded you. ⁶Be strong and be bold. Don't be afraid and don't be scared in front of them, because YHWH, your God: He is the one going with you. He won't let you down and won't leave you."

⁷And Moses called Joshua and said to him before the eyes of all Israel, "Be strong and be bold, because *you* will come with this people to the land that YHWH swore to their fathers to give to them, and *you* will get it for them as a legacy. ⁸And YHWH: He is the one who is going in front of you. He will be with you. He won't let you down and won't leave you. You shall not fear, and you shall not be dismayed."

⁹And Moses wrote this instruction and gave it

שָׁנָה אָנֹכִי הַיּוֹם לֹא־אוּכַל עוֹד לָצֵאת וְלָבוֹא
וַיהוָה אָמַר אֵלַי לֹא תַעֲבֹר אֶת־הַיַּרְדֵּן הַזֶּה:
³יְהוָה אֱלֹהֶיךָ הוּא ׀ עֹבֵר לְפָנֶיךָ הוּא־יַשְׁמִיד אֶת־
הַגּוֹיִם הָאֵלֶּה מִלְּפָנֶיךָ וִירִשְׁתָּם יְהוֹשֻׁעַ הוּא עֹבֵר
לְפָנֶיךָ כַּאֲשֶׁר דִּבֶּר יְהוָה: ⁴וְעָשָׂה יְהוָה לָהֶם
כַּאֲשֶׁר עָשָׂה לְסִיחוֹן וּלְעוֹג מַלְכֵי הָאֱמֹרִי וּלְאַרְצָם
אֲשֶׁר הִשְׁמִיד אֹתָם: ⁵וּנְתָנָם יְהוָה לִפְנֵיכֶם וַעֲשִׂיתֶם
לָהֶם כְּכָל־הַמִּצְוָה אֲשֶׁר צִוִּיתִי אֶתְכֶם: ⁶חִזְקוּ
וְאִמְצוּ אַל־תִּירְאוּ וְאַל־תַּעַרְצוּ מִפְּנֵיהֶם כִּי ׀ יְהוָה
אֱלֹהֶיךָ הוּא הַהֹלֵךְ עִמָּךְ לֹא יַרְפְּךָ וְלֹא יַעַזְבֶךָּ:
פ ⁷וַיִּקְרָא מֹשֶׁה לִיהוֹשֻׁעַ וַיֹּאמֶר אֵלָיו לְעֵינֵי כָל־
יִשְׂרָאֵל חֲזַק וֶאֱמָץ כִּי אַתָּה תָּבוֹא אֶת־הָעָם הַזֶּה
אֶל־הָאָרֶץ אֲשֶׁר נִשְׁבַּע יְהוָה לַאֲבֹתָם לָתֵת לָהֶם
וְאַתָּה תַּנְחִילֶנָּה אוֹתָם: ⁸וַיהוָה הוּא ׀ הַהֹלֵךְ לְפָנֶיךָ
הוּא יִהְיֶה עִמָּךְ לֹא יַרְפְּךָ וְלֹא יַעַזְבֶךָּ לֹא תִירָא
וְלֹא תֵחָת:
⁹וַיִּכְתֹּב מֹשֶׁה אֶת־הַתּוֹרָה הַזֹּאת וַיִּתְּנָהּ אֶל־הַכֹּהֲנִים

wordplay on his finishing (יכל) in v. 1 and his saying "I'm not able (אוכל) to go out and come in anymore" in v. 2.

31:7. Be strong and be bold . . . *you* will get it for them as a legacy. This, finally, is the culmination of what Moses told the people in chapter 3. He had told them that God was angry at him, that he was not permitted to enter the land, and that God told him to "command Joshua and strengthen him and make him bold, because . . . he will get them the land that you'll see as a legacy" (3:28). Moses has now instructed the people in the laws and exhorted them to be faithful to the covenant, and so he turns to the task that he was assigned: he passes the leadership to Joshua. Note that it is not just that Moses dies and Joshua replaces him. Rather, during his lifetime, publicly, Moses himself identifies Joshua as his successor, charges him with his task, and *encourages* him to be successful. Although one can easily imagine Moses envying Joshua, who is replacing him for the fulfillment of the promises, Moses acts in Joshua's favor: preparing him and enhancing his stature in the people's eyes. One who begrudges his successor does not understand time and history.

31:9. And Moses wrote this instruction (and 31:24. "And it was when Moses finished writing the words of this instruction on a scroll"). This "instruction" (Hebrew *tôrāh*) does not refer to the entire five books, which came to be known as the Torah

to the priests, sons of Levi, who were carrying the ark of YHWH's covenant and to all of Israel's elders. 10And Moses commanded them, saying, "At the end of seven years, at the appointed time of the year of the remission, on the Festival of Booths, 11when all Israel comes to appear before YHWH, your God, in the place that He will choose, you shall read this instruction in front of all Israel in their ears. 12Assemble the people— the men and the women and the infants and your alien who is in your gates—so they will listen and so they will learn and will fear YHWH, your God, and they will be watchful to do all the words of this instruction. 13And their children who have not known will listen and learn to fear YHWH, your God, all the days that you're living on the land to which you're crossing the Jordan to take possession of it."

14And YHWH said to Moses, "Here, your days to die have come close. Call Joshua, and stand up in the Tent of Meeting, and I'll command him."

בְּנֵי לֵוִי הַנֹּשְׂאִים אֶת־אֲרוֹן בְּרִית יְהוָה וְאֶל־כָּל־ זִקְנֵי יִשְׂרָאֵל: 10וַיְצַו מֹשֶׁה אוֹתָם לֵאמֹר מִקֵּץ ׀ שֶׁבַע שָׁנִים בְּמֹעֵד שְׁנַת הַשְּׁמִטָּה בְּחַג הַסֻּכּוֹת: 11בְּבוֹא כָל־יִשְׂרָאֵל לֵרָאוֹת אֶת־פְּנֵי יְהוָה אֱלֹהֶיךָ בַּמָּקוֹם אֲשֶׁר יִבְחָר תִּקְרָא אֶת־הַתּוֹרָה הַזֹּאת נֶגֶד כָּל־יִשְׂרָאֵל בְּאָזְנֵיהֶם: 12הַקְהֵל אֶת־הָעָם הָאֲנָשִׁים וְהַנָּשִׁים וְהַטַּף וְגֵרְךָ אֲשֶׁר בִּשְׁעָרֶיךָ לְמַעַן יִשְׁמְעוּ וּלְמַעַן יִלְמְדוּ וְיָרְאוּ אֶת־יְהוָה אֱלֹהֵיכֶם וְשָׁמְרוּ לַעֲשׂוֹת אֶת־כָּל־דִּבְרֵי הַתּוֹרָה הַזֹּאת: 13וּבְנֵיהֶם אֲשֶׁר לֹא־יָדְעוּ יִשְׁמְעוּ וְלָמְדוּ לְיִרְאָה אֶת־יְהוָה אֱלֹהֵיכֶם כָּל־הַיָּמִים אֲשֶׁר אַתֶּם חַיִּים עַל־הָאֲדָמָה אֲשֶׁר אַתֶּם עֹבְרִים אֶת־הַיַּרְדֵּן שָׁמָּה לְרִשְׁתָּהּ: פ 14וַיֹּאמֶר יְהוָה אֶל־מֹשֶׁה הֵן קָרְבוּ יָמֶיךָ לָמוּת קְרָא אֶת־יְהוֹשֻׁעַ וְהִתְיַצְּבוּ בְּאֹהֶל מוֹעֵד וַאֲצַוֶּנּוּ

---

long after this chapter was written. Those who began claiming that Moses was the author of the entire Torah created much confusion and misinformation by claiming more for Moses than the Torah itself ascribed to him. It became a firmly established doctrine by the rabbinic period, and many great teachers, including Rashi and Ramban, followed it. Ibn Ezra raised subtle doubts about it, Spinoza openly challenged it, and Jewish, as well as Christian, scholars came to reject it in the nineteenth and twentieth centuries. Orthodox Jews still accept it.

The instruction that Moses writes here appears to be most of the law code that begins in Deuteronomy 12 and ends at 26:15. It may also be understood to include the list of blessings and curses in Deuteronomy 28. That concluding list of curses especially would account for the strong reaction that is ascribed to King Josiah when he hears the words of the scroll of the Torah centuries later (see the comment on 31:26).

31:10. **seven years.** The biblical requirement was to read "this torah" (the law code of Deuteronomy) once every seven years, on the holiday of Sukkot. Later the Jewish practice became to read the entire Torah (all of the Five Books of Moses), once every year or every three years, and in weekly portions rather than all at once.

31:10. **the remission.** See Deut 15:1ff.

31:12. **your alien.** Five times in the Torah, laws about aliens in Israel say "*your alien*" (compare "*your* poor" in the Covenant Code; Exod 23:6)—including in the Decalogue in both Exodus and Deuteronomy.

And Moses and Joshua went and stood up in the Tent of Meeting. 15And YHWH appeared in the tent in a column of cloud, and the column of cloud stood at the entrance of the tent.

16And YHWH said to Moses, "Here, when you're lying with your fathers, this people will get up and whore after foreign gods of the land into which it is coming, and it will leave me and break my covenant that I've made with it. 17And my anger will flare at it on that day, and I'll leave them, and I'll hide my face from them, and it will become prey, and many bad things and troubles will find it. And it will say on that day, 'Isn't it because my God is not present in me that these evils have found me?' 18But I: I'll *hide my face* on that day over all the bad that it has done, because

וַיֵּ֤לֶךְ מֹשֶׁה֙ וִיהוֹשֻׁ֔עַ וַיִּֽתְיַצְּב֖וּ בְּאֹ֥הֶל מוֹעֵֽד: 15וַיֵּרָ֨א
יְהוָ֤ה בָּאֹ֙הֶל֙ בְּעַמּ֣וּד עָנָ֔ן וַיַּעֲמֹ֛ד עַמּ֥וּד הֶעָנָ֖ן עַל־
פֶּ֥תַח הָאֹֽהֶל: ס 16וַיֹּ֤אמֶר יְהוָה֙ אֶל־מֹשֶׁ֔ה הִנְּךָ֥
שֹׁכֵ֖ב עִם־אֲבֹתֶ֑יךָ וְקָם֩ הָעָ֨ם הַזֶּ֜ה וְזָנָ֣ה ׀ אַחֲרֵ֣י ׀
אֱלֹהֵ֣י נֵֽכַר־הָאָ֗רֶץ אֲשֶׁ֨ר ה֤וּא בָא־שָׁ֙מָּה֙ בְּקִרְבּ֔וֹ
וַעֲזָבַ֕נִי וְהֵפֵר֙ אֶת־בְּרִיתִ֔י אֲשֶׁ֥ר כָּרַ֖תִּי אִתּֽוֹ: 17וְחָרָ֣ה
אַפִּ֣י ב֣וֹ בַיּוֹם־הַה֗וּא וַעֲזַבְתִּ֜ים וְהִסְתַּרְתִּ֤י פָנַי֙ מֵהֶ֔ם
וְהָיָ֣ה לֶֽאֱכֹ֔ל וּמְצָאֻ֛הוּ רָע֥וֹת רַבּ֖וֹת וְצָר֑וֹת וְאָמַ֣ר
בַּיּ֤וֹם הַהוּא֙ הֲלֹ֗א עַ֣ל כִּֽי־אֵ֤ין אֱלֹהַי֙ בְּקִרְבִּ֔י
מְצָא֕וּנִי הָרָע֖וֹת הָאֵֽלֶּה: 18וְאָנֹכִ֗י הַסְתֵּ֨ר אַסְתִּ֤יר פָּנַי֙
בַּיּ֣וֹם הַה֔וּא עַ֥ל כָּל־הָרָעָ֖ה אֲשֶׁ֥ר עָשָׂ֑ה כִּ֣י פָנָ֔ה

31:16–18. **it**. God repeatedly speaks of the people in the singular in this passage—and quotes the people as speaking of itself in the singular as well: "not present in *me* . . . these evils have found *me*." The hiding of the face of God, which is predicted here, is understood to be the fate of the entire people, not of individuals. Divine hiddenness is not an individual's unique experience, and it is not based on an individual's behavior. It is the experience of a *community* and possibly of an *era*. At the time that I am writing this, it is such an era.

31:17,18. **I'll hide my face**. These words come twice in the passage that contains the last words that God speaks to Moses before summoning him to die. They occur in the song that God tells Moses to teach the people as a witness for the future as well (32:20), and this expression occurs nearly thirty times more in the *Tanak* after that. These words here predict a time in which God will be hidden. It is more frightening than divine punishment: It is one thing for a parent to punish a child; it is far worse if the parent becomes hidden from the child, so the child does not know if the parent is present or not. The child feels vulnerable, unprotected. The child cries for the parent, but there is no answer. It is terrifying.

The expression *hestēr pānîm*, the hiding of the face, became a known idiom in rabbinic literature, and in theological thinking to this day. I have written about how it develops through the Bible (in *The Hidden Face of God*). The *Tanak*'s story moves from a time of extraordinary divine involvement—creation, flood, personal contact, splitting sea, hearing God's voice at Sinai—to a time in which humans are left on their own. God is not pictured as speaking or appearing in the books of Ezra and Nehemiah and is never mentioned in Esther. The prediction at the end of the Torah comes true at the end of the *Tanak*. Humans are left not knowing if God exists or not. Thus the *Tanak* tells a story of a development from a world of direct communication with God to the world we have known ever since: in which the existence of God is a matter of faith, or doubt, or search.

it turned to other gods. ¹⁹So now write this song and teach it to the children of Israel. Set it in their mouths, so this song will become a witness for me among the children of Israel. ²⁰When I'll bring it to the land that I swore to its fathers, flowing with milk and honey, and it will eat and be full and get fat and turn to other gods, and they will serve them and reject me, and it will break my covenant, ²¹then it will be, when many bad things and troubles will find it, that this song will testify as a witness in front of it, because it won't be forgotten from its seed's mouth. Because I know its inclination that it is doing today even before I bring it to the land that I swore."

²²And Moses wrote this song on that day, and he taught it to the children of Israel.

²³And He commanded Joshua, son of Nun, and said, "Be strong and bold, because you will bring the children of Israel to the land that I swore to them, and I shall be with you."

²⁴And it was when Moses finished writing the words of this instruction on a scroll to their end, ²⁵and Moses commanded the Levites, who carried the ark of the covenant of YHWH, saying, ²⁶"Take this scroll of instruction and set it at the side of the ark of the covenant of YHWH, your God, and it will be there for you as a witness.

אֶל־אֱלֹהִים אֲחֵרִים: ¹⁹וְעַתָּ֗ה כִּתְב֨וּ לָכֶ֜ם אֶת־הַשִּׁירָ֣ה הַזֹּ֗את וְלַמְּדָ֤הּ אֶת־בְּנֵֽי־יִשְׂרָאֵל֙ שִׂימָ֣הּ בְּפִיהֶ֔ם לְמַ֨עַן תִּֽהְיֶה־לִּ֜י הַשִּׁירָ֥ה הַזֹּ֛את לְעֵ֖ד בִּבְנֵ֥י יִשְׂרָאֵֽל: ²⁰כִּֽי־אֲבִיאֶ֜נּוּ אֶל־הָאֲדָמָ֣ה ׀ אֲשֶׁר־נִשְׁבַּ֣עְתִּי לַאֲבֹתָ֗יו זָבַ֤ת חָלָב֙ וּדְבַ֔שׁ וְאָכַ֥ל וְשָׂבַ֖ע וְדָשֵׁ֑ן וּפָנָ֞ה אֶל־אֱלֹהִ֤ים אֲחֵרִים֙ וַעֲבָד֔וּם וְנִ֣אֲצ֔וּנִי וְהֵפֵ֖ר אֶת־בְּרִיתִֽי: ²¹וְ֠הָיָה כִּֽי־תִמְצֶ֨אןָ אֹת֜וֹ רָע֣וֹת רַבּוֹת֮ וְצָרוֹת֒ וְ֠עָנְתָה הַשִּׁירָ֨ה הַזֹּ֤את לְפָנָיו֙ לְעֵ֔ד כִּ֛י לֹ֥א תִשָּׁכַ֖ח מִפִּ֣י זַרְע֑וֹ כִּ֧י יָדַ֣עְתִּי אֶת־יִצְר֗וֹ אֲשֶׁ֨ר ה֤וּא עֹשֶׂה֙ הַיּ֔וֹם בְּטֶ֣רֶם אֲבִיאֶ֔נּוּ אֶל־הָאָ֖רֶץ אֲשֶׁ֥ר נִשְׁבָּֽעְתִּי: ²²וַיִּכְתֹּ֥ב מֹשֶׁ֛ה אֶת־הַשִּׁירָ֥ה הַזֹּ֖את בַּיּ֣וֹם הַה֑וּא וַֽיְלַמְּדָ֖הּ אֶת־בְּנֵ֥י יִשְׂרָאֵֽל: ²³וַיְצַ֞ו אֶת־יְהוֹשֻׁ֣עַ בִּן־נ֗וּן וַיֹּ֨אמֶר֙ חֲזַ֣ק וֶֽאֱמָ֔ץ כִּ֣י אַתָּ֗ה תָּבִיא֙ אֶת־בְּנֵ֣י יִשְׂרָאֵ֔ל אֶל־הָאָ֖רֶץ אֲשֶׁר־נִשְׁבַּ֣עְתִּי לָהֶ֑ם וְאָנֹכִ֖י אֶֽהְיֶ֥ה עִמָּֽךְ: ²⁴וַיְהִ֣י ׀ כְּכַלּ֣וֹת מֹשֶׁ֗ה לִכְתֹּ֛ב אֶת־דִּבְרֵ֥י הַתּוֹרָֽה־הַזֹּ֖את עַל־סֵ֑פֶר עַ֖ד תֻּמָּֽם: ²⁵וַיְצַ֤ו מֹשֶׁה֙ אֶת־הַלְוִיִּ֔ם נֹשְׂאֵ֕י אֲר֥וֹן בְּרִית־יְהוָ֖ה לֵאמֹֽר: ²⁶לָקֹ֗חַ אֵ֣ת סֵ֤פֶר הַתּוֹרָה֙ הַזֶּ֔ה וְשַׂמְתֶּ֣ם אֹת֔וֹ מִצַּ֖ד אֲר֥וֹן בְּרִית־יְהוָ֣ה אֱלֹהֵיכֶ֑ם וְהָֽיָה־שָׁ֥ם בְּךָ֖ לְעֵֽד:

31:21. I know its inclination. Again an essential point from the Torah's beginning returns at its conclusion. The flood story starts and ends with God's recognition that humans' *inclination* is toward doing bad: "I won't curse the ground on account of humankind again, for the inclination of the human heart is bad from their youth" (Gen 6:5; 8:21). The word "inclination" (*yēṣer*) then does not occur again in the Torah until here. God states that He knows, even before the people enter the land, that this will be a problem, and so He has them learn a song that refers to their rebellion and to the hiding of the face of God so that they will know that they were warned.

31:26. it will be there for you as a witness. The scroll that Moses has written stays there beside the ark for six hundred years until the reign of King Josiah. Apparently it has long been ignored by then. The priest Hilkiah says there, "I've found the scroll of instruction (*sēper hattōrāh*) in the house of YHWH." When it is read to King Josiah, he tears his clothes and says, "YHWH's fury is great that has ignited at us because our fathers didn't listen to this scroll's words, to act according to everything that's written about us!" (2 Kings 22:8-13). Especially in light of the curses in Deuteronomy 28, Josiah's reaction is understandable. And so it is understood that these laws go ignored

27Because I know your rebellion and your hard neck. Here, while I'm still alive with you today, you've been rebelling at YHWH, so how much more after my death! 28Assemble all the elders of your tribes and your officers to me so I may speak these things in their ears and call the skies and the earth to witness regarding them, 29because I know, after my death, that you'll be *corrupted*, and you'll turn from the way that I've commanded you. And the bad thing will happen to you in the future days when you'll do what is bad in YHWH's eyes to provoke Him with your hands' work."

30And Moses spoke in the ears of all the community of Israel the words of this song to their end:

27כִּי אָנֹכִי יָדַעְתִּי אֶת־מֶרְיְךָ וְאֶת־עָרְפְּךָ הַקָּשֶׁה הֵן בְּעוֹדֶנִּי חַי עִמָּכֶם הַיּוֹם מַמְרִים הֱיִתֶם עִם־יְהוָֹה וְאַף כִּי־אַחֲרֵי מוֹתִי: 28הַקְהִילוּ אֵלַי אֶת־כָּל־זִקְנֵי שִׁבְטֵיכֶם וְשֹׁטְרֵיכֶם וַאֲדַבְּרָה בְאָזְנֵיהֶם אֵת הַדְּבָרִים הָאֵלֶּה וְאָעִידָה בָּם אֶת־הַשָּׁמַיִם וְאֶת־הָאָרֶץ: 29כִּי יָדַעְתִּי אַחֲרֵי מוֹתִי כִּי־הַשְׁחֵת תַּשְׁחִתוּן וְסַרְתֶּם מִן־הַדֶּרֶךְ אֲשֶׁר צִוִּיתִי אֶתְכֶם וְקָרָאת אֶתְכֶם הָרָעָה בְּאַחֲרִית הַיָּמִים כִּי־תַעֲשׂוּ אֶת־הָרַע בְּעֵינֵי יְהוָה לְהַכְעִיסוֹ בְּמַעֲשֵׂה יְדֵיכֶם: 30וַיְדַבֵּר מֹשֶׁה בְּאָזְנֵי כָּל־קְהַל יִשְׂרָאֵל אֶת־דִּבְרֵי הַשִּׁירָה הַזֹּאת עַד תֻּמָּם: פ

---

for generations and then are rediscovered. Josiah has the scroll read aloud to the entire people, and he institutes a renewal of the covenant and a tremendous religious reform. The narrative concludes: "And before him there was not a king like him, who came back to YHWH with all his heart and with all his soul and with all his might, according to all of Moses' instruction, and after him none rose like him" (2 Kings 23:25). All the kings in the books of 1 and 2 Kings are measured by whether they fulfilled the laws of Deuteronomy, and Josiah is rated the highest. Above all, Josiah institutes the practice of public reading of the Torah, which prevails to the present day. And, to this day, the measure of a leader among the Jews must be the degree to which he or she lives by the Torah and draws others to do so as well.

31:28. **call the skies and the earth to witness**. Moses will do this in the opening words of the song (32:1): "Listen, skies, so I may speak; and let the earth hear what my mouth says." Ancient Near Eastern treaties include a summoning of witnesses, usually the gods of the parties to the agreement. The biblical covenant cannot include pagan gods as witnesses, but it must have eternal witnesses since the covenant is meant to last forever. Therefore, the earth and sky are called on as witnesses. This summoning of earth and sky rather than gods in an early poem is further evidence that monotheism existed early in Israelite history.

31:29. **you'll be *corrupted***. Another term from the Torah's beginning returns at its end: the *Hiphil* of the root *šḥt* with the sense of humans becoming corrupt was used to introduce the flood: "All flesh had corrupted its way on the earth" (Gen 6:12). It does not occur again with this meaning until Deut 4:16 and then again here, where Moses says he *knows* that the people will someday become corrupted. That is, he understands that the susceptibility to corruption has been part of human nature from the beginning.

LISTEN

32

¹Listen, skies, so I may speak
 and let the earth hear what my mouth
  says.

2 Let my teaching come down like showers;
 let my saying emerge like dew,
 like raindrops on plants
 and like rainfalls on herbs.

3 When I call YHWH's name,
 avow our God's greatness.

4 The Rock: His work is unblemished,
 for all His ways are judgment.
 A God of trust, and without injustice,
 He's virtuous and right.

5 It corrupted at Him—not His children,
  their flaw—
 a crooked and twisted generation.

6 *Is it to YHWH* that you repay like this?!
 Foolish people and unwise!
 Isn't He your father, who created you,
 He who made you and reared you?

7 Remember the days of old.
 Grasp the years through generations.
 Ask your father, and he'll tell you,
 your elders, and they'll say to you:

הַאֲזִינוּ

32 ¹הַאֲזִינוּ הַשָּׁמַיִם וַאֲדַבֵּרָה
וְתִשְׁמַע הָאָרֶץ אִמְרֵי־פִי:
²יַעֲרֹף כַּמָּטָר לִקְחִי תִּזַּל כַּטַּל אִמְרָתִי
כִּשְׂעִירִם עֲלֵי־דֶשֶׁא וְכִרְבִיבִים עֲלֵי־עֵשֶׂב:
³כִּי שֵׁם יְהוָה אֶקְרָא הָבוּ גֹדֶל לֵאלֹהֵינוּ:
⁴הַצּוּר תָּמִים פָּעֳלוֹ כִּי כָל־דְּרָכָיו מִשְׁפָּט
אֵל אֱמוּנָה וְאֵין עָוֶל צַדִּיק וְיָשָׁר הוּא:
⁵שִׁחֵת לוֹ לֹא בָּנָיו מוּמָם דּוֹר עִקֵּשׁ וּפְתַלְתֹּל:
⁶הֲ־לַיהוָה תִּגְמְלוּ־זֹאת עַם נָבָל וְלֹא חָכָם
הֲלוֹא־הוּא אָבִיךָ קָּנֶךָ הוּא עָשְׂךָ וַיְכֹנְנֶךָ:
⁷זְכֹר יְמוֹת עוֹלָם בִּינוּ שְׁנוֹת דּוֹר־וָדוֹר
שְׁאַל אָבִיךָ וְיַגֵּדְךָ זְקֵנֶיךָ וְיֹאמְרוּ לָךְ:

32:2. plants. This word, too, occurs among the first words of the Torah and does not occur again until its appearance here. In Genesis, God causes the earth to produce plants by His word (Gen 1:11–12). Now Moses turns this image and sings of his words dropping like rain on the plants.

32:4. The Rock. The first letter of the word is oversized in the Torah, possibly to distinguish it from other uses in the song. The song plays on this word, using it seven more times with several different meanings.

32:5. It corrupted at Him—not His children, their flaw. The noun, Hebrew *mûm*, means an injury of the sort that makes a man unacceptable for the priesthood, or an animal unacceptable for sacrifice. Here I understand it to be some such damage in humans' nature, as God and Moses have just said (31:21,27,29). It is not humans, "His children," as such, but rather this inherent shortcoming in their nature that brings about corruption in the eyes of the deity.

32:6. *Is it to YHWH . . . ?!* The first letter (the Hebrew interrogative h, which makes the line a question) is oversized in many manuscripts. This seems to underscore the question, to make it incredible: "You'd repay *God* this way?!"

8 When the Highest gave nations legacies,
   when He dispersed humankind,
He set the peoples' borders
   to the number of the children of Israel.

8בְּהַנְחֵל עֶלְיוֹן גּוֹיִם בְּהַפְרִידוֹ בְּנֵי אָדָם
יַצֵּב גְּבֻלֹת עַמִּים לְמִסְפַּר בְּנֵי יִשְׂרָאֵל:

32:8. dispersed humankind. The term "dispersed" refers to the separation of humankind into nations in Genesis (10:5,18,32; 25:23).

32:8. to the number of the children of Israel. In light of the other occurrences of the phrase "to the number" in the *Tanak* (Josh 4:5,8; Judg 21:23), it means here "equal to the number of the children of Israel." This makes little sense: that the number of nations is equal to the number of the children of Israel. Traditional commentators have taken this to mean that there are seventy nations (as in Genesis 10), matching the seventy souls of Jacob's (Israel's) family who go to Egypt (Exod 1:5), or that there are twelve Canaanite peoples, matching Israel's twelve sons.

Contemporary scholars have taken account of a Qumran (Dead Sea) scroll (4QDeutj) that says instead: "to the number of the children of the gods" (or "children of God"—*běnê ʾĕlōhîm*). The phrase "children [or: sons] of the gods" normally means: the gods. Scholars have hypothesized that this was the original reading of this verse and that later scribes or editors were distressed by this meaning so they changed "children of the gods" to "children of Israel." If so, then the original meaning was that God allotted a nation to each of the gods—and He took Israel as His own people. Thus the next verse reads: "YHWH's portion is Israel." One may take this to mean that the author of this song believed that there were in fact other gods but that YHWH was supreme. (This is known as henotheism, a step between polytheism and monotheism.) Or one may understand it to mean that the author's view was that YHWH allotted the peoples their gods in whom to believe, but that these gods did not really exist.

To complicate this picture further, the Greek text reads "to the number of the angels of God." And there are cases in which the *běnê ʾĕlōhîm* are thought to be the angels (Gen 6:2; Job 1:6). It is likely that the Greek translator had the "children of the gods" reading and changed it to "angels of God" to establish that these were in fact the angels and not the pagan gods. On this understanding of the *běnê ʾĕlōhîm*, God allots a nation to each of the angels but retains Israel for Himself.

I believe that Psalm 82 is particularly relevant to this matter. It pictures the following: "God is standing in the divine council. He judges among the gods" (82:1). In this extraordinary scene, God criticizes the gods for failing to judge justly, and He takes away their immortality, condemning them to die like humans: "I had said you are gods, children of the Highest, all of you; but you shall die like a human!" (82:6). Whether meant literally or figuratively, this psalm tells a myth of the death of the gods. And note that it refers to God as "the Highest" (*ʿelyôn*), as in our verse here in the Song of Moses (and it refers to the gods as the children of the Highest); and it ends with God giving *legacies* to the nations (82:8)—which is also what our verse here says: "When the Highest gave nations legacies. . . ." It is likely, therefore, that the passage in the Song of Moses reflects the idea of Psalm 82: that there once were lesser gods along with YHWH, and that each was the god of a people, but they were inadequate, and

9 For YHWH's portion is His people.
　Jacob is the share of His legacy.

10 He found it in a wilderness land
　and in a formless place, a howling desert.
　He surrounded it. He attended to it.
　He guarded it, like the pupil of his eye.

11 As an eagle stirs its nest,
　hovers over its young,
　spreads its wings, takes it,
　lifts it on its pinion,

12 YHWH, alone, led it,
　and no foreign god with Him.

13 He had it ride over earth's high places
　and fed it the field's bounties
　and had it suck honey from a rock
　and oil from a flint rock

14 and curds of cattle and milk of the flock
　and fat of lambs
　and Bashan rams and he-goats
　with fat of innards of wheat
　—and from grape's blood you drank wine.

15 And Jeshurun got fat and kicked
　—you got fat, you got wide, you got
　　stuffed!—

9 כִּי חֵלֶק יְהֹוָה עַמּוֹ יַעֲקֹב חֶבֶל נַחֲלָתוֹ:
10 יִמְצָאֵהוּ בְּאֶרֶץ מִדְבָּר וּבְתֹהוּ יְלֵל יְשִׁמֹן
יְסֹבְבֶנְהוּ יְבוֹנְנֵהוּ יִצְּרֶנְהוּ כְּאִישׁוֹן עֵינוֹ:
11 כְּנֶשֶׁר יָעִיר קִנּוֹ עַל־גּוֹזָלָיו יְרַחֵף
יִפְרֹשׂ כְּנָפָיו יִקָּחֵהוּ יִשָּׂאֵהוּ עַל־אֶבְרָתוֹ:
12 יְהֹוָה בָּדָד יַנְחֶנּוּ וְאֵין עִמּוֹ אֵל נֵכָר:
13 יַרְכִּבֵהוּ עַל־בָּמֳותֵי אָרֶץ וַיֹּאכַל תְּנוּבֹת שָׂדָי
וַיֵּנִקֵהוּ דְבַשׁ מִסֶּלַע וְשֶׁמֶן מֵחַלְמִישׁ צוּר:
14 חֶמְאַת בָּקָר וַחֲלֵב צֹאן עִם־חֵלֶב כָּרִים
וְאֵילִים בְּנֵי־בָשָׁן וְעַתּוּדִים עִם־חֵלֶב כִּלְיוֹת חִטָּה
וְדַם־עֵנָב תִּשְׁתֶּה־חָמֶר:
15 וַיִּשְׁמַן יְשֻׁרוּן וַיִּבְעָט שָׁמַנְתָּ עָבִיתָ כָּשִׂיתָ

32:13 קְ בָּמֳתֵי

---

they no longer exist. This may have been believed literally, or it may have been conceived as an answer to those who asked, "What happened to the gods we used to worship?" Or it may have been conceived as a metaphor for the replacement of the belief in many gods by the belief in one.

32:10. **a formless place.** Hebrew *tôhû*. The word has not occurred since its mention at the very beginning of the Torah: "the earth had been formless and shapeless" (Gen 1:2). Now Israel's environment in the wilderness is pictured comparably to the condition of the universe prior to the acts of creation: a condition of chaos.

32:11. **hovers.** This word, too, occurred in Gen 1:2 (see the preceding comment) and never again in the Torah until its appearance here. YHWH's protection of Israel in its infancy in the wilderness (like an eagle hovering over its young) is pictured comparably to the divine spirit hovering over the still-shapeless waters in which the earth and skies will be formed.

32:15. **Jeshurun.** Israel.

32:15. **got fat.** This is a pun. The Hebrew consonants *yšmn* are the same as in the word "desert" (*yĕšîmōn*) in v. 10. But the wordplay is that the same words consonantally have nearly opposite meanings: the people ironically go from a desert (*yšmn*) to getting fat (*yšmn*).

668

and it left God who made it
and took its saving rock for granted.

16 They made Him jealous with outsiders.
   With offensive things they made him
      angry.
17 They sacrificed to demons, a non-god,
   gods they hadn't known;
   new ones, they came of late;
   your fathers hadn't been acquainted with
      them.
18 The rock that fathered you, you ignored,
   and you forgot God who bore you.
19 And YHWH saw and rejected
   from His sons' and His daughters'
      angering.
20 And He said, "Let me hide my face from
      them;
   I'll see what their future will be.
   For they're a generation of overthrows,
   children with no trust in them.
21 They made me jealous with no-god.
   They made me angry with their nothings.

וַיִּטֹּשׁ אֱלוֹהַּ עָשָׂהוּ וַיְנַבֵּל צוּר יְשֻׁעָתוֹ׃
16 יַקְנִאֻהוּ בְּזָרִים בְּתוֹעֵבֹת יַכְעִיסֻהוּ׃
17 יִזְבְּחוּ לַשֵּׁדִים לֹא אֱלֹהַּ אֱלֹהִים לֹא יְדָעוּם
   חֲדָשִׁים מִקָּרֹב בָּאוּ לֹא שְׂעָרוּם אֲבֹתֵיכֶם׃
18 צוּר יְלָדְךָ תֶּשִׁי וַתִּשְׁכַּח אֵל מְחֹלְלֶךָ׃
19 וַיַּרְא יְהוָה וַיִּנְאָץ מִכַּעַס בָּנָיו וּבְנֹתָיו׃
20 וַיֹּאמֶר אַסְתִּירָה פָנַי מֵהֶם אֶרְאֶה מָה אַחֲרִיתָם
   כִּי דוֹר תַּהְפֻּכֹת הֵמָּה בָּנִים לֹא־אֵמֻן בָּם׃
21 הֵם קִנְאוּנִי בְלֹא־אֵל כִּעֲסוּנִי בְּהַבְלֵיהֶם

32:20. **Let me hide my face.** See the comment on Deut 31:17.

32:20. **I'll see what their future will be.** Hebrew 'aḥărît, often understood as "end," does not mean this in the sense of humankind's coming to an end. Rather, it refers to what will happen in the distant future, the long run. There are two sides to the hiding of the face. It is a fearful period of estrangement from their creator. It has been called divine eclipse, *Deus Absconditus*, and "death" of God. But, after living through it, humans are forced to grow up, to become more responsible for their world. The words of the Song of Moses declare that God is not simply hiding His face to bring His relationship with humans to an end. There are rather two halves to the statement: "I'll hide my face from them; I'll see what their future will be." God gives humans responsibility for their world. And the only way that they can be forced to take that responsibility is if God is hidden. At whatever price (even world wars, even the holocaust?!) and with whatever successes (rebuilding Israel, conquering diseases, discovering secrets of the creation of the universe), humans must grow up. And God will see what their destiny will be.

The Torah does not end with the natural conclusions of the story: the promised land has not been reached, but it is in sight. Everything lies in the future: finding a home, fulfillment of the promises, bringing blessing to all the families of the earth. The divine words resound: "I'll see what their future will be." The Torah ends leaving us looking forward to what we can do and what we can be.

And I: I'll make them jealous with
    no-people.
I'll make them angry with a foolish
    nation.

22 For fire has ignited in my anger
    and burned to Sheol at bottom
    and consumed land and its crop
    and set the mountains' foundations
        ablaze.

23 I'll mass bad things over them.
    I'll exhaust my arrows on them,

24 sapped by hunger and devoured by
        flame.
    And bitter destruction
    and animals' teeth I'll let loose at them
    with venom of serpents of the dust.

25 Outside: a sword will bereave,
    and inside: terror,
    both young man and virgin,
    suckling with aged man.

26 I'd say, 'I'll erase them.
    I'll make their memory cease from
        mankind,'

27 if I didn't fear the enemy's anger,
    in case their foes would misread,
    in case they'd say, '*Our* hand was high,
    and it wasn't YHWH who did all this!'

28 For they're a nation void of counsel,
    and there's no understanding in them.

29 If they were wise they'd comprehend this;
    they'd grasp their future.

30 How could one pursue a thousand
    and two chase ten thousand

וַאֲנִי֙ אַקְנִיאֵ֣ם בְּלֹא־עָ֔ם בְּג֥וֹי נָבָ֖ל אַכְעִיסֵֽם׃

22 כִּי־אֵשׁ֙ קָדְחָ֣ה בְאַפִּ֔י וַתִּיקַ֖ד עַד־שְׁא֣וֹל תַּחְתִּ֑ית
וַתֹּ֤אכַל אֶ֙רֶץ֙ וִֽיבֻלָ֔הּ וַתְּלַהֵ֖ט מוֹסְדֵ֥י הָרִֽים׃

23 אַסְפֶּ֥ה עָלֵ֖ימוֹ רָע֑וֹת חִצַּ֖י אֲכַלֶּה־בָּֽם׃

24 מְזֵ֥י רָעָ֛ב וּלְחֻ֥מֵי רֶ֖שֶׁף וְקֶ֣טֶב מְרִירִ֑י
וְשֶׁן־בְּהֵמֹת֙ אֲשַׁלַּח־בָּ֔ם עִם־חֲמַ֖ת זֹחֲלֵ֥י עָפָֽר׃

25 מִח֥וּץ תְּשַׁכֶּל־חֶ֙רֶב֙ וּמֵחֲדָרִ֣ים אֵימָ֔ה
גַּם־בָּחוּר֙ גַּם־בְּתוּלָ֔ה יוֹנֵ֖ק עִם־אִ֥ישׁ שֵׂיבָֽה׃

26 אָמַ֖רְתִּי אַפְאֵיהֶ֑ם אַשְׁבִּ֥יתָה מֵאֱנ֖וֹשׁ זִכְרָֽם׃

27 לוּלֵ֗י כַּ֤עַס אוֹיֵב֙ אָג֔וּר פֶּֽן־יְנַכְּר֖וּ צָרֵ֑ימוֹ
פֶּן־יֹֽאמְרוּ֙ יָדֵ֣ינוּ רָ֔מָה וְלֹ֥א יְהוָ֖ה פָּעַ֥ל כָּל־זֹֽאת׃

28 כִּי־ג֛וֹי אֹבַ֥ד עֵצ֖וֹת הֵ֑מָּה וְאֵ֥ין בָּהֶ֖ם תְּבוּנָֽה׃

29 ל֥וּ חָכְמ֖וּ יַשְׂכִּ֣ילוּ זֹ֑את יָבִ֖ינוּ לְאַחֲרִיתָֽם׃

30 אֵיכָ֞ה יִרְדֹּ֤ף אֶחָד֙ אֶ֔לֶף וּשְׁנַ֖יִם יָנִ֣יסוּ רְבָבָ֑ה

32:24. **serpents of the dust**. Or: things that crawl in the dust. This is reminiscent of
the story of Eden, in which the snake and its descendants are condemned to be leg-
less, going on their bellies and eating dust (Gen 3:14); and in which the descendants
of the humans and the snake are cursed with mutual enmity, so that the snake will
bite the human's heel (3:15).

32:26. **erase them . . . make their memory cease**. To capture the full irony and horror of these words, one must recall that this is what is supposed to happen to Amalek,
the people who symbolize Israel's worst enemies: "wipe out the memory of Amalek"
(Deut 25:19).

if not that their rock had sold them,
that YHWH had turned them over?"

31 For their rock is not like our rock,
though our enemies are the judges.

32 For their vine is from Sodom's vine
and from Gomorrah's fields.
Their grapes are poison grapes.
They have bitter clusters.

33 Their wine is serpents' venom
and cruel poison of cobras.

34 "Isn't it stored with me,
sealed in my treasuries?

35 Vengeance and recompense are mine,
for the time their foot will slip;
for the day of their ordeal is close
and comes fast: things prepared for them."

36 For YHWH will judge His people
and regret about His servants
when He'll see that their strength is gone
and there's none: held back or left alone.

37 And He'll say, "Where are their gods,
the rock in whom they sought refuge,

38 who would eat the fat of their sacrifices,
would drink the wine of their libations?
Let them get up and help you!
Let that be a shelter over you.

39 See now that I, *I* am He,
and there is no god with me.

אִם־לֹא כִּי־צוּרָם מְכָרָם וַיהוָה הִסְגִּירָם:

31 כִּי לֹא כְצוּרֵנוּ צוּרָם וְאֹיְבֵינוּ פְּלִילִים:

32 כִּי־מִגֶּפֶן סְדֹם גַּפְנָם וּמִשַּׁדְמֹת עֲמֹרָה
עֲנָבֵמוֹ עִנְּבֵי־רוֹשׁ אַשְׁכְּלֹת מְרֹרֹת לָמוֹ:

33 חֲמַת תַּנִּינִם יֵינָם וְרֹאשׁ פְּתָנִים אַכְזָר:

34 הֲלֹא־הוּא כָּמֻס עִמָּדִי חָתֻם בְּאוֹצְרֹתָי:

35 לִי נָקָם וְשִׁלֵּם לְעֵת תָּמוּט רַגְלָם
כִּי קָרוֹב יוֹם אֵידָם וְחָשׁ עֲתִדֹת לָמוֹ:

36 כִּי־יָדִין יְהוָה עַמּוֹ וְעַל־עֲבָדָיו יִתְנֶחָם
כִּי יִרְאֶה כִּי־אָזְלַת יָד וְאֶפֶס עָצוּר וְעָזוּב:

37 וְאָמַר אֵי אֱלֹהֵימוֹ צוּר חָסָיוּ בוֹ:

38 אֲשֶׁר חֵלֶב זְבָחֵימוֹ יֹאכֵלוּ יִשְׁתּוּ יֵין נְסִיכָם
יָקוּמוּ וְיַעְזְרֻכֶם יְהִי עֲלֵיכֶם סִתְרָה:

39 רְאוּ עַתָּה כִּי אֲנִי אֲנִי הוּא
וְאֵין אֱלֹהִים עִמָּדִי

32:30. turned them over. This is the same word that is used to refer to turning an escaped slave over to his master (Deut 23:16). The preceding colon, which parallels this, refers to *selling* the people. That is, both lines convey an image of God selling Israel back into slavery, when it was God who had freed them from slavery in the first place. Like the last curse of the list in Deuteronomy 28, it is the ultimate horror for Israel: to return to slavery.

32:39. there is no god with me. It is *possible* that this might mean that other gods exist but that they just do not happen to be present with YHWH at this time, but that seems to me to be a stretch. Where would a god be who is not in YHWH's presence?! The plain sense of these words (and other passages on which I have commented) is monotheistic. It comes in a context of calling on gods to show themselves if they exist: "Where are their gods. . . . Let them get up and help you!" And this poem shows well-known linguistic signs of being an early composition. The persistent view in biblical scholarship that monotheism is a late development in biblical Israel (coming during or after the Babylonian exile) is contrary to such explicit statements as this.

I cause death and give life.
I've pierced, and *I'll* heal.
And there's no deliverer from my hand,

40   when I raise my hand to the skies,
and I say, 'As I live forever,

41   if I whet the lightning of my sword,
and my hand takes hold of judgment,
I'll give back vengeance to my foes
and pay back those who hate me.

42   I'll make my arrows drunk with blood,
and my sword will eat flesh
from the blood of the slain and captured,
from the head of loose hair of the
enemy.'"

43   Nations: cheer His people!
For He'll requite His servants' blood
and give back vengeance to His foes
and make atonement for His land, His
people.

44And Moses came and spoke all the words of
this song in the people's ears, he and Hoshea son
of Nun.

45And Moses finished speaking all these things
to all of Israel. 46And he said to them, "Pay attention to all the things that I testify regarding you
today, that you'll command them to your children, to observe and to do all the words of this instruction. 47Because it's not an empty thing for
you, because it's your *life.* And through this thing
you'll extend days on the land to which you're
crossing the Jordan to take possession of it."

48And YHWH spoke to Moses in this very day,
saying, 49"Go up to this mountain of Abarim,
Mount Nebo, which is in the land of Moab,
which is facing Jericho, and see the land of Canaan, which I'm giving to the children of Israel
for a possession. 50And die in the mountain to
which you're going up, and be gathered to your

אֲנִ֧י אָמִ֣ית וַאֲחַיֶּ֗ה מָחַ֙צְתִּי֙ וַאֲנִ֣י אֶרְפָּ֔א
וְאֵ֥ין מִיָּדִ֖י מַצִּֽיל׃
40כִּֽי־אֶשָּׂ֥א אֶל־שָׁמַ֖יִם יָדִ֑י
וְאָמַ֕רְתִּי חַ֥י אָנֹכִ֖י לְעֹלָֽם׃
41אִם־שַׁנּוֹתִי֙ בְּרַ֣ק חַרְבִּ֔י וְתֹאחֵ֥ז בְּמִשְׁפָּ֖ט יָדִ֑י
אָשִׁ֤יב נָקָם֙ לְצָרָ֔י וְלִמְשַׂנְאַ֖י אֲשַׁלֵּֽם׃
42אַשְׁכִּ֤יר חִצַּי֙ מִדָּ֔ם וְחַרְבִּ֖י תֹּ֣אכַל בָּשָׂ֑ר
מִדַּ֤ם חָלָל֙ וְשִׁבְיָ֔ה מֵרֹ֖אשׁ פַּרְע֥וֹת אוֹיֵֽב׃
43הַרְנִ֤ינוּ גוֹיִם֙ עַמּ֔וֹ כִּ֥י דַם־עֲבָדָ֖יו יִקּ֑וֹם   פ
וְנָקָם֙ יָשִׁ֣יב לְצָרָ֔יו וְכִפֶּ֥ר אַדְמָת֖וֹ עַמּֽוֹ׃
44וַיָּבֹ֣א מֹשֶׁ֗ה וַיְדַבֵּ֛ר אֶת־כָּל־דִּבְרֵ֥י הַשִּׁירָֽה־
הַזֹּ֖את בְּאָזְנֵ֣י הָעָ֑ם ה֖וּא וְהוֹשֵׁ֥עַ בִּן־נֽוּן׃ 45וַיְכַ֣ל מֹשֶׁ֗ה
לְדַבֵּ֛ר אֶת־כָּל־הַדְּבָרִ֥ים הָאֵ֖לֶּה אֶל־כָּל־יִשְׂרָאֵֽל׃
46וַיֹּ֤אמֶר אֲלֵהֶם֙ שִׂ֣ימוּ לְבַבְכֶ֔ם לְכָל־הַדְּבָרִ֔ים אֲשֶׁ֧ר
אָנֹכִ֛י מֵעִ֥יד בָּכֶ֖ם הַיּ֑וֹם אֲשֶׁ֤ר תְּצַוֻּם֙ אֶת־בְּנֵיכֶ֔ם
לִשְׁמֹ֣ר לַעֲשׂ֔וֹת אֶת־כָּל־דִּבְרֵ֖י הַתּוֹרָ֥ה הַזֹּֽאת׃ 47כִּ֠י
לֹֽא־דָבָ֨ר רֵ֥ק הוּא֙ מִכֶּ֔ם כִּי־ה֖וּא חַיֵּיכֶ֑ם וּבַדָּבָ֤ר
הַזֶּה֙ תַּאֲרִ֣יכוּ יָמִ֔ים עַל־הָ֣אֲדָמָ֔ה אֲשֶׁ֨ר אַתֶּ֜ם עֹבְרִ֧ים
אֶת־הַיַּרְדֵּ֛ן שָׁ֖מָּה לְרִשְׁתָּֽהּ׃   פ
48וַיְדַבֵּ֤ר יְהוָה֙ אֶל־מֹשֶׁ֔ה בְּעֶ֛צֶם הַיּ֥וֹם הַזֶּ֖ה
לֵאמֹֽר׃ 49עֲלֵ֡ה אֶל־הַר֩ הָעֲבָרִ֨ים הַזֶּ֜ה הַר־נְב֗וֹ
אֲשֶׁר֙ בְּאֶ֣רֶץ מוֹאָ֔ב אֲשֶׁ֖ר עַל־פְּנֵ֣י יְרֵח֑וֹ וּרְאֵה֙ אֶת־
אֶ֣רֶץ כְּנַ֔עַן אֲשֶׁ֨ר אֲנִ֥י נֹתֵ֛ן לִבְנֵ֥י יִשְׂרָאֵ֖ל לַאֲחֻזָּֽה׃
50וּמֻ֗ת בָּהָר֙ אֲשֶׁ֤ר אַתָּה֙ עֹלֶ֣ה שָׁ֔מָּה וְהֵאָסֵ֖ף אֶל־

32:44. **Hoshea**. Joshua.

32:47. **it's your *life*.** Again we are reminded here at the end of the Torah that these
things are a path back to the tree of life that was lost at the Torah's beginning. See the
comment on Deut 30:19.

people, as Aaron, your brother, died in Mount Hor and was gathered to his people, [51]because you made a breach with me among the children of Israel at the waters of Meribah of Kadesh at the wilderness of Zin, because you didn't make me holy among the children of Israel. [52]Because you'll see the land from opposite, but you shall not come there, to the land that I'm giving to the children of Israel.

עַמֶּיךָ כַּאֲשֶׁר־מֵת אַהֲרֹן אָחִיךָ בְּהֹר הָהָר וַיֵּאָסֶף אֶל־עַמָּיו: 51עַל אֲשֶׁר מְעַלְתֶּם בִּי בְּתוֹךְ בְּנֵי יִשְׂרָאֵל בְּמֵי־מְרִיבַת קָדֵשׁ מִדְבַּר־צִן עַל אֲשֶׁר לֹא־קִדַּשְׁתֶּם אוֹתִי בְּתוֹךְ בְּנֵי יִשְׂרָאֵל: 52כִּי מִנֶּגֶד תִּרְאֶה אֶת־הָאָרֶץ וְשָׁמָּה לֹא תָבוֹא אֶל־הָאָרֶץ אֲשֶׁר־אֲנִי נֹתֵן לִבְנֵי יִשְׂרָאֵל: פ

AND THIS IS THE BLESSING

וזאת הברכה

33 [1]And this is the blessing with which Moses, the man of God, blessed the children of Israel before his death. [2]And he said:

YHWH came from Sinai
and rose from Seir for them.
He shone from Mount Paran
and came from ten thousands of the
	holy,
slopes at His right, for them.

3　Also loving peoples,
all holy ones are in your hand.
And they knelt at your feet;
they bore your words.

4　Moses commanded us instruction,
a possession, community of Jacob.

5　And He was king in Jeshurun
when the people's heads were
	gathered:
Israel's tribes together.

6　Let Reuben live and not die,
but his men will be few in number.

33 1וְזֹאת הַבְּרָכָה אֲשֶׁר בֵּרַךְ מֹשֶׁה אִישׁ הָאֱלֹהִים אֶת־בְּנֵי יִשְׂרָאֵל לִפְנֵי מוֹתוֹ: 2וַיֹּאמַר יְהֹוָה מִסִּינַי בָּא וְזָרַח מִשֵּׂעִיר לָמוֹ הוֹפִיעַ מֵהַר פָּארָן וְאָתָה מֵרִבְבֹת קֹדֶשׁ מִימִינוֹ אֵשְׁדָּת לָמוֹ: 3אַף חֹבֵב עַמִּים כָּל־קְדֹשָׁיו בְּיָדֶךָ וְהֵם תֻּכּוּ לְרַגְלֶךָ יִשָּׂא מִדַּבְּרֹתֶיךָ: 4תּוֹרָה צִוָּה־לָנוּ מֹשֶׁה מוֹרָשָׁה קְהִלַּת יַעֲקֹב: 5וַיְהִי בִישֻׁרוּן מֶלֶךְ בְּהִתְאַסֵּף רָאשֵׁי עָם יַחַד שִׁבְטֵי יִשְׂרָאֵל: 6יְחִי רְאוּבֵן וְאַל־יָמֹת וִיהִי מְתָיו מִסְפָּר: ס

33:2 קֹ אֵשׁ דָּת

33:2. **slopes at His right**. No one knows what this line means. (Frank Cross and David Noel Freedman once wrote, "Conjectures are almost as numerous as scholars.") I followed the consonantal text, taking Hebrew 'šdt as "slopes," which is what it means in its only other occurrences in the Torah (Deut 3:17; 4:49). In both of those occurrences it refers to the slopes of Pisgah, east of the Dead Sea. In this verse, YHWH shines like the sun coming from the east over Seir and Paran, in which case the slopes of Pisgah would in fact be at His right.

33:6. **few in number**. The territory of Reuben was the most vulnerable of any tribe:

7 And this for Judah—and he said:
    Hear, YHWH, Judah's voice,
    and bring him to his people.
    With his hands he strove for himself,
    and you'll be a help from its foes.

8 And for Levi he said:
    Your Tummim and your Urim are your
       faithful man's,
    whom you tested at Massah,
    disputed with him over Meribah's water.

9 Who said of his father and his mother:
    "I haven't seen him,"
    and didn't recognize his brothers
    and didn't know his children,
    for they observed what you said
    and kept your covenant.

10 They'll teach your judgments to Jacob
    and your instruction to Israel.
    They'll set incense at your nose,
    entirely burnt on your altar.

11 Bless, YHWH, his wealth
    and accept his hands' work.
    Pierce his adversaries' hips,
    and those who hate him, so they won't
      get up.

12 For Benjamin he said:
    Beloved of YHWH,
    he'll dwell in security by Him.
    He shelters over him all day
    as he dwells between his shoulders.

7וְזֹאת לִיהוּדָה֮ וַיֹּאמַר֒
שְׁמַ֤ע יְהוָה֙ ק֣וֹל יְהוּדָ֔ה וְאֶל־עַמּ֖וֹ תְּבִיאֶ֑נּוּ
יָדָיו֙ רָ֣ב ל֔וֹ וְעֵ֥זֶר מִצָּרָ֖יו תִּהְיֶֽה: ס
8וּלְלֵוִ֣י אָמַ֔ר
תֻּמֶּ֥יךָ וְאוּרֶ֖יךָ לְאִ֣ישׁ חֲסִידֶ֑ךָ
אֲשֶׁ֤ר נִסִּיתוֹ֙ בְּמַסָּ֔ה תְּרִיבֵ֖הוּ עַל־מֵ֥י מְרִיבָֽה:
9הָאֹמֵ֞ר לְאָבִ֤יו וּלְאִמּוֹ֙ לֹ֣א רְאִיתִ֔יו
וְאֶת־אֶחָיו֙ לֹ֣א הִכִּ֔יר וְאֶת־בָּנָ֖ו לֹ֣א יָדָ֑ע
כִּ֤י שָֽׁמְרוּ֙ אִמְרָתֶ֔ךָ וּבְרִֽיתְךָ֖ יִנְצֹֽרוּ:
10יוֹר֤וּ מִשְׁפָּטֶ֙יךָ֙ לְיַעֲקֹ֔ב וְתוֹרָֽתְךָ֖ לְיִשְׂרָאֵ֑ל
יָשִׂ֤ימוּ קְטוֹרָה֙ בְּאַפֶּ֔ךָ וְכָלִ֖יל עַֽל־מִזְבְּחֶֽךָ:
11בָּרֵ֤ךְ יְהוָה֙ חֵיל֔וֹ וּפֹ֥עַל יָדָ֖יו תִּרְצֶ֑ה
מְחַ֨ץ מָתְנַ֧יִם קָמָ֛יו וּמְשַׂנְאָ֖יו מִן־יְקוּמֽוּן: ס
12לְבִנְיָמִ֣ן אָמַ֔ר
יְדִ֣יד יְהֹוָ֔ה יִשְׁכֹּ֥ן לָבֶ֖טַח עָלָ֑יו
חֹפֵ֤ף עָלָיו֙ כָּל־הַיּ֔וֹם
וּבֵ֥ין כְּתֵיפָ֖יו שָׁכֵֽן: ס

—————
33:9 קְ בָּנָֽיו

---

located east of the Dead Sea, cut off from the tribes that were west of the Jordan. It virtually ceased to exist by the tenth century B.C.E.

33:9. father . . . mother . . . brothers . . . children. This has been taken in a narrow sense (by Rashi and others) to refer to the golden calf episode, in which Moses tells the Levites to "kill, each man, his brother and, each man, his neighbor and, each man, his relative" (Exod 32:27,29). And it has been understood more broadly, to refer to the Levites' single-minded performance of their priestly duties, neither being distracted by one's family nor showing favoritism to them. Alternatively, it might refer to the requirement that the high priest may not touch any dead bodies, even of his own parents (Lev 21:11).

33:10. entirely burnt on your altar. The term for "entirely burnt" (*kālîl*) is used in connection with the offering that the priests make on the day of the high priest's anointing (Lev 6:12–16). It thus especially symbolizes the priestly status of Levi.

13 And for Joseph he said:
    Blessed of YHWH is his land,
    from the skies' abundance, from dew,
    and from the deep, crouching below,

14 and from the abundance of the sun's
        produce
    and from the abundance of the moon's
        output

15 and from the top of the ancient
        mountains
    and from the abundance of the hills of
        antiquity

16 and from the abundance of earth and
        what fills it
    and the favor of the one who dwelt in
        the bush.
    May it be on Joseph's head,
    on the top of the head of the one
        separate from his brothers.

17 His firstborn bull: it has majesty.
    And its horns are a wild ox's horns.
    It will gore peoples with them,
    together, the ends of the earth.
    And they're Ephraim's ten thousands,
    And they're Manasseh's thousands.

18 And for Zebulun he said:
    Rejoice, Zebulun, when you go out,
    and Issachar in your tents.

19 They'll call peoples to the mountain.
    There they'll offer the sacrifices of
        virtue.
    For they'll suck the seas' bounty
    and the sand's hidden treasures.

20 And for Gad he said:
    Blessed is one who enlarges Gad.
    Like a feline, abiding
    and tearing an arm and the top of a
        head,

וּלְיוֹסֵף אָמַר13
מְבֹרֶכֶת יְהוָֹה אַרְצוֹ מִמֶּגֶד שָׁמַיִם מִטָּל
וּמִתְּהוֹם רֹבֶצֶת תָּחַת:
וּמִמֶּגֶד תְּבוּאֹת שָׁמֶשׁ וּמִמֶּגֶד גֶּרֶשׁ יְרָחִים:14
וּמֵרֹאשׁ הַרְרֵי־קֶדֶם וּמִמֶּגֶד גִּבְעוֹת עוֹלָם:15
וּמִמֶּגֶד אֶרֶץ וּמְלֹאָהּ וּרְצוֹן שֹׁכְנִי סְנֶה16
תָּבוֹאתָה לְרֹאשׁ יוֹסֵף וּלְקָדְקֹד נְזִיר אֶחָיו:
בְּכוֹר שׁוֹרוֹ הָדָר לוֹ וְקַרְנֵי רְאֵם קַרְנָיו17
בָּהֶם עַמִּים יְנַגַּח יַחְדָּו אַפְסֵי־אָרֶץ
וְהֵם רִבְבוֹת אֶפְרַיִם וְהֵם אַלְפֵי מְנַשֶּׁה: ס
וְלִזְבוּלֻן אָמַר18
שְׂמַח זְבוּלֻן בְּצֵאתֶךָ וְיִשָּׂשכָר בְּאֹהָלֶיךָ:
עַמִּים הַר־יִקְרָאוּ שָׁם יִזְבְּחוּ זִבְחֵי־צֶדֶק19
כִּי שֶׁפַע יַמִּים יִינָקוּ וּשְׂפֻנֵי טְמוּנֵי חוֹל: ס
וּלְגָד אָמַר20
בָּרוּךְ מַרְחִיב גָּד כְּלָבִיא שָׁכֵן
וְטָרַף זְרוֹעַ אַף־קָדְקֹד:

33:16. **May it be**. Following Cross and Freedman, I have read the Hebrew תבואתה
on the likelihood that it conflated two readings: "May it come" (תבוא) and "May it be"
(תה). The latter is preferable on the basis of comparison with the parallel blessing of
Joseph in Gen 49:26.

21 so he saw the foremost for himself,
for a ruler's share was kept there.
And the heads of the people came.
And he did YHWH's justice
and His laws with Israel.

22 And for Dan he said:
Dan is a lion's whelp
that leapt from Bashan.

23 And for Naphtali he said:
Naphtali is full of favor
and filled with YHWH's blessing.
He'll possess west and south.

24 And for Asher he said:
Blessed out of the sons is Asher.
Let him be favored by his brothers
and dipping his foot in oil.

25 Your lock is iron and bronze,
and your strength is as much as your
days.

26 There's none like the God of Jeshurun,
riding skies to help you
and clouds in His majesty.

27 The ancient God is a refuge;
and below: the arms of the eternal.
And He drove out an enemy before you
and said, "Destroy!"

28 And Israel will dwell secure,
Jacob dwells alone.
To a land of grain and wine;
and its skies drop dew.

21וַיַּרְא רֵאשִׁית֙ לֹ֔ו כִּי־שָׁ֛ם חֶלְקַ֥ת מְחֹקֵ֖ק סָפ֑וּן
וַיֵּתֵא֙ רָ֣אשֵׁי עָ֔ם צִדְקַ֤ת יְהוָה֙ עָשָׂ֔ה
וּמִשְׁפָּטָ֖יו עִם־יִשְׂרָאֵֽל׃ ס

22וּלְדָ֣ן אָמַ֔ר
דָּ֖ן גּ֣וּר אַרְיֵ֑ה יְזַנֵּ֖ק מִן־הַבָּשָֽׁן׃

23וּלְנַפְתָּלִ֣י אָמַ֔ר
נַפְתָּלִי֙ שְׂבַ֣ע רָצ֔וֹן וּמָלֵ֖א בִּרְכַּ֣ת יְהוָ֑ה
יָ֥ם וְדָר֖וֹם יְרָֽשָׁה׃ ס

24וּלְאָשֵׁ֣ר אָמַ֔ר
בָּר֥וּךְ מִבָּנִ֖ים אָשֵׁ֑ר יְהִ֤י רְצוּי֙ אֶחָ֔יו וְטֹבֵ֥ל
בַּשֶּׁ֖מֶן רַגְלֽוֹ׃

25בַּרְזֶ֥ל וּנְחֹ֖שֶׁת מִנְעָלֶ֑יךָ וּכְיָמֶ֖יךָ דָּבְאֶֽךָ׃

26אֵ֥ין כָּאֵ֖ל יְשֻׁר֑וּן רֹכֵ֤ב שָׁמַ֙יִם֙ בְּעֶזְרֶ֔ךָ
וּבְגַאֲוָת֖וֹ שְׁחָקִֽים׃

27מְעֹנָה֙ אֱלֹ֣הֵי קֶ֔דֶם וּמִתַּ֖חַת זְרֹעֹ֣ת עוֹלָ֑ם
וַיְגָ֧רֶשׁ מִפָּנֶ֛יךָ אוֹיֵ֖ב וַיֹּ֥אמֶר הַשְׁמֵֽד׃

28וַיִּשְׁכֹּן֩ יִשְׂרָאֵ֨ל בֶּ֤טַח בָּדָד֙ עֵ֣ין יַעֲקֹ֔ב
אֶל־אֶ֖רֶץ דָּגָ֣ן וְתִיר֑וֹשׁ אַף־שָׁמָ֖יו יַֽעַרְפוּ־טָֽל׃

33:21. **he saw the foremost for himself.** Neither the length nor the content of this verse suits the tribe of Gad, which is covered in the previous verse. My colleague David Noel Freedman has suggested that it is rather intertribal and that the specific references are to Moses as the leader of the confederation of the tribes. This matches the picture of Moses in vv. 4–5.

33:22. **Dan is a lion's whelp.** But in Jacob's blessing "*Judah* is a lion's whelp"! (Gen 49:9). Why are these two tribes described this way? Dan is the northernmost tribe, and Judah is the southernmost. So this produces an image of Israel protected by lions on either side. (Actually, Simeon is the southernmost tribe, but Simeon is unaccountably left out of this song.)

33:23. **west and south.** But Naphtali is located in the *north* and *east* of Israel. So this verse is understood to refer to the west and south of the Sea of Galilee (known also as Sea of Tiberias, or Sea of Kinneret).

29 Happy are you, Israel!
Who is like you,
a people saved by YHWH,
your strong shield
who is your majestic sword?!
And your enemies will fawn to you.
And you: you'll step on their high places.

אַשְׁרֶיךָ יִשְׂרָאֵל מִי כָמוֹךָ עַם נוֹשַׁע בַּיהוָה29
מָגֵן עֶזְרֶךָ וַאֲשֶׁר־חֶרֶב גַּאֲוָתֶךָ
וְיִכָּחֲשׁוּ אֹיְבֶיךָ לָךְ
וְאַתָּה עַל־בָּמוֹתֵימוֹ תִדְרֹךְ: ס

34 1And Moses went up from the plains of
Moab to Mount Nebo, the top of Pisgah,
which is facing Jericho. And YHWH showed him
all of the land, Gilead to Dan, 2and all of Naphtali and the land of Ephraim and Manasseh and
all the land of Judah to the far sea 3and the
Negeb and the plain, the valley of Jericho, city of
the palms, to Zoar.

4And YHWH said to him, "This is the land
that I swore to Abraham, to Isaac, and to Jacob,
saying, 'I'll give it to your seed.' I've caused you to
see it with your eyes, but you won't pass there."

5And Moses, YHWH's servant, died there in

וַיַּעַל מֹשֶׁה מֵעַרְבֹת מוֹאָב אֶל־הַר נְבוֹ 34
רֹאשׁ הַפִּסְגָּה אֲשֶׁר עַל־פְּנֵי יְרֵחוֹ וַיַּרְאֵהוּ יְהוָה
אֶת־כָּל־הָאָרֶץ אֶת־הַגִּלְעָד עַד־דָּן: 2וְאֵת כָּל־
נַפְתָּלִי וְאֶת־אֶרֶץ אֶפְרַיִם וּמְנַשֶּׁה וְאֵת כָּל־אֶרֶץ
יְהוּדָה עַד הַיָּם הָאַחֲרוֹן: 3וְאֶת־הַנֶּגֶב וְאֶת־הַכִּכָּר
בִּקְעַת יְרֵחוֹ עִיר הַתְּמָרִים עַד־צֹעַר: 4וַיֹּאמֶר
יְהוָה אֵלָיו זֹאת הָאָרֶץ אֲשֶׁר נִשְׁבַּעְתִּי לְאַבְרָהָם
לְיִצְחָק וּלְיַעֲקֹב לֵאמֹר לְזַרְעֲךָ אֶתְּנֶנָּה הֶרְאִיתִיךָ
בְעֵינֶיךָ וְשָׁמָּה לֹא תַעֲבֹר: 5וַיָּמָת שָׁם מֹשֶׁה עֶבֶד־

33:29. Happy are you, Israel! These are the last words that the people hear from
Moses. Strange: The first half is understandable as his final words, "Happy are you . . .
a people saved by YHWH." The second half is not what we might have expected: God
is their strong shield and sword! "And your enemies will fawn to you. And you: you'll
step on their high places." Why does he end with the defeat of enemies? Apparently
an assurance that Israel does not have to fear enemies was important—and so it has
in fact turned out in the people's history in the three millennia following Moses. The
presence of enemies has been a sad, constant fact of life. But Moses' last words are an
assurance that Israel will survive to fulfill the destiny that was the first promise to
Abraham: to be a source of blessing for all the earth's families.

33:29. high places. See the comment on Lev 26:30.

34:4. Abraham, Isaac, and Jacob. This is the last mention of them in the Torah. The
Torah returns to them and to the promises to them, but it does not end with those
promises fulfilled. It ends with Moses looking out at the land, with the fulfillment
lying in the future. Some have said that the original unit was the Hexateuch rather
than the Pentateuch; that is, that the story more properly concludes in the book of
Joshua, when the people come to live in the land that was promised to Abraham,
Isaac, and Jacob. But the Torah ends here, with the future, with the story still to be
told. It is a message to the reader that this is not meant to be just a story of the past.
I wrote at the beginning of this commentary that the Torah's story is rich in background, always presuming what has come before it (and I shall discuss below how it
is also enriched by its reader's knowledge of what is coming later in the story). Now I

the land of Moab by YHWH's mouth, 6and He buried him in the valley in the land of Moab opposite Beth Peor. And no man knows his burial place to this day. 7And Moses was a hundred twenty years old at his death. His eye was not dim, and his vitality had not fled.

יְהוָה בְּאֶרֶץ מוֹאָב עַל־פִּי יְהוָה: 6וַיִּקְבֹּר אֹתוֹ בַגַּיְ בְּאֶרֶץ מוֹאָב מוּל בֵּית פְּעוֹר וְלֹא־יָדַע אִישׁ אֶת־קְבֻרָתוֹ עַד הַיּוֹם הַזֶּה: 7וּמֹשֶׁה בֶּן־מֵאָה וְעֶשְׂרִים שָׁנָה בְּמֹתוֹ לֹא־כָהֲתָה עֵינוֹ וְלֹא־נָס לֵחֹה: 8וַיִּבְכּוּ

---

would add that it has a third perspective in that it always points beyond itself, to the destiny of Israel and humankind in the rest of the *Tanak* that follows, and, for millions of readers, in their continuing life beyond the conclusion of the Bible.

34:6. **He buried him**. This is usually understood to mean that God buries Moses. We should note that Qumran, Septuagint, and some manuscripts of the Samaritan tradition read *"they buried him."* This presumably means that the people bury him. That would imply a completely different picture of Moses' death. He does not die alone on the mountain. After he sees the land from the top of the mountain he goes down to a lower part of the mountain, where he dies with others around him, and then his people bury him. It is remarkable that a scribal difference of a single letter (a *waw* at the end of the word ויקבר, making it plural: "they buried") leaves open such a significant point: Does Moses end his life with God or with his fellow human beings? Perhaps it is meaningful (and appropriate?) that some scribes understood it one way, and other scribes understood it the other way. Moses lives his life in a zone between God and humans. We saw in the matter of the golden calf at Sinai that when Moses speaks to God he represents the people, and when he speaks to the people he represents God. (See the comment on Exod 32:19.)

34:6. **no man knows his burial place to this day**. Ancestor veneration is linked with the actual grave site. One can go to the so-called tombs of Rachel and David in Israel today and see people praying to Rachel and David there to answer their prayers or to intercede with God. In this report of the nonknowledge of Moses' burial place, therefore, the concern is that such veneration and prayer for intercession is not possible with Moses. It comes as a sharp contrast to all the other reports about burials in the family tomb in the Torah and elsewhere in the Bible.

If we understand the first part of this verse to read *"He buried him,"* then it would suggest that God does not desire such things to take place at Moses' tomb. If we read *"they buried him,"* it is harder to interpret why the Israelites themselves would make his burial site unknown. One possibility is that their leaders, in particular the high priest Eleazar, likewise do not want veneration at Moses' tomb. Another is that they are burying Moses in Moab, outside the land of Israel, and so they fear that the grave would be mistreated by foreign people. They cannot take Moses' body to the promised land with them because of the biological necessity of immediate burial. The bodies of Jacob and Joseph are carried back to Israel for burial, but in those cases we are specifically informed that the bodies have been embalmed (Gen 50:1,26).

34:7. **a hundred twenty years old**. Moses gets the maximum that anyone can live according to YHWH's decree in Genesis: "My spirit won't stay in humankind forever, since they're also flesh; and their days shall be a hundred twenty years" (Gen 6:3).

8And the children of Israel mourned Moses in the plains of Moab thirty days. And the days of weeping, the mourning of Moses, ended. 9And Joshua son of Nun was full of the spirit of wisdom because Moses had laid his hands on him, and the children of Israel listened to him. And they did as YHWH commanded Moses.

10And a prophet did not rise again in Israel like Moses, whom YHWH knew face-to-face, 11with all the signs and the wonders that YHWH sent him to do in the land of Egypt to Pharaoh and to all his servants and to all his land, 12and with all the strong hand and with all the great fear that Moses made before the eyes of all Israel.

בְּנֵי יִשְׂרָאֵל אֶת־מֹשֶׁה בְּעַרְבֹת מוֹאָב שְׁלֹשִׁים יוֹם וַיִּתְּמוּ יְמֵי בְכִי אֵבֶל מֹשֶׁה: 9וִיהוֹשֻׁעַ בִּן־נוּן מָלֵא רוּחַ חָכְמָה כִּי־סָמַךְ מֹשֶׁה אֶת־יָדָיו עָלָיו וַיִּשְׁמְעוּ אֵלָיו בְּנֵי־יִשְׂרָאֵל וַיַּעֲשׂוּ כַּאֲשֶׁר צִוָּה יְהוָה אֶת־מֹשֶׁה: 10וְלֹא־קָם נָבִיא עוֹד בְּיִשְׂרָאֵל כְּמֹשֶׁה אֲשֶׁר יְדָעוֹ יְהוָה פָּנִים אֶל־פָּנִים: 11לְכָל־הָאֹתוֹת וְהַמּוֹפְתִים אֲשֶׁר שְׁלָחוֹ יְהוָה לַעֲשׂוֹת בְּאֶרֶץ מִצְרָיִם לְפַרְעֹה וּלְכָל־עֲבָדָיו וּלְכָל־אַרְצוֹ: 12וּלְכֹל הַיָּד הַחֲזָקָה וּלְכֹל הַמּוֹרָא הַגָּדוֹל אֲשֶׁר עָשָׂה מֹשֶׁה לְעֵינֵי כָּל־יִשְׂרָאֵל:

34:10. face-to-face. This does not appear to be meant literally. See the comments on Exod 33:11 and Deut 5:4.

34:12. that Moses made. Here at the end of the Torah, for the first time, the strong hand and the fear are ascribed to Moses himself rather than, as usual, to God (Deut 3:24; 4:34)! This is a surprise because Moses has so often told the people that it is God, not himself, who has done these things. Perhaps it is a final tribute to Moses.

Closing comment:

We should appreciate the significance of the Jewish practice of returning immediately to Genesis 1 anew after completing the reading of Deuteronomy. It conveys the point, with each new reading of the Torah, that the Torah (and the entire Bible, as well) is a whole, that our concern is with the totality as well as the individual parts. That may seem obvious, but it is easy to lose sight of because we are used to studying the text in small units. The weekly reading is only a few chapters. Then the rabbi is constrained by time to comment on only a small portion of that reading. Both the Christian and the Jewish sermon are thus limited to a small corner of the tapestry. Likewise in Bible study groups and in Hebrew and Sunday school classes, we usually deal with a single verse or story. We would do well to learn from Rashi, who never lost sight of the whole while making comments on the parts. His commentary implicitly reminds us at its outset that the word TaNaK (Tōrāh, Nĕbî'îm/Prophets, Kĕtubîm/Writings) stands for a whole-composed-of-parts, because in commenting on Gen 1:1 Rashi brings in citations from all parts of the Bible: from Torah (Genesis and Exodus), the Prophets (Isaiah, Jeremiah, Hosea, and Amos), and the Writings (Psalms and Proverbs). Even the seemingly obvious fact that Jews study the weekly readings in order, rather than commenting on whatever passage one chooses each week, reinforces the idea that, even as we focus on the component, our concern ultimately is with the full narrative, with continuity, with context—with Torah.

At the beginning of this commentary, I emphasized the point that the Bible is rich in *background*, that the events in the first reading, Parashat Bereshit, remain as an essential substratum in all that follows in the Bible's story. Every biblical scene will be laden—artistically, theologically, psychologically, spiritually—with all that has come before. The broad concern with the earth that is established in the first parashah remains. So when the story narrows to the divine relationship with Abraham, it is still with the ultimate aim that this will be "a blessing to all the families of the earth." Now I want to add the opposite point: that one also has a finer sense of what is happening in each biblical episode, starting with the creation, if one reads it with consciousness of what is *coming*.

For example: the Sabbath is set in the very structure of the universe, but for most readers the Sabbath draws its significance in Genesis 2:1–3 not only from its being a feature of the creation but from the readers' knowledge that it is to be a prime commandment later, one of the Ten Commandments, and will be identified as the *sign* of the relationship between God and the Israelites (Exod 31:16–17). Just try to read about the seventh day in Genesis 2 without thinking about what Shabbat comes to mean later.

Some things change dramatically over the course of the Hebrew Bible's story: from an undefined divine-human relationship in Parashat Bereshit to a series of covenants in the books that follow; from a depiction of all humankind in Genesis 1–11 to a focus specifically through Israel for many books thereafter; from explicit depiction of divine power in Genesis 1 to divine hiddenness in Ezra, Nehemiah, and Esther; and as the face of God becomes more hidden through the course of the narrative, humans grow up and must take ever more responsibility for their world.

When I go to a movie or play, I prefer to know as little as possible about its story in advance. Few of us are able to come to the Bible that way. It is too well-known. But few of us experience our knowledge of things that come later in the Bible as spoiling Bereshit for us the way it might spoil a mystery story to know "who done it." When we read the difficult account of the divine beings and the human women in Genesis 6, which results in the deity's setting a 120-year limit on human life (6:3), we gain rather than lose something by knowing that the Torah will end with an announcement that Moses lives the maximum and dies at the age of 120 (Deut 34:7).

Likewise, we can have a richer appreciation of the story of Cain and Abel if we know that fratricide will become a recurring theme—Jacob and Esau, Joseph and his brothers, Abimelek and his brothers, Absalom and Amnon, the woman of Tekoa's story of two brothers—culminating in Solomon's executing his brother Adonijah and thus establishing the stability of the Davidic line on the throne of Israel. It is no longer just a tale of Cain's fate; it is rather an introduction and first installment in an ongoing, agonizing biblical treatment of the envies, rivalries, and affections of siblings.

And we can better understand humankind's loss of the tree of life as the price of gaining knowledge of good and bad if we know that life and death, and good and bad, will become crucial themes in Moses' last speech in Deuteronomy. And we understand it better still if we know that later, in the book of Proverbs, the highest form of knowledge of good and bad in the Bible—wisdom—will be characterized this way: "It is a *tree of life!*" (Prov 3:18). And so Jews sing this passage from Proverbs when they return

the Torah to the ark after reading it each week. The garden of Eden and the tree of life are not destroyed in Genesis; they are rendered inaccessible. The initial divine-human alienation that is marked by the eviction from paradise, therefore, is not necessarily to be understood as final. The possibility of human return to a condition in which the creator is so close as to be perceived as walking among humans in the breeze of the day (Gen 3:8) is left open. Cherubs guard the path back to the tree of life, but this, too, can be understood better if one knows what is coming: golden cherubs will spread their wings over the ark and its contents inside the Temple. The cherubs keep watch over the path to the tree of life, and their images symbolically keep watch over the keys to the path back: covenant, Torah, knowledge, wisdom.

How does the end of the Torah indeed lead us back to the beginning (as well as on to Joshua)?

At the beginning of the Torah, the tree of life is lost, and death becomes the fate of all humans. Now the Torah ends with the death of Moses. At the beginning, Cain worries that "I'll be hidden from your presence" (literally, from your face). Now God tells Moses, "Let me hide my face from them; I'll see what their future will be." Back in Genesis, God promises a land to Abraham for his descendants. Now God shows Moses the land that God promised. In Genesis, Abraham "passes" through the land. Now God tells Moses: you won't "pass" there (34:4). In Genesis, Isaac's eyes were dim. Now we are told that Moses' eye was not dim. Genesis ends with Jacob's blessing of twelve sons (The Blessing of Jacob, Genesis 49). Now the Torah ends with Moses' blessing of twelve tribes (The Blessing of Moses, Deuteronomy 33). Genesis recounts the first merging of "spirit" and "wisdom" in a man: Joseph (Gen 41:38–39). Now these two words are applied to Joshua (Deut 34:9); and Joshua, coming from the tribe of Ephraim, is a descendant of Joseph.

We find all of these (and many more) reminiscences and denouements at the end of the Torah that remind us of things we found at the beginning. But this look backward is only half of what we get—because our custom is to start over immediately, going back to Genesis. So we begin the Torah looking forward. Now when we go back to Genesis and read about the 120-year limit on human life, we will think of how Moses arrived at it. Now when we read about the divine promise of the land to Abraham in Genesis, we may think of Moses' reminder to the people that this promise is about to come true at the end of Deuteronomy.

And note: the promise to Abraham is not fulfilled at the end of the Torah. It is fulfilled in Joshua. So the last chapter of the Torah invites us to do both: to turn back to Genesis and to read on in Joshua.

The Torah thus involves a looking forward and a looking back, a linking of past and future. It is a strange concept of time: linear and cyclical at the same time, historical and timeless at the same time. It is the first known work of history on earth: telling a record of events through a progression of time on a line. Yet we read that record in a cyclical manner, always returning to the beginning. And so Returning becomes one of the central concepts of Judaism.

This work contains the Hebrew text as well as the English translation.

Following the pattern of the Hebrew language, this book opens and reads from right to left.